1 CORINTHIANS

ZONDERVAN
Exegetical
Commentary
ON THE
New Testament

PAUL GARDNER

CLINTON E. ARNOLD
General Editor

ZONDERVAN®

ZONDERVAN

1 Corinthians
Copyright © 2018 by Paul D. Gardner

Requests for information should be addressed to:
Zondervan, 3900 *Sparks Dr. SE, Grand Rapids, Michigan 49546*

Library of Congress Cataloging-in-Publication Data
Names: Gardner, Paul, 1950- author.
Title: 1 Corinthians / Paul Gardner.
Other titles: First Corinthians | Zondervan exegetical commentary on the New Testament.
Description: Grand Rapids, Michigan : Zondervan, [2018] | Series: Zondervan exegetical commentary on the New Testament / Clinton E. Arnold, General editor | Includes bibliographical references and indexes.
Identifiers: LCCN 2017036437 | ISBN 9780310243694 (hardcover)
Subjects: LCSH: Bible. Corinthians, 1st—Commentaries.
Classification: LCC BS2675.53 .G36 2018 | DDC 227/.207—dc23 LC record available at https://lccn.loc.gov/2017036437

Cover design: Tammy Johnson
Interior design: Beth Shagene

Printed in the United States of America

18 19 20 21 22 23 24 25 26 27 28 /DCI/ 12 11 10 9 8 7 6 5 4 3 2 1

Contents

Series Introduction

This generation has been blessed with an abundance of excellent commentaries. Some are technical and do a good job of addressing issues that the critics have raised; other commentaries are long and provide extensive information about word usage and catalogue nearly every opinion expressed on the various interpretive issues; still other commentaries focus on providing cultural and historical background information; and then there are those commentaries that endeavor to draw out many applicational insights.

The key question to ask is: What are you looking for in a commentary? This commentary series might be for you if

- you have taken Greek and would like a commentary that helps you apply what you have learned without assuming you are a well-trained scholar.
- you would find it useful to see a concise, one- or two-sentence statement of what the commentator thinks the main point of each passage is.
- you would like help interpreting the words of Scripture without getting bogged down in scholarly issues that seem irrelevant to the life of the church.
- you would like to see a visual representation (a graphical display) of the flow of thought in each passage.
- you would like expert guidance from solid evangelical scholars who set out to explain the meaning of the original text in the clearest way possible and to help you navigate through the main interpretive issues.
- you want to benefit from the results of the latest and best scholarly studies and historical information that help to illuminate the meaning of the text.
- you would find it useful to see a brief summary of the key theological insights that can be gleaned from each passage and some discussion of the relevance of these for Christians today.

These are just some of the features that characterize the new Zondervan Exegetical Commentary on the New Testament series. The idea for this series was refined over time by an editorial board who listened to pastors and teachers express what they wanted to see in a commentary series based on the Greek text. That board consisted of myself, George H. Guthrie, William D. Mounce, Thomas R. Schreiner, and Mark L. Strauss along with Zondervan senior editor at large Verlyn Verbrugge, and former Zondervan senior acquisitions editor Jack Kuhatschek. We also enlisted a board of consulting editors who are active pastors, ministry leaders, and seminary professors to help in the process of designing a commentary series that will be useful to the church. Zondervan senior acquisitions editor Katya Covrett has now been shepherding the process to completion, and Constantine R. Campbell is now serving on the board.

We arrived at a design that includes seven components for the treatment of each biblical passage. What follows is a brief orientation to these primary components of the commentary.

Literary Context

In this section, you will find a concise discussion of how the passage functions in the broader literary context of the book. The commentator highlights connections with the preceding and following material in the book and makes observations on the key literary features of this text.

Main Idea

Many readers will find this to be an enormously helpful feature of this series. For each passage, the commentator carefully crafts a one- or two-sentence statement of the big idea or central thrust of the passage.

Translation and Graphical Layout

Another unique feature of this series is the presentation of each commentator's translation of the Greek text in a graphical layout. The purpose of this diagram is to help the reader visualize, and thus better understand, the flow of thought within the text. The translation itself reflects the interpretive decisions made by each commentator in the "Explanation" section of the commentary. Here are a few insights that will help you to understand the way these are put together:

1. On the far left side next to the verse numbers is a series of interpretive labels that indicate the function of each clause or phrase of the biblical text. The corresponding portion of the text is on the same line to the right of the label. We have not used technical linguistic jargon for these, so they should be easily understood.

2. In general, we place every clause (a group of words containing a subject and a predicate) on a separate line and identify how it is supporting the principal assertion of the text (namely, is it saying when the action occurred, how it took place,

or why it took place?). We sometimes place longer phrases or a series of items on separate lines as well.

3. Subordinate (or dependent) clauses and phrases are indented and placed directly under the words that they modify. This helps the reader to more easily see the nature of the relationship of clauses and phrases in the flow of the text.

4. Every main clause has been placed in bold print and pushed to the left margin for clear identification.

5. Sometimes when the level of subordination moves too far to the right—as often happens with some of Paul's long, involved sentences!—we reposition the flow to the left of the diagram, but use an arrow to indicate that this has happened.

6. The overall process we have followed has been deeply informed by principles of discourse analysis and narrative criticism (for the Gospels and Acts).

Structure

Immediately following the translation, the commentator describes the flow of thought in the passage and explains how certain interpretive decisions regarding the relationship of the clauses were made in the passage.

Exegetical Outline

The overall structure of the passage is described in a detailed exegetical outline. This will be particularly helpful for those who are looking for a way to concisely explain the flow of thought in the passage in a teaching or preaching setting.

Explanation of the Text

As an exegetical commentary, this work makes use of the Greek language to interpret the meaning of the text. If your Greek is rather rusty (or even somewhat limited), don't be too concerned. All the Greek words are cited in parentheses following an English translation. We have made every effort to make this commentary as readable and useful as possible even for the nonspecialist.

Those who will benefit the most from this commentary will have had the equivalent of two years of Greek in college or seminary. This would include a semester or two of working through an intermediate grammar (such as Wallace, Porter, Brooks and Winbery, or Dana and Mantey). The authors use the grammatical language that is found in these kinds of grammars. The details of the grammar of the passage, however, are discussed only when it has a bearing on the interpretation of the text.

The emphasis in this section of the text is to convey the meaning. Commentators examine words and images, grammatical details, relevant OT and Jewish background to a particular concept, historical and cultural context, important text-critical issues, and various interpretational issues that surface.

Theology in Application

This, too, is a unique feature for an exegetical commentary series. We felt it was important for each author not only to describe what the text means in its various details, but also to take a moment and reflect on the theological contribution that it makes. In this section, the theological message of the passage is summarized. The authors discuss the theology of the text in terms of its place within the book and in a broader biblical-theological context. Finally, each commentator provides some suggestions on what the message of the passage is for the church today. At the conclusion of each volume in this series is a summary of the whole range of theological themes touched on by this book of the Bible.

Our sincere hope and prayer is that you find this series helpful not only for your own understanding of the text of the New Testament, but as you are actively engaged in teaching and preaching God's Word to people who are hungry to be fed on its truth.

CLINTON E. ARNOLD, general editor

Author's Preface

My love for biblical studies really began while running a candle-making business in Cambridge with Dr. Jim Hurley, who was studying 1 Corinthians at Tyndale House for his PhD! We both needed the extra money, and my wife and I were trying to save enough money to go to seminary in the United States. Eventually doors were opened, and I was able to study at Reformed Theological Seminary where I met Dr. Simon Kistemaker. Later he wrote the commentary on 1 Corinthians in the Hendriksen New Testament Commentary series. His excellent, pastorally centered, New Testament teaching and his strong personal encouragement confirmed me in my desire to go on to a PhD. I returned to Cambridge where professor Morna Hooker accepted me as a student with 1 Corinthians 8–10 as the area of study. I remain so grateful for her deep scrutiny of each step of that doctoral work.

Following ordination, I taught Greek, New Testament, and homiletics at Oak Hill Theological College, an Anglican seminary in north London. First Corinthians again figured in the schedule. Since then I have returned to the Oak Hill library for times of study and am thankful for the facilities they have let me use. I also owe a great debt of gratitude to the wardens and staff at Tyndale House Library, who provided a place to study and invaluable advice during the PhD writing and in later sabbaticals. Without them I could never have completed this work.

I am also most grateful to three bishops who, over many years, constantly encouraged me in various writing and teaching projects while pastoring churches under their oversight: the Rt. Revds. Michael Baughen, Michael Langrish, and Dr. Peter Forster. While pastoring churches in the UK and the United States, I have taken a couple of opportunities to preach through the whole of this wonderful epistle and have taught it at various seminaries. All Scripture is profitable for all God's people in all times, but in a society that above all prizes knowledge and wisdom and affords most recognition to the best educated and most articulate, in a society that is preoccupied with status and with individualistic approaches to life, in a society that serves many gods with the deepest of idolatries, this epistle seems to say it all as God speaks to our generation.

It is mainly for this reason that I have been encouraged in the long process of writing a commentary while serving full-time in a church. This series affords me the opportunity to examine the Greek text exegetically but also to offer possible applications of this text on the understanding that God's word is for the church of all generations.

I am most grateful to the general editor of this series, Dr. Clint Arnold, for his many kind encouragements and his detailed helpful comments on the work, and to Dr. George Guthrie, who has provided invaluable and meticulous help with the grammatical charting and other areas of the work. This work could not have been completed without the gracious support of the elders and congregation of Christ-Church Presbyterian in Atlanta and of my assistants, especially Ms. Jessica Hudson, who has helped proofread and sort footnotes and bibliography with such attention to detail. Above all the support of Sharon, my wife, has been unstinting and wonderfully encouraging, particularly during those times when I have been tempted to give up. Always she has been there for me in every area of our joint ministry. Together we have sought to live our lives determined "to know nothing . . . except Jesus Christ and him crucified" (2:2). At times we have fallen far short, but in the end we know we are "known by God" (8:3), and so we pray that this commentary will in some small way serve his glory.

PAUL GARDNER

Abbreviations

AB	Anchor Bible
ANF	*The Ante-Nicene Fathers*. Edited by Alexander Roberts and James Donaldson. 10 vols. Edinburgh: T&T Clark, 1866–72.
AcBib	Academia Biblica Series (SBL)
ACCS	Ancient Christian Commentary on Scripture
AGJU	Arbeiten zur Geschichte des antiken Judentums und des Urchristentums
AJA	*American Journal of Archaeology*
AnBib	Analecta Biblica
ANTC	Abingdon New Testament Commentaries
ASV	American Standard Version
AThR	*Anglican Theological Review*
AV	Authorized Version
AYBC	Anchor Yale Bible Commentaries
BDAG	Danker, Frederick W., Walter Bauer, William F. Arndt, and F. Wilbur Gingrich. *Greek-English Lexicon of the New Testament and Other Early Christian Literature*. 3rd ed. Chicago: University of Chicago Press, 2000.
BDF	Blass, Friedrich, Albert Debrunner, and Robert W. Funk. *A Greek Grammar of the New Testament and Other Early Christian Literature*. Chicago: University of Chicago Press, 1961.
BECNT	Baker Exegetical Commentary on the New Testament
BT	*The Bible Translator*
BR	*Biblical Research*
BTB	*Biblical Theology Bulletin*
BZ	*Biblische Zeitschrift*
CBC	Cambridge Bible Commentary
CBET	Contributions to Biblical Exegesis and Theology
ConBNT	Coniectanea Biblica: New Testament Series
CBQ	*Catholic Biblical Quarterly*
CGTC	Cambridge Greek Testament Commentary

CNT	Commentaire du Nouveau Testament
CRINT	Compendia Rerum Iudaicarum ad Novum Testamentum
DFTC	Dissertationes ad gradum magistri in Facultate Theologica vela in Facultate Iuris Canonici consequendum conscriptae
EKKNT	Evangelisch-katholischer Kommentar zum Neuen Testament
ESV	English Standard Version
ET	English translation
EvQ	*Evangelical Quarterly*
ExpTim	*Expository Times*
HAR	*Hebrew Annual Review*
HibJ	*Hibbert Journal*
HNT	Handbuch zum Neuen Testament
HNTC	Harper's New Testament Commentaries
HTR	*Harvard Theological Review*
HUT	Hermeneutische Untersuchungen zur Theologie
ICC	International Critical Commentary
ISBE	*International Standard Bible Encyclopedia*. Edited by Geoffrey W. Bromiley. 4 vols. Grand Rapids: Eerdmans, 1979–1988.
JB	Jerusalem Bible
JBL	*Journal of Biblical Literature*
JETS	*Journal of the Evangelical Theological Society*
JSNT	*Journal for the Study of the New Testament*
JSNTSup	Journal for the Study of the New Testament Supplement Series
JTS	*Journal of Theological Studies*
L&N	Louw, Johannes P., and Eugene A. Nida, eds. *Greek-English Lexicon of the New Testament: Based on Semantic Domains*. 2nd ed. New York: United Bible Societies, 1989.
LCL	Loeb Classical Library
Leg.	*Legum allegoria* [Philo]
LNTS	Library of New Testament Studies
LSJ	Liddell, Henry George, Robert Scott, Henry Stuart Jones. *A Greek-English Lexicon*. 9th ed. with revised supplement. Oxford: Clarendon, 1996.
LXX	Septuagint (the Greek Old Testament)
𝔐	Majority text
MM	Moulton, James H., and George Milligan. *The Vocabulary of the Greek Testament*. London, 1930. Repr., Peabody, MA: Hendrickson, 1997.
m. Pesahim	Mishnah: Pesahim
NA	Nestle-Aland, *Novum Testamentum Graece*
NAC	New American Commentary

NASB	New American Standard Bible
NCB	New Century Bible
NEB	New English Bible
NIBCNT	New International Bible Commentary on the New Testament
NICNT	New International Commentary on the New Testament
NICOT	New International Commentary on the Old Testament
NIGTC	New International Greek Testament Commentary
NIV 1984	New International Version (1984)
NIV 2011	New International Version (2011)
NIVAC	NIV Application Commentary
NJB	New Jerusalem Bible
NKJV	New King James Version
NovT	*Novum Testamentum*
NovTSup	Supplements to Novum Testamentum
NRSV	New Revised Standard Version
NSBT	New Studies in Biblical Theology
NTL	New Testament Library
NTS	*New Testament Studies*
NTT	New Testament Theology (Cambridge University Press)
Num. Rab.	Numbers Rabbah
𝔓	Papyrus (manuscript)
PNTC	Pillar New Testament Commentaries
P. Oxy.	*Oxyrhynchus Papyri*. Edited by Bernard P. Grenfell, Arthur S. Hunt, et al. London: Egypt Exploration Fund, 1898–.
Prov.	*De providentia* [Philo]
PTMS	Pittsburgh Theological Monograph Series
RB	*Revue biblique*
REB	Revised English Bible
RevExp	*Review and Expositor*
RSV	Revised Standard Version
RTR	*Reformed Theological Review*
SBG	Studies in Biblical Greek (Lang)
SBL	Society of Biblical Literature
SBLDS	Society of Biblical Literature Dissertation Series
SBLMS	Society of Biblical Literature Monograph Series
SBT	Studies in Biblical Theology
SNT	Studien zum Neuen Testament
SNTSMS	Society for New Testament Studies Monograph Series
SP	Sacra Pagina
T. Jud.	Testament of Judah

T. Levi	Testament of Levi
t. Sukkah	Tosefta: Sukkah
TDNT	*Theological Dictionary of the New Testament.* Edited by Gerhard Kittel and Gerhard Friedrich. Translated by Geoffrey W. Bromiley. 10 vols. Grand Rapids: Eerdmans, 1964–1976.
TEV	Today's English Version (= Good News Bible)
THKNT	Theologischer Handkommentar zum Neuen Testament
TJ	*Trinity Journal*
TNTC	Tyndale New Testament Commentaries
TOTC	Tyndale Old Testament Commentaries
TynBul	*Tyndale Bulletin*
UBS[5]	*The Greek New Testament*, United Bible Societies, 5th ed.
VC	*Vigiliae Christianae*
WBC	Word Biblical Commentary
WTJ	*Westminster Theological Journal*
WUNT	Wissenschaftliche Untersuchungen zum Neuen Testament
ZECNT	Zondervan Exegetical Commentary on the New Testament
ZNW	*Zeitschrift für die neutestamentliche Wissenschaft und die Kunde der älteren Kirche*

Introduction

Paul's Corinthian epistles have fascinated, encouraged, and challenged Christians throughout the centuries. From the earliest times they have stimulated pastoral exposition and the writing of many commentaries and, in more recent years, the multiplication of articles in both the popular Christian press and the most erudite journals. The topics upon which Paul touches as he writes have undoubtedly generated much of this continued interest across the generations.

While 1 Corinthians is rightly first to be seen as a product of an apostle's concern for a particular church and its attendant problems, there is no doubt that the wider church through the ages has been attracted to this epistle because so much of its teaching appears easily and immediately applicable in any generation. This letter has been employed through generations of the church's teaching on matters as diverse as marriage and singleness, sexual conduct and immorality, idolatry, use of spiritual gifts, the last things, the wisdom of the world and its impact on the church, pride, problems between the wealthy and the poor, church unity, and many other subjects.

Apart from the obviously practical messages of the letter, it is also replete with episodes of great theological depth. It contains Paul's longest exposition on the nature of love as the marker par excellence of true faith, through to his longest theological treatment of the resurrection. Above all, perhaps, the reader cannot fail to see how underlying everything that Paul writes is his humble and total commitment to a *theologia crucis*, "to know nothing among [them] except Jesus Christ and him crucified" (2:2). Communicating and upholding this gospel of the Lord Jesus Christ is Paul's "compulsion," laid upon him by God (9:16–17). Here he expounds and applies that gospel, sometimes even drawing upon his own Christian experience to illustrate the implications of its content for the individual believer and for the church. His application of the gospel to the church's life is offered at times with joy and encouragement but also at times with strong admonition, as he reveals his grave concern for a people who have easily been drawn back into the "wisdom of this age" (2:6). Yet even when this is the case and Paul seems to be chastising the Corinthians, it is clear he does so from a position of deep love for his "brothers and sisters" and as one who also sees himself as their "father in Christ Jesus" (4:15 ESV), and them as "beloved children" (4:14 ESV).

Of course, it is probably fair to say that the text can hardly bear the weight of all the teaching notionally based upon it, but there is no doubt that for the interested Christian this book feels at times as if it might have been written for the twenty-first century church. In fact, as pastors and students examine the socio-historical and religious background into which Paul wrote, as they study Paul's emphasis on "the Lord Jesus Christ" against a backdrop of his own society, as they examine Paul's intriguing use of Scripture, and as they examine the development of Paul's arguments, they will at once find depths that may not have been immediately apparent and, in God's providence, speak even more clearly than they might imagine to today's world. After all, this too is a generation which needs to be reminded that the "the folly of God is wiser than the wisdom of men and women and the weakness of God is stronger than the strength of men and women" (1:25).

The Author

That the apostle Paul was the author of this epistle is not disputed. The inclusion of the cosender is rare in Greek letters, being found in only a very few papyri letters of the hundreds now available. However, it is not uncommon in Paul's own letters as, for example, with the mention of Timothy and Silvanus in 1 Thessalonians 1:1 and 2 Thessalonians 1:1. Here in 1 Corinthians 1:1 Paul mentions Sosthenes (see comments on 1:1), who may well be the Sosthenes who suffered persecution in Corinth in Acts 18:17 and is referred to as "the ruler of the synagogue." Sosthenes may have been the amanuensis, or it may simply be that Paul wants to be clear that Sosthenes is with him and aiding him in his ministry and, like him, has love and concern for the church at Corinth.

Paul in Corinth

Acts 18 provides a secondary source for understanding the nature of Paul's original evangelistic mission to the city. Allowing that the sequence of Paul's journeys as recounted in Acts is accurate, then we can see Paul's first arrival in Corinth as occurring on his second extensive missionary journey. This journey began in Antioch before moving on to Derbe, Lystra, and Iconium, across the Aegean Sea to Philippi, then south to Thessalonica, Berea, and eventually Athens where Paul preached first in the Jewish synagogue and then to Stoic and Epicurean philosophers at the Areopagus (17:16–34). Luke then informs the reader that Paul "left Athens and went to Corinth" (18:1). In Corinth Paul once again taught and reasoned first in the synagogue. Whether he met Aquila and Priscilla through the synagogue or while seeking to carry out his trade of tent making[1] is not clear (18:3). They were Jews who had

---

1. "Tent making" probably involved working with leather. Other less likely meanings of the word σκηνοποιός include "maker of stage properties" and "weaver of tent cloth." See the extensive discussion in BDAG 928–29.

been forced to leave Rome under an edict from the Emperor Claudius, and they worked at the same trade as Paul. If they were not Christians when they arrived in Corinth, they certainly were by the time Paul left (18:26; 1 Cor 16:19). Though the majority of Jews rejected the message, we read of the conversion of Crispus, a "ruler of the synagogue," and of Titius Justus, who lived next door to the synagogue and was a "worshipper of God" (18:7–8). Many other Corinthians were converted. However, it seems something caused Paul to think of moving on, at which point the Lord directly intervened through a vision and told him not to be afraid but to keep on speaking. The message of the vision hints at the fact that Paul may have been thinking of leaving as he saw the opposition building against him and the recent converts.

The Lord promised he would be with Paul and that there were yet many people who would come to faith (vv. 9–10). So Paul stayed in Corinth for a further eighteen months—in all, perhaps two years (v. 11). In the end, largely inspired by the Jewish people, serious persecution broke out during the time of Gallio, the proconsul (vv. 12–16). The synagogue leader Sosthenes, mentioned above (see also 1 Cor 1:1), was seized and beaten by the Jews, probably because he too had become a Christian (Acts 18:17). Even after this we read Paul stayed on for "many days," but eventually set sail for Syria with Priscilla and Aquila (v. 18). The account Luke gives provides every indication that a church of a number of converts had been well established by the time Paul left. It would have contained both the converted Jews mentioned in Acts but also the "many" of the Greek, pagan society who also had come to faith. In 1 Corinthians 3:6 Paul refers to having "planted" this church.

Date and Occasion of the Epistle

It is likely that this epistle, which was written from Ephesus, was penned sometime in AD 54 (or perhaps AD 55), perhaps a little before Pentecost (16:8).[2] Acts 18:2 refers to Priscilla and Aquila having "recently" arrived from Italy where they had been subject to the emperor's order for Jews to leave Rome. That decree probably was issued in AD 49.[3] This ties in reasonably well with Acts 18:12. There Luke tells us that Gallio was the proconsul in Achaia, when Paul was preaching there. This provides the more secure date by which to anchor Paul's dates in Corinth.[4] Gallio most likely

---

2. Although the date of AD 53 has occasionally been espoused, it is our view that, given the amount of activity to do with the church in Corinth that we know about (see below), pre-Pentecost AD 53 would be too early. If Fitzmyer (see note 5 below) is correct about the dating of Gallio's time in Achaia, then it is certainly too early.

3. The expulsion order is mentioned by Suetonius in his *Lives of the Caesars* (*Divus Claudius* 25.4).

4. In the Delphic inscription of Claudius, seven fragments of which were discovered between 1905 and 1910 and two

further fragments in 1967, Claudius refers to Gallio as "Junius Gallio my friend and [pro]consul." The inscription refers to the twelfth year of Claudius's reign (AD 41–54). See a translation and reconstruction of the relevant inscription in C. K. Barrett, *The New Testament Background: Writings from Ancient Greece and the Roman Empire That Illuminate Chrisatian Origins*, rev. ed. (San Francisco: HarperCollins, 1989), 51–52. Also J. Murphy-O'Connor, *St. Paul's Corinth: Texts and Archaeology* (Wilmington, DE: Glazier, 1983), 149ff.

took over his responsibilities in June or July AD 51 or AD 52 and did not last a full two years. Since Gallio must have been reasonably established in his role by the time he encountered Paul (18:14–15), and Paul seems to have been there eighteen months by that time (18:11) and then stayed on "many days" in Corinth after this encounter, it is reasonable to assume that Paul left Corinth in late AD 51 or spring/summer AD 52 after nearly two years of ministry.[5] A number of factors then suggest the passing of perhaps two-and-a-half years before this letter is written.

As we read 1 Corinthians, it is clear that during the intervening period between Paul's leaving Corinth and the writing of this letter, the church had continued to advance, probably both in numbers and in its impact upon the city. At some stage during that time, Apollos had spent time with the church and had "watered" the work (1 Cor 3:5–7). No doubt Apollos had helped teach in the church and contributed to its long-term establishment. Paul was at pains to say that Apollos's work was in line with his own and that he and Apollos were not divided (3:8–9). Indeed, Paul had urged Apollos to visit the church again (16:12).

Also, during this intervening period Paul had written another letter (5:9), in which he had clearly expressed concern for the way the Corinthian Christians had been associating with sexually immoral people.[6] Since 1 Corinthians 5 deals with incest being tolerated in their midst, the previous letter may have addressed that specific issue. It is difficult to imagine that such sin would have arisen while Apollos was in Corinth, and some time must be allowed for such an attitude to sin to develop in the congregation.

In terms of the occasion of our epistle, even if in some sense it is a follow-up to the letter mentioned in 5:9, the reason for writing is broader. First Corinthians clearly indicates that Paul had received considerable information about the church, probably over some period of time, from at least three sources. First, he has heard reports from "Chloe's people" (1:11). She may have been a business woman based either in Ephesus or in Corinth. Clearly Paul trusted her emissaries. Parts of the epistle seem closely related to these oral reports; for example, 1:11–4:5, 11:17–34, and chapter 15:12–34. A second source for his information was a letter from the Corinthian church. It would seem that an official or semi-official delegation from the church made up of Stephanas, Fortunatus, and Achaicus might have carried this letter to Paul (16:17). Again, parts of the epistle, especially those sections starting

---

5. Joseph A. Fitzmyer, *First Corinthians: A New Translation with Introduction and Commentary*, AYBC 32 (New Haven: Yale University Press, 2008), 37–45, examines the evidence for the dating of Paul's stay in Corinth in great detail. He concludes that Paul would have been brought before Gallio sometime in mid AD 52. Given Paul's subsequent lengthy travels and stay in Ephesus, he posits that 1 Corinthians was written "sometime before Pentecost . . . probably early in the year 57 (but the end of the year 56 is possible)." Fitzmyer is surely correct in recog-

nising the need for some considerable time to elapse between Paul's leaving Corinth and the writing of 1 Corinthians. On the detail of Gallio's ruling and its impact on the case brought against Paul and on Paul's future use of Roman law, see Bruce W. Winter, "Gallio's Ruling on the Legal Status of Early Christianity (Acts 18:14–15)," *TynBul* 50.2 (1999): 213–24. For further detail and reconstruction of dating, see Jerome Murphy O'Connor, *Paul: A Critical Life* (Oxford: Clarendon, 1996).

6. This may have been written during the latter part of AD 52.

with the phrase "now concerning," probably address that letter (7:1, 25; 8:1; 12:1; and perhaps 16:1). Finally, given that Paul has clearly talked with Apollos about the situation in Corinth (4:6; 16:12), it is safe to assume Apollos had been a source for some of Paul's concern for the church.[7]

Divisions in the Church

Nearly every analysis of the letter faces first the issue of the divisions in the church at Corinth (1:10–17; 3:3–9). For some, these divisions are the primary occasion for this letter. Paul specifically mentions members of the church who see themselves as "of Paul . . . of Apollos . . . of Cephas . . . of Christ" (1:12).[8] Although some commentators have tried to lay the blame for some problems at the feet of the "Peter" group and others at the feet of the "Apollos" group, in fact Paul never does that, and it is important to remember that the groups are not mentioned again as the source of the later problems that Paul confronts. Indeed, Johannes Munck in a major work on Paul entitled a chapter "The Church without Factions" because he rightly believed that interpreters had pressed these divisions too far.[9]

Furthermore, arguing that the groups of 1:12 provide the major occasion of this epistle tends to minimize other divisions within the church to which Paul pays significant attention. In chapter 8 Paul refers to some who are "weak," as opposed to those he is obviously addressing at that point who might be called the "strong" (although he does not call them this in 1 Corinthians). Paul isolates a further division between rich and poor in his discussion of the Lord's Supper (11:17–22). That division had led to an abuse of the Lord's Supper. What is clear is that something had caused this church to divide itself up into groups at many points in the church's life. However, it is important not to read into every situation that Paul addresses a particular group situation. For example, it is highly doubtful that 1 Corinthians 2 provides enough information to suggest that the problem of wisdom is fundamentally an issue concerning the group that followed Apollos.[10] This conclusion is largely drawn from Acts 18:24, which says that Apollos was "an eloquent man, well-versed in the scriptures" (NRSV), while Paul apparently says almost the opposite of himself in 1 Corinthians 2:1.

---

7. The extent of these communications between Paul and the church that help contribute to the occasion of this epistle provide some basis for regarding its dating in AD 53 as probably a little too early.

8. The suggested nature of these divisions is discussed in more detail in the commentary, especially at 1:12.

9. Johannes Munck, *Paul and the Salvation of Mankind* (Richmond: John Knox, 1959). Fee's assessment is still largely valid: "It is probably quite wrong to envisage the church as split into 'parties' at all, since nothing in the letter itself gives much in the way of hints as to how these might be viewed" (Gordon D. Fee, *The First Epistle to the Corinthians*, rev. ed., NICNT [Grand Rapids: Eerdmans, 2014], 5). Munck's chapter is reprinted in the excellent collection of essays by Edward Adams and David G. Horrell, eds., *Christianity at Corinth* (Louisville: Westminster John Knox, 2004).

10. See J. C. Hurd, *The Origin of 1 Corinthians* (SCM: London, 1965).

Having said that the divisions of 1:12 can be overplayed, and acknowledging (see comments on 1:12) that there is no secure evidence of what this group or that group actually taught, it is still important to note that the divisions in the church are significant matters in this epistle and the unity of the church is high on Paul's agenda as he writes. Paul is utterly dismayed at the splits and conflicts (1:10–11; 3:3; 11:18) among these Christians.

Integrity of the Epistle

The integrity of this epistle as we now have it has been challenged by some. The question has been raised largely due to Paul's own mention of other letters he had written (1 Cor 5:9; 2 Cor 2:3–4, 7:8 refer to at least two other letters). Some commentators have suggested that the letters we now know as 1 and 2 Corinthians are in fact, to a lesser or greater degree, composite texts redacted to include parts of those "other letters." Various apparent internal textual problems have been used as indications of places where texts may have been inserted or conflated. Some of the observed indications of textual redaction, it is said, include the following: 1) apparent breaks and sudden changes of subject (e.g., the lack of transition between the subjects of 1 Corinthians 8 and 9 and other such questions of transition especially notable in 2 Corinthians); 2) suggested difficulties that arise when the extant letters to Corinth are compared with the account in Acts 18 of Paul's dealings with the church; 3) a supposed distinction between so-called "rigorous" and "lenient" passages (e.g., sections of 1 Corinthians 8–10); 4) a possible contradiction between 1 Corinthians 4:19 and 16:5–9; 5) questions regarding the links between the apostolic defense found in 1 Corinthians 4 and 9.[11] Some have then gone on to attempt to reconstruct the epistolary history and argue for which sections in the extant letters belong to which "original" correspondence. Whilst reconstructions of various complexities are found in commentators from J. Weiss (1910) onwards,[12] in 1948 Jean Héring sought to simplify matters, arguing for only two letters to be found in the extant 1 Corinthians. However, that work was dismissed by W. Schmithals in the presentation of one of the most complex reconstructions of all. Though Schmithals himself changed his mind over a number of years, in 1971 he argued for six pieces of correspondence between Paul and the Corinthians, parts of which are to be found in 1 and 2 Corinthians.[13]

---

11. These headings are partly drawn from the work of Schmithals and from Héring's summary of "critical observations." Walter Schmithals, *Gnosticism in Corinth: An Investigation of the Letters to the Corinthians*, trans. John E. Steely (Nashville: Abingdon, 1971), 90–101; Jean C. Héring, *The First Epistle of Saint Paul to the Corinthians*, trans. A. W. Heathcote and P. J. Allcock (London: Epworth, 1962), xiii. Héring argues for two letters: letter (a) is defined as "1–8, 10:23–11:1, 16:1–4,

10–14" and letter (b) is therefore "9, 10:1–22, 11–15, the remainder of 16 (13 being a special addition, on any view)" (ibid., xiv).

12. A helpful English-language summary of Weiss's division of 1 Corinthians is found in Hans Conzelmann, *1 Corinthians: A Commentary on the First Epistle to the Corinthians*, trans. J. W. Leitch, Hermeneia (Philadelphia: Fortress, 1975), 3.

13. His method is well demonstrated in *Gnosticism in Corinth*, 90–101.

Of Héring's more simple analysis he said, "To be sure, [it is] based on astoundingly narrow observation and is correspondingly superficial."[14]

The problem with all such hypotheses is that they are subjective. A hypothesis that seeks to respond to the textual issues such as those listed above without resort to literary and source criticism is to be preferred because it deals with the evidence already in hand. Conzelmann summarizes well the view taken in this commentary: "There is no conclusive proof of different situations within 1 Corinthians. The existing breaks can be explained from the circumstances of its composition."[15]

Others have sought to address questions of internal integrity and continuity of argument within the extant epistles by positing sometimes complex reconstructions of Paul's dialogue with the Corinthian church. One of the most detailed of these, found in the work of J. C. Hurd, may be mentioned here simply by way of example. He attempted to offer a total hypothesis concerning the origin, structure, and situation at Corinth and its related Pauline correspondence.[16] He suggests that the apostolic decree (Acts 15) forced a compromise upon Paul that led him to change his position somewhat with regard to certain rights and freedoms. In his first visit, Paul had taught the Corinthians about "wisdom" and "knowledge," but now in the light of the compromise Paul had to revisit his position. The Corinthians responded with anger and incomprehension. The main section from 7:1–11:1 deals with problems raised by the church. Verses that commentators believe are quotations from the Corinthian letter Hurd suggests are former Pauline sentences, which the Corinthians now quote back to him in disbelief that he seems to have changed his position. An example from chapters 8–10 reveals how Hurd's thesis seeks to explain a number of matters. He suggests that in the founding mission (stage 1) Paul had preached 1) "Christians have knowledge," 2) "an idol is nothing," 3) "there is no God but one," and 4) "all things are lawful." In his conduct, Paul had eaten meat from the public market. Into this situation Paul then wrote the "previous letter" (stage 2) that said, "Do not eat idol meat." Perplexed and annoyed, the Corinthians replied (stage 3) with the points already made by Paul: 1) "But we have knowledge," 2) "but an idol is nothing," etc. To this they added, "Do you mean to say that we may not even buy meat in the market or eat with our friends?" Paul's response to this (stage 4) is to be found in 8:1–11:1: 1) "yes, but knowledge puffs up," 2) "yes, but there are so-called gods," 3) "yes, but not all have this knowledge," 4) "yes, but not all things build up." And regarding his conduct, he replied: "Am I not free? Am I not an apostle?" (9:1) and "eat whatever is sold in the market or served at banquets" (10:25).

This hypothetical reconstruction is attractive because it suggests a single original problem occasioning 1 Corinthians, that is, the previous letter (5:9). It also suggests the various problems were not random or disconnected matters, but issues

14. Ibid., 88n8.   16. Hurd, *Origin of 1 Corinthians*.
15. Conzelmann, *1 Corinthians*, 4.

Paul himself had raised in the previous letter. The problem with this reconstruction as with other similar attempts, however, is that it is not easy in the text itself to see where Pauline thought gives way to Corinthian thought. Since we actually do not have the previous letter, and the only thing we know for certain is that it addressed immorality in the church, the reconstruction becomes further and further removed from the text we actually possess. Hurd himself was no doubt correct when, commenting on his "stage 2," he said, "The further we venture from our text, 1 Corinthians, (stage 4), the more precarious becomes our investigation."[17] But it must also be asked whether it is probable that Paul would have changed his view on substantive matters in such a short period of time. Moreover, Hurd's reconstruction in effect requires a different dating of Paul's life from that seen in Acts. For example, the Council of Jerusalem (Acts 15) must be placed after Acts 18.

Various reconstructions of Paul's correspondence with the Corinthians have been offered by some commentators with the purpose of attempting to help explain the progression of or aspects of Paul's argument in the epistle. Hurd highlights for the reader some of the matters that do require explanation if we are to understand what Paul is saying and how it is to be interpreted. However, we believe along with most recent major commentaries[18] that these can be explained from the progression of the epistle we have before us without resort to reconstructing an epistle we have never seen. Occasionally, and only where necessary, we tentatively reconstruct possible backgrounds for Paul's comments as he interacts with the Corinthian church but seek to do so drawing on what he writes more broadly in the epistle itself.

Corinth: The City

Though inhabited fairly consistently during the Mycenaean civilization (ca. 1600–1100 BC), it was not until around 800 BC that the city of Corinth seems to have emerged again as a strong and wealthy cosmopolitan town. By 400 BC it was one of the largest Greek cities with perhaps about ninety-thousand inhabitants. However, in 146 BC it fell to Roman invaders, was completely destroyed,[19] and was not reestablished until 44 BC when it was rebuilt by Julius Caesar. It was soon made the provincial capital of Greece and the seat of the Roman proconsul who governed the province of Achaia (27 BC). Gallio, mentioned in Acts 18:12–17, was one such proconsul. The city's position on the isthmus connecting mainland Greece and the Roman province of Achaia (the modern Peloponnese) and its harbor and port provision for major shipping routes connecting Adriatic and Mediterranean trade led

---

17. Ibid., 213.

18. E.g., see Fee, *1 Corinthians*, 16; Anthony C. Thiselton, *The First Epistle to the Corinthians: A Commentary on the Greek Text*, NIGTC (Grand Rapids: Eerdmans, 2000), 36–38; Fitz-

myer, *1 Corinthians*, 48–53; Mark Taylor, *1 Corinthians*, NAC 28 (Nashville: Broadman & Holman, 2014), 21.

19. Pausanias, *Description of Greece* 2.1.2.

to its strategic importance and its general prosperity. Strabo describes it like this: "Corinth is said to be prosperous because [it is] a place of commerce."[20] In terms of its economic status, Theissen draws attention to Corinth as a banking center and a center for "production from artisans."[21]

Though the emperor Nero later started to build a canal, linking the two sides of the isthmus (at its widest point about four miles or 6.4 km), it was never completed,[22] and in Paul's day cargo may have been hauled by land between the two port cities of Cenchreae (Rom 16:1) to the east and Lechaeum to the north on an ancient stone pathway known as the *diolkos*.[23]

The Social Context

By the time Paul arrived the city was composed of a mixed population of Greeks, numerous Romans, and many other arrivals from countries far and near. There may have been as many as one-hundred thousand inhabitants. It is therefore not surprising, as Bruce Winter reminds us, that the general social climate of the new city owed more to Rome than to Greece.[24] Even Corinthian architecture and city design imitated Rome with the temple dedicated to the emperor being of Roman design and raised above the level of others at the head of the forum.[25] Intriguingly, many inscriptions have been found in the excavations at Corinth, but virtually all from the time of the early church in Corinth are in Latin rather than Greek.[26]

When Paul writes that "not many of you were wise by human standards; not many were influential; not many were of noble birth" (1:26), he may well be reflecting upon the general social makeup of the city and not simply the church. The early Roman settlement of Corinth involved large numbers of freedmen,[27] that is, of former slaves who would have been relatively poor and, though coming largely from Rome itself, probably also came from places as far away as Egypt. One writer commenting on the

20. Strabo, *Geography*, trans. Horace Leonard Jones, 8 vols, LCL (Cambridge: Harvard University Press, 1917–32), 8.6.20.

21. Gerd Theissen, *The Social Setting of Pauline Christianity: Essays on Corinth*, ed. and trans. with an introduction by John H. Shultz (Philadelphia: Fortress, 1982), 101. Wayne A. Meeks, *The First Urban Christians: The Social World of the Apostle Paul* (Newhaven: Yale University Press, 1983), 48 and n265, draws attention to the city's well known bronze work, citing Pausanias, *Description of Greece* 2.2.1–4 and Pliny, *Natural History* 34.1, 6–8.

22. A canal was finally built in the late 1800s. However, it is too narrow for modern ships.

23. It is believed this stone structure that has become known as the *diolkos* was built in the late-seventh or early-sixth century BC. In a detailed article relating to the archaeology of this site, David K. Pettegrew has argued that the route was unlikely to have been frequently used to transport commercial goods. He argues that it was occasionally used for the haulage of warships, but also for moving "heavy building materials" from one side to the other of the isthmus and for enabling the "easy movement of goods produced on the isthmus . . . for export to market" (David K. Pettegrew, "The Diolkos of Corinth," *AJA* 115 [2011]: 549–74).

24. Bruce W. Winter, *After Paul Left Corinth: The Influence of Secular Ethics and Social Change* (Grand Rapids: Eerdmans, 2001), 7.

25. Ibid., 9.

26. J. H. Kent, *Corinth VIII.3: The Inscriptions, 1926–1950* (Princeton: American School of Classical Studies at Athens, 1966).

27. Strabo records that the new city had been settled "with people that belonged for the most part to the freedmen class" (*Geography* 8.6.23 [Jones, LCL]).

city said this: "What inhabitants, O luckless city, have you received, and in place of whom? Alas for the great calamity to Greece!"[28] However, the implication of what Paul writes is that some were indeed wealthy. This was a city open to entrepreneurs like Paul and Priscilla and Aquila. It was no doubt a place where fortunes were made by some and lost by others, all contributing to a complex world in which social status took on great prominence.

In writing his letter to the Romans from Corinth, Paul sends these greetings in Romans 16:23: "Gaius, who is host to me and to the whole church, greets you. Erastus, the city treasurer, and our brother Quartus, greet you" (NRSV). (The same Erastus may be in mind also in 2 Tim 4:20.) It is possible that Paul draws attention to these men because they were important community leaders, and it is worth noting their Latin names. As a city official, this Erastus was probably reasonably wealthy. The name and person has taken on special significance after inscriptions were found near the theater in Corinth. One reads, "Erastus in return for aedileship[29] laid this stone at his own expense," and another inscription may point to the same man: "The Vitelli, Frontinus, and Erastus [dedicate this] to. . . ."[30] In 1 Corinthians the listing of names such as "Chloe's people," Fortunatus, Achaicus, and Stephanas, may also indicate wealthier Christian business people with wide-ranging business interests (1:11; 16:17). The flourishing trade of the city is revealed in excavations of the central square where several small shops have been discovered. It would have been a shop like these that Paul and Priscilla and Aquila may have shared in their tent making.

Along with the influx of the many tradesmen and seafarers, every two years the city hosted the Isthmian Games.[31] This brought in many hundreds more people from far and wide and expanded business activity. Since it appears these games may have taken place during Paul's residency in the city, his illustration of the athlete in 9:24–27 would be especially relevant. Murphy O'Connor suggests that these games ranked below the Olympic games but above the games at Delphi and Nemea (see comments on 9:24–26). All of this meant that even during Paul's time this was a city growing in wealth and power and therefore was a vital place in which to establish the church of Christ. From here others would join the apostolic missionary enterprise and take the gospel far and wide.

It is likely that the tragic divisions between the wealthy and the poor, so noticeable in the eating of the Lord's Supper (11:17–22), simply reflected the ways in which

---

28. Crinagoras, *Greek Anthology* 9.284 (Murphy-O'Connor, *St. Paul's Corinth*, 49).

29. The office of aedile included maintaining the public infrastructure such as streets and the forum. It also involved collecting business taxes.

30. For detail on these inscriptions, see D. W. J. Gill, "Eras-

tus the Aedile," *TynBul* 40 (1989): 293–301, and A. D. Clarke, "Another Corinthian Erastus Inscription," *TynBul* 42 (1991): 146–51. Also see A. D. Clarke, *Secular and Christian Leadership in Corinth: A Socio-Historical and Exegetical Study of 1 Corinthians 1–6*, AGJU 18 (Leiden: Brill, 1993), 47–57.

31. Aelius Aristides, *Orations* 46.23.

people of different socio-economic backgrounds would have treated each other in the city. Much as in the modern world, wealth and learning would have brought increased social status. As people moved up the social ladder, they would have left behind those less fortunate, turning their back on their previous status and embracing their newly found social status. Paul's repeated concern in the epistle with the boasting of the elite is well understood against this background of society's scramble for public recognition and honor.

In recent years much has been written about social stratification in Hellenistic society and about how this may have impinged on the matters faced by Paul in the Corinthian congregations. In the 1970s Gerd Theissen wrote a series of influential articles relating the social context of first-century Hellenism to Paul's writings. One of the most significant starts with Paul's own comments on the social makeup of the Corinthian church in 1:26–29 and then seeks to set this within a Hellenistic literary and social framework to elucidate the importance of social stratification in order to understand the people and problems he encountered.[32] Another influential social description of the Hellenistic environment may be found in a volume by Wayne Meeks from 1983.[33] In many ways this set the scene for the more recent works referred to below in the commentary by Ben Witherington and Andrew Clarke.

Like most seaports today, Corinth was known for its immorality. Yet Corinth had a worse name than most. The name of the town even became a byword for sexual promiscuity, and to be a "Corinthiastes" was to be a profligate. There was even a proverb in both Greek and Latin: "Not for everyman is the voyage to Corinth."[34] However, as far as may be determined, much of this reputation is from the earlier Greek city, and it is important not to read too much into the letter simply because at one stage it was a particularly immoral town. For example, the accounts drawn from Strabo, mentioned in some earlier commentaries, of the temple of Aphrodite having a thousand temple prostitutes are surely from a time before the Roman conquest of the town.[35] It would be anachronistic to imagine that when Paul addresses activity in idol temples in 1 Corinthians 10, he has in mind such practices. Even so, as we learn from his correspondence, immorality was a serious matter. Indeed, if the epistle to the Romans was written from Corinth, then the vices listed in Romans 1:18–32 no doubt were to be found in towns like Corinth.

---

32. These articles are collected in the English volume already mentioned (Theissen, *Social Setting of Pauline Christianity*). See esp. ch. 2, "Social Stratification in the Corinthian Community: A Contribution to the Sociology of Early Hellenistic Christianity," 69–120.

33. Meeks, *First Urban Christians*.

34. Strabo, *Geography* 8.6.20 (Jones, LCL). Also cf. Horace, *Epistles* 1.17. However, Richard A. Horsley, *1 Corinthians*, ANTC (Nashville: Abingdon, 1998), 31, probably correctly notes that this likely referred to the intense "commercial competition" rather than to the unbridled sexual appetites of the city.

35. The original claim is made by Strabo, *Geography* 8.6.20; see also 12.3.36. Murphy-O'Connor, *St. Paul's Corinth*, 55–56, points out that it does not appear that there is any temple to Aphrodite that is of sufficient size from the Roman period for such a number of temple prostitutes.

The Religious Context

The social and religious contexts of the Corinth in which Paul had preached and to which he was writing can hardly be separated in the way the modern person might wish to do. Any society where religious practices so dominate the day-to-day life of citizens, as they did in the ancient Roman world, finds religion directly impinging on everything from trade to social acceptance and social status. A visitor walking down the main streets of any city in Paul's day would have been reminded of the plurality of the gods worshipped in the Roman Empire. First, there were the pillars that lined most main streets every few meters. On top of these would have been representations of the famous and noble people, but also of gods. Then there were multiple temples and shrines in all Greek and Roman cities, with certain temples and their gods having higher status in the city than others. The statues of deities could differ from city to city. An example found in Scripture is the notable Ephesian worship of Diana (Artemis in the Greek pantheon). She was the patron god of that city, but was worshipped in most others. In Corinth, excavations have revealed numbers of temples both extensive and small in size.

As the Romans rebuilt the city, they both accommodated the ancient Greek gods and drew some into their own pantheon or effectively equated some of their own with the ancient Greek gods. They also gradually introduced the imperial cult. While the extent of emperor worship in the early AD 50s is not clear, statues and images of Augustus and later emperors have been found in the ruins of ancient Corinth, and the Roman temple at the head of the forum was dedicated to the emperor. Other temples evidenced in the environs of the city include those dedicated to the ancient Greek gods Apollo (god of healing and prophecy) and his twin sister, Artemis (Diana in the Roman pantheon). Asclepius, son of Apollo and god of medicine, was also worshipped, as was Aphrodite, the god of love (Venus in the Roman pantheon). Poseidon (Neptune), the god of the sea, unsurprisingly had a significant temple in this port area. Other temples included those dedicated to the female gods Kore (also called Persephone) and her daughter Demeter, and the Egyptian gods Serapis and Isis, representatives of the mystery cults. Some decades later Pausanias writing in the second-century AD speaks of having seen twenty-six places of worship in Corinth.[36] But this should not be seen as exceptional. In Acts 17:16 when the apostle Paul was in Athens, we read that his heart was provoked by a city full of idols. When he visited the Areopagus, Acts 17:21–22 makes it clear that those with whom he engaged in conversation were "very religious" and particularly interested in any novel talk of gods.

The pervasive nature of religion in every area of life meant that temples served as places where business people and tradespeople would network and encounter friends. Indeed, it would have been difficult to conduct business without considering

---

36. Pausanias, *Description of Greece* 2.2.1–4.1.

the patron god. For example, the temple of Kore and Demeter and the Asclepius shrine both had a number of dining rooms. Early papyri offer examples of invitations to dinners, some in temple dining areas. In some examples, dinner invitations seem to be for nonreligious gatherings.[37] However, in others, the invitation is actually to dine in the temple of a god, or is even issued in the name of the god.[38] That the apostle had to face questions on how to behave in such a society was surely inevitable. Numerous questions relating to social gatherings in different contexts, religious and supposedly nonreligious, must have raised their heads as Christians sought to be a holy people in the midst of a world where, as Paul describes it in Romans 1:23, people had "exchanged the glory of the immortal God for images resembling a mortal human being or birds or four-footed animals or reptiles" (NRSV). The discussion in 1 Corinthians 8 and 10 of different approaches to different meals are well explained against this background.

It quickly becomes apparent in 1 Corinthians that Paul writes to those who were converted both from Judaism and paganism. The evidence for Jewish converts in the church is clear. He had preached first in the synagogue. His colleagues Priscilla and Aquila, among others, were Jews. Crispus, a leader in the synagogue, was the first convert (Acts 18:8; 1 Cor 1:14). Circumcised believers are also mentioned in 7:18. Paul also makes it clear that as he preached "to the Jews [he] became as a Jew, in order to win Jews" (9:20 NRSV). Part of a lintel has been found in the Corinthian excavations with the inscription "synagogue of the Hebrews," which offers external evidence for what was probably a substantial Jewish community in the city. Philo also refers to this Jewish community in Corinth.[39] Meanwhile, there is also evidence for numbers of converted pagans. It is for them that Paul expresses most concern in 8:7. Some church members, probably those with roots in paganism, were being invited to meals with unbelievers. Some were prepared to enter idol temples (8:10), something that could hardly be imagined of those who had grown up in Judaism. Others, again most likely those with Roman or Greek roots rather than Jewish, were happy to take advantage of the local court system (6:1). Unbelievers, most probably pagans, seem to have been invited in or wandered in to watch the church at worship (14:24–25).

There is no doubt the previous religious convictions of those who made up the church would have added to the complexity of the issues Paul addresses. More generally, though, whether from a Greek or Jewish background, converts were being influenced by their surrounding society. Social aspirations and pride of status in society, mixed with the ever-present religious aspect to all social, political, and business intercourse, no doubt led to enormous temptations to compromise for the sake of

---

37. E.g., *P. Oxy.*, 926.

38. Thus, for example, *P Coll Youtie* 51–55, cited in G. H. R. Horsley, *New Documents Illustrating Early Christianity*, vols. 1–4 (Sydney: The Ancient History Documentary Research Centre of Macquarie University, 1981–87), 1:5, is an invitation to dine at a "banquet of Lord Serapis." In *P Köln* 57 it is actually the god who invites (ibid.).

39. Philo, *On the Embassy to Gaius*, 281–83.

community acceptance and belonging. Paul's response is to point to Christ crucified, to the humility modeled at the cross, and to disciplined self-sacrifice for the gospel and for the sake of the holiness required of a people who must bring all glory to Christ the Lord.

In short, Paul's opening sentences addressing the Corinthians as "sanctified in Christ Jesus," as those "called to be his holy people" who "call on the name of our Lord Jesus Christ," and as having a God who is "faithful" and will sustain them to "the day of our Lord Jesus Christ" reveal both Paul's deep concern for a compromised people, but also the confident grounds for his hope (1 Cor 1:2–9). Their desire for status and their desire for acceptance and belonging must now all be found in Christ and in his church rather than in the values and attitudes of a self-obsessed, status-seeking, idolatrous paganism.

The Rhetorical and Literary Context

In recent years, much has been made of Paul's use of forms of classical rhetoric in his writing. This is noted at various points in this commentary. However, before we touch on the literary and oratory context in which he writes, it must be remembered that in the text itself the apostle reminds the reader that he stands apart, not just from the content of what other teachers and philosophers of his generation were promoting, but also from the manner in which such messages were normally persuasively communicated to an audience. Thus, in 2:1 he says he came not "with eloquence or human wisdom." He deliberately avoids certain sophistic conventions (see commentary on 2:1–5). Paul insists that the content of what he preaches, "Christ crucified," and the manner in which he preaches must not be separated. Any power in what he says is due to God's work and not his rhetoric. Nevertheless, it is clear that Paul writes with great care, occasionally using various epistolary and rhetorical conventions. Ben Witherington speaks of some of this as "micro-rhetoric," by which he means "the use of rhetorical devices within the NT documents—for instance the use of rhetorical questions, dramatic hyperbole, personification, amplification, irony, enthymemes (i.e., incomplete syllogisms), and the like."[40] However, as he readily admits, it is a different matter to go on to claim, as he and others have done recently, that a letter like 1 Corinthians may exhibit all or some of the characteristics of the formal rhetorical divisions of ancient speeches.

Aristotle's work *Rhetorica* is the oldest full treatise on rhetoric and influenced the whole Graeco-Roman period. In the first-century AD, Quintilian's *Institutio oratoria*[41] provides us with a detailed description of the principles of rhetoric and its

---

40. Ben Witherington III, *New Testament Rhetoric: An Introductory Guide to the Art of Persuasion in and of the New Testament* (Eugene, OR: Cascade, 2009), 7. For his outworking of some of this material in the exposition of 1 Corinthians, see *Conflict and Community in Corinth: A Socio-Rhetorical Commentary on 1 and 2 Corinthians* (Grand Rapids: Eerdmans, 1995).

41. This work was probably published in the last decade of the first century.

pervasive influence in the Roman Empire. Quintilian refers to rhetoric as "the good man, speaking well."[42] The three different categories of ancient speech rhetoric include: 1) "forensic" or "judicial" rhetoric, which was used both to accuse and to defend in legal cases and largely focused on past events; 2) "deliberative" rhetoric which, focusing largely on the future, was used widely in political debate to persuade an audience either toward or against some particular action; 3) "epideictic" or ceremonial rhetoric, which focused on the present and was frequently used in public gatherings to eulogize a person, whether in a funeral or for some city honor. These broader types of rhetoric could be further broken down into six divisions: the *exordium*, the *narratio*, the *propositio*, the *probatio*, the *refutatio*, and the *peroratio*.

Of special note with regard to the analysis of 1 Corinthians in terms of formal rhetoric is Margaret Mitchell's work on the epistle. This is a masterful contribution to the exegesis of the epistle and offers another strong argument in favor of viewing the letter as a single unit. However, her insistence that the epistle is "throughout a deliberative argument" for church unity probably overstates the matter and perhaps especially overemphasizes Paul's quest for church unity as the primary driving force of his argument.[43] More recently Bruce Winter has sought to locate Paul's correspondence in an opposition to the broader philosophical and rhetorical context of the sophistic movement.[44] His work also analyzes texts in 1 Corinthians in terms of their rhetorical character and seeks to demonstrate how Paul (and Philo) interacted with the movement, both countering it—specially by reference to the Old Testament—and yet also adopting some of its method.

In this commentary Paul's use of rhetorical devices are noted in a number of places. The possibility of viewing chapter 15 as a good example of deliberative rhetoric is commented upon, as is the advantage of seeing chapter 13 as an example of epideictic rhetoric. Beyond this, though, we believe the text functions more broadly than other examples of extended deliberative rhetoric and that viewing it solely in this way overly restricts the content and varied personal and corporate applications Paul provides in the letter. This lengthy letter, though undoubtedly read aloud to the church, is above all a personal communication and, in style, far from a piece of persuasive public oratory.

This epistle should primarily be read for what it is, a letter. Numbers of ancient letters are available for comparison, and certainly this sits well within the accepted

---

42. Quintilian, *Institutio oratoria* 12.1.1.

43. Margaret M. Mitchell, *Paul and the Rhetoric of Reconciliation: An Exegetical Investigation of the Language and Composition of 1 Corinthians* (Louisville: Westminster John Knox, 1991).

44. Bruce W. Winter, *Philo and Paul among the Sophists: Alexandrian and Corinthian Responses to a Julio-Claudian Movement*, 2nd ed. (Grand Rapids: Eerdmans, 2002), 188. See further in comments on 1:17. Sophists were trained in the "art" of rhetoric. Young sophists were taught how to speak as public orators. Training of this sort was a prerequisite in the first century AD for those entering the professional classes. In describing the sophistic movement in Corinth, Winter insists "Corinth was flush with sophists, orators and poets, and the intense rivalry which seemed to arise wherever two or three were gathered together . . . the sophists, because of their educational prowess, believed that they knew more than others" (ibid., 128).

norms of letter writing of Paul's day, although his is a much longer letter than other examples available to us. While Hellenistic epistolary conventions are briefly noted in the exegesis below, they are of little help in interpretation beyond the conventions of letter introductions and conclusions. The introduction and conclusion of this letter largely follow those conventions. Thus, in the introduction the name of the correspondent is given and the addressee is mentioned, followed by greetings and sometimes a thanksgiving for the one to whom the letter is written. In the conclusion, contemporary letters may include travel plans, but they almost always include further greetings, an autograph, and a final blessing. As noted in the commentary, Paul made use of these conventions but clearly adapted them to his Christian intent.

Interpreting 1 Corinthians: One Underlying Problem?

Given that it is difficult to say with any certainty that the group divisions give rise to most of the content of this epistle,[45] there is a need to ask whether some other underlying problem might provide a coherent understanding of the occasion for this epistle. The attempts at historical reconstruction have sought to do this but become too speculative. In reading this epistle, four main alternatives present themselves. The first two have been noted above, namely, that either the underlying problem is to be found in the four groups of 1:12, or that the problem may lie in Paul's own dealings with the Corinthians and their misunderstanding of his position, or the change in his position (as per Hurd).

A third view sees the letter largely as a loose arrangement of a number of basically unrelated problems with which Paul feels he has to deal. Then, fourthly, it is suggested that there probably was some underlying theological matter that had led to much wrong thinking and many wrong practices. The problems with the first and second possibilities have been noted. The idea that the epistle is an arrangement of basically unrelated ideas gives a dissatisfying picture of the church as a whole and fails to do justice to several themes that do recur, several of which are laid out in the opening few verses. If each problem is unconnected, we are also left with a view that Paul made an incredible mess of his eighteen months of teaching there.

It has been noted above that more recent commentators have tended to examine this epistle and interpret it in the light of its literary form and the social and religious milieu in which it was written. However, it is worth noting briefly how modern interpretation has drawn upon and yet also moved on from earlier work. Before the nineteenth century, scholars usually viewed the epistle as a response to a series of different issues connected by two factors: 1) the desire of Satan to split a church, and 2) leaders who had been corrupted by a desire for prominence.[46] In the nineteenth

---

45. E.g., it is hard to see how a particular group was to blame for the "disgraceful" behavior of women in church (14:35), or

for encouraging incest (ch. 5), or for eating idol meat (ch. 8).

46. See, e.g., John Chrysostom, *The Homilies of S. John*

century, however, commentators sought to reconstruct the historical situation in Corinth in the attempt to find a common factor behind these individual problems. Thus, in 1831 F. C. Baur attempted to define the characteristics of the "parties" mentioned in 1:12. He argued that two groups existed in the church: the one being Paul/Apollos and the other Christ/Peter. He believed that Paul faced Judaizers in Corinth as he had done in Galatia. The attacks on Paul were seen, then, as a new step in the Judaism/Paulinism controversy.[47] While, as we noted above, there are places that indicate Paul's congregation was partly Jewish, the fact that Jewish problems did arise does not necessitate the presence of a "Judaizing" group.[48] Further, there is no evidence of an ongoing battle of such proportions between a Pauline and Petrine Christianity as Baur's reconstruction requires.[49] Many at the end of the nineteenth century expressed dissatisfaction with Baur's thesis. In connection with 1 Corinthians, Godet claimed that some Hellenistic influence was present among Paul's opponents, but he still viewed the Christ-party as Judaizers, arguing that "nothing authorizes us to ascribe to Peter a conception of the Gospel opposed to that of Paul."[50] The Peter party was distinct and conceded more liberty than the legalists in the Christ party, but even the rigorists were people involved in "unsound speculations" rather than pharisaical Jews. Godet also suggested a likely parallel among gnostic writers.[51] This takes us on to those who believe that Gnosticism provided the background against which 1 Corinthians should be read.

In 1908 Lütgert argued, *contra* Bauer, that Paul was being attacked by antinomian hyperpneumatics, even Gnostics. They were the Christ party. Lütgert saw only this one camp opposing Paul: a pneumatic, hyper-Paulinist and gnostic group.[52] He also attempted to connect this pneumatic group with Paul's own preaching of liberty

---

Chrysostom, Archbishop of Constantinople, on the First Epistle of St. Paul the Apostle to the Corinthians, 2 vols, Library of Fathers of the Holy Catholic Church (Oxford: Parker, 1839), 1:2; John Calvin, *The First Epistle of Paul the Apostle to the Corinthians*, trans. John W. Fraser, ed. David W. Torrance and Thomas F. Torrance (Edinburgh: Oliver & Boyd, 1960), 9. Chrysostom regards the given names of the apostles in 1:12 as "masks" behind which pompous leaders hide. There is no separate "Christ" group, for Paul "added this of himself, wishing to make the accusation the more grievous, and to point out that by this rule Christ must be considered as belonging to one party only" (*Homilies on First Corinthians*, 1:24–25). Calvin also takes this position (*First Corinthians*, 24–25).

47. F. C. Baur, "Die Christus Partei in der Korinthischen Gemeinde," *Tübinger Zeitschrift für Theologie* 5 (1831): 61–206; cf. Baur, *The Church History of the First Three Centuries*, 3rd ed., 2 vols. (Edinburgh: T&T Clark, 1878), 1:61ff.; Baur, *Paul, the Apostle of Jesus Christ*, 2 vols. (London: Williams and Norgate, 1876), 1:269ff. This reflects his dialectical understanding of history: "Principle stood opposed to principle; and only the future development of Christianity could decide which of the

two principles would acquire the predominance over the other" (Baur, *Church History*, 1:63).

48. Cf. Conzelmann, *1 Corinthians*, 14n108. Luther laid some of the groundwork for seeing problems arising from a Judaizing Christianity. See Martin Luther, *Luther's Works, Vol. 28: Commentaries on 1 Corinthians 7, 1 Corinthians 15; Lectures on 1 Timothy* (Saint Louis: Concordia, 1973), 7.

49. H. J. Schoeps, *Paul: The Theology of the Apostle in the Light of Jewish Religious History* (Philadelphia: Fortress, 1959), 78ff. also suggests the controversy centers on Judaizing elements.

50. F. L. Godet, *Commentary on St. Paul's First Epistle to the Corinthians*, trans. A. Cusin, 2 vols. (Edinburgh: T&T Clark, 1889–90), 1:33–34; in 1:63–82 he allows for the existence of four separate groups at 1:12.

51. Ibid., 72–77.

52. D. W. Lütgert, *Freiheitspredigt und Schwarmgeister in Korinth: Ein Beitrag zur Charakteristik der Christuspartei* (Gütersloh: C. Bertelsmann, 1908). See especially pp. 49ff. for criticisms of Baur.

by suggesting that Paul's original gospel had been radically affected by Hellenistic thought in the Corinthian situation and had moved from its original content. He further argued that the Corinthian correspondence gave no indication of Judaizing problems. The Corinthians despised rather than feared Paul because he was not imposing and because the evidence of power and Spirit seemed to be missing.

Schlatter built on Lütgert's hypothesis of Jewish-gnostic opponents (influenced by their Hellenistic environment) but believed that their theology had been derived from a speculative Palestinian Judaism.[53] New leaders from Jerusalem arrived in the church and claimed they belonged to Peter. However, they were not Judaizers in the accepted sense. As the influence of these new leaders increased, so their criticism of Paul became sharper. When the Corinthians appealed to Paul or even Peter, the new leaders responded with an appeal to Christ. This was their expression of spiritual independence. Schlatter saw the difference between Paul and the opponents as a "different conception of the Gospel." The Corinthians substituted wisdom for faith.[54] This wisdom was not specifically Greek in conception but rather reflected Jewish "wisdom" ideas that came to prominence under syncretistic Hellenistic pressures. Paul's letter therefore spoke against the self-centered theology of the "wise" men. The wise expressed their wisdom through freedom. Paul did not discourage freedom but showed how in specific situations freedom should be balanced by love, thus avoiding an "autonomous ethic." Schlatter's emphasis on 4:6 and 4:8 and their specific association with a pneumatic group partly laid the basis for later talk of "over-realized eschatology."[55]

The desire to see one main theological problem arising from one set of opponents, who were gnostic, laid the basis for many others. Notably, W. Schmithals argued that Gnosticism provided the context for 1 Corinthians but refused to accept that it arose in Palestinian Judaism. Gnosis, he believed, was a *terminus technicus* of all religious language of Paul's day.[56] He found the root of the idea in the *Corpus Hermeticum*. Although others had presented hypotheses based on gnostic ideas, none achieved the detail presented by Schmithals. Certainly Schmithal's view does take seriously the existence of a religious vocabulary that appears only rarely elsewhere in Paul's letters, but the likelihood of a developed Gnosticism existing Corinth at the time of Paul's writing is widely dismissed today.[57] In the light of this, some have preferred to talk of "enthusiasts" or "spirituals," thereby partly leaving open the questions of the

---

53. Adolf von Schlatter, *The Church in the New Testament Period*, trans. Paul P. Levertoff (London: SPCK, 1955), 174ff.

54. Ibid., 174.

55. Many have argued that part of the problem Paul faced at Corinth was that of "realized eschatology." See R. M. Grant, *An Historical Introduction to the New Testament* (London: Collins, 1963), 204. "Over realized eschatology" is a phrase perhaps popularised by Thiselton. See Anthony C. Thiselton, "Realized

Eschatology at Corinth," *NTS* 24.4 (1978): 510–26.

56. Schmithals, *Gnosticism in Corinth*, 146.

57. Conzelmann, *1 Corinthians*, 15; Fee, *1 Corinthians*, 11–12; Birger A. Pearson, *The Pneumatikos-Psychikos Terminology in 1 Corinthians: A Study in the Theology of the Corinthian Opponents of Paul and Its Relation to Gnosticism*, SBLDS 12 (Missoula, MT: Scholars Press, 1973); E. Yamauchi, *Pre-Christian Gnosticism: A Survey of the Proposed Evidences*, 2nd ed. (Grand

provenance of these ideas, whether from mystery cults or from Gnosticism.[58] Others have talked of proto-Gnosticism.[59]

Multiple commentators have since added their voice to the views stated above, often disputing and sometimes defending previous conclusions. Certainly, the quest for a unifying theme or cause of the problems Paul faced with the Corinthian church has brought many benefits, not least that most scholars these days see the letter as a unit that deals with more than a series of random matters. In different ways, this commentary is indebted to many of the scholars mentioned, and this is noted through the text.

However, it is also our view that a particular *religious* problem to do with "community markers" provides the best understanding of the whole letter. Most communities have badges or markers of some sort that denote whether someone is part of the community or not part of it. Thus, some groups will have membership requirements; for example, a person has to live in a certain geographical region to be part of one community or else they belong to another. Some wealthy golf clubs may require a large financial deposit that will identify people as participants or members in their community. In religious circles, various "markers" can be seen around us on a daily basis. For example, women in Islam may be required to wear a head covering. Sikh men wear their hair long beneath a turban. In worldwide Christianity, the boundary marker for the community as people enter is that they must be baptized. Yet exactly what continues to mark them as members of the church, or as spiritual people, once they are "in" the church is part of the discussion Paul has here with the Corinthians. For Paul, it will come down to imitating Christ and be primarily seen in the outworking of love. However, it is easy to see how in almost any community these so-called "community markers" or "boundary markers" could become a source of pride and arrogance. After all, they are not just markers of who is "in," but they are also exclusive. Those who do not possess them are not part of the community, or not part of some inner or elite group within the community. In this Corinthian church, part of the problem Paul addresses is that some are insisting on the wrong "markers" and so have become arrogant and puffed up. The way Paul handles this, with his insistence on Christ crucified and on the authenticating nature of love, is therefore relevant to any who are tempted to seek Christian community markers or status in the wrong places. Below we normally use the word *marker* to identify this issue.

In our view Paul confronts a church of converts both from Judaism and from

Rapids: Baker, 1984); A. J. M. Wedderburn, "Gnosticism and Paul's First Letter to the Corinthians" (diss., Cambridge college fellowship competition, 1969), 189ff.

58. See, e.g., G. Bornkamm, *Paul* (London: Hodder and Stoughton, 1971), 71ff.; E. Käsemann, *New Testament Questions of Today* (London: SCM, 1969), 125ff.; R. A. Knox, *Enthusiasm: A Chapter in the History of Religion; with Special Reference to the XVII and XVIII Centuries* (Oxford: Clarendon, 1950), 9ff.

59. Proto-Gnosticism is merely descriptive of possible thought forms and words that were later used in Gnosticism. Thus, hypotheses accepting this background vary considerably; e.g., in emphasizing the Jewish or Greek background or taking different stances on the "groups," etc.

paganism. However, both groups lived in the same city and worked in the same business, social, and religious environment. That environment provided ample pressure on all to compromise in many areas of life. The seeking after knowledge and sophistry, and the desire for community status, belonging, and acceptance formed a formidable temptation. Without much deliberation, the wisdom and knowledge of the Christian faith, with their background in the Old Testament and their prominence in the grace-gifts, could quickly be accommodated to pagan values. As society sought markers and indicators of status and specially prized knowledge and wisdom, so did some of the Corinthian Christians. The only answer from Paul's perspective had to be a return to the gospel he had preached with its center in Christ crucified and the living out of the love that Jesus had modeled.

In this commentary, and again in common with several commentators, it is suggested therefore that the main underlying issue that Paul addresses concerns the possession of wisdom and knowledge. We will argue that the Corinthians regarded these as spiritual gifts and gave them a significance and importance that caused spiritual arrogance among some. In one way or another this gave rise to much of what Paul addresses. Paul's response is to return to the humbling centrality of the gospel message in which Christ is preached as the crucified Lord. In the end, while Corinthian arrogance "puffs up," it is only love that will reflect true commitment to the crucified Lord (8:1; 13:1–13). It will be seen that much of this epistle concerns standing in the community and before God in one form or another. For Paul, pride should have no place in this. Questions of status are not to be answered by appeal to God's gifts of wisdom, knowledge, or any other. Humble worship of the Lord and the humble building up of the church are what matters.

Outline of 1 Corinthians

Select Bibliography

Commentaries

Allo, Ernest B. *Saint Paul: Première Épître aux Corinthiens*. 2nd ed. Paris: J Gabalda, 1956.

Barclay, William. *The Letters to the Corinthians*. Revised edition. Philadelphia: Westminster, 1975.

Barrett, Charles K. *A Commentary on the First Epistle to the Corinthians*. 1st ed. HNTC. New York: Harper & Row, 1968.

Bengel, Johann Albert. *Gnomon of the New Testament*. Volume 3. Edinburgh: T&T Clark, 1877.

Best, Ernest. *Critical and Exegetical Commentary on Ephesians*. ICC. Edinburgh: T&T Clark, 1998.

Betz, Hans Dieter. *Galatians: A Commentary on Paul's Letter to the Churches in Galatia*. Philadelphia: Fortress, 1979.

Bittlinger, Arnold. *Gifts and Graces: A Commentary on I Corinthians 12–14*. London: Hodder & Stoughton, 1967.

Blomberg, Craig. *1 Corinthians*. NIVAC. Grand Rapids: Zondervan, 1994.

Bray, Gerald Lewis. *1–2 Corinthians*. ACCS. Downers Grove, IL: InterVarsity Press, 1999.

Bruce, Frederick F. *1 and 2 Corinthians*. NCB. Grand Rapids: Eerdmans, 1984.

Calvin, Jean. *The First Epistle of Paul the Apostle to the Corinthians*. Translated by John W. Fraser. Edited by David W. Torrance and Thomas F. Torrance. Edinburgh: Oliver and Boyd, 1960.

Chrysostom, Saint John. *The Homilies of S. John Chrysostom, Archbishop of Constantinople, on the First Epistle of St. Paul the Apostle to the Corinthians*. Library of Fathers of the Holy Catholic Church. Oxford: Parker, 1839.

Ciampa, Roy E., and Brian S. Rosner. *The First Letter to the Corinthians*. PNTC. Grand Rapids: Eerdmans, 2010.

Collins, Raymond F., and Daniel J. Harrington. *First Corinthians*. SP 7. Collegeville, MN: Liturgical Press, 1999.

Conzelmann, Hans. *1 Corinthians: A Commentary on the First Epistle to the Corinthians*. Hermeneia. Philadelphia: Fortress, 1975.

Dunn, James D. G. *1 Corinthians*. New Testament Guides. Sheffield: Sheffield Academic Press, 1995.

Edwards, Thomas Charles. *A Commentary on the First Epistle to the Corinthians*. London: Hamilton, Adams, & Co., 1885.

Ellicott, C. *St. Paul's First Epistle to the Corinthians, with a Critical and Grammatical Commentary*. London: Longmans, Green, & Co., 1887.

Fee, Gordon D. *The First Epistle to the Corinthians*. NICNT. Rev. ed. Grand Rapids: Eerdmans, 2014.

Fitzmyer, Joseph A. *First Corinthians: A New Translation with Introduction and Commentary*. AYBC 32. New Haven: Yale University Press, 2008.

Furnish, Victor Paul. *The Theology of the First Letter to the Corinthians.* NTT. Cambridge: Cambridge University Press, 1999.

Garland, David E. *1 Corinthians.* BECNT. Grand Rapids: Baker Academic, 2003.

Godet, Frédéric Louis. *Commentary on St. Paul's First Epistle to the Corinthians.* Translated by A. Cusin. 2 vols. Edinburgh: T& T Clark, 1889–90.

Hays, Richard. *First Corinthians.* Interpretation. Louisville: Westminster John Knox, 1997.

Héring, Jean. *The First Epistle of Saint Paul to the Corinthians.* Translated by A. W. Heathcote and P. J. Allcock. London: Epworth, 1962.

Hodge, Charles. *An Exposition of the First Epistle to the Corinthians.* New York: Robert Carter and Brothers, 1860.

Horsley, Richard A. *1 Corinthians.* ANTC. Nashville: Abingdon, 1998.

Kistemaker, Simon. *Exposition of the First Epistle to the Corinthians.* Grand Rapids: Baker, 1993.

Lias, J. J. *The First Epistle to the Corinthians.* The Cambridge Bible for Schools. Cambridge: Cambridge University Press, 1881.

Lightfoot, Joseph Barber. *Notes on Epistles of St. Paul from Unpublished Commentaries.* New York: Macmillan, 1895.

Lindemann, Andreas. *Der Erste Korintherbrief.* Handbuch zum Neuen Testament 9/1. Tübingen: Mohr Siebeck, 2000.

Luther, Martin. *Luther's Works, Vol. 28: Commentaries on 1 Corinthians 7, 1 Corinthians 15; Lectures on 1 Timothy.* Saint Louis: Concordia, 1973.

Meyer, H. A. W. *Critical and Exegetical Commentary on the New Testament. 1 Corinthians.* Edinburgh: T&T Clark, 1873–82.

Moffatt, James. *The First Epistle of Paul to the Corinthians.* London: Hodder & Stoughton, 1938.

Montague, George T. *First Corinthians.* Catholic Commentary on Sacred Scripture. Grand Rapids: Baker, 2011.

Morris, Leon. *The First Epistle of Paul to the Corinthians: An Introduction and Commentary.* Tyndale New Testament Commentaries. Grand Rapids: Eerdmans, 1958.

Murphy-O'Connor, Jerome. *1 Corinthians.* New Testament Message 10. Dublin: Veritas, 1980.

Orr, William F., and James Arthur Walther. *I Corinthians: A New Translation.* AB 32. Garden City, NY: Doubleday, 1976.

Parry, Reginald St. John. *The First Epistle of Paul the Apostle to the Corinthians.* Cambridge: Cambridge University Press, 1937.

Ridderbos, Herman. *The Epistle of Paul to the Churches of Galatia.* NICNT. Grand Rapids: Eerdmans, 1953.

Robertson, Archibald, and Alfred Plummer. *A Critical and Exegetical Commentary on the First Epistle of St. Paul to the Corinthians.* ICC. Edinburgh: T&T Clark, 1911.

Ruef, John S. *Paul's First Letter to Corinth.* Pelican New Testament Commentaries. Philadelphia: Westminster, 1977.

Sampley, J. Paul. "The First Letter to the Corinthians." In vol. 10 of *The New Interpreter's Bible.* Edited by Leander E. Keck. 12 vols. Nashville: Abingdon, 2002.

Schrage, Wolfgang. *Der erste Brief an die Korinther.* EKKNT Bd. 7:1–4. Neukirchen-Vluyn: Neukirchener, 1991–2001.

Senft, Christophe. *La Première Épître de Saint Paul aux Corinthiens.* CNT. Geneva: Labor et Fides, 1990.

Soards, Marion L. *1 Corinthians.* NIBC. Peabody, MA: Hendrickson, 1999.

Talbert, Charles H. *Reading Corinthians: A Literary and Theological Commentary on 1 and 2 Corinthians.* New York: Crossroad, 1987.

Taylor, Mark. *1 Corinthians*. NAC 28. Nashville: Broadman & Holman, 2014.

Thiselton, Anthony C. *The First Epistle to the Corinthians: A Commentary on the Greek Text*. NIGTC. Grand Rapids: Eerdmans, 2000.

Thrall, Margaret E. *I and II Corinthians*. Cambridge Bible Commentary. Cambridge: Cambridge University Press, 1965.

Walvoord, John F., and Roy B. Zuck, eds. *The Bible Knowledge Commentary: An Exposition of the Scriptures*. New Testament edition. Wheaton: Victor, 1983.

Weiss, Johannes. *Der erste Korintherbrief*. Göttingen: Vandenhoeck & Ruprecht, 1970 [1910].

Wolff, Christian. *Der erste Brief des Paulus an die Korinther: Zweiter Teil: Auslegung der Kapitel 8–16*. THKNT 7/2. Berlin: Evangelische Verlagsanstalt, 1982.

Other Works

Adams, Edward, and David G. Horrell, eds. *Christianity at Corinth: The Quest for the Pauline Church*. Louisville: Westminster John Knox, 2004.

Agnew, Francis H. "The Origin of the NT Apostle-Concept: A Review of Research." *JBL* 105.1 (1986): 75–96.

Arnold, Clinton E. *Ephesians*. ZECNT. Grand Rapids: Zondervan, 2010.

Asher, Jeffrey R. "Speiretai: Anthropogenic Metaphor in 1 Corinthians 15:42–44." *JBL* 120.1 (2001): 101–22.

Aune, David Edward. *Prophecy in Early Christianity and the Ancient Mediterranean World*. Grand Rapids: Eerdmans, 1983.

Baker, David L. "Interpretation of 1 Corinthians 12–14." *EvQ* 46 (1974): 224–34.

Barclay, John M. G. *Paul and the Gift*. Grand Rapids: Eerdmans, 2015.

Barrett, C. K. *Essays on Paul*. London: SPCK, 1982.

———. *The New Testament Background: Writings from Ancient Greece and the Roman Empire That Illuminate Christian Origins*. Revised Edition. San Francisco: HarperCollins, 1989.

Barré, Michael L. "To Marry or to Burn: Pyrousthai in I Cor 7:9." *CBQ* 36.2 (1974): 193–202.

Bartchy, S. Scott. *[Mallon Chrēsai]: First-Century Slavery and the Interpretation of 1 Corinthians 7:21*. SBLDS 11. Missoula, MT: SBL, 1973.

Barth, Markus. *Ephesians 4–6*. AB 34A. New York: Doubleday, 1974.

Bassler, Jouette M. "1 Cor 12:3: Curse and Confession in Context." *JBL* 101.3 (1982): 415–18.

Baur, F. C. "Die Christus Partei in der Korinthischen Gemeinde." *Tübinger Zeitschrift für Theologie* 5 (1831): 61–206.

———. *The Church History of the First Three Centuries*. 3rd ed. 2 vols. Edinburgh: T&T Clark, 1878.

———. *Paul, the Apostle of Jesus Christ*. 2 vols. London: Williams and Norgate, 1875–76.

Beasley-Murray, George Raymond. *Baptism in the New Testament*. Grand Rapids: Eerdmans, 1990.

Bedale, Stephen. "Meaning of *Kephalē* in the Pauline Epistles." *JTS* 5.2 (1954): 211–16.

Beekman, John, and John Callow. *Translating the Word of God, with Scripture and Topical Indexes*. Grand Rapids: Zondervan, 1974.

Beker, Johan Christian. *Paul the Apostle: The Triumph of God in Life and Thought*. Philadelphia: Fortress, 1984.

Bilezikian, Gilbert G. *Beyond Sex Roles: What the Bible Says about a Woman's Place in Church and Family*. Grand Rapids: Baker Academic, 2006.

Bock, Darrell L. *Jesus according to Scripture*. Grand Rapids: Baker, 2002.

Bornkamm, Günther. *Early Christian Experience*. New York: Harper & Row, 1969.

———. *Paul*. London: Hodder & Stoughton, 1971.

Bosch, Jorge S. *"Gloriarse" Segun San Pablo. Sentido Y Teología de* Καυχάομαι. AnBib 40. Rome: Biblical Institute Press, 1970.

Boswell, John. *Christianity, Social Tolerance, and Homosexuality: Gay People in Western Europe from the Beginning of the Christian Era to the Fourteenth Century*. Chicago: University of Chicago Press, 1981.

Bourke, M. M. "The Eucharist and Wisdom in I Corinthians." Pages 2:267–81 in *Studiorum Paulinorum Congressus Internationalis Catholicus 1961: Simul secundus Congressus Internationalis Catholicus de Re Biblica: completo undevicesimo saeculo post S. Pauli in urbem adventum*. 2 vols. AnBib 17–18. Rome: Pontificio Instituto Biblico, 1963.

Brown, Alexandra R. *The Cross and Human Transformation: Paul's Apocalyptic Word in 1 Corinthians*. Minneapolis: Fortress, 1995.

Bruce, F. F. *Paul: Apostle of the Heart Set Free*. Grand Rapids: Eerdmans, 1977.

Bultmann, Rudolf. *Theology of the New Testament*. Vol. 1. Translated by Kendrick Grobel. Scribner Studies in Contemporary Theology. New York: Scribner, 1951.

Burke, Trevor J., and J. K. Elliott, eds. *Paul and the Corinthians: Studies on a Community in Conflict: Essays in Honour of Margaret Thrall*. NovTSup 109. Leiden: Brill, 2003.

Byrne, Brendan. "Sinning against One's Own Body: Paul's Understanding of the Sexual Relationship in 1 Corinthians 6:18." *CBQ* 45.4 (1983): 608–16.

Byron, John. *Slavery Metaphors in Early Judaism and Pauline Christianity: A Traditio-Historical and Exegetical Examination*. WUNT. Tübingen: Mohr Siebeck, 2003.

Campbell, Constantine R. *Basics of Verbal Aspect in Biblical Greek*. Grand Rapids: Zondervan, 2008.

———. *Verbal Aspect, the Indicative Mood, and Narrative: Soundings in the Greek of the New Testament*. SBG 13. New York: Peter Lang, 2007.

Campbell, R. Alastair. "Does Paul Acquiesce in Divisions at the Lord's Supper." *NovT* 33.1 (1991): 61–70.

Carson, Donald A. *Exegetical Fallacies*. Grand Rapids: Baker, 1984.

———. *From Sabbath to Lord's Day: A Biblical, Historical, and Theological Investigation*. Grand Rapids: Zondervan, 1982.

———. *Showing the Spirit: A Theological Exposition of 1 Corinthians 12–14*. Grand Rapids: Baker, 1987.

Castelli, Elizabeth A. *Imitating Paul: A Discourse of Power*. Louisville: Westminster John Knox, 1991.

Cervin, Richard S. "Does *Kephalē* Mean 'Source' or 'Authority over' in Greek Literature: A Rebuttal." *TJ* 10.1 (1989): 85–112.

Cheung, Alex T. *Idol Food in Corinth: Jewish Background and Pauline Legacy*. JSNTSup 176. Sheffield: Sheffield Academic, 1999.

Chow, John K. *Patronage and Power: A Study of Social Networks in Corinth*. JSNTSup 75. Sheffield: JSOT, 1992.

Clarke, Andrew D. "Another Corinthian Erastus Inscription." *TynBul* 42 (1991): 146–51.

———. *Secular and Christian Leadership in Corinth: A Socio-Historical and Exegetical Study of 1 Corinthians 1–6*. AGJU 18. Leiden: Brill, 1993.

———. *Serve the Community of the Church: Christians as Leaders and Ministers*. First-Century Christians in the Graeco-Roman World. Grand Rapids: Eerdmans, 1999.

Coffin, Charles Porter. "The Meaning of 1 Cor 15:32." *JBL* 43.1–2 (1924): 172–76.

Cotterell, Peter. *Linguistics & Biblical Interpretation.* Downers Grove, IL: InterVarsity Press, 1989.

Cullmann, Oscar. *Christ and Time: The Primitive Christian Conception of Time and History.* Rev. ed. with a new introductory chapter. London: SCM, 1962.

———. *The Early Church.* Abridged ed. London: SCM, 1966.

Dana, Harvey E., and Julius R. Mantey. *A Manual Grammar of the Greek New Testament.* New York: Macmillan, 1957.

Danker, Frederick W., Walter Bauer, William F. Arndt, and F. Wilbur Gingrich. *Greek-English Lexicon of the New Testament and Other Early Christian Literature.* 3rd ed. Chicago: University of Chicago Press, 2000.

Danylak, Barry. *Redeeming Singleness: How the Storyline of Scripture Affirms the Single Life.* Wheaton, IL: Crossway, 2010.

Daube, David. "Κερδαίνω as a Missionary Term." *HTR* 40.2 (1947): 109–20.

Davies, William D., and David Daube. *The Background of the New Testament and Its Eschatology.* Cambridge: Cambridge University Press, 1956.

Deissmann, Adolf. *Light from the Ancient East: The New Testament Illustrated by Recently Discovered Texts of the Graeco-Roman World.* Rev. ed. New York: George H. Doran, 1927.

DeMaris, Richard E. "Corinthian Religion and Baptism for the Dead (1 Corinthians 15:29): Insights from Archaeology and Anthropology." *JBL* 114.4 (1995): 661–82.

Deming, Will. *Paul on Marriage and Celibacy: The Hellenistic Background of 1 Corinthians 7.* 2nd edition. Grand Rapids: Eerdmans, 2004.

Derrett, J. Duncan M. "Judgment and 1 Corinthians 6." *NTS* 37.1 (1991): 22–36.

DeYoung, Kevin. *What Does the Bible Really Teach about Homosexuality?* Wheaton, IL: Crossway, 2015.

Dio Chrysostom. *Discourses 1–11.* Translated by J. W. Cohoon. LCL 257. Cambridge: Harvard University Press, 1932.

———. *Discourses 12–30.* Translated by J. W. Cohoon. Loeb Classical Library 339. Cambridge: Harvard University Press, 1932.

———. *Discourses 31–36.* Translated by J. W. Cohoon and H. Lamar Crosby. LCL 358. Cambridge: Harvard University Press, 1940.

———. *Discourses 61–80. Fragments. Letters.* Translated by H. Lamar Crosby. LCL 385. Cambridge: Harvard University Press, 1951.

Dodd, Brian J. *Paul's Paradigmatic "I": Personal Example as Literary Strategy.* JSNTSup 177. Sheffield: Sheffield Academic, 1999.

Dodd, Charles H. *The Meaning of Paul for Today.* New York: Meridian Books, 1965.

Duff, Arnold M. *Freedmen in the Early Roman Empire.* New York: Barnes & Noble, 1958.

Dunn, James D. G. *Baptism in the Holy Spirit: A Re-Examination of the New Testament Teaching on the Gift of the Spirit in Relation to Pentecostalism Today.* SBT 15. London: SCM, 1970.

———. *Christology in the Making: A New Testament Inquiry into the Origins of the Doctrine of the Incarnation.* 2nd edition. Grand Rapids: Eerdmans, 1996.

———. *Jesus and the Spirit: A Study of the Religious and Charismatic Experience of Jesus and the First Christians as Reflected in the New Testament.* Philadelphia: Westminster, 1975.

———. *Romans 1–8.* WBC 38A. Dallas: Word, 1988.

———. *The Theology of Paul the Apostle.* Grand Rapids: Eerdmans, 1998.

———. *Unity and Diversity in the New Testament: An Inquiry into the Character of Earliest Christianity.* London: SCM, 1977.

Dupont, Jacques. *Gnosis: La Connaissance Religieuse dans les Épîtres de Saint Paul.* Dissertationes ad gradum magistri in Facultate Theologica vel in Facultate Iuris Canonici consequendum conscriptae 2.40. Louvain: Nauwelaerts, 1949.

Ellingworth, Paul. "Translating 1 Corinthians." *BT* 31.2 (1980): 234–38.

Ellis, E. Earle. *Paul's Use of the Old Testament.* Grand Rapids: Eerdmans, 1957.

———. *Prophecy and Hermeneutic in Early Christianity: New Testament Essays.* WUNT 18. Tübingen: Mohr Siebeck, 1978. Repr., Grand Rapids: Eerdmans, 1978.

English, Adam C. "Mediated, Mediation, Unmediated: 1 Corinthians 15:29: The History of Interpretation, and the Current State of Biblical Studies." *RevExp* 99.3 (2002): 419–28.

Epictetus. *Discourses, Books 1–2.* Translated by W. A. Oldfather. LCL 131. Cambridge: Harvard University Press, 1925.

———. *Discourses, Books 3–4. Fragments. The Encheiridion.* Translated by W. A. Oldfather. LCL 218. Cambridge: Harvard University Press, 1928.

Eriksson, Anders. *Traditions as Rhetorical Proof: Pauline Argumentation in 1 Corinthians.* ConBNT 29. Stockholm: Almqvist & Wiksell, 1998.

Fee, Gordon D. *God's Empowering Presence: The Holy Spirit in the Letters of Paul.* Peabody, MA: Hendrickson, 1994.

———. *Pauline Christology. An Exegetical-Theological Study.* Peabody, MA: Hendrickson, 2007.

Finlan, Stephen. *The Background and Content of Paul's Cultic Atonement Metaphors.* AcBib 19. Atlanta: SBL Press, 2004.

Fishbane, Michael A. "Through the Looking Glass: Reflections on Ezek 43:3, Num 12:8 and 1 Cor 13:8." *HAR* 10 (1986): 63–75.

Fitzgerald, John T. *Cracks in an Earthen Vessel: An Examination of the Catalogues of Hardships in the Corinthian Correspondence.* SBLDS 99. Atlanta: Scholars Press, 1988.

Fjärstedt, Biörn. "Synoptic Tradition in 1 Corinthians: Themes and Clusters of Theme Words in 1 Corinthians 1–4 and 9." Diss., Teologiska Institutionen of Uppsala, 1974.

Forbes, Christopher. "Comparison, Self-Praise and Irony: Paul's Boasting and the Conventions of Hellenistic Rhetoric." *NTS* 32.1 (1986): 1–30.

———. *Prophecy and Inspired Speech in Early Christianity and Its Hellenistic Environment.* WUNT 75. Tübingen: Mohr Siebeck, 1995.

Fotopoulos, John. *Food Offered to Idols in Roman Corinth: A Social-Rhetorical Reconsideration of 1 Corinthians 8:1–11:1.* WUNT 151. Tübingen: Mohr Siebeck, 2003.

Gagnon, Robert A. J. *The Bible and Homosexual Practice: Texts and Hermeneutics.* Nashville: Abingdon, 2001.

Gardner, Paul Douglas. *The Gifts of God and the Authentication of a Christian: An Exegetical Study of 1 Corinthians 8–11:1.* Lanham, MD: University Press of America, 1994. Repr., Eugene, OR: Wipf & Stock, 2017.

Gärtner, Bertil E. *The Temple and the Community in Qumran and the New Testament: A Comparative Study in the Temple Symbolism of the Qumran Texts and the New Testament.* SNTSMS 1. Cambridge: Cambridge University Press, 1965.

Gill, D. W. J. "Erastus the Aedile." *TynBul* 40 (1989): 293–301.

Grant, R. M. *An Historical Introduction to the New Testament.* London: Collins, 1963.

Gray, Patrick. *Opening Paul's Letters: A Reader's Guide to Genre and Interpretation.* Grand Rapids: Baker Academic, 2012.

Grudem, Wayne A. "Does *Kephalē* ('head') Mean 'Source' or 'Authority over' in Greek Literature: A Survey of 2,336 Examples." *TJ* 6.1 (1985): 38–59.

———. *The Gift of Prophecy in 1 Corinthians.* Lanham: University Press of America, 1982.

———. *The Gift of Prophecy in the New Testament and Today.* Rev. ed. Wheaton: Crossway, 2000.

———. "The Meaning of *Kephalē* ('head'): A Response to Recent Studies." *TJ* 11.1 (1990): 3–72.

———. "The Meaning of *Kephalē* ('head'): An Evaluation of New Evidence, Real and Alleged." *JETS* 44.1 (2001): 25–65.

Gundry, Robert H. "Ecstatic Utterance (NEB)." *JTS* 17.2 (1966): 299–307.

———. *Sōma in Biblical Theology: With Emphasis on Pauline Anthropology.* SNTSMS 29. Cambridge: Cambridge University Press, 1976.

Guthrie, George H. *2 Corinthians.* Grand Rapids: Baker Academic, 2015.

Hans-Joachim Schoeps. *Paul: The Theology of the Apostle in the Light of Jewish Religious History.* Philadelphia: Westminster, 1961.

Hanson, Anthony Tyrrell. *Studies in Paul's Technique and Theology.* London: SPCK, 1974.

Harrill, J. Albert. "Paul and Slavery: The Problem of 1Cor 7:21." *BR* 39 (1994): 5–28.

Harris, Murray J. *Slave of Christ: A New Testament Metaphor for Total Devotion to Christ.* NSBT 8. Downers Grove, IL: InterVarsity Press, 2001.

Harrison, James R. *Paul's Language of Grace in its Graeco-Roman Context.* WUNT II.172. Tübingen: Mohr Siebeck, 2003.

Hawthorne, Gerald F., Ralph P. Martin, and Daniel G. Reid, eds. *Dictionary of Paul and His Letters.* Downers Grove, IL: InterVarsity Press, 1993.

Hays, Richard B. "Relations Natural and Unnatural: A Response to J. Boswell's Exegesis of Rom 1." *Journal of Religious Ethics* 14.1 (1986): 184–215.

Heil, John Paul. *The Rhetorical Role of Scripture in 1 Corinthians.* Atlanta: SBL Press, 2005.

Hengel, Martin. *The Atonement: The Origins of the Doctrine in the New Testament.* Philadelphia: Fortress, 1981.

———. *Crucifixion in the Ancient World and the Folly of the Message of the Cross.* London: SCM, 1977.

Higgins, A. J. B. *New Testament Essays: Studies in Memory of Thomas Walter Manson, 1893–1958.* Manchester: Manchester University Press, 1959.

Hill, C. E. "Paul's Understanding of Christ's Kingdom in I Corinthians 15:20–28." *NovT* 30.4 (1988): 297–320.

Hooker, Morna D. "Authority on Her Head: An Examination of 1 Cor 11:10." *NTS* 10.3 (1964): 410–16.

———. "'Beyond the Things Which Are Written': An Examination of 1 Cor 4:6." *NTS* 10.1 (1963): 127–32.

———. "Hard Sayings: I Corinthians 3:2." *Theology* 69.547 (1966): 19–22.

———. *Jesus and the Servant: The Influence of the Servant Concept of Deutero-Isaiah in the New Testament.* London: SPCK, 1959.

Horrell, David G. *The Social Ethos of the Corinthian Correspondence: Interests and Ideology from 1 Corinthians to 1 Clement.* Edinburgh: T&T Clark, 1996.

Horsley, G. H. R. *New Documents Illustrating Early Christianity.* Vols. 1–4. Sydney: The Ancient History Documentary Research Centre, Macquarie University, 1981–87.

Howard, J Keir. "Baptism for the Dead, a Study of 1 Corinthians 15:29." *EvQ* 37.3 (1965): 137–41.

———. "Christ Our Passover: A Study of the Passover-Exodus Theme in 1 Corinthians." *EvQ* 41.2 (1969): 97–108.

Hull, Michael F. *Baptism on Account of the Dead (1 Cor:15:29): An Act of Faith in the Resurrection.* AcBib 22. Atlanta: SBL Press, 2005.

Hurd, John Coolidge. *The Origin of I Corinthians.* Macon, GA: Mercer University Press, 1983.

Hurley, James B. *Man and Woman in Biblical Perspective.* Grand Rapids: Zondervan, 1981.

Instone-Brewer, David. "1 Corinthians 7 in the Light of the Graeco-Roman Marriage and Divorce Papyri." *TynBul* 52.1 (2001): 101–15.

———. "1 Corinthians 7 in the Light of the Jewish Greek and Aramaic Marriage and Divorce Papyri." *TynBul* 52.2 (2001): 225–43.

———. "1 Corinthians 9:9–11: A Literal Interpretation of 'Do Not Muzzle the Ox.'" *NTS* 38.4 (1992): 554–65.

Jeremias, Joachim. *The Eucharistic Words of Jesus.* New Testament Library. London: SCM, 1966.

———. "'Flesh and Blood Cannot Inherit the Kingdom of God' (1 Corinthians 15:50)." *NTS* 2.3 (1956): 151–59.

———. *Infant Baptism in the First Four Centuries.* Library of History and Doctrine. Philadelphia: Westminster, 1960.

———. "This Is My Body." *ExpTim* 83.7 (1972): 196–203.

Jewett, Robert. *Paul's Anthropological Terms: A Study of Their Use in Conflict Settings.* AGJU 10. Leiden: Brill, 1971.

Johanson, Bruce C. "Tongues, a Sign for Unbelievers: A Structural and Exegetical Study of I Corinthians 14:20–25." *NTS* 25.2 (1979): 180–203.

Jones, Stanton L., and Mark A. Yarhouse. *Homosexuality: The Use of Scientific Research in the Church's Moral Debate.* Downers Grove, IL: InterVarsity Press, 2000.

Josephus. *Jewish Antiquities, Volume I: Books 1–3.* Translated by H. St. J. Thackeray. LCL 242. Cambridge: Harvard University Press, 1930.

———. *Jewish Antiquities, Volume IV: Books 9–11.*

Translated by Ralph Marcus. LCL 326. Cambridge: Harvard University Press, 1937.

Jourdan, George Viviliers. "KOINŌNIA in I Corinthians 10:16." *JBL* 67.2 (1948): 111–24.

Käsemann, Ernst. *New Testament Questions of Today.* Philadelphia: Fortress, 1969.

Kim, Seyoon. *The Origin of Paul's Gospel.* 2nd edition. WUNT II.4. Tübingen: Mohr Siebeck, 1984. Repr., Eugene, OR: Wipf & Stock, 2007.

———. *Paul and the New Perspective. Second Thoughts on the Origin of Paul's Gospel.* Grand Rapids: Eerdmans, 2002.

Kim, Yung Suk. *Christ's Body in Corinth. The Politics of a Metaphor.* Minneapolis: Fortress, 2008.

Kinman, Brent. "'Appoint the Despised as Judges!' (1 Corinthians 6:4)." *TynBul* 48.2 (1997): 345–54.

Klassen, William. "The Sacred Kiss in the New Testament: An Example of Social Boundary Lines." *NTS* 39.1 (1993): 122–35.

Klein, William W. "Noisy Gong or Acoustic Vase: A Note on 1 Corinthians 13:1." *NTS* 32.2 (1986): 286–89.

Kloppenborg, John S. "Analysis of the Pre-Pauline Formula 1 Cor 15:3b–5 in Light of Some Recent Literature." *CBQ* 40.3 (1978): 351–67.

Knox, R. A. *Enthusiasm: A Chapter in the History of Religion; with Special Reference to the XVII and XVIII Centuries.* Oxford: Clarendon, 1950.

Kovach, Steven D., and Peter R. Schemm Jr. "A Defense of the Doctrine of the Eternal Subordination of the Son." *JETS* 42 (1999): 461–76.

Kreitzer, Larry J. *Jesus and God in Paul's Eschatology.* JSNTSup 19. Sheffield: JSOT, 1987.

Kubo, Sakae. "I Corinthians 7:16: Optimistic or Pessimistic?" *NTS* 24.4 (1978): 539–44.

Kuck, David W. *Judgment and Community Conflict: Paul's Use of Apocalyptic Judgment Language in 1 Corinthians 3:5–4:5.* NovTSup 66. Leiden: Brill, 1992.

Lampe, Geoffrey W. H., and K. J. Woollcombe. *Essays on Typology.* SBT 22. Naperville, IL: AR Allenson, 1957.

Levertoff, Paul P. *Midrash Sifre on Numbers: Selections from Early Rabbinic Scriptural Interpretations.* Translations of Early Documents. Series III, Palestinian-Jewish and Cognate Texts (Rabbinic). London: SPCK, 1926.

Liddell, Henry George, Robert Scott, Henry Stuart Jones. *A Greek-English Lexicon.* 9th ed. with revised supplement. Oxford: Clarendon, 1996.

Lietzmann, Hans. *An die Korinther I–II.* 4th ed. HNT 9. Tübingen: Mohr Siebeck, 1949.

Lindars, Barnabas. *New Testament Apologetic: The Doctrinal Significance of the Old Testament Quotations.* London: SCM, 1961.

Louw, J. P., and Eugene A. Nida. *Greek-English Lexicon of the New Testament: Based on Semantic Domains.* 2nd ed. New York: United Bible Societies, 1989.

Lütgert, D. W. *Freiheitspredigt und Schwarmgeister in Korinth: Ein Beitrag zur Charakteristik der Christuspartei.* Gütersloh: C. Bertelsmann, 1908.

MacDonald, Margaret Y. "Women Holy in Body and Spirit: The Social Setting of 1 Corinthians 7." *NTS* 36.2 (1990): 161–81.

Macgregor, George H. C. *Eucharistic Origins: A Survey of the New Testament Evidence; Bruce Lectures, 1928.* London: J Clarke, 1929.

Malina, Bruce J., and John J. Pilch. *Social-Science Commentary on the Letters of Paul.* Minneapolis: Fortress, 2006.

———. *The New Testament World: Insights from Cultural Anthropology.* Rev. ed. Louisville: Westminster John Knox, 1993.

Marshall, I. Howard. *Last Supper and Lord's Supper.* Grand Rapids: Eerdmans, 1981.

Martin, Dale B. *The Corinthian Body.* New Haven: Yale University Press, 1995.

———. *Sex and the Single Savior: Gender and Sexuality in Biblical Interpretation.* Louisville: Westminster John Knox, 2006.

———. *Slavery as Salvation: The Metaphor of Slavery in Pauline Christianity.* New Haven: Yale University Press, 1990.

Martin, Ralph P. *The Spirit and the Congregation: Studies in 1 Corinthians 12–15.* Grand Rapids: Eerdmans, 1984.

McArthur, John. *Strange Fire: The Danger of Offending the Holy Spirit with Counterfeit Worship.* Nashville: Thomas Nelson, 2013.

Meeks, Wayne A. *The First Urban Christians: The Social World of the Apostle Paul.* New Haven: Yale University Press, 1983.

———. "'And Rose up to Play': Midrash and Paraenesis in 1 Corinthians 10:1–22." *JSNT* 16 (1982): 64–78.

Meier, John P. "On the Veiling of Hermeneutics (1 Cor 11:2–16)." *CBQ* 40, no. 2 (1978): 212–26.

Metzger, Bruce M. *A Textual Commentary on the Greek New Testament.* 2nd ed. Stuttgart: Deutsche Bibelgesellschaft/German Bible Society, 1994.

Mickelsen, Alvera. *Women, Authority & the Bible.* Downers Grove, IL: InterVarsity Press, 1986.

Mitchell, Alan C. "Rich and Poor in the Courts of Corinth: Litigiousness and Status in 1 Corinthians 6.1–11." *NTS* 39.4 (1993): 562–86.

Mitchell, Margaret M. *Paul and the Rhetoric of Reconciliation: An Exegetical Investigation of the Language and Composition of 1 Corinthians.* HUT 28. Tübingen: Paul Siebeck, 1991.

Mitton, Charles L. "New Wine in Old Wineskins." *ExpTim* 84.11 (1973): 339–43.

Moloney, Francis J. *A Body Broken for a Broken People: Eucharist in the New Testament.* Peabody, MA: Hendrickson, 1997.

Motyer, J. Alec. *The Prophecy of Isaiah: An Introduction and Commentary.* TOTC. Leicester: Inter-Varsity Press, 1993.

Moule, Charles F. D. *An Idiom Book of New Testament Greek*. 2nd edition. Cambridge: Cambridge University Press, 1959.

———. "The Judgment Theme in the Sacraments." Pages 464–81 in *The Background of the New Testament and Its Eschatology*. Edited by W. D. Davies and D. Daube. Cambridge: Cambridge University Press, 1956.

———. *Miracles: Cambridge Studies in Their Philosophy and History*. London: A. R. Mowbray, 1965.

Moulton, J. H., and G. Milligan. *The Vocabulary of the Greek Testament: Illustrated from the Papyri and Other Non-Literary Sources*. London, 1930. Repr., Peabody, MA: Hendrickson, 1997.

Mullins, Terence Y. "Greeting as a New Testament Form." *JBL* 87.4 (1968): 418–26.

Munck, Johannes. *Paul and the Salvation of Mankind*. Richmond, VA: John Knox, 1959.

Murphy-O'Connor, Jerome. "1 Corinthians 11:2–16 Once Again." *CBQ* 50.2 (1988): 265–74.

———. "Interpolations in 1 Corinthians." *CBQ* 48.1 (1986): 81–94.

———. *Keys to First Corinthians: Revisiting the Major Issues*. Oxford: Oxford University Press, 2009.

———. *Paul: A Critical Life*. Oxford: Oxford University Press, 1996.

———. *Paul: His Story*. Oxford: Oxford University Press, 2004.

———. "Sex and Logic in 1 Corinthians 11:2–16." *CBQ* 42.4 (1980): 482–500.

———. *St. Paul's Corinth: Texts and Archaeology*. Wilmington, DE: Glazier, 1983.

———. "Tradition and Redaction in 1 Cor 15:3–7." *CBQ* 43.4 (1981): 582–89.

———. "Works without Faith in 1 Cor 7:14." *RB* 84.3 (1977): 349–61.

Murray, John. *Collected Writings of John Murray*. Edinburgh: Banner of Truth Trust, 1977.

Niccum, Curt. "The Voice of the Manuscripts on the Silence of Women: The External Evidence for 1 Cor 14:34–35." *NTS* 43.2 (1997): 242–55.

O'Brien, Peter T. *Introductory Thanksgivings in the Letters of Paul*. NovTSup 49. Leiden: Brill, 1977.

Odell-Scott, David W. "Editorial Dilemma: The Interpolation of 1 Cor 14:34–35 in the Western Manuscripts of D, G and 88." *BTB* 30.2 (2000): 68–74.

———. "In Defense of an Egalitarian Interpretation of 1 Cor 14:34–36: A Reply to Murphy-O'Connor's Critique." *BTB* 17.3 (1987): 100–103.

———. "Let the Women Speak in Church: An Egalitarian Interpretation of 1 Cor 14:33b–36." *BTB* 13.3 (1983): 90–93.

Økland, Jorunn. *Women in Their Place: Paul and the Corinthian Discourse of Gender and Sanctuary Space*. JSNTSup 269. London: T&T Clark, 2004.

Osborne, Robert E. "Paul and the Wild Beasts." *JBL* 85.2 (1966): 225–30.

Oster, Richard. "When Men Wore Veils to Worship: The Historical Context of 1 Corinthians 11:4." *NTS* 34.4 (1988): 481–505.

Paige, Terence. "1 Corinthians 12:2: A Pagan Pompe?" *JSNT* 44 (1991): 57–65.

Panikulam, G. *Koinōnia in the New Testament: A Dynamic Expression of Christian Life*. AnBib 85. Rome: Biblical Institute, 1979.

Patterson, Orlando. *Slavery and Social Death: A Comparative Study*. Cambridge: Harvard University Press, 1982.

Payne, Philip B. "Fuldensis, Sigla for Variants in Vaticanus, and 1 Cor 14.34–5." *NTS* 41.2 (1995): 240–62.

Pearson, Birger A. *The Pneumatikos-Psychikos Terminology in 1 Corinthians: A Study in the Theology of the Corinthian Opponents of Paul and Its Relation to Gnosticism*. SBLDS 12. Missoula, MT: Scholars Press, 1973.

Perriman, Andrew C. "The Head of a Woman: The Meaning of *Kephalē* in 1 Cor 11:3." *JTS* 45.2 (1994): 602–22.

Peterman, Gerald W. *Paul's Gift from Philippi: Conventions of Gift-Exchange and Christian Giving.* SNTSMS 92. Cambridge: Cambridge University Press, 1997.

Pettegrew, David K. "The Diolkos of Corinth." *AJA* 114 (2011): 549–74.

Petzer, J. H. "Contextual Evidence in Favour of *Kauchēsōmai* in 1 Corinthians 13:3." *NTS* 35.2 (1989): 229–53.

Philo. *Allegorical Interpretation of Genesis 2 and 3.* Translated by F. H. Colson and G. H. Whitaker. LCL 226. Cambridge: Harvard University Press, 1929.

———. *On Abraham. On Joseph. On Moses.* Translated by F. H. Colson. LCL 289. Cambridge: Harvard University Press, 1935.

———. *On Providence.* Translated by F. H. Colson. LCL 363. Cambridge: Harvard University Press, 1941.

———. *On the Confusion of Tongues. On the Migration of Abraham. Who Is the Heir of Divine Things? On Mating with the Preliminary Studies.* Translated by F. H. Colson and G. H. Whitaker. LCL 261. Cambridge: Harvard University Press, 1932.

———. *On the Decalogue. On the Special Laws, Books 1–3.* Translated by F. H. Colson. LCL 320. Cambridge: Harvard University Press, 1937.

———. *On the Special Laws, Book 4. On the Virtues. On Rewards and Punishments.* Translated by F. H. Colson. LCL 341. Cambridge: Harvard University Press, 1939.

Phipps, William E. "Is Paul's Attitude toward Sexual Relations Contained in 1 Cor 7:1?" *NTS* 28.1 (1982): 125–31.

Phua, Richard Liong-Seng. *Idolatry and Authority: A Study of 1 Corinthians 8.1–11.1 in the Light of the Jewish Diaspora.* LNTS 299. London: T&T Clark, 2005.

Piper, John, and Wayne A Grudem. *Recovering Biblical Manhood and Womanhood: A Response to Evangelical Feminism.* Wheaton, IL: Crossway, 1991.

Plato. *Lysis. Symposium. Gorgias.* Translated by W. R. M. Lamb. LCL 166. Cambridge: Harvard University Press, 1925.

———. *Republic, Volume II: Books 6–10.* Translated by Christopher Emlyn-Jones and William Preddy. LCL 276. Cambridge: Harvard University Press, 2013.

Plevnik, Joseph. *Paul and the Parousia: An Exegetical and Theological Investigation.* Peabody, MA: Hendrickson, 1997.

Plutarch. *Lives, Volume I: Theseus and Romulus. Lycurgus and Numa. Solon and Publicola.* Translated by Bernadotte Perrin. LCL 46. Cambridge: Harvard University Press, 1914.

———. *Moralia.* Translated by F. Babbitt, W. Helmbold, P. De Lacy, et al. 15 vols. LCL. Cambridge: Harvard University Press, 1927–69.

Poythress, Vern S. "Linguistic and Sociological Analyses of Modern Tongues-Speaking: Their Contributions and Limitations." *WTJ* 42.2 (1980): 367–88.

———. "Nature of Corinthian Glossolalia: Possible Options." *WTJ* 40.1 (1977): 130–35.

Prothro, James. "Who is 'of Christ'? A Grammatical and Theological Reconsideration of 1 Cor 1.12." *NTS* 60 (2014): 250–65.

Reitzenstein, Richard. *Hellenistic Mystery-Religions: Their Basic Ideas and Significance.* PTMS 18. Pittsburgh: Pickwick, 1978.

Ridderbos, Herman N. *Paul: An Outline of His Theology.* Grand Rapids: Eerdmans, 1975.

Roberts, Alexander, and James Donaldson, eds. *Ante-Nicene Christian Library: Translations of the Writings of the Fathers down to A.D. 325.* Edinburgh: T&T Clark, 1867.

Robertson, A. T. *A Grammar of the Greek New Testament in the Light of Historical Research.* Nashville: Broadman, 1934.

Robinson, John A. T. *The Body: A Study in Pauline Theology.* SBT 5. London: SCM, 1952.

———. *Twelve New Testament Studies.* London: SCM, 1962.

Rosner, Brian S. *Greed as Idolatry: The Origin and Meaning of a Pauline Metaphor.* Grand Rapids: Eerdmans, 2007.

———. *Paul and the Law: Keeping the Commandments of God.* NSBT 31. Downers Grove, IL: InterVarsity Press, 2013.

———. *Paul, Scripture and Ethics: A Study of 1 Corinthians 5–7.* AGJU 22. Leiden: Brill, 1994. Repr., Grand Rapids: Baker, 1999.

———. *Understanding Paul's Ethics: Twentieth-Century Approaches.* Grand Rapids: Eerdmans, 1995.

Sampley, J. Paul. *Pauline Partnership in Christ: Christian Community and Commitment in Light of Roman Law.* Philadelphia: Fortress, 1980.

Sanders, E. P. *Paul and Palestinian Judaism: A Comparison of Patterns of Religion.* Philadelphia: Fortress, 1977.

Savage, Timothy B. *Power through Weakness: Paul's Understanding of the Christian Ministry in 2 Corinthians.* SNTSMS 86. Cambridge: Cambridge University Press, 1996.

Scanzoni, Letha. *All We're Meant to Be: Biblical Feminism for Today.* 3rd ed. Grand Rapids: Eerdmans, 1992.

Schaff, Philip, ed. *The Principal Works of St. Jerome.* Vol. 6 of *Nicene and Post-Nicene Fathers*, second series. Translated by W. H. Fremantle. Buffalo, NY: Christian Literature, 1893.

Schlatter, Adolf von. *The Church in the New Testament Period.* London: SPCK, 1955.

Schmidt, Thomas E. *Straight & Narrow? Compassion & Clarity in the Homosexuality Debate.* Downers Grove, IL: InterVarsity Press, 1995.

Schmithals, Walter. *Gnosticism in Corinth: An Investigation of the Letters to the Corinthians.* Translated by John E. Steely. Nashville: Abingdon, 1971.

Schnackenburg, Rudolf. *Baptism in the Thought of St. Paul: A Study in Pauline Theology.* Oxford: Blackwell, 1964.

Schoeps, H. J. *Paul: The Theology of the Apostle in the Light of Jewish Religious History.* Philadelphia: Fortress, 1959.

Schreiner, Thomas R. *Paul, Apostle of God's Glory in Christ: A Pauline Theology.* Downers Grove, IL: InterVarsity Press, 2001.

Scroggs, Robin. *The New Testament and Homosexuality: Contextual Background for Contemporary Debate.* Philadelphia: Fortress, 1983.

———. "Paul: *Sophos* and *Pneumatikos*." NTS 14.1 (1967): 33–55.

Segal, J. B. *The Hebrew Passover: From the Earliest Times to A.D. 70.* London Oriental Series 12. London: Oxford University Press, 1963.

Seneca. *Epistles, Volume II: Epistles 66–92.* Translated by Richard M. Gummere. LCL 76. Cambridge: Harvard University Press, 1920.

Shanor, Jay. "Paul as Master Builder: Construction Terms in First Corinthians." NTS 34.3 (1988): 461–71.

Smit, Joop F. M. *"About the Idol Offerings": Rhetoric, Social Context, and Theology of Paul's Discourse in First Corinthians 8:1–11:1.* CBET 27. Leuven: Peeters, 2001.

———. "Two Puzzles: 1 Corinthians 12:31 and 13:3: A Rhetorical Solution." NTS 39.2 (1993): 246–64.

Stacey, David. *The Pauline View of Man in Relation to Its Judaic and Hellenistic Background.* New York: Macmillan, 1956.

Stanley, Christopher D. *Paul and the Language of Scripture: Citation Technique in the Pauline Epistles and Contemporary Literature.* Cambridge: Cambridge University Press, 1992.

Storms, Sam. *The Beginner's Guide to Spiritual Gifts*. Minnesota: Bethany House, 2012.

Tertullian, Minucius Felix. *Apology. De Spectaculis. Minucius Felix: Octavius*. Translated by T. R. Glover and Gerald H. Rendall. LCL 250. Cambridge: Harvard University Press, 1931.

Theissen, Gerd. *Psychological Aspects of Pauline Theology*. Philadelphia: Fortress, 1986.

———. *The Social Setting of Pauline Christianity: Essays on Corinth*. Edited, translated and with an introduction by John H. Shultz. Philadelphia: Fortress, 1982.

Thielman, Frank. *Paul & the Law: A Contextual Approach*. Downers Grove, IL: IVP Academic, 1995.

Thiselton, Anthony C. "Realized Eschatology at Corinth." *NTS* 24.4 (1978): 510–26.

Tischendorf, Constantin von. *Novum Testamentum Graece*. Editio Stereotypa sexta decima ad editionem viii maiorem compluribus locis emendatem conformata. Lipsiae: B. Tauchnitz, 1904.

Tomson, Peter J. *Paul and the Jewish Law: Halakha in the Letters of the Apostle to the Gentiles*. CRINT. Assen: Van Gorcum/Minneapolis: Fortress, 1990.

Turner, Max. *The Holy Spirit and Spiritual Gifts: In the New Testament Church and Today*. Rev. ed. Peabody, MA: Hendrickson, 1998.

Vanhoozer, Kevin J. *Is There a Meaning in This Text? The Bible, the Reader, and the Morality of Literary Knowledge*. Grand Rapids: Zondervan, 1998.

Verbrugge, Verlyn D. *Paul's Style of Church Leadership Illustrated by His Instructions to the Corinthians on the Collection*. Lewiston, NY: Mellen, 1992.

Vines, Matthew. *God and the Gay Christian: The Biblical Case in Support of Same-Sex Relationships*. New York: Convergent, 2014.

Walker, William O. "1 Corinthians 2:6–16: A Non-Pauline Interpolation?" *JSNT* 47 (1992): 75–94.

Wallace, Daniel B. *Greek Grammar beyond the Basics: An Exegetical Syntax of the New Testament with Scripture, Subject, and Greek Word Indexes*. Grand Rapids: Zondervan, 1996.

Warfield, Benjamin Breckinridge. *Counterfeit Miracles*. New York: Charles Scribner, 1918.

Watson, Francis. *Agape, Eros, Gender: Toward a Pauline Sexual Ethic*. Cambridge: Cambridge University Press, 2000.

———. "The Authority of the Voice: A Theological Reading of 1 Cor 11.2–16." *NTS* 46.4 (2000): 520–36.

Wedderburn, A. J. M. "Gnosticism and Paul's First Letter to the Corinthians." Diss., Cambridge college fellowship competition, 1969.

Weima, Jeffrey A. D. *Neglected Endings: The Significance of the Pauline Letter Closings*. JSNTSup 101. Sheffield: JSOT Press, 1994.

Westerholm, Stephen. *Justification Reconsidered: Rethinking a Pauline Theme*. Grand Rapids: Eerdmans, 2013.

Westermann, William Linn. *The Slave Systems of Greek and Roman Antiquity*. Philadelphia: American Philosophical Society, 1955.

Whiteley, Denys E. H. *The Theology of St. Paul*. Philadelphia: Fortress, 1964.

Williams, Guy. "An Apocalyptic and Magical Interpretation of Paul's 'Beast Fight' in Ephesus (1 Corinthians 15:32)," *JTS* 57 (2006), 42–56.

Willis, Wendell Lee. *Idol Meat in Corinth: The Pauline Argument in 1 Corinthians 8 and 10*. SBLDS 68. Chico, CA: Scholars Press, 1985.

Winter, Bruce W. "1 Corinthians 7:6–7: A Caveat and a Framework for 'the Sayings' in 7:8–24." *TynBul* 48.1 (1997): 57–65.

———. *After Paul Left Corinth: The Influence of Secular Ethics and Social Change*. Grand Rapids: Eerdmans, 2000.

———. "Civil Litigation in Secular Corinth and the Church: The Forensic Background to 1 Corinthians 6:1–8." *NTS* 37.4 (1991): 559–72.

———. "Gallio's Ruling on the Legal Status of Early Christianity (Acts 18:14–15)." *TynBul* 50 (1999): 231–24.

———. "Lord's Supper at Corinth: An Alternative Reconstruction." *RTR* 37.3 (1978): 73–82.

———. *Philo and Paul among the Sophists: Alexandrian and Corinthian Responses to a Julio-Claudian Movement.* 2nd ed. Grand Rapids: Eerdmans, 2002.

———. "Puberty or Passion? The Referent of ΥΠΕΡΑΚΜΟΣ in 1 Corinthians 7:36." *TynBul* 49.1 (1998): 71–89.

———. *Roman Wives, Roman Widows: The Appearance of New Women and the Pauline Communities.* Grand Rapids: Eerdmans, 2003.

———. "Secular and Christian Responses to Corinthian Famines." *TynBul* 40.1 (1989): 86–106.

———. *Seek the Welfare of the City: Christians as Benefactors and Citizens.* First-Century Christians in the Graeco-Roman World. Grand Rapids: Eerdmans, 1994.

———. "St Paul as a Critic of Roman Slavery in I Cor 7:21–23." *Proceedings of the International Conference on St Paul and European Civilization.* Παύλεια 3 (1998): 339–54.

Wire, Antoinette Clark. *The Corinthian Women Prophets: A Reconstruction through Paul's Rhetoric.* Minneapolis: Fortress, 1990.

Witherington III, Ben. *Conflict and Community in Corinth: A Socio-Rhetorical Commentary on 1 and 2 Corinthians.* Grand Rapids: Eerdmans, 1994.

———. *New Testament Rhetoric: An Introductory Guide to the Art of Persuasion in and of the New Testament.* Eugene, OR: Cascade, 2009.

———. "Not So Idle Thoughts about Eidolothuton." *TynBul* 44.2 (1993): 237–54.

———. *Women and the Genesis of Christianity.* Cambridge: Cambridge University Press, 1990.

———. *Women in the Earliest Churches.* SNTSMS 59. Cambridge: Cambridge University Press, 1991.

Wright, J. Robert. "Boswell on Homosexuality: A Case Undemonstrated." *AThR* 66.1 (1984): 79–94.

Wright, Nicholas Thomas. *Paul and the Faithfulness of God.* Christian Origins and the Question of God 4. Minneapolis: Fortress, 2013.

———. *The Resurrection of the Son of God.* Christian Origins and the Question of God 3. Minneapolis: Fortress, 2003.

———. *Surprised by Hope: Rethinking Heaven, the Resurrection, and the Mission of the Church.* New York: Harper, 2008.

Yamauchi, E. *Pre-Christian Gnosticism. A Survey of the Proposed Evidences.* 2nd ed. Grand Rapids: Baker, 1984.

Zuntz, Günther. *The Text of the Epistles: A Disquisition upon the Corpus Paulinum.* Schweich Lectures, 1946. London: Oxford University Press, 1953.

1 Corinthians 1:1–9

Literary Context

Paul's letter to the Corinthian church begins in a form similar to that found in various Hellenistic letters. An initial greeting mentions the sender and those who are being addressed and often includes some form of thanksgiving. However, Paul expands on this form in a distinctively Christian manner. He draws attention to the fact that both sender, Paul, and recipients, the Corinthians, are called by God in service of the Lord Jesus Christ (vv. 1–2). His greeting functions more like a prayer (v. 3). Paul desires that the Corinthian Christians should remember and experience the grace and peace that they have received from God and from Christ.

The expansion of the thanksgiving then emphasizes the grace they have received in Christ. This "enrichment" included gifts from God. Mention of these allows Paul in his introduction to touch upon a subject to which he will return in due course (specially in chs. 8–14) and which, in one way or another, will underlie most of the letter. Though specific gifts have been abused by the Corinthians, the opening greeting functions to draw all attention to God and the Lord Jesus rather than to either the sender or the recipients. It also reminds the readers of their current context in which they await "the day of our Lord Jesus Christ" (v. 8). Since it is God alone who can sustain them in this wait, Paul concludes this opening by reminding them that God is faithful.

➡ **I. Introduction to the Letter (1:1–9)**
   II. Paul's Dismay at the Lack of Unity (1:10–17)
   III. A Radically Different Perspective Shaped by the Cross (1:18–2:5)

Main Idea

Paul and Sosthenes, the senders of this letter, greet the Corinthian church as God's called and sanctified people. Paul thanks God for his grace evident among them in their calling and in the grace-gifts they have received in Christ. He affirms Christ's lordship and God's faithfulness in regard to his people.

Translation

1 Corinthians 1:1–9

1a	Correspondent	**Paul,**
b	Assertion of authority	called [to be] an apostle of Christ Jesus
c	Agency	through the will of God
d	Correspondent #2	and **Sosthenes [our] brother**
2a	Recipients	to the church of God that is in Corinth,
b	Apposition	to those sanctified in Christ Jesus,
c	Apposition	[to those] called [to be] saints,
d	Expansion	together with all who call upon the name of our Lord Jesus Christ
e	Place	in every place,
		their [Lord] and ours:
3a	Greeting	**grace and peace** **to you**
b	Source of 3a	from God our Father and the Lord Jesus Christ.
4a	Thanksgiving	**I give thanks to my God always for you**
b	Reason	because of the grace of God given you in Christ Jesus,
5a	1st explanation of 4b	for in everything you ✍
		were made rich in him
b	Expansion	in all speech and all knowledge,
6a		because the testimony to Christ was ✍
		confirmed among you,
7a	Result of 5a	so that you may not ✍
		lack any grace-gift
b	Temporal	while awaiting the revealing
		of our Lord Jesus Christ;
8a	2nd explanation of 4b (the grace given them)	and he will establish you until the end
b	Description of 8a	unimpeachable on the day of our ✍ Lord Jesus Christ.
9a	Assertion	**God is faithful,**
b	Means (also agency)	through whom you were called
c	Location	into covenant participation with his Son,
d	Apposition	Jesus Christ our Lord.

Structure

This opening section of the epistle is carefully constructed in a way that provides for the conventional mention of sender, recipient, and greeting (including thanksgiving) and yet draws the readers' attention to God and to Christ, the source of all grace and peace. Drawing attention away from self toward God and Christ will later form part of Paul's appeal that they should stop their boasting and factionalism. The repetition of "Jesus Christ" (or other forms of the name such as "Christ Jesus") and of "God" serve to emphasize this. Thus, we see reference to "God" six times and reference to "Jesus" eight times in these nine verses.

Both Paul and the recipients are identified by their "calling" (vv. 1, 2, 9). In v. 2 a series of datives indicates the people to whom the apostle is writing, with v. 2b expanding upon v. 2a, and v. 2c in apposition to v. 2b. God the Father and Jesus Christ are both seen to be the source of grace and peace (v. 3).

The main clause of vv. 4–8 is "I give thanks . . ." (Εὐχαριστῶ). This is followed by a number of subordinate clauses, each further expanding upon the reasons why Paul gives thanks for them. It is in these clauses that Paul gently raises the issue of "gifts" that will become important through the letter. He specifically mentions "speech and knowledge."

The emphasis (v. 9) on God being "faithful" (πιστός), together with the following subordinate clause of agency, usefully summarize this opening section by insisting that God is the one who "called" them and that their future is dependent upon his sovereign grace. However, the mention of being called into "covenant participation with his Son" (εἰς κοινωνίαν τοῦ υἱοῦ αὐτοῦ) also functions to prepare the readers for what is to come, for Paul is about to talk of their divisions and will later return to the nature of this "fellowship" in more detail in chapter ten.

Exegetical Outline

→ **I. Introduction to the Letter (1:1–9)**

    A. The Greeting (1:1–3)

        1. God's Calling (1:1–2)

            a. Paul's Calling as Apostle (the Sender) (1:1)

            b. The Corinthian Calling (the Recipients) (1:2)

        2. God's Grace (1:3)

    B. Thanksgiving (1:4–9)

        1. For the Riches of God's Grace in Christ Jesus (1:4–7)

        2. For God's Faithfulness to Them (1:8–9)

Explanation of the Text

1:1 Paul, called [to be] an apostle of Christ Jesus through the will of God and Sosthenes [our] brother (Παῦλος κλητὸς ἀπόστολος Χριστοῦ Ἰησοῦ διὰ θελήματος θεοῦ, καὶ Σωσθένης ὁ ἀδελφός). Both Paul and Sosthenes are the senders of this letter, though after these first three verses, the first-person singular dominates,[1] and it becomes clear that Paul himself is writing or at least dictating. He describes himself as called by God to be "an apostle."

The emphasis on Paul's calling opens this section and leads into a discussion of the calling of the Corinthians (vv. 2, 9). Most of Paul's letters, except Philippians and Philemon, open with this affirmation of authority. While the word "apostle" can refer to one who is sent out, or a messenger (cf. 2 Cor 8:23; Phil 2:25),[2] in the New Testament it generally refers to those originally chosen by Jesus as disciples (Mark 3:14–15) and to just a few others. An apostle was an eyewitness of the risen Lord Jesus and so especially called by God to "become an official witness to his [Jesus's] resurrection and who has been commissioned by him to preach the word in a way fundamental to its spread."[3] Paul's calling has come "through the will of God," referring probably to his unique vision of the risen Lord Jesus on the Damascus Road (Acts 9:1–7; 1 Cor 9:1; Gal 1:12). In this epistle Paul will appeal strongly to the authority inherent in this calling as he both encourages and rebukes the church (1:10; 9:1–27; 15:7–9; cf. 4:9; 12:28–29).[4]

Sosthenes is not identified as an apostle, but the fact that he is called "brother" suggests he was known to the Corinthians. He may have been the leader of the synagogue in Corinth when Paul was preaching the gospel of Christ in the town (Acts 18:17). If so, he must now have been working at Paul's side and may have been his amanuensis and even carried the letter to the Corinthians.

"Through the will of God" (διὰ θελήματος θεοῦ) indicates agency, that is, *by* God. Paul is clear that his calling lies deep within the plans and purposes of God himself. He does not write as one who became an apostle by a leading that he felt within him, nor even because of his desire to serve the Lord, but because God willed the gospel of Jesus Christ to be delivered through apostles. This is a statement about the nature of apostolic authority that is founded in the purposes of God himself.[5] Paul returns to issues raised by his apostolic authority in 2:6–13, 4:9–16, and in 9:1–27.

To have been "called" (κλητός) by God to be an apostle of "Christ Jesus" and thus to have a foundational role in proclaiming, interpreting, and demonstrating the gospel of Jesus Christ in his life might have been regarded as an arrogant claim, even a boast. Yet the Corinthians' complaint about Paul was that he was not like this, and his bearing was hardly that of a person who had the "authority" of Christ. In fact, Paul was not boastful. Rather, he presented the gospel in weakness of speech (1:17) and also through what appeared to be a weak life (see 2 Cor 10–11). In doing this he both spoke and lived out the message of Christ, following in his footsteps and even in his sufferings. This opening is, then, a strong claim to authority founded

---

1. The first plural is first used in 2:6, but it is unlikely that Paul is referring there to Sosthenes. Rather, he is referring to the other apostles or to the apostolic witness generally.

2. See further discussion at 9:4.

3. F. H. Agnew, "The Origin of the NT Apostle-Concept: A Review of Research," *JBL* 105 (1986): 75–96 (see 77).

4. For a lengthy discussion on Paul's apostolic authority and the way he used this, see J. D. G. Dunn, *The Theology of Paul the Apostle* (Grand Rapids: Eerdmans, 1998), 571–80.

5. This recalls a similar though stronger statement in Gal 1:1.

in both God the Father and in Jesus Christ. Paul will develop further the nature of this calling as he speaks against the divisive Corinthian view of power and wisdom.

1:2 to the church of God that is in Corinth, to those sanctified in Christ Jesus, [to those] called [to be] saints, together with all who call upon the name of our Lord Jesus Christ in every place, their [Lord] and ours: (τῇ ἐκκλησίᾳ τοῦ θεοῦ τῇ οὔσῃ ἐν Κορίνθῳ, ἡγιασμένοις ἐν Χριστῷ Ἰησοῦ, κλητοῖς ἁγίοις, σὺν πᾶσιν τοῖς ἐπικαλουμένοις τὸ ὄνομα τοῦ κυρίου ἡμῶν Ἰησοῦ Χριστοῦ ἐν παντὶ τόπῳ, αὐτῶν καὶ ἡμῶν). Paul now identifies the recipients of the letter and greets them. He is writing "to the church of God" (τοῦ θεοῦ—a genitive of possession). This is an important statement in light of what will follow. Right at the start Paul reminds them that they are *God's* church. "The church does not 'belong' to any of its in-groups or leaders, but to God."[6] When Paul tackles them head-on in 3:9–17, it is notable he repeats "of God" some eight times (θεοῦ and τοῦ θεοῦ). God has brought into being *his* church "that is in Corinth" (adjectival participle τῇ οὔσῃ ἐν Κορίνθῳ). This gathering of people who believed in Jesus Christ probably met together in houses for worship, but here the use of the singular "church" helps identify the very unity which they are failing to reflect. The church is not, of course, a building but the people who believe. Thus, Paul further expands upon the nature of those to whom he writes.

First he writes "to the sanctified in Christ Jesus" (ἡγιασμένοις). This perfect passive participle functions as a noun (substantive). As Paul moves from the singular "church" to the plural, so he talks to all

the people who make up this one united organism of the church at Corinth. The designation of God's people as "sanctified" recalls the people of Israel who were called out by God to be a "holy" nation (Exod 19:6 LXX; ἔθνος ἅγιον). That is, they were a people who were "set apart" to God for his own possession, belonging to a holy God who is perfect in righteousness. God's people were called into being to reflect who he is, including his holiness. In 1 Corinthians 6:11 Paul reminds the Corinthians that they gained their status as "sanctified" people in the past when they came to faith in Christ. Just as "you were washed" and "justified," he says, so "you were sanctified" (aorist passive: ἡγιάσθητε). But here in 1:2 the perfect tense points to the present outcome of God's past action (note the passive voice). What happened "in Christ Jesus" results in a new community of people who are to be the "holy" people they have been called to be.

Thus, secondly, Paul adds that he writes "[to those] called [to be] saints"[7] (κλητοῖς ἁγίοις). Just as Paul was called by God to be an apostle, so now Paul reminds the Corinthians that God has called them as well to a specific role in which they will reflect a holiness of community and life. Perhaps the LXX of Leviticus 11:44 lies behind Paul's thinking here, as the Israelites are told that they will be a "sanctified" people and are also challenged to be "holy" (καὶ ἁγιασθήσεσθε καὶ ἅγιοι ἔσεσθε). Notably, Paul will pursue the issue of the need for a sanctified people actually to behave as a holy people in 1 Corinthians 6 and 7.

Thirdly, Paul further expands upon this constituency of those who are "called to be saints." It is not that Paul is expanding the scope of this letter so

---

6. Thiselton, *1 Corinthians*, 74.

7. Some, e.g., Fee, *1 Corinthians*, 29, object to translating ἅγιοι as "saints" on the grounds that the word is misleading these days. It is often used of those who may seem *extra* holy, like *Saint* Paul, for example. However, provided it is understood, the word refers here to *all* who "call upon the name of our Lord Jesus Christ in every place," then there can be no real reason for trying to find a substitute. In fact, the word should be reclaimed from its misleading connotations.

that it is now "to all in every place." This would be a tortuous rendering of the Greek. Rather, Paul is saying that many others are called to be saints, not just the Corinthians. Indeed, all those who "call" upon the name of the Lord Jesus Christ belong to him. This present participle of the verb "to call" (ἐπικαλέω) is in the middle voice and usually describes calling upon God or the gods to perform something.[8] Thus, in Acts 2:21 we read "everyone who calls upon the name of the Lord" shall be saved (ὃς ἂν ἐπικαλέσηται τὸ ὄνομα κυρίου—aorist, middle subjunctive). Calling on the name of the Lord is drawn here from Joel 2:32 (3:5 LXX; "And everyone who calls on the name of the LORD will be saved"). In its original context Joel looks forward to the day when the Spirit will be poured out on all flesh (v. 28) and the Lord will come to judge and to deliver his people out of the hands of their enemies. Here Paul interprets the verse in terms of Christ's saving lordship. It is this strong, covenant, protecting "lordship" that Paul seems to have in mind here as he speaks of the "name of the Lord." Calling on his name, therefore, indicates having faith in him and worshipping and serving him but also being obedient to him. "Name" here refers to all that he is. The fact that there are people "in every place" who call on the Lord serves to remind the Corinthians of the great geographic expansion of God's church. They are not the center of the universe as far as God is concerned!

The final phrase of this verse "their [Lord] and ours" (αὐτῶν καὶ ἡμῶν) could possibly be taken with "place,"[9] but this seems strained and makes little sense. It is more likely to be an expansion of "our [ἡμῶν] Lord Jesus Christ . . . their [Lord] and ours."

This simple addition further reminds the Corinthians, whom we later discover are divided and self-obsessed, that they are under the same Lord as any other local congregation of God's people.

1:3 grace and peace to you from God our Father and the Lord Jesus Christ. (χάρις ὑμῖν καὶ εἰρήνη ἀπὸ θεοῦ πατρὸς ἡμῶν καὶ κυρίου Ἰησοῦ Χριστοῦ). Thus, having identified in detail those to whom the letter is sent, Paul greets them with the simple expression, "grace and peace." Although derived from a traditional greeting at the start of letters, this greeting is peculiarly Christian. After mentioning the sender and the recipient, letters of Paul's day would often simply contain the word "greetings" (χαίρειν).[10] We see this usage in a letter in Acts 15:23. However, Paul transforms the idea into something much deeper than simple greetings. This is a "wish-prayer"[11] in which grace and peace are invoked upon those to whom he writes.

Grace. Here in v. 3, the word is defined by Paul's reference to its origin, "from God our Father and the Lord Jesus Christ." Both God's calling and his continued provision for his people (v. 2) are surely in mind in this prayerful greeting. However, since Paul uses the word "grace" again in v. 4, it is best to examine the word in a little more detail at this point. The grace to which he refers here is, again, not simply the grace received so that people may come to faith, but the grace that has "enriched" them in order to benefit the community. Paul looks back to its origin in God as he uses the aorist passive, "was given" (v. 4).

The word "grace" (χάρις) is one of the most loved of all Christian words. Its origins lie in the

---

8. It is unlikely there is any intensifying force in this middle voice, such as is discussed by David E. Garland, *1 Corinthians*, BECNT (Grand Rapids: Baker Academic, 2003), 29n6.

9. Witherington, in *Conflict and Community*, 80, regards "place" as referring to "meeting place" and suggests "theirs and ours" therefore is to be taken as descriptive of different meeting places.

10. E.g., *P. Oxy.* 932: "Thais to her Tigrios, greetings." For further examples of salutations in first-century letters, see Patrick Gray, *Opening Paul's Letters: A Reader's Guide to Genre and Interpretation* (Grand Rapids: Baker, 2012).

11. Thiselton, *1 Corinthians*, 81.

idea of favor. In Classical usage it could refer to the favor of the gods. As it is used in the New Testament and specially by Paul, however, it often becomes effectively a shorthand for all God's loving care for his people and for all that believers receive from God and the Lord Christ, especially their salvation. In modern Christendom, the English word "grace" is normally understood as referring to the entirely *undeserved* mercy and forgiveness of God toward sinful humanity that issues from his love and from his purposes to redeem a people for himself. However, it is important to realise that the word itself (χάρις) is embedded in the terminology relating to the giving of gifts. Indeed, on occasion its most natural English translation will simply be "gift" (cf. 1 Cor 16:3), or "act of giving" (2 Cor 8:6–7; NIV: "grace of giving"). Gifts can indeed be utterly undeserved, but they can also be given for a whole variety of other reasons. For example, they can be given to people by way of reciprocation for a gift received, or given to a person to curry favor, or because someone has done something to deserve it. In understanding this, it becomes important to examine carefully the context, which alone may reveal whether such gift-giving is in some sense deserved or undeserved. Frequently this will be tied into the relationship between the giver and the one receiving the gift. In an outstanding treatise on the subject of gift and grace, John Barclay has demonstrated how varied can be the meaning of this word, even in relation to God's various giftings of his people. That grace that is given without reference to the recipient's status, worth, or otherwise he refers to as "incongruous" grace.[12] In v. 4 the word is defined in relation to the saving and sustaining work of God in Christ, the Lord. Here it surely carries the sense of an undeserved gift that elicits great thankfulness from the apostle as he sees among them the gift of God in their calling, in what he has given them for the encouragement and benefit of the church, and in the way God will ensure they are found "not guilty" on the day of the Lord (v. 8).

The use of the conjunction (καὶ) here in v. 3 indicates the equality of Father and Son as the originators or source[13] of the grace and peace. The self-sufficiency of the Corinthians together with their boasting may make this prayer even more applicable.

Peace. The word "peace" (εἰρήνη) does not appear in traditional-Greek letter writing in introductory formulae. However, Paul uses it in all his letters as part of the greeting and in a number of his closing benedictions. Its roots lie in the Old Testament. Peace (*shalom*; שָׁלוֹם) describes the inheritance and experience that come with being God's people. It summarizes the blessings of the covenant and thus is far more than a prayer that the Corinthians should feel peaceful. Its objective content includes peace with God as a result of justification (Rom 5:1), but it also summarizes the covenant security that belongs to God's people (Ezek 34:25). The word even has a missionary thrust, since part of the "covenant of peace" is that God's people will "multiply" (Ezek 37:26). It is not surprising, then, that this word is used to summarize the eschatological hope of Israel, as for example in Isaiah 66:12. Since the "gospel" is described as good news of "peace" in Isaiah 52:7 and Nahum 1:15, we may see Paul's wish-prayer as simply that the

---

12. John M. G. Barclay, *Paul and the Gift* (Grand Rapids: Eerdmans, 2015). For a summary of his conclusions, see his prologue and ch. 18. This work examines Paul's understanding of gift and grace primarily against a vast panorama of literature reflecting Second Temple Judaism, before examining the themes in terms of Paul's theology in Galatians and Romans.

Throughout, Barclay interacts in detail with both historic and modern theological expositions of Paul's understanding of grace.

13. This is not a particularly common use of ἀπό +genitive, but is found in a number of greetings, such as in 2 Cor 1:2 and Phil 1:2. See also a similar use of the construction in 1 Cor 6:19.

Corinthians should continue to experience Christ daily as the one who brings them to the Father and the one who secures them with the rich blessings of salvation (see also Eph 6:15). It stands to reason, therefore, that they must live in peace and not be quarrelsome or divided.

1:4a I give thanks to my God always for you (Εὐχαριστῶ τῷ θεῷ μου πάντοτε περὶ ὑμῶν). Paul now moves to an extended thanksgiving to God for those to whom he writes. This lengthy sentence must therefore be held together if the relationship between the subordinate clauses is to be understood. The main clause discussed here stands at the beginning: "I give thanks to my God always for you." "Always" (πάντοτε) modifies the verb, reminding the readers that Paul has a continuing and long-standing concern and care for this church. Paul probably intends to make it clear that he prays for them whenever he is praying.[14]

Unlike the opening thanksgiving sections of other ancient letters, which were simply polite greetings, Paul uses the thanksgiving not to praise the Corinthians or even to draw attention to his own deeds but rather to give thanks to God.[15] Here we see a deliberate focus on God the Father, on Jesus Christ, and on the grace that has been given them in Christ. It is said that Paul often begins his letters by finding good things to say about those to whom he writes, but this is only partially true. Because Paul is writing to a part of *God's* church, it is God who is thanked for the grace *he* has shown to his people. There is no need to see this as a rhetorical *exordium*, using praise of people in order "to secure the good will of the listeners while encapsulating the main themes of the speech or letter."[16] While Paul does indeed take this opportunity to introduce the matter of grace-gifts that will later be seen to be at the heart of some of the Corinthian problems, here Paul straightforwardly establishes that their gifts come from God and Jesus Christ, who are to be thanked for such riches. Indeed, these riches are necessary for God's people, who await the return of Christ.

1:4b–5 because of the grace of God given you in Christ Jesus, for in everything you were made rich in him in all speech and all knowledge (ἐπὶ τῇ χάριτι τοῦ θεοῦ τῇ δοθείσῃ ὑμῖν ἐν Χριστῷ Ἰησοῦ, ὅτι ἐν παντὶ ἐπλουτίσθητε ἐν αὐτῷ, ἐν παντὶ λόγῳ καὶ πάσῃ γνώσει). These clauses present two reasons for Paul's thanksgiving. The first subordinate clause (v. 4b) can be translated "because of the grace . . ." (ἐπὶ τῇ χάριτι). The second (v. 5a) also begins with a word that can mean "because" (ὅτι). How these two clauses relate to each other and how best to translate them has been the subject of some discussion. The Greek prepositional phrase (ἐπὶ + dative) is used in a variety of ways. The question here is whether it introduces the first reason for giving thanks ("because"), which is then followed by "that" or "for" (ὅτι), further explaining the content of the grace that was given.[17] The alternative is that the phrase (ἐπὶ + dative) here provides the ground for that which Paul now gives thanks. In this case it is the second clause (ὅτι . . . ; v. 5a) that gives the first reason for thanking God ("I always give thanks . . . on the ground of God's grace . . .

---

14. Elsewhere Paul reveals the depths of his prayer life on behalf of the churches (Phil 1:4, 9; Col 1:9; 1 Thess 1:2; 2 Thess 1:11).

15. See P. T. O'Brien, *Introductory Thanksgivings in the Letters of Paul*, NovTSup 49 (Leiden: Brill, 1977).

16. Suggested by Witherington, *Conflict and Community*, 87. Witherington argues that the knowledge and speech mentioned here in 1:5 (understood as Greek *sophia* with its atten-

tion to rhetoric and eloquent discourse) were the cause of the problems in Corinth and that their mention here is "inexplicable" unless what Paul writes has a rhetorical purpose of securing "the goodwill of the listeners while encapsulating the main themes of the . . . letter. The Corinthians seem to have assumed that eloquence in speech *was* wisdom" (82).

17. So NIV, RSV, and ESV. See also Fee, *1 Corinthians*, 36n13, and Héring, *First Corinthians*, 3.

because you were made rich").[18] In the translation above the view has been taken that v. 4b gives the first reason for which Paul gives thanks to God for them. It is "because" they have received God's grace which "was given" (δοθείση) to them.

It is God who is thanked because this grace[19] was given "in Christ Jesus" (ἐν Χριστῷ Ἰησοῦ). This is more than an instrumental dative. It is not simply that Christ is the one who has mediated God's grace to them, though that is true. It is that this grace was received as they were identified with Christ and came to find themselves represented by him and part of his community.

Verse 5a explains further the content of the grace. God's grace meant that they were made rich in every way "in him," that is, in Christ.[20] The aorist suggests that this happened at a time in the past. This does not imply they are somehow no longer rich, but it may gently be reminding the Corinthians that the gifts they exhibit have not come upon them more recently or that they come and go depending on their spiritual maturity. Paul talks of God's grace as "riches" and "treasure" in various places[21] and is always deeply thankful for and most amazed at what God does for his people and provides for them "in Christ." As the Corinthians are tempted to boast of their gifts, Paul draws attention to their source, God, and recognizes that these gifts are truly riches of his grace.

A further subordinate clause (v. 5b) now amplifies the nature of the riches to which Paul especially wishes to draw attention: they were enriched "in all speech" and "in all knowledge." In light of the reference in v. 7a to not lacking any grace-gifts (χαρίσματα), it is most likely that Paul is referring here to the grace-gifts of "speech" (λόγος) and "knowledge" (γνῶσις), gifts which he again mentions in a thoroughly positive light in 12:8; 14:2–19.[22] Since Paul later reminds the Corinthians that not every member has all the individual gifts of the Spirit (12:4–11), it may be assumed that these two gifts were especially prominent in the church and that they are therefore singled out for mention and for thanksgiving to God. Drawing attention to them at this stage, and thanking God for them, will serve to remind the Corinthians that Paul's problem with their "knowledge" has to do with the *way* they use the gift and let it function in their community, rather than with this gift of God's grace per se.

It is difficult, if not impossible, to define accurately what these gifts looked like. It is to be noted that the word "knowledge" (γνῶσις) occurs much more frequently in this letter than elsewhere in the New Testament. As we saw in the introduction, this fact—together with the appearance of words like "spiritual" (πνευματικός) and "wisdom" (σοφία)—has encouraged speculation that Paul faced some form of Gnosticism. However, such a background hardly seems to fit with what Paul actually says about knowledge as his letter progresses, and moreover should be discounted on the grounds of dating.[23]

Nevertheless, the prominence of "wisdom" and "knowledge" in Greek society and, indeed, in some

---

18. So H. E. Dana and Julius R. Mantey, *A Manual Grammar of the Greek New Testament* (New York: Macmillan, 1957), 106. See also Thiselton, *1 Corinthians*, 84.

19. See comments on v. 3 above for more on the word "grace" in this verse.

20. The use of the pronoun here, referring back to "in Christ Jesus" in v. 4, is another reason for believing that v. 5a explains v. 4b.

21. See, e.g., Rom 2:4; 9:3; Eph 1:7; 2:7.

22. Fee, *1 Corinthians*, 38; *contra* Thiselton, *1 Corinthians*, 92–93.

23. See further discussions on the gift of "knowledge" in comments on 2:12; 8:1–2, 7; 12:8; 13:2. For a detailed discussion of possible backgrounds for 1 Corinthians and of the nature of gnosis, see Paul D. Gardner, *The Gifts of God and the Authentication of a Christian: An Exegetical Study of 1 Corinthians 8–11:1* (Lanham, MD: University Press of America, 1994; repr., Eugene, OR: Wipf & Stock, 2017), 6–10, 23–27.

Jewish wisdom traditions may help us understand why the Corinthians seemed to have especially emphasized these gifts. Perhaps they came to regard these grace-gifts as the Christian equivalent of the very things that their own society most valued. There the art of rhetoric was highly valued. The power of persuasion and the use of logic were prized forms of communication. As Munck argued, probably correctly, what Paul encountered was a compromised and distorted gospel, centered on a Corinthian theology owing much to "a mixture of philosophy and sophistry typical of that age." Here, he says, we meet a "popular . . . mixture of philosophy, religion and rhetoric."[24] More recently Winter has examined the first-century Sophists and their influence on the world into which Paul was writing in considerable detail.[25] He maintains that the Corinthians had absorbed much of the sophistic attention to careful rhetoric, wisdom, and knowledge and that Paul's teaching is specifically countering this tendency. Thus, from these early verses of the epistle the emphasis on God's gifts of wisdom and knowledge must be seen against a background in which such skills are to be admired and are indications of a status possessed by an elite. Knowledge of the gods and of spirituality was highly regarded. Later, Paul will show how distorted the Corinthian understanding and use of these gifts really was. For now, he simply thanks God for what they have received from the riches of his grace.

1:6 because[26] the testimony to Christ was confirmed among you (καθὼς τὸ μαρτύριον τοῦ Χριστοῦ ἐβεβαιώθη ἐν ὑμῖν). Paul is talking to the whole Christian community at Corinth ("among you"). It was in the confirming of the gospel, the

testimony to Christ (τοῦ Χριστοῦ; objective genitive), that God poured out the riches of his gifts. It is not that the gifts somehow established the gospel but that the establishment of the gospel among the Corinthians led to God's grace-gifts being made available to all.

1:7 so that you may not lack any grace-gift while awaiting the revealing of our Lord Jesus Christ (ὥστε ὑμᾶς μὴ ὑστερεῖσθαι ἐν μηδενὶ χαρίσματι, ἀπεκδεχομένους τὴν ἀποκάλυψιν τοῦ κυρίου ἡμῶν Ἰησοῦ Χριστοῦ). As part of his thanksgiving, Paul is reminded that they were made rich in Christ with the result that they do not lack in any "grace-gift."[27] This result clause is best seen as modifying v. 5a. Nothing should be read into the fact that this is put negatively. Verse 5a ("for in everything you were made rich") was explicitly positive, so this is probably simply stylistic and unlikely to reflect a "deft swipe at [the Corinthians'] undue pride."[28] Later, in 1 Corinthians 12 Paul will make it clear that each one has a grace-gift and that the Spirit gives to the body the gifts the body needs. None will be lacking since God knows what is best for his church and is rich in his grace.

Paul further qualifies this with a reminder of the age in which Christians live. It is a time of waiting for Christ's glorious coming, "the revealing of our Lord Jesus Christ" (taking ἀπεκδεχομένους as a temporal participle). The gifts are given to help the church live appropriately until the time when they shall see "face to face" (13:12). It is not necessary to view this as specifically speaking against some form of realized eschatology in the Corinthians' own teaching. Rather, Paul simply continues to thank God that the Corinthian Christians are

---

24. Munck, *Paul and the Salvation of Mankind*, 153.
25. Winter, *Philo and Paul among the Sophists*, 180–85.
26. The word καθώς here is a causal adverbial conjunction.
27. The chosen way here of translating χάρισμα is "grace-

gift." On the problem of the interpretation of this word, see the discussion below entitled, "In Depth: Understanding the Word Χάρισμα."

28. Garland, *1 Corinthians*, 34.

kept by him and given grace to help them survive while they await "the day" (v. 8). Later Paul suggests that some of the Corinthians feel they have already "arrived," and this opening may be partly setting things up for that discussion, but Paul remains most concerned to remind Christians of the goal ahead of them and that God guarantees their arrival. This is what he moves to in the next verse.

1:8 and he[29] will establish you until the end unimpeachable on the day of our Lord Jesus Christ (ὃς καὶ βεβαιώσει ὑμᾶς ἕως τέλους ἀνεγκλήτους ἐν τῇ ἡμέρᾳ τοῦ κυρίου ἡμῶν Ἰησοῦ [Χριστοῦ]). The content of God's grace for which Paul gives thanks is that the Corinthians have been called by God, given great riches in Christ (grace-gifts), and that God will ensure they will be found "not guilty" on the day of the Lord. In the Exegetical Outline for this section, we have suggested that this now forms the second main subordinate clause explaining v. 4b.

The waiting "until the end" (ἕως τέλους) refers to the time of Christ's "revealing" (v. 7b). At that time the Corinthian Christians will be established "unimpeachable."[30] In other words, by God's grace in Christ Jesus they will be free of any charge when Christ returns to judge. "The day of our Lord" is drawn from Old Testament texts. The prophets warned about the day with some foreboding. Joel talks of "sounding an alarm" and of people who should "tremble" for the "day of the Lord is coming." Ezekiel and Amos refer to it as the time when God will return to judge and vindicate his name.[31] Paul's Christ-centered eschatology awaits that day as the day when Christ will return to judge and to save. He refers to it again in 1 Corinthians 5:5.[32]

In the thanksgiving section of this letter, Paul focuses on God's grace in Christ for the Corinthian Christians. Whatever their faults and even their sin, Paul thanks God that his grace has been at work among them in giving them the grace-gifts necessary for this present age and in securing their position on judgment day as unimpeachable at the court of the living Lord.

IN DEPTH: Understanding the Word Χάρισμα

The word χάρισμα, as it appears in 1 Corinthians, is translated in a variety of ways by the English versions and by commentators. Partly this relates to apparently different meanings in different contexts where the word is used, and partly because commentators tend to want to acknowledge a difference in this epistle between Paul's use of the word and his use of the word "spiritual things" (πνευματικά). The NRSV, NIV, and NET translate the word as it first appears at 1:7 as "spiritual gift," and then in 7:7 and occurrences in chapter 12 as simply "gift" (cf. RSV). The AV, NJB, REB, and ESV translate the word as "gift" in each case, while

---

29. It is unclear to whom the pronoun "he" (ὅς) refers. Is it "and *Christ* will establish you" or "and *God* will establish you"? Thiselton rightly suggests that it cannot properly be known from the Greek, but this does not affect the sense of the passage in which Paul is concerned with "the promises of God-in-Christ." Thiselton, *1 Corinthians*, 101.

30. Archibald Robertson and Alfred Plummer, *A Critical and Exegetical Commentary on the First Epistle of St. Paul to the Corinthians*, ICC (Edinburgh: T&T Clark, 1911), 7.

31. See especially Ezek 30:2–3; 36:22–33; Joel 2:1–2; Amos 5:18–20.

32. See also 3:13 and comments on 15:23–24.

the TEV uses "blessing" (1:7) "gift" (7:7) and "spiritual gift" (12:4). Calvin refers to "gifts" and expands upon this with the word "graces."[33] In this commentary we have chosen to translate the word consistently as "grace-gift" and below are some reasons for doing so. I first encountered this translation for the word χάρισμα in Professor James Moffatt's commentary. Although his translation refers to the Corinthians lacking no "spiritual endowment" (v. 7), he explains this as a "'grace-gift' to fit them for their course."[34] D. A. Carson has employed the translation "grace-gift," and more recently it is used by David Garland in his commentary on the epistle.[35] The substantive question of the translation of this word is raised well in Carson's statement about the χάρισμα of chapter 12: "For the apostle who so delights to discuss grace, it is eminently appropriate that he should devote attention to the things of grace, to the concretizations of grace, to grace-gifts."[36]

The word appears in the New Testament on seventeen occasions with only one occurrence outside the Pauline corpus (1 Pet 4:10). Philo employs the word twice in *Legum allegoriae* 3:24, otherwise it is very rare in other Greek literature, with the "earliest assured occurrence of the word . . . from the second century AD (Alciphron *Ep.* 3.17.4)."[37] It is derived not from the word "grace" (χάρις) but from the verb χαρίζομαι, which means "to give graciously"[38] or "to give freely." The -μα ending can refer to the result or outcome of an action, and so here the word indicates the gift that has been graciously given. It is important to note therefore that the noun in itself does not denote "*spiritual* gift." For it to indicate this meaning either the adjectival qualifier "spiritual" will be needed, or the context will need to make this abundantly clear. Thus, for example, in Romans 1:11 Paul desires to impart to the Romans some "spiritual gift" (χάρισμα ὑμῖν πνευματικὸν). However, in Romans 5:15, 16 the word χάρισμα means simply "gift," and to avoid repetition Paul uses two virtual synonyms that we also translate as "gift" (δωρεά and δώρημα).[39] Thus, just as care must be taken with the

---

33. Calvin, *First Corinthians*, 22.

34. James Moffat, *The First Epistle of Paul to the Corinthians* (London: Hodder and Stoughton, 1938), 7.

35. D. A. Carson, *Showing the Spirit: A Theological Exposition of 1 Corinthians 12–14* (Grand Rapids: Baker, 1987), 19–22; Garland, *1 Corinthians*, 31–32, 271–72, 575–78, and passim.

36. Carson, *Showing the Spirit*, 19.

37. James R. Harrison, *Paul's Language of Grace in its Graeco-Roman Context*, WUNT II.172 (Tübingen: Mohr Siebeck, 2003), 280. See further on the subject, 279–83.

38. *Contra* Gordon D Fee, *God's Empowering Presence: The*

Holy Spirit in the Letters of Paul (Peabody, MA: Hendrickson, 1994), 33, who says "the noun has been formed from χάρις (grace)." See Max Turner, *The Holy Spirit and Spiritual Gifts: In the New Testament Church and Today*, rev. ed. (Peabody, MA: Hendrickson, 1998), 264. See also BDAG 1081.

39. N. T. Wright is surely correct in saying of this multiplication of words in these two verses that "there are no doubt fine distinctions between these terms." He goes on to say of these verses that "part of Paul's reason for choosing different words . . . is to avoid repetition" ("Romans," in *The New Interpreter's Bible Commentary*, ed. Leander E. Keck, vol. 10 [Nashville: Abingdon, 2002], 524).

word "spiritual" in relation to the "gift" of which Paul talks, so it is also important not to assume that the word χάρισμα *necessarily* involves connotations of Paul's expansive teaching of God's *grace* in Christ each time he employs the word. Again, only the context will allow us to deduce whether Paul specifically has in mind that this "gift" is one given freely of God's grace.

Here in 1 Corinthians 1, it is immediately clear that the "gifts" to which Paul refers come from God "in Christ" (v. 4). These opening verses are full of God's favor toward his people revealed to them in Jesus Christ, and so the apostle says that he gives thanks to God for them "because of the grace [χάρις] of God given you [δίδωμι] in Christ Jesus." This grace of God is then expounded in terms of gifts that "enriched" them, with two being mentioned by name: "for in everything you were made rich in him in all speech and all knowledge" (v. 5). Indeed, Paul is thankful that the result of God's gifting has been "that [they] may not lack any [χάρισμα] while awaiting the revealing of our Lord Jesus Christ" (v. 7).

The emphasis on "the grace of God" that "was given" to them and to their enrichment by God "in Christ" all speak to what will be developed later; namely, these "gifts," at least in this epistle, should be understood as part of God's *gracious* activity for his people in and through Jesus Christ. Although in 7:7 it is clear that Paul refers to a "gift" that seems different from the gifts of "speech and knowledge" and others like prophecy or tongues, nevertheless the context once again is of a gift received directly "from God." As the argument of the epistle builds, it becomes clear that the "gifts" to which Paul refers in this epistle with the word χάρισμα are all designed to build up the community in unity, love, and service of the Lord. They are given by the God who has been gracious to them and who graciously gives them with a purpose in mind. In 2:12 where this point is made again, it is the Spirit who helps the church understand the true nature of "what is given" to us.

Paul contrasts that which comes freely from God as a "gift" with the boasting of the Corinthians concerning their prowess or spirituality. Paul's own calling enabled him to lay the foundation of the church like a "master-builder" (3:10). This he speaks of as "the grace (χάρις) of God given to me" (v. 10). In challenging the Corinthian boasting he asks, "For what do you have that you have not received? If then you received it, why do you boast as if you did not receive it?" (4:7). Finally, in chapter 12 as Paul expounds upon the proper purpose of the gifts in building up the community, he makes it clear that they are all given by and empowered by God and his Spirit.

As we study the epistle, we shall see that it is this emphasis on *God's* gifting of his people that Paul is specifically contrasting with the Corinthian pride in what they see as *their* spiritual achievements. All has been given, and all has been given in Christ, and so Paul give thanks for God's *grace* seen among them in these gifts.

In this epistle Paul faces a people who pride themselves in being "spiritual" and who pay great attention to "spiritual things." Paul has to redefine both what it is to be "spiritual" and the fact that true "spiritual things" are gifts of God's grace and favor rather than skills or attributes in which to boast. Part of his redefinition involves his use of the word χάρισμα. This gracious gift is more than simply another "gift." In the light of this, our translation of χάρισμα as "grace-gift" seems reasonable. No doubt it may feel clumsy, but it avoids the artificially introduced word "spiritual," which in this epistle could be very confusing.

1:9 God is faithful, through whom you were called into covenant participation[40] with his Son, Jesus Christ our Lord (πιστὸς ὁ θεὸς δι᾽ οὗ ἐκλήθητε εἰς κοινωνίαν τοῦ υἱοῦ αὐτοῦ Ἰησοῦ Χριστοῦ τοῦ κυρίου ἡμῶν). This final verse of the thanksgiving section of Paul's letter provides both a summary of the greeting and a bridge into what follows. Paul first affirms God's faithfulness. The words "God is faithful" (θεὸς πιστός) appear twice in the Septuagint (LXX) at Deuteronomy 7:9 and 32:4. We also find the phrase "the Holy One of Israel is faithful" in Isaiah 49:7 LXX (πιστός ἐστιν ὁ ἅγιος Ισραηλ). Each of these passages are especially concerned with the covenant relationship formed between God and his people.[41] God's people are "called" or "chosen" by him, and he promises to remain faithful to them. Through his prophets God warns his people of the dangers of sin and rebellion, but he always does this in the context of his

faithfulness to his covenant promises. God will forgive. Indeed, it is only in God's faithfulness that there is any possibility of being "established" until judgment day and being found "unimpeachable" (1 Cor 1:8). Like the writers of old, the apostle Paul knows that the human situation is hopeless if the one who first "called" his people does not remain faithful to them.[42]

Grammatically, the prepositional phrase (δι᾽ οὗ) should be understood in the same manner as in v. 1. It is that *calling* "by him [God]"[43] into a covenantal relationship with the Lord to which Paul now refers. The passive voice (ἐκλήθητε) reminds the reader that sharing in the blessings of God's community (his church) only occurs through his sovereign work of calling. This is the goal of God's work with his people, that they should have "covenant participation"[44] (κοινωνία) with the one who has all authority, "Jesus Christ our Lord."

---

40. See the discussion in "In Depth: The Meaning of the Word Κοινωνία" at the end of comments on this verse.

41. See further comments on πιστὸς ὁ θεός and its covenantal references in 10:13.

42. For more detail on Paul's exposition of and dependence upon the wilderness traditions and especially Deut 32 as it relates to 1 Corinthians, see Gardner, *Gifts of God*, 115–33, 153–54.

43. Charles F. D. Moule, *An Idiom Book of New Testament Greek*, 2nd ed. (Cambridge: Cambridge University Press, 1959), 57, 204.

44. See Victor P. Furnish, *The Theology of the First Letter to the Corinthians*, NTT (Cambridge: Cambridge University Press, 1999), 34–35. The difficulty of translating the word κοινωνία has been discussed in many places (see my summary in Gardner, *Gifts of God*, 159–65). Using the phrase "covenant participation" reminds us that the word is at the very heart of the gospel message and of what the church is all about (Acts 2:42). It has to do with participating or sharing in the benefits of being God's people. As we shall see in our examination of 1 Cor 10:16, 18, this translation of the word also helps in

Paul has referred again and again to Christ, usually using the longer designation stressing Christ's lordship, "Lord Jesus Christ," or simply calling him "Lord" (v. 2 twice; vv. 3, 7, 8, 9). Christ is, above all, "Lord." Finally, Paul ends this section with the longer title, "Jesus Christ our Lord." When Christ returns, judgment will take place, but those who are his will not be found guilty. He is the source of grace, and those who participate in his covenant community find themselves as recipients of his riches now and are utterly secured in the future. The next section begins with an appeal in the name of "our Lord Jesus Christ" (v. 10). Paul will there argue that participation in the Lord's own community has its requirements. The people of God are to reflect the unity of their calling. It is to this that the apostle now turns.

IN DEPTH: The Meaning of the Word Κοινωνία

It is perhaps tempting to delay the discussion of the importance of Paul's concept of κοινωνία until we explore 1 Corinthians 10. In that one chapter the word appears four times and is critical to his understanding of why Christians cannot have dealings with idolatry, and what religious activity is taking place at meals eaten in the pagan temples. However, much as that passage is key to how this word is to be understood and translated, it is vital not to miss its importance as an underlying assumption that guides all Paul's dealings with the Corinthian church. This word, which we translate "covenant participation" (for reasons that will become clear), is first found in 1:9 and speaks to a theological theme in Paul's thinking that influences the whole way he writes about the church as God's people and their relationship to Christ, the Messiah. Indeed, if there is one driving idea in this epistle that energizes Paul and his quest for unity in the church at Corinth, his quest for a sanctified and humble people and for a people who understand the lordship of Christ in all things, it is surely this. For Paul, being "called into covenantal participation with . . . Jesus Christ our Lord" (1:9) is to be called into the people of God who share with their Lord the great benefits that belong to this community. The participation is therefore both, as it were, "vertical" with God in Christ and "horizontal," that is, a joining with others who also bow to the covenant Lord, Jesus Christ (cf. 1:2).

Paul finds inspiration for this description of the church as a covenant community from his understanding of Scripture and its account of God's dealings with his people Israel. Each carefully chosen description of the church is one that has its parallels in the Old Testament, except that what is new is that God's chosen King, the Lord Jesus Christ, has now come. Paul knows the church has come into being at the "call" of God (1:2, 9, 24, 26) and at his determination or deliberate

an understanding of what is going on in that passage. The inadequacy of the usual translation "fellowship," the "covenant" context of most of the biblical uses of the word, and the "sharing" or "participating" involved in the word's connotation are examined below.

that Jesus is their king and is the covenant Lord to whom they owe allegiance and whom they must obey.

This covenantal aspect of Paul's thought is further seen, *firstly*, in the fact that in 1:9 κοινωνία is the outcome, the goal, of God's choosing for himself a people who will be a community in relationship with the Lord Jesus Christ. Indeed, Currie has argued that a survey of the use of κοινωνία in the New Testament indicates that it was always at the heart of the gospel and of God's electing purpose.[48] This has echoes of God's calling of Israel as he binds himself in covenant to them (Deut 14:2; Isa 43:1; 48:12; cf. Isa 42:6). Then, *secondly*, it should also be noted that this "covenantal participation" is focused in the "Lord Jesus Christ." The emphasis on Christ as the "*Lord* Jesus Christ" is striking in these opening verses (vv. 2, 3, 7, 8, 9, and 10). Lordship requires allegiance, not just a partnership, as v. 2 ("their [Lord] and ours") makes clear. First Corinthians 10 significantly develops a contrast of different "lordships"—Christ or demons (10:21–22). Lordship was fundamental to the workings of the covenant relationships God formed with his people. Obedience to the "Book of the Covenant" meant obedience to God as Lord (Exod 24:7). Covenant lordship also meant the lord would secure his people and bless them (1 Cor 1:8; cf. Exod 34:10) as they followed and obeyed him and that he would judge them if they did not (1 Cor 11:31–32; Deut 7:9–10). This is precisely what Paul sees happening in the church, and it gives rise to Paul's concern for the Corinthians. They are God's *covenant* people, and so Christ, the King (Lord) will come either to bless (1 Cor 1:8) or to judge, just as he did the Israelites (10:11–12). Turning to other gods (ch. 10) or even causing disunity by dividing one covenant member from another would mean judgment for breaching the covenant terms. Thus, it is not surprising to read that Paul regards the stories of the covenantal dealings of God with his people Israel as having been "written down for our instruction" (10:11 ESV).

Thirdly, in 1:9 it is significant that this calling into "covenantal participation" with the Lord is at the behest of the "God [who is] faithful" (πιστὸς ὁ θεός). This phrase is used again in 10:13 (cf. 2 Cor 1:18) and specifically carries connotations of God's covenant faithfulness in calling into being a community who would be his people. The phrase has its background in two notable covenantal passages in the Old Testament (LXX Deut 7:9; 32:4). In Deuteronomy 7, Moses reminds the people that the Lord (Yahweh) has "chosen" them to "be a people" (v. 6) because he loves them (vv. 7–8). He then says, "You will know that the Lord your God, he is God, the faithful God [θεὸς πιστός] who maintains covenant and

---

48. Stuart D. Currie, "Koinonia in Christian Literature to 200 AD" (PhD diss., Emory University, 1962), 14.

mercy [ὁ φυλάσσων διαθήκην καὶ ἔλεος] with those who love him and keep his commandments, to a thousand generations, and who repays those who hate him" (v. 9). The importance of Deuteronomy 32 for Paul's thinking about Christ as Lord must also be noted (see commentary on ch. 10). Here too it is God's faithfulness as covenant Lord to his people that is at issue with a reminder that he chose them, but they have rejected him as Lord, leading to their judgment.

In 1 Corinthians 10 the covenant themes are explicit (see commentary). "They," the Israelites, were "our fathers" (v. 1)! Those under Moses had, as it were, their own baptism as they came through the sea. They were given great blessings (gifts) as they escaped the slavery of Egypt and as God fed them and nourished them in the wilderness. The tragedy they faced was that they had turned to other gods, thus directly disobeying the covenant law (Exod 34:12–15). They even worshipped other gods in cultic meals (Exod 32:6; 1 Cor 10:7), and so "with most of them God was not pleased" (10:5 ESV). As Paul develops this idea, he thinks of the cultic meal that all Christians know: communion. And here we find Paul applied the term κοινωνία to that which was created by or occurred through eating both the Christian meal (v. 16) and the Israelite/pagan meal (vv. 18–20). The Christian meal has to do with the covenant established through the death of Christ. It is where God's people covenantally participate in the blood of Christ and in the body of Christ. Here is where on-going community identity is established. How much more then should the covenant community at Corinth, under the Lord Jesus Christ, recognise that getting involved in the sacrificial meals, celebrated in the temples of idols, will reflect membership of a *different* covenant community, one that follows and serves other lords, that is, demons (10:20–21). Participating in two covenant communities is an impossibility. As Jesus himself said: "No one can serve two masters" (Matt 6:24).

In sum, as Paul uses the word κοινωνία (and cognates) in 1 Corinthians 1:9 and 10:16, 18, 20, his framework of reference is the God-created community of Israel in its relationship with Yahweh. Yahweh had come to his people in love, offering a covenantal relationship (Gen 12:1–3; 15:18; Exod 34:10). In such a relationship the Lord is to be obeyed (Gen 17:9; Exod 19:5) and, as God, to be worshipped (Exod 34:14). As Willis says, "They are a cultic community."[49] In turn the covenant Lord will bless and offer security to his faithful people, but he will judge those who rebel and do not obey for he is a "jealous God" (Exod 34:14; cf. 1 Cor 10:22). Paul sees the Corinthian Christians as having been called by God to participate in this covenant relationship with and "in Christ." Huge joys and blessings have already been seen in this community (1:1–9) for "God is faithful"

---

49. Willis, *Idol Meat in Corinth*, 187.

to his covenant, but clouds loom because some of the people have been less than faithful in various ways. For them Paul's loving concern is that judgment may await.

Theology in Application

The opening verses of this epistle are full of the joys of God's grace as he calls his people and works among them in Christ. They lay a firm basis for all that follows in this letter, and the teacher or preacher may wish to dwell proportionately rather longer on this section to establish some of the theology that Paul briefly touches upon and yet which later is seen to undergird much of what he says. For example, whatever the problems Paul knows he must address in this epistle, their secure status in the Lord and at Christ's second coming is established here. Furthermore, even though some of the gifts of the Spirit may be abused within this church, their existence in the church is entirely of God's grace and he is to be thanked for them. Above all, the God who in Christ called Paul to be an apostle and called this church into being remains faithful and will sustain his people.

Facing up to Individualism

Several theological matters here will be of particular challenge to much of the modern Western church. With its emphasis on individualism, the modern church often fails to pay enough attention to the corporate identity of those who are called by God ("in Christ") to be his church. Symptomatic of this is the way churches are often described with reference to the name of their leader or senior pastor rather than with reference to God and his calling in Christ. The fact that many congregations see "church" as what they "do" on Sunday morning for seventy minutes is another symptom of this common problem. Discovering what it is to be the "church of God in . . . ," to be corporately "the sanctified," to be corporately "called into covenant participation with his Son" is surely one of the greatest needs the church faces. At least at the local level there is a need to allow these verses to lift people's eyes beyond the individual to see each other as part of the total work of Christ in producing his church, and to lift the eye of the local church still further to understand that it is but a small part of the global church. To miss out on Paul's ecclesiology here is to miss out on much that will ultimately strengthen the church's witness to and service of the Lord, as well as the commitment of individual believers to each other.

The goal of God's calling is that Christians may be a sanctified people who belong to his *church* and together have covenant participation with Christ. It is only when this corporate nature and goal of the church is truly grasped that the discussion of grace-gifts, of church discipline, etc., fall into place. Paul's stress on God's initiating work of calling people into the covenant community of Christ and of God's sustaining of his people until the day of the Lord draws further attention to God's sovereign purposes and goal for his church.

Many would say that the most attractive churches for those who have no faith and, humanly speaking, the most "successful" churches are those that best understand and work out God's calling to *covenant-community participation* (κοινωνία). These days some evangelists are saying that the only way of reaching large numbers of those without faith in Christ is through church planting. Mainly this is because church plants are usually small communities of the most dedicated Christians who have learned to work together and rely on each other's gifts. Pragmatically this may be true, but it is a sad reflection on the great majority of churches that have been around for many years. At times in the Corinthian correspondence the reader is left with the feeling that Paul might have preferred to start another church without all the problems that had arisen (in a relatively short period of time). But such is not the answer. The church is the church. It is called by God and must rediscover "in Christ" its calling to be a covenant community in which Christ is the Lord and each individual, enabled by the Spirit, has his or her part and works to further the calling of God. What is said here about the church is later built upon in a number of ways, not least with the appeal to a godly life in chapters 5 and 6 and the body metaphor in chapter 12. In fact, the unity established in God's sanctifying purposes for his church provides the basis for all of Paul's later appeals to the Corinthians, whether it be the appeal for unity or for better behavior within the community.

Trusting that God is Faithful to His Church

The importance attached to the faithfulness of God with regard to his church must be recognized. It is all too easy for individual believers to despair of the church. Currently, I am teaching an oft-repeated course to those interested in the Christian faith. Time and again the first thing people wish to make clear is that they have given up on the "institutional church." When they give their reasons, most Christians in the room usually feel embarrassed and despondent as they recognize an all-too-accurate description of many churches, and yet at the same time they know that what is described is a distortion of what the church is supposed to be. However, Paul's view of the church is such that giving up on it is not an option, for it is *God's church*. He is faithful (v. 9). No doubt recalling God's extraordinary and repeated forgiveness of Israel despite her rebellion, Paul insists that God's faithfulness means he will continue to forgive, sanctify, and sustain the church to the end when Christ returns. God's goal is that his church will be sustained in such a comprehensive way that it will be presented on the last day as "unimpeachable" (v. 8). Many church-planting efforts in Western societies are a positive offshoot of churches that desire to fulfill their calling to be a light and witness to the world. Yet here there is also a call to all churches to remember what they have been called to, to remember God's sustaining power, and to become again the people who love God and one another other and are winsome and welcoming as they go out to serve.

Thankfulness for God's Grace-Gifts to His People

Paul's insistence here on being thankful for the grace-gifts of God given to the people at Corinth should stimulate modern thinking about the church. Too often this discussion has been beset by debates between charismatics and those who are non-charismatics.[50] Sometimes these debates have centered on the question of whether God's Spirit gives new revelation today or not.[51] These are serious and proper debates for the church to have, but sadly both sides often seem to miss out on the joy and thankfulness that Paul has here as he speaks of the Lord's work in giving grace-gifts to the Corinthian church. Paul will go on to show that the use of the grace-gifts at Corinth had often been distorted and this had led to divisions in the church and to distorted theology. Nevertheless, he does not then suggest the gifts should be ignored. There is a reflection of the church at Corinth in parts of the modern church whenever the function of the grace-gifts is distorted and the gifts are abused. In another section of the church, the gifts are ignored altogether for fear of their abuse. The apostle criticizes the distortion of the use of the gifts later in his epistle, but he does not then ignore them. Rather, he teaches more about their right and proper function. Here in the opening verses he lays the theological groundwork. The grace-gifts are liberally dispersed by God's Spirit to all members of God's church. Their purpose is to empower and enable the church to follow its calling while it waits for the revelation of Christ.

Knowing How to Give Thanks

Finally, in this opening there is Paul's example of thanksgiving. This section of thanksgiving is not simply about being nice to the Corinthians before launching into criticism, nor is it simply a rhetorical device. Rather, it reflects the grace of God at work in Paul, causing him to know how to give thanks even when there is much that disturbs him about this church. Learning to look for what God is doing among his people is a lesson all Christians must learn (cf. Phil 4:11). It is then that the blessings and grace of God among his people are truly appreciated.

---

50. At a popular level, see John McArthur, *Strange Fire: The Danger of Offending the Holy Spirit with Counterfeit Worship* (Nashville: Thomas Nelson, 2013); Sam Storms, *The Beginner's Guide to Spiritual Gifts* (Minnesota: Bethany House, 2012).

51. See, for example, Benjamin B. Warfield, *Counterfeit Miracles* (New York: Charles Scribner, 1918).

1 Corinthians 1:10–17

Literary Context

In introducing his letter with a greeting and with thanksgiving to God for the grace the Corinthians have received in Christ, Paul has reflected briefly on a number of matters that will resurface as the letter proceeds. He has thanked God for the grace-gifts they have received and for the fact that God remains faithful to his people. Christ's lordship has been highlighted, and Paul has reminded them that God called them into the Lord's own community.

Paul now comes to the substance of the letter. It will deal with several issues that concern him deeply. In the first instance, in 1:10–17 Paul is concerned with the lack of unity in the church. He has set this up with his affirmation at the end of the last section that they were called into Christ's covenant community, the church (v. 9). A series of rhetorical questions in v. 13 drives home the seriousness of the issue and serves to move the argument on to a discussion of the implications for unity of a gospel message that centers in the cross of Christ. This is developed in vv. 18–25 and illustrated from the calling of the Corinthians themselves in vv. 26–31. The discussion of unity and the problem of divisions continues now through to the end of chapter 4.

Main Idea

Paul expresses his dismay at the lack of unity in the church and pleads with the Corinthians that they should be united in thought and purpose. Nothing less than this is required by the gospel of the cross of Christ that Paul has preached among them.

λόγου, ἵνα μὴ κενωθῇ ὁ σταυρὸς τοῦ Χριστοῦ). As a summary of this section, this verse also prepares the reader for that which follows. Paul insists that the power of the gospel does not lie in how eloquently he presents it. Indeed, to be pretentious in any way might cause the real message of the cross to be obscured. It is worth noting that "not in wisdom of speech" modifies "to preach." It is therefore part of Christ's commission and not simply part of Paul's preferred way of speaking.[34] So Paul indicates that the way of expression itself affects the success or otherwise of a proper reception of the message of the gospel. Thus Paul says "lest the cross . . . be emptied" (ἵνα μὴ κενωθῇ). If the gospel is communicated "in wisdom of speech," then not only is its content lost but its very *power* is lost.[35] Thus, as we move to v. 18, we see that "the word of the cross" changes lives because in it God is at work in power to effect the calling of people to worship the Lord Christ.

What, then, does "with wisdom of speech" (ἐν σοφίᾳ λόγου) mean? One problem, as many have noted, is that both the words "wisdom" (σοφία) and "word" (λόγος) have wide ranges of meaning. "Word" (λόγος) can mean anything from a word to a speech or statement and so on. Indeed, Paul has already used the word to describe a grace-gift of the Spirit in 1:5, though it is clear that is not what he has in mind here because the one is commended and the other is scorned.

"Wisdom" (σοφία) can be used to describe intelligence. When used in a biblical context, wisdom is often seen to be that which God gives to his people so they come to understand his will, but it also has a deliberately practical bent to it. In other words, the wise person is one who not only knows the will of God but *does* it. This is particularly seen in Old Testament wisdom literature and specially in the many aphorisms of the Book of Proverbs. However, in 1:22 it becomes clear that the sort of wisdom to which Paul refers here is especially in the domain of the Greeks. For them wisdom involved impressive thinking and philosophical enquiry. It concerned the realm of ideas. But there was much more to it, for part of being a "wise person" was being able to communicate and argue with fine standards of rhetoric. There is some evidence that occasionally the rhetoric of an argument, its sophistication of presentation, became more important than the content itself.[36] No doubt the clever rhetoric was aimed at convincing people of a particular position or belief, but the ability to persuade through the argument, structure, and form of the oratory or writing was in itself highly prized. This in turn fed into the constant desire in Hellenistic society for status and being highly regarded by all. Bruce Winter has argued that Paul was facing a community in Corinth where the philosophy and attitudes of the Sophists held special sway.[37] They were known for their ability in oratory that would "secure a public following and attract students to their schools."[38]

Looking now at what Paul says in this passage and how he contrasts this "wisdom of speech" with

---

34. Interestingly, most commentators point out that there is a contrast here in the methods of presentation of the gospel. Yet they do not seem to make the grammatical link in the text that makes it most likely Paul regarded the method as inherent in the message, and part of the totality of his apostolic calling.

35. The gospel presented *in the right way* (as God commissioned and in the power of the Spirit) has *illocutionary* force. See K. J. Vanhoozer, *Is There a Meaning in This Text? The Bible, the Reader, and the Morality of Literary Knowledge* (Grand

Rapids: Zondervan, 1998), 427–28. For further discussion of speech-act theory and its application to this verse, see Thiselton, *1 Corinthians*, 146 (also 51–52). See also Alexandra R. Brown, *The Cross and Human Transformation: Paul's Apocalyptic Word in 1 Corinthians* (Minneapolis: Fortress, 1995), 14–29.

36. Winter, *Philo and Paul among the Sophists*, 188.

37. Winter, *Philo and Paul among the Sophists*.

38. Ibid., 4.

the "word of the cross" (v. 18) and the "wisdom of God" (v. 21), we see that Paul is arguing that the gospel itself simply turns the way that the world views wisdom on its head. The cross of Christ, understood as the "gospel"—the full revelation of God in Christ—carries within itself the ultimate "wisdom," that is, the mind and plan of God for this world. It also carries within itself the "power of God" (v. 18). Human teachers and preachers are but the vessels that carry God's powerful message. Clever rhetoric will simply serve to obscure the power of God's word. To elevate the manner of delivery is to give a profile to the one who preaches, and this is not the focus of the gospel. Conversely, to elevate the content (the "wisdom of God"), which is the plan of God in Jesus Christ, inevitably diminishes the human voice that brings the message. Therefore, in sending Paul to preach the gospel, Christ gave him a task that, as with John the Baptist before him, would mean that he would always be decreasing while Christ would always be increasing (John 3:30). No doubt Paul would have joined with John in saying, as Christ was exalted, "This joy of mine is now complete" (John 3:29 ESV).

The emptying of the power of the gospel would have occurred when delivered through "wisdom of speech." Instead of the gospel being heard and understood by all—from the educated to the uneducated, the elite of society to the dregs of society—it would have only been appreciated by the elite, those brought up to understand sophistic rhetoric and philosophy. In modern terms, it would have been like saying that the gospel can only be heard in a university town from a highly sophisticated professor! In every way, Paul is saying, the calling to evangelize involves turning the world's values upside down.

With the themes of "wisdom" and of the "cross" having been introduced, this verse now links directly into the section that follows. The "cross of Christ" (ὁ σταυρὸς τοῦ Χριστοῦ) becomes a shorthand for the content of the preached gospel.

IN DEPTH: The Gospel

The "gospel" (τὸ εὐαγγέλιον) or "good news" refers primarily to the content of the preaching of the Christian faith with regard to Christ's saving work. The fact that Paul can use the word in the absolute on occasion, with no further explanation, suggests the word was already in use in Christian vocabulary. Probably his use of the word derives from Christ's own use as found in the Gospels. There both the substantive and verbal form of the word are especially tied to Christ himself, his person and presence on earth, and his own preaching and teaching of the kingdom of God (e.g., Matt 4:23; Mark 1:1; Luke 3:18; 4:18). Response must be made to the gospel message by following the command of Jesus to "repent and believe the good news" (Mark 1:15). These ideas, in turn, reflect the prophetic idea of good news from God being announced to his people. The verbal form of "preaching good news" (εὐαγγελίζω) as found in Isaiah 40:9, 52:7, and 61:1–2 is particularly significant. In Isaiah 40:9 the prophet speaks of God being revealed in his saving power and the gathering of his people together to shepherd them and care for them. In Isaiah 52:7 the emphasis is also on the salvation of God's

1 Corinthians 1:18–25

Literary Context

Paul has now introduced the substance of this letter. The lack of unity has been the first matter to be mentioned, and this will resurface throughout the epistle. He has also introduced the problem that individuals seem to be identifying with specific leaders. This was occurring perhaps because they were baptized by them or simply because, in line with the society of the day, it was to their apparent benefit to identify with a patron and thus to gain some sort of acceptance and status in the community. Paul has begun to challenge what is going on by constantly referring to Christ, to his lordship, and to "the cross of Christ" that stands against "the wisdom of speech." In the next main section (1:18–2:5), Paul expands upon the distinction of v. 17 between the eloquence and elitism of secular wisdom and the power of the cross of Christ. He draws out several contrasts between the understanding of "wisdom" that has sucked in the Corinthians and the wisdom that is from God. The cross is regarded either as "folly" or as "God's power." God's wisdom deliberately made foolish the wisdom of this world. Even in his weakness God is stronger than men; even in his "folly" God is wiser than men.

The section of 1:18–25 addresses the power of "the cross of Christ" and how it functions to destroy and to save different people. Both Jew and Gentile are impacted by the gospel and react in different ways. How could something that seems so absurd in the world's eyes—a crucified king—ever be regarded as "wisdom?" In 1:26–31 Paul establishes his point by illustrating the (strange) impact of this gospel among the Corinthians themselves, most of whom were not "wise" and did not have power or status by worldly standards. In 2:1–5 Paul further illustrates his message by pointing to the (strange) phenomenon that God worked through him despite his weakness and lack of "words of wisdom." In this way Paul argues that at every point in their hearing the gospel and responding to it, God's wisdom has been seen to be stronger and more effective than human wisdom. Even the way the gospel was presented would have been shunned by the "wise" of this world, for Paul had appeared weak and had not used sophisticated rhetoric. The gospel has cut right through everything to which the Corinthians were committed: their boasting, arrogance, and their tendency to look for status the way the surrounding culture did.

Main Idea

The message of Christ crucified seems foolish to the world and yet enshrines the power of God to save people. Despite the influences of contemporary thinking about what is wise and what is foolish, the message of the cross reveals God's power and his wisdom to those who are being saved. In light of this, the wisdom and strength of men and women are reduced to nothing.

Translation

1 Corinthians 1:18–25

18a	Assertion	For **the word of the cross is foolishness**
b		to those who are perishing, but
c		to us who are being saved
d	Contrast	**it is the power of God**
19a	Verification of 18a–b	For **it is written:**
b	Quotation	"I will destroy the wisdom of the wise and
c		the intelligence of the intelligent I will nullify." [Isa 19:14]
20a	Rhetorical questions	**(1) Where is the wise person?**
b	Series	**(2) Where is the scribe?**
c	Series	**(3) Where is the debater of this age?**
d	Series conclusion	**(4) Has not God made foolish the wisdom of the world?**
21a		For in the wisdom of God
b	Causal of 21c–e	since … the world did not know God
c	Means	| by means of wisdom,
d	Assertion	**it pleased God … to save those who believe.**
e	Means	through the foolishness of preaching

Continued on next page.

Continued from previous page.

22a	Assertion	For since **Jews ask for signs**
b		and **Greeks seek wisdom,**
23a	Assertion	so **we preach a crucified Christ**
b	Description	to the Jews a stumbling block and
c		to the Gentiles folly, but
24a	Contrast	to the called,
b	Apposition	both Jews and Greeks,
c		Christ
d	Description	the power of God and
e		the wisdom of God.
25a	Assertion	For **the folly of God is wiser than** [the wisdom of] **men** [and women]
b		and **the weakness of God is stronger than** [the strength of] **men** [and women].

Structure

Paul's main thesis in this section is presented in v. 18, though the entire section (1:18–2:5) offers an extended development of v. 17. In vv. 18–21 the power of the gospel is regarded, as it were, from God's perspective. The world regards the word of the cross as folly, but people divide into two classes as they respond in radically different ways. Paul writes that it is God's intention, by means of the folly of the message of the cross, to thwart those who feel they might reach God by means of their own wisdom (vv. 19–21). He supports this by appeal to Scripture (v. 19) and an allusion to Scripture with three forceful rhetorical questions (v. 20). Verse 21 further develops the point (ἐπειδὴ γὰρ) that in God's *wisdom* the world did not come to know him in its own way but that, in the same event of preaching, people who believe are saved. Despite these two responses purposed by God, the next subsection reveals that the gospel will be and must be preached to all (both Jew and Gentile; vv. 22–24). In a series of contrasts Paul shows that among Jews and Gentiles there will be a negative response. He carefully balances the negative reaction of some Jews to the negative reaction of some Gentiles (v. 23). Jews look for signs and to them a crucified king is a stumbling block. Gentiles look for wisdom and to them a crucified king is folly. In contrast, those who are called (κλητοί) will encounter the wisdom and power of God (v. 24). Verse 25 uses comparative clauses to summarize this section by showing that God's way of salvation has revealed how much wiser and stronger he truly is than are human beings. This opens the way for Paul to turn to the example of how God's wisdom has actually been put into effect among the Corinthians themselves (vv. 26–31).

Exegetical Outline

Explanation of the Text

1:18 For the word of the cross to those who are perishing is foolishness, but to us who are being saved, it is the power of God (Ὁ λόγος γὰρ ὁ τοῦ σταυροῦ τοῖς μὲν ἀπολλυμένοις μωρία ἐστίν, τοῖς δὲ σῳζομένοις ἡμῖν δύναμις θεοῦ ἐστιν). Having explained in v. 17 how he had been called to preach in a manner that would not take anything away from the power of the "cross of Christ," in this verse Paul now begins to address the nature of the power to be found in gospel proclamation. This power may be seen in how some are being saved while others perish. "For" links this to v. 17. Paul had talked of preaching "not in wisdom of speech." Now he talks of the "word of the cross" (Ὁ λόγος . . . ὁ τοῦ σταυροῦ), which he insists is experienced as God's power among those being saved. The wide range of meaning for the Greek term "word" (λόγος) was noted above. Here the contrast between "the word of the cross" and "wisdom of speech" in v. 17 could not be clearer. The latter exudes human skill, acumen, and creativity; the former is all of God. The word of the cross is a synecdoche for the proclamation of the gospel of salvation to be found in Christ

crucified. This proclamation, as we see elsewhere in Paul and in the New Testament, would have included the announcement of God's judgment upon sin, the need for repentance if forgiveness is to be received, and the way in which the salvation is achieved as Christ died on the cross "for you" (1:13; cf. 15:1–7). The death, resurrection, and exaltation to glorious lordship would all have been part of this full message.[1] Yet because of the centrality of the cross, the ignominy of this part of the message, the humiliation of the one who claims to be Lord, and the appalling horror of death by crucifixion, the whole message ends up dividing people.

Death on a cross was regarded with horror and disdain by Jews and Gentiles alike. For many Jews, as Paul makes clear, it is a cause of "stumbling" (see further comments at v. 23). Jewish law had taught that death "on a tree" meant a person was cursed, that is, damned by God (Deut 21:23; cf. Gal 3:13; 5:11). Yet for Jew and Gentile alike it was the sheer horror of this form of death that made the whole idea of preaching about one who had been crucified, let alone a crucified king, seem madness or

---

1. See the above essay, "In Depth: The Gospel."

folly (μωρία; v. 18). Hengel writes of crucifixion, "At relatively small expense and to great public effect the criminal could be tortured to death for days in an unspeakable way."[2] It is thus unsurprising that within the confines of human wisdom this all seemed incredible. Yet with extraordinary brevity Paul describes these incredulous people as those "who are perishing" (ἀπόλλυμι). The present middle participle indicates that these people "go toward destruction."[3] It is possible that the middle voice implies God is the agent or cause of this. This would fit with the general theme that the "word of the cross" itself divides people and has within itself both the power of God to save as well as to cause to perish.

With equal brevity Paul states the vital contrast, comparing two groups of people: to the one group the word of the cross is "foolishness," but to the other group the word of the cross "is the power of God" (δύναμις θεοῦ ἐστιν). The two dative participles define those to whom the cross is the one or the other (μέν . . . δέ). It is thus in people's reaction to a king who had died on a cross that God reveals those who are perishing or being saved.

The present participle, "who *are being* saved" (σῳζομένοις), reminds us that salvation will only be fully realized in the great eschatological climax of history. As Paul will need to tell the Corinthians later, they have not yet arrived. Of course, "God is faithful" (1:9; 10:13), and he will keep and guard his people, but they have not yet arrived. Final judgment and salvation remain on the eschatological horizon.

The phrase "the word of the cross" is thus rather more than just the preaching of a message about how to be saved, though it is certainly that. It is also the announcement by God that the end of the ages has come (1 Cor 10:11). God's promises to the prophets are being fulfilled. He is on his way to judge, vindicate his name, and be revealed in power and glory. The judgment of God is seen when Christ died on the cross. The end times have come upon the world, and everyone is caught up in it either for salvation or for destruction.

It might have been expected that Paul would compare "foolishness" with "wisdom" here. Instead he compares "foolishness" with "power," reminding the reader that the proclamation is the way that God powerfully changes lives. In v. 24, Paul does use the phrase "wisdom of God" where it is virtually synonymous with "power of God." However, Paul's point here in v. 18 is vital. The way of this world compares foolishness and wisdom. When dealing with the cross we have a different comparison, that between achieving nothing and the *power* that provides salvation and thus also grants true standing in God's community.

1:19 For it is written: "I will destroy the wisdom of the wise and the intelligence of the intelligent I will nullify" (γέγραπται γάρ, ἀπολῶ τὴν σοφίαν τῶν σοφῶν, καὶ τὴν σύνεσιν τῶν συνετῶν ἀθετήσω). Using a quotation from Isaiah 29:14 (LXX),[4] Paul provides support for what he has been saying. In the cross of Christ, God's declared intention to destroy the wisdom of the wise finds its fulfillment. "It is written" (γέγραπται) traditionally introduces quotations from Scripture.[5] The perfect tense indicates that which was written in the past but which has continuing force. Paul quotes some fourteen times from Scripture in this epistle and alludes to many other Scriptures. In its original context, Isaiah 29:14 looks forward to a time of judgment

---

2. Martin Hengel, *Crucifixion in the Ancient World and the Folly of the Message of the Cross* (London: SCM, 1977), 87.

3. Héring, *First Corinthians*, 8; cf. Horsley, *1 Corinthians*, 48.

4. The final word in the LXX of Isa 29:14 is κρύψω ("I will hide") rather than Paul's ἀθετήσω ("I will nullify"). For possible reasons for this change, see Thiselton, *1 Corinthians*, 161.

5. E.g., Matt 4:4; Acts 1:20; Rom 1:17.

when God will move against his people for the way their plans and actions have been done in the darkness and contrary to his ways (v. 15). The "wise" whose plans will be destroyed are likely to have been the king's advisors. God complains that they have set themselves up as gods (v. 16), making themselves the creator rather than recognizing they are but the creature. They have even complained that God "has no understanding" (v. 16). But God will show that he is the wise one and is in control. As he goes on to show in Isaiah 30:1–2, the plans of the "wise" to form a treaty with Egypt to stave off invasion from Assyria will come to nothing. In fact, God will so reverse those plans that the alliance itself effectively scares Assyria into invading before, from their point of view, it gets too difficult. God's salvation of his people comes through a plan that seems weak. His people are invaded. They are subdued and humbled in the process, yet out of this comes God's deliverance. The text thus ably suits what Paul is saying to the Corinthians. It is as though, as God's people, they have come to rely upon the wisdom of the world and not recognized that God's wisdom is different. In (apparent) weakness will true power be found. In the humiliation of the cross alone they find God's final and decisive answer for the defeat of sin and the overturning of the wisdom of the world.

The use of a quotation with the future tense "I will destroy" (ἀπολῶ) further establishes the eschatological context for what Paul is teaching and reinforces the present tense of 1:18 ("are perishing"; ἀπολλυμένοις). Paul is saying this was always God's intention to destroy all other wisdoms that were not his and to bring about salvation in his way. Paul's

use of the future "I will nullify" (ἀθετήσω) carries with it the idea that the wisdom of this world is not just another way of looking at the world but is diametrically opposed to God and so needs "nullifying" or setting aside. It is those possessing this worldly wisdom and intelligence who will be destroyed, as in Isaiah's prophecy. Such "wisdom" cannot be abstracted from the people who conceive it, teach it, and act on it.

1:20a Where is the wise person? Where is the scribe? Where is the debater of this age? (ποῦ σοφός; ποῦ γραμματεύς; ποῦ συζητητὴς τοῦ αἰῶνος τούτου;). Three rhetorical questions continue the appeal to Scripture, though only by allusion. The repetition strengthens still further the impact of what Paul is saying. The crucified Christ destroys all forms of the wisdom of "this age." It is possible that he was using a preexisting collection of verses such as Isaiah 19:12, 33:18, and 44:25 or something similar.[6] Though it is unlikely and not essential to his argument, it is possible that Paul did intend a reference here to three specific types of person.[7]

1. The "wise person" (σοφός) might refer to a Greek Sophist or philosopher of the sort mentioned earlier;[8]
2. the "scribe" (γραμματεύς) might refer to a person well versed in the law, perhaps Jewish (which would introduce the coming references to Jews and Greek in vv. 22–23);
3. the "debater [συζητητής] of this age" might refer to the general enjoyment of philosophical debate and discussion for its own sake that prevailed among some.

The phrase "of this age" (τοῦ αἰῶνος τούτου) is more significant to Paul's concern. It describes

---

6. See, for example, C. K. Barrett, *A Commentary on the First Epistle to the Corinthians*, HNTC (New York: Harper and Row, 1968), 52–53.

7. That all three of these persons were Jewish because of the Old Testament quotations is unlikely. See Munck, *Paul and the Salvation of Mankind*, 146–53, for a detailed examination of

Paul's use of the Old Testament in this section.

8. So Robertson and Plummer, *First Corinthians*, 19, disagreeing with Charles Ellicott, *St. Paul's First Epistle to the Corinthians, with A Critical and Grammatical Commentary* (London, 1887), who sees this as generic (for Jew and Gentile).

this present world that "is passing away" (7:31; παράγω). Paul's understanding of the "age" is Jewish, not dualistically Greek. While "this age" is essentially synonymous with "of the world" (1:20–21; 2:12; cf. 3:19) and it is "passing away" (7:3; cf. 2:6), there is no suggestion that the Christian should seek to escape through asceticism or the like. In Jewish thought the present age gives way eventually to the age of the Messiah, the time of God's salvation. Texts like Daniel 9:24–27 and Psalms of Solomon 17:1–4, 42–46; 18:5–6 speak to that great developing messianic expectation of Second Temple Judaism. God would send the king, his messiah, who would conquer his enemies, gather his people, and rule on earth in a kingdom of everlasting righteousness. Thus, for Paul and the early church who recognise Jesus as the Messiah, the end of this current world order has begun with the coming of Christ, his death, resurrection, and ascension. The ascended and enthroned king has begun his rule.[9] This event has destroyed the wisdom of the wise. Those who belong to Christ belong already to the new age. It is here that Paul's eschatology differs from the Judaism of his day. The Messiah is on David's throne and rules forever, but *two ages currently exist side by side*. The work of God in Christ reveals that, of course, these dominions are not in any sense equal. Indeed, already the word of the cross reveals this truth: people are *already* perishing and *already* being saved. Christ (and him crucified) *is* the power of God.

1:20b Has not God made foolish the wisdom of the world? (οὐχὶ ἐμώρανεν ὁ θεὸς τὴν σοφίαν τοῦ κόσμου;). For the sake of the argument, Paul assumes he carries with him the Christians he is addressing. The question (with οὐχί) expects the answer "yes." The verb "has made foolish" (ἐμώρανεν; an aorist) shows the conclusion arrived at in the last paragraph to be correct. God "made foolish" the wisdom of the world. This happened with Christ crucified. The phrase "of the world" is a possessive genitive. The wisdom that belongs to the world, that is, "of this age," is therefore set to perish.

1:21 For since in the wisdom of God the world did not know God by means of wisdom, it pleased God, through the foolishness of preaching, to save those who believe (ἐπειδὴ γὰρ ἐν τῇ σοφίᾳ τοῦ θεοῦ οὐκ ἔγνω ὁ κόσμος διὰ τῆς σοφίας τὸν θεόν, εὐδόκησεν ὁ θεὸς διὰ τῆς μωρίας τοῦ κηρύγματος σῶσαι τοὺς πιστεύοντας). Paul continues with a summary and expansion of his argument that insists on the God-ordained relationship between preaching and God's wisdom, even as the world's wisdom regards gospel preaching as folly. To see the sentence structure clearly, the main sentence is separated below from the subordinate clauses.

It pleased God . . . to save those who believe. The verb "it pleased God" (εὐδόκησεν; an aorist) reminds the reader that God has deliberately, and with pleasure, laid out his way in which people should come to salvation. God planned both that people would be saved and the means by which this would be achieved. The idea of what has "pleased God," referring to his deliberate plan, may be seen in New Testament texts such as Matthew 17:5; Luke 12:32; Galatians 1:15 (cf. Col 1:19; Eph 1:5), and, negatively, in 1 Corinthians 10:5.[10]

The present participle (πιστεύοντας) is significant. Those who are being saved (v. 18) are those who "are believing" (v. 21). Continued faith[11] in and commitment to Christ crucified is the defining

---

9. For more on Paul's approach to the two "ages," see Wright, *Paul and the Faithfulness of God*, 1061–73, esp. 1069.

10. See G. Schrenk, "εὐδοκέω," *TDNT* 2:740–42.

11. While the context will always determine whether a pres-

ent participle should be regarded as having continuative force, the substantival participle, "those who believe" (πιστεύοντας), here seems to have this force. In other words, Paul and others did see continual believing as evidence of salvation (cf. 14:22;

issue. This requires a deliberate turning away from human wisdom and a wholehearted commitment to the effective plan of God for salvation through the death and resurrection of Christ. Paul adds emphasis by placing his main clause at the end of the sentence. In the wonderful plan of God, people will be saved. The means by which God decreed salvation would happen is "through the foolishness of preaching."

Through the foolishness of preaching. This contrasts with the high value placed on rhetoric and cleverness of speech in Corinthian circles. But the "preaching" is not just a reference to a form of communication so much as a reference to the *content*. The word "proclamation" could be used. Paul will go on to say, "We preach Christ crucified" (v. 23). It is the content of the message that, above all, causes this preaching to be regarded, humanly speaking, as "foolishness." Now we may return to the first part of the sentence, which serves as the link between what has been said about God's destruction of human wisdom and how God in fact reveals his own true wisdom.

While Paul has spoken before of the "power of God" in contrast to the world's "wisdom" (vv. 18–19), he now talks of "the wisdom of God" (possessive genitive).[12] The content of this wisdom is in fact spelled out in the main clause ("it pleased God"). It is none other than God's decree to save believing men and women through the death of Christ. This *is* God's wisdom, and it is, as Paul goes on to demonstrate, a wisdom that is utterly alien to the wisdom of "this age" (3:18).

In v. 19 we saw that the world's wisdom is to be destroyed by God. This idea of God's predetermined plan for the world's wisdom is picked up in the main clause: "It pleased God . . . ." Now the introductory clause falls into place: *"For since in the wisdom of God, the world did not know God by means of wisdom . . . ."* The use of "since" (ἐπειδή) here is causal. Part of God's destruction of the world's wisdom is effected by God "since" the world's wisdom did not enable people to know God.[13] Paul thus reminds the Corinthians that it is an established fact that men and women have not known God through their own devices and their own strategies ("by means of wisdom"). Knowing God is not just knowing *about* God. All people know something about God (Rom 1:19–21). Rather, it is about identifying with the Lord as the only one who can save. It is about "call[ing] upon the name of our Lord Jesus Christ" (1:2). Above all, it is about coming into a relationship with God in such a way that a whole new way of seeing, a new mind-set, pertains. Paul expands on this in 2:6–16, which ends with the statement, "We have the mind of Christ." (See also comments on 8:2–3.)

1:22 For since[14] Jews ask for signs and Greeks seek wisdom (ἐπειδὴ καὶ Ἰουδαῖοι σημεῖα αἰτοῦσιν καὶ Ἕλληνες σοφίαν ζητοῦσιν). By taking these two main religious divisions of the world, Paul is now able to show that no one is excluded from what he has been saying. Even working from within different religious frameworks, both Jews and Greeks have not known God. It is not that some religious viewpoints are closer than others, but that all

---

Rom 3:22; 4:11, 24). See also comments in Daniel B. Wallace, *Greek Grammar Beyond the Basics: An Exegetical Syntax of the New Testament with Scripture, Subject, and Greek Word Indexes* (Grand Rapids: Zondervan, 1996), 621n22.

12. Moule, *Idiom Book of New Testament Greek*, 40.

13. The aorist "did not know" (οὐκ ἔγνω) is consummative or resultant. This use involves the viewing of an event in its entirety with specific regard to its end results. See A. T. Robert-

son, *Grammar of the Greek New Testament in the Light of Historical Research* (Nashville: Broadman, 1934), 834; Dana and Mantey, *Manual Grammar*, 195. In terms of verbal function, it may be seen as "summary."

14. "Since" (ἐπειδή) introduces an elaboration on what Paul has said in v. 21 and looks toward v. 23: "Since Jews ask . . . so we preach . . . ."

people everywhere have suffered under the same delusion that they can reach God by *their* preferred means. Hence, later Paul clearly states, "Let no one deceive himself" (3:18). In the end, this means that people tend to create a god after their own image. This god may be mighty and "other" but will always act in the way people want. The very demand for proof from both parties means they "set themselves up as an authority that can pass judgment on God."[15] This is nothing less than idolatry.

Paul states that Jews ask for "signs." At great points in their history, Israel had experienced their covenant Lord acting in their midst with powerful signs. Thus, for example, great signs surrounded the exodus (Exod 10:1; Deut 10:4) and the encounter of the people with God at Mount Sinai. Signs were seen in the days of Elijah (1 Kgs 17–18; cf. Luke 4:25) and at the opening of the temple in Solomon's day (2 Chr 7:1). Signs had thus become part of the messianic expectation (Deut 18:15; Isa 64:1–4; Jer 31:31–33; Acts 7:37). But instead of trusting in God and waiting for him to operate in whatever way he wished, the Jewish people had come to see signs as proof of God. Their demanding of such proofs had been condemned even in the Old Testament (e.g., Deut 6:16). But Jesus had also despaired of the seeking after signs in Matthew 12:38–45. There the religious leaders came to test him and asked him to show them a sign. Jesus's response was to say that all they would see was the sign of Jonah, a reference to his death and resurrection. Jesus was pointing to the fact, now understood by the apostle Paul, that the one great sign was to be found in what appeared as folly, what appeared as no sign at all, the crucifixion. To test God by

seeking signs was simply to show that they did not trust his way but that they wanted a god who would perform at their behest. Jesus called them an "evil and adulterous generation" (v. 39 ESV), and this, in effect, is the point Paul makes here. They are no different in their demands from the Greeks.

"Greeks" are synonymous, as v. 23 shows, with Gentiles.[16] Greeks seek wisdom, says Paul, by which he means that this is a characteristic of their society. We have already seen how prominent and highly esteemed a commitment to wisdom was in the Hellenistic world in which the Corinthians lived. Paul is thus both criticizing the elitism of their wisdom and its content. Paul's own encounter with the heart of this civilization at the Areopagus in Athens would probably have continued to influence his thinking here (Acts 17:16–34). There he had talked to Epicureans and Stoics and many others.[17] What he saw was that their wisdom had led to great religiosity and yet resulted in nothing less than ignorance of God, even as they multiplied gods. Paul regarded this fact as culpable and requiring repentance (vv. 31–32).

1:23a so[18] we preach a crucified Christ (ἡμεῖς δὲ κηρύσσομεν Χριστὸν ἐσταυρωμένον). Into this world where no one, Jew or Gentile, has attained true knowledge of God, Paul says, "We preach a crucified[19] Christ." The perfect tense suggests Paul contemplates the continuing significance of Christ having been crucified. The passive reminds us that this was done to Christ. Paul now sets up a series of contrasts. The first two audiences, Jew and Gentile, are negative in their assessment of the gospel of a crucified Christ. The third is positive in its assessment.

---

15. Conzelmann, *1 Corinthians*, 47.

16. Winter, *After Paul Left Corinth*, 23–24: "The term Ἕλληνες should be translated consistently in 1 Corinthians as 'Gentiles,' for that is to whom he was referring."

17. Luke's gloss on this provides an interesting insight into what the effect of this constant searching after wisdom might

have looked like in day-to-day life (Acts 17:19–21).

18. The particle δέ is usually translated here as "but." This means not translating ἐπειδή in v. 22. Since δέ is simply continuative and ἐπειδή in v. 21 parallels the word here in v. 22, we have translated "since . . . so we preach."

19. The participle ἐσταυρωμένον functions as an adjective.

1:23b to the Jews a stumbling block (Ἰουδαίοις μὲν σκάνδαλον).[20] As noted, these two groups of Jews and Greeks (Gentiles) end up in the same place of rejecting a crucified Christ, but they get there by different means. For Jews the crucified Christ is a "stumbling block" (σκάνδαλον), which refers to that which causes stumbling.

The concept of stumbling and causing to fall will become an important theme in this letter, especially in chapters 8–10. It is widely accepted that Isaiah 8:14 and 28:16 stand behind Paul's thinking here. Both passages are addressed to a rebellious Israel. The Israelites who "believed" in and "feared" the Lord were the ones who would not stumble but be kept safe. Isaiah 8:14 describes God as either a "sanctuary" to those who believe or a "stone of offense" (ESV; LXX: λίθου προσκόμματι) to those who refuse him. The upshot of these texts in Isaiah is that God lays down the stone, which becomes a test. It is in effect an article of belief. Thus, as Paul uses these ideas, *he sees the preaching of the crucified Christ as the testing stone, the article of belief.* As Isaiah warned the "wise" and "arrogant" Israel of his day not to fall, so in Paul's day Israel is seen to have stumbled on the stone (Christ) rather than seeking sanctuary in him.[21]

IN DEPTH: The Theme of Stumbling

Paul's use in this letter of words relating to the idea of a stone that causes stumbling is of considerable importance, especially in 1 Corinthians 8–10 (πρόσκομμα, σκάνδαλον, σκανδαλίζω, ἐγκοπή, and ἀπρόσκοπος).[22] The concept of a "stumbling block" (σκάνδαλον) was introduced in 1:23. It is widely accepted[23] that the background for the use of this word in the New Testament lies in the so-called "stone texts" of the LXX.[24] In fact, the same Old Testament texts also provide the background for the word "stumbling block" (πρόσκομμα) in 8:9. For our purposes, it is useful to draw attention to certain ways those texts *function* since this helps illuminate the way Paul draws on them in 1 Corinthians.

Both in Old and New Testament texts, the "stone" concept is often used in discussions related to apologetics.[25] In these cases the idea functioned in two ways. A "stone" might cause stumbling and destruction, or it might become a secure sanctuary or foundation. The function of the stone in this respect related

---

20. The μέν . . . δέ construction introduces the comparison, so the δέ does not need translating. "To the Jews . . . to the Gentiles" are datives of reference; so also "to the called" at v. 24.

21. This is more than an "affront" caused by the proclamation of a crucified criminal (Thiselton, *1 Corinthians*, 171). It is a God-intended way of revealing the true religious and faith commitment of the Jews who hear the message.

22. See 1 Cor 1:23; 8:9, 13; 9:12; 10:32. It is doubtful that Paul distinguishes between the "stumbling stone" and that which can cause the falling (πρόσκομμα and σκάνδαλον). Cf. Rom 9:33 where both words are used adjectivally (σκάνδαλου and προσκόμματος).

23. G. Stählin, "σκάνδαλον," *TDNT* 7:344, writes: "Both formally and materially the NT use of σκάνδαλον and σκανδαλίζω is exclusively controlled by the thought and speech of the OT and Judaism." Cf. Conzelmann, *1 Corinthians*, 148n28.

24. See Isa 8:14; 28:16; Ps 117:22 (LXX; 118:22 ET); cf. Rom 9:33.

25. See Barnabas Lindars, *New Testament Apologetic: The Doctrinal Significance of the Old Testament Quotations* (London: SCM, 1961), esp. 169ff., for a detailed study of links between the "stone" texts and their use in New Testament apologetics. Cf. G. Stählin, "προσκόπτω," *TDNT* 6:745–58.

to the response of the people and whether they responded in faith or not. The stone would then indicate whether a person belonged to God's people (for example, as a member of the "remnant" in Isaiah, or "the called" in Paul) or whether a person would be destroyed.

The word translated as "cause of stumbling" in 8:13 (σκανδαλίζω)[26] was probably not used in pre-LXX Greek literature or in Philo or Josephus, though a related word meaning "trap" (σκανδάληθρον) occasionally occurred. The noun "stumbling stone" (πρόσκομμα)[27] was also rare outside the LXX, not appearing in Philo or Josephus.[28] In the LXX it is used to translate different words, but is exclusively metaphorical, meaning a "trap" or "cause of destruction" brought about by sin.[29] Of special interest for the text of 1 Corinthians 8–10 is the idea of being led to worship other gods by a "snare" or "stumbling block" (LXX—πρόσκομμα) in Exodus 23:33 and 34:12. Thus, that which causes stumbling is what causes sin against God.

Two Old Testament texts in particular played a key role in the development of the "stumbling stone" and the "foundation" and/or "cornerstone" themes. Both Isaiah 8:14 and 28:16 were addressed to a *rebellious* Israel. The Israelites who "believed" in and "feared" the Lord were the ones who would be kept safe and would not stumble. They would find that the Lord was their sanctuary. Isaiah 8:14 describes God as a "sanctuary" (ἁγίασμα), a "stone of stumbling" (λίθου προσκόμματι), and a "rock of stumbling" (πέτρας πτώματι). Though God might cause such stumbling (many would stumble and fall—πίπτω, Isa 8:15 LXX), he was also a sanctuary. In Isaiah 28:16 God laid a "foundation" and a precious and tested cornerstone in Zion in which a person had to believe lest they should be "shamed" (LXX).[30]

Both these texts attach the idea of testing to the stone. In Isaiah 8:14 it is a snare, and in 28:16 it is a "stone" in which people must believe or be "shamed." The question confronted in both texts was whether those being addressed would be destroyed or whether they would find God a sanctuary. Isaiah 28–29 emphasizes that God must be the basis for Israel's salvation rather than humans and their wisdom, while Isaiah 8 shows what a problem such a view of salvation really was for a proud and arrogant Israel.[31] In that these chapters in Isaiah face

26. The verb appears twenty-two times in the LXX and the noun four times.

27. It occurs eleven times in the LXX (five are in Sirach).

28. It is found in Quintus Curtius Rufus, *Historia Alexandri Magni*, where it refers to Darius of Macedonia, whom Alexander cannot conquer and so flees (recensio γ, book 2:15; recensio ε, 16).

29. Exod 23:33; 34:12; Jdt 8:22; Isa 8:14; 29:21; Jer 3:3.

30. The possibility of destruction is seen in the "shaming" and the "falling."

31. Herman N. Ridderbos, *Paul: An Outline of His Theology*, trans. John Richard DeWitt (Grand Rapids: Eerdmans, 1975), 142.

the issue of who among the Israelites were really God's people, it is perhaps not surprising that the texts were used in *Christian* apologetics. As Lindars has so carefully shown, in the New Testament apologetic of response, "the stone is first of all an article of belief, belief in Christ, the crucial test between belonging to the New Israel or being rejected from it."[32]

In Romans 9:33 Paul brings together Isaiah 8:14 and 28:16. There, in dealing with God's destiny for Israel, Paul shows it was Christ who was the stone of stumbling and the rock of stumbling. Significantly, Paul added "in him" in v. 33b: "And the one who believes *in him* [i.e., Christ] will never be put to shame." In this way Paul faced the Jewish problem head-on. If Israel was to be destroyed, or non-Israel to be saved, the determining factor was to be found in the response to Christ, the stone. Belief in him determined whether a person belonged to the people of God.[33]

As we study 1 Corinthians, it is important to see that Paul works within this apologetic framework. The point Paul stressed at Corinth did not concern the place of physical Israel in God's plans, but he did face the same basic *religious* issue of "who are the people of God?" or "what is it that identifies people as belonging to God?" The contrast Paul draws in chapter 1 lies between the wisdom the Corinthians claim to have and the gospel message centered in Christ. This message of Christ crucified (1:23) was a "stumbling block" (σκάνδαλον).[34] This "stone" led to the "wisdom of the wise" (1:19) being confounded but also to some people "being saved" (1:18). Both aspects of the way in which the stone functioned were "simply variations on the no less biblical principle that *God and His gifts can bring either salvation or perdition.*"[35] In essence, the only difference between this scandal in 1:23 and the scandal/stone discussions of Isaiah 8 and 28–29 is the christological content.[36] Was their confidence "before God" (1:29) to be found in human wisdom or in Christ? Would they be part of the folly that God put to "shame" (1:27–28)? Or would Christ be their foundation stone? It

---

32. Lindars, *New Testament Apologetic*, 177.

33. These "stone" themes occur also in 1 Pet 2:4–10. The stone was precious to believers but would cause stumbling and falling to those who were disobedient. The Israelites stumbled and fell (vv. 7–8). However, the true people of God were those who had believed and had received mercy (vv. 9–10). In 2:7 the writer employed a third OT "stone" text (Ps 118:22) to show that Christ was that stone.

34. It is unnecessary to distinguish greatly between the effect of preaching Christ crucified on Jews or Gentiles. The σκάνδαλον of the cross was that it caused a rethinking for both Jew and Gentile (in different ways) of the sphere within which salvation, or God's grace, was manifest.

35. G. Stählin, "προσκόπτω," *TDNT* 6:750 (emphasis added). This arose, no doubt, from the dual function of the stone in Isa 8:14. The context of Isa 28:16 also discusses two responses: in one the stone becomes a θεμέλιον; in the other the wisdom of the wise is destroyed (Isa 29:13; Cf. 1 Cor 1:19).

36. The move from seeing God as a potential stone on which to stumble (πρόσκομμα) to seeing Christ in this way was probably quite natural to a faith that saw Christ as fulfilling many of the functions fulfilled by God in the OT. Also, note the "law" was a potential cause of stumbling (σκάνδαλον) in Ps 118:165 (LXX), and a transfer to Jesus Christ may also have been prompted by this route.

is this contrast that is precisely the contrast that Paul makes as he moves in 3:10–11 to his use of the building metaphor. That metaphor then gives rise to his use of the word "build" ([ἐπ]οικοδομέω) both there and in chapter 8.

We will suggest that in using the building metaphor Paul had a number of Old Testament texts in mind that talked of rebuilding or "building up" the temple and cities in the messianic era. In 3:10 and 11 the word "foundation" (θεμέλιος) is used. Given the way Paul personalized the foundation, making it refer to Christ (see Rom 9:33), it is quite possible that Isaiah 28:16 was also in mind. Paul does not discuss the stumbling stone while writing about the foundation, but the line of thought is similar to Romans 9:33 and 1 Peter 2:6–8 where Isaiah 8:14 and 28:16 are conflated. In both Romans and 1 Peter the stone laid was the "cornerstone" of Isaiah 28:16, and in both it resulted in both stumbling and salvation. This was Paul's purpose in his Corinthian epistle. He has preached Christ as the foundation of God's building. Acceptance of this foundation identifies those who are God's, and Paul emphatically reminds them that they *are* God's temple and the Spirit *does* dwell in them (3:16–17; cf. Ps 117:22–24 LXX [118:22–24 ET]).[37]

1:23c and to the Gentiles folly (ἔθνεσιν δὲ μωρίαν). Paul writes of "Gentiles," indicating again that he thinks of Gentiles and Greeks (v. 22) as the same. We have already seen why they would regard this as "folly" (see comments on v. 17). To them the crucifixion was the ultimate in humiliating deaths. It was not something that any civilized people would normally wish to see. For those whose natural inclination was to seek wisdom in brilliant rhetoric or sophisticated religious and philosophical debate, as at the Areopagus (cf. Acts 17:16–34), then a crucified Christ was simply "folly," to be rejected out of hand. However, if the first two groups end up in the same place of rejecting Christ, but for different reasons, there is a third group who see things differently.

1:24 but to the called, both Jews and Greeks, Christ the power of God and the wisdom of God (αὐτοῖς δὲ τοῖς κλητοῖς, Ἰουδαίοις τε καὶ Ἕλλησιν, Χριστὸν θεοῦ δύναμιν καὶ θεοῦ σοφίαν). Those who are called have come to see, believe, and experience that in the crucified and risen Lord Christ lies God's power to transform, forgive, and create a people who will be his forever. That power continues to be seen across the world as the gospel is preached and people come to repentance and faith. This was God's plan. This was his "wisdom." As J. Fitzmyer puts it, "By linking 'power' and 'wisdom,' Paul is showing that wisdom is not merely speculative, but is a manifestation of God's dynamic action."[38] The phrase "to the called" (τοῖς κλητοῖς) is another dative of reference: "We preach a crucified

---

37. Cf. 1 Pet 2:4–10. Lindars, *New Testament Apologetic*, 179ff., shows how this verse relates to Isa 28:16, suggesting that the whole metaphor of Christ as a stone depends on Ps 117:22 (LXX; 118:22 ET). Isa 28:16 is then used as a comment on Ps

117:22 LXX. Note also that Ps 117:22 is quoted by Peter in 1 Pet 2:7 as part of the conflation mentioned above.

38. Fitzmyer, *1 Corinthians*, 160.

Christ . . . with reference to the called . . . the power of God." Those who are "called" are those who "believe" (v. 21) and those who are "being saved" (v. 18). They are the ones who enjoy "covenant participation" in Christ (v. 9). And this group is not distinguished by race, education, wealth, or background, for in God's great design ("it pleased God"; v. 21) he called all types of people, Jew and Greek. These people perceive and understand things differently. They have come to recognize that what fails to meet the world's criteria of "wisdom," that is, a crucified Christ, is in fact both "the power of God" and "the wisdom of God."[39] Paul has yet much to say on the wisdom of God, but here both phrases, which stand in apposition to "a crucified Christ" (v. 23), have been seen before. A concluding sentence seems hardly necessary for this section, but Paul summarizes again for emphasis and uses it to introduce the next section.

1:25 For the folly of God is wiser than [the wisdom of] men [and women] and the weakness of God is stronger than [the strength of] men [and women] (ὅτι τὸ μωρὸν τοῦ θεοῦ σοφώτερον τῶν ἀνθρώπων ἐστίν, καὶ τὸ ἀσθενὲς τοῦ θεοῦ ἰσχυρότερον τῶν ἀνθρώπων). The point of the verse is that what God is and what he does cannot be compared with what humans might be or do. In fact, God turns the ways of men and women on their head, for he is wiser than could ever be imagined or conceived, and he is stronger in bringing his plans into effect than could ever be envisioned. Nothing will thwart him, even when his plans incorporate the supposed weakness of the crucified king. This conclusion is arrived at by use of comparisons. The comparison here is expressed with a comparative adjective followed by the genitive (sometimes here called the ablative): "Stronger than [the wisdom] of men [and women]."[40]

Theology in Application

The Cross as a Countercultural Proclamation

Being sucked into the world's way of thinking is always a problem for the church of all ages and all cultures. Often we are unaware of how much our culture affects the way we think and the priorities in our thinking. The problem of a church becoming self-centered and even arrogant should not surprise us, but the extraordinary similarities between some of the problems Paul faced in Corinth and the problems of many modern churches may surprise us. It is commonplace in contemporary society to value education, wisdom, wealth, and especially power. Time and again churches end up valuing these things because this is what members value in their day-to-day work. Thus, in congregations where elders are appointed, we may find that they are chosen more because of their position in society or their wealth or educational background than because they are the most spiritually mature in the church. Elsewhere churches will sometimes talk about the "power of God" but then look for the signs of this in miracles, signs and wonders, or in rapidly growing numbers in

---

39. "Wisdom" and "power" or "might" are brought together as God's attributes in various texts (e.g., Jer 10:12; 51:15; Dan 2:20, 23; cf. Isa 11:2).

40. Moule, *Idiom Book of New Testament Greek*, 98, points out that "the wisdom" (τῆς σοφίας) is to be understood here and so inserted in the English.

the congregation. There may be a great emphasis on the "power of the Spirit" in a congregation where this can be seen in how "spiritual" the members appear to be or how much they "do" for the Lord or witness for him. So much is the understanding of power now limited to the extraordinary, the wealthy, the evidence of community status, or human activity that some teachers no longer even attempt to spend time talking about the cross. Interestingly, when the redemptive events are taught, it is often the resurrection or the sending of the Holy Spirit that receive most treatment. These are events which, from a human point of view, seem to be the most powerful. But the apostle Paul turns to the cross. Of course, in preaching Christ crucified Paul also speaks clearly on the resurrection and the Holy Spirit, but he deliberately chooses the cross as the focus of the gospel.

The cross is so important that this center of redemption that seems so humiliating, so full of sadness, and so uninspiring to the world is seen for what it is. It is the "power of God." Understanding that it is God who works through the preaching of Christ crucified helps the Christian see afresh that it is by grace that a person is saved. The more that teachers and those preaching see that this uncomfortable message transforms lives as it is taken up and used by God for that purpose, the more they humble themselves in the task of teaching. In God's economy, it is by such preachers teaching this message that the true life-changing power of God's grace will be revealed. For those called by God to teach and preach and yet know that they will never be the orators that some of the best known and media-savvy preachers are, here is hope and comfort. God takes weak, uninspiring people and changes the course of history as he uses them. Indeed, there is a long pedigree in the biblical story of God working in this way through those who seem weak in the world's eyes or who are even fearful in their own eyes due to their lack of ability or power. To name but a few we may recall Moses, Elijah, David, and Isaiah.

For those on the receiving end of teaching week by week where Christ crucified figures at the heart of all that is said, then even if the one speaking is not the best speaker in the world, there is the reassurance that God will be at work in them and among them. Both leaders and congregations need to be challenged to ask themselves where the true center of their gospel lies. Asking this question of newcomers can provide a salutary reminder that Christians are not always heard to be majoring on what they think is their core message.

A Message That Causes Stumbling

This passage also reminds us how human beings always wish to make gods after their own image. Paul speaks of Jews demanding signs and Greeks wisdom. Their respective cultures, histories, and religions have caused them to expect these things of their god or gods. However, Christ crucified cuts right across these demands. No one ever demanded a crucified god! Yet even as this is read by Christians, so they too need to be aware that the temptation is always the same: to change Christ crucified into something more palatable for our age. This can be done in all sorts of ways, and the problem becomes even more acute because usually the distortion of the gospel is done with the best of intentions and often by using *some* elements of gospel truth. So, for example, Christ is preached as the one who answers all our needs. He does, but to those listening this can often mean that they can ask of him whatever they want and they will receive it. "Christ crucified" is thus lost beneath half-truths expressed in a way designed to appeal to modern men and women. The "slot-machine" society creates a "slot-machine" god.

The presentation of a gospel that truly causes stumbling and is regarded as folly is a humbling act in any culture and in any age. It is only when the church understands with Paul that this is God's chosen way—his wisdom, his way to save, his power—that Christians will find confidence to bring the crucified Christ to the world. Christians may feel weak and powerless and unable to speak of Christ in a persuasive way to neighbors, colleagues, friends, or family, yet they may indeed be confident in God. Even in the face of antagonism, we should "with gentleness and respect" (1 Pet 3:15), and as best we can, speak of Christ as king and of his love in giving his life for the forgiveness of sins.

CHAPTER 4

1 Corinthians 1:26–31

Literary Context

In 1:18–25 Paul has addressed the question of how something that seems absurd in the world's eyes, a crucified Christ, could ever be regarded as "wisdom." He has shown that the world can be divided into two types of people, those who find a crucified Christ foolish, and those who find that in Christ lies the power and wisdom of God himself to call and to save. The section ended by pointing to God's power and wisdom as greater than anything that anyone might conceive.

Paul now gives two examples of how these truths have played out in the experience of the Corinthians themselves. In 1:26–31 he addresses the (strange) impact of the gospel on the Corinthians themselves. God in his wisdom did not choose those that might have been expected to be chosen. The Corinthians embody in their number people who lack learning, status, or power. Yet God chose them, and they came to faith. They can only boast in the Lord, for this has happened by his power. In the following section (2:1–5), Paul will proceed to apply the teaching of the nature of God's power and wisdom to himself as one who proclaims the gospel.

Main Idea

The Corinthian Christians themselves provide evidence for Paul's argument that people are called by God in Christ through God's choosing and according to his purposes. They demonstrate that God's wisdom triumphs over human wisdom, and so there is only one ground left on which to boast: the Lord himself, who has done it all.

Translation

1 Corinthians 1:26–31

26a	Illustration of 25a	**Reflect upon your call, brothers** [and sisters],
b	Circumstance of call	that not many [of you were] wise according to the flesh,
c	List	not many powerful,
d	List	not many wellborn,
27a	Contrast	but
		God chose the foolish things of the world
b	Purpose	in order to shame the wise and
c	List	**God chose the weak things of the world**
d	Purpose	in order to shame the strong and
28a	List	**God chose** **the insignificant things of the world** and
b	List	the despised things,
c		the things that are not,
d	Purpose	in order to bring to nothing the things that are,
29a	Purpose (summative) 1	so that no human being might boast before God.
30a	Cause	Now because of him [God]
b	Assertion	**you are in Christ Jesus,**
c	Expansion	who became wisdom for us from God, and
d		righteousness, and sanctification, and redemption,
31a	Purpose (summative) 2	so that as it is written:
b	Quotation	"Let the one who boasts, boast in the Lord." [Jer 9:23]

Structure

To the called, Christ has been seen to be the power and wisdom of God (v. 24). Paul uses the experience of the Corinthian Christians themselves as a powerful *ad hominem* argument. In vv. 26–29, he asks them to reflect upon *their* calling. He begins by stating the type of people, from a worldly point of view, that they were (v. 26). Then he talks of how God chose them despite their lowliness and insignificance (vv. 27–28), with the result that no one can boast of their part in what has happened in their calling (v. 29). Paul then summarizes this example by showing again the centrality of Christ who is in himself wisdom from God (vv. 30–31).

The text becomes even more powerful as Paul builds two series of three statements to reinforce his point. Thus, in v. 26 three statements begin with "not many...," and these contrast with a list of three (vv. 27–28) that begin, "God chose...." The emphatic threefold repetition of "God chose" (ἐξελέξατο ὁ θεός) and the concluding phrase "before God" (ἐνώπιον τοῦ θεοῦ) in v. 29 further emphasize Paul's insistence that in their calling *all* were dependent upon God. Notably, then, the first list of the three matters of status is seen to be overturned in the second list as Paul draws the focus back to God and to Christ in v. 30. The whole is rounded off with another biblical quotation that summarizes Paul's message (v. 31).

Exegetical Outline

> **III. A Radically Different Perspective Shaped by the Cross (1:18–2:5)**
>   A. The Word of the Cross (1:18–25)
> ➡ **B. Illustrated in the Calling of the Corinthians (1:26–31)**
>   1. They Had Little Status in the World When Called (1:26)
>   2. God Still Pursued His Purpose in Their Call (1:27–29)
>   3. God Has Given Them New Status "in Christ" (1:30)
>   4. They Should Boast in the Lord (1:31)
>   C. Illustrated in Paul's Preaching (2:1–5)

Explanation of the Text

1:26a Reflect upon your call, brothers [and sisters][1] (Βλέπετε γὰρ[2] τὴν κλῆσιν ὑμῶν, ἀδελφοί). In an *ad hominem*[3] argument, Paul now asks the Corinthians to "reflect" on their calling, that is, to reflect on how they came to faith and their status and condition in society when they did so.[4] Calling has figured significantly in Paul's argument thus far. He has talked of his own call in 1:1, of the Corinthians' calling (1:2), of their calling into "covenant participation" (1:9), and again to the calling of those to whom he writes (1:24). The significance Paul attaches to the word "calling" (κλῆσις) is considerable because it refers not just to God's

summons but to the accompanying transforming power of God. It is the circumstances surrounding the total package of how they became Christians that Paul wants them to reflect upon. They are to look again at God's gracious working among them in an undeserved love and calling. As his "brothers and sisters" Paul identifies with them. He will reflect on his own calling shortly (2:1–5), which is a further magnificent demonstration of God's grace.

"Reflect upon" (Βλέπετε) could be either indicative or imperative, but the context here in introducing an example for consideration suggests it is imperative. The usual meaning of this verb is "to

---

1. For "brothers" (ἀδελφοί) see 1:10.
2. "For" (γάρ) links to the next stage of Paul's argument and need not be translated.
3. Fitzmyer, *1 Corinthians*, 161.
4. See comments on calling at 1:2–3.

look at" or "to see." Used metaphorically like this the translations "reflect upon" or "consider" are both appropriate. Conzelmann points to the paradox here. They are being asked to "look where 'nothing' is to be seen."[5]

1:26b that not many [of you were] wise according to the flesh, not many powerful, not many wellborn (ὅτι οὐ πολλοὶ σοφοὶ κατὰ σάρκα, οὐ πολλοὶ δυνατοί, οὐ πολλοὶ εὐγενεῖς). As they reflect on their calling, Paul asks them to note the contrast between the "wisdoms" of which he has been writing. Thus, he draws attention to the social status of believers in Corinth. "That" (ὅτι) introduces three clauses that describe the circumstances of the "calling." The verb "to be" must be inserted for sense in English in at least the first of the three clauses. Thus "wise" (σοφοί), "powerful" (δυνατοί), and "wellborn" (εὐγενεῖς) are complements of the verb "to be."

While he has already spoken of power and wisdom, the introduction of the word "wellborn" (εὐγένης) makes it clear that Paul is primarily thinking sociologically and describing, as truly lowly, the social standing of *most* of the Christians in this church. The three words describe those elements of society that were most esteemed in Hellenistic Roman societies.[6] Generally, the "wise" were regarded as the clever in the community, probably especially well-read and capable in public speaking. The "powerful" were those who could exercise power in society, perhaps a power that came from learning, wealth, or political standing. The "well-born" were those offspring of the powerful and those with social standing and wealth. Whether Winter is correct in suggesting that all Corinthians would immediately have recognized these three words as coming specifically from the arena of sophistic training is perhaps questionable. Nevertheless, he amply demonstrates how widespread were the ideas that social status lay in wisdom, power, being wellborn, and wealthy. He suggests that "the wise" (σοφοί) were those taught by the Sophist educators, while the "powerful" (i.e., those of influence) and "wellborn" would have described their parents, since most Sophist teachers came from well-to-do families.[7]

There is no doubt that Paul's concern is that the Corinthians were in danger of succumbing to the idolatry of the age. The irony on which Paul builds is that "not many" (οὐ πολλοί) of these people came from that sector of society. Put positively, many were called and came to know God despite *not* coming from an elite social group. Indeed, their existence as Christians who belong to God proves the point made in 1:21 that the world "did not know God by means of wisdom." For the "not many" who did have that background, the visible evidence around them of what Paul was saying was that the majority who had come to faith still possessed no significant status in society. Paul thus succeeds in humbling those who did consider themselves wise, powerful, and wellborn since in the church they fraternized with a majority with whom they would normally have had little social contact. The fact that Paul says "not many" implies

---

5. Conzelmann, *1 Corinthians*, 49.

6. In various contexts, the words and the ideas they represent are to be found in Greek literature. Munck, *Paul and the Salvation of Mankind*, 162n2, provides numerous examples. He correctly emphasizes that each of these three words spoke to attributes prized by the Sophists. Cf. Plutarch's *Moralia* 1.58C–E, writing of the Stoics who "call the wise man at the same time rich, handsome, well-born, and a king" (LCL). Philo in *Virtues* 187–226, writes in some depth about his opinion of those who are deemed wellborn. Thucydides, *History of the Peloponnesian War* 1.126.3, describes Cylon as "both well born and powerful." See further comments and citations in Winter, *Philo and Paul among the Sophists*, 191.

7. Winter, *Philo and Paul among the Sophists*, 190. In this he follows Munck, *Paul and the Salvation of Mankind* (ibid., 161ff.). Cf. Clarke, *Secular Christian Leadership in Corinth*, 41–45.

that *some* did have worldly status in Corinth. There is some limited evidence of this in the text of Scripture. It is just possible that Stephanas, mentioned in 1:16 and again with others in 16:15–18, was one such person. "Chloe's people," Aquila and Priscilla, and others were probably business people who travelled far and wide (1:11; 16:19). Crispus was likely the noted synagogue leader (1:14). By implication Paul points to the fact that this urban congregation was socially diverse.[8]

Paul describes the "wise" as wise "according to the flesh" (κατὰ σάρκα). This phrase is used on a number of occasions by Paul with a variety of sometimes subtly different connotations. In the Corinthian correspondence it occurs twice in this epistle (see also 10:18) and a further six times in 2 Corinthians (1:17; 5:16 [2x]; 10:2, 3; 11:18). It can simply refer to the historical flesh and blood of the people (Rom 4:1; 9:5).[9] More broadly in Paul's writings, however, the phrase or even on occasion the simple use of the word "flesh" (σάρξ) has a spiritual significance and contrasts with what is of the Spirit or from God. This means that it is often offered as part of an assessment on a spiritual condition or situation.[10] In the immediate context here, different spiritual conditions are being discussed. Paul is contrasting the wisdom of this world with that of God. At one level Paul may be seen as neutrally stating what was presumably obvious: many were

not wise "according to the flesh," that is, in terms of their natural abilities, just as many were not powerful. However, as Paul makes his point this fact contrasts dramatically with how these same people are to be viewed given their status as Christians. In 2:12, as the argument develops, Paul directly sets "the spirit of the world" against the "Spirit of God." This is the heart of Paul's contrast of wisdoms that he has introduced here in chapter 1. We take it therefore that Paul uses the phrase "according to the flesh" with a spiritually negative connotation here. After all, as Schreiner points out those mentioned as wise in 1:26 "will be rejected at the judgment because their wisdom is of this world (1 Cor 1:20; 3:18–20) and in accordance with 'the rulers of this age' (1 Cor 2:6, 8)."[11] One of Paul's concerns is that the Corinthians are making judgments even among their own number based on the world's perceptions of how things should be rather than God's. In 2 Corinthians 1:17 Paul faces up to the fact that in the way the Corinthians are reacting to him it is almost as if they are saying *he* is unspiritual! Thus, he rhetorically asks: "Do I make my plans according to the flesh?" (ESV). In other words, he asks whether they believe he works in a "worldly," deceptive way or honestly and in a godly way.[12] The intention of the phrase when it is used in 1 Corinthians 10:18 raises the same question. Is Paul denoting "simply physical kinship,"[13] or does

---

8. An account of the diversity of the early urban church is found in Meeks, *First Urban Christians*, esp. 51–73. Munck's comment that "the extreme top and bottom of the Greco-Roman social scale are missing from the picture" is to overstate the evidence (*Paul and the Salvation of Mankind*, 73.) See also Theissen, *Social Setting of Pauline Christianity*, esp. ch. 2; and Clarke, *Secular and Christian Leadership in Corinth*, 45n25, where he takes issue with Munck.

9. Even these verses, however, appear in contexts where Paul eventually makes clear spiritual divisions between those who belong to Christ and those who do not.

10. Some clear examples of this use are to be found in Rom 8:5, 12–13; Gal 4:23, 29.

11. Thomas R. Schreiner, *Paul, Apostle of God's Glory in Christ: A Pauline Theology* (Downers Grove, IL: InterVarsity Press, 2001), 144.

12. See further uses of the phrase in 2 Corinthians: 5:16 [2x]; 10:2, 3; 11:18. In 5:16 the contrast is between the old and the new creation. Christians are not to be regarded "according to the flesh" for the old has passed away, and they are now "a new creation" (5:17 ESV).

13. So Dunn, *Theology of Paul*, 65. See Dunn's excellent analysis of Paul's "anthropological presuppositions" and his use both of the word σάρξ and of the phrase κατὰ σάρκα (ibid., 62–73).

he, even in this context, imply a spiritual assessment of Israel? In our comments there, we argue he is making a spiritual assessment of historic Israel.

Thus in 1:26 Paul asks the Corinthians to reflect the thinking of God as they assess "wisdom" rather than the thinking of a godless and fallen society. It is ironic that those who, as we discover later (especially in 3:1ff.), clearly think they are spiritual are making judgments based on the values of a sinful and status-conscious society.

As Paul makes his appeal to the Corinthians to reflect on God's power and wisdom and its contrast with the power and wisdom of this world, it is easy to miss his deeper argument. True spiritual maturity will involve thinking *biblically*. Paul has called them back to Scripture several times already in this opening chapter, since in God's word lies wisdom. In vv. 18–19 he has both quoted and alluded to verses from Isaiah to show that his critique of secular wisdom in the light of Christ crucified is not new but follows in the older prophetic critique of the views of the world that are at odds with God's wisdom. Here, Jeremiah 9 provides the framework for his thinking, and in 1 Corinthians 1:31 he concludes with a quotation (Jer 9:24). While parallels in Greek to what Paul writes here have been shown above, it is more likely that the threefold negative assessment of v. 26 draws on Jeremiah's threefold negative assessment in Jeremiah 9:23 (9:22 LXX)— "Thus says the LORD: 'Let not the wise man boast in his wisdom, let not the mighty man boast in his might, let not the rich man boast in his riches'" (ESV). As Alexandra Brown points out, "Jeremiah 8:4–10:25 is characterized, as is 1 Corinthians 1–4, by the recurrent themes of 'knowing' and being

'wise.'"[14] The context in which Jeremiah wrote and in which Paul saw a parallel with Corinth involved God's people and their leadership claiming to be "wise" when they were not (Jer 8:8). Of these people the prophet had written, "The wise will be put to shame" (8:9 ESV). These people did not want "to know [God]" (9:6 ESV [9:5 LXX]) as they should have done. They had not seen the covenant law or the covenant Lord as the source of God's wisdom but had looked to their own power, wisdom, and riches. Their circumcision was not of the heart but simply of the flesh (9:25–26 [9:24–25 LXX]). For Paul, just as God had put to shame the "wise" of old, so he will do again, as vv. 27–28 make clear.

1:27 but God chose the foolish things[15] of the world in order to shame the wise and God chose the weak things of the world in order to shame the strong (ἀλλὰ τὰ μωρὰ τοῦ κόσμου ἐξελέξατο ὁ θεὸς ἵνα καταισχύνῃ τοὺς σοφούς, καὶ τὰ ἀσθενῆ τοῦ κόσμου ἐξελέξατο ὁ θεὸς ἵνα καταισχύνῃ τὰ ἰσχυρά). The contrast is set up with the strong adversative "but" (ἀλλά). What a difference there is between what human beings (κατὰ σάρκα) see as important and what God sees as important, demonstrated in the way God has acted. That "God chose" (ἐξελέξατο ὁ θεός) his own way of doing things is given strong emphasis, as subject and verb are repeated three times (including the occurrence in the next verse). This second triad contrasts with the three types of people Paul has just identified in v. 26.

God's choice involves his sovereign decision to grant his love and grace to whomever he pleases. Those who may have been humbled by what Paul has just written are now shown what a privilege is

---

14. In an analysis of Paul's use of Jeremiah in 1 Cor 1:26–31, it is surprising that Alexandra Brown does not make anything of Jer 8:8–9. It seems to me these verses may provide Paul's reason for using Jer 9 (Alexandra R. Brown, *The Cross and Human Transformation: Paul's Apocalyptic Word in 1 Corinthi-* ans [Minneapolis: Fortress, 1995], 87–96).

15. Paul writes of *people* but uses neuter substantival adjectives τὰ μωρά, τὰ ἀσθενῆ; see also in v. 28. Barrett, *First Corinthians*, 58, suggests this is "to generalize" and "perhaps . . . to spare the Corinthians too blunt a description of themselves."

theirs as the chosen of God. While elsewhere God's choice is clearly embedded in his eternal decree to save those whom he would save, here Paul looks more immediately at the impact of that choice. The argument is almost curt in its forthrightness. He is calling some of the Corinthians "foolish" as to the world's standards. *Yet* God chose them. Paul knows the depths of God's grace and love and is saying to his audience that if they will only reflect on what God has done with them, they too will see that God's loving priorities are utterly distinct from those of humanity.

Here in v. 27 a purpose clause picks up on the first of the three groups of people mentioned in 1:26: the "wise." God's work of choosing set out "to shame" these people. Paul alludes to Jeremiah 8:9, "The wise men shall be put to shame" (cf. 1 Sam 2:10 LXX). In Jeremiah (LXX) the agent of the passive verb ἠσχύνθησαν is clearly God. Thus, Paul makes God the subject here in 1 Corinthians 1:27 (ἵνα καταισχύνη τοὺς σοφούς). While "shame" would have been deeply humiliating in the status-ridden Greek society,[16] Paul is still concerned with teaching a biblical view of two wisdoms set in opposition to each other and showing that God will overthrow the wisdom of the world. Not only does Jeremiah talk of wise men being put to shame, but it is interesting that the same verb "to shame" is used in Isaiah 28:16 (LXX), the passage that lay behind the "stumbling block" of 1:23. In Isaiah 28 a person who "believes" in the "foundation stone" will not be "shamed," that is, face destruction (ὁ

πιστεύων ἐπ᾽ αὐτῷ οὐ μὴ καταισχυνθῇ). In Romans 9:32–33, speaking of Israel Paul writes: "They stumbled over the stumbling stone. As it is written: 'See, I lay in Zion a stone that causes people to stumble and a rock of that makes them fall, and the one who believes *in him* will never be put to shame [καταισχυνθήσεται].'" Thus Paul shows that God's choice of "the foolish things" is part of his deliberate council to "shame," that is, to bring upon the unbelieving "wise" God's judgment of destruction. In 1:21 Paul had put this the other way around: "It pleased God through the foolishness of preaching to save those who believe."

Paul's second description of the Corinthian Christians in v. 26 was that not many were "powerful." So in v. 27 Paul repeats "God chose" and speaks of "the weak things" (τὰ ἀσθενῆ). Many of the Christians were simply weak in terms of power, influence, and status in the community. But God's deliberate purpose (repeating a purpose clause) was to "shame the strong" (meaning the same as shaming the wise).

1:28 and God chose the insignificant things of the world and the despised things, the things that are not, in order to bring to nothing the things that are (καὶ τὰ ἀγενῆ τοῦ κόσμου καὶ τὰ ἐξουθενημένα ἐξελέξατο ὁ θεός, τὰ μὴ ὄντα, ἵνα τὰ ὄντα καταργήσῃ). The third group in v. 26 was those who were not "wellborn." Now in the third of Paul's contrasting statements he writes that God chose "the insignificant things" (τὰ ἀγενῆ).

---

16. See the essay, "In Depth: Shame," following comments on 6:5–6. By definition, shame is humiliating in all societies. In the Greco-Roman world of Paul's day there was perhaps an even greater consciousness of status than we find today. It was difficult to rise up through any social tiers in society. People then, as now, loved to be honored or to be named with respect. In Corinth there are great numbers of inscriptions honoring citizens of repute; see Witherington, *Conflict and Community*, 8, who also writes that "Corinth was a city where public boasting and self-promotion had become an art form . . . where the

worst thing that could happen was for one's reputation to be publicly tarnished." Honor and respect allow people to "boast" of their success, status, achievements, wisdom, etc. Shame is what is experienced by those who find they are torn down publicly and have nothing left in which to "boast." Shame serves to confirm a person's inadequate community standing. However, the Old Testament background in Paul's use of the word points to God's judgment, not just to social embarrassment or abasement in society.

The word in this context provides an opposite to "wellborn"; thus, it might be translated as "not wellborn" or "born in humble circumstances." Yet in this case the contrast is made much stronger by two additional descriptions, "the despised things" (τὰ ἐξουθενημένα) and "the things that are not" (τὰ μὴ ὄντα).

People who were not wellborn would have been regarded as insignificant in the eyes of the world. Such people are also "despised" (ἐξουθενημένα). These are the very people God chose contrary to all that the world would count valuable. Paul summarizes the list by reference to "the things that are not" (τὰ μὴ ὄντα). In modern English we can talk of being a "no one" or, in slang, of being a "zero." This is what Paul has in mind here. This is how many of the Corinthian Christians were regarded by the society around them. Epictetus writes in a similar way; he says he expects others to despise him and imagines them saying, "Epictetus was a nothing" (οὐδὲν ἦν ὁ Ἐπίκτητος).[17] Paul has shown that in his choosing God has comprehensively demolished the values of the world. Yet he has also pointed toward ideas, not yet developed at this point, of God being involved in a new creation in Christ. The "things that are not" have been taken by God and fashioned for his purposes. A new people has been brought into being. Now he shows the purpose for this.

The final purpose clause of the series parallels the previous two clauses in vv. 27b ("to shame the wise") and v. 27d ("to shame the strong"). Paul says God has chosen in this manner "to bring to nothing [or 'destroy'] the things that are" (ἵνα τὰ ὄντα καταργήσῃ). This verb ("to bring to nothing"; καταργέω), like the verb "to shame," indicates judgment and destruction in a number of biblical contexts. These ideas are more explicit in 2:6, 6:13, and especially 15:24 where the word is examined in greater detail. The preaching of Christ crucified completely upends what the world values. Through this gospel God works his purposes of salvation and judgment. He raises up that which seems foolish and weak and "nothing" in the world's eyes and judges (brings to shame and nullifies) that which the world deems of value.

1:29 so that no human being might boast before God (ὅπως μὴ καυχήσηται πᾶσα σὰρξ ἐνώπιον τοῦ θεοῦ). If the purpose of God's choosing is that the people who are considered "something" in the world's eyes are ultimately brought to judgment and destruction, there is also a final summative purpose that concerns all people, including those who are being saved. The end of God's choosing (introduced by ὅπως[18]) is that "no human being might boast before God." Here πᾶσα σὰρξ (lit., "all flesh") refers to all humanity. The unbelievers will have nothing to boast of as they are brought to destruction, but neither will those who are being saved.

"Boasting" is developed as a theme later in this epistle (see the discussion at 9:15). The concept was a commonplace in the Greek world.[19]

---

17. Epictetus, *Discourses* 3.9.14 (Oldfather, LCL). Theissen, *Social Setting of Pauline Christianity*, 71, lists a number of sayings from Greek writers where the wellborn are brought to nothing or contrasted with those who are nothing.

18. BDF §369.4 suggests that ὅπως is used in this purpose clause for stylistic reasons since ἵνα has been used previously.

19. Philo in *Worse* 32–35 allegorizes the OT figure of Cain to refer to the self-seekers of his day who are proud of their learning and wealth. See also Plutarch's *Moralia* 7.539–47 for his treatise on proper and improper self-glorification. Plutarch demonstrates an ambivalence with regard to self-praise. On the one hand, he talks of "the abhorrence of self-praise," and, on the other hand, he talks of a right place for talking about oneself, such as when the truth about oneself must be told (7.539.E) or when avoiding self-pity (7.541.A–B; LCL). This last section offers an extreme contrast with the apostle Paul's "boast" in his misfortunes in 1 Cor 4:8–13 and 2 Cor 11:21–30. Paul's thought world is a far cry from Plutarch's approval of "self-glorification" when avoiding self-pity. "So the man cast down by fortune . . . using self-glorification to pass from a humbled

Though Hellenistic writers did see occasion for "self-glorification" (περιαυτολογία),[20] on the whole boasting was despised. According to Bosch, there were at least four reasons that "boasting" was regularly denigrated: (a) because it was offensive to the gods, (b) because it was offensive to people, (c) because it sounded bad in company, and (d) because the basis of the boast was not considered worthy.[21] As Paul uses the term here, undoubtedly the Corinthians would have understood his criticism of them. With their grasping after status in the church and their flaunting of the grace-gifts they would surely have felt offended by this. However, while they might have felt personally attacked here, Paul's mention of "no human being" (μὴ . . . πᾶσα σὰρξ) would help them see that he was making a much deeper theological point. He was arguing that the trouble with *all people* "before God" (ἐνώπιον τοῦ θεοῦ) is their tendency to promote their own accomplishments and achievements. God's choosing negates any appeal to human endeavor of any sort.

It is important to see here that Paul's definition of boasting redefines the Hellenistic concept in the light, once again, of biblical thought on the matter. The importance of Jeremiah 8–9 to Paul's perspective on what is going on at Corinth and the appeal to Jeremiah 9:23 (9:22 LXX) for his triad in 1 Corinthians 1:26 makes it unremarkable that he should continue to keep the same prophetic text

in mind. Paul has identified the issue as standing "before God." In the text of Jeremiah, the Lord insists in 9:23 (9:22 LXX) that wisdom cannot help, and the people must not "boast" in these things. However, in 9:24 (9:23 LXX) they *can* and *should* boast in the fact that they "understand and know that I am the Lord" (συνίειν καὶ γινώσκειν ὅτι ἐγώ εἰμι κύριος). Not all boasting is to be seen as something to be disdained! In v. 31 Paul offers his summary redefinition of "boasting" as he quotes this text. Thus we find Paul advocating a positive use of the word. Paul so redefines the idea (biblically) that while most boasting remains wrong, there is a boast that is right and proper. This seems to have no background in Hellenistic thought, but Paul insists there is a way in which standing before God is possible and that it is through belief in Christ crucified. Since this is all of grace, of God's wisdom and God's choice, it is appropriate to boast in the Lord.[22]

1:30a–b Now because of him [God] you are in Christ Jesus (ἐξ αὐτοῦ δὲ ὑμεῖς ἐστε ἐν Χριστῷ Ἰησοῦ). This verse is first and foremost a reminder of God's *grace* in Christ. There is a substantial contrast in this verse with what has gone before. Paul has talked of things that "are not" (v. 28). Now, by contrast he says because of [God] *"you are"* (ὑμεῖς ἐστε). "Because of him" (ἐξ αὐτοῦ) suggests that

---

and piteous state to an attitude of triumph . . . strikes us not as offensive or bold, but as great and indomitable" (7.541.A–B; LCL). In similar vein, see the study of the Hellenistic view that comparison of oneself with those who are greater helps develop self-knowledge in Christopher Forbes, "Comparison, Self-Praise and Irony: Paul's Boasting and the Conventions of Hellenistic Rhetoric," *NTS* 32 (1986): 1–30.

20. Plutarch, *Moralia* 7.539.E.

21. Jordi Sanchez Bosch, *"Gloriarse" según San Pablo: sentido y Teología de* Καυχάομαι, AnBib 40 (Rome: Biblical Institute Press, 1970), 4ff. See also Gardner, *Gifts of God*, 85–87, for multiple examples of "boasting" being regarded in a pejorative way.

22. Paul's redefinition of the concept of boasting in the

light of texts such as Jer 9:23 explains why he can use the idea positively on a number of occasions in 2 Corinthians (e.g., 2 Cor 1:14; 5:12). In 2 Corinthians Paul finds himself having to commend himself to the Corinthians because of the negative comparisons they make in their assessment of him. As he goes on to talk of his "boast," however, he speaks only of his ministry and how he has followed the Lord. While the Corinthians put themselves forward in terms of their own abilities, Paul refuses such comparisons but writes of his work in terms of his submission to God. See the useful summary of the different way that Paul commends himself to the Corinthians to what they were doing in their "boast" and what they expected of Paul in George H. Guthrie, *2 Corinthians* (Grand Rapids: Baker Academic, 2015), 488–90.

God is the effective *cause* of their Christian status in Christ, but the phrase may also indicate that God is the *source* of their being in Christ. The use of the personal pronoun with the verb (ὑμεῖς ἐστε) and its position in the sentence give emphasis.

The worldly emphasis on wisdom and knowledge providing status and honor had led some in Corinth to emphasize grace-gifts like "knowledge" or "wisdom of word" as evidence of their standing in the Christian community. They had simply "spiritualized" and then imported the values of their society into the church. Therefore, Paul has systematically undermined those values and has reminded the Corinthians that there is *no* standing before God, no "boast" (v. 28), to be found in any of this. *Nevertheless*, they do have a standing before God; not through their grace-gifts or great rhetoric or wisdom of word but simply because God has *caused* them to have it. Even though the word *grace* is not used here, Paul's whole argument depends on God's grace. He is the source and cause of their standing and of the fact that they do "belong" because he has provided the King who, representing his people, has brought about their salvation through his crucifixion and resurrection. In fact, if "wisdom" gives standing in the pagan community, then, says Paul, Christians should understand that they too know a wisdom—albeit different from the world's—that is revealed by grace and is possessed by all who are "in Christ."[23]

1:30c–d who became wisdom for us from God, and righteousness, and sanctification, and redemption (ὃς ἐγενήθη σοφία ἡμῖν ἀπὸ θεοῦ, δικαιοσύνη τε καὶ ἁγιασμὸς καὶ ἀπολύτρωσις).

It was in Christ's death and resurrection that the possibility of true objective status before God became available to those who believe. Christ is the one who shows forth and has lived out the plan of God, bringing in his person the fulfillment of the covenant blessings and curses. He *is* wisdom, but not as understood by the world. He is the manifestation of the great plan of God to save and to judge. He is the only way that anyone can have the standing that ultimately matters, standing "before God" (ἐνώπιον τοῦ θεοῦ; v. 29). Paul now includes himself with these Christians as he moves to the first-person plural. The aorist passive looks back to a time in the past when Christ became wisdom. The dative "for us" (ἡμῖν) is a dative of advantage. "From God" (ἀπὸ θεοῦ) refers back to God as the ultimate source.[24]

As he builds toward the Jeremiah quotation in v. 31, Paul now adds three words: "righteousness," "sanctification," and "redemption." Each have to do with standing before God, though each carries a distinct meaning.[25] They partly explicate the content of "wisdom" as it relates to believers.[26] Once again there is a partial parallel from the prophecy. Following Jeremiah, Paul refers to "righteousness" (δικαιοσύνη). In the original context in Jeremiah, righteousness has to do with God who practices steadfast love, justice, and righteousness; he has pleasure in these things and expects them of his people (9:24 [9:23 LXX]). In this part of Jeremiah, God's righteousness has to do with God's faithful verdict upon his people that, unless they heed his warnings, will be one of judgment. For Paul also, the idea of divine verdict is present. The crucified king who died for his people (cf. 1:13) has been

---

23. Much of the commentary on chapter 2 will attend to this in more detail.

24. The subject of a passive verb is normally indicated by ὑπό + genitive; ἀπό + genitive is less frequent (see also 1 Cor 11:32). God is the "ultimate agent" (Wallace, *Greek Grammar*, 433).

25. N. T. Wright suggests they indicate "broadly, a status, a process and an event" (Wright, *Paul and the Faithfulness of God*, 950).

26. The NIV makes this obvious by inserting "that is, our righteousness."

vindicated by God, evidenced in the resurrection. As the representative king of all who believe, Christians find that "in Christ" that which was not true of them—that they could stand before the Lord—is now true. Paul does not say here how this happens in the crucifixion and resurrection of Christ, but he surely has in mind that Jesus died under the judgment reserved for those who sin; that is, for those who breach covenant (cf. Gal 3:3). On the cross, as 2 Corinthians 5:21 puts it, "For our sake he made him to be sin who knew no sin" (ESV). Christians thus find that "in Christ" they do indeed have covenantal standing before God. They, like him, have been found "righteous." Present Christian community status is thus assured, but not in the way the world had imagined. This assurance of the "not guilty" verdict anticipates the resurrection of all who believe when their vindication will be as evident as Christ's was in his resurrection. Paul will later show that this has important ethical implications for the lives of believers, but that is not his point here.

"Sanctification" (ἁγιασμός) also has to do with the objective status that Christians find they have "in Christ" (as in 6:11, where the aorist tense is used of having been sanctified by the Spirit). Often sanctification is held up to the Christian as a lifetime process through which he or she becomes more Christlike, more holy. However, that rightful call for a holy life, which plays such an important role in this letter, arises from the *prior* work of God in Christ in which Christians find they are a set-apart people "chosen" by God. It is this to which Paul has drawn attention in vv. 27–28 with his threefold repetition of "God chose." Thus "sanctification" here continues to have a distinctly Old Testament or covenantal feel to it. "In Christ" the King, Christians find they are caught up with God's

people of old to whom God said, "Now therefore, if you will indeed obey my voice and keep my covenant, you shall be my treasured possession among all peoples, for all the earth is mine; and you shall be to me a kingdom of priests and a holy nation" (Exod 19:5–6 ESV). The King has obeyed and kept covenant, and so his people find themselves truly to be "a holy people."

Finally, Paul speaks of "redemption" (ἀπολύτρωσις). This might have been expected to be first in the list as a word that well summarizes the whole of the work of Christ on behalf of his people, but its position at the end of the list may give it a certain emphasis (cf. Rom 3:24–25). The picture comes from the world of slavery and the payment of a purchase price for a slave.[27] This price might have bought freedom, but it often indicated the transfer from one master to another. Once again the Israel of old provides the backstory. The freedom of Israel from Egypt and its entry into the promised land was seen as God's "redemption" (e.g., Ps 111:9). Of course, this deliverance was freedom from a particular form of slavery, and so "freedom" is the right term to use. Yet in fact a transfer took place as Israel became the fully formed people belonging to God. In redemption Paul has in view once again that which has happened in the past in Christ.[28] Of course, it looks forward to "the day of redemption" when Christ returns, but here it reflects what Paul elsewhere refers to as being "sealed" for that day (Eph 4:30). The aorist "became for us" (ἐγενήθη) still governs this description. It was in Christ's total work on the cross and in the vindication of his resurrection that Christians were gathered up "in Christ," freed from the domain of sin and its consequent judgment by God and transferred into God's own kingdom (Col 1:13–14).

---

27. See the essay, "In Depth: Slavery as Metaphor and the Transfer of Lordships" at 7:24.

28. See further comments on the purchase price for redemption at 6:20.

Since those who *were not* now *are* in Christ Jesus, their status before God is established and confirmed. Through no action on their own part, through no degree of human wisdom or plan, God worked in Christ crucified to accomplish all that was necessary to allow them to stand before God.

1:31 so that as it is written, "Let the one who boasts, boast in the Lord" (ἵνα καθὼς γέγραπται, Ὁ καυχώμενος ἐν κυρίῳ καυχάσθω). God's work in Christ brings this quotation from Jeremiah to fulfillment. Christ crucified has shown that there is only one possible boast, for it is all "from God" and it is in the Lord. This construction introducing a quotation from Scripture (ἵνα καθὼς) is elliptical and difficult to understand, but it is likely that this is a further summative purpose clause similar to 1:29. The flow of vv. 30–31 becomes clearer with the help of a paraphrase: "You are in Christ Jesus, who became wisdom for us from God . . . in order that (it may be noted) just as is written (in Scripture), 'Let the one who boasts, boast in the Lord.'" In this sense, the quotation is not a "proof" of the argument thus far but evidence of "fulfillment."

We have noted from the context of Jeremiah 9:23–24 reasons why Paul should have turned to this text beyond just the mention of "boasting." In 9:12, Jeremiah questions who may be "wise" enough to understand what the Lord is doing with Israel. The Corinthians seem by their actions not to have understood what God has done with them. In the end, all participation in God's church, all *belonging*, all status before the covenant Lord is entirely "because of him [God]" (v. 30). There is therefore a legitimate boasting. There can be no self-glorying, for all glory is due the Lord.

Theology in Application

Proclaiming the Gospel to All

The Corinthian Christians seem to have been making judgments about their leaders, about each other, and about those coming to the faith that were based more on the values of the world than on the gospel of Christ crucified. Such is sinful human nature that people seem almost bound to do this whatever their own background at the point of their conversion. This point is well inferred from Paul's use of Jeremiah. There people boasted in their wisdom, a reliance upon Torah, and race. Yet Paul sees Jeremiah's critique of such boasting as offering a parallel to what he sees in a church influenced largely by a Greek society. This provides an important warning for the modern church. The fact of the matter is that God chooses (repeated three times for emphasis in 1:27–28) whom he wills for deliberate reasons. While it is his intention to save from among all peoples and all types of people, it is also his intention to "shame" and destroy that which is proud, strong, self-sufficient, and arrogant. He will not allow anything or anyone to usurp his place as God of gods. In reaching those who are unwise and weak from a worldly point of view, God is not ignoring those who are rich and wise, but he is making a statement about himself. He is not prejudiced or bigoted. (*Some* were wise, v. 26!) His justice and mercy and grace extends to all people regardless of their background. God teaches this important fact about himself by ensuring that those who are saved often reflect in considerable numbers those whom the world might despise.

In the modern church there is a need to ask how this heart of the gospel is reflected in evangelistic methods, in the amount of time dedicated to different sociological groupings, and so on. Many groups concentrate upon evangelism among the highly educated and those who influence the world. Some college-student ministries concentrate on the "high fliers" and the more prestigious universities and colleges rather than others. The reasoning seems fair enough. If the influential people of this world become Christians, they are more likely to be able to change society or to bring larger numbers of others to the Lord. The aim is good, but is the effectiveness of the message of Christ crucified being limited? That some are called to witness to such groups is no doubt part of God's plan. However, the vast majority of the world today who are coming to the faith live in countries where education is not that good, where there is not much wealth, and where people feel weak and exploited. It is easy to dismiss this on the grounds that people in such need are more likely to turn to Christ. Surely Paul would ask us to examine the nature of the gospel and of God himself to see that it is in God's purposes that the wise shall be shamed, even as God chooses the low and the despised and brings to nothing the things that are. Even as Paul writes of the gospel that centers on a crucified King, he must have recalled Deuteronomy 7:7–8: "The LORD set his love on you and chose you . . . . But it was because the LORD loves you" (ESV).

To what extent does the church unknowingly hide something of the very gospel she preaches when she spends more time seeking the wealthy, educated, and influential than the poor, disillusioned, and exploited of society? It is clear from what Paul says that in the early days of the church it was culturally and sociologically diverse. Many who were not highly regarded by society for one reason or another were converted. It is doubtful that Paul targeted these people; it is more likely that he simply, indiscriminately, and without prejudice spoke of Christ to all he encountered. More than that, he must have deliberately had a policy of ensuring he put himself in places where all types of people could hear the message. All of this has huge implications for the way we do evangelism or reach out to our communities. In fact, this has implications for how local churches delineate their "community" in the first place.

Humility in Proclamation

The passage also contains warnings and challenges for those called to pastor and teach in churches. With such an emphasis on further degrees and lengthy theological study, worthy as this may be, there can be an arrogance that attends this such that the nature of the gospel and its heart and center in Christ crucified may be obscured. It is the preached gospel of Christ that reveals and *is* the power of God to move men and women to faith. It is not the eloquence or learning of the preacher or teacher even when, in God's grace, such learning is used by God. The need to keep the focus, as Paul does, on "Christ crucified" is at one and the same time a call to simplicity and clarity in word and life, together with much hard work and preparation. These truths are deeply humbling. Just as those who are Christ's and were "nothings" become "something" in Christ, so the messenger—as we see with John the Baptist (John 3:30)—must decrease and become "nothing" as Christ is exalted.

Toward a Biblical Self-Esteem

It is also worth noting in an age that speaks so much of self-esteem that this passage points clearly to both a sinful self-esteem and a godly self-understanding. There can be no boasting from anyone that they have become a follower of Christ. Salvation is of grace in Christ. Paul insists that this does not take place because of who that person "was" or "is" but happens through the work of God in Christ as he chooses those who often are "nothing" in the world's eyes. Too frequently, modern worldly psychology is drawn into the church, a psychology that seeks to build up individuals, to "empower" them, to emphasize how good or how gifted they really are, and therefore how valuable they are to this world and to God. Such self-esteem is often based upon favorable comparisons with other people or upon a greater stress on "self." What Paul says in this passage shows that the gospel undercuts all such ideas of self-esteem. To begin with, the gospel leaves people with nothing. All people are "nothings," often in the world's eyes, but certainly in God's eyes until he mercifully extends his electing love.

On the other hand, this passage points the way forward for a people who feel alienated and undervalued in society and by family and friends. It offers a way forward that provides a realistic and godly way of self-appreciation and self-assessment. Christ crucified reminds the individual that Christ himself was not regarded well by anyone and that he was prepared to be humiliated for the sake of the Father's will. As Christians seek to have the mind of Christ and to apply this passage to themselves, so the world's assessment of self-esteem is turned upside down. Instead of fighting for it, instead of constantly feeling weighed down and even incapacitated by a low self-esteem, Christians can look to their calling and to the Father who chose them. Then they will see what he has now made them and the status he has given them as part of his family. Whatever the world may say of us, or even whatever other church members may think, it is all irrelevant when a person realizes the power of the words, "you are in Christ Jesus" (v. 30). The divine verdict is favorable ("righteousness"), redemption is established, the plan of God ("wisdom" in Christ) has been worked in the Christian, and he or she has status as part of the sanctified people of God. This is where self-understanding must lie for the Christian. This is what pastors and leaders must lead people toward, to drink not at the well of the world's wisdom but from the depths of the well of God's mercy, love, and compassion.

1 Corinthians 2:1–5

Literary Context

In 1:18–25 Paul, speaking in the first-person plural, had shown how the gospel centers on Christ crucified. This way of salvation is God's wisdom, however poorly it may sit with those who have an entirely different, "worldly" view of wisdom. In 1:26–31, Paul switched to the second-person plural and addressed the Corinthians to show that they themselves provide evidence of the power of God in the word of the cross. They were not "wise" or of great repute in society, yet God had called them to their present status "in Christ Jesus" (v. 30). They who had no status now have status. They had been "nothings," and so it was all entirely of God, who had made them his. In themselves, therefore, they bear witness to the power of God's wisdom in the preaching of the gospel of Christ crucified. Now, in 2:1–5, using the first-person singular, Paul offers himself as a second example to make a similar point, amplifying his passing comments of 1:17. Paul's own preaching was not powerful by worldly standards. It was neither he nor his words that had persuaded them of the gospel. Rather, God's Spirit and the power of God had enabled them to believe. This section serves as a bridge to the next major section of this epistle, in which Paul addresses the nature of true wisdom (2:6–4:21).

III. A Radically Different Perspective Shaped by the Cross (1:18–2:5)
  A. The Word of the Cross (1:18–25)
  B. Illustrated in the Calling of the Corinthians (1:26–31)
→ **C. Illustrated in Paul's Preaching (2:1–5)**
  IV. Mature Christians Pursue God's Wisdom (2:6–4:21)

Main Idea

Though weak, fearful, and not coming to Corinth with the great rhetorical skills that many in Greek society might have expected, Paul's gospel proclamation demonstrated both God's Holy Spirit and the power of God in such a way that people came to faith. Thus, in himself and in the fact that people have come to faith, Paul offers further proof that God's wisdom prevails over that of human beings.

Translation

1 Corinthians 2:1–5

1a		And I,
b	Temporal	when I came to you, brothers [and sisters],
c	1st personal example	**did not come to you**
d	Manner	with loftiness of speech or wisdom,
e	Content	proclaiming the testimony from God
2a	Explanation	For **I decided to know**
b	Content	**nothing among you** except
c	Content	Jesus Christ and him crucified.
3a		And
b	Manner	in weakness and in fear and in much trembling
c	2nd personal example	**I came to you,**
		and
4a	Content (negative)	**my speech and my proclamation were not in persuasive words of wisdom** ⟳
		but rather
b	Contrast (positive)	**[my speech and my proclamation were] in demonstration of the Spirit and** ⟳ **power,**
5a	Purpose (negative)	in order that your faith may not be [based] in the wisdom of men but rather
b	Contrast (positive)	[based] in God's power.

Structure

Paul's own testimony to the power of God in the gospel is clearly designed to show that the manner of his delivery reflects and amplifies the gospel's power. This is reflected in the structure in which Paul begins two sections, addressing his manner of presentation, with an autobiographical "and I" (κἀγώ; vv. 1, 3), and places between these a comment on the content of what he preached (v. 2). The manner of his proclamation and the content of the message are integrally intertwined.

He begins with a negative assessment of the manner in which he conducted his ministry. He did not come to promote his own wisdom or prowess (2:1). Secondly, he speaks of the *content* of his message—Christ crucified (v. 2). Then thirdly, he returns to his manner of ministry, speaking of his fear and repeating his comments about his delivery and speech (vv. 3–4a). Finally, Paul comments on the results of this preaching. He concludes with a strong contrast reinforced by a double reference to the power of God present in both the manner with which he has preached (v. 4b) and in the content that he has preached (v. 5). In his preaching, there was a demonstration of the Spirit and of God's power that meant their faith had to be rooted in God's power.

In this way Paul concludes the section that began at 1:18, in which he has demonstrated how, in the gospel, God has undermined the wisdom of the world. He has shown that this has been achieved through Christ crucified, who is the content of the gospel. In this gospel *God's* power and *his* wisdom have been revealed, and they stand in sharp contrast with the power and wisdom so sought after in Corinth. In the next section to the end of chapter 2, Paul will expand upon the nature of *God's* wisdom which must be pursued by all spiritual people.

Exegetical Outline

III. A Radically Different Perspective Shaped by the Cross (1:18–2:5)

    A. The Word of the Cross (1:18–25)

    B. Illustrated in the Calling of the Corinthians (1:26–31)

➡   **C. Illustrated in Paul's Preaching (2:1–5)**

        1. The Manner of His Preaching (2:1)

           a. Not with Lofty Speech

           b. Not with Wisdom

        2. The Content of His Preaching (2:2)

           a. Only Jesus Christ

           b. And Him Crucified

        3. The Manner of His Preaching (2:3–4a)

           a. In Weakness

           b. Not in Words of Wisdom

        4. The Results of His Preaching (2:4b–5)

           a. A Demonstration of the Spirit and power

           b. A Faith Resting on God's Power

Explanation of the Text

2:1 And I,[1] **when I came to you,**[2] **brothers [and sisters], did not come to you with loftiness of speech or wisdom, proclaiming the testimony from God** (Κἀγὼ ἐλθὼν πρὸς ὑμᾶς, ἀδελφοί, ἦλθον οὐ καθ' ὑπεροχὴν λόγου ἢ σοφίας καταγγέλλων ὑμῖν τὸ [μαρτύριον][3] τοῦ θεοῦ). Employing the first-person singular, Paul moves the argument on. He is now the subject of consideration rather than the Corinthians themselves. As he turns to his own preaching of the gospel by way of further example of how God's wisdom is greater than that of humans, he refers back to his earlier preaching in the city. The aorist, temporal participle (ἐλθών) suggests he is thinking of his first visit to Corinth.

Unlike the travelling philosophers and sophists of that age who knew first impressions were vital if they were to succeed and therefore would have spoken in high rhetoric with a pretense at superiority and a flamboyant style,[4] Paul came without "loftiness of speech." The Greek word "loftiness" (ὑπεροχή) is uncommon but can mean "preeminence" or "superiority."[5] In 1 Timothy 2:2 Paul uses it to describe people of high dignity or in high places. However, Paul's use of the word here seems to have a tinge of sarcasm in it, something along the lines of "high and mighty rhetoric" or even "highfalutin speech." The phrase "with loftiness of speech" is most naturally linked to his "coming" rather than to the proclaiming, with the present participle "proclaiming" being complementary to the main verb "I did not come."

Did Paul say that he came proclaiming the "testimony of God" (τὸ μαρτύριον τοῦ θεοῦ) or the "mystery of God" (τὸ μυστήριον τοῦ θεοῦ)? Above, it is translated as "testimony" (μαρτύριον), which we take as the more likely reading. However, a significant textual variant appears here. There are almost equal numbers of scholars choosing each option, although most recently more have opted for "mystery."[6] A further question is raised by the genitive "of God" (τοῦ θεοῦ). If this is objective, then Paul refers to the "testimony about God." If it is subjective, then Paul refers to the "testimony from God." We take it as a subjective genitive, thus giving the sense that Paul proclaimed a testimony (the gospel itself) that he received from God about Christ crucified.[7]

Thus Paul begins his autobiographical illustration

---

1. "And I" (κἀγώ) takes up the next example.

2. "To you" (πρὸς ὑμᾶς) is the most natural reading since πρός + accusative usually means "to" or "toward."

3. On this text-critical decision, see the discussion that follows on this verse.

4. Winter, *Philo and Paul among the Sophists*, 147–48, 155–64, points to particular "sophistic conventions" that would have been expected of a philosopher who wanted to be well received upon first coming to a city. It may be that these are what Paul conscientiously lays aside in 2:1–5.

5. BDAG 1034.

6. According to the NA[28], the textual support for μαρτύριον (*pace* Metzger, *Textual Commentary*, 480) is strong: ℵ[2] B D F G L P Ψ 33. 81. 104. 365. 630. 1175. 1241. 1505. 1506. 1739. 1881. 2464 𝔐 b vg sy[h] sa (see NA[28] for key to abbreviations). The textual evidence for μυστήριον is potentially earlier, though note that the evidence of 𝔓[46] is no more than a probability: 𝔓[46vid] ℵ* A C ar r sy[p] bo; Hipp BasA Ambst (see NA[28] for key to

abbreviations). Metzger argues that μυστήριον "here prepares for its usage in ver. 7," whereas μαρτύριον recalls its use at 1:6. However, as Fee notes it is too distant from that verse for that to be the cause, and it is highly unlikely that scribes of later centuries who were used to Paul's understanding of "mystery" would substitute "witness." For further arguments see Fee, *1 Corinthians*, 96. Winter, in *Philo and Paul among the Sophists*, 156, suggests "witness" may also be correct if Paul had in mind "the sophist's μάρτυς as a sign of the truth of his method." Versions and commentators opting for "testimony" include the following: NA[25], AV, ASV, RSV, ESV, NIV; Barrett, *First Corinthians*, 62–63; Fee, *1 Corinthians*, 96; and Craig Blomberg, *1 Corinthians*, NIVAC (Grand Rapids: Zondervan, 1994), 54. Those opting for "mystery" or its equivalent include the NA[28], NRSV, TEV; Héring, *First Corinthians*, 15; Thiselton, *1 Corinthians*, 207; and Garland, *1 Corinthians*, 83.

7. So J. B. Lightfoot, *Notes on Epistles of St. Paul from Unpublished Commentaries* (London: Macmillan, 1895), 171.

by speaking to the manner of his presentation of the gospel, which is a testimony from God. He refused human conventions relating to good communication and refused even the suggestion that he was promoting himself. Nevertheless, he spoke God's word clearly as he proclaimed the gospel and spoke of Christ. The result was that people came to faith and, as he will show, this was due to the power of God.

2:2 For I decided to know nothing among you except Jesus Christ and him crucified (οὐ γὰρ ἔκρινά τι εἰδέναι ἐν ὑμῖν εἰ μὴ Ἰησοῦν Χριστὸν καὶ τοῦτον ἐσταυρωμένον). In this second point Paul refers to the content of the "testimony from God" that he proclaims. Paul had made a deliberate decision that, when proclaiming the testimony, he would concentrate on one subject alone, namely, Jesus Christ and him crucified.[8] The use of the word "to know" (εἰδέναι) here again draws together the content of Paul's teaching with his manner of teaching. "I decided to *know*" indicates that Paul was not only Christ and cross-centered in the way he spoke or the words he used but that, in his entire demeanor and comportment, his life was decisively settled on Christ. He has already described the centrality of Christ crucified in 1:18–25. In the midst of much discussion about what rhetoric or speaking styles Paul relinquished, it is often forgotten that his emphasis here is on what he *did* preach. This whole section from 1:18 to 2:5 is above all a description of the way the gospel is the power of God for salvation through Christ crucified (cf. Rom 1:16).

2:3 And in weakness and in fear and in much trembling I came to you (κἀγὼ ἐν ἀσθενείᾳ καὶ ἐν φόβῳ καὶ ἐν τρόμῳ πολλῷ ἐγενόμην πρὸς ὑμᾶς). Paul now returns to what he has been saying in v. 1 about the manner of his presentation of the gospel

when he arrived in Corinth. This is indicated by the repetition of κἀγώ ("and . . . I"). In his own person Paul has appeared weak and fearful. He did not put on airs, nor was he full of self-confidence. He had a confidence in God and in the gospel message, but he knew that his style and personality would not of themselves gather crowds of supporters. The aorist "I came" (ἐγενόμην) indicates that he is still talking of his original appearance among them. "To you" (πρὸς ὑμᾶς) is the same as in 2:1.

Though Paul had probably remained weak and fearful among them, it is not this to which he draws attention here. His example still looks back to how the Corinthians became believers when he first came to them. Humanly speaking, it was weird that such an unimpressive man, who did not fulfill any of the conventions that might have drawn crowds, was still involved in powerful ministry. The power was God's.

Many recent discussions of this section have tended to emphasize Paul's contrast with contemporary rhetoricians to such an extent that the implication is that the whole of Paul's behavior among them is a deliberate choice on his part to give up what he otherwise could easily have done, that is, to "play the sophistic game." There is surely no doubt that Paul was a great scholar, as well as a good debater when needed as, for example, at the Areopagus (Acts 17:19–34). However, as has been noted, running throughout this whole section from 1 Corinthians 1:10 onward, Paul is saying something much deeper, and this verse spells it out clearly. By the will of God, Paul was called to be an apostle (1:1). The content of what Paul preaches is a stumbling block and a folly to people (1:23). Those at Corinth who have come to faith mostly do not come from a background of high repute. And so it is with Paul. He is a fearful and unimpressive

---

8. More closely to the Greek: "This crucified one" (τοῦτον ἐσταυρωμένον).

man. He does not speak with great eloquence in the Greek style. This is who he *is*. It is not just that he decides to *appear* like this for the sake of the comparison with worldly wisdom. Paul knows that God has deliberately called him despite his many inadequacies, fears, failings, and weaknesses to proclaim the gospel. What Paul has come to realize is that this is actually part of his calling. God has chosen a person like him in order that Christ crucified will be the one who is seen and heard rather than the messenger.

In several places Paul makes the point about his weakness or inadequacy and not always in contexts where he might be fending off the Hellenistic "wisdom of word." For example, in Galatians 4:13–14, Paul speaks of preaching to them at the start while ill. Interestingly, where some Corinthians might well have despised him for this, he notes the Galatians did not despise him. It is interesting that even when he speaks of persecutions and outward hurts and sufferings, Paul sees them as something that God has given or allows in order that Christ crucified may be seen in the lives of those who preach him. His emphasis on having the treasure in "jars of clay" and "always carry[ing] in our body the death of Jesus" further establishes this principle (2 Cor 4:7–10).

The phrase "in fear and much trembling" (ἐν φόβῳ καὶ ἐν τρόμῳ πολλῷ) adds further to Paul's self-description. There is little doubt that this demeanor would have contrasted strongly with the self-presentation of the sophistic teachers, but that does not adequately explain the nature of the fear or its overall gospel impact. An attractive option

is that this fear and trembling could refer to Paul's deep sense of awe at being entrusted by God with the gospel.[9] Similar ideas are occasionally found in the Old Testament (e.g., Pss 2:11; 55:5 [54:6 LXX]; cf. Heb 12:20–21). But Luke's account of Paul's first visit to Corinth offers a more likely reason for reading the phrase straightforwardly as referring to genuine fear. Luke makes it clear that Paul found that first visit to Corinth to be an exceedingly difficult time. He was "opposed and reviled" (Acts 18:6 ESV) and left the synagogue (v. 7). Clearly Paul was physically afraid, and with good reason, for the Jews made a united attack upon him and dragged him to court (v. 12). Sosthenes was also caught and beaten (v. 17). But most indicative of this was the fact that, uniquely at Corinth (as far as we know), God had to intervene with a vision for Paul in which he specifically addressed the fear that men might attack and harm him (Acts 18:9–10). It was this that persuaded Paul to stay a further eighteen months in the city (v. 11). Chrysostom makes the delightful statement, "I for my part on this account admire [Paul]; because being in fear, and not simply in *fear*, but even in trembling, at his perils, he so ran as ever to keep his crown."[10]

Paul thus pulls together all the evidence he can from what the Corinthians will remember of him from that time when he first came to them. He was truly fearful and physically weak, but he also did not fit the standards of a travelling philosopher or speaker. He now returns to this point.

2:4a and my speech and my proclamation were not in persuasive words of wisdom[11] (καὶ ὁ λόγος

---

9. Roy E. Ciampa and Brian S. Rosner, *The First Letter to the Corinthians*, PNTC (Grand Rapids: Eerdmans, 2010), 116, following Timothy B. Savage, *Power through Weakness: Paul's Understanding of the Christian Ministry in 2 Corinthians*, SNTSMS 86 (Cambridge: Cambridge University Press, 1995), 73.

10. Chrysostom, *Homilies on First Corinthians*, homily 6 (pp. 68–69).

11. Some manuscripts add "human" (ἀνθρωπίνης) before "wisdom" (among others: ℵ² A C L P Ψ 81, 104, 365, 630, 𝔐; see NA²⁸ apparatus). Metzger, *Textual Commentary*, 481, regards this as an "explanatory gloss." The phrase πειθοῖς σοφίας is found in 𝔓⁴⁶ F G, but 𝔓⁴⁶ does not include λόγοις. The variants at this point do not significantly affect the thrust of Paul's argument. The fact that πειθοῖς does not appear elsewhere

μου καὶ τὸ κήρυγμά μου οὐκ ἐν πειθοῖ[ς] σοφίας [λόγοις]). Paul returns to the other characteristic of his presence among them at that first visit: his personal lack of sophisticated argument and delivery when proclaiming the gospel. Once again, the content of what is being proclaimed and the manner of delivery cannot be separated. In the context, "speech" and "proclamation" (λόγος and κήρυγμα) mean the same thing. The duplication may be stylistic in the light of "fear and trembling" and does add a certain emphasis. Paul proclaims the word, but it is not with "loftiness of speech" (2:1) and, coming back to where he started, nor is it "in persuasive words of wisdom." The word "persuasive" (πειθοῖς) qualifies "words" (λόγοις). Paul here thinks of the art of persuasion by means of rhetorical devices. Paul is clearly able to do this in his writing, as we note in a number of places in this epistle, but this is not what he depended on as he preached, and, by way of comparison with those who did depend on such devices, he appeared weak. It is not that Paul deliberately "dumbed down" the gospel so much as he did not hide it behind an unnecessarily loquacious and pretentious form of words. However, what was delivered was as deep and as powerful and life-changing as anything spoken on earth. Thus, Paul continues with a strong contrast we translate as "but rather."

2:4b–5a but rather [my speech and my proclamation were] in demonstration of the Spirit and power, in order that your faith may not be [based] in the wisdom of men (ἀλλ᾽ ἐν ἀποδείξει πνεύματος καὶ δυνάμεως, ἵνα ἡ πίστις ὑμῶν μὴ ᾖ ἐν σοφίᾳ ἀνθρώπων). Despite all that Paul has said about his weakness and his speech, his procla-

mation demonstrated the work of the Holy Spirit and the presence of genuine power. The subject of the contrasting sentence, "my speech and my proclamation" (ὁ λόγος μου καὶ τὸ κήρυγμά μου), is taken from the previous sentence. The word "demonstration" (ἀπόδειξις) can have to do with "demonstrating" an argument or "proving" something to be true.[12] Indeed, Winter suggests the word should be understood in a technical way as the demonstration or "proof" of the persuasive argument that faith rests in the power of God (v. 5).[13] Paul insists that, although some Corinthians might want the reliability of his proclamation to be evidenced through his grand oratory and persuasive rhetorical power, it is in fact demonstrated or proved through the work of the Holy Spirit and in the power of God, since it is this that has resulted in the changed lives of the Corinthians themselves.

As will be seen in 1 Corinthians 3, above all the Spirit's work reveals Christ. He powerfully transforms believers to follow Christ. "Power" (δύναμις) is not referring to "[powerful] works" (as in 12:28) but to the fact that, surprisingly from a human point of view, Corinthian people really did come to faith when Paul preached the gospel among them. Their faith becomes the proof that the Spirit of God is at work in power when the gospel is preached in *non*-powerful ways.

Paul is at pains in many places in his writings to insist that coming to faith in Christ is a miraculous work of God that takes place entirely by his grace. For example, in Ephesians 2:4–5 he insists that "it is by grace you have been saved" and that this is all because of God's "great love" and "mercy." Here, Paul shows that God's powerful grace is involved

---

in Greek literature may have contributed to some of the textual confusion. Note also the detailed textual analysis in Fitzmyer, *1 Corinthians*, 172. See BDAG 791. Here ἐν is used instrumentally.

12. L&N 28.52, ἀπόδειξις: "'To demonstrate, to show' . . . the means by which one knows that something is a fact— 'proof, evidence.'" See further discussion of backgrounds for this idea in Thiselton, *1 Corinthians*, 218–22.

13. Winter, *Philo and Paul among the Sophists*, 159–60.

at all stages, even in the (humanly speaking) inadequate preaching of the word. For faith comes by hearing and hearing by the word of Christ (Rom 10:17). And it is to that faith that Paul now turns. Faith itself is a product of the power of God.

The opening clause of v. 5 expresses Paul's purpose for presenting the gospel in the way he has. In his presentation there can be no possible appeal to "the wisdom of men" (ἐν σοφίᾳ ἀνθρώπων). This broad expression summarizes the whole way in which humanity might wish to see a preacher or philosopher behaving and speaking: with words of eloquent wisdom (1:17), with the wisdom the Greeks are said to seek (1:22), and with persuasive words of wisdom (2:4).

However, that Paul has presented himself and his message in this way must not be separated from *God's purpose* in choosing Paul and *in giving him this message to proclaim in this way*. It is God's purpose that faith should not be based in what are no more than the clever arguments of people. Paul reiterates this in 1 Thessalonians 1:5: "Our gospel came to you not only in word, but also in power and in the Holy Spirit and with full conviction" (ESV).

In conclusion, Paul makes his point with a further strong contrast.

2:5b but rather [based] in God's power (ἀλλ' ἐν δυνάμει θεοῦ). God's power alone is to be the basis for faith in Christ. It is all of grace. "Faith" (πίστις) is about trust and commitment to Christ. It is the God-empowered result of the "speech and demonstration" of Christ crucified. It thus has an objective content yet also indicates the internal response that has taken place in the transformation of believers. As John Murray has put it, "Faith itself is the whole-souled movement of the person in entrustment to Christ."[14]

As Paul draws this example to an end, he brings everything back to God and his power. Paul was a living example of how God is involved at every stage in drawing people to himself. The best of clever argumentation may draw some to the preacher but not to Jesus Christ. Paul shows that a message that is folly to many and a stumbling block to others has been presented in a manner that seems to reflect the message: devoid of rhetorical flourishes and sophistication and of powerful signs. The messenger himself is weak and fearful. Given that the content of the message, the way in which it is communicated, and the person doing the communication will not be well regarded in the eyes of the world, then the results of his initial visit to the city ("when I came"; v. 1) can only be attributed to the power of God and the working of the Holy Spirit. It is God who has taken the word of the good news of Christ and has applied it in power through his Spirit in the lives of those who are being saved.

Theology in Application

Personal Frailty, a Humbling Advantage for the Preacher?

Paul's personal example provides a profound challenge to those who proclaim the gospel today. More widely in the biblical narrative we discover he is not unique in his apparent weakness, for on other occasions God also chose leaders for his people

---

14. John Murray, *Collected Writings of John Murray*, vol. 2 (Edinburgh: Banner of Truth, 1977), 262–63.

from those who might not naturally be seen to be the best for the job. In Exodus 4:10 we read, "Moses said to the LORD, 'Oh, my Lord, I am not eloquent, either in the past or since you have spoken to your servant, but I am slow of speech and of tongue'" (ESV). In Jeremiah 1:6 we read, "Then I said, 'Ah, Lord GOD! Behold, I do not know how to speak, for I am only a youth'" (ESV). The Lord did and does choose those who will communicate his gospel, but modern preachers should be encouraged to know that it will be in the faithful preaching of Christ crucified that they will see the true power of the Spirit at work in people's lives. Too often younger preachers are to be found seeking to imitate even the voice inflexions of one of the so-called great preachers they hear on the internet or at conferences. While there may be much to learn, there is surely even more to learn and to be encouraged by as we look at Paul and how God used him. In 1 Corinthians 4:16, after speaking of the "fools for Christ" that he and the apostles have been and how much he personally has been and is suffering for Christ, Paul appeals for them to "imitate me." If this is true for all Christians as they live in the light of Christ, how much more so should it be for gospel preachers and pastors. God does not need someone powerful and clever to achieve his ends with the gospel. He does not need the myriad of anecdotes and jokes that are heard in pulpits around our nation today. He needs people who are servants of Christ and who model humility and frailty as they preach of one who was despised and rejected and who suffered even death on a cross.

An Obsession with Christ

Preaching with such frailty and humility will require a complete commitment to the Lord Jesus Christ in everything, not just in the words spoken. In 2:2 it would be easy to believe Paul was writing with a degree of hyperbole when he wrote, "I decided to know nothing among you except Jesus Christ and him crucified." Yet, having read the first chapter, we know that for Paul this meant total life commitment to the gospel of Jesus. His words, his actions, his lifestyle, his ability to endure ridicule and persecution, and the content of his preaching are all driven by the one who is the Messiah, the God-King, who gave his life for his people. Paul expounds this later in the epistle, but it is the fact that the Messiah was vindicated in the resurrection and that he is ushering in a new creation that enables Paul to see so clearly through the suffering to the glory. Paul's obsession with Christ is visible at every turn, and it is something that all who preach the gospel need to emulate. When Christ is first in all things, then it is possible to know nothing except Christ crucified since this will be the attitude of one who especially understands the nature of Christ's role as servant. As Paul says in 2 Corinthians 4:5, "For what we proclaim is not ourselves, but Jesus Christ as Lord, with ourselves as your servants for Jesus' sake" (ESV). Too many preachers end up obsessing about themselves and are disheartened that they do not live as well as other preachers do or that they have not seen "success" as others.

Many become preoccupied with being well thought-of, or obsess about the numbers of worshippers each Sunday. Paul said, "I am compelled" to preach the gospel (9:16), and he obsessed about Christ and his calling from God. Surely, Christ first and Christ last should be the objective of all called by God and seeking to proclaim the gospel.

1 Corinthians 2:6–16

Literary Context

Paul has written of the unifying nature and content of the gospel. Its focus is Christ crucified (1:18–25). It stands opposed to all human ideas of what is worthy and of value. Nevertheless, the Corinthians themselves are evidence that this is the way God's power has been working (1:26–31). Paul has spoken of himself who, despite weakness and fear and his lack of great rhetorical skill, was used by God so that people came to faith. He has asserted that this has happened only through the wisdom and power of God (2:1–5).

Having established that they are, like him, part of the fellowship of God's people not by their own power or wisdom but by the wisdom and power of God, Paul moves forward with his challenge to the divided Corinthians. Their boasting and status-seeking has all the hallmarks of a worldly wisdom since they are seeking to establish their spiritual credentials and status in the community on the wrong basis altogether. Thus, in a lengthy section that runs through to 4:21 Paul sets out what "spiritual" people should look like as they seek to discern God and his ways. They will understand that even the grace-gifts are given by God to whom he will and so cannot function to establish spiritual status. In particular, they will come to see that church leadership must reflect the qualities of servanthood and humility that should mark all Christians.

Thus, moving back to the first-person plural, Paul speaks of the nature of the true wisdom that the apostles preach. He describes its origin and its impact as he contrasts true wisdom with the wisdom of this age and Christian with unbeliever. In a line of argument similar to 1:18–25, he begins to redefine Corinthian thinking and vocabulary. Many words here vary from Paul's usual vocabulary, prompting considerable comment. Yet Paul's Hellenistic readers of both Jewish and pagan background would have been accustomed to using them in their own religious conversation.[1] For his part, Paul imposes new content upon them. The new content is a natural conse-

---

1. See Pearson, *Pneumatikos-Psychikos Terminology in 1 Corinthians.* Robin Scroggs in "Paul: Σοφός and Πνευματικός," *NTS* 14 (1967): 33–55, looks for the background to Paul's teaching here in Jewish Wisdom categories.

quence of what he has been saying already, but it is also heavily indebted to biblical thought. Paul develops a Christ-centered view of wisdom and explains why some believe and some do not. He speaks of the nature of true maturity. For Paul the key to all that he is saying is the Spirit of God. This allows Paul to tackle another word that needs careful definition: the word "spiritual" (πνευματικός). Paul applies this to people, to things that need to be discerned properly in the light of Christ crucified, and to the work of the Spirit who enables all of this to happen. In 1 Corinthians 3, the apostle will go on to apply what he has taught in this section to the specific problems he encounters among the Corinthians.

The style of this passage and its contrast with what precedes has caused a few commentators to discuss whether the whole should be seen as an interpolation that did not come from Paul,[2] or whether Paul used some preexisting "midrash."[3] The issue of the move from the singular to the plural, the apparent ease with which the passage could sit independently from the text and have a meaning of its own,[4] and the vocabulary have all contributed to the debate. Murphy-O'Connor has provided strong arguments against the separation of this text from its context, though Walker's article unsuccessfully sought to rehabilitate the idea.[5] More recently Murphy-O'Connor has returned to a defense of the passage's integrity,[6] and Thiselton has offered a sustained argument for the same.[7] It is in the exegesis of the text itself in its greater context that it will be seen how this passage both makes sense in the flow of Paul's argument and substantially moves it forward.

III. A Radically Different Perspective Shaped by the Cross (1:18–2:5)

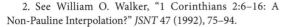 **IV. Mature Christians Pursue God's Wisdom (2:6–4:21)**

    A. Paul Proclaims God's Wisdom (2:6–13)

    B. God's Wisdom Characterizes Those Who Are "Spiritual" (2:14–16)

    C. The Corinthians Are Spiritually Immature (3:1–9)

    D. Wise Leadership Acts with Spiritual Discernment (3:10–4:21)

---

2. See William O. Walker, "1 Corinthians 2:6–16: A Non-Pauline Interpolation?" *JSNT* 47 (1992), 75–94.

3. E. E. Ellis, *Prophecy and Hermeneutic in Early Christianity: New Testament Essays*, WUNT 18 (Tübingen: Mohr Siebeck, 1978; repr., Grand Rapids: Eerdmans, 1978), 156, argues that this section is in the "literary form of a midrash . . . probably created within a (Pauline) group of pneumatics prior to its use [by Paul in this epistle]."

4. Hence, Ellis's discussion (ibid.). Or it could perhaps be explained as an attempt by the Corinthian "spirituals" to provide their own position against Paul's and so was added separately to the letter (Walker, "1 Corinthians 2:6–16," 75–94).

5. Jerome Murphy-O'Connor, "Interpolations in 1 Corinthians," *CBQ* 48 (1986): 81–84.

6. Jerome Murphy-O'Connor, *Paul: A Critical Life* (Oxford: Oxford University Press, 1996), 282–84. However, though Paul is indeed redefining his opponents' language here and is sarcastic, it is unwarranted to say that "Paul is playing a cruel intellectual game with his opponents. His whole purpose is to mystify them and thereby reduce them to confused silence amid the laughter of all others who hear the letter read aloud" (ibid., 283). This would hardly be the action of one who believed he had made himself a "slave to all" to "win" people for Christ (1 Cor 9:19 NRSV).

7. Thiselton, *1 Corinthians*, 36–41, 224–26, 239–40.

Main Idea

Paul defines true wisdom and speaks of its origin in God and its revelation through the Holy Spirit. He addresses what it is to be "spiritual," contrasting the "mature" person who possesses the Holy Spirit, with the "unspiritual" person who does not. The unspiritual person has not understood God's wisdom in Christ; the spiritual person has received and understood it and has come to have spiritual discernment and to have the mind of Christ.

Translation

1 Corinthians 2:6–16

6a	Assertion	But **we do**	**speak** **wisdom**
b	Location		among the mature, but
c	Contrasting assertion	**[we do] not [speak] the wisdom**	
d	Explanation		of this age or of the rulers of this age,
e	Description		who are doomed to come to ↵ nothing.
7a	Adversative	But rather	
b	Assertion	**we speak God's wisdom**	
c	1st description of wisdom		in a mystery and hidden,
d	2nd description		which God foreordained
e	Temporal		before the ages
f	Ultimate goal/ advantage		for our glory,
8a	3rd (negative) description		which none of the rulers of this age understood,
b	Condition		for if they had understood ↵ [this wisdom]
c	Contrasting assertion		they would not have crucified the Lord of glory.
9a	Evidence	Rather, as it is written,	
b	Scripture quotation		"What things eye has not seen and ear has not heard and the ↵ human heart has not conceived,
c			[these] things God has prepared for those who love him." [Isa 64:4, 65:16]
10a	Assertion	For **to us God has revealed**	**[these things]**
b	Means		through the Spirit.
c	Explanation of 10a	For **the Spirit searches**	**all things,**
d	Expansion		even the depths of God.

11a	Basis for v. 10	For **who has known from among people**	the things	of a person
b	Rhetorical question	except	the spirit	of a person which is in him?
c	Conclusion	So also **no one knows**	the things	of God
d		except	the Spirit	of God.
12a	Assertion (negative)	But **we have not received**	the spirit	of the world;
b	Contrast (positive)	rather, **we have received**	the Spirit	of God,
c	Purpose	in order that we might know	the things	
d	Source		that were graciously given to us by God.	
13a	Assertion (negative)	And **we do not speak**	these things	
b	Instrument	in words taught by human wisdom but		
c	Contrast	[in words] taught by the Spirit,		
d	Manner	evaluating spiritual matters for spiritual people.		
14a	Assertion 1	**Now the unspiritual person does not receive the things**		
b	Source	of the Spirit of God,		
c	Reason for assertion 1	for **they are** ☞ **foolishness to him**		
d	Addition to assertion 1	**and he is not able to come to know** [them]		
e	Reason	because they are judged spiritually.		
15a	Contrasting assertion 2	But **the spiritual person** **judges all things,** and		
b	Additional assertion	**is himself judged by no one.**		
16a	Scripture quotation	"For who has known the mind of the Lord,		
b		so that he should instruct him?" [Isa 40:13 LXX]		
c	Concluding assertion	But **we have the mind of Christ.**		

Structure

In 2:6–13 Paul proclaims God's wisdom as he develops the contrast between Christians and non-Christians with a series of antitheses. What may have appeared as foolishness to the world around is in fact "wisdom" to the "mature"—that is, to Christians.

2:6–7. In the first contrast wisdom is imparted to Christians, *but* it is not the wisdom of this age. It is a wisdom decreed from before the ages.

2:8–10. Those of "this age" have not understood this wisdom, *but* this has been revealed to Christians through the Spirit.

2:11–13. No one knows the things of God *but* those who have received the Spirit. Therefore, spiritual things are for spiritual people.

2:14–16. Paul reflects on the differences between the unspiritual and the spiritual person. The first does not understand what comes from God, *but* the spiritual person discerns the things of God and has the mind of Christ. God's wisdom thus characterizes those who are "spiritual."

Exegetical Outline

→ **IV. Mature Christians Pursue God's Wisdom (2:6–4:21)**

    A. Paul Proclaims God's Wisdom (2:6–13)

        1. True Wisdom Is Distinct from the Wisdom of This Age (2:6–9)

            a. What Was "Secret" and "Hidden" Has Been Revealed (2:7)

            b. It Is Not Understood by the Rulers of This Age (2:8)

            c. It Is God's Gift for Those Who Love Him (2:9)

        2. True Wisdom Is Revealed by the Holy Spirit (2:10–13)

    B. God's Wisdom Characterizes Those Who Are "Spiritual" (2:14–16)

        1. The Unspiritual Person Does Not "Discern" Spiritual Things (2:14)

        2. The Spiritual Person "Judges" All Things (2:15–16)

Explanation of the Text

2:6a–b But we do speak wisdom among the mature (Σοφίαν δὲ λαλοῦμεν ἐν τοῖς τελείοις). Having spent time examining the difference between his gospel proclamation and what the world would expect of him and count as wisdom, Paul now returns to examine "wisdom." We have seen that Paul is concerned because the Corinthians are placing a high value on what he has called the world's wisdom. They have been judging people and making decisions concerning their community status by this benchmark rather than by their commitment to Christ crucified. Paul must clarify the nature of true wisdom as seen from God's perspective.

"But" (δέ) moves the discussion forward and is mildly adversative as he moves to the first-person plural. This switch is partly stylistic after using himself as a specific example in the preceding paragraph. More importantly, though, Paul is probably linking himself to all who preach the gospel,[8] perhaps especially the apostles. In the light of the mention of Peter (1:12) and Apollos (1:12 and 3:5), Paul may already be preparing the ground to show that he and they do the same thing as they bring the wisdom of God to people, for there can be no different types of "wisdom" among those who preach Christ crucified. As the passage moves on, the first-person plural also draws in all the Corinthian believers, since they are "spiritual."

His redefinition of the Corinthian understanding of wisdom is entirely focused, as already noted in 1:17, 24, 30, on the salvific gracious work of God in Christ. It therefore comes as something of a surprising contrast to read Paul saying that despite the world's wrong understanding of these things, "we do speak wisdom" (Σοφίαν δὲ λαλοῦμεν). The precise meaning of "wisdom" must be determined by the context. Thus far in this epistle the godly wisdom Paul has described has virtually been a shorthand for the way in which salvation is found in Christ. It is given by God to all so that, believing, they may come to faith in Christ crucified. Paul now rather enigmatically adds to his description of wisdom by saying he does impart wisdom "among the mature."

"The mature" or "the perfect" (τέλειοι) is a word

---

8. Garland, *1 Corinthians*, 91, rightly says that "all who proclaim the Christian gospel speak this wisdom."

used in the mystery religions, in Gnosticism, and in apocalyptic Jewish writings, thus generating some discussion as to which background directs Paul's thinking and how the Corinthian elitists would have regarded the term. In Hellenistic mystery religions "the mature" can refer to those initiated into the deeper secret teachings of the cult. The word can take on the idea of reaching a state of spiritual perfection. Conzelmann and Senft are among several commentators who suggest Paul is indebted to these mystery cults. Conzelmann says that the word "belongs to the sphere of the language of the mysteries" and that, especially in the light of v. 10, Paul hints at "additional pieces of knowledge that he has so far withheld from the Corinthians."[9] Others suggest the vocabulary is essentially gnostic and that either this is the Corinthian background for the word or Paul's own. In sum, the "mature" would be those who have reached fulfillment through receiving special or additional "knowledge" from the Spirit. Some therefore conclude that Paul is talking of a message he speaks only to a spiritual elite, thus distinguishing between two types of Christians, or that he is arguing against some Corinthians who make these distinctions.[10]

However, any view that suggests Paul differentiated between groups of Christians, in the sense that some have "attained the goal" (τέλειοι) and others have not, flies in the face of all that Paul has said thus far and specially against what he says later in 4:6–21. In fact, the nature of Paul's differentiation between peoples immediately becomes apparent in this passage.

Since Paul's contrast of wisdoms (his and the world's) hinges on Christ crucified, Paul contrasts those who crucified "the Lord of glory" with those who believe in him (2:8). In v. 7 Paul talks of God's decree for *our* glory, thus identifying with the Corinthian Christians as a whole. Paul's wisdom concerns what God has prepared for all "those who love him" (2:9), that is, all those who possess the Holy Spirit (2:12). In 12:13, all Christians are seen to possess the Spirit. The second half of 2:6 then contrasts the mature with those who are doomed to pass away, not with those who are less mature in their faith! The "mature" are therefore the Christians to whom he is writing, those who have received the "wise" message of Christ crucified.[11] Paul does not contrast one group of Christians with another, for that is precisely what the Corinthians were doing. Nevertheless, Paul will later make a distinction between what many of these Christians *are* and how they are behaving—between their identity and their behavior. They may be "mature," that is, true Christians with community status, yet they are behaving as "babies" (3:1).

So, in this verse Paul is addressing the type of wisdom that *he* preaches. It becomes apparent that God's wisdom is about more than simply *believing* in Christ crucified. The whole gospel, that is, the whole wisdom and plan of God includes understanding the practical implications of that belief and behaving as a church in a way that follows a crucified Christ. Paul had shown this in his own life in the opening verses of the chapter. Earlier he had looked back to Jeremiah for his teaching about

9. Conzelmann, *1 Corinthians*, 61; cf. Christophe Senft, *La Première Épître de Saint Paul aux Corinthiens*, CNT (Geneva: Labor et Fides, 1990), 49. See also Richard Reitzenstein, *Hellenistic Mystery Religions: Their Basic Ideas and Significance*, trans. John E. Steely, PTMS 18 (Pittsburgh: Pickwick, 1978).

10. Schmithals, *Gnosticism in Corinth*, 150–55, sees Paul countering the Christ group who were (Jewish) gnostic and for whom this word and others had technical meanings of having

received an esoteric knowledge from the Spirit. Barrett, *First Corinthians*, 69, writes that "in the paragraph as a whole . . . there is gnostic language."

11. Chrysostom, *Homilies on First Corinthians*, homily 7.1, says: "'Wisdom' is the name he gives to the Gospel, to the method of salvation, the being saved by the Cross. 'The perfect' [τέλειοι] are those who believe."

wisdom and boasting, and again here what he says recalls Old Testament wisdom ideas. His contrast is not between supposed enlightened and unenlightened Christians but between those who are learning what it is to be a Christian (the "mature"—τέλειος) and those who are not bothering to learn. Fee sums it up: "Those 'in Christ' (1:30) are 'the mature', and thus the Corinthians are included."[12] Paul now offers four qualifications of "wisdom" that help open up the concept from his perspective.

2:6c–e but [we do] not [speak] the wisdom of this age or of the rulers of this age who are doomed to come to nothing (σοφίαν δὲ οὐ τοῦ αἰῶνος τούτου οὐδὲ τῶν ἀρχόντων τοῦ αἰῶνος τούτου τῶν καταργουμένων). First, Paul defines his wisdom negatively. It is not the wisdom of this age or the rulers of this age. The verb is drawn from the first half of the verse (λαλοῦμεν). Paul speaks with the eschatological perspective that was noted back in 1:7–8 and 1:20. The "wisdom" of God has been contrasted with that which belongs to "this age" (see discussion of τοῦ αἰῶνος τούτου in 1:20) and which Paul now says is followed by "the rulers of this age" (τῶν ἀρχόντων τοῦ αἰῶνος τούτου). The cross has doomed this age and all who belong to this age to come to nothing, to perish.[13] Godly wisdom will not be regarded as wisdom by those "who are doomed to come to nothing." As in 1:18

Paul's contrast is between those of this age who are being destroyed and those "who are being saved."

The "rulers" may refer to the political leaders of the day,[14] or to demonic powers,[15] or to both demonic forces and their human agents.[16] While all are possible, the fact that Paul goes on specifically to talk of the crucifixion does suggest that actual political rulers are uppermost in Paul's mind. These would have included all associated with the crucifixion and must include undifferentiated Jewish and Gentile rulers from the Pharisees, to Herod, Pilate, and, behind it all, Caesar. As Wright notes, these crucified the Christ "only to find that they had signed their own death warrant."[17] Elsewhere in the New Testament, political "rulers" (ἄρχοντες) are associated with the crucifixion (e.g., Luke 23:35; Acts 3:17; 4:8). In Romans 13:3 "rulers" refers clearly to present political leaders. However, it would seem less than natural for Paul, working in this eschatological and apocalyptic framework of the passing age, to separate political rulers entirely from the forces of evil for whom they work (see also 1 Cor 15:24). Such a merging of ideas is surely present in Romans 8:38–39. It may also be that Paul is taking a swipe at the influential people of honor who were so admired by Corinthian society and yet who rejected Christ. Either way, these rulers have nothing to offer Paul when it comes to wisdom.

---

12. Fee, *1 Corinthians*, 110.

13. The present, passive participle καταργουμένων agrees with τῶν ἀρχόντων ("the rulers"). See comments on 15:24 for more on the verb "to come to nothing" (καταργέω); cf. 1:28.

14. Chrysostom, *Homilies on First Corinthians*, homily 7.1, writes: "Now by 'rulers of the world,' here, he means not certain demons as some suspect, but those in authority." So also Calvin, *First Corinthians*, 53; Horsley, *1 Corinthians*, 8.

15. In the note above, Chrysostom, loc. cit., may have been referring to Origen, *Fr. Lam.* 4.11 where Origen regards Babylon's rulers as demonic representatives. See also Origen, *De principiis* 33.3 where we read: "So . . . we are to suppose is the working of the world's princes in whom various spiritual

powers have been assigned the rule over the nations and who for this reason are called the princes of this world." See also Moffatt, *First Corinthians*, 29: "Paul sees supernatural powers of evil at work." Héring, *First Corinthians*, 16; Barrett, *First Corinthians*, 70.

16. See Cullmann, *Christ and Time* (Northampton: SCM, 1951), 191: "By 'the rulers of this age' Paul manifestly means *both* the invisible 'princes of this world' . . . and their actual instruments, Herod and Pilate." For analysis of Cullmann's perspective here and his influence on other writers, see Thiselton, *1 Corinthians*, 237–38. Ciampa and Rosner, *First Corinthians*, 125, also see Paul as referring to "both."

17. Wright, *Paul and the Faithfulness of God*, 1284.

2:7a–c But rather we speak God's wisdom in a mystery and hidden (ἀλλὰ λαλοῦμεν θεοῦ σοφίαν ἐν μυστηρίῳ τὴν ἀποκεκρυμμένην). With a strong adversative, Paul sets up the positive statement, thus emphasizing the fact that what he speaks is *God's* wisdom (possessive genitive). Again, two words here have provoked much discussion. The use of the phrase "in a mystery" and talk of a "hidden" wisdom have prompted speculation about the influence of the mystery cults or of gnostic ideas that were mentioned above.[18] Neither is any more likely here than when we considered them in v. 6. In the end, however, more important than any possible background for words that may have emanated from the Corinthian religious vocabulary is what Paul himself means by "wisdom." He offers four descriptions.

First, "in a mystery" (ἐν μυστηρίῳ) describes the nature of God's wisdom, thus functioning adjectivally. It does not modify the verb "we speak" (λαλοῦμεν). In other words, Paul is not saying that he speaks mysteriously or in a hidden way in order that only the mature or spiritually elite may understand what is going on. Rather, God's wisdom is "in a mystery" and "hidden" to those who are of "this age." If there were religions around in Corinth where much was made of "mystery" or of the fact that only the educated or sophisticated elite could understand the deeper matters of religion, then Paul is redefining the words in accordance with what he has already taught in 1 Corinthians 1. The context, especially v. 8, clearly defines "the rulers of this age" as those for whom God's wisdom remains a mystery. For those who know only the wisdom of this age and are doomed to come to nothing, then the things of which Paul speaks remain a mystery, however clearly and simply he actually preaches.

In Paul the word "mystery" (μυστήριον) appears twenty times in various contexts, but regularly addresses the fact that "in Christ" God's way of salvation has been revealed. On a number of occasions it also specially speaks to the revelation of how salvation has come to the Gentiles (Rom 11:25; Eph 3:1–9; Col 1:26–27). It is this "mystery" of which Paul, the one who knows nothing among them "except Jesus Christ and him crucified" (v. 2), has been called to be a steward (4:1). Paul preaches the truth of the gospel, which is that God has sent the long promised Messiah-King to redeem his people and that he delivers them, not in the way the world might expect of the "Lord of glory" (τὸν κύριον τῆς δόξης; v. 8), but through his crucifixion. Of course, the mystery also shows how the Messiah and his people are vindicated with the resurrection. But "in Christ" the saving purposes of God have been revealed. Yet the "mystery" as Paul understands it has been declared by God himself in Christ and so has within itself, as we have seen in 1 Corinthians 1, the power of God to deliver those who believe and to destroy the wisdom of the wise. The mystery that is revealed includes God's actual salvation of people in Christ, not merely some theoretical knowledge that is now understood.[19] Indeed, in Paul's eschatological framework not even the future remains a full-blown mystery, for we know Jesus as the "Lord of glory," that already those who believe "are being saved," and that Christ will come in glory to this earth for his people. We may still see as "in a mirror dimly" and long for the joy of seeing "face to face" (13:12 ESV), but God's wise plan for his people, which was in a mystery and hidden, has been revealed. Therefore, the way the future will turn out for the redeemed is known.

Secondly, the word "hidden" is added and also qualifies "wisdom" (τὴν ἀποκεκρυμμένην).[20] The use of the *perfect* passive suggests that Paul is

---

18. See discussion in Schmithals, *Gnosticism in Corinth*, 138–40.

19. G. Bornkamm, "μυστήριον," *TDNT* 4:820–21.
20. This participle functions as an attributive adjective.

thinking of the continuing consequences of God's revealed wisdom in Christ crucified. This wisdom is hidden, not because God or Paul has only made it available to the few, but because those of "this age" have not understood. In fact, the Spirit has "revealed" to us (2:10) what has remained hidden to those of "this age" (v. 6). It is the privilege of all Christians that they have had these mysteries of salvation revealed to them by the Holy Spirit (v. 10). The corollary is that no one group of Christians can therefore claim to have received more *hidden* things than any other. To have received the revelation of Christ crucified is what it is to be a Christian.

2:7d–f which God foreordained before the ages for our glory (ἣν προώρισεν ὁ θεὸς πρὸ τῶν αἰώνων εἰς δόξαν ἡμῶν). Thirdly, Paul adds another qualification of "wisdom." God "foreordained" (προορίζω) this wisdom. In other words, Christ and his work on the cross was planned in advance by God. Paul stresses this fact by adding "before the ages" (πρὸ τῶν αἰώνων). The idea, though more directly and forcefully stated, means the same as the clause "it pleased God" in 1:21. It was God's great and wonderful wisdom from "before the foundation of the world" (Eph 1:4 RSV), now revealed to all who believe, that he should meet people in love and with mercy and forgiveness in Christ. It is this that has been "hidden" from all eternity until the time when Christ was revealed. Again, an extraordinary contrast lies between those who know their end is "glory" and those who find themselves "shamed" and "brought to nothing."

Paul then adds another remarkable statement. God's plan "to save those who believe" (1:21) was "for *our glory*."[21] In the next verse, Christ is called

"the Lord *of glory*." It was God's purpose that his people would share in the glory of Christ. This is the opposite of "shame" (1:27). Where the latter has eschatological connotations of destruction and judgment, "glory" has all the connotations of final redemption and salvation in the presence of God's own glory. The glory will be fully realized at the resurrection (15:42–43), a reminder that when Paul proclaims Christ crucified he speaks of the resurrection and ascension as essential to its content. Christians already have a foretaste, as the glory of what has been prepared for them has been revealed to them (vv. 9–10). They have understood God's plan of salvation; they know the risen Lord of glory, experience his love, and know that they are "joint heirs with Christ" (Rom 8:17 NRSV).

2:8 which[22] none of the rulers of this age understood, for if they had understood [this wisdom] they would not have crucified the Lord of glory (ἣν οὐδεὶς τῶν ἀρχόντων τοῦ αἰῶνος τούτου ἔγνωκεν, εἰ γὰρ ἔγνωσαν, οὐκ ἂν τὸν κύριον τῆς δόξης ἐσταύρωσαν).[23] A fourth qualification is now added to wisdom as Paul returns to the reaction of unbelievers to God's wisdom in Christ (v. 6). The fact that this wisdom in Christ has not been understood by the rulers of this age is evidenced in the fact that they crucified the "Lord of glory." The truth of the crucified King, who is followed by a people who themselves must follow him in suffering (Rom 8:17; 2 Cor 4:16–17), has been hidden from them so that they have not "understood" what is going on. This lack of understanding on the part of those who crucified the Lord is seen by Paul as culpable; hence their "shame" (1 Cor 1:27). Jesus himself viewed his persecutors in this way as he prayed from the cross: "Father, forgive them,

---

21. The εἰς + acc. here indicates goal.

22. "Which" (ἣν) qualifies "wisdom" and introduces another relative clause.

23. For "the rulers of this age," see 2:6. That historical rulers

are in mind rather than demons is clearer here. In the Gospels, the demons are among only a few who seem to understand who Jesus really is! The rulers referred to here did not understand who he is.

for they do not know what they are doing" (Luke 23:34). Here, the perfect of the verb "to know" (ἔγνωκεν; here translated as "understood"[24]) prepares the way for the example that follows. Paul has in mind that which happened in the past with the crucifixion of Christ and which has ongoing implications among all rulers of this age.

Lord "of glory" (τῆς δόξης, a descriptive genitive; cf. Jas 2:1) reminds the reader of that which belongs to the heavenly realms and describes God. As Fitzmyer writes, "He is the 'God of glory,' because by his resurrection he has entered the glorious presence of the Father and so been glorified."[25] Kistemaker notes that Paul provides here the answer to the question of Psalm 24:8, "Who is this King of glory?"[26] The phrase is used in 1 Enoch in a number of places to describe Yahweh himself (e.g., 1 En. 25:3; 27:3–5). First Enoch 63:2 looks forward to the day of judgment when the leaders of this earth are pleading to be spared God's judgment. They call out to "the Lord of glory and the Lord of wisdom."[27] Though it is unlikely Paul draws upon Enoch, he addresses the phrase to Christ as a title that could only have previously been meant for God.[28] Once again Paul takes that which would be expected to apply to Lord "Yahweh" and applies it to the Lord "Christ." As 1 Chronicles 16:10 says of Yahweh, "Glory in his holy name." This too is surely part of what the rulers of this age have never understood but which has now been revealed. In Christ, Yahweh has come.

Paul uses a contrary-to-fact condition (εἰ γὰρ . . . οὐκ ἂν . . .), with the aorist tense being used in both the protasis and apodosis to demonstrate his point that the rulers of this age have not understood

God's wisdom. The very juxtaposition of "the Lord of Glory" with crucifixion is precisely what is totally incomprehensible. This fitted neither with Jewish ideas of God's wisdom and what the Messiah might look like and how he might come, nor with Hellenistic ideas of "glory." As Paul made clear in 1:23, both groups, Jews and Greeks representing all people, rejected this wisdom in favor of their own.

The great irony of God's wisdom here is that in following *their* wisdom, the rulers of this age in fact carried out God's wisdom as they crucified the Lord. Truly, God has destroyed "the wisdom of the wise" (1:19). This extraordinary teaching is not presented to the Corinthians in any triumphalistic manner. It is not just about the triumph of God's plan over the plan of those who are "doomed to come to nothing" (2:6). In fact, the whole teaching serves as wonderful encouragement to those Christians who are being tempted to view things in a worldly way, that they too should not be deceived by appearances. For those who love God, the way of the cross is the way of glory; it is the way of true wisdom. No one could have imagined that God would work for the glory of those who love him in such a way.

2:9 Rather, as it is written, "what things eye has not seen and ear has not heard and the human heart has not conceived, [these] things God has prepared for those who love him." (ἀλλὰ καθὼς γέγραπται, ἃ ὀφθαλμὸς οὐκ εἶδεν καὶ οὖς οὐκ ἤκουσεν καὶ ἐπὶ καρδίαν ἀνθρώπου οὐκ ἀνέβη, ἃ ἡτοίμασεν ὁ θεὸς τοῖς ἀγαπῶσιν αὐτόν). Paul now concludes this section and introduces the next with a quotation from Scripture. The general thrust of what Paul writes is clear enough. He summarizes

---

24. With RSV, ESV, NIV, NRSV, NASB, and others.

25. Fitzmyer, *1 Corinthians*, 177.

26. Simon J. Kistemaker, *Exposition of the First Epistle to the Corinthians* (Grand Rapids: Baker, 1993), 83.

27. James H. Charlesworth, ed., *The Old Testament Pseudepigrapha*, 2 vols. (New York: Doubleday, 1983), 1:44.

28. *Contra* Conzelmann, there is nothing to suggest that "in his descent through the cosmos [the Lord of glory] has disguised himself" (*1 Corinthians*, 63).

the content of what he "speaks" (2:7), namely, "wisdom," which he refers here to as "what things" (ἅ). He has called this wisdom God's hidden mystery, but it is for "our glory." And he has said that humanity of "this age" does not understand (2:8). But Scripture, he concludes, confirms the wonder of what he speaks. Thus, in paraphrase we may put it like this: "We speak wisdom that, as Scripture says, involves things that neither eye had seen nor ear heard and that the human heart had not conceived; it is these things God had prepared for those who love him." We have used the past tense to reflect the aspect of the Greek aorist that is suggested by the context; that is, God's wisdom is all now revealed.[29] Paul is reiterating that what was once a mystery is now "spoken." Christ came and was crucified. He is the Lord of Glory. It is he who is now revealed to all who are his in the preaching of the gospel. Thus what is "prepared" does not look forward to the eschatological blessings of which Paul speaks later but refers to the revelation of Christ of which Paul has yet more to say in what follows.[30]

The adversative (ἀλλά) contrasts the action of those who crucified Christ with the strangeness of God's plan. On "it is written" see 1:19. "What things" (ἅ) is a translation of the neuter, plural pronoun and provides the object of the first two clauses: concerning what things have been seen and heard. Problematically, there is no obvious subject for the third clause. "In the heart of man" may be the best translation (ἐπὶ καρδίαν ἀνθρώπου). The verb (ἀνέβη), like the previous two, is in the aorist singular. Robertson suggests that whereas "what things" is accusative (object) with "eye has seen" and "ear has heard," it functions *also* as nominative neuter with "conceived"; thus, giving the translation "what has not entered (been conceived by) the heart of man."[31] But this is still uncomfortable, and certainly the Greek here is at best unclear. The second occurrence of the phrase "what things" probably has a greater demonstrative weight, so it is rendered "these things."

Finally, where does this quotation come from?[32] Clearly at least the first couple of clauses have Isaiah 64:4 (64:3 LXX) in mind. Isaiah 65:16 may offer the closest parallel to the third clause. It is also speculated that Paul is quoting from a previously existing composite of Old Testament texts.[33] Certainly Paul can put texts together and quote them (cf. Rom 3:10–18). However, the quotation is given as Scripture and confirms the point Paul has been making of the depths of God's wisdom and how wonderful it is for those "who love him" (τοῖς ἀγαπῶσιν αὐτόν is a dative of advantage). This phrase further indicates that Paul is addressing all Christians and not just some who happen to be "mature." A similar idea occurs in Romans 8:28.

At this stage, Paul does not discuss the centrality of love as *the* marker that should characterize all Christians.[34] However, this quotation's reference to

---

29. In Christ God has revealed these things that now may be viewed as a whole, all of which were revealed in Christ but which no one had imagined would be like this.

30. In Matt 25:34 the same idea of preparation does point to the yet-to-be-received eschatological blessings of the kingdom. Yet here the emphasis is on the revelation of Christ who has been revealed.

31. Robertson and Plummer, *First Corinthians*, 40. Also see Thiselton, *1 Corinthians*, 248–49.

32. It has occasionally been suggested that this might be a saying that came from Jesus. There is nothing to indicate this in the text or in the Gospels. The suggestion has recently found favor among those seeking parallels between Paul and other noncanonical material. Cf. Tuckett's examination of the possible relationship between this "saying" and similar phraseology in the Gospel of Thomas (Christopher Tuckett, "Paul and Jesus Tradition: The Evidence of 1 Corinthians 2:9 and the Gospel of Thomas 17," in *Paul and the Corinthians: Studies on a Community in Conflict: Essays in Honor of Margaret Thrall*, ed. Trevor J. Burke and J. K. Elliott, NovTSup 109 [Leiden: Brill, 2003], 109).

33. Fee, *1 Corinthians*, 115.

34. See the essay at 13:3 entitled, "In Depth: Love, Its Function and Background."

"those who *love* him" serves to introduce the theme that will be developed in detail in 1 Corinthians 8–13. We have seen that for the Corinthians status in the community was vital. The desire for such recognition was, no doubt, the result of a compromise with the values of surrounding society, with the wisdom of "this age." It is likely that some Corinthian Christians did see themselves as superior to other Christians. Some were claiming to be "spiritual," as we shall see later in chapters 2 and 3. Some probably looked to the grace-gifts of "wisdom" or "knowledge" as evidence of their standing before God and within the Christian community. For Paul, it is vital that they understand that the true mark of a Christian is love.

God prepared all these things for our glory. The scriptural citation in support of this makes it clear that the "us" are all who "love him." It is this love for God and love for neighbor, found in Old Testament law, that is foundational for anyone seeking to understand what marks out or authenticates Christian community status. For Paul, as we shall see in more detail later, love for God grows out of the prior love of God for his people. However, love for God is also dependent upon the work of the Holy Spirit in a person's life. If one is to look for a true marker of belonging to God's people—a marker of a spiritual person—then one need look no further than to see whether they live a life of love for God and for others. Paul's understanding of the process involved here is perhaps most clearly expressed in Romans 5:5: "God's love has been poured out into our hearts through the Holy Spirit, who has been given to us." To all this Paul will return later. For now, he begins to talk about this work of the Spirit in the life of those who love God.

2:10 For[35] to us God has revealed [these things] through the Spirit. For the Spirit searches all things, even the depths of God (ἡμῖν δὲ ἀπεκάλυψεν ὁ θεὸς διὰ τοῦ πνεύματος· τὸ γὰρ πνεῦμα πάντα ἐραυνᾷ, καὶ τὰ βάθη τοῦ θεοῦ). In this verse Paul insists that the deep things of God include the very revelation that Paul has been talking about, the self-revelation of God in Christ crucified. The Spirit alone can penetrate the depths of God's purposes and his self-sacrifice in Christ. He alone enables people to understand something the rulers of this age are unable to comprehend. Grammatically, the preposition "to us" (ἡμῖν) is emphatic in its position, while "these things" is brought forward from the quotation of Scripture. The quotation thus completes the previous discussion but serves also to introduce the next section concerning the work of the Holy Spirit in this revelation. By using "us" with emphasis here, Paul seeks to bring on side all the Corinthian Christians, but especially to identify them with "those who love him [God]." "We" therefore stands in direct contrast with those mentioned in v. 8 to whom what is hidden has remained hidden.

It was God's predetermined purpose to reveal these things to those who love him. This is what God has prepared, and the means by which these things have been revealed is "through the Spirit" (διὰ τοῦ πνεύματος). Having introduced the role of the Holy Spirit in the matter of the revelation of God's purposes in 2:4, the Spirit now dominates the discussion through until the end of chapter 2. There is little doubt that some Corinthian Christians were making a great deal of being spiritual. Paul tackles this by helping them see, first of all, the role of the Holy Spirit in revelation. How is it that

---

35. The Nestle-Aland text starts the verse with "but" (δέ). We believe "for" (γάρ) has stronger support, including 𝔓⁴⁶, B, 6, 365, inter alia, and so is the adopted reading here.

some have received "Christ crucified" and some have not? It is down to the work of the Spirit.

In the second half of this verse, "for" (γάρ) is explanatory. "Even" (καί) should be taken as intensive. The context suggests that Paul is describing the ongoing work of the Spirit, and so here it is legitimate to see the present active "searches" (ἐραυνᾷ) as customary: this is what the Spirit does and continues to do. Paul's argument follows a standard Greek argument that "like may be known by like."[36]

The Spirit bridges, as it were, the distance between human beings and the depths of God. An interesting parallel to Paul's ideas on the "deep things of God" is suggested by 1 Enoch 63:2–3. There we read: "Blessed is the Lord of the spirits . . . the Lord of glory and the Lord of wisdom . . . deep are all your mysteries, and numberless" (cf. 2 Bar. 14:8–9).[37] Of course, since both these works are likely to postdate Paul (especially 2 Baruch, which is likely second-century AD), all this reveals is that the ideas were not unknown in Jewish apocalyptic writings and so they may have been known to Paul in a general sense.

The (Holy) Spirit fully knows God. He alone has access to and understanding of the deep things of God. However, in the same way that "God's wisdom in a mystery and hidden" (v. 7) did not refer to some special revelation shared with a few "spiritual" people, neither does the term "depths" (τὰ βάθη). They are not the deeper content of the mystery religions or some gnostic special knowledge. They are things shared with all those who have the Spirit (v. 12), those who love God, that is, all Christians.[38] The Spirit "searches all things"

(πάντα ἐραυνᾷ) in the sense that he seeks out and knows what is the plan and purpose of God. He does this to communicate it with and activate it among "those who love him" (v. 8).

2:11 For who has known from among people the things of a person except the spirit of a person which is in him? So also no one knows the things of God except the Spirit of God (τίς γὰρ οἶδεν ἀνθρώπων τὰ τοῦ ἀνθρώπου εἰ μὴ τὸ πνεῦμα τοῦ ἀνθρώπου τὸ ἐν αὐτῷ; οὕτως καὶ τὰ τοῦ θεοῦ οὐδεὶς ἔγνωκεν εἰ μὴ τὸ πνεῦμα τοῦ θεοῦ). This verse is the basis for what Paul has said in v. 10. Just as human beings know the truth of the first part of this verse, so they should see and immediately understand the truth of the second part. Only God's Spirit can truly know God himself—his ideas and plans and purposes and innermost desires.[39] The upshot is that if 2:10a is true, that the deep things of God have been revealed to us through the Spirit, these things could *only* have been revealed by the Spirit of God since he alone knows them.

Paul is not thinking with some Greek dualistic frame of reference here. The "spirit of a person, which is in him" describes that which is not evident to an outsider. Barrett describes this as "his self-consciousness,"[40] but it is more than this. Paul's point is that an individual is the only one who truly knows himself.

The reference to "things" (τά) perhaps deliberately recalls the "what things" (ἅ) of v. 9.

2:12a–b But we have not received the spirit of the world; rather, we have received the Spirit of God (ἡμεῖς δὲ οὐ τὸ πνεῦμα τοῦ κόσμου ἐλάβομεν

---

36. Garland, *1 Corinthians*, 98.

37. Charlesworth, *Old Testament Pseudepigrapha*, 1:44. 2 Bar. 14:8–9: "Who can explore the depth of your way?"

38. Thiselton, *1 Corinthians*, 257, argues that in the light of v. 11 and its emphasis on self-knowledge, Paul's sense may perhaps best be caught in the paraphrase "the depths of God's own self."

39. Paul is not making a statement about anthropology, nor is he speaking about the nature of God as he refers to "spirit." This is simply an analogy. As I know myself, God knows himself.

40. Barrett, *First Corinthians*, 74.

ἀλλὰ τὸ πνεῦμα τὸ ἐκ τοῦ θεοῦ). Paul continues building his argument that there are two classes of people who must be distinguished: those following "the spirit of the world" (τὸ πνεῦμα τοῦ κόσμου) and those who have received "the Spirit of God" (τὸ πνεῦμα τὸ ἐκ τοῦ θεοῦ).[41] God is the one from whom the Spirit comes. This is a primary focus of differentiation: What "spirit" does a person have? The differentiation is neither to be based on a social status nor on the "wisdom" the world counts as valuable. It is not to be based on who has received gifts from the Spirit such as "knowledge" or "word." All Christians are the "mature" and "those who love God" and must therefore be those who "have received the Spirit of God." The aorist "received" (ἐλάβομεν) looks back to the time when they came to faith as, for example, in Galatians 3:2 and 2 Corinthians 11:4.[42] All of this leads to a completely different mindset and approach to life for the Christian. It will be a way of existence, as Paul has already begun to show, that focuses on Christ and recognizes that all that a Christian has and is depends on God's work alone, upon grace. It is this differentiation based on which spirit a person possesses that will allow Paul to talk about what is or is not "spiritual." It will also allow him to begin to address questions of maturity of Christian life and ethics without dividing Christians into those who are "superspiritual" and those who are not (something the Corinthians seemed keen to do).

2:12c–d in order that we might know the things that were graciously given to us by God (ἵνα εἰδῶμεν τὰ ὑπὸ τοῦ θεοῦ χαρισθέντα ἡμῖν). As Paul continues to redefine Corinthian Christian think-

ing, he returns to the question of knowledge. He has been scathing of the sort of knowledge and wisdom that they have imported from the world. Nevertheless, there is a wisdom (v. 7) that has been revealed and is for "us" all who have the Spirit of God (v. 11). Again, Paul assumes all who have believed in Christ crucified *do* have the Spirit. The Spirit, he insists, has been received precisely "in order that we might *know*"! The object of the verb *to know* is expressed with the neuter plural accusative (τὰ χαρισθέντα).[43] Thus, Paul talks of us knowing the things that were graciously given to us "by God" (ὑπὸ τοῦ θεοῦ, denoting agency). We have used the word "graciously" to include the "grace" (χάρις) aspect of this verb.[44]

Paul achieves a double purpose in this statement. First, he continues to show that it is "us" who possess the Spirit and therefore we can indeed "know." Christians are those who can understand and evaluate what is from God because of the indwelling Spirit. Secondly, Paul shows that "we" can only know that which God has graciously chosen to give and to reveal.

There is something truly humbling throughout these verses as they continue to show that human wisdom has achieved none of what Christians possess. Christians possess the wondrous things promised in Isaiah, God's gifts centering on all that "Christ crucified" entails. In its broadest sense, they possess salvation. Yet more specifically as we shall see, what Paul refers to includes the "grace-gifts" so evident among the Corinthians, to which Paul referred with joy back in 1:7. These things have been revealed by God's Spirit, who comes from God to show Christians all that God has done

---

41. The phrase ἐκ τοῦ θεοῦ is a partitive genitive (Lightfoot, *Notes on Epistles*, 180).

42. Dunn, *Theology of Paul*, 324, points out that Paul's aorists "again and again recall his readers to that initial stage [of experiencing grace] and to its character as determinative for their on-going discipleship."

43. This substantival participle is aorist passive.

44. For further reflection on the context in which Paul sees all that is "given" by God to his church, see the essay, "In Depth: Understanding the Word Χάρισμα," following comments on 1:8.

for them and given them. It is grace from start to finish, something that this verse tells us the Spirit helps us "know."

2:13a–c And we do not speak these things in words taught by human wisdom but [in words] taught by the Spirit (ἃ καὶ λαλοῦμεν οὐκ ἐν διδακτοῖς ἀνθρωπίνης σοφίας λόγοις ἀλλ᾽ ἐν διδακτοῖς πνεύματος). The contrast between human wisdom and that given by the Spirit continues as Paul describes the manner of his own teaching in a way that recalls what he said in v. 4. The conjunction "and" (καί) connects this to the previous sentence, while the whole thought picks up on the description of Paul's gospel wisdom in vv. 6–7. This instrument or means by which the gospel is delivered has nothing to do with "human wisdom," but is proclaimed by the enabling of the Spirit.[45] The "things" (ἃ is accusative and functioning as the object) that "we speak" are therefore the things that were given by God, which the Spirit has enabled Paul—and all of "us"—to "know."

The hidden wisdom of which Paul speaks (vv. 6–7) is not only revealed by the Spirit (v. 10) but is also delivered by Paul in words "taught by the Spirit" (ἐν διδακτοῖς πνεύματος). That is, these "depths" or "deep things" of God relating to salvation and the work of Christ are beyond being accounted for by the normal discourse arising from human wisdom, yet even their communication through Paul requires the Spirit's intervention. It may well be that Paul has in mind here not just the Spirit's enabling power for the preacher but also the Spirit's enabling of the ears, eyes, and hearts of those who will receive the message.

The next clause has evoked much discussion.

2:13d evaluating spiritual matters for spiritual people (πνευματικοῖς πνευματικὰ συγκρίνοντες). Paul is speaking about the evaluation of what is or is not of the Spirit or who is or is not of the Spirit. This is the differentiation he has been making through the passage. There are some who understand and some who do not and are doomed to pass away. The gospel that Paul preaches under the direction of the Spirit is precisely *divisive*. As it is God's "wisdom," it reveals that which is not "wisdom." It "shames" the one group and is "for the glory" of the other. This has been a recurring theme in this epistle since 1:18. Thus the word (συγκρίνοντες) is translated here as "evaluating." It is essential for Christians to understand they, as "spiritual people," have the Spirit to help them evaluate whether things are or are not "spiritual"—that is, of or from the Spirit.

However, exegetical questions arise here. Is the dative plural of "spiritual" (πνευματικοῖς) masculine or neuter? And what does "evaluating" (συγκρίνοντες) mean? First, it seems clear grammatically that this clause continues to qualify the positive side of what "we speak" (v. 13a). Secondly, the meaning of the verb (συγκρίνω) must be determined.[46] Because the word is used for interpreting dreams in the LXX, the translation "interpret" is favored by many.[47] However, in the New Testament the word is only used once elsewhere (2 Cor 10:12), where it refers to an evaluative judging or comparison between Paul and the other leaders in Corinth. This is not dissimilar to what Paul means here. In the context, he is concerned that Christians make the right or "spiritual" evaluation of all things.

Thirdly, is the word "spiritual" (πνευματικοῖς) in this context to be translated as "spiritual things"

---

45. "In words taught" (ἐν διδακτοῖς . . . λόγοις) is taken as an instrumental clause.

46. For a detailed examination of the words συγκρίνω and πνευματικός as Paul uses them in this letter see Gardner, *Gifts of God*, 73–74, 137–43.

47. Cf. Gen 40:16, 22; 41:12; Num 15:34; Dan 5:8 (5:7 LXX).

(neuter) or "spiritual people" (masculine)? We have already noted above that Paul is comparing how two groups of *people* evaluate spiritual things. The emphatic position in the clause of "spiritual matters" (πνευματικά) seems to lead into the comparison in v. 14 where the nonspiritual *person* (ψυχικός) is seen *not to receive* "the things of the Spirit" (τὰ τοῦ πνεύματος). We therefore take the word πνευματικοῖς as masculine in this instance, thus referring to "spiritual people" for whom "spiritual things" must be evaluated.[48]

Paul's concern, then, is that the Corinthians understand he is rightly evaluating and then describing "spiritual things" for those who are spiritual, *unlike* what is happening with the self-designated "wise." "Spiritual things" for Paul is virtually a shorthand for the gospel, provided gospel is defined broadly enough in terms of its focus on Christ and its addressing of covenantal life and obedience (see also 9:11). That is, Paul wants them to see that their salvation has been given to them by God and that their status within the Christian community is because of God's plan in Christ for them. Their "wisdom" is God's wisdom; their enrichment with all speech and knowledge are *gifts* of the Spirit. Since what is "spiritual" is always Christ-centered or points to Christ, it stands to reason that "Christ crucified" is a message that is understood by people who are "spiritual," that is, who possess the Spirit.

As Paul continues it will become evident that he always understands this word "spiritual" to be that which, or the one who, points to Christ. The spiritual person will see Christ as "wisdom" (1:30). This person will also properly evaluate what gives status in the Christian community, seeing that status is conferred as a gift from God in Christ rather than being provided to those who have the recognition of the surrounding society. A "spiritual person" will see Christ before they see themselves because it is the Spirit's work to reveal spiritual matters, that is, the revelation provided in Christ Jesus. In the last analysis, the spiritual person will be able to say with Paul, "We have the mind of Christ" (2:16).

2:14a–c Now the unspiritual person does not receive the things of the Spirit of God, for they are foolishness to him (ψυχικὸς δὲ ἄνθρωπος οὐ δέχεται τὰ τοῦ πνεύματος τοῦ θεοῦ, μωρία γὰρ αὐτῷ ἐστιν). This verse recalls earlier comments about the "foolishness" of those who have rejected Christ crucified (see 1:18, 21, 23) when Paul writes that this unspiritual person is one for whom things from the Spirit are "foolishness" (μωρία). Given the context, such a person might have been called "the person of this age," where belonging to "this age" is seen as not belonging to Christ and therefore coming under judgment (1:20). Although there has been some debate about the meaning of "unspiritual" (ψυχικός), the contrast between the "unspiritual person" and the "spiritual person" of v. 15 (and "the spiritual persons" of v. 13) is so strong that the "unspiritual person" must refer to those who have no "spiritual" understanding at all, that is, to those who are not Christians.[49]

The use of the habitual present tense "does not receive" (οὐ δέχεται) indicates Paul sees this as a continuing characteristic of such people. Paul emphasizes this point in the second half of the verse when he says that this person "is not able to" to understand. Here "the things of the Spirit" of God (τὰ τοῦ πνεύματος)[50] are the "spiritual things" (πνευματικά) mentioned in v. 13, and these are

---

48. *Contra* NIV; Garland, *1 Corinthians*, 100; with the ESV, RSV, and NRSV.

49. E. Schweizer, "ψυχικός," *TDNT* 9:662–63; Pearson, *Pneumatikos-Psychikos Terminology in 1 Corinthians*; Scroggs,

"Paul: Σοφός and Πνευματικός," 52.

50. Genitive of source. This is sometimes referred to as an ablative.

the things this person will not entertain. What comes from the Spirit and points to Christ will be regarded as "foolishness" (1:23). This "unspiritual person" (the ψυχικός) cannot understand that a crucified Christ could be "wisdom." This person cannot discern the difference between what is of God and what is of the world and simply ignores the things of God. The word ψυχικός is used in Jude 19 of those who are "devoid of the Spirit," and James uses this word as an adjective to describe a wisdom which is "earthly" and "demonic" (Jas 3:15).

In 3:1 Paul speaks to *Christians*, some of whom are living as they should, evaluating and discerning the mind of Christ as they discern the things of the Spirit, and others who are not living as they should and seem to behave as if they were not Christians at all. There, Paul does not use the word "unspiritual" (ψυχικός) to contrast with "spiritual" (πνευματικός), and the reason seems clear. He seeks out a word that will help him describe a differentiation among *Christians*. There he uses the word "fleshly people" (σαρκινοί).

For Paul the reason the things of the Spirit are not received by the "unspiritual" is that such things need "spiritual" evaluation. They require the presence of the Holy Sprit since he alone enables such understanding (v. 12). It is precisely for this reason, as Paul now argues, that the matter of judgment and discernment becomes so prominent in the epistle. The very people who claim to have knowledge and wisdom demonstrate their lack of these attributes in their inability to discern the things of the Spirit. This is what Paul now explains.

2:14d–e and he is not able to come to know [them] because they are judged[51] spiritually (καὶ οὐ δύναται γνῶναι, ὅτι πνευματικῶς ἀνακρίνεται). Paul writes that the unspiritual person "is not able to come to know" (οὐ δύναται γνῶναι)[52] that which is from the Spirit of God. It is God's wisdom to destroy the wisdom of the wise and to nullify "the intelligence of the intelligent" (1:19). This is what he does in decreeing that the things of God will be known only by those who belong to him, to those who possess his Spirit. As Paul has already argued, the things of God need the Spirit of God to reveal them and enable them to be properly judged.[53] We take the verb "to judge," or "to discern" (ἀνακρίνω) to have a forensic connotation here in 2:14. Thus Paul is saying something like this: "The unspiritual person rejects the things given by the Spirit of God and is unable to understand them because their true nature can only be judged by someone who is spiritual, who possesses the Spirit."[54] Therefore, the judgment talked of here would result in one of two verdicts. Either the things of God will be judged "folly" or they will be judged to be "of God." Paul's point is that unspiritual people make seriously *false* judgments, resulting in their destruction (1:18). It is not the case that if these people had tried harder to come to understand deeper spiritual matters, they would have "come to know" what Paul speaks of in Christ crucified. Rather, such knowledge is simply unavailable to those who do not have the Spirit.

2:15 But the spiritual person judges all things, and is himself judged by no one (ὁ δὲ

---

51. The verb ἀνακρίνεται is singular passive. A neuter plural subject normally takes a singular verb. Wallace, *Greek Grammar*, 399–401.

52. The aorist infinitive γνῶναι is an ingressive aorist; thus the translation "to come to know."

53. Conzelmann, *1 Corinthians*, 69, suggests it is "wisdom" that is spiritually judged. We take it that it is more generally "the

things of the Spirit of God" that have to be judged spiritually.

54. Though Fee, *1 Corinthians*, 125, translates the word "discern" he reaches more or less the same conclusion as here: "'Discern' in the sense of being able to make appropriate 'judgments' about what God is doing in the world." See also Reginald St. John Parry, *The First Epistle of Paul the Apostle to the Corinthians* (Cambridge: Cambridge University Press, 1957), 14.

πνευματικὸς ἀνακρίνει [τὰ] πάντα, αὐτὸς δὲ ὑπ᾽ οὐδενὸς ἀνακρίνεται).[55] By way of contrast with the "unspiritual person," the "spiritual person" (ὁ πνευματικός) can "judge" (ἀνακρίνω), and so can make right judgments and know "all things" (v. 10) that the Spirit has revealed "to us." This person "knows" the things that are grace-gifts from God and the "spiritual things." Such people see Christ at the center of all these things and will avoid making inappropriate or false judgments based on the values of this age. Especially, they will not judge other Christians according to which leader they follow or what esoteric knowledge or wisdom they seem to show. Spiritual people will rightly judge that, by grace and because of Christ crucified, the Christian community must be undivided since all have status before God as people who "are being saved" (1:18).

Not only that, but this spiritual person himself (αὐτός) "is not judged by anyone" (ὑπ᾽ οὐδενὸς ἀνακρίνεται). This sentence has received various explanations. However, if, as we have suggested, there is a genuine problem among the Corinthians that they are judging each other and considering some to be more spiritual than others, then Paul is here affirming that Christians, who are spiritual people because they have received the Spirit, cannot be judged by others. Once more, this suggests the verb "judge" has a forensic sense here, and Paul intends something quite similar to what he writes in 1 Corinthians 4:3–5. There Paul is clear that the Corinthians are making judgments about him. To them he responds with the theology of this verse. "It is the Lord who judges me [ἀνακρίνω]. Therefore, do not judge anything . . . before the time, before the Lord comes" (vv. 4–5). In effect Paul writes something along the lines of what he says in Romans 8:33: "Who will bring any

charge against those whom God has chosen? It is God who justifies." At present in chapter 2, Paul is pointing out the difference between Christian and non-Christian. As he enters the next stage of his argument in chapters 3 and 4, he will apply the same lessons to people who make judgments against each other *within* the church. Another quotation from Scripture concludes the chapter.

2:16 "For who has known the mind of the Lord, so that he should instruct him?" But we have the mind of Christ (τίς γὰρ ἔγνω νοῦν κυρίου, ὃς συμβιβάσει αὐτόν; ἡμεῖς δὲ νοῦν Χριστοῦ ἔχομεν). With this appeal to Scripture, there is a conclusion to Paul's lengthy argument that began back in 1:18. He quotes from Isaiah 40:13 (LXX), though he leaves out the middle clause of the verse, thus leaving "who" (ὅς) without an antecedent in this quotation. Robertson points out this is "a particularly good example" of how the relative pronoun can function in a consecutive sense.[56] Thus, in line with most translations we have inserted "so that" to carry the consecutive idea and the sense of the quotation Paul uses.

In the Old Testament, the answer to the question "who has known the mind of the Lord?" can only be "God." But Paul's argument has taken the reader further. He has said that the Spirit of the Lord knows the mind of the Lord and that therefore those who possess the Spirit can know all that the Spirit reveals. Therefore, he can conclude, "We have the mind of Christ." This is another of those occasions in Paul's writings where a verse originally applied to Yahweh (LXX, κύριος) in the Old Testament is seen as applying now to Christ.[57] This is in fact precisely an example of what Paul means when he says that "hidden" things are revealed. It

---

55. The first "but" (δέ) carries a mild adversative force, and the second is conjunctive to the first clause.

56. Robertson, *Grammar of the Greek New Testament*, 724.
57. Paul also employs the quotation in Rom 11:34.

is about understanding what has been graciously given by God to his people (2:12), and it all focuses upon Christ.

To have "the mind of Christ" (νοῦν Χριστοῦ) must be defined by the context here. It is the summary statement of a lengthy argument. Paul has shown that this "mind," this understanding or knowledge, is something all Christians should have because they have the Spirit.[58] It stands in direct contrast to the mind of this world, which judges people on their abilities, their status in the community, their prowess in communication, and so on. The mind of Christ is one that has understood that Christ crucified is what life is all about. That is, the Christian life is to be one of humility and one of accepting that all that Christians may have is by grace and from God. The mind of Christ does not make superficial judgments about people, for that is Christ's work on the last day. The mind of Christ is able to discern that which is of God's wisdom and that which is of the world's wisdom. In other words, this mind is one that is in tune with the "wisdom of God" to the extent that it follows the Lord's will rather than human will.[59] It is truly "to think God's thoughts after him."

As we shall see in the next section, this passage has frequently been distorted to the verge of heresy in its application and the way it has been preached. But it stands as an extraordinary reminder of just how much Christians have received through God's gracious revelation in Christ and by his Spirit. This passage has shown that the triune God himself has indeed been at work in fulfillment of his decree *for* his people and *for* "our glory" (2:7).

Theology in Application

Joy for Those Who Love God

Paul has shown how changed lives, as a result of the preaching of the gospel, are entirely due to the power of God (2:5). The believer's faith has its foundation in God's calling and the work of the Spirit as the word of the cross is proclaimed. The foundation for faith is not and cannot lie in anything dreamed up by humanity, no matter how "spiritual" it might seem. God's work is complete in the sense that Christ "became wisdom for us from God, and righteousness, and sanctification, and redemption" (1:30). Paul thus addresses believers as the "mature." This cannot mean "perfect" or "having arrived" because Paul insists that even he and the apostles are not that in 4:8! Yet it does refer to the status that all Christians enjoy from the moment they come to faith. In Colossians 1:13 Paul explains that they have moved from one kingdom to another. Here it is a move from being those "who are perishing" to those "who are being saved" (1 Cor 1:18). To know that God has had those who are Christians in his mind and purposes since "before the ages" (2:7; cf. Eph 1:4) is more than we can fathom. With this should come immense joy. This is hinted at in 2:9 as Paul refers to Scripture. Both the verses in Isaiah 64 and 65 to which Paul likely ap-

---

58. It seems most unlikely that here Paul is referring only to himself and "faithful ministers" (*contra* Calvin, *First Corinthians*, 64). The context seems to require that all Christians are being addressed.

59. Taylor, *1 Corinthians*, 96, reflects that having the mind of Christ "is synonymous with God's hidden wisdom. One cannot help but note the strong trinitarian focus in Paul's interplay with the Old Testament text."

peals speak of joy. As Christians come to understand more of this wisdom and realize they belong fully to God, then their joy should overflow. God has revealed his love in Christ and the way of salvation that is theirs. He has revealed the power and work of the Holy Spirit for *their* glory in this world. He has enabled people to be able to understand what has happened in the death of Christ and to know that his death was *for them*. He has shown that it is possible to live for God and that God has enabled people to love him. Above all, he has enabled Christians to have the mind of Christ. This means that Christians, because they possess the Spirit, *can* distinguish between what is and is not of the Lord and how to live and speak for him. Often the Christian life is portrayed as one long list of laws to be followed and as a largely depressing existence until Christ comes in glory. This is not the picture Paul paints here. We as Christians have so much already. We have Christ, we understand God's plan of salvation in him and experience that salvation. We enjoy the covenant-community participation that is ours in Christ, and we are able to judge between what is of the Lord and what is not. This means we can look and see just how much has been freely given us so graciously by God (2:12). This is joy, and it is beyond what anyone's heart could even imagine.

The Spiritual and the Unspiritual Person

The Bible as a whole divides humanity into two groups. These groups are given a variety of names in Scripture. Christ refers to "sheep and goats" (Matt 25:32). Paul speaks in 1 Corinthians 14:24 of those who are "unbelievers or outsiders" as opposed to those who do believe and are inside the church. In Hosea 1:9–2:1 God speaks of those who are "not my people" and those who are "my people." In our passage in 1 Corinthians, the distinction is made between those who have received the Spirit from God and those who do not accept the things of God's Spirit. God also distinguishes between those who are "unspiritual" and "spiritual." It is this distinction between two—but only two—groups among men and women that is fundamental to much of what Paul will say in this epistle. Too often today this distinction is blurred. People are quicker to distinguish between different types of Christians—whether new or older, whether deeper or more superficial, whether less holy or more holy— than ever they are to make the one and only critical distinction between themselves as Christians and others who are not. Making such a distinction is often today referred to as being "judgmental," and, of course, it can be that. It is not the place of a Christian to judge a person to hell, nor is it the place to appear as "holier than thou." In fact, in this letter this distinction is not about making unbelievers feel inferior; rather, it is about helping believers to understand who they are as God's people. Since they are "in Christ," their thinking and their whole approach to life, including their priorities and attitude to sin and holiness, should be entirely different from that of the unspiritual person. To the unspiritual person Paul preaches the gospel and trusts in the power and wisdom of God to deliver people from judgment. To the spiritual person Paul is saying, "So how can you think of living as unspiritual people do? How can you think of making judgments among people in the way they do?"

In the modern church the call to be in the world is often strong enough, but the challenge to be the holy people of God with the mind of Christ and possess great spiritual discernment is less often heard. Jesus himself prays for this shortly before his death. "I do not ask that you take them out of the world, but that you keep them from the evil one. They are not of the world, just as I am not of the world" (John 17:15 ESV). The challenge for God's people as they live under the rule of Christ and yet alongside the kingdom of darkness was always going to be hard. However, the Spirit has been given to enable, among other things, proper judgment and discernment so that God's people may understand what it is to be "not of the world" while still living in the world as his covenant community.

Having the Mind of Christ

Sadly, on occasion, parts of this passage have been badly abused by Christians as they have misunderstood what is being said and have wrongly applied it to themselves or to others in the church. Even though through his letter Paul constantly argues against those who would show any form of elitism or who would suggest any one group of Christians is more spiritual than another, some have still applied the passage as if that is precisely what Paul means. Taking the "mature" to refer to Christians who have understood mysterious deeper things of God and equating them with the "spiritual" has led to applications that undermine Paul's theology. On this reading, some Christians are therefore not "spiritual" or among "the mature." It is sometimes suggested that such "spiritual" people are above reproach since they should not be judged by anyone. Others suggest that some Christians need a further experience of God beyond coming to faith before they become "mature," and that means that they must yet have to receive the Spirit of God. This is not the place to enquire into the many ways this passage has been applied in support of such ideas, but it is the place to note how easily Scripture may be wrested from its context. Certainly, as we have seen, this is not the easiest of passages to understand. Sometimes we will need to be cautious as we seek to apply verses that may not immediately be entirely clear. Here, for example, words like "mature" and "unspiritual" need careful examination, and yet this must be done, first, within the framework of Paul's theology. As Paul speaks of "we" who have "received the Spirit who is from God," he addresses all Christians to whom he writes. When he speaks of having "the mind of Christ," he speaks of himself but aligns himself with all who are "spiritual," that is, *all* Christians. In 4:8 he makes it clear that this is not a claim to having arrived or to being "kings." It is not a claim to elitism. Strangely, because it is so different from the wisdom of this age, it is a deeply leveling statement. What is true for Paul is true for all Christians, and so they should act upon it and live by it. Since they possess the Spirit and are therefore capable of making Christ-like judgments on how to live and what to believe and not to believe, they too should be able to speak of having the mind of Christ.

God's people need as much encouragement now as they did in Paul's day to think as Christ thinks. No area of life is exempt from the challenge. Therefore, to be "spiritual" should not be understood, as it often is today and was in Paul's day, in a dualistic way. To be spiritual is to live for Christ and think like Christ among his people and in his world. It is to live under his rule always.

1 Corinthians 3:1–9

Literary Context

In 1:18–2:16 Paul has presented an extended attack on the wisdom of this world and contrasted it with knowing Christ crucified, who is the wisdom of God. The wisdom of this world judges people by their status, by their learning, by the gifts they exhibit, by their rhetoric, etc. These two wisdoms are diametrically opposed to each other. In what the world counts as foolishness, the crucified Christ, lies the power and wisdom of God. It is Christ who represents God's plan from before the foundation of the earth for the salvation and the glory of his people. If the Corinthian Christians wish to be divided among themselves and talk about status in the Christian community, then Paul insists that they must return to basic principles. The division between those who have wisdom and those who do not is a distinction between those who know Christ and those who do not. The attitudes of the wisdom of this world must not be allowed to judge who are or are not God's people.

Paul shows this by talking of Christians as "spiritual" (a word almost certainly being used by the Corinthians). He points out that the wisdom of God can only be discerned "spiritually." That is, these things of God can only be understood if the Holy Spirit reveals them since he alone knows the mind of God. Thus, Paul redefines the word "spiritual" not to indicate levels of "spirituality" but to indicate the basic division between those who are the Lord's and those who are "unspiritual" and have not followed him or understood him.

Christians are judged by no one (except the Lord). Their status is secure because they possesses the Spirit. Now, having established the essential divisions of people and shown that Christians cannot be divided into those with standing before God and those without, Paul will directly tackle the Corinthian church's problems. In 3:1–4:21 he returns to the question of the divisions among the Corinthians, examining in detail how a Christian teacher should or should not be judged. He speaks to Corinthian Christians who, he says, behave as "fleshly." Though they have received the Spirit of God (2:12), their lives and behavior reflect more of this world's wisdom than God's. This must be changed.

In 3:1–4 Paul shows that their jealousy and divisions are unacceptable and are behavior that belongs to the world of the flesh rather than the world of God's Spirit. To do this Paul introduces a new contrast. Now the spiritual people themselves are referred to as "babies" (3:1; νήπιος).[1] The contrast formerly was between those who were believers (the spiritual) and those who are not (the unspiritual). Now this contrast is between what spiritual people (believers) ought to be, and how they actually appear in Corinth. They are part of the family, but they have a lot of growing up to do!

In 3:5–9, Paul takes the ministries of himself and Apollos and shows that the differences of ministry have to do with God's calling, not with who is the greater between them. This section thus serves as a bridge into a more lengthy examination of the nature of Christian leadership and ministry (3:10–4:21).

IV. Mature Christians Pursue God's Wisdom (2:6–4:21)

    A. Paul Proclaims God's Wisdom (2:6–13)

    B. God's Wisdom Characterizes Those Who Are "Spiritual" (2:14–16)

➡   **C. The Corinthians Are Spiritually Immature (3:1–9)**

    D. Wise Leadership Acts with Spiritual Discernment (3:10–4:21)

Main Idea

The Corinthian Christians need to behave as the spiritual people they are. Their jealousy and quarrelling, especially over leadership and their teachers, reveal they are still just babies in Christ. Paul uses himself and Apollos to show what a spiritual perspective on different ministries and callings should look like.

Translation

1 Corinthians 3:1–9

1a	Addressees	And **I,** brothers [and sisters],	
b	Assertion 1	**was not able to speak to you**	**as spiritual people** but rather
c	Contrast		as fleshly [people],
d	Apposition		as babies in Christ.
2a	Assertion 2	**I gave you** **milk to drink,**	
b	Contrast		not [solid] food;

Continued on next page.

---

1. See BDAG 671. The word νήπιος, here used metaphorically, refers to a very young child or infant. Cf. 1 Cor 13:11 where it is used non-metaphorically.

Continued from previous page.

c	Basis for assertion 2	for **you were not yet able [to eat it];**
d	Temporal contrast	indeed, **not even yet are you able [to eat it],**
3a	Explanation	for **still you are fleshly people.**
b	Basis (location) for ...	For where jealousy and strife [exist] among you,
c	Rhetorical question 1 (a)	**are you not fleshly people**
d	Restatement question 1 (b)	and **are you not living according to human ways?**
4a	Basis (temporal) for ...	For when someone says, "I am of Paul," and another, "I am of Apollos,"
b	Restatement question 1 (c)	**are you not being [simply] human?**
c	Examples ...	So
5a	Rhetorical question 2	**what is Apollos?**
		And
b	List	**what is Paul?**
c	Assertion (response)	[They are] servants
d	Agency	through whom you believed,
e	Expansion	as the Lord assigned to each one.
6a	Clarification of response	**I planted,**
b	Progression	**Apollos watered,**
c	Contrast	but **God was causing the growth.**
7a	Consequence	Thus, neither the planter is something, nor the waterer, but God causes the growth.
b	Recapitulation	
8a	Expansion of v. 7a	And **the one who plants and the one who waters are one,**
b	Further expansion	and **each will receive their own wage**
c	Manner	according to their own labor.
9a	Conclusion	For **we are God's fellow workers;**
b	Conclusion	**you are God's field,**
c	Expansion	**God's building.**

Structure

Paul takes up the word "spiritual" (πνευματικός) from the preceding chapter. He has shown the Corinthians that they are spiritual if they love God and so have the Spirit. The argument then proceeds as follows: (1) they are babes in Christ acting in a "fleshly" manner (3:1–2); (2) their jealousy and competitive strife proves this (3:3–4); (3) they therefore must learn from the example of Paul and Apollos (3:5–9). Here there is no jealousy; they are God's fellow workers with different jobs *under God as he has assigned*. This then opens the way for the further investigation of the nature of the work of God's assigned teachers and, specifically, the place of these workers within the church at Corinth.

Exegetical Outline

    IV. Mature Christians Pursue God's Wisdom (2:6–4:21)

        A. Paul Proclaims God's Wisdom (2:6–13)

        B. God's Wisdom Characterizes Those Who Are "Spiritual" (2:14–16)

➡   **C. The Corinthians Are Spiritually Immature (3:1–9)**

           1. Their Factions Reveal They Are Not Living as "Spiritual People" (3:1–4)

                a. They Can Only Be Fed Milk (3:1–2)

                b. They Are "of the Flesh" (3:3)

                c. Their Factionalism Centers on Church Leaders (3:4)

           2. Church Leaders Are God's Servants (3:5–9)

                a. God Assigns Their Work (3:5–6a)

                b. God Brings Fruit from That Work (3:6b-7)

                c. God Provides Their Wages (3:8)

                d. God's Field and God's Building Are Their Workplace (3:9)

Explanation of the Text

3:1 And I, brothers [and sisters], was not able to speak to you as spiritual people but rather as fleshly [people], as babies in Christ (Κἀγώ, ἀδελφοί, οὐκ ἠδυνήθην λαλῆσαι ὑμῖν ὡς πνευματικοῖς ἀλλ᾽ ὡς σαρκίνοις, ὡς νηπίοις ἐν Χριστῷ). Paul returns to the first-person singular as he takes them to task. While he affirms that they are all "spiritual," their behavior suggests otherwise. "And I" (κἀγώ) gives emphasis to this change of tack (see 2:1, 3 above).

Here the word "spiritual" (πνευματικοῖς) is clearly masculine. The point of comparison is made by the double use of the particle "as" (ὡς). Calling them "brothers and sisters" (ἀδελφοί) is kindly and reminds them of his relationship to them in Christ. What is about to come may appear as harsh, and

certainly Paul has to challenge them strongly. Yet, throughout he does so with conscious reminders to them that *together* they are God's family and that he loves and cares for them (1:10, 11, 26; 2:1; 4:6, 14–15; 7:24; 10:1; 11:33).

Paul has argued that the Corinthian Christians are "spiritual" (they are indeed "brothers and sisters"). However, they are not behaving or living as if they are. Thus, the contrast between the first and second parts of this sentence is clear. "But rather,"[2] says Paul, he speaks to them "as fleshly" (ὡς σαρκίνοις). The following clause is in apposition to "as fleshly," thus explaining that he speaks to them as "babies in Christ" (ὡς νηπίοις ἐν Χριστῷ).

As we noted above, Paul does not use the word

---

2. Taking ἀλλά as a strong adversative.

"unspiritual" (ψυχικός) to describe them. The reason seems clear. He seeks out a word that will describe someone who is behaving in a worldly way, as if following the "wisdom of this age," and yet who actually is a Christian and is therefore "spiritual."

Paul's use of the imagery of an immature child (or baby) is straightforward. If the Corinthians have been talking of the "mature" (τελείοι; 2:6) and making judgments about whether some in the church have arrived and some not, Paul has had to say that all have "arrived." They all are "mature" in a strict sense because they belong to the Lord and they are his. Once they are in Christ, they are *not* among those who are doomed to come to nothing. The Corinthians need to hear that status in the covenant community of Christ is secure for all who are his and is not dependent upon the judgments of those who follow a different worldview. They *are* holy, and they *do* belong. However, it is one thing to say that their status and standing before God is secure and altogether another to say that they evidence this in their lives.

This apparent desire to divide into groups of the "spiritual" and those who are not is something Paul will not tolerate, and so, in a blunt opening salvo, he now speaks to those who consider themselves spiritually superior to others (this attack becomes even more explicit in 4:8). He tells them that whatever they may think about their superior status in the community, he could not talk to them as "spiritual people" (ὡς πνευματικοῖς).

They are behaving as thoroughly immature Christians. For those who termed themselves "mature" now to hear themselves referred to as "babies" would surely have stung, but they are behaving with one another in the sort of inconsiderate and aggressive way that is so typical of immature children. Just as young children will often leave others out of their games, so the Corinthians exclude each other and put each other down.

However, this infantile existence is worse than it might at first appear, because they are behaving as people who have a *non*-Christian mindset. Their behavior, their words, and their whole mindset is fleshly. It derives from that worldview that cannot understand the centrality of Christ crucified rather than from a mindset transformed by the Holy Spirit. As Garland notes, there is a great irony here, especially in the light of Jesus's own teaching and what Paul has already said in 1:18–2:16. In reference to Matthew 11:25–27 Garland writes, "Jesus thanked God for hiding 'these things' from 'the wise and understanding' and revealing them to 'infants.'"[3]

We have kept the translation "fleshly" (σαρκινοί), but recognize that in some Christian circles it may have rather narrower connotations than Paul means it to have here. In the modern church the word is sometimes reduced to denoting immoral behavior or to licentiousness or generally doing things most Christians would not want to do! For Paul, the idea is much wider than this. It is about a whole way of life or, as it is sometimes called, a "worldview." Part of being "fleshly" for these people is precisely that they are prepared to make judgments about Christian leaders and their followers that their commitment to Christ should have shown them are not theirs to make. Being "fleshly" is about ending up being divisive in the church and quarrelling together. It is about judging some Christians to be superior than others, and so barely allowing some to be counted as part of the community at all. In other words, it means they follow their natural instincts rather than those formed in the believer by God's Spirit.

This is not some pleasant discourse from Paul

---

3. Garland, *1 Corinthians*, 107.

encouraging them to grow in the faith. This is a dramatic and pointed challenge to the very basis on which they are operating as God's people. Their problem arises from their supposed "wisdom" (1 Cor 3:18) and their "cunning" (v. 21), both attributes one would expect of those who are not Christians, the unspiritual. It is certainly an attack on those who would say in their puffed-up arrogance (8:1), "We all have knowledge!"

3:2–3a I gave you milk to drink, not [solid] food; for you were not yet able [to eat it]; indeed, not even yet are you able [to eat it], for still you are fleshly people (γάλα ὑμᾶς ἐπότισα, οὐ βρῶμα, οὔπω γὰρ ἐδύνασθε. ἀλλ᾽ οὐδὲ ἔτι νῦν δύνασθε, ἔτι γὰρ σαρκικοί ἐστε). Despite all the boasting and claimed sophistication of some of the Corinthian Christians, they are behaving childishly and must grow up. They have failed to examine properly the "meat" of the gospel of Christ crucified. They are still not able to do so (οὐδὲ ἔτι νῦν δύνασθε) in the sense that they are still looking for what Hooker has called "synthetic substitutes."[4] Paul has thus been obliged to adjust the way he addresses them. Using the aorist (ἐπότισα), he again looks back to his coming among them when he gave them "milk" to drink. He continues to use the picture of a baby. As new converts, they were not given solid food. During that time, they were unable to eat it since they were not ready for it. This is what might have been expected, but the strong contrast of the second half of this verse is biting in its sarcasm. "Indeed" seeks to reflect the strong contrast (ἀλλά), which is also continuative. "Not even" (οὐδὲ ἔτι) intensifies that contrast, as Paul moves to the present tense. Even "now" (νῦν) they cannot eat solid food,

because they are still fleshly. There is something of a play on words in vv. 1–2. Paul says he "was not able to speak" to them because they were "not yet able [to eat]"; indeed, they are "not even yet able [to eat]."

It is important to understand what Paul means by "milk" and "food." The terms appear together and are used both metaphorically and non-metaphorically elsewhere. For example, Philo talks of milk as food for babies (νηπίοι) and bread for adults (τελείοι) and commonly uses milk and bread in metaphorical passages.[5] However, Paul's "milk" and "food" are used in a particular way here. He has laid out very clearly his gospel in the opening chapter. It centers in Christ crucified. This is the very "wisdom" of God. Surely, in every sense, this is "solid food." Life commitment to this message could hardly be called a commitment to "milk"! Given Paul's distaste for the Corinthian categorizing of people, he surely would not have held back on "deep teaching" only to give it later as people seemed ready for it.[6] This would have created the very divisions in the community that he opposes throughout his letter.

It is perhaps better to concentrate on the main metaphor here rather than on the milk and food, which serve to further the main picture. Paul fed them with the gospel of Christ crucified and so gave them the very "wisdom of God" (1:24) and revealed in that gospel "the power of God" (2:5). He has made the point earlier in a number of places that he did this when he "came among them" (2:1). He did not hold part of the message back. But new Christians ("babies in Christ") do have to grow. They need to study and apply themselves to the

---

4. Morna D. Hooker, "Hard Sayings: 1 Cor. 3:2," *Theology* 69 (1966): 21.

5. The metaphor of spiritual food is found in a number of places in Philo and elsewhere. See examples in J. Behm, "βρῶμα," *TDNT* 1:643n7.

6. Barrett, *First Corinthians*, 81, suggests that the wisdom Paul speaks to the mature "rests on the word of the cross, but is a development of this." One cannot help but think that this would suggest the problem lay with the teacher!

message, which has implications for the whole of life. It is a message that will lead them deeper into the word of God as they seek to understand better what has been revealed in Christ. They themselves would have been expected to look at Scripture and come to the same conclusions for life that Paul has. This is not some "deeper" truth that has been withheld until people reach a "spiritual" status where they are competent to hear such things. Rather, it is part of the expected growth process when the original message is absorbed ever more deeply. In other words, milk and food are the same thing; they keep people alive. But the one is the natural progression of the other. One true sign of a Christian—and often this is to be noticed among young Christians—is their great desire to know more and more about Christ and to go ever deeper into the same original gospel message. That message is not added to, but is now examined in the light of Scripture and lived out in ways which ever more deeply reflect "the mind of Christ." Luke offers an interesting aside on the Berean Christians in Acts 17:11, where they are complimented for assessing the Scriptures daily to see "if these things were so" (ESV). It is surely this commitment to the church's continued study of God's word after they had "received the word with all eagerness" (17:11 ESV) that Paul would have wished to see among the Corinthians. The Bereans were making judgments or assessing what they were hearing in the light of Scripture, and this is the difference between those who are "infants" and those who are behaving as adults.

The Corinthians are eating at the trough of the wisdom of this age rather than of God in Christ. One of the things they most need to realize, as Paul will show so clearly later in the letter, is that each one has gifts of the Spirit with which to build up the community. In Christ's church there are many different people from whom to learn and from whom much can be gained. Just like with the reception of the gospel in the first place, these gifts will not just be the domain of those who seem great by the world's standards.

Here Paul uses a slightly different word for "fleshly" from the one he used in v. 1. (There it was σαρκινοί. Here it is σαρκικοί.) It is not at all clear that there is a difference of meaning between them. Some have suggested there is a different connotation for each word. Fee suggests that one (v. 3; σαρκικοί) has clearer ethical overtones, while the other (v. 1; σαρκινοί) relates more to the physical side of their existence than to the spiritual.[7] Conzelmann, among others, says the words are synonymous, the view taken here.[8]

3:3b–d For where jealousy and strife [exist] among you, are you not fleshly people and are you not living according to human ways? (ὅπου γὰρ ἐν ὑμῖν ζῆλος καὶ ἔρις, οὐχὶ σαρκικοί ἐστε καὶ κατὰ ἄνθρωπον περιπατεῖτε;). At this point Paul makes it clear that the aspect of their "fleshly" behavior that most concerns him is the jealousy that has led to divisions. This is no better than would be expected of the unbelieving world. Thus, the conjunction "for" (γὰρ) introduces a further explanation and example of what it is to be fleshly and childish. "Jealousy" is a typically childish behavior and has to do with fighting for and arguing over one's status and possessions (ζῆλος can mean "zeal," but here it is used with strongly negative overtones). Galatians 5:13–26 contains a some-

---

7. Fee, *1 Corinthians*, 135–36. Garland, *1 Corinthians*, 109, suggests that "the-ικος suffix connotes 'characterized by'" and says "it refers to an individual's values, attitudes and judgments, which manifest themselves in self-centeredness."

8. Conzelmann, *1 Corinthians*, 72. See also Thiselton, *1 Corinthians*, 293.

what similar argument in which Paul speaks of the works of "the flesh" (v. 13; σάρξ) and asks them to "walk by the Spirit (v. 16; πνεύματι περιπατεῖτε). There Paul lists the works he considered typically to reflect "the flesh," and they included sexual immorality, idolatry, and strife and jealousy (Gal 5:19–20). Jealousy will naturally bring about strife as people compare themselves negatively with each other or seek to establish their superiority over another (cf. Rom 13:13; 2 Cor 12:20). "Strife" (ἔρις) was used before at 1:11 when Paul was introducing his subject matter.

Paul's question expects the answer "yes" (with οὐχί) as he expands upon what it means to be "fleshly." Paul has in mind their quarrels and petty jealousies over status and leadership and their attitudes to each other, which indicate they are living "according to human ways" (NRSV: "according to human inclinations").[9] Paul's understood contrast here is between living in a fundamentally human way and living a spiritual life "according to the Spirit" (Gal 4:29 ESV; κατὰ πνεῦμα).

3:4 For when someone says, "I am of Paul," and another, "I am of Apollos," are you not being [simply] human?[10] (ὅταν γὰρ λέγῃ τις, Ἐγὼ μέν εἰμι Παύλου, ἕτερος δέ, Ἐγὼ Ἀπολλῶ, οὐκ ἄνθρωποί ἐστε;). With another explanatory conjunction, Paul applies this directly by returning, at least partly, to the groupings to which he referred in chapter 1. The emphatic position of the pronoun "I" (ἐγώ), the genitive of relationship, and the lack of the verb are the same as noted in 1:12. The possible constituency of these groups is also discussed there and in the introduction.

However, Paul mentions here just himself and

Apollos as he narrows down his argument. The two of them will now become his chosen examples to illustrate how spiritual adults regard things and how they behave. The text does not reveal why Apollos, rather than Cephas, is the chosen exemplar.[11] It may be that the fact that Apollos was known for his eloquence (Acts 18:24) and that Paul has insisted he has not spoken with "words of eloquent wisdom" (1:17) make him the obvious choice here. In human terms, he and Paul seem to be quite different and can be judged accordingly. In fact, both work together for the Lord, understanding their different callings with no edge of jealousy or strife. More simply, it may simply be that Apollos and Paul were better known by a majority of the church since they are the two who have preached in Corinth.

3:5 So what is Apollos? And what is Paul? [They are] servants through whom you believed, as the Lord assigned to each one (Τί οὖν ἐστιν Ἀπολλῶς; τί δέ ἐστιν Παῦλος; διάκονοι δι' ὧν ἐπιστεύσατε, καὶ ἑκάστῳ ὡς ὁ κύριος ἔδωκεν). In this next section Paul takes himself and Apollos by way of example. He will show that there is no rivalry between them as leaders, for they are God's fellow workers. He starts with two rhetorical questions that set up the next few verses. The first point Paul makes is that he and Apollos are "servants" (διάκονοι). Secondly, he says each was given (assigned) his work by the Lord. The use of "to each one" (ἑκάστῳ) prepares the way for a number of points that Paul will wish to make through this letter, of which he and Apollos serve as examples. First, they have *different* callings and assignments of gifts, as he will show in the verses that follow (cf. 9:15–17). Secondly, each

---

9. The phrase κατὰ ἄνθρωπον means "living as fleshly people." "According to human ways" seeks to capture the implicit contrast between the godly way and the fleshly way of living. The verb περιπατέω is commonly used for living life, as Gal 5:16 noted above.

10. Again, Paul uses "human" (ἄνθρωποι) as a synonym for "fleshly"; cf. 3:3.

11. Fitzmyer, *1 Corinthians*, 188: "Mention of two groups is made only by way of example, not because of a difference in his relations with Apollos or Cephas."

of them has been "given" what they have by God. Later, he will show that this is in fact true of *all* Christians. In 12:4–11 Paul will insist for everyone that there are varieties of gifts and yet to *each one* a service has been given. He will also insist that such assignments are all given by God and through his Spirit. Then, in 12:29 he will also make it clear that not all have the same roles within the church but that God has appointed all of them.

Paul reminds the Corinthians that they did "believe" *through* the work of Paul and Apollos.[12] From a human point of view this might have generated attachment to a figurehead. However, Paul immediately leads away from that conclusion as he insists that they are simply "servants" (διάκονοι). The impact of Paul's rhetoric here is dismissive of any who might have thought otherwise. Their work for Christ among the Corinthians was given to them by God, and as obedient servants they followed his calling. This is the life of the person who has come to see God's wisdom in the crucifixion of the King. Modeling such servanthood and obedience reveals "the mind of Christ" (2:16).

Thus, this verse firstly serves the immediate function of helping the Corinthians to see how leadership according to the Spirit should be regarded. Secondly, it begins a number of contrasts that Paul will make as he drives home his message. He will argue that working for the Lord is all about knowing that God has taken the initiative, God has called, God has assigned the task, God gives growth to the work, and God gives any rewards there might be.

3:6 I planted, Apollos watered, but God was causing the growth (ἐγὼ ἐφύτευσα, Ἀπολλῶς ἐπότισεν, ἀλλὰ ὁ θεὸς ηὔξανεν). As we noted in the exegetical outline above, Paul's argument in vv. 5–9

can be broken down in a way that demonstrates the main point he makes, thus challenging the Corinthian "fleshly" way of seeing things. All is of God; therefore, there can be no grounds for boasting when it is the Lord's work with which they are involved. Verse 5 has indicated the key theological motif: *Paul and Apollos are God's servants, and this is how all church leaders should be regarded* (4:1; 9:19; cf. 2 Cor 4:5; 6:4). In vv. 5–6a God assigns both to different work. For both, any fruit from their work is because God provides the growth, and it does not mean they are "something" (vv. 6b–7). There is a unity to the work of those called by God, and he is the one that gives out wages (v. 8). Finally, Paul makes it clear that the two of them are God's workers, while the Corinthian church is God's field that must be worked and his building that must be built (v. 9). By his repetition of "God" Paul leaves the audience in no doubt of his point.

Changing the analogy, Paul now uses the picture of farming. The aorist verbs still look back to those early days when Paul came among the Corinthians. As they look back at what has happened in their midst, Paul wants them to look at the *work* that was done among them for the Lord. Paul planted. He was the first there, and he sowed the seed of God's word among them. Apollos did some follow-up work but also planted, as some had come to faith through him (v. 5). Though the content of Apollos's work is not discussed, it probably involved further teaching of the faith and expounding of Scriptures among them. But whatever either of them did is precisely *not* important to Paul. "Rather" (ἀλλά is a strong adversative, introducing the key to Paul's thought here), what is important is that it was "God" who "was causing growth" (ηὔξανεν)[13] throughout the time Paul planted and Apollos wa-

---

12. The διά + genitive is used here to indicate agency.

13. The imperfect carries a continuative force here.

tered.[14] God's work continued whatever Paul and Apollos had done by way of service to the Lord among this people. Thus, Paul talks of two leaders and of two different works. However, it is *God* who is the one on whom people should focus, and he continues to do the work even as leaders come and go as he assigns them various tasks. In the analogy, the very idea that the one who planted might be at odds with the one who watered or that one was needed and not the other is absurd, and so Paul continues.

3:7 Thus, neither the planter is something, nor the waterer, but God causes the growth (ὥστε οὔτε ὁ φυτεύων ἐστίν τι οὔτε ὁ ποτίζων ἀλλ᾽ ὁ αὐξάνων θεός). The first point Paul draws from the agricultural or horticultural picture is that the only person who counts for anything in the whole process is God. The Corinthians' "fleshly" ways of regarding their leaders meant that *who* they were and *what* they had done were given importance. They could point to their special leaders, whom they held in high honor, and mention their name and their work. For Paul *God* is all that matters. When seen in the light of God and his work in Christ, then all others are "nothing." Just as colloquially we might say today, "He's really *something!*" so the Corinthians did the same with those they esteemed. Paul would much rather have them say, "God is really *something!*" (The use of τι here is an emphatic use of the indefinite pronoun, as in Acts 5:36).

Paul thus offers a wonderful and humbling reminder to all that God's work continues with or without us. Yet his words also offer great encouragement that, in his grace, God does use his people to further his work. On the one hand, ministries in God's church are not what make it all "happen"; on the other hand, God has given each person the enormous privilege of taking part in the work of the master farmer.

3:8–9 And the one who plants and the one who waters are one, and each will receive their own wage according to their own labor. For we are God's fellow workers; you are God's field, God's building (ὁ φυτεύων δὲ καὶ ὁ ποτίζων ἕν εἰσιν, ἕκαστος δὲ τὸν ἴδιον μισθὸν λήμψεται κατὰ τὸν ἴδιον κόπον. θεοῦ γάρ ἐσμεν συνεργοί· θεοῦ γεώργιον, θεοῦ οἰκοδομή ἐστε). The second point Paul makes from the agricultural picture is that the two workers with different jobs to do "are one" (ἕν εἰσιν). Paul argues that he and Apollos are "one"— that is, they are both "fellow workers" belonging to God (θεοῦ is a possessive genitive). It is pointless to ask whether they are one in status or in the work they have been asked to do. The two things cannot be separated. They are clearly one in status, whatever they do. This is what Paul has shown of all Christians earlier in his argument. Here, though, Paul also shows that they are about one work, in which both fulfill what the Lord has assigned to them. In the Corinthian mind, they are far from "one." Leaders are judged differently. Some have good presentations of the message that exhibits an acceptable "wisdom" to the world around. Others seem to have more important teachings or roles than others. Constantly, they are *judging*. Yet Paul says of himself and Apollos that they are both nothing (v. 7) and that they are one. Once again, note the triple repetition of *God*, which is where the focus is placed.

The third point Paul makes is that he and Apollos are "fellow workers." There is a unity between

---

14. These aorists (ἐφύτευσα and ἐπότισεν) are complexive or constative aorists (see BDF §332). Wallace, *Greek Grammar*, 557, describes this as viewing the action as a whole. The imperfect (ηὔξανεν) contrasts with the aorist and draws attention to Paul's point that it was always God who gave the growth.

them that, in order for Paul to appeal to it, must have been visible to the Corinthians. The genitive "of God" (θεοῦ) is likely possessive, making the servanthood involved even clearer. These servants belong to God and work together with each other to carry out God's work. It is less likely that Paul was thinking at this point of being a coworker *with God* and more likely that both he and Apollos were servants belonging to God. However, it is possible that this word (συνεργοί), which he used regularly,[15] had a dual reference in Paul's mind; that is, he was contemplating both the unity of the workers *and* the fact that God was with them as they worked. In 16:15–16 Paul warmly commends Stephanas and his household and all the true fellow workers in the church who were devoted to "the service of the Lord's people."

A fourth point Paul makes is that there will be one differentiation between the person who plants and the person who waters, but this will be *entirely in the hands of God*. "Each one will receive their own wage" (ἕκαστος . . . τὸν ἴδιον μισθὸν λήμψεται) does suggest a difference between Paul and Apollos, but not one of which they are aware. It is only in respect to how God views the work. The future tense of "receive" (λήμψεται) looks forward to judgment day, something Paul will expand upon in 3:13–14. The "labor" (κόπος) to which Paul refers is the hard work of the Christian laborer in the field. It is a work that God's people must endure despite its difficulties. Later he will urge the Corinthians themselves to abound in "the work of the Lord" (15:58). Paul puts the word in the list of his trials in 2 Corinthians 6:5. He can refer to his labor and hardship (2 Cor 11:27; Gal 6:17). Even as he wrote this, he was probably thinking of the "toil" involved in having to write this letter to a people

who had come to faith when he had preached and yet who were now looking down on him. However, in a real sense for Paul this was "all in a day's work," and one day his work would be evaluated by the one person who could do so justly and in full view of all the circumstances.

The word "wage" (μισθός) often has an eschatological connotation, especially in Paul.[16] He looks at those from Corinth with the honor they give to certain people and the status some claim for themselves and then thinks of the contrast with the genuine gospel of a Christ crucified. Perhaps he recalls the teaching of Jesus. His own teaching certainly moves in the same direction as the Lord's (and he will say more on this in ch. 9). In Matthew 6:2 the Lord sees those who flaunt themselves to be honored by others; "they have their 'reward' [μισθός] in full." But the Father "sees what is done in secret" and he "will reward" (6:4). Paul has more to say on this in 1 Corinthians 3:14–15. For now, we note that it is not for the "field," that is, the church in Corinth, to judge!

Finally, having talked of himself and Apollos by way of example, he continues with the analogy but now slightly changes the angle of view: "You are God's field" (θεοῦ γεώργιον). The mention of planting, watering, and now the field recalls aspects of a picture long used of God's people (e.g., Ps 80:8; Isa 5:7; Jer 31:27–28; 42:9–10; Amos 9:14). The prophet Ezekiel had used it as a picture of God's planting of Israel, while contemplating the possibility that Israel would not survive when judgment came (Ezek 17:5–10). Paul may even see his call to gospel work in similar terms to the call Jeremiah had received, where both building and planting come together in God's commission: "See, I have set you this day over nations and over kingdoms . . . to build and to

---

15. Cf., e.g., Rom 16:3, 9, 21; 2 Cor 8:23; Phil 4:3; Phlm 1.

16. See further the essay, "In Depth: What Reward?" at 3:15.

plant" (Jer 1:10). Again, the emphasis is on *God's* field and *God's* building. And it is to the picture of a building that Paul now turns.

"You are . . . God's building." The "you are" (ἐστε) is again emphatic and contrasts with "we are" in v. 9a. Paul's point is that the very ones who are so proud and so judgmental of each other and their leaders are fields and buildings that need much work. It is the "building" (οἰκοδομή) meta-

phor that will now come to the fore and continue to be touched on throughout the epistle. Paul will talk of each person needing to "build up" (οἰκοδομέω) the others in the fellowship, and this will be a theme he introduces in the next few verses. This brings Paul's example from and comparison with his own and Apollos's ministries to a close. He will move next to examine the nature of this "building" ministry.

Theology in Application

The Need for Spiritual Growth

God's people throughout history have always had a tendency to assume that once they are God's people they have nothing more to learn or that they need no further instruction. The temptation is that, once people have evidence in their own lives of God's blessing, they need nothing more. They begin to see their status before God as secure. Different people and different generations have appealed for this "security" to various aspects of the gospel calling or message. Some turn to the doctrine of election and argue that as "saved" people they are safe and do not need to worry about going much deeper into the faith. In ancient Israel the appeal was often to the possession of God's gracious gift of Torah and also to the sign of circumcision. Torah possession and the sign of circumcision thus came to be seen as a guarantee of community status, and so it did not matter too much what they then did with their lives. Thus, one of the great prophetic appeals called upon people to "circumcise your hearts" (Deut 10:16; cf. Jer 4:4). In Corinth some were appealing to the spiritual gifts as evidence of their secure status as superior or mature Christians, and so they did not believe that they needed much else. The problem, of course, is always that there is some truth to these positions. God's blessings—whether through Torah or grace-gifts, whether through election or baptism—all point to the Spirit's work in the believer.

Yet throughout Scripture it is seen that the true believer and the godly church will be committed to continual feeding by God. In the church this means being committed to learning more of God and his work in Christ from his word in Scripture. It is only this commitment that will ultimately prevent divisions as disciples grow together in humility before God and his word. It is only in this commitment to seeking after "solid food" that people will find how to bring glory to God in every area of their life. As a church is committed to this "solid food," so it will have a greater appreciation for the whole work to which it is called both in building up the people of God as well as in outreach with the gospel.

Many churches faithfully preach the gospel and call for conversions week by week and yet do not take people further into the purposes of God. For example, too few people have learned a biblical view of the church and its central role in "this age." So they become divided or move from one church to another to receive "what their itching ears want to hear" (2 Tim 4:3). They find churches that always make them feel good or where other aspects of worship or ministry rather than the preached word are given priority. Sadly, of course, church ministers and leaders get pulled into this as they long to be well liked by their people. One complaint that a message was "too heavy" results in them reverting to a lighter "milk" from the pulpit that will not help the congregation grow into the world-impacting church they should be. Church members should be at the forefront of asking for good teaching that builds on the foundation of Christ crucified and leads to their own spiritual growth. It is this that will result in a Christ-focused church of real influence in this world.

Servants with a Mission

The multiple repetition of "God" in these verses has put the emphasis where it should be. God owns his people, and he calls them and guides them and, if he is so pleased, brings fruit from their labors. Thus, Paul has emphasized that he and Apollos are servants of God. The background for this idea of God's people—especially the leaders—being "servants" finds its roots in the Old Testament. Moses was regularly referred to as "the servant of the Lord" (e.g., Deut 34:5; Joshua 1:1, 13; 2 Chr 24:6). David is addressed in the preface of certain psalms in this way (e.g., Pss 18:1; 36:1), and years later Mary the mother of Jesus referred to herself in this way (Luke 1:38). In large part, it was a term specially reflecting a person's *faithful* commitment to the service of God (see Isa 20:3 [Isaiah]; 22:20 [Eliakim]; Isa 37:35 [David]). Even the nation of Israel itself is, at times, designated as God's "servant." It is therefore not surprising that prophecies in Isaiah speak of the "servant" (see 42:1, 19 [2x]; 43:10; 44:1, 2, 21 [2x]) and that in the end it is Jesus who ultimately fulfills perfectly this understanding of "servant" and is, above all others, *the* servant (Matt 12:18; Acts 3:13, 26; 4:27; Phil 2:7). Christian servanthood is thus known and experienced in the imitation of Christ through faithfulness to him.

However, Christians can easily nod to this idea of servanthood as what should characterize their lives without it making any difference practically in how they live. First, Paul knows that servanthood is something that is a foundational truth of the gospel. It is not an optional extra. Since Christ was a servant, so his people must be servants. Secondly, Paul sees servanthood as tied up with God's calling, just as it was for Christ. This means that it will take on different practical forms for different Christians, depending on their calling. Paul planted and Apollos watered, but both did this in obedient service to the Lord's calling. Because this is the way servanthood works itself out, it becomes clear why divisions among Christians or the putting one person on a pedestal above another should never happen in the church. Thirdly, there is a unified mission that constantly provides the framework for each person's obedience and service according to their calling. The mission is the building up of God's people. This is why each is given grace-gifts and why each is said to be a member of the body. Thus, each member, however lowly they are humanly speaking, has significance in the church and in God's work in Christ.

At times, most true Christians will ask themselves whether they are growing in the Lord. Are they progressing in their faith? Do they love the Lord more deeply and serve him more intently? In this section, Paul has pointed to essential and foundational truths that all Christians must know and understand if they are to be able to answer those questions satisfactorily. They do not progress in their faith, grow in the Lord, come to love him more deeply, or serve him more intently unless they are becoming ever more immersed in what he says to them in his word.

1 Corinthians 3:10–17

Literary Context

In 3:1–9 Paul has told the Corinthians that, however much they may boast in some leaders and in the degree of "spirituality" they think they have, Paul can only deal with them as babies in the faith. They are behaving in a purely human way and not in a way that reveals the Holy Spirit within and among them. Thus, they may be spiritual (after all, they are Christians), but their lives do not reflect this. They are fleshly. In 3:6–9 Paul briefly compared himself and Apollos to show that there is an entirely different way of looking at church leadership. Its focus must be on God, who calls each one to different tasks to work in God's field and with God's building.

In 3:10–17, Paul takes the picture of the building somewhat further. He talks about the need to ensure that the right foundation, Jesus Christ, is the only one that is laid. He insists on the need to examine carefully what is built on it. Builders are ultimately responsible to God alone and will be held accountable by him. This building is *God's* temple.

Paul then draws together his argument thus far by returning to the matters of wisdom and spiritual discernment as Christians judge each other and dare to assess Christian leadership and ministry. He warns that people should assess themselves properly before God and not with the eyes of the world. He then addresses the right way of assessing Christian teachers, especially applying what he says to how they have judged him.

Main Idea

The Corinthian Christians are God's building, and the Holy Spirit dwells among them. Subsequent builders need to pay careful and appropriate attention to the foundation. Any attempt to destroy the temple of God will lead to that individual's destruction.

Translation

1 Corinthians 3:10–17

10a	Manner	According to the grace of God given to me as a wise master builder,
b	Assertion	**I laid a foundation,** and
c	Assertion	**another is building [on it].**
d	Exhortation	Now **let each one build with care.**
11a	Basis for exhortation	For no other foundation can be laid
b	Contrast	than the one that is in place,
c	Explanation	which is Christ Jesus,
12a	Condition 1 (protasis)	Now if anyone builds upon the foundation
b	Manner	with gold, silver, precious stones, wood, hay, or straw
13a	Assertion (apodosis)	**each person's work will become evident,**
b	Reason	for the Day will disclose it,
c	Explanation	because it is revealed through fire
d	Expansion	and each person's work, what sort it is,
e	Assertion	**the fire itself will test.**

Continued on next page.

Continued from previous page.

14a	Condition 2 (protasis)	If anyone's work lasts,
b	Description	which he has built,
c	Assertion (apodosis)	**he will receive a reward.**
15a	Condition 3 (protasis)	If anyone's work is burned up,
b	Assertion (apodosis)	**he will suffer loss,**
c	Expansion	but **he himself will be saved** but
d	Manner	only as through fire.
16a	Rhetorical questions	**Do you not know**
b		that you are God's temple and
c		the Spirit of God dwells in you?
17a	Condition 4 (protasis)	If anyone destroys God's temple
b	Assertion (apodosis)	**God will destroy him;**
c	Basis for assertion	for **the temple of God is holy,** and
d	Expansion	you are the temple!

Structure

The previous section ended by saying that the Corinthians are *God's building*. This section (3:10–17) ends by saying that they are *God's temple*. It is this picture of a building that is now developed. In 3:10–15 Paul shows the work of teachers in the church. Paul, as a master builder, laid the foundation, and others build on it but must do so carefully (v. 10). They cannot lay again the foundation, which is Jesus Christ (v. 11). The necessity for careful building will become evident at judgment day. In the second subsection, 3:16–17, Paul shows that the building is in fact the temple of God. Any attempt to destroy this temple will be met with judgment because this is God's temple and God's Spirit dwells there. The Corinthians are the temple.

Exegetical Outline

IV. **Mature Christians Pursue God's Wisdom (2:6–4:21)**

    A. Paul Proclaims God's Wisdom (2:6–13)

    B. God's Wisdom Characterizes Those Who Are "Spiritual" (2:14–16)

    C. The Corinthians Are Spiritually Immature (3:1–9)

➡   D. **Wise Leadership Acts with Spiritual Discernment (3:10–4:21)**

        1. **Illustration: A Building and a Wise Master Builder (3:10–15)**

            a. Lays No Other Foundation but Jesus Christ (3:10–11)

            b. Builds a Building That Will Stand When Tested by God (3:12–15)

        2. **The Building Is God's Temple in Which His Spirit Dwells (3:16–17)**

            a. The Corinthian Christians Are the Temple (3:16)

            b. Destroying the Temple Leads to God's Judgment (3:17)

IN DEPTH: Building Up the Church

1 Corinthians 3:9 concludes with a reference to "God's building" (θεοῦ οἰκοδομή). The development of this building metaphor now becomes crucial to substantial parts of Paul's instruction in this epistle. Especially from chapter 8 onward, this is ultimately the main metaphor to which Paul turns as he seeks to explain the beneficial purpose of the grace-gifts of the Spirit. The right use of these gifts builds up God's church, while the wrong use, as seen among the self-proclaimed "mature" or elitists at Corinth, leads to great harm among God's people. At this point, it is therefore worth taking a deeper look at the background and use of the metaphor.

In 3:10 Paul speaks of having laid the foundation for this local church at Corinth. The local church is thus the main referent of Paul's "building." As we see below, he commands anyone who builds on it to use proper materials (3:10–15). In other words, anyone now developing the gospel on which the church was founded must ensure that all that is said and taught only expands on the same message and does not change that message. As chapter 3 progresses, it is not entirely clear whether the building metaphor gives rise to Paul calling the Corinthians "the temple of God" (3:16) or vice versa. To us it seems likely that it is the temple imagery that precedes the building imagery, at least in Paul's composition of his argument. No doubt Paul's thoughts were driven by the knowledge that they lived in the messianic age (see especially his treatment of the present age in chapter 15), an age in which the Spirit had come (3:16) and an age that was moving toward the day of judgment (3:13). Unsurprisingly, therefore, Paul says the foundation he laid was Christ (3:11).

The metaphor itself is drawn from the Old Testament,[1] where rebuilding or "building up" the temple and the cities was regarded as part of God's future blessings for Israel. Indeed, the goal of the building was the completion of the promises of God.[2] Paul regarded the church as that renewed temple, built on its messianic foundations, within which the Spirit of God dwelt.[3]

For Paul, as he extended the metaphor, "building up" spoke to what helped the church and the individuals who comprised the whole to become what they were. They were the holy temple of God (3:16–17). Any building that took place therefore had to follow God's wisdom and plans, not a human's (2:16), and the attitude with which such building was to take place had to be one of service to Christ (4:1). Second Corinthians 5:1–5 is a reminder that Paul regarded the Spirit as a guarantee of an eternal building (cf. 1 Cor 3:16).

While the use of the verb "to build up" (οἰκοδομέω) in 1 Corinthians 8:1b is not a specific allusion to the Old Testament temple theme seen in chapter 3, the word probably did come to Paul's mind because of his earlier comparison of his own building work with that of the Corinthian leaders (3:10–15). Parallels between chapters 3 and 8 make this likely. In chapter 3 Paul had mentioned wrong building leading to destruction.[4] In 8:10–11 the wrong application of "building" (based on "knowledge") to eating idol food in a pagan temple could also lead to destruction (ἀπόλλυμι). People who built incorrectly perhaps thought they were "wise" (3:18) or that they had "knowledge" (8:2), but they had yet to become wise (3:18) and did not yet know as they ought to know (8:2).

In light of this, when we look at chapter 8, we cannot ignore Paul's earlier discussion of the subject since at the heart of the metaphor was Paul's concern for the *church*—a church that was Christ's and should be united in service to Christ rather than divided. Thus, the outworking of theory into practice was to be tested by examining the type of building that was occurring. In a statement that lays the groundwork for chapter 13, Paul shows in 8:1 that love, in practice, builds up the church; yet knowledge, in practice, puffs up the individual. This

---

1. This is demonstrated in various studies. See Pierre Bonnard, "L'Église corps de Christ dans le Paulinisme," *Revue de théologie et de philosophie* 8 (1958): 268–82; Ridderbos, *Paul*, 429–32.

2. In Acts 15:16 James's speech drew on this picture; using Amos 9:11 and Jer 12:15.

3. Ridderbos, *Paul*, 430. Cf. Isa 28:16; 65:21–22; 66:1; Ezek 36:10, 36; 37:24–28; Jub 1:17. Barrett, *First Corinthians*, 90; Héring, *First Corinthians*, 24; Conzelmann, *1 Corinthians*,

77–78, among others, also argue that Paul draws on these ideas in 1 Cor 3. See also Burtil E. Gärtner, *The Temple and the Community in Qumran and in the New Testament*, SNTSMS 1 (Cambridge: Cambridge University Press, 1965), 56–60, who demonstrates parallels between this section in Paul and ideas in the Qumran texts.

4. The word is φθείρω. See BDAG 857 ("punish with eternal destruction"). Cf. 2 Pet 2:12; Jude 10, 11 (with ἀπόλλυμι).

theme will be still further developed in chapter 14 where Paul takes the examples of two grace-gifts, prophecy and speaking in a tongue, and contrasts them by showing that when used in the gathered congregation one "builds up" the people of God and the other does not (14:2–3). The specifics of the content he expects of a gift that "builds up" are examined in the comments on 14:2–5 where Paul speaks of "encouragement" and "consolation."

So, for Paul, as the church replaces the temple as the place where God's Spirit dwells, it is the job of Christians to build it up. This will mean upholding its purity, encouraging its members, and seeking to ensure that all who are part of the building truly become the holy temple that God desires for his dwelling place.

One final point may be added. Another theme that is important to Paul in this epistle is that of the "stumbling block" or the "scandal." Of course, this is also closely related to temple themes, messianic passages, and the question of building and destruction (see "In Depth: The Theme of Stumbling" at 1:23).

Explanation of the Text

3:10a–c According to the grace of God given to me, as a wise master builder, I laid a foundation, and another is building [on it] (Κατὰ τὴν χάριν τοῦ θεοῦ τὴν δοθεῖσάν μοι ὡς σοφὸς ἀρχιτέκτων θεμέλιον ἔθηκα, ἄλλος δὲ ἐποικοδομεῖ). Here Paul replicates what he has said in 3:6a, but he uses the metaphor of builder rather than planter. The main verb is "I laid" (ἔθηκα). The aorist again looks back to when Paul first preached among them. The participle in the attributive position indicates the gift nature of God's grace (τὴν χάριν . . . τὴν δοθεῖσάν). Given the meaning of "grace," this expression seems redundant, but Paul has just been insisting that the whole work is *God's*, and this now reinforces the point that anything he has done is all because of the grace he has received from God for

this work. There may be a slight sense of irony in describing himself as a "wise master builder."[5] It is the nature of wisdom and what it looks like that is part of the dispute between Paul and the Corinthians. However, "wise" (σοφός) here may simply indicate being "skilled."

The "foundation" is Jesus Christ (3:11; cf. 2:2). Paul's use of the word "foundation" (θεμέλιος) is important. The influence of two texts on his theology was examined when we looked at the theme of the "stumbling stone" (σκάνδαλον).[6] Those texts are Isaiah 8:14 LXX and 28:16 LXX. In the first, God is spoken of as either a sanctuary (ἁγίασμα) for those who believe or a stone of stumbling for those who don't. In 28:16 the word for a foundation stone (θεμέλιος; cf. NRSV) appears. One must

---

5. Jay Shanor, "Paul as Master Builder: Construction Terms in First Corinthians," *NTS* 34 (1988): 461–71, examines many ancient descriptions and contracts for the construction of buildings in the ancient Greek world and draws comparisons with Paul's development of the building metaphor in this sec-

tion. He shows that in a building's construction the "general supervision of day-to-day work fell to the ἀρχιτέκτων" (ibid., 465).

6. See commentary on 1:23 and "In Depth: The Theme of Stumbling" at 1:23b. See also Lindars, *New Testament Apologetic*, 169ff.

believe in this stone or else be put to shame (see comments on "shame" at 1:27). In both texts in Isaiah, it is *God's* stone to lay. Paul is acutely conscious of this in his strong insistence that it is God's grace that lets him have a part in this. But in Isaiah it is the reaction to the foundation stone that is crucial, and this is what Paul built on in 1:23–25 and has in mind here. There is no other foundation than Jesus Christ. Acceptance of this one foundation is what identifies those who are God's, and Paul emphatically reminds them that they *are* God's building (3:9) and they *are* his temple and the Spirit *does* dwell in them (3:16–17).

To summarize, then, Paul is saying that, in line with the prophecies, God's own foundation of his Son, Jesus Christ, has indeed been laid. They *do* believe in him and so are a holy place, God's "temple"—a point to which he is building in 3:16. Since Paul has laid the right foundation in the right way, it is now vital that it is built upon in such a way that leaders do not later introduce a new "stumbling block." In the context, "another" (ἄλλος) who is building on the foundation cannot be Apollos. He is not now in Corinth, and Paul has already said that he and Apollos are united in their mission to fulfill God's calling and that God has given growth to both (3:6). Rather, Paul presently seems to speak rather vaguely of "another," though later he will be concerned with those who are doing this work badly.[7]

3:10d Now let each one build with care (ἕκαστος δὲ βλεπέτω πῶς ἐποικοδομεῖ). "Each one" (ἕκαστος)

reminds the readers that there will be a number of such people who are called to build. Paul may have in mind here only those leaders currently working in Corinth, yet what is missed by many is that what he says applies to *all* Christians. Later, using the word "to build" (οἰκοδομέω)[8] Paul will show that all Christians have gifts from God for building up the church (8:10; 10:23; 14:17). All Christians are thus challenged as to how they "build." However, the specific issue right now is more focused on what is being taught about status in the community by the current leaders. With the imperative "watch out" (βλεπέτω), Paul warns each builder to be careful. Hence the translation "build with care."

3:11 For no other foundation can be laid than[9] the one that is in place, which is Christ Jesus (θεμέλιον γὰρ ἄλλον οὐδεὶς δύναται θεῖναι παρὰ τὸν κείμενον, ὅς ἐστιν Ἰησοῦς Χριστός). Paul repeats the vital message of 1:23 and 2:2. Christ alone is the basis on which any church must be built. The description of the foundation as one that "is in place" (κείμενον) seeks to convey a present participle that carries a passive sense. Some translate this with a past tense ("already has been laid"), but the present tense carries with it the idea that this foundation is the one that is always laid[10] and must therefore always go on being built upon in appropriate ways. It recalls the present tense of "we preach" in 1:23.

3:12–13 Now if anyone builds upon the foundation with gold, silver, precious stones, wood, hay, or straw each person's work will become evident,

---

7. There has been considerable discussion about whether "another" is indeed a general reference (e.g., Thiselton, *1 Corinthians*, 309; Garland, *1 Corinthians*, 115), or whether it refers to those who are doing a *bad* job of the building (e.g., Fee, *1 Corinthians*, 149), or to Apollos (e.g., Lightfoot, *Notes on Epistles*, 189–90).

8. The difference between "to build" (οἰκοδομέω) and "to build upon" (ἐποικοδομέω) is negligible. The latter (with ἐπί, "upon") is used in contexts where a foundation is specifically

mentioned. Later in this letter, "building up" (οἰκοδομέω) is contrasted with being "puffed up" (8:1), and the building metaphor remains strong throughout the epistle.

9. In a comparison, παρά + accusative is best translated as "than," especially with ἄλλος, rather than the usual "beside." Dana and Mantey, *Manual Grammar*, 108 (§116 [3rd meaning]). See also BDF §236.3.

10. This assumes a gnomic present here. This foundation is the one that is always laid as the gospel is proclaimed.

for the Day will disclose it, because it is revealed through fire and each person's work, what sort it is, the fire itself will test (εἰ δέ τις ἐποικοδομεῖ ἐπὶ τὸν θεμέλιον χρυσόν, ἄργυρον, λίθους τιμίους, ξύλα, χόρτον, καλάμην, ἑκάστου τὸ ἔργον φανερὸν γενήσεται, ἡ γὰρ ἡμέρα δηλώσει· ὅτι ἐν πυρὶ ἀποκαλύπτεται, καὶ ἑκάστου τὸ ἔργον ὁποῖόν ἐστιν τὸ πῦρ [αὐτὸ] δοκιμάσει). Paul now proceeds to discuss the judgment that will fall upon those who build wrongly and the reward that will come to those who build appropriately. He uses here the first of four simple conditions (see vv. 14–17 for the other three).[11] Paul assumes that some people's work will last (v. 14) and that some people's work will be burned up (v. 15).

In each of these conditional clauses, the subject is "anyone" (τις). As Paul uses the building analogy, he is concerned with the people who are building. The materials are not so much of individual significance except that some materials may be burned up and others not. In other words, as Fee puts it, Paul's concern is with "the *imperishable* quality of some [building materials] over against the others."[12] Thus, there is no need to seek great detail on the particular building that Paul may have in mind as he talks of these materials. Fitzmyer comments, "The materials mentioned for the superstructure are symbolic."[13]

The whole argument here demonstrates how deeply Paul sees the activity of laying the church's foundation and building upon it as an activity of the last days. This entire enterprise has a great eschatological goal. It is that people should be presented "standing" before God on that final day. The building as the temple of God is to reflect now what will be: God's people with God in their midst. The time will come when we see "face to face" (13:12), but even now God's Spirit dwells in his church (3:16).

As Paul thinks of God's people as a building and as God's temple (v. 16), perhaps he recalls David's commission of his son, Solomon (1 Chr 22:6–16). Solomon was told to build the house of the Lord and to do so with "understanding" (σύνεσις) and "wisdom" (σοφία; v. 12 LXX). David had stored up the best of materials for this work, including gold, silver, bronze, and stone (v. 14). Just as Solomon had the task of building the temple beautifully and carefully, so do those whom Paul is addressing. "Wood" (ξύλον), "hay" (χόρτος), and "straw" (καλάμη) are mentioned in Paul's list to offer examples of that which may be burned up. Each person will be held accountable.

Thus, it is to "the Day" (ἡ ἡμέρα) that Paul looks. Here is where the final vindication will be seen in the battle of the "wisdoms." The day will make things clear. Paul has already referred to it as "the day of our Lord" in 1:8, where it is seen positively as the day when God's people will appear "unimpeachable" before the Lord's judgment seat (see also 5:5). "The Day" is drawn from an Old Testament background and looks forward to the time of judgment.[14] Its link to a refining, eschatological judgment of fire is seen in Isaiah 66:15–16, Zephaniah 1:17–18, and Malachi 3:2–3. In the New Testament this "Day" is the time when Christ returns to save and to judge.[15]

---

11. Simple conditions usually assume the truth of the protasis and can take any tense of an indicative verb in either part of the sentence. In other words, this is not a vague supposition that one might expect to find with a conditional clause using a subjunctive or optative in the protasis.

12. Fee, *1 Corinthians*, 150.

13. Fitzmyer, *1 Corinthians*, 198. Fitzmyer writes that Paul is referring to subsequent preaching of the gospel which may

"be of fine quality (the gospel itself) or of very poor quality (stories and anecdotes of human wisdom), and that in time that difference would become apparent."

14. See, e.g., Isa 34:8; Jer 46:10; Joel 2:11; 3:14; also in later material, cf. Pss. Sol. 15:4–6; 2 Bar. 48:39–41.

15. See, e.g., 1 Cor 1:8; 5:5; Luke 17:30; Rom 13:12; 1 Thess 5:4; 2 Pet 3:10.

Verse 13 (the apodosis of the condition of v. 12) develops what Paul means when he says that each one's work will become "evident" (φανερός, an adj.; the verb φανερόω appears in 4:5 where Paul mentions the final judgment day). The basis upon which he says this (γάρ) is that the Day "will disclose it" (δηλώσει), and the reason (ὅτι) this will happen is that the work of building and its materials are revealed for what they are through fire (ἐν πυρί is instrumental).[16]

From earliest times fire has been linked in the Scriptures with the awesome presence of God as one who is holy and who reveals himself as Judge and Savior. He pledged himself in his covenant relationship with Abraham, as a smoking fire pot passed between the pieces of the sacrificed animal (Gen 15:17). He judged Sodom and Gomorrah with fire (Gen 19:24). He appeared to Moses in a flaming bush (Exod 3:2) and descended upon Mount Sinai in fire (19:18). In Hebrews 12:29 God is said to be a "consuming fire." Therefore, to say in the New Testament that *fire* judges or tests is to say that the Lord himself will judge and test. It does not point to the judgment of hellfire because the fire in question also reveals who is good (cf. 1 Pet 1:7). The picture here is like that spoken of in Revelation 3:18 where Jesus counsels the Laodicean church to "buy from me gold refined in the fire." As all gold is assayed to determine its quality, so the quality of the work of building Christ's church will be assayed by the Lord at his coming. This will clearly show the quality of the work (ὁποῖος, a pronoun: "what

sort it is") that has been built on the foundation of Christ crucified.

3:14–15 If anyone's work lasts, which he has built, he will receive a reward. If anyone's work is burned up, he will suffer loss, but he himself will be saved but only as through fire (εἴ τινος τὸ ἔργον μενεῖ ὃ ἐποικοδόμησεν, μισθὸν λήμψεται· εἴ τινος τὸ ἔργον κατακαήσεται, ζημιωθήσεται, αὐτὸς δὲ σωθήσεται, οὕτως δὲ ὡς διὰ πυρός). As Paul's argument continues from the previous two verses, he indicates that the builder whose work lasts, that is, survives the test, will receive a reward. The one whose work "is burned up"[17] will suffer loss, although the individual concerned will himself be saved. Thus, the second and third simple conditions here serve to expand on what Paul has been saying. It is notable, despite this judgment by fire, that Paul does not go back on his teaching earlier that these people at Corinth *are* God's people. Even any teacher to whom he speaks will "himself" (αὐτός) be saved, but "only as *through* fire."[18] In other words, the Christian teacher *is* a Christian and God is faithful (1:8–9), but the teacher will barely survive. It is the work that is burned up, not the teacher him or herself. The reference to the person concerned being "saved" (σωθήσεται) indicates salvation in the face of God's final judgment. Bad work does not void a person's salvation, which cannot depend on the preacher's merit. Clearly, therefore, "salvation" itself is not the reward Paul has in mind.

Though the matter of rewards and losses has

---

16. In v. 13 "it will be revealed by fire" could refer to "the Day" rather than the "work" being revealed. So, among others, Robertson and Plummer, *First Corinthians*, 63; Barrett, *First Corinthians*, 88. This is argued on the grounds that the "Day" is spoken of as being revealed by fire in, for example, 2 Thess 1:7–8; 2:8; Dan 7:9–11. It is also said that if "it" refers to "the work" then the next clause is repetitive. However, the next clause, "each person's work, what sort it is, the fire itself will test," can also be seen as explicative. With Fitzmyer, *1 Corinthi-*

ans, 199, it is more natural to see "the work" itself ("what sort it is") being revealed by this judgment of fire than the Day itself.

17. The future passive of κατακαίω looks to the time when it will happen.

18. The διά +genitive construction here means "through" a place (cf. 1 Pet 3:20). Robertson and Plummer, *First Corinthians*, 65, write: "The fire is so rapid in its effects that the workman has to rush *through* it to reach safety."

provoked much discussion, here, as in 3:8, the reward or "wage" should be viewed within Paul's eschatological framework (see below). It is the hope and expectation of God's faithful people that they will receive this at Christ's coming. Later in this letter Paul writes of the "prize" for which he aims (see comments on 9:24–27). Yet this is not to deny the possible experience of reward in this life and before the end. As Ciampa and Rosner well summarize, "The reward for faithful service is the master's pleasure and his confidence, which leads to a further entrusting of responsibility."[19]

IN DEPTH: What Reward?

The idea of rewards, especially rewards for the work of the gospel, has often raised questions for Christians, who are rightly keen to preserve the biblical teaching that all salvation and standing before God is entirely of grace. In this particular context of 3:14–15, the type of reward is not specified, and this has led to a variety of different views as to what Paul is referring.

First, it is important to notice that this text does not introduce some notion of purgatory. Whatever one may say about that doctrine to which some subscribe, Paul is here dealing with the *work* being tested by fire, not the person. Neither is the fire so much about purifying a work (as if God is now making good through fire what was previously flawed), as judging a work that may be burned up.[20]

Secondly, this passage does not in any way undermine all that Paul has been saying about grace. If builders build in a way that lasts, then they do so by grace alone. They are simply doing what God has called and equipped them to do as God's servants. After all, when Paul referred in v. 8 to the wages of the agricultural laborer, he went on to stress in v. 9 that the workers, the field, and the building were all *God's*. In v. 7 he had made it clear that it is only *God* who causes the growth. In 15:58 Paul further insists that it is only in the Lord that labor is not in vain. However, neither the nature of the loss nor of the reward is easily defined.

It has been suggested that preaching the gospel is its own reward and this is part of what Paul alludes to here. It has also been suggested that rewards only make sense for "voluntary" work, otherwise they come to be regarded as "wages."[21] In chapter 9, however, where Paul speaks of his "prize" (v. 24) he

---

19. Ciampa and Rosner, *First Corinthians*, 157.

20. From a Roman Catholic perspective on the matter of purgatory and its relationship to this verse, see George T. Montague, *First Corinthians*, Catholic Commentary on Sacred Scripture (Grand Rapids: Baker, 2011), 75–76. (Montague does not believe this verse reveals anything about purgatory.) So also Fitzmyer, *1 Corinthians*, 201. However, the verse is used as a text supporting the doctrine in various medieval Roman Catholic documents. In the modern church, 1 Cor 3:13 is cited as scriptural evidence for the doctrine of purgatory in *The Catechism of the Catholic Church*, 2nd ed. (Vatican City: Libreria Editrice Vaticana, 1994), para. 1031n607.

21. Kistemaker, *First Corinthians*, 114.

hardly sees his work as voluntary. Rather, it is a compulsion laid upon him (v. 16). Indeed, both the words translated as "reward" (μισθός) and "suffer loss" (ζημιόω) can appear in contexts where financial remuneration is in mind. Jay Shanor has demonstrated how both terms were used in ancient Greek building contracts.[22] This could provide a background for Paul's use of the words here since the metaphor with which he works concerns building. Yet while such use of the words may have prompted Paul to speak like this, the context of the apostle's teaching here on rewards predominantly arises from his understanding of the *eschatological expectation* for God's people.

Part of that expectation allows Paul to write of the "prize" for which he aims (see comments on 9:24–27). Perhaps we can say little more of the prize or reward than this: good work will receive the "praise" from God (ὁ ἔπαινος) to which Paul refers in 4:5. Yet elsewhere Paul opens up a further idea, for he looks forward to the final day when he will see *the people themselves to whom he has preached* as his "crown of boasting," glory, and joy (1 Thess 2:19–20 ESV). In this sense the results of the gospel will themselves be part of the joy or reward on that final day when the work is seen to stand before God.

Paul's view of that end-time reward coheres well with Christ's own teaching in the Gospels. There the work of the gospel and faithfulness to the calling to follow Christ are to be rewarded. Several parables and some paraenetic passages directly address the matter. In Matthew 5:12 Jesus teaches that those who are persecuted should rejoice because "great is your reward [ὁ μισθὸς ὑμῶν] in heaven." Parables like that of the faithful steward in Matthew 25:23 conclude with the same idea: "Well done, good and faithful servant. You have been faithful over a little; I will set you over much. Enter into the joy of your master" (ESV). Other passages such as Matthew 6:1 and Luke 6:35 also speak to rewards. So, while it is not entirely clear what Paul imagined as he anticipated the crown and rewards, it is probably well summed up by Jesus's words: "Enter the joy of your master."[23] Part of that joy will be the viewing of the work that has survived the judging fire of the last day. The very sight of the Thessalonian or Corinthian church on that last day, standing before the Lord, may indeed be what Paul imagines in 4:5 when he refers to the commendation or praise (ἔπαινος) from God.

Serving the Lord faithfully in the good work of disseminating the gospel in word and in life brings the rewards of which Paul and Jesus speak. Paul well summarizes this in Colossians 3:23–24: "Whatever you do, work at it with all your

---

22. Shanor, "Paul as Master Builder," 468–69.
23. Matt 25:23. Cf. Luke 6:23. Hebrews 12:2 shows Jesus's own life and death in the light of the "joy that was set before him" (ESV).

heart, as working for the Lord, not for human masters, since you know that you will receive an inheritance from the Lord as a reward. It is the Lord Christ you are serving."[24]

Perhaps "loss" lies in the exact opposite direction: poor work will simply disappear from before the teacher's eyes. The sorrow and sadness of seeing that a life's work has achieved little or nothing for the Lord and his gospel will be devastating. The challenge is vital for all Christians. We may imagine that some of today's leaders who have replaced a theology of the cross (Christ crucified) for a triumphalist, preacher-centered church may find, however large the church has grown, that even though their people have been saved by God's grace, nothing remains at the judgment day at which the minister can look and say, "Ah, by God's grace, I had a hand in that!" As Paul has shown, the work that will survive and stand at the last day is that which has been built appropriately on the "foundation" (θεμέλιος; 3:10–12). That work, and that alone, will truly be the work of God's grace delivered through his people. See further at comments on 9:18.

3:16 Do you not know that you are God's temple and the Spirit of God dwells in you? (Οὐκ οἴδατε ὅτι ναὸς θεοῦ ἐστε καὶ τὸ πνεῦμα τοῦ θεοῦ οἰκεῖ ἐν ὑμῖν;). Before coming to the fourth, final, and most serious of the conditional clauses (v. 17), Paul breaks off to re-emphasize the point that the Corinthian church is to be regarded as God's temple and therefore is obliged to present itself as unified in Christ. They are God's temple *because* the Spirit of God dwells among them. "Do you not know?" (Οὐκ οἴδατε) is a rhetorical question, but he certainly expects them to agree with what he says. He uses this question (Οὐκ οἴδατε) on a number of occasions in this epistle[25] in a way that appears slightly sarcastic, given that some think they are superior to others because they have "knowledge" (8:1). The question usually introduces a section in which Paul is especially concerned about their practice or behavior in the Christian life. It often occurs where he makes a theological statement that they should know but appear to be ignoring in the way they live. The main impact of the rhetorical device, however, is that it makes it clear that Paul regards what he is saying as foundational theology to be accepted by all, even if some at Corinth have apparently missed the point.

The "temple" (ναός) refers not to the whole temple precinct with its courtyards but to the building itself, the holy place.[26] This is the picture of God's people that Paul paints. They are God's building (3:9). That God dwells in his temple is explained as Paul says that it is "in you" (ἐν ὑμῖν, plural) where the Spirit of God has his residence. Later he will appeal to individuals to refrain from immorality and there will speak of an individual's body being the temple of the Holy Spirit (6:19), but this is not his point here. Here he wants teachers, leaders, and the people to understand the significance of the

---

24. See also Mark 9:41; Luke 6:35–36; 2 John 8.

25. Paul especially uses this rhetorical form in ch. 6, in vv. 2, 3, 9, 15, 16, 19; see also 9:13, 24.

26. Cf. Jdt 4:2: τοῦ ναοῦ κυρίου θεοῦ αὐτῶν ἐταράχθησαν ("they were alarmed . . . for the temple of the Lord their God" [NRSV]).

church. The key to this is that the Spirit is among them. When they gather together, they even experience "the power of our Lord Jesus" (5:4).

Here is the ultimate argument for unity. They are *one* temple that belongs to God (θεοῦ is a possessive genitive), and *together* they are the place where the one Spirit dwells. But this is also the ultimate argument for building well. They are building the place where God dwells. This probably carried all the connotations of the care with which the Solomonic temple had to be built.[27] This image is more likely than that Paul was picturing the building of pagan temples in Corinth. Thus, Paul demonstrates that the divisions, factions, and disputes about leadership are not just a sad episode in a church's life but fundamentally represent a failure to understand the significance and nature of the local church as God's temple. Thus, Paul's fourth and final conditional clause is the strongest.

3:17a–b If anyone destroys God's temple, God will destroy him (εἴ τις τὸν ναὸν τοῦ θεοῦ φθείρει, φθερεῖ τοῦτον ὁ θεός). This somber warning is like a decree. There may be some leaders in this church of whom Paul is thinking as he writes, people who have gone much further than others in their factionalism and their causing of divisions, certainly further than those mentioned in the preceding verses. Paul has moved from talking about the works of the leaders being judged or rewarded. Now he speaks of the destruction of anyone who

has been involved in the destruction of the church. Yet the warning is for the whole church. Some leaders may be destroyed for their actions, but it appears that much of the church has been seduced with the wisdom of this world and has been tempted to look to certain leaders for their status and sense of belonging and honor in the church. They too need to see how serious this all is. Leaders will soon change or leave if they have no one who listens to them! If a congregation recognizes the danger and looks for leaders who promote not themselves but Christ crucified, then those are the leaders whom they will find and the church will become healthy again.[28]

The judgment warning follows the "eye for an eye" approach to justice. The verb translated "destroy" (φθείρω) picks up the imagery of a building that is being pulled down. The future tense of the apodosis looks forward to the Day that Paul has been speaking of when each person's work will be revealed by God. Theologically, Scripture elsewhere makes it clear that God's church cannot be overcome, yet that is not to say a local church cannot end up being destroyed. Paul has already said that though their work may be judged individuals may ultimately be saved. Nevertheless, destruction at that time can mean only one thing: final judgment and damnation. The words of Christ through John in the book of Revelation help illuminate Paul's concern. The Laodicean church may

---

27. Noting the emphasis on the holiness of the temple in v. 17 below, this passage is then easily compared with 2 Cor 6:16–18. There Paul calls for the holiness of "we [who] are the temple of the living God," and it is notable that he appeals directly to Old Testament ideas of the temple found in Exod 6:7, Lev 26:12, and Jer 31:33. N. T. Wright addresses in some detail the way Paul's two "major and closely combined themes" of holiness and the Spirit's dwelling among his people run through his teaching. As he clearly demonstrates, "the holiness of the *ekklesia* comes to be, in itself, a central part of Paul's positive symbolic world . . . this community is the transformed new reality to which Paul saw the Jerusalem Temple itself as the

advance signpost" (Wright, *Paul and the Faithfulness of God*, 357–58).

28. Shanor, "Paul as Master Builder," 469–70, argues on the basis of various inscriptions that the idea of destruction (v. 17, φθείρω) is to be understood as "damage." He suggests the word "destroy" is too strong. In some ancient contracts a worker who "damaged" the building (φθείρω) would be "fined" (ζημιόω, as in 3:15). This may or may not be how Paul is using the word, but it hardly makes sense to say then that God "will damage him." The context has a more definite eschatological sense than this translation would allow for.

have reflected some of the same problems of pride and arrogance and self-sufficiency as the church of Corinth. There Jesus describes himself as effectively having been left outside the church. The vivid picture is one of the Lord of the church, who is supposed to dwell in his temple by his Spirit, standing outside and knocking to see if he can get in (Rev 3:20)! Jesus warns, "I will spit you out of my mouth" (3:16). At the time of writing to Laodicea there is still time to "be zealous and repent" (v. 19), as there is here in 1 Corinthians 3:17. This is a strong warning to the church at Corinth, and the church has been left in no doubt about how serious matters are.

3:17c–d for the temple of God is holy, and you are the temple! (ὁ γὰρ ναὸς τοῦ θεοῦ ἅγιός ἐστιν, οἵτινές ἐστε ὑμεῖς). If further explanation was needed, Paul extends his argument from v. 16 and presents it again by way of summary: the temple is

holy because that is where God dwells. Then Paul emphatically states, "*You* are that temple" (cf. 3:9, 16). The plural relative pronoun (οἵτινές) is not easy grammatically. It picks up "the temple" (singular) as its reference from the previous clause but is plural (by attraction) because it looks back to those who make up that temple, that is, "you" Corinthians (v. 16). The "you" (ὑμεῖς) in the second clause is unnecessary in Greek with the verb in the second plural and so gives emphasis.

The addition in this verse to what Paul is saying is his description of the temple as "holy" (ἅγιός). It has certainly been implied throughout this section. Where God is, that place is always holy. (See comments above on v. 16.) The "temple" (ναός) contained the "Most Holy Place" (e.g., Exod 26:33; Lev 16:2) and attention is now drawn to this. The sacrilege that would be involved in destroying this needs no further comment. The severity of Paul's warning is established.

Theology in Application

Knowing Only Christ Crucified

In this section Paul has laid out still more of the implications in church work of "Jesus Christ and him crucified" (2:2). Thus, these verses offer a radical challenge to all Christian ministry as we are reminded that God sees and discerns all that is being achieved in the world. That this work may or may not be seen to stand under God's judgment indicates that careful attention must be paid not only to the focus of the message that is preached, but also to strategy in the application of gospel work. The application of what Paul says here to the modern church may take many different forms. Undoubtedly, all of us in church leadership will need to look first at ourselves. Do we know only Christ crucified among our people? A couple of comments may provoke that self-examination a little. In many places, especially younger ministers are planting churches these days rather than seeking to pastor an existing church. Sometimes this is with the best of intentions, believing that this is the quickest way to win more for Christ and grow a church numerically. Yet I have met some for whom the choice to church plant is more about forging their own way in designing church life according to their own preferences. Many questions are asked about everything from the demographics of an area, to how the work will be funded, through to the type of music that will be preferred. Even the dress code is addressed. Lengthy discussions on matters such as these crowd out the simple and most basic question: "Is Jesus Christ the only foundation for this church?" Many churches—and not just church plants—become centered on the original minister and his vision. If this is a vision to know nothing but Christ crucified, then may God be praised. But it requires humility and a servant's heart to ask this question genuinely of ourselves and our churches. For those in more established churches, the same question arises but often in a different way. Many churches become relatively well-oiled machines after several years, specially those that have been around a long time. The whole "machine" with all its traditions and its often unspoken arrogance that "nothing needs to change" can be a deep hindrance to asking honestly whether the church still knows nothing but Christ crucified in all its ministry.

The Local Church

In today's Western church, in particular, many have lost all sense of the importance of the local church. The idea that it is the community in which God has chosen to dwell and which offers the world a genuine life alternative has all but disappeared. Many churches offer little more than a short Sunday meeting that has to be kept to seventy minutes lest people be discomforted or arrive late to a meal! The view that Paul presents here of an alternative society in which the crucified and resurrected King and Lord dwells by his Spirit and in which there is a foretaste of the new heavens and earth is often almost unknown. As with the Corinthians, the values and priorities of the world around us dominate people's thinking. That is why it is a genuine danger that the local manifestation of the place where God dwells could be destroyed.

Building Where Another Has Planted

Recognising different gifts and callings among the leaders of God's people has always been difficult in practice. The problems of the relationship between Moses, Aaron, and Miriam (Num 12) offer just one example of several in Scripture. Paul's complete acceptance that he had a calling to plant the church at Corinth and Apollos had a different calling to come in and take the church on to its next step in spiritual growth is an amazing example, for accepting the Lord's different callings among church ministers and leaders is critical for the growth of any church. Again, often humility will be required by church and leader to acknowledge this. One may be called to plant a church, another to be a "senior" minister in an established church, another to evangelism, and yet another to pastoring the flock. We see this happening in various places in the New Testament, not least in this passage but also in a passage like Acts 6. In practice some are gifted to preach, others in expounding and teaching the gospel in a personal way to individuals, and others at applying the gospel in pastoral care. The fact that often leaders can do at least some or all of these things should not mean the question remains unasked: "But to what has God called and for what has he truly given you his grace-gifts?" Congregations need carefully to consider the same. Is the church planter humble enough to know when his specialized gifts have reached their limit so it is time to let an "Apollos" come in and "water"? Can a church part with someone they have come to love and under whom many of them have been converted, or are they wedded to that person's "group"?

God's Gracious Rewards

We noted above that it is sometimes difficult to imagine rewards and yet still understand all that we ever receive to be only of God and his grace. Surely the greatest of motivations to work for Christ in humble obedience as his servants is that we know all that he has done for us. Our deepest motivation is the response of love. It is this that surely gives rise to the two "great" commands to love God and love our neighbor. That which God has done for us is what we seek to imitate, and he *first* loved us. In this context, though, the Scriptures do speak of rewards, and it is wrong to ignore these as a *further* motivation to live and work for the Lord. These rewards are offered to those who are already Christians, who have been redeemed by God's grace, and who are committed to his service. The issue for the Christian is that with humble servanthood comes responsibilities. It is our response to these God-given responsibilities that is assessed by God both in the present to some extent and on "the Day" in full. The teaching Paul uses in this section concerning "loss" and "reward" reminds us of the seriousness of using properly the gifts we have received (by grace) in the Lord's service. As the apostle puts it in Ephesians 2:10, "We are his workmanship, created in Christ Jesus for good works, which God prepared beforehand, that we should walk in them" (ESV). That we are God's workmanship is by his grace. That we are "created for good works in Christ Jesus" is by God's grace. That he has prepared in advance things for us to do is by his grace. That he has, according to 1 Corinthians, given us "grace-gifts" with which to do these things is by his grace, and it is entirely by his grace when we take our calling seriously and he chooses to reward his people. The reward may be seen primarily in the covenant blessings that await us at Christ's coming, which will include seeing him "face to face" and enjoying the new creation. They are best summed up in the word "joy" (Matt 25:23; Luke 6:23). The writer to the Hebrews speaks of Jesus also being motivated by "joy" as he fulfilled his calling to be the crucified Christ: "Looking to Jesus, the founder and perfecter of our faith, who for the joy that was set before him endured the cross, despising the shame, and is seated at the right hand of the throne of God" (12:2 ESV). Yet there is also an indication in Jesus's teaching that rewards for taking seriously our responsibility as the Lord's servants will mean that in the future we will be rewarded with further responsibility. This too will be a great joy, but it can never be seen as "what I have earned" or in any sense a matter of meritorious works. Rather, it is yet another glorious aspect of God's grace that remains with us as a challenge to be the people he has called us to be.

1 Corinthians 3:18–4:5

Literary Context

Paul has spoken of one foundation being laid, Jesus Christ. People must build carefully upon this, for the building is the temple of God and the Christians in Corinth are that temple. The dangers of causing divisions and fragmenting the people of God are serious. Builders will be held responsible.

In 3:18–4:5 Paul now draws together his argument thus far. He first warns that people should judge *themselves* properly before God (and not with the eyes of the world), and then he addresses the right way of assessing Christian teachers, especially applying what he says to how they have judged him. The eschatological context of all that he is saying continues here. The judgment at Christ's return will reveal all. Building on 3:10–17, Paul shows this will include rewards as each receives praise from God (4:5). In this summary, Paul's style changes somewhat and proceeds by way of a series of five commands or exhortations, each of which are developed from what Paul has already taught concerning matters such as wisdom, boasting, and judgment. Three exhortations have to do with how they should assess themselves. Returning to the contrast of wisdoms, Paul says that they should not deceive themselves; they should become like fools if they want to become wise, and they should not boast. Two further exhortations concern how they should assess Paul and the apostles themselves. They should be regarded as servants of Christ. The Corinthians should not make judgments upon them as leaders before the time of Christ's return. By turning matters back to how the Corinthians judge their leaders and specifically picking up on their relationship with him, Paul prepares the ground for what follows in 4:6–21. This point is made clear in 4:16: "Be imitators of me."

IV. **Mature Christians Pursue God's Wisdom (2:6–4:21)**

    A. Paul Proclaims God's Wisdom (2:6–13)

    B. God's Wisdom Characterizes Those Who Are "Spiritual" (2:14–16)

    C. The Corinthians are Spiritually Immature (3:1–9)

    D. Wise Leadership Acts with Spiritual Discernment (3:10–4:21)

        1. Illustration: A Building and a Wise Master Builder (3:10–15)

        2. The Building Is God's Temple in Which His Spirit Dwells (3:16–17)

➡   **3. Leadership Must Be Seen in the Light of God's Wisdom (3:18–23)**

        4. Wise Leadership Will Be Commended by God Alone (4:1–5)

        5. Paul and Apollos as Models to Imitate (4:6–21)

    V. Lack of Spiritual Wisdom Has Led to Grievous Sin (5:1–6:20)

Main Idea

The Corinthian Christians must forget their supposed wisdom and their boasting in certain leaders and assess their own status properly as people who belong to Christ. Furthermore, they must recognize that church leaders also belong to Christ, as servants who must be found trustworthy. Since Christ is their Lord, he alone will judge and the Corinthians should not rush in to do the Lord's work before he returns. Wise leadership will be commended by God.

Translation

1 Corinthians 3:18–4:5

18a	1st exhortation	**Let no one deceive himself.**
b	Condition (protasis)	If anyone among you thinks he is wise in this age
c	2nd exhortation (apodosis)	**let him become a fool**
d	Purpose	in order that he may become wise.
19a	Basis for exhortation	For **the wisdom of this world is foolishness** in the presence of God
b	Verification/proof	for it is written,
c	Scripture citation 1	"He catches the wise in their cunning," [Job 5:13]
20a		and again,
b	Scripture citation 2	"The Lord knows the opinions of the wise
c		that they are futile." [Ps 94:11, LXX 93:11]
21a	Inference	So then
b	3rd exhortation	**let no one boast in people.**
c	Basis for exhortation	For **all things are yours—**

22a	List	whether	Paul, or Apollos, or Peter, or
b			the world, or life, or death, or
c			the present, or the future—
d	Repetition	**all things are yours;**	

| 23a | Assertion | now **you are Christ's, and Christ is God's.** |

4:1a	4th exhortation	**Let a person regard us in this way,**
b	Manner	as servants of Christ and
c	Expansion	stewards of the mysteries of God

2a	Place	In this position, furthermore,
b	Assertion	**it is required of stewards that they be found faithful.**

3a	Assertion	But **for me it is a very small matter that I should be judged**
b	Agency	by you or
c	Agency	by any human court;
d	Assertion (intensified)	in fact, **I do not even judge myself.**
4a	Assertion	Now **I am not aware of anything against myself,**
b	Contrast	but **I am not acquitted for that reason.**
c	Ultimate basis	**It is the Lord who judges me.**
	Inference	Therefore,
5a	5th exhortation	**do not judge anything**
b	Time	before the time,
c	Expansion	before the Lord comes,
d	Description	who will shine light on the hidden things of darkness and
e		will reveal the purposes of our hearts.

| f | Result | Then **each will receive praise from God.** |

Structure

In 3:16–17 Paul had shown the danger of destroying God's temple through bad workmanship that is not in accord with its foundation, Jesus Christ. The next section draws together what Paul has been saying and makes his application specific. It falls naturally into two parts, with the flow of Paul's thought indicated by his use of five imperatives.

The first section (3:18–23) is introduced with an imperative ("let no one deceive himself"; v. 18), which returns the thought to the comparison of "wisdoms." The Corinthians are asked to be honest in their self-assessment. Self-deception can only be overcome by facing up to the reality that what is wise in the world's eyes is foolishness to God. Two further imperatives drive the point home: "Let him become a fool" (v. 18) and "Let no one boast" (v. 21a). Those who think they are wise in the world's eyes should first become fools to become truly wise. Any who wish to boast in human leaders should remember they belong to Christ.

The second section (4:1–5) shows that ultimately only God commends wise leadership. It is introduced by another imperative that exhorts the Corinthians to think about apostolic leadership in terms of service for Christ. These servants must be found trustworthy, but they are accountable to their "lord" and him alone. Paul's application by means of a fifth imperative in the series is that it is not for them to judge. The Lord will reveal all when he comes.

Exegetical Outline

IV. Mature Christians Pursue God's Wisdom (2:6–4:21)

    A. Paul Proclaims God's Wisdom (2:6–13)

    B. God's Wisdom Characterizes Those Who Are "Spiritual" (2:14–16)

    C. The Corinthians are Spiritually Immature (3:1–9)

    D. Wise Leadership Acts with Spiritual Discernment (3:10–4:21)

        1. Illustration: A Building and a Wise Master Builder (3:10–15)

        2. The Building Is God's Temple in Which His Spirit Dwells (3:16–17)

    ➡   **3. Leadership Must Be Seen in the Light of God's Wisdom (3:18–23)**

            a. Let Them Not Be Deceived (3:18)

            b. Let Them Become "Fools" (3:19–20)

            c. Let Them Not Boast in Their Leadership (3:21–22)

            d. They Belong to Christ (3:23)

        4. Wise Leadership Will Be Commended by God Alone (4:1–5)

            a. The Apostles Should Be Regarded as Servants of Christ (4:1)

            b. Christ's Servants Are Required to Be Trustworthy (4:2)

            c. Christ's Servants Are Judged Only by the Lord (4:3–5)

        5. Paul and Apollos as Models to Imitate (4:6–21)

Explanation of the Text

3:18 Let no one deceive himself. If anyone among you thinks he is wise in this age let him become a fool in order that he may become wise (Μηδεὶς ἑαυτὸν ἐξαπατάτω· εἴ τις δοκεῖ σοφὸς εἶναι ἐν ὑμῖν ἐν τῷ αἰῶνι τούτῳ, μωρὸς γενέσθω, ἵνα γένηται σοφός). With another simple condition, Paul picks up the main problem he has been addressing and returns to the comparison of "wisdoms." Now he addresses individuals (τις) in the church. The pro-

tasis is assumed true. Paul knows that people at Corinth *do* think they are wise. But Paul is ironic here, not just with the use of a conditional clause but because he adds "in this age."[1] The two wisdoms are polar opposites. Each thinks of the other as "foolishness." Each turns the other upside down, as Paul makes clear in what follows. To be wise in God's way of seeing things means becoming a fool in this age. Thus, as Kuck puts it, in 3:18–23 Paul

---

1. The ἐν + dative construction introduces a temporal clause.

"recapitulates much of the argument of 1:18–2:16 from the perspective of God's judgment of human wisdom."[2]

The first imperative, "let no one deceive himself" (Μηδεὶς ἑαυτὸν ἐξαπατάτω) is abrupt and challenging, and it sums up much of what Paul has said in 1:18–3:17. The problem is that people may "think" themselves to be wise, yet this is no more than self-deception. Many have claimed a community standing on the back of their supposed "wisdom" and are content to boast about this, but they are talking of what it is to be "wise in this age,"[3] and God views things very differently. As Christians, there is a need to "have the mind of Christ" (2:16). Paul has spoken of what is needed to survive the last day and the Lord's judgment (3:10–17), so self-deception about one's status before God must be regarded as serious. The theme of "judging" and especially God's judgment is thus being summarized. To arrive at that day of judgment and to think one "stands" only to find otherwise would be horrific (cf. 10:12).

In 6:9 and 15:33, though using a different verb, Paul also urges the Corinthians not to be deceived (μὴ πλανᾶσθε). In both places the problem is that people can always deceive themselves into thinking that wrong is right and right is wrong, but God is never deceived. In chapter 15 the problem of self-deception centers on the resurrection. In 6:9 the problem is self-deception in the area of morality. For Paul, if they deceive themselves about true wisdom, there is no doubt they will deceive themselves

in a variety of other areas as well. His second imperative provides the only way through: "Let him become a fool." That is, those who think they are wise in this age need to become fools with regard to this age. The reason for this is now spelled out.

3:19–20 For the wisdom of this world is foolishness in the presence of God for it is written, "He catches[4] the wise in their cunning," and again, "The Lord knows the opinions of the wise that they are futile" (ἡ γὰρ σοφία τοῦ κόσμου τούτου μωρία παρὰ τῷ θεῷ ἐστιν· γέγραπται γάρ, ὁ δρασσόμενος τοὺς σοφοὺς ἐν τῇ πανουργίᾳ αὐτῶν· καὶ πάλιν, Κύριος γινώσκει τοὺς διαλογισμοὺς τῶν σοφῶν ὅτι εἰσὶν μάταιοι). Paul now repeats his point from God's perspective: if the cross seems foolishness to the Gentiles (1:23), this world's wisdom is foolishness before God. "Before God" (παρὰ τῷ θεῷ) means "in his presence," that is, before his throne of judgment.[5] Paul then cites two further Scripture verses to demonstrate the truth that human wisdom stands under God's judgment. For "it is written" (γέγραπται), see comments on 1:19. The first part of the quotation is from Job 5:13 (where the participle, ὁ δρασσόμενος, does not appear). The broad context of the Job quotation is ideal for Paul's purposes with its discussion of jealousy and strife and of the "fool" and the "wise." There, Eliphaz (wrongly) argues that no one can be right before God. In the process, he (rightly) talks of those who are not right before God as perishing "without wisdom" (4:21). He talks of the "fool" (the one who does not do the will of the Lord) as being

---

2. David W. Kuck, *Judgment and Community Conflict: Paul's Use of Apocalyptic Judgment Language in 1 Corinthians 3:5–4:5*, NovTSup 66 (Leiden: Brill, 1992), 196.

3. Paul continues to think in terms of "this age" (1:20; 2:6, 8) as the present time in which people are dismissive of God or in rebellion against him. It describes the contrast between those who have the spirit of the world and those who have the Spirit of God (2:12).

4. The participle translated "he catches" (ὁ δρασσόμενος) is

an "independent nominative" or a form of "nominative absolute" and is to be noted with proverbial expressions (e.g., 2 Pet 2:22). Dana and Mantey, *Manual Grammar*, 70 (§83[4]). Also cf. Wallace, *Greek Grammar*, 55.

5. This phrase refers elsewhere to standing before the judgment of God in Rom 2:11, 13; Gal 3:11; Eph 6:9; 1 Pet 2:20. Kuck, *Judgment and Community Conflict*, 192, says that "there is a fundamental dichotomy between standing before the tribunal of this world and standing before God."

slain by envy (5:1–2). He then says that the Lord "frustrates the devices of the crafty. . . . He catches the wise in their own craftiness" (5:12–3 ESV). Eliphaz thus urges Job to commit his cause to God, exactly what Paul is doing with those who may be deceiving themselves.

Paul then adduces a second quotation, from Psalm 94:11 (93:11 LXX). Here he simply changes the words "of men" (τῶν ἀνθρώπων) to "of the wise" (τῶν σοφῶν). The irony is that God, who knows the "foolishness" of the so-called "wise," uses their own devices against them to capture them. God sees through it all, and it is futile. The word "futile" (μάταιοι) suggests the fruitlessness of all their wise plans and opinions. God knows they are achieving nothing and going nowhere. What a contrast this is with the wise plan of the Lord, whose end-time goal has been and is being brought about through Christ crucified. On his predetermined "Day" he will reveal all things.

3:21a–b So then let no one boast in people (ὥστε μηδεὶς καυχάσθω ἐν ἀνθρώποις). "So then" (ὥστε)[6] introduces a consequence of what Paul has just written. Thus, we reach the third imperative of Paul's application to the Corinthians: "Let no one boast" (μηδεὶς καυχάσθω).[7] Here Paul summarizes and applies 1:28–31, but he is also returning to his original appeal in 1:10. Any "boast" will only ever be in the Lord himself for those who truly have understood the message of Christ crucified. Paul's aim is unity, but this means above all understanding God and his ways, and so he returns to his theological basis once more as he states why any human dependence upon human wisdom must be eliminated from the thinking of God's people. The next sentence begins with "for," indicating the reason for not boasting in human leaders and their ways.

3:21c–23 For all things are yours—whether Paul, or Apollos, or Peter, or the world, or life, or death, or the present, or the future—all things are yours; now you are Christ's, and Christ is God's (πάντα γὰρ ὑμῶν ἐστιν, εἴτε Παῦλος εἴτε Ἀπολλῶς εἴτε Κηφᾶς εἴτε κόσμος εἴτε ζωὴ εἴτε θάνατος εἴτε ἐνεστῶτα εἴτε μέλλοντα, πάντα ὑμῶν, ὑμεῖς δὲ Χριστοῦ, Χριστὸς δὲ θεοῦ). All attempts to appeal to some human leader or to want to belong to some superior spiritual group miss the glorious light of the gospel. In the wisdom of God in Christ everything that has been done for God's people has had them in mind from start to finish. The crucified Christ may seem foolish to the world, but this has been God's way to give his people all that he has planned for them to enjoy in the present and the future, in life or in death. These last two and-a-half verses of the chapter need to be held closely together, for the last two clauses (v. 23) help explain what is meant in vv. 21c–22. They provide a glorious statement of the privileges that belong to God's people as they find themselves belonging to God in Christ and to his church.

Paul returns to his illustrative list of leaders, mentioning Peter again for the first time since 1:12. This mention of Peter probably simply serves to draw everything together. It is unlikely, as noted above on 1:12, that there was a specific group of people following Paul or Peter. What is noticeable here is how expansive and wide reaching this list is. Paul moves his readers far beyond thinking of particular leaders to thinking about what is the total inheritance of God's people. Instead of the individualistic approach of saying something like "I am of Paul," the church is told, "All things are yours!"

Paul and everyone else and everything else are to be understood in relationship to the church.[8] Paul will develop this when he tells the Corinthi-

---

6. The word frequently introduces an imperative.

7. See comments on 1:29 for the word's theological roots.

8. It is natural in English to translate the genitives here as possessive, "all things are yours," in the sense of belonging to.

ans that they need to regard their leaders as "servants of Christ" (4:1). In this new perspective "all things" are defined in association with the church, meaning ultimately the church in its relationship to Christ and to God. As Robertson says, "The Church is not the property of the Apostles; Apostles are ministers of the Church."[9] All things are caught up in God's great purposes for his church. The leaders are there to serve the church, but even what happens in the world—even life or death, present or future (perhaps Paul means beyond the grave), "all things" are for the benefit of the church, the temple where the Spirit of God dwells. They are therefore "yours" (πάντα ὑμῶν), or "for your benefit." At the end of Romans 8 Paul relates something similar as he lists the things that cannot separate God's people from the love of God in Christ (Rom 8:35–39). Perhaps the best summary of what Paul has in mind here is in Romans 8:28: "We know that all things work together for good for those who love God, who are called according to his purpose" (NRSV). All things are thus brought into the service of the Lord's people and so belong to them.

Paul has started from the perspective of the Corinthian church. This is their situation, and he works from them to God. But he could have started with God. Paul used the name "God" (θεός) five times for emphasis in 3:16–17 alone, so it is appropriate that he should finish this section with "God." Christ is God's. He is God's Son and Messiah,[10] the one who comes to this earth for the sake of the church. The church is Christ's. Since all things belong to God and to the Son, so all things are for the benefit of the church. This relationship between God and his church, in which the church belongs to God and to Christ and is brought into being by Christ, is why "all things" are for them. How can status matter in such a community? They are Christ's! They have got it all the wrong way around. Each Christian is part of the church and so has status beyond anything the world can offer: the status of "standing before God." Let the Corinthians consider, then, who *they* are. In Ephesians 1:18 Paul captures something of all this from God's perspective as he refers to *God's* "glorious inheritance in the saints" (ESV). They belong to God, and God views them as *his* glorious inheritance. They are *for* him.

4:1a–b Let a person regard us in this way, as servants of Christ (Οὕτως ἡμᾶς λογιζέσθω ἄνθρωπος ὡς ὑπηρέτας Χριστοῦ). Once they understand who *they* are, Paul can ask the Corinthians, by way of application of 3:5–9, to consider again just who they think their *leaders* are. In this second summarizing section, Paul talks about church leadership and then narrows it down to the specific concern that they are making judgments about him. In the fourth exhortation Paul uses the present imperative of the verb "to count" (λογίζομαι). Metaphorically it means to evaluate, reckon, or regard. We have translated "let a person" to carry the force of this fourth imperative; "this is how one should" (RSV; ESV) or "men ought to regard us" (NIV) do not carry the weight of what Paul is saying. Paul is not making a suggestion that may help the Corinthians see things in a better light. Rather, this is the way it is in God's church. Leaders are servants who work for Christ, and so they should be regarded in this way. "Servants" and "stewards" (4:1c) both introduce clauses in apposition to "us"

However, this genitive is at times hard to distinguish from the Greek genitive of relationship (see comments on 1:12). The point of what Paul is saying is that "all things" have a relationship to God's people that is *for their benefit* and is in their interests.

9. Robertson and Plummer, *First Corinthians*, 72.

10. Paul is not here discussing an ontological relationship of Father and Son. His point relates to the function of the Son in relationship to the Father in regard to the church. There is a functional subordination.

(hence the accusatives in Greek). The word "servant" (ὑπηρέτης) is not used elsewhere in Paul's writings. In 3:5 Paul used a more common word (διάκονος). The word here can simply mean "subordinates."[11] But as the second phrase shows, Paul's thought centers on serving Christ in his household.

4:1c and stewards of the mysteries of God

(καὶ οἰκονόμους μυστηρίων θεοῦ). A "steward" (οἰκονόμος) was someone who was given charge in a household.[12] Paul seeks to achieve two ends at the same time. He must make it clear, firstly, that he and the other apostles or leaders are servants of Christ, and therefore people should not look to them as some form of guru who is to be followed because of their great giftedness or communication skills. They serve a "Lord" (vv. 4 and 5) and are answerable to him for their work.[13] But, secondly, he must keep the way open to being able to exercise a genuine apostolic leadership among them. These two clauses taken together help Paul achieve that. They stress that he is a servant, takes orders, and is there to serve Christ and his church. Yet they also reinforce that, as in any household where there would have been many servants, Paul holds a position of oversight. Specifically, he and the other apostles are stewards of "God's mysteries" (θεοῦ is a possessive genitive). As was seen in 2:7, "mysteries" (here in the plural) refer to God's purposes for salvation that are revealed in Christ, especially with reference to the drawing in of the Gentiles. The apostles have brought the message and revealed the "wisdom" of God in Christ crucified to Jew and Gentile in Corinth and the world. This was their sacred duty as servants called to be stewards

in God's mission. Simply put, they are preachers of the gospel.

4:2 In this position, furthermore, it is required of stewards that they be found faithful (ὧδε λοιπὸν ζητεῖται ἐν τοῖς οἰκονόμοις ἵνα πιστός τις εὑρεθῇ). Any steward of a household will be expected to be found "faithful" (πιστός). It is possible here that Paul thinks back to the fact that "God is faithful" (1:9; cf. 10:13). The stewards of the mysteries of God need to be like him. "In this position," that is, given their involvement in this type of work, something more is required. The final clause providing the object of the verb "to require" is in the third singular. An English plural translation as above is most natural, though an alternative in the singular might be "that one be found faithful." The verb "be found" (εὑρεθῇ) suggests that trustworthiness is a requirement for the job, giving the basis on which the steward's work may be judged.

It is a pity that some translations use different words to translate πιστός ("faithful") in 1:9 and here in 4:2, for it means that a connection is lost. God is faithful in the sense that he is utterly to be trusted; yet, more than that he carries through on whatever he chooses to do. The apostles must also be found faithful and trustworthy in both these realms. People should not be able to find any dissimulation in them or inconsistency between life and word, but they must also be faithful in delivering what they have been called by God to do. They cannot hold back on preaching the gospel and on teaching the churches about Christ crucified and what that entails for life.

Of course, what is said here actually applies to all Christians in their various callings. Christians

---

11. See BDAG 1035. See ὑπηρέτης elsewhere, e.g., Mark 14:54; John 7:32; Acts 5:22.

12. Thiselton's translation of "estate managers" may go a little far, but clearly connotes the responsibility of this position (*1 Corinthians*, 336).

13. Clarke, *Secular and Christian Leadership in Corinth*, 122, says Paul's "use of this term serves to focus Paul's argument once again not on the person but on the task."

are to be found faithful because God is faithful. Here, though, in talking about "stewards" Paul specifically has himself and other apostles or senior leaders of the church in mind. The question of such faithfulness in stewardship can easily be "judged," and so Paul now turns to the way the Corinthians have set about this and applies what he is saying directly to the way they have judged him.

4:3 But for me it is a very small[14] matter that I should be judged by you or by any human court; in fact, I do not even judge myself (ἐμοὶ δὲ εἰς ἐλάχιστόν ἐστιν, ἵνα ὑφ᾽ ὑμῶν ἀνακριθῶ ἢ ὑπὸ ἀνθρωπίνης ἡμέρας· ἀλλ᾽ οὐδὲ ἐμαυτὸν ἀνακρίνω). Paul is not suggesting that some Corinthians have already considered bringing him to some ecclesiastical trial! However, they are making judgments about leaders and clearly have been doing so about Paul. "That" (ἵνα) introduces the complement clause of the sentence. The aorist, passive subjunctive "I should be judged" (ἀνακρίνω) speaks of a hypothetical situation.

In making such judgments, they were probably imitating once again the world's wisdom, for in secular Corinthian society the assessment of a person's success in the political world was indeed carried out in public, following which the person would be recognized as one of society's leaders.[15] Paul has a different perspective altogether, and this should be their perspective as well. He is the Lord's servant and steward, so his great concern is with the Lord, who has every right to judge him and will indeed do so in due course (vv. 4–5). In other words, Paul's perspective remains one embedded in his Christology (Christ is Lord) and in his eschatology (God's own judgment is coming). The

Corinthians, in line with their society, have been seeking after status and stature in the community that were based on deeply false assumptions about what it is to be spiritual. While they have looked to what grace-gifts leaders have received, to rhetorical abilities and the like, Paul has shown them another way, God's way.

In 2:13 Paul said he had not spoken in words taught "by *human* wisdom" (ἀνθρωπίνης σοφίας). Here he points out that God will judge him rather than a *human* court (ἀνθρωπίνης ἡμέρας).[16] Human wisdom stands or falls in the human court. Wisdom from God stands or falls in God's court. So Paul directly applies this to the Corinthians, saying he will not be judged "by you" and then adding "or by any human court." This last clause stands in apposition to "by you." Thus, Paul makes the serious comment that he considers the Corinthians to be a human court since they live by and are judging by human wisdom.

The strong adversative (ἀλλά) functions here, as it frequently does, not to express something that is contrary to what has gone before but to intensify the additional thought; thus the translation "in fact" ("indeed" would also work). Paul now goes further. He does not even judge himself.

This important theme of judgment, running throughout the epistle, was examined earlier, and the use of the word "judge" (ἀνακρίνω) was remarked upon (2:14–15). Paul went on to say that the spiritual person "is himself judged by no one" (2:15). There we suggested that Paul was making the point that all Christians are "spiritual" because they possess the Spirit and therefore there is no sense in which someone can judge another

---

14. "Very small" translates ἐλάχιστος, which is used as the superlative of μικρός.

15. Clarke, *Secular and Christian Leadership in Corinth*, 121.

16. Note the translation "court" for "day" (ἡμέρα), which is adopted by almost all translations. In this passage the human

"day" stands in contrast with *the* "Day," which refers to God's court of judgment (3:13). See BDAG 347. Fee helpfully refers to the similar English expression "having one's day in court" (Fee, *1 Corinthians*, 175).

Christian to be less "spiritual." Here Paul directly applies this to himself. The Corinthians are not entitled to make judgments about Paul as to how "faithful" he is for two reasons. First, this is God's prerogative alone. Secondly, the very type of judgment and evaluation in which they are involved is based on the world's understanding of degrees of spirituality and standing in the community. Christians have that standing by grace alone because they have the Spirit of God. By grace they have been called to work for the Lord, and by grace they have been given the gifts to do the work to which he has called them. Paul stands or falls before his master, the Lord. He believes he is doing what he has been called to do. He believes that he will be found faithful. The worldly judgment of some of the elitists had in effect put Paul "in the dock," and they were rendering a judgment about his standing that was for God alone to do.

4:4 Now I am not aware of anything against myself, but I am not acquitted for that reason.[17] It is the Lord[18] who judges me (οὐδὲν γὰρ ἐμαυτῷ σύνοιδα, ἀλλ᾽ οὐκ ἐν τούτῳ δεδικαίωμαι, ὁ δὲ ἀνακρίνων με κύριός ἐστιν). The Corinthian elitists have been judging Paul on the basis of his grace-gifts, knowledge, wisdom, and leadership. Paul refuses this altogether as the basis for judgment. Being judged on how he has fulfilled his stewardship is something only God can do. When he thinks of his stewardship, Paul is not aware of having been unfaithful. His own self-awareness makes him believe that there is probably not anything against him. But if he is to be found faithful this,

too, is by the Lord's grace. He says just this in 7:25: "As one who by the Lord's mercy is trustworthy."

The verb "I am not aware of" (σύνοιδα) is in the perfect tense with a present meaning—a "defective" verb. We have translated it "aware" because its connotation largely has to do with "self-awareness."[19] The relevance here is simply this. Paul is not saying, "My conscience is clear" (NIV) as if he was searching for something he may have done wrong or felt guilty about. He is simply saying that, as far as he can assess himself, he has been faithful in his service to the Lord.

However, Paul must add yet more, for the effect of the judgments being made by the Corinthians was to exclude or virtually to exclude people from the category of "spiritual." As Paul has shown, doing this would in the end exclude *them* from the people of God because being "spiritual" is defined (by Paul) as having the Spirit. People who have the Spirit *are* the Lord's. So the result, even if unintended by the Corinthians, is that they are making judgments that parallel the judgment of the last day when the Lord comes.

Thus, Paul thinks of the judgment day and talks of being "justified" or "acquitted" (δεδικαίωμαι is perfect passive; the agent is the Lord as the next verse shows). Paul's self-awareness is not what finally counts. It is simply a guide as he seeks to be faithful. What counts is the judgment of God, and for that he must rely on God's mercy and grace. It is interesting here and in the next verse to note that he uses the title "Lord." As the covenant Lord who "comes" (v. 5), he alone has the authority to pronounce judgment.

---

17. Moule, *Idiom Book of New Testament Greek*, 51, for use of ἐν τούτῳ.

18. Colwell's rule: predicate nouns before the verb are [usually] definite even if they do not have the article.

19. Later in chapter 8, Paul will have much to say about συνείδησις, usually translated "conscience." This commentary

on that chapter argues that a better meaning for the word—one regularly found in Koine Greek—is "self-awareness" rather than what these days is thought of as a "moral conscience." For more on this, see the essay, "In Depth: The Meaning of the Word 'Conscience' (συνείδησις)" after comments on 8:7. Also see Gardner, *Gifts of God*, 42–48.

4:5a–c Therefore, do not judge anything before the time, before the Lord comes (ὥστε μὴ πρὸ καιροῦ τι κρίνετε, ἕως ἂν ἔλθῃ ὁ κύριος). On that last day the Lord's judgment will expose everything. It will reveal whether a person really did belong to the Lord, but it will also, as Paul has said in 3:14–15, reveal the lasting value or otherwise of a leader's work. "Therefore" (ὥστε) introduces the consequence of what is being said and the last and most important of the five imperatives of this section. The imperative "do not judge" (μὴ . . . κρίνετε) is required by the context, though the verb grammatically could be indicative or imperative. "Before the time" (πρὸ καιροῦ)[20] is then expanded in the next clause to "before the Lord comes" (ἕως ἂν ἔλθῃ ὁ κύριος). The Greek indicates that the timing of the coming is indefinite.[21] And so Paul continues to describe further the activity of the Lord on that day.

4:5d–f who will shine light on the hidden things of darkness and will reveal the purposes of our hearts. Then each will receive praise from God (ὃς καὶ φωτίσει τὰ κρυπτὰ τοῦ σκότους καὶ φανερώσει τὰς βουλὰς τῶν καρδιῶν· καὶ τότε ὁ ἔπαινος γενήσεται ἑκάστῳ ἀπὸ τοῦ θεοῦ). The Lord will shine his light in such a way that he will reveal the things "of darkness" (τοῦ σκότους is a descriptive genitive). "The purposes of our hearts" (τὰς βουλὰς τῶν καρδιῶν) are part of the "hidden things" (τὰ κρυπτὰ). These are not open to public scrutiny, for only God sees the heart. In other words, God will reveal the truth about a person's relationship with the Lord. Motivations and preoccupations, desires and lusts will all be disclosed, as will a person's pride or humility, attitude toward others, or desire to fragment or unite the church. But Paul ends this whole section on a positive note, for he looks to that time as a time when rewards will be given, picking up on 3:8 and 3:14. Here he also describes what that reward will look like. What more could be desired than that praise should be given God's people in God's presence ("from God"; ἀπὸ τοῦ θεοῦ])! It is not necessary to look for another meaning to the word "praise" (ἔπαινος) to account for the possibility that some will not receive praise at that time. For those who follow Paul's teaching here and take seriously his five summary exhortations there will be praise.

In this way Paul closes this part of the application of his teaching to the church. He has asked them to consider first who they are. With three imperatives he has told them not to deceive themselves with who they are, to become "fools" in the eyes of the world, and not to boast in people. He further reminded them that they are Christ's. They belong and have a status with God as his people, which is more than they seem to have ever imagined. Paul then moved on to talk of their understanding of leadership and especially his own leadership. With two imperatives Paul insists that he and the apostles must be regarded as "servants of Christ" and are therefore answerable to their Lord. Therefore, the church must not pronounce judgment on him since this is the prerogative of the Lord on the final day. Paul ends on a note of encouragement, for commendation from the Lord's judgment throne awaits the faithful servant.

---

20. The preposition πρό takes the genitive and here is temporal.

21. The conjunction ἕως with the particle ἂν takes the aorist subjunctive in a number of places in the NT, suggesting a timing that is indefinite.

Theology in Application

The Problem of Self-Deception

Self-deception must be one of humanity's most common sins. It can be found in every walk of life. In Jeremiah 37:9 the Lord warns Israel of the dangers of the self-deception involved in imagining he will not carry out his word of judgment. In James 1:22 there is also a warning against the self-deception of hearing God's word but doing nothing about it. In similar vein, Paul later addresses the self-deception of those caught up in immorality, in adultery, or in sexual relationships of various sorts outside heterosexual marriage (6:9–10). How much greater is that self-deception when it is a Christian who thinks such behavior is unimportant yet has been explicitly told that those who practice such things will not "inherit the kingdom of God" (6:10). Each of these instances highlights the general principle that people have deceived themselves into believing that *their* wisdom, *their* way of life, and *their* priorities without regard to God are adequate for life. Paul insists that this wisdom is folly before God. Self-deception can only be remedied by repentance, renewed faith in Christ crucified, and in recognising that in Christ alone lies the true wisdom of God. Such repentance comes at the expense of our pride and greed and of a life that is self-centered and lived for self-gratification. Such a life is replaced by a life that knows Christ alone as Lord. This is a life prepared to follow him into ignominy, disrepute, suffering, and even persecution. Yet it is also a life that looks forward in the end to the glory of hearing the commendation of God on the last day.

Faithful Stewards

Paul has spoken of himself and church leaders as stewards. The idea of overseeing the household of God is formidable and humbling for any church leader. The apostles had a special role in this, but all those who teach in the church have a parallel calling since they preach, teach, and build upon the foundation of Christ crucified. Speaking more generally of church leaders, the writer to the Hebrews talks of them as "keeping watch over your souls, as those who will have to give an account" (13:17 ESV). There is a huge responsibility laid on such people, and it leads them either to bring great glory to God's name or, for some, into arrogance or pride. It is not surprising that James wrote in 3:1, "Not many of you should become teachers, my fellow believers, because you know that we who teach will be judged more strictly."

Such service among God's people needs enormous spiritual support from God's people, especially in the form of regular prayer. The lack of such prayer probably reflects the pervasive impact of the wisdom of this age in our churches. In effect the people are saying, "There is no need to rely on God when we can rely on our appointment of such an excellent pastor!" Then, of course, the same people blame the minister when things are not as "successful" as they had hoped. Paul is showing that the church and its stewards are integrally and intimately tied together into the building up of the church. "All things are yours!"

The need for church people to insist that right building takes place on the foundation of Christ crucified requires not just a theologically attuned minister but a godly and committed people who pray for the stewards whom God has put in place. Such a people will also recognize the authority that God has given his stewards among his people. This is not an authority of the sort that worldly wisdom would recognize, but is one born of God's word being brought to bear among them.

Leaders are called to be faithful stewards. Their joy will be found in many ways, but the respect in which they are held by God's people will play a large part in helping them become the servants they should be. In Hebrews 13:17 we read, "Obey your leaders and submit to them, for they are keeping watch over your souls, as those who will have to give an account. Let them do this with joy and not with groaning, for that would be of no advantage to you" (ESV). In 1 Thessalonians 5:12 Paul urges the people "to respect those who labor among you and are over you in the Lord and admonish you" (ESV). The role of a faithful steward is never easy, as the apostle Paul reveals in his own life, but it can be a joyous one as steward and people work and pray together for God's purposes to be worked out among them.

At the Lord's Coming

The judgment day is often regarded in Scripture as a fearful day. Even in this passage there has been talk of the danger of self-deception and the judgment of God on such people. Yet Paul also sees it as the day when God's faithful people stand before a God who is faithful and who blesses his people, so that "each one will receive his praise before God." Understanding the balance between fear and great joy at the thought of the day of the Lord is difficult. Warnings are warnings and must never be understated, and they are here in this epistle in abundance. However, God's people are entirely redeemed and justified by God's grace. They labor at the work to which God has graciously called them and for which he has graciously given them gifts. They work with the gift of God's Spirit guiding and enabling in power day by day. Therefore, it is good for Christians, and specially for leaders who view themselves as insignificant and unsuccessful, to remember that it is not the judgment of this age that matters, but it is the standing that we have as God's people before the Lord that matters. He has promised "each one will receive praise before God."

10

1 Corinthians 4:6–21

Literary Context

In 3:18–4:5, Paul exhorted his readers to examine the nature of wise leadership and to assess themselves properly before God. He then also asked them to consider how they should regard their leaders, especially Paul himself. The greater context within which they live and work is one of Christ's return. There is no place for making judgments about leaders, which rightly belong to God on the last day. Meanwhile, God's stewards are to be faithful to the Lord.

Paul now returns to the matter of the grace-gifts of God that he introduced as a matter for thanksgiving back in 1:4–7. There he especially noted the gifts of "speech" (λόγος) and "knowledge" (γνῶσις). Paul alluded to this again in 2:4 where he said his "speech" (λόγος) may have seemed to be lacking in "wisdom" but was in fact a demonstration "of the Spirit and of power." Later, as he defined what an authentic spiritual person looks like, he emphasized that he or she possesses the Spirit of God but also has gifts from God (2:10–12). Paul now returns to the question of the gifts and the Corinthian belief that they seemed to attest to some sort of spiritual maturity or evidence of "having arrived." The section of 4:6–21 contains heavy sarcasm, but Paul is not here defending his apostleship.[1] Far from it. The Corinthians might have expected the apostles of all people to be highly regarded and have a grand status in the church and perhaps even in the society. Paul's point here is that there is no difference between the apostles and the normal church member (4:7). They have all received gifts, but such gifts do not function to authenticate spiritual maturity. If they look for an outward authentication of the reality of the Christian faith, it will be seen in the life that follows Christ and has a deep commitment to a theology of the cross with all the hardship and sadness and toil that it will involve. At the end of the day, the presence of God's kingdom is not seen in "speech" (λόγος) but in "power" (δύναμις), the power of God himself. Later, especially from chapter 8 onward, Paul will have much more to say about how the gifts of the Spirit were being allowed to

---

1. *Contra* Fee, *1 Corinthians*, 179. He calls this whole section, "The Marks of True Apostleship."

function (wrongly) in the Corinthian church. The theme of arrogance that is so prominent in this passage then allows Paul to move to discuss the arrogance of their behavior with regard to morality in chapter 5.

IV. Mature Christians Pursue God's Wisdom (2:6–4:21)

    A. Paul Proclaims God's Wisdom (2:6–13)

    B. God's Wisdom Characterizes Those Who Are "Spiritual" (2:14–16)

    C. The Corinthians are Spiritually Immature (3:1–9)

    D. Wise Leadership Acts with Spiritual Discernment (3:10–4:21)

        1. Illustration: A Building and a Wise Master Builder (3:10–15)

        2. The Building Is God's Temple in Which His Spirit Dwells (3:16–17)

        3. Leadership Must Be Seen in the Light of God's Wisdom (3:18–23)

        4. Wise Leadership Will Be Commended by God Alone (4:1–5)

        5. Paul and Apollos as Models to Imitate (4:6–21)

   V. Lack of Spiritual Wisdom Has Led to Grievous Sin (5:1–6:20)

Main Idea

God's gracious gifts do not provide evidence that authenticates Christian maturity. The Corinthians have not yet arrived and must cease their arrogance. They should look at Paul, whose life and teaching reflects the humiliation of Christ crucified.

Translation

1 Corinthians 4:6–21

6a		Now brothers [and sisters],
b	Assertion	**I have applied these things to myself and Apollos**
c	Advantage	for your benefit
d	Purpose	that, by considering our case, you may learn not to go beyond what is written,
e	Result	so that none of you may be puffed up one against another.
7a	Rhetorical question	For **who judges between you?**
b	Rhetorical question	For **what do you have that you have not received?**
c	Condition (protasis)	If then you received it,
d	Rhetorical question (apodosis)	**why do you boast as if you did not receive it?**

Continued on next page.

Continued from previous page.

8a	Exclamation	**Already you are filled!**
b	Exclamation	**Already you have become rich!**
c	Assertion	
	(further exclamation)	**You have come to reign without us.** And
d	Wish	indeed **I wish you did reign,**
e	Purpose	so that we might reign with you!
9a	Explanation	For it seems to me,
b	Assertion	**God has exhibited us apostles last of all**
c	Manner	as men sentenced to death
d	Reason	because we have been made a spectacle to the world,
e	Apposition	to both angels and human beings
10a	Series, contrasting illustrations	We are fools for Christ's sake, but
b	Contrast	you are wise in Christ.
c	Illustration	We are weak, but
d	Contrast	you are strong.
e	Illustration	You are held in honor, but
f	Contrast	we are dishonored.
11a	Time	Up to the present hour
b	Further illustrations	**we are hungry**
c	List	**and thirsty**
d		**and are poorly dressed**
e	List	**and beaten and homeless**
12a		**and we grow tired**
b	Instrumental	working with our own hands;
c	Event (series, illustrations)	when scoffed at,
d	Response	**we speak kindly;**
e	Event (series, illustrations)	when persecuted,
f	Response	**we endure;**
13a	Event (series, illustrations)	when slandered,
b	Response	**we entreat with kindness;**
c	Summation	**we have become** like the scum of the world,
d	Expansion	the refuse of all to this very day.
14a	Assertion	**I do not write these things**
b	Purpose (negative)	**to make you ashamed,** but rather
c	Purpose (positive)	**to warn you as my dearly loved children.**
15a	Condition (protasis)	For if you had perhaps ten-thousand teachers in Christ,
b	Assertion (apodosis)	**certainly you do not have many fathers,**
c	Sphere	for in Christ Jesus
d	Assertion	**I fathered you through the gospel.**
16a	Exhortation	Therefore, **I urge you, be imitators of me.**

17a	Cause	For this reason	
b	Assertion	**I have sent Timothy to you,**	
c	Description	who is my beloved child and faithful in the Lord;	
d	Expansion	**he will remind you of my ways in Christ Jesus**	
e	Description	just as I teach them everywhere in every church.	
18a	Circumstance	Now, as if I were not coming to you,	
b	Assertion	**some have become puffed up;**	
19a	Assertion	but **I will come to you soon,**	
b	Wish	if the Lord wills,	
c	Purpose	and **I will find out not**	**the speech of the puffed up but their power;**
20a	Basis	For **the kingdom of God is not a matter**	**of speech but**
b	Contrast		**of power.**
21a	Rhetorical question	**What do you desire?**	
b	Rhetorical question	**Shall I come to you**	
c	Manner (instrumental)	with a rod, or	
d	Manner (instrumental)	in love and in a spirit of gentleness?	

Structure

This section of 4:6–21 may be broken down into three subsections. Subsection 4:6–8 forms a bridge from what has gone before with the discussion of Corinthian arrogance based on gifts of the Spirit. First, Paul speaks against the competitive spirit that has caused some to think they are greater than others and that has led to boasting. Secondly, he asserts that all that they have they have received as gifts from God. Thirdly, Paul writes with some irony and sarcasm, insisting that the Corinthians think they have arrived. Paul suggests they are behaving and thinking like kings.

In the next subsection of 4:9–13, Paul presents a dramatic contrast as he describes the life and work of the apostles. God has called them to be a "spectacle" to the world, reminding the reader of Christ, who was also made a spectacle on the cross. The apostolic message is of Christ crucified, and they live a life that reflects this theology of the cross. This subsection may be further broken down as Paul is seen in v. 10 as offering three contrasts between the apostles and the Corinthian leaders. Then he offers six ways in which the apostles suffer (vv. 11–12a) before returning to three further contrasts (vv. 12b–13a). The brief summary of the subsection is that the apostles are therefore regarded as scum (v. 13).

In the third subsection of 4:14–21, Paul returns to a more gentle pastoral role of "father in God" to them. He asserts that he has no desire to shame them but rather wants to warn them of the dangers of the arrogance of some. Picking up on his comments that they have become "kings," he reminds them that the kingdom of God is not found in their "speech" (whether a gift of the Spirit or not) but in the power of God.

Exegetical Outline

Explanation of the Text

4:6a–c Now brothers [and sisters], I have applied these things to myself and Apollos for your benefit (Ταῦτα δέ, ἀδελφοί, μετεσχημάτισα εἰς ἐμαυτὸν καὶ Ἀπολλῶν δι᾽ ὑμᾶς). Paul explains why he has employed himself and Apollos as examples of leadership in the church. "Now" (δέ) is continuative. The meaning of the verb translated "I have applied" (μετασχηματίζω) has proved controversial. One reason for the difficulty is that this is a more or less unique use of the word. Below, we take the word to indicate that Paul has written about himself by way of a figure of speech, hence the translation, "I have applied these things to myself."[2] However, the discussion of Paul's meaning here usually begins with Chrysostom's comments on this passage. In a nutshell, he argued that Paul had used a literary

---

2. With RSV, NRSV, NIV. See BDAG 642 (3). The word is used by Paul in Phil 3:21 where it denotes the "transformation" of the body from that which is lowly to that which is glorious. Thiselton, *1 Corinthians*, 349, discusses four approaches to the word.

"disguise" in his teaching by applying his criticisms and arguments to himself and Apollos.[3] Paul's target was in fact the divisive leaders in Corinth who remain anonymous, but he softens the attack by applying it to himself and Apollos. Many have followed this interpretation. One of its obvious difficulties is that there is nothing else, apart perhaps from this word, that really suggests Paul is using himself and Apollos as "disguises" for something else. Robertson and Plummer, who follow this view, put it like this: "I have transferred these warnings to myself and Apollos for the purpose of a covert allusion, and that for your sakes, that in our persons you may get instruction."[4] One of the supporting arguments for this position among some is that it is impossible to imagine Paul seriously considering that he or Apollos might destroy God's temple (3:16). But, as we have suggested, there does seem to be a change of tack between 3:15 and 3:16–17, including the move to the second-person plural at that point. However, there is no doubt even from within chapter 3 that Paul sees himself as having to give account on the last day for the work he has done. Others propose a variety of meanings, largely centering on the view that in 4:6 Paul is making reference to the images he has used in chapter 3 for planting, building, and so on.[5] Most agree that part of what Paul is doing here is saying that he uses himself and Apollos by way of example in order not to cause an immediate backlash from those at Corinth to what he is saying about leadership. There is some ground in the text for suggesting that Paul was trying to avoid this sort of reaction to

his teaching in 4:14–16. There he refers to them as his "dearly loved children" and states that he does not wish to make them "ashamed" but to warn or admonish them as a "father."

As noted, the position taken here is to translate the verb in line with the NIV, RSV, NRSV, and ESV: "I have applied," yet not to ignore the fact that Paul is using a literary device. This device does not need to be so complicated or disguised that all that has been said does not apply to him and Apollos. Rather, it seems that Paul has used himself and Apollos as people who, precisely in their ministries and callings, have shown how to apply what Paul now wants the Corinthians to learn about leadership. Paul is quite prepared here to put himself "in the dock," but only before God. Paul and Apollos have worked together with different callings. They have placed Christ crucified at the center of all. They have constantly been concerned that they are faithful stewards and have sought humbly to be servants of Christ in their ministries. They live in anticipation of reward on the final day but also see that day as a motivation for faithful commitment.

4:6d–e that, by considering our case, you may learn not to go beyond what is written, so that none of you may be puffed up one against another (ἵνα ἐν ἡμῖν μάθητε τὸ μὴ ὑπὲρ ἃ γέγραπται, ἵνα μὴ εἷς ὑπὲρ τοῦ ἑνὸς φυσιοῦσθε κατὰ τοῦ ἑτέρου). Paul draws attention to the way he and Apollos have worked together. This humility, and their lack of boasting or contrasting themselves with each other, points to their Christ-centered ministry. The second half of this verse contains

---

3. Chrysostom, *Homilies on First Corinthians*, homily 12: "Signifying that if he had applied his argument in their persons, they would not have learnt all that they needed to learn, nor would have admitted the correction, being vexed at what was said. But as it was, revering Paul, they bore the rebuke well." In 2 Cor 11:13, 14, 15 the middle form of the verb indicates those who have deceitfully "disguised" themselves as apostles.

4. Robertson and Plummer, *First Corinthians*, 80. See also J. Schneider, "μετασχηματίζω," *TDNT* 7:958. More recently Fitzmyer, *1 Corinthians*, 215, has taken the word in this way, arguing for the sense of the sentence employing this "normal meaning."

5. So, for example, Morna D. Hooker, "'Beyond the Things Which Are Written': An Examination of I Corinthians 4:6," *NTS* 10 (1963): 127–32.

two purpose clauses. Fee argues that the overall purpose of what Paul is saying is found in the second clause.[6] This one is easily understood. Paul desires that they should learn not to boast, not to "be puffed up." The verb "puffed up" (φυσιοῦσθε, a passive subjunctive) appears six times in this letter and otherwise only once elsewhere in Paul's writings (Col 2:18). It indicates a flaunting of something or of oneself over *against* another (hence κατά). Paul's concern is with a *deliberate* effort among the Corinthians to contrast one with another.[7] This is what is breaking up the community. Paul will go on to speak about gifts from God not being a cause for boasting or differentiation. The Corinthians cannot and must not become puffed up against each other on the basis of the grace-gifts they have received (v. 7). However, the first clause has priority and, for a number of reasons, seems more likely to be Paul's first and main purpose in all that he has been saying.

First, some grammatical points need to be noted. "By considering our case" (ἐν ἡμῖν μάθητε) is an example of what Moule calls the exemplary dative, which is an extension of the instrumental dative.[8] Another example of this occurs in 9:15. "Beyond" (ὑπέρ + accusative) could also mean "above." The neuter pronoun (τό) provides another difficulty. Sometimes when it appears on its own, as here, it can introduce indirect speech or a quotation. Thus, some have translated "that you may learn the meaning of the saying 'do not go beyond.'"[9] However, it is not necessary to go so far as to suggest that the Corinthians might have

recognized this as a saying. Simple indirect speech is sufficient, as we have translated above. As a verb form, "written" (γέγραπται) is exclusively used by Paul to refer to what is written in Scripture (see on 1:19). Paul customarily uses "as it is written" (καθὼς γέγραπται) or "for it is written" (γέγραπται γάρ). The combination here with "the things" (ἃ γέγραπται) is unique. However, the exclusive use of the perfect passive elsewhere to refer to what is written in *Scripture* makes it a reasonable assumption that this is also what Paul has in mind here.

Secondly, the meaning of the phrase "not to go beyond what is written" needs to be interpreted. Conzelmann wrote, "The phrase . . . is unintelligible. [Most] do not get beyond guesswork."[10] But this is unduly pessimistic. Most agree that Paul is referring to Scripture. Paul's point is that the Corinthians should learn from the example of Paul and Apollos not to go beyond what Scripture says (i.e., what is written). The question then is, "Which Scriptures?" The whole of Scripture has been suggested; that is, Paul is referring generally to the need to apply Scripture to their existence as the people of God after the manner of Paul and Apollos.[11] Others have suggested that Paul has in mind specifically his citations from Scripture already used in the epistle thus far.[12] In fact, the context here helps us somewhat. We have suggested that this is Paul's main purpose clause. At the end of the day, they must follow Scripture in their approach to "status" and "belonging" and what is "spiritual" and so on. If they do this, then the immediate problem (there are others Paul will deal with later) will be resolved.

---

6. Fee, *1 Corinthians*, 175.

7. Paul criticizes this comparing one against another even more firmly in 2 Cor 10:12.

8. *Idiom Book of New Testament Greek*, 77.

9. Barrett, *First Corinthians*, 106; Fee, *1 Corinthians*, 181; Moule, *Idiom Book of New Testament Greek*, 111, are among a number who take this view. Also NRSV and NIV, but not RSV, ESV or NASB.

10. Conzelmann, *1 Corinthians*, 86.

11. This is the position taken by F. F. Bruce, *1 and 2 Corinthians*, NCB (Grand Rapids: Eerdmans, 1984), 48, who paraphrases it, "Keep to the Book," which he regards as the gospel of Christ; also Barrett, *First Corinthians*, 106–7.

12. So especially Hooker, "'Beyond the Things Which Are Written,'" 127–32.

Hence, we have the second, but ultimately subsidiary, purpose clause, that they should not be "puffed up." It is precisely their going beyond Scripture, that is, going further than Scripture says, that has led to the divisions. They are going further than Scripture when they insist that the grace-gifts of the Spirit reveal status and authenticate Christian maturity. They are going further than Scripture in judging leaders with a judgment that belongs to the Lord alone.

One test of whether this is the right way of looking at the meaning here is to look at the quotations Paul has used so far. The first quotation in 1:19 speaks against human wisdom on which many of the Corinthians seem to depend. The quotation serves to show them that they have put themselves beyond what this verse has said. The quotation in 2:9 speaks against the limitation of God's wisdom to a few elite people who are "spiritual." Paul is asserting that to say otherwise is to go beyond the plain teaching of Scripture. The quotation in 2:16 has the same impact. In 2:19–20 Paul shows that the Lord has no place for human wisdom, regarding it as "folly." Again, this is an area where the Corinthians were clearly going beyond Scripture, giving more value to such wisdom than Scripture allows. Such a brief survey cannot do justice either to the quotations or to the force of what Paul is saying here. However, there is no reason to give up on the meaning of what Paul writes. Paul's concern is that gifts of God are not made to function in the community in a way that they do not function in Scripture. This will be a major part of his argument in 8:1–14:40. But it is also the main thrust of chapters 1–4. If the Corinthians have been blessed by

God with "speech" (λόγος) and "wisdom" (σοφία) and "knowledge" (γνῶσις), then they should thank God, for Scripture reveals that these things, properly understood, come from God. However, Scripture does not equate these gifts with "wisdom" and "knowledge" as they are seen in the world, and it does not allow these gifts to function as authenticators of spiritual maturity or status in the Christian church.[13]

To summarize: Paul has shown how he and Apollos work in Christian ministry together. Paul has even been prepared to put himself in the dock by way of example in 4:3–5, not because the Corinthians were so antagonistic to him but because he wanted them to see the broader eschatological context of his ministry. How he fulfills his calling and uses his gifts will be judged by his Lord. So Paul now urges the Corinthians to think again. They should look at Paul and Apollos and see a theology of the cross, a theology that is humble. They should see men who are sometimes humiliated and understand that this is true discipleship. Anything less goes far beyond what Scripture ever tolerates or points toward.

4:7 For who judges between you? For what do you have that you have not received? If then you received it, why do you boast as if you did not receive it? (τίς γάρ σε διακρίνει; τί δὲ ἔχεις ὃ οὐκ ἔλαβες; εἰ δὲ καὶ ἔλαβες, τί καυχᾶσαι ὡς μὴ λαβών;). We may paraphrase this verse thus: "Reflect on this: Who *can* judge you? After all, is not whatever spiritual gifting you have something you received from God?" "That you have not received" (ὃ οὐκ ἔλαβες) gives the content of the "what" (τί) of the

---

13. We therefore agree with Hooker, "'Beyond the Things Which Are Written,'" 130, that people at Corinth were preaching something additional "to Paul's message of Christ-crucified in the form of a wisdom-based spirituality." However, we believe that this wisdom largely centers around the gifts of the

Spirit mentioned in 1:9 of "speech" and "knowledge." They had taken these gifts and made them special because they seemed to be the ones most likely to convey status and indicate levels of spirituality in a society preoccupied with such concepts.

second question. Three rhetorical questions now get to the heart of what is wrong for the church at large ("Who?" "What?" "Why?"). In this verse alone the questions move to the singular, allowing any individual to apply this to his or her position in the church. Even those who are coming off badly in the church because they are given a poor assessment by those who boast are still asked, "Who judges you?" Why does anyone in the church allow this to happen to them? Every person judging or being judged needs to see the whole process as misconceived. So why boast as if it were not all a gift in the first place?

This is Paul's first use in this epistle of another verb (διακρίνω), which can be translated as "to judge" or "evaluate." It is closely related to the other verbs we have already noted with the Greek root κρίνω. But here the prefix διά especially calls attention to the dividing nature of such a judgment. For example, in 6:5 Paul appeals for someone to settle a dispute, to differentiate legally, between two brothers who have gone to court. A similar use of the word is found in 14:29 where some differentiate between prophecies to see what is of value. Back here at 4:7, the NRSV translates it in context as "Who sees anything different in you?" This carries clearly the meaning of differentiation between people. But the translation does not carry quite the weight of *judgment* that is going on here.[14] Paul is concerned not just about differentiation but about *differentiation that results in a positive or negative judgment or evaluation*. It is this that he views as wrong and going beyond Scripture. Of course, people will see something "different" as they look at different Christians. Some have one gift and some another (Paul himself makes this point with force in ch. 12), but Paul refuses to allow that this

"seeing something as different" provides grounds for judging status or spirituality. There *are* differences between Christians, and these have been noted. How those differences are approached is what concerns Paul. His next sentence addresses this. Meanwhile, we translate the verb, probably inadequately, as "judges between," which we hope connotes differentiation but also judgment that ends in a verdict for better or worse.

They had nothing that they had not "received" (ἔλαβες). The aorist tense suggests that Paul looks back to their conversion when they received the Holy Spirit and the gifts that God gave them. "You" (singular) received things as a gift. This is where there is no differentiation. They did not earn their gifts. They do not grow into this gift or that. There is no opportunity here for triumphalism or elitism. Whatever they have, they received from God by grace. If this is true, Paul goes on, then how can they boast? The repetition of the final clause, "as if you did not receive it" (ὡς μὴ λαβών) simply reinforces the point that what they have is a gift.

4:8a–c Already you are filled! Already you have become rich! You have come to reign without us! (ἤδη κεκορεσμένοι ἐστέ· ἤδη ἐπλουτήσατε· χωρὶς ἡμῶν ἐβασιλεύσατε). This section of vv. 8–13 is deeply ironic and even sarcastic. Paul now demonstrates the vast difference of approach to life between the way of the cross, followed by Paul and the apostles, and the way of those who consider themselves spiritually superior in the Corinthian church. This much is obvious. The use of "already" (ἤδη) is emphatic at the start of the sentences and serves to introduce the tenor and style of what Paul is about to say. By using the phrase "without us" (χωρὶς ἡμῶν), Paul points out that the "spirituals"

---

14. This is also true of translations such as "Who distinguishes you?" (Garland, *1 Corinthians*, 131) or "Who makes you different from anyone else?" (Ciampa and Rosner, *First* *Corinthians*, 174), which carry in English the connotation of division but not of forensic judgment that is Paul's concern in the context.

say they have or experience something even the apostles do not.

However, it is less obvious just what it is that these "superior" people really did believe (the plural "you" probably does not refer to all the Corinthian Christians). Thiselton has been the clearest proponent in recent years of those who argue that the issue Paul addresses is an overrealized eschatology. The use of "already" (ἤδη), he says, is a "clear signal" of this.[15] By this he means that the Corinthians believed that the kingdom of God had already arrived. He quotes Barrett: "For them there is no 'not yet' to qualify the 'already' of realized eschatology."[16] One of the problems with this view is that it assumes a rather coherent theology on the part of the Corinthians, and the evidence for this is perhaps not as clear as is suggested.

There is no doubt that Paul's argument in 1:18–25 is a deep "theology of the cross." This sets the tone and basis for Paul's criticism of the Corinthians. However, Paul then talks much about the *practice* of the Christian life in Corinth. They are dividing people and boasting in leaders. They are suggesting some are more spiritual than others, and they are undoubtedly advocating a view of "status" or "standing" in the body of Christ that leaves out some Christians. But it is precisely here that there may be a flaw in the view that the Corinthian spirituals held a full-fledged theology of a realized eschatology. Paul does not have to ask them, "Do you not know there is yet more to come?" He says, "Do you not know that you are God's temple and the Spirit of God dwells in you?" (3:16). This statement would surely be in danger of *confirming* an overrealized eschatology. Certainly they knew this. Their division of the church was not so much between those who had "arrived" (in an eschatological sense) and those who had not (after all, even the "spirituals" still saw other Christians as part of the church) but between those who claimed a higher level of standing because of their particular grace-gifts. Paul's response is to force the Corinthians to think through the logic of their position. If all have the Spirit, all must be spiritual. To say some are not is thus, in effect, to say that such people do not belong because they are not actually Christians! This is the logic also of Paul's sarcasm in what follows. He is forcing the elitists to think more deeply about what they are *really* saying of others if they claim this super spirituality for themselves.

It is therefore their theology of "belonging" (the theology of the Spirit's indwelling presence in the believer) and of "maturity" with which Paul is most concerned. This is why his response to the problems he sees at Corinth has to do with the "markers" of the Christian faith and with ethics.[17] The Corinthians are *behaving as if* they have achieved the highest spiritual status and so are *behaving as if* the cross no longer mattered.

The argument that follows really only works if it is assumed, as we have done thus far in this commentary, that the Corinthians did not despise Paul and were not in head-to-head combat with him. Otherwise, Paul's argument would surely confirm them in their position. Paul still talks to them as one who is their father, who thinks of them as beloved children and who expects them to respond to him as children to a father. He clearly believes that his relationship with them is deep and sufficiently personal, and that he carries enough authority that they will not only listen but will heed his call to "imitate me" (4:16). Paul knows his sarcasm will

---

15. Thiselton, *1 Corinthians*, 357–59. See also, Anthony C. Thiselton, "Realized Eschatology at Corinth," *NTS* 24 (1978): 510–26.

16. Barrett, *First Corinthians*, 109.

17. The question of Paul's ethics and his response to the Corinthians is pursued by Kuck, *Judgment and Community Conflict*. More recently, Garland, *1 Corinthians*, 137–39, has also challenged the "overrealized eschatology" position.

therefore be hurtful to them, but it is not designed to undermine or destroy them (see on vv. 14–16).

The three rhetorical questions talk of being "filled" (κεκορεσμένοι), having become "rich" (ἐπλουτήσατε), and "having come to reign" (ἐβασιλεύσατε). The aorists are ingressive,[18] that is, they emphasize the starting point of what has happened or is happening. The "images are descriptive of thoroughly secularized leadership."[19] These leaders have "arrived" not so much in a theological sense but in a secular sense that the Corinthian world around them would have recognized. They truly reflect the values of the wisdom of this age.[20] How different this is from the apostles, who must take a "shameful place at the end of the procession" (see below on v. 9).[21]

4:8d And indeed I wish you did reign, so that we might reign with you! (καὶ ὄφελόν γε ἐβασιλεύσατε, ἵνα καὶ ἡμεῖς ὑμῖν συμβασιλεύσωμεν). As his rather sarcastic comment continues, Paul expresses a wish that will not be fulfilled. If they "reign," he wishes he also reigned!

While the Corinthians see life in these terms because they are so secular and so arrogant in their worldly thinking, Paul knows that there is a time that has not yet arrived when God's people *will* be "filled" (cf. Ps 63:5; Luke 1:53) and "become rich" (cf. Pss 21:3; 112:3) and "reign" with God (cf. Dan 7:27; 2 Tim 2:12; Rev 20:6). Paul, the suffering apostle, must indeed have wished that they really "reigned" so he could also do so, but that time has yet to come. What the Corinthians needed to understand was that such glory awaits Christ's glo-rious coming and bears no relationship to secular notions of glory.[22] Though they might behave as if they had it all and had, as it were, arrived, they must understand that they do not yet reign either in the church or, especially, in their contemporary society. This is not the way of the kingdom of God, a matter to which Paul will return in v. 20.

4:9 For it seems to me,[23] God has exhibited us apostles[24] last of all as men sentenced to death because we have been made a spectacle to the world, to both angels and human beings (δοκῶ γάρ, ὁ θεὸς ἡμᾶς τοὺς ἀποστόλους ἐσχάτους ἀπέδειξεν ὡς ἐπιθανατίους, ὅτι θέατρον ἐγενήθημεν τῷ κόσμῳ καὶ ἀγγέλοις καὶ ἀνθρώποις). Paul now begins a series of contrasts between the way the apostles live and how they appear to the world around them, and how the "spirituals" in Corinth live and appear to those around them.

It is easy to miss Paul's point here. It is not just that the apostles have one lifestyle and the Corinthians another, one which is not as beneficial or God-serving. Paul shows that what the apostles' lives look like is *the work of God*. God is the subject of the sentence, and it is he who "has exhibited" (ἀπέδειξεν) the apostles in this way. God has put the apostles "on show" like men doomed to die. This is "because" (ὅτι introduces the reason), says Paul, "we have been made" a "spectacle" (θέατρον; see Acts 19:29, 31; cf. our word "theatre"). Thus, Paul is not talking about a voluntary ascetic lifestyle that he has adopted but of what God has called him and the apostles to *be* in Christ. They carry about the gospel of Christ crucified, not just in word but also

---

18. Moule, *Idiom Book of New Testament Greek*, 11.

19. Clarke, *Secular and Christian Leadership in Corinth*, 123.

20. Winter, *Philo and Paul among the Sophists*, 198–99, shows how the terms that Paul uses of the elitists, "full, rich and reigning" are those that find obvious parallels in the boasting of the Sophists. See Philo, *Worse* 33–34.

21. Ibid.

22. In 6:1–3 Paul urges the Corinthians to handle grievances between people in the church wisely in this age given that, in the next, God's people will not only reign with him but also judge with him.

23. "I think" (δοκῶ), when used to introduce a main clause of a sentence as here, comes to mean "I think of it like this," or, "It seems to me," in common English.

24. For "apostles" see on 1:1.

in their bodies. They are living pictures of the one they follow. (Paul also develops this perspective in 2 Cor 4:12.) What is of note, however, is that Paul insists here that this is not just an apostolic calling. In these matters, all believers are to imitate the apostles (v. 17) since all are called to follow Christ, even in taking up their cross (Luke 9:23).

The picture Paul paints may recall a procession of the "worthies" of society behind whom, at the very end (ἐσχάτους; "last") come those who are about to enter the arena where they will be killed.[25] The adjective here functioning as a noun, "sentenced to death" (ἐπιθανατίους) only appears here in the New Testament. In its one use in the LXX (Bel 31–32) it describes those who are thrown to the lions. Here in 1 Corinthians 4:9, the apostles have become a spectacle to the world, and Paul expands this in the final phrase "to both angels and human beings" (καὶ ἀγγέλοις καὶ ἀνθρώποις; datives of reference). In doing this he reminds the Corinthians not so much of the cosmic significance of *apostolic* suffering but of the cosmic significance of the Christ who suffered. It is Christ's sufferings that the apostles reflect, and it is "for Christ" that they are fools (v. 10).

In the verses that follow, the apostle lays out three contrasts between the apostles and the Corinthian leaders. He then points to six ways in which the apostles suffer and returns to three further contrasts. His summary is that they are regarded as no better than refuse (v. 13).

4:10 We are fools for Christ's sake, but you are wise[26] in Christ. We are weak, but you are strong. You are held in honour, but we are dishonored (ἡμεῖς μωροὶ διὰ Χριστόν, ὑμεῖς δὲ φρόνιμοι ἐν Χριστῷ· ἡμεῖς ἀσθενεῖς, ὑμεῖς δὲ ἰσχυροί· ὑμεῖς

ἔνδοξοι, ἡμεῖς δὲ ἄτιμοι). Paul builds on his opening exposition of "foolishness" and "wisdom," and with heavy irony he takes the world's view of wisdom as his starting point. On this view, the lives of the apostles appear as foolish as the teaching of a Christ crucified (1:18–25). From that perspective, the Corinthian leaders seem "wise in Christ." "For Christ's sake,"[27] Paul and other apostles are fools. The "we" (ἡμεῖς) refers to Apollos and Paul and probably the other apostles (v. 9). These three abrupt contrasting statements have no verb in Greek, though a verb is needed to provide the sense in English. The terseness that this produces makes Paul's statement pointed.

The apostle insists one group seems "weak," the other "strong." In the light of his introduction (see more detailed comments at 1:26–27) in which he had said that God chose the weak and was shaming the strong, this contrast is filled with irony.[28] Put simply, Paul is saying that God is for him and judging them. The third contrast is just as strong: the one is "held in honor" and the other "in dishonor" (cf. 12:22–24). To be "honored" (ἔνδοξος) was what Corinthian society sought. It contrasts with what Paul had noted in 1:26; that is, that when they came to faith not many were "well born." Now they claim "honor," while the apostles continue to be dishonored. In v. 11 we see how this disrepute is publicly observed.

4:11–12b Up to the present hour we are hungry and thirsty and are poorly dressed and beaten and homeless and we grow tired working with our own hands (ἄχρι τῆς ἄρτι ὥρας καὶ πεινῶμεν καὶ διψῶμεν καὶ γυμνιτεύομεν καὶ κολαφιζόμεθα καὶ ἀστατοῦμεν καὶ κοπιῶμεν ἐργαζόμενοι ταῖς ἰδίαις χερσίν). Paul introduces his list of sufferings with

---

25. Dio Chrysostom, *Orations* 31.121 describes the contests of the arena in Corinth.

26. Note that Paul uses φρόνιμοι here, meaning "sensible" or "wise," rather than σοφοί "wise." This is probably stylistic.

27. διά + accusative; cf. v. 6.

28. See the essay entitled, "In Depth: Shame," after comments on 6:5–6.

a temporal phrase. "Up to the present hour"[29] reminds the Corinthians that things have not changed in his life since he left them. The suffering is not some temporary phase that apostles grow out of as they become more "spiritual." Rather, even as he writes, he and others among them are experiencing suffering for the sake of Christ. This point is made stronger by the final repetition of a temporal clause (ἕως ἄρτι) at the end of the list in 4:13.

His list of sufferings is revealing. Today, to talk of "suffering for the gospel" tends to refer to persecution or occasionally to privations that missionaries make as they travel. But here Paul puts together all the sufferings that are related to his life as an apostle. In other words, he does not distinguish between grades of suffering. For example, the beatings are not more significant than having to work for his own support. He describes the general unpleasantness of life that distinguishes him from the well-honored citizen of Corinth, who would not be beaten and would not have to work with his own hands.

Though much has been made of supposed parallels in other literature to Paul's list of sufferings,[30] they are of little value in helping interpret what Paul is doing here. Paul is talking about his own real-life experiences, and he offers them by way of example for the Corinthians to follow.[31] Through these verses Paul evokes memories of the teaching of Christ. He perhaps specifically has this in mind as he looks at what Christ taught and matches his own life and experience up against that teaching. Christ had taught the need to "take up the cross" and deny oneself in following him (Mark 8:34). It is this that Paul models in his life. Being "hungry

and thirsty" may reflect the fact that Paul refused sophisticated patronage from the wealthy, but it is more likely to reflect his experience as he travelled with the gospel and endured imprisonments (e.g., Phil 4:10–14).

Jesus speaks of the disciples having "hunger" and so being "satisfied" (Luke 6:21). He further speaks of his disciples being "hated" and "excluded" and "reviled" by society (Luke 6:22), and this is precisely what Paul and the apostles are experiencing. The Corinthian leaders are not experiencing this. "To be poorly dressed" (γυμνιτεύω) does not appear elsewhere in the New Testament. More commonly the word meant "to go lightly armed." The so-called "wise" would no doubt have been well dressed in a manner suitable for their elevated status in the community. The verb "to beat" (κολαφίζω; here a passive) can mean being beaten up or being ill or even mistreated in the way that would be a common experience for those who were dishonored (v. 10). Any of these meanings would suit the context, but after the "hunger" and "thirst" it may be better to see this as actual bodily harm received either from crowds or in prison. "Homeless" is the lot of a missionary who is constantly travelling. We are reminded of Jesus who had nowhere to call home (Matt 8:20). We should also recall that Paul holds this up as part of what they should imitate in him. The word can mean "vagabond," and hence one who wanders from place to place "without a permanent residence."[32] It contrasts therefore with those in the Corinthian community who have their fine houses and are well-settled citizens of this world rather than of the kingdom of God.

Finally, in this list Paul says "we grow tired

---

29. ἄχρι + genitive τῆς ὥρας, which is qualified by ἄρτι functioning as an adjective.

30. See Horsley, _1 Corinthians_, 71. For a full discussion of this list of sufferings in the light of other literature and the attitudes to suffering in the Hellenistic world in which Paul lives, see John T. Fitzgerald, _Cracks in an Earthen Vessel: An_

Examination of the Catalogues of Hardships in the Corinthian Correspondence, SBLDS 99 (Atlanta: Scholars Press, 1988).

31. Paul's most extended exposition of his sufferings is found in 2 Cor 11:23–29. See also 2 Cor 4:8–12; 6:4–10.

32. BDAG 145; Thiselton, _1 Corinthians_, 362.

working with our own hands."[33] In one sense this was probably simply the genuinely felt experience of one who not only spent much time teaching and preaching, often until late at night, but who also had a "day job" that kept him busy. Paul makes a point of this elsewhere (1 Thess 2:9; 4:11; 2 Thess 3:6–10). A further implication in what he was saying, though, would have been significant to those to whom he was writing. Many looked down on manual work. It would not have been expected of the sophisticated of society.

In this way Paul concludes a list of six descriptions of apostolic ministry that would not have fitted well into the thinking of the "spirituals" in leadership positions in Corinth. He concludes this forceful argument with a further series of three descriptions of their behavior. The apostolic response to their own situation is not one of annoyance or of feeling that they were entitled to greater respect. Rather, it was to seek to be Christ-like through everything.

4:12c–13b when scoffed at, we speak kindly; when persecuted, we endure; when slandered, we entreat with kindness (λοιδορούμενοι εὐλογοῦμεν, διωκόμενοι ἀνεχόμεθα, δυσφημούμενοι παρακαλοῦμεν). Paul reflects again in his behavior what Christ has held out both in teaching and by way of example (Luke 6:28; 23:34). The adverbial participles here (all present, passive nominatives) are usually translated as temporal: "When reviled . . ." (NIV, RSV, NRSV, ESV). However, they could also be translated as concessive, in effect forming the protasis of a concessive sentence: "If we are reviled . . . ."[34] The choice here makes little difference. The word "scoff at" (λοιδορέω) can mean "revile." The apostle Peter uses the same word in speaking of Jesus: "When he was *reviled*, he did not revile in return" (1 Pet 2:23 ESV). The apostolic

response to reviling and scoffing is to bless, that is, to "say something good" (εὐλογέω). Their response to persecution is to endure. They do not fight back.

Since the apostles suffered in this way, Paul, like Peter, was probably consciously following the Lord's teaching that Christ's disciples would be persecuted and that in enduring they would find life (Luke 21:12–19; using a different word for endurance in v. 19: ὑπομονή). "To slander" (δυσφημέω) means making false accusations against someone, to which Paul says they respond by "entreat[ing] with kindness." This verb (παρακαλέω) has a wide range of meaning. It is what the Holy Spirit does in coming alongside the believer (John 14:16). The word also can carry the connotation of putting forward a legal case, or it may simply refer to the offer of friendship. Thus, the RSV has "we try to conciliate" and the ESV "we entreat." What Paul means here is that as the apostles are slandered so they continue to speak truthfully of Christ, *entreating people with kindness*, despite the deliberate distortion of their position presented by the slanderers.

In retrospect, for those of us with the whole of Scripture before us, it is almost impossible to read this passage without thinking of the one whom Paul sought to imitate at all points, the one who "was oppressed, and he was afflicted, yet he opened not his mouth; like a lamb that is led to the slaughter, and like a sheep that before its shearers is silent, so he opened not his mouth" (Isa 53:7 ESV). Just as Philip expounded this passage to the Ethiopian eunuch in Acts 8:32, so all the apostles sought to live out the life of the Christ they preached. Thus, Paul comes to a final summary of the experience of life that is the apostles' experience.

4:13c–d we have become like[35] the scum of the world, the refuse of all to this very day (ὡς

---

33. The participle ἐργαζόμενοι is complementary and the dative ταῖς ἰδίαις χερσίν is instrumental: "with" our own hands).

34. Moule, *Idiom Book of New Testament Greek*, 150.
35. "Like" translates the comparative particle (ὡς).

περικαθάρματα τοῦ κόσμου ἐγενήθημεν, πάντων περίψημα ἕως ἄρτι). Paul's summary is that when seen from the world's perspective, the apostles are the very least of the least. The temporal phrase "to this very day" (ἕως ἄρτι) received comment in 4:11 and so serves to enclose this subsection. The genitive "of the world" (τοῦ κόσμου) recalls 1:20, 27, and 2:12.

The two words "scum" and "refuse" mean more or less the same thing.[36] They carry the sense of that which is scraped off or wiped away. The words are used as a term of abuse. Neither appears elsewhere in the New Testament. However, both words can sometimes refer to an expiatory sacrifice, since purification is achieved through the removal of that which is "scraped off" (περικάθαρμα). This is possibly the meaning of LXX Proverbs 21:18.[37] In Tobit 5:19 "scapegoat" may be the right translation of περίψημα.[38] Soards views this as significant, suggesting that Paul ends this series not on two negative notes, but on a note that points to the reason for the suffering and is thus positive. He says, "Paul may mean to offer two positive images of ransom in apposition." Pointing to Paul's constant referral back to Christ and his suffering on the cross which brings salvation, he says that "it makes good sense" to believe that in naming the apostles as the scum of the earth, Paul also "names them as God's agents in salvation." He thus translates: "Being slandered, we call out, having become like scum—an expiation for the world, refuse—a ransom for all until now."[39] The difficulty with this view is that the evidence for this meaning is very limited; yet, more significantly it does not easily fit with what Paul

is actually saying here. He is arguing throughout that "even to this point" his life reflects the dregs of society. He goes on to say that he does not write these things to make them ashamed. It is most unlikely therefore that Paul, suddenly at the end of this list, turns around and makes something positive of all that he has been saying. He continues to speak from the viewpoint of this world's wisdom, and thus the apostles remain "the scum." Nothing will change that.

4:14 I do not write these things to make you ashamed, but rather to warn you as my dearly loved children (Οὐκ ἐντρέπων ὑμᾶς γράφω ταῦτα, ἀλλ' ὡς τέκνα μου ἀγαπητὰ νουθετῶν).[40] Some commentators argue that the tone changes now.[41] But what follows is very much part of the same message that has gone before. Paul has written much. His contrasts between the apostles and the Corinthian leadership have been hard hitting. Nonetheless, throughout his description Paul has been concerned for them as a father with his children. He has talked on a number of occasions to them as "brothers and sisters" (1:10, 26, 2:1; 3:1; 4:6), but now he passionately insists that the purpose of his writing is to warn them as a father might warn his children. Fathers sometimes have to warn children forcefully, but they do so because they love their children, and Paul wants to ensure that the Corinthians understand this and will remain in this relationship with him. These verses again speak against the idea that Paul was the subject of a strong attack from the Corinthian leadership. It is written by one who clearly still has a

---

36. G. Stählin, "περίψημα," *TDNT* 6:84–93.

37. BDAG 801.

38. BDAG 808.

39. Soards, *1 Corinthians*, 98, 100. With Barrett, *First Corinthians*, 113, he believes that Paul may have had in mind a deliberate *double entendre*.

40. The variant readings of νουθετῶ[ν] (see NA[28]) do not materially affect the meaning of this verse. The participle form is more likely grammatically. It could be argued that the form νουθετῶ would be the harder reading.

41. Conzelmann, *1 Corinthians*, 91; also Brian J. Dodd, *Paul's Paradigmatic 'I': Personal Example as Literary Strategy*, JSNTSup 177 (Sheffield: JSOT Press, 1999), 65.

relationship of love, leadership, and authority in the community. Plainly, some of the leaders must have been puzzled or even in disagreement with Paul about the matters he has been addressing with them, but Paul does so from a position of love and acceptance, and he expects to be heard because of this relationship with them.

"These things" (ταῦτα) refers to all that Paul has said thus far, not just the last few verses. Two contrasting purpose clauses follow. First, Paul speaks negatively. The participle provides the purpose clause (ἐντρέπων). He does *not* write to "shame" them.[42] (Note this is not the verb καταισχύνω that was discussed in 1:27 with its connotations of God's judgment.) In a status-conscious community in which appearances matter more than they should, Paul wants to be clear that he is not deliberately seeking to make them feel "put down." His intention is not publicly to insult or demean them in front of each other or before the world. His intention throughout has been to seek to help them see that their "belonging," their status, is safe and secure, yet "in Christ" this will be seen in ways that the world does not recognize. In today's terminology, their "self-esteem" should not lie in what they look like, what gifts they have received, or how sophisticated their speech and behavior are. It should be found simply in the grace and love of the Lord. So Paul does not write to undermine them as people, but rather to warn them as his "dearly loved children" and as one who is their "father" in Christ (v. 15).

With a strong adversative Paul says, "but rather [ἀλλά] . . . [I write] to warn" (νουθετῶν, another purpose participle). This verb "to warn" or "admon-

ish" (ESV) is used in a variety of contexts, but is used elsewhere of what a father does for his children (see Wis 11:10 LXX). In this sense, such warnings are not threats but words and actions designed to help a person mature as behavior changes.[43]

Paul's gentle pastoral heart is on view for all to see here. It is one of the sadnesses of the modern world that our tendency is always to equate genuine love with softness of speech and character. Paul's true love for these people is to be seen at its clearest in the verses that have preceded this. Here we see Paul's understanding that as one who is loved by them and as one who loves them, his words will hurt. So he reinforces and builds on the relationship that *alone* actually allows him to be able to say what he has said and still receive a hearing. If they did not actually grant this relationship, then Paul's words would fall on deaf ears.

4:15a–b For if you had perhaps ten-thousand teachers in Christ, certainly you do not have many fathers (ἐὰν γὰρ μυρίους παιδαγωγοὺς ἔχητε ἐν Χριστῷ ἀλλ᾽ οὐ πολλοὺς πατέρας).[44] Pedagogues (παιδαγωγός), or "teachers" were well-known figures in Hellenistic society.[45] They were usually trusted slaves who would keep a child of a wealthy family at his studies. Often pictured with a stick in hand, they were regarded as something of a taskmaster. Paul contrasts himself and his loving, fatherly behavior with those who carry a stick. In v. 21, with a degree of ironic humor he will ask them whether this is what they want or whether they would prefer the stick! "Certainly"[46] introduces the apodosis of the conditional sentence.

Paul's appeal to fatherhood here is not simply a metaphor concerning his love for the church,

---

42. See the essay entitled, "In Depth: Shame," following comments on 6:5–6.

43. See, for example, Rom 15:14; Eph 6:4; 1 Thess 5:12, 14.

44. "For" (γάρ) is continuative. The ἐὰν + subjunctive construction introduces the protasis of the condition, which is indefinite; hence our addition of "perhaps." Though the sub-

junctive (ἔχητε) is in the present tense, the remote hypothetical nature of the condition translates readily using the past in English.

45. Conzelmann, *1 Corinthians*, 91n10.

46. The word ἀλλά here fulfills its intensifying function (Dana and Mantey, *Manual Grammar*, 240).

though it is partly that.[47] In fact, Paul's role among them did involve bringing them into being or "bearing" them, as the next sentence shows.[48] However, it is quite beyond the evidence of the text and the tone of this section to see Paul presenting himself here "as the *one* who 'in Christ Jesus' had become their 'father through the gospel,' as opposed to myriads of 'guardians' or baby-sitters (another put down of Apollos!)."[49] Paul does not speak like this of Apollos, whom he always sees as an associate in gospel ministry.

4:15c–d for in Christ Jesus I fathered you through the gospel (ἐν γὰρ Χριστῷ Ἰησοῦ διὰ τοῦ εὐαγγελίου ἐγὼ ὑμᾶς ἐγέννησα). Paul goes back once again to those early days when many came to faith. The whole work was "in Christ." It was by Christ and through Christ, but the Lord used Paul in that work as he preached the gospel. "Through the gospel" (διὰ τοῦ εὐαγγελίου) expresses the means by which this happened. So he says that by means of the gospel, in Christ I "bore you" or "fathered you" (γεννάω). The "gospel" is shorthand for the content of the preaching of Christ and salvation through his incarnation, death, resurrection, and exaltation.[50] It is from *within* this special relationship with the Corinthians that Paul can now add his appeal.

4:16 Therefore, I urge you, be imitators of me (παρακαλῶ οὖν ὑμᾶς, μιμηταί μου γίνεσθε). Paul wants the Corinthians to reflect the Christ in whom they believe. His own life, so strange to the worldly-wise, can help them see what this means in practice day by day. The appeal looks both back-

ward and forward in Paul's argument. "Therefore" (οὖν) builds not just on the appeal to his fatherhood in Christ but to his previous argument, especially to what he has said about the apostles and their life as scum of the earth. The exhortation encloses the whole section from 1:10 where Paul started out with the words "I urge you." In comments on 1:10, the meaning of "to urge" (παρακαλέω) was discussed. It was suggested there that Paul uses the word by way of "firm encouragement" but not as harsh rhetoric. This is the father talking to his children. He is passionate but loving as he "urges" them to look at him, yet the "therefore" (οὖν) reminds us that his example is in fact no more than what is seen among all the apostles (vv. 9–13). He is the one to imitate, for he is *theirs*.

The idea of *imitation* here does not imply a simple copying of all that Paul does or says. As this letter makes clear, in God's economy some are apostles and some are not. All have gifts from God, but they vary in purpose and intent for the community. Paul's concern is that the Corinthians imitate him in the sense that they follow both his teaching and his practice in whatever life they have been called to lead. (See also comments at 11:1.) Paul wants their lives to reflect the saving gospel of Christ, and that means not a life of triumphalism, elitism, sophistic arrogance, or status seeking but rather *a life that reflects the crucified Christ*.

This great appeal from Paul has been sadly distorted as some have read it as arrogant or paternalistic and others as manipulative.[51] In fact Paul wants nothing but the best for those who came to

---

47. On Paul's use of familial terms in this letter, see Trevor J. Burke, "Paul's Role as 'Father' to his 'Children' in Socio-Historical Context (1 Cor. 4:14–21)," in Burke and Elliott, *Paul and the Corinthians*, 95–113.

48. Andrew D. Clarke, *Serve the Community of the Church: Christians as Leaders and Ministers*, First-Century Christians in the Graeco-Roman World (Grand Rapids: Eerdmans, 2000), 218–23.

49. *Contra* Horsley, *1 Corinthians*, 72.

50. See comments on 15:1.

51. Horsley, *1 Corinthians*, 72. Thiselton, *1 Corinthians*, 370–73, looks more deeply at some of the criticisms not just of Paul as manipulator but also his supposed paternalism and authoritarianism. He interacts specifically with the arguments of Elizabeth A. Castelli, *Imitating Paul: A Discourse of Power* (Louisville: Westminster John Knox, 1991), suggesting that exegetical and even philosophical evidence speaks against her position.

faith as he preached the gospel to them. Looking at him, they will have one example that should guide them, for he is their father in Christ. The children will have different callings and different gifts, but they have enough evidence before them to look again at their own lives and ask what these should look like. In practice, given what Paul has been saying, if they do imitate him then they too will be regarded as the scum of the earth and as "fools."[52] They will also likely recognize Paul's sufferings for the gospel—both his physical deprivations and his suffering at the hands of those who would persecute him. All of this he is asking them to imitate.

4:17a–d For this reason I have sent Timothy to you, who is my beloved child and faithful in the Lord; he will remind you of my ways[53] in Christ Jesus (διὰ τοῦτο ἔπεμψα ὑμῖν Τιμόθεον, ὅς ἐστίν μου τέκνον ἀγαπητὸν καὶ πιστὸν ἐν κυρίῳ, ὃς ὑμᾶς ἀναμνήσει τὰς ὁδούς μου τὰς ἐν Χριστῷ [Ἰησοῦ][54]). Paul has sent Timothy to them "for this reason" (διὰ τοῦτο), that is, to help them understand everything that he has been saying to them. The two clauses introduced by the relative pronoun "who" (ὅς) are descriptive of Timothy. The first describes his relationship to Paul and the second his action on Paul's behalf with regard to the Corinthians. For clarity in English, we translate the second pronoun (ὅς) as a personal pronoun, "he."

The type of aorist used here (ἔπεμψα) is debated. It could be "epistolary" where the writer places himself at the viewpoint of the reader. In English this could become, "I am sending Timothy with my letter" or "I have sent Timothy with my letter." Another possibility is to take this as a more stan-

dard constative aorist and assume that Timothy had visited the Corinthians recently and that this letter was sent following that (recent) visit. A third possibility, which seems more likely in the light of 16:10, is that Paul has now sent Timothy, but he has not yet arrived at Corinth. See comments on 16:10. (This could then be a culminative or effective aorist.) It was likely that Timothy's time of arrival was indefinite rather than his actual travel to Corinth being uncertain. Thus, putting 4:17 together with 16:10, we might paraphrase: "I have sent Timothy to you . . . he will remind you of my ways in Christ . . . whenever he [actually] arrives."

Whatever the case, Timothy had a long-standing relationship with Paul as one of his thoroughly trusted co-workers. This text is an indication that Paul held him in high regard in relation to his behavior as well as his understanding of doctrine and teaching. The son of a Jewish woman and a Greek father, Paul met him in Lystra, where he was "well spoken of," and asked him to travel with him (Acts 16:1–4 ESV). Timothy then travelled widely, sometimes with Paul and sometimes on errands for him. In Paul's second letter to the Corinthians, we discover that Timothy was involved with Paul and Silvanus in the proclamation of the word in Corinth, is one of the senders of that letter, and had an established relationship with the congregation (2 Cor 1:1, 19; cf. 1 Thess 1:1; 2 Thess 1:1).

If the Corinthians want to understand how Paul would like them to be, then Timothy will remind them. He too is Paul's "beloved child" (compare 4:14). Paul had talked of the need for "faithful" (πιστός; 4:2) stewardship, and Timothy is "faithful in the Lord" (πιστὸν ἐν κυρίῳ). If there has been

---

52. Mitchell, *Rhetoric of Reconciliation*, 222: "For each of the comparisons in 4:1–13 by which the Corinthians fared so badly, they are to seek to emulate Paul's behavior. Each type of behavior there . . . is an example of humility and self-effacement as opposed to fractious boasting and self-interest seeking."

53. This is an example of a double accusative (ὑμᾶς . . . τὰς ὁδούς) used with a verb of reminding or teaching. Moule, *Idiom Book of New Testament Greek*, 33. See BDF §155.

54. The textual variants either include "Christ" or do not. The meaning is unaffected. However, the early witnesses of 𝔓[46] and ℵ speak for its inclusion.

any doubt about how Paul viewed the Corinthians, then in Timothy they will find what Paul is seeking of them too. He has grasped what Paul is talking about. If clarification is needed, he will explain it, yet above all he will model it. In Timothy they will be reminded of Paul's "ways in Christ" (τὰς ὁδούς μου τὰς ἐν Χριστῷ). The use of the word "ways" (ὁδοί) probably has a Jewish background to its meaning for Paul. The *halakah*, or "walk" of rabbinic teaching, concerned deeply practical guidance for life.[55] Paul is concerned with how he and Timothy and the Corinthians live their lives "in Christ."[56] The point will reappear in v. 19.

4:17e just as[57] I teach them everywhere in every church (καθὼς πανταχοῦ ἐν πάσῃ ἐκκλησίᾳ διδάσκω). In the light of his comments on the way of life of the apostles as a group, it may reasonably be assumed that Paul is teaching nothing that would not have been taught by any of the other apostles. The phrase "just as everywhere" (καθὼς πανταχοῦ) is adverbial, modifying the present verb "I teach" (διδάσκω). Paul insists that there is nothing novel in what he seeks of the Corinthians. This way of life is exactly what he has taught in all the churches that he has founded. In Paul's writings the word "church" (ἐκκλησία) normally refers to the local church, but here we see how Paul's thinking does not easily separate the local from the wider group of churches. The church as a whole, in all its gath-

erings, is to be characterized by a lifestyle, a morality, and an attitude toward others that reflect the Christ she worships, the Christ "crucified."

4:18 Now, as if I were not coming to you, some have become puffed up (ὡς μὴ ἐρχομένου δέ μου πρὸς ὑμᾶς ἐφυσιώθησάν τινες). In Paul's absence some have become truly conceited and are flaunting their pride. In verses 18–19 Paul warns them he will come to visit. A genitive absolute (ἐρχομένου . . . μου) is introduced by a particle (ὡς) meaning "as if." The main clause then picks up on 4:6 and reminds the readers that some[58] leaders have "become puffed up" (ἐφυσιώθησάν) enough to ignore all that is being said to them, so their arrogance deeply concerns Paul. He simply asserts that what he has said must be listened to and he will visit to ensure that his fatherly advice has been followed by the children he loves. Paul again here and in v. 19 uses the derogatory verb "puff up" (φυσιόω) that he had first used in 4:6 to describe the arrogant (see also 5:2; 8:1; 13:4). Later, in 8:1 Paul will specifically call attention to the way in which they have let the gift of "knowledge" become a cause of being "puffed up."

4:19 but I will come to you soon, if the Lord wills, and I will find out not the speech of the puffed up but their power (ἐλεύσομαι δὲ ταχέως πρὸς ὑμᾶς, ἐὰν ὁ κύριος θελήσῃ, καὶ γνώσομαι οὐ

---

55. In Deut 8:6 the Israelites are urged to walk "in [the] ways" of God (ESV; cf. Deut 10:12 and multiple references in the LXX to walking in God's ways. See especially Ps 119 where these ways are set against false ways.)

56. See Alfred Seeberg, "Moral Teaching: The Existence and Contents of 'the Ways,'" in *Understanding Paul's Ethics: Twentieth Century Approaches*, ed. Brian S. Rosner (Grand Rapids: Eerdmans, 1995), 161–63. Seeberg takes a substantially different view of Paul's intent here. He argues that Paul's intent in calling for this imitation is not directly related to his conduct. He asks why Timothy would be needed to remind them of his conduct when he had laid it out for them even in the immediately preceding verses. He argues that "the ways" "are not Paul's

way of life but rather designate the *name of the Christian moral teaching*, which was Paul's moral teaching, insofar as he made use of it in his ministry . . . (my ways) should therefore be considered in the same sense as τὸ εὐαγγέλιόν μου (my gospel; Rom 2:16, 2 Tim 2:8)." This, he suggests, makes much better sense of what Paul means when he goes on to say in v. 17, "As I teach them everywhere in every church."

57. Continuing Seeberg's interpretation (see note above) here involves taking καθὼς as meaning "in the manner, in which" or "of the content, which content." Paul is thus referring to a body of moral teaching he gives everywhere.

58. The subject of the main clause is "some" (τινες).

τὸν λόγον τῶν πεφυσιωμένων ἀλλὰ τὴν δύναμιν). Paul will come "speedily" (ταχέως). The nature of this visit is further expanded in 16:1–8 where we find that it was somewhat delayed. Its purpose, as chapter 16 indicates, is multifaceted. Here, though, Paul spells out that when he comes he will find out or "come to know"[59] what is going on with these people. The simple conditional "if the Lord wills" does not express indefiniteness in Paul's intention, but it allows that the providence of God may intervene. It is a common expression among Christians even today. Paul will come soon.

He refers to their "speech" (τὸν λόγον). The translation "speech" is not as smooth here as "talk," which most versions prefer. But this loses the important connection with the word as it has appeared before in this epistle where it can be translated "speech." These links help us understand what is going on in Paul's thinking, yet they also return us to the fundamental issue for the "spirituals." How do the gifts of the Spirit, especially speech, wisdom, and knowledge—all the gifts that would be especially valued in their Hellenistic society—function among them? Paul has thanked God for their grace-gift of "speech" in 1:5. He has spoken of this gift elsewhere. He has contrasted the world's "speech" or "word" with that of Christ and his own (1:17–18; 2:1, 4, 13). The test that Paul sets for those who claim "speech" as a gift is the test he will set for all Christians since all have grace-gifts. Does it build up? In other words, what do these people *do*? If these gifts genuinely come from the Spirit, then the power of the Spirit will be at work as they are used. If not, then they are simply self-serving products of the value system of "this age." Paul's own "speech" (λόγος) among them had been far from impressive, humanly speaking, but the Spirit

had moved with "power" (δύναμις) and people had come to faith (2:3–5). Here in vv. 19–20 Paul is in effect saying he will "call their bluff"!

4:20 For the kingdom of God is not a matter of speech but of power (οὐ γὰρ ἐν λόγῳ ἡ βασιλεία τοῦ θεοῦ ἀλλ' ἐν δυνάμει). The basis on which Paul will call their bluff is the nature of the kingdom of God itself, which manifests the power of God through the Spirit of God. The adversative (ἀλλά) and lack of verb intensify the contrast and make it terse. Paul is speaking of God's dynamic rule, his reign in kingly power, and the fulfillment of *his* purposes of salvation that will one day reach the great consummation in the return of the King himself.[60] Paul takes the idea of "the kingdom of God" as a given when writing to the Corinthians. Herein lies the source of the power of which he has been talking. This kingdom has been inaugurated by King Jesus, the Messiah. One day when "the end" comes, Christ will deliver "the kingdom to God the Father after destroying every rule and every authority and power" (15:24–25 ESV). The present rule of Christ among the people will only be seen if the power of God is evident in the church.

When Paul comes to Corinth, he will be seeking to discover evidence that God in Christ is at work through these leaders. He fears that their grace-gifts, abused to buy them status and honor within the community, will offer no such evidence. The irony is that real evidence will be offered as people's lives are so changed that they become Christ-like and even "apostle-like," as has been described earlier. It is in weakness, in being the scum of the earth and yet living for God and his rule that kingdom power will be manifest. This is what Paul desires to see, and so he ends with a statement that is regarded by most as harsh or heavy-handed.

---

59. The middle voice of γινώσκω gives the sense of "coming to know."

60. See the essay, "In Depth: The Kingdom of God," following comments at 6:9a.

4:21 What do you desire?[61] **Shall I come to you with**[62] **a rod, or in love and in a spirit of gentleness?** (τί θέλετε; ἐν ῥάβδῳ ἔλθω πρὸς ὑμᾶς ἢ ἐν ἀγάπῃ πνεύματί τε πραΰτητος;). As Paul comes to the end of a hard but loving reprimand of his beloved children, there is surely a note of compassionate humor here. Of course the children would prefer that he come in love and with a spirit of gentleness, that is, without the rod!

The main question with this verse is whether Paul concludes with a "threat"[63] or with a more gentle attitude.[64] If it is assumed throughout that Paul is in head-on confrontation with the Corinthians, then this may well be read as a summary threat at the end of this section. However, we have seen little if any evidence for such complete confrontation. Paul's appeal has depended throughout on the fact that even the leaders with whom he disagrees still have enough of a respect for him that they will listen. Another way of viewing this verse is to remember that, thus far, Paul has used a considerable amount of irony, especially in 4:8–13, following which he denied that he wished to make them feel ashamed. Rather, he wanted them to understand that they were being admonished as children. He has referred to a pedagogue or teacher, often seen by both the Greeks and in the Old Testament as the one with a stick or rod,[65] and now he offers them a choice. He can play the pedagogue with them and come with a rod, or he can be the father! There is, we suggest, a degree of ironic humor here. This does not undermine the serious nature of what the apostle has been talking about, especially in light of the immorality that he will go on to address in the next chapter.

Theology in Application

Like the Scum of the Earth?

There is little doubt that if a modern preacher, especially in Western countries, were to say what Paul says here about being treated as the scum of the earth, about hungering and thirsting, being poorly dressed, being weak and held in disrepute, we would dismiss them as deluded. Even if we thought they were great biblical teachers, we would still probably comment along the lines of "his hyperbole was a bit overboard today!" The problem for us is that this is the apostle Paul, and as best as we know from here and other Scriptures this was his real experience. So, we have no cause to doubt him. Indeed, there are many Christians in the world who can well identify right now with what Paul describes here. The difficulty for all, though, is that after his description of such hardships he then says that people should imitate him. The challenge of such a passage is therefore far stronger than perhaps we often imagine it. This is not just a call to lead a sacrificial life of servanthood but truly a call to model what we proclaim. Minimally, this must surely mean that we are constantly asking ourselves with our various gifts and different callings in life what this

---

61. The interrogative pronoun (τί) can be used in New Testament Greek to introduce alternatives; thus here it can imply the meaning "which of the two?"

62. The three datives (with ἐν) are all instrumental of manner.

63. Fee, *1 Corinthians*, 209.

64. The genitive "of gentleness," πραΰτητος, is descriptive.

65. The word "rod," ῥάβδος, is used in the LXX for correction and discipline. See, for example, Exod 21:20; Prov 10:13.

means for us. What is it to be so concerned for presenting Christ in our lives that we are not concerned for our own prosperity and our own standing among our friends or at work?

As we look at Scripture as a whole, we see men and women who fully served the Lord and had social standing among believers and even among those in the world at large. The apostle Paul clearly had standing even among the other apostles, given the way he was treated in Jerusalem (Acts 15:4–26; Gal 2:1–10) and given that Peter was later able to refer to Paul's writings as Scriptures (2 Pet 3:15–16). However, it is Paul's attitude to ministry that stands out here, as it does in his autobiographical example in chapter 9. As we hear Paul recounting the way things are for him and the things he has suffered, we know at the same time it was not always like this for him. Yet Paul was prepared at anytime for whatever would come his way as he lived and spoke for the Lord as his servant. It is that *whatever comes* that is the true challenge. *If* God called us to suffer as Paul did, *would we?* In Hebrews 11 the author lists a host of famous biblical characters who were noted for the faith, many of whom were called to suffer for it. What Paul presents is not a unique picture, but his challenge is as personal as any in Scripture. One might almost imagine that Paul kept re-running in his mind clips from the film *The Passion of the Christ*[66] and asking himself, "How can I best speak for and live out the message of this anointed king before the world at large?" Paul's challenge is a profound reminder that we need the Holy Spirit to continue his life-transforming work among us.

Examples to Follow

Paul holds himself up as an example for the Corinthians to follow. Naturally, he is a model as well for all Christians. The seriousness of such modeling of the godly life is seen in multiple passages of Scripture. Theologically, the idea is surely embedded in God's command to his people to "be holy for I am holy" (Lev 11:44–45; 19:2; 1 Pet 1:16). The Old Testament call to holiness, especially for those who lead God's people, means that the challenge that Paul raises with the leadership of this church finds a number of parallels in the charges leveled by the Old Testament prophets at Israel's priesthood. For example, Malachi's challenge of the priesthood (Mal 2) is aimed not only at the way their instruction has led people to stumble but also at their arrogance and sinful lifestyles. The priests were supposed to teach without favoritism and demonstrate God's law in how they lived. It was always expected that God's people would have models before them, even as they listened to God's law. In Jesus that model is seen in full perfection; thus, the imitation of Christ is paramount (1 Cor 11:1).

---

66. A 2004 film directed by Mel Gibson detailing the final hours and crucifixion of Christ and vividly depicting his suffering.

However, the need for Christians to have examples of other Christians to look up to and to learn from is a vital part of growth to maturity in Christ.[67] It can be a humbling experience to look around for people we respect and who we feel, despite their faults, live their lives in ways that reflect Christ. Today, much is said about "mentoring" or "discipling" in Christian circles. This can be helpful for many, but for those who like these things to be more natural and spontaneous, the process of simply looking out for that maturer Christian, befriending them, and then enjoying that friendship provides an ideal place to learn, watch, and imitate. The family picture of a father with his children allows Paul also to talk of "admonishing" them (4:14). To have such respect for a brother or sister in Christ that a person would allow themselves to be "admonished" when necessary is a privilege too few Christians enjoy, yet it is one all should seek out if possible. Conversely, too many Christians who are maturer in their faith and perhaps older—and so have more experience of a life lived with Christ—retreat away from the younger members of churches. Once again, the family model encourages us all to be self-aware and see what God is calling us to. We should make ourselves available for each other that all may grow in Christ.

The Need to Be Accepted

Life would be so much easier for all Christians if they were highly regarded by the societies in which they live. The temptation to be highly regarded affects Christians in all ages, including the present. If it was the reception of certain gifts of the Spirit, such as "speech," "wisdom," or "knowledge" that married up well with the expectations of Hellenistic society, today it may be gifts such as the wealth to give liberally (Rom 12:8), or the gift of teaching, or the gift of good communication that, for the modern church, helps it marry up and consequently compromise with its secular society. There is only one "theology" that will truly challenge the church as it seeks respect and acceptance, and that is the theology of the cross. In many churches a theology of the cross is almost entirely missing. The idea of weakness, of self-sacrifice, of humbling oneself, and of accepting persecution for the Lord is barely heard. Instead, matters of status in the world around concern people more than becoming Christ's obedient servants. Christians act as if they have become rich and have come to reign, and they seek the affection and respect of people who are rooted in the wisdom of this age. Though the kingdom of God is certainly revealed in power, this is God's power in Christ. Thus, a people who truly want to see this must decide, like Paul, "to know nothing among [those around] except Jesus Christ and him crucified" (1 Cor 2:2 ESV).

---

67. Cf. Phil 3:17; 2 Thess 3:7–9; Heb 13:7.

1 Corinthians 5:1–13

Literary Context

Paul has addressed the Corinthians' preoccupation with status, which they have based on what God has given them (4:7). With some sarcasm, the apostle has commented on their demeanor as being like rich people and "kings." They are boasting in their status, something that Paul sees as the behavior of those who follow the wisdom of the world. He has described his own life and presented it in stark contrast to the lives of many in the Corinthian church. He has urged them to listen to him but also to look at his life, and imitate the way he lives for Christ.

It is God's wisdom revealed in the crucified Christ that alone guarantees the status of God's people as a holy people and a covenant community. Truly mature Christians will understand this and pursue God's wisdom. In these opening chapters, Paul has stressed that this sort of wisdom will reflect good discernment and that by it the Corinthians will be able to make right judgments about people, about the nature and function of spiritual gifts, and about what it is to be God's people. In chapters 5–6, Paul addresses grievous sins in which the people, by means of their inaction or tolerance, have revealed their lack of godly wisdom and maturity. In chapter 5 Paul tackles the sin of incest that has been tolerated within the church. He does this in a way that continues to reveal his view of the church as a covenant community that, like Israel before, is called to be holy or else face the Lord's judgment. As he addresses the subject, it is likely that he has in mind passages such as Leviticus 18:8, 20:11, Deuteronomy 22:22, 30, and Deuteronomy 27:20. The expulsion of the sinful from the Israelite community becomes the model for expulsion from the Christian community.

The continuity in chapters 5–6 with what has gone before is revealed in several ways, and the following are a few of these. Firstly, the themes of being "puffed up" and boasting recur (5:2, 6; 6:12). Secondly, the theme of the need for right judgment and discernment recurs (5:3, 9–13; 6:1–6, 12, 15–16, 19). Thirdly, the appeal to the crucified and raised Christ reappears (5:7; 6:14, 20). Fourthly, the ongoing concern with status within and without the church returns (5:10–12; 6:4, 10–11, 17, 20), as does the notion that God's people are themselves the temple of God (6:19). This leads to Paul's development of the theme of holiness, also noted earlier in chapters 1 and 3, as part of the nature of Christian community identity (5:9–13; 6:9–11).

IV. Mature Christians Pursue God's Wisdom (2:6–4:21)

➡ **V. Lack of Spiritual Wisdom Has Led to Grievous Sin (5:1–6:20)**

　　A. A Case of Incest Must Be Resolved (5:1–8)

　　B. Community Identity Requires Holiness (5:9–13)

　　C. Lawsuits between Christians Must Be Resolved without the Courts (6:1–8)

　　D. Community Identity Requires Holiness (6:9–11)

　　E. Immorality Is Incompatible with Union with Christ (6:12–17)

　　F. Community Identity Requires Holiness (6:18–20)

VI. Marriage, Celibacy, Divorce, and Widowhood in Relation to Community Status (7:1–40)

Main Idea

The lack of godly discernment among those who arrogantly assume they possess an elite spiritual status is tragically revealed in their acceptance of immorality in their midst. The church for whom Christ died is to be a holy people, with the presence and power of the Lord Jesus being seen among them. A mature spirituality, arising from the wisdom of God, will properly discern evil in the church's midst and deal with it appropriately through the expulsion of the evil person.

Translation

1 Corinthians 5:1–13

1a	Assertion	**It is actually reported that**
	Place	among you
b		**there is sexual immorality,** and
c	Description	sexual immorality of such a kind that is not even ⏎ tolerated among the pagans.
d	Expansion	Someone is having sex with his father's wife.
2a	Exclamation	And **you are puffed up!**
b	Rhetorical question	And yet **should you not rather have mourned**
c	Result	so that he who has done this might be ⏎ removed
d	Separation	from your midst?

3a	Emphasis	For **I,**
b	Circumstance	though absent
	Sphere	in the body
c	Circumstance	but present
	Sphere	in the spirit,
d	Action	**I have already judged**
		as present
e	Description	**the person** who has done this in this way.

4a	Means	In the name of our Lord Jesus,
b	Time	when you are assembled and my spirit is with you
c	Means	with the power of our Lord Jesus,
5a	Command	**hand over such a man to Satan**
b	Anticipated result	for the destruction of the flesh,
c	Purpose	so that his spirit may be saved in the day of the Lord.

6a	Assertion	**Your boasting is not good.**
b	Rhetorical question	**Do you not know that a little leaven makes the whole batch of dough rise?**
7a	Command	**Clean out the old leaven,**
b	Purpose	so that you may be a new batch,
c	Cause	since you really are unleavened,
d	Basis for command	for Christ our Passover lamb has been sacrificed.
8a	Exhortation	Therefore **let us celebrate the festival,**
b	Manner	not with old leaven or
c	Expansion	leaven of malice and evil, but
d	Manner/contrast	with the unleavened bread of sincerity and truth.

9a	Assertion	**I wrote to you in the letter**
b	Purpose	**not to associate** **with sexually immoral people—**
10a	Explanation	not at all meaning with the sexually immoral of this world or
b	List	with the greedy and thieves or idolaters,
c	Basis	since you would then need to leave the world.

11a	Contrast with 9a	But **now I write to you**
b	Purpose 1	**not to associate with anyone**
c	Description	called a brother [or sister]
d	Condition	if that person goes on being evil or greedy or
e	List	an idolater, or slanderer,
		or a drunkard or thief,
f	Purpose 2	**nor even to eat with such a person.**

12a	Rhetorical question 1	For **what is it to me to judge outsiders?**
b	Rhetorical question 2	**Is it not those inside whom you are to judge?**
13a	Assertion/response 1	**God judges those outside.**
b	Command/proof ...	
c	Citation/(response 2)	"Banish the evil person from among yourselves." [Deut 17:7, 12 inter alia]

Structure

Chapter 5 divides most simply into two parts.

In the first part (vv. 1–8) the question of incest is raised by Paul as a matter of the deepest concern. Such behavior is not even tolerated by pagans, and the fact that it is tolerated by the church reveals the very arrogance of which he has been speaking (4:18–19; 5:1–2a). The imperative of v. 2b indicates at the start Paul's main goal: this evil person must be expelled from the community. He then makes this point in various ways in vv. 5, 7, 9, 11, 13. In vv. 3–5 the process of expulsion is discussed, and in vv. 6–8 an analogy provides a theological basis for the expulsion.

In the second section (vv. 9–13) Paul insists on holiness being one of the vital boundary markers of God's people, referring to the fact that he has already written about this (v. 9). Paul is not concerned with the people of the world (vv. 9–10) but with the Christian community from which the evil person must be expelled (vv. 11–13).

Exegetical Outline

→ **V. Lack of Spiritual Wisdom Has Led to Grievous Sin (5:1–6:20)**
  A. A Case of Incest Must Be Resolved (5:1–8)
    1. The Action the Church Should Take (5:1–2)
    2. The Process of Expulsion (5:3–5)
    3. The Theological Basis for This Action (5:6–8)
  B. Community Identity Requires Holiness (5:9–13)
    1. The Church Is Not to Concern Itself with the Immoral of This World (5:9–10)
    2. The Church Must Concern Itself with the Immoral in Its Own Number (5:11–13)
  C. Lawsuits between Christians Must Be Resolved without the Courts (6:1–8)
  D. Community Identity Requires Holiness (6:9–11)

Explanation of the Text

5:1a–c It is actually reported that among you there is sexual immorality, and sexual immorality of such a kind that is not even tolerated among the pagans (Ὅλως ἀκούεται ἐν ὑμῖν πορνεία, καὶ τοιαύτη πορνεία ἥτις οὐδὲ ἐν τοῖς ἔθνεσιν). "Sexual immorality" (πορνεία) is introduced as a subject here for the first time in this epistle and is addressed through chapters 5–6 and parts of chapter 7. In Koine Greek the word can refer to general immorality, but it was most often related to payment for prostitutes or occasionally to fornication.[1] Paul reveals his shock at what seems acceptable in the Corinthian church. The passive "it is reported" (ἀκούεται) may refer to further information provided by Chloe's people (1:11), or it may have come to Paul's attention from other sources. "Actually"

---

1. F. Hauck and S. Schulz, "πόρνη," *TDNT* 6:579–95.

(ὅλως) expresses his dismay and shock at what he has heard. In terms of Paul's argument, this matter becomes clear evidence that unless they pull themselves together and act as the Lord's people, he may well have to come with them "rod in hand" (4:21). In the second part of the sentence, a verb must be supplied for translation, hence "there *is* sexual immorality" among them.

The world of Paul's day had an ambiguous approach to what we would call "immorality." On the one hand, heterosexual marriage was protected in law, and on the other there was a general view that regarded "sexual intercourse as just as natural, necessary and justifiable as eating and drinking. . . . Even the married man was permitted extra-marital intercourse as he pleased as long as he did not violate a civil marriage."[2] Thus, with a fairly lax approach among the citizens of Corinth to sexual mores, Paul's words strongly impact the reader as he insists that so bad is this sexual immorality that it is "not even"[3] "tolerated"[4] "among pagans" (ἐν τοῖς ἔθνεσιν; locative). In fact there is evidence to show that incestuous relationships, which included having sex with one's stepmother or father, was prohibited by law.[5]

From Paul's perspective, however, and from that of the converted Jews in the church, "sexual immorality" (πορνεία) had a broader meaning. Working within the framework for sexual relationships provided by Scripture, immorality referred to any sexual behavior outside of heterosexual marriage as indicated by creation itself and by the Mosaic law. Thus, the LXX uses the word to describe Tamar's prostitution in Genesis 38:24, the immoralities of Jezebel in 2 Kings 9:22, prostitution and immo-

rality in Hosea 1:2, 2:4, etc. Biblical law offered much clearer definitions concerning the rights and wrongs of sexual activity outside of marriage than anything in the Greco-Roman world. Whether it be acts of adultery, prostitution, bestiality, incest, homosexuality or sexual acts linked with idolatry, all are condemned in some detail in the pages of the Old Testament (e.g., Exod 20:14; 22:16; Lev 18; 19:29; Ezek 23:36–49, etc.). It is therefore important to understand the full extent of Paul's horror at what is going on among them and how it is being tolerated. It goes without saying that those of Jewish background would find incestuous activity despicable, but "even" the Gentiles would not accept this behavior. And so, the apostle succinctly describes what is going on.

5:1d Someone is having sex with his father's wife (ὥστε γυναῖκά τινα τοῦ πατρὸς ἔχειν). The dreadful immorality not acceptable even to pagans is a case of incest. The initial conjunction (ὥστε), if translated at all, may mean "that is" or "for." "Someone" (τινα) is indefinite, indicating either that Paul did not know the name of the people involved or, more likely, that he wants to make the serious point out of the incident that immorality of any sort must not be tolerated. It is possible that this case was widely enough known that he could simply refer to it and then build on it in terms of general application in vv. 6–13.

The present infinitive (ἔχειν) indicates that this is an ongoing relationship that is being ignored by the Corinthians. Commentators speculate on the background of the incestuous relationship. From Paul's point of view, the Scriptures are definitive. In Leviticus 18 several incestuous relationships are

---

2. Ibid., 6:582–83.

3. The use of "not even" (οὐδὲ) emphasizes the extraordinary nature of the case about which Paul has heard.

4. The Greek here has no verb. Barrett, *First Corinthians*, 121, translates "such fornication as *is not practised* even

among. . . ." For our translation, see also ESV and Thiselton, *1 Corinthians*, 385. RSV has "of a kind that is not found."

5. Useful detail on the prevailing attitude toward incest among pagans and in the law of the day is provided by Clarke, *Secular and Christian Leadership in Corinth*, 77–84.

outlawed; especially see 18:8: "Do not have sexual relations with your father's wife; that would dishonor your father" (NIV). The court of the Old Testament would have led to the death penalty for this crime if proven. In Paul's thinking the gathered congregation of God's people must pronounce judgment as a court, and the penalty must be expulsion from the community (vv. 2–5).

The problem of incest may have been acute since so many lived in extended households. Scripture protects families by stating clearly that certain relationships, those which would destroy families and trust between husband and wife, are banned. Today it is known that incest can lead to later, serious medical and genetic problems, but Paul's concern here is that God's law for the family has been broken. The fact that this law was also upheld in pagan society allows Paul to argue *how much more* dreadful is it that Christians should turn a blind eye to such things. The precise relationship between the woman and man concerned is unclear. Paul does not say "having sex with his *mother*" but with "his father's wife." Thus, some assume that this must mean "stepmother." However, it is just as likely that Paul used the term "father's wife" to match what appears in Leviticus 18:8 where the actual "mother" is probably indicated. Certainly, such relationships occurred in ancient times as much as they do in modern times.[6]

5:2a–b And you are puffed up! And yet should you not rather have mourned (καὶ ὑμεῖς πεφυσιωμένοι ἐστέ, καὶ οὐχὶ μᾶλλον ἐπενθήσατε). Now Paul links the problem back to the issues he has been addressing in the earlier chapters. Here, "you are puffed up" (πεφυσιωμένοι)[7] could simply

mean "you are arrogant," but the translation "you are puffed up" connects this use to the same verb used in 4:6, 18, and 19. Where they should have mourned over their sin, their self-confident pride in their status before God meant they had ignored evil in their midst.

The nature of this arrogance has been much discussed, especially in light of 6:12 (see the discussion there).[8] In that verse a Corinthian slogan, "all things are lawful for me," is cited by Paul and then critiqued. Is it that the "spirituals" thought they were beyond the need to worry about morality and matters of the flesh? In other words, was this some form of dualism in which bodily matters were regarded as insignificant? Indeed, could it be that the actual demonstration of the so-called freedom helped establish their great "spirituality"? This view suggests that what Paul means in this verse is that some Corinthians were actually boasting in this man's relationship. But that seems to go well beyond what Paul actually says.

In the light of chapter 4, it is more likely that this problem arises not so much from a form of dualism or from some realized eschatology but simply from ignoring the whole matter of *behavior* in the community. What dominates their worldview is their "spirituality" witnessed in their "speech" and "knowledge." They believe their community status is secure, and they are proud and arrogant in this. There is perhaps a modern resonance with their position in the expression, now sadly heard widely even in some Christian circles, "Who cares what men and women get up to in the privacy of their own home/bedroom?" The answer for Paul is, of course, that such behavior is utterly incompatible

---

6. In his interesting examination of Roman legal and literary attitudes to incest, Clarke suggests that a possible motivation for adultery might be financial and related to the intricacies of Roman dowry law after divorce or the death of a spouse (ibid., 84–85).

7. This is a periphrastic perfect passive, implying an ongoing effect.

8. Clarke, *Secular and Christian Leadership in Corinth*, 74–76.

with God's law and with being God's people. Moreover, it brings disrepute upon the church and thus upon Christ himself.

The exclamation is linked with "and yet" (καὶ οὐχί) to a rhetorical question.[9] He asks whether they should not have "mourned" (πενθέω). As in chapter 4 where the reader was reminded of the teachings of Christ himself on being reviled and persecuted, so here there may be an allusion to the second beatitude, "Blessed are those who mourn [πενθέω], for they will be comforted" (Matt 5:4). In the LXX the verb is used to describe mourning over another's sin, which makes sense of Paul's use of the word here. Those in the church should themselves have mourned before God over the sin in their midst and repented and called the couple to repentance. One of the most notable examples of mourning over sin is found in Ezra 10:6 where Ezra mourns for the faithlessness of the exiles. This passage then refers to the expulsion from the community of those who would not be challenged and changed by the law of God and who persisted in sin (10:7–8). It also calls upon the godly community to separate itself from the ways of the peoples of the land (cf. Neh 1:4; Dan 10:2; 1 Esd 9:2). Mourning for sin in Ezra's time was as much a public spectacle as mourning over a family death would have been.

Paul's rhetorical question expects an affirmative answer. The Corinthians should have reacted with deep confession of sin on behalf of the whole community. The whole community cannot carry on rejoicing in their status while in their midst an event is happening, uncommented upon, which breaches the law of the Lord.

5:2c–d so that he who has done this might be removed from your midst? (ἵνα ἀρθῇ ἐκ μέσου ὑμῶν ὁ τὸ ἔργον τοῦτο πράξας;). The result of such mourning would have been the recognition of the heinous nature of this sin and the subsequent removal[10] of the culprits from the Christian community in Corinth. This clause introduced by "so that" (ἵνα) has been variously interpreted. It may simply be a purpose clause or perhaps, as we have translated here, a result cause. Though a rarer use of the particle ἵνα, this use certainly appears in the New Testament and makes sense here.[11] This sort of mourning for sin *results* in action. This action will be the same as that which followed Ezra's mourning—the banishment from their midst of the offender.

Paul's immediate concern therefore with this immorality is for the holiness of the church itself. Whether they have ignored this behavior in their midst because the man concerned has a high status in the community or simply because they have no desire "to rock the boat," the result is horrendous. How can they be "puffed up" about their status and their gifts and yet ignore immorality and God's law?

5:3 For I, though absent in the body but present in the spirit, I have already judged as present the person who has done this in this way (ἐγὼ μὲν γάρ, ἀπὼν τῷ σώματι παρὼν δὲ τῷ πνεύματι, ἤδη κέκρικα ὡς παρὼν τὸν οὕτως τοῦτο κατεργασάμενον). "I" is emphatic. While the Corinthians are "puffed up" (v. 2), Paul is decisive. His judgment is straightforward and in line with Old Testament precedent: the person must be excluded from the covenant community. Paul has "judged" (κρίνω) the person concerned as one who is present. The perfect of this verb implies that this judgment, probably made as soon as he heard the circumstances, stands in the present as they read the letter.

---

9. Here καί is used to emphasize in the second clause or sentence something noteworthy or unexpected (see BDAG 495).

10. "Be removed," ἀρθῇ (from αἴρω), is an aorist, passive subjunctive.

11. Cf. John 9:2; Rom 11:11.

The phrases "in the body" (τῷ σώματι) and "in the spirit" (τῷ πνεύματι) raise a number of questions. Since they qualify the present participles of being "absent" and being "present," they could be either dative of place or dative of manner. The latter seems most likely. Paul describes the manner in which he is either not present (ἄπειμι) or present (πάρειμι). His manner of presence with them is not to be physically present since he is elsewhere at the time. But his judgment to expel the man is made as one who is present (not "as if" present; ESV). Thus, what precisely he means when he says he *is* with them "in the spirit" needs examination.

Some have suggested it simply means being present in a nonbodily way.[12] For example, we might say, "Our thoughts are with you," or, "I feel like I am with you as I say this." This suggests Paul is thinking in a sort of dualistic way: the body is absent but the spirit (in some way) is "as if" present. However, v. 4 points to something rather more profound than this. There Paul talks about them being assembled "in the name of our Lord Jesus" with Paul's "spirit" present and "with the power of our Lord Jesus." Paul has already written that "we" have all received "the Spirit of God, in order that we might know the things that were graciously given to us by God" (2:12). The Spirit of God brings knowledge and understanding to the church, and Paul is part of the church and with them possesses the Holy Spirit. In 6:17 Paul says that "anyone united to the Lord becomes one spirit with him" (NRSV). Thus, perhaps Paul means here that as the Spirit of the Lord is among them as they gather and because Paul is also at one with the Spirit, so he too is present. Garland puts it this way: "United to Christ in spirit, he is present with them through Christ's presence."[13] But perhaps there is still more here, for Paul writes with apostolic authority and

his words come from the Holy Spirit. He therefore speaks with the authority of the Spirit and so pronounces judgment, and expects that the congregational meeting will immediately agree with his verdict.

5:4 In the name of our Lord Jesus, when you are assembled and my spirit is with you with the power of our Lord Jesus (ἐν τῷ ὀνόματι τοῦ κυρίου [ἡμῶν] Ἰησοῦ, συναχθέντων ὑμῶν καὶ τοῦ ἐμοῦ πνεύματος σὺν τῇ δυνάμει τοῦ κυρίου ἡμῶν Ἰησοῦ). When the assembly of the Lord's people meet together with Paul in spirit and in the Lord's name and with his power, Paul expects them to render the same verdict as he has rendered and to carry out the banishment of the person committing incest. The genitive absolute was seen in 4:18. Here it means "when you are assembled" (συναχθέντων ὑμῶν). Given the word order, the phrase "in the name of our Lord Jesus" might, in theory, be placed with "the person" (v. 3). Thus, it could mean that Paul passed judgment on "the person who had done this in this way in the name of the Lord Jesus." This would imply the incestuous man had appealed to the Lord for justification of his actions, perhaps claiming a special "knowledge" to do so. In chapter 8, there are good grounds for assuming that the Corinthians were indeed hiding behind their so-called knowledge and behaving in inadvisable ways. Here, though, Paul is not dealing with something that is inadvisable but something that is so serious the person should be banished. Secondly, unlike in chapter 8, Paul does not tackle the theology of what is being done or said here. Here it is simply the unacceptable action that is the focus of his attention.

A second possibility is that it is Paul who has already judged "in the name of the Lord Jesus"

---

12. Paul is more likely to have this in mind in Col 2:5. See Barrett, *First Corinthians*, 123.

13. Garland, *1 Corinthians*, 165.

(RSV, NRSV),[14] but the phrase is too far removed from the verb for this to make easy sense. More than that, Paul is not doing this on his own. He has judged, but he expects the Corinthian church to agree with and implement the judgment.

It is more likely that this phrase goes with what immediately follows. Paul reminds the Corinthians that when gathered as a church they gather in the Lord's name. In other words, they are his body on earth and carry out his will with his power. Thus, two prepositional phrases help explain each other. Together they explain the means by which the assembled church may make such a serious judgment. They do so, firstly, "in the name of our Lord Jesus," and secondly this is amplified by "with the power of our Lord Jesus."

As noted in the comments under 1:2, "name" here means calling upon all that the Lord is. The background in Joel 2:32 was also noted where Joel looks forward to the day when the Spirit will be poured out on all flesh and the Lord will be seen in mighty power coming to judge and to save. Both the "name" and the "power" can carry connotations of the Lord's judgment (or salvation). The church thus operates under the Spirit's guidance and with confidence in the apostle's own view of the matter, but it does so acting *as Christ*. Of course, the decision of the church in the Lord's name does not usurp the right of the Lord to make the final judgment. The church's judgment of this sort is always with restoration in mind—even with such a serious case as this. Thus, in v. 5 Paul will add "that his spirit may be saved in the day of the Lord," referring to Christ's coming and final judgment.

The action Paul is insisting upon thus links up

with Jesus's own teaching in Matthew 18:17–18 where the role of the whole church in dealing with sin in their midst is firmly established. As here in 1 Corinthians 5, the one mentioned in Matthew 18 who does not repent is to be cast out, that is, regarded by the church as "a pagan or a tax collector."

5:5 hand over such a man to Satan for the destruction of the flesh, so that his spirit may be saved in the day of the Lord (παραδοῦναι τὸν τοιοῦτον τῷ Σατανᾷ εἰς ὄλεθρον τῆς σαρκός, ἵνα τὸ πνεῦμα σωθῇ ἐν τῇ ἡμέρᾳ τοῦ κυρίου). For reasons mentioned above, it seems likely that Paul sees his own judgment as being made together with the assembled church. Banishment must take place with the goal of the individual's final restoration and salvation. It is probably best to regard the infinitive (παραδοῦναι) as an imperative. Most translations take it this way with some variation of the command, such as "you are to hand over" (NRSV) or "hand over" (NIV). A plural subject would also make sense, with Paul then saying, "Let us hand over such a man."[15]

"Handing over" concerns a formal judgment of putting the man outside the community. As Robertson and Plummer write, "The offender is sent back to his domain."[16] A person who sins in this way needs to be placed among those who belong to the realm of darkness, even if he himself will ultimately be restored. His behavior is not fitting for "the kingdom of God" (4:20), and so he can have nothing to do with the Lord's people while he maintains his evil position. It was noted in discussion of the opening ten verses of this epistle just how vital to Paul's thinking is his view of the lordship of Christ. This man was not obeying the Lord

---

14. Fee, *1 Corinthians* (first edition), 206. In his revised edition (228) Fee argues that "in the end the best answer lies with seeing the phrase basically as modifying the entire sentence." See Garland, *1 Corinthians*, 166.

15. If all the action of making the judgment is Paul's, then παραδοῦναι could be seen as an infinitive of indirect speech. A translation might go like this: "I judged this person in the name of our Lord Jesus . . . that you are to hand over . . . ."

16. Robertson and Plummer, *First Corinthians*, 99.

Jesus Christ, and so, until he repents, he must live in the world where another lord holds sway.

Talk of different "lordships" can seem alien to the modern reader, but Paul understands Satan to have real power. It is limited by the "Lord of lords," but in "this world" and "this age" his power and influence are real enough. He is the "god of this world" (2 Cor 4:4). Satan tempts Christians (7:5). He has designs against God's people (2 Cor 2:11; 11:14; 12:7), and some have followed him (1 Tim 5:15). In 1 Timothy 1:19–20, there is mention of an instance not dissimilar to the one mentioned here. Some have made a wreck of their faith, and two have been "handed over to Satan to be taught not to blaspheme." Again, the purpose is restoration. The sense is that such people will once again "taste the other side," as it were, and so come to regret their actions and return in repentance and faith to the Lord. Two goals are therefore achieved with such a judgment. First, the community itself, which is Paul's first concern here, behaves as it should in taking action to cleanse itself, ensuring it does not appear to condone that which is against the Lord's will. It thereby seeks to keep itself "holy" (1:2). Secondly, the individual finds that he goes from a position where he thinks he has status and belongs to a position in which he does not and is cast out. This will draw him back to the community, God willing.

Two further clauses need explanation. The first concerns the "destruction of the flesh" (ὄλεθρον τῆς σαρκός). Is this the "purpose" of the handing over (thus, does εἰς introduce a purpose clause)? This could mean that there are two purpose clauses, the second beginning with "that" (ἵνα). Also, it is important to ask what the "destruction of the flesh" means.

Taking the grammatical question first, the sense demands that the second clause is indeed "pur-

pose." Paul's desire for "such a person" (τοιοῦτον) is that at that final day the man might be "saved" (σωθῇ). This is the purpose of the judgment. It is ultimately restorative. The meaning of the first clause, "to hand over *for*..." (εἰς) is less clear. While it could also be a purpose clause, Fee points out that a double purpose clause expressed in this way is uncommon and that it is more likely to indicate the "anticipated result." He suggests that "the 'destruction of his flesh' is the anticipated result of the man's being put back out into Satan's domain, while the express purpose of the action is his redemption."[17]

The meanings of "flesh" and "spirit" are important in seeking to understand Paul's point. Often the word "flesh" has been taken as the physical body. "Destruction" (ὄλεθρος) therefore means that the person will die in his body, but will still be "saved" in his spirit at the final judgment day. It has been suggested that Paul envisaged a person suffering, dying, and perhaps repenting during that process, so that he would in the end be saved. This view suggests that something akin to what is described in Romans 1:24–27 is happening. There Paul speaks of unbelievers being handed over by God to their sin and receiving the penalty of their sin in their own persons. Another indication that Paul may have in mind the suffering of the physical body is to be found in 1 Corinthians 11:30 where members of the congregation have become ill and died because of their abuse of the Lord's Supper. However, even though there may be links to this way of thinking, in both Romans 1 and 1 Corinthians 11 the action comes from God and is not part of a decision by a congregation. Furthermore, Paul does not use the word "spirit" or the word "flesh" in either of those passages.

In 1:26 Paul has talked of the "wise according to the flesh" and uses Israel "according to the flesh"

---

17. Fee, *1 Corinthians*, 230. See also BDAG 290 (4.e).

as an illustration in 10:18. In 1:26 it was noted that Paul uses the word "flesh" virtually as a synonym for "this age." "Flesh" in this connotation has to do with following that which is not of God but is of the domain of darkness or Satan. Fleshly actions would be those which are not God-serving but self-serving, and ultimately done in service of Satan. If we understand "flesh" in this way, then Paul—saying that his purpose is the salvation of this man's spirit—may be intending that this "handing over" is so that the *ways of the flesh* will be destroyed. That is, he believes that immersion once again in the world, rather than remaining in the Christian community, will indeed lead to repentance. Repentance will then be seen in a changed life in which the flesh, that is, the behavior and life of darkness, is destroyed. "The spirit" (τὸ πνεῦμα) would therefore represent that existence in which, fully separated from sin, he would be able to come through the final judgment day and be saved. It is a realm of existence that Paul has been talking about that is enabled and guaranteed by having received "the Spirit of God" (2:12). An objection to this view is that it implies that it is Satan who enables the man to find salvation. However, this is to misunderstand God's sovereignty as it is seen repeatedly in Scripture. Satan's power is limited. What Satan may intend for evil God can intend for good. This is clearly seen in the life of Joseph (Gen 50:20), but it is also seen in different circumstances with Paul where his "thorn in [the] flesh" is regarded as a "messenger of Satan," and yet helps Paul learn that God's grace is sufficient (2 Cor 12:7–10).

If this view is correct, then Paul's reference to the ways of "the flesh" does indeed find parallels in Romans 1. This is true even though the situation is entirely different, for the people spoken of there in vv. 26–27 are not Christians at all. Their being given over to sin is seen as their receiving judgment from God in the present, pointing toward

their ultimate state. Yet even there it seems that such an action on God's part probably is designed to lead some to repentance. Here in 1 Corinthians 5 a Christian is handed over so that he too may experience the ongoing judgment of the Lord, yet because he is the Lord's the *purpose* can confidently be expressed as "that [he] may be saved in the day of the Lord."

This corporate judgment has two great motivations: the holiness and protection of God's people and the salvation of this individual. In vv. 3–5, it is the individual who has been the focus of the judgment. This judgment by the church, however alien it may feel to Christians in the twenty-first century, is radical and even judicial. Yet it is ultimately restorative and is not intended to usurp the place of the Lord himself on the final judgment day. In the verses that follow, Paul will show why this judgment is vital for the sake of the church in its corporate identity.

5:6–7 Your boasting is not good. Do you not know that a little leaven makes the whole batch of dough rise? Clean out the old leaven, so that you may be a new batch, since you really are unleavened, for Christ our Passover lamb has been sacrificed (Οὐ καλὸν τὸ καύχημα ὑμῶν. οὐκ οἴδατε ὅτι μικρὰ ζύμη ὅλον τὸ φύραμα ζυμοῖ; ἐκκαθάρατε τὴν παλαιὰν ζύμην, ἵνα ἦτε νέον φύραμα, καθώς ἐστε ἄζυμοι. καὶ γὰρ τὸ πάσχα ἡμῶν ἐτύθη Χριστός). In vv. 6–8 an analogy drawing upon the Passover now provides a theological basis for the expulsion. Paul states the obvious and reminds the readers of what he has said about boasting in 5:2 (cf. 4:18–19). "Not good" (Οὐ καλὸν) could sound trite, but it is far from this since it indicates Paul's deep concern that their whole approach to the matter of immorality is altogether wrong. The problem lies not just with one individual but with the whole community. The behavior of the one affects the entire congregation.

However, their self-centered arrogance and their confidence in their spiritual status have produced a lethal combination. They have been ignoring the community as a whole and especially the relationship between the individual and the church. The image of the leaven that permeates bread is appropriate, not just because of how a small amount can have a dramatic effect on the whole batch of dough but also because it is replete with ideas drawn from the Old Testament that concern sin and lack of holiness.[18]

Paul again begins a section with a rhetorical question: "Do you not know . . . ?" (οὐκ οἴδατε). The answer ought to be, "Of course we do!" This question is used ten times in the epistle; see comments on 3:16. Paul orders them (v. 7) to "clean out" (ἐκκαθαίρω) the old yeast with the purpose (ἵνα) that they should actually become what they are. "Since you really are unleavened" (καθώς is used in a causal sense)[19] provides the basis for the imperative, and the final clause gives the underlying theology centered once again in Christ crucified. Paul refers to the sacrificial offering, the Passover lamb (τὸ πάσχα). The word ζύμη, sometimes translated as "yeast" (NIV, NRSV) and sometimes as "leaven" (RSV, ESV) is better translated as "leaven."[20] For the modern household, which rarely makes its own bread, the distinction may seem unimportant. Even where households do make their own bread today, pure yeast is bought, often in little sachets, and little is understood of what goes on in the process of bread making as the dough begins to rise. At the time of Paul's writing, the baking of bread, both leavened and unleavened, would have been a daily experience, but rarely would people have acquired anything approaching a pure yeast. Most baking would keep aside a little of the raw dough containing the yeast cultures so this could be added to the next batch. During the time it was put aside, it would begin to ferment and so would rapidly infect the new dough and cause it to rise. This leftover fermenting dough is the "leaven."

The ease with which this can be used as a negative image is obvious. The effectiveness of leaven depends on contamination of the pure dough. With yeasts and fermentations of different sorts going on rapidly, especially in warmer climates, there needed to be regular times when the leaven was cleared out completely and a fresh start was made; otherwise there would be a real danger of sickness caused by lack of hygiene and contamination from other organisms. The Feast of Unleavened Bread, in the cycle of Jewish festivals, was one of the seasons when this was done each year. Any leaven had to be removed from houses for seven days. At the heart of this festival, described in Exodus 12:14–20 and 13:3–10, was the picture of separation and redemption of God's people from Egypt. This festival, with its direct relationship to the Passover, no doubt accounts for Paul's movement from the picture of the leaven to the Passover sacrifice itself. The people were no longer contaminated by the gods of Egypt but were holy to the Lord.

This clearing out of the old also provided a useful picture for the changing from old to new. Just as a new nation is formed at the exodus and its formation is recalled in the Passover and the Feast of Unleavened Bread, so the Christian church at Corinth is a new community. There can be no going back. Here Paul draws on both those pictures of clearing out and of the change from old to new.

The immorality of the individual has been ignored by the leaders of the congregation. The consequences of the actions of one or two people, a

---

18. This picture also appears in Gal 5:9.

19. BDAG 391. "Really" is added to help interpret the emphasis of the clause.

20. An extensive discussion of the meanings and distinctions is to be found in Charles Leslie Mitton, "New Wine in Old Wineskins; IV, Leaven," in *ExpTim* 84 (1973): 339–43.

"little" leaven, may not seem that important but are in fact disastrous for all (v. 6; "little," μικρά, is in an emphatic position). For Paul, the community markers of the Christian church are settled by being "in Christ." Such people follow the way of Christ crucified, live lives in accordance with the law of God, and reveal a community of the new era, the age ushered in by Christ in his death and resurrection. This new society is made up of a people who are holy and serve Christ as Lord and Master. They are a people greatly blessed with grace-gifts from God and who will be found "unimpeachable" on the final day (1:8). They have left behind the old way of life and have taken on a new one. Paul made it clear in his opening nine verses of the epistle that this *is* who the Corinthians are. Here he makes the point again: "Since you really are unleavened" (καθώς ἐστε ἄζυμοι). Holiness and purity are therefore at the very heart of what defines a Christian community: a holy God has a holy people made holy in Christ Jesus (1:2, 30). This is why ignoring impurity in such a grave and obvious breach of holiness is so serious. The foundation of the community identity "in Christ" is being undermined. Those whom God has called specifically to be holy are showing scorn for the calling.

However, what Paul indicates here about the holiness of the community has an added dimension in light of what he has already said about the church being "God's temple" (3:16–17), an idea to which he returns in 6:19. This community is where God dwells by his Spirit, and as such it must be kept "cleansed" or "holy" just as the tabernacle and the temple of the Lord in Israel had to be holy (cf. Pss 5:7; 11:4; Ezek 43:12; Hab 2:4). In Israel, the temple or sanctuary was simply the physical place representing the deeper truth that God dwells among his people. Thus Exodus 29:45 reads, "I will dwell among the people of Israel, and I will be their God" (NRSV). Then in 29:46 this is even seen as the purpose for God bringing them out of Egypt: "I am the LORD their God, who brought them out of the land of Egypt *that I might dwell among them*" (NRSV; cf. 25:8; Ezek 11:16; 37:26–28). Thus, the cleansing of the physical temple at times of revival such as under King Hezekiah and King Josiah was designed to reflect the cleansing of the community at its corporate heart with the representative king taking the lead. In both cases the kings opened the doors of the temple that had been neglected for years, and, following various sacrifices for cleansing, the great Passover feast was celebrated (2 Chr 29–30; 34–35; cf. Ezra 6).[21]

As noted above, Paul is likely to have thought of Deuteronomy 22:30 (23:1 LXX) as he contemplated the incestuous couple. In that context, also, the presence of God among his people is to the fore, as law is laid down about who shall be driven from the assembly and who is to be allowed to be among the people (Deut 23:1–8). In Deuteronomy 22:13–30 there is a repeated call to "purge the evil from" Israel (vv. 21, 22, 24; cf. 13:5; 17:7, 12; 19:19; 21:21; 24:7). Thus, with a multifaceted background found in God's dealings with his covenant community of Israel, Paul's own thinking is clear: God dwells in his temple among the Corinthian believers, and it is essential that they be cleansed and holy, especially since the Passover has already happened in the sacrifice of Christ, the Passover lamb (γὰρ τὸ πάσχα ἡμῶν ἐτύθη Χριστός).

The theological impact goes still further. In Christ's crucifixion sin was paid for at great price in order that God might have a holy people. To ignore sin is therefore to diminish and even undermine

---

21. Rosner points out that even Jesus's own cleansing of the temple is immediately followed by the Passover celebration (Mark 11:15–18; Mark 14). Brian S. Rosner, *Paul, Scripture and Ethics: A Study of 1 Corinthians 5–7*, AGJU 22 (Leiden: Brill, 1994; repr., Grand Rapids: Baker, 1999), 61–93.

the whole redemptive event of Christ's sacrificial death, resurrection, and ascension. Therefore, ethics matter because they reflect the theology of the church, its soteriology, and even its Christology. Nothing could make this clearer than the final sentence in this verse speaking of the sacrifice of Christ, which reminds the reader of the opening exposition of Christ crucified in 1 Corinthians 1.

The death of Christ is expounded in a number of different ways by the New Testament writers. As Christ was seen to be the goal (τέλος) of the law (Rom 10:4), so it was understood that the whole sacrificial system pointed toward him. The lamb sacrifice of the Passover (τὸ πάσχα) was but one part of that sacrificial system, but it is a vital one for Paul's argument here. In fact, the link between Christ's sacrificial death and the Passover probably seemed natural, given the likelihood that the Lord's Supper was understood to have arisen in the context of the celebration of the Passover (see comments on 11:24). The shed blood of the Passover lamb involved a costly sacrifice made by each family that was to be saved from the destroying angel. The angel "passed over" those houses where the blood of the sacrificed lamb had been painted on the door posts and lintel.

The Israelites were identified as the people of God in the action of the sacrifice, the shedding of the lamb's blood, and its appropriation through the painting on the doors. The Passover and Feast of Unleavened Bread are the festivals of nation formation and nation identity *par excellence* for the Israelites, as is made clear by God when they have entered the wilderness and escaped Egypt (Exod 12–13). Significantly, this newly formed nation sees God bringing judgment not just on the firstborn of Egypt but "on all the gods of Egypt" (Exod 12:12). In what may be described as the "the battle of the gods," played out between the one true God, Yahweh, and Pharaoh as representing the gods of

this age, the Lord decisively wins. In doing so, he separates his people from all other gods.

For Paul it is the immensely costly redemptive sacrifice of Christ that is "nation forming." In Christ the people of God find they "were bought with a price" (6:20). They were saved from the gods of this world and are to live lives reflecting the purity and holiness of the one they now serve. Christ's work on the cross secures a people for God, and the Corinthians *are* members of that people. Paul's Christology, soteriology, and ecclesiology come together here as a basis for his appeal to right living and casting out the sinner from their midst.

5:8 Therefore let us celebrate the festival, not with old leaven or leaven of malice and evil, but with the unleavened bread of sincerity and truth (ὥστε ἑορτάζωμεν, μὴ ἐν ζύμῃ παλαιᾷ μηδὲ ἐν ζύμῃ κακίας καὶ πονηρίας, ἀλλ᾽ ἐν ἀζύμοις εἰλικρινείας καὶ ἀληθείας). The view of Christ as the Passover lamb being sacrificed for the people allows Paul to move naturally to the idea of celebration. Just as the Passover festival celebrated redemption from Egypt, the victory of the true God over the false gods of the Egyptians, and the nation-forming event of the exodus, so the whole Christian life is to be viewed in this way. It is to be a festival of rejoicing that God's people have been redeemed, the gods of the world have been dealt with by Christ, and a new people exists. However, just as the Passover festival had to be celebrated in an appropriate way that reflected properly what God had done through the sacrifice for and redemption of his people, so it should be for the church. Their lifelong celebration should be as a holy people, separated from the nations, not contaminated with the old leaven of immorality and the ways of their former existence but having all that "cleared out" (v. 7; ἐκκαθαίρω).

"Therefore" (ὥστε) indicates the movement toward Paul's conclusion. The command "let us celebrate" (ἑορτάζωμεν, a hortatory subjunctive) suggests this celebration should continue. The two words "malice" (κακία) and "evil" (πονηρία) are really synonyms here and are descriptive genitives expanding upon the meaning of "old leaven" (ζύμη παλαιά). The celebration will have to root out that which contaminates the community: not just immorality but all that is evil and belongs to this age. Thus, with a strong adversative (ἀλλά) Paul draws the contrast. The alternative to the contamination is described in terms of unleavened bread "of sincerity and of truth" (εἰλικρινείας καὶ ἀληθείας, descriptive genitives). These arrogant, puffed-up people need to look again at Christ and be sincere rather than self-deceiving. The word "sincerity" (εἰλικρίνεια) only appears in the Corinthian correspondence. In 2 Corinthians 1:12 Paul compares the description of his own behavior as "godly sincerity" with "fleshly wisdom." In 2 Corinthians 2:17 Paul likewise compares himself and other apostles as "men of sincerity" with "peddlers" of God's word. When using this word, Paul seems to have in mind the contrast between that which would be expected in terms of fleshly wisdom and that which is of the Spirit. There can be no dissimulation, no distorting the truth, no playing up the message simply to make an impression. In fact, there should be a genuine innocence and openness in the way people live and act. Thus "truth" (ἀλήθεια) is also characteristic of this celebration of the new life. Truth is suppressed by the wickedness of those who reject God (Rom 1:18). For those who are absorbed with themselves and not with Christ, truth is often an early casualty of their boasting. Arrogant exaggeration leads on to ever greater deceit and especially to self-deception.

In summary, Paul's call is to a holy life in which God's people celebrate his goodness and their calling as people who are "sanctified in Christ Jesus" (1:2). The transformation is so radical that it is likened to the new start experienced by the Israelites at the exodus and remembered in the Passover sacrifice and celebration. There can be no going back to the past, no compromising with the past life, no tolerating evil in the midst of the community. There must also be an active commitment to godly, sincere, and truthful living since the redemption that led to their belonging to this covenant community came at great cost. "For Christ our Passover lamb was sacrificed."

5:9 I wrote to you in the letter not to associate with sexually immoral people (Ἔγραψα ὑμῖν ἐν τῇ ἐπιστολῇ μὴ συναναμίγνυσθαι πόρνοις). Paul does not change the subject in vv. 9–13. Rather, he seeks to ensure there is no misunderstanding of what he is saying: Christian community identity *requires* holiness, and that means dissociating itself from the sexually immoral. The aorist "I wrote" refers to a previous letter ("in the letter"), which does not now exist. His purpose of that writing, expressed with the infinitive, was "not to associate with" (μὴ συναναμίγνυσθαι) such people.

Banishing the immoral person from the church does not mean that Paul desires the church to become a Christian "ghetto." He is not looking for any church to become an isolated monastic community that keeps itself pure by having no contact with sexually immoral people. Otherwise, how would many of the Corinthians themselves have encountered the gospel? For as Paul says in 6:11, "Such were some of you" (ESV). But Paul is saying that those who claim to be part of the covenant community must be who they are, that is, God's holy people. Therefore, internal community discipline around the markers or boundaries of the community is essential.

First, then, in vv. 9–10 he makes it clear that the church is not to concern itself with the immoral of this world. The verb "to associate with" (συναναμίγνυμι) also appears in v. 11 and otherwise only elsewhere in the New Testament in 2 Thessalonians

3:14.[22] The fact that Paul says in v. 11 that they should "not even . . . eat with such a person" helps to explain what is in mind. The Corinthians are to look at ways in which it will be made clear to the individual, but also to the outside world, that *this* community is different and does not allow immorality. Eating a meal together may have meant the communion meal, but this is unlikely. Rather, meals generally were places of fellowship and intimacy. In idol temples, as will be seen in chapter 8, eating the meal could imply acceptance of that particular idol. Paul's exhortation therefore has to do with being seen to belong to the community, so he expects the Corinthians to look at the ways that belonging is expressed as the community gathers. It is from those places that the person is to be excluded. But this may all have been misunderstood from the previous letter, or perhaps the previous letter was being misused, as leaders defended their behavior in ignoring sexual immorality. There is insufficient information in the text of this letter to be sure about circumstances. So Paul expands on what he means by not associating with such people.

5:10 —not at all meaning with the sexually immoral of this world or with the greedy and thieves or idolaters, since you would then need to leave the world (οὐ πάντως τοῖς πόρνοις τοῦ κόσμου τούτου ἢ τοῖς πλεονέκταις καὶ ἅρπαξιν ἢ εἰδωλολάτραις, ἐπεὶ ὠφείλετε ἄρα ἐκ τοῦ κόσμου ἐξελθεῖν[23]). Here is Paul's explanation or clarification of what he meant in his previous letter. Furthermore, it is also an amplification of what he has said here regarding the immoral person in the congregation. Paul insists he is not advocating withdrawal from this world. The word "world" (κόσμος) in this verse means something slightly different on the two occasions it is used. In the first instance "this world" is more than simply the physical sphere in which we all live. It relates back to Paul's use of the word previously in the epistle. There he had talked of the "foolish things of the world" (1:27) and Christians not having received "the spirit of the world" (2:12). For Paul, sexual immorality, greed, and the vices he lists here are part and parcel of what it is to be "of this world." "This world is passing away" (7:31), but Paul is not asking that Christians should part from this world. The second use of this word has more to do with the sphere. This is where God's people, though indeed an alternative society and under a different lordship, have been called to live. Peter refers to Christians as "foreigners and exiles" in the land (1 Pet 2:11–12), but they are to maintain such good lives "among the pagans" that they too may eventually glorify God. This is Paul's theology here. God has called his church to be a witness in the world to the one true Lord. Sincerity and truth must characterize her. He has not called her to depart from this world but to bring the gospel to bear, continually revealing Christ crucified, even when this teaching is regarded as foolishness. It would be a gospel nonsense if he were asking the Corinthians not to mix with the people of this world characterized by much sin.

It is suggested that Paul's particular list of vices here is paralleled in other Greek literature. Sometimes this leads to the conclusion that the vices mentioned are therefore more "example" than they are an actual description of Corinthian life.[24] However, from what we learn of Corinthian life in this epistle, the vices would surely all have been eminently recognizable in Corinth. There is a case of

---

22. The verb is also used in two passages where there is concern that Israel is mixing with foreigners and becoming defiled by idolatry in LXX Hos 7:8 and Ezek 20:18.

23. The aorist infinitive "to leave" (ἐξελθεῖν) provides the

object clause for the verb "would need" (ὀφείλω), and the datives are still governed by the main verb "associate with."

24. See the excursus in Conzelmann, *1 Corinthians*, 100–101.

sexual immorality in the church that is the cause of Paul's concern here. In chapter 8 we discover there are serious issues of compromise with idolatry. We are then left asking how "the greedy" (πλεονέκτης) and "thieves" (ἅρπαξ) fit in. There can be little doubt, following the studies of Clarke, Witherington, and others, that this society that espoused elitism and status was full of those who constantly wanted more. Money brought power and status, and thus greed grew and multiplied.[25] It is not a big step to see stealing as simply an extension of greed. The word "thief" (ἅρπαξ) normally refers to a person who steals by cheating, that is, one who is a swindler.[26] Rosner suggests that "the first word [πλεονέκτης] focuses on the grasping aspect of avarice, and the latter [ἅρπαξ] on the violent and dishonest means of carrying it out."[27]

However, Paul's understanding of the church as a holy people who are called by God is, as we have seen, clearly dependent on much Old Testament teaching. In the Old Testament the sorts of sins mentioned here are regularly regarded as breaches of the covenant with the Lord. We have noted the sexual sins of Leviticus 18. We may note the constant emphasis that idolatry will bring God's judgment and "banishment" upon the Israelites (e.g., Deut 32:21; 2 Kgs 17:15–18). What is not so often noted, perhaps because it is a sin so prevalent in the modern church, is that greed and extortion are seen in the same light in Scripture as these other sins. Where God's people are involved in these things, they come under his judgment. Thus, for example, in a remarkable passage in Ezekiel 16 the sin of Israel is described as worse than that of Sodom. The sin of Sodom is described as pride, having an excess of food and prosperity, and so not

helping the poor. The Lord judged them. There are many places in the Old Testament where the prophets speak against the people "of the world" and against the Israelites themselves because of sexual sin, idolatry, greed, extortion, and exploitation. Rosner surely rightly argues that the "representative list of sinners [in vv. 10–11] . . . is in one sense a list of covenantal norms which, when broken, automatically exclude the offender." He points to how the LXX of Deuteronomy lists five offenses that may be "roughly compared with five of the six items in Paul's list."[28] He refers to Deuteronomy 22:21 for sexual immorality, to 17:3, 7 for idolatry, to 19:18–19 for malicious false testimony (a reviler), to 21:20–21 for the drunkard, and to theft in 24:7. This covenantally framed theology of the community and of expulsion clarifies the particular choice of quotation with which Paul concludes in v. 13b (see below).

Even given this background, Paul probably specifically picked these particular vices because each one would have been recognized as a problem in the Corinthian society and therefore a problem for the people of the church, who were so tempted by the wisdom of this world. Thus, in line with what he has seen in Corinth, what he has heard from Chloe's people, and what in the light of Scripture he knows to be so dangerous for the covenant community, Paul lists these particular vices. Yet he insists in v. 10 that the Christian is not expected to avoid mixing with such people, for that would mean having to "leave this world" (ἐκ τοῦ κόσμου ἐξελθεῖν). There will be no Christian ghetto.

5:11 But now I write to you not to associate with anyone called a brother [or sister] if that person goes on being evil or greedy or an idolater,

---

25. See also Theissen, *Social Setting of Pauline Christianity*, 131.

26. BDAG 109. Thiselton, *1 Corinthians*, 411, helpfully translates as "people who practice extortion."

27. Brian S Rosner, *Greed as Idolatry: The Origin and Meaning of a Pauline Metaphor* (Grand Rapids: Eerdmans, 2007), 109.

28. B. Rosner, *Paul, Scripture, and Ethics*, 69–70.

**or slanderer, or a drunkard or thief, nor even
to eat with such a person** (νῦν δὲ ἔγραψα ὑμῖν μὴ
συναναμίγνυσθαι ἐάν τις ἀδελφὸς ὀνομαζόμενος ᾖ
πόρνος ἢ πλεονέκτης ἢ εἰδωλολάτρης ἢ λοίδορος
ἢ μέθυσος ἢ ἅρπαξ, τῷ τοιούτῳ μηδὲ συνεσθίειν).
Paul's concern with community identity and its
boundaries continues as his exhortation takes a direct focus. They are not to "associate with" any person who "is called a brother [or sister]" (ἀδελφὸς
ὀνομαζόμενος) if that person continues in sin. In
writing this he continues to generalize from the
specific of one man's immorality to the situation
that many may continue in sin in any of these areas.

"I wrote" (ἔγραψα; an aorist) is taken here as
an epistolary aorist here, unlike v. 9. Hence the
present-tense translation with the majority of recent commentators and versions.[29] The addition of
"now" (νῦν) seems to confirm this. Not all agree,
however. Paul's use of a present tense when referring to the current letter in 4:14 could speak against
this. Moreover, the RSV, for example, takes ἔγραψα
at 5:11 as a genuine past tense and sees Paul thus
moving on to explain what he meant in that first
letter. Assuming an epistolary aorist, Paul is saying
"now I write to you," forming a contrast between
the current letter and the past one (v. 9), which may
have been misunderstood.

The present subjunctive and the way the offenses
are described indicate Paul has in mind that which
is habitual or ongoing as sin. Just as he has shown
that such sin is typical of those who are of this
world, Paul addresses those for whom this sort of
sin is typical and who claim to be "inside" (ἔσω) the
church (v. 12). In other words, Paul is not suggesting that at the first evidence of sin, or of falling into
temptation, the only way forward is to be banished
from the community. Rather, he is writing about
those whose sin is known and whose sin continues.
What one might expect of many of this world cannot be allowed of those within the church.

Here Paul adds two to his list of vices: "slanderer" and "drunkard." The background in Deuteronomy was discussed above. The verb "to slander"
or "scoff at" (λοιδορέω) was encountered in 4:12.
Paul responded to those who scoffed at him with
"kindly words." Clearly Paul has in mind another
vice that he knows is commonplace in Corinth.
In their high esteem for rhetoric and status, those
who were not of that class were scoffed at. In these
verses, Paul indicates that he was on the receiving
end of this. However, it is not just a personal matter
that concerns Paul. Within the church the scoffing
and slander would be focused on people like Paul,
who spoke what the world considered folly. It is
not possible for someone who claims to be part of
the Lord's covenant community to continue in that
community while slandering or scoffing at the one
who bears the message of the Lord himself.

"Drunkard" (μέθυσος) is a new category and describes one who is regularly drunk. There is not
much evidence either way to suggest whether this
was a special problem at Corinth. However, it is
possible that there is an allusion to drunkenness
as a church problem in the Old Testament quotation in 10:7 (from Exod 32:6). Pagan feasts were
noted for their orgy-like atmospheres, and drunkenness and immorality would go hand in hand as
they often do today. In 11:21 Paul indicates there
are cases of drunkenness even at the Lord's Supper, suggesting that some approached the Supper
in much the same way as they had approached a
pagan temple feast in their former life. In Paul's
writings self-control is seen to be an important
fruit of the Spirit.[30] Drunkenness therefore stands

---

29. E.g., ESV, NIV, NRSV, but RSV, REB, and NJB use a
past tense.

30. See Gal 5:23. In this epistle, note 7:5, 9; 9:25. See also
the list of vices in 2 Tim 3:3 where being "without self-control"
is listed. See also 2 Tim 1:7: "God gave us a spirit of . . . self
control" (ESV).

in stark contrast to the one who is supposed to give evidence in his or her life to the possession of the Holy Spirit.

Finally, Paul adds a second part to his command "not to associate with anyone." They are "not even" (μηδέ) to eat together with such a person. This sentence is explanatory in the sense that it develops what Paul means by not "associating with." It is likely that the single most important application of the injunction not to eat with them involved excluding them from the communion meal. But it is not entirely clear how much further this meal exclusion was to be extended. In a similar exhortation in 2 Thessalonians 3:14, it is equally unclear how far Paul intends the exclusion to extend. However, as in many cultures today, in Paul's day eating with people had to do with social bonding and the establishment of deeper relationships. Meals were the places where friendships were established and even where contracts were made. These are times when people form the lasting relationships and commitments to one another in which dependency is expressed. All of this is entirely appropriate within the Christian community and much to be encouraged. Church members are to love one another and are indeed dependent on each other. However, Paul is saying that such expressions of depth of fellowship are inappropriate when a person is coming under discipline and being banished from the community. Calvin makes the comment that "the authority of the Church [in excommunication] would count for nothing if individuals were allowed to invite to their own tables those who have been debarred from the Lord's table."[31]

In today's church, there would be a need to look at what cultural expressions of closeness and community dependence would have to be avoided, but social contact will have to be approached cautiously. This explanation does help the church understand, however, that Paul is not asking the impossible. It is not that there should be no contact of any sort with such a person. In fact, it is that the church should treat this person as one who is now thoroughly outside the community.

5:12–13 For what is it to me to judge outsiders? Is it not those inside whom you are to judge? God judges those outside. "Banish the evil person from among yourselves" (τί γάρ μοι τοὺς ἔξω κρίνειν; οὐχὶ τοὺς ἔσω ὑμεῖς κρίνετε; τοὺς δὲ ἔξω ὁ θεὸς κρινεῖ. ἐξάρατε τὸν πονηρὸν ἐξ ὑμῶν αὐτῶν). Lest there be any confusion, Paul again insists that he is concerned with the sinful person *within* the Christian community. God, he says, will judge those outside.[32] As Paul now moves toward his conclusion, the structure of these last two verses is clear. It takes the shape of AB-AB. The first rhetorical question (5:12a) receives a response in the assertion of an action in 5:13a. Paul will not judge outsiders because it is not his job to do so and neither is it the job of the Corinthians. "God judges those outside" (τοὺς δὲ ἔξω ὁ θεὸς κρινεῖ). The second rhetorical question of 5:12b calls for judging of those inside and receives a response in 5:13b commanding action: "Banish the evil person . . ." (ἐξάρατε).

The protection of the community from God's judgment requires the expulsion of the evil person concerned. Paul thus clarifies the responsibilities that lie upon the church of God with regard to discipline. However "spiritual" they may be, it is not their duty to judge (κρίνειν) "the outsiders" (τοὺς ἔξω). Again, it is the boundary of the community that must be understood, and this involves right judgment or discernment. Those "outside" are

---

31. Calvin, *First Corinthians*, 114.
32. The opening clause requires a verb when translated to

English: "For what [is it] to me" (with μοι ["to me"] functioning as a dative of personal interest).

those who are not in the church. They are non-Christians and unbelievers. In the covenant terms of the Pentateuch this is the equivalent of the nations around Israel who do not acknowledge Yahweh. They belong in God's hands for his judgment (Ps 82:8; cf. Rev 18:4–8). Time and again the threat to the Israelites is that they will be punished by being put "outside" the camp or the people; that is, their punishment will be to become as the nations (e.g., Lev 22:10; 24:14; Num 12:14–15).

Christians meeting as a church are, however, to judge those inside. The RSV adds "inside *the church*." This provides a climax to the whole matter of judgment and discernment that Paul sees as such a vital issue for those concerned with membership and status within the community. This serious area of judgment is one where they have dramatically failed, yet they judge each other over trivialities in wrongful ways. The judgment needed here requires them firstly to see that sin has indeed entered the community in a dramatic and serious manner, and then secondly to act to eject the person concerned. Paul completes this section with a quotation that is repeated several times in the same

section of Deuteronomy to which he has been alluding. There the Greek expression in the LXX is "you shall banish the evil from the midst of you" (AT; ἐξαρεῖς τὸν πονηρὸν ἐξ ὑμῶν αὐτῶν; see Deut 17:7; 19:19; 21:21; 22:21, 24; 24:7; see also 17:12; 22:22). To suit the way his argument is phrased, Paul has changed the future indicative of the LXX to the aorist imperative.

Paul has concluded his discussion of the church's approach to the matter of incest in their midst in dramatic and clear-cut style. The covenantal obedience required by the Lord of those who are his has been deliberately ignored. The holiness of the temple community in which God's Spirit dwells has been damaged, and so the church must act if it is not to find itself under God's judgment of the sort seen in Israel in the past. Just as Israel was required to banish the willful and unrepentant sinner from the camp, so the church must do the same. Paul will return to examples of the Lord's judgment upon Israel in chapter 10. There, he will explicitly say that "[these things] were written down for our instruction, on whom the end of the ages has come" (10:11 ESV).

Theology in Application

Sexual Immorality in the Church

The danger of a church tolerating sexual immorality among its own members is clearly seen in this chapter.[33] At his chosen time God will judge, for sexual immorality is portrayed throughout all Scripture as offensive to God. Though often the modern church will point out and speak about certain sins such as adultery or pornography, the biblical theology of the matter is rarely heard. Yet it is in the flow of Scripture as a whole with regard to this subject that we discover why it is such an important matter. Well-intended teaching on immorality may leave Christians in no doubt about what is impermissible behavior, yet it often can seem simply arbitrary. Many are left feeling "we do not do this because we are not allowed to" rather than

---

33. On the great significance Paul attaches to the dangers of greed and idolatry for the church (5:10), see comments on that verse. See also the section under Theology in Application following comments on 6:1–11 ("Idolatry and Greed").

being able to make a case from Scripture that the Lord's commands are far from arbitrary. Indeed, it is often as people begin to see the biblical theology of the act of sexual intercourse as part of heterosexual marriage that they finally understand why God insists on certain behavior.

Paul followed in the tradition of all biblical writers that the place for sexual activity was laid down by God at creation. It was only when Adam finally looked on God's creation of woman that he had the right partner to fulfill the command to "be fruitful and multiply" (Gen 1:28 ESV; see 2:23). It is *after* that, when the right partners were together, that we are told of marriage. Indeed, marriage is introduced as a consequence of having the right partners to fulfill God's creation mandate in place: "*Therefore* a man shall leave his father and his mother and hold fast to his wife, and they shall become one flesh" (Gen 2:24 ESV). Yet, additionally, as the biblical narrative progresses it becomes clear that this marriage relationship was placed in creation by God in order that there might be in human life a picture of his relationship with his people. It is not that God looked around and saw marriage and decided that it could be a good picture of his love for his people, but that he created marriage so that people would have a better understanding of his love for his people and what their love for him should be like.

This is why it is also possible for God to use the distortion of the picture as evidence of what happens when people turn away from him to idols. Adultery comes to picture the breakdown of his people's relationship with him. Divorce likewise no longer upholds the picture of creation that God loves his people and is faithful to them. The book of Hosea and multiple passages of Scripture, such as Ezekiel 16 and Jeremiah 3, draw on the same ideas. Perhaps the clearest of all passages to draw out the creational and biblical-theological understanding of marriage is Ephesians 5:21–33. There Paul moves backward and forward between speaking of the love of Christ for the church and that of husband for wife, and between the love of the church for Christ and that of the wife for the husband. There the picture is laid out for us in its full glory. It concludes remarkably with a quotation of Genesis 2:23 that is then applied directly to Christ and the church (Eph 5:29–30). Perhaps even more remarkable is that in quoting Genesis, Paul specifically links the act of sexual intercourse to this picture of God and his people: "The two shall become one flesh." At the point of deepest possible intimacy between a man and a woman lies the depth of the picture God placed in creation.

Given that God intended marriage to be this picture and the breach of marriage to portray something akin to idolatry or to forsaking God, then the many laws about sexual activity laid down in the Pentateuch take on much more than simple pragmatic intent. No doubt when the law of the Lord was kept then, pragmatic advantages were seen; illnesses of various sorts were avoided (cf. Rom 1:27), lust was controlled, children had two parents, and other practical benefits were experienced within family life. However, we can immediately see that, for example, bestiality was wrong because Adam had deliberately rejected the animals and God had made a special creation for Adam in Eve. This enabled them to enjoy fulfilling the creation mandate even as they enjoyed each other's bodies. Incest was also wrong because it involved the *same* family and was not about leaving one family and starting another (leaving father and mother; Gen 2:24). The "differentness" of God and his people is reflected in husband and wife in a way in which it is not in homosexual "marriage" relationships. Of course, vastly more than this is indicated in Scripture as to why sexual activity is limited to heterosexual marriage and why anything else is sexual immorality, but it is this biblical theology that is so rarely taught. The result is that many Christians are left thinking that this is all arbitrary on God's part. They are thus even more vulnerable to tolerating unbiblical behavior. The sin is ultimately most serious in the church because it reflects a rejection of the teaching that God has made his people his temple and that they must therefore be a holy place.

The Discipline of Excommunication

The demand that God's people be holy as God dwells among them runs right through Scripture. In this passage Paul's dependence on similar themes from the Old Testament is clear. The comparison Paul makes between the Christian community and the Israelites is at times implicit in this epistle and at other times explicit, and it is this that forms the background for the idea of community banishment for the sinner who lives in rebellion against God's law. For Paul, this judgment that the community is required to pass on those who continue to deliberately flout the demand for holiness is an aspect of the discernment he expects of those who follow Christ and are led by his Spirit. This sort of spiritual discernment is as sadly lacking in much of the modern church as it was in Corinth. The final judgment of an individual is always left in the Lord's hands, but the church's judgment should demonstrate the Lord's own displeasure at willful, continuing sin among his people. Today, as in Corinth, immorality, greed, drunkenness, slander, and much else is tolerated without comment. Recently, a young professional woman spoke to me of the church she had just started attending. She expressed surprise that her peers joked at the back of church about how drunk they had been the night before and of their sexual exploits with different "dates." Her special concern was that she saw church leaders on the edge of these conversations who never said anything to any of them. None were ever challenged about holiness.

Today there is often no real sense of the church as a covenant community responsible to the covenant Lord God *as a people* and therefore also having a right to be responsible for each other spiritually. The emphasis on individualism means that each person will be left to choose his or her own way before the Lord. If others recognise that an individual needs to repent of serious sin, something may be said, but then it will be left to him or her as to whether repentance occurs. The impact of that sin on the body is never even contemplated or discussed. While the leaders of that woman's church may not have agreed with or even liked the behavior being discussed and were in fact concerned for the souls of these individuals, they clearly were not overly concerned for the holiness of the church.

Today's church also wrestles with the strong secular emphasis on toleration of others. When this is imported into the church as "we must all tolerate and love each other and so not judge each other," the church again finds itself unable to act in concert against the sin of an individual. To do so is seen to be authoritarian and unloving. Often people will add comments like, "And who are we to judge?" The Bible's answer is of course multifaceted to these sorts of questions but, at heart it is that the church is a "body" that should act in unity under the leadership of the Holy Spirit to become the holy place that it really is. Holiness matters.

What we call "excommunication" or banishment from the community must surely be seen as the ultimate step of discipline by the church on a member who needs to repent and to be forgiven by the Lord. It is designed to lead to the restoration of the individual and will be the culmination of various intermediate steps designed to restore people to holiness. Christians are encouraged to admonish their brothers and sisters who are wandering from the life they should be living in holiness and the service of Christ (cf. Matt 18:15–16; 1 Thess 5:12–15; 2 Thess 3:15), much as Paul himself did (Acts 20:31; 1 Cor 4:14). In Ephesians 5:11–14 the apostle describes a form of discipline or action against those who follow the "works of darkness" that is more than warning but prior to full excommunication and involves publicly exposing sin (cf. 1 Tim 5:20).[34] There Paul insists that Christians are not to fellowship with such people, but to draw attention to or expose their sin in order that the immature Christian or recent convert may change their way of life toward holiness.

In the end, of course, church discipline is about more than simply getting the ethics of Christian life correct, because it is about the holiness of a people called by God to be a place fit for him to dwell. Ultimately, this serious step of banishing people from the fellowship of the church will only make sense if both aspects are taught in the church and understood by the people. That is, the church must see such measures as restorative for the individual and as maintaining the holiness of the place where God dwells.

A lack of holiness among God's people means that strangers walking into a church simply see a reflection of the world they already know. God has determined that his people should be in the middle of their society but living as a holy people in a way that will be recognizable by all.

---

34. For further comment on the application of what Paul says in Eph 5 on this matter, see Clinton E. Arnold, *Ephesians*, ZECNT (Grand Rapids: Zondervan, 2010), 338–40.

12

1 Corinthians 6:1–11

Literary Context

In chapter 6 Paul continues to address certain behaviors and attitudes among the Corinthians that reflect their lack of judgment, their arrogance, and their divisions. Their toleration of immorality in their midst, discussed in chapter 5, is but one example of the tragic behavior of a church and its leadership that wrongly believes their status before God is virtually unassailable. Paul ended that section by reminding the Corinthians that Christian community identity requires holiness. Though priding themselves in their wisdom and their spiritual gifts, Paul now points to another area in the church's life that reveals their lack of godly wisdom and concern and care for each other. This section begins and ends with vocabulary that reminds Paul's readers of their true status before God and how it is achieved. They are "saints" (6:1–2), and they "were washed" (v. 11), and they are inheritors of the kingdom of God (vv. 9–11).

However, despite this, members are taking each other to court. The irony of this example is acute. Judgment in civil legal cases requires the practice of wisdom. Can it be that those who claim to be wise are unable even to help guide members of their own church as to what is fair or just? Where is the wisdom they so flaunt if they have to go before unbelievers for judgments even on minor civil cases? In 6:9–11 Paul makes it clear that their lack of discernment raises serious questions about their status before God. Again, the irony of this must not be lost. They take pride in their status and power, which they regard as secured in the manifestation of their gifts, especially their wisdom and knowledge. This is why Paul reminds them of what he had said at the start of the epistle: their status is dependent on God's grace. The use of the passive tenses in v. 11 helps make the point. In 6:12–20, Paul will take up yet another matter from the life of the church in which their judgment on moral issues has been seriously amiss.

Main Idea

Christians are saints, and their community should reflect who they are. Their divisions and the ease with which they resort to a worldly court system are both wrong. As inheritors of the kingdom of God, they should reflect their God-given status in their love for each other and in using their grace-gift of wisdom in a godly way to resolve any legal problems between members.

Translation

1 Corinthians 6:1–11

1a	Rhetorical question 1	**Dare anyone of you,...**
b	Explanation	having a [legal] grievance against another,
c		**... go to law**
d	Place	before the unrighteous instead of
e	Contrast	the saints?
2a	Rhetorical question 2 (basis)	Or **do you not know that the saints will judge the world?**
	Argument from greater to lesser	And
b	Condition (protasis)	if the world is judged
c	Agency	by you,
d	Rhetorical question 3 (apodosis)	**are you not competent to try minor cases?**
3a	Rhetorical question 4	**Do you not know that we judge the angels?**
b	Argument from greater to lesser	How much more cases pertaining to this life!

Continued on next page.

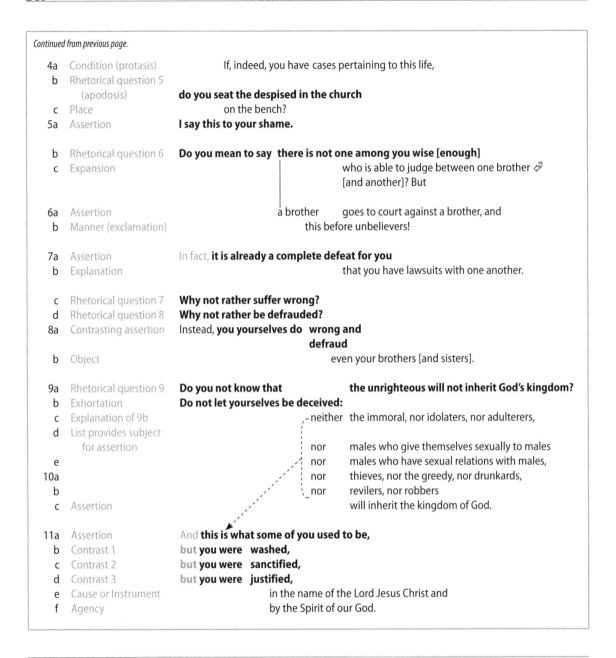

Continued from previous page.

4a	Condition (protasis)	If, indeed, you have cases pertaining to this life,
b	Rhetorical question 5 (apodosis)	**do you seat the despised in the church**
c	Place	on the bench?
5a	Assertion	**I say this to your shame.**
b	Rhetorical question 6	**Do you mean to say there is not one among you wise [enough]**
c	Expansion	who is able to judge between one brother ↺ [and another]? But
6a	Assertion	a brother goes to court against a brother, and
b	Manner (exclamation)	this before unbelievers!
7a	Assertion	In fact, **it is already a complete defeat for you**
b	Explanation	that you have lawsuits with one another.
c	Rhetorical question 7	**Why not rather suffer wrong?**
d	Rhetorical question 8	**Why not rather be defrauded?**
8a	Contrasting assertion	Instead, **you yourselves do wrong and defraud**
b	Object	even your brothers [and sisters].
9a	Rhetorical question 9	**Do you not know that the unrighteous will not inherit God's kingdom?**
b	Exhortation	**Do not let yourselves be deceived:**
c	Explanation of 9b	–neither the immoral, nor idolaters, nor adulterers,
d	List provides subject for assertion	nor males who give themselves sexually to males
e		nor males who have sexual relations with males,
10a		nor thieves, nor the greedy, nor drunkards,
b		nor revilers, nor robbers
c	Assertion	will inherit the kingdom of God.
11a	Assertion	And **this is what some of you used to be,**
b	Contrast 1	**but you were washed,**
c	Contrast 2	**but you were sanctified,**
d	Contrast 3	**but you were justified,**
e	Cause or Instrument	in the name of the Lord Jesus Christ and
f	Agency	by the Spirit of our God.

Structure

This section begins and ends with an affirmation of the status before God of those to whom Paul writes. The forward momentum of the passage is maintained through a series of identical rhetorical questions previously used in 3:16 and 5:6: "Do you not know . . . ?" (6:2, 3, 9). Further rhetorical questions emphasize the message (6:1, 5, 7).

The first section (6:1–8) is structured to begin and end with the problem: one brother takes another to court (note the use of the word translated here as "to go to law" and as "to judge" [κρίνω] in v. 1 and v. 6 and its repetitive use in these verses). Three main reasons are proposed for why Christians should not go to court (vv. 1–3, 4–6, 7–8).

In the second section (6:9–11), Paul broadens the message away from the people who are taking each other to court to a more general challenge to the conduct of the whole church. As in chapter 5, the appeal to community holiness now reappears as the focus. The imperative "do not be deceived" (v. 9) stands at the heart of this section. The repetition of the related words translated here variously as "unrighteous" and "wrong" also serves to maintain the forward movement of the argument (6:1, 7, 8, 9; ἄδικος/ἀδικέω).

Exegetical Outline

V. Lack of Spiritual Wisdom Has Led to Grievous Sin (5:1–6:20)

    A. A Case of Incest Must Be Resolved (5:1–8)

    B. Community Identity Requires Holiness (5:9–13)

➡   **C. Lawsuits between Christians Must Be Resolved without the Courts (6:1–8)**

       1. Because They Will Eventually Judge the World (6:1–3)

       2. Because They Are Supposed to Possess Godly Wisdom (6:4–6)

       3. Because This Action Reveals Their Unrighteousness (6:7–8)

    D. Community Identity Requires Holiness (6:9–11)

       1. The Unrighteous Do Not Inherit the Kingdom of God (6:9–10)

       2. The Righteous Have Been Changed by God (6:11)

Explanation of the Text

6:1 Dare anyone of you, having a [legal] grievance against another, go to law before the unrighteous instead of the saints? (Τολμᾷ τις ὑμῶν πρᾶγμα ἔχων πρὸς τὸν ἕτερον κρίνεσθαι ἐπὶ τῶν ἀδίκων, καὶ οὐχὶ ἐπὶ τῶν ἁγίων;). This translation is not the most fluent English but seeks to maintain the expression of deep surprise, if not shock, that Paul communicates as he begins to address the next issue of believers taking believers to court. The initial interrogative verb is forceful. "Anyone"

(τις) is normally indefinite, but it is possible here that there is only one such legal case in the congregation, in which case the translation could be, "Does one of you dare . . . ?" If Paul has in mind just one individual, then it is likely to be the plaintiff who is being addressed[1] before the argument is broadened out in v. 2 to address the whole church. Given the usual indefinite connotation of "anyone" and the plural verbs in the following verses, it seems preferable to assume that Paul is referring

---

1. Fee, *1 Corinthians*, 255.

to a number of unnamed people in the church who were taking their fellow brothers or sisters to court. The participial clause qualifies "anyone." "Grievance" (πρᾶγμα) is a word that usually simply means "deed" or "action." In this context and with this construction, it takes on a specific connotation of a legal action or lawsuit.[2] The present, middle infinitive of the verb "to judge" (κρίνω) plus the preposition "before" (ἐπί + genitive) provides the idea of a person to be judged; hence the translation "go to law."

Paul's introduction to this further example of inappropriate behavior among God's people is stark. It seems he cannot believe that those whom he congratulates for not lacking in any grace-gift—particularly that of "knowledge" (1:4–7)—are so ready to turn to others outside the community (the ἄδικοι) when it comes to matters of law or to grievances and arguments between believers.

Recalling his opening remarks, Paul again calls the Christians "saints."[3] Thus, even as the Corinthians are bragging about their human status and speaking of their wisdom, power, and many gifts, Paul reminds them of the only status that truly matters—their standing before God. The fact that he has in mind their status by referring to them as "saints" becomes clear from the context. In vv. 2–3, it is their status as judges of the world and of angels that speaks against their resorting for judgment to those who have no such status. Paul's eschatology frames his argument here. The future status of both groups, the "saints" (ἅγιοι) and the "unrighteous" (ἄδικοι; v. 1), is in mind in vv. 2–3 where the "saints will judge the world" and "judge the angels" and in v. 9 where the "unrighteous will not inherit God's

kingdom." The one group has standing within God's community; the other group is outside.[4]

Furthermore, Paul's specific contrast of "saints" with the "unrighteous" also suggests that spiritual status is the issue. The more usual contrast in Scripture is between the "righteous" (δίκαιος) and the "unrighteous" (ἄδικος), which may simply distinguish between believer and nonbeliever (e.g., Matt 5:45; Acts 24:15)[5] or, on occasion, provide a moral contrast between the deeds performed by individuals (e.g., Rev 22:11). Of course, the moral dimension of the comparison between the "saints" and the "unrighteous" cannot be ignored. Paul's concern through these chapters is that people with the status of "saints" seem to remain unaffected by this when it comes to their behavior. The holy are acting like the unrighteous, like unbelievers. Indeed, the unrighteous are characterized by their immoral behavior (6:9).

Nevertheless, the appeal to the future status of the saints as judging the world (v. 2), the use of "unbelievers" as a synonym for "unrighteous" (v. 6), the reference to inheriting the kingdom of God (v. 9), and the passive voice appealing to the status of the believers in v. 11 all suggest that Paul's main concern is that it is simply *wrong* for those who are saints to seek legal redress against each other before those who are not saints, that is, who have no standing in the Christian community.

Caution needs to be exercised, therefore, before jumping to the conclusion that Paul's problem with outside judges mainly concerns the fact that they were *unfair* as judges. Of course, it is possible that the proclivity of judges or magistrates to render unjust judgments contributes to Paul's consider-

---

2. *P. Oxy.* 743.19. See BDAG 858 and examples from the papyri quoted in MM 532.

3. See comments on 1:2.

4. Bruce J. Malina and John J. Pilch, *Social-Science Commentary on the Letters of Paul* (Minneapolis: Fortress, 2006),

82, is right when they refer to the groups as "insiders" and "outsiders."

5. Barrett, *First Corinthians*, 135, on this verse says "possibly 'non Christians' and 'Christians' . . . would be preferable."

able sarcasm in v. 5, when he asks whether there is anyone in the Christian community capable of deciding between Christian brothers and sisters. Yet some have seen in Paul's description of the judges as "unrighteous" (ἄδικοι) not so much a statement about their status as non-Christians but rather a moral reference to the lack of fairness in their judgments or even to their supposed inherent bias toward the rich or powerful.[6] Certainly the Roman courts were not always known for their judicial rectitude. Dio Chrysostom, writing at the end of the first century, refers to lawyers in Corinth who perverted justice.[7] Thiselton goes so far as to translate as "seek judgment at a court where there is *questionable justice.*"[8] Winter has also contended for the view that "unrighteous" refers to "unfair" or "unjust" judgments, extensively examining much of the Corinthian civil-litigation system and commenting on the wealthy using the courts as a means of exercising their power to manipulate justice in their favor. This he argues is possibly what the elite, wealthy, Christian Corinthians were doing as they took brothers and sisters to court.[9] Garland largely follows this argument, suggesting that "Paul is not simply exasperated that any Christian would take a case involving a brother to nonbelieving judges but that they would take it to those biased in favor of the rich and powerful."[10]

While much of this examination of Corinthian and Greek systems for litigation—and their cor-

ruption and manipulation by the powerful to suit their own ends—adds to our understanding of the experience of those who took small cases before a corrupt judiciary in Corinth, it still seems from the text to be more likely that Paul's concern would have been just as deep had the judiciary among the unbelievers been the best in the world! Paul cannot accept that disputes among Christians need to be resolved in this way at all because Christians work with a completely different worldview governed by the gospel, by love, and by appeal to the Lord (cf. 6:7). Mature, spiritual, and grace-gifted Christian believers, even those unschooled in the law, should have the necessary understanding to handle such dissensions. The contrast between those within and those outside the covenant community of Christ has deep consequences for Paul in the whole way that life itself is approached, including when it comes to matters that might otherwise have been taken to civil litigation.

6:2–3 Or do you not know that the saints will judge the world? And if the world is judged by you,[11] are you not competent to try minor cases? Do you not know that we judge the angels? How much more cases pertaining to this life! (ἢ οὐκ οἴδατε ὅτι οἱ ἅγιοι τὸν κόσμον κρινοῦσιν; καὶ εἰ ἐν ὑμῖν κρίνεται ὁ κόσμος, ἀνάξιοί ἐστε κριτηρίων ἐλαχίστων; οὐκ οἴδατε ὅτι ἀγγέλους κρινοῦμεν, μήτι γε βιωτικά). Paul's argument is now brought to a

---

6. Cf. Horsley, *1 Corinthians*, 84; Garland, *1 Corinthians*, 195–96.

7. Dio Chrysostom, *Orations* 8.9, writing with great sarcasm about those who gathered around the Isthmian games, said: "Many fortune-tellers interpreting fortunes, lawyers innumerable perverting judgment," who were used to exercising their power in that way and would have been expected to win.

8. Thiselton, *1 Corinthians*, 418 (emphasis added).

9. Bruce W. Winter, "Civil Litigation in Secular Corinth and the Church: The Forensic Background to I Corinthians 6:1–8," *NTS* 37 (1991): 559–72.

10. Garland, *1 Corinthians*, 197. Also Witherington, *Con-

flict and Community, 164, and John K. Chow, *Patronage and Power: A Study of Social Networks in Corinth*, JSNTSup 75 (Sheffield: Sheffield Academic Press, 1992), 181–82, conclude that it is likely it was the wealthy in the church who were going to court to settle their grievances because they were more likely to receive favorable judgment.

11. "By you" (ἐν ὑμῖν) is the best translation here, though in the Greek this construction (ἐν with the dative) rarely expresses agency. However, see 6:11 below ("by the Spirit of our God"). Wallace, *Greek Grammar*, 374, regards 6:2 as the only clear example of this. BDF §219.1 adds, "Properly 'before the forum of.'" This latter would imply a locative use of the dative.

climax as he argues from the greater to the lesser. It is precisely because of the high status of God's covenant people, even with regard to the final judgment, that judgment in this life should, as is colloquially said, "be a piece of cake!" Since God has given his people extraordinary competencies to judge, surely they can judge small matters among themselves. On the rhetorical question "do you not know that . . . ?" (οὐκ οἴδατε ὅτι), see comments on 3:16. Here again the rhetorical question communicates a tone of sarcasm. The future tenses look forward to the eschatological judgment at the time of the King's return. "If" (εἰ) introduces a first-class condition, with the present, middle indicative (κρίνεται). The protasis thus assumes, for the sake of the argument, that the saints will judge the world. "To try minor cases" translates the objective genitives (κριτηρίων ἐλαχίστων).[12]

As Paul continues, he uses both irony and sarcasm. The irony lies in the fact that those who will share with Christ in the most serious and fearful judgment of all time are unable to trust each other to sort out minor legal cases within the Christian community. Whether it is one or several going to court, the cases are described in 6:2 as "trivial" or "the least" (ἐλαχίστων). These cases would have been smaller cases brought under civil law. The ending of the word translated "to try cases" (-τηρίων) may denote the place where judgment is given. Thus, Robertson translates: "Are ye unworthy of the smallest tribunals?"[13]

Why some should have pursued these court cases is a matter of some discussion, but the text gives little information. Part of the answer may be found in the recurring problem in the church of the exercise of power. As has been noted, status in the Corinthian pagan society was based upon wealth, power, wisdom, and patronage. The courts were often biased toward these people. It would not be surprising to find that converts, used to getting their way in society because of this status, should try to achieve their goals in a similar way within the community of the church. The rich and powerful would have been expected to win in the lower civil courts and probably resorted to these rather more speedily than would happen in the modern world.[14] Such an abuse of power and community status by richer Christians, however, would simply add to Paul's horror of what is going on. Paul's concern is that they should know better ("Do you not know . . . ?"). Their status now has a different foundation. They have a status "in Christ Jesus" (1:30) where "the least" among people have the same standing as all others who enjoy covenantal participation in him and with his people. Their problems must now be resolved in different ways. Their new status requires that they be content with ideas such as being prepared to "suffer wrong" or even to "be defrauded" (6:7). What they are doing is indeed "a serious breach of community,"[15] and surely, with all their spiritual gifts, they had people in their midst who could deliver good and godly mediation between people who should have love for one another.[16]

---

12. It is the adjective "not competent" (ἀνάξιοί) that produces the genitives (κριτηρίων ἐλαχίστων) here. BDF §182.2 refers to this under the rubric of "genitive of price." Matthew 3:8 offers an example where ἄξιος takes a genitive object.

13. Robertson and Plummer, *First Corinthians*, 112. For a detailed discussion of the type of case and court that may be in mind, see J. Duncan M. Derrett, "Judgment and 1 Cor 6," *NTS* 37 (1991): 22–36. Also Bruce W. Winter, *Seek the Welfare of the City: Christians as Benefactors and Citizens* (Grand Rapids: Eerdmans, 1994), 105–21.

14. In his "Civil Litigation," 561ff., Winter argues that only the powerful would have gone to court. See also idem, *Seek the Welfare of the City*, 106–21. It is speculation to suggest that the divisions of 1 Cor 1 under different church leaders had led to court cases between them (contra Winter, *Seek the Welfare of the City*, 118).

15. Witherington, *Conflict and Community*, 164–65.

16. The emphasis on "love" as *the* community marker is developed at greater length by Paul in chapters 8 and 13, but the idea is ever present as Paul discusses the behavior of God's people.

So Paul develops his argument *from the greater to the lesser*. With three rather sarcastic-sounding rhetorical questions followed by a summary exclamation, the point is driven home. The "saints will judge the world,"[17] so surely as "saints" they are competent to judge minor civil cases (κριτηρίων ἐλαχίστων).[18] The saints will also "judge the angels" (ἀγγέλους κρινοῦμεν), so how much more should they be able to judge "cases pertaining to this life" (βιωτικά)![19] The argument is made more personal as Paul specifically identifies the Corinthians as "the saints" ("by you" [ἐν ὑμῖν] in v. 2), thus still identifying them, even in their wretched inadequacies of understanding, as covenant participators "in Christ." Similarly, in v. 3 Paul makes the application personal as he now identifies with the Corinthians in their status as eschatological judges, using the first-person plural (κρινοῦμεν). In this way, the argument from the *greater to the lesser* reaches its climax. If these Corinthian Christians will even

judge angels one day, how much more should they be able to solve minor cases that arise among the people of God.

The power of this argument from eschatology could hardly have been lost on the Corinthians. The end time to which Paul refers reveals a complete reversal of the current scene, in which he has described even the apostles as "made a spectacle [by God] to the world, to both angels and men" (4:9). The true status of believers is not at once apparent to this world or even to angels anymore than Christ's kingship was at once apparent when he walked this earth or went to the cross. But just as Jesus lived in a manner befitting his status as the Son of God and Messiah, so Christians should live in a manner befitting their status as God's people (in the present) and as those who will one day rule and judge. For the time being, that status is best seen in the preparedness of the Christian, out of love for the brother or sister, to suffer wrong.

IN DEPTH: The Saints and the Judgment of the World

It is likely that the background to the claim that the saints will judge the world and the angels lies in the LXX of Daniel 7:22 where we read "he gave judgment to the saints of the Most High" (καὶ τὴν κρίσιν ἔδωκε τοῖς ἁγίοις τοῦ ὑψίστου). Wisdom of Solomon 3:8–9 and Sirach 4:14–15 also give a similar perspective that God's people (the Jews in this case) shall judge the nations.[20] Other texts that show similar ideas in intertestamental writings and in the Qumran documents provide further context for Paul's statement.[21] While in some of these references

---

17. See above, "In Depth: The Saints and the Judgment of the World."

18. Winter, *Seek the Welfare of the City*, 107–8, argues that this phrase requires us to understand these were minor *civil* cases. He also points out that "generally, lawsuits were conducted between social equals who were from the powerful (οἱ δυνατοί) of the city, or by . . . [one of] superior social status and power against an inferior." These court cases are thus run-of-the-mill disputes that constantly crop up between people, whereas the more serious court cases would go before a Roman judge.

19. This word refers to "matters of daily life." See BDAG 177.

20. Wis 3:8–9: "They shall judge the nations"; and Sirach 4:14–15: "Those who serve her [wisdom] minister to the Holy One, and the Lord loves those who love her. Whoever obeys her rules the nations."

21. 1 En. 1:9, 38 (where the "holy ones" are probably angels); 38:1; 98:12; 108:12–13; Jub. 24:29; 1QpHab 5:4–5; 4Q161 8–10:20. See also Jude 14–15.

the "holy ones" appear in fact to be angels rather than God's people, the vision of Daniel 7 seems to have dominated in these texts to the extent that N. T. Wright can say, "It seems clear that by the first century this passage [Dan 7:18, 22, 27] was being read in terms of the faithful Jewish people as a whole."[22] He also comments that this would explain passages like the ones referred to above in Wisdom 3 and Sirach.

For Paul and the early church, it is a given that God's judgment will be carried out by the Christ who is himself the "Lord." This will happen as he comes in divine glory at the end of this age (cf. Luke 21:27; Acts 17:31). Indeed, that is why Paul has urged the Corinthians not to judge him since that should wait until the time when "the Lord comes" (4:5). Building on the scriptural heritage, Paul believes that God's people are involved with the work of their Lord and caught up in his status, being found "in Christ" and *participating* covenantally with him. They are involved in his work and are incorporated in him as they are represented by him. Just as Paul is able to say that "we [Christians] have died with Christ" (Rom 6:8), "we will also live with him" (2 Tim 2:11), and "it is no longer I who live, but Christ who lives in me" (Gal 2:20), so he can envisage God's people caught up in all that is true of the Lord Christ. If Christ is judge of the world, it stands to reason that those "in Christ" will judge the world, just as it seems Daniel had seen in his vision. In other words, this is another consequence of the apostle's theology of God's people's "participation with [God's] Son, Jesus Christ our Lord" (1:9).[23]

The same realm of ideas is also present elsewhere in the New Testament. For example, Jesus himself promises the disciples they will sit on thrones with Christ and will judge the twelve tribes of Israel (Matt 19:28).[24] Revelation 20:4 speaks of those given authority to judge being seated on thrones. Those who are raised with Christ will also "reign with him" (20:6; cf. Rom 5:17). Indeed, all that the suffering Son of God inherited when the Father brought him again to glory is shared with his people. Even now "in Christ" believers share many things with him, not least "his sufferings" (2 Cor 1:5). Yet they will share much more with Christ when God brings them to glory. This will include his rule and dominion for which humanity has been created from the beginning (Gen 1:28). Part of that rule will be to join the Lord of glory in his judgment. Ironically, the

---

22. Wright, *Paul and the Faithfulness of God*, 1090n208.

23. See the essay, "In Depth: The Meaning of the Word Κοινωνία" at the end of 1:9.

24. Whatever this particular judgment may refer to, the realm of ideas remains the same: the followers of the King will be involved in and with his judgment at the last day. There is no need to distinguish between "making judicial decisions" and administering "God's judgments" (so Garland, *1 Corinthians*, 202, suggesting that the supposed background texts only refer to the latter). For Paul, the exalted people of God have the mind of Christ. Their will is finally in line with the will of God himself, and they are fully participating in the work of the covenant Lord. Paul's appeal is to the eschatological status of God's people (so Fee, *1 Corinthians*, 257–58).

elitist Christians had it all wrong. They believed they had "become kings" (1 Cor 4:8). Paul ironically said he would like to share such rule with them, but the apostle knows that this final rule is as yet spurious. One day, though, he and they will share in their Lord's rule!

The reference to judging the angels (6:3) also refers to the final judgment day and therefore to fallen angels who will be judged by Christ. Their judgment is a recurring idea in apocalyptic thought.[25] In 15:24–27 Paul speaks of the destruction of every "rule and authority and power" by Jesus before he hands the kingdom to his Father. Christ will reign until every enemy is overcome. Again, it is likely that Paul assumes that the saints are ruling with Christ and involved in this great eschatological judgment even of the angels themselves. There is little point in speculating about which angels or what type of judgment Paul has in view.[26] In the context it is all part of the general judgment in which God's people take part along with their Lord. The argument from the greater to the lesser is potent. If all this is to happen in the future, how can some of these Christians not resolve lesser, internal church disputes right now!

6:4 If, indeed, you have cases pertaining to this life, do you seat the despised in the church on the bench? (βιωτικὰ μὲν οὖν κριτήρια ἐὰν ἔχητε, τοὺς ἐξουθενημένους ἐν τῇ ἐκκλησίᾳ τούτους καθίζετε;). Paul continues his ironic and critical rhetorical questions. He cannot understand why those with the status of "saints," the holy people of God, should even consider turning for judgments to those pagans who should be regarded in the church as "despised." This verse, however, raises a few substantial interpretative difficulties. Clearly it is necessary to decide whether the verb "to seat" (καθίζω) appears here as a present indicative or a present imperative. Also, a decision regarding the punctuation must be made. Is it a question or a statement/command? Moreover, who are the "despised"? Are they members of the church or the outside judges to whom some in the church are resorting? The arguments surrounding these questions are considerable.

Some take the verse as another in the series of rhetorical questions.[27] The verb is therefore taken as present indicative, and the "despised" refer to the pagan judges who should have no place at all within this eschatological community. Thus, it may be read, *"If, indeed,[28] you have cases pertaining to this life, do you sit those despised by the church on the bench?"* This interpretation is supported in a number of ways. The series of rhetorical questions

---

25. See, for example, Jude 6; 2 Pet 2:4; cf. Matt 25:41.

26. There has been some question as to whether Paul envisages both good and bad angels being judged. Godet, *First Corinthians*, 1:288, argues from 15:24 that Christ's judgment of "every power" would include the judgment of "evil" angels. This would accord with 6:2 and the judgment of the "world," understood as the world set against God. He disputes Meyer's view that Paul refers to the judgment of "good" angels whose works will be held to account. Meyer refers to Heb 1:13–14 for

support, but that passage says nothing about the saints judging the angels.

27. Agreeing with the punctuation of UBS[5]. So RSV, NJB, NASB. For modern commentators taking this view, see Barrett, *First Corinthians*, 137; Héring, *First Corinthians*, 39; Fee, *1 Corinthians*, 260; Thiselton, *1 Corinthians*, 432; Fitzmyer, *1 Corinthians*, 252; see also Meeks, *First Urban Christians*, 94.

28. Taking οὖν in its intensifying force; see MM 465; BDAG 736.

is maintained. The first question of v. 2a provides the basis for the following ironic question of v. 2d. The question of v. 3a provides the basis for the following ironic question of v. 4b–c. The irony and building sense of sarcasm are established and lead naturally into the high sarcasm of the rhetorical question in v. 5. It is highly unlikely that Paul himself would refer to some of the Corinthian congregation as "despised" even if he acknowledges that in the view of the world the whole church consists of the "despised" (1:28). It is more likely that the verb, when placed at the end of the sentence in this way, is indicative rather than imperative. The interpretation is also supported by reference to the problems with the alternatives. However, there are problems with this view as well. Would Paul have spoken in such a disparaging way of non-Christians? Nowhere else does he do so. Was the Christian church in any position to "seat" the secular judges, that is, to appoint them? The phrase "in the church" is awkward. Does it effectively mean "despised *by* the church" or "despised *among* those in the church"?

Some take the verse as a command; thus the verb is understood as an imperative.[29] Thus, it may be read, *"If, indeed, you have cases pertaining to this life, seat those despised in the church on the bench."* In this case, the "despised" must refer to Christians because it is inconceivable, following Paul's train of thought, that he should command them to do the very thing he finds so extraordinary! This view is also supported in a number of ways. The word "despised" (ἐξουθενημένους) is used in 1:28 and refers to the world's attitude to *Christians*. This is also how it is used of Jesus who was "despised" by Herod and by the Jewish people in Luke 23:11 and

Acts 4:11. Elsewhere the word is used by Christians of Christians.[30] If Christians are in mind here, then it is they who are to be seated in the place of judgment ("on the bench"), and thus Paul is pointing again to the reversal of the world's values that should be expected in the Christian community. Christians may be "despised" by the world, but they are the "saints" and will one day sit in judgment on the world; therefore, even the least of them should be prepared to offer guidance and judgments right now within their own community. Moreover, even the wealthiest among them should be prepared to submit to their brothers. In doing this the church will both reveal its different way of doing things—a way that reflects God's righteousness and in which even the poor receive justice—and also prove to be a testimony to the world that needs to see "grace at work."[31] Two problems with this view are that it is most unlikely that an imperative verb would be placed right at the end of the sentence. And, secondly, it is unlikely that Paul would himself have referred to some Christians as "despised." It would seem particularly unlikely in this section of his argument where he is appealing to the *exalted* status of believers as those who will judge the world and angels. In effect, he would be admitting to a social stratification in the church that he consistently rejects. Of course, for the sake of irony he could be admitting to these social distinctions without commending them, but this could easily have been misunderstood by the Corinthians and have seriously undermined his general argument that they are all equal within the community of Christ's church.

The arguments for and against these two main positions concerning v. 4 are often detailed and complicated. The position that this is another rhe-

---

29. So AV and NIV. For modern commentators taking this view, see Kistemaker, *First Corinthians*, 181; Clarke, *Secular and Christian Leadership in Corinth*, 71; Garland, *1 Corinthians*, 204–7; Brent Kinman, "'Appoint the Despised as Judges!' (1 Corinthians 6:4)," *TynBul* 48 (1997): 345–54. Kinman makes

the point that these "despised" may be lowly members of this church who are despised by the powerful and wealthy in the church.

30. E.g., 1 Cor 16:11; Rom 14:3, 10; 2 Cor 10:10; Gal 4:14.

31. So Murphy-O'Connor, *Paul: A Critical Life*, 285.

torical question seems to have the greater weight, especially in terms of the grammar, and so it is adopted here, but not without admitting to the strangeness of having Paul speak of outsiders as "despised" people. Perhaps it serves further to emphasize to the Corinthians that *they* are an exalted eschatological community and should not give up their place to secular leaders and judges, who, in fact, because they are outside the covenant community are the ones who should be regarded as "despised."

A further detail should be noted about the sentence structure. Starting the verse with the same word (βιωτικά) that concluded the previous verse gives great emphasis to "cases pertaining to this life." The sentence takes the form of a third-class condition. In using this construction, which can often imply a lack of certainty in its fulfillment, Paul perhaps raises the point that it is surprising to find Christians having such cases at all.[32] In other words, he is expressing continued surprise that there should be such quarrels and problems among these Christians. At the end of the day, their position as saints who will one day judge the world and angels should surely serve as a reminder to them that they can make righteous and godly decisions among themselves right now. This leads naturally into his next statement.

6:5–6 I say this to your shame. Do you mean to say there is not one among you wise [enough] who is able to judge between one brother [and another]? But a brother goes to court against a brother, and this[33] before unbelievers! (πρὸς ἐντροπὴν ὑμῖν λέγω. οὕτως οὐκ ἔνι ἐν ὑμῖν οὐδεὶς σοφὸς ὃς δυνήσεται διακρῖναι ἀνὰ μέσον τοῦ ἀδελφοῦ αὐτοῦ; ἀλλὰ ἀδελφὸς μετὰ ἀδελφοῦ κρίνεται καὶ τοῦτο ἐπὶ ἀπίστων). The first sentence of v. 5 more naturally looks backward while setting up the next question.[34] It is to their great shame that those who will judge the world have turned for judgments even in trivial civil cases to those whom they will one day judge. So serious is the matter that Paul now rubs salt in the wound. The adverb (οὕτως), "do you mean to say,"[35] summarizes what has gone before and now moves the argument to the next point. Paul asks his sixth rhetorical question. It assumes the answer is "yes indeed, there are some wise people among us." But this furthers the irony of what Paul is saying. They might have responded in the affirmative, but their actions of going to outside courts indicate a mistrust at least of the wisdom of those in the church, a wisdom that Paul has shown is provided to them "in Christ" (1:30). This should shame them. Paul's argument is still founded upon his discussion of wisdom in 3:18–20 (see comments there). They have been proud of their supposed "wisdom." However, Paul has consistently viewed such wisdom (σοφός) in a negative light and called it a wisdom "of this age,"[36] which he has contrasted with the wisdom of God provided in Christ. The former he had said is "foolishness in the presence of God" (3:19). It is even more shameful, at a human level, to suggest that none of them has any wisdom of either sort! In turning to pagan courts for help, the Corinthian elite are simply demonstrating publicly (and so to their shame) that they have not "become wise" (3:18)!

The future tense of the verb "to be able" (δυνήσεται) is idiomatic and best translated in the

---

32. See Wallace, *Greek Grammar*, 696–97. We thus take this as a future-more-probable condition. *Contra* Fee, *1 Corinthians*, 258n201, and Fitzmyer, *1 Corinthians*, 252, who take it as a present-general condition.

33. καὶ τοῦτο is adverbial and therefore intensive.

34. If v. 4 is taken as a command, then it is difficult to see how this sentence could look backward. It must look forward.

35. This translates the adverb in the way suggested in BDAG 741.

36. Alan C. Mitchell, "Rich and Poor in the Courts of Corinth: Litigiousness and Status in 1 Corinthians 6:1–11," *NTS* 39 (1993): 562–86.

present in English. But it does add further irony since Paul has talked much of the power (δύναμις) that the Corinthian Christians have in Christ (e.g., 1:18, 24; 4:19). Should they not, then, have a spiritual aptitude given them by God to judge?! The use of the word "brother" here cannot easily be translated "believer" with the NRSV. This translation, as a number of commentators point out, fails to communicate the family relationship that pertains to those who are "in Christ." While that relationship is clearly not gender specific (women may have also been going to court and were certainly part of the Christian community), we are left searching in modern English for any way to be gender neutral and still be faithful to the singular used here and to the familial point at stake. If, as may be the case, Paul has in mind the dominical discussion of "brother" sinning against brother and the way this should be handled (Matt 18:15–18), then "believer" is even less helpful as a translation.

In 4:14 Paul states that his purpose is not to shame these Christians. In a community so infected with concern for status and position, Paul had no intention of putting anyone down. Rather, he acted as a father would with his children (see comments on 4:14). However, the situation he has been addressing in chapter 6 is decidedly different. It has revealed again the arrogance of some in this church and the wrongful exercise of power by some over others. For a community that prides itself on its "knowledge" and "wisdom," Paul sarcastically reveals the true bankruptcy of such pride. This should indeed bring shame upon them, and Paul has no compunction as he insists upon this. They should not go to court against each other since they are supposed to reflect godly wisdom. At the heart of all that Paul writes here remains his concern for community distinctiveness and holiness. Horsley summarizes the matter well: "As indicated in 6:2–3, Paul's concern here is that the assembly, as the eschatological people of God, stands over against 'the world,' which stands under God's judgment."[37]

IN DEPTH: Shame

The idea of "shame" (ἐντροπή) no doubt involves a particularly hard-hitting condemnation in a culture where status, self-esteem, and good community standing meant so much. Shame is specially concerned with a person's or a community's public status or worth. Indeed, in 4:14 Paul reveals how sensitive this word may be when he uses the verb "to shame" or "to put to shame" (ἐντρέπω) and writes, "I do not write these things to make you ashamed but rather to warn you as my dearly loved children." There he emphasized his loving and fatherly approach to this church. Here, his tone is stronger. Even in the public view there is surely shame attached to their inability to judge trivial cases in their own church community. Paul only uses the noun itself here at 6:5 and in 15:34. The verb also appears in Paul's writings in 2 Thessalonians 3:14 and Titus 2:8. In both these latter references the public nature of the shaming involved is clear from the context. Thus, Paul entirely undermines their supposed wisdom with this word "shame." As Malina puts it, "To be or get shamed is to be

---

thwarted or obstructed in one's personal aspiration to worth or status, along with one's recognition of loss of status involved in this attempt."[38] The status of the "knowledgeable" or "wise" in the church is being challenged at the point where it hurts most.

There is little doubt that in Corinth, the tendency of Greco-Roman culture toward pride and an emphasis on social status was carried to an extreme. As Witherington points out, both the civic and individual emphasis on pride is reflected in the "staggering" number of inscriptions that were erected even by slaves, let alone by those who wanted the world to know of their status in and beneficence toward the society. He continues: "The Corinthian people thus lived with an honor-shame cultural orientation . . . where the worst thing that could happen was for one's reputation to be publicly tarnished."[39]

However, the concept of shame is not just something that makes sense within the Greek culture of Corinth. Paul may also have been drawing significantly on the Old Testament concept of spiritual shame. There is a shame before the world of which the righteous need not be embarrassed. This comes to them because of their righteous living and gives rise to the call that God's people should be vindicated (Pss 34:26; 68:8, 20, where LXX uses ἐντροπή). But there is also the shame that is illegitimate and causes embarrassment to God's people. Frequently, this shame is caused by Israel's idolatry, as in Hosea 10:6 (cf. Isa 42:17) where idolatry leads to the "shame" (LXX: αἰσχύνω) of Ephraim and Israel before God and her enemies. Paul's "shaming" of the Corinthians, while carrying a potency in the Corinthian cultural milieu, may well have had this fuller biblical understanding behind it. Their shame was not just before friends and society but also before God.

6:7–8 In fact, it is already a complete defeat for you that you have lawsuits with one another. Why not rather suffer wrong? Why not rather be defrauded? Instead, you yourselves do wrong and defraud even your brothers [and sisters] (Ἤδη μὲν [οὖν] ὅλως ἥττημα ὑμῖν ἐστιν ὅτι κρίματα ἔχετε μεθ᾽ ἑαυτῶν· διὰ τί οὐχὶ μᾶλλον ἀδικεῖσθε; διὰ τί οὐχὶ μᾶλλον ἀποστερεῖσθε; ἀλλὰ ὑμεῖς ἀδικεῖτε καὶ ἀποστερεῖτε, καὶ τοῦτο ἀδελφούς). Paul now develops a third argument. They should not take each other to court at all because this reveals their own unrighteousness. There is another way, a way that may involve suffering and better reflects a gospel of Christ crucified. "In fact" conveys the intensifying force of the Greek (μὲν οὖν).[40] The plural "you" of these verses may refer to the plaintiffs, but it seems

---

38. Bruce J. Malina, *The New Testament World: Insights from Cultural Anthropology*, 3rd ed. (Louisville: Westminster John Knox, 1983), 46.

39. Witherington, *Conflict and Community*, 8.

40. The two words together are used in classical Greek but only here in the New Testament. See MM 450. The word οὖν is missing from various manuscripts such as 𝔓46, ℵ*, D*. It is included in ℵ2, A, B, C, and D.

more likely that Paul's argument is with the whole church that allows this even though one case may have been in mind in v. 1. We suggested that Paul had opened the possibility to this theme with his earlier use of the subjunctive in the third-class condition of v. 4 ("If, indeed, you have cases pertaining to this life . . ."). Paul is now explicit. They have "already" (ἤδη), that is, even before considering the results of any court case or the damage they are doing to the community, suffered a "complete defeat" (ὅλως ἥττημα). But in what sense have the Corinthians suffered defeat by taking out lawsuits against other brothers? The defeat may here refer to a "failure" in the sense of a failure to perceive what their status is before God and what is the nature of their inheritance in Christ. This is the way the word (ἥττημα) is used in Rom 11:12 where Paul expounds on what Israel has failed to understand and receive of its inheritance in Christ. In this sense, it is indeed "moral failure."[41] (Christians should never have been fighting each other anyway, and they have revealed their self-centeredness, pride, and lack of concern for the community.) Yet it is more than this. It is also a complete failure of spiritual wisdom and insight. Like Israel in Romans 11, the Corinthians have failed to see their true inheritance of the kingdom of God with all its blessings. These blessings make any win at court pale into insignificance. In fact, the way they are pursuing their grievances leads them into the same unrighteousness and the same wrongdoing and defrauding so typical of the world around them. Both the moral and the spiritual failure involved in taking brothers and sisters to court means, says Paul, that the people going to court, believing they are

the ones who have been wronged, have themselves now wronged and defrauded "even [their] brothers [and sisters]" (καὶ τοῦτο ἀδελφούς).[42]

Paul offers an alternative way forward that is in line with the teachings of Christ and reflects the wisdom and power of God in Christ (1:18, 21, 24). He has already indicated this approach in 4:12–13: "When scoffed at, we speak kindly; when persecuted, we endure; when slandered, we entreat with kindness; we have become like the scum of the world, the refuse of all to this very day." This is the outworking of Matthew 5:39 and Christ's teaching to "not resist one who is evil" and to "turn the other cheek."[43] It is true that such teaching is not without its parallels among Greek writers. Notably in Plato we read, "We say that to do wrong is the greater evil, to suffer wrong the lesser."[44] Other examples from the Greeks demonstrate a line of teaching that the wise would rather be wronged than wrong others.[45] Nevertheless, in the context of this letter with the eschatological framework Paul has presented and the emphasis on the effect of the work of Christ in the life of the believer and community (repeated at the close of this section), it is evident that Paul's teaching has its basis solidly within the Christian tradition.

In summary, it is the way of the cross—the wisdom that the world regards as "folly" (1:23)—that is fully worth pursuing. Thus, Paul makes his point with two brief rhetorical questions that offer alternative behavior, both beginning with "Why not rather . . . ?" (διὰ τί οὐχὶ μᾶλλον . . .)[46] He calls upon those who would pursue a case to court against a brother to let it be. Is it so wrong to be cheated or defrauded? Surely not when the per-

---

41. Thiselton, *1 Corinthians*, 436.

42. The word τοῦτο, "this," refers to the wronging and defrauding. It serves to emphasize the wrongdoing by repetition, but does not need to be translated here.

43. See also Rom 12:17.

44. Plato, *Gorgias* 508E (Lamb, LCL).

45. Mitchell, "Rich and Poor," 562–68.

46. The middle voice of the two verbs (ἀδικέω and ἀποστερέω) implies the notion of "allowing oneself to. . . ."

spective is that of the "kingdom of God" (v. 9). As Christ gave himself up for his people (folly in the world's eyes), so his people should give themselves up for each other. This would hardly enhance their status in church or in the world, but instead of the defeat they have already experienced it would lead to the blessing of the inheritance of the kingdom of God. In 13:4–7 Paul identifies this approach to life with love.

Verse 8 begins with the strong adversative (ἀλλά) and takes Paul into the most forceful part of his argument. The fact of the matter is that at least one member of the church, and perhaps more, has actually gone to court. Given the likely injustice of the system and the way it was used to enhance status and exercise power, this must have inevitably led to the weaker or less powerful person suffering wrong and even being defrauded. "Even" (τοῦτο) is used to particularize the matter at hand. That "saints" should do this to "saints," given the eschatological reality, is unbelievable.

6:9a–b Do you not know that the unrighteous will not inherit God's kingdom? Do not let yourselves be deceived (ἢ οὐκ οἴδατε ὅτι ἄδικοι θεοῦ βασιλείαν οὐ κληρονομήσουσιν; μὴ πλανᾶσθε). With a ninth rhetorical question this part of the argument reaches its conclusion. Once more, Paul begins, "Do you not know that . . . ?" (see comments on 3:16). The eschatological context set up by the rhetorical question of v. 2 is now expounded further. In v. 1 the "unrighteous" were contrasted negatively with the "saints." In vv. 9–10 the "unrighteous" are shown not to inherit God's kingdom. The implicit contrast is that the "saints" will indeed inherit "God's kingdom."[47] "The unrighteous," as Paul speaks of them here, are thus more than just

people involved in the type of immorality and ungodliness he will go on to describe. They are a category of people outside the covenant community. They are not "in Christ" and thus will not inherit all that has been promised to God's people (see also Gal 5:21). The juxtaposition in the Greek of "the unrighteous" with "God's kingdom" serves to heighten the contrast between those who will and will not inherit. However, one of the ways of identifying this category of people, the unrighteous, is by their life and works, just as the saints should be able to be identified by their life and works.

Herein lies the power of Paul's argument. *It is possible for people to be deceived about their status.* Paul's command to these church members is brief and to the point: "Do not let yourselves be deceived!" (μὴ πλανᾶσθε; also 15:33). They should know that their life and works provide an important indicator to them of their community status. The holy distinctiveness of God's people must be clearly evident to all. Paul laid the groundwork for this particular point about the danger of self-deception back in 3:18: "Let no one deceive himself" (ἐξαπατάω). There, like here, the issue concerns their standing in the community and what is needed to survive on the last day (3:12–15). They deceive themselves by relying on their (worldly) wisdom, which is foolishness with God (3:19). Here, their lack of wisdom has led them to be worldly in their approach to all that is "unrighteous." After listing some of the behaviors that may be apparent among those who are unrighteous and repeating that they will not inherit the kingdom of God (vv. 9c–10), Paul argues that Christians should be changed people because of the work of Christ in their lives (v. 11).

---

47. See below the essay, "In Depth: The Kingdom of God."

IN DEPTH: The Kingdom of God

In 6:9–10 the phrase "kingdom of God" focuses on the eschatological kingdom. The theme is developed further in chapter 15 (see discussion there, especially on 15:50). In 15:50 Paul states that "flesh and blood are not able to *inherit* the kingdom of God." There Paul is concerned with the transformation epitomized in the resurrection. There is a radical differentiation to be made between those who are to inherit the imperishable and future kingdom that reaches its fulfillment at the last day, and those who will not inherit the great blessings summarized by words such as "imperishable," "immortality," and "victory" (15:52–57). As Paul says of that time, speaking of all Christians, "We shall be changed" (v. 52). It is to all this that the future tense in 6:9 is referring. It is all this that will *not* be experienced by the unrighteous. However, as Paul has made clear in 4:20 where he uses the present tense, the kingdom is not just future, it is also present. The "saints" are the people of the kingdom now. The present nature of the kingdom is most frequently discussed in the Gospels, especially in Matthew where it is normally called the "kingdom of heaven" and appears more than fifty times. It is a phrase found on the lips of Jesus on many occasions. The concept draws on the kingship that is ascribed to Yahweh in the Old Testament. He not only rules as king and has full authority over his people in particular but also over all creation (Judg 8:23; Ps 47:2; Isa 6:5; 43:15; Mal 4:1). In 1 Chronicles 28:5 King Solomon is Yahweh's representative in this role as the one chosen "to sit on the throne of the kingdom of the LORD" (LXX: βασιλεία κυρίου; so also 2 Chr 13:8). In the New Testament the aspirations of the prophets reach fulfillment as Jesus himself comes to rule. In his person the rule of God has come (Matt 4:8, 23; 12:28; Luke 17:21). To accept the gospel message is to accept Jesus Christ (Mark 1:1), and accept that the kingdom is *at hand*, and accept the need for repentence (Mark 1:15). Time and again Jesus preaches about the type of faith, behavior, and life that will characterize those who are of the kingdom (under the rule of God and of Christ). Notably in the Beatitudes he talks of both the life that is expected and the inheritance that follows (Matt 5:3–12). The fact that the apostle Paul can refer simply in passing in 4:20 to the kingdom of God and to what is expected of those who participate in it no doubt is an indication that the Lord's teaching was widely known and understood.

With a background in Old Testament teaching and especially in the tradition being handed to the churches from the Lord's teaching, it is not surprising that Paul's argument assumes that the saints are already committed to the king and his rule and are therefore to reflect this in their lives (just as Jesus had taught). Such people, the ones who will one day "inherit the kingdom of God," are to be readily identifiable as under the rule of Christ already now. Christians who do not think these matters are important, perhaps because they feel secure before God, need to watch out lest they deceive themselves.

6:9c–10 neither the immoral, nor idolaters, nor adulterers, nor males who give themselves sexually to males nor males who have sexual relations with males, nor thieves, nor the greedy, nor drunkards, nor revilers, nor robbers will inherit the kingdom of God (οὔτε πόρνοι οὔτε εἰδωλολάτραι οὔτε μοιχοὶ οὔτε μαλακοὶ οὔτε ἀρσενοκοῖται οὔτε κλέπται οὔτε πλεονέκται, οὐ μέθυσοι, οὐ λοίδοροι, οὐχ ἅρπαγες βασιλείαν θεοῦ κληρονομήσουσιν). Paul now lists those whose way of life must be considered utterly incompatible with the kingdom of God. This list is exemplary rather than exhaustive, but examples of such people were probably known within the Corinthian congregation. Six sins characterizing some people have already been listed in 5:9–11. There they appear in a different order (the sexually immoral, greedy, idolaters, thieves, revilers, and drunkards). On these six, see the explanation in the comments on 5:9–11. In this passage four new categories are listed. Two of these, "adulterers" (μοιχοί), and "thieves" (κλέπται) already stand condemned under the Ten Commandments that Paul repeats in Romans 13:9 (Exod 20:14–15 [20:13–14 LXX]). The term "adulterer" applies specifically to those who are unfaithful to their spouses (see also Rom 7:2–3). The Lord

himself speaks to this sin in Matthew 5:27 where he quotes the command and reveals its deeper intent. In the parable of the tax collector and the Pharisee (Luke 18:9–14), the "righteous" Pharisee mentions this as a sin that he does not commit, along with distinguishing himself from the unrighteous (ἄδικοι). The denotation of "thieves" is clear.

Paul then employs two words that address those involved in homosexual practices.[48] However, the meaning of these two words has become, mostly in recent years, a matter of controversy.[49] The translations "males who give themselves sexually to males" (μαλακοί) and "males who have sexual relations with males" (ἀρσενοκοῖται) are an attempt to communicate the apparent difference between the types of homosexual activity to which Paul draws attention. The first word in its adjectival form (μαλακός) can simply mean "soft" (e.g., of cloth in Matt 11:8). But in ancient Greek the adjective was sometimes used of men; thus, in English, "effeminate." The word also took on a more specifically sexual meaning, denoting the passive male partner in homosexual activity.[50] The juxtaposition of this word with the second word (ἀρσενοκοῖται), which is a compound of "male" and "bed" (ἄρσην and κοίτη), makes this clear.[51] Though the word does

---

48. BDAG 613.

49. See the essay, "In Depth: The Matter of Homosexual Practice and 1 Corinthians 6:9," following comments on 6:11.

50. Cf. Diogenes Laertius, *Lives of Eminent Philosophers* 7.173; Dio Chrysostom, *Orations* 66.25.

51. For detailed examination and examples, see Robert A. J. Gagnon, *The Bible and Homosexual Practice: Texts and Hermeneutics* (Nashville: Abingdon, 2001), 306–32. Gagnon summarizes his lengthy examination of the meaning of μαλακός thus: "In 1 Cor 6:9, the term *malakoi* has most in view males who ac-

tively seek to transform their maleness into femaleness in order to make themselves more attractive as receptive or passive sexual partners of men; *arsenokoitai* has most in view men who serve as the active partners of the *malakoi*" (ibid., 338). Also cf. D. F. Wright, "Homosexuals or Prostitutes? The Meaning of ARSENOKOITAI (1 Cor. 6:9, 1 Tim. 1:10)," *VC* 38 (1984): 125–53; Brian S Rosner, "The Origin and Meaning of 1 Corinthians 6,9–11 in Context," *BZ* 40 (1996): 250–53; Fitzmyer, *1 Corinthians*, 256–58.

not appear in any earlier Greek writings, it almost certainly has its origins, for Paul, in the commands of the Old Testament and especially the holiness code in which "if a man lies with a male as with a woman" (κοιμηθῇ μετὰ ἄρσενος κοίτην γυναικός; Lev 20:13 LXX) he was to be put to death. Thus, Paul refers to men involved in homosexual acts. First, Paul describes the passive male recipient in the sex act and then the one who performs the penetrative act. This is the traditional understanding of the words Paul uses here and remains the most widely accepted view among the majority of modern scholars and English versions. It is the one adopted here.

As Paul lists people whose lives are caught up in sinful sexual practices, he has given a broadbrush picture of the unrighteous and their behavior and life choices, that is, of people living outside God's covenant community. These people must not deceive themselves about their true status as to whether they are "saints" or not. He has been forthright in condemning some in the church for going to court against fellow believers. The problems Paul has noted with their behavior are several, but he concluded by saying that those who have gone to court in this way have even wronged and defrauded their own Christian brothers. Since this behavior is characteristic of the "unrighteous," Paul has indicated they are a people who have no standing before God and so will not inherit the kingdom of God. This is not how it should be among the saints because their status is different, and hence

their behavior and lifestyle should be different. After all, "saints" in whom the King resides by his Spirit (6:19–20), who will be raised bodily from the dead—witnessing to the victory over sin and death (15:53–56) and having the status to judge with Christ when he comes in kingly glory (6:2–3)— must reflect *now* the King they serve and the status he has already given them.[52] It is to that different status that Paul now returns.

6:11 And this is what some of you used to be, but you were washed, but you were sanctified, but you were justified, in the name of the Lord Jesus Christ and by the Spirit of our God (καὶ ταῦτά τινες ἦτε· ἀλλὰ ἀπελούσασθε, ἀλλὰ ἡγιάσθητε, ἀλλὰ ἐδικαιώθητε ἐν τῷ ὀνόματι τοῦ κυρίου Ἰησοῦ Χριστοῦ καὶ ἐν τῷ πνεύματι τοῦ θεοῦ ἡμῶν). In the past, "this is what" some of the Corinthians Christians "used to be" (ἦτε)[53] like, but they have been washed.[54] "Some" (τινες) allows for the possibility that there were people in the congregation, perhaps converted Jews who had followed Scripture, who had never lived in these ways as "unrighteous." Nevertheless, all of them had experienced the work of God in ways that Paul insists should have dramatic implications for the way they live. He lists three of God's actions that bear upon his argument. Each verb is passive,[55] because this is the work of God effected in the life of the believer in Christ and by the Spirit, as becomes apparent at the end of the verse.

First, "you were washed" (ἀπελούσασθε). Paul is referring here to the event of repentance and faith

---

52. This "imaging" of God remains imperfect until the perfect comes (13:10), but with the Spirit's indwelling presence it still witnesses to the covenant Lord God himself. This accounts for Paul's frequent appeal for people to "imitate" Christ. Since he is imitating Christ in the way that we are all called on to do, he can also urge people to "imitate" him (4:6, 11; cf. 1 Thess 1:6; 3:9; Eph 5:1).

53. The imperfect here expresses a state of being.

54. The demonstrative adjective "these things" (ταῦτά),

translated "this is what," suggests that he is thinking of "all of the above" and that he regards the whole with horror. Wallace, *Greek Grammar*, 331, captures this: "The neuter is used to express the horror of depravity, as if they had been subhuman before conversion."

55. ἀπελούσασθε is aorist *middle*, and this may imply a degree of causation ("you let yourself be . . ."); yet here it probably has passive intent. Almost all English translations translate it as passive.

that results in sin being "washed" away. While baptism points to this, baptism is not in mind here.[56] Rather, in mind is the work achieved by Christ in the life of the believer and the church, as with the following two passives. Ephesians 5:25b–27 offers a useful parallel. There Paul refers to Christ giving himself for the church to sanctify her, "having cleansed her by the washing of water with the word . . . that she might be holy" (καθαρίσας τῷ λουτρῷ τοῦ ὕδατος ἐν ῥήματι). See also Titus 3:5; cf. John 15:3. As they heard the word of Christ and received it in conversion, they were "washed" clean of the evil of their former lives that were lived away from the lordship of Christ. *This is their status: a washed people.*

Second, "you were sanctified" (ἡγιάσθητε). This looks back to the end of 1 Corinthians 6:1 and back to the start of the epistle (see comments on 1:2, 30). This refers to that part of the redemptive act of Christ through which believers become part of the holy people of God ("saints"). This was discussed in the comments on 1:2 where "the sanctified" stands in apposition to "the church of God." They have been called out and set apart by God from their previous way of life. *This is their status: a holy people of God.*

Finally, "you were justified" (ἐδικαιώθητε). This speaks again to their status, that is, a status of now being in a right relationship with God. There is little reason to distinguish the meaning here from that in Romans 5:18 where God's people are acquitted and granted life by "one man's act of righteousness." It is at the judgment seat of God that all must stand (see comments on 1:30). "In Christ" this has happened for those of faith and it is entirely of grace.[57] Given the local context of the sins mentioned, the fact that previously some of the Corinthians followed the way of life typical of the unrighteous, and that the saints will sit in judgment on such people, there is good reason to assume that Paul has in mind *the judgment seat of God.* In Christ the "saints" who will judge have themselves already been judged and acquitted. It is seemingly rather a false dichotomy to seek to separate the fully forensic imagery, so necessary for the Corinthians to grasp, from the fact that, having grasped this truth, they find themselves further established in their status as saints.[58] *This is their status: a people judged righteous before God.*

All of this happened "in the name of the Lord Jesus Christ."[59] This prepositional phrase qualifies all three of the preceding verbs. It is important not

---

56. For the view that this refers to baptism, see Beasley-Murray, *Baptism in the New Testament,* 162–67. Cf. Fitzmyer, *1 Corinthians,* 258. For an exposition of the view presented here, see James D. G. Dunn, *Baptism in the Holy Spirit: A Re-Examination of the New Testament Teaching on the Gift of the Holy Spirit in Relation to Pentecostalism Today,* SBT 15 (London: SCM, 1970), 120–23.

57. It is worth noting that this is the only place where the work of the Holy Spirit is directly linked to Christians' justification.

58. Thiselton, *1 Corinthians,* 455, seems too quick to dismiss what he calls Paul's supposed appeal to "narrow imagery of forensic acquittal." The imagery may be narrow, as is the imagery of "washing" and "sanctification," but the implications of such radical works of Christ in the life of his people are far from narrow. His detailed note entitled "Justification by Grace in 6:11 and in the Epistle" is an outstanding resource, but it is

doubtful, given the preceding verses and the arguments above, that Paul's declaration to the Corinthians may be summed up quite so boldly as "Paul declares: You are accepted! You belong! You have privileged status. But all this comes from God as his free, sovereign gift. He tells them . . . to accept that they are accepted. . ." (ibid., 455–58). It is granted their problem is status, but this final verse appeals to status more by way of reprimand than by way of encouragement. The Corinthians should know all this, but they are acting as if they do not. The repetition of the conjunction "but" (ἀλλά) before each verb provides additional force to Paul's emphasis that they are not living in the light of their status.

59. Some manuscripts, including A, D², 𝔐, omit "Christ" and have the shortest reading. Some add *"our* Lord Jesus *Christ."* The early papyri 𝔓[11 vid], 𝔓[46] as well as ℵ and D* support "Jesus *Christ."*

to confuse this with baptism "in the name of. . . ." Paul is not saying that all this happened at baptism.[60] Rather, he here has in mind the whole work of Christ on behalf of his people. "In" may perhaps be construed causally or even instrumentally. The "name" as noted in 1:10 is a way of representing all that the Lord is. It especially connotes Christ's authority and lordship over the believer. These people have been transformed and brought into the covenant community of the Lord because of (or by) the person and work of the Lord himself. It is applied to them "by the Spirit of our God" (with ἐν understood as in 6:2 as expressing agency). It is interesting to note the mention of God, of Christ, and of the Spirit in this verse. The whole of the

Trinity is involved in the plan, and the effecting of the plan, to bring about a holy people for God.

Wresting believers away from their former way of life received regular emphasis from the apostolic writers. Paul lists some of the changes that have taken place in the life of a believer as a result of the redemptive work of Jesus, but these have to be worked out and lived out in that person's life and in the life of the church as a whole. The Lord requires this. For a people who pride themselves in their wisdom and grace-gifts, Paul carefully reminds them of the work of the Spirit in bringing about their new status. It is by the Spirit that they have been changed. It is by the Spirit, who indwells them (6:19), that they must now live.

IN DEPTH: The Matter of Homosexual Practice and 1 Corinthians 6:9

Over the ages there has been little dispute that homosexual activity is condemned by New Testament Scripture in verses such as Romans 1:26–27, 1 Corinthians 6:9, and 1 Timothy 1:10. These texts have mostly been seen as building on Old Testament teaching, especially the creation story and passages such as Leviticus 18:22 and 20:13. However, in recent years a number of commentators have sought to demonstrate in various ways either that Scripture does not address the matter of *faithful* homosexual relationships that involve a commitment of one person to another, or that various New Testament texts actually mean something different from the traditional way they have been understood. Often both these, and other arguments, are made at the same time. A brief summary of these matters is all that is possible here and only as they relate to 1 Corinthians 6:9. Reference to three writers will help highlight some of the main areas of contention today.

John Boswell's influential thesis sought to argue that early Christianity, like the Roman society of that era, was not intolerant of homosexuality.[61] Such intol-

---

60. In Paul's writings baptism is always "into" (εἰς), as already seen in this epistle (1:13, 15; also 10:2). In Acts this is also normally true (e.g., Acts 8:16; 19:3, 4, although Luke once in Acts 2:38 uses the preposition ἐπί, perhaps with a causal idea: "on the basis of"). The only instance in which we read

"baptized in" (ἐν) is in Acts 10:48.

61. John Boswell, *Christianity, Social Tolerance, and Homosexuality: Gay People in Western Europe from the Beginning of the Christian Era to the Fourteenth Century* (Chicago: University of Chicago Press, 1980).

erance, he argued, emerged much later as the political power of the church grew. He reasoned that the New Testament does not address homosexual sexual acts themselves. On 6:9, he suggested that the two terms (μαλακός and ἀρσενοκοῖται) must not be taken together. The first he proposed refers to "general moral weakness, with no specific connection to homosexuality." Ultimately, he argued, it may refer to those who, lacking self-discipline, masturbate. He suggests that "this was the unanimous tradition of the church through the Reformation," a point that has been decisively contradicted by several other studies. The second word he claims "does imply an active sexual role, but not necessarily in homosexual intercourse."[62] He suggests Paul is much more concerned with the whole question of prostitution, which may or may not include homosexual activity. He dismisses the idea that Paul's list of vices relates back to Leviticus or Old Testament law.[63] Almost every area of Boswell's arguments has been disputed with regard to 1 Corinthians 6:9.[64] What is particularly notable is his extraordinary insistence that the early Christian church would not have assumed that sexual sins condemned in Leviticus would be relevant to working out their own views of the rights and wrongs of sexual activity. Reflecting a surprising lack of understanding of early-church hermeneutics, he argues that because the early church ignored some laws from Leviticus, they would never have turned to other such texts to guide them on ethical matters.[65] However, the proximity of Paul's chosen subjects in both Leviticus 18 and 20 is remarkable and helps refute Boswell's assertion (incest, Lev 18:7–18 and 20:11–12; sexual immorality, widely in both chapters; adultery, Lev 18:20 and 20:10; homosexuality, Lev 18:22 and 20:13).[66]

Robin Scroggs suggests that Paul's vice list in 6:9–10 probably has its background in early Hellenistic Judaism. However, he argues that such vice lists functioned simply to build up a sense of the importance of what the author was writing rather than suggesting that the writer was concerned about those particular sins *per se*. Thus he argues that "what Paul cites in 1 Cor. 6:9–10 is a stereotyped literary form, which may or may not reflect his own sense of priorities."[67] Paul's priorities, he urges, are in fact the case of incest (5:1–5), church

---

62. Ibid., 340–41.

63. Ibid., 113.

64. For a refutation of substantial parts of Boswell's work on 1 Cor 6:9, see a review article by J. Robert Wright, "Boswell on Homosexuality: A Case Undemonstrated," *ATR* 66 (1984): 79–94; cf. Gagnon, *Bible and Homosexual Practice*; Richard B. Hays, "Relations Natural and Unnatural: A Response to John Boswell's Exegesis of Romans 1," *Journal of Religious Ethics* 14 (1986): 184–215. Many pastors will also find a good resource in Kevin DeYoung, *What Does the Bible Really Teach about*

Homosexuality? (Wheaton, IL: Crossway, 2015).

65. Boswell, *Christianity, Social Tolerance, and Homosexuality*, 106.

66. Paul's ability to appeal to Leviticus is also probably seen in Rom 1:27; 8:3; 12:19; 13:9; Gal 5:14.

67. Robin Scroggs, *The New Testament and Homosexuality: Contextual Background for Contemporary Debate* (Philadelphia: Fortress, 1983), 107–8. For a summary of various views on the "prehistory" of these vice lists, see Rosner, *Greed as Idolatry*, 52–53. Whatever the possible source for such a list

members going to court against each other (6:1–8), and church members going to female prostitutes (6:12–20). He adds, "Obviously, homosexuality is not an issue, the sexual sins are heterosexual."[68] Having argued thus, he then links up this conclusion with his examination of Paul's two words (μαλακός and ἀρσενοκοῖται).

In combination, he suggests, these words in fact point to those who sin in exploitative relationships of pederasty.[69] The second term (ἀρσενοκοῖται) refers, he argues, to the active sexual partner who exploits or hires the weaker partner, probably a younger man or boy. He reads the exploitative perspective so deeply into the text that he suggests the first term (μαλακός) denotes "effeminate call-boys," meaning those who imitate women, comport themselves in an effeminate way, and offer themselves as the passive partner. Even in Romans 1:26–27, which Scroggs agrees refers to homosexuality as a sin to be abhorred, he adds, "I close with the observation that Paul thinks of pederasty, and perhaps the more degraded forms of it, when he is attacking homosexuality."[70] However, as many have noted, another Greek word exists that denotes pederasty (παιδεραστής), while neither of Paul's words in 1 Corinthians 6:9 do this. Also to be noted is that in Romans 1:27 Paul explicitly says that both women and men had "passion for one another" (NRSV). This hardly suggests an exploitative relationship in that passage. Commenting on Scrogg's interpretation of Romans 1:28, Dunn writes, "Paul's indictment seems to include all kinds of homosexual practice, female as well as male, and was not directed against one kind of homosexual practice in distinction from another."[71] This would be in line with the dictates of Leviticus against several sexual sins.

The limiting of the sin to pederasty is not established but, as with Vines (below) it is used by some today as an argument that Paul regarded exploitative sexual acts as wrong and was not addressing faithful and loving homoerotic behavior. There is an irony to this position that is not often noticed. While the effeminate male who dresses and behaves as a woman is almost universally condemned in Greek literature, pederasty is actually upheld as a loving relationship in some writings and was not universally regarded as either wrong or exploitative.[72]

In the third sampling of modern views on this verse, we turn to Matthew

---

might be, Paul himself contextualizes it with direct reference to the Corinthian church by adding "and such were some of you" (6:11). The existence of other somewhat comparable lists cannot be used to suggest that these matters were simply generic examples of sinful people.

68. Scroggs, *New Testament and Homosexuality*, 103.

69. Ibid., 101–9.

70. Ibid., 117.

71. James D. G. Dunn, *Romans 1–8*, WBC 38A (Dallas: Word, 1988), 65.

72. For several examples, see Gagnon, *Bible and Homosexual Practice*, 350–60.

Vines's book, *God and the Gay Christian*. This has vastly outsold the more academic publications on the subject and has popularized some highly tendentious understandings of 1 Corinthians 6:9 and of Paul's understanding of homosexuality more generally. Most pastors will need to be aware of this volume. Vines, who is gay and an evangelical, begins by saying that his "larger argument is this: Christians who affirm the full authority of Scripture can also affirm committed, monogamous same-sex relationships."[73] The book is full of personal, sometimes extremely painful anecdotes of rejection, dismissal, and hurt often emanating from the church or Christians. Six main biblical passages are discussed. Many comments and conclusions lack hermeneutical rigor. For example, he refers to the fact that Leviticus prohibits same-sex sexual activity in the same passage as the prohibition of eating shellfish, and since one is not now followed it is unlikely Paul would have based his sexual ethics on that section of Leviticus. Elsewhere he suggests that Jesus's comment, "If something bears good fruit it cannot be a bad tree," can become *an ultimate arbiter for moral behavior*. Thus, since "good fruit," he suggests, comes from loving, stable, same-sex relationships, they cannot be sinful. In a further example, he says that "mandatory celibacy for gay Christians *is* more than many [gay people] can bear" and therefore 1 Corinthians 10:13 shows that such a demand could not actually be asked by God of Christians.[74]

In chapter 7 he addresses 1 Corinthians 6:9. Citing Dale Martin, he argues for the meaning of "soft" for μαλακός.[75] Quoting Seneca, he says this word was used of some men who are womanizers and self-indulgent people without self-control. This lack of self-control might apply to those being passive in sexual relations or to a man who was too doting on his wife. He concludes that the word must ultimately be translated as done by Hays: "Those who lack self-control."[76] On the second word (ἀρσενοκοῖται), again he follows Dale Martin. He accepts Martin's argument that the context must define a word and that as many contexts as possible must be found, but then proceeds effectively to deny the context of 6:9 as in any way determinative of meaning. Instead, he reads the context of two other later uses of the word (both of which he probably misunderstands) back into 6:9. He allows that the word has a possible background in Leviticus but then talks (with Scroggs) of pederasty as the major problem in such sexual relationships in the ancient world. That is self-evidently not the case in Leviticus, and he allows no possibility that Paul could be thinking biblically.

---

73. Matthew Vines, *God and the Gay Christian* (New York: Convergent, 2014), 2.

74. Ibid., 11.

75. Dale B. Martin, *Sex and the Single Savior: Gender and Sexuality in Biblical Interpretation* (Louisville: Westminster John Knox, 2006).

76. Hays, "Natural and Unnatural," 218–21.

Then, because of a few later examples of the use of the word, he concludes the word most likely refers to economic exploitation. In the end he writes, "Even if Paul *had* intended his words to be a condemnation of both male partners in same-sex relations," Paul's context was quite different from our context today.[77] Thus, even if the traditional understanding of the words were to be upheld, for Vines that would not be enough to sustain the idea that Paul could have spoken of *all* homoerotic relationships as sinful. The twenty-first century, he writes, provides a different context in which to understand some of these relationships. Now it is known that they can potentially be faithful or "covenantal" commitments. The book thus becomes a well-written polemic, born out of the true, personal hurt of a gay man seeking to remain true to Scripture. But the arguments on 6:9 and on other texts is subtly confusing. Nowhere does he interact with the serious scholarship that has shown Dale Martin's views to be, in many ways, misconceived, but he sows enough doubt about the meaning of all the biblical texts he addresses to confuse readers. Once there is confusion on the meaning of the texts, the emotional and unproven argument—that loving same-sex relationships were not known in the New Testament—gains strength. He concludes his examination of the biblical texts and states, "We looked at the disputed Greek terms that appear in 1 Corinthians 6:9 and 1 Timothy 1:10. While *malakoi* and *arsenokoitai* could encompass forms of same-sex behavior, the behavior they might describe bears little resemblance to the modern relationships of lesbian, gay, bisexual, and transgender Christians."[78]

Above we argued in line with most recent commentators that Paul's words (μαλακός and ἀρσενοκοῖται), taken together, do indeed indicate homosexual activity. In the immediate context we have suggested Paul has drawn upon Leviticus 18 and 20 to discuss incest. Paul's sexual ethics usually find their background in Old Testament Scripture, so this should not come as a surprise. It is interesting that Vines does not deal with Gagnon's careful exegesis of 1 Corinthians 6:9. Neither does he deal with Gagnon's and others' refutation of many of the exegetical points made by Martin, Scroggs, and Boswell on whose work Vine builds.

In conclusion, the modern suggestion that if Paul had known about same-

---

77. Vines, *God and the Gay Christian*, 126.

78. Ibid., 129. Again, it is important to remember that it is simply *wrong* to suggest that ancient writers knew nothing of love or permanence in homosexual relationships. For example, in his speech on love in Plato's *Symposium* (181 B–D), Pausanias distinguishes between a "common" love where men first fall in love with women and a "heavenly" love that "first of all does not partake of the female but only the male." Talking of men falling in love with men who are beyond puberty, he writes that such men are "prepared to love in the expectation that they will be with them all their life and will share their lives in common." Pausanias also distinguishes between this and pederasty. For this and several other lengthy quotations from the ancients espousing homosexual love, see Gagnon, *Bible and Homosexual Practice*, 351–60. Hellenistic Judaism, on the other hand, universally condemned homosexual activity.

sex love and commitment as we do today he would not have condemned it is simply speculative and even fanciful. In Romans 1:27 where Paul condemns homosexuality as a distortion of God's created order, he speaks of a man's desire for a man as mutual "in their passion for one another" (ἐν τῇ ὀρέξει αὐτῶν εἰς ἀλλήλους). There is no suggestion here of exploitation. Furthermore, if only exploitative relationships or pederasty are in mind, why does he mention women with women? In 1 Corinthians Paul is well aware of strong sexual urges and their consequent temptations (e.g., 7:2, 5, 9). He does not condemn the urges *per se* but argues for self-control in order that God's order may be maintained. For Paul self-control is a fruit of the Spirit (Gal 5:23), indicating that he did not regard it as something automatically and "naturally" occurring among all peoples. When sexual desires arise within heterosexual marriage, each partner is to oblige the other (7:2–3); when such desires arise outside of that relationship, then either self-control is urged or a heterosexual marriage should take place (7:9, 36). In the modern era where sexuality is bound up with identity, Paul's prohibition of homoerotic behavior will always be disavowed by many. Yet in Scripture the teaching is embedded in God's purposes for creation, and the distortion of those purposes is almost invariably linked with idolatry. In Paul's worldview, a believing person's identity is to be found only "in Christ," and it is by his Spirit alone that the obedient believer will find power to live as God desires of him or her. There is nothing in Scripture to suggest that a person's desires or temptations will be entirely removed. Rather, it is incumbent upon the church to speak with greatest fervor of the living Christ who calls "all who labor and are heavy laden" to come to him for help (Matt 11:28 ESV) and to remind all Christians that "God is faithful, and he will not let you be tempted above what you are able, but with the temptation he will also provide a way out, so that you can bear up under it" (10:13).[79]

Theology in Application

Legal Matters

For Paul, the idea that God's people would look outside the covenant community for judgment on conflicts arising within the community defies logic. A people with the "wisdom of God" should not need to do this. The irony is not lost on the reader that this is a people claiming to possess the grace-gift of "wisdom." Theologically,

---

79. For further study, see Thomas E. Schmidt, *Straight and Narrow? Compassion and Clarity in the Homosexual Debate* (Downers Grove, IL: InterVarsity Press, 1995); Stanton L. Jones and Mark A. Yarhouse, *Homosexuality: the Use of Scientific Research in the Church's Moral Debate* (Downers Grove, IL: InterVarsity Press, 2000).

this too has always been God's concern for his people. They were always expected to judge carefully, justly, and wisely whether in small matters or large. It was Solomon's prayer that he would be given an "understanding mind" to govern and the ability to discern good and evil that "pleased the Lord" (1 Kgs 3:7–8). Interestingly, even in Leviticus 19 in the midst of the sections on adultery, incest, homosexuality, idolatry, and other sins, we read: "You shall do no injustice in court. You shall not be partial to the poor or defer to the great, but in righteousness shall you judge your neighbor. . . . You shall not hate your brother in your heart, but you shall reason frankly with your neighbor, lest you incur sin because of him. You shall not take vengeance or bear a grudge against the sons of your own people, but you shall love your neighbor as yourself: I am the LORD" (vv. 15–18 ESV). Sadly, among many Christians the notion implied by the questions "Why not rather suffer wrong? Why not rather be defrauded?" would likely be greeted with the same response of laughter and incredulity as it would in the world at large.

There are surely going to be cases that Christians, even those worshipping in the same church, will finally be forced to take to outside or "secular" courts. In divorces or property rights, for example, legally binding rulings that are recognized in society will have to be made. Many other examples could be offered. Nevertheless, surely this matter of litigation has become another area of life in which many Christians behave like those in the surrounding society. Instead of seeing disputes between Christians as matters to be hammered out fairly and with the Spirit's help by godly men and women, they resort to the courts all too easily. As in Paul's day it is much easier for the wealthy to threaten the poor with court proceedings, and so for justice to become partial based on wealth and influence. In recent years, many groups have been formed to help Christians reach reconciliation or to help bring justice to a conflict. But most churches would probably agree that whether in business or personal relationships, too often people resort to the secular court system as if God's wisdom had nothing to add.

Self-Deception

Paul sees evidence already in the Corinthian church of the great danger that has beset the church through the centuries: *self-deception*. Through a desire for selfish pleasure or under the influence of their former lives or simply because of the constant pressure of the society in which they live, Christians come to excuse sin. Perhaps they justify sin by appealing to their lofty spiritual status or, as is argued in this commentary, by appealing to a security they believe is evidenced by their possession of certain grace-gifts. Either way, self-deception is so serious in the Christian community because it obscures the dreadful truth that such people will not inherit the kingdom of God. Whether it be in the common self-deception that our sexual activity outside heterosexual marriage is not really immoral, or the self-deception that our greed is not really greed, or that which is most important in our lives is not really idolatry, the end result, without repentance, is that we may not inherit the kingdom of God.

Becoming like the Nations

What was a problem for the Corinthian church is as much a problem for the modern church. Part of the reason that Christians can so easily fall into self-deception is that they rarely understand the impact of the world on their thinking and behavior and so find it hard to see where their holiness has become compromised. This is seen in many ways, whether it be in the convoluted discussions about the type of sexual activity that is or is not permitted in Scripture, or simply in ignoring the seriousness of greed or the question of injustice in society. As Christians confront a secular society, they face the same temptations to conform that the Corinthian church faced and were faced by Israel of old. This was the temptation of Israel in its relation to the women of Moab (Num 25:1–2), or to the cult prostitutes of Canaan (1 Kgs 14:24; 15:12). They became like the nations around them (2 Kgs 17:15; cf. Ezek 20:32). The likelihood of succumbing to the temptation to be like the surrounding society is made the worse for God's people because they often seem almost incapable of being self-critical and discerning of the Lord's will. We have seen how this lack of discernment is key to Paul's concern with the Corinthian church, but again it has always been a common problem for God's people through the ages (cf. Deut 32:28–29; Isa 44:18–20; Hos 14:9). Special pleading for a cause close to our hearts, even one we find contradicted in Scripture, is all too common. No wonder Paul urges, "Do not be deceived!"

Idolatry and Greed

Because of the current debate, much has been said above about homosexuality, but greed (so closely linked to the tenth commandment) surely affects almost all Christians and yet is rarely talked about. (See 5:10 for further comments on greed.) The way Paul places greed in a list alongside sexual immorality and idolatry in both 5:10–11 and 6:9–10 clearly indicates just how serious of a sin it is in the life of the church.[80] It is interesting to contemplate the modern church's reaction to sexual immorality or clear-cut idolatry and compare it to her reaction to the subject of greed. The first two will, in many churches, lead to some degree of church discipline. Personally, I have not heard of greed provoking the same reaction! How easily greed can be justified in terms of "legitimate ambition" or the need to have a better car or house or clothing for the sake of one's children or to form an impression in business. Once

---

80. Rosner says that "to brand greed as idolatry is a most striking and effective means of emphatic condemnation." In Excursus 1 he summarizes how greed is condemned in ancient Judaism and early Christianity (*Greed as Idolatry*, 157–59).

again, for the church it is the temptation to become "like the nations," and it is surely one of the most difficult areas of life in which to become self-critical and on which to shine the light of God's word. We have seen how idolatry is linked in Scripture to sexual sin, but it is also closely linked to most sin, including greed (e.g., Jer 6:13–15). In Habakkuk 2:5–19 greed, drunkenness, and idolatry are linked, as in 1 Corinthians 6:10. The placing of oneself as the arbiter of what is or is not greed or coveting is the core of such idolatry. It can only be imagined what a transformation might be seen in the church at large if modern forms of greed, theft, swindling, and drunkenness were the subject of such discussion as is currently happening with homosexuality.

1 Corinthians 6:12–20

Literary Context

In 6:12–20 Paul continues his section that began in 5:1, discussing the dangers of tolerating sin within the Christian community. He has taken on specific matters that have come to his attention: the case of incest (5:1–13) and the case of taking a Christian brother or sister to court (6:1–11). He has shown that both toleration of such sin and participation in it is utterly incompatible with the status of God's people as saints. Paul concludes in this last section (6:12–20) his immediate concern with the toleration of sin within the church. Once again the repeated appeal to community holiness summarizes Paul's argument (vv. 19–20; cf. 5:9–13; 6:9–11). In doing this, he addresses yet another grave danger they seem to face, namely, sexual immorality and the matter of resorting to prostitutes. While the passage has a concluding force, so it also opens up matters of import that the apostle will address through the rest of the epistle. As Lightfoot has noted, "The case of incest . . . did not stand by itself (see 2 Cor xii. 21): the sin of sensuality was the scourge of the Corinthian church."[1]

The opening slogan, "all things are lawful for me," is repeated in 10:23 in the discussion of eating meat offered to idols. Scripture regularly links immorality and idolatry as two sides of the same coin, and Paul follows suit in suggesting that this linkage is evidenced in the behavior tolerated by this church. Two similar commands highlight the overlap of these two sins: "Flee sexual immorality" (6:18) is followed by "flee idolatry" (10:14).[2] Paul's theological argument against the union formed by having sex with a prostitute—that a person is joined to the Lord and one spirit with him—anticipates the same basic argument for not becoming involved in idolatry since they are part of one body, the body of Christ (10:16–17). Paul's reference to the body as the "temple of the Holy Spirit" (6:19) also anticipates the discussion about idolatry, while simultaneously looking back to his discussion in 3:16–17 that with the indwelling of the Spirit God's people have become God's holy temple.

The example of prostitution prepares the ground for chapter 7 and the discussion of marriage that, in part, provides an answer to the temptations to sexual immorality

---

1. Lightfoot, *Notes on Epistles*, 213.

2. See the essay, "In Depth: Sexual Sin, Idolatry, and the Covenant Community," at 6:20.

(7:2, 9). Paul's appeal to Christ's redemptive act, "You were bought with a price" (6:20), becomes a foundational appeal for appropriate behavior before the Lord and is repeated in 7:23. Even the appeal to the resurrection in 6:14 anticipates the lengthy discussion of the place of the body at the time of the resurrection in chapter 15. Thus, Paul writes a section that, although deeply practical for what is undoubtedly an actual problem in the community, seems to have a more didactic and theological feel to it. Paul remains deeply concerned that the community would tolerate this sort of sexual sin in their midst, but he also provides a greater explanation of his views and the reasons why immorality must be eschewed.

IV. Mature Christians Pursue God's Wisdom (2:6–4:21)

V. Lack of Spiritual Wisdom Has Led to Grievous Sin (5:1–6:20)

    A. A Case of Incest Must Be Resolved (5:1–8)

    B. Community Identity Requires Holiness (5:9–13)

    C. Lawsuits between Christians Must Be Resolved without the Courts (6:1–8)

    D. Community Identity Requires Holiness (6:9–11)

➡   **E. Immorality Is Incompatible with Union with Christ (6:12–17)**

    F. Community Identity Requires Holiness (6:18–20)

VI. Marriage, Celibacy, Divorce, and Widowhood in Relation to Community Status (7:1–40)

Main Idea

Christians belong to the Lord who bought them at a price. They must recognize that they have been incorporated into one body with Christ. Therefore, what they do with their bodies matters before the Lord. Any form of sexual immorality indicates an abuse of the body and an obscuring of community holiness.

Translation

1 Corinthians 6:12–20

12a	Quotation/assertion	**"All things are lawful for me,"**
b	Assertion/response	but **not all things are beneficial.**
c	Quotation/assertion	**"All things are lawful for me,"**
d	Assertion/response	but **I will not be enslaved by anything.**

13a	Quotation/assertion	"Food is	for the stomach and
		the stomach	for food,
b	Assertion	but **God will destroy**	
		both	**the one and**
			the other."
c	Contrast/assertion	But **the body is not**	**for sexual immorality** but
d	Explanation	**is**	**for the Lord,** and
e	Further explanation		**the Lord is**
f			**for the body,**
14a	Assertion	and **God raised**	**the Lord** and
b		**will raise**	**us**
c	Means	through his power.	
15a	Rhetorical question	**Do you not know that your bodies are members of Christ?**	
b	Rhetorical question	**Shall I** therefore,...	
	Circumstance	taking away the members of Christ,	
c		**... make them members of a prostitute?**	
d	Exclamation	**Never!**	
16a	Rhetorical question	**Or do you not know that a person ... is one body [with her]?**	
b	Description	who is joined to a prostitute	
c	Proof for 16a, b	For it is written,	
d	Biblical quotation	"The two will become one flesh." [Gen 2:24]	
17a	Contrast (with 16a, b)	But **a person ... is one spirit [with him].**	
b	Description	who is joined to the Lord	
18a	Command	**Flee sexual immorality.**	
b	Assertion/basis for 18a	**All [other] sin that a person commits is outside the body,**	
c	Basis for 18a continued	but **the sexually immoral person sins against his own body.**	
19a	Compound rhetorical question, part 1	Or **do you not know**	
		that your body is the temple of the Holy Spirit	
b	Place	within you	
c	Source	whom you have from God and	
d	Compound rhetorical question, part 2	**that you are not your own?**	
20a	Basis of 19d	For **you were bought with a price.**	
b	Exhortation	So indeed **glorify God**	
c	Manner	in your body.	

Structure

In this section, the command "flee sexual immorality" (6:18) marks a pivotal point, much as the command "do not let yourselves be deceived" (6:9) did in the preceding section. Immorality involves sinning against one's own body. Paul begins by qualifying two slogans that appear to emanate from the Corinthians (6:12–13). Three further rhetorical questions beginning "do you not know . . ." (vv. 15, 16, 19) serve to introduce Paul's theologically based appeal to give the body the place it deserves as they live under the lordship of Christ. However, there is less polemic here than in the previous section. The careful structure of v. 13 helps reveal the progression of Paul's argument. Thus, we see the structure in this way:

A. Food is for the stomach	the stomach for food
B. God will destroy the stomach	God will destroy food
A. The body is for the Lord	the Lord is for the body
B. God raised the Lord	God will raise us

In this structure, "food is for the stomach and the stomach for food" sets up the following in which "the body is . . . for the Lord [and not for immorality], and the Lord for the body." This reveals Paul's main concern here, for he then adduces a series of three arguments to show why sinning against the body, evidenced in immorality involving prostitutes, is completely at odds with the Christian life: (1) the body is for the Lord (witness the resurrection, vv. 13–14); (2) the bodies of believers are members of Christ (v. 15); and (3) believers are one spirit with him (vv. 16–17). This is followed by the command to flee immorality (v. 18), which leads into a further summary call to community holiness based on the presence of the Spirit and the work of Christ: (1) their bodies are the temple of the Holy Spirit (v. 19), and (2) they were bought at a price (v. 20). The argument concludes with a final exhortation to glorify God with the body. This appeal forms an apt conclusion to a section that began with an example of extraordinary immorality (5:1) and is an apt introduction to how husbands and wives should respect each other's bodies (7:2–4).

Exegetical Outline

V. Lack of Spiritual Wisdom Has Led to Grievous Sin (5:1–6:20)

A. A Case of Incest Must Be Resolved (5:1–8)

B. Community Identity Requires Holiness (5:9–13)

C. Lawsuits between Christians Must Be Resolved without the Courts (6:1–8)

D. Community Identity Requires Holiness (6:9–11)

→ **E. Immorality Is Incompatible with Union with Christ (6:12–17)**

1. Christian Freedom Has Its Boundaries (6:12–13)
2. The Body is Not for Sexual Immorality but for the Lord (6:13–17)
   a. The Body Is for the Lord (6:13)
   b. The Lord Will Raise the Body (6:14)
   c. Bodies Are Members of Christ and Not to Be Joined to Another (6:15–17)

F. Community Identity Requires Holiness (6:18–20)

1. Sexual Sin Is Sin against the Body (6:18)
2. The Body Is the Temple of the Holy Spirit (6:19)
3. The Body Is to Glorify God (6:20)

Explanation of the Text

6:12 "All things are lawful for me," but not all things are beneficial. "All things are lawful for me," but I will not be enslaved by anything (Πάντα μοι ἔξεστιν, ἀλλ᾽ οὐ πάντα συμφέρει. πάντα μοι ἔξεστιν, ἀλλ᾽ οὐκ ἐγὼ ἐξουσιασθήσομαι ὑπό τινος). Paul now addresses the question of the boundaries set around Christian freedom. Community holiness will only be established once the church (and individual Christians) understand that the principles of "building up" and benefitting the community are to be given priority. The first part of the opening sentence is commonly assumed to be a quotation that Paul then proceeds to qualify. It is repeated again in this verse and then also repeated twice in 10:23. Paul's first qualification ("but not all things are beneficial") is also repeated in 10:23. This passage begins to open up a discussion that comes to the fore from chapter 8 onward. It also picks up on the opening four chapters and develops in more detail the question of what it is precisely that marks out the true Christian. If status or standing in society is so important to these Corinthians, Paul wants them to understand that status is also fundamental to Christian theology. Nonetheless, the marker of such community identity for the believer is entirely different from what an unbelieving society seeks.

Firstly, Paul has argued that they should remember that "wisdom" does not authenticate or mark out their membership in the church. *Secondly,* he has insisted that what they think is "wise" must be judged against a number of important theological "givens." Since, as Paul will make clear in the pivotal thirteenth chapter, *love* is the defining marker of membership in the Christian community, it is not surprising that Paul here sees the test of true wisdom as whether its product is "beneficial." *Thirdly,* while the slogan "all things are lawful" sounds liberating, its wise and godly application will always question whether the Christian might become "enslaved" to a way of life or a behavior that is ungodly.

Since the slogan precedes Paul's horror that some should consider turning to prostitutes, it seems the Corinthians regarded the saying as an unqualified truth. Perhaps it was taken from the society around. Perhaps it derived from a distortion of Paul's own teaching on freedom from the law, but the way it is being applied leads to an immediate challenge from Paul introduced by the strong adversative "but" (ἀλλά). "Not all things are beneficial." The Greek word (συμφέρω) implies a "bringing together," but its meaning in this context is really an outworking of his repeated discussion in this letter of what "builds up." Thus, for example, in 10:23 the verb "build up" is simply explicative of "benefits" ("'All things are lawful,' but not all things are *beneficial* [συμφέρω]. 'All things are lawful,' but not all things *build up* [οἰκοδομέω]." Mitchell points to the frequent use of this word in deliberative rhetoric as an appeal to advantage.[3] An orator or the writer of a deliberative letter would have a number of ways of arguing that a particular course of action was advantageous, and this appeal to what was beneficial was one of them. Undoubtedly, if this convention was widely understood by Paul's readers, then it adds to the weight of Paul's argument.

It is not until chapters 8–14 that Paul will explain his thinking on all this in much greater detail. Here, he is primarily concerned with the matter of sexual immorality being tolerated by the church, but the later chapters certainly help explain his thinking here. In 8:1 we read for the first time about what we will call the "marker," the true identifier of status in the Christian community: love.[4] There Paul makes a straightforward point that "knowledge puffs up"—it is one of the possessions that have made the Corinthians arrogant—but that "love builds up" (see comments on 8:1). One of the tests of their slogan must be whether something is of (loving) benefit to brothers and sisters in Christ. At various levels, there is some degree of freedom in being "in Christ," whether it be freedom from the law, freedom from the realm of darkness, and so on. In chapter 9 Paul starts off by asking the rhetorical question and expecting an affirmative answer, "Am I not free?" (using the Greek word ἐλεύθερος). But Paul insists all of this is meaningless if it does not function to the benefit or edification of the church.

The second challenge to the slogan in this verse

is not dissimilar. Again, the later chapters are of help. In the Greek there is a play on the words "lawful" and "enslaved" (ἔξεστιν and ἐξουσιασθήσομαι, from ἐξουσιάζω). The verb translated as "enslaved" has to do with a person's "authority" or "power" or "(legal) right" to do something (see 7:4). Perhaps translating this as "all things are lawful for me, but I will not be fettered by anything" is a way of capturing the idea that Paul will refuse to be shackled by anything, even if it might of itself be something that in some circumstances could be useful. Thus, in chapter 9 we read at length of Paul's preparedness to give up all of his rights rather than have any of them become an impediment to the gospel (ἐξουσία; 9:4–6, 12, 18; cf. 8:9).

6:13–14 "Food is for the stomach and the stomach for food, but God will destroy both the one and the other." But the body is not for sexual immorality but is for the Lord, and the Lord is for the body, and God raised the Lord and will raise us through his power (τὰ βρώματα τῇ κοιλίᾳ, καὶ ἡ κοιλία τοῖς βρώμασιν· ὁ δὲ θεὸς καὶ ταύτην καὶ ταῦτα καταργήσει. τὸ δὲ σῶμα οὐ τῇ πορνείᾳ ἀλλὰ τῷ κυρίῳ, καὶ ὁ κύριος τῷ σώματι· ὁ δὲ θεὸς καὶ τὸν κύριον ἤγειρεν καὶ ἡμᾶς ἐξεγερεῖ διὰ τῆς δυνάμεως αὐτοῦ). With a quotation from the Corinthians, Paul insists that sexual immorality is totally inconsistent with God's design for the body—a body that will eventually be raised and is designed for union with Christ. Once more most commentators and Bible versions treat either the first part or the whole of the opening sentence (v. 13) as a quotation. We take the whole sentence to be a quotation (v. 13a–b; i.e., all of A and B as discussed in "Structure" above). Paul employs datives of advantage (for the benefit of), so *"for the stomach . . . for food"* (τῇ κοιλίᾳ . . . τοῖς βρώμασιν). "The one" refers to the stomach (ταύτην agrees with κοιλία), and

---

3. Mitchell, *Rhetoric of Reconciliation*, 29–31.   4. This has been hinted at in 2:9.

"the other" refers to the food (ταῦτα agrees with βρώματα). In v. 13c–f the same is true of the datives in v. 13: "*For* the Lord . . . *for* the body." The qualification of v. 13b that "God will destroy" is abrupt.[5] It may be Paul's reaction to the slogan, but it is probably part of the whole expression that was used to argue the irrelevance of the stomach when it comes to what is important for God.[6] It is possible that the Corinthians used this or similar arguments to defend immorality, though there is no proof of this.[7] Wherever we put the quotation marks here, or even if we assume that this is a known saying that Paul himself brings to bear on the subject, it is Paul's continuing argument that matters.

Paul's concern is that the relationship of stomach to food and vice versa is *not* the same as the relationship between the body and sexual immorality ("the body is *not* for sexual immorality"; v. 13c). The stomach and food work together for a specific purpose until God destroys both at the end of life. But the body also works for a specific purpose within God's creative order and that is "for the Lord." The body has been created with a special relationship that is as close to the Lord as the stomach's relationship is close to food.[8] As Wright says, "In the present time the 'body' is the locus and means of obedience, and as such is to be 'presented' to God the creator for his service."[9] What

God has created should be used for the purpose given by God. Most definitely, the body was not created for sexual immorality (πορνεία).

Paul's teaching at this point is broad. The body is truly significant in the purposes of God; therefore, any sexually immoral act involving the body is wrong. There can be no dualism in which the body, as matter, has no existence or significance beyond the phenomenal. This is not the worldview with which Paul works. In chapter 15 he will speak of the present body and the future body, to which he also refers here in v. 14. There is both continuity and discontinuity. One is described as perishable and the other as imperishable (15:42), yet both are "body." It is the Lord who was raised by God,[10] and so it is truly we who shall be raised in the future "by his power," that is, God's power (v. 14). It is the *body* that must put on the imperishable and the immortal. It does not become something other than "body."

Nonetheless, Paul speaks here about more than just continuity with the future and that the body will not be destroyed. He says that it is *for the Lord*. That is, just as the body is not designed for immorality, it *is* designed for union with Christ and for being joined to the Lord (v. 17) and for bringing God glory (v. 20). The Lord is *for the body* in the sense that Paul develops in the next few verses, that is, that the Spirit indwells the body (v. 19) and that

---

5. On the meaning of this verb (καταργέω), see comments on 15:24.

6. Jerome Murphy-O'Connor, "Corinthian Slogans in 1 Cor 6:12–20," *CBQ* 40 (1978): 394–95.

7. Some suggest this seems to make sense of why Paul should talk about the stomach at all. Thus, just as the saying tells people that the stomach does not matter ("God will destroy the stomach"), so they have been arguing that the body does not matter ("God will destroy the sex organs"); so Fee, *1 Corinthians*, 280; Rosner, *Paul, Scripture, and Ethics*, 129. This is bolstered by some on the basis that "stomach" (κοιλία) can refer to the womb and by extension perhaps to the sexual organs (neither BDAG nor MM offer any such examples of this extension of meaning, and the examples offered by Garland, *1 Corinthians*, 230, can all the more probably be translated sim-

ply as "belly"; e.g., offspring coming from the "loins" or "belly" in LXX 2 Sam 7:12; Ps 131:11, etc.). While some Corinthians might have seen a linkage between a saying about the stomach not mattering and sex organs not mattering, it must be remembered that the word clearly does *not* mean "sexual organs" here.

8. Furnish, *Theology of the First Letter to the Corinthians*, 58, captures this well: "Food and the stomach can only fulfill their respective roles when they do so in relation to one another. Similarly, the body is only itself when it acts in accord with its relationship to Christ."

9. Wright, *Paul and the Faithfulness of God*, 491.

10. Note that God is the subject and therefore is the one who will "destroy" in v. 13, who raised Christ, and will do the raising of us as the Lord's people in v. 14.

the Lord unites it with himself so that the person is "joined" to him (v. 17).

There is considerable discussion about what "body" (σῶμα) means in Paul's writings. Whiteley helpfully summarizes some of the possible meanings of the word in Paul's writings, especially with regard to Christ. Firstly, there is the earthly, physical body. Applied to Christ, this is the "body of Christ in his earthly life," which belonged to the natural order and is to be taken in a literal manner. Secondly, "the resurrection body," which, Whiteley says, belongs "to the supernatural order," although the language again refers to an actual body. Thirdly, "the church," where the word may be understood metaphorically but indicates both the "natural" (today's church) and what he calls the "supernatural" (the church at the resurrection).[11]

A further question is discussed in great detail by many but need not delay us here. Rudolf Bultmann, followed by many, has argued that in Paul's writing the word "body" generally equates with "self" or "person." In dealing with 1 Corinthians 6:13–20 he suggests that this meaning underlies a variety of uses of the word.[12] In v. 13 the body is "the seat of sex-life, [and so] is not to be defiled by immorality." Yet he goes on to say that the word can scarcely mean the same when Paul writes of the body being "for the Lord, and the Lord for the body." There and in v. 14 he says that the idea of "self, person" is once again present. For Bultmann the meaning of "body" (σῶμα) throughout this section seems to swing back and forth between the meanings of physical "body" and "person" or "self."[13] This view was severely taken to task by Ernst Käsemann. He argued that Bultmann's interpretation of giving different meanings in this passage to the word "becomes involved in inextricable contradiction." He rightly and strongly affirms that "the coherence of Pauline soteriology is destroyed once we modify in the slightest degree the fact that for Paul all God's ways with his creation begin and end in corporeality."[14]

In these verses, it does seem most natural to read the word "body" (σῶμα) as simply denoting the physical body of a person which, unsurprisingly, Paul sees as being under Christ's lordship. Although "whole person" or "person" might be possible in vv. 13, 15, and 16, it is the physical act between two bodies that forms the illegitimate union that undermines Paul's teaching that the Spirit lives in that body (v. 19). Paul's argument is that our *physical bodies* matter and what we do with them physically as bodies indicates whether we take seriously the lordship of Christ in all areas of life, including our physical actions. The church must not tolerate sin. The sin of sexual immorality is wrong because there is an integral relationship between the body and the Lord, who created the body for a purpose.

The importance of this physical body continues in Paul's teaching that a body can be raised, as Christ's was (v 14), to be truly a physical body that is recognizable as such and yet be spiritual and imperishable.[15] Paul now turns to the specific matter of the use of prostitutes and appeals to Scripture as a witness to the truth that he writes.

6:15–16 Do you not know that your bodies are members of Christ? Shall I therefore, taking away the members of Christ, make them members of a prostitute? Never! Or do you not know

---

11. D. E. H. Whiteley, *The Theology of St. Paul* (Philadelphia: Fortress, 1971), 197.

12. Rudolph Bultmann, *Theology of the New Testament*, 2 vols. (London: SCM, 1952), 1:194–95.

13. Ibid.

14. Ernst Käsemann, *Perspectives on Paul* (Philadelphia: Fortress, 1971), 18–19.

15. For example, compare how Christ's physical, resurrected body can eat food and be immortal (cf. Luke 24:42–43; 1 Cor 9:1; 15:42–55).

that a person who is joined to a prostitute is one body [with her]? For it is written, "The two will become one flesh" (οὐκ οἴδατε ὅτι τὰ σώματα ὑμῶν μέλη Χριστοῦ ἐστιν; ἄρας οὖν τὰ μέλη τοῦ Χριστοῦ ποιήσω πόρνης μέλη; μὴ γένοιτο. [ἢ] οὐκ οἴδατε ὅτι ὁ κολλώμενος τῇ πόρνῃ ἓν σῶμά ἐστιν; Ἔσονται γάρ, φησίν, οἱ δύο εἰς σάρκα μίαν). As Paul builds his theological argument against sexual immorality, he has said, first, that the body is for the Lord. He has demonstrated this by reference to the power of God in raising Christ and then in the promise that we too will be raised. This resurrection is a bodily resurrection. In vv. 15–17 two further arguments are made. In v. 15 Paul appeals to the fact that believers are members of Christ and in v. 17 that believers are one spirit with the Lord and are joined to the Lord. In the midst of this, he introduces the matter of prostitution and shows why prostitution is so serious a sin for the Christian.

Another question in the series of rhetorical questions begins this verse (see on 3:16). If the last few verses have been less polemical and more didactic, Paul now indicates how deeply distressed he is by the behavior of some in the church but also by a church that is prepared to tolerate such sin. To talk of bodies as "members" (μέλη), though an accurate translation (NIV, ESV, NASB, and most others), does not immediately convey Paul's picture. Just as a body has members, that is, arms, legs, eyes, and so on, so Paul is saying that Christ has the same and that the bodies of Christians are those "members." In 12:12–27, Paul takes this analogy further and looks more deeply at what it means in the Christian community (see also Rom 12:4–5). The picture is fairly straightforward. Each Christian's body serves some function (as a "member" of our own body might) when joined to the "body" of Christ. Elsewhere Paul explains that individual Christians, as "members," do not serve the same function in the community any more than an eye serves the function of an ear (ch. 12). All are vital and are committed to the service of Christ. In chapter 12 and Romans 12, Paul is more concerned about how the members relate to each other. Here, his main purpose is to speak of how Christians relate to Christ himself, the one who has been raised bodily from the dead. In our bodies we are to be *for him*.

The structure helps reveal the progression of thought. The bodies are members of Christ, so they cannot be joined to a prostitute's body. Joining a body to a prostitute involves a union with her; joining a body to Christ means union with him. A structure of ABBA emerges: A, the body in relation to Christ; B, the body in relation to a prostitute. The statement against prostitution is enclosed by the theology. The issue at stake is the relationship between the Christian and Christ and the nature of that union. It is a union in which the body that God created serves a purpose.

The second question starts with a circumstantial participle, "taking away" (ἄρας). The aorist carries no *past* implication here but indicates the whole action of taking oneself away from Christ in favor of a prostitute. The main verb ("shall I . . . *make* them"; ποιήσω) may be either an aorist subjunctive or a future indicative. Taking it as future makes it a more dogmatic question. This future tense then helps interpret the participle. "Shall I therefore, taking away the members of Christ, make them members of a prostitute?" After most rhetorical questions starting with "do you not know . . . ?" Paul has used the second or third person to make the polemic more direct. Here he changes to the first-person singular. In doing this, Paul seems to make the scene even more unimaginable by speaking of himself. Would they expect him ("Shall I . . . ?") to take his own body or the bodies of others and join them through sex to a prostitute? "Never!" (μὴ γένοιτο) is the only possible response.

Paul's concern is with the liability of each believer to recognize that his or her body *belongs* to Christ and may be used only in Christ's service. Using a prostitute for immoral sexual intercourse is to be joined to her and to be one body with her. Paul uses a quotation from Genesis 2:24 to make the point. The sexual intercourse that ensues in the husband-wife relationship of total commitment is referred to as becoming "one flesh." It is as though, in this act of sex, Christians are to recall that, at creation, woman was taken from man and so once they were indeed "one flesh."

The concept of being "joined" (κολλώμενος) can mean "to bind closely," "to cling to," or even "to glue."[16] In this context, though, the meaning follows the LXX of Genesis 2:24 (where the longer form προσκολλάω is used). It refers there to sexual intercourse, as in Matthew 19:5 where the same verse is quoted from the LXX but uses the shorter form of the verb. Since God is the creator and is the one who has joined husbands to wives and people to the Lord, the problem with visiting a prostitute is more than simply infidelity to a spouse, though that is serious enough. It is to "unglue," as it were, that which God has joined. In causing a rupture of the union that God created between a man and a wife and, in fact, causing a different "joining," the Lord is rejected. But since this marital joining is a God-created picture of the other "joining" he does of himself to his people, turning to a prostitute is also to reject the Lord in this area as well. It is to this that v. 17 now speaks.

6:17 But a person who is joined to the Lord is one spirit [with him] (ὁ δὲ κολλώμενος τῷ κυρίῳ ἓν πνεῦμά ἐστιν). The structure reveals the lack of symmetry between the joining involved with a prostitute and that with the Lord: "A person . . . is one body [with her]" (v. 16), "a person is . . . is one spirit [with him]" (v. 17). Much has been made of this difference. Gundry, among many others, has forcefully argued against those like Bultmann and Robinson, who suggest that Paul follows a dualism between body and spirit in which the body is inferior to the spirit.[17] Rather, Paul continues to think about the body and its role in the Christian's relationship with Christ. That relationship involves the believer being "one spirit" with Christ. Paul likely has in mind the fact that the Holy Spirit is involved in the creation and sustaining of this relationship. He has just said as much in v. 11 where the Spirit was the agent of the transformation that occurred on becoming a Christian. Then in v. 19 the body is his "temple" (see also 3:17). The relationship on being joined to the Lord is by and with the Spirit and leads to a union Paul describes as "one spirit" with the Lord.

Paul has in mind traditional biblical imagery that draws on the creation story and the sexual union of a husband and wife in order to picture the depth of the relationship of God to his people. It is therefore irrelevant to suggest that Paul "does not intend to conjure up the image of a nuptial relationship with Christ."[18] Paul's argument is the opposite. He has assumed that the nuptial image distorted by sex with a prostitute *should*, for the right-thinking Christian, conjure up the image of a broken relationship with the Lord. The image of sexual relations is so frequently used in this way in Scripture that this is surely why Paul uses the intense rhetoric of "do you not know . . . ?" in v. 15. Time and again, as we have already seen, sexual immorality is linked to idolatry. We will return to this in 10:7–9. It is not a coincidence that false reli-

---

16. BDAG 555; MM 352.

17. Robert H. Gundry, *SOMA in Biblical Theology with Emphasis on Pauline Anthropology*, SNTSMS 29 (Cambridge: Cambridge University Press, 1976), 66–69; see Bultmann, *The-ology of the New Testament*, 1:194–95, and John A. T. Robinson, *The Body: A Study in Pauline Theology*, SBT (London: SCM, 1952), 29.

18. Garland, *1 Corinthians*, 235.

gions regularly have different approaches to sexual morality, even to the extent that some have encouraged (temple) prostitution.[19]

The union of one spirit with the Lord does not involve a separation of body and spirit. The body is part of the person, who is to be wholly committed to the Lord and is continually offered up in the Lord's service. Part of that service is to obey the Lord in the area of sexual relations in order that men and women may truly (in their bodies) image God in his love, faithfulness, and holiness. The following command then comes as no surprise at all in summarizing Paul's intent.

6:18 Flee sexual immorality. All [other] sin that a person commits is outside the body, but the sexually immoral person sins against his own body (φεύγετε τὴν πορνείαν· πᾶν ἁμάρτημα ὃ ἐὰν ποιήσῃ ἄνθρωπος ἐκτὸς τοῦ σώματός ἐστιν, ὁ δὲ πορνεύων εἰς τὸ ἴδιον σῶμα ἁμαρτάνει). While the imperative "flee" (φεύγετε) is emphatic and summarizes Paul's reaction to the problem of prostitution, it probably also looks back to the case of incest as Paul concludes this section by calling for community holiness. The only way of dealing with this immorality is to run in the other direction as if fleeing an enemy. Immorality is the domain of a different lord, and it is dangerous to go there since it leads to judgment. Perhaps Paul recalled Joseph's flight from Potiphar's wife in Genesis 39:12; leaving

his coat in her hand, Joseph "fled and went outside" (ἔφυγεν καὶ ἐξῆλθεν ἔξω).

What Paul intends by the following statement is not readily apparent. While most translations speak of "all *other* sin,"[20] the Greek simply reads "every sin" (so AV, NRSV). The introduction of the word "other" allows for the contrast implied by the argument between sin generally and the specific sin of sexual immorality. However, the second half of the sentence is clear enough. Those committing sexual immorality sin against their own bodies (εἰς here used as in Luke 12:10, meaning "against"). As Paul has argued, in the action of sexual intercourse a "joining" occurs. God created it thus (Gen 2:24). If this physical bonding or joining with another is not what the body was intended for, then by definition it is a sin against the body.

Returning to the first half of this sentence, questions arise.[21] Does Paul imply that somehow sexual immorality is worse than any other sin or perhaps qualitatively different from all other sin? What does it mean that "all [other] sin that a person commits is outside [ἐκτός] the body"? Are commentators and versions correct to add the word "other" to make this first part of the sentence contrast with the second, that is, that there is one sin that is not "outside" the body, namely, sexual immorality? In different ways, a number of commentators both ancient and modern have sought to show the uniquely different nature of sexual sin

---

19. While there is possibly reliable evidence for a form of sacred temple prostitution at Corinth in the earlier era before the destruction of Corinth in 146 BC, there is no definitive evidence from the time when Paul writes. Therefore, it is possible but unlikely that Paul had cult prostitution in mind. He might also have had "normal" prostitution in mind, given that this was, as today, common in most cities and particularly in port cities. Given Paul's emphasis in this passage on the body being a "temple" and the clear link earlier in the chapter and in ch. 10 between idolatry and sexual promiscuity generally, Paul may also have had in mind secular prostitutes who frequented idolatrous temple feasts. Since these feasts are a matter of concern in ch. 10 along with their attendant promiscuous sexual

behavior, the Corinthian Christians who attended those meals may also have taken advantage of the prostitutes. Winter (*Seek the Welfare of the City*, 174) comments: "There were peripatetic brothel keepers who supplied prostitutes for grand occasions and it may have been that they provided services at dinners."

20. E.g., NIV, RSV (changed to "every sin" in NRSV), TEV, NASB.

21. There have been multiple attempts to decipher the meaning of this sentence in the context here of Paul's teaching. Space precludes evaluating each. For a helpful summary, see Bruce N. Fisk, "Porneuein as Body Violation: The Unique Nature of Sexual Sin in 1 Cor 6:18," *NTS* 42 (1996): 540–58.

when compared with other sin. Thus Calvin, while readily admitting that many members of the body are stained by different sins, writes, "The hand is stained by theft or murder," nevertheless, "those other sins do not leave anything like the same filthy stain on our bodies."[22] Kistemaker takes a similar view. To the question raised by many as to whether other sins are not also "against the body," such as drug addiction, he responds: "The sin of fornication which arises in the spirit seeks gratification of the physical body itself and thus is confined to the body. In a sense this sin is different from all other sins, because it stays within the body."[23]

An alternative way of viewing this text is to assume that Paul here quotes a Corinthian slogan or at least summarizes *Corinthian* thinking. Thus, they say, "All sin that a person commits is outside the body" (and therefore the body is morally irrelevant, having nothing to do with sin). Paul then qualifies this by saying that one sin is an exception to the dictum, namely, sexual sin.[24] There are problems with this view, though. The command to flee sexual immorality has been decisive. It is at the heart of Paul's argument here and is set firmly between two rhetorical questions ("do you not know that . . . ?"; vv. 16, 19). It seems unlikely that Paul would seek to handle a different argument in the middle of a discussion concerning the sin of immorality. It may well be that the Corinthians regarded their bodies to be more or less irrelevant when it came to their spiritual status before the Lord and thus believed that sexual sin was not a matter of concern for the church. However, Paul's argument

has been that the body *does* matter, and he has argued this on theological grounds, offering scriptural evidence to support his view. Verse 18 is more naturally read as an extension of Paul's argument concerning the nature of the relationship formed by the body during sexual sin. Furthermore, it is unlikely that the "but" (δέ; v. 18c) can take the weight of being as contrastive as is suggested. In v. 12, where we have argued for a Corinthian slogan, a strong adversative is employed (ἀλλά, which actually helps in a decision about whether there is a slogan in that verse or not). As Garland points out, if this is a slogan, then "the response in 6:18b is hardly an adequate refutation."[25]

Even if the first half is taken as a slogan, it is not apparent why Paul should agree with it at all unless he actually does believe there is a *qualitative* difference of some sort between sexual sin and all other sin. It is this view that ultimately makes most sense, but in what sense is this sin an exception? Calvin and others in their discussions, referred to above, explained the dire consequences of sexual sin. All this may be true, but it is best to examine Paul's own argument thus far to see if he has hinted at such a distinction between sins.

Paul has been speaking about the nature of sexual immorality and using prostitution as his example. The sin has been described in detail as causing a "joining" of bodies with the woman involved, whereas the body is actually *for* the Lord. Under the lordship of Christ and in accord with his creative purposes, the body in its sexual activity has a purpose that cannot be destroyed. This

---

22. Calvin, *First Corinthians*, 131–32.

23. Kistemaker, *First Corinthians*, 201. See also Barrett, *First Corinthians*, 151; Fee, *1 Corinthians*, 290.

24. Murphy-O'Connor, "Corinthian Slogans," 391–96. See also Leon Morris, *The First Epistle of Paul to the Corinthians: An Introduction and Commentary*, TNTC (Grand Rapids: Eerdmans, 1958), 103; Horsley, *1 Corinthians*, 92; Fitzmyer, *1 Corinthians*, 269.

25. Garland, *1 Corinthians*, 236. Brendan Byrne, "Sinning against One's Own Body: Paul's Understanding of the Sexual Relationship in 1 Corinthians 6:18," *CBQ* 45 (1983): 608–16. Byrne comes to a similar conclusion that here "there is something about fornication that strikes at one's own 'body' in some particularly direct way." His explanation of why this should be is convoluted and unnecessary. Following Käsemann, he argues that σῶμα must here be understood as an "instrument of personal self-communication" (ibid., 613).

purpose is to reflect certain aspects of the image of God, including his faithfulness to his people and his love and commitment to them, as noted above. To indulge in sexual sin is therefore very specifically a sin *against the body* in the sense that it is a sin against the created purpose of the body's sexual functions. It speaks against the union of the Lord with his people and the way the Lord has used the physical body itself to further that union and to help explain that union.[26] Taken in this way, the next rhetorical question ("do you not know . . . ?" as in v. 16a) simply forces home the message.

6:19 Or do you not know that your body is the temple of the Holy Spirit within you whom you have from God and that you are not your own? (ἦ οὐκ οἴδατε ὅτι τὸ σῶμα ὑμῶν ναὸς τοῦ ἐν ὑμῖν ἁγίου πνεύματός ἐστιν, οὗ ἔχετε ἀπὸ θεοῦ, καὶ οὐκ ἐστὲ ἑαυτῶν;). In yet another summary call to community holiness, Paul now mentions a fourth reason why immorality involving prostitutes is completely at odds with the Christian life. The body is where the Holy Spirit has taken up residence. The rhetorical question governs the two following statements. First, it presupposes that they did of course know or certainly should have known that "your body is the temple of the Holy Spirit within you." Secondly, they should have known that they are not their own but belong to the Lord.

The first rhetorical question earlier in this series, "Do you not know . . . ?" (see comments on 3:16), also raised the question of their understanding of themselves as "God's temple." There we noted that Paul was talking of God's presence indwelling the church by his Holy Spirit. There Paul speaks of the temple as holy and warns of destruction to anyone who would destroy the temple. Here in chapter 6 the emphasis is on the individual in whom the

Spirit dwells (ἐν ὑμῖν). Thus, Paul can speak of a person's "body" also being the temple of the Spirit because this is where he has taken up residence. In Romans 8:11 Paul links this indwelling of the Holy Spirit to the Spirit's involvement in the resurrection of Jesus. This is the Spirit who indwells us, says Paul, and who "will also give life to your mortal bodies." So here, Paul writes of the body being inhabited by the Spirit and that God "will raise us through his power" (ἡμᾶς ἐξεγερεῖ διὰ τῆς δυνάμεως αὐτοῦ; v. 14). The agent is the Spirit who is "within you," that is, resides in the body of the believer. For a believer to be "joined" to another is to ignore the very presence of God in one's life.

Paul makes a further vital point here. He appeals to God's grace. He uses a relative clause qualifying the Holy Spirit: "Whom you have from God." God is the source and the giver of the Holy Spirit. The Holy Spirit of God takes up residence in the life of the community and the life of the individual believer entirely of God's initiative and grace. Paul started his letter by giving thanks for the grace of God that they had received in Jesus Christ (1:4). In 1:9 we saw that the goal of God's calling of people to himself was that they should have "covenant participation" (κοινωνία) with the one who has all authority, "Jesus Christ our Lord" (see comments on 1:9). The giving of the Holy Spirit enables and witnesses to the transfer of lordships that allowed Paul to contrast the life of Christians with the life of those "of this age." In 2:12 he introduced the point he builds on here that disciples have not received the spirit of the world "but the Spirit of God." This Spirit enables the Christian to "have the mind of Christ" (2:16). This is God's grace: his amazing gift to his people. To abuse the body in the way Paul has described in chapter 6 is therefore a rejection of the grace of God and a fracturing of the covenant

---

26. See the essay, "In Depth: Sexual Sin, Idolatry, and the Covenant Community," at the end of this chapter.

relationship established by the work and presence of the Spirit who indwells the believer's body.

Now Paul moves to a final argument in his call for community holiness, which further shows why sinning against the body with prostitutes is at odds with the Christian life. It is that Christians, and therefore their bodies, belong to the Lord. Grammatically it is important to note that the clause "you are not your own" (ὅτι . . . καὶ οὐκ ἐστὲ ἑαυτῶν) is a second object clause in response to the rhetorical question ("Do you not know that . . . you are not your own?"). This reminds them that they belong to the Lord. They have entered into "covenant participation" with God's "Son, Jesus Christ our Lord" (1:9). They are not independent agents (and never were), nor do they belong to "the rulers of this age" (2:6–8). As Paul said in 3:16 and 3:23, "You are God's temple," and, "You are Christ's." But it is in v. 20a that he explains what he has in mind.

6:20 For you were bought with a price. So indeed glorify God in your body (ἠγοράσθητε γὰρ τιμῆς· δοξάσατε δὴ τὸν θεὸν ἐν τῷ σώματι ὑμῶν). Since Christians were purchased for God through the death of Christ, Paul insists that all bodily activity must have a goal of bringing glory to God. The "for" (γάρ) makes it clear that this is an explanation of what he has just said. The passive voice, "you were bought" (ἠγοράσθητε) again draws attention to God's action. "With a price" (τιμῆς)[27] hearkens back 1:30 and redemption in Christ. Paul's imagery of purchasing people draws upon the world of slavery.[28]

As Thiselton argues, this is not a matter of a person's *freedom* being purchased.[29] In other words, the metaphor is not about gaining a slave's independence. Rather, Paul has in mind a transfer of ownership or transfer of lordships. This is altogether clear from the text since Paul is expanding upon the statement "you are not your own." In 7:23 Paul makes an identical statement about Christians, "you were bought with a price." The context there (see comments on 7:17–24) helps us better understand Paul's point here. There, against the Corinthian desire for status and social climbing, Paul argues for a different approach to status. When people become Christians, they are to live and work for God no matter what their condition at the time (slave or free). He speaks to slaves in 7:21–22 and, while encouraging a slave to take their freedom if offered it, moves on to speak of that person being the "Lord's freed person." But this remains a genitive of possession ("the Lord's"). Thus, Paul speaks of a person who is free when called by God now being "Christ's slave" (7:22). This leads him straight into "you were bought with a price" and the command, "Do not become slaves of men" (7:23).

Paul was concerned back in 6:12 that nothing should "enslave" him (ἐξουσιασθήσομαι). Throughout his writing this has been his concern. The covenant participation established with Christ and through his work has established the rights of lordship for Christ over the life of the believer. The believer has relinquished their rights (see comments on ch. 9) for the sake of the Master who purchased him (see also Eph 6:9; Col 4:1).[30]

The purchase price was the death of Christ. Paul

---

27. An adverbial genitive of value.

28. See the essay, "In Depth: Slavery as Metaphor and the Transfer of Lordships," at 7:24.

29. Thiselton, *1 Corinthians*, 476–77. See comments on the word "redemption" at 1:30.

30. Martin urges that we see the slavery to Christ in terms of upward mobility; that is, being a slave to Christ is a higher status of slavery. But this carries a danger of underestimating the power of the total transfer of lordships. Christ's lordship is not just superior or of greater status but is altogether *different* since it works in a different dominion. See Dale B. Martin, *Slavery as Salvation: The Metaphor of Slavery in Pauline Christianity* (New Haven: Yale University Press, 1990), 64–65.

wrote in 5:7, "Christ, our Passover lamb, has been sacrificed" (see comments on 5:7). "Christ crucified" is the very heart of the gospel message (1:18, 23). It is through that sacrificial death that God made Christ "our redemption" (see comments on 1:30). With the transfer of the person to the lordship of Christ, everything about them belongs to the Lord, including the body. As a consequence, "so indeed" (δή), Paul moves from the indicative ("your body is the temple of the Holy Spirit . . . you are not you own . . . you were bought with a price") to the concluding imperative: "Glorify God *in your body*" (δοξάσατε δὴ τὸν θεὸν ἐν τῷ σώματι ὑμῶν).[31]

Paul has put forward five arguments against Christian toleration of sexual immorality, and he has done so by showing the significance and purpose of the body: (1) the body is for the Lord, (2) our bodies are members of Christ, (3) we are one spirit with him, (4) our bodies are temples of the Holy Spirit, and (5) we were bought with a price.

The final command is thus virtually inevitable. To "glorify God" (δοξάσατε, an aorist imperative)[32] means to draw attention to God so that honor may accrue to him. However, Paul adds "in your body" (ἐν τῷ σώματι ὑμῶν). Here "in" (ἐν) may be taken instrumentally, "with your body." This imperative contrasts with the previous "flee sexual immorality" (v. 18). The use of the body for immoral purposes serves one lord, while the Christian should use his or her body in the service of the one who bought them with a price. Setting the glory of God as the goal of all the body's activity would have prevented this church from tolerating any form of immorality, whether the case of incest, homosexuality, prostitution, or other. The first step for the Corinthians was to remember the place of the body in God's redemptive purposes. God will raise his people bodily through his power, for the body is a member that belongs to Christ. Meanwhile, the body is indwelt by the Holy Spirit.

IN DEPTH: Sexual Sin, Idolatry, and the Covenant Community

In 5:1 Paul began to tackle a serious case of sexual immorality (πορνεία). He urged God's holy people to distance themselves from any in the Christian community who were sexually immoral or idolaters (5:10). In 6:9, 13, and 18 the matter of sexual immorality is raised again, as it is in 7:2 and 10:8. In 5:11, 6:9, and 10:7–8 sexual immorality is directly linked with idolatry (cf. Gal 5:19–20). While obviously these two matters can and often are dealt with separately by Paul (e.g., Rom 13:13; 1 Thess 4:3), it is worth examining why both are frequently addressed together and are equally and strongly condemned by Paul.[33] The

---

31. "So indeed" (δή) is used only five times in the New Testament. This postpositive particle usually appears with imperatives or hortatory subjunctives and serves to intensify the command (e.g., Luke 2:15; Acts 13:2; 15:36).

32. On this useful example of a constative aorist, see Wallace, *Greek Grammar*, 721. It is not that this has not been happening, but as a command it must take on a new urgency.

33. Cf. also Eph 5:3–5; Col 3:5. Paul has much to say of those who sin in other ways, but idolatry and sexual immorality dominate not just in this epistle but in others as well. A case could be made that people who sin are usually involved in one or other of these two broad seemingly *great* sins. For example, greed is described as idolatry in Col 3:5. See also 1 Sam 15:23 where the sin of "presumption," that is, presuming upon God, is described as "idolatry" (ESV).

answer lies in the way these two sins are particularly destructive to the covenantal relationship Christians have both with their Lord and with each other.

It is notable in 6:9 that Paul has in mind the way *people* live. This is not simply a list of vices but, as in 5:10, Paul lists sinful people identified by their sin (see comments on 5:10 and 6:9). Thus, Paul refers to sexually immoral *people* (πόρνοι), not to some abstract idea of sexual immorality. Likewise, he refers to *idolaters* (εἰδωλολάτραι), not to some abstract idea of idolatry. The importance of this can easily be missed. Throughout this letter Paul has been concerned about the community of God's people, the "saints" in Corinth. This community, termed here a "covenant community," lives in a relationship with the Lord ("in Christ") that requires them to "image" their God to each other and to the world. In effect, this means they are being asked to be the community that Adam and Eve should eventually have formed had sin not entered the garden: a community of love for God and neighbor and submissive entirely to the will of God in true, joyful obedience. This community will not be perfected until the Lord comes in glory and all things are made new (Rev 21:5). Yet God's people find themselves already "in Christ." They are represented by the Lord, who has already been raised from the dead, who is the firstfruits of all believers who themselves will one day be raised from the dead to inherit the earth. The representative head of all Christians is *already* the "last Adam" (1 Cor 15:45). It is for this reason that in 15:49 Paul can say "just as we have borne the image of the man made of dust, let us also bear the image of the man of heaven."[34] Bearing his image is to reinstate what humanity was created for, that is, to image God (Gen 1:26–27; 5:3; Wis 2:23).

Idolatry is clearly a direct affront to this understanding of how Christians are to live out their covenant relationship with the Lord, who must be imaged. The Decalogue makes this point strongly. When "the LORD our God made a covenant with [them] at Horeb" (Deut 5:2), his law was clear: There shall be no other gods and no carved images (5:7–9). In Deuteronomy 4:16 a partial explanation for these prohibitions is given: God did not reveal himself in any form at Horeb, and so the people shall not make any "image" (εἰκών) of man or woman or of any creature. The fact is that, as the Books of Moses tell the story, the only image of God needed was the image of men and women as God had made them in Eden. If true humanity is the only permissible image of God and (since the fall) has only been seen in its perfection in Jesus, then idolatry is not only that which seeks to usurp God's place but is fundamentally *dehumanizing*. The covenant

---

34. See comments below on 15:48–49 for Paul's argument concerning the representative nature of the first and the last Adam. Also note arguments there for the hortatory subjunctive in 15:49.

Lord is *truly God*; he is Yahweh who has come as the God-King, and so idolatry of any form seeks to replace him at the head of his community, thus causing a breach of God's covenant with his people. Yet there is more going on here. In Christ, the covenant Lord has come as king on earth as a *true human being* and therefore as one who alone truly "images" the creator. Any other "image" thus holds before people a complete deception. "Do not let yourselves be deceived" (6:9; cf. 15:33), says Paul, for such deception is the work of demons (10:20). Idolatry ultimately destroys a person's ability to be what they were created to be: a true human being, the only true image of God. Paul therefore insists, "My beloved, flee from idolatry" (10:14).

Sexual immorality is also a direct affront to the call to covenantal obedience. The apostle sees sexual intercourse as much more than simply a matter of personal gratification, for it pictures the intimacy of the relationship between the Lord who is "abounding in steadfast love and faithfulness" and his people and who says to them, "You shall love the LORD your God with all your heart and with all your soul and with all your might" (Exod 34:6 and Deut 6:5 ESV; cf. Mark 12:30). Thus, as with idolatry in 10:14, Paul insists in 6:18, "Flee sexual immorality." Once again, Paul sees both the creation story and God's covenant with his people as pivotal in understanding the problem with immorality.

Paul is concerned that each believer recognizes that they *belong* to Christ and may be used only in Christ's service. This service includes the *body*. The covenant, creator Lord has *ownership* rights, and the body is his ("The body is not for sexual immorality but is for the Lord, and the Lord is for the body"; 6:13). Once again Paul thinks of the creation story as he reflects on how the covenant people should live in preparation for the time when all things are made new, including and especially the body.

It should not therefore surprise the reader that Paul turns in 6:16 to Genesis 2:24 to make his point that immorally using a prostitute in a sexual relationship is to be "joined" to her and to be "one body [with her]." In the creation story, Eve is created for Adam out of Adam's body because "it was not good" that man should be alone (2:18). She is "flesh of my flesh," says Adam in Genesis 2:23, the perfect helper "corresponding" to him (2:18). Genesis 2:24 then speaks of a man leaving his father and mother and holding fast to his wife. In sexual intercourse it is as if the couple recall that there was once one flesh, Adam, from which the woman, Eve, was taken. There is a closeness of *bodies* that is more profound than in any other human activity. Scripture does not seem to suggest that God in some way looked at human activity and decided that sexual intercourse, performed in an atmosphere of love, would provide a suitable picture of his love for people and their love for him. The indication in Scripture is far more profound. It is that God actually *planned* that human beings should enjoy this sexual relationship with their spouse *in order that* there should be a picture, at the deepest level of human relationships, of the bond between God and his people. In other words, the metaphor or picture is formed first in the mind of God, whose creative purpose is to bring a man and a woman together in this particular way. As Jesus says in Matthew 19:6, where he also quotes Genesis 2:24, "What God has joined together, let no one separate." This is a likely reason why Paul picks on Genesis 2:24 to support his case rather than, say, the specific injunctions against sexual immorality found elsewhere (Exod 20:14; Lev 19:29; 21:7; Deut 5:18; Prov 23:27).

Sexual immorality is thus understood to deny the whole goodness of creation and so indicates disobedience to the way in which God is to be imaged. Any sexual activity outside the marriage of a husband and wife, whether adultery, incest, homosexual activity, or other is covenant breaking and thus sinful activity (6:9). It is not how things were created to be, and it breaks the picture of the covenant relationship between God and his people. The fact that at times idolatrous worship seemed to have involved sexual immorality as well only sharpens the focus (10:7–8). Negatively, those who go after other gods can therefore be described as adulterers. This provides the substance to Hosea's prophecy and to many passages where Israel is accused by the prophets of adultery with other gods (Jer 3:9; Ezek 16; cf. Rev 2:22).

Theology in Application

The Danger of Tolerating Sexual License

Paul remains horrified that sexual license is being tolerated in the church, yet it appears this is being justified in the church on the basis of a claim to all things being lawful. Paul so radically qualifies this statement here, and even more so in chapter 10, that it is hard to concur with some commentators who hold that Paul agreed with this "slogan" despite his qualification of it. In effect Paul's qualifications render the slogan worthless.

Everyone should know that there are enormous boundaries set on a Christian's liberty. Perhaps the line from a famous Anglican prayer sums it up best when, in praying to God it says "Whose service is perfect freedom."[35] That service is, as Paul

---

35. The "Collect for Peace" at Morning Prayer in *The Book of Common Prayer*. The ancient Latin prayer from which this is drawn is perhaps more remarkable. It reads: cui servire, reg-nare est ("whom to serve is to reign"). That is, living in God's service and being subject to him is in fact to rule with him!

will show, a service of the Lord. Among the Lord's people only things that benefit or build up the community should be promoted. The biblical link between imaging God and the way men and women were created is part of the underlying rationale here (Gen 1:26–27). The church must be a place where people are edified so they can better image the Lord in the world and live for him in humble service.

When churches tolerate sexual license in their midst or any sexual activity outside of that described in Genesis 2 as between man and wife, they may be moving with the times, but they are being disobedient to Scripture. One of the ways God planned that he should be imaged to the world is being distorted, if not destroyed, and the temple of the Holy Spirit has become an unholy place. Prostitution is so commonplace in our age that many Western countries have already legalized it. For many Christians, such relationships become tempting in a world where often they can feel lonely and isolated. There is little doubt the church should do far more to help people with such needs and temptations, but it must be with better imaging of the love of the Lord rather than with tolerance of activity that will only serve to further alienate people from the knowledge and love of the Lord.

The Possibility of Change

In many of the modern discussions about sexual activity, Christians get sucked into arguments that suggest there are some activities in life from which people should not ever be asked to refrain. This idea dominates much of the thinking of the current generation. It is assumed that the practical expression of a person's sexual desires or preferences is so wrapped up with who they *are* that they must be expected to engage in sexual activity. The acceptance of such a view among Christians reflects an ever-decreasing understanding of the nature of the miracle of *conversion*. In a day when conversion is mostly seen in whether people have spoken a particular prayer to Jesus as Savior and whether they (occasionally) go to church, the transformation of the whole being described in the New Testament has been largely discarded. This has also contributed to the diminishing emphasis on holiness in the modern church. The constantly negative presentation of Christian ethics, even within the church, has only exacerbated the problem. That is, the church is often heard by its people simply to be saying "no" rather than teaching Christian ethics that have their foundation in the God who loves and cares for them and who has a purpose for them as they live for him. While the temptations to compromise with the ways of this world will always be acute, the nature of God's calling to image him and to evidence his transformative power that enables this to be achieved are encouraging and positive messages when properly taught. These are the messages that will "build up" rather than tear down. It is good to recall the unity we have with the Lord, being "one spirit [with him]" (6:17). It is vital to recall the extraordinary power of the Holy Spirit to change even our nature as he resides within each of us (6:19). As Paul said to the Ephesians, "[You were taught] to put on the new self, created after the likeness of God in true righteousness and holiness" (4:24 ESV). Again, in 2 Corinthians 5:17 the contrast between new and old is explicit: "If anyone is in Christ, he [or she] is a new creation. The old has gone, the new is here!" It is surely time to renew an emphasis on the radical miracle that occurs in the life of one coming to faith. This miracle can even change what we may see as someone's "nature." The process that ends in glory has already begun as the Spirit works in us, for "we all, with unveiled face, beholding the glory of the Lord, are being transformed into the same image from one degree of glory to another. For this comes from the Lord who is the Spirit" (2 Cor 3:18 ESV).

1 Corinthians 7:1–9

Literary Context

Having written of the dangers he sees in the way the Corinthian church tolerates sin within its community, Paul now begins a new section of his epistle in which he takes up concerns raised by the Corinthians in a letter they have sent him (7:1). It seems likely, given his use of the introductory formula "now concerning" (περὶ δέ) in 7:1 and its repetition in 8:1 and 12:1, that their questions have fallen into three broad categories: matters related to marriage and celibacy (ch. 7), matters related to idolatry (chs. 8–11), and matters related to the use of spiritual gifts (chs. 12–14). Into the discussion of marriage and celibacy he incorporates teaching on remaining single, on the place of widows, on being married to a nonbeliever, on divorce, and, at the heart of his message, on remaining in the same marital status as at the time of conversion.

Though the subject is new and suggested by Paul's response to the Corinthian letter, nevertheless themes and ideas that were previously introduced are picked up in this passage and provide a degree of continuity. Paul remains concerned about the temptation to "sexual immoralities" (τὰς πορνείας; 7:2), a dominating concern in the latter part of chapter 6. He draws on his understanding of the place of a "grace-gift" (7:7; cf. 1:7). He is concerned with a person's "calling" (7:17–24; cf. 1:9, 24–26) and again raises the matter of a person's "authority" or "rights" (7:4; cf. 6:12). He writes further on the nature of Christian freedom and being a "slave" to Christ, who "bought" his people (7:22–24; cf. 6:12, 20).

However, the tone of this section of the letter is rather different. Gone are the rhetorical questions ("do you not know . . . ?"). Rather, there is a more subtle tone. Some of the matters about which they have written do indeed raise serious issues, but Paul is also concerned to demonstrate that all Christians have a responsibility to follow the life for which the Lord has gifted them and to ensure they do not fall into temptation.

Paul has voiced great concern about those in the congregation who seem to be spiritually arrogant. In this passage, it appears that some of those may have held to a form of asceticism in which bodily activities, such as sexual intercourse, are regarded as nonspiritual.

Main Idea

In response to a matter raised by the Corinthians suggesting that some among them regarded sexual abstinence in marriage as the more spiritual position to adopt with regard to sexual relations, Paul insists that they face up to temptations to immorality. He affirms the value and mutuality of sexual relations within marriage partnerships and of self-control for the unmarried.

Translation

1 Corinthians 7:1–9

1a	Circumstance	Now **concerning the things about which you wrote:**			
b	Quotation		**"It is good for a man not to touch a woman."** ⬏		
2a	Basis	But	because of sexual immoralities		
b	1st exhortation (1st part)	**let each man have**	**his own wife** and	(A, man)	
c	(2nd part)	**each woman**	**her own husband.**	(B, woman)	
3a	2nd exhortation (1st part)	**Let**	**the husband give**	to his wife her [sexual] rights, and likewise	(A)
b	(2nd part)		**the wife**	to her husband.	(B)
4a	1st basis for v. 3 (1st part)		**The wife**	**does not rule over her own body**	(B)
b	(2nd part)		but **the husband**	**[does]**, and likewise	
c	2nd basis for v. 3 (1st part)		**the husband**	**does not rule over his own body**	(A)
d	(2nd part)		but **the wife**	**[does].**	

5a	Exhortation	**Do not deprive each other**
b	Concession	unless perhaps by mutual agreement for a time
c	Purpose (positive)	so that you may devote yourselves to prayer, and then
d	Exhortation	be together again
e	Purpose (negative)	lest Satan tempt you
f	Manner	through your lack of self-control.
6a	Explanation of concession at 5b	**I say this**
b	Manner	by way of concession
c	Manner	not by way of command.
7a	Wish	**I wish all were as I myself am.**
b	Assertion	But **each has his own grace-gift from God,**
c	Description	one of one kind and
		one of another.
8a	Assertion	**I say**
b	Addressees	to the unmarried and the widows
c	Content	**that it is good for them to remain [single]** as I do.
9a	Concession (protasis)	But if they are not showing self-control,
b	Assertion (apodosis)	**let them marry,**
c	Basis	for **it is better to marry than to burn** [with passion].

Structure

In chapter 7 Paul begins to address matters raised by the Corinthians (see also 7:25; 8:1; 12:1). Verse 1 is likely to contain a quotation from or reference back to the expressed opinion of at least some in the congregation. The first nine verses may be divided into three sections. The first (vv. 1–5) addresses married couples and their sexual relationship. The matter of sexual temptation encloses the argument with the opening phrase "because of sexual immoralities" (v. 2) and the closing "lest Satan tempt you" (v. 5). The verses are carefully balanced as both husband and wife are addressed alternately. (See a more detailed structural breakdown of vv. 2–4 demonstrating this balance in the comments on v. 2.) This is followed by a personal note (vv. 6–7), which forms a bridge into the third section.

The third section (vv. 8–9) begins with Paul drawing attention to his authority (also seen in vv. 10, 12, 25, 26). Here he addresses the unmarried, including widows. Paul recognizes their sexual desires and speaks to them. Either remaining single (v. 8) or marrying (v. 9) are the options available to the unmarried. Again, the section ends with reference to sexual temptation.

Exegetical Outline

> VI. Marriage, Celibacy, Divorce, and Widowhood in Relation to Community Status (7:1–40)
>
> ➡   A. Married and Unmarried Should Pursue God's Calling (7:1–24)
>
> 1. Married Couples and Sexual Relations (7:1–5)
>   a. The Corinthian Slogan (7:1)
>   b. Mutuality in Sexual Relations between Husband and Wife (7:2–5)
> 2. Paul's Preference for Remaining Single (7:6–7)
> 3. Unmarried People and Sexual Desires (7:8–9)

Explanation of the Text

7:1 Now concerning the things about which you wrote: "It is good for a man not to touch a woman" (Περὶ δὲ ὧν ἐγράψατε, καλὸν ἀνθρώπῳ γυναικὸς μὴ ἅπτεσθαι). Paul turns to the matter of sexual relations and their appropriate place in marriage. In doing so, he also addresses multiple other situations for people who are not married. The statement, "it is good for a man not to touch a woman," in v. 1b is taken here as a quotation from the Corinthian correspondence with Paul. Paul will go on to offer such strong qualifications of this statement that it is rendered virtually meaningless. The introductory words, "now concerning" (περὶ δέ), which appear on six occasions in the epistle (7:1, 25; 8:1; 12:1; 16:1, 12; cf. 8:4), indicate he is taking up issues identified by both parties as matters of concern.[1] Some Corinthians seem to espouse a dualism that regards abstinence from sexual intercourse (in marriage) as of spiritual value. Paul denies this. "To touch" (ἅπτεσθαι) a woman refers to having sexual relations with her.[2] The verb is used in this way in Ruth 2:9 (LXX) where Boaz orders the young men not to

sexually molest Ruth as she gleans, and in Proverbs 6:29 (LXX), which speaks against adultery with a neighbor's wife.

Whether this sentence is to be regarded as a quotation has prompted some debate. In the light of Paul's comments in vv. 2–5, it seems to make little sense unless it is regarded as a quotation. However, two other interpretations deserve examination. The first takes v. 1b to be a question ("Is it good for a man not to touch a woman?"). The understanding of the passage changes little by adding the question mark, except that it might suggest the Corinthians had written a less confrontational letter to Paul and were seeking his advice rather than stating their position. Another possibility would be to regard this as Paul's rhetorical question introducing the new subject matter in the light of some (unknown) reference to it in the Corinthian correspondence. Either way, Paul's answer denies the absolute nature of this proposition since in marriage sexual relations are not to be denied but are even to be encouraged.

---

1. It is not altogether clear whether each use of "now concerning" refers to a letter in the way it clearly does in 7:1. See below as each occurrence of the phrase (περὶ δέ) is addressed in the commentary (7:25; 8:1; 12:1; 16:1, 12).

2. Ciampa and Rosner, *First Corinthians*, 273–75, offer an

alternative understanding of "touched" (ἅπτεσθαι). They examine a number of uses of the word and conclude that it should probably be translated as "it is good for a man not to use a woman for sexual gratification" or "it it is good for a man not to have sex with a woman for the sake of pleasure."

A second approach views v. 1b as a simple statement that comes from Paul.[3] It is then assumed that Paul qualifies the statement in the next verses. The main problem with this is simply that the assertion of v. 1b seems to fly in the face of vv. 2–5, which are surely more affirming of sexual relations in the right context than simply a *concession*. Moreover, since the apostle's fundamental view of marriage is drawn from the Old Testament and specifically from the creation narrative, it is unlikely he would countenance the assertion of v. 1b even if he was intent on qualifying it. For him, Genesis 2:18 would have provided a background. There God says, "It is *not* good for the man to be alone. I will make a helper suitable for him." That culminates in the man and the woman becoming one flesh (Gen 2:24), which ends the "good" story of creation. The statement in v. 1b, if a simple statement, would thus seem to deny the goodness of sexual relations as part of creation itself by suggesting that it *is* good for a man not to be with a woman. Moreover, v. 1b might then imply a body/spirit dualism typical of Greek thought but not of biblical or Pauline thought. Sadly, at times in history the statement has been used to justify an asceticism that has more in common with Greek dualistic spirituality than with a biblical view of the whole person, body and soul, living in every area of life to God's glory.[4]

Many reasons are adduced for regarding v. 1b as an assertion emanating from Corinth rather than reflecting Paul's own view of the matter. First, it provides a simpler way to understand the logic of these verses and removes from Paul's lips a statement that seems out of line with the rest of his argument. It permits the view that in fact Paul

disagrees with the statement (hence vv. 3–5), while allowing, in certain specific situations, that celibacy can be a good and spiritual calling. However, as we shall see, he allows for the goodness of celibacy on a different basis, not because it is not good for a man to have sexual relations with a woman. Secondly, the fact that 7:1 begins with a reference to a Corinthian letter and is introduced with "now concerning" may well indicate a forthcoming quotation. (There are significant similarities with 8:1 where the same formula is used and is followed by a statement that also seems most unlikely to have come from the apostle.) Then it is to be noted, thirdly, that the assertion of v. 1b refers to a "man" and does not speak to the actions or thoughts of a woman. This is not how Paul continues his own teaching in this chapter where he specifically touches upon the mutuality (ἐκ συμφώνου, 7:5) of responsibilities and obligations of both a man *and* a woman (7:2–5, 12–13). This is true even in those places where he affirms celibacy (e.g., 7:32–34).

A further point of discussion centers on the meaning of the word "good" (καλόν). In brief, most of those commentators who take v. 1b as a statement made by Paul, which he then qualifies, take "good" as simply pragmatic in meaning. If a man can control himself, it is good, perhaps even "better," to remain celibate. However, the word may also be seen as an ideal or a moral or philosophical "good,"[5] in which case this statement could be seen as generic. If this is how it is to be read, then all Paul's qualifications would have to be regarded as second-best options. This would be inconceivable if the statement is attributed to the apostle. He would never have seen marriage and the creation

---

3. AV; RSV; TEV; NIV (1984); NASB. Barry Danylak, *Redeeming Singleness: How the Storyline of Scripture Affirms the Single Life* (Wheaton, IL: Crossway, 2010), 173–211. Calvin, *First Corinthians*, 134; Conzelmann, *1 Corinthians*, 115–16.

4. W. E. Phipps, "Is Paul's Attitude toward Sexual Relations Contained in 1 Cor. 7:1?," *NTS* 28 (1982): 125–31.

5. From earliest times some commentators have taken it in this way. For example, Tertullian, *Monogamy* 3:2; Jerome, *Jov.* 1:7. Also see Will Deming, *Paul on Marriage and Celibacy: The Hellenistic Background of I Corinthians 7*, SNTSMS 83 (Grand Rapids: Eerdmans, 2004), 110–15.

mandate as a "second best," with the ideal "good" being to abstain from sexual intercourse at all times.

However, if we take this as a Corinthian slogan, we are forced to ask what the Corinthians meant by it. Given the way Paul proceeds either to qualify the statement severely or even to deny it in the next few verses, it is likely that the Corinthians regarded this as a spiritual or moral "good." For some of them, given their dualism and reliance upon a Greek view of "wisdom" and "knowledge," abstinence from sexual relations was the best way of existence. Paul will have nothing of this.

In what follows, Paul will speak both of marriage and celibacy with enthusiasm. For him, one is not a superior moral good; rather, what is good is to follow God's calling and gifting for life (v. 17). He will allow that one course of action can, for pragmatic reasons, be better than another, but even this will be subject to God's calling. Since Paul takes the argument altogether out of the realm of an idealized spiritual existence, we do not find it convincing to argue that Paul accepts the Corinthian slogan but then qualifies it. Rather, it seems Paul mentions the slogan because it was used in the Corinthian letter, but uses it to speak of marriage and celibacy in an entirely different way. Paul will argue that the moral or spiritual "good" is to be seen in living life as the Lord has granted it. The pragmatic good will be determined by the need to serve and obey the Lord in all situations.

7:2 But because of sexual immoralities let each man have his own wife and each woman her own husband (διὰ δὲ τὰς πορνείας ἕκαστος τὴν ἑαυτοῦ γυναῖκα ἐχέτω, καὶ ἑκάστη τὸν ἴδιον ἄνδρα ἐχέτω). In their sexual relationship, husband and wife find

a specific way of avoiding sexual immorality. Paul now moves the discussion in a different direction from the one implied by the slogan. He offers a strong qualification, if not denial, of it. The phrase "sexual immoralities" (τὰς πορνείας) reminds the reader of the previous chapter and its discussion of prostitution and the command to flee from immorality (6:18). While some suggest that Paul here is not rejecting the Corinthian position outright (because he has a high regard for celibacy),[6] it seems more likely that he is indeed rejecting it. The argument, though developing in a different direction, continues from chapter 6 where he had addressed the problem of immorality and licentiousness. However, the ascetic argument from some in the Corinthian church is equally problematic for Paul. If one is to glorify God in the body (6:20), marriage is precisely a God-given way in which men and women may do so. We might paraphrase the argument in this way: "*'It is good for a man not to touch a woman.' On the contrary,[7] it is precisely because of the sexual immoralities of which we have been speaking that a man must have his own wife and a wife her own husband.*"

For Paul there will be time enough to speak of celibacy, but the very fact that it is vv. 2–6 rather than v. 8 that follow v. 1 suggests here that he is all but completely refuting the slogan. The present imperative "let [each man/each woman] have" (ἐχέτω) reinforces this view. Paul does not here offer a concession.[8] Rather, this is his command concerning the way forward for husbands and wives wishing to avoid the temptations of society that were laid out so clearly in chapter 6.[9] "Each man" does not refer to every single man so much as to each one who is married.

In contrast with the slogan that refers simply to

---

6. Cf. Garland, *1 Corinthians*, 255.

7. Thiselton, *1 Corinthians*, 501, suggests this translation for the adversative.

8. Contra Conzelmann, *1 Corinthians*, 116.

9. The use of the article, "*the* immoralities" (τὰς πορνείας), may refer back to the specific incidents described in ch. 6.

a *man*, Paul is careful to construct the following few sentences with a structure that shows the mutuality of husband and wife and that highlights their responsibilities to each other. A number of suggestions have been made about the chiastic structure involved in these verses. It is certainly useful to note how Paul uses structure here to demonstrate the mutuality in the husband and wife relationship. Taking v. 2b as the starting point, the husband (A) is first addressed, then this is followed by the wife (B) being addressed. In this way we see the interesting pattern noted in the opening diagram:

A (2b) let each *man* have his own wife
   B (2c) and each *woman* her own husband
A (3a) let the *husband* give to his wife
   B (3b) likewise the *wife* to the husband
   B (4a) the *wife* does not rule over her body (the husband does; 4b)
A (4c) the *husband* does not rule over his own body (the wife does; 4d)

This is followed in v. 5 by an insistence on a deep degree of mutual agreement.

The restrictions of the context of chapter 6 and the slogan of 7:1 mean that Paul is not here describing all that he believes about marriage. The context does not allow the deduction that Paul favors asceticism or sees marriage as second best, as suggested by some. Elsewhere Paul clearly articulates deeper reasons for viewing marriage as important to all of life. Theologically it is a picture of the love between Christ and his church, and it is a fulfillment of the creation ordinance (Eph 5:24–31; cf. 1 Cor 11:3, 11–12; 2 Cor 11:2). Yet here the immediate problem of sexual immorality is still to the fore in his mind. Chapter 7 must not be separated from chapter 6 just because it begins with "now concerning."

Paul is moving on to discuss marriage and celibacy, but the backdrop remains a church that has tolerated sexual immorality.

The feminine and masculine demonstrative adjectives (ἕκαστος . . . ἑκάστη) provide the subject for the imperatives. The imperative "let [each man/each woman] have" (ἐχέτω) may connote "hold fast to," but it is unlikely to mean "have sexual relations with," given Paul's use of the same verb in 7:12 where it simply means to "have a wife" (i.e., be in a state of marriage).[10] The use of two reflexive pronouns, "his *own* wife" (τὴν ἑαυτοῦ γυναῖκα) and "her *own* husband" (τὸν ἴδιον ἄνδρα), indicates that Paul is not here ordering all men and all women to be married but rather that all married men and all married women ensure they hold fast to their own spouses rather than take off with another into sexual immoralities. Paul will expound this specifically in relation to sexual intercourse in the next three verses. As such, Paul begins a straightforward denial of the slogan. It is indeed right and proper that a husband and wife cling to each other and have sex with each other (vv. 2–5) rather than seek out other immoral relationships.

7:3 Let the husband give to his wife her [sexual] rights, and likewise the wife to her husband (τῇ γυναικὶ ὁ ἀνὴρ τὴν ὀφειλὴν ἀποδιδότω, ὁμοίως δὲ καὶ ἡ γυνὴ τῷ ἀνδρί). The sentence might be translated as "let him pay [ἀποδιδότω] to his wife what is owed" (τὴν ὀφειλὴν). Though some have found this idea of a "debt" in marriage to be strange, it reminds the reader that biblical marriage has always contained covenantal ideas that involve contractual responsibilities and duties. Right from the creation story in which a man and a woman make a public statement of moving away from parents to be

---

10. Garland, *1Corinthians*, 256, is wrong to argue that the verb (ἔχω) cannot mean the same in v. 2 as it does in v. 12 on the grounds that, if it means "to have" in v. 2, Paul would be contradicting himself in vv. 8–9 where he advocates celibacy.

The command in v. 2 is not that each man must have a wife and vice versa, but that each must have his or her *own* husband/wife.

together (in marriage), the contract has involved sexual relations: "And they shall become one flesh" (Gen 2:24). The "duty" involved here in no way implies a lack of love or lack of (sexual) desire on the part of either party. It is simply a part of what marriage *is*. In this context in which some have been saying that it is good for a man not to have sexual relations with a woman, Paul is demonstrating that, in marriage, this would be a breach of the covenantal obligations of the relationship.[11]

In this way Paul orders husbands and wives to fulfil their (sexual) obligations to each other. Again, the quotation from the Corinthian letter is untenable. Having sexual intercourse with one's spouse is to be encouraged as part of the commitment of marriage. But it is also the natural way to avoid the immoralities of chapter 6. The way Paul argues is that the existence of the temptations to immorality expounded upon in chapter 6 indicate both the normality of marriage but also the absurdity of the Corinthian statement itself. Something that may have sounded pious and "spiritual" to those seeking a form of greater "spirituality" through asceticism (perhaps because of a dualistic worldview) could in fact lead to immorality and lack of holiness (licentiousness). For Paul marriage is seen here as the normal mode of existence.[12] It also is the way in which, in the area of sexual relations, a person may with his or her body still bring glory to God (6:20; cf. 1 Thess 4:3–5).

We have already noted how the structure of these verses emphasizes the mutuality of activity and decision making involved in the relationship between wife and husband. The word "likewise" (ὁμοίως) makes this point linguistically. In this area of sexual intimacy husband and wife have equal rights, which is a concept that would probably not have been typical in the world of Paul's day but which reflects the "one flesh" union of biblical teaching on the matter.[13] This is further highlighted in v. 4.

7:4 The wife does not rule over her own body but the husband [does], and likewise the husband does not rule over his own body but the wife [does] (ἡ γυνὴ τοῦ ἰδίου σώματος οὐκ ἐξουσιάζει ἀλλὰ ὁ ἀνήρ· ὁμοίως δὲ καὶ ὁ ἀνὴρ τοῦ ἰδίου σώματος οὐκ ἐξουσιάζει ἀλλὰ ἡ γυνή). Paul adds that in marriage the partners' bodies belong to each other, thus affording them "rights" over each other. The argument is developed in a stark way. The word "rule over" (ἐξουσιάζω) has already been employed by Paul in a wordplay in 6:12. The noun "authority" or "right" (ἐξουσία) is picked up in 8:9 and becomes a significant subject of discussion in chapter 9. But the discussion there only contributes to an understanding of this verse in this way: part of the problem the Corinthian church seemed to manifest was its appeal to "rights." That Corinthians appeal to "rights" reflected their spiritual arrogance. Here, in the example of marriage Paul himself is prepared to talk about such rights or du-

---

11. The fact that this particular "duty" refers to the sexual relationship is clear when it is understood that vv. 3–5 are a unit. Verses 4–5 speak specifically of the partner having a right over the spouse's "body," and v. 5 refers to depriving the partner. The word in v. 5 for "deprive" (ἀποστερέω) is used in Exod 21:10 (LXX) which speaks of how a man must not deprive his (first) wife of "her food, clothing and marital rights." "Marital rights" can refer in both the Hebrew (עֹנָה) and the Greek (ὁμιλία) here to sexual intercourse.

12. This point is well made by Soards, *1 Corinthians*, 138, who also argues that Paul does not make a concession to mar-

riage in v. 2 but assumes that "marriage is a normal, natural necessity. [Paul] recognizes the potential problem of immorality in order to explain and to verify his basic understanding that marriage is the rule, not the exception."

13. See Witherington, *Conflict and Community*, 170–75. Soards, *1 Corinthians*, 139, says of v. 4, "There is little to no historical or cultural precedent for what Paul says. While male-dominant society was the predominant culture of antiquity, Paul understands the dynamics of marital relations in a strikingly egalitarian way."

ties. However, for him these "rights" do not provide grounds for someone to laud it over another. The reverse is true. Paul insists that when married, a man or a woman does not rule over his or her own body. The spouse does. While in Roman society the first part of this verse might have been expected, the second part in which the man is said *not* to "rule over his own body" stands out as remarkable for a largely patriarchal society. Indeed, in many sectors of our own Western society in which men exercise power over women, often to their great detriment and pain, we might say that vv. 4c–d still stands out as remarkable. There is no need to discuss how it is possible that "one's own" body can be under someone else's rule and no need to add the word "alone" (NIV 1984: "The wife's body does not belong to her *alone*") as if, without the word "alone," it is implied that the man has total power over the woman's body and vice versa. This seems to miss the point.[14] The context makes clear that the "body" here refers to the body *as participating in sexual intercourse.*

Even though this mutuality of obligation in marriage may start within the biblical and legal understanding of the duties of marriage, it would be wrong to suggest that Paul ignores love as he spells out this further command. The emphasis on mutuality and on each person's sexual desires and needs points to a loving and respectful relationship.

7:5 Do not deprive each other unless perhaps by mutual agreement for a time so that you may devote yourselves to prayer, and then be together again lest Satan tempt you through your lack of self-control (μὴ ἀποστερεῖτε ἀλλήλους, εἰ μήτι ἂν ἐκ συμφώνου πρὸς καιρόν ἵνα σχολάσητε τῇ προσευχῇ καὶ πάλιν ἐπὶ τὸ αὐτὸ ἦτε, ἵνα μὴ πειράζῃ

ὑμᾶς ὁ Σατανᾶς διὰ τὴν ἀκρασίαν ὑμῶν). "Deprive" (ἀποστερέω) implies theft or defrauding[15] and harks back to the mutual obligation and duty in marriage for husband and wife. Neither is to rob the other of sexual relations. To do so might lead to a lack of self-control brought about by the work of Satan. Paul then introduces a gentle caveat to what he has said. There might be occasion when both devote themselves to a time of sexual abstinence for concerted prayer.

The translation "unless perhaps" (εἰ μήτι ἂν) reflects the hesitancy of the Greek phrase.[16] "For a time" (πρὸς καιρόν) suggests a specific, but short, time. The two main purpose clauses (ἵνα and ἵνα μὴ) modify "deprive each other . . . by mutual agreement." The first purpose clause is divided into two parts. The first part speaks to the possible purpose for mutually agreeing to suspend sexual relations: that they might "devote" themselves (σχολάσητε) to prayer. The second speaks to the end purpose of the "mutual agreement": that they may "be" (ἦτε)[17] "together again" (lit., "to the same place"; ἐπὶ τὸ αὐτό). The second main purpose clause is expressed negatively. The mutual decision is made "lest Satan tempt" them (ἵνα μὴ; lit., "in order that [Satan] may not"). Given the emphasis on being together again, the danger of temptation, and the hesitancy about the concession in the first place it seems clear that the apostle Paul is far from enthusiastic about even this degree of concession to abstinence.

The potential temptation to lack of self-control has its source in Satan. Paul probably has in mind that too long a time without sexual activity in marriage may lead to a loss of self-control and so being tempted by the immoral behavior mentioned in

---

14. *Pace* Thiselton, *1 Corinthians*, 505, who adds the word "exclusive."

15. See 1 Cor 6:7.

16. BDF §376.

17. Some texts substitute the imperative "come together" (συνέρχησθε) for "be" (ἦτε). Since the former simplifies the latter, it is less likely to be original; despite support from 𝔓[46] most evidence is later.

chapter 6 or the "sexual immoralities" of v. 2. It is thus wrong in a Christian marriage to expose one's spouse or oneself to possible sexual temptation by deprivation of normal marital sexual activity. No doubt Theissen makes a valid suggestion when he refers also to the temptation of sexual fantasies when a married person is deprived by his or her partner of their marriage rights.[18]

This verse provides further evidence that the catchphrase of v. 1 emanated from the Corinthians. Here in v. 5 Paul barely even grants that prayer is a good reason for abstention from sexual intercourse between husband and wife. In the mutuality of the marital relationship, in which each may legitimately expect to have their sexual desires satisfied by their partner, abstention must also be a joint decision taken together. Of course, there would be a sad irony if this same temptation were to occur when a couple had mutually decided to forgo sex for the sake of prayer. This is why even Paul's concession is qualified by a fixed (short) period of time. Perhaps since the decision is to be mutual, Paul may have in mind a time of prayer when husband and wife are praying together, perhaps for their own family needs.

Throughout his writings Paul regards prayer as vital to Christian life and urges that it be "constant."[19] Clearly the prayers of husband and wife together do not normally, to Paul's mind, require abstention from sexual intercourse. However, he allows that an occasional time of concentrated prayer might benefit from a cessation of sexual activity. It is interesting to reflect on why this might be the case. Paul does not think dualistically like the society around or even like some of the Corinthians themselves.[20] For Paul it is not that one activity, prayer, is "spiritual" and the other, sexual intercourse, is not. Paul may have imagined a time of close and intimate prayer in which husband and wife come before the Lord together for a lengthy period. In the intimacy of this closeness, as they open up to each other and to the Lord together, so their love for each other would deepen. If this closeness found in prayer were to go for long, then sexual desire would likely deepen. Satan's temptation might then come through sexual fantasies or simply result in the prayer time itself becoming a frustration.

7:6 I say this by way of concession not by way of command (τοῦτο δὲ λέγω κατὰ συγγνώμην, οὐ κατ᾽ ἐπιταγήν). The personal note of vv. 6–7 forms a bridge between the discussion of married people

---

18. Gerd Theissen, *Psychological Aspects of Pauline Theology*, trans. John P. Calvin (Philadelphia: Fortress, 1986), 172.

19. Rom 12:12; 15:30; 2 Cor 1:11; Eph 6:18; 1 Thess 5:17.

20. There has been much discussion about the origins of the asceticism implied by the Corinthian quotation in 7:1 (see comments on 7:1). It is likely that some of the Corinthian Christians did distinguish "spiritual" activities such as prayer as being more "holy" and therefore more confirming of a spiritual status in the community. Indeed, for some sexual abstinence itself may have become a matter of spiritual pride. Such views were not uncommon even in Hellenistic Judaism. For example, Philo, *Moses* 2.14 talks of Moses's restraint with regard to food and sexual activity as he awaited visions from God (cf. Horsley, *1 Corinthians*, 96–98, who suggests that the Corinthians may have been motivated to asceticism in the light of some in Greek society who left their spouses in order to be fully devoted to *Sophia*, "whom they consider to be their spiritual life-mate"). There is some considerable attraction

to this in the light of our belief that the Corinthians held the gift of "wisdom" to be especially significant as an indicator of a mature or sophisticated spirituality. Yet other alternative backgrounds for their withdrawal from sexual relations have been suggested. For example, some Jewish thinking of the day also spoke of possible temporary suspension of the physical relationship with a woman for the sake of a time of prayer: "There is a time for intercourse with his wife, and a time [for a man] of continence for his prayer" (*T. Naph.* 8:7–10, quoted in Deming, *Paul on Marriage and Celibacy*, 120). Certainly, the general climate of Greek dualistic thought lent itself to those who would argue that their abstention from sexual activity demonstrated their higher spiritual status, perhaps even their greater "knowledge" or "wisdom." They may have believed that this would strengthen their claim to superior status in the community. Narrowing down the precise religious or philosophical background that gives rise to this form of Corinthian Christian asceticism is perhaps impossible.

and the unmarried. Paul refers to the concession of v. 5. He insists that he makes no command for abstinence. This is simply a concession, perhaps even a reluctant one! Paul reiterates the hesitancy he has just expressed about speaking of such an exception at all.

While this seems to make the most logical sense of the meaning of "I say *this*" (τοῦτο), some have suggested "this" may refer to part or the whole of vv. 2–5, while others have suggested it looks forward to what follows beginning at v. 7.[21] The imperatives of vv. 2–3 and the assertions of v. 4 make it unlikely that Paul is thinking of all he has said in those verses as "by way of concession." Among others, Orr and Héring have suggested that the sentence looks forward.[22] Recently Winter and Garland have developed this view in more detail.[23] In a lengthy exegetical article Winter argues that after a verb of saying, "this" refers to what follows. Garland suggests that if the concession refers backward it can only refer to abstinence during prayer (our position), but then questions why Paul would offer a concession for something like this when there must be a number of other reasons in any relationship for a couple to experience "cycles of quiescence in their sexual relationship."[24] He then follows Winter. However, a number of problems pertain to this view. First, the problem Paul faced was not simply allowing a "cycle of quiescence" for prayer but the problem of abstinence regarded as something extra "spiritual" without regard for the temptations of Satan. Paul allowed no deliberate abstinence based on any such slogan as spelled out in v. 1 except—by way of concession—an occa-

sional interruption of normal relationships for the sake of a defined period of prayer. Secondly, it is not possible to build such a strong argument that "this" refers forward. First Corinthians 7:35 offers just one example where the pronoun "this" refers backward. Furthermore, Thiselton suggests that the use of "concession" (συγγνώμη) in v. 6 deliberately recalls "mutual agreement" (σύμφωνος) in v. 5, giving further weight to the view that v. 6 looks back to Paul's hesitant concession of v. 5.

7:7 I wish all were as I myself am. But each has his own grace-gift from God, one of one kind and one of another (θέλω δὲ πάντας ἀνθρώπους εἶναι ὡς καὶ ἐμαυτόν· ἀλλὰ ἕκαστος ἴδιον ἔχει χάρισμα ἐκ θεοῦ, ὁ μὲν οὕτως, ὁ δὲ οὕτως). In the light of what Paul has said, he reminds his readers that there are advantages to singleness. It is not, however, for all. This sentence is best read as a conclusion to the argument of the previous six verses, though it certainly opens the way for discussing the unmarried. Paul had started with a slogan from the Corinthians, "It is good for a man not to touch a woman" (v. 1), but he had refused to accept this. Husbands and wives are commanded to have sexual relations and are told they have rights over each other's bodies. They may only desist by mutual agreement and for a short while, lest their self-control break down under the temptation of Satan. This could lead to the very sexual immoralities mentioned in v. 2 and in chapter 6. Now, as Paul concludes this section he turns to his own position and his own preferences.[25]

---

21. Some who think that it refers backward also assume that the slogan of v. 1b is from Paul. Then in vv. 2–5 Paul speaks for marriage, but he does *this* only by way of concession (Robertson and Plummer, *First Corinthians*, 132–35; see also Conzelmann, *1 Corinthians*, 118; Morris, *First Corinthians*, 107; Ernest B. Allo, *Saint Paul: Première Épître aux Corinthiens* [Paris: Gabalda, 1956], 159).

22. William F. Orr and James A. Walther, *I Corinthians*, AB 32 (Garden City: Doubleday, 1976); Héring, *First Corinthians*, 58.

23. Bruce Winter, "I Corinthians 7:6–7: A Caveat and a Framework for 'the Sayings' in 7:8–24," *TynBul* 48 (1997): 57–65. Cf. Garland, *1 Corinthians*, 269–70.

24. Garland, *1 Corinthians*, 269–70.

25. Those who take v. 1 as a statement made by Paul in favor of celibacy regard this verse as a summary of that argument, but, as we have seen, this is unlikely for a number of reasons, especially given Paul's commands in vv. 2–5.

Paul himself is single as v. 8 makes clear. Whether he is single because his wife died, or left him, or because he has never been married is unclear. However, his appeal to his "grace-gift" (χάρισμα; see 1:7 and 12:4) suggests he may have never been married. It is interesting that the apostle should believe it is a gracious gift from God that enables life to be lived as a single person. God has enabled him to live without needing a wife, without the trappings and time commitments that go with a marriage (7:33–34), and without the need for a sexual relationship. However, Paul acknowledges that marriage is also a "grace-gift" when he speaks of "each one" (ἕκαστος) having a grace-gift "one of one kind and one of another" (ὁ μὲν οὕτως, ὁ δὲ οὕτως). Singleness and marriage are not simply down to an individual's choice or preference. Grace-gifts of God enable men and women to live as God has called them to live. Later on in his argument, Paul refers to the life that the Lord has assigned to "each one" and appeals to people to remain "in the condition in which [they were] called" (v. 20; 7:17–24). The Lord assigns a life of marriage or singleness, but then by his grace provides grace-gifts that enable that life. As we shall see in v. 8, part of the grace-gift for singleness has to do with being able to show "self-control" and not burn with passion, but it probably also includes the ability to focus on the work of the gospel and on learning to be content in this situation (Phil 4:11).[26] We may speculate that Paul would consider faithfulness to one partner, giving one's whole self to another person, turning away from any form of immorality, and lifetime love to be among the characteristics that necessitate a "grace-gift" from God for marriage.

At what level, then, are we to construe Paul's wish in v. 7a? Clearly he is not advocating celibacy for the married, but he is advocating celibacy for those who find this is the life the Lord has assigned them (see v. 8c). The tone of this verse, however, continues to reflect the attitude of concession seen in v. 6. Paul makes no command here. We shall see later (7:34) that he has good reasons to suggest that singleness has its advantages, but it is not for everyone, and it has nothing to do with some dualistic notion of a higher plain of spirituality.

7:8–9 I say to the unmarried and the widows that it is good for them to remain [single] as I do. But if they are not showing self-control, let them marry, for it is better to marry than to burn [with passion] (Λέγω δὲ τοῖς ἀγάμοις καὶ ταῖς χήραις, καλὸν αὐτοῖς ἐὰν μείνωσιν ὡς κἀγώ· εἰ δὲ οὐκ ἐγκρατεύονται γαμησάτωσαν, κρεῖττον γάρ ἐστιν γαμῆσαι ἢ πυροῦσθαι). Paul proceeds to address those who are at present single in the church, the "unmarried" and the "widows." Singleness can be "good," but marriage is appropriate in some circumstances. The word "unmarried" (ἄγαμος) appears only in this chapter within the New Testament. Here it seems to refer to both men and women, while in v. 11 it refers to divorced women and in v. 32 to unmarried men and in v. 34 to unmarried women. It has been suggested that the word in v. 8 may refer only to single men generally or, more specifically, to widowers in the light of the following mention of "widows."[27] However, Paul's discussion proceeds to examine examples of single men and women who should not marry or who might be best to marry and, even though it is not immediately apparent why he should specify "widows" right here, it seems to make more sense

---

26. Thiselton, *1 Corinthians*, 513.

27. Fee, *1 Corinthians*, 318–19, argues that Paul mostly refers to men and women together in each of his arguments and so there is no reason why this verse should be read differently.

He also argues that there was no ready Greek word to describe "widowers" and so he refers to single men who are defined by the context as being widowers.

of the whole argument if "unmarried" is regarded as a general description of all single people.

"It is good" (καλόν) need not imply a moral good here. Paul is not going back on all that he has said but is amplifying, by way of example, what he has said in v. 7. Paul has not commanded singleness and is not doing so now. Nevertheless, singleness is good as a state of existence, and hence Paul says, "As I do" (ὡς κἀγώ). But it does require its own grace-gift. Lack of that gift will be shown by a lack of self-control and a burning with passion.

Most commentators and translations believe that Paul's concern here is that while singleness is good and has its advantages (v. 32), it is "better" to marry if a person is unable to control his or her sexual desires. The person should under no circumstances "burn [with passion]." This implies that Paul imagines marriage to be mainly about providing an outlet for an uncontrolled sexual desire. Yet two important questions are raised by this interpretation. First, to what does "burn" (πυροῦσθαι) refer? It has been suggested that it might mean "burn [in hell]." This could make sense if sexual intercourse was already taking place outside of marriage (5:1–5; and perhaps in ch. 6). The verb "to burn" is used in this way on occasion in the LXX (cf. Sir 23:17) but also in 2 Peter 3:12,[28] so God's judgment may be in mind. But the word is also used metaphorically to describe intense emotion (see 2 Cor 11:29; 2 Macc 4:38), and it is perhaps more natural to take it this way here; hence the translation "burn [with passion]." Secondly, is the lack of self-control hypothetical or actual? The former is rather more likely to imply that marriage is the answer for uncontrolled sexual desires. However, the present tense "not showing self-control" (οὐκ ἐγκρατεύονται) suggests Paul may have in mind actual situations in which some unmarried people are having sexual relations with people to whom they are not married. Since Paul sees marriage as a calling and needing a grace-gift from God and not simply as an outlet for repressed sexual tensions, this may be more likely.

It is worth noting that in the New Testament "self-control" does not simply refer to holding evil desires in check. In 1 Corinthians 9:25 an athlete's exercise of "self-control" (RSV; NRSV; ESV) is used as an example of the way a Christian should set his eyes on the goal of God's blessings. "Self-control" (ἐγκράτεια) is also listed as one of the fruits of the Spirit (Gal 5:23). Thus, though lack of such control may refer to a specific matter, such as not being able to control one's sexual desires, it also has a broader connotation for Paul. Marriage is not simply a "way out" for a person without such control but is actually the path of self-control when a person sets their mind on God's calling and pursues it. Marriage is not here regarded as some less good option for a person who is not as spiritual as someone else. Rather, it is the right option for those who are called, hence the aorist imperative: "Let them marry" (γαμησάτωσαν).

---

28. BDAG 899. Michael L. Barré, "To Marry or to Burn: πυροῦσθαι in 1 Cor. 7:9," *CBQ* 36 (1974): 193–202.

Theology in Application

Mutuality in Marriage

The idea that a person's body might belong to another is fraught with difficulties. Wrongly understood, it might appear to condone the exploitation and abuse seen in so many relationships. Many pastors have seen such abuse even in Christian marriages, most frequently on the part of the man over the woman, but also at times on the part of the woman over the man. However, the crime of abuse and horrific exploitation that is so common in today's world should not be allowed to mask the beauty of the mutuality of marriage called for in Scripture. This starts with creation itself as husband and wife are created to be perfectly complementary to each other. "Bone of my bones and flesh of my flesh . . . and they shall become one flesh" (Gen 2:23–24) points clearly toward the language that Paul uses here in discussing the sexual relationship between husband and wife. Since the unity of their relationship is most clearly seen in this bodily act as they become "one flesh," the idea that the one belongs to the other and that the one has "rights" over the other's body makes profound sense. It speaks to their created purpose for each other but also to their calling to a covenantal, God-imaging, self-sacrificial relationship of faithfulness and love. In the marriage relationship Paul envisions, when it comes to sexual relations the spouse should consider their body as belonging to the partner. Equally, the partner has the right to assume this other body belongs to them. This is what it is to be "one flesh." Nowhere is the unity of the couple more clearly seen than in the sex act. Nowhere can the partners be more giving to each other, more acknowledging of the other's position in his or her life than in the unashamed nakedness and vulnerability of this relationship. Paul's words speak of complete vulnerability and openness. It is no wonder that later in the Ephesian correspondence it is this becoming one flesh that is seen so clearly to reflect the oneness of Christ and his people (Eph 5:31–32).

In an evangelical church that often seems to see the sexual relationship as providing for little more than procreation and for the control of (mostly male) sexual urges, this passage speaks of so much more. It reminds those who refuse to acknowledge it that women also have sexual desires that they need to be able to satisfy with their God-given partner in marriage. It reminds men and women of the mutuality of the sex act itself as each gives him or herself to the other in love, seeking the joy of the partner and so finding their own joy. "Do not deprive one another" is a strong reminder that there is no place in marriage for using sex as a tool for manipulation. In Scripture the most remarkable poetic exposition of this sort of physical love is to be found in the Song of Songs. There the lover and the beloved both describe each other's bodies with ecstatic language (e.g., the woman: 5:10–16; the man: 6:4–7; 7:1–5) and both cry out in their desire for fulfillment of their love in sexual intercourse (e.g., the woman: 3:1–5; 4:16b; 8:1–3; the man: 4:1–16; 7:8–9). The need for the church to preach a positive message on these matters and to spend as much time, or preferably more, on these verses as she does on the one verse of 6:9 is critical for the spiritual (and physical) health of all Christian women and men.

Lack of Self-Control

The call to the unmarried and widows to remain single, if they can, is a hard call for many, especially in today's society, which so often links a person's sexual activity or lack of it to their personhood. Paul clearly recognizes the problems that may be encountered with sexual temptations. Yet he can also envisage another way of living in a fulfilled and joyful way. As we noted in comments on chapter 6, the powerful transformation of the Christian through the miracle of conversion is often overlooked or deliberately ignored in some church circles. Paul assumes the power of God to change people. "Self-control" is thus not a hopeless and overly optimistic aspiration but a behavioral attitude to life that is attainable in Christ. His appeal to self-control is a common theological thread in his writings. In Galatians 5:23 he reminds us that it is a product of God's work in the life of a believer, calling it a "fruit of the Spirit." In chapter 6 he has insisted on the fact that the Spirit indwells all believers. However, this fruit of the Spirit is often separated from the other fruit. All too often self-control is regarded as something altogether negative. It is about what should *not* be done, of *refraining* from certain actions or saying "*no*" to parts of life that people would rather say "*yes*" to. This is not how Paul sees it. As a fruit of the Spirit, the exercise of self-control is seen to be God-glorifying and a witness to the image of Christ in this world. It enables service to the Lord in love and obedience, and it brings joy to the individual who lives as God desires them to live. Indeed, self-control allows a person to receive an imperishable wreath (9:25). There is no doubt that this fruit of the Spirit, like others, must be "fanned into flame," but this is one of the reasons the Spirit was given: "For God gave us a spirit not of fear but of power and love and self-control" (2 Tim 1:6–7 ESV). This is part of a positive and joyful life that Christians ought to experience daily. It is a counsel of despair for the church to assume such fruit is unattainable and so to downplay God's power in the believer's life.

1 Corinthians 7:10–16

Literary Context

Continuing from the questions of promiscuity and sexual immoralities addressed variously in chapters 5–6, Paul began to answer a Corinthian question about sexual relationships between husband and wife in 7:1–7. In vv. 8–9 Paul addressed those unmarried people who may be contemplating marriage, encouraging both singleness and marriage depending on the context. His discussion now rapidly touches upon a variety of relationships. There should be no divorce, not even if a person is married to an unbeliever when that unbeliever is prepared to live in the marriage. If divorce does happen, then the person divorced should remain single. The unbelieving husband or wife and even the children in a mixed marriage (Christian and non-Christian) experience a special relationship to the faith and the Lord. It is possible the unbelieving spouse will be saved and come to faith. The principle guiding what he says of these various relationships will be laid out in the following verses (vv. 17–24).

Main Idea

Christians should remain married and not be divorced from their spouses. Even if married to a non-believer, Christians should remain married unless the nonbeliever breaks up the marriage. Such marital faithfulness to an unbelieving spouse may lead to his or her salvation.

Translation

---

1 Corinthians 7:10–16

10a	Addressees	Now to the married
b	Command	**I charge** ...
c	Parenthesis	(not I but the Lord)
d	Content of command	... **a wife not to be separated from her husband.**
11a	Exception: concession	But ... if she separates,
b	command	... let her remain single or
c	command	be reconciled to her husband. And
d	Content of command	... **a husband is not to divorce his wife.**
12a	Addressees	To the rest
b	Assertion	**I say**
c	Parenthesis	(I, not the Lord)
d	Condition (protasis)	if any brother has an unbelieving wife and she agrees to live with him,
e	Content for 12b (apodosis)	**he is not to divorce her.**
13a	Condition (protasis)	And if a woman has an unbelieving husband and he agrees to live with her,
b	Content for 12b (apodosis)	**she is not to divorce her husband.**
14a	Basis for 13b	For **the unbelieving husband is made holy**
b	Agency	**through his [believing] wife and**
c	Basis for 12e	**the unbelieving wife is made holy**
d	Agency	**through the [believing] brother.**
e	Analogy	Otherwise **your children would be unclean,**
f		but in fact **they are holy.**
15a	Exception: condition	But if the unbeliever separates,
b	command	**let him [or her] separate.**
c	explanation	**The brother or the sister is not enslaved**
d	circumstance	in such cases.
e	Assertion	**God has called you to peace.**
16a	Rhetorical question	For wife, **how do you know whether you will save your husband?**
b	Rhetorical question	Or husband, **how do you know whether you will save your wife?**

Structure

Paul's structure is clear and logical as his thought progresses from the unmarried believers and widows in v. 8 to those believers who should get married in v. 9. Verses 10–11 are then directed to the married, specifically addressing the matter of divorce. Finally, Paul writes for the "rest" (vv. 12–16), that is, believers married to unbelievers. This section can be further broken down as, first, Paul urges that neither the Christian husband or wife of an unbeliever should get a divorce (vv. 12–13). Then he speaks of the influence the believer may have on the life of the unbelieving spouse (vv.14–16). Paul's theological justification for all that he is saying will be developed in vv. 17ff.

Exegetical Outline

VI. Marriage, Celibacy, Divorce, and Widowhood in Relation to Community Status (7:1–40)

   A. Married and Unmarried Should Pursue God's Calling (7:1–24)

      1. Married Couples and Sexual Relations (7:1–5)

      2. Paul's Preference for Remaining Single (7:6–7)

      3. Unmarried People and Sexual Desires (7:8–9)

➡   **4. Married Couples Are to Remain Married (7:10–16)**

         a. Separation and Divorce Should Not Happen (7:10–11)

         b. Christians Married to Unbelievers Should Not Seek Divorce (7:12–13)

         c. The Believing Spouse May Lead the Unbeliever to Salvation (7:14–16)

Explanation of the Text

7:10–11 Now to the married I charge (not I but the Lord) a wife not to be separated from her husband. But if she separates, let her remain single or be reconciled to her husband. And a husband is not to divorce his wife (Τοῖς δὲ γεγαμηκόσιν παραγγέλλω, οὐκ ἐγὼ ἀλλὰ ὁ κύριος, γυναῖκα ἀπὸ ἀνδρὸς μὴ χωρισθῆναι—ἐὰν δὲ καὶ χωρισθῇ, μενέτω ἄγαμος ἢ τῷ ἀνδρὶ καταλλαγήτω—καὶ ἄνδρα γυναῖκα μὴ ἀφιέναι).[1] In vv. 7–8 Paul gave his directions for the "unmarried" and the "widows."

In vv. 10–11 Paul speaks "to the married" (Τοῖς δὲ γεγαμηκόσιν), and his argument is simple. Married Christian believers should not separate or divorce. If a wife has separated, then she should either remain unmarried or be reconciled. Presumably Paul is concerned that if she remarried she would be committing adultery. The teaching is stark, but it is the same as Christ's own teaching in Mark 10:7–12. It is probably unwise to speculate here as to why the problem of separation had become an issue

---

1. These verses offer a useful comparison of anarthrous nouns in the main clauses—"wife" and "husband" (γυναῖκα and ἄνδρα)—where simply a class of people is being identified, and a noun with its article in the subordinate clause where a specific person is in mind, "her husband" (τῷ ἀνδρί).

worthy of Paul's comments; ultimately, this cannot be known. Since he spoke about some abstaining wrongly from sexual relations (v. 5), it is possible that some couples had not just given up sexual relations but had separated from each other to avoid temptation. Since the woman is addressed first, it is possible that some women had become ascetics in their dedication to Christ,[2] but there is little evidence for such a tradition of asceticism among groups of women. It is more likely that men and women were separating and divorcing simply because they came from a Greco-Roman background in which divorce was commonplace and extremely easy to secure. It simply required a consent between the partners to leave the marriage or even a unilateral statement that the relationship was at an end. This would help explain Paul's "charge" or command here, for he continues to be concerned through this epistle with the Corinthian church's inability to distinguish itself sufficiently from the sin of the surrounding culture. In this case, they are also clearly flouting the teaching of Christ himself.

These two verses must be taken together as one sentence with a parenthesis between the two commands that Paul gives, first to the wife and then to the husband. The perfect participle (γεγαμηκόσιν) speaks to the ongoing state of being married. The command stands in stark contrast to his concessions and desires in the first few verses of this chapter. The Lord himself has spoken on the matter of divorce and Paul seeks to apply that teaching now to Corinthian Christian husbands and wives. The two verbs translated as "separated" (χωρίζω) and "divorce" (ἀφίημι) are virtually synonyms. Both imply separation or departure away from someone. However, the latter is sometimes used in legal con-

texts and therefore is perhaps better understood as "divorce."[3] The word is applied to men here and in v. 12, which may reflect the fact that in Judaism men alone sued for divorce,[4] but the context and its application to women in v. 13 (μὴ ἀφιέτω τὸν ἄνδρα) makes this unlikely. Paul probably here recalls the teaching of Jesus recorded in Mark 10:2–12 and perhaps especially v. 9: "Therefore what God has joined together, let no one separate [ἄνθρωπος μὴ χωριζέτω]." The phrase "not I but the Lord" (οὐκ ἐγὼ ἀλλὰ ὁ κύριος) is introduced because Paul will go on to say "I, not the Lord" in v. 12.

Some commentators have sought to distinguish two levels of authority here: Paul's and the Lord's. The suggestion is that Paul's words in 7:10 where he appeals to the Lord are to be seen as more significant than the words that he claims are from him and "not the Lord" in v. 12. This is entirely to misunderstand the apostle's understanding of his own authority. Paul simply means that, on this subject, the Corinthian Christians will be aware that the Lord has spoken. In vv. 10–11 Paul speaks to believers who are married. For them Jesus's saying remains unchanged. Divorce is unacceptable. However, Paul will move on in vv. 12–16 to discuss separation and divorce in a new set of circumstances for which he has no saying of Christ upon which to draw. There he addresses the "rest" (v. 12); that is, people who are married to unbelievers. He thus makes it clear that when it comes to this second group it is he who is now speaking. Nevertheless, the authority of this teaching is not thereby diminished in any way. Rather, Paul applies his mind to a new situation and does so knowing that he is "someone who by the Lord's mercy is trustworthy" (ὡς ἠλεημένος ὑπὸ κυρίου πιστὸς

---

2. A view taken by Horsley, *1 Corinthians*, 96; also Margaret Y. MacDonald, "Women Holy in Body And Spirit: The Social Setting of I Corinthians 7," *NTS* 36 (1990): 161–81.

3. BDAG 156. However, not too much should be made of

this difference between the two words. MM 696 suggests that "separate" (χωρίζω) "has almost become a technical term in connection with divorce, as in 1 Cor 7:10, 11, 18."

4. Barrett, *First Corinthians*, 162.

εἶναι; 7:25) and that he speaks as one who has "the Spirit of God" (7:40). With apostolic authority Paul goes on to explain the mind of Christ in a new situation (cf. 2:16).

Despite the clear command, Paul remains pastorally sensitive. In some cases of separation or divorce it will not be possible for the wife to be reconciled to her husband. For example, divorce may have led to another marriage to someone else. Yet whatever might cause divorce, if it has happened, the wife should remain unmarried, says Paul. Just as wives should not separate, so husbands also must not divorce their wives. Whoever has walked out on whom, divorce must not be pursued. Meanwhile, Christian couples should strive for reconciliation, which may take much work but is the right course.

7:12–13 To the rest I say (I, not the Lord) if any brother has an unbelieving wife and she agrees to live with him, he is not to divorce her. And if a woman has an unbelieving husband and he agrees to live with her she is not to divorce her husband (Τοῖς δὲ λοιποῖς λέγω ἐγώ, οὐχ ὁ κύριος· εἴ τις ἀδελφὸς γυναῖκα ἔχει ἄπιστον, καὶ αὕτη συνευδοκεῖ οἰκεῖν μετ᾽ αὐτοῦ, μὴ ἀφιέτω αὐτήν· καὶ γυνὴ εἴ τις ἔχει ἄνδρα ἄπιστον, καὶ οὗτος συνευδοκεῖ οἰκεῖν μετ᾽ αὐτῆς, μὴ ἀφιέτω τὸν ἄνδρα). Paul now addresses a different subgroup of the "married." The "rest" (λοιποί) are those Christians married to unbelievers. The believer should not initiate divorce. Paul again maintains his careful balance of addressing men and women alternately. Having addressed the wife first in the previous couplet of verses, he now addresses the husband first in these two verses, which should also be held together. This time, however, he does not refer to a specific teach-

ing of Jesus: "I say (I, not the Lord)."[5] This is Paul's pastoral advice concerning marriage relationships that were not addressed by Jesus. The contrast between the believer and unbeliever (ἄπιστος) is accentuated in the first couplet in which the believing husband is referred to as "brother" (ἀδελφός) and the unbelieving wife as simply "wife" (γυνή). In the second couplet the context has already been established, and so it is unnecessary to refer to the wife as "sister" (ἀδελφή),[6] though that is evidently what she is.

It is unlikely that a Christian would have married an unbeliever, but Paul did face marriages in which a spouse has come to faith after marriage. In 7:39 Paul instructs widows to marry "only in the Lord," and Old Testament teaching clearly forbade mixed marriages, even advocating divorce in some situations (Deut 7:3; Ezra 10:3). Indeed, this biblical teaching may have provided the incentive for Christian spouses to feel that it would be right to divorce a partner who was not a believer. With the emphasis on spiritual status and perhaps a degree of spiritual dualism, divorce may have seemed an apt and "spiritual" way forward to some. However, Paul again views matters differently in the light of the gospel of Christ. Neither Christian husbands nor Christian wives are to divorce their unbelieving partner while that person agrees to live with the Christian. The English translation of the imperative needs to carry the weight of a command: "He/she is not to divorce" (μὴ ἀφιέτω). The NIV captures this with "must not divorce." The ESV and NRSV "should not divorce" is inadequate. The reasons for this injunction will be spelled out in vv. 14 and 16. Paul thus addresses a practical situation, still experienced frequently in the modern church, in which one partner becomes a Christian while

---

5. See comments above on v. 10.

6. For the use of "sister" (ἀδελφή) referring to a believing woman, see Rom 16:1 and 1 Cor 9:5, where the nouns "sister" and "wife" are placed side by side so that "sister" in effect becomes an adjective, hence the translation "believing wife" (so also NIV, ESV, NRSV).

the other does not. Staying married will mean that Christ is brought into the home with benefits for all (v. 14), and perhaps, in due course, the spouse will come to faith (v. 16).

7:14 For the unbelieving husband is made holy through his [believing] wife and the unbelieving wife is made holy through the [believing] brother. Otherwise your children would be unclean, but in fact they are holy (ἡγίασται γὰρ ὁ ἀνὴρ ὁ ἄπιστος ἐν τῇ γυναικί, καὶ ἡγίασται ἡ γυνὴ ἡ ἄπιστος ἐν τῷ ἀδελφῷ· ἐπεὶ ἄρα τὰ τέκνα ὑμῶν ἀκάθαρτά ἐστιν, νῦν δὲ ἅγιά ἐστιν). This verse offers Paul's first reason why it is better for a Christian to remain married to an unbelieving spouse if the spouse will have it. It is because the unbeliever "is made holy" (ἡγίασται) by the Christian partner. We shall suggest that, while not indicating their salvation, this means unbelieving spouses experience at close quarters the impact of the Holy Spirit's presence on Christians around them. They are thus in a privileged position as they benefit from the tangible reflection of Christ lived before them day by day. The perfect indicates that it is the present results of this action with which the writer is concerned. This statement has created much debate. In what sense might it be true that an unbeliever could be said to be "sanctified" *by* or *through* or *in* an unbeliever? The problem is not made any easier by the possible different meanings of the preposition here (ἐν τῇ γυναικί . . . ἐν τῷ ἀδελφῷ).

Paul has been counseling against a Christian divorcing an unbelieving spouse. The possible reasons for such a divorce have been mentioned in the comments on vv. 12–13. Since it is likely that Christians were afraid that union in marriage with an unbeliever was unspiritual and were perhaps using Old Testament texts to support this view, they probably feared that the union itself rendered

them unholy. This view could further be supported from Paul's own teachings that their "bodies are members of Christ" (6:15) and that the "body is a temple of the Holy Spirit" (6:19; cf. 3:17). Additionally, given the general condemnation of relationships with prostitutes, they may have assumed that the same would apply to any sexual relationship with unbelievers.

Paul argues from a different perspective. Rather than the Christian becoming unholy in this setting, the unbeliever "is made holy" (ἡγίασται). In Paul's writings the word "holy" is normally a description of believers (see 1:2) and is their status by virtue of being "in Christ" and through the work of the Holy Spirit in their lives (6:11; Rom 15:16). Behind this meaning lies the Old Testament concept of holiness as separation unto God. God's people are called by him out of unbelief into the community of believers. However, this cannot be the meaning here since this would mean that the spouse had become one of God's people and a believer through being married to one, as if holiness were somehow a transferable substance through the act of marriage. Even if this could happen, Paul would no longer call such a person an "unbeliever," and v. 16 would be rendered redundant.

Calvin argued that Paul is thinking of the relative spiritual power or status of the one who follows Christ over against the one who does not believe. He supposes that a Christian might become "unclean from contact with an unbelieving husband" (or wife) but adds: "Yet it turns out differently. For the godliness of one does more to 'sanctify' the marriage than the ungodliness of the other to make it unclean. . . . In the meantime this sanctification is of no personal benefit to the unbelieving partner."[7] Garland, following part of Calvin's argument, has suggested that this marriage follows God's design for marriage and is therefore holy, unlike the

---

7. Calvin, *First Corinthians*, 148.

relationship with a prostitute, which breaks that creation ordinance of marriage. This marriage involving a Christian is thus a place where God's own holiness is experienced and a sphere in which his transforming power is present.[8] Jerome Murphy-O'Connor views this holiness mainly from its ethical dimension: "Although the pagan has not committed him/herself to Christ in faith, he or she nonetheless exhibits a pattern of behavior that is analogous to the conduct expected of the *hagioi*."[9]

There can be no doubt that having a Christian spouse can open up new ways of living for the unbeliever. The behavior, values, and Christ-inspired love of the Christian will be likely to have its effect in the marriage, either in leading to rebellion on the part of the unbeliever and consequent divorce or to quiet and appreciative acquiescence on their part. As Paul indicates in v. 16, this may even lead to salvation. This approach necessitates taking the preposition ($\dot{\epsilon}\nu$) as having an instrumental force, thus reading: "Is made holy *through* his [believing] wife . . . is made holy *through* the [believing] brother" (cf. NRSV, NASB).

However, in our opinion, these scenarios still only partly explain Paul's thinking as he says that the spouse "is made holy" or that the children of the Christian parent are "holy" rather than "unclean" ($\dot{\alpha}\kappa\dot{\alpha}\theta\alpha\rho\tau\alpha$). Some therefore have turned more specifically to a covenantal framework of ideas to provide an explanation. Calvin cites Romans 11:16: "If the dough offered as firstfruits is holy, so is the whole lump, and if the root is holy, so are the branches" (ESV). Whatever may be said of this approach to children, the context of Romans 11 is about the place of Jews and Gentiles among the *holy* people of God, Israel. Some who were "in"

are eventually broken off because of their unbelief (Rom 11:17–18). Fee also turns to these verses in Romans,[10] arguing that the use of the word *holy* is similar there and here in that covenantal ideas are present, and the *holy* group incorporates those who are not yet saved but whom Paul hopes will be saved. That Paul can address Israel and the church as "holy" even when both contain those he later identifies as not being in Christ is evident in a number of places.

How do these covenantal ideas work for Paul? Though we shall examine more of this in chapter 10, Romans 3 seems to provide some help. There, after Paul has proved from Scripture that all, Jew and Gentile, have sinned and are to be found unrighteous before God, he asks the rhetorical question: "Then what advantage has the Jew?" (Rom 3:1). He lists a number of great benefits that they possess, including "the oracles of God." In Romans 9:4–5, speaking of the Israelites, he adds detail to this: "To them belong the adoption, the glory, the covenants, the giving of the law, the worship, and the promises; to them belong the patriarchs, and from them, according to the flesh, comes the Messiah" (NRSV). This is the amazing context within which God's people live and operate. These are among the huge benefits of being within God's covenant community. But then in 3:9–10 Paul asks a second rhetorical question, "What then? Are we [Jews] any better off? No, not at all . . . both Jews and Greeks are under the power of sin" (NRSV). Ultimately, salvation is not guaranteed by experiencing the covenant benefits of community membership nor even in receiving the mark of that community's membership, circumcision. Salvation comes through faith in the covenant Lord, Jesus

---

8. Garland, *1 Corinthians*, 289; see Calvin, *First Corinthians*, 149. Cf. Rosner, *Paul, Scripture, and Ethics*, 169–170.

9. Jerome Murphy-O'Connor, "Works without Faith in 1 Corinthians 7:14," in *Keys to First Corinthians: Revisiting the*

Major Issues (Oxford: Oxford University Press, 2009), 49 [The essay was first published in *RB* 84 (1977): 349–61].

10. Fee, *1 Corinthians*, 331–32.

Christ. This, we believe, is how Paul thinks here in 1 Corinthians. The presence of a believing spouse brings to the marriage relationship all that is theirs under the lordship of Christ. The instrumental "through" (ἐν), "made holy *through* his wife . . . *through* the brother," indicates Paul's understanding that the believer is the means by which unbelievers find themselves to be "holy." It is thus inevitable that the whole relationship will be affected by this. If the wife is the believer, then she will submit to her husband "as to the Lord"; if the husband, then he will love his wife "as Christ loved the church and gave himself up for her" (Eph 5:22–25 ESV). Unbelievers will indeed have all the advantages of living under the influence of and hearing the Scriptures, of hearing about the covenant promises, of understanding the nature of worship, and even of having a tangible reflection of Christ in front of them. This is of huge advantage. They will benefit in similar respects to the ways in which the Lord expected aliens to benefit from living among the Israelites (cf. Exod 23:12; Ezek 47:22). They are indeed "set apart" with great advantages over their fellow unbelievers. But they are not yet people of faith. As Paul will show in chapter 10, this may be true of many who in one way or another are part of the covenant community.

With regard to the children, the same is true. Paul assumes this because they form the analogy by which he can argue for the "holy" unbeliever. For children with a Christian parent or parents the advantage of being in a home where the covenant Lord rules and is worshipped, his word taught and understood, his promises explained, and they are brought up to know the need for faith and to worship is great indeed. It is again the great advantage of the Jew over the Gentile as Paul described in Romans, with more besides, for now the covenant Lord is known as King Jesus.[11] As with his deepest desire to see his fellow Jews come to faith in Christ (Rom 9:1–3; 10:1), so also here Paul challenges the believing wife and believing husband with the hope and real possibility of salvation for the unbelieving spouse (7:15–16).

7:15–16 But if the unbeliever separates, let him [or her] separate. The brother or the sister is not enslaved in such cases. God has called you to peace. For wife, how do you know whether you will save your husband? Or husband, how do you know whether you will save your wife? (εἰ δὲ ὁ ἄπιστος χωρίζεται, χωριζέσθω· οὐ δεδούλωται ὁ ἀδελφὸς ἢ ἡ ἀδελφὴ ἐν τοῖς τοιούτοις· ἐν δὲ εἰρήνῃ κέκληκεν ὑμᾶς ὁ θεός. τί γὰρ οἶδας, γύναι, εἰ τὸν ἄνδρα σώσεις; ἢ τί οἶδας, ἄνερ, εἰ τὴν γυναῖκα σώσεις;). The logic of Paul's argument from v. 14 continues directly in v. 16, with v. 15 being a logical continuation of vv. 12–13. We therefore turn to v. 16 first. Paul uses his *covenantal optimism*, based within the workings and promises of God, to encourage the believer to persevere in the marriage if possible. With two identical rhetorical questions, "How do you know . . . ?" (τί οἶδας), Paul indicates that for both a Christian wife or a Christian husband, there is a possibility that the unbeliever will be saved. Despite arguments that propose the contrary, it seems likely that Paul would indeed have been hopeful of the possibility of salvation for an unbelieving spouse.[12] Of course, the fact is that the

---

11. However, though for some it may make logical sense to suggest that if they are part of a covenant family and hence part of the covenant community they should therefore receive the covenant sign of baptism, this is not what Paul says here nor is he addressing the matter.

12. Here the rhetorical question is understood to be an expression of hope, thereby giving another reason for the

Christian partner not to divorce unless the unbeliever insists on separation. This would continue the general approach of this passage and specifically v. 14 that divorce is not the best way forward. In Tertullian, *To His Wife* 2.2.3 and Augustine, *Adulterous Marriages* 1.13, both understood the text in this way. Lightfoot, *Notes on Epistles*, 227, supported this interpretation of the questions on linguistic grounds, that "how do

Christian spouse cannot know for certain that this will happen since salvation is in the hands of God. But God uses his people in his work, and where there is a witness to Christ and the word of Christ is seen and heard, there is real hope that God will work his salvation.

The text reads consistently and clearly if vv. 15a–d is seen as a parenthesis. Verses 12–14 address Christians with nonbelieving spouses, and v. 16 continues this line of thinking. But now we must return to v. 15. This parenthesis also deals with Christians married to non-Christians, but it now views the marriage from the perspective of the non-Christian taking the initiative to divorce. Thus, the reader is not taken far from the issue at hand. Paul takes a moment to admit that some unbelieving spouses will not be content to live with a Christian. If such a person separates from a Christian "brother" or "sister," Paul says, "Let him [or her] separate" (χωριζέσθω). Even though the Christian approach to marriage is that it should be indissoluble, the Christian need not stand in the way of this separation that is initiated from outside the faith. This much is relatively straightforward.

However, a further discussion surfaces in translation here as Paul uses the word "enslaved" (ESV) or "bound" (NIV; NRSV; δουλόω). Is he referring to being freed from the "slavery" of a marriage or the "slavery" of the laws of marriage? If it is the latter, as some argue, then the "freed" Christian would potentially be in the same position as the "widow" described in 7:39 and hence able to remarry, though of course "only in the Lord."[13] The word "enslaved" can also mean "bound" as in "bound like a slave."[14] However, the usual word used to describe being "bound" under law and the word that Paul uses in 7:39 (cf. Rom 7:27) is distinct (δέω). The difference becomes significant when it is asked whether Paul intends simply to state that when someone has divorced he or she is no longer enslaved in marriage with an unbelieving partner or whether Paul wants to emphasize that the marriage arrangements, the legal ties, no longer enslave or bind the believer.

Two potential problems arise if the idea of enslavement is taken to refer to the state of marriage. First, it is difficult to imagine that Paul could speak of being "enslaved" to a marriage. Given his description of marriage in Eph 5:22–33 and the high regard for marriage throughout Scripture, Paul is unlikely to have seen marriage as any form of enslavement.[15] Marriage is a place where God's will for men and women can be fulfilled in a relation-

---

you know . . . ?" (τί οἶδας) is used in a context of hope in 2 Sam 12:22, Joel 2:14, and elsewhere. This so-called "optimistic" understanding of the question is well expressed in the NRSV translation: "Wife, for all you know, you might save your husband" (see also NEB). The main alternative takes these rhetorical questions as implying doubt that the spouse will be converted, and so adds to the argument of v. 15 in favor of separation. To paraphrase: "If the unbeliever separates, let them separate, for how can you know whether you will save the unbeliever?" In this view, the idea of saving the unbeliever is regarded as unlikely and so does not provide a reason for holding the marriage together. For a defense of this view, see Sakae Kubo, "1 Cor 7:16: Optimistic or Pessimistic?," *NTS* 24 (1978): 539–44. A third position is held by Fee, *1 Corinthians*, 337–38, who believes that the questions are ambiguous but that "almost certainly" the flow of thought suggests they go with vv. 12–14, not with v. 15ab.

13. This is sometimes referred to as the "Pauline privilege."

14. BDAG 260 gives the first meaning as "enslave" and a second meaning of "cause to be like a slave" or "bound" and lists 7:15 in this category.

15. Two possible backgrounds have been suggested that might have enabled Paul to speak of marriage as "slavery." First, Deming has argued that there is evidence among the Stoic-Cynic philosophers of discussions of marriage in terms of slavery. He quotes numerous texts to support this. For example, when Philo describes the Essenes he speaks of their "true and only freedom" found within a celibate community. When a man marries he becomes "a slave in the place of a freeman" (Quoted in Deming, *Paul on Marriage and Celibacy*, 147, from Philo's *Hypothetica*). He also develops an argument from their understanding of freedom that involves the "power" of a person to do whatever he wants. We do not have to follow Deming's subsequent speculation about the way the Corinthians saw marriage and his speculation about their view of "power" in relationship to an unbeliever to accept that in the Hellenistic world of ideas

ship that reflects the love of Christ for his people. Secondly, read like this, the statement seems somewhat redundant. If the unbeliever has divorced the believer, it is clear the believer cannot any longer be in the "enslavement" of marriage. Recalling the flow of Paul's argument is important. He has spoken of an unbeliever being willing to live with a believer and has insisted that, in this case, there is no cause for the Christian to initiate divorce. He has spoken of how covenant categories may give some cause for optimism in this relationship. He makes this clear by way of summary in v. 16. Yet as he speaks of the unbelieving partner (v. 14), he needs to clarify that if *this* person walks out on the marriage then a different situation pertains altogether. The Christian must let the partner separate him or herself.[16] The word used here (χωρίζω) is the same word Paul used back in 7:10–11. There he addressed a Christian partnership and insisted that if a Christian couple separates, the husband or wife should not remarry. The text of 7:15 is notable because it breaks away from this general argument that divorce should not be an option and that the ongoing consequence of marriage means the partner should not normally remarry.[17] In the situation of v. 15, there was nothing that a Christian partner could have done anyway to maintain the marriage since the unbelieving spouse has separated him or herself. Whereas in the Christian situation the rule of "no remarriage" looks for reconciliation (v. 11c), here the unbeliever has no such demands laid upon him or her. Thus, we may see a clear contrast whether or not we like the word "enslaved"! In a Christian marriage one might appeal either to the state of marriage (the enslavement) or to the binding of the law to argue for no remarriage and for the spouses to pursue reconciliation. In the situation of v. 15a, neither the state of marriage (the "enslavement"?) pertains nor, since now there is no marriage, do the Christian rules about divorce or remarriage still "bind." It is our view that this sad situation of an unbeliever walking out of a marriage to a Christian and forcing a divorce leaves the man or woman as if their partner was dead and hence, under certain strict conditions, available for remarriage.

One further sentence needs comment. In what sense have Christians been "called" by God "to" (ἐν) peace? Two main interpretations are offered. First, the appeal to peace here may look backward and be a reinforcement of what has just been said. The Christians being addressed ("you")[18] should not fight against an unbeliever's desire to divorce. To the extent they can, all Christians are called to live in peace in all their interactions with others

---

marriage was sometimes spoken of as "slavery." Secondly, it has been suggested that the background lies within the Old Testament and Judaism, not in regarding the state of marriage as "slavery" but that the deed of divorce itself had its roots in Exod 21:10–11, which deals with the rules surrounding the divorce of a slave wife. See two articles by David Instone-Brewer, "1 Corinthians 7 in the Light of the Graeco-Roman Marriage and Divorce Papyri," *TynBul* 52 (2001): 101–15 and "1 Corinthians 7 in the Light of the Jewish Greek and Aramaic Marriage and Divorce Papyri," *TynBul* 52 (2001): 225–43. Whether or not we maintain that either of these backgrounds could have influenced Paul's vocabulary, neither is especially helpful in determining Paul's view of the end result of this divorce. Even if it is freedom from the slave-state of marriage, that very freedom makes the slave a free person presumably with the legal rights of a free person and so, by analogy, the Christian divorcee has

the rights of one who is not a slave, the rights to start again with free choices.

16. The middle indicative is followed by the middle imperative (χωρίζεται and χωριζέσθω). This emphasizes that the initiative lies with the unbeliever. If he separates himself, let him separate himself from the relationship.

17. *Contra* Fee, *1 Corinthians*, 334.

18. The word "you" (ὑμᾶς) is rated "B" by UBS being found in ℵ* A C K 81 1175 among others. "Us" (ἡμᾶς) appears in 𝔓46 ℵ2 B D F G Ψ 33 𝔐 among others. The latter manuscript evidence is strong and would mean that Paul was appealing to the general requirement on all Christians to live in peace in all their relationships with others. Héring, *1 Corinthians*, 53, follows this reading. Metzger (*Textual Commentary*, 489) argues that scribes were more likely to generalize "the reference of aphorisms" and so widen an application.

(Rom 12:18; 14:19). Otherwise, it may present another argument for not divorcing an unbelieving partner, in which case the particle (δέ) is taken as adversative, as "but" rather than the consecutive/causal "for." In this case, 7:15e must be separated from the thought of the rest of the verse and put with v. 16.[19] In our view, either position makes sense—both of the thought line and of the Greek. However, it is worth noting that "peace" is full of covenant overtones. It summarizes all that God wants for his people, and so here Paul may indeed have in mind that this peaceableness of the believer and the peace experienced by the believer will feed into the making "holy" of the unbeliever (cf. 2 Cor 13:11). In this case the sentence looks forward to v. 16, as discussed above, where Paul gives his second main reason for refraining from divorce.

Following this mention of God's calling, Paul proceeds in the next section to talk about how this calling is vital for understanding whether singleness or marriage or even remarriage is the appropriate course of action (vv. 17–24).

Theology in Application

The Permanence of Marriage

Many years ago, while at seminary I heard a lecture from an amazing Indian theologian and Christian leader. It has lived with me ever since. She was lecturing on "cultural Christianity." To illustrate her point that we are all tempted to play down Scripture that does not suit our cultural perspectives, she drew on the example of the rampant divorce largely accepted by many Christians in the USA. Times have changed in India, but at the time she spoke she pointed out that most Indian Christians would never conceive of divorce as a possible choice for their lives nor, she said, would the general population since neither the church, nor Islam, nor Hinduism generally allowed divorce. The apostle Paul works on the same assumption, one which is found throughout Scripture: divorce is not God's will. The biblical emphasis on the permanence of marriage goes back to Genesis 2:21–25. Both the emphasis on becoming "one flesh" and the leaving of father and mother and "holding fast" to the spouse assume the lifetime commitment. Though the possibility of divorce was opened up in the law of Moses (cf. Deut 24:1–4), it was allowed only for obvious sin like adultery, which by definition had already breached the relationship's permanence and sanctity. Jesus addressed the matter with equal clarity, driving down to the intent of the law and reminding the teachers that even the permission granted by Moses "was not this way from the beginning" (Matt 19:8). It is this biblical and theological background that Paul reflects as he applies the teaching to the new pastoral context that he faced, in which those who had become Christians found themselves married to unbelievers. The Western church in particular, as it faces so many cultural challenges to the biblical view of marriage, needs a renewed call to the permanence of this institution.

---

19. So Garland, *1 Corinthians*, 292.

Paul introduces a new argument that further promotes the permanence and value of marriage (cf. v. 39), even in marriages where one is not a believer. He argues that the unbeliever will be influenced by the faith of the Christian spouse and possibly be saved. In today's world, such "mixed" relationships are regularly encountered in church life. Often the (newly?) believing spouse is hurting and finding life extremely difficult with their spouse, perhaps even meeting real antagonism. Yet the default position Paul encourages is one of "stay together." Churches need to endorse this whenever they can and encourage their new Christians with the gospel hope that rings through Paul's words. This means Christian leaders will need to be proactive in helping Christian spouses know what it is to live an effective Christian family life in such a way that the unbelieving spouse does indeed want the marriage to continue. For women, the advice in 1 Peter 3:1–4 is no doubt helpful. Surely 1 Peter 3:1–2 will also speak to Christian men with an unbelieving wife, as does 1 Peter 3:7a. However, though Paul's preference is clearly for couples to remain together in line with the teaching of the permanence of marriage, it is important to note that Paul does allow for the possibility of divorce if it is initiated by the unbelieving spouse. Such circumstances are beyond the Christian's control. There is a great and often unrecognized need in these cases for the church to gather around and encourage the divorced Christian. Unlike most modern divorces, divorce for this reason is often experienced by the individual as a suffering for the faith and, as many of us have seen too frequently, can leave a young Christian spouse questioning their newfound faith. The tendency for churches to lump all divorces together and view either all as wrong or, more likely, all as commonplace and unworthy of comment leaves many whose spouses have walked out because of their faith feeling unsupported.

Covenant Children

It is important not to build a whole theology of children and their relationship to the Lord on this one verse (v. 14), but it is certainly notable that Paul's reference to the children of a believing parent is used by way of analogy. In other words, the truth of what Paul expresses is assumed, and he expects the Corinthians to understand what he is saying. The sphere in which children are brought up is important throughout Scripture. From the Mosaic instructions that God's law (which is to "be on the heart" of the adult) shall be taught to the children as parent and child sit together, walk together, lie down together, and rise together (Deut 6:7), to the "enrolling" of the priests' children in the Lord's service during the revival in Hezekiah's time (2 Chr 31:16), to the Lord's drawing children to his knee (Matt 18:2–5; 19:13–14), children are to be regarded as part of God's covenant people. We have noted that this does not mean such children are necessarily regenerate, but it does suggest a way of bringing up children that encourages them to see themselves as belonging to God and that enables them gradually to be able to articulate the faith as their own in ever clearer and age-appropriate ways. For those Christian parents who have not grown up in Christian homes, which in America and Europe is now the majority of those we see converted in our churches, this is an area where much encouraging teaching is needed and where those married to unbelievers must find help and encouragement from Christians in the church.

1 Corinthians 7:17–24

Literary Context

Paul has addressed various relationships between men and women. With the discussion of divorce temporarily suspended (7:10–16), Paul now lays out a principle that helps explain his perspective on marriage, divorce, singleness, and widowhood. This principle should guide Christian men and women in their choices and actions in their relationships with the opposite sex. It is summarized simply in v. 17. People should remain in the state in which they found themselves when God called them to faith, that is, either as unmarried or married. Christians must see that any decision to change that status, either from married to unmarried or unmarried to married, should not be made on the assumption that one state is less or more spiritual than another. Rather, the fact that God has called them is critical. If Christians look at their lives in terms of having graciously been called by God to live as part of his holy people and enabled by him with grace-gifts, then they will note great benefits as the Lord leads them in life. Using two illustrations, one from the ritual of circumcision (7:18–19) and one from the realm of slavery (7:21–23), Paul urges his audience three times to remain in the state in which they found themselves when they were called to faith (7:17, 20, 24). The two illustrations seem far removed from the question of marriage to which he returns in v. 25. However, both demonstrate that Christians should not change their status for so-called *spiritual* reasons. Just as neither circumcision nor uncircumcision provide spiritual or religious merit before God, so neither does marriage or singleness. God's gracious call comes regardless of social status. This does not mean that Christians cannot change their social status. The slave can take advantage of the offer of freedom (7:21), and the unmarried can get married, but this is always to be done in the recognition that the Lord must lead.

V. Lack of Spiritual Wisdom Has Led to Grievous Sin (5:1–6:20)

VI. Marriage, Celibacy, Divorce, and Widowhood in Relation to Community Status (7:1–40)

A. Married and Unmarried Should Pursue God's Calling (7:1–24)

1. Married Couples and Sexual Relations (7:1–5)

2. Paul's Preference for Remaining Single (7:6–7)

3. Unmarried People and Sexual Desires (7:8–9)

4. Married Couples Are to Remain Married (7:10–16)

➡ **5. Each Person Should Lead the Life Assigned by the Lord (7:17–24)**

B. The Benefits of Remaining Unmarried (7:25–40)

Main Idea

Each person should lead the life the Lord has appointed for them. Conversion is the critical point from which social relationships must now be viewed. The Lord is now Lord, and life must be led according to his assignment and will.

Translation

1 Corinthians 7:17–24

17a	Circumstance	Just as the Lord has assigned to each person, and
b		as God has called each person,
		thus
c	Command	**let him [or her] live.**
d	Assertion	And thus
		I order [things]
e	Place	in all the churches.
18a	Illustration 1 (condition)	If a circumcised person was called,
b	Exhortation	**let him not remove the mark of circumcision.**
c	Condition	If a person was called in uncircumcision,
d	Exhortation	**let him not be circumcised.**
19a	Assertion (negative)	**Circumcision is nothing,**
b		and **uncircumcision is nothing,**
c	Assertion (positive)	rather **[what matters is] keeping the commands of God.**
20a	Exhortation	**Let each one remain**
b	Sphere	in the condition
c		in which he was called.

21a	Illustration 2 (condition)	If you were a slave when you were called,
b	Exhortation	**let it not concern you**
c	Parenthesis	(but
	Condition	if indeed you can gain freedom,
		by all means
	Assertion	**make use of [the opportunity for freedom]).**
22a	Basis for 21b	For **the one who was called** ...
b	Sphere	in the Lord
c	Circumstance	as a slave
d	Assertion	**... is the Lord's freed person,**
		likewise
e	Further basis for 21b	**the one who was called** ...
f		as free
g	Assertion	**... is Christ's slave.**
23a	Assertion	**You were bought with a price.**
b	Exhortation	**Do not become slaves of human beings**
24a	Concluding summary	Brothers [and sisters],
b	Circumstance	in the condition in which each was called,
c	Exhortation	**let him or her remain there at God's side.**

Structure

The centrality of 7:17–24 to the whole argument of chapter 7 is specially notable when we recognise that the norm of remaining either single or married is so frequently asserted (7:2, 8, 10–11, 12–16, 26–27, 37–38, 40). The principle is stated in full in v. 17. The social relationships at the point of God's call, whether single or married, are to be maintained. The principle also concludes the section in v. 24, thus forming an *inclusio*. Its restatement in v. 20 serves to bridge the two illustrations of circumcision (vv. 18–19) and slavery (vv. 21–23). The first illustration is taken from the realm of Jewish and Gentile interaction and the question of circumcision (vv. 18–19). The second is taken from the world of slavery (vv. 21–23). The first provides an example of the need to remain as "called" (v. 20). The second, by admitting the possibility of freedom, allows for the possibility of change if it is really necessary.

Exegetical Outline

Explanation of the Text

7:17 Just as the Lord has assigned to each person, and as God has called each person, thus let him [or her] live. And thus I order [things] in all the churches (Εἰ μὴ ἑκάστῳ ὡς ἐμέρισεν ὁ κύριος, ἕκαστον ὡς κέκληκεν ὁ θεός, οὕτως περιπατείτω· καὶ οὕτως ἐν ταῖς ἐκκλησίαις πάσαις διατάσσομαι). The first sentence defines the context of this section. Paul exhorts people to consider two related principles when making decisions about how to live their lives. These principles concern the need to understand that the Lord has assigned them the wherewithal to live their Christian lives and the nature of God's call. The exhortation is thus qualified by two subordinate clauses containing these principles. The sentence opens with a conditional phrase (εἰ μὴ) which does little more than offer a mild contrast with what has gone before.[1] Colloquially we might say, "Just keep in mind."

The first principle concerns what the Lord has divided out or assigned to each person (ἐμέρισεν). The content of what has been "assigned" has generated discussion. Two possibilities are most likely. Either Paul may be considering the particular circumstances of life in which God has placed each individual,[2] or he may have in mind the particular grace-gifts that the Lord has assigned to each.[3] Deciding between these two is not simple. One argument against this referring to grace-gifts is that Paul usually uses the verb "to give" when speaking of them as, for example, in 12:7–8.

However, before taking a view on this, it is important to note the second principle: "As God has called each person." The prevalence in these verses of the verb "to call" (καλέω; nine times between vv. 15 and 24) is remarkable. (The noun "call" [κλῆσις] also appears in v. 20.) God is the subject of the verb

---

1. It is too strong to translate this with "nevertheless" (NIV). The contrast lies simply in the move from practical advice to the underpinning principles on which Paul has based his advice, which he will now elucidate. The translation "only" (RSV, NASB) is satisfactory.

2. So Godet, *First Corinthians*, 1:353–54; Barrett, *First Corinthians*, 168; Fee, *1 Corinthians*, 341; Thiselton, *1 Corinthians*, 548.

3. So Calvin, *First Corinthians*, 151; Conzelmann, *1 Corinthians*, 125.

"to call" here in v. 17. As in 1:9 and elsewhere in the Pauline writings, the call of God has to do with being brought into the sphere of salvation, with conversion (e.g., Rom 4:17; 8:30; 9:24; Gal 1:6, 15; 1 Thess 2:12). Yet some have suggested that this calling has more to do with the vocation or social situation in the culture in which people were found when they came to faith.[4] The question that these different emphases pose is whether Paul is saying specifically that each person should remain in the "calling" (married, unmarried, etc.) they had when they came to faith or whether each person, whatever their social context or state of marriage, should see their conversion/calling as the defining matter. The exhortation to "live" in this manner either then means they should go on living as "married" or "unmarried" or that they should simply ensure that, married or not, divorced or not, God's call to serve him governs all decisions. Of course, these positions are not so easily separated in Paul's argument, as Thiselton makes clear.[5] Following God's call means following him in obedience (v. 19c) and in recognition of the new status of "slave" to Christ (v. 22).

The verses that follow help resolve the point. The person who is converted ("called") has his spiritual status changed by that call, not by seeking to change social status. To those who may have felt that divorce of an unbelieving spouse would better their spiritual position, Paul reminds them of their original call. There is no requirement to change social situations to prove spiritual status. The example of circumcision and of slavery both make this point. Indeed, the emphasis on "each person" (ἕκαστος) in v. 17 itself draws attention to the fact that God calls to himself on an individual basis

and from many different backgrounds. The status change happens "in the Lord" (ἐν κυρίῳ), as v. 22 makes clear. This means that each person can remain living with the spouse he or she had on being called, that is, when they were converted. Thus, if the Corinthians have been arguing that certain grace-gifts and certain lifestyles or actions bring them into a more "spiritual" state, then Paul denies this by arguing that all are dependent on living as befits a person called to belong to the Lord. This view also points to an understanding of the first clause to which we now return.

We have said that at first glance the clause "as the Lord has assigned" may not seem to refer to the grace-gifts received from Christ but rather to the different circumstances to which God has assigned his people. Apart from the question mentioned above as to whether grace-gifts are "assigned" or "given," some have looked to Romans 12:3 as a parallel in which Paul seems to be talking about how God has assigned (μερίζω) people's circumstances. However, in no way is this a true parallel. While Romans 12:3 actually speaks of God assigning "the measure of faith" and this might possibly refer to the faith necessary for the circumstances in which people find themselves, this interpretation seems most unlikely in the context. In fact, the only parallel that Romans 12:3 offers is in the use of the verb "to assign" (μερίζω). Furthermore, in Romans 12:3 God is the subject, whereas in 7:17 the Lord is the subject and that which is "assigned" is not even mentioned.

In 1 Corinthians 1:4–8 Jesus imparts the grace of God and the "grace-gifts" in abundance. Earlier in 7:7 Paul has spoken of his own "grace-gift" (χάρισμα) in connection with how he lives in God's

---

4. Héring, *First Corinthians*, 55; Fitzmyer, *1 Corinthians*, 307.

5. Thiselton, *1 Corinthians*, 549. Thiselton is careful to say that "called" in vv. 18, 20b, and 22 is controlled by the meaning

"when you became a Christian." But then he draws attention to the use of the noun, "the call" (κλῆσις), in v. 20 and remarks that this "comes very close to the notion of a *calling* to a specific state or role."

calling and of how "each one" is given their gift to enable them to live as married or unmarried. It thus seems likely that here in 7:17 Paul is talking of the Lord assigning the converted (those whom God calls) the wherewithal, through his grace-gifts, to live in accordance with the call. The imperative "thus let him [or her] live" (περιπατείτω) expresses Paul's exhortation that following God's call, aided by the Lord's grace, is the way Christians are to live. If they are a Jew or Gentile convert, or slave or free, the Lord's grace is sufficient for them to continue in whatever their social circumstances. They do not need to make changes in their marital relations or social status to "remain there at God's side" (μενέτω παρὰ θεῷ; v. 24; cf. 20). Paul adds weight to this injunction by indicating that this is the way he orders things "in all the churches" (ἐν ταῖς ἐκκλησίαις πάσαις). On three other occasions, he refers to what happens in other churches to emphasize the apostolic authority of his teaching (4:17; 11:16; 16:1; cf. 14:33).

7:18–19 If a circumcised person was called, let him not remove the mark of circumcision. If a person was called in uncircumcision, let him not be circumcised. Circumcision is nothing, and uncircumcision is nothing, rather [what matters is] keeping the commands of God (περιτετμημένος τις ἐκλήθη; μὴ ἐπισπάσθω. ἐν ἀκροβυστίᾳ κέκληταί τις; μὴ περιτεμνέσθω. ἡ περιτομὴ οὐδέν ἐστιν, καὶ ἡ ἀκροβυστία οὐδέν ἐστιν, ἀλλὰ τήρησις ἐντολῶν θεοῦ). Paul's illustration is straightforward. If[6] a person was "called" (ἐκλήθη; the passive indicates God's initiative) into God's kingdom, then whether or not he is circumcised is irrelevant and he should not seek to hide the mark of circumcision. Nor should the uncircumcised seek circumcision. The word (ἐπισπάσθω) implies stretching the skin over

the tip of the penis as if forming another foreskin. Such actions to cover a person's Jewishness appear to have taken place from time to time. For example, 1 Maccabees 1:15 describes this happening as part of the Hellenizing process of some Jews, especially with regard to the athletic games in which men would participate unclothed. No doubt this was part of a desire to be more acceptable in the society. Perhaps it also enabled a greater, upward social mobility.[7] The fact that this illustration "works" for Paul is a good enough indication that the congregation contained converted Jews and Greeks as much as it had those who were slaves or free (vv. 21–23). Just as removing the marks of circumcision is unnecessary, so is the reverse. No one should be circumcised just because when he became a Christian he was an uncircumcised Gentile. The essential spiritual-status change takes place through God's call, that is, in becoming a Christian. It is not established by being marked with circumcision, any more than by marriage or the lack of it.

In the final clause Paul writes, "Rather [what matters is] keeping the commands of God" (ἀλλὰ τήρησις ἐντολῶν θεοῦ). The adversative (ἀλλά) is strong; hence our translation "rather." The ellipsis requires some form of words in English that indicate the contrast with the "nothing" of the first half; hence our translation (with NASB) "what matters is." The contrast is clear and noteworthy. In Jewish thinking circumcision and the Mosaic law were tantamount to synonyms. After all, it was part of the law to have a male child circumcised, so this statement provides us with an insight into the remarkable change that has taken place in Paul's hermeneutic, as well as his theological appreciation for the place of the law in light of his encounter with Christ and his becoming Christian. While this cannot be the place to examine Paul's understand-

---

6. This follows the punctuation of UBS[5]. The sentence is punctuated as a question by most commentators: "Was a person circumcised . . . ?" The difference is immaterial.

7. Winter, *Seek the Welfare of the City*, 147–52.

ing of the Mosaic law in detail, a few comments are needed if we are to understand Paul's intention in his adding the final clause, "rather [what matters is] keeping the commands of God." Circumcision or lack of it provides him with an example of a defining social, ethnic, and *religious* separation between two groups of people, Jews and Gentiles. This sort of separation matters not at all in the Christian faith anymore than one's status as married or unmarried. Such ethnic or religious markers do not reveal anything about the depth of a person's spirituality or standing with God.

However, though it is God's gracious call and the indwelling Spirit that truly matters, it must not be forgotten that the call itself is to the obedient service of the Lord. Thus v. 19c seems to be added lest the Corinthians should imagine that Paul was abrogating God's law by saying circumcision does not matter. Given the direct breaches of God's law that had been occurring in this church, especially in the area of sexual sin, Paul could not allow his example of circumcision to be exploited for antinomian purposes.

Though the meaning of the illustration and final clause is thus clear and provided by the context, what Paul meant by "the commandments of God" (ἐντολῶν θεοῦ) still needs clarification. Similar phrases were used in the Pentateuch to refer broadly to the commands God gave the Israelites (Lev 4:22; Deut 4:2) and in the Psalms to refer to the whole Mosaic law (Pss 78:7 [77:7 LXX]; 119:115 [118:115 LXX]). But many argue this cannot be Paul's intention here. It would imply Paul was saying something like, "Circumcision [which was part of the "commandments"; Lev 12:3; cf. Sir 32:23] does not count, but keeping the commandments does."[8] Most commentators therefore understand this to be a more general reference to God's law, which is best expressed by Paul himself in Galatians 5:14: "For the whole law is fulfilled in one word: 'You shall love your neighbor as yourself'" (ESV). So, for example, Hodge quotes Galatians 5:6 by saying that the only thing that counts is "faith expressing itself through love." This, he says, is the same thing as keeping God's commands.[9] This is probably correct, yet on what grounds are some laws, like circumcision, to be ignored?

Galatians 6:15 provides further help, for there it is notable that Paul's point of contrast is with the "new creation." He writes, "For neither circumcision counts for anything, nor uncircumcision, but a new creation" (RSV). It is this new eschatological status granted by God when an individual is called and comes to faith in Christ that turns out to be determinative in Paul's discussions about the place of the law and the question of religious status. The "new creation" overrides all other attempts to claim any higher spiritual status or to authenticate status before God. Questions of birth or nationality mean nothing, for in Christ a person is a new creation and, as Paul says in 2 Corinthians 5:17, "the old has passed away, behold, the new has come" (RSV). Regarding certain social relationships or conditions as determinative of spiritual status is to revert to what is "old" and to view people "according to the flesh" (2 Cor 5:16 ESV).

In the new-covenant community, none of "the commands of God" can authenticate status. In

8. Traugott Holtz, "The Question of the Content of Paul's Instructions," in Rosner, *Understanding Paul's Ethics*, 65. Referring to this crux in 7:20 Holtz says, "Here we are confronted by one of the central problems of the theology of the Law not only for Paul, but for the New Testament generally." In his introductory essay in this work ("That Pattern of Teaching"), Rosner offers a helpful overview of different understandings or approaches to Paul's ethics and its roots. The essays contained in the work by and large reflect different approaches to Pauline ethics.

9. Charles Hodge, *An Exposition of the First Epistle to the Corinthians*, 7th ed. (New York: Robert Carter and Brothers, 1860), 122–23.

the greatest of ironies, circumcision, which many believed authenticated their religious status before God, ended up pointing to their judgment, and it was only in Christ that the answer was to be found. In his redemptive work (his death, resurrection, ascension, and sending of the Spirit), Christ is revealed as the "goal" (τέλος) of the law (Rom 10:4). Indeed, in him circumcision reached its own goal since in his representative death, in his "circumcision" as the king of his people,[10] the curse-judgment of the law was carried out. For those who have faith in this king, there is no more curse or need to be identified as a people who may be judged by God. Circumcision is gone. Rather, they have received the Holy Spirit who indwells people as they come to faith in the Messiah, and this is revealed to all in the practice of love (see below on 1 Cor 8:1 and ch. 13). Of course, even under the old covenant, "love" is the command of God and a summary of all other commands (Deut 10:12; 11:1, 13; Mark 12:30–31) but, as the old always anticipated, the Spirit has now written the law on the heart and empowered God's people to live it out (Jer 31:33; Heb 8:10; 10:16). Physical circumcision had always pointed toward the need for the heart to be right before God lest judgment come (cf. Deut 10:16; Jer 4:4; 9:25). In Christ, judgment has come and is passed, and the Spirit is at work in and on the heart. "Love," so beautifully seen in its full glory in the King, thus becomes the authenticator of religious status before God, and it is available to all who have faith in Christ.

In this context, for Paul God's commands do not lose their significance or importance. Rather, they are to be understood afresh in the light of the King's work and the indwelling presence of his Spirit. They belong to God's people, written on their hearts, and they continue to function in a "community-shaping and community-defining" manner.[11] God's people are still to be "holy." Their approach to life, to the poor, to justice, to each other, and above all to the King will all be guided by the laws of God. Yet those laws that do not reflect the unity of peoples achieved through Christ's saving work, which speak to distinctions between Jew and Gentile, have indeed been superseded for the Christian.

7:20 Let each one remain in the condition in which he was called (ἕκαστος ἐν τῇ κλήσει ᾗ ἐκλήθη ἐν ταύτῃ μενέτω). This verse forms a center to Paul's argument (see structure above). Lying between the two illustrations of circumcision (vv. 18–19) and slavery (vv. 21–23), it summarizes the lesson Paul teaches. It is a relationship with God and with Christ that establishes the spiritual status of Christians. As we saw above, "he was called" is likely to refer to conversion, and so the exhortation is for believers to remain in the social "condition" (ἐν τῇ κλήσει)[12] in which they found themselves at the time they came to faith. No change is needed.

7:21 If you were a slave when you were called, let it not concern you (but if indeed you can gain freedom, by all means make use of [the opportunity for freedom]) (δοῦλος ἐκλήθης, μή σοι μελέτω· ἀλλ' εἰ καὶ δύνασαι ἐλεύθερος γενέσθαι, μᾶλλον χρῆσαι). For his second example, Paul turns to another matter of social status, slavery.[13] Despite the complications of translation in this verse, the point remains clear and is the same as that made with the

---

10. Col 2:11–12.

11. Wright, *Paul and the Faithfulness of God*, 1036.

12. We have used "condition" (cf. NRSV, ESV) rather than "call" (κλῆσις) by way of translation to avoid confusion. The same idea is evident in 1:24–26 where Paul asks the Corinthi-

ans to think about the position they held in society when they were called by God to the faith.

13. On Paul's ethics and the matter of slavery, see Dunn, *Theology of Paul*, 698–701.

example of circumcision: the change of one's spiritual status takes place at the point of God's call; that is, when a person comes to faith. Other changes in social conditions do not affect this status one way or another. Thus, whether or not one is a slave does not matter. However, Paul provides a qualification. If freedom is available, a slave may take advantage of that freedom. In either condition, as slave or free, God can be fully served.

The difficulties of translation in this verse are considerable. The example of slavery is not presented in exactly the same form as that of circumcision. In the first place, it is noticeable that in this second illustration Paul uses the second-person singular rather than the indefinite third person. It is not clear whether there is any significance in this, but it may be that slavery was already a point of discussion in this church, while circumcision was a more hypothetical example. Paul uses the second person again in vv. 27–28. Secondly, to be the same this formulation would have to say something like, "If you were a slave when called, do not seek your freedom," when actually Paul says, "Let it not concern you." Moreover, he would have had to add, "If you were free when called, do not seek slavery." This would be absurd since no one would seek slavery! In fact, the changes Paul therefore is obliged to make in using this second example serve to further his argument. There is little doubt that many slaves would have been preoccupied with gaining the status of freed person. For many the goal was to achieve this by the age of thirty. The illustration thus becomes particularly pertinent for those who seem to be preoccupied with their spiritual status as Christians. Just as their state of slavery should not be a matter of spiritual concern for Christian slaves, so neither should the state of marriage or singleness be of concern with regard

to status before God. In both cases, God's call to obedience and the service of Christ is what matters (v. 22c). Thirdly, unlike the example of circumcision Paul here adds a qualification: "But if indeed you can gain freedom" (ἀλλ᾽ εἰ καὶ δύνασαι ἐλεύθερος γενέσθαι).

The structure of the Greek in this verse raises further matters. As in v. 18, some have unnecessarily[14] punctuated the opening clause, making it a rhetorical question ("Were you a slave when called?"; so NRSV and NIV). Nestle-Aland[28] punctuates it as a simple clause, thus reading it as a form of first-class condition in which the apodosis is in the imperative ("if you were a slave . . . let it not concern you"). Given the structural balance of the sentence in which the second half of the verse also contains a condition followed by an aorist imperative, this is most likely correct.

However, given the lack of a direct object, it is still unclear what it is that Paul urges the slave to "make use of" (χρῆσαι)? Above, we have translated by inserting "the opportunity for freedom" (in which case the Greek might have read τῇ ἐλευθερίᾳ). This position has been taken by many across the centuries from Erasmus and Calvin to the ESV, which translates, "But if you can gain your freedom, avail yourself of the opportunity." In a nutshell, if this is correct, Paul's qualification to remaining in the condition in which one was called to Christ is that a slave may take his freedom if offered it. Nevertheless, another alternative presents itself. It can be argued, against our translation, that the "opportunity" provided by their *slavery* is what they should "make use of" rather than their freedom (in this case the Greek might have read τῇ δουλείᾳ). This position has been taken by many from Chrysostom to the NRSV, which translates, "Even if you can gain your freedom, make use of

---

14. BDF §494.

your present condition [as slave] now more than ever." Context and grammar have been used to promote both positions.

The second position is well supported. First, contextually it fits with the stress in 7:17, 20, and 24 on people remaining in the condition in which they found themselves when called. It is also suggested that this makes better sense of the "for" (γάρ) at the beginning of v. 22. Verse 22 then becomes a reason why a person should be prepared to make use of their slavery, that is, because what really matters is that they are the *Lord's* freed person. Secondly, grammatically the protasis is introduced by an adversative "but" (ἀλλ'). This may suggest a strong contrast with the previous sentence. The phrase "but if also" or "but even if" (ἀλλ' εἰ καί) is then rendered as a concession: "Let it not concern you, *but even if* you should be able to gain your freedom, rather make use of your present condition." This argument is bolstered by regarding "rather" (μᾶλλον) as adversative and introducing therefore something unexpected.[15] In this view, Paul offers a certain comfort to Christian slaves: even as they continue in slavery they must remember that "in the Lord" they are "free." Furthermore, they can perhaps use their position for God as the believing spouse might do with an unbelieving partner.[16]

The first position is also well supported. First, contextually, as already mentioned, it is important to note that Paul obviously cannot use the slavery illustration in exactly the same way as he used circumcision. Also, in the examples of circumcision (v. 18) and of marriage (v. 27), Paul uses imperatives to order people to stay in the condition in which they find themselves. Here the imperative

is different and relatively gentle, as Deming has noted.[17] "Let it not concern you" (μή σοι μελέτω) certainly indicates that Paul believes that even slavery is a matter of indifference and that slaves can learn to be content in their position as they serve the Lord. Yet it does open the door for the qualification that follows. Qualifying what he has said here would not be strange, since in other statements in this passage Paul also offers certain qualifications to his commands. For example, in v. 5 there is an exception that allows for conjugal restraint by "mutual agreement" for the purposes of prayer. In v. 9 there is an exception to the unmarried remaining single "if they are not showing self-control." In v. 15 Paul argues that Christians are not to divorce their spouses and then enters an exception: "But if the unbeliever separates. . . ." Yet another example is found in vv. 27–28. Contextually, then, that Paul provides a qualification to an already gentle command need not surprise us. In fact, the only example *without* any exception being offered is that of circumcision.

Secondly, there is further grammatical support for believing Paul has in mind slaves taking advantage of an offer of freedom. First, when a word or object in a sentence is missing, it is normal to look elsewhere in the same sentence to supply it. Here in the immediate context the word "freedom" is provided. Then, secondly, the concession introduced in this form (εἰ καί) carries a degree of emphasis, "if indeed."[18] Examples of this are found in 4:7; 7:28; 2 Cor 4:3; 11:6. The adversative (ἀλλά) may then still be given its usual stronger force with the use of "but" or "however" or "rather." The comparative (μᾶλλον) often appears as an intensive and so

---

15. BDAG 613 (2.a: "rather" or "sooner").

16. Conzelmann, *1 Corinthians*, 127; Deming, *Paul on Marriage and Celibacy*, 156n210. K. H. Rengstorf, "δοῦλος," *TDNT* 2:272–73.

17. Deming, *Paul on Marriage and Celibacy*, 156–57. Deming argues for a number of parallels between Paul's argument and Stoic forms of diatribe.

18. Dana and Mantey, *Manual Grammar*, 292 (§278.3), speaks of an "emphatic concession."

can be translated, "by all means." Thirdly, a number of scholars have noted that if Paul had been speaking of remaining in a *present* condition (of slavery), a present imperative would have been more natural. The aorist imperative (χρῆσαι) is more likely to assume one action rather than the continuation of an action.[19]

In conclusion, it seems to us that Paul is allowing an exception to his main argument, just as he does on other occasions. The main argument remains that which insists there is no justification for divorce for reasons of spiritual status. The condition of slavery offers another example, for even this should not cause concern. What matters is that a person belongs to the Lord. Consequently, vv. 22–23 now reinforce the main argument but with reference to slavery.

7:22–23 For the one who was called in the Lord as a slave is the Lord's freed person, likewise the one who was called as free is Christ's slave. You were bought with a price. Do not become slaves of human beings (ὁ γὰρ ἐν κυρίῳ κληθεὶς δοῦλος ἀπελεύθερος κυρίου ἐστίν· ὁμοίως ὁ ἐλεύθερος κληθεὶς δοῦλός ἐστιν Χριστοῦ. τιμῆς ἠγοράσθητε· μὴ γίνεσθε δοῦλοι ἀνθρώπων). These two verses now give further explanation of Paul's thinking and follow naturally from v. 21a (understanding v. 21c to be a parenthetical exception, as argued above). Again "called" (κληθείς) here looks to conversion. The one who at the time of their conversion was a slave should recognize that in the Lord's economy they are a "freed person."[20] While one who was "free" (not a slave) when converted is now the Lord's slave since they have been "bought with a price." All other lordships and status relationships

become inconsequential in the light of a person's relationship with Christ following their conversion. A person's conversion ("who was called in the Lord") has forever changed that individual's status and brought them under an altogether different dominion. The new relationship with Christ is what truly matters.

Paul then addresses the person who is not a slave but is "free" and reminds them that each is "Christ's slave" (v. 22). This point is accentuated with the statement of v. 23 that Christians have been "bought with a price" (τιμῆς ἠγοράσθητε; cf. 6:20). They are now in a contractual position of service to the Lord himself. This position of "the Lord's freed person" (ἀπελεύθερος κυρίου) carries many privileges and is one that is to be sought after for those who do not yet belong to the Lord. However, with it come requirements to serve, obey, and worship. All who are "in the Lord" are in fact his "slaves," for they were bought with a price. This recalls both the redemption from the slavery of Egypt (Exod 6:6) and the redemption that results in the freedom from and forgiveness of sin (Isa 44:23; Titus 2:14). Christians must focus on serving the King and on understanding that they live under his dominion as slaves; yet they are *loved* slaves, who were bought by the death of Christ. Christians *belong* to Christ the Lord. They are his and, unless providentially moved on, are to serve him in the social position in which they found themselves when they came to faith.

In 6:20 we noted that some modern commentators would have us see Paul's argument in terms of upward mobility; that is, Paul suggests the true upward mobility for Christians is to see themselves as

---

19. Robertson and Plummer, *First Corinthians*, 148; Garland, *1 Corinthians*, 310, whose cautions on overstating the role of the aorist are wise. While care must be used in looking at the role of the aorist here, it seems likely to have in mind a new action and may well be an ingressive aorist.

20. See further on "freed person" and on Paul's metaphor of slavery for those who belong to the Lord in the essay, "In Depth: Slavery as Metaphor and the Transfer of Lordships," following comments on 7:24.

belonging to the Lord, not to a slave master. Some then develop these views when they examine these verses. For example, Thiselton follows Martin[21] in rejecting the view that Paul here refers to eschatological freedom or freedom from sin. He points to the use of "freed person" (ἀπελεύθερος) as a technical term rather than simply a description of freedom, suggesting that becoming a freed person reflected upward mobility in society. Thus, it may be argued that the real issue for Paul here is not freedom but status. For the slave, becoming *Christ's* "freed person" is the best of all "upward mobility" and makes all other designs on increased social status irrelevant. But Paul also talks in this verse of a free person becoming "Christ's slave." Thus, also following Martin, Garland can say, "This assertion does not level the ground between slaves and free but actually places the free person on a lower rung on the ladder. It reverses the normal status of slave and free."[22]

However, this is to go further than Paul intends. It is indeed useful to see how the social patterns of Roman household hierarchies functioned. The significance of becoming a freed person must not be overlooked as people ascended the social ladder. It is also good to remember that being a freed person still involved obligations and responsibilities to the (now) patron of whom the freed person could be proud. Yet, to admit that Paul here contrasts human positions of status with the newly found status under Christ's lordship is not to say that Paul assumes the *reversal* of human hierarchies in the household of the Lord. In v. 23a the reference to being "bought with a price" refers to *both* free and slave. In v. 23b the contrast implied by "do not

become slaves of human beings" is that they are already *all* slaves of someone else, the Lord. Paul will not allow differentiation of social status within the household of God. He wishes to ensure that slave and free see their status as *different* because the rule under which they find themselves is now profoundly different. As we said at 6:20, we must take care here for there is a danger *of underestimating the power of the total transfer of lordships. Christ's lordship is not just superior or of greater status; it is altogether different for it works in a different dominion.* So, while it is probably true that Paul is concerned to have the Corinthians regard their conversion as the great event that achieves an "upward mobility" (they are now under the authority of a much greater master and patron) and thus relativizes all such desires for increased social status in this world's societies, *the new dominion is so utterly different that in Christ freed person and slave contain no connotation of status at all* (cf. 1 Cor 12:13; Gal 3:28).

Paul was a Roman citizen and enslaved to no one. Yet for him being a "slave [δοῦλος] of Christ" was the greatest of all privileges and even became a self-designation. The idea is found in a number of places[23] and no doubt still has Old Testament ideas lying behind it, but the Lord's own teaching probably also provided a likely background, especially in the parallelism of Jesus's words in John 15:20: "A servant [or slave] is not greater than his master. If they persecuted me, they will persecute you also. If they obeyed my teaching, they will obey yours also."

In the two sentences of v. 23, Paul emphatically reinforces this contrast of lordships. Anyone who was free and is now a "slave of Christ" must not

---

21. Thiselton, *1 Corinthians*, 559–61, mostly following Martin, *Slavery as Salvation*, 63–68.

22. Garland, *1 Corinthians*, 315, who quotes Martin, *Slavery as Salvation*, 66.

23. It is found at Rom 1:1; 14:18; 16:18; 1 Cor 7:22; Gal 1:10; Eph 6:6; Phil 1:1; Col 4:12; 2 Tim 2:24 (the Lord's slave);

cf. Rom 6:22 ("enslaved to God" [NRSV]) and 1 Thess 1:9 ("to serve the living and true God [as slaves]"). Also note the use of "fellow slave" in Col 1:7; 4:7 (AT). See Murray J. Harris, *Slave of Christ: A New Testament Metaphor for Total Devotion to Christ*, NSBT 8 (Downers Grove, IL: InterVarsity Press, 2001).

become a slave to someone else since "you were bought with a price." While it may seem unlikely that anyone would want to become a slave, in the Roman empire some forms of slavery provided housing, employment, and a set of privileges.[24] So Paul addresses here those Christians who are free people but seek these relationships with "human masters" (NRSV) in order to better their social position and hence further their upward mobility in society. To seek this status enhancement is wrong enough for the Christian, but to do so through commitment to a human master in some form of slavery would be deeply ironic and a living denial of the reality that Christ alone is Lord and that he is the provider and patron *extraordinaire*.

7:24 Brothers [and sisters], in the condition in which each was called, let them remain there at God's side (ἕκαστος ἐν ᾧ ἐκλήθη, ἀδελφοί, ἐν τούτῳ μενέτω παρὰ θεῷ). This verse concludes the section, summing up what Paul has been saying. He has used two illustrations, circumcision and slavery. They have been considerably different from each other in some respects, but Paul's main point, still addressed to marriage, is that a person's situation or "condition" is completely overshadowed by belonging to the Lord. Each person should therefore set their mind to remaining there ("in the condition") at God's side (the word παρά with the dative indicates "at" or "by the side of" or "beside"). Christians do not live on in their situation of marriage or singleness or slavery, etc., *alone*. They can live day by day, even in difficult circumstances, knowing they are at God's side or that he is beside them.

IN DEPTH: Slavery as Metaphor and the Transfer of Lordships

The two illustrations Paul chooses in chapter 7 of circumcision and slavery are a good indication of the social and ethnic diversity found among the believers at Corinth. Slaves were found throughout the Roman Empire in Paul's day. Their social status was the lowest of the low. Despite the fact that they could rise to be powerful people in large households and even have slaves of their own, and despite the fact that many would have had greater security in their households than the poor freedmen of that age, they had no legal rights. Many slaves, especially in Italy, were acquired through war, but the birth of slaves within households also provided for many more. Estimates for the number of slaves in cities like Corinth vary from a third of the population through to a half.[25]

---

24. See the section, "Social Mobility: 1 Cor 7:17–24," in Winter, *Seek the Welfare of the City*, 146–47.

25. There are many studies of Roman slavery, their legal rights, their numbers in the first-century AD, and their social status and work environments. See, among others, Orlando Patterson, *Slavery and Social Death: A Comparative Study* (Cambridge: Harvard University Press, 1982); William L. Westermann, *The Slave Systems of Greek and Roman Antiquity* (Philadelphia: American Philosophical Society, 1955); Arnold

M. Duff, *Freedmen in the Early Roman Empire* (Oxford: Clarendon, 1928). A work addressing this section of 1 Corinthians and examining much material on slavery is S. Scott Bartchy, *First-Century Slavery and the Interpretation of 1 Corinthians 7:21*, SBLDS 11 (Atlanta: Scholars Press, 1973). Also, J. Albert Harrill, "Paul and Slavery: The Problem of 1Cor 7:21," *BR* 39 (1994): 5–28; Bruce W. Winter, "St Paul as a Critic of Roman Slavery in 1 Cor 7:21–23," *Pauvleia* 3 (1998): 339–54.

They were regarded as property and were not even allowed a legal marriage. Owning slaves was not merely a matter of cheap labor and hence of financial advantage to the owner, but it also provided the owner with a greater status in society. Slavery was thus one of the more obvious areas in which social status was provided by the exercise of power of one person over another.

Though the apostle Paul would not apparently have encountered much slavery in Tarsus, he would certainly have been exposed to it in his travels.[26] In Jerusalem he would have seen domestic and civil slaves, "both Jew and Gentiles; and he probably was acquainted with the special stone set close to the cattle market, from which slaves were auctioned."[27] As he worked with Priscilla and Aquila in Ephesus (see comments on 16:19), he may well have worked in close contact with slaves in the same industry. Historically, there is good evidence that slaves in Judaism had more rights and were better treated than slaves in Roman society.[28]

It inevitably seems strange to the modern reader that Paul did not make a point of urging slave owners to free their slaves or, as here in 7:21, of more enthusiastically encouraging slaves to seek their freedom. Partly this has to do with Paul's theology. Just as God's people had once been freed at the time of the exodus from slavery in Egypt so, in due course when the King returns, Paul anticipates all finding themselves in that amazingly paradoxical situation of being established forever as servants to their covenant Lord yet in a relationship that will reveal the essence of true freedom and joy. Roman slavery, an institution that at its best had the tendency to _dehumanize_, will be replaced with a new slavery to the Creator-King that will truly _humanize_ all people as they become fully what they were created to be. It is to Paul's theology of lordship, ownership and belonging, and _status-that-matters_ that we must look if we are to understand how Paul approaches real slavery. This is especially so in 7:21–23, for then it is possible to see how he can use slavery positively and negatively in a metaphorical manner.

Unlike the elitists at Corinth, Paul does not look down on those less wise or educated or with less prominent spiritual gifts than himself. Rather, his concern is to demonstrate that in the kingdom of God _status_ is established by God's gracious calling (1:2, 26–31). As the Spirit of the Messiah takes up residence in the church, so he does in the individuals within the church (cf. 3:16; 6:19; 12:27). Thus, Paul can say in 12:13, "For indeed in one Spirit we were all baptized

---

26. Bartchy, _First-Century Slavery_, 50, suggests that "many of the tasks performed by slaves in other places . . . were the jobs of freemen in Tarsus."

27. Ibid., 50–51. Bartchy describes Paul's probable contact

with slavery with evidence from most of the major cities he visited. His discussion of the existence of slavery in Judaism and Jerusalem is enlightening (ibid., 31–35).

28. Ibid., 52.

into one body, whether Jews or Greeks or slaves or free, and all were made to drink of one Spirit" (cf. Gal 3:28; Col 3:11). However, the result of such freedom in Christ is achieved by the transfer of lordships, and so in what may appear initially to be rather ironic, the end status for Christians is that they are now *all* slaves.

Such an understanding of who God's people are has its roots, for Paul, in the exodus event. The history of Israel in its liberation from Egyptian slavery is also the history of the church. God called and chose a people in his covenant with Abraham. Later, in remembrance of this covenant (Exod 6:5–6), the Lord came to free them from slavery and from the kingship of Pharaoh, and he placed them under his own rule. He chose to live among them and to make a covenant with them, elaborating on the ancient covenant with Abraham. In this covenant, as delivered by Moses, it is immediately apparent that one king has been replaced by another (Num 23:21–22). Moses's final blessing sums this up, describing the love of the Lord in coming to his people and concluding: "Thus the LORD became king in Jeshurun" (Deut 33:2–5 ESV). On a number of occasions the Lord calls for obedience to his commands with a preface similar to this one: "You shall remember that you were a slave in the land of Egypt, and the LORD your God brought you out. . . . Therefore . . . [you are commanded] . . ." (Deut 5:15 ESV; cf. 6:12–15; 13:5; 15:15, etc.). In Colossians 1:13–14 the apostle describes this transfer of lordships or of kingdoms in this way: "He has delivered us from the domain of darkness and transferred us to the kingdom of his beloved Son, in whom we have redemption, the forgiveness of sins" (ESV).

The text of 1 Corinthians 7:21–23 takes its place against this background. The status for the slave within the Roman social system has become meaningless because a greater lordship is at stake. Being called "in the Lord" provides no greater or lesser social status among people in the church. Coming under this dominion is to come under the God-King himself, so all else must pale into insignificance. Each Christian has become "a freed person of the Lord" (ἀπελεύθερος κυρίου). Notably, Paul does not say that each Christian is "free." In using the word "freed person" (ἀπελεύθερος), Paul draws on his evident knowledge of the Roman practices of manumission. Most slaves would have expected to eventually gain their freedom. And this may have been why many were indeed "concerned" (7:21). Epictetus wrote, "It is the slave's prayer that he be set free immediately. Why? . . . it is because he fancies that up till now he is hampered and uncomfortable, because he has not obtained his freedom from slavery."[29] Even so, those who were freed did not find themselves free in the

---

29. Epictetus, *Discourses* 4.1.33 (Oldfather, LCL).

way we might expect it today. Most were not able, for example, simply to move away to another country or city. Some would have been too poor to do so anyway. However, they would have enjoyed a degree of more control over their lives, especially with regard to spending their own money. Yet when slaves were freed, their *paranomé*, or continuing contract of work obligation, which often lasted between two and ten years, would sometimes require the freed person to remain with his former owner until one of them died. Frequently it seems that part of the conditions of manumission would have included the slave having to swear an oath to offer certain services on a certain number of days to the slave master. The freed person would even take on the master's name.[30] All this clarifies Paul's thought here. The actual freedom a slave may desire is worth having, and so Paul is happy for Christian slaves to take the opportunity of manumission should it arise. Indeed, it often arose for slaves whose work had been especially useful or productive, and Christian slaves might especially have hoped they would receive this privilege. However, more important than how they are viewed by society is the fact that Christian slaves are "freed" in the Lord. That is, they have a contract of continuing obligation to the Lord who is above all other masters. Their freedom is a joyous one that makes all other forms of manumission fade in significance.

Theology in Application

Marrying a Christian

Paul's emphasis on remaining in the same marital state that believers were in when they became Christians will raise questions for many today. For some married Christians, the idea that an unbelieving spouse might want a divorce would be met with surprise. Yet many pastors will have experienced this among their church converts. Increasingly, the conversion of one spouse is meeting with substantial opposition from the other, and church members should be aware of this so they can give support and pastoral encouragement to those who encounter it. Sadly, since a surprising number of Christians today have chosen to marry unbelievers, the sensitivities to the position of such newly converted Christians may be much diminished.

Reading this section of the epistle should provide a great challenge to a generation of Christians who are often complacent about marriage to unbelievers. Second Corinthians 6:14 is frequently cited as a verse that speaks against a Christian mar-

---

30. For extensive detail see Bartchy, *First-Century Slavery*, 72–82. See also John Byron, *Slavery Metaphors in Early Judaism and Pauline Christianity: A Traditio-Historical and Exegetical* *Examination*, WUNT 162 (Tübingen: Mohr Siebeck, 2003), 236–37.

rying an unbeliever. While that is not the immediate issue Paul is addressing in that chapter, it can be appropriate to use the verse as a theological principle that would also cover marriage. However, this text in 1 Corinthians 7 is a powerful statement that confirms that Christians are expected to marry Christians. The type of mutuality that Paul considers here, for example, abstaining for a short while from sexual intercourse that both may be dedicated to a time of prayer, assumes that their faith is held in common. The understanding that both partners in marriage should see themselves as called by God to remain together, to give their bodies to each other, and by God's grace to live out his desires for marriage all point to reasons for stressing the need to marry someone who worships the same Lord. There is remarkably little emphasis on this in the modern church, and what there is may often be viewed negatively. This passage lays out several positive results and privileges that arise from a Christian marrying only another Christian.

The Possibility of the Conversion of Non-Christian Spouses

Paul does not promise that a faithful and loving Christian husband or wife will see the unbelieving partner come to faith, but he holds it out as a real possibility. As Peter makes clear (1 Pet 3:1–2), this will often require a self-sacrificial life. Such mixed marriages are probably even more commonplace today than they were in the early church. Such a possibility, though, can never be used as an excuse for someone who is a Christian to deliberately decide to marry someone who is not, since that would be to presume on God's grace (cf. 1 Sam 15:23 ESV). With those who become Christians after they are married, the church must be gentle, respectful, and welcoming as they seek to help the wife or husband show the love of Christ to the unbelieving spouse. As Peter continues in 1 Peter 3:8–9, "Finally, all of you, have unity of mind, sympathy, brotherly love, a tender heart, and a humble mind. Do not repay evil for evil or reviling for reviling, but on the contrary, bless, for to this you were called, that you may obtain a blessing" (ESV).

Escaping Slavery

We are told that today there is more slavery in the world than in any previous generation. The slavery that forces people to work, often in adverse conditions, is rightly regarded as utterly wrong not just by Christians but by much of the secular Western world. Yet in the past some Christians have defended slavery. As I write I am doing so from a home in Atlanta, Georgia, a "Southern state" where slaves were once held by many Christians. Various theological or biblical arguments have been used to defend the practice, including Paul's lack of insistence that a slave should claim his or her freedom as a right and the fact that slavery was allowed under some circumstances in the Old Testament. Here in 1 Corinthians 7, the fact that Paul speaks of slaves and encourages people to remain in the condition in which they were called has been used as evidence for the defense of slavery. We have seen that this text can hardly be used in this way in any legitimate sense. However, a case for the abolition of slavery can hardly be made from this text either! That case will be better made at a biblical-theological level. There is not the space to do this here, but some pointers may be useful. In the light of the deliverance of God's people from slavery in Egypt and the adoption of the same motif to describe deliverance from sin in the New Testament, a solid theological basis was laid for the church's further examination of its attitude to slavery itself. Paul's own writings might not advocate freeing all slaves, but they clearly indicate that slaves should take their freedom if they can, while still living within the social constraints of the time. Furthermore, his argument in Philemon shows that he preferred people to have their freedom rather than go on living as slaves. It also shows that Christian slave masters should see their Christian slaves as "brothers," which suggests an entirely different relationship.

The biblical case for the abolition for slavery will be augmented by appealing to the way in which throughout history Scripture challenges ever more deeply the way slaves are treated and when and how they should be freed. The vision for freedom is born out of the constant refrain that once "you were a slave in the land of Egypt" (e.g., Deut 15:15 ESV; cf. Lev 26:11–13). The extraordinary rules in Israel for the freeing of slaves every seven years and letting them depart with gifts point to God's concern that all be treated well and, if enslaved, that they be granted their freedom after a few years (Deut 15:12–18; cf. Exod 21:2–5).

The critical themes of humanity made in God's image and the necessity that all people should be treated with justice and equity, that there should be no favoritism in the judgment between peoples, that the worker should receive a fair wage, and so on all contribute in the end to a strong belief, now shared by almost all Christians, that slavery was and is wrong and must be abolished wherever it is possible to do so. Today, most Christians find it difficult to believe there could ever have been a Christian defense of the institution. However, it serves as a vivid reminder that we are all deeply influenced by the ideas of our own age from which it is often so hard to stand back. The "wisdom of this world" all too easily impacts how we interpret Scripture and what we seek to justify and what we are therefore most reluctant to change in our lives and in our churches.

1 Corinthians 7:25–40

Literary Context

Having written of marriage, divorce, and sexual relationships, Paul has argued that those who are married should strive to remain married and those who are unmarried should not normally feel they need to seek marriage. Neither the married nor unmarried states are of any spiritual advantage or disadvantage. For those married to unbelievers, special circumstances may prevail that lead the unbeliever to desire a divorce. However, divorce should be avoided if possible, for real benefits accrue to the children of believers and a real possibility of salvation exists for the unbelieving spouse. Generally, Christians should exercise great caution in seeking to change the marital status in which they found themselves when converted. Change is not forbidden, but it should be carefully considered in the light of Paul's advice and in the light of the life to which the Lord has called the Christian.

In the section that follows, verses 25–40, Paul addresses advantages of remaining unmarried, writing mainly with specific reference to those who have never been married ("virgins"). Though the advantages to being single are considerable, including the ability to be more committed to the affairs of the Lord, this does not mean that marriage is wrong. In the last two verses, Paul returns to talk of a widow (cf. 7:8), who, though free to marry, may be more blessed if she remains as she is (vv. 39–40). Paul's goal is that each person should understand that "undivided devotion to the Lord" (v. 35) should guide these decisions and that such a stance benefits the whole church.

Main Idea

Undivided devotion to the Lord should guide decisions about whether to remain single or to marry, but other factors, which point to the value of remaining unmarried, should all be considered.

Translation

1 Corinthians 7:25–40

25a	Circumstance	Now concerning the virgins
b	Assertion	**I do not have a command from the Lord,**
c	Assertion	**but I give my judgment**
d	Expansion	as someone who by the Lord's mercy is trustworthy.
26a	Assertion	Therefore, **I think** **this is good** ...
b	Basis	because of the present distress—
d	Repetition	that it is good
e	Content	for a man to remain as he is.
27a	Explanation of 26/ question	**Are you bound to a wife?**
b	Exhortation/response	**Do not seek to be released.**
c	Question	**Are you released from a wife?**
d	Exhortation/response	**Do not seek a wife.**
28a	Concession	But if you should marry
b	Assertion	**you have not sinned,**
c	Concession	and if a virgin should marry
d	Assertion	**she has not sinned.**
e	Basis for concession	Yet **such people will have trouble**
f	Time	in this life,
g	Desire	and **I would spare you that.**
29a	Assertion	Now **this I affirm,** brothers [and sisters],
b	Content	**The time is shortened;**
c	Result	so that ...
	Time	from now on
d	Illustrations, series	... those who have wives should live as though they had none, and
30a		those who mourn as though they were not mourning, and
b		those who rejoice as though they were not rejoicing, and
c		those who buy as though they did not possess, and
31a		those who use the world as though they did not make full use of it.

b	Basis of 29b	For **the form of this world is passing away.**

32a	Assertion	Now **I want you to be free from** **concerns.**
b	Explanation of 32a	**The unmarried man is** **concerned** about the things of the Lord,
c	Expansion	how he may please the Lord.
33a	Explanation cont./ contrast	But **the married man is** **concerned** about the things of the world,
b	Expansion	how he may please his wife, and
34a	Outcome	[his attention] is divided.

b	Explanation cont.	Also, **the** **unmarried woman or**
c		**virgin is concerned** about the things of the Lord,
d	Expansion of v. 34d	that she may be holy
e	Manner	both in body ↵
		and in spirit.
f	Explanation cont./ contrast	But **the married woman is** **concerned** about the things of the world,
g	Expansion	how she may please her husband.

35a	Summary	Now **I say this**
b	Advantage	for your own benefit,
c	Purpose (negative)	not to lay a restriction on you but rather
d	Purpose/goal of vv. 32–34	with a view to [what is] appropriate and
e	Expansion	to an undivided devotion to the Lord.

36a	Condition part 1 (protasis)	If anyone thinks he is behaving inappropriately towards his betrothed,
b	Condition part 2 (protasis)	if his passions are strong and consequently it must happen,
c	Permission	**let him do what he wishes;**
d	Assertion	**he does not sin.**
e	Exhortation	**Let them marry.**

37a	Contrast with v. 36	Now **whoever stands**
b	1st of four conditions (criteria)	steadfast in his heart,
c	2nd	being under no necessity but
d	3rd	having control over his own desire, and
e	4th	determines this in his own heart
		to keep his own betrothed,
f	Assertion	**he will do well.**

38a	Conclusion to vv. 36–37	So then, **he who marries his betrothed does well,**
b		and **he who does not marry will do better.**

Continued on next page.

Continued from previous page.

39a	Assertion	**A wife is bound**
b	Time	as long as her husband lives.
c	Condition (protasis)	But if the husband dies,
d	Apodosis	**she is free to be married**
e	Expansion	to whom she wants,
f	Qualification	only in the Lord.
40a	Circumstance/repetition (see v. 25c)	But, in my judgment
b	Assertion	**she is happier**
c	Condition	if she remains as she is.
d	Assertion	And **I also think that I have the Spirit of God.**

Structure

Paul now writes in vv. 25–40 of the benefits of remaining unmarried. He refers to "virgins" (παρθένος) six times. The change of topic is introduced in v. 25 by another use of "now concerning" (περὶ δέ). The first main section (vv. 25–38) examining matters related to the unmarried may be divided into three. First, in vv. 25–31 Paul presents the matter of end-time living, referring to "the present distress" and to the "passing away" of the present world. This context for life relativizes questions of marriage and singleness. Secondly, in vv. 32–35 Paul speaks of the great value of the undivided commitment both unmarried men and women can offer to the Lord. Thirdly, in vv. 36–38 Paul then addresses betrothed men and urges marriage, if they are finding it unduly hard to control their sexual desires. In a short second section (vv. 39–40) Paul briefly comments on matters related to widows.

The whole unit of text continues the theme of "remaining as you are" (vv. 26–27, 37–38, 40; cf. 7:2, 8, 10–11, 12–16). It begins (v. 25) and ends (v. 40) with mention of Paul's own "judgment" (γνώμη). In both those verses Paul emphasizes his right to make such judgments, first because he is trustworthy (v. 25) and then because he possesses the Spirit of God (v. 40). Further, careful structures reinforcing Paul's arguments are especially to be noted in the comments on vv. 29d–31 (five illustrations) and vv. 32b–34 with its careful balance between the married and the unmarried man and the married and unmarried woman.

Exegetical Outline

Explanation of the Text

7:25 Now concerning the virgins I do not have a command from the Lord, but I give my judgment as someone who by the Lord's mercy is trustworthy (Περὶ δὲ τῶν παρθένων ἐπιταγὴν κυρίου οὐκ ἔχω, γνώμην δὲ δίδωμι ὡς ἠλεημένος ὑπὸ κυρίου πιστὸς εἶναι). "Now concerning" introduces the new topic (περὶ δέ, see comments on 7:1). Continuing his broad discussion of marriage and singleness, Paul addresses the unmarried and begins with those he calls "virgins." While it is clear in 7:1 that Paul is picking up on a subject about which the Corinthians wrote to him, that is not so clear here. Paul may simply be extending the previous discussion in a somewhat different direction, but it remains most likely that at some point the Corinthians had at least mentioned the matter of "virgins." Though the word "virgin" in a context of marriage or celibacy is uncommonly used in modern English where we might be more likely to speak of the "married" or "unmarried," it is good to remember that actual virginity would have been assumed for all those who were unmarried and had not been married previously. Simply to trans-

late this as "the unmarried" fails properly to set the scene for vv. 36 where sexual passion is being discussed. This whole discussion assumes the unmarried should remain "virgins" and that they should resist temptation to become sexually active outside of marriage. We should also note that the modern English word "virgin" is almost always used of girls and women and rarely of men. In these verses (vv. 28, 34, 36, 37, 38) the word is used with the feminine article and clearly speaks of women or girls. In v. 25 the plural could refer to women and/or men.[1] Further complicating matters is the fact that the word appears to be used in v. 34 in a slightly more restricted sense. There "the unmarried woman" (ἡ γυνὴ ἡ ἄγαμος) is presented as a different category apparently from "the virgin" (ἡ παρθένος). At that point, for reasons we shall note later, it seems best to translate the word as "betrothed."

So we are left with some questions. Are the "virgins" referred to all women, or does Paul also have in mind unmarried men, at least in part of his discussion? Who are the female virgins? Are they simply all the unmarried (probably mostly young)

---

1. Some cite the fact that men are called virgins in Rev 14:4, but this is not strictly relevant since "virgin" there is a metaphor for those who have not indulged in idolatry.

women? Or does the word include those engaged or betrothed to be married but not yet sexually active because not yet married? Or are they some specific category of women that the Corinthians would have recognized? On the matter of virgins Paul says, "I do not have a command from the Lord" (ἐπιταγὴν κυρίου οὐκ ἔχω), recalling his comments in vv. 10 and 12. In v. 10 Paul and the Corinthians knew that the Lord had spoken on the subject. In v. 12 there were no specific comments from the Lord, so Paul speaks. Here in v. 25 Paul has no specific command that has been handed down to the church from Christ; rather, he offers his own "judgment" (γνώμη). He does so, however, as one who is "faithful" (πιστός; cf. 4:2). God is a "faithful" God (10:13), and so through his mercy Paul's word can be trusted (cf. 2 Cor 1:17–22). Paul always associated God's mercy with his calling to be an apostle and with his preaching of the gospel (1 Cor 15:10–11; 2 Cor 4:1), so it is to this calling and this working of God in his life that Paul now appeals, asserting that his word can be trusted. Although Paul addresses a variety of different situations in this chapter and though the advice or judgment that Paul gives is given as an apostle, how he arrives at this advice serves as a model for all Christians. There are no direct commands in the Old Testament or from the Lord on some of these matters, and so Paul speaks from general biblical principles. Times are stressful (v. 26), so it is good for people to stay as they are. All believers are to serve the Lord. If this can be done better when unmarried or when married, then that becomes a genuine criterion for decision making. If a person is tempted to immoral behavior and marriage is the answer, then the decision is again guided by vital biblical principles.

7:26–27 Therefore, I think this is good because of the present distress—that it is good for a man to remain as he is. Are you bound to a wife? Do not seek to be released. Are you released from a wife? Do not seek a wife (Νομίζω οὖν τοῦτο καλὸν ὑπάρχειν διὰ τὴν ἐνεστῶσαν ἀνάγκην, ὅτι καλὸν ἀνθρώπῳ τὸ οὕτως εἶναι. δέδεσαι γυναικί; μὴ ζήτει λύσιν· λέλυσαι ἀπὸ γυναικός; μὴ ζήτει γυναῖκα). There is an echo here of the Corinthian slogan in 7:1, "It is good for a man not to touch a woman." But it is no more than an echo, probably made for rhetorical effect to maintain interest and to form the link with the main subject of the chapter. Paul, as we have seen, does not agree with their slogan. But here he speaks to a particular situation. The issue is not about whether it is good to have sex or not or to have a physical relationship or not; far from it. For Paul marriage may be right, and celibacy may be right. The condition in which people find themselves when they come to faith, as he has been saying in the last section, is what must be determinative. People should remain as they are. "To remain as he is" (τὸ οὕτως εἶναι) looks forward to v. 27: it is good for a man to remain married, if married, or if not, not to seek a wife. But Paul now remarks upon another reason why singleness remains a viable, even a favored option: "Because of the present distress."

The word "present" may mean "imminent" or even "impending." Its regular New Testament usage may indicate that Paul speaks eschatologically, that is, that he thinks of the "distress" as evidence of the last days. The word (ἐνίστημι) is used in a few such contexts, for example, 2 Timothy 3:1 (in the future) and 2 Thessalonians 2:2 (in the perfect). Similarly, it is used of "the present [evil] age" in Galatians 1:4 and of this "present time" in Hebrews 9:9 (both perfect participles, as here; cf. Rom 8:38 and 1 Cor 3:22). Here it is hard to avoid the view that Paul is speaking of a "present" distress since this is his normal use of the word. Yet he probably also has in mind an eschatological schema of the present ("this age"; 1:20; 2:6–8; 3:18) and the future age.

The word "distress" (ἀνάγκη) adds to this view that Paul has a broader frame of reference than simply an immediate and localized discomfort that the Corinthians were facing. This word has a broad semantic range. It can mean "compulsion" or "necessity" (e.g., see discussion of 9:16 where Paul is "compelled" or "pressured" to preach). But it also refers to calamity and distress. Luke uses the word to describe the distress of the last days when times will be desperate for pregnant women and those nursing babies (Luke 21:23). In this sense it becomes effectively a synonym for "tribulation" (θλίψις; cf. 1 Thess 3:3–4, 7), a word also used here in v. 28 and that can also refer to the troubles of the last days (cf. Matt 24:29). Thus, an eschatological frame of reference is possible for all three words: "present" (ἐνίστημι), "distress" (ἀνάγκη), and "tribulation" (θλίψις; vv. 26, 28). This is made more likely by Paul's reference to the fact that the "time is shortened" (v. 29) and that the present "form of this world" is passing away (v. 31). For Paul the coming of Christ has meant that "the end of the ages" has come upon us (10:11), a fact that he will return to on several occasions later in this epistle.

So what difference does this make to an understanding of this passage? It suggests that though Paul addresses serious and practical pastoral issues, he sees these as part of a broader picture. All the things that the Corinthian Christians face in their day-to-day lives can be seen as indicators of living in the last days. While offering his trustworthy opinion on particular matters, more generally he is talking about living in "this age," an age whose rulers are doomed to pass away (2:6). He regards the inheritance of the kingdom of God as more important than all else (6:9). The "present distress" (τὴν ἐνεστῶσαν ἀνάγκην) has to be endured "at

God's side" (παρὰ θεῷ, v. 24) and living to serve him must be life consuming. Changing one's status as married or unmarried will end up producing its own set of anxieties and so becomes a mere distraction in the great aim of pleasing the Lord (v. 32).

In an article examining first-century famines in Corinth, Bruce Winter cites evidence of what appears to have been a particularly bad famine in the Empire in AD 51 and suggests this may account for the specific "present distress." He quotes a number of early writers about the acute social upheaval and even riots that often ensued from famine. He argues that there is every likelihood even as Paul wrote this epistle that Corinth was experiencing the social dislocation of a severe famine. The questions of marriage and whether to have children or not would naturally have raised their heads at such a time. Yet, more than that, theologically the Corinthian Christians could hardly have been unaware of the regular linking of famines and earthquakes, etc., with the coming of God's judgment, that is, of the last days. As Winter puts it, famines would have been seen as part of "the beginning of the eschatological birthpangs"[2] (cf. Mark 13:8). If we put this together with the vocabulary Paul employs in these verses, it seems Paul's advice to a person to remain "as he is" may have been given against a background of the "distress" of an actual famine. In turn, this would have served to remind everyone that God's people live in this age and so must rest not in the "wisdom of men but in God's power" (2:4).

In this context, marriage and singleness are once again relativized. Paul refuses to accept what seems to have been the Corinthian view that singleness or abstinence is more "spiritual." Rather singleness or marriage are both about following the

---

2. Bruce W. Winter, "Secular and Christian Responses to Corinthian Famines," *TynBul* 40 (1989): 86–106 (93). This need not mean, of course, that Paul anticipated Christ's return as immediately imminent. So also see Wright, *Paul and the Faithfulness of God*, 562.

Lord obediently. Some will be married and some not, but, given the "present distress," Paul makes his point. "Are you bound [δέδεσαι][3] to a woman? Do not seek to be released. Are you released from a woman? Do not seek a wife." The words "bound" and "released" (λύσις; "released" in the sense of being loosed from a binding contract) are not the usual words for marriage and divorce. It is thus likely that Paul means to incorporate two types of "binding" relationships that were possible between a man and a woman. He has already addressed marriage. The other, about which he will say more and which is the main focus here, is a legal betrothal or "engagement." It must be remembered that such betrothals carried a heavier legal commitment of one party to the other than modern engagement usually does. This is why we have used the word "released" instead of "free" (RSV). In modern English we may talk of a breakup or a release from the promises of a marriage or an engagement. So Paul says to the man who is betrothed, "Do not seek to be released." To one who is married he says in effect, "Don't breakup." To a person who is neither betrothed to a woman nor married he says, "Do not seek a wife."[4] It is to the first point that Paul now addresses himself. If a man is betrothed to a woman, Paul is telling him *not* to break up, that is, to seek release from the contract.

7:28 But if you should marry you have not sinned, and if a virgin should marry she has not sinned. Yet such people will have trouble in this life, and I would spare you that (ἐὰν δὲ καὶ γαμήσῃς, οὐχ ἥμαρτες· καὶ ἐὰν γήμῃ ἡ παρθένος, οὐχ ἥμαρτεν. θλῖψιν δὲ τῇ σαρκὶ ἕξουσιν οἱ τοιοῦτοι, ἐγὼ δὲ ὑμῶν φείδομαι). By means of a conditional clause that speaks to the lack of certainty that such action will be pursued, Paul makes it clear that this decision to marry or not is up to the individual virgin (v. 25), who should keep in mind what he has been saying. Paul's pastoral application is clear as he moves to the second-person singular "you should marry" (γαμήσῃς). It is important for the one who must decide whether to proceed with marriage or not to be clear. If he does marry, he is told, "You have not sinned" (οὐχ ἥμαρτες; taking the aorist as ingressive).

Having addressed the unmarried man, as usual in this chapter Paul balances the argument by making the same point for a virgin. Likewise, "she has not sinned." Since Jewish thought advocated the ideal of marriage so strongly, the idea that getting married might ever have been conceived of as a "sin" is extraordinary. Almost certainly, therefore, Paul is again counteracting the Corinthian position that "it is better not to touch a woman." He does not wish to be misunderstood. Both he and some of the elitist Corinthians have their reasons for suggesting people should not marry. Yet for Paul this has nothing to do with its morality or that marriage is wrong in any sense. His reasons for suggesting celibacy are pastoral. There is no command from the Lord or in Scripture suggesting otherwise.

However, Paul does have a further concern with this course of action that anyone deciding to marry should consider. "Such people" (οἱ τοιοῦτοι) will have "trouble" (θλῖψις) in this life. In this context, "in the flesh" (lit.; τῇ σαρκὶ) simply refers to the bodily life lived on earth (thus our translation "in this life" above). Again, the context suggests that

---

3. The perfect, being imperfective in verbal aspect, here depicts a state of being and so can be said to be stative. It is translated as a present in view of the present ongoing state of being "bound." For the relationships between the perfect (and pluperfect), its verbal aspect, and the possibility of a stative *Aktionsart*, see Constantine R. Campbell, *Basics of Verbal Aspect in Biblical Greek* (Grand Rapids: Zondervan, 2008), 103–7, esp. 106.

4. In the context of this statement the Greek γυνή indicates a "wife," while "woman" is used in the other statements to indicate Paul is speaking probably to the betrothed.

this "trouble" cannot be separated from the general fact of living in the times of suffering of this age. Paul, however, does not indicate the particular sufferings that may present themselves to the married that would not arise for the single person. If famine was an issue, it might be the feeding of the family that would be more difficult. Or it may be the time-consuming and all-involving nature of marriage that he has in mind, since later he refers to the married person's attention being "divided" (μερίζω) and to being "anxious" (μεριμνάω) about pleasing the spouse rather than being able to concentrate on the Lord's service (v. 34). At his pastoral best, Paul simply says that he would spare them such trials if he could.

7:29a–b Now this I affirm,[5] brothers [and sisters], the time is shortened (τοῦτο δέ φημι, ἀδελφοί, ὁ καιρὸς συνεσταλμένος ἐστίν). Paul does not develop the nature of the troubles to which he has referred, nor does he give further reasons for the advantages of remaining single. Rather, he expands an argument that becomes more general. His concern is that all Christians understand the nature of the age in which they live. The coming of Christ means that they live in the end times and "the form of this world is passing away" (v. 31). Though people should remain in their state of marriage or singleness, their priorities in life are to reflect this new reality. Christ is the focus and goal of all things, and all human activity must reflect this perspective. Robertson and Plummer well capture this when they paraphrase the apostle, "But, though I counsel none to change their state,

I do counsel all to change their *attitude toward* all earthly things."[6] Controlling this perspective, says Paul, is the fact that "the time is shortened" (ὁ καιρὸς συνεσταλμένος ἐστίν).

There is considerable discussion about what this clause means. Is the line of reasoning that Christ will return imminently and so there is essentially little point in taking time with the otherwise normal human activities of marriage, doing business, etc.? Are some terrible sufferings or "tribulations" about to be poured out as an immediate precursor to Christ's coming? The difficulty with seeing Paul's argument in this way is that he does not appeal to Christ's coming to make his point. Moreover, he clearly does *not* suggest that people give up their regular life activities because of the imminence of Christ's coming. Nevertheless, what Paul writes about the "time" is indeed driven by an eschatological frame of reference in which the Christ has come and will come. Paul works with a view of history that sees these two points in history as enclosing an "age." He refers to this in 10:11 where he speaks of "us, upon whom the end of the ages has come." For Paul, this age is the last period of history for this world as it now exists, and its present form is passing away (v. 31). The age that began with Christ's death, resurrection, and exaltation will come to an end at his "coming" (cf. 15:24).[7] It is this "time" that has been "shortened" (συστέλλω), which may simply mean that it is short. However, the word can also mean "shortened" in the sense of "limited." Thus Paul may have in mind that God has deliberately restricted the time "for the sake of the elect" to spare them the worst of a period of

---

5. The verb "I affirm" (φημι) has a number of meanings. It sometimes simply means "I say," and at other times it introduces a quotation (e.g., 6:16). Occasionally it can be used to explain what has been said before (as in 10:19). This is how the NIV, NRSV, ESV and other versions take it here. However, it can also imply confirmation; hence, to "affirm" something (so Thiselton, *1 Corinthians*, 579). In this sense it also serves

to move the argument on to the nub of Paul's concern that the time is short. Paul uses a periphrastic participle, "is shortened" (συνεσταλμένος ἐστίν) to qualify the "time."

6. Robertson and Plummer, *First Corinthians*, 154 (emphasis theirs).

7. The age may also be seen as commencing at the coming of the King at his incarnation (so possibly Heb 1:1–2).

extreme sufferings (Mark 13:20; though note the different word for "shorten"—κολοβόω). Or it may mean that it is "shortened" in the sense that because of Christ it is now known that the end will come and so Christians must live in the light of this fact. Thiselton, building on Cullmann, suggests that "the time" (καιρός) is a "critical time," not necessarily to be limited only to some particular distress or affliction, such as a famine, but is a general "time of opportunity" that Christians must take advantage of.[8] In the light of the emphasis on a person following his or her "calling," this makes good sense of the chapter.

Here we take the view that Paul believes God has deliberately limited or shortened this time, in line with the Lord's teaching, and that therefore the time is one of special opportunity and challenge. What Paul builds from this, though, in no way reflects what we might today call "short-termism." Paul is not suggesting the suspension of normal human activity because the end may come tomorrow. Even though all Christians live in anticipation of that coming day (the letter ends in 16:22 with the Aramaic prayer *marana tha* ["come, Lord!"]), Paul asks that such life activity now be framed in an appropriate manner and lived with priorities appropriate to gospel people who have been called by God. As Christians come to understand that this age will pass away (7:31), so they are to gain a certain urgent perspective on life's priorities in this age. Christ is Lord. He is to be followed as a matter of priority over everything else in life.

7:29c–31 so that from now on those who have wives should live as though they had none, and those who mourn as though they were not mourning, and those who rejoice as though they were not rejoicing, and those who buy as though they did not possess, and those who use the world as though they did not make full use of it. For the form of this world is passing away (τὸ λοιπὸν ἵνα καὶ οἱ ἔχοντες γυναῖκας ὡς μὴ ἔχοντες ὦσιν, καὶ οἱ κλαίοντες ὡς μὴ κλαίοντες, καὶ οἱ χαίροντες ὡς μὴ χαίροντες, καὶ οἱ ἀγοράζοντες ὡς μὴ κατέχοντες, καὶ οἱ χρώμενοι τὸν κόσμον ὡς μὴ καταχρώμενοι· παράγει γὰρ τὸ σχῆμα τοῦ κόσμου τούτου). Paul proceeds to offer five illustrations of how a "shortened" time will affect people as they live lives prioritized around the service of Christ and his return. Escapism is by no means an option, but this world's occupations should not absorb the Christian's life. "From now on" (τὸ λοιπόν) is adverbial, modifying the ensuing lengthy clause. Each illustration is introduced by the "so that" (ἵνα) and the present subjunctive "they might be" (ὦσιν). This is more likely to be a result clause than a rare example of an imperatival (ἵνα) clause.[9] Thus Paul is saying, "The time is short with the result that from now on those having wives might be as though . . . ."

In Depth: Possible Backgrounds for Ideas in 7:29–31

It is suggested that some of the clauses in these verses may have a background in or reflect the influence of Stoic thought. Certainly some similarities of content are apparent. For example, Epictetus writes of Socrates: "Take Socrates and

---

8. Thiselton, *1 Corinthians*, 581–83, building on Oscar Cullmann, *Christ and Time: The Primitive Christian Conception of Time and History* (London: SCM, 1962).

9. With Fee, *1 Corinthians*, 373n298; contra BDF §387.3; cf. Robertson, *Grammar of the Greek New Testament*, 994.

observe that he had a wife and children, but he did not consider them as his own; that he had a country . . . friends and kinsmen also, but he held all in subjection to law and to the obedience due to it. For this reason he was the first to go out as a soldier, when it was necessary; and in war he exposed himself to danger most unsparingly."[10] Seneca writes of using possessions with caution "as if they were given for safe-keeping and will be withdrawn. Anyone who does not employ reason in his possession of them never keeps them long; for prosperity of itself, if uncontrolled by reason, overwhelms itself. If anyone has put his trust in goods that are most fleeting, he is soon bereft of them, and, to avoid being bereft, he suffers distress."[11] Though both examples here provide some overlap with what Paul says, Paul's thoughts are moving in a very different direction from the Stoic.[12] Paul is not concerned in the examples he gives with a self-control and determination that flow from reason, which can overcome the weakness of emotions. Paul does not see the goal of the spiritual person as personal freedom from the determinism of the world order, nor does he see separation from the world's possessions enabling a person to achieve "freedom." Rather, Paul lives and thinks within a specifically Christian eschatology that arises from within biblical teaching. Christ is Lord, and a person's calling in this passing age is what matters. Priorities of life must therefore always be followed in the light of what is pleasing to the coming King (v. 32).

Others have suggested that Paul's thought draws on terms from Jewish apocalyptic and cite passages such as Ezekiel 7:10–13 (LXX), in which there is talk of "the day" of doom coming and therefore it is said, "Let the buyer not rejoice, and let the seller not mourn" (v. 12).[13] Closer verbal parallels are found in 4 Ezra 16:41–44 where the judgments of the last days are coming upon people. We read: "Let the one who sells be as one who flees away, and the one who buys, as one who will lose. Let the one who does business be like one who makes no profit, and the one who builds a house as one who does not live in the building, and the one who sows as one who does not reap . . . those who marry as those who will have no children, and those who do not marry like those who are widowed." However, as Fee rightly insists, Paul is far from advocating "the apocalyptist's 'escape' from the world."[14]

---

10. Epictetus, *Discourses* 4.1 (Oldfather, LCL).

11. Seneca, *Epistles* 74:18 (Gummere, LCL).

12. Both these examples and many other parallels with Paul's writing here are examined in detail in Deming, *Paul on Marriage and Celibacy*, 187 (but see 178–88).

13. Ibid., 174–78, also examines texts from Jewish apocalyptic works that appear to offer some degree of parallel with Paul's rhetoric here in 1 Cor 7. "In the final analysis," he says, "we must reckon with a high degree of integration between Stoic and apocalyptic materials here."

14. Fee, *1 Corinthians*, 375.

Marriage is the first of five illustrations from the normal day-to-day experience of Christians, which are provided to make the point that all activity is relativized in the light of the age in which they live. These illustrations are enclosed by the insistence that "the time is shortened" and "the form of this world is passing away."

Marriage. Marriage has been the main subject of this chapter and now provides the first illustration. The immediate context reminds us that the issue is the priority of serving the Lord in every area of life. The broader context (cf. vv. 2–5) makes it clear that Paul is not advocating celibacy or any form of spiritual asceticism. He is not denying human sexual passion (cf. vv. 8–9) nor advocating divorce. Marriage does not last beyond this age (v. 39; cf. Luke 20:34–38), and so it must not be regarded as decisive in life. The contrast between the married and unmarried man in vv. 32–33 indicates what Paul intends here. What *is* decisive is pleasing the Lord and remaining undistracted from his service. Even those who are married must understand that, while marriage is fine (v. 2) and sexual intercourse within marriage is to be encouraged (vv. 3–5), a person's preoccupation should be with the Lord. To "live as though they had [no wife]" is thus careful and considered hyperbole, making the point.

Mourning and Rejoicing. Paul is not suggesting that Christians should live void of the normal emotions of life (cf. Rom 12:15). He himself is able at different times both to rejoice (2 Cor 7:13) and to weep (2 Cor 2:4). However, in the light of Christ all mourning is relativized, for nothing shall "separate us from the love of God" (Rom 8:39). Though Paul does not quote Isaiah on this subject, he no doubt worked on the understanding that at Christ's return

God will take away all mourning (Isa 35:10; 51:11; 65:19; cf. Rev 21:4). Wallowing in sadness now can only be a distraction from the present calling to serve the Lord. Likewise, even rejoicing is relativized. In fact, in the light of Christ Christians know that the joy of laughter and fun in this age will be short-lived but that eternal joy awaits the one who follows the Lord. Both mourning and rejoicing are now driven by the context of a preoccupation with service to the Lord.

Purchasing and Business Dealings. All business dealings are equally to be treated as passing. Neither buying goods nor being involved in business should be so all-absorbing that the priority of serving Christ becomes diminished. The word translated here as "possess" clearly reveals Paul's intention throughout these examples. Paul speaks of those who "buy" but says they should be "as though they did not possess" (or "hold"; κατέχοντες). In 1 Thessalonians 5:21 the word is translated "hold fast" (NRSV; "hold fast to what is good"). It is this connotation of possessing in the sense of clinging on to something (cf. 15:2) that helps us see the nature of Paul's concern both for those who buy things as well as for those who conduct business. The contrast between using the world but not making *full* use of it again reveals that Paul is far from escapist in his eschatological view of the world.[15] The present world must be lived in and used and enjoyed. Commercial and social business must be conducted, but they must not absorb the person.[16]

The illustrations thus come to an end with a reminder that it is the eschatological context that has given rise to what Paul says ("for"; γάρ). The present "is passing away" (παράγει), meaning that this process of world decay has already begun.

---

15. The prefix κατά has the effect of intensifying the meaning of χράομαι. Thiselton, *1 Corinthians*, 583–84, discusses a play on the words χρώμενοι and καταχρώμενοι.

16. Those who see the world as passing inevitably contrast directly with those who deny the resurrection and do not look to the future. The latter concentrate on making full use of the here and now: "Let us eat and drink, for tomorrow we die" (15:32).

However, here Paul's thought is not so much of the problem faced by creation (to which he speaks in Rom 8:19–22) but rather about the "form" (σχῆμα) or the way things are. The shape of this world as it is now experienced in terms of marriage, crying, laughing, business, etc., is on its way out to be replaced with a new earth (cf. Isa 65:17; 2 Pet 3:13).

7:32–34 Now I want you to be free from concerns.[17] The unmarried man is concerned about the things of the Lord, how he may please the Lord. But the married man is concerned about the things of the world, how he may please his wife, and [his attention] is divided. Also, the unmarried woman or virgin is concerned about the things of the Lord, that she may be holy both in body and in spirit. But the married woman is concerned about the things of the world, how she may please her husband (Θέλω δὲ ὑμᾶς ἀμερίμνους εἶναι. ὁ ἄγαμος μεριμνᾷ τὰ τοῦ κυρίου, πῶς ἀρέσῃ τῷ κυρίῳ· ὁ δὲ γαμήσας μεριμνᾷ τὰ τοῦ κόσμου, πῶς ἀρέσῃ τῇ γυναικί, καὶ μεμέρισται. καὶ ἡ γυνὴ ἡ ἄγαμος καὶ ἡ παρθένος μεριμνᾷ τὰ τοῦ κυρίου, ἵνα ᾖ ἁγία [καὶ] τῷ σώματι καὶ τῷ πνεύματι· ἡ δὲ γαμήσασα μεριμνᾷ τὰ τοῦ κόσμου, πῶς ἀρέσῃ τῷ ἀνδρί). The goal of Paul's advice in vv. 32–34 is identified by the summary of v. 35d–e. *His desire is for an undivided devotion to the Lord.* The discussion thus follows on clearly from his argument in the previous verses. The depth of concern for the things of the world and the things of the Lord will inevitably be affected by whether a person is married or unmarried. "Now" (δέ) is adversative only in the sense that it starts a new but related narrative

segment. It might be translated "that is" or even "so," thus leading into a related discussion.[18]

Paul's argument is clear and reinforced by its structure. In a fashion to which we have become accustomed in this chapter, he balances married and unmarried, woman and man. He speaks of (a) the concerns of the unmarried man (v. 32), (b) the concerns of the married man (v. 33), (c) the concerns of the unmarried woman and of the virgin (v. 34b–e), and (d) the concerns of the married woman (v. 34f–g). His point is that it is difficult to serve the Lord fully when a person "is divided." We have inserted the words "his attention," but the Greek simply says "and he is divided" (μεμέρισται). The division is between giving oneself to the Lord and to other, potentially conflicting activities. Being married inevitably means, for either husband or wife, that some of his or her attention will be focused on the spouse. Being single, whether man or woman, means that particular concerns of the marriage relationship are removed so that there is more possibility of *un*divided attention in the Lord's service.

The things of this world are neither wrong nor irrelevant; however, even in matters to do with singleness and marriage, the normal day-to-day life should always be lived before and in the service of the Lord, whom all his people should seek to "please" (ἀρέσκω; v. 32). Paul's line of thought here has nothing to do with the Stoic concept of freedom from anxiety nor with the Cynic approach to celibacy in marriage, which allows for a more devoted contemplation of virtue and a better road to self-sufficiency.[19] Rather, the apostle draws on the

---

17. The word "concerns" (ἀμερίμνους) is found only here and in Matt 28:14 and may be translated as "anxiety." However, the frequently negative connotation of "anxiety" in English is unhelpful. The "concern" that the unmarried man has with the things of the Lord is a positive preoccupation with serving the Lord. The apparent play on words provided by the next sentence (μεριμνάω and μερίζω ["divided"]) also suggests the

meaning of the word is better conveyed by the English word "concern," which can have both positive and negative connotations. In 12:25 Paul urges positive "concern" for one another in the body of Christ (cf. Phil 2:20).

18. For this use, see 1 Cor 10:11. BDAG 213 (2).

19. For detailed examples from the Cynics and Stoics of similar styles of argument to the apostle's here, see Deming,

Old Testament teaching, reiterated by Christ himself, that the Lord God is to be loved with all the heart, soul, and might (Deut 6:5; Mark 12:30). This love is revealed especially in the preoccupation of the individual with the Lord in life and service (cf. Matt 10:37; Mark 8:34).

Being "divided" (μεμέρισται, a perfect passive) is the problem. As husbands and wives think about bringing pleasure to and looking after their spouses, they will find their thoughts, actions, and their time less concentrated on "the things of the Lord" (τὰ τοῦ κυρίου). Paul is not finding fault with being married or with having to look after a relative. In 1 Timothy 5:8 Paul instructs Timothy: "Whoever does not provide for relatives, and especially for family members, has denied the faith and is worse than an unbeliever" (NRSV). Nor is the apostle reversing his teaching earlier in chapter 7 that the husband and wife have responsibilities to each other. Rather, as he states in v. 35, both men and women, married and unmarried, must recognize that their lives are to be devoted to the Lord. They must recognize both the advantages and disadvantages of the state in which they find themselves and in which they have been told to remain (v. 24).

The "things" people should be concerned about are spelled out for unmarried women[20] in terms of being holy both in body and in spirit. As usual, Paul is concerned for the whole person, who is to live her life devoted to the Lord.[21] This statement expounds what is said of unmarried men in v. 32c that they are concerned "how to please the Lord" (πῶς ἀρέσῃ τῷ κυρίῳ). The comments on married women directly parallel those on married men in v. 33. As Paul writes, he surely still has in mind the particular grace-gift that each has (v. 7). Assuming that these unmarried men and women are able to exercise self-control (v. 9), then Paul continues to insist that theirs is a calling that allows a greater devotion of time and activity to the Lord's service. By no means is he agreeing with the asceticism implicit in the position of some of the Corinthians (v. 1). Paul's contrast between being concerned about the "things of the world" and "about the things of the Lord" views the calling to be married or to remain unmarried *pragmatically* in terms of service and dedication to the Lord.[22]

7:35 Now I say this for your own benefit, not to lay a restriction on you but rather with a view to [what is] appropriate and to an undivided devotion to the Lord (τοῦτο δὲ πρὸς τὸ

Paul on Marriage and Celibacy, 193–201. Epictetus, *Discourses* 3.22.69 is often cited for its mention of celibacy removing the "distraction" of marriage and a family in the service of God: "Is it not fit that the Cynic should without any distraction be employed only on the administration of God, able to go about among men, not tied down to the common duties of mankind, nor entangled in the ordinary relations of life . . . ?" (Oldfather, LCL).

20. The "unmarried woman or virgin" (καὶ ἡ γυνὴ ἡ ἄγαμος καὶ ἡ παρθένος) may be read in different ways. Three translations are possible. First, the two nouns may form a compound subject. Thus, they probably refer to two slightly different groups of women: (1) unmarried women, perhaps the widows and divorcees, and (2) those younger women who have never been married or are, as yet, only betrothed. The problem lies with the use of the singular verb "is concerned." This problem may be overcome by using "or," as we have done above. The

singular is probably used because this is a "collective category" (Thiselton, *1 Corinthians*, 590). More dubiously the NRSV simply makes the verb plural: "The unmarried woman and the virgin are anxious. . . ." Secondly, "the virgin" may be epexegetical of "the unmarried woman." This requires the translation, "the unmarried woman, that is, the virgin." A third possibility is that "unmarried" and "virgin" are used adjectivally to describe "woman"; thus, "the unmarried and virginal (or chaste) woman."

21. Conzelmann writes that "σῶμα, 'body' and πνεῦμα, 'spirit', are not dualistic concepts. They designate together the whole man" (*1 Corinthians*, 134n32).

22. There is no warrant for seeing the holiness of "body" as solely about remaining chaste. Nor is it necessary to postulate with Barrett (*First Corinthians*, 181) that this phrase is quoted from "the Corinthian ascetical party" since elsewhere it is clear that Paul demands holiness of body of all Christians.

ὑμῶν αὐτῶν σύμφορον λέγω, οὐχ ἵνα βρόχον ὑμῖν ἐπιβάλω, ἀλλὰ πρὸς τὸ εὔσχημον καὶ εὐπάρεδρον τῷ κυρίῳ ἀπερισπάστως). Here Paul provides a summary of his purpose (ἵνα) in writing these last few verses. His goal is that each in his or her state of marriage or singleness may understand that the most important aspect of living life in the present relates to the degree of devotion to the Lord. "Undivided devotion to the Lord" (εὐπάρεδρον τῷ κυρίῳ ἀπερισπάστως) benefits the whole church. However, what he has written could be misread as a new legalism, so Paul insists his purpose is not to restrict them.[23] Rather, if they follow what he is saying, it will be to their benefit. Paul has in mind their spiritual benefit in that they will be better able to serve the Lord and fulfill his calling. It is important to bear in mind that, throughout, Paul considers the community and not just the individual. The obedience and holiness of the married and unmarried is of "benefit" (σύμφορος) to the community.[24]

The negative purpose clause is followed by a strong contrast, "but rather" (ἀλλά). The two phrases that now follow (introduced by πρός) expound on the idea of the "benefit" that is theirs. Paul speaks for their benefit, that is, *with a view to* or perhaps *with the object of* (πρός) an "appropriate" (εὔσχημων)[25] devotion to the Lord that is fully "undivided." The position of this adverb "undivided" (ἀπερισπάστως) at the end of the sentence has occasioned a number of comments. Whether great force can be attributed to the word simply

because of its position is probably doubtful, but it certainly provides a clear concluding summary of Paul's argument. All Christians should be *undividedly* committed to living for the Lord, whether married or not.

Throughout the chapter Paul's teaching has been concerned with a life lived in devotion to the Lord. This will be determined by a person's calling and his or her grace-gifts. But the way this is worked out in a person's life must be by constant reference to an appropriate holiness of life and a pragmatic (rather than dualistic) understanding of how marriage and singleness impinge on that devotion. After such affirmation of singleness Paul returns to address what is or is not "appropriate" behavior for certain single people.

7:36 If anyone thinks he is behaving inappropriately toward his betrothed, if his passions are strong and consequently it must happen, let him do what he wishes; he does not sin. Let them marry (Εἰ δέ τις ἀσχημονεῖν ἐπὶ τὴν παρθένον αὐτοῦ νομίζει ἐὰν ᾖ ὑπέρακμος, καὶ οὕτως ὀφείλει γίνεσθαι, ὃ θέλει ποιείτω· οὐχ ἁμαρτάνει· γαμείτωσαν). Paul desires devotion to the Lord and that men and women are free from "concerns" (v. 32). While the unmarried man and woman may be free from such concerns (vv. 32–34) and so better able to be preoccupied with the "things of the Lord," Paul now identifies in v. 36 a set of circumstances that will militate against this. He speaks

---

23. The clause "to lay a restriction on you" (βρόχον ὑμῖν ἐπιβάλω) refers to the tightening of a rope on an animal as in a halter or rein.

24. The verb or its substantive form (συμφέρω and σύμφορος) is also used in 6:12; 10:23, 33; 12:7. In discussing 6:12 we noted that for Paul this idea of spiritual "benefit" is virtually synonymous with the idea of "building up" the community.

25. The word εὐσχήμων has been variously translated as "good order" (NRSV); "as it should be" (JB); "what is proper" (Thiselton); "with seemliness" and "what is seemly" (Barrett,

Fee, and Garland). The negative form of the cognate verb in the next verse (ἀσχημονέω) provides a good indication of the semantic value here. In v. 36 Paul refers to one who acts in an improper or inappropriate way toward his virgin. We have translated the word in v. 35 as "appropriate" since this can include the idea of suitable moral behavior, but it also can indicate that undivided attention to the Lord is *appropriate* behavior to be expected of any servant of the Lord. Because this is an articular adjective, most translations add a verb. Thus NRSV adds, "*to promote* good order."

of the betrothed man whose conduct is leading toward inappropriate behavior with his fiancée because his passions are strong. Presumably, such a person would be one who does not have the "grace-gift" for celibacy spoken of in v. 7.

Few verses in this book have provoked such discussion, due largely to difficulties with the Greek construction and meaning. The above translation is the one that seems to make the most sense to us, both of the Greek and of the context. "And consequently it must happen" (καὶ οὕτως ὀφείλει γίνεσθαι) speaks to what Paul sees as the inevitable outcome for this couple. Applying the principles of what he has said earlier in the chapter, he reminds the man that marriage is not a sin and that he should do as he wishes. The imperative "let them marry" (γαμείτωσαν) suggests that Paul does not see this in terms of concession on this occasion. For a person in this state of raised passion it is in fact "appropriate" to marry to fulfil devotion to the Lord. This understanding of the verse also leads very naturally into v. 37 where the unmarried man whose passions *are* under control is said to do well in not marrying the one to whom he is betrothed. Verse 38 then offers a summary of Paul's view of the possible actions to be taken by men with regard to their fiancées. However, it is important to note a number of exegetical points on which commentators differ and to see why these have arisen.

Firstly is the matter of our translation strong "passions" (ὑπέρακμος). Two alternative translations present themselves: (1) Some translate this as "if she is past [her] prime." The article in BDAG states that the noun (ἀκμή) refers to the "highest point or prime of a person's development," and hence the word may mean "beyond that point."[26]

(2) Some translate as done in the present commentary: "[strong] passions." BDAG usefully explains how this interpretation arises: "Other interpreters focus on the ascensive force of [the preposition] ὑπέρ, 'exceedingly'. . . . In our [passage], then, ὑπέρακμος means *at one's sexual peak* . . . and hence *with strong passions*."[27]

The interpretation that Paul intends to speak of the woman (or possibly man) who is past her prime, as in (1) above, has an ancient pedigree. Some of the church fathers follow it, and later Calvin and Luther do likewise. In line with this view, the AV translates thus: "If any man think that he behaveth himself uncomely toward his virgin, if *she pass the flower of her age*, and need so require. . . ." As recently as 1995, the NASB adopted a similar translation. The reading that Paul intends to speak of a man whose passions run high, as in (2) above, has been adopted by many modern commentators. The NIV (2011) translates as "if his passions are too strong." The ESV translates, "If his passions are strong." Winter strongly defends the view that sexual passions are at stake, pointing out sources where the word is used of puberty in a woman and of sexual passions in a man.[28] It is this view that we adopt here.

Secondly, commentators have debated who the "anyone" (τις) is at the start of the verse. In the summary of v. 38 the normal verb Paul has used for "to marry" (γαμέω) is changed to one normally meaning "to give in marriage" (γαμίζω),[29] and this has given rise to a long tradition of interpretation that has assumed "anyone" must be a father who is giving his "virgin (daughter)" in marriage. Thus, it is suggested that Paul turns now to the concern of some fathers. In the light of the "present crisis,"

---

26. BDAG 1032.
27. Ibid.
28. Bruce W. Winter, "Puberty or Passion? The referent of ΥΠΕΡΑΚΜΟΣ in 1 Corinthians 7:36," *TynBul* 49 (1998): 71–89.

29. In vv. 9, 10, 28, 33, 34, 36, and 39 the more usual verb for "to marry" (γαμέω) is used.

should they still give their daughters in marriage? Given that it was the father's duty to decide upon or arrange his daughter's marriage, v. 36 may then address a father's action regarding his virgin *daughter* who has either reached "puberty," or "has reached her prime" or is "past her prime" (see the various translations of ὑπέρακμος mentioned above). The NASB takes this interpretation, which is common among the church fathers. Calvin's translation well demonstrates this perspective: "If any man judges it unseemly for his virgin daughter, and if she passes the flower of her life, and it is necessary to do so; let him do what he wants; he does not sin; let them marry. . . . Therefore, he who gives in marriage does well, and he who does not give, does better."[30] A number of problems may be noted with this interpretation, however. First, it would be unusual to use "virgin" in this context when the word "daughter" would simply suffice. Secondly, why is the word "father" not used if the subject is now changing from the previous verses? In fact, only one subject naturally presents itself from the previous verses for the indefinite "anyone" (τις): the unmarried man of v. 32. Thirdly, and more significantly, we may ask why Paul uses the third-person plural "let them marry" in v. 36 rather than "let *her* marry." The plural would more naturally point to the "anyone" and his daughter. Clearly Paul is not saying "let the *father* and daughter marry!" Fourthly, in light of Paul's previous instructions to a "virgin" in v. 28, these verses would seem redundant. There has been no mention at all in this passage about a parents' involvement with the marriages being contemplated. Finally, it is not at all clear that such a distinction can be made between the verbs "to marry" and "to give in marriage" in Koine Greek. Paul's choice of verb (γαμίζω) in v. 38

may simply relate to the fact that it is here used as a transitive verb, while the alternative verb (γαμέω) is used elsewhere in the chapter intransitively. In summary, it seems to be a more natural reading to see "virgin" as referring to a single woman who is not yet married, as in v. 28. Since "he" may not be behaving appropriately to "his virgin," it seems reasonable to assume the couple are engaged or betrothed to be married. The plural imperative at the end of v. 36 thus also makes good sense.

Thirdly, commentators have debated who the "virgin" is. We have already suggested that it seems to refer to an unmarried woman engaged to be married. However, some have suggested a third option: *a married woman who has remained a virgin*. This view assumes the existence of so-called "spiritual marriages." The suggestion is that couples lived together while committed to celibacy. In principle, it is entirely possible to believe that some of the Corinthians—caught up in a strong Greek dualism that regarded some behavior as spiritual and some more "earthy" behavior, like sex, as "unspiritual"—could have engaged in such a practice. It might provide further evidence of how far the Corinthians were prepared to take the slogan of v. 1b, "It is good for a man not to touch a woman." Some couples adopting this worldview might therefore have sought to avoid what could be seen as "worldly" activity in their marriage out of devotion to the Lord. To them Paul says that they should marry if the man's sexual appetite cannot be restrained, presumably meaning they should consumate their marriage as normal married people. Thus Moffatt translates, "If any man considers he is not behaving properly to the maid who is his spiritual bride, if his passions are strong." However, attractive as it might be to regard the "virgin"

---

30. Godet, *First Corinthians*, 1:389: "The apostle means: 'He [the father] might, no doubt, have done better for his child's happiness; but he has not made himself liable to any reproach.'"

as a kind of "spiritual bride," there is no evidence that such a form of marriage existed either within the church or outside in the society of that day. If this form of marriage had existed, then surely Paul would have condemned it anyway in the light of what he has said already in 7:3–4.

In summary, to a betrothed couple where sexual passions are running strong, Paul says they should marry lest they behave inappropriately.[31] Most likely this refers to the possibility of them having sexual intercourse outside of marriage. It contrasts with Paul's vision for "appropriate" behavior in v. 35, which is summed up in an undivided devotion to the Lord. The clause "he does not sin" (οὐχ ἁμαρτάνει) is probably added because Paul himself is the one who has been promoting celibacy rather than because the couple themselves may have seen marriage as sinful. Paul wants them to be clear that, though celibacy is a preferable option in some circumstances, it is not so here. Getting married will not in any way be sinful. More than that, they *should* marry.

7:37 Now whoever stands steadfast in his heart, being under no necessity but having control over his own desire, and determines this in his own heart to keep his own betrothed, he will do well (ὃς δὲ ἕστηκεν ἐν τῇ καρδίᾳ αὐτοῦ ἑδραῖος, μὴ ἔχων ἀνάγκην, ἐξουσίαν δὲ ἔχει περὶ τοῦ ἰδίου θελήματος, καὶ τοῦτο κέκρικεν ἐν τῇ ἰδίᾳ καρδίᾳ, τηρεῖν τὴν ἑαυτοῦ παρθένον, καλῶς ποιήσει). Paul now explains when a man may indeed choose *not* to marry his betrothed. He is to be convinced in the core of his being that he is not making this decision due to outside pressure and that he is able to live a celibate life, being sure he has control over his (sexual) de-

sires. Undoubtedly this person, therefore, will have examined himself to see whether he has the gift of celibacy (7:7). The ABBA chiastic structure of the verse shows clearly the conditions Paul lays out for the betrothed man remaining celibate. "Whoever" is the one who "will do well" (καλῶς ποιήσει). Four criteria are given that will enable this decision to remain single to be made.

The first criterion is "whoever stands[32] steadfast in his heart" (ὃς δὲ ἕστηκεν ἐν τῇ καρδίᾳ αὐτοῦ ἑδραῖος). The "heart" (καρδία) here refers to the man's whole will and does not just refer to his emotions as it might in English. It is the "source of resolves."[33] If a betrothed man is not to marry, then he must have a truly settled and established position on this matter. The adjective "steadfast" (ἑδραῖος) adds considerable force to this idea. Clearly he must be in a position in which he will not be swayed from his decision by outside pressures, whether in the form of sexual desires or social pressures, perhaps coming from the woman's parents.

The second criterion, "being under no necessity" (μὴ ἔχων ἀνάγκην) is interpreted by the third, "having control over his own desire" (ἐξουσίαν . . . θελήματος). Though it is possible to understand the pressures and necessities referred to here in the sense of social pressures, the most likely reference is to sexual pressures. This has been a recurring issue in this chapter, especially in the opening verses. "Desire" is thus a better translation than "will" in this instance, and we may compare it with the clear sexual connotation of the noun in John 1:13. Thus the negative, that there should be no compulsion from outside, is balanced by the pos-

---

31. The verb "behave inappropriately" (ἀσχημονέω) is only found here and in 13:5 in the New Testament. It refers to inappropriate or rude moral behavior.

· 32. The present tense translates a perfect indicative (ἕστηκεν). The intensive perfect in Greek is often best trans-

lated with a present tense in English because it is the present state or result from a past action that is being emphasized. We have translated "determines" (κέκρικεν, also a perfect) in the same way in this verse for the same reasons.

33. J. Behm, "καρδία," *TDNT* 3:612.

itive, that he should have "control"[34] over his own desire. Above all, the man cannot allow himself to be pressured in a way that will lead to inappropriate and therefore sinful behavior with regard to the fiancée.

The fourth criterion is that he "determines this in his own heart to keep his own betrothed." The addition of "his own" (ἴδιος) emphasizes again that his decision is not to be influenced by external factors, whether events or people. The decision must be firmly made that he should keep the woman in a betrothed rather than a married relationship. In other words, the man makes up his mind to "keep" the woman a virgin and not have sexual relations with her.

If the man has determined that he fulfills these four criteria, then the decision will be a good one; "he will do well" (καλῶς ποιήσει). What is good in this decision is not so much the actual decision one way or another but that the man will have determined what the Lord has assigned for him (v. 17). The previous verse had concluded with the somewhat less affirming "he does not sin." Throughout, Paul is being practical and is concerned that Christians do what is right as they seek to live holy lives while being devoted to Christ. Verse 26 may explain why Paul seems more affirming in this verse. Here he has been talking about a decision that leaves both man and woman in the state in which they currently find themselves, something he has advocated wherever possible. In the following verse Paul summarizes the argument of vv. 36–37.

7:38 So then, he who marries his betrothed does well, and he who does not marry will do better (ὥστε καὶ ὁ γαμίζων τὴν ἑαυτοῦ παρθένον καλῶς ποιεῖ, καὶ ὁ μὴ γαμίζων κρεῖσσον ποιήσει). "So

then" (ὥστε καί) brings the discussion of the last two verses to a summary conclusion. Now Paul establishes firmly that both getting married, for the reasons outlined in v. 36, and not getting married, for the reasons outlined in v. 37, are good positions. Both are acceptable to the Lord and reflect a concern to be devoted to the Lord and for holiness of life. The use of the comparative adverb "better" (κρεῖσσον) is not of great significance, but it does still reflect Paul's stated preference for people to remain in the state in which they currently find themselves (v. 26) and his understanding that the unmarried will face fewer distracting concerns in their devotion to the Lord (vv. 32–34).

Significantly, the fact that the one who gets married "does well" (καλῶς ποιεῖ) provides further strong support for believing the opening sentence of this chapter is a Corinthian statement with which Paul profoundly disagrees (v. 1; καλὸν . . . μὴ ἅπτεσθαι).

7:39 A wife is bound as long as her husband lives. But if the husband dies, she is free to be married to whom she wants, only in the Lord (Γυνὴ δέδεται ἐφ᾽ ὅσον χρόνον ζῇ ὁ ἀνὴρ αὐτῆς· ἐὰν δὲ κοιμηθῇ ὁ ἀνήρ, ἐλευθέρα ἐστὶν ᾧ θέλει γαμηθῆναι, μόνον ἐν κυρίῳ). Having addressed issues related to unmarried men and women in vv. 36–38, Paul now addresses a circumstance concerning women and marriage and asserts the indissolubility of marriage other than when the husband dies.[35] This verse also introduces the new subject of remarriage after a husband's death. Paul has already spoken to widows in v. 8 where he has recommended that they remain unmarried.

Paul begins by affirming the principle established in v. 10, based in the teaching of the Lord, that the married should not separate or divorce.

---

34. On the translation and possible origins of the word ἐξουσία, see "In Depth: 'Rights' and 'Freedom'" at 8:9.

35. There is, thus, a strong attachment with what has gone before. These last two verses are not an afterthought!

Being "bound" refers, in the first instance, to the legal binding of marriage. The intensive, perfect passive (δέδεται) is rightly translated with an English present tense.[36] It is the present situation affected by the past legal binding of the marriage ceremony that is in view here. However, it is likely that Paul thinks more broadly here than simply the legal requirements. He anticipates that Christians will not divorce or separate because of their commitment to the Lord (see comments on vv. 10–13).

The legal situation is altogether changed by death. Paul expounds on this fact in Romans 7:1–4 where he uses the legal binding of marriage and then the freeing from the law's obligations at death as an illustration of how Christ's death has led Christians to having "died to the law" (v. 4). Here Paul is not concerned at the illustration this may offer but the sad facts faced by many women who would often be left without support or home. With a third-class conditional clause, Paul introduces a discussion of the implications for the wife if her husband dies. In common with a number of statements in the New Testament about death, the euphemism "sleep" is used (cf. 1 Cor 11:30; 15:6, 18, 20, 51; three times in 1 Thess 4:13–15). The theological significance of this euphemism must not be underestimated. For those in Christ, the sleep of death points to the awakening of the resurrection. See also comments below on 1 Corinthians 15:18, 20.

If her husband dies, she is "free" (ἐλευθέρα), that is, free from the legal requirements of marriage and therefore able to make other choices, namely, to remain single or to remarry. Paul addresses the question of remarriage. This is now permissible, and she is free to be married "to whom she wants to be married" (ᾧ θέλει γαμηθῆναι). Though few

comment on this clause, it is notable that this continues in the line of Paul's general discussion of the advantages and disadvantages of marriage. She is in fact now free to discern the route of God's will for her future. She must not be pressured by others into marriage and, should she decide to remarry, then will need to seek God's will regarding her new partner.

It is probable that the pressure within the Christian community to remarry was less than that experienced outside the community. The commitment of Christians to care for the widows in their midst was explicit from the earliest days of the church (see Acts 6:1–6; cf. 1 Tim 5:3, 16; Jas 1:27). The explicit recommendation in 1 Timothy 5:11–15 that younger widows should consider remarrying does not negate what Paul says in this verse. The advice in that passage simply reflects the practical issues of passion and of the desire for children that the younger widow will need to consider as she examines her calling and resists temptation to be drawn away from Christ.

The only qualification Paul imposes here is that she remarry "only in the Lord" (μόνον ἐν κυρίῳ). Though this phrase has occasioned a degree of discussion, its general intent is clear. The new marriage must be within the framework of a life devoted to the Lord as discussed throughout this chapter. It therefore must at least imply that it will be a marriage to a fellow Christian believer.

7:40 But, in my judgment she is happier if she remains as she is. And I also think that I have the Spirit of God (μακαριωτέρα δέ ἐστιν ἐὰν οὕτως μείνῃ, κατὰ τὴν ἐμὴν γνώμην, δοκῶ δὲ κἀγὼ πνεῦμα θεοῦ ἔχειν). In the light of his comments in v. 38 regarding the single man marrying and his use of

---

36. Wallace, *Greek Grammar*, 581, lists this perfect as one of the rare occurrences of the "gnomic perfect" ("it has a distributive value"). This aspect of the verb speaks to something

that will happen on many occasions or for many individuals. It remains intensive.

the comparative "better," Paul now speaks similarly to widows. As far as Paul is concerned, remaining single will reduce the concerns of life of which he wrote in v. 32 and thus more readily enable an undivided devotion to the Lord. This time the comparative "happier" (μακαριωτέρα) is used. We discussed Paul's reference to his own "judgment" (γνώμη) in matters like this back in v. 25. Paul still gives the Christian woman a clear choice. He does not force his view of these matters on anyone but does remain concerned that people think through the practical issues of how best to serve the Lord and be devoted to him in these stressful times.

"Happier" (μακαριωτέρα) could refer to being "more blessed" in the theological sense of being blessed by God and hence to the joy that goes with such blessing. This use is seen in the beatitude form of Romans 14:22. When a person who makes a decision on "ethical matters has no reason for self-reproach," they are "blessed" by God rather than "condemned" (see Rom 14:23).[37] However, it seems unlikely that Paul has this in mind here. Singleness is not more blessed by God than marriage, but the individual may encounter less stress in the current crisis and will find herself with more time to devote to the Lord's service by remaining single and so be "happier" in her state of mind.

The final sentence indicates again that Paul probably has certain self-styled spiritual people in his sights. They claim the Holy Spirit's leading in what they say. It has led to statements like "it is good for a man not to touch a woman" (7:1). Paul speaks humbly as he says, "I also think that I have the Spirit of God" (δοκῶ δὲ κἀγὼ πνεῦμα θεοῦ ἔχειν). To widows, and indeed to other men and women throughout the chapter, Paul has offered a carefully nuanced theological argument concerning living the life to which the Lord has called and for which he has assigned grace-gifts. He has discussed this side by side with temptations and the concerns of life at times of crisis. His advice has been deeply practical and called for the exercise of discernment on the part of married and single men and women. Learning what principles to apply in these various situations in life and how to apply them will lead to the maturity that Paul longs for among the Corinthian Christians (3:1). It will also reveal the truly spiritual person, who is able to discern practically in the midst of the ups and downs of day-to-day life what is the "mind of Christ" (2:15–16).

Theology in Application

Contentment with Life

Paul encourages Christians to see their default position regarding marriage and singleness as "remain as you are." In a world where, for so many, their "choice" to lead exactly the life they desire is almost their definition of freedom, this will sound unbearably restricting. Given the use of slavery as the illustration, many may think their worst fears are well founded, and that this Pauline injunction cannot be followed in today's world. For many single people, it seems an unbearable possibility that God might desire that they remain single, and for many married people it may seem unbearable, for utterly different reasons, that they should be expected to remain

---

37. F. Hauck, "μακάριος," *TDNT* 4:369. The word is also taken as referring to God's blessing by Fitzmyer, *1 Corinthians*, 329.

with their spouse. Regarding the married, we know that Jesus allowed for divorce in certain circumstances of sexual sin (Matt 19:3–9). Paul in this passage allows also for divorce for a further reason (7:15). The request to remain together must be seen against a background in which it is known that divorce may be allowed in various, serious circumstances. Regarding the single, Paul clearly stipulates that it is not wrong to marry and gives reasons for marriage.

Nevertheless, for the Christian man or woman who so longs to be married, the idea that God may have called him or her to singleness is more than many can even consider. Yet it is time the church stopped making it seem as though marriage is the only way for a Christian person to find contentment in life. More than ever in our oversexualized society, where identity is often caught up in sexual activity, it is important that the church teaches clearly what the grace-gift of singleness might look like and what the benefits in serving the Lord may be. The idea that somehow a man or woman is only "complete" when married (a comment regularly heard in some evangelical circles) is simply unbiblical. Without pointing to the obvious fact that Jesus himself was single and totally "complete" (whatever that might mean!), this passage speaks to the obvious ministry advantages that a single person might have.

However, understanding Paul's theological underpinning for successful Christian marriage and successful Christian singleness is vital if the message of this chapter is to be well taught. First, the whole of life is to be lived with the constant empowering and enabling of the Holy Spirit. The fact that the Lord has called and has assigned grace-gifts to enable the life of the believer to be lived to God's glory is one of the most wonderfully freeing teachings of Scripture. The Lord even gives such gifts for marriage and singleness so that each may live the life to which the Lord has called (7:7, 17). Secondly, this chapter reminds us that the goal of marriage or singleness is not, first and foremost, lasting feelings of joy though, of course, all long for that! The goal is to be the slave of Christ wherever he wants us and so glorify God in the present age (7:22). Paul writes of this principle in different ways. The Christian is to seek to be free from the pressures or concerns of this world, but only so he or she can be concerned to "please the Lord" (v. 32) and maintain undivided devotion in serving him (v. 35). Thirdly, the broader eschatological context must be kept constantly in mind. "This world" is "passing away" and the time is shortened (vv. 29, 31). What people imagine are the most significant matters and decisions of their whole life are but fleeting in the plan of God. With these principles in mind, Paul can appeal to Christians in the way he has, because he knows that he is not offering a counsel of despair. With the Spirit *of the Lord*, Christians can survive a difficult marriage, and a single person can endure what perhaps is an undesired celibate life, bringing glory to God by seeking contentment in the Lord. This may not come easily, and even Paul had to "learn" it, but in Philippians 4:11 he was able to write, "I have learned to be content whatever the circumstances" (cf. 2 Cor 12:10).

Indeed, when people come to faith, this may mean them having to learn to be quiet and humble in a marriage relationship that may prove increasingly difficult. On the other hand, it may mean a new Christian moving out of her boyfriend's house or breaking up a long-term relationship because it is now recognized not to be what the Lord has assigned her. Paul is aware of the difficulties of what he is saying, but his theological principles guide him and he trusts the enabling power of God's Spirit to produce fruit in the individual's life.

CHAPTER 18

1 Corinthians 8:1–13

Literary Context

Paul has been concerned in various ways throughout the epistle about how a faction of this church has arrogantly insisted on its superior status in the community. In this commentary we have suggested that behind the appeal to their status lies their view that the gifts of the Spirit and especially those of "wisdom" and "knowledge," gifts which would have been so admired in the Greco-Roman society of that day, authenticate their status before God. This theme continues in chapter 8 as Paul now addresses another subject, probably from a Corinthian letter, with the phrase "now concerning" (περὶ δέ; see 7:1). At this point in the epistle he begins to address directly the question of their so-called "knowledge," a subject introduced in 1:5. He will demonstrate that they use this knowledge to encourage behavior that can lead to other less-confident Christians stumbling in their faith, a stumbling that could even lead to their destruction. Paul is prepared to forgo "knowledge" for the sake of brothers and sisters in Christ. In chapter 9 he will develop the idea that Christians can give up much to which they may feel they are entitled, either for the gospel's sake or for the building up of the body of Christ. In chapter 10 he will continue speaking of the problem of the arrogant Christians and where their overconfident view of status may lead *them*. In chapter 11 Paul addresses specific instances in which the love and care of others has taken second place to people's insistence on their rights and status even during times of coprorate worship. Then in chapter 12 Paul will address the right function of the gifts of the Spirit as opposed to the way in which the elitists of the Corinthian church were using them. Chapter 13 forms a pivotal summary to this argument. Whatever gifts a person may have (even "knowledge") are worthless without love. The reason for this is that love is in fact the true marker or authenticator of spiritual maturity and status in the Christian community.

"Knowledge" here relates to Spirit-given understanding about how to live and *practice* the Christian life. Paul's problem is not with the gift *per se* but with the activities and teachings that some Corinthians are putting forward based on their gift. Hence, for example, their "knowledge" says "an idol is nothing" *with the result that* meat offered to idols can be eaten. So, Paul's argument against the way the elitists behave takes two tracks that are closely intertwined. First, he questions the actual nature of the "knowledge" relating to idol meat and introduces the subject of love and the theme of being "built up" (8:1, 5–6). Then he demonstrates that through their "knowledge" they are leading brothers and sisters into sin (8:10–13). The chapter, though complicated in structure, sees Paul roundly challenging the elitists at each point.

VI. Marriage, Celibacy, Divorce, and Widowhood in Relation to Community Status (7:1–40)
➡ **VII. Status, Knowledge, Freedom, and Food Offered to Idols (8:1–11:1)**
   A. Knowledge and Love Contrasted (8:1–3)
   B. Knowledge concerning the Existence of "gods" and "lords" (8:4–6)
   C. Knowledge regarding the Eating of Idol Food in an Idol Temple (8:7–13)
   D. Status and Rights Should Be Subordinated for the Sake of the Gospel (9:1–27)

Main Idea

Paul warns that the "knowledge" of the Corinthian elitists regarding participation in the eating of idol food is wrong and can prove dangerous for Christians. Food has nothing to do with standing before God. The alternative to this "puffed-up" emphasis on the grace-gift of knowledge is the practice of love.

Translation

(See pages 364–65.)

Structure

This chapter divides into three parts. The first (8:1–3) examines the Corinthian question concerning eating food offered to idols. Paul contrasts "knowledge," which puffs up, with love that builds up. The second section (8:4–6) addresses the Corinthian "knowledge" that idols do not exist and that there is only one God. Here Paul lays out the Corinthian position (v. 4) and then his own (vv. 5–6). Paul thus challenges both the content of this "knowledge" and the elitists' deduction from this. In the third section (8:7–13), the apostle examines the possibly serious detrimental effect of eating food offered to idols on those who formerly believed in idols (8:7, 9–13), and the reason for the Corinthians' belief that they should eat this food (8:8).

1 Corinthians 8:1–13

1a Topic Introduction   Now   concerning food offered to idols:

b Quotation from
   Corinthians   **"We know that we all possess knowledge."**

c Assertion/response   **Knowledge   puffs up,**
                                but

d Assertion/response   **love   builds up.**

2a Condition (protasis)   If anyone thinks that he knows,

b Apodosis
   (contrast with 1c)   **he does not yet know** as he ought to know.

3a Condition   But   if anyone loves [God],

b Apodosis   **this one is known [by him].**

4a Circumstance   With reference to the eating of food offered to idols,

b Quotation from
   Corinthians   **"we know that an idol is nothing in the world** and

c Cont.   **that   there is no   God but one."**

5a Concession   For indeed   if   there are so-called "gods" either in heaven or ✍
                                                                                     on earth—

b Parenthesis/affirmation   as indeed there are many   "gods" and many "lords"—

6a Apodosis (pt. 1),
    confession   certainly **for us there is one God,**
                                                             the Father,
b Apposition   from whom are all things and
c Expansion   to whom we go, and
d Advantage

e Apodosis (pt. 2)   **one Lord,**
f Apposition   Jesus Christ,
g Expansion   through whom are all things and
h Expansion   through whom we [come to God].

7a Denial of 1b, 4b, c   However, **this knowledge is not possessed by all,**
b Explanation   but **some ...**
c Reason   because of their association until recently with an idol
d Assertion   **... [still] eat [this food]**
e Manner   as food offered to idols.

f Assertion   And **their self-awareness, being weak, is defiled.**
8a Basis   For **food will not prove our standing before God:**
b Expansion,
   series (protasis)   neither if we abstain from eating
c Assertion (apodosis)   **do we lack anything [before God]**

d Expansion, series
   (protasis)   nor   if we do eat

e	Assertion (apodosis)	**do we gain [divine approval].**
9a	Entreaty	**Now take care**
b	Content	that this right of yours does not become a stumbling block to the weak.
10a	Basis for v. 9; Condition	For
		if someone sees you
b	Description	who has knowledge
c	Circumstance	reclining to eat
d	Place	in an idol's temple
e	Assertion	**will he not be built up,**
f	Further condition	if his self-awareness is weak,
g	Content	to eat the food offered to idols?
11a	Result	For **this weak person is destroyed**
b	Means	by your knowledge,
c	Apposition to 11a	**the brother [or sister] for whom Christ died.**
12a	Manner	And	in this way
b	Explanation of 12a	sinning against your brothers [and sisters] and
c	Explanation of 12a	inflicting a blow to their self-awareness
d	Time	when it is weak,
e	Assertion	**you are sinning against Christ.**
13a	Summary	Therefore,
b	Condition	if food causes my brother [or sister] to stumble,
c	Assertion/conclusion	**I will never eat meat,**
d	Result (negative)	lest I cause my brother to stumble.

Exegetical Outline

→ **VII. Status, Knowledge, Freedom, and Food Offered to Idols (8:1–11:1)**

  A. Knowledge and Love Contrasted (8:1–3)

   1. Knowledge Is Temporary and Puffs Up (8:1a–c)

   2. Love Builds Up (8:1d)

   3. Loving God Is to Be Known by God (8:2–3)

  B. Knowledge concerning the Existence of "gods" and "lords" (8:4–6)

   1. The Elitist Position: Idols Do Not Exist (8:4)

   2. Paul's Position: For Us One God, but Demons Exist (8:5–6)

  C. Knowledge regarding the Eating of Idol Food in an Idol Temple (8:7–13)

   1. Recent Converts May Be Drawn into Sin (8:7)

   2. Such Eating Gains No Advantageous Status before God (8:8)

   3. Such Eating May Lead to a Person's Destruction (8:9–13)

Explanation of the Text

The "weak" and the elitists. Two groups of people emerge in this chapter even more clearly than in earlier chapters. Paul refers to the "weak" (8:7). These weak, as we shall see later, are those who are weak in their self-awareness (συνείδησις). They are insecure in their standing before God and lack confidence in community membership. How can they be sure they are part of God's rescued covenant community? This means that they are open to being misled by others who would claim to be secure in their status. The second group of people is normally referred to as "the strong," though Paul does not use that term here. Variously in this commentary this group is referred to as "the elitists," "the arrogant," "the knowers." Mostly we have avoided the term "the strong" because of the very real concern that this group should not be identified with the "strong" of Romans 14–15. In Romans 15:1 Paul refers to himself as "strong." In this passage, he distances himself almost entirely from the group. In using various terms, we are also seeking to reflect our belief that these people do not have a settled theological position to defend but rather have a deficient understanding of how their standing before God and membership in his community are to be demonstrated and authenticated. We shall see more on this in 8:7.

8:1 Now concerning food offered to idols: "We know that we all possess knowledge." Knowledge puffs up, but love builds up (Περὶ δὲ τῶν εἰδωλοθύτων, οἴδαμεν ὅτι πάντες γνῶσιν ἔχομεν. ἡ γνῶσις φυσιοῖ, ἡ δὲ ἀγάπη οἰκοδομεῖ). "Now concerning" introduces the new topic. In light of our comments on the same phrase in 7:1, it is likely that this subject was also raised in the letter the Corinthians had sent to Paul. The concern raised has to do with eating food that has had some association with idolatry. Clearly the early church had always sought to distance itself from the surrounding culture with its pervasive worship of idols. This had even been one of the issues on the agenda of the Council of Jerusalem recounted in Acts 15. Since most meat available to the consumer would have been slaughtered in some religious setting, eating such meat was likely often the cause of some discussion, especially with those who had recently exited the pagan religions to become Christians.[1] It seems most likely, as we shall see, that the question here especially related to the social context in which this food was eaten. Some seemed to be saying that there was nothing amiss in eating food offered by way of sacrifice to idols *in the temples* of the idols or at least in closely related social settings.[2] However, the matter is complicated because, initially, Paul seems to change the subject of discussion from idol food to a discussion of "knowledge" and "love." The precise link between "food offered to idols" and "knowledge" and "love" will only be understood as the whole argument unfolds, but four interpretative questions immediately arise: (1) What exactly is "food offered to idols"? (2) If Paul quotes the Corinthian letter, what is the extent of that quotation? (3) What is the "knowledge" referred to and how does it function in the community to cause "puffing up"? (4) What is the "love" referred to and how does it function in the community to cause "building up"? We will take each issue in turn below.

---

1. There is no evidence (*pace* Alex T. Cheung, *Idol Food in Corinth: Jewish Background and Pauline Legacy*, JSNTSup 176 [Sheffield: Sheffield Academic Press, 1999], 109) that this issue had been a specific subject of discussion at an earlier time between these Christians and the apostle.

2. See further on comments at 8:10.

Regarding issue (1), "food offered to idols" (εἰδωλόθυτα) translates a neuter, plural noun that is made up of a combination of the words "idol" (εἴδωλον) and "offered" as in a sacrifice (θύω). As 8:4 and 8:10 make clear, it is the *eating* of this food that is the issue that Paul and the Corinthians are discussing here and hence our general translation "*food* offered to idols." Some simply translate the word as "idol meat." As I have suggested elsewhere, this is a word that was probably coined in the earliest Christian circles to describe the sort of food offered in pagan temple sacrifices that Christians, for all their new-found freedom, normally felt unable to eat. Specifically, this would be food being eaten in a temple.[3] In 8:10 Paul speaks of someone who has "knowledge" being seen eating "in an idol's temple." Eating food in this context would certainly have been unacceptable generally to Christians even given a theology that said idols do not exist (8:4). The question presented by this section of the epistle is not likely to have simply been the general matter of whether food from the market could have been eaten, even if it had been originally offered as a sacrifice, but whether food or meat with specific links to idol worship could be eaten as, for example, a Christian entering a temple to eat it. In the light of 8:10 and further discussion in 10:20–21 the real question seems to have involved the (temple) context in which such sacrificial food

was eaten.[4] Whether Paul only has in mind "meat" here is not entirely clear. While he refers generally to "food" (βρῶμα) in 8:8–13, his use of the word "flesh" (κρέας) in 8:13 may indicate he was speaking of animal sacrifices and hence "meat."

Regarding issue (2), the majority of commentators agree that 8:1b contains a quotation from the Corinthian letter to Paul mentioned in 7:1. However, there is no unanimity on where that quotation begins. Most argue that Paul is concurring with the Corinthian quotation when he says "we know that"[5] and that the actual quotation is therefore "we all possess knowledge." The problem with this is that 8:7a then seems to be a direct contradiction. First, Paul agrees "all of us possess knowledge," but then in 8:7 he writes, "However, this knowledge is not possessed by all." A number of solutions to this apparent contradiction have been suggested. For example, Conzelmann joins others by suggesting that in 8:1 Paul agrees that the Corinthians "have objective knowledge" and that this consists of certain "theoretical principles," whereas in 8:7 Paul is concerned with the *practice* of this knowledge.[6] Such a distinction between theory and practice or emotional assimilation is strained at best. Paul never seems to make this separation even if the Corinthians did. He is concerned with how "knowledge" is being used by the Corinthian so-called "strong."

---

3. The normal Greek word for this food (ἱερόθυτος) is used in 10:28. The word εἰδωλόθυτος seems to have become a technical Jewish-Christian word describing the food sacrificed in the temple and probably eaten there or in the environs of the temple. Several works examine the nature of this sacrificed food. See Gardner, *Gifts of God*, 15–63, also 183–85; Willis, *Idol Meat in Corinth*; Joop F. M. Smit, "*About the Idol Offerings*": Rhetoric, Social Context and Theology of Paul's Discourse in First Corinthians 8:1–11:1, CBET 27 (Leuven: Peeters, 2001).

4. Ben Witherington, "Not so Idle Thoughts about Eidolothuton," *TynBul* 44 (1993): 237–54. For further detailed discussion of the background of idolatrous meals and Paul's response, see Richard Liong-Seng Phua, *Idolatry and Authority: A Study*

of 1 Corinthians 8:1–11:1 in the Light of the Jewish Diaspora, JSNTSup 299 (Edinburgh: T&T Clark, 2005) and John Fotopoulos, *Food Offered to Idols in Roman Corinth: A Social-Rhetorical Reconsideration of 1 Corinthians 8:1-11:1*, WUNT II.151 (Tübingen: Mohr Siebeck, 2003).

5. The ὅτι is taken as recitative, introducing a quotation.

6. Conzelmann, *1 Corinthians*, 146; Also cf. Barrett, *First Corinthians*, 194; Jerome Murphy-O'Connor, *1 Corinthians*, New Testament Message 10 (Dublin: Veritas, 1980), 80, speaks of "the difference between theoretical acceptance and emotional assimilation. The Weak mouthed the words but in their hearts were still influenced by the conditioning of decades (v. 7), and emotionally they held the 'gods' of their past in awe."

An alternative approach offered by Thiselton still suggests the quotation starts with "we all possess," but translates the preceding clause (οἴδαμεν ὅτι) as "we are fully aware that (as you say) 'All of us possess . . . .'"[7] Paul is thus simply admitting that some of the Corinthians are making this statement but not actually agreeing with it. In not specifically identifying with what these Corinthians were saying, Thiselton suggests that Paul therefore remains fully free to make his strong comments on such "knowledge" in 8:2 and 8:7.

A third approach is to take the whole sentence as a quotation: "We know that we all possess knowledge." Those who follow this interpretation point out that the clause "we know that"[8] appears only here and in 8:4 and cannot confidently be said to be an introductory clause to a quotation. They also assume therefore that the same clause in 8:4 is to be taken as part of the Corinthian quotation, "we know that an idol is nothing in the world." This third view is the one followed here. It seems to let Paul's argument flow more clearly and, as we shall see, avoids a tension with 8:7. It also avoids the need to separate theory and practice. In other words, (1) not all people did grant them this fact, and (2) the knowledge being referred to was a *particular* spiritual knowledge (the nature of which is discussed below). The tone of these Corinthians was probably defensive: "This is what we know we all possess (whatever anyone else may say)." In 8:7 Paul simply points out, in line with much of what he says in 1 Corinthians 12 and 14, that all do *not* possess "this knowledge."

Regarding issue (3), how the word "knowledge" (γνῶσις) is understood will influence how this chapter is read. The view adopted here is that the

Corinthian elite were flaunting the gifts of the Spirit ("grace-gift"; χάρισμα) and using them as authenticators or indicators of their security and standing before God. Paul has acknowledged that the Corinthians have many grace-gifts, including "knowledge" (1:5). The elitists arrogantly insist they all possess this particular gift. Paul asserts that the way they regard this gift "puffs [them] up" (8:1c). In 8:1d he contrasts this with "love" that "builds up" (οἰκοδομέω). That both Paul and the Corinthians were thinking of the grace-gift of "knowledge" is further supported by the argument of chapter 13. The linking of "grace-gifts" (12:31) with "tongues" and "prophetic powers" (13:2) and the description of their bankruptcy when compared with possessing "love" (13:1–3) is surely a vivid summary of the issues Paul addresses here in chapter 8.

Regarding issue (4), the meaning of "love" (ἀγάπη) and the function it serves in Paul's mind is also crucial to understanding the nature of Paul's concern with the elitist position.[9] The idea of "love," in contrast with "knowledge" and grace-gifts, is introduced here and lies behind much of the discussion through to the end of chapter 14, which begins with "pursue love" (14:1). Of course, chapter 13 is the great exposition of love. Given the link in 8:1 between "love" and its manifestation in being "built up," it is right to assume that wherever Paul speaks of activities that build up he is also thinking of the demonstration of love. For Paul, love for God is the sure sign that the person is "known by God" (8:3). This builds on the Old Testament teaching that God "knew" his people in an electing way (cf. Num 16:5; Jer 1:5 LXX). For Paul "knowledge" fares poorly in contrast with love, for the former is a gift that "not all possess"

---

7. Thiselton, *1 Corinthians*, 621.

8. For οἴδαμεν δὲ ὅτι and οἴδαμεν γὰρ ὅτι see Rom 2:2; 3:19; 2 Cor 5:1. Willis, *Idol Meat in Corinth*, 70, and Gardner, *Gifts of God*, 22–23.

9. See at 13:3 the essay, "In Depth: Love, Its Function and Background."

(8:7) and is only partial at best (13:12). Since not all Christians possess it, it can hardly be a marker of election or of standing before God. Yet neither can it be a sign of greater spiritual maturity, as the elitists seemed to believe. For Paul, only love functions as a marker or authenticator of a Christian or a Christian's maturity. This love becomes the bedrock that produces Christians who are concerned for the community and who build it up in a way that reflects respect and love for neighbor.

First Corinthians 8:1 therefore introduces both the main topic for chapters 8–10 but also Paul's main theological concern. Taking the whole sentence, "we know that we all possess knowledge" (οἴδαμεν ὅτι πάντες γνῶσιν ἔχομεν), as a quotation, the double use of a first-person plural verb ("we know," "we possess") draws attention to those who have raised the issue of food offered to idols: "We [the truly 'spiritual people' at Corinth] know that we all possess knowledge." Being "puffed up" (φυσιόω) involves the flaunting of something for one's own benefit or to stress one's own status. So here in v. 1 Paul offers a sober and deliberately deflating perspective on the way their "knowledge" was functioning in the community. As a marker, it had become a cause of pride and of differentiation between Christians.

What the church should most seek is that which "builds up," love. Being built up refers first to edification of the community, but it also refers to the edification of the individual in his or her faith.[10] Thus, love is truly a "marker," and yet it is *not puffed up* (13:4). Paul will need to show in chapter 13 what love looks like in practice. At the outset,

then, Paul contrasts the different *functions* in the community of "knowledge" and "love."

8:2 If anyone thinks that he knows,[11] he does not yet know as he ought to know (εἴ τις δοκεῖ ἐγνωκέναι τι, οὔπω ἔγνω καθὼς δεῖ γνῶναι). Two conditional sentences expand the last sentence of 8:1 as Paul develops his strong challenge to the elitists who claimed "knowledge." The first picks up on the matter of knowledge and the second on love. The irony inherent in the grace-gift of knowledge is that it reveals how little Christians do know, or how much is yet to be known. Since "knowledge" is incomplete and partial, it can hardly function as a marker of status before God, so flaunting it brings no benefit at all. However, those who love God reveal in themselves that they are indeed authentically the Lord's, for they reveal that they "are known" (v. 3).

Paul's use of the perfect tense, "that he knows" (ἐγνωκέναι) is significant. It suggests that the Corinthians imagined or thought (δοκέω) that, having once received "knowledge," they then possessed the gift of knowledge going forward. Perhaps such experiences of the gift were often repeated (12:8), but they were being used as the basis for arguing that certain people now "had knowledge."[12] They see themselves, as Cheung puts it, as "knowers."[13] Yet Paul implies that because knowledge is incomplete it will need to be tested. The testing would probably have to take much the same form as it seems to have done with other gifts, such as prophecy. It would be tested against Scripture and against the teaching of the apostles (14:37) and tested to

---

10. See "In Depth: Building Up the Church" at 3:10.

11. A number of textual variants in 8:2–3 should be noted. 𝔓⁴⁶ and Ambrosiaster omit the word "something" (τι) in 8:2. This omission makes good sense. It is knowledge *qua* knowledge that the Corinthians eulogize, not knowledge about something specific. Likewise, for Paul it is "love" *qua* love that should be sought, and the omission of an object provides a bet-

ter correspondence to the first conditional sentence. A person should exhibit love over knowledge. If an object for the verb were needed, then it would be summed up in the commands of Scripture to love God and neighbor.

12. Paul does not allow this deduction in 8:2b where he uses an ingressive aorist.

13. Cheung, *Idol Food in Corinth*, passim.

see that it built up the church (14:26). Moreover, it would be subjected to appraisal by others in the church (14:29, 32). Of course, Paul has already listed a number of areas of life and belief where the Corinthians did not seem to know what they should have known, and thus the irony of Paul's earlier rhetorical questions, "Do you not know?" (οὐκ οἴδατε), becomes still more pointed (3:16; 5:6; 6:2, 3, 9, 15, 16, 19, etc.).

The theological challenge that Paul poses to this arrogant group continues in various ways right through chapter 13. There he makes it clear that all gifts of the Spirit, including knowledge, are to be viewed as partial and as impermanent. Their temporary nature becomes clear in the light of Christ's return, which is the coming of the "perfect" (τὸ τέλειον; 13:10). Now "we know in part" (v. 9), but even when the "partial will be abolished" (at Christ's coming; v. 10), the gift of knowledge will also pass (v. 8). Meanwhile, the Corinthians must not attribute to knowledge or to any gift of the Spirit a potency that it cannot possess. It cannot mark out or authenticate a Christian when that is not its purpose. Like all gifts, knowledge is given to build up the church until her Lord returns, and during that time it provides useful, practical but partial knowledge for God's people.

8:3 But if anyone loves [God], this one is known [by him][14] (εἰ δέ τις ἀγαπᾷ τὸν θεόν, οὗτος ἔγνωσται ὑπ᾽ αὐτοῦ). Verse 3 may now be seen in its full irony. The Corinthians' elitist approach to knowledge has led to some Christians being "puffed up" and overly confident of their status

before God. In fact, however, it is love that is the authenticator of the Christian's standing before God. It is not the one who says "I know" who can be confident that they belong ("is known") but the one who says "I love." The copyists who added the words "by him" were surely correct in understanding the sentence. The idea recalls Numbers 16:5 (LXX): "God knows those who are his [καὶ ἔγνω ὁ θεὸς τοὺς ὄντας αὐτοῦ] and who are holy . . . and whom he has chosen for himself."[15]

Elsewhere Paul refers to love as one of the "fruits" of the Spirit (Gal 5:22), and unlike the gifts love lasts into all eternity (1 Cor 13:8, 13). Paul's emphasis on the centrality of love builds to its exciting climax in chapter 13, but it is important to remember in this chapter, as Paul addresses idolatry and its associated sacrifices and meals, that the authenticating function of "loving God" appears in the first of the Ten Commandments, which is actually a command against idolatry. "You shall have no other gods before me. . . . I the Lord your God am a jealous God, visiting the iniquity of the fathers on the children to the third and fourth generation of those who hate me, but showing steadfast love to thousands of *those who love me* and keep my commandments" (Deut 5:7–10 ESV; cf. Exod 20:2–6; Deut 7:1–10). Given that in the next verse (1 Cor 8:4) part of the Corinthian argument is drawn from the Shema (Deut 6:4–5), continuing, "You shall love the Lord your God . . . ," it should surely have been clear to God's people that the authentic child of God will be one who exhibits love for God and for fellow human beings. Numerous

---

14. Two further variants are to be noted. 𝔓[46] omits "God" (τὸν θεόν) and 𝔓[46], ℵ, and 33 omit the words "by him" (ὑπ᾽ αὐτοῦ). The omission may well have been original and would balance the conditional sentences. The use of the passive "is known" (ἔγνωσται) may have caused other scribes to have inserted "him" (understood to be God) as the agent. This is further complicated by the possibility that the perfect verbal form should be regarded as the middle rather than the passive

mood. If it was originally intended to be a middle form of the verb, then the meaning would be clear: "If a person loves, this person knows" (or "has experienced true knowing"; see Thiselton, *1 Corinthians*, 625–27). See Fee, *1 Corinthians*, 402. The translation adopted here again follows 𝔓[46]. With Fee, *1 Corinthians*, 402n28, we believe "this has all the marks of being the original text."

15. Note Paul's quotation of this text at 2 Tim 2:19.

times throughout Scripture, love is seen to be the marker of the one who belongs to God. Jesus himself had said, "By this all people will know that you are my disciples, if you have love for one another" (John 13:35 ESV).

Ironically, the elitists at Corinth had failed to "know" that love is the only clear marker of authentic Christianity and maturity of faith. It is love, practiced in their love for God and for each other, that they should be pursuing (14:1; cf. 16:22). This contrasts starkly with "knowledge," which is being practiced in a way that divides people and even leads some back to other gods.

8:4 With reference to the eating of food offered to idols, "we know that an idol is nothing in the world and that there is no God but one" (Περὶ τῆς βρώσεως οὖν τῶν εἰδωλοθύτων οἴδαμεν ὅτι οὐδὲν εἴδωλον ἐν κόσμῳ, καὶ ὅτι οὐδεὶς θεὸς εἰ μὴ εἷς). Paul now returns to the matter raised in v. 1. There is another question here about the extent of a possible quotation from the Corinthians. In line with our view of v. 1, we take it that the quotation includes the words "we know that . . ." (οἴδαμεν ὅτι). The single sentence of 8:5–6, though incomplete grammatically (an anacoluthon), is then Paul's cautious but clear response to the Corinthians.

The Corinthians offer theological support for their position of eating this food, probably in temples (8:10), by appealing to their monotheism. That "there is no God but one" (οὐδεὶς θεὸς εἰ μὴ εἷς) is an affirmation of the Shema and of the foundational commitment of Judaism and of Christianity. The nonexistence of idols can clearly be drawn from biblical teaching. This probably allowed them to say that going to temples and eating food, even in an idol temple itself, was a matter of indifference since idols did not exist. If this is their "knowledge," then it is more than simply the words

of Scripture! "Knowledge" as the gift of the Spirit has to do with the *understanding* needed for the *practice* and *application* of the truth. It seems likely that they believed God's Spirit has enabled them to be "enlightened" to understand that certain truths of Scripture (if that is what they are) in fact allow them to eat this idol food. More than that, they seem to have suggested that an authentic or mature Christian would *deliberately* eat this meat or food because that would demonstrate possession of the gift of "knowledge." This reconstruction helps explain why Paul later sarcastically talks of a "weak" person being "built up" to eat idol meat and consequently being "destroyed" (vv. 8–11).

It is not surprising, therefore, that Paul needs to qualify what these elitists are saying, especially with regard to idols. It is one thing to say with Scripture that idols are "nothings," but that is not the same as suggesting that no evil spiritual entities lie behind the idols. In Isaiah 44:9 the idol *makers* are, like the things they make, "all nothings" (πάντες μάταιοι), but only when set in contrast with the true God who is creator (Isa 44:6–8). In Isaiah 41:29 the works of the gods are "nothing." In fact, the Israelite *perspective* is to be that false gods and their idols are "nothing" and that only the true God can do anything for them.[16] In truth, other verses suggest that behind these idols lie demons or "gods." In 1 Corinthians 10, especially vv. 19–22, Paul draws on Deuteronomy 32 where, in a chapter that establishes the concept of "no gods" and foolish worship, there is mention of "strange gods" and sacrifices "to demons" (32:16–18, 21). Scripture repeatedly warns of the dangers of idolatry and demons and the worship of other gods.

So Paul establishes his critique of the Corinthian position in two ways. Firstly, he objects to the way they were allowing "knowledge" to *function* in

---

16. Gardner, *Gifts of God*, 35–37.

the community. It cannot be a marker of the sort they believed it was. Only "love" could be this. Secondly, their knowledge is simply *wrong*. Their behavior regarding food offered to idols is based, at best, on incomplete understanding. Monotheism is true, but to deny the spiritual realities involved with idolatry and the eating of food offered to idols is wrong. This is what Paul now argues in the next two verses, which, we believe, reflect the apostle's position as distinct from the Corinthian position.

8:5–6 For indeed if there are so-called "gods" either in heaven or on earth—as indeed there are many "gods" and many "lords"—certainly for us there is one God, the Father, from whom are all things and to whom we go, and one Lord, Jesus Christ, through whom are all things and through whom we [come to God] (καὶ γὰρ εἴπερ εἰσὶν λεγόμενοι θεοὶ εἴτε ἐν οὐρανῷ εἴτε ἐπὶ γῆς, ὥσπερ εἰσὶν θεοὶ πολλοὶ καὶ κύριοι πολλοί, ἀλλ' ἡμῖν εἷς θεὸς ὁ πατήρ, ἐξ οὗ τὰ πάντα καὶ ἡμεῖς εἰς αὐτόν, καὶ εἷς κύριος Ἰησοῦς Χριστός, δι' οὗ τὰ πάντα καὶ ἡμεῖς δι' αὐτοῦ). A paraphrase of 8:4–6a might read like this: "You say, in support of eating food offered to idols, 'We know that an idol does not exist in the world and there is no God but one,' but, while you question whether there are gods (and I assure you there are), certainly [ἀλλά][17] for *us* there is one God, the Father." This helps reveal the careful structure of what *Paul* says:

8:5a	indeed if	there are so-called
8:5b	*as indeed*	*there are*

		"gods" either in heaven or on earth
		many "gods" and
		many "lords"

8:6a	Certainly for *us*	
	there is	*one God,*
	the Father,	from whom are all things and
	to whom we go, and	
		one Lord,
	Jesus Christ,	through whom are all things and
		through whom we [come to God].

As Paul begins this part of his argument, he refers to "so-called gods" (λεγόμενοι θεοί) and affirms that there are "indeed many 'gods' and many 'lords,'" thus taking a different position from the Corinthians. He begins with the rare phrase, "for indeed if" (καὶ γὰρ εἴπερ), which implies that the supposition agrees with the fact.[18] The supposition is that there *are* so-called gods, which he further affirms by saying, "Indeed there are many 'gods' and many 'lords.'" However, the apodosis of 8:6 offers the qualification by adding that "certainly for *us*," that is, for Christians, there is only one God,[19] whom we know as Father.[20]

So how can the difference between Paul and the

---

17. BDF §448.5. Here ἀλλά introduces the apodosis after εἴπερ. As in a similar construction with ἐάν in 4:15, it can be translated as "certainly" or "at least."

18. LSJ 489. Thayer suggests a translation "provided that" (Joseph H. Thayer, *A Greek-English Lexicon of the New Testament* [New York: Harper & Brothers, 1889], 172). Robertson, *Grammar of the Greek New Testament*, 1026, writes that "the truth of the principal sentence is stoutly affirmed in the face of this one objection." The "one objection," we suggest, is offered

in the apodosis (8:6), beginning with "certainly" (ἀλλά). See below.

19. Hurd, *Origin of 1 Corinthians*, 122, rightly calls this a "henotheistic-sounding statement." However, this is not henotheism because Paul views these "gods" as "so-called." In fact, they are not gods but demons.

20. Again, there is a strong indication that Paul has Deut 32 in mind through much of this section and into ch. 10. In Deut 32:6 there is one of the rare Old Testament uses of the word

Corinthians here be explained more accurately? Conzelmann suggests that Paul's view is that "gods *become* gods by being believed in, and faith in the *one* God and the *one* Lord creates freedom no longer to recognize these powers."[21] But that seems to be more like the Corinthian position than Paul's, and we have seen in v. 5b that these gods and lords *do* exist. Neither can we say that because 8:6 begins with "for us" therefore 8:5 is stating something that was only true for *them* (the "weak") *subjectively*. This distinction between an "objective" Christian view that gods do not exist and a "subjective" view in the minds of pagans that gods do exist seems far from Paul's mind. In 8:7 Paul's concern is with *real* defilement with idols and idol meat. If it were not, then there would be no need for the strong statements of 8:9–13.

It is not until 10:14–22 that the distinction Paul makes here becomes fully explicit. However, his point is simply this: while idols are "nothing" when compared with God the Father who creates all things ("from whom are all things") and the one Lord, Jesus Christ, who sustains us and all things, nevertheless demons do indeed exist and can truly be worshiped. The "demons" of 10:14–22 are the "gods" and "lords" of 8:5. The Christian view of these matters is therefore the traditional Jewish view: for *us* there is only one God who is true and who is the Father of those who are his. When God's people compare him and his works with anything else at all, the rest is "nothing." If Christians should forget this at any point, then they are vulnerable to demons (10:14–22). Truly he is "God of gods and Lord of lords" (Deut 10:17).

In the midst of this main argument, in 8:6 Paul expounds briefly but most profoundly on

the saving and sustaining work of the Father and of Jesus Christ. It has been suggested that this is one of the earliest affirmations of Christ's preexistence. Again, Deuteronomy 32, which Paul quotes in 10:20, 22, provides background. In Deuteronomy 32:6 the Israelites are challenged, "Is this the way you repay the LORD, you foolish and unwise people? Is he not your Father, your Creator, who made you and formed you?" The creating work of God is seen in bringing his people into being and is why God is here called "Father." The passage then describes how the Israelites rejected God and "made him jealous with strange gods. . . . They sacrificed to demons . . . . You were unmindful of the Rock that bore you; you forgot the God who gave you birth" (vv. 16–18 NRSV). What Paul writes here in 8:6 is close to this. Paul will always insist that idolatry, demons, and worship of idols is dangerous for Christians just as it was for the Israelites. Nevertheless, part of the way in which Christians will fight off temptations to idolatry and participation in idol worship is by remembering that the one sovereign God brought all things into being and uniquely brought his people into being. He is known therefore as Father. From him (ἐξ οὗ) come all things for his people and to him (εἰς αὐτόν) we go.[22] Thiselton offers a paraphrase that speaks of God as "the goal of our existence."[23] All that we are and all we do must be for our God.

The mediator of the one God's work is the one Lord. It is Jesus "through whom" (δι᾽ οὗ) are all things and "through whom" (δι᾽ αὐτοῦ) *we*, as Christians, continue our existence and service before God in order that we might arrive at the goal of our existence ("through whom [we come to God]"). Therefore, belonging to God in Christ

---

"Father" applied to God. Here Paul uses the word "Father" of God with its customary Old Testament connotation. God is "Father" of his people in bringing them into being and in his electing love for them (Deut 32:6; Isa 63:16; Jer 3:19; 31:9; cf. Ps 89:26).

21. Conzelmann, *1 Corinthians*, 145.
22. Literally, "we to him." Barrett, *First Corinthians*, 192: "And to whom our own being leads."
23. Thiselton, *1 Corinthians*, 638.

clearly requires the avoidance of all idolatry. Our whole existence must be for and about him. Christ brought us into being as God's people just for this. Yet this great teaching about us being sustained as God's family with him as our Father also has clear consequences for how the family should live together. It is this to which Paul now turns.

8:7 However, this knowledge is not possessed by all, but some because of their association until recently[24] with an idol [still] eat [this food] as food offered to idols. And their self-awareness, being weak, is defiled (Ἀλλ᾽ οὐκ ἐν πᾶσιν ἡ γνῶσις· τινὲς δὲ τῇ συνηθείᾳ ἕως ἄρτι τοῦ εἰδώλου ὡς εἰδωλόθυτον ἐσθίουσιν, καὶ ἡ συνείδησις αὐτῶν ἀσθενὴς οὖσα μολύνεται). Paul now refuses to adopt the standpoint of the elitists by challenging the *content* of their knowledge. They are simply wrong to suggest that the knowledge they claim to have is possessed by everyone. It is not. Some who have recently converted from paganism[25] are seeking to build their self-awareness and confidence in this new-found status among God's people. If the knowledge of the elitists really does demonstrate the standing of Christians before God and authenticate that status, then it is not surprising that the "weak" will seek to follow them. After all, they too want to feel secure before God. However, far from these weaker and newer Christians being built up, they find themselves being defiled and drawn (back) into sin.

8:7 begins with the strong adversative "however" (ἀλλ᾽) and an emphasis on the negative "not" (οὐκ). It may be that Paul meant simply that the gift of the Spirit called "knowledge" was not possessed by all the Christians. This would make sense in the light of his use of the body metaphor in chapter 12 and would still be a direct contradiction of their statement in 8:1 that "we know we all possess knowledge." However, it is more likely that 8:7 refers here to the claimed manifestations of knowledge in all three of the statements that we suggest are theirs. Those statements are: (1) "We know that we all have knowledge"; (2) "We know that an idol is nothing"; and (3) "There is no God but one." Paul denies that all possess this knowledge, not as theory but as statements upon which the behavior of the Corinthian elitists may be justified.

Paul's mention of "*this* knowledge"[26] refers, then, to the matters the Corinthians are raising. To this Paul responds with criticism of all three of their statements: (1) not all have knowledge; (2) not everyone possesses the knowledge that an idol is nothing *with the result that* they can eat idol meat sacrificed to idols; and (3) not everyone possesses knowledge that there is "no God but one" *with the result that* they can go to idol temples and eat. Indeed, Paul does not possess this knowledge! As we have seen, neither v. 4c nor v. 6a can be regarded as theoretical statements of monotheism. They are, in effect, contrary "words of knowledge." Paul's words in v. 6 center on what God has done in Christ and on understanding better the place of Christ as founder and sustainer of his people. It clearly does

---

24. "Recently" or "just now" is a relatively common meaning for ἄρτι; see, e.g., Matt 9:18; Rev 12:10; "just before the time in which we are speaking" (Thayer, *Greek-English Lexicon*, 75).

25. Some have suggested that the "weak" are those who have Jewish sensibilities to eating idol meat. Thus, the "until now" may be paraphrased, "until now accustomed to believing idols to be real because they were Jewish," and therefore having pangs of conscience about eating something they used to think was wrong. See Jacques Dupont, *Gnosis: La Connaissance Religieuse dans Les Épîtres de Saint Paul* (Louvain: E. Nauwlaerts,

1949), 532–33. Also Adolf von Schlatter, *The Church in the New Testament Period* (London: SPCK, 1955), 174ff. While in the end the *religious* problem Paul addresses here would remain the same whether he was writing to converts from Jewish or pagan backgrounds, we believe for reasons given in various places through the commentary that it is more likely that the "weak" were Gentile converts.

26. The definite article functions as a demonstrative adjective.

not "puff up" Paul, but it does "build up" the Christian church.

Thus, Paul's response to the Corinthians continues.[27] However theoretical the Corinthian statement about the nature of God and idolatry may sound to the modern ear, their knowledge has never been simply theoretical, as some have suggested. In fact, even making this suggestion is to misunderstand the purpose of the gifts of the Spirit. As we have seen, the gift of knowledge took biblical (or other) truth and *applied* it to the current church situation for its edification. Thus, a true exposition of "knowledge" would be one that involved the Holy Spirit's revelation of an application or a meaning of Scripture for the present church's edification. In fact, the very test of this and any of the gifts of the Spirit will be whether or not edification of Christ's church takes place (14:26). Clearly, some are not being built up. In fact, this so concerns Paul that he resorts to extreme irony in 8:10–11, saying that some will be so "built up" to eat sacrificed idol food that they end up being "destroyed" by the so-called "knowledge" of the elitists.

Paul now states that their self-consciousness or self-awareness, being "weak, is defiled" (ἀσθενὴς οὖσα μολύνεται).[28] That is, they will be caused to sin. Paul develops this at greater length in vv. 8–13. He is concerned for those who have recently come out of paganism. They had been accustomed to worshipping idols and eating sacrificed food as part of that religious worship. While in chapter 10 Paul will insist that there is a serious danger for all Christians from becoming mixed up in eating idol meat in sacrificial settings, here he begins to show the folly of this "knowledge." Such may be the temptation and the confusion among these former pagans as they re-enter these social settings centered on idolatrous feasts that they may be sucked back into pagan worship and activities.

Those "weak" in their "self-awareness" (συνείδησις) were people who, reflecting on their own actions and feelings, felt insecure as God's people. Their weakness was not in moral decision making. As those who "until recently" (ἕως ἄρτι) were pagans, their weakness in self-awareness is easily understood, and it would be compounded if they were told that the gift of knowledge (which some did not have) indicated status before God.

IN DEPTH: The Meaning of the Word "Conscience" (συνείδησις)

We have translated the word "conscience" (συνείδησις) as "self-awareness" or "self-consciousness." The modern meaning of "conscience" as an inward moral knowledge or consciousness that can restrain people from sin was only just

---

27. There is much discussion about the relationship between 8:1 and 8:7. If Paul agrees in 8:1 that "all possess knowledge," how does this fit with him saying "not all of us possess this knowledge"? Fee, *1 Corinthians*, 417, and Conzelmann, *1 Corinthians*, 146, suggest that the difference is best explained by differentiating between knowledge at a theoretical level (which all have—8:1) and knowledge at the experiential and emotional level (that not all have—8:7). But as we have seen, there is little evidence that Paul, *or the Corinthians*, would have separated theory and practice in this way. The gift of knowl-

edge seems to have involved specifically their *practice* of their understanding of God's will. By taking the whole sentence in 8:1, "We know that we all possess knowledge," as a quotation from the Corinthians the problem with 8:7 is substantially reduced. Verse 7 is Paul's summary of his view that what the Corinthian elitists have claimed is simply wrong at a number of levels. See below.

28. The word "defiled" (μολύνω) means "stained (with sin)." Cf. 2 Cor 7:1.

developing at the time Paul was writing. Until the first century the word was, as Maurer puts it, "more often used for self-consciousness in a non-moral sense," indicating that the connection with moral decision making was only secondary.[29] However, when a word's meaning is changing, it is the context that can most help our understanding. Here in chapter 8 it is evident that, for three reasons, the idea of a "moral conscience" does not make sense. The people for whom Paul is concerned he calls "weak" in conscience. Firstly, if this is a "moral conscience," then these "weak" people seem to have had too *strong* a conscience, one which made them feel guilty for attending idol temples. Secondly, if "moral conscience" was the issue, then it was the "strong" whose "conscience" was actually weak. After all, they were the ones Paul showed had to become aware (morally) of their sin (8:12). Thirdly, Paul never criticized the "weak" in this passage. He accepted them as they were and condemned those who would have changed them.[30] This approach was in line with how Paul reminded the arrogant that they were not "powerful" (1:26) and that the "weak" were chosen by God (1:27). Paul had even argued that he was "weak" in comparison with those who believed themselves to be "strong" (4:10). Furthermore, had the issue been a matter of lax or inadequate *moral* consciousness, Paul would never have condoned it. This is evident in 9:19–23 where Paul was prepared to be "weak" to those who were "weak," but in doing so would not break the "law of Christ."

Given the above and the fact that the weak desired to be *seen* to be like the elitists, even to the point where they were led into real idolatry (8:7, 10), we believe a so-called "weak conscience" simply means having a lack of knowledge or self-awareness of oneself in relation to the community. This is a perfectly possible meaning for the word in Greek and best fits the context. In the first place, Paul has already shown that the main issue surrounding the problem with "knowledge" was one of belonging (8:3). If the "weak" were doubtful about their belonging or status before God, that would provide ample motivation to do something known to be wrong. Much-desired group recognition could easily lead to doing many unwise things. If they were persuaded that eating idol meat in temples would demonstrate that they were "known," then their motivation to do so is well understood. Secondly, this would also explain why the elitists were keen to see the weak follow them. They wanted to see the weak "built up" to be like them, thus giving them a greater sense of security before God.

---

29. C. Maurer, "συνείδησις," *TDNT* 7:898–919.

30. It is because Paul clearly implies that "the weak" need to mature in their faith in Rom 14 that some imagine he must inevitably feel the same about these "weak." However, as mentioned above, 1 Cor 8 addresses a different matter.

8:8–9 For food will not prove our standing before God: neither if we abstain from eating do we lack anything [before God] nor if we do eat do we gain [divine approval].[31] Now take care that this right of yours does not become a stumbling block to the weak. (βρῶμα δὲ ἡμᾶς οὐ παραστήσει τῷ θεῷ· οὔτε ἐὰν μὴ φάγωμεν ὑστερούμεθα, οὔτε ἐὰν φάγωμεν περισσεύομεν. βλέπετε δὲ μή πως ἡ ἐξουσία ὑμῶν αὕτη πρόσκομμα γένηται τοῖς ἀσθενέσιν). This verse has generated much discussion.[32] However, there is no difficulty with this verse if it is viewed as all part of Paul's response.[33] The elitists did indeed believe that eating this food could prove their status before God because it demonstrated their possession of "knowledge." Paul is determined that both the elitists and the "weak" need to understand that eating this idol food has no effect on their status before God.

Murphy-O'Connor rightly suggests, "The importance that the Corinthians attached to *charismata* needs no emphasis. Such gifts were of divine origin (1 Cor 12:6). Consequently, they could be used as a tangible test of one's standing before God."[34] However, Paul had already shown that this was not how the grace-gifts were to function. In 1:5 he had acknowledged that the Corinthians were enriched with God's gifts and that none was "lacking" (ὑστερέω) any grace-gift (1:7). Nevertheless, though it is clear that Paul saw the richness of the gifts as part of God's blessings in the present

era until the parousia, he was also clear that it was not the gifts but the Lord who would sustain them guiltless on the day of the Lord (1:7–9).[35] So here in chapter 8 Paul responds with great clarity. To paraphrase, Paul says, "You are wrong. Food does not prove your standing before God. Neither *not eating* nor *eating* helps us in this matter at all. Not eating does not mean we lack anything in our relationship with God; similarly, we gain nothing if we do eat."

The word "standing" (8:8a, παρίστημι) confirms that the issue for the Corinthians concerns status before God. The word can mean to "demonstrate" or "prove" something, but most likely here it means "to bring to stand before a judge." As Héring says, "There is a clear allusion to the Judgement."[36] The opposite of standing is "stumbling" (πρόσκομμα), which has to do with failing to stand before God and which now becomes another important theme Paul develops through the next few verses.[37] It is thus very important to see how Paul emphatically moves to the second person as he speaks of "*this* right[38] [or authority] of *yours*" (ἡ ἐξουσία ὑμῶν αὕτη). Paul does not at all identify with what they are calling a "right to eat." There is no indication here that Paul accepts this so-called "right" of these elitists; rather, he does not approve of their approach. As Garland says, the phrasing "sounds contemptuous."[39] What is a right for the elitists is, for Paul, no more than a "stumbling block" to the weak. The second-person plural imperative

---

31. BDAG 805.

32. Barrett, *First Corinthians*, 195, assumes the first clause "is clearly consistent with the position of the strong." He and many others believe the "strong" (not a word used in this passage) would have regarded eating idol meat as adiaphorous and of no consequence one way or the other. Gordon Fee, "Εἰδωλόθυτα Once Again: An Interpretation of 1 Corinthians 8–10," *Bib* 61 (1980): 190, has said "this text is as puzzling as it is abrupt." This has led to suggestions that parts of 8:8 may contain further quotations from the Corinthian strong.

33. Paul's return to the first-person plural (ἡμᾶς) adds to the likelihood that this is him speaking.

34. Murphy-O'Connor, "Food and Spiritual Gifts in I Corinthians 8:8," in *Keys to First Corinthians*, 81.

35. Cf. the eschatological context of "to lack" or "fall short" (ὑστερέω) in Rom 3:23; Heb 4:1; 12:15.

36. Héring, *First Corinthians*, 73. Also Johann Albrecht Bengel, *Gnomon of the New Testament*, vol. 3 (Edinburgh: T&T Clark, 1877), 253; Allo, *Première Épître aux Corinthiens*, 204; Barrett, *First Corinthians*, 195. See 2 Cor 4:14 and Rom 14:10.

37. See "In Depth: The Theme of Stumbling" at the end of 1:23.

38. See below.

39. Garland, *1 Corinthians*, 387.

(βλέπετε) drives home his order to the elitists that they must not cause another to stumble in sin. The second person continues through to the end of 8:13 as Paul continues to address the elitists. As he goes on to say in 8:11–12, the one who causes a brother or sister to stumble in this way sins against Christ; moreover, the weak brother or sister may be destroyed.

IN DEPTH: "Rights" and "Freedom"

The word "right" (ἐξουσία) as Paul uses it in chapters 8 and 9 is difficult to define, and no single English word can fully capture its meaning, especially since it seems slightly to change as Paul uses it.[40] Of the ten occurences in this epistle, six are to be found in chapter 9. It is often translated as "authority," although in 8:9 the NRSV has "liberty" and in 9:4, 5, 6, and 12 it has "right" (at v. 12 it is also translated as "rightful claim"). The word's prominence and use in chapter 9 undoubtedly aids an understanding of the word in chapter 8. Both the translations "authority" and "right" mentioned above draw on a legal understanding of the word found in the LXX (e.g., 1 Macc 10:38; Ps 113:2; Wis 10:14). Given that background and especially the way Paul uses the word in 9:9 where he calls upon the law of Moses for support, we might translate with a phrase like "the exercise of your legal right (given your membership in a group of people)."[41] Thus, the elitists or "strong" were part of a group having "knowledge" and exercising what they believed to be their "rights." In chapter 9 when Paul speaks of his "rights," it is notable that he does so specifically as one of the (group of the) apostles.

A translation along the lines of "the exercise of your legal rights (given your membership in a particular group of people)" certainly makes sense of the word's use in chapter 9 but also provides a satisfactory understanding of the word in 8:8. This definition is consistent with the word's use on some occasions in other Greek literature. The Greek word stems from the idea of an "ability" to perform an action because "there are no hindrances in the way."[42] The legal or political right to do something seems to predominate even when the best translation may be "power," for that power is often understood as pertaining to the one with sufficient power to enforce their will.[43]

In sum, "this right of yours" (ἡ ἐξουσία ὑμῶν αὕτη), of which Paul talks almost

---

40. For more detail see Gardner, *Gifts of God*, 55–56.

41. See also comments on 6:12 and 10:23 where the slogan of the Corinthian elitists in "all things are lawful" (πάντα ἔξεστιν) bears an obvious similarity to the word ἐξουσία when it appears in 8:9. See also comments on 7:4.

42. W. Foerster, "ἐξουσία," *TDNT* 2:562. Foerster sees Paul's freedom being exercised as freedom from the Jewish law (ibid., 566).

43. The following examples help to demonstrate the different meanings of the word within this category. In Plutarch, *Lycurgas* 3.14, we read of "royal power" (LCL; καὶ βασιλικὴν ἐξουσίαν ἔχοντι; cf. Thucydides, *History of the Peloponnesian War* 6.31.4; 7.69.2) and of freedmen not receiving the "rights of suffrage" in his *Publicola* 7.8 (LCL; ἐξουσίαν ψήφου). Also cf. Epictetus, *Discourses* 1.29.11 (καὶ τίς σοι ταύτην τὴν ἐξουσίαν δέδωκεν; Ποῦ δύνασαι νικῆσαι δόγμα ἀλλότριον;).

disdainfully in 8:8, is not some theoretical possibility but involved *practice*. In their belief that eating in an idol temple was their right, the "strong" caused the destruction of the weak person. Therefore, Paul was not prepared to allow it as a "right" (ἐξουσία) of the Christian community. Rather, it was a stumbling block (v. 9; πρόσκομμα).[44]

8:10–11 For if someone sees you who has knowledge reclining to eat in an idol's temple, will he not be built up,[45] if his self-awareness is weak, to eat the food offered to idols? For this weak person is destroyed by your knowledge, the brother [or sister] for whom Christ died (ἐὰν γάρ τις ἴδῃ σὲ τὸν ἔχοντα γνῶσιν ἐν εἰδωλείῳ κατακείμενον, οὐχὶ ἡ συνείδησις αὐτοῦ ἀσθενοῦς ὄντος οἰκοδομηθήσεται εἰς τὸ τὰ εἰδωλόθυτα ἐσθίειν; ἀπόλλυται γὰρ ὁ ἀσθενῶν ἐν τῇ σῇ γνώσει, ὁ ἀδελφὸς δι᾽ ὃν Χριστὸς ἀπέθανεν). Paul now reveals the real nature of the problem. It was not a matter of whether to buy meat in the marketplace that had been slaughtered in some sacrificial rite, nor simply of some urging their "weaker" brothers or sisters in Christ that food is adiaphorous and they can eat this food with impunity. The person with a weak "self-awareness," for better or worse, is being "built up" as he watches the elitists eat meat *in* a temple where an idol is worshipped. No doubt those doing the eating were deliberately drawing attention to this display of their "knowledge" in

order to draw in the "weak" and "build them up" to a confidence in their status before God.[46] The very verb "recline to eat" (κατακείμενον) suggests the enjoyment of fellowship in the eating at the temple more than the simple word "eat" (ἐσθίω) that Paul uses when he speaks more generally in 8:13.[47] With great irony Paul insists that if a "weak" person follows those eating in this way, instead of being built up to secure status before God they "will be built up" (οἰκοδομηθήσεται) to idolatry. They will eat the sacrificial food as an offering to an idol, thus eating in such a way that they sin. Far from having their status in God's people authenticated by their action, they end up back in idolatry in a way that leads to their destruction.

The full repercussions of the wrongful use of this so-called "right" are that a person "is destroyed" (ἀπόλλυμι). Paul does not mince his words here. The verb "to destroy" is placed, possibly for emphasis, to the front of the sentence. In the apostle's writings it is a word that always refers to eternal ruin. Conzelmann says the verb "must not

---

44. Gardner, *Gifts of God*, 56.

45. This is not the smoothest English translation, but is used here deliberately to draw attention to Paul's purposeful and continuing use, here ironic, of the verb οἰκοδομέω. Others, for example, translate as "be encouraged to" (NRSV) or "emboldened to" (NIV).

46. Garland, *1 Corinthians*, 387, argues against my view that this was a deliberate policy on the part of the elitists to make the weak follow them (*Gifts of God*, 24, 30–31, 50–51, etc.). He rightly points out that Paul uses a "probable future condition" (οἰκοδομηθήσεται) which has not yet occurred. However, he ignores the impact of the combinations of the words "puffed up" and "built up" as Paul uses them here and later in the epistle.

Paul is concerned for the "weak" precisely because the elitists are flaunting their activity and so trying to draw others into their activity, which Paul argues will end in destruction for the one who follows. The future probable anticipates the end result of eating this meat as espoused by the elitists *if* it continues unchecked. Garland is right that Paul does not suggest here that some have already fallen so far that they will inevitably be "destroyed."

47. The verb (κατάκειμαι) describes the common position in which people would recline on a couch to eat, usually in someone's house. Inevitably a degree of intimacy is implied here. Cf. Jesus in Mark 2:15 and Luke 7:37.

be taken in a weakened sense of moral ruin; here as elsewhere it means eternal damnation."[48] Paul contemplates the whole question of eating this meat and the matter of "standing" or "falling." If these arrogant men and women had supposed that eating this idol meat would help guarantee the standing of the weak before the judgment seat of God, exactly the opposite will probably happen.

In 8:11 we see again that the underlying issue concerns the function of the gifts of the Spirit. It is "by your knowledge" (ἐν τῇ σῇ γνώσει) that the destruction happens. The tragedy is that this distortion of the function of the gift means that, far from it proving a person's standing before God, it may end with the destruction of a brother or sister "for whom Christ died" (δι᾽ ὃν Χριστὸς ἀπέθανεν). In this way Paul shows that the saving work of Christ in establishing a Christian's identity as "brother," or sister, is challenged by such thinking.

A person's identity as "brother," as a member of the community, was established on and through the one foundation of Christ crucified (1:23; 3:11; 8:6). Back in 1:31 Paul had shown that the only "boast" that Christians could have was "in the Lord" because "in Christ Jesus" they were "set apart" (1:2). Participation in the community of God's people and having a standing before him was by being "called into covenant participation with his Son, Jesus Christ our Lord" (1:9). This point is developed further in chapter 10. But here in the final part of v. 11, Paul establishes that even those without "knowledge" enjoy full community status, summed up in the word "brothers." They are all, men and women, part of the family that has God as its Father and that has been brought into being through Christ (8:6), who died for this family. They belong to God and his church simply by God's grace and Christ's redemptive work on

the cross. Paul now insists that to suggest otherwise or to cause Christians to doubt the security that is theirs through Christ's death is not just a sin against the brother or sister but also against Christ.

8:12–13 And in this way sinning against your brothers [and sisters] and inflicting a blow to their self-awareness when it is weak, you are sinning against Christ. Therefore, if food causes my brother [or sister] to stumble, I will never eat meat, lest I cause my brother to stumble (οὕτως δὲ ἁμαρτάνοντες εἰς τοὺς ἀδελφοὺς καὶ τύπτοντες αὐτῶν τὴν συνείδησιν ἀσθενοῦσαν εἰς Χριστὸν ἁμαρτάνετε. διόπερ εἰ βρῶμα σκανδαλίζει τὸν ἀδελφόν μου, οὐ μὴ φάγω κρέα εἰς τὸν αἰῶνα, ἵνα μὴ τὸν ἀδελφόν μου σκανδαλίσω). The way in which the elitists sin against their brothers and sisters has been shown in 8:10–11. Paul, repeats the word "brother" twice more for emphasis. The verb "to sin" (ἁμαρτάνω) is emphasized as it begins and ends the sentence of v. 12, for sin is the undoubted result of eating in this way in an idol's temple. The sin of "inflicting a blow" (τύπτω) or wounding their weak self-awareness (τὴν συνείδησιν ἀσθενοῦσαν) is that they have been led away by the pressure of idolatry from trust in Christ and his death as the sole grounds for their security. Thus the sin is not just against the weak brother or sister but ultimately against Christ himself. What a contrast with the love of Christ who died for the weak brother or sister! Paul has nothing good to say of their knowledge here, as he moves in 8:13 to speak of his own actions by way of example.

The nature and function of love in the Christian community will be outlined in detail in chapter 13, but here Paul begins to open up his own life in a way that will show how love should be exercised in the community, a theme that will continue through

---

48. Conzelmann, *1 Corinthians*, 149n38.

chapter 9. Paul's concern is that "knowledge" should always be subjected to love and concern for others in the community. To stress how far this must affect a person's actions, he emphatically writes that he is prepared to "never eat meat" at all (οὐ μὴ φάγω κρέα εἰς τὸν αἰῶνα) if a believer should be caused to "stumble" (σκανδαλίζω) by such eating. "Meat" (κρέας) has been broadened away from the food eaten in an idol's temple to any meat at all, just as the "reclining to eat" of 8:10 in the intimate setting of a temple has given way to the more general "eat." The effect of this is to create strong hyperbole. Even though we know in chapter 10 that Paul is actually prepared to eat different types of meat, the reader here is left in no doubt what matters most to Paul. He will give up anything rather than risk the destruction of a brother or sister. In chapter 10 Paul used the wilderness events to illustrate the danger. *The particular association of the "stumbling stone" or "snare" (πρόσκομμα) with the Israelites turning to other gods may have given the word added significance in 8:9.*[49]

We have already seen that the word "to stumble" (σκανδαλίζω) is closely related to the idea of the "stumbling block" (8:9; πρόσκομμα). It has to do with what Paul has been saying about the possibility of a brother or sister being destroyed. A closely related word was first encountered in 1:23 where Paul referred to "Christ crucified" as a "cause of stumbling" (σκάνδαλον). When confronted with the gospel of Christ crucified, the wisdom of the wise is confounded, and some find they "are perishing" while others find they "are being saved" (1:18–19). Paul is categorically clear: nothing must cloud the gospel that Christ died to bring salvation. No other cause of stumbling must ever be admitted, even if a person has to give up much! What Paul has written in this chapter relativizes "knowledge." The claimed grace-gift will need to be challenged as to *content* and *function*. When it no longer "builds up" a person to enjoy their standing before God but rather "builds up" toward sin and idolatry, it is no longer a grace-gift. This final verse thus becomes a summary of all that Paul has said in chapter 8, but it also provides the opening for Paul to begin to offer himself as an example in chapter 9. He is prepared to give up his "rights" so that love for the brother or sister will trump all.

Theology in Application

The Desire to Show Off Community Status

Like the danger facing all Christians of all ages, the Corinthians had succumbed to interpreting their faith in a manner amenable to the society in which they lived. Their society greatly valued knowledge and wisdom as spiritual virtues, and their grace-gifts fitted well in this cultural milieu. As a result, they became "puffed up" and arrogant. The danger of conceit and pride in one's religious affections is addressed repeatedly in Scripture. Both ascetic practices on the one hand, or licentious behavior on the other can provide a basis for pride, as one person or group distinguishes themselves from another and begins to consider themselves more "spiritual" than others (cf. 1 Cor 4:6; 8:1; Gal 6:13; Col 2:18). *The underlying theological problem*

---

49. Exod 23:33; 34:12–13.

has to do with losing sight of God's grace in Christ. When men and women look to themselves for their spiritual status before God, they immediately devise means by which to demonstrate that they belong to the church and are deeply "spiritual." Paul's response is to say that he will "boast" in or take pride in nothing except "Jesus Christ and him crucified" (2:2) or "the cross of our Lord Jesus Christ" (Gal 6:14). Since status before God lies entirely in God's grace in Christ and his love for his people, then faith cannot be allowed to rest in anything other than the power of God (2:5). It is therefore the "law of faith" that will completely exclude boasting (Rom 3:27 NRSV).

This danger of finding things related to one's spiritual life in which to take pride is one all Christians face. In 1 Timothy 3:6 it provides a reason for not appointing a recent convert to the office of elder. As happened in the Corinthian church, it is all too easy to take something imparted to us in God's loving mercy and make that into something of which we can be proud. The prophet Jeremiah addressed this specially in Jeremiah 9:23–24. God may graciously give wisdom, riches, or might, but the wise or rich or powerful should know that there is nothing here in which to boast other than in the gracious and loving activity of the Lord in their life. The danger of this temptation to become proud is acute in the modern church. Whether it be the preacher, the music leader, or the person with some other notable spiritual gift, anyone can easily fall prey to forgetting that all Christians have is of grace.

Encouraging Assurance

Many Christians wonder whether their faith is secure, and perhaps inevitably this means they look around for visible or practical evidences to which they can appeal to provide them assurance of their standing before God. A poor understanding or "weak self-awareness" regarding our position among God's people can easily be exploited by those who have become puffed up and boastful of their own supposed community standing. Paul does not suggest that the position of the "weak" is wrong. Rather, he uses this passage to teach of the danger of them being led by other Christians back into their old, sinful way of life. That such "weak" people should be "built up" in the faith and in their assurance of their standing before God goes without saying. In chapter 12 Paul will demonstrate that this is precisely why grace-gifts have been given: to build up people in their faith in Christ and so they can better see themselves as part of the body of Christ. All Christians need this edification, but it must be built on the foundation of Christ rather than on seeking to copy some other Christian who seems to have the outward signs of status. Those who think they are "something" need to realize they can end up leading others into sin. When they no longer see love for God and love for neighbor as the true markers of community standing, then they will behave arrogantly toward others and will replace what is good and of the Lord with what is at best inadequate. This arises from people's desire to place themselves and their actions at the center of their spiritual lives. The ability of Christians to give up what they see as their community rights and privileges—even things they enjoy—for the sake of a Christian brother or sister is ultimately the test of the presence of love. Assurance for those who lack it is found first in looking again to the love of Christ who was crucified for them, but it is then reinforced by a people who build each other up in the faith through their love for one another.

19

1 Corinthians 9:1–27

Literary Context

Paul has argued that the elitists are so flaunting their "knowledge," especially regarding their right to eat meat sacrificed to idols, that the "weak" who once worshipped idols were being led back into idolatry. Chapter 8 ended with Paul insisting that he willingly would give up eating meat altogether to avoid leading anyone to destruction. For Paul, the Lord and the gospel will always take priority in life. It is this that provides the link into chapter 9, in which Paul exemplifies from his own life how he prioritizes the gospel. As an apostle he has certain rights that he can exercise, but he has been prepared to give these up "for the sake of the gospel" (9:23). Structurally the link between this chapter and the previous is therefore to be found in 8:13. Here Paul moves from the rights of the elitists and the danger that their behavior may lead the weak person to destruction to talking about himself and his actions, which are designed to avoid leading brothers and sisters into such stumbling. The Corinthians were likely leading the weak astray through the exercise of what they saw as a "right" to eat food that had been sacrificed to idols in an idol temple. Following illustrations from his own life, Paul will return in chapter 10 to further examples from history where the weak ended up being destroyed and to a more detailed discussion about specific dangers of meat sacrificed to idols.

VI. Marriage, Celibacy, Divorce, and Widowhood in Relation to Community Status (7:1–40)

VII. Status, Knowledge, Freedom, and Food Offered to Idols (8:1–11:1)

    A. Knowledge and Love Contrasted (8:1–3)

    B. Knowledge concerning the Existence of "gods" and "lords" (8:4–6)

    C. Knowledge regarding the Eating of Idol Food in an Idol Temple (8:7–13)

➡   **D. Status and Rights Should Be Subordinated for the Sake of the Gospel (9:1–27)**

    E. Israel's Abuse of Spiritual Gifts Provides a Warning (10:1–13)

Main Idea

The gospel of Christ must take priority in the life of all believers, especially in their dealings with other people. While certain "rights" may be attached to the membership of any group of people, yet for Christians these must always be exercised with extreme caution lest for others they become a stumbling block to the gospel itself. Paul's life is always lived in a way that prioritizes the gospel.

Translation

1 Corinthians 9:1–27

1a	1st rhetorical question	**Am I not free?**
b	2nd rhetorical question	**Am I not an apostle?**
c	3rd rhetorical question	**Have I not seen Jesus our Lord?**
d	4th rhetorical question	**Are you not my work in the Lord?**
2a	Negative condition	If I am not an apostle to others,
b	Assertion	certainly **I am to you;**
c	Basis	for **you are the seal of my apostleship** in the Lord.
3a	Assertion/defense	**My defense to those who would evaluate me is this:**
4a	1st defense/ rhetorical question	**Do we not have a right to eat and drink?**
5a	2nd defense/ rhetorical question	**Do we not have a right to bring along a believing wife**
b	list	as [do] the rest of the apostles and
c	list	the brothers of the Lord and
d	list	Cephas?
6a	3rd defense/ rhetorical question	Or **is it I alone and Barnabas who have no right to refrain from working for a living?**
7a	1st illustration of 6a (rhet. quest.)	**Who** **serves as a soldier**
b	Manner	at his own expense?
c	2nd illustration of 6a	**Who** **plants a vineyard and**
d	/rhetorical question	**does not eat its fruit?**
e	3rd illustration of 6a	**Or who** **tends a flock and**
f	/rhetorical question	**does not drink the flock's milk?**

Continued on next page.

Continued from previous page.

8a	4th defense/ rhetorical question	**I am not saying these things from a human perspective,** am I?
b	Expansion	**Does not the law also say these things?**
9a	Basis	For **it is written in the law of Moses,**
b	Quotation	"You shall not muzzle an ox while it threshes the grain." [Deut 25:4 LXX]
c	Explanation of 9b	**Is it for oxen that God is concerned?**
10a	Assertion/ rhetorical question	Indeed, **does he not by all means speak for our sake?**
b	Repetition	Yes, **it is written for our sake,**
c	Explanation	because the one who ploughs ought to plough in hope and
d	Series	the one who threshes in hope of partaking [of the crop].
11a	Rhet. quest. in conditional form	If we have sown spiritual things among you,
b	Conclusion of defense	**is it too much that we reap material things among you?**
12a	Rhet. quest. in conditional form	If others partake of the rights you [give them],
b	Conclusion of defense	**should not we even more?**
c	Assertion (contrast)	Nevertheless, **we have not made use of this right,**
d	Assertion	but rather **we put up with all things,**
e	Negative purpose	lest we put a stumbling block
f	Place	in the way of the gospel of Christ.
13a	Rhetorical question	**Do you not know**
b	Content	that those employed in temple duties eat from the temple food, and
c	Content	those serving at the altar share together in [food from] the altar?
14a		And likewise
b	Assertion, climax	**the Lord commanded**
c	Content	that those preaching the gospel should live by the gospel.
15a	Conclusion (contrast)	But **I have not used any of** these things.
b	Negative assertion	And **I am not writing** these things
c	Negative purpose	so that this might thus happen to me;
d	Partial basis	for **it would be better for me to die than—**
e	Assertion	**no one will make empty my boast.**
16a	Concession	For though I preach the gospel,
b	Assertion	**I have nothing to boast in.**
c	Basis for 15e, 16b	For **I am under compulsion.**
d	Basis for 16c (apodosis)	For **woe to me**
e	Condition (protasis)	if I do not preach the gospel!

17a	Condition (positive)	For	if I accomplish this
b	Means		of my own initiative,
c	Assertion (apodosis)		**I have a reward;**
d	Condition (negative)	but	if　not of my own initiative,
e	Assertion (apodosis)		**I have [simply] been entrusted with a stewardship.**

18a Question (summary)　　So **what is my reward?**
 b Response　　　　　　That in preaching **I may make the gospel free of charge,**
 c Result　　　　　　　　　　　　with the result that I do not make use of my right in the gospel.

19a Basis for 19b　　　For,　　being free　from　all,
 b Assertion　　　　**I have enslaved myself　to　　all**
 c Purpose　　　　　　in order that I might win more.

20a 1st illustration,
　　advantage　　　　　　　　　　　　To　　the Jews
 b Assertion　　　**I became**
　　　　　　　　　like　　　　　　a Jew
 c Purpose　　　　so that I might win　the Jews;
 d 2nd illustration,
　　advantage　　　　　　　　　　　　to　　those under the law
 e Assertion　　　　like　　　　　　[one] under the law
 f Purpose　　　　so that I might win　those under the law
 g Parenthesis　　(though not myself being　under the law);

21a 3rd illustration,
　　advantage　　　　　　　　　　　　to　　those outside the law
 b Assertion　　　　like　　　　　　[one] outside the law
 c Parenthesis　　(though not being　outside God's law but
　　　　　　　　　　　　　　　　　under Christ's law)
 d Purpose　　　　so that I might win　those outside the law;

22a 4th illustration,
　　advantage　　　　　　　　　　　　to　　the weak
 b Assertion　　　**I became weak**
 c Purpose　　　　so that I might win　the weak.

 d Assertion　　　**I have become　　all things**
 e Advantage　　　　　　　　　　　to　　all people,
 f Purpose　　　　so that …　　　by all means
　　　　　　　　… I might save　some.

23a Assertion　　　Now **I do all things**
 b Advantage　　　　**for the sake of the gospel**
 c Purpose　　　　so that I might participate in it.

Continued on next page.

Continued from previous page.

24a	Rhetorical question	**Do you not know**
b	Content	that in a race all the runners run but
		one receives the prize?
c	Entreaty, consequence of 24a–b	**So run**
d	Purpose	that you may receive it.
25a	Assertion	Now **every athlete is self-controlled** in all things.
b	Expansion	Indeed, **they do this**
c	Purpose	in order to receive a perishable crown, but
d	Contrast	we [to receive] an imperishable [crown].
26a	Consequence	Hence,
b	Assertion	**I do not run**
c	Manner	in an aimless way,
d	Assertion	**nor do I box**
e	Result	such that I beat the air.
27a	Contrast	Rather,
b	Assertion	**I punish my body**
		and **enslave it,**
c	Purpose (negative)	lest after preaching to others I myself might be disqualified.

Structure

Chapter 9 divides into three sections. Throughout the chapter Paul offers himself as an example of one who is prepared to sacrifice his "rights" for the sake of any Christian who might be led away from the gospel. The style changes somewhat between chapters 8 and 9. A series of fifteen rhetorical questions now make this passage vivid and clear.[1]

The first main section is 9:1–18, which can be divided further into two subsections. Verses 1–12a argue for Paul's right to support as an apostle. Verses 1–2 are not a defense of Paul's apostleship, as some have suggested. Rather, through four rhetorical questions and a strong assertion he establishes the premise for the ensuing argument. The whole argument of this chapter requires that the reader grant the premise that he is an apostle and apostles have certain rights. His purpose is to demonstrate that apostles and the exercise of their rights can offer a general analogy for Christians and the exercise of their rights.[2] Thus, how Paul handles his rights provides an example for how the elitists should handle their so-called "rights." In 9:3–12a Paul argues that he has the apostolic right to financial or logistic support.

---

1. Paul Ellingworth, "Translating 1 Corinthians," *BT* 31.2 (1980): 234–38. Such questions, as we have seen, are not at all uncommon in this epistle. Indeed, there are nearly a hundred of them.

2. If there is any apostolic "defense" at all here, it is only that some of the "elite" Christians may have looked down on Paul because he was not making use of his rights and, therefore, did not radiate the charisma of a leader that perhaps they expected. However, there is no clear evidence in the text that this is the case.

He speaks generally of others in apostolic circles who receive support, illustrates this, and then also appeals to the Mosaic law (vv. 8–10) and concludes that for the sake of the gospel he has made no use of this right (v. 12a). In the second subsection (vv. 12b–18) Paul insists that the gospel is to be offered to all "free of charge" and that he is compelled of divine necessity to preach it.

The second main section (9:19–23) provides further examples of relinquishing rights for the sake of the gospel. The governing principle is that more people may be won for Christ (v. 19). A list of three groups of people follows in which Paul shows how he himself accommodated to them to enable more to be won. In v. 20 he speaks of Jews, in v. 21 of Gentiles, and finally in v. 22 of the "weak." Thus, at the end of the argument Paul comes back to a direct example from his own life of the problem raised at the end of chapter 8—the way the "weak" should be helped rather than caused to stumble. The priority of the gospel is again stressed (v. 23, cf. vv. 12, 16).

In the third and final section (9:24–27), Paul summarizes his message as he uses the metaphor of the athlete and writes of the self-control and self-imposed restrictions necessary, even for an apostle, if an "imperishable crown" is finally to be received.

Exegetical Outline

VII. Status, Knowledge, Freedom, and Food Offered to Idols (8:1–11:1)

    A. Knowledge and Love Contrasted (8:1–3)

    B. Knowledge concerning the Existence of "gods" and "lords" (8:4–6)

    C. Knowledge regarding the Eating of Idol Food in an Idol Temple (8:7–13)

➡   **D. Status and Rights Should Be Subordinated for the Sake of the Gospel (9:1–27)**

        1. Paul Has Subordinated His Own Apostolic Status and Rights (9:1–18)

            a. Paul's Premise: He Is Free and an Apostle (9:1–2)

            b. As an Apostle, He Has a Right to Support (9:3–12a)

                (1) Other apostles exercise this right (9:3–6)

                (2) Even soldiers are entitled to support (9:7)

                (3) The Mosaic law grants him the right to support (9:8–12a)

            c. As One Who Is Free, He Has Relinquished the Right to Support (9:12b–18)

                (1) He will put no stumbling block in the way of the gospel (9:12b–15)

                (2) He is under compulsion to preach the gospel (9:16–18)

        2. Paul's Principle: Win More for Christ (9:19–23)

            a. He Has Become a Servant to All (9:19–22)

                (1) an example from his work to win Jews (9:19–20)

                (2) An example from his work to win Gentiles and others (9:21–22)

            b. He Has Done All for the Sake of the Gospel (9:23)

        3. Paul's Purpose: To Receive an Imperishable Wreath (9:24–27)

            a. An Illustration from an Athlete's Disciplined Life (9:24–25)

            b. Paul's Own Self-Discipline (9:26–27)

Explanation of the Text

9:1–2 Am I not free? Am I not an apostle? Have I not seen Jesus our Lord? Are you not my work in the Lord? If I am not an apostle to others, certainly I am to you; for you are the seal of my apostleship in the Lord (Οὐκ εἰμὶ ἐλεύθερος; οὐκ εἰμὶ ἀπόστολος; οὐχὶ Ἰησοῦν τὸν κύριον ἡμῶν ἑόρακα; οὐ τὸ ἔργον μου ὑμεῖς ἐστε ἐν κυρίῳ; εἰ ἄλλοις οὐκ εἰμὶ ἀπόστολος, ἀλλά γε ὑμῖν εἰμι· ἡ γὰρ σφραγίς μου τῆς ἀποστολῆς ὑμεῖς ἐστε ἐν κυρίῳ). Four rhetorical questions establish the premise that Paul is an apostle. He will argue from this premise throughout the rest of this chapter. These questions are reinforced by the assertion that, of all people, the Corinthians will surely grant his apostleship since they are the direct result of his apostolic ministry.

The Rhetorical Questions. Given the number of rhetorical questions in this chapter, it is important to understand how these function in Paul's discussion. Some commentators, while acknowledging that these four questions are indeed a rhetorical device, proceed to treat the questions as *real* questions and so suggest that Paul is here having to defend the fact that he is an apostle.[3] On this view, "Am I not an apostle?" is therefore a real question, as are all four. The Corinthian reader, it is suggested, was expected to answer "yes."[4] However, the functional difference between real and rhetorical questions is that real questions are used to elicit information or specific response while rhetorical questions are used "to convey or call attention to information."[5] The questions in themselves, then,

provide no evidence that Paul was seeking to defend his apostleship against some who were either criticizing or denying it. Rather, they are a useful device to make a strong assertion of the premise for the following argument. Paul is an apostle, and apostles have certain rights that in his case and for the sake of the gospel he has chosen to forgo.

The reference to "freedom" (ἐλεύθερος) initially seems strange.[6] Paul had used the word for freedom from slavery in 7:21 and had then talked of slaves being free in the Lord and those who are "free" being slaves of Christ (7:22). However, the freedom that Paul refers to here specifically belongs to him as an apostle and is a direct contrast with what he had just said about himself in 8:13. There he had seriously restricted himself, if necessary for the sake of the gospel, to not eating some types of food! Now he insists that he is "free." Not unlike the argument of 7:21–22, Paul is showing that true freedom in the Lord can produce surprising results that even seem to contradict the whole idea of "freedom." How different was Paul's behavior to that of the so-called strong! For Paul, to be "free" in the Lord was to be a "slave" in the service of Christ. This is a point he makes again in 9:19.

The second question, like the first, seems rather unexpected. Fee has argued that this question "gets immediate attention" and that "this is the first statement in the letter that his apostleship itself is at stake in Corinth."[7] However, this seems thoroughly unlikely. First, it takes the rhetorical ques-

---

3. Fee, *1 Corinthians*, 435–37, for example, assumes the questions provide further evidence for the supposed confrontation on each question raised. However, there is no need to assume that any answer is expected for genuine rhetorical questions. They function simply as a strong assertion of fact.

4. A question containing the particle οὐκ expects an affirmative response.

5. See John Beekman and John Callow, *Translating the Word of God* (Grand Rapids: Zondervan, 1974).

6. Textual variants found in D F G Ψ 𝔐 place the second question, "Am I not an apostle?" before the first. But the NA[28] text is well attested: 𝔓[46] B D F G 33 inter alia. It may be that some copyist felt the second question was the more important and so transposed the questions.

7. Fee, *1 Corinthians*, 436.

tions as real questions rather than simply as neutral but strong assertions. Secondly, the statement on apostleship is little different to the one in Romans 1:1 and other places where Paul affirms his own calling. Thirdly, while some Corinthians were arrogant (4:18), possibly against Paul specifically, Paul still called them "dearly loved children" (4:14) and seemed more concerned with their behavior than with their attitude to him. Finally, it is dubious, if Paul's authority as an apostle was an important issue between him and the Corinthians, that he would have waited until 9:1 to make the first clear statement of that fact. Each question, including this one, simply reaffirms his claim in 1:1 to be an apostle but now establishes that he therefore has certain rights. The questions assume that the assertions are unremarkable and to be taken as a given. The third question reminds the readers that he had seen the Lord (cf. 1 Cor 15:8) and so met an early criterion required by the apostles when they replaced Judas (Acts 1:22; 2:32).[8] He is likely to be recalling his encounter with the risen Lord on the road to Damascus (Acts 9:3–6).[9]

The final question in this series refers to the fact that he was the founder of the church in Corinth. This is reinforced by the assertion of v. 2 in which Paul makes it clear that he does not expect the Corinthians to take issue with his apostleship. Even if others might not see him as an apostle, the Corinthians surely will since their existence sets the seal on it. After all, they are the result of Paul's work of gospel proclamation. The word "seal" (σφραγίς) attests to something that is legally valid. It is a word that is used metaphorically of circumcision and Abraham's "righteousness by faith" in Romans 4:11 and there

legally attests to his membership in the covenant people. In 2 Timothy 2:19 it is used as an attestation of membership in God's people. Here Paul indicates that the existence of the Corinthian church attests to his apostleship. However, the seal is provided by the fact that all his work has been "in the Lord" (ἐν κυρίῳ). In fact, the conversion of the Corinthians has been the work of the Lord and has been brought about according to his will (1 Cor 1:4–8).

9:3 My defense to those who would evaluate me is this: (Ἡ ἐμὴ ἀπολογία τοῖς ἐμὲ ἀνακρίνουσίν ἐστιν αὕτη). While some have suggested this verse looks back to vv. 1–2,[10] it more likely looks forward to the following discussion. The use of legal words such as "defense" (ἀπολογία) and "evaluate" (ἀνακρίνω) reminds us that Paul has been speaking of the exercise of a person's legal rights. However, Paul has already criticized the Corinthians at length for not making adequate spiritual judgments (2:14–15; 4:3–4). In chapters 2–4 Paul had begun to apply the problem of judging and evaluating people to himself and to Apollos. Now he specifically asks them to "evaluate" or judge him. They need to evaluate his behavior as one who is an apostle. If they do, they will find it is thoroughly different from the sort of behavior in which they are engaged. Paul's main concern is that they should see that just as the exercise of an apostle's "rights" do not authenticate apostleship (he is an apostle whether he exercises his "rights" or not), so the exercise of certain other rights that the elitists claim to have do not authenticate those who are God's.

9:4–6 Do we not have a right to eat and drink? Do we not have a right to bring along a believing

---

8. In Gal 1:16, Paul also appeals to his eyewitness testimony.

9. See 1:1 for comments on "apostle." See Kim, *Origin of Paul's Gospel*, 7ff.; 55ff.

10. Among others, Fitzmyer, *1 Corinthians*, 357, and Robertson and Plummer, *First Corinthians*, 179, suggest it looks

backward to v. 2. The position of "this" (αὕτη) at the end of the sentence may point forward. However, the "evaluation" Paul refers to concerns not his apostleship but the use he makes of his "rights," and that is the topic he is about to address in the following verses.

wife as [do] the rest of the apostles and the brothers of the Lord and Cephas? Or is it I alone and Barnabas who have no right to refrain from working for a living? (μὴ οὐκ ἔχομεν ἐξουσίαν φαγεῖν καὶ πεῖν; μὴ οὐκ ἔχομεν ἐξουσίαν ἀδελφὴν γυναῖκα περιάγειν, ὡς καὶ οἱ λοιποὶ ἀπόστολοι καὶ οἱ ἀδελφοὶ τοῦ κυρίου καὶ Κηφᾶς; ἢ μόνος ἐγὼ καὶ Βαρναβᾶς οὐκ ἔχομεν ἐξουσίαν μὴ ἐργάζεσθαι;). A lengthy illustration from Paul's own life begins. "We" refers at first to the group of apostles who have "rights" but then specifically to Paul and Barnabas. The first "right" (ἐξουσία)[11] or what perhaps could be called "entitlement" to which Paul refers is that of financial or material support as apostles conduct their ministry. It is introduced with another series of three rhetorical questions that provide evidence for the case Paul is building. The points made by the questions are assumed to be obvious to the readers, and the double negative makes them seem even stronger (μὴ οὐκ). *Of course they are entitled to these things. Of course Paul and Barnabas are not to be excepted from this right.* Paul is not saying anything controversial. The rhetoric serves once again simply to assert positively the nature of the entitlements and the fact that all the people in the group have these rights. The appeal to Peter ("Cephas") by name may reflect the fact that he was well known to them (cf. 1:12).

The mention of eating and drinking in the first question reflects back on chapter 8 and the subject of food originally raised by the Corinthians themselves. They have tried to insist on their right to eat any food anywhere (ch. 8), a matter to which Paul

will return in chapter 10. So Paul talks of his apostolic rights regarding food, rights for which he will further argue in vv. 7–11 and vv. 12–14.

The second question concerns an apostle's right to take along a wife with him on his journeys. It would appear from the way the passage reads that neither Paul nor Barnabas had wives. Yet the point to be assumed, given the strength of the rhetorical questions, is this: apostles may expect not only to be supported themselves but also to receive material support for their wives. The phrase "believing wife" (ἀδελφὴν γυναῖκα) might be read as "sister wife" (cf. AV).[12] Most commentators assume that "sister" refers to being a Christian sister (cf. 7:15) and so qualifies "wife"; hence, "Christian wife " (TEV) or "believing wife" (most modern versions). It is most unlikely that Paul is here thinking back to his discussion in chapters 5–7 of sexual relationships with spouses.[13] That would introduce a subject well out of line with the rest of this section. Rather, he is simply making the point that *if* an apostle is accompanied by a wife, they are both entitled to food and financial support for their needs. This reference provides an interesting passing insight into the fact that couples were involved together in missionary work from earliest times and that at least some couples were receiving material support.

It is unlikely that "the brothers of the Lord" (ἀδελφοὶ τοῦ κυρίου) were a separate category of church leadership from the apostles. But it does raise the question as to whether Paul is here using the term "apostle" (ἀπόστολος) as a more general description of the better known early missionar-

---

11. Hans Lietzmann, *An Die Korinther I–II*, 4th ed., HNT 9 (Tübingen: Mohr Siebeck, 1949), 40, does not sufficiently allow for the progression in Paul's argument when he translates "right" here and in vv. 5, 6, and 12 as "freedom" ("Freiheit"). "Freedom" in the first rhetorical question (v. 1) reflects the choice that Paul has in exercising his right (ἐξουσία). "Freedom" and "right" are not the same thing. In v. 19 he rightly translates as "right" ("Recht").

12. It has been suggested by some early commentators (e.g., Tertullian, *Monogamy* 8; Jerome, *Jov.* 1.26), possibly influenced by the growing commitment to celibacy among priests, and by one or two more recent scholars (cf. Allo, *Première Épître aux Corinthiens*, 214) that the woman in question was perhaps a deaconess or female apostolic assistant.

13. *Contra* Ciampa and Rosner, *First Corinthians*, 401.

ies ("messengers") or in its more technical sense of the Twelve plus one or two. In Mark 6:3 James, Joseph, Judas, and Simon are mentioned as the Lord's brothers. In Galatians 1:9 James is named by Paul as "the Lord's brother" and apparently referred to as one of the apostles. Since Paul has already referred to his having "seen Jesus our Lord" (v. 1), it is likely that the Lord's brothers were generally granted the same sort of status in the early church as the apostles chosen by the Lord, though there is no way of being certain of this. However, the mention of these people, all of whom knew the Lord, is a reminder that Paul was probably well aware of the Lord's own teaching on the matter he now addressed. In Matthew 10 the Twelve are sent out by Jesus. They are told not to take provisions "for," says Jesus, "the laborer deserves his food" (v. 10 ESV).[14]

The final question insists that Paul and Barnabas do, like the rest of the apostles, have the entitlement to receive material support rather than having to earn their own living while preaching the gospel. The choice of Barnabas is significant. It was he who had introduced Paul to the apostles and vouched for the fact that he had "seen the Lord" (Acts 9:27), and who had sought out Paul in Tarsus to bring him to Antioch (11:25–26). He also accompanied Paul on missionary journeys. Perhaps even more significantly in terms of relinquishing "rights," Barnabas had earlier been prepared to sell property for the sake of the church (4:36–37).

9:7 Who serves as a soldier at his own expense? Who plants a vineyard and does not eat its fruit? Or who tends a flock and does not drink the flock's milk?

(τίς στρατεύεται ἰδίοις ὀψωνίοις ποτέ; τίς φυτεύει ἀμπελῶνα καὶ τὸν καρπὸν αὐτοῦ οὐκ ἐσθίει; ἢ τίς ποιμαίνει ποίμνην καὶ ἐκ τοῦ γάλακτος τῆς ποίμνης οὐκ ἐσθίει;). Having shown that he is due the same rights that belong to the other apostles, Paul broadens the discussion with three further rhetorical questions that provide brief illustrations of the same principle for which he has been arguing but which are applied to other groups of people.[15] Paul continues to think about food here rather than specifically about wages. But he thinks also about a person's activity in pursuing their calling. Thus, he does not talk of a soldier or a shepherd or a vinedresser, but of one who engages in these activities. One who goes to war is not expected to provide his own food[16] as he serves in an army. One who plants a vineyard will eat some of its fruit, and one who shepherds sheep will take for himself ("eat"; ἐσθίω) some of the sheep's milk. Each of these callings has a deep biblical background. Though it may not be uppermost in Paul's mind here, his readers must have noted that Paul had already written of his "planting" the field as one of "God's fellow workers" (3:6–9). The more general point about certain activities entitling those involved to certain privileges reinforces the specific point that apostles also have certain entitlements to provisions for their work. Paul has given three common and well-understood examples or illustrations of the link between certain activities and the entitlements that normally pertain to them. Yet

---

14. Though Paul does not employ a saying of the Lord here, the overlap in ideas and vocabulary between Luke 10, Matt 10, and 1 Cor 9 suggests Paul was probably aware of the Lord's teaching. Jesus speaks to the disciples of their authority or right (ἐξουσία; Matt 10:1; Luke 10:19) but also speaks of them "eating [ἐσθίω] and drinking [πίνω] what [the hosts] provide, for the laborer deserves his wages [μισθός]" (Luke 10:7 ESV). For a more detailed discussion, see Biörn Fjärstedt, *Synoptic Tradition in 1 Corinthians: Themes and Clusters of Theme Words in*

1 Corinthians 1–4 and 9 (Uppsala: Rotobeckman, 1974); also Peter J. Tomson, *Paul and the Jewish Law: Halakha in the Letters of the Apostle to the Gentiles*, CRINT (Assen: Van Gorcum/ Minneapolis: Fortress, 1990), 125–31.

15. On the possible Stoic-Cynic and rabbinic traditions lying behind these particular illustrations, see Tomson, *Paul and the Jewish Law*, 126.

16. The term ὀψώνιον can mean wages but also "provisions" (LSJ; also Thayer, *Greek-English Lexicon*, 471).

Paul does not leave it here, for he now adduces biblical support to affirm that this is truly a legal right, drawing on the Mosaic law.

9:8 I am not saying these things from a human perspective, am I? Does not the law also say these things? (Μὴ κατὰ ἄνθρωπον ταῦτα λαλῶ, ἢ καὶ ὁ νόμος ταῦτα οὐ λέγει;). Paul now appeals to the law to make his point. This rhetorical question would normally expect the answer "no"; hence the attempt to capture this in the translation here. However, the question again simply serves as a positive assertion: *I'm not just speaking these things from a human standpoint!* The phrase "from a human perspective" (lit., "according to man"; κατὰ ἄνθρωπον) also appears in 3:3 where it has a negative connotation. Here it is a neutral statement. Paul has just defended his rights by means of an appeal to three human occupations. Now he goes further in making the same point. Though Paul can sometimes use "the law" to speak broadly of parts of Scripture, in the following verse it becomes clear that he refers to the "law of Moses," the Torah, as he quotes from Deuteronomy 25:4.

9:9 For it is written in the law of Moses, "You shall not muzzle an ox while it threshes the grain." Is it for oxen that God is concerned? (ἐν γὰρ τῷ Μωϋσέως νόμῳ γέγραπται, Οὐ κημώσεις βοῦν ἀλοῶντα. μὴ τῶν βοῶν μέλει τῷ θεῷ). The point of this quotation is clear. It is simply that an ox involved in pulling around the great stone that mills the grain should not be muzzled in a way that does not allow it to eat some of it as it labors. Since God is surely not "concerned"[17] with oxen (the question expects a negative answer) but rather with humans, then it is reasonable to see it as legal proof (because it is in the law) that an apostle should not be unreasonably hindered from receiving provisions as he carries out his work.[18] However, the use Paul makes of this verse and what he goes on to write in 9:10 has led to much discussion.

9:10 Indeed,[19] does he not by all means speak for our sake? Yes,[20] it was written for our sake, because the one who ploughs ought to plough in hope and the one who threshes in hope of partaking [of the crop]. (ἢ δι᾽ ἡμᾶς πάντως λέγει; δι᾽ ἡμᾶς γὰρ ἐγράφη, ὅτι ὀφείλει ἐπ᾽ ἐλπίδι ὁ ἀροτριῶν ἀροτριᾶν, καὶ ὁ ἀλοῶν ἐπ᾽ ἐλπίδι τοῦ μετέχειν). With strong emphasis Paul insists that "by all means" (πάντως)[21] Moses wrote "for our sake" (δι᾽ ἡμᾶς). Paul applies the quotation to the apostles[22]

---

17. This is a gnomic present used of a timeless fact or in proverbial statements (Wallace, *Greek Grammar*, 523–24).

18. Paul quotes this verse on one other occasion at 1 Tim 5:18. There he links it directly with the quotation, "The laborer deserves his wages." In the context, this qualifies Paul's comment that elders who rule well, especially those who labor in teaching and preaching, are worthy of double honor (τιμή). Given this context and this quotation, it is surely right to suggest that Paul meant "double wages" rather than "double honor"!

19. The context alone can indicate the meaning of the particle ἤ, which is not always easy to translate. It can mean "or" as a disjunction between clauses. It can also simply function as a separator between clauses, in which case it will often not be translated into English. However, it is also often used "to introduce and to add rhetorical questions" (BDAG 432). In 9:7 it is used with an interrogative after a previous interrogative sentence where it need not be translated. In 9:15 it is used as part

of a comparative construction: "I would rather die than . . . ," Cf. Matt 10:15; 1 Cor 14:19. Here in 9:10, it may function adverbially and so may be translated as "truly" or even "indeed" (BDAG 433); this is made more likely given the emphatic "by all means" (πάντως).

20. The word γάρ is used on occasion to affirm an answer to a question. Cf. 1 Thess 2:20. See BDF §452.2.

21. The ESV has "certainly," and the NIV "surely."

22. This assumes the first plural "we" is exclusive, relating only to the apostles whose rights Paul is seeking to establish, *contra* Conzelmann, *1 Corinthians*, 155. See Wallace, *Beyond Basics*, 398. The phrase "for us" or "for our sake" could possibly mean "for all human beings like us" as opposed to oxen. However, the second occurrence of the phrase and its application to the one who ploughs suggests it refers to the apostles around whom Paul's argument has been established. The "we" of v. 11 may in fact be even more exclusive and refer only to Barnabas and Paul.

and their rights. However, several questions immediately present themselves. Is this a legitimate use of Scripture? Is Paul arbitrarily employing a text as a "proof text"? Is he allegorizing the law in a fashion similar to Philo, as some commentators suggest? In the light of the oft-repeated claims that God cares for all his creation (e.g., Gen 1:24; Ps 50:10–11; Luke 12:6), can Paul truly mean that God is not concerned for oxen?

Lietzmann and others suggest that Paul's use of this quotation is similar to the sort of allegorizing found in Philo.[23] Conzelmann, followed by Senft, explains, "God's concern is with higher things" leading to the detail of the law being "allegorically expounded."[24] Philo's comment is cited by several: "For the law does not prescribe for unreasoning creatures, but for those who have mind and reason."[25] Another group of commentators suggests that Paul is using the text in a more "real" way but in rabbinic style, arguing from the lesser to the greater: *if this is true of oxen how much more so of humans.* In this case the text on the ox is used as an analogy.[26]

Paul's use of the Old Testament often provokes questions of this sort, and it is always good to start by looking at the original context in the Old Testament of the verse quoted since frequently this can help explain why he chose the passage. The context for Deuteronomy 25:4 has to do with the way in which men and women are treated. It especially has to do with the care of certain people. To go back no further than 24:14, the passage first speaks to the need to pay workers what they are due. Workers must not be oppressed, and wages must be paid on the day they are due (24:14–15). Only the sinner himself should be punished for a crime, not the children or other relatives (24:16). The widow and sojourner are to be cared for appropriately in terms of justice (24:17–18) but also with the principle of gleaning firmly established in the fact that the fields are not to be fully stripped of their harvest (24:19–22). Justice is to be compassionate and clear with no person's punishment to degrade them in the sight of others (25:1–3). In 25:5–10 the rights of a widow are established with the laws of levirate marriage. Clearly then, at face value 25:4, which speaks apparently of the rights of an ox, is somewhat incongruent! This suggests that even in its original context it served as an illustration of the justice and fairness with which humans were to be treated rather than specifically of the matter of the treatment of oxen! In fact, this is the way most Jewish exegesis spoke of it.[27] As an illustration of this sort it serves both as a statement about the treatment of an ox as it labors, yet it is legitimately and contextually used by Paul as referring to people.

The second part of v. 10 is not a quotation. The word ὅτι is not recitative, and there is no Scripture that might have given rise to a quotation. However, Instone-Brewer notes that "this is almost a paraphrase of *m.B.Mes.* 7.2: 'These may eat [of the crop in which they labour] by virtue of what is enjoined in the Law: he who labours on what is still growing after the work is finished [ie. from ploughing to reaping], and he who labours on what is already gathered before the work is finished

---

23. Lietzmann, *An Die Korinther I–II,* 41, cites numerous examples from Philo. For a detailed review of the different positions commentators have taken on what Paul is doing here with this quotation, see David Instone-Brewer, "1 Corinthians 9:9–11: A Literal Interpretation of 'Do Not Muzzle the Ox,'" *NTS* 38 (1992): 554–65.

24. Conzelmann, *1 Corinthians,* 154–55, and Senft, *Première Épître de Saint Paul aux Corinthiens,* 119.

25. Philo, *Spec. Laws* 1.260 (Colson, LCL).

26. For a detailed presentation of the rabbinic material, see Anthony T. Hanson, *Studies in Paul's Technique and Theology* (London: SPCK, 1974), 162–66. "All this evidence goes to show that Deut. 25.4 was a very familiar text with the rabbis . . . it was very freely applied in an analogical sense, though no rabbi suggests that the literal meaning can be ignored."

27. See Tomson, *Paul and the Jewish Law,* 127n160, 129.

[i.e. threshing].'"[28] Nevertheless, it is speculative to suggest that it "seems likely that Paul had this specific Mishnah in mind." Rather, with rhetorical precision, Paul moves from the matter of the grain raised by the quotation to explaining how it can be said that this is written "for our sake." It is "because" (ὅτι) anyone who ploughs must plough with real hope of a harvest, given that they cannot be sure of the harvest, and thresh with the hope of receiving a share of the end product. Thus, Paul makes his point yet again. A person working with grain, sowing it and then threshing it, will expect to enjoy the fruit of their hands. It is now a minor matter, as Smit says, to switch "to agricultural laborers in the figurative sense" for "finally this brings [Paul] to the preachers of the gospel, some of whom . . . have sown, while others have only threshed."[29] The Corinthian elitists are to see that Paul had hope in planting (3:6–9) and so has a right to share in the fruit of the work, which includes material support.

Though raising a number of exegetical issues and interpretative questions, the place of vv. 9–10 is now clear in Paul's discussion of his "right" as an apostle to material support. The law supports Paul and all that he has argued with the rhetorical questions of v. 7. He is entitled to such support. The law speaks to Paul's generation and to gospel preachers. Moving on from the ox to the people who produce the crop that eventually must be threshed, Paul adds that these also clearly wait for a share of the threshed grain. He has now most carefully set up the next part of his argument, namely, that he has sown and so he too can rightly expect to share in what is reaped.

9:11–12b If we have sown spiritual things among you, is it too much that we reap material things

among you? If others partake of the rights you [give them], should not we even more? (εἰ ἡμεῖς ὑμῖν τὰ πνευματικὰ ἐσπείραμεν, μέγα εἰ ἡμεῖς ὑμῶν τὰ σαρκικὰ θερίσομεν; Εἰ ἄλλοι τῆς ὑμῶν ἐξουσίας μετέχουσιν, οὐ μᾶλλον ἡμεῖς;). Paul has talked of his ministry in Corinth as "planting" (3:5–8) and will refer to conversions as the fruit when he speaks of the "household of Stephanas" being the "firstfruits" of the work in Achaia (16:15). So truly, Paul has sown "spiritual things" (τὰ πνευματικὰ) among them as he preached the gospel and imparted wisdom that focused on the crucified Christ. Paul's use of the word "spiritual" (πνευματικός) was examined in 2:13. There we suggested that it referred to that which was revealed by the Spirit and always pointed to Christ. Here, Paul simply has in mind what he summarizes at the end of v. 12 as "the gospel of Christ." The "material things" (τὰ σαρκικά) are not to be viewed in any dualistic way. Rather, they are simply material benefits flowing from those who have come to faith in Christ.[30]

Paul employs yet another rhetorical question to make this point, though this time it is in a conditional form and contains more than a hint of irony as the apodosis begins: "Is it *too much* . . ." (μέγα). Thiselton interprets this well in modern idiom: "Is it any Big Deal if we reap . . . ."[31] The reader is left feeling some amazement that these two matters, "spiritual things" and "material things," should even be compared at all! As Paul returns to the first-person plural, he drives home the fact that he certainly deserves his apostolic right of financial and material provision for the work he does.

The conditional clause presumably refers to an actual situation so, interestingly, while Paul argues for apostolic rights, he now acknowledges

---

28. Instone-Brewer, "1 Corinthians 9:9–11," 558.

29. Smit, *About the Idol Offerings*. See also John P. Heil, *The Rhetorical Role of Scripture in 1 Corinthians*, SBLMS 15 (Atlanta: SBL Press, 2005), 139.

30. Cf. Rom 15:27 where the sharing in spiritual things ["spiritual blessings"; NRSV] elicits the duty of being of service to others in material things.

31. *1 Corinthians*, 688.

that the Corinthians have already granted a certain right of financial help to "others" (ἄλλοι). In agreement with Thiselton, Héring, and Robertson and Plummer the genitive (ὑμῶν) is taken as subjective, and hence the translation of the clause, "partake of the rights you [give them]" (τῆς ὑμῶν ἐξουσίας μετέχουσιν).[32] Since the rights others have exercised are more likely to be associated with issues of power and patronage (see below), the exact opposite of what Paul has been arguing for, the objective genitive is less likely. The NRSV takes it as objective: "If others share this rightful claim on you, do not we still more?" But Paul does not say "this," and there is no reason to suggest that Paul, who is claiming a God-ordained right for apostles (vv. 9–10), should see the rights of others "over the Corinthians" as anything like what he is asking for. The last thing on Paul's mind is exercising some authority "over" them. The point of comparison is simply that the Corinthians do not appear to have refused financial help for "others."

Who the "others" are whom Paul believes have already been granted some "right" to financial help from the Corinthians is unclear. They may well be the leaders of the factions mentioned in chapter 1. Garland suggests Apollos may be one of the others, since he is the one who "waters" the work that Paul planted and is mentioned by Paul as also being a "fellow worker" who will "receive [his] own wage" for his labor (3:5–9).[33] However, it is at least possible that some wealthy members held power in the church through patronage, thus providing income for the leaders they preferred. Paul has made it clear that such patronage is unacceptable to him

(1:12–14). He does not want this support on the grounds of status as a leader nor on the grounds of patronage, but for the sake of the gospel and because the fruit of the gospel is already being reaped in Corinth.

9:12c–f Nevertheless, we have not made use of this right[34], but rather we put up with all things, lest we put a stumbling block in the way of the gospel of Christ (Ἀλλ' οὐκ ἐχρησάμεθα τῇ ἐξουσίᾳ ταύτῃ, ἀλλὰ πάντα στέγομεν ἵνα μή τινα ἐγκοπὴν δῶμεν τῷ εὐαγγελίῳ τοῦ Χριστοῦ). Paul now moves on to show that the gospel must be presented "free of charge." This has led him to relinquish his rights to financial support (vv. 12c–15). It then moves him to point to the "compulsion" he has to preach (vv. 16–18). "Nevertheless" (ἀλλά) forms a strong contrast with what has gone before. Having spent verses establishing the apostolic "right" to support, Paul now states in advance the conclusion to his argument and, in doing so, reveals exactly how this whole section directly continues to address the subject raised in chapter 8. Paul has been and always will be determined that nothing at all should get in the way of the gospel of Christ, and if this apostolic "right" to financial assistance should do so, he will never take up his entitlement. Thus, the Corinthians must learn that if they have so-called "rights," theirs too are always to be subordinated to the gospel of Christ. In vv. 13–14 Paul briefly returns to a further example in support of his own "right" before developing at length (vv. 15–23) the application of his conclusion in terms of how he subdues every claim he may have for the sake of winning some for Christ.

---

32. Fee, *1 Corinthians*, 453, argues, with many, that it is objective. Thiselton's response to Fee is significant (*1 Corinthians*, 690).

33. Chow, *Patronage and Power*, 173, writes: "It looks likely that [there] were those in the church who provided material support for other apostles (1 Cor. 9.12a), that is, the rich pa-

trons who had money to spend on their inferiors"; see also his comments on pp. 107–9. See also Clarke, *Secular and Christian Leadership in Corinth*, 31–32, 125, 133.

34. Note the verb χράομαι used here and in v. 15 takes the dative. Robertson, *Grammar of the Greek New Testament*, 532–33.

The idea of "putting up with" (στέγω)[35] reminds the reader that Paul's refusal to exercise his rights carries with it a cost (cf. 13:7a: "Love puts up with all things"). He will suffer ignominy and perhaps even hunger and lack of good clothing, but none of this matters when placed alongside the call of God to preach the gospel (see 1:17) and win people for Christ (see below). This offers a stark contrast with the elitists, who were not prepared to give up rights and so ran the danger of "sinning against" their brothers and sisters and even seeing them "destroyed" (8:8–12). In using the word "stumbling block" (ἐγκοπή) to refer to an obstacle placed in the way of the person understanding the gospel and its implications, Paul makes a further direct link back to chapter 8.[36] This apostolic "right" is something he has refused to exercise because of "the gospel of Christ" so that no stumbling block is placed in peoples' way. The elitists should imitate him.

9:13 Do you not know that those employed in temple duties eat from the temple food, and those serving at the altar share together in [food from] the altar? (Οὐκ οἴδατε ὅτι οἱ τὰ ἱερὰ ἐργαζόμενοι [τὰ] ἐκ τοῦ ἱεροῦ ἐσθίουσιν, οἱ τῷ θυσιαστηρίῳ παρεδρεύοντες τῷ θυσιαστηρίῳ συμμερίζονται;). Verses 13–14 seem almost to be an afterthought as Paul returns to illustrate the fact that apostles have this "right" of support. Yet it is important to remember the care with which Paul has penned this whole section from 8:1–11:1. As a master rhetorician Paul has given his conclusion before providing two final and most powerful examples. In the first example of priests eating the food from temple sacrifices he probably thinks of this as further biblical evidence establishing his point (v. 13). But it is the second example that carries the final authority for all that he is saying: the words of Jesus (v. 14). Paul's argument is long and detailed but builds in power. The strongest authority for Paul's insistence that the apostles have "rights" to support is reserved till last. Jesus himself had spoken of the matter. It is important also to remember that the rhetoric of this larger section of text is leading toward the recapitulation of the injunction, "Be imitators of me as I am of Christ" (11:1; cf. 4:16).

In the Old Testament, as they sacrificed the offerings brought by the people, the priests were allowed to eat some of the grain offerings and even parts of the animal sacrifices (Lev 6:14–18; 10:14).[37] This was probably true in the pagan temples as well.[38] (On "do you not know . . . ?" see 3:16.) This appeal to temple practice could have been little more than a truism in the age in which Paul was writing. The second sentence in this compound sentence probably explains the first. The idea of "sharing together in [food from] the altar" (τῷ θυσιαστηρίῳ συμμερίζονται) also serves to help set up Paul's later discussion in 10:18. Once again the rhetorical question functions as a clear assertion of fact and assumes the reader must agree: temple priests can partake of the food offered in sacrifices.

---

35. The verb "to put up with" (στέγω) can be translated "endure." The meaning would be the same. However, in 13:7 a virtually synonymous word meaning "endure" (ὑπομένω) is used side by side with this word. See comments on 13:7 for details. To demonstrate the clear link in Paul's thinking between 9:12b and what he says in 13:7, we have translated στέγω as "to put up with" in both places, thus allowing us to use the word "endure" for ὑπομένω.

36. The themes of the "stumbling block," "scandal," or "cause of stumbling" were examined in detail at 8:13. Also see, "In

Depth: The Theme of Stumbling," following comments on 1:23.

37. The proximity of the words θυσιαστήριον and μερίς in LXX Lev 6:7–10 makes it possible that Paul has these verses in mind.

38. The fact that the verb "to serve [as a priest]" (παρεδρεύω) is a hapax legomenon in the NT and is not found in the LXX with reference to serving priests (though cf. Prov 1:21; 8:3), yet does appear in secular writings regarding pagan offerings is not conclusive in determining that Paul is thinking of pagan priests.

9:14 And likewise the Lord commanded that those preaching the gospel should live by the gospel (οὕτως καὶ ὁ κύριος διέταξεν τοῖς τὸ εὐαγγέλιον καταγγέλλουσιν ἐκ τοῦ εὐαγγελίου ζῆν). Paul's final and decisive authority for his "right" to financial support as an apostle is to be found in the words of the Lord Jesus himself. By saying "And likewise" (οὕτως καὶ) Paul may mean that the same thing can be learned from Jesus's words as from the practice seen in the occupations mentioned above, the law of Moses, and the way temple priests get their living. However, given that it is the climax of Paul's argument, the phrase may be rather more significant. If Paul sees his previous example as *God* ordering the way the priests manage their life (drawing on God's commands in Leviticus), then it is *in the same way* that Jesus orders the life of those who preach the gospel. God speaks, then Jesus speaks with the same conclusive authority. Either way, the two final references of vv. 13–14 are both based on the highest possible authority.

Paul writes, "The Lord *commanded*" (ὁ κύριος διέταξεν). In all the previous examples and illustrations, parallels are to be drawn and lessons learned that justify Paul's insistence that as an apostle he has "rights." Now, however, Paul concludes by insisting this is also about *obedience*. The word translated "commanded" (διατάσσω) can mean to "direct" or "order" and is used frequently of soldiers giving instructions or putting things in order. In Acts 18:2 it is used of Claudius "ordering" the Jews to leave Rome (RSV: "commanded"). Paul does not quote Jesus's words here, but many dominical sayings would have served to guide the common life and belief of the early church, and this was no doubt one of them. The closest the Gospel texts come to such a command from Jesus is found in Mark 6

and its approximate parallels in Matthew 10 and Luke 9 and 10. Jesus's orders are included in those given to the Twelve (Mark 6:7; Matt 10:5; Luke 9:1) or to the Seventy-Two (Luke 10:1) as they are sent out on their mission. Two aspects of Jesus's instruction become evident, and Paul makes use of both in his writing. The first aspect is that the disciples are told to "acquire no gold or silver or copper for your belts, no bag for your journey, or two tunics or sandals or a staff, *for the laborer deserves his food.*" (Matt 10:9–10 ESV) The second aspect is that the people are expected to provide room and board for those who preach the gospel: "Remain in the same house, *eating and drinking what they provide*, for the laborer deserves his wages; do not go from house to house. Whenever you enter a town and they receive you, eat what is set before you" (Luke 10:7–8 RSV; cf. 9:4).

Though Paul appeals to these instructions of the Lord, at first sight it seems that in his practice he chooses to disobey them. After all, he makes an issue of the fact that he is *not* taking Corinthian support. But that is to misunderstand the way Paul is arguing. As Fee so clearly notes, "As 'command' the word of Jesus referred to here does not have to do with *his* (Paul's) action but *theirs*. . . . The command is not given *to* missionaries but *for* their benefit."[39]

9:15 But I have not used any of these things. And I am not writing[40] these things so that this might thus happen to me; for it would be better for me to die than—no one will make empty my boast (Ἐγὼ δὲ οὐ κέχρημαι οὐδενὶ τούτων. Οὐκ ἔγραψα δὲ ταῦτα ἵνα οὕτως γένηται ἐν ἐμοί, καλὸν γάρ μοι μᾶλλον ἀποθανεῖν ἤ—τὸ καύχημά μου οὐδεὶς κενώσει). In v. 15 Paul reaches the climax of his

---

39. Fee, *1 Corinthians*, 456n280. In this note he takes issue with Dungan, who at length argues that Paul deliberately set aside a clear command from the Lord.

40. An epistolary aorist translated as present.

discussion and a turning point in his argument as he says, "But I have not used any of these things." Paul has "rights" to financial support that are fully established. He can now make his simple but profound point: he has not exercised *any* of his rightful entitlements. The sentence is made more emphatic as he returns to the first singular (last used in vv. 1–3) and uses two negative forms, "not . . . none" (οὐ and οὐδενί). The perfect tense (κέχρημαι) indicates that Paul continues to operate in this way. "These things" (ταῦτα) refers to his whole preceding argument establishing his right. At this point, Paul's writing becomes more complex and abbreviated in its language. Thus, Paul returns to his earlier undeveloped conclusion in v. 12.

The purpose clause indicates what Paul is *not* hoping will happen (γίνομαι—to "happen" or "to come into being")! He is not writing to ensure he receives his rights. Exactly the opposite. He is offering himself as an example of one who gives the gospel absolute priority as he lives his life. The next clause is the first of five that begin with the word "for" or "because," each amplifying the previous sentence.

The reason he is not writing to secure provision is "because he would rather die than . . ." (γάρ μοι μᾶλλον ἀποθανεῖν ἤ . . .). As this highly emotional climax is reached, Paul fails to complete the comparison. Here the reader is left to fill in the blank. Given the judgment "woe" of v. 16 and the whole of this context, we may legitimately speculate that Paul might have said, "I would rather die than place a stumbling block in the way of the gospel . . . woe to me if I do not preach the gospel." In context, this seems to make best sense of Paul's argument as a whole. Alternatively—and also speculatively—several translations simply force the comparison to link up with the next sentence about Paul's boast-

ing. Thus, for example, the RSV reads: "For I would rather die than have any one deprive me of my ground for boasting."

The fact that Paul might have gone on to speak of the gospel in this unfinished comparison is given weight by what he *does* say. He insists that no one will take away his "boast." It is important to note here that he assumes that if he were to receive payment this would remove his boast. In other words, in his relationship with this congregation, in which power plays were all too evident amid bad theology and unhelpful patronage, taking money would remove his boast. That is, taking money would impede the gospel.

Furthermore, it must be remembered that *his* boast is solely "in the Lord." In 1:29–31 Paul introduced the idea of "boasting," which some translate as "glorying" (see discussion of 1:29–31 above).[41] By way of background it was noted that under the influence of the Sophists it was likely that Greco-Roman society saw boasting as something rather distasteful. But we also noted how Paul went further than the Sophists by suggesting that the trouble with *all people* "before God" is their tendency to promote their own accomplishments and achievements. Drawing on the Old Testament, however, Paul had turned this idea around. There could be no boasting in what humans achieved or in their wisdom. Nevertheless, *there was a good boast*, summarized in the quotation derived from Jeremiah 9:24 (9:23 LXX), "Let the one who boasts, boast in the Lord." In the LXX, approval is given to boasting that arises out of a loving response to a gracious God. Therefore, it is unsurprising that Scripture encourages people to boast in God himself or in his "name." An example of how this works can be found in Deuteronomy 10 where we read that the Lord requires love of his people. They are

---

41. In that discussion, we point to the links to Paul's talk of boasting in various parts of 2 Corinthians.

to "circumcise [their] hearts" (v. 16), and because he made them a nation, God is to be their "boast" (v. 21 AT; LXX: καύχημα). Psalm 89:17 (88:17 LXX) offers another example of the use of the word in the way Paul is prepared to use it: "For you are the boast [καύχημα] of their strength."

When Paul speaks of his boast, therefore, he is making two points both here and in chapter 1. Firstly, Paul deliberately contrasts what *he* wants to boast in with what the elitists have been boasting in with their arrogant words and behavior. They have been boasting in outward wisdom and spiritual gifts. This sort of boasting is condemned in Jeremiah 9 and by Paul. Secondly, in expounding upon his own "boast," which is in the Lord and in a God-centered grace revealed in Christ crucified, he points to his total dependence on Christ. Paul's boast arises not from his brilliant gospel preaching or his wisdom but simply from his love for the one who had died for them.

9:16–17 For though I preach the gospel, I have nothing to boast in. For I am under compulsion. For woe to me if I do not preach the gospel! For if I accomplish this of my own initiative, I have a reward; but if not of my own initiative, I have [simply] been entrusted with a stewardship (ἐὰν γὰρ εὐαγγελίζωμαι, οὐκ ἔστιν μοι καύχημα· ἀνάγκη γάρ μοι ἐπίκειται· οὐαὶ γάρ μοί ἐστιν ἐὰν μὴ εὐαγγελίσωμαι. εἰ γὰρ ἑκὼν τοῦτο πράσσω, μισθὸν ἔχω· εἰ δὲ ἄκων, οἰκονομίαν πεπίστευμαι). These four sentences begin with "for" and thus amplify

the previous sentence. The two third-class conditions give rise to the subjunctives. Even Paul's evangelizing,[42] fruitful as it has been in Corinth, does not provide him with anything in which to boast, and the reason for this (the third "for") is the Lord. Paul says he is "under compulsion," by which he means that God has called him and imposed on him this duty. It is so much a divine obligation that he describes the horror of possible judgment should he not fulfill his obligation to preach.

This talk of "compulsion" (ἀνάγκη) has provoked much discussion.[43] In effect Paul says he does not have a choice in the matter. If he does have a choice (v. 17), that is, if he does this through his own initiative (ἑκών),[44] then he already has his reward. If it is *Paul* who has done something, then he could boast of what he has done. If it is not of his own initiative (ἄκων), then he can claim no more than that this is a "stewardship" (οἰκονομία) entrusted to him by God. In this latter case the only boast would therefore be in the Lord. As Barrett indicates, Paul probably viewed his own apostolic calling and the compulsion and duty to preach as similar to the calling of a prophet (cf. Jer 20:9; Amos 3:8: "The Sovereign LORD has spoken—who can but prophesy?").

It is highly likely that Paul uses the word "woe" (οὐαί) in v. 16 in an eschatological sense (see examples in Jer 23:1; Zech 11:17; Luke 6:26). Because of this compulsion from God, Paul sees himself in danger of God's judgment should he not fulfill his calling. He always has before him the goal and the

---

42. "Preach the gospel" could be translated as "evangelize," the English word derived directly from the verb used here (εὐαγγελίζω).

43. Ernst Käsemann succinctly summarizes the different positions taken on this subject ("A Pauline Version of the 'Amor Fati,'" in *New Testament Questions of Today* [Philadelphia: Fortress, 1969], 217–35).

44. For a detailed examination of the words ἑκών and ἄκων, see Gardner, *Gifts of God*, 91–93. They are sometimes translated as "willingly" and "unwillingly" or "voluntarily" and "in-

voluntarily." Even though Paul saw his preaching as a divine necessity or "compulsion" (ἀνάγκη), he would never have said he was "unwilling" to preach the gospel. Far from it! He has a clear passion for this calling. Nor does he do it "involuntarily," as if he were being forced to do something he did not want to. It is for this reason that we have translated the words as "of [his] own initiative" and "not of [his] own initiative." So Margaret E. Thrall, *Corinthians I and II*, CBC (Cambridge: Cambridge University Press, 1965), 69. Cf. Byron, *Slavery Metaphors*, 252–53.

prize (vv. 24–27), and his determination is that he should not be disqualified. As a steward or servant to whom a great commission has been "entrusted" (πεπίστευμαι),[45] Paul knows he will be held accountable by his Master.

9:18 So what is my reward? That in preaching I may make the gospel free of charge, with the result that I do not make use of my right in the gospel (τίς οὖν μού ἐστιν ὁ μισθός; ἵνα εὐαγγελιζόμενος ἀδάπανον θήσω τὸ εὐαγγέλιον, εἰς τὸ μὴ καταχρήσασθαι τῇ ἐξουσίᾳ μου ἐν τῷ εὐαγγελίῳ). This verse fills out the argument of the previous two verses in a manner that draws the section to a close. If the reward for preaching is not to be found in the immediate praise of men and women for the apostle's great initiative and brilliance in delivery, then where is it to be found? Paul's response is that his reward lies (for now) simply in seeing the gospel of Christ crucified being received by all people "free of charge" (ἀδάπανος), for this is the commission that he fulfills as the Lord's steward, who makes himself a slave "to all" (v. 19). No one must have to pay to receive the message or to jump through certain hoops to receive it. They cannot and must not be compelled to believe the same as the elitists.

For Paul, presenting the gospel free of charge is itself, in one sense, a reward that he receives now in the present. It lies in the joy that comes in fulfilling the task he has been given. However, this can hardly be all that Paul means, for he has already told the reader where the true reward lies for the one who builds on the foundation of Christ. It lies in the future when "the Day will disclose it" (3:13).

Only then will a "wage" or "reward" (μισθός) be given (3:8, 14 where future tenses are used).[46]

Paul's understanding of rewards is similar to what is taught in Matthew 6:1–6, 16. There Jesus distinguished between the intentionally self-flaunting acts of the hypocrites and the quiet works of the righteous. The former "receive" (ἀπέχουσιν, present tense) their "reward" (μισθός), while the Father "will reward" (ἀποδώσει, future tense) the righteous. Just as the "woe" of v. 16 looked forward to the future, so Paul now shows that he anticipates "reward" rather than judgment (see again vv. 24–27).[47]

We must not lose sight of the fact that throughout this discussion Paul holds himself up as an example to the "knowers" who claim to have "rights" (see 11:1). Paul is one who has true "rights," as opposed to the so-called "rights" that the elitists claim. But even if their rights are granted, Paul has demonstrated the appropriate and godly attitude toward them. While he has clearly shown he has a right to financial provision "in the gospel," he will not "make use of [his] right" (καταχρήσασθαι). "In the gospel" likely means the right that is inherent in the role of gospel preaching.

9:19 For, being free from all, I have enslaved myself to all in order that I might win more (Ἐλεύθερος γὰρ ὢν ἐκ πάντων πᾶσιν ἐμαυτὸν ἐδούλωσα, ἵνα τοὺς πλείονας κερδήσω). As the passage moves into its next section (9:19–23), it is the word "free" that stands out with dramatic emphasis. Paul is "free" (ἐλεύθερος), and yet now he will demonstrate from personal examples how he has been prepared to relinquish this freedom and his "rights" so that more people may be won for Christ.

---

45. The perfect passive reminds us that this was a calling from God (perhaps Paul was thinking of the Damascus road experience) that continued to be worked out throughout his life.

46. See "In Depth: What Reward?" following comments on 3:15.

47. In v. 17 the present tense makes it clear that it is present rewards that are available to people who do things in their own power and of their own initiative. However, in v. 18 Paul subtly shifts the focus to his main goal, eschatological reward.

Since people come to faith through the preaching of the gospel, Paul uses examples of different groups of people he has worked among and for whom he has been prepared to sacrifice his rights. After the introduction in v. 19, which looks both backward and forward, Paul will talk specifically about his work among the Jews (v. 20), among the Gentiles (v. 21), and among the "weak" (v. 22). Verse 23 then reminds his readers of his purpose in relinquishing his rights. It is all "for the sake of the gospel."

Many translate the first clause as concessive: "Though I am free . . ." (Ἐλεύθερος γὰρ ὤν . . . ; e.g., NIV; ESV; NRSV). A participle can carry this meaning sometimes, but here the context suggests that it is a contemporaneous participle of time.[48] Paul *is* free. This means the main clause deliberately comes as a surprise. He is free yet has deliberately enslaved himself. The third clause gives the purpose or goal for this enslavement, which is to win more. The comparative (πλείονας) qualified by the article (τούς) suggests "the more" and so perhaps suggests the translation "to win as many as possible" (with the NIV; cf. TEV).

Slavery is of course tied into Paul's understanding of his "compulsion" (v. 16; ἀνάγκη). The slave is not free to do as he wishes, but Paul's slavery is deliberate. It is to the Lord, first, but therefore also to his calling to preach the gospel. He does this, as he has noted earlier in the epistle, in response to the love of God for him in Christ Jesus. It is a vision of God's grace that inspires Paul to understand his calling and to be passionate for it even though, as a slave, he will never be able to forsake it. Furthermore, it will take him on a route marked with pain and suffering (2 Cor 1:5–7). In many ways, as Paul will make clear in 11:1, what is seen in Paul is an imitation of Christ. Of Christ, Paul later wrote, "For you know the grace of our Lord

Jesus Christ, that though he was rich, yet for your sake he became poor, so that you by his poverty might become rich" (2 Cor 8:9 ESV). So when Paul says he is free "from all" (ἐκ πάντων) and enslaved "to all" (πᾶσιν), what is he referring to? In being free from all it is not clear whether he is thinking of things or people. Both alternatives make sense. On the one hand, Paul is free from people who wish to tell him he must exercise his "rights"; on the other hand, he is free to subordinate his "rights" to the calling itself. In fact, there is no reason to separate these two. Paul is free from both people and their ideas. He is free from following what certain dogmatic elitists are telling him he must do, and he is also free from having to pursue the legitimate "rights" he knows he has. The argument is thus not dissimilar to 7:17–24 where Paul exhorts the Corinthians not to become "slaves of men," while the context reveals that Paul means no one should be enslaved to the *ideas* of people, such as the necessity of circumcision.

Paul does all this to "win" people (κερδαίνω, vv. 19, 20 [twice], 21, and 22). This is the only place where Paul uses this verb in this way. (The one other occurrence of the word in his writing is in Phil 3:8 where he writes of "gaining" Christ.) In modern Christian vocabulary, this word is used primarily of conversion. Someone is "won" for Christ "from" darkness, or the world, etc. In fact, the Greek word can mean "to gain or acquire by investment."[49] Even so Fee says this: "Such language as the interchange with 'save' in v. 22b makes clear, can only refer to evangelizing."[50] There is little doubt that the word can mean winning people in terms of their conversion. This is the more natural reading in vv. 20–21 where Paul says "to the Jews I became like a Jew . . . to those outside the law like [one] outside the law," but this meaning

---

48. Wallace, *Greek Grammar*, 623 (temporal participles); cf. 634 (concessive participles).

49. BDAG 541.
50. Fee, *1 Corinthians*, 471.

is less likely in v. 22 where Paul says "to the weak I became weak." This will be examined in detail as the verses are considered below.

This "free" man has thus given up everything to which he is entitled and become a "slave" for the Lord. No doubt all this would have had quite an impact as it was read aloud for the congregation in Corinth. Paul was definitely siding with the weak and identifying with them. He was humbling himself by refusing to appeal to the rights granted him by virtue of his apostleship and siding with those who were being hurt by the elitists. Even in his attitude to eating, drinking, and money, he was siding with the "weak" and with those who found themselves regularly "humiliated" in the church because they "had nothing" (11:20–22). So now Paul pushes home, by way of example from his own life, what the effects of this slavery have been.

9:20–21 To the Jews I became like a Jew so that I might win the Jews; to those under the law like [one] under the law so that I might win those under the law (though not myself being under the law); to those outside the law like one outside the law (though not being outside God's law but under Christ's law) so that I might win those outside the law (καὶ ἐγενόμην τοῖς Ἰουδαίοις ὡς Ἰουδαῖος, ἵνα Ἰουδαίους κερδήσω· τοῖς ὑπὸ νόμον ὡς ὑπὸ νόμον, μὴ ὢν αὐτὸς ὑπὸ νόμον, ἵνα τοὺς ὑπὸ νόμον κερδήσω· τοῖς ἀνόμοις ὡς ἄνομος, μὴ ὢν ἄνομος θεοῦ ἀλλ' ἔννομος Χριστοῦ, ἵνα κερδάνω τοὺς ἀνόμους). In vv. 20–22a three groups of people are listed: Jews (those under the law), those outside the law (meaning Gentiles), and the "weak." In each case the purpose clause shows Paul's purpose in accommodating to them: *it is in order to win them*. In general the sense of each of these examples from his practice in life is clear. Paul was

concerned not to let cultural or other differences become a stumbling block when speaking of the gospel to people. Thus, he would not let his work among the Gentiles become a stumbling block to the gospel when he was with Jews. Likewise, when among the Gentiles, Paul would not allow his Jewish background to hinder them seeing the full intent of the gospel.

However, though the general thrust of these verses seems relatively clear, they do raise a number of exegetical questions. Is there a difference between "Jews" and "those under the law"? Why does "law" so dominate here (vv. 20b–21)? Why does Paul talk about being "like" a Jew and "like one outside the law" and yet of *being* "weak"? What does it mean to be "like a Jew" when he is a Jew? What does to "win" or "gain" (κερδαίνω) mean here?

The answer to the last question feeds off the context but also will enable a better understanding of what Paul is saying. Above, it was noted that the verb is often simply understood as "to win" in terms of winning people for Christ; in other words, it is a reference to conversion. Yet rarely in Greek does the word simply mean "to win." Its normal meaning is "to gain" or "to make a profit."[51] The question of meaning arises here because thus far Paul has not talked of non-Christians at all. He has been talking of people within the church at Corinth, that is, of some who seem to be arrogant and elitist and some he has called "weak," but they are all *within* the church. The fact of the matter seems to be that Paul used his accommodation as a strategy to win the unconverted, but found that it was *also* the behavior required in God's church if people were not to fall away. *It was thus the behavior required of all Christians to ensure that those who were falling away were won back for Christ.*[52]

---

51. Mark 8:36; Matt 16:26; Luke 9:25; Jas 4:13. See BDAG 541.

52. Though the context is different, this concept is not dis-

similar at a religious level from the teaching in Jude 22–23: "Be merciful to those who doubt; save others by snatching them from the fire." Garland, *1 Corinthians*, 433, misses the

IN DEPTH: The Meaning of "To Win" in 9:20–21

A number of arguments are used to suggest that Paul has now moved to talking of "winning" in the sense of winning people for Christ.[53] First, it is possible that because here he is simply offering *examples*, Paul could be drawing on a completely different area of ministry and so be talking about his missionary policy. Secondly, there is little doubt that Paul did adopt an attitude of accommodation when he evangelized. So if this is about winning people for Christ, we know that this was his practice. Indeed, the very fact that in chapter 10 he can even contemplate eating meat offered to idols rather than meat killed according to Jewish law shows his ability to accommodate. It is clear, too, that he is perfectly capable of justifying this approach to non-Christians theologically in much of his writing as, for example, in the account of his confrontation with Peter in Galatians 2:11–14. In much of this discussion Daube's work examining the background of the word has been influential.[54] He argues that the word "to win/gain" (κερδαίνω) refers to conversion. This is further supported by a number of commentators who point to Paul's use of the word "save" in v. 22 (σῴζω) in his summary of the previous examples.

However, there are reasons to support the view that it refers to "winning" or "gaining" those who are *already* part of the church. First, there is the word itself. Daube acknowledges that, in the Hebrew background he examines, the usual meanings are "gathering in," "gaining advantage," etc. Of one set of rabbinic examples he examines, he acknowledges that "the masses which God 'gains' in the chain of texts just examined are Israelites condemned and reprieved, 'won back,' not Gentiles 'won over.'"[55] In fact, he offers little clear evidence of any rabbinic background to the word that implies the conversion of *outsiders*. Then there is Jesus's use of the word in Matthew 18:15 where it refers to winning back God's people: "If your brother sins against you, go and tell him his fault, between you and him alone. If he listens to you, you have *gained* your brother" (ESV). Of course, it is likely that the word κερδαίνω can

---

point when he says that these arguments only "appear to make sense . . . if the problem over idol food is delineated as a conflict between the strong and the weak." That is certainly not the argument here. These arguments make sense in the context of an apostle teaching the sort of behavior *Christians* should exhibit as they work together to build each other up in the faith, yet who is always wary lest any brother or sister in Christ be so compromised that he or she should be "disqualified." This is a concern he has for himself no less than for others (9:27).

53. G. Bornkamm, "The Missionary Stance of Paul in 1 Corinthians 9 and in Acts," in *Studies in Luke-Acts: Essays*

Presented in Honor of Paul Schubert, eds. L. Keck and J. Martyn (Nashville: Abingdon, 1966), 194–98, following this approach, believed that vv. 19–23 were an indication of Paul's "missionary practice."

54. David Daube, "Κερδαίνω as a Missionary Term," *HTR* 40 (1947): 109–20. He examines a number of Hebrew words in the rabbinic record and suggests that they possibly provide the background to Paul's use of κερδαίνω as speaking of drawing in those *outside* the faith.

55. Ibid., 117.

refer to *both* conversion and the winning back of those who may have gone astray or are going astray.[56]

Nevertheless, it seems that here in 1 Corinthians 9:19–22, the idea of "winning" or "gaining *back*" has been too quickly dismissed. It is an understanding of someone being "won back to the Lord" that makes most sense of what Paul says here. Indeed, context provides a solid second reason for viewing the word in this way. Paul has not been speaking about converts. He has, however, been exhibiting deep concern for the brother or sister who might be "disqualified" (8:11) and for the elitists who are "puffed up" and "sinning against [their] brothers [and sisters]" (8:12). Thirdly, the modern emphasis on individual conversion has often overstressed a sole meaning of the *English* verb "to save" and "to win." For Paul, the proclamation of the gospel, which is his "compulsion" and divine call, does not cease at the point of conversion! The very fact that we have his epistles is a clear indication that Paul saw the proclamation of the gospel in much broader terms. He knew that being won for Christ was just the start of a process of being "won," as the former ways give way to Christ's ways and as people mature in their faith. For Paul "salvation" concerned the eschatological destiny of the people of God, as well as initial conversion.[57] Paul has already used the verb "to save" in just this way of Christian teachers in 1 Cor 3:15: "If anyone's work is burned up, he will suffer loss, but he himself will be saved but only as through fire."

Finally, it is vital to see that 10:31–33 offers an enlightening parallel with 9:19–23. It comes toward the end of Paul's larger argument (8:1–11:1). Paul sums up all he has been saying by talking of seeking the "benefit" of "the many," giving no offense "to Jews or to Greeks or to the church of God" (10:31–32), "*in order that they might be saved*" (v. 33). The "church of God," clearly Christians, are at least part of what Paul has in mind here, and in the modern individualistic sense of "save" as the point of conversion, they are by definition already there! Paul is speaking much more broadly of bringing people to faith. He earnestly desires to ensure that they remain in the covenant community. In fact, we may say that he has *perseverance* in mind. And this is surely more likely contextually in 9:20–22, especially as we already know "the weak" are indeed part of God's church and that is why Paul is so worried for them.

---

56. E.g., possibly 1 Pet 3:1.

57. Cf. 1 Cor 1:18–21; 2 Cor 1:6; 6:1–3; 1 Thess 5:8–9. See also E. P. Sanders, *Paul and Palestinian Judaism: A Comparison of Patterns of Religion* (Philadelphia: Fortress, 1977), 447–74.

Another exegetical question now arises: In what sense could Paul, the Pharisee and Jew (cf. Phil 3:4b–7), "become *like* a Jew" (ὡς Ἰουδαῖος)? In fact, the first thing to note here is just how far Paul distances himself from his heritage in order to write like this. As Hays comments, it reflects how deeply Paul regarded the fact that "in Christ" he now "transcended all cultural allegiance." It is truly remarkable that this Jew could now see his work among fellow Jews as an "accommodation." He was a new creation in which the old had passed and in which "circumcision counts for nothing" (2 Cor 5:17; Gal 6:15).[58] But what did this mean in practice? Certainly here and in the example that follows, Paul is talking of the place of the Jewish law in his life and what he will and will not do. It has been suggested that Paul is prepared to practice Jewish customs but not to teach the law as a way of salvation.[59] But it is doubtful that Paul would ever have taught the law as a way to salvation even before he became a Christian.[60] The key here is that Paul is revealing the extent to which he has adopted the stance of a servant "to all" (v. 19). For Paul servanthood for Christ is the driving force. Thus, he is prepared to "become all things to all people" (9:22). This means Paul no longer has a "relationship to God which is *evidenced* by *possession* of the law."[61] This is not the "marker" of his faith as it was for a Jew. Nevertheless, when he is working among Jewish converts or among Jewish people who have not yet come to the faith, he is still prepared to follow Jewish customs even if those customs are embedded in Jewish law. No doubt he was prepared to eat in the way they did, pray as they did, and perhaps even dress as

they would have expected. One example is offered in Acts 21:15–24 where Paul was prepared to help fellow Jews take part in the ceremony of a Nazirite vow. For some believing Jewish people, keeping the law, especially circumcision, was the "marker" of the "saved," as Acts 15:5 makes clear: "But some believers who belonged to the party of the Pharisees rose up and said, 'It is necessary to circumcise them and to order them to keep the law of Moses'" (ESV; cf. Acts 15:1). This is what Paul would not have. This is why he adds the parenthesis, "though not myself being under the law" (1 Cor 9:20). And it is this attitude that gives rise to the different ways in which Paul handles Timothy, whom he circumcises because he was working among Jews and his mother was a Jew (Acts 16:3), and Titus, who was not forced to be circumcised even though he was a Greek (Gal 2:3–5). When keeping the law is considered a "marker" and necessary as evidence for Paul's identity as one of the "saved," then Paul is no longer a Jew. When the law is considered culturally and as generally useful for the sake of the gospel, he will accommodate himself. As Fee indicates, it is likely that Paul especially has in mind food laws here since this is the general issue running through chapters 8–10.[62] N. T. Wright writes: "Being a 'Jew' was no longer Paul's basic identity, for that is no longer 'who he was' at the deepest level."[63]

The next issue is what "those outside the law" (τοῖς ἀνόμοις) refers to. Some have suggested that this may refer to Gentiles who have become God-fearers. In other words, they have come under Jewish law and so have lived as Jews in relation to the law. Others have suggested Paul is simply saying

---

58. Richard Hays, *First Corinthians*, Interpretation (Louisville: Westminster John Knox, 1997), 153.

59. Conzelmann, *1 Corinthians*, 160.

60. It is more likely that Jewish theology of Paul's day did not see salvation as being *attained* by the law but *evidenced* through obedience to it. There continues to be considerable debate about this and *how* salvation was achieved in Judaism of

that age. See my brief summary in Gardner, *Gifts of God*, 100, esp. 100n194 and references to others there.

61. Sanders, *Paul and Palestinian Judaism*, 550 (his emphasis).

62. Fee, *1 Corinthians*, 473.

63. Wright, *Paul and the Faithfulness of God*, 1436.

the same thing in a different way. It matters little to Paul's argument either way. However, the fact that Paul does not in fact say "to the Gentiles I became like a Gentile" does reveal more clearly that the issue here for Paul has to do with the law. How does he, a "free" apostle, deal with the law when it is looked to as evidence of salvation? Again, Paul's response is the same as it was to working among Jews.

However, Paul takes the opportunity here to confront the potential accusation that he is antinomian. Using a concessive participle, he adds as a parenthesis, "Though not being outside God's law but under the Christ's law" (μὴ ὢν ἄνομος θεοῦ ἀλλ᾽ ἔννομος Χριστοῦ). With a play on words (ἄνομος used in two senses and followed by ἔννομος), Paul insists that he may be outside the law but is not lawless (ὡς ἄνομος; μὴ ὢν ἄνομος). The function of the law remains at issue. Paul is outside in the sense that he is not bound to follow it to be identified as a Christian, but he still follows the "law of Christ" and law still matters. The phrase "under Christ's law" could mean a number of things, but it is important to realize that Paul is not saying that there is now a new "Christian law." Rather, Paul still concerns himself with the centrality of Christ. In 11:1 he says, "Be imitators of me as I am of Christ." His concern is not with a set code, but he is thinking quite broadly about obedience to Christ in day-to-day service. As a servant to all, Paul is first and foremost a servant of Christ. This means, of course, that there are things he will not do even for the sake of "winning" people for Christ. He will not do what Christ would not do! In this context, among other things, he would not take part in idolatrous rites or meals.

9:22 to the weak I became weak so that I might win the weak. I have become all things to all people, so that by all means I might save some (ἐγενόμην τοῖς ἀσθενέσιν ἀσθενής, ἵνα τοὺς ἀσθενεῖς κερδήσω· τοῖς πᾶσιν γέγονα πάντα, ἵνα πάντως τινὰς σώσω). In v. 22a the Greek structure and the use of a purpose clause follows the previous two verses, except that Paul does not say that he has become "like" the weak (ὡς) but simply that he *has become* weak. Paul continues to make his point about accommodation and care for the weak and why the exercise of "rights" without consideration of other people can lead to their "stumbling" and even to their "destruction" (8:11, 13). To "win" them has most likely meant, as it has with the Jews and "those without the law," gaining them back for Christ if they are falling away or have stumbled or are now moving on a pathway toward destruction. These were the "weak" for whom Paul was concerned in 8:11–12. Their community self-awareness was weak. They were suffering at the hands of the elitists and were regarded by them as less than adequate. Paul has thus referred to them as weak. *They are "weak" as he has made himself weak. They do not flaunt their status.* They may not have much by way of material possessions. Or they may have followed Paul and deliberately avoided things in their society like "wisdom," "knowledge," financial power, or patronage that would have taken them away from Christ. This is why Paul can say, "to the weak I became weak" (ἐγενόμην τοῖς ἀσθενέσιν ἀσθενής). Paul has no problems with being weak for the gospel's sake. He has no problems with refusing anything that would give him status or power or indicate that he is better than other Christians. For example, as he has shown, he has refused apostolic rights. But he does this *for the sake of the gospel.*

There *is* a difference in how Paul can identify with Jews and the weak. He can be *like* a Jew as pertains to certain customs and cultural and religious practices, but he cannot live as one who believes the law is a requisite marker to be considered a member of the people of God. On the other hand, he can *become* weak because there is nothing wrong with being "weak." After all, they are only weak in the eyes of the elitists. Indeed, their whole problem is that they do not flaunt community markers. Paul has no problem with this. In fact, it is how he himself lives. He will show later there is just one marker that reveals the Christian as a Christian, and that is love.

Nevertheless, Paul does still need to gain them back (κερδαίνω). They are in danger of being led astray by the arrogant in the church. If they are falling away to destruction, they need saving. In the end, the difference between Paul's weakness and theirs is that "weakness" does not worry Paul. He is secure in Christ and in his love for Christ, whatever others may say about him. He can give up his "rights" because his security lies in the Lord, and he will boast in Christ alone. The weak, on the other hand, are unsure of their standing before the Lord and among his people.

The sum of what Paul says is that he will do whatever it takes, without disobeying the law of Christ, in order to gain people for Christ, whether that means keeping in the community those who seem to be driven out or bringing in those who are new to the faith.[64]

IN DEPTH: The Weak

Paul has used the word "weak" to describe a people who have been made to feel inferior because they are not exercising certain rights related to gifts of the Spirit, such as wisdom or knowledge. These people are looked down upon by the elitists or "knowers" and so have been made to feel weak. Yet, in God's eyes the so-called "weak" belong to him even without these (merely) human markers, and Paul can happily identify with that! It is to read too much into the text to insist that these people must be poorer people not in receipt of patronage, even though some might be so. Defining them as they are defined in chapter 8 works well in this context and explains why Paul omits the word "like" (ὡς). It would be exceedingly strange if Paul introduced at this point a different set of people known as "the weak."

Therefore, the word "weak" should not be seen as a derogatory term or even a description of a people who are basically inadequate in one way or another. In chapter 8 Paul sided with the weak, and ever since 1:27 "weak" has been a term that has been used to contrast one group of people against the arrogant. From the start, Paul has ensured that this has been a contrast that favors the weak. Sadly, though, their self-awareness as members of the body of Christ is depleted and poor. If they also have no status in the world's eyes, no power, no

---

64. Paul's principle of accommodation here is of course not one that can be taken out of its context in 1 Cor 9 and applied in all situations. For example, Paul does not accommodate the "strong." He will not accommodate their acceptance of incest or their understanding of status. In the next chapter, he is clear that eating food in an idol's temple is unacceptable. He insists that there can only be one κοινωνία and that must be with the Lord, not with demons (10:2–21). His accommodation is in fact defined by his obedience to Christ, who "gave himself up" for him (Eph 5:2). It is therefore all about self-denial "under Christ's law."

patronage, no great wealth, then this may make them feel even more "weak" in the church. Yet, for Paul they reflect the very evidence that "God chose what is weak in the world to shame the strong; God chose what is low and despised in the world, even things that are not, to bring to nothing things that are, so that no human being might boast in the presence of God" (1:27 ESV). Indeed, Paul has even called himself "weak" in comparison with the strong in 4:10.

9:23 Now I do all things for the sake of the gospel so that I might participate in it (πάντα δὲ ποιῶ διὰ τὸ εὐαγγέλιον, ἵνα συγκοινωνὸς αὐτοῦ γένωμαι). A summary verse draws this subsection to a close. It is the gospel that must drive everything. Paul does "all things" for its sake, and it is his passion and total preoccupation. He has said he would rather die than cause anyone to fall away from Christ, so it is no wonder he gives up his rights for the gospel's sake and no wonder he becomes weak for the gospel's sake! He does all this so that as many people as possible will be drawn to Christ and then also so they are kept faithful and find their security, not in wisdom or knowledge or the law or the gifts of the Spirit or any other "marker," but in Christ alone. It has already become clear that "gospel" for Paul is much more than simply the evangelizing message, for it is also the message about being God's people, about covenantal participation with God's people "in Christ."

Paul then ends by saying that he does all for the sake of the gospel so *he* can be a "participant" in it. This final purpose clause (ἵνα συγκοινωνὸς αὐτοῦ γένωμαι) is somewhat ambiguous. In the previous six purpose clauses in vv. 19–22, Paul has been

concerned to see *others* being "won" and kept from stumbling. Here it seems as if Paul is suddenly concerned for himself. Conzelmann writes, "This has a utilitarian sound: by behaving thus, Paul secures his own personal salvation," but he then goes on to say that "Paul has the community and his own divine commission in view."[65] "That I might participate in it" may mean participating in the benefits or blessings of the gospel (NIV, NRSV, TEV), or it may mean participating in the work of gospel proclamation. Barclay translates, "I do this because of the good news, that I may share it with all men."[66] Godet suggested that the clause be understood as "partaking with all other believers in the blessings which it [the gospel] confers, and in those it promises."[67] However, in the context Paul has been describing the subordination of his "rights" for the sake of the gospel, so it is unlikely that here he should turn to *his* blessings. The way of the gospel that Paul preaches and lives is the way of the cross, not the way of power and status. Paul knows that he must identify with the weak, for this is living out the gospel of Christ who suffered and died.[68]

As we noted above at 1:9,[69] while the concept of "participation/sharing in" (κοινωνός) in Paul may

65. Conzelmann, *1 Corinthians*, 161.

66. William Barclay, *The Letters to the Corinthians* (Philadelphia: Westminster, 1975), 82; cf. Johannes Weiss, *Der erste Korintherbrief* (Göttingen: Vandenhoeck & Ruprecht, 1970 [1910]), 246.

67. Godet, *First Corinthians*, 2:42.

68. Horrell, *Social Ethos of the Corinthian Correspondence*,

216, rightly summarizes: "Paul is determined to avoid the hindrance which would, in his view, result from his removal of himself from membership of the group he calls 'the weak.'... His solidarity with this social group is demonstrated in two ways: by his self-image as one who is the scum of the earth, and by his manual labour."

69. See "In Depth: The Meaning of the Word Κοινωνία."

include both the idea of fellowship and sharing here, as in 1:9 and chapter 10 it is likely to include ideas of "covenantal participation." In v. 23 Paul reveals that giving up his "rights" in his life among "all people" and becoming "weak" has meant that he has both lived and modeled the gospel, and so he exhibits his true covenantal status before the Lord.[70]

9:24–26 Do you not know that in a race all the runners run but one receives the prize? So run that you may receive it. Now every athlete is self-controlled in all things. Indeed, they do this in order to receive a perishable crown, but we [to receive] an imperishable [crown]. Hence, I do not run in an aimless way, nor do I box such that I beat the air (Οὐκ οἴδατε ὅτι οἱ ἐν σταδίῳ τρέχοντες πάντες μὲν τρέχουσιν, εἷς δὲ λαμβάνει τὸ βραβεῖον; οὕτως τρέχετε ἵνα καταλάβητε. πᾶς δὲ ὁ ἀγωνιζόμενος πάντα ἐγκρατεύεται, ἐκεῖνοι μὲν οὖν ἵνα φθαρτὸν στέφανον λάβωσιν, ἡμεῖς δὲ ἄφθαρτον. ἐγὼ τοίνυν οὕτως τρέχω ὡς οὐκ ἀδήλως, οὕτως πυκτεύω ὡς οὐκ ἀέρα δέρων). In this final section (vv. 24–27), Paul does not digress but appeals to another concluding example in which people are prepared to forgo entitlements for the sake of a goal. The example functions as a summary and conclusion.

Athletes and runners are people who will forgo much in order to win a competition or race. They cannot afford to be overconfident. In the same way, there can be no overconfidence in the Christian life of the sort shown in the behavior of the elitists.[71] Paul draws attention to four parallels between the Christian life and the example drawn from the world of athletics. In the first place, like athletes, Christians are seeking a "prize" (βραβεῖον, though an imperishable prize). Secondly, to win will mean "enslaving" (δουλαγωγέω; v. 27) oneself to the task. Thirdly, just as the weak could be in danger of disqualification as they tried to follow the elitists, so all Christians can face disqualification. This includes Paul and, most certainly, those who think they are secure. Fourthly, the world of athletics speaks again to the cost and pain of what Paul is proposing. The Christian life involves following Christ (and following Paul as he follows Christ; 11:1), and this is the way of sacrifice and often of pain. While the elitists seem to think their knowledge guarantees the prize, Paul once again insists that their status is not at all confirmed in this way. Simply saying one is an athlete does not guarantee any prize. Prizes must be worked for, and the way is hard and humbling and painful. Neither the Corinthians nor Paul have yet crossed the finishing line. In chapter 10 Paul will use the Israelites, whom God had brought out of Egypt under Moses, as an example of people who likewise thought they were secure and yet many were "destroyed."

While Paul starts off in v. 24 by making it clear that he intends the Corinthians to apply this to themselves (a plural imperative is used), in v. 26, as he reverts to the first-person singular, he reiterates that he is not asking them to do things he does not do himself. In his own life he provides them with an example of how to live since he imitates Christ (11:1).

---

70. It has been noted that Paul may exhibit here an inconsistency between his own actions of accommodation and his condemnation of Peter in Gal 2:11–14. However, the two situations are quite different. For detailed discussion of a possible inconsistency, see D. A. Carson, "Pauline Inconsistency: Reflections on 1 Corinthians 9.19–23 and Galatians 2.11–14," *Churchman* 100.1 (1986): 6–45.

71. Many commentators see the issue of these last verses as one of the danger of overconfidence among the "strong" or "knowers." A number see the problem being one of overconfidence in the sacraments. However, there is no evidence here to suggest the subject has suddenly changed. Paul has not said anything at all about sacraments. These commentators assume that in ch. 10 Paul is concerned with the sacraments. This is most likely not the case. Among those who regard the problem as one of sacraments, see Barrett, *First Corinthians*, 216; Whiteley, *Theology of St. Paul*, 172–73; Fee, *1 Corinthians*, 477.

The rhetorical question "Do you not know?" has been repeated several times (see on 3:16). What Paul says about athletes is to be taken as noncontroversial. As today, there were numerous athletic competitions in Paul's day. In the Roman Empire there were both international and local "games." Among the better known were the Isthmian Games held in the city of Corinth, which would have included running and boxing and other sports. Murphy-O'Connor suggests that these games ranked below the Olympic games but above the games at Delphi and Nemea. They were a huge event held every two years,[72] and Paul may have been in Corinth during one of these festivals since they took place in AD 49 and 51. Like the modern Olympic Games, though on a much smaller scale, wealthy patrons would sponsor the games at huge expense, even giving free food and drink to the crowds. The games also brought in a great deal of money for the local economy, as visitors poured into the city from all over.[73] Dio Chrysostom, writing in the latter part of the first century describes the games as a time of great fun and intense competition, but also a time of religious festivities and cultural activities. He mentions some of the main events in which men and women took part. They "sprint or wrestle or jump . . . box, throw the spear, and hurl the discus."[74]

The games and their various sports were used as a metaphor for life by various first and early second-century writers. Examples from both Philo[75] and Epictetus abound. The latter writes of the progress of a philosopher as he puts "into practice his guiding principles, as the runner does when he applies the principles of running."[76] On one occasion he urges the potential philosopher to think carefully about things and not to rush into ideas and then give them up. He urges discipline like that of an athlete and says, "You must have turned yourself over to your trainer precisely as you would to a physician." But then, thinking of those who want to follow after multiple, fanciful philosophical ideas, he compares them to children playing at being athletes. "Sometimes [the children] play athletes, again gladiators, again they blow trumpets. . . . So you too are now an athlete, now a gladiator, then a philosopher . . . yet with your whole soul nothing."[77]

The contrast between a "perishable" (φθαρτός) wreath or crown or "imperishable" (ἄφθαρτος) is also one that would have been well understood in Corinth, where the wreaths given to athletes were made of celery! Plutarch, living in first-century Corinth, wrote about the wreath for athletes at the Isthmian Games, saying that historically it had been a "pine wreath . . . but later, when the context was made more sacred, they adopted the celery crown from the Nemean games."[78] This is just one of many indications from the writers of the time how much temple worship and religious activities were caught up in the Games. With this background it is clear that Paul's final illustration would have been understood by all, both from the Games that regularly took place in the city but also from the general metaphorical language of philosophy and spirituality.

Paul's use of the analogy of running a race is designed to make one simple point: "run" for the prize.[79] In v. 24 the "runners" are the image Paul uses for all the people in the church. They are run-

---

72. Aelius Aristides, *Orations* 46.23.

73. Murphy-O'Connor, *St. Paul's Corinth*, 14–17. This book cites many intriguing texts relating to the city of Corinth with enlightening comments on what Paul may have experienced.

74. Dio Chrysostom, *Orations* 8.6–16 (Cohoon, LCL).

75. E.g., Philo, *Moses* 1.48; *Spec. Laws* 4.99.

76. Epictetus, *Discourses* 1.4.20 (Oldfather, LCL).

77. Ibid., 3.15.6–7.

78. Plutarch, *Moralia* 5.3.1–3 (LCL).

79. The aorist of the word τρέχω is ἔδραμον from the obsolete verb δράμω.

ning toward a "prize" and should be running in a way designed to obtain it. They are to remember that there is only "one prize." This, of course, does not mean that only one Christian will ever receive a prize. Rather, the one prize is the inheritance of eschatological glory and is attained by all who complete the race (cf. 1 Thess 2:19). This means learning from the athlete (v. 25), whom Paul describes as exercising self-control in all things. He is not speaking here about the general life of an individual believer who elsewhere is told to abstain from sin (cf. 1 Thess 4:3; 5:22), nor is the word being used here as it is in 1 Corinthians 7:9. Indeed, there is certainly no call here to any sort of asceticism. Rather, Paul is still addressing the rights that he has given up and the rights that the elitists should be content to give up. Not to give these things up for the sake of the gospel may lead to a forfeiture of the race itself. Exercising self-control (ἐγκρατεύομαι) as an athlete will be hard and sacrificial work. Yet athletes will put themselves through great deprivations and painful practice simply to receive a "perishable crown" of celery! How much more should "we" (Paul and the Corinthians) be prepared to exercise this self-control in restricting "rights," whether legitimate or not, for the sake of the imperishable prize.

In v. 26 Paul moves from the first plural, in which he has recognized that all the Christians at Corinth have the same goal and prize in mind, to the first singular as he returns to talking about the example his own life must offer. He does not run aimlessly (ἀδήλως). The word can mean "uncertainly," but here Paul simply means that he does not run as one *without* a goal in mind. He knows where he is going, and this must guide all his actions. The image of the boxer who boxes the air serves his purposes well. Dio Chrysostom wrote of the boxer Melancomas that "he was even more remarkable for his self-control and moderation . . . boxing was his specialty . . . he had trained so rigorously and went so far beyond others in toilsome exercise."[80] This is the sort of boxer Paul says he is. Yet for the elitists with all their rights and pretensions it is as if they are boxing the air. They entirely miss the fact that what should mark them out should be their humble love for God and neighbor. It can hardly be lost on the readers that those whom Paul thinks are in fact boxing the air (ἀέρα δέρων) are "puffed up" (4:6; 8:1)!

Paul's deep concern for other brothers and sisters in the Lord, evidenced in how he will even give up his rights for their sake, is none other than a fulfillment of the second "great commandment." There can be no place in the kingdom of the Lord for any arrogance, for there always remains the possibility of "destruction" (8:11), of "stumbling" (8:13), and of "disqualification" (9:27). Thus, the possibility of running in vain disturbs Paul. He mentions it again in Galatians 2:2 and in Philippians 2:16. Instead, he will run in such a way that he will "press on" toward the goal (Phil 3:13–14).

9:27 Rather, I punish my body and enslave it, lest after preaching to others I myself might be disqualified (ἀλλὰ ὑπωπιάζω μου τὸ σῶμα καὶ δουλαγωγῶ, μή πως ἄλλοις κηρύξας αὐτὸς ἀδόκιμος γένωμαι). This verse reveals clearly that the section from vv. 24–27 is both looking backward to the rest of chapters 8–9 as well as introducing the example of Israel in chapter 10. The use of the verb "to enslave" (δουλαγωγέω) recalls Paul's comment that he has made himself a slave to all (δουλόω; v. 19). He has cautiously refused to exercise his rights for the sake of the gospel. He has been especially insistent that no one who is in the community should be caused to stumble. The behavior of the elitists

---

80. *Orations* 28.6–7.

was likely to do just that and had perhaps already done that. Paul is now saying that the person who causes someone to stumble and so be "destroyed" is himself or herself in danger of being "disqualified" (ἀδόκιμος). He or she will not win the prize or arrive at the goal. In fact, the end of that person will be the same as the end of the one who has stumbled to the point of destruction. Israel offers the perfect example. Marked out as God's people by their exodus from Egypt and by the constant presence of God with them in the wilderness, they felt secure and unassailable. Yet God would not tolerate the sin in which they indulged so that in the end many were "destroyed" (10:10).

It is because this is such a serious matter that Paul reminds his readers that, even as an apostle, he lives daily as one who "punishes" and enslaves his body.[81] This is the conclusion of the analogy drawn from athletics. Just as the athlete forces his body to perform amazing feats by a regime of "punishing" training, so Christians should pay similar detailed attention to their behavior. For Paul it is important to show that this message that he preaches to many comes as a daily challenge to himself as well. Though vital theologically, what Paul is saying is also profoundly personal. He is prepared for a punishing regime of self-control for the sake of the gos-

pel and wishes that the self-satisfied Corinthians saw life in the same way.

One final point may be made here. Since this lengthy section from 8:1 to 11:1 begins and ends with the matter of whether food offered to idols should be eaten, it may well be that Paul is using this final part of the analogy to cause people to think again about what they *eat*. Paul's main concern, as has been seen, is with a serious religious problem to do with "rights." It is an abuse of so-called rights that has led to the question about sacrificial food. But even as Paul thinks of the apostolic rights he has given up for the sake of the gospel, he may also be thinking of the dangers of certain types of food and certain contexts for eating and drinking. The athlete analogy lends itself to considerations of serious dietary decisions, as we know even today. In the first century, Epictetus spoke about the life of a would-be philosopher and compared it with being an Olympic athlete. He wrote, "You have to submit to discipline, follow a strict diet, give up sweetcakes, train under compulsion, at a fixed hour, in heat or in cold; you must not drink cold water, nor wine just whenever you feel like it."[82] As Paul leads into chapter 10, he may already be thinking of the verse he will shortly quote: "The people sat down to eat and drink and stood up to play" (10:7).

Theology in Application

Proper Support for Those Who Proclaim the Gospel

In 9:1–14 Paul makes a series of arguments that those engaged in gospel proclamation, together with their family members (spouse and probably children) should be properly recompensed by other Christians. Even though Paul makes his case with a view to speaking forcefully about giving up this "right" to support, his cumulative arguments are powerful and persuasive and form the most prolonged argument in

---

81. The modern English word "punish" is often used of the harsh conditions athletes have to endure as they practice. Though the word ὑπωπιάζω can mean "discipline," Paul proba-

bly has more in mind the *pain* endured for the sake of the goal. See BDAG 1043.

82. Epictetus, *Discourses* 3.15.2–4 (Oldfather, LCL).

Scripture for the support of all engaged in gospel ministry. The final claim that Jesus himself commanded this (v. 14) reminds everyone that this is a serious matter that the church must address. As Paul makes clear, such care for those serving the Lord in their evangelizing and teaching can be traced right back to the way God ordered the Israelite tribes. The tribe of Levi and its priesthood was God's "gift" to his people (Num 18:1–7). The whole tribe, committed and called by God to serve and lead in the Lord's worship and to teach his people, was provided for by taxes placed upon the other tribes and through the regular sacrifices the people made to the Lord. What was given to the Lord was handed back by the Lord to the priesthood (e.g., Lev 7:28–36; 24:9; Num 18:8–24). At times of revival in Israel's history, it is notable that offerings and tithes poured into the temple, enabling the priesthood to recover, priestly teachers to travel the nation, and worship itself to be revitalized (2 Chr 29–31 [esp. 31:4–5]; 34:1–35:19).

In the modern Western church, such support for ministers, missionaries, and others engaged full time in the church's gospel ministry is normal. However, often ministers are treated paternalistically by their congregations, as if to say their remuneration is a "favor" from the people. In fact, Paul's argument here, and the analogy provided by the Old Testament priesthood and treatment of the tribe of Levi, should remind congregations that the true "favor" is the one God has done for the church. He has gifted the church with teachers and evangelists much as he gave the Levites as a gift to Israel (Eph 4:11–14). When congregations see their ministers in this way, there will be no sense of helping them with some paternalistic and condescending discussion of how much they are worth. Rather, there will be a joy in the giving and support that enable them to live and serve without worry for provision. It is worth remembering that revivals have often brought increased financial support and general care by God's people for their ministers. Indeed, it may be argued that the spiritual life of a congregation can be measured by their attitude to and treatment of their gospel ministers.

Having said this, it is an obvious deduction from what Scripture teaches and what most concerns Paul here that neither church nor minister should boast of what they have. In some denominations, all ministers receive more or less the same "stipend," adjusted for local cost of living. Provided this income is adequate for housing and a life devoid of major financial concerns that would detract from ministry, then this can help prevent competition between churches in seeking to attract the "best" ministers. It can also help ministers more clearly seek God's calling to a church rather than choosing one above another for worldly reasons of income.

While gospel ministry must be properly supported and ministers, evangelists, and missionaries have a "right" to such support, provided with care and love by the local church, they should remember that they have not been promised great treasures in this life! It is significant that while in many ways the Old Testament priesthood were probably better off than most in Israel, especially at times of revival, they had no inheritance in the land. As the Lord said to Aaron: "You shall have no inheritance in their land, neither shall you have any portion among them; I am your portion and your inheritance among the people of Israel" (Num 18:20 RSV). Those called to serve the Lord in this way as evangelists, teachers, missionaries, etc., will do well to look at the point Paul makes from this passage. "For the sake of the gospel" he will give up such rights. The need for ministers to model a life-commitment to the Lord must run deeply into their attitudes to money, to lifestyle, and even to inheritance. Trusting the Lord to provide for all things, whether it be for raising a family with less income than most in the congregation enjoy, or for retirement, or, in some countries, urgent medical care can be truly humbling.

In some places an opposite situation may also be challenged by what Paul teaches here. Some poor congregations pay their minister much more than the average salary of the congregation. This may show a wonderful love and respect for gospel ministry, but ministers may have to ask themselves about self-sacrifice and modeling the gospel in the area to which they have been called. Those of us in ministry would do well to examine again the true extent of Paul's preparedness to humble himself and rely on the Lord's provision, so that we may know firsthand what Paul means when he says that preaching gives us no grounds for boasting but rather "woe to us, if we do not preach the gospel!"

Accommodation for the Sake of the Gospel

Paul's prioritizing of the gospel was revealed clearly in his ability to move socially between different peoples in ways that enabled the maximum number of people to hear of Christ without giving them grounds to "stumble" other than on the truth of Christ crucified. The word "accommodation" is widely used of what Paul speaks to in 9:19–23, and it is not inappropriate, provided it is understood what it means and does not mean. Paul does everything "for the sake of the gospel." He will not distort the gospel. For example, he refuses to accommodate the message of the wisdom of Christ to the prevailing Greek understanding of wisdom (something the Corinthian church has clearly done). Paul does not back away from confrontation either with Christians or society over, for example, sexual ethics or participation in idolatry. Rather, he has a deep, biblical understanding that the coming of the King is news for all people. It must not be hidden behind laws regarding eating certain foods or behind human "boasts" in status or power or behind certain assumed cultural norms. As he enters various, different communities, it appears that Paul is constantly on the lookout for anything in his actions or life that might cause people's ears to close against the gospel. Even as he works among Christians and seeks to win some back to a deeper trust in Christ, still Paul refuses to let anything clutter the vision of Christ of whom he speaks and whom he seeks to imitate.

The message of the Lord Christ, crucified and raised, who demands love and the obedience of faith, must not be changed (Gal 1:9–11). Many will turn away from this message, and many who appear to believe will eventually walk away (Luke 8:9–15; 2 Cor 4:3), but Paul is content to leave that in God's hands (1 Thess 1:4–5). However, he is prepared to sacrifice his personal social and cultural preferences if they might cloud the message of Christ. The modern church has all too often accommodated the message in its desire to be heard. Christ has been reduced to a palatable mixture of love, kindness, and ethical propriety. In some parts of today's American Christianity the message of Christ has been so accommodated to the prevailing political voice of so-called evangelicalism that anyone with a divergent political view will no longer listen to the message of the gospel. Whatever Paul's political views or his likely disdain for much of Greek and Roman civilization around him, he speaks only of biblical truth and of the Christ to whom the whole of Scriptures point. It would be good to see the modern church looking more carefully at what this might mean in practice. Undoubtedly there would be more pushback against the message by many. However, many others might much more readily give it a proper hearing once they find they no longer have to get past all the baggage of either liberal or conservative cultural Christianity.

20

1 Corinthians 10:1–13

Literary Context

Some have suggested that in the transition from chapter 9 to chapter 10 there is a change from letter B (ch. 9 or parts of it) to letter A (ch. 10:1–23).[1] However, as the exegesis will show, chapter 10 fits well into the whole context of 8:1–11:1. The problem of eating meat previously sacrificed to idols has been set by Paul within the framework of a discussion of the issue of status in the community of God's people. How is this "standing" authenticated? Eating this meat, Paul demonstrates, is a serious matter since it has involved a false understanding of how community status is authenticated. This is why Paul moved directly in 8:1 from the problem of food offered to idols to the question of "knowledge." The elitists saw grace-gifts such as knowledge as markers of their elevated status in the church. In chapter 9 Paul talked about standing in the community and, by way of example, the rights that accrue to his own apostolic status. He would rather die than have his rights present an obstacle or stumbling block to gospel proclamation. Paul insisted that he behaved like an athlete (9:24–27), always with an eye to the prize, and this had to mean being prepared to give up "rights" for the sake of Christ. Indeed, with hyperbole Paul wrote at the end of chapter 8 that he would give up meat altogether rather than cause one to stumble. Now in chapter 10, Paul plays a trump card.

He now presents an example of people who were indeed part of the community of God and who even had their own "spiritual gifts," yet they discovered these did not offer the evidence of standing and security that they imagined. As a result, many of them ended up "stumbling," and finally many were destroyed. The example is taken from Israel during its wilderness wanderings. The Israelites were God's people. Their spiritual gifts included provision of manna and water by God (10:1–5). They too were arrogant, took advantage of God, and sinned in ways that offer parallels to what is going on in Corinth. Verse 12 then goes to the heart of Paul's message about status: "Therefore if you think you stand, take heed lest you fall." They must not presume

---

1. See Introduction. Also Schmithals, *Gnosticism in Corinth*; cf. Hurd, *Origin of 1 Corinthians*, 45.

upon God's grace-gifts. Paul then will proceed to show precisely why eating meat sacrificed to idols is, in some circumstances, deeply dangerous.

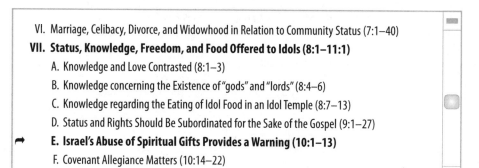

VI. Marriage, Celibacy, Divorce, and Widowhood in Relation to Community Status (7:1–40)

VII. Status, Knowledge, Freedom, and Food Offered to Idols (8:1–11:1)

  A. Knowledge and Love Contrasted (8:1–3)

  B. Knowledge concerning the Existence of "gods" and "lords" (8:4–6)

  C. Knowledge regarding the Eating of Idol Food in an Idol Temple (8:7–13)

  D. Status and Rights Should Be Subordinated for the Sake of the Gospel (9:1–27)

➡   **E. Israel's Abuse of Spiritual Gifts Provides a Warning (10:1–13)**

  F. Covenant Allegiance Matters (10:14–22)

Main Idea

The community of Israel, established by God and given gifts by God, still sinned and was judged. It thus offers a salutary example for the community of Christians at Corinth. They must watch out lest they too, thinking they stand, sin and fall. Ultimately, only dependence upon God's faithfulness will enable them to bear up under temptation.

Translation

1 Corinthians 10:1–13

1a	Desire	For **I do not want you to be ignorant,** brothers [and sisters],
b	Content	that our fathers were all under the cloud, and
c	Series	all passed through the sea, and
2a		all were baptized into Moses
b	Sphere	in the cloud and
c		in the sea, and
3a	Series	all ate the same spiritual food, and
4a		all drank the same spiritual drink.
b	Basis	For **they drank from the spiritual rock**
c	Description	that followed them,
d	Identification	and **the rock was Christ.**
5a	Assertion	Nevertheless, **God was not pleased with most of them,**
b	Basis	for **they were killed**
c	Place	in the wilderness.

Continued on next page.

Continued from previous page.

6a	Assertion	Now **these things are an example**
b	Advantage	for us,
c	Purpose	so that we might not have evil desires
d	Comparative illustration	as they desired [evil things].
7a	Entreaty 1	**Do not take part in idolatry,**
b	Comparative illustration	as some of them did;
c	Evidence	as it is written,
d	Quotation	"The people sat down to eat and drink and stood up ↵ to play." [Exod 32:6]
8a	Series	Neither
b	Entreaty 2	**should we indulge in sexual immorality,**
c	Comparative illustration	as some of them indulged, and
d	Expansion	in one day twenty-three thousand fell.
9a	Series	Neither
b	Entreaty 3	**should we test Christ,**
c	Comparative illustration	as some of them tested [him] and
d	Expansion	were destroyed
e	Agency	by the serpents.
10a	Series	Nor
b	Entreaty 4	**should you grumble,**
c	Comparative illustration	as some of them grumbled, and
d	Expansion	were destroyed
e	Agency	by the Destroyer.
11a	Assertion/expansion	Now **these things were happening to them**
b	Cause	by way of example,
c	Assertion	and **it was written as a warning**
d	Advantage	for us,
e	Expansion	upon whom the ends of the ages have come.
12a	Warning	Therefore, **let anyone who thinks he stands take heed lest he fall.**
13a	Assertion	**No temptation has overtaken you**
b	Exception	except what is common to a human being.
c	Assertion	**God is faithful,** and
d	Assertion	**he will not let you be tempted**
e	Extent	above what you are able,
f	Circumstance	but with the temptation
g	Assertion	**he will also provide a way out**
h	Purpose	so that you can bear up under it.

Structure

The heart of this section of chapter 10 is found in the admonition in v. 12. The issue of people thinking that they are standing before God, when in fact they should watch out lest they fall, provides the reason for Paul's introduction of the example from the Israelites in the wilderness. The passage may then be broken down in various ways or simply treated as one long exposition and application of the wilderness story. A straightforward structure sees vv. 1–5 as the first section in which the main wilderness story is related with its link to Christ (v. 4). The recounting of this short part of the wilderness story says all that needs to be said. God's people had reason to believe they were secure, but many were killed by God (v. 5). Verses 6–11 then provide a second section. An *inclusio* is formed by vv. 6 and 11, which both talk of these things happening as "examples" for us. This section makes explicit Paul's concern that his own generation of Christians realize a lesson must be learned: *do not desire sin as they did.* Verses 7–10 then list four of the sins of Israel that find some parallel in the Corinthian church: idolatry, sexual immorality, putting Christ to the test, and grumbling. The concluding admonition (v. 12) and its qualification (v. 13) complete the section.[2]

Throughout this passage, the wilderness description is applied directly to Christians who are the people "upon whom the ends of the ages have come" (v. 11). The correspondence that Paul sees between the events of the wilderness and the behavior of the wilderness generation is carefully and repeatedly brought out in the text. This happens both implicitly and explicitly. In v. 2 it is implicit with the reference to an Israelite "baptism." In v. 4, it is explicit as the wilderness rock from which water flowed is identified as Christ. In vv. 6–10 it is once again explicit, as Paul uses a series of imperatives to tell the Corinthians they must not follow the pattern of the Israelites.

IN DEPTH: Paul's Typology and the Exodus Events

Before a more detailed exegesis, it is important to examine generally how Paul is using the Old Testament story. Collins refers to 10:1–13 as a "sustained midrashic exposition." He says that Paul's way of using the text from Numbers "bears similarity to rabbinic *haggadah* (the story) and *halakah* (the behavioral imperative)."[3] Meeks says that vv. 1–13 "are a literary unit, very carefully composed prior to its use in the present context."[4] In the text itself the apostle uses

---

2. Meeks overstates the careful structure when he suggests that the five positive clauses containing "and all" in vv. 1–4 are paralleled by five negative clauses containing "as some of them" (vv. 6–10). Wayne A. Meeks, "'And Rose Up to Play': Midrash And Paraenesis In 1 Cor 10:1–22," *JSNT* 16 (1982): 64–78.

3. Raymond F. Collins, *First Corinthians*, Sacra Pagina 7 (Collegeville, MN: Liturgical Press, 1999), 364–65.

4. Meeks, "And Rose Up to Play," 64.

the word "type" (τύπος, v. 6; cf. v. 11) which makes the modern reader think of "typology." Furthermore, the use of the word "spiritual" might suggest to some modern readers that this section contains some deeper or metaphorical use of Scripture. The most useful approach is simply to look at *this* text and see what Paul is doing as he draws on Scripture by way of example.

It is evident that in Paul's theological framework there was a definite and providential correspondence between the old events of the wilderness and the new in the church at Corinth. That's why he is able to say in v. 11, "These things were happening to them by way of example [τυπικῶς]." Further, Paul saw the significance of the relationship between the old and the new as for those "upon whom the ends of the ages have come." The Old Testament was being viewed by Paul from the perspective of the messianic age, the age of Christ, "the power of God and the wisdom of God" (1:24). From this perspective "hidden" realities were revealed (2:9–12, 16), for it was the age of the "new covenant" in which, through Christ, the "veil" was removed even from the reading of the "old covenant" (2 Cor 3:6, 14–16). Paul saw a correspondence between the attitude of the Israelites and that of the Corinthians toward the gifts God had given them. Thus, Paul may be said to have used the Old Testament as an "example" or "warning." However, these words fail to adequately convey Paul's attention to the providential, historical framework of revelation. From Scripture Paul showed a correspondence between old and new that was visible because God had now revealed how he had worked in redemptive history. Paul's generation had received the revelation of Christ and through him was able to discern a deliberate contemporary purpose for the recounting of events providentially overseen by God in the past. All upon whom "the ends of the ages have come" can and must learn from these events and from the people of Israel in the Old Testament, for they live in continuity with them. They are "our fathers" (οἱ πατέρες ἡμῶν; 10:1). Indeed, Paul's approach to God's people and their redemption and salvation has been referred to as the "new exodus," something to which various prophetic Scriptures, including Isaiah 61:1–5, seemed to point.[5]

As the Israelites were led by God out of Egypt and slavery into the freedom and inheritance of the promised land, as they saw his protective and guiding presence in the cloud and pillar of fire, and as they were distinguished as a separate and holy nation in the crossing of the Red Sea, so God's people of the new covenant find themselves caught up in a parallel story. Christians are the continuation of this people of the past. They are also being led out of the

---

5. E.g., see Wright, *Paul and the Faithfulness of God*, 1069ff., 1334ff.

nations to be a new and separate and holy people, freed from sin and its enslavement, into the inheritance that will eventually be fulfilled in the new earth. The same Lord is present with them by his Spirit as he was with the "fathers." By the baptism of water and the Spirit, those who trust in and owe allegiance to Christ are seen to be his people. He is with them by his Spirit as he was with the Israelites in the cloud and the fire. The presence of God, seen in the tabernacle placed at the center of the community, is now seen as the Spirit resides in the midst of the people (3:16–17; 2 Cor 6:16). In the wilderness God gave Israel gifts by his Spirit as he now does the church. However, the Israelites took these gifts for granted, ignored them, and even despised them. So, the same danger exists for those caught up in the "new exodus." God's people need to live as a holy people who obey and love their covenant Lord.

Throughout, as Paul works with this framework he assumes that the Israelites in the wilderness were expected to see beyond their hunger and thirst. That is why many were destroyed in the wilderness. It was also important for later generations that they, too, should respond correctly to God, who still talked to them through those past events (Deut 8:1–3).

Two principles of interpretation must not be neglected in this discussion. The first is that the original events, such as the exodus, were important in themselves as evidence of God's redemptive purposes among his people.[6] The "old" should not be regarded as of secondary importance.[7] The second is that later revelation from God was not always to be seen as a straightforward application of the events to a later generation in some "spiritual" manner. Rather, God revealed more about how things actually were. This new understanding of what happened then could now be shown, providentially, to parallel events of the day in which the reader lived. Woolcombe suggests that this is particularly evident in the Pauline corpus: "Paul proceeded to show that the events . . . directly corresponded to the events which he and his contemporaries were experiencing because Christ was the prime mover in both . . . the historical pattern of the Old Covenant exactly corresponds to the historical pattern of the New Covenant, because both are the work of the Word and Wisdom of God."[8]

As Paul writes he wants his readers to understand that the coming of Christ means that they may expect a greater understanding of how events actually

---

6. Although, of course, the people often failed to recognise this or "forgot" what God had done.

7. Ellis writes, "Although the 'type' has its own historical value, its real significance typologically is revealed only in the 'anti-type' or fulfillment" (E. E. Ellis, *Paul's Use of the Old Testament* [Grand Rapids: Eerdmans, 1957], 128).

8. G. W. H. Lampe and K. J. Woollcombe, *Essays on Typology*, SBT 22 (London: SCM, 1957), 66; this is a position similar to what Ellis calls "covenant typology" (Ellis, *Prophecy and Hermeneutic*, 166).

were and so see more clearly their own place in this story. Thus, as Paul looks at the wilderness story and events, he does not just see analogies or symbols but comes to see that Christ was present in the wilderness and that *he* gave gifts to the people. This is the new wisdom of the new covenant where all that is "spiritual" is seen to focus on Jesus. However, in the light of some common teachings in the church today, it is important to understand that Paul's teaching gives no warrant to suggest that the Israelites themselves knew Jesus! That Jesus was present is precisely the heart of what is new about what Paul is doing in expounding this Old Testament text.

Exegetical Outline

VII. Status, Knowledge, Freedom, and Food Offered to Idols (8:1–11:1)

   A. Knowledge and Love Contrasted (8:1–3)

   B. Knowledge concerning the Existence of "gods" and "lords" (8:4–6)

   C. Knowledge regarding the Eating of Idol Food in an Idol Temple (8:7–13)

   D. Status and Rights Should be Subordinated for the Sake of the Gospel (9:1–27)

➡ **E. Israel's Abuse of Their Spiritual Gifts Provides a Warning (10:1–13)**

   1. Israel: A Community with Spiritual Gifts (10:1–4)

      a. The Israelites Established as God's People (10:1–2)

      b. The Israelites Received Spiritual Gifts (10:3–4)

   2. Israel: Many Were Judged (10:5)

   3. Israel: An Example for "Us" (10:6–11)

      a. They Desired Evil (10:6)

      b. They Were Idolaters (10:7)

      c. They Were Sexually Immoral (10:8)

      d. They Tested Christ (10:9)

      e. They Grumbled (10:10)

      f. They Provide an Exemplary Warning (10:11)

   4. Application: Stand Firm (10:12–13)

      a. Watch Out Lest You Fall (10:12)

      b. Remember God Is Faithful (10:13)

Explanation of the Text

10:1–2 For I do not want you to be ignorant, brothers [and sisters], that our fathers were all under the cloud, and all passed through the sea, and all were baptized into Moses in the cloud and in the sea (Οὐ θέλω γὰρ ὑμᾶς ἀγνοεῖν, ἀδελφοί, ὅτι οἱ πατέρες ἡμῶν πάντες ὑπὸ τὴν νεφέλην ἦσαν καὶ πάντες διὰ τῆς θαλάσσης διῆλθον, καὶ πάντες εἰς τὸν Μωϋσῆν ἐβαπτίσαντο ἐν τῇ νεφέλῃ καὶ ἐν τῇ θαλάσσῃ). "For" (γάρ) is omitted by some (e.g., NRSV, TEV) but is important because it clarifies to the reader that what is now said follows on from and illustrates what has just been said. There is a need for these "brothers [and sisters]" to run the race as Paul is doing. Using a common forceful rhetorical device,[9] Paul starts the section by insisting the Corinthians should take note of what he is saying. "All" (πάντες) is repeated five times in vv. 1–4 and refers to every member of the Israelite people. This will be important in Paul's argument as he goes forward. It is not just the weak or one particular part of the community of Israel that Paul will show were subjected to judgment.

As Paul here moves from examples taken from his own life to expounding Scripture, the first two verses establish a premise for what Paul is about to teach from the story of the wilderness generation. "All" were indeed covenant-community members. This is seen in the fact that they all experienced the presence of the Lord in the cloud and all came through the Sea. Historically Paul is describing the formation of the people of Israel as an independent nation, separated from the nations (notably Egypt). As a covenant community under God's protection, they naturally offer a comparative model for the new-covenant community, who are also a separated people of God and under God's protection (1:2, 8). Thiselton notes that the events offer a "paradigm of redemption." This he outlines as "*from* bondage, *by* God's saving act, *to* a new lifestyle and reality."[10] Earlier it was mentioned that this can be regarded as a second or new exodus.

Paul begins the story with "our fathers" (οἱ πατέρες ἡμῶν). Time and again the story of the exodus and wilderness wanderings was repeated through Israelite history. On many occasions the recounting of these stories began with the words "our fathers" (NIV: "our ancestors" or "our parents"; cf. Deut 5:3; Josh 24:17; Judg 6:13; 1 Kgs 8:53; Neh 9:9, 16; Ps 78:3). The accounts often rejoiced in God's deliverance, but on other occasions they drew attention to the sin of that generation as Paul will do in this section. The fact that the traditions can be used both to point to God's protection and his provision and yet also be used to warn a later generation of judgment means the traditions lend themselves exactly to Paul's purposes here as he instructs the Corinthians.

Of course, "our fathers" (which might be translated in the modern idiom as "our ancestors") refers to past generations of the people of *Israel*. Since this letter is written to a predominantly Gentile congregation, its meaning has generated considerable discussion. Thus, some suggest that "our fathers" refers generally to *Christians* in Corinth whom Paul regarded as children and therefore inheritors of the Old Testament people of faith. Others have suggested that talk of "our fathers" provides evidence that the "strong" were composed

---

9. A litotes. In Paul's writing this same clause is always attached to "brothers" and is used in 12:1; also in Rom 1:13; 11:25; 2 Cor 2:11; and 1 Thess. 4:13. "Forceful"—note the double negative of Οὐ with ἀγνοεῖν.

10. Thiselton, *1 Corinthians*, 724.

of converted *Jewish* Christians. However, that Paul should draw on the Israelite traditions is not surprising. It is certainly no indication that his audience or the intended audience for this part of what he was writing was Jewish. From the start of the Christian church, the continuity of God's people was preached to the Gentiles. God's activity among his people in Israel helps explain his activity among his people "in Christ." This meant that as the gospel was expounded, (Old Testament) Scripture was taught from the beginning to all people. The gospel revelation of the Christ who died and was raised was to be understood in terms of what had happened with Israel. It is the story of God's grace to his people.

The description of the Israelites as "all" being "under the cloud" (πάντες ὑπὸ τὴν νεφέλην) and having "passed through the sea" (διὰ τῆς θαλάσσης διῆλθον) refers to their protection by God who was present in the cloud[11] as they left Egypt and walked on dry ground across the Sea. There are very few places in the traditions where the "cloud" and the "sea" are linked. When they are, it is usually Exodus 14:19–22 that is recalled. There the cloud manifesting the presence of God comes to stand between the Egyptians and the Israelites while the Israelites cross the sea in safety. Paul maintains the same order: cloud covering followed by passing through the sea. Following the destruction of the Egyptians in the sea through the presence of God, the Israelites then "believed in the LORD and his servant Moses" (Exod 14:31 NRSV; cf. Ps 106:7–12, esp. vv. 7, 12). When Philo used the wilderness traditions, he allegorized them. Thus, the cloud coming between the Egyptians and the Israelites revealed the separation of good and evil.[12] But Paul does not do this. His aim is to establish that this great, gracious work and sign of God established his people as a people and nation. "All" Israelites were part of this.

It is this gracious incorporation of his people into the covenant community of Israel, through redemption from Egypt, that enables Paul to talk of this as a "baptism" (v. 2). Paul says that in the cloud and through the sea "all were baptized into Moses" (πάντες εἰς τὸν Μωϋσῆν ἐβαπτίσαντο). The "water" of the sea may have given rise to the analogy with "baptism." Certainly, the word "baptism" has no Jewish precedent in this context of the wilderness accounts. Combine the water of the Sea with the typological understanding of God's redemption under Moses's leadership and with the need for the people to believe in him (Moses) and God,[13] and the language of "baptism" is surely understandable. For Christians, baptism is applied as evidence of God's gracious redemptive work in their lives and that by this and through faith in Christ they have become members of the covenant community of God's people (the church).

However, some still ask whether Paul is talking about baptism. In other words, has Paul now moved on to the subject of sacraments? If he has, then is it to be understood that the arrogance of the elitists, at least in part, can be put down to overconfidence in the sacraments? The view outlined above is that Paul is talking about God's grace in bringing about the formation of a covenant community. He therefore views the comparison between the Israelites and the Christian community in *covenantal* terms.

The majority view undoubtedly is that the issue Paul faced with the elitists could be traced back to a false reliance on the sacraments. William Barclay concisely sums up this position: "[The Corinthian] point of view was, 'we have been baptized and are therefore one with Christ; we have partaken of the

---

11. Exod 14:24: "The LORD in the pillar of fire and of cloud looked down on the Egyptian forces" (ESV). Cf. Josh 24:7 and Ps 105:39.

12. See, e.g., Philo, *Heir* 202–4. Cf. *Moses* 1.178–79; 2.254.
13. Exod 14:31.

sacrament and so of the body and blood of Christ; we are in him and he is in us; therefore we are quite safe; we can eat meat offered to idols and take no harm.' So Paul warns of over-confidence."[14] This commentary has frequently suggested there was a problem of arrogance born of overconfidence among the elitists in Corinth, but *not* that this was caused by an abuse of the sacraments. The sacraments have not been mentioned at all until now (and, as such, are probably not mentioned here either). Even in the opening five verses of this chapter, they are still not the subject of discussion. There is little doubt, of course, that the phrase "baptized into Moses" was arrived at by analogy with "baptism into Christ." But it is more likely, as indicated above, that uppermost in Paul's mind was not the sacrament and its abuse but the *result* of the rite. The result was a community of people to which "all" belonged, just as the exodus through the Sea resulted in the community of Israel. This is suggested firstly by the repeated use of "all" in vv. 1–2. Paul wants the Corinthians to know that "all" the people were identified in a *single* community. Secondly, the experiences of the cloud and sea related to the *identification* of the Israelites as a people or nation. Thirdly, the nation-forming events meant that *all* experienced the same protection by God and *all* received his gifts, as Paul will go on to say. There were no distinctions between the Israelites, no elitists who were given water while others were not, etc. All were part of the community. All received gifts (vv. 3–4), and all found they could be judged (v. 5). So Paul's intended comparison is that *all* who are baptized into Christ and in his Spirit belong to the covenant community. All receive God's gifts, and all will find they can be judged

by God. Thus vv. 1–2 serve to indicate *why* Paul is going to use the wilderness traditions (one covenant people speaks to their successors) and *how* he is going to use them.

It is also worth noting that the matter of "over-confidence" exhibited by some can scarcely be said to start here with mention of the sacraments. It has been a problem noted throughout the epistle. What has become more explicit in the discussion of idol meat is that the overconfidence is found among those claiming to be "knowers" and that Paul identified them as having the gift of "knowledge" (which "puffs up"). One further and surely somewhat obvious point, often completely ignored by those who see the matter as "sacraments," is that it is not "bread and wine" in the wilderness. It is "bread and *water*."

In summary, it is preferable to see in these opening verses that Paul emphasizes the same points that the accounts of the wilderness traditions in Jewish history have emphasized. Notably, the Israelites were identified as God's covenant people by the separation from Egypt in crossing the sea (a "baptism"). No Israelite was exempted as they "believed in God and in Moses." As a people, *all* benefitted from his "spiritual" gifts of manna and water. Even so, as a people, many were judged for their sin because they desired evil. Significantly, this is the classic way these stories were used by Jewish traditions, a point missed by most commentators.[15] Paul's comparison then builds on these points, as will be seen in the next few verses. *All* Christians are identified as covenant people in baptism as they believe in God and in Christ. As his people, *all* benefit from his spiritual gifts. None is exempt. In the same way, Christians who desire evil will

---

14. Barclay, *Letters to the Corinthians*, 87. Also see Bengel, *Gnomon of the New Testament*, 268–73; Fee, *1 Corinthians*, 487ff., clearly reads vv. 14–22 back into vv. 1–5.

15. See below "In Depth: Paul's Use of the Wilderness Traditions of Water and Food." See also Gardner, *Gifts of God*, 121–35 (a section entitled, "The Function of the Wilderness Traditions in Judaism").

face judgment (v. 6). It is the parallel with "desiring evil" that Paul will first take time to elaborate upon in vv. 6–12.

10:3–4a and all ate the same spiritual food, and all drank the same spiritual drink (καὶ πάντες τὸ αὐτὸ πνευματικὸν βρῶμα ἔφαγον, καὶ πάντες τὸ αὐτὸ πνευματικὸν ἔπιον πόμα). The emphasis on "all" continues. It is not just some Israelites who received "spiritual food" and "spiritual drink." All the Israelites did. The reference is to the manna and water that God supplied the Israelites when they found themselves without in the wilderness. Once again, some have said that Paul regards this food and drink of the old covenant to parallel the food and drink of the communion meal in the new covenant. As we have noted, this seems rather unlikely.[16]

The possibility that Paul is truly thinking of the sacrament of communion here becomes even less likely if we examine how the manna and water from the rock *function* in the Jewish traditions themselves, for it is likely Paul uses them in the same way. In those traditions, the manna and the water from the rock were consistently regarded as God's gifts or blessings for his people. As the stories were retold, their emphasis was not on the eating or drinking that the Israelites enjoyed but on the gift nature of God's providential care of his people. This is what Paul draws on as a parallel for God's provision for the people of the new covenant. His use of the word "spiritual" is the key indicator that the parallel he wishes to draw between old and new centers not on the covenant meal but on God's gifts to his covenant people. This makes sense of the local and the greater context.

IN DEPTH: **Paul's Use of the Wilderness Traditions of Water and Food**

So how do the wilderness traditions that Paul draws upon here *function* through the history of Israel? Manna is first mentioned in Exodus 16. In the wilderness of Sin a lack of meat caused the Israelites to grumble against Moses, but the Lord brought quail and manna. The tradition emphasizes both the miraculous nature of the manna that Yahweh gave them to eat (Exod 16:4, 8, 12, 15, 32, 35) and the murmurings that Moses said were "not against us but against the LORD" (v. 8 ESV). In Numbers 20 the Israelites again blamed Moses for the lack of water. Moses used his rod to bring water from the rock (the passage to which Paul turns in 1 Cor 10:4). The harshness of the Egyptian rule experienced by "our fathers" is recalled. Then, as the Israelites committed acts of immorality with the Moabites and offered sacrifices to other gods (Num 25), so God destroyed many (probably the passage to which Paul turns in v. 8). These stories are told again

---

16. The *possibility* that Paul here introduces a new subject of overconfidence in the sacraments cannot be ruled out. However, it seems that often too much is made of the word "spiritual," which some seem to imbue with the meaning of "mystical" or sacramentally efficacious. Horrell, *Social Ethos of the Corinthian Correspondence*, 144, follows the majority when he writes, "The main aim of the passage is to warn against the complacent assumption that through sharing in baptism and the Lord's Supper, people are irrevocably confirmed as God's people."

in Deuteronomy. Even though the Israelites had evidence of God's blessings, yet "in spite of this word [they] did not believe the LORD [their] God" (1:32 ESV) and were presumptuous. Mighty signs were performed by God so that they "might know that the LORD is God; there is no other beside him" (4:35 ESV). In the covenant renewal ceremony of Deuteronomy 29 the people are judged because they do not "understand" (εἰδέναι, v. 4 [v. 3 LXX]). They failed to discern the nature of the "signs" and "great wonders" of God's provision in the wilderness (v. 3). They are warned again about the great danger of relying on a false sense of security even as they indulge in sin, as "one who blesses himself in his heart, saying, 'I shall be safe, though I walk in the stubbornness of my heart.' This will lead to the sweeping away of moist and dry alike" (Deut 29:19 ESV). So once again the blessings and the curses of the covenant are laid before the people (Deut 27:9–28:68).

The next account is given in Deuteronomy 32. As noted, it may have been on Paul's mind in 1 Corinthians 8, and he quotes from it in 10:20–22. Here God's faithfulness, justice, and goodness are extolled. God himself is called "Rock," emphasizing the permanence and faithfulness of the God who chose them (Deut 32:15, 18; also Isa 44:8). They are described as growing "fat" and resisting God (Deut 32:15). Again, they are accused of not "understanding" or "discerning" God's works among them (v. 29). We return to this passage further on in 1 Corinthians 10.

Nehemiah 9 recounts the great covenant-renewal ceremony for those who had returned from the captivity. Again, the wilderness traditions of food and water figure prominently, and lessons must be learned from their history. They are told that "our fathers" were presumptuous, stiff-necked, and disobedient (vv. 9, 16). They forgot God in spite of the law given on Sinai and the *bread* "from heaven" (LXX: ἐξ οὐρανοῦ) and *water* "from the rock" that God had given (v. 15). Then the golden calf incident is remembered, and God's forgiveness is recalled (vv. 18–19). Then there follows a most significant statement in v. 20, especially as we consider how these traditions are used in 1 Corinthians 10. The text reads: "You gave your good Spirit to instruct them and did not withhold your manna from their mouth and gave them water for their thirst" (Neh 9:20 ESV). References to the Holy Spirit are rare enough in the Old Testament, but this is the first instance of the Holy Spirit being directly associated with God's gifts of manna and water in the wilderness and the understanding of these gifts necessary for God's people. All the traditions emphasize that the origin of the manna and water is with God or from heaven, and most indicate that the people needed to "discern" or "understand" their significance. In the end, though, the people became arrogant and presumptuous and "became fat" (v. 25 ESV). Nevertheless, in another link to 1 Corinthians 10 (v. 13) this passage, like all the other passages that recount the stories, stresses the faithfulness of God (Neh 9:7, 17, 20, 22, 28). Isaiah 63 also looks to the work of the Holy Spirit both for the future of God's people but also in looking back to the wilderness days with Moses. In the wilderness they were said to have "grieved his Holy Spirit" (v. 10). As the prophet recalls the passage through the Sea, he asks the rhetorical question: "Where is he who put in the midst of them his Holy Spirit, who caused his glorious arm to go at the right hand of Moses, who divided the waters before them . . . ?" (63:11–12 ESV).

Many other accounts of the same traditions all reveal the same main issues.[17] One final passage worth mentioning here is Psalm 78. This Psalm is a *mashal* that reveals lessons for the present drawn from the past. Once again those who heard this Psalm were not to be like "their fathers" who suffered for "not keep-[ing] God's covenant" (Ps 78:8, 10 ESV). Hyperbole describes the water coming from the rock like "streams" (vv. 15–16, 20). The sin of "testing" God through "craving" (v. 18) was interpreted as not having faith in God or trusting his salvation (v. 22). They were punished for their lack of belief. Yet in their punishment the people "remembered" God, their "Rock" and "Redeemer" (v. 35). Despite their rebellions, God remained faithful. The manna "rained down" from opened "doors of heaven" and is called the "bread of the angels" (vv. 23–25 ESV).

The link in Nehemiah and Isaiah of God's Spirit with the gifts of manna and water and the discernment necessary to understand the gifts or use them appropriately is significant. These three gifts (water, manna, and understanding or discernment) are mentioned in almost all the accounts as coming "from heaven" or from God, so it is not surprising that Nehemiah would explain this in terms of the Holy Spirit. This is the key link to Paul and 1 Corinthians 10. Paul uses the stories in the whole of chapter 10 in a similar way. Manna and water are "spiritual." Since gifts to the covenant community come from God's Spirit (are "spiritual") and need to be discerned in terms of their meaning and use, then Paul is saying the same thing as Nehemiah. That is, the manna and water are gifts from God's Spirit (1 Cor 10:3–4), and judgment awaits those who abuse them by failing to discern their proper intent in the community. Constantly, the people who received these gifts were said to have become presumptuous or arrogant or fat. They became overly secure, and in the end they turned to other gods and were judged. Yet all the traditions also talk in the same context about God's faithfulness (e.g., Neh 9:7, 17, 20, 22, 28; Ps 78:67–72). These are just the

---

17. For further detail on the function of the traditions in the Psalms, the prophets, Qumran, Philo, the wisdom literature, John 6, etc., see Gardner, *Gifts of God*, 127–33.

points that it seems Paul draws from these traditions (1 Cor 10:6–10). God gave each member ("all") of his (new) covenant community spiritual gifts as they were baptized into Christ, just as his Spirit had given gifts to the older covenant community when they were baptized into Moses and became a covenant people. Some of his new-covenant people have felt these gifts guaranteed a security such that they could do things that in the end lead them away from the Lord. They have become arrogant and overconfident. This is what happened among the Israelites. The people are called upon to repent. God is then always seen to be faithful when they do repent, as the traditions recount. Paul makes the same points that repentance is needed and that God is faithful (v. 13).

10:4b For they drank from the spiritual rock that followed them, and the rock was Christ (ἔπινον γὰρ ἐκ πνευματικῆς ἀκολουθούσης πέτρας· ἡ πέτρα δὲ ἦν ὁ Χριστός). Paul continues to draw upon the wilderness traditions, except that here the rock is identified with Christ. "For" (γάρ) reminds the reader that this is a further explanation of what has been said in the previous sentences. In the wilderness traditions it is God or the Holy Spirit who are seen to be the providers of the water. Here, for Paul it is Jesus. This is a distinctively Christian interpretation of the traditions.

Paul is determined to make clear that genuine parallels can be drawn between old and new-covenant communities and that the Christian community must learn essential lessons from what happened in the past. He has done this with the word "baptized," he has done it with his use of the word "spiritual," and now he does it by this direct identification of Christ with the rock. It is more than likely that, once again, Paul has in mind the Jewish way in which these traditions were told, especially perhaps in a text like Deuteronomy 32, to which he returns on a number of occasions. In Deuteronomy 32:4 God is the giver of the manna and water but is also called "Rock," a description of his faithful and consistent character. As the poem recalls, God guided his people and provided for them, but Israel

"scoffed at the Rock of his salvation" (v. 15 ESV). So they turned to other gods and sacrificed to demons and "were unmindful of the Rock that bore [them]" (v. 18 ESV). The poem comes to an end by saying that "their rock is not as our Rock" as it compares the gods of the enemies with the true God. Psalms 78 and 95 also talk of water coming from the rock and later refer to God as the "rock" of his people (78:35; 95:1). Thus, seeing Christ as the provider for the covenant people is readily understandable in the light of the new (Christian) understanding that Christ is in fact the covenant Lord.

Many have sought other links between Christ and the rock to explain especially the idea of the rock that "followed" them. To some extent it must be said that this quest, though producing some interesting ideas from Jewish thought, has proved largely unhelpful. The wilderness traditions were used widely in all ages of Jewish history for various purposes but mostly for the purposes noted above. At times the description of God's providence in the wilderness, especially with the provision of food and water from the rock, is restated with considerable poetic hyperbole (e.g., Pss 78:16; 81:16), and later Jewish expositions of the traditions further that hyperbole. Given that the function of these traditions, as seen above, was in part to remind the Israelites of God's great faithfulness to them and provision for them, it is not surprising that ideas might develop that the giving of the water continued throughout their time in the desert much as the manna continued for many years.[18]

In what sense did the apostle think of Christ being present in the wilderness or in the rock? Some have suggested that this is allegory of the sort found in Philo, but this is unlikely. Neither is it likely that Paul arrived at the idea from literature such as Sirach or Wisdom. In Wisdom the gifts were given by wisdom, and the rock was wisdom. Bourke has suggested that Paul thus arrives at the idea that since wisdom was the rock and Christ is wisdom therefore Christ was the rock.[19] Perhaps more likely is that Paul draws on the epithet "Rock" for God as found in Deuteronomy 32. Since "Rock" speaks to God's covenant faithfulness to his people, Paul could therefore simply be applying the rock idea to Christ in much the same way as he was able to take the Old Testament "Lord" (Yahweh; LXX: κύριος) and apply it to Christ.

Paul saw Christ as the fulfillment of God's faithfulness and the embodiment of his grace (1:4). "In Christ Jesus" the Corinthians received every spiritual gift (1:4–7). In line with Old Testament teaching, Paul regarded the manna and water as gifts from the faithful God who was called "Rock." But Paul had a new "spiritual" understanding of this. Christ was the source of the water, water that was "spiritual" in that it pointed back to Christ. To ask questions about the *manner* in which this was true misses Paul's point and is a question perhaps more prompted by anachronistic sacramental discussions than by v. 4. Paul was direct. The rock *was* Christ. Detailed analysis of how Christ was there is not addressed. For Paul, the fact is that he *was*, and that is God's revelation to Paul. It is thus meaningless to ask whether the Israelites should have seen Christ in the wilderness, for that understanding is precisely what is new to Paul. It is not that "Paul's readers should see the rock then as an equivalent to Christ now"[20] but rather that they should look

---

18. Some of the sources that get closest to this idea in Jewish writings are mostly based on Num 21:16–20. In Targum Neofiti on Num 21:16ff the names of the places past which the Israelites travelled were interpreted literally: Beer was taken to refer to a "well," Mattanah referred to a "gift," Nahaliel to a "torrent," Bamoth to "high places," and so on. This resulted in an interpretation of Numbers that the "well" was a "gift" that became a "torrent" that went up to the "high places" and down to the valleys (A. Diéz Macho et al., *Neophyti I*, 6 vols. [Madrid and Barcelona: Consejo Superior de Investigaciones Cientificas, 1968–79]). Another Targum adds that the well went around the entire camp of Israel and gave a drink to each person at his tent door (see Diez Macho, *Neophyti I*, 4:582n2 (*Pseudo Jonathan*). These ideas may have given rise to the idea that the source of water followed the Israelites, but for our purposes we must remember they talk of the *well*, not a rock, and Paul refers to Christ as the "following" rock. Others cite Numbers Rabbah 1.5 on 21:17: "How was the well constructed? It was rock-shaped like a kind of bee-hive and wherever they journeyed it rolled along. . . . When the standards halted . . . that same rock would settle" (translation from *Midrash Rabbah*, eds. H. Freedman and M. Simon, 10 vols. [London: Soncino, 1961]). The writer also wrote of the well having been "given" as evidenced in the text "he opened the rock." The idea of water

following the Israelites was present in earlier traditions. *Sifre* on Numbers 11:21 reads, "Did not a brook follow them in the wilderness and provide them with fat fish?" (This work was probably edited in the fourth-century AD, but it represents traditions of Tannaitic rabbis. See Paul P. Levertoff, *Midrash Sifre on Numbers: Selections from Early Rabbinic Scriptural Interpretations* [London: SPCK, 1926], 77.) In t. Sukkah 3:11 we read, "So the well which was with Israel in the wilderness, was like a rock . . . travelling with them . . . and it made mighty streams." (This text also mentions the well going up the mountains and down valleys. See online Safaria Library, https://www.sefaria.org/texts.) However, not even Philo mentions a "following" rock. Paul was drawing attention to God's continued care with "spiritual gifts" for "all" the people of Israel. It may be that the type of text referred to above gave him the idea of a "following rock." Certainly, the reference to "following" conveys the idea of the continuing nature of God's supply for his people.

19. M. M. Bourke, "The Eucharist and Wisdom in First Corinthians," in *Studiorum Paulinorum Congressus Internationalis Catholicus, Vol 1*, AnBib 17 (Rome: Pontifical Biblical Institute, 1963), 376–81, esp. 376–77. For an extended discussion on Christ as "wisdom" in relation to what Paul says here, see Thiselton, *1 Corinthians*, 728–29.

20. *Contra* Dunn, *Christology*, 184.

at Scripture and see a directly parallel example to their own situation, for the covenant Lord is with his people now as he was with Israel.

10:5 Nevertheless, God was not pleased with most of them, for they were killed in the wilderness (ἀλλ᾽ οὐκ ἐν τοῖς πλείοσιν αὐτῶν εὐδόκησεν ὁ θεός, κατεστρώθησαν γὰρ ἐν τῇ ἐρήμῳ). The wilderness traditions had almost always contained the salutary reminder of how God had judged the Israelites despite his gracious gifts among them. They had become "fat" and presumptuous, and so many of them were killed by God in judgment in the wilderness. The strong adversative (ἀλλά) reminds the reader that this is not what might have been expected. God had been gracious but was now judging them. Psalm 78:29–31 is but one place that recounts the eating and immediately describes God's judgment of the wilderness generation. It may be that Paul is thinking of the death of the twenty-three thousand to which he refers in v. 8, where he looks back to Numbers 25:9. But when Paul says "with most of them" (ἐν τοῖς πλείοσιν αὐτῶν), he may be thinking of the overall experience of the Israelites in the wilderness. If this is the case, as Garland says, it is an "understatement since only two, Joshua and Caleb, survived and entered the promised land."[21]

This is Paul's concern for the Corinthians. He sees parallels and patterns at multiple levels between the covenant community of the wilderness generation and that in his day in Corinth. Both communities have been mightily blessed by God, who has poured out his gifts on both. The Corinthians lacked no grace-gift and had been enriched "in all speech and all knowledge" (1 Cor 1:5). But God killed many of the Israelites in judgment. Now

Paul will write of the reasons why they were judged and show the parallels yet again, for the Corinthians face the very same dangers. Ellis rightly says that Paul, having presented God's grace in 10:1–4, moves in the verses that follow to "judgment typology."[22]

10:6 Now these things are an example for us, so that we might not have evil desires as they desired [evil things] (Ταῦτα δὲ τύποι ἡμῶν ἐγενήθησαν, εἰς τὸ μὴ εἶναι ἡμᾶς ἐπιθυμητὰς κακῶν, καθὼς κἀκεῖνοι ἐπεθύμησαν). "These things" (ταῦτα) both looks backward to the gracious gifts God has given and to Christ's presence with the community and forward to the examples of community judgment laid out in vv. 6–11. Paul says they are an "example for us" (τύποι ἡμῶν).[23] Of course, he is not suggesting that they were *only* written for the people of the new covenant. In themselves they were evidence of God's redemptive and judging purposes among his people. Yet in the apostolic use of events like this, their new understanding of what happened *then* could now be shown providentially to parallel events of the day in which the reader lived. As Hays puts it, "Paul reads Scripture in the conviction that its narratives and prophecies all point to his own time . . . in which all of God's past dealings with Israel and the world have come to their climactic point."[24]

"Us" is Paul and all Christians "upon whom the ends of the ages have come" (v. 11). The problem is sin. Paul's use of the first-person plural is a reminder that he was always able to admit that he too was a sinner and also had evil desires (εἰς τὸ μὴ εἶναι ἡμᾶς ἐπιθυμητὰς κακῶν). The problem of the wilderness generation was that they "desired" (ἐπιθυμέω) evil things. This verb is the one used

---

21. Garland, *1 Corinthians*, 458. See Num 14:2–33.

22. Ellis, *Prophecy and Hermeneutic*, 168.

23. The word τύπος here means little more than "example." It is unlikely that Paul has any technical meaning in mind,

though of course he does see these examples as tools for his teaching.

24. Hays, *First Corinthians*, 162.

in the Ten Commandments and translated there as "covet" (Exod 20:17). Because of this link to the Ten Commandments, it may be that the word "desiring" or "craving" came to be a prominent and general description of sin. Paul sets out the sin of "desiring evil" in four examples of sin that feature prominently in the Old Testament stories of the wilderness: idolatry, immorality, testing Christ (though it is "God" or "the Lord" in the Old Testament), and grumbling.[25]

These are spelled out in the next few verses. All the sins or particular desires he mentions are, of course, sins that the Corinthians are involved with. The fact that these sins have happened in both the wilderness and Christian communities further highlights the close model that is provided for the present Christian generation by the past wilderness generation. The Corinthians must learn the lessons that God's people throughout history have had to learn. When self-confidence leads to sin, God will judge.

10:7 Do not take part in idolatry as some of them did; as it is written, "The people sat down to eat and drink and stood up to play" (μηδὲ εἰδωλολάτραι γίνεσθε, καθώς τινες αὐτῶν· ὥσπερ γέγραπται, Ἐκάθισεν ὁ λαὸς φαγεῖν καὶ πεῖν, καὶ ἀνέστησαν παίζειν). The first of the four sins is idolatry. The issue of "food offered to idols" remains the key issue (8:1). This is the special matter that they have raised with Paul and that Paul is directly concerned about. They have arrived at this place of sin through overconfidence and presumption about their community status, but the presenting problem must itself also be addressed.

The wilderness traditions, once again, are excellent for Paul's paraenetic purposes. The verse that Paul quotes (Exod 32:6) is in a passage recounting the incident of the golden calf. The word "to play" (παίζειν) is a New Testament *hapax legomenon*. It refers here to the cultic use of dance and games that in their licentiousness may have had an erotic content. In Exodus 32 the Hebrew word also probably connotes sexual revelry. It is possible that the Corinthian idolatrous rites may also have involved various sexual sins. On the other hand, it may be that since Paul has already addressed sexual sin (1 Cor 5:1–2, 10–11; 6:9, 13, 18) he was thinking more widely than simply about the idol feasts of the cult.

The command is clear. There must be no taking part in the sort of cultic idolatry that is referred to in the account of Exodus 32. If there was any "innocence" on the part of the elitist Corinthians in somehow thinking that they could get involved with activities in the pagan temples that were religiously neutral, Paul dispels the idea immediately. If, as seems likely, this came from their so-called "knowledge," then the knowledge is plainly *wrong* and deeply dangerous. Since Paul is later going to address the matter of "participation" in demons (vv. 18–20), Thiselton is surely rightly to suggest that the Greek command γίνεσθε means "do not take part in."[26] Idolatrous cultic rights and the behavior attached to them have been judged by God in the past and it will happen again. This is a classic case in which the self-control of which Paul has been speaking in 9:25–27 is vital for the believer.

10:8 Neither should we indulge[27] in sexual immorality, as some of them indulged, and in one

---

25. The noun (ἐπιθυμητής) is used in Num 11:34 where Israelites are judged by God and die at Kibroth Hattaavah ("tombs of the cravers") because of their "craving." They die even as they begin to eat the "meat" (v. 33; LXX: τὰ κρέα; cf. 1 Cor 8:13), that is, the quail that the Lord provides.

26. Thiselton, *1 Corinthians*, 736.

27. As the list of imperatives continues, the meaning of the repeated particle (μηδὲ) with the negative imperative is best translated as "neither" (thus, "do not," v. 7, is followed by "neither" in vv. 8–9 and "nor" in v. 10). The hortatory subjunctive (πορνεύωμεν) in the first plural is used as in v. 9 (ἐκπειράζωμεν). As in v. 6, Paul uses the first-person plural and so includes him-

day twenty-three thousand fell (μηδὲ πορνεύωμεν, καθώς τινες αὐτῶν ἐπόρνευσαν, καὶ ἔπεσαν μιᾷ ἡμέρᾳ εἴκοσι τρεῖς χιλιάδες). It is possible that Paul could be referring here to the immorality (πορνεία) he has highlighted earlier in the epistle.[28] However, this second imperative does seem closely related to the first (v. 7) and is part of the continuing exposition of the wilderness narratives. Thus, it is likely that Paul thinks of how Israelite idolatry led to sexual license and so here insists that Christians must not indulge in sexual immorality. Idolatry and sexual promiscuity are mentioned together in a number of places.[29]

Paul's example is taken from Numbers 25:1–9 where sexual sin and idolatry are explicitly linked. That passage also addresses the matter of eating in the presence of idols, to which Paul turns in 1 Corinthians 10:18–22. In Numbers 25, illicit sexual relations between the men of Israel and Moabite women led to idolatry. The women invited the Israelites to sacrifice to their gods "and the people ate and bowed down to their gods. So Israel yoked himself to Baal of Peor" (vv. 2–3 RSV). The end of this idolatry and sexual sin is, once again, the

severe judgment of God: twenty-four thousand[30] died from a God-given plague (v. 9). Once again Paul's point is clear. "Some of them" died under God's judgment even though they were identified as "Israel," and this happened because they desired evil (v. 6).

10:9 Neither should we test Christ, as some of them tested [him] and were destroyed by the serpents (μηδὲ ἐκπειράζωμεν τὸν Χριστόν,[31] καθώς τινες αὐτῶν ἐπείρασαν, καὶ ὑπὸ τῶν ὄφεων ἀπώλλυντο). In an elliptical construction that omits the object for the verb, Paul says that the Israelites "tested [him]," that is, Christ. This had led to their destruction. The sin of "testing" (πειράζω) God was also prominent in the wilderness accounts and often linked to "craving" or "desiring" (Exod 17:2; Deut 6:16; Pss 78:18; 95:8–9; 106:14). Paul, as one "on whom the ends of the ages have come" (v. 11), could talk of *Christ* being "tested" instead of God. This change may have been facilitated by the LXX of Numbers 21 where the people were sinning against the "Lord" (κύριος). However, in v. 4 Paul has already established the presence of Christ among God's people in the wilderness.

---

self in carefully applying lessons from the wilderness. In UK English the negative imperative might simply be translated, "neither must we . . ." (i.e., "we must not").

28. For example, in his summary exhortation in 6:18: "Flee sexual immorality."

29. See "In Depth: Sexual Sin, Idolatry, and the Covenant Community" at 6:20. In Rev 2:14, 20 the writer makes reference to Balaam and Balak, employing similar vocabulary to Paul's in 1 Corinthians. Balak put a "stumbling block" (σκάνδαλον) before the people of Israel so they ate "food sacrificed to idols" (εἰδωλόθυτα) and indulged in "sexual immorality" (πορνεύω; cf. also Philo, *Moses* 1.301–2). Wisdom 14:12 says, "For the idea of making idols was the beginning of fornication [πορνεία]" (NRSV).

30. Paul mentions twenty-three thousand and Num 25 speaks of twenty-four thousand people dying in the plague. Many suggestions are offered to resolve this tension. Lietzmann, Barclay, Barrett, and others suggest that Paul is quoting from memory. Calvin (*First Corinthians*, 208–9) assumes that

neither Moses nor Paul were that concerned to make "an exact count of individuals" but rather gave approximate numbers: "Moses gives the upper limit, Paul the lower, and so there is really no discrepancy." Collins and Kremer believe Paul is influenced by the reference in Num 26:61–62 where, in another time of judgment, twenty-three thousand are mentioned. There is no obvious solution to the puzzle, but it makes no difference to Paul's point at all, and Calvin's is as good as any answer that carefully respects the trustworthiness of Scripture.

31. "Christ" (Χριστόν) has strong early support (𝔓[46] D F G K L Ψ 630. 1241. 1505. 1739. 1881 𝔐 latt sy co; Ir[lat] Or[1739mg]) and is the harder reading since the manner of Christ's presence in the wilderness needs to be explained. Some variants replace "Christ" with "Lord" (κύριον; א B C P 33. 104. 326. 365. 1175. 2464 sy[hmg]), and others replace with "God" (θεόν; A 81). These changes also bring the text into alignment with some verses of the LXX where the Israelites tested "God" (cf. Pss 78:18 [77:18 LXX]; 106:14 [105:14 LXX]) or "the Lord" (cf. Exod 17:7). Metzger, *Textual Commentary*, 494, rates this a "B".

Once again, this serious sin of the people led to their judgment by God, and some of them were destroyed by the serpents. The incident is recorded in Numbers 21:4–6 where, because of the lack of food, the people became "impatient" and "spoke against" God and Moses. In a probable reference to this incident, Psalm 78:18 [77:18 LXX] talks of them "test[ing] [ἐκπειράζω] God in their heart by demanding the food they craved" (ESV).

"Testing" God describes the sin of not trusting him for his provision or not trusting in his promises. Yet it is more than this. The Israelites did not trust the Lord to provide, but even then, when he did provide, they held his provision in contempt: "We detest this miserable food" (Num 21:5). It is this contempt for the Lord and his gifts and provision for the community that draws down immediate judgment in the form of the snakes (v. 6). Once again, the result is that many died.

10:10 Nor should you grumble,[32] as some of them grumbled, and were destroyed by the Destroyer (μηδὲ γογγύζετε, καθάπερ τινὲς αὐτῶν ἐγόγγυσαν, καὶ ἀπώλοντο ὑπὸ τοῦ ὀλοθρευτοῦ). "Testing" the covenant Lord, especially as they "grumble" (γογγύζω), will provoke his judgment. The switch to the second-plural imperative amplifies the direct application to the Corinthians of what Paul is saying (note the repeated "as some of them," τινὲς αὐτῶν). Paul insists that the Corinthians must see how similar they are to the Israelites and understand that these wilderness accounts are given as warnings for the Christian community. He returns to this in v. 11. There is no Old Testament text that directly links "the Destroyer" with the "grumbling" of the Israelites. However, Psalm 106:23–25 probably provides Paul with the link he

wants. There the verb "to destroy" (ἐξολοθρεύω; Ps 105:23 LXX) appears twice in proximity to "grumbling," as the psalmist recounts the sin of the Israelites in the wilderness (the same form of the verb "they grumbled" [ἐγόγγυσαν] is used in Ps 105:25 LXX). Furthermore, the specific incident the psalmist is recounting at this point is the sin of the golden calf, to which Paul has just referred in v. 7.

"Grumbling" in the wilderness stories was directed against Moses and God, though in the end all grumbling is in fact grumbling against God (e.g., Exod 16:7; Num 16:41). The problem with grumbling was similar to the problem of testing God. It reflected the tendency of the Israelites to look back to Egypt with longing and hence to desire sin. This becomes explicit when we read Exodus 17:2–3: "Moses said to them, 'Why do you quarrel with me? Why do you *test* the LORD?' But the people thirsted there for water, and the people *grumbled* against Moses and said, 'Why did you bring us up out of Egypt, to kill us and our children and our livestock with thirst?'" (ESV). The problem of returning to the past is one of Paul's chief concerns here. The arrogant believe they are safe in their salvation, evidenced by the Spirit's grace-gifts among them. But they want to have their cake and eat it. With a complete lack of discernment and despite their "knowledge," they are prepared to "partake at the table of the Lord and at the table of demons" (v. 21).

These last few verses of examples of judgment reveal how concerned Paul is that these arrogant Corinthians have truly never considered that they might be subject to judgment. Paul has provided examples of God's people receiving his gifts and yet finding themselves, because of their sin, under his severest judgment. The use of the verb "to destroy"

---

32. A variant makes this a first plural in line with the first plural in 10:9 (ℵ D F G 33 bo). Nevertheless, the text is the harder reading and has strong support: A B C K L P Ψ 81 𝔐 lat sy sa, among others.

in both vv. 9 and 10 (ἀπόλλυμι)[33] and the noun "destroyer" in v. 10 recall the warning of destruction in 8:11 and demonstrate the result of the "sin against Christ" in 8:12.

10:11 Now these things were happening to them by way of example, and it was written as a warning for us, upon whom the ends of the ages have come (ταῦτα δὲ τυπικῶς συνέβαινεν ἐκείνοις, ἐγράφη δὲ πρὸς νουθεσίαν ἡμῶν, εἰς οὓς τὰ τέλη τῶν αἰώνων κατήντηκεν). This verse summarizes why the Corinthians should take note of what Paul has been writing. The adverb, "by way of example" (τυπικῶς), is not found elsewhere in the New Testament or the LXX, but means following after a model or pattern. In v. 6 a similar statement was made (see comments there). However, in v. 6 Paul says the examples are "for us," while in this verse the events happened by way of example "to them." As Thiselton notes, the continuous imperfect in this verse is significant (συνέβαινεν). The pattern or model being offered in the wilderness was one of continuing events from which the people of Israel should have been learning.[34] Each successive judgment should have served as a warning to them. They were not *all* destroyed as a result of a single event. At different times "some of them" were destroyed as a result of various rebellions against God. Paul's point is that the same judgments can happen to the Christian community "upon whom the ends of the ages have come."

For Paul, this is the age toward which all history and all God's activities with his people have been leading. He sums this up by describing Christians as those "upon whom the ends of the ages have come." The perfect tense (κατήντηκεν) emphasizes the continuing implications for God's people of the arrival of this age. In line with other New Testament writers, Paul understands the coming of Christ to have inaugurated the "last days" (cf. Acts 2:17; Heb 1:2; Jas 5:3; 2 Pet 3:3). Yet the plural "ends of the ages" (τὰ τέλη τῶν αἰώνων) is strange and has given rise to some discussion. It may simply be, as Bruce suggests, that the plural here is by attraction to the plural of the word "ages."[35] It is difficult to see how Paul could mean that one age has come to an end and another begun simply because "the ends" can hardly refer to the beginning of an age![36] Of course, the age of the Messiah and the last days overlaps with the old (cf. 2:6–8; 3:18), but Christians are the ones who, in Christ, have come to understand the significance of the new that has arrived. It is for this reason that what Paul says is so vital. Christians need to know that God judges and will judge even his people if they fail to heed the gospel of Christ.

---

33. In v. 9 the third-plural imperfect is used while in v. 10 it is the aorist that is used as in the previous verses. The imperfect may add a certain vividness to the narrative as the event is "presented as unfolding before the eyes of the reader." In other words, it may not be so much *tense* as spatial *aspect* that indicates the reason for its use. See Constantine R. Campbell, *Verbal Aspect, the Indicative Mood, and Narrative: Soundings in the Greek of the New Testament*, SBG 13 (New York: Peter Lang, 2007), 84.

34. Thiselton, *1 Corinthians*, 746.

35. Bruce, *1 and 2 Corinthians*, 93.

36. Robertson and Plummer, *First Corinthians*, 207, quote Hort who, in commenting on 1 Pet 1:20 and the word "times," says it "denotes successive periods in the history of humanity, and perhaps also the parallel periods for different nations and parts of the world." He goes on to say that this speaks more simply of Paul's word "ages" (αἰῶνες). In this view, various ages of history, including Jewish ages—perhaps of Moses, the law, etc.—and ages of humankind generally, have come to their goal as the new age of the last days begins.

IN DEPTH: Further Comments on the Use of Scripture in 10:1–11

The idea that Scriptures will need further, detailed interpretation in the future may have its origins in the Old Testament itself. Some have suggested that passages like Isaiah 8:16–17 or sections of Daniel point in the direction that some writing in Scripture had a meaning that was yet to be revealed (cf. Dan 12:4 where words are "sealed until the time of the end" [NRSV]). However, none of this is a necessary background for what Paul says here. In a typically Jewish way that may be rightly described as a midrash, Paul structured a paraphrase of various Old Testament texts in vv. 1–5 around the word "all" (πάντες). In vv. 6–10 he then expounded and applied the text, adding an additional text in v. 7. But the great difference from a standard Jewish midrashic approach of explaining and applying a text to the current situation is that Paul's exposition is dependent on the new wisdom and perspective provided by Christ's coming. As we have seen, when Paul looks back at the wilderness traditions and expounds them, they are not just an analogy "for us" today. With the revelation of Christ, Paul sees *Christ* present in the wilderness and giving gifts to God's people. The people (Israelites and Christians) are the same, God's covenant people. The covenant Lord is the same, Christ. Christ was at work then and now in the "exodus" of his people. God's people then and now are to learn and to understand. In this sense, all that has been written in the past serves as more than simply "warning" or "example" or even "pattern," even though these words are useful and help with translation.

10:12 Therefore, let anyone who thinks he stands take heed lest he fall (ὥστε ὁ δοκῶν ἑστάναι βλεπέτω μὴ πέσῃ). The word "therefore" (ὥστε) shows the centrality of this short verse, and the direct application forms the climax to the argument. *This is the Corinthian problem.* Some feel secure and think they "stand" safely in the covenant community without fear of judgment. They are arrogant in that they do indeed "think they stand." Paul insists with an imperative (βλεπέτω) that they must "watch out!" or "take heed" lest they fall. The

danger is real and deeply disturbing for Paul, as he has made clear.

Paul again demonstrates he thinks in "covenant" categories as he writes of "standing" and "falling." The verb "to stand" (ἵστημι) invariably carries theological weight when used by Paul. Though it can mean "established" or "stand secure" (Rom 3:31; cf. 2 Cor 13:1), it normally refers to standing before God. People can stand before God by faith (Rom 11:20; 2 Cor 1:24), but it is the Lord himself who enables this standing.[37] This means that judg-

---

37. It is unlikely that Paul is here thinking of "standing in the faith" (1 Cor 16:13) where a different Greek word is used (στήκω) and the issue being addressed is different.

ment on such a person belongs to God alone (Rom 14:4). Once justified by faith, a person "stands" in grace (Rom 5:2). This covenant understanding of the word was also clearly present in the LXX where "stand" (ἵστημι) is used to translate the same ideas. God's covenant "stands" secure (e.g., Ps 105:10 [104:10 LXX]). In Jeremiah 7:8–15 those who seek after other gods cannot "stand" before God in his house (v. 10). This is why "falling" is theologically the opposite of "standing" before the covenant Lord. There is surely considerable irony here in that the elitists, who thought they stood but were causing people to "stumble" (8:8, 11), were in fact themselves in danger of "falling." Paul's comment, "anyone who thinks he stands" (ὁ δοκῶν ἑστάναι) provides another link back to 8:2, "if anyone thinks he knows" (εἴ τις δοκεῖ ἐγνωκέναι). This person in 8:2 is the arrogant "knower" who is reminded by Paul that he does not yet know as he ought. The person in 10:12 is surely the same: those who think they stand must be reminded that they are in danger of falling.

10:13 No temptation has overtaken you except what is common to a human being. God is faithful, and he will not let you be tempted above what you are able, but with the temptation he will also provide a way out so that you can bear up under it (πειρασμὸς ὑμᾶς οὐκ εἴληφεν εἰ μὴ ἀνθρώπινος· πιστὸς δὲ ὁ θεός, ὃς οὐκ ἐάσει ὑμᾶς πειρασθῆναι ὑπὲρ ὃ δύνασθε, ἀλλὰ ποιήσει σὺν τῷ πειρασμῷ καὶ τὴν ἔκβασιν τοῦ δύνασθαι ὑπενεγκεῖν). Verse 13 is not difficult to locate logically in Paul's argument, once it is realized that he was using the wilderness traditions *as they had normally been used in Jewish history*. The function of v. 13 is the same as the function of the stress on God's covenant faithfulness in those traditions. The logic goes like this:

God "tested" (πειράζω) his people so that they would learn to rely on him (cf. Deut 8:2). When they failed this test, they were guilty of "tempting" (ἐκπειράζω) or "proving" God (Ps 78:18 [77:18 LXX]; cf. 1 Cor 10:9). Thus, the whole situation was hopeless if God himself, who had originally chosen them, did not remain faithful to them. This was what Paul had acknowledged in 1:8–9, but it needed repeating if the warnings against arrogance and false security from the past were to be understood.

At first glance this verse seems out of place. Verse 14 could follow reasonably easily from v. 12. Godet commented, "This verse is undoubtedly one of the most difficult of the whole Epistle, at least as to the logical connection joining it to what precedes and to what follows."[38] However, the problem is greatly diminished when it is remembered that the faithfulness of God, despite the people's rebellion, is common to almost all the accounts of the wilderness events. Earlier it was suggested that the idea of Christ as the "rock" (10:4) was drawn from the epithet "Rock" that was applied to God, especially in Deuteronomy 32. It served clearly as a reference to the covenant Lord's faithfulness in providing for his people in the wilderness.[39] In fact, the description of God as "the faithful God" appears only twice in the LXX. In Deuteronomy 7:9 God is called "a faithful God" (θεὸς πιστός), "who keeps covenant and steadfast love." Then in Deuteronomy 32:4 we read, "God ["the Rock" in Hebrew], his work is true, and all his ways are justice, a faithful God [θεὸς πιστός], and without unrighteousness, just and right is the Lord." The covenant ideas abound here. Even as the Israelites are warned of God's judgment, God's nature to be faithful to and protective of his people is emphasized. Thus, the exodus, when God brought them

---

38. Godet, *First Corinthians*, 2:68.
39. The importance of Deut 32 to Paul was mentioned

above and will be examined more closely when looking at 10:20–22.

out of Egypt and brought his people through "test-ing," all the while remaining faithful to them, is stressed.

The temptation Paul has in mind may be the general sin of "desiring evil" (v. 6) or the more specific sin of idolatry (v. 7). This would then lead easily into v. 14: "Flee from idolatry." However, though the sin of idolatry is indeed addressed next, it seems more likely that in this sweeping text Paul is thinking generally of the sin of self-pride seen in those who believed they "stood" when they did not. For his covenant people, however, God faith-fully provides the "way out" (ἔκβασις) of this sin.

God's kind faithfulness to his people will enable them "to bear up under" (ὑπενεγκεῖν) the temp-tation; that is, it will prevent them from "falling." The special faithfulness of God is seen in the way God providentially oversees the life of his people so that they will not be tempted "above what they are able" (ὑπὲρ ὃ δύνασθε). In other words, the sin of which Paul speaks is not inevitable. Paul is not describing a counsel of despair and hopelessness. Rather, as they return to the Lord, he not only for-gives but also enables by his Spirit the life of holi-ness to which he calls them (cf. Rom 8:4, 13; 1 Cor 6:19; Gal 5:16, 25; cf. 2 Pet 1:3).

Theology in Application

Knowing "Our" History

In Acts 17:10–12 Luke recounts how the Jews in Berea examined the Scriptures daily to test whether what Paul and Silas were teaching was true. As a result, "many of them believed" (v. 12). Jewish converts realized immediately that their Jewish history of God's dealings with their ancestors had led to the coming of the Messiah and that their history now helped interpret the apostolic gospel. Indeed, the test of the new was whether it met with God's word of old. What is fascinating is how quickly Gentiles were brought into this story and began to make it "their" story as well (Acts 13:44–49). Theologically, this is much more profound than simply the Gentiles beginning to look at what we call the Old Testament and finding useful ma-terial in it or seeing in Christ the fulfillment of some specific prophecies. It is about taking on board the whole biblical story of the world from Adam and Eve, through (especially) Abraham in whom the nations were to be blessed, through the revela-tion of God's presence and law in his redemption of Israel, through the judgment they received for their rebellion, and into the steadfast love they experienced in the Lord's patience and the coming of the Messiah. It is about seeing God's calling of one covenant people that was always looking outward to all nations. It is about being able to say, "This is what happened to *our* fathers." The emphasis on the teaching of (Old Testament) Scripture to those early Greek and pagan converts is evident in many places (e.g., Acts 18:11; Rom 15:4; 1 Cor 15:3–8; 1 Tim 4:13). Sadly, in the modern church much of this is missing; our whole story is often not told. Those who teach in seminary will often comment on the "biblical illiteracy" of otherwise enthusiastic Christians, meaning that they know little or nothing of the wonderful God-story that is their inheritance. The frequent modern lack of understanding of the relationship between law and grace can often be traced back to a simple lack of understanding of how holiness and love function in the covenant community and what their purpose is. The need for church teaching that tells the story of "our fathers" in such a way that it grips each generation and so teaches each generation is critical. There is little doubt that constant topical preaching will never achieve this. Learning to preach narrative is but one of the preaching skills that is often neglected.

Social Life and Idolatry

It is interesting to note that the two examples of the Israelite problem of idolatry that Paul chooses in 1 Corinthians 10:7–8 (drawn from Exod 32:1–6 and Num 25:1–3) both arose in communal settings. In the first passage, recounting the incident of the golden calf, it seems almost as if the whole community simply drifts into idolatry due to the lack of leadership (Moses is away). The cultic use of dance and games, mentioned above, perhaps with an erotic content, proved to be seductive temptations. In Numbers 25 the illicit sexual relations between the men of Israel and Moabite women clearly did not happen in a vacuum. It seems that much of the community on both sides, Moabite and Israelite, were caught up in what was going on, and it led to social attendance together at the sacrifices to the Moabite gods. Again, the temptation of the sexual aspects of the worship may have been directly related to the "whoring with the daughters of Moab" described in 25:1 (ESV). Likewise, for the Corinthians the eating of food offered to idols in a temple was clearly, as early sources readily show us, a community affair.

Often there is an emphasis on individual sin in modern worship, and this is right and biblical. Each person is responsible for his or her own sin, but it is important to see how often in Scripture and in the history of the church people are led into sin *communally*. This is more than simply what might be termed "peer pressure." The power of community to turn wrong into right and to draw people into activities and ways of thinking that are contrary to God's word is evident all around the modern Western world. It is community life in the twenty-first century that has encouraged sexual behavior among so many that is contrary to Scripture. Likewise, it is in community that people are drawn to the celebration and worship of the gods of consumerism and materialism. The biblical answer to this is multifaceted, but a vital part of the answer is the *community* to which Christians actually belong. It is in the church, the community of the followers of the covenant Lord, where people can build each other up to love and good works and where they can hold each other accountable. It is here that they can offer an entirely different way of living that can be described as "holy" and God honoring. The apostle sees the church as a safe alternative community where God is worshipped and where other gods must not be tolerated.

Many Christians fail to see the seriousness of getting involved in activities that are directly related to different forms of idolatry and are guilty of failing to see how other Christians may be drawn into even deeper sin than they are. Understanding how potent social activities and communities can be for good or for bad can be a great help in keeping people from idolatry. Unfortunately, social activities are often not neutral and can draw many into sin.

The problem with idolatry has always been that it involves a professed allegiance to another god. It has been the problem of all humanity ever since the fall. Sinful men and women are tempted to follow and to worship other gods, and when a whole community finds nothing wrong in this, the temptation can seem unbearable. In today's world, the gods that could be listed are many, but consumerism, materialism, and philosophies promoting the individual self all produce their own forms of worship and all are heartily encouraged by the society in which we find ourselves.

An Escape from Temptation?

Many Christians have wondered what Paul intended by verse 13. Is there always a way out of temptation? The context here is important. Paul is making the point that the true grounds for security ("standing") before God lie in the faithful God himself. He is the faithful covenant Lord who protects and cares for his people. If people look to God alone (instead of arrogantly relying on themselves and their supposed spirituality), then he is always faithful to his people and they are indeed secure in their "standing" before him. However, this will mean a humble submission to the Lord and a commitment to follow him. It will mean travelling the way of the cross, as Paul was prepared to do, and the way of discipline like an athlete. Such people will be fully secure since they are trusting in God and his promises and not in their own prowess or status. When people rely arrogantly on what God has graciously given but become self-centered in the belief they are so secure that behavior matters little, then no such security is guaranteed. The escape from temptation becomes possible, always, because God is faithful and powerful. Such escape, however, depends on people understanding their sin and depending on the faithful God for the help they need.

1 Corinthians 10:14–22

Literary Context

The elitists have become arrogant because of their possession of "knowledge" and "wisdom" (1:5–7; 8:1, 11). Paul has shown how the wilderness events and the behavior of the Israelites provide a clear warning. All of the Corinthians should therefore take heed lest, thinking they "stand" before God, they find that like so many of the Israelites they "fall" (10:12). However, God is always faithful and will provide a way out of every temptation for those who look to him alone to preserve their community status. The God who called his people is the only one who can keep and protect his people from sin. Now in 10:14–22, Paul continues to think in covenantal terms as he addresses the specific matter of eating food offered to idols that was first raised in 8:1. Taking part in idolatrous meals is to be involved in idolatry. Thus, the section begins by warning against idolatry and ends with the danger of provoking the Lord to jealousy (v. 22). God's hatred of idolatry and of any attempt to replace him with other gods is seen in the description, drawn from the Old Testament, of him as a "jealous God." The problem with the idolatrous meals is explained, again in covenantal terms, by means of the example of the Lord's Supper (vv. 16–17). In that meal, there is a "participation in Christ." Why should it be any less the case when they participate in meals in the presence of idols (vv. 18–21)? The section concludes with the caustic comment that some are claiming to be stronger than the Lord himself! In other words, they act as if they can withstand his jealousy or that it does not matter (v. 22). The following section (10:23–11:1) speaks more generally to the question of how to approach the eating of sacrificial meat that is available in the marketplace.

Main Idea

Some of the Corinthians have been drawn into idolatry by eating sacrificial food at tables where offerings are being made to idols. As the Lord's Supper demonstrates, covenant meals involve real participation in the God or gods in whose honor they are held. This will provoke the Lord's jealousy just as the Israelites' idolatry in the wilderness provoked him to covenantal jealousy and judgment.

Translation

1 Corinthians 10:14–22

14a		Therefore, my beloved,
b	Command	**flee from idolatry.**
15a	Assertion	**I speak as to sensible people;**
b	Entreaty	**judge yourselves what I say.**
16a	Rhetorical question/ assertion	**The cup of blessing**
b	Description	**that we bless,**
c		**is it not a covenant participation in the blood of Christ?**
d	Rhetorical question/ assertion	**The bread**
e	Description	**that we break,**
f		**is it not a covenant participation in the body of Christ?**

17a	Inference from 16d–f	Because [there is] one bread,
b	Assertion	**we who are many are** **one body,**
c	Basis	for **we all partake of the** **one bread.**
18a	Negative illustration	**Consider the Israelites according to the flesh:**
b	Rhetorical question	**Are not those who eat the sacrifices [covenantal] participants in the altar of ☙ sacrifice?**
19a	Expansion	**What then do I affirm?**
b	Content	That food offered to idols is anything or
c	Rhetorical question	that an idol is anything?
20a	Assertion	No, rather [I affirm]
b	Content	that what they sacrifice, ☙ they sacrifice
c	Quotation	to demons and not to God. [Deut 32:17 LXX]
d	Desire	**I do not want you to become covenant participants with demons.**
21a	Negative assertion	**You cannot drink**
b	Content	the cup of the Lord and
c		the cup of demons,
		and
d	Negative assertion	**you cannot partake**
e	Content	at the table of the Lord and
f		at the table of demons.
22a	Rhetorical question	Or **shall we make the Lord jealous?**
b	Rhetorical question	**Are we stronger than he?**

Structure

The section focuses on the opening command to "flee from idolatry" (v. 14), with the concluding rhetorical question about idolatry provoking the Lord to jealousy summing up the matter (v. 22). Paul's concern is that the covenant relationship that Christians have with the Lord requires their total allegiance. Loyalties cannot be divided. The section stands as one argument, but it can usefully be divided into two by noting that 10:20b–22 is a specific application of the first section. The first section (10:14–20a) develops a strong argument. It should be noted that the Lord's Supper is introduced as an example of the way in which a participant in the meal actually "participates" in or with the "lord" whose meal it is (vv. 16–17). While this section may contribute in a general way to an understanding of how sacramental meals function, that is not Paul's purpose at this point. Rather, as the argument develops he promptly returns to drawing out lessons from the wilderness traditions (v. 18). When the Israelites turned to idolatry in the wilderness, they became participants in demons as they joined in the sacrificial meals. They broke covenant. In appealing to Deuteronomy 32, Paul then demonstrates that while other gods do not exist, demons do, and the idolatry of the Israelites was real (vv. 19–22). Thus, both the Lord's Supper and the example of Israel provide a context in which the "jealousy" of the Lord makes complete sense since, as covenant Lord, he asks for and expects total allegiance. This allegiance cannot be compromised (vv. 20b–22). A series of seven rhetorical questions repeat Paul's favored way of arguing in these chapters.

Exegetical Outline

VII. Status, Knowledge, Freedom, and Food Offered to Idols (8:1–11:1)

    A. Knowledge and Love Contrasted (8:1–3)

    B. Knowledge concerning the Existence of "gods" and "lords" (8:4–6)

    C. Knowledge regarding the Eating of Idol Food in an Idol Temple (8:7–13)

    D. Status and Rights Should Be Subordinated for the Sake of the Gospel (9:1–27)

    E. Israel's Abuse of Spiritual Gifts Provides a Warning (10:1–13)

➡   **F. Covenant Allegiance Matters (10:14–22)**

        1. Covenantal Allegiance Is Indicated in Pagan Sacrifical Meals (10:14–20a)

           a. Flee Idolatry (10:14)

           b. Consider Covenant Allegiance in the Lord's Supper (10:15–17)

           c. Consider the Israelite Breach of Covenant in Pagan Meals (10:18)

           d. Pagans Are Participants with Demons (10:19–20a)

        2. Allegiance to the Lord Cannot Be Compromised (10:20b–22)

           a. Do Not Participate in Demons (10:20b)

           b. Do Not Participate at Both the Table of Demons and of the Lord (10:21)

           c. Do Not Provoke the Lord to Jealousy (10:22)

Explanation of the Text

10:14 Therefore, my beloved, flee from idolatry (Διόπερ, ἀγαπητοί μου, φεύγετε ἀπὸ τῆς εἰδωλολατρίας). This verse forms a bridge between what Paul has written thus far in chapter 10 and what he will now write about idolatrous meals. "Therefore" (διόπερ) indicates that the command to "flee idolatry" is an unambiguous consequence of what Paul has been saying as he has urged the Corinthians to heed lessons from the wilderness generation. The present imperative (φεύγετε) suggests Paul regards this as a continuing need for Christians. Brash self-confidence has led some of them into real and present danger, for they are being drawn into idolatry.[1] Paul's kind reference to "my beloved" (ἀγαπητοί) gives an added passion to what he says and indicates that he is determined to per-

---

1. On idolatry as Paul may have encountered it, see Richard L. Phua, *Idolatry and Authority*.

suade them of the danger in a way that is caring yet unambiguous (cf. 4:14; 15:58).

Many commentators have noted the striking parallels between the way Paul handles the matter of idolatry here and the way he handled the matter of sexual sin in chapter 6:

10:14/6:18	Flee from idolatry/sexual immorality
10:17/6:18–19	One body because we partake of one bread/the body is the temple of the Holy Spirit
10:21/6:15	Cannot have dual loyalties—cannot participate at the table of the Lord and demons/cannot be members of Christ and of prostitutes

10:15 I speak as to sensible people; judge yourselves what I say (ὡς φρονίμοις λέγω· κρίνατε ὑμεῖς ὅ φημι). Paul now presents a carefully constructed argument that he assumes will persuade the Corinthians, whom he describes as "sensible people" (φρόνιμοι).[2] Since Paul has repeatedly been concerned at the lack of discernment shown by some of the Corinthians, and since the question of "judging" and discerning spiritual matters properly has been so much a part of the epistle thus far, this comment may be somewhat ironic.[3] However, it is also possible that at this point Paul is simply stating the obvious; these "thinking people" should pay attention to what he is saying and "judge" it carefully for themselves. The addition of "yourselves" (ὑμεῖς) lays the burden firmly on them to begin to think like Paul thinks as he expounds on the nature of certain religious meals leading to idolatry.

Understanding the likely background(s) to what Paul says about the communion meal in vv. 16–17 and the pagan meals in vv. 18–20 can greatly help the interpreter understand what Paul intends in this section. Two main views emerge. Some suggest Paul draws on a background from Jewish religious meals, while others say that he draws on ideas from pagan cult meals. It seems more likely to us that Paul in fact draws on the Jewish meals associated with covenant renewal and the Passover.

IN DEPTH: Possible Backgrounds to the "Meals" of 10:16–20

Some have sought to explain what they see as Paul's "sacramental" attitude to the Lord's Supper (vv. 16–17) and the pagan meals (vv. 18–20) against the background of Hellenistic, pagan mystery cults. This approach was generally led by earlier scholars from the *religionsgeschichtliche Schule* (history-of-religions school). For example, Loisy argued that Christians "do not only commemorate this [the death of Jesus]; we may say they go over it again for themselves, as the votaries of Osiris or of Attis renewed for themselves the death of their god."[4] In his commentary, Lietzmann has a significant excursus on what he calls "cult meals," in which he adduces numerous apparent parallels between the

---

2. NASB and AV: "Wise men."

3. Weiss, *Der erste Korintherbrief*, 256, but cf. Conzelmann, *1 Corinthians*, 171n12, who says this "is not ironical."

4. A. Loisy, "The Christian Mystery," *HibJ* 10 (1911/12): 54.

cult meals and the Lord's Supper.[5] However, he also notes that in 1 Corinthians 11:23–26 the more likely background is that of a Jewish meal (*haburah*). This, he argued, was a basic table meal that the Corinthians enjoyed, while Paul himself had followed a more "sacramental" meal in the manner of the pagan cult meals. He therefore suggests that part of Paul's problem with the Corinthian attitude to the Lord's Supper was that they had too "low" a view of all cultic meals. An obvious problem with this approach is that Paul assumes with his rhetorical questions in 10:16–19 that his view of the Supper does *not* differ from that of the Corinthians! His problem with them is that they have not realized that the pagan meals functioned in a similar way to the Lord's Supper in bringing the participants into a covenantal relationship with the divinity.

Moreover, as many have noted the problems with believing that Paul drew upon pagan cult meals for his understanding of the Lord's Supper are considerable. Rightly, MacGregor points out that not only are there problems of anachronism, but the cult meals did not seem central to the pagan cults anyway.[6] Furthermore, it is doubtful that the crude idea of "eating God" (argued by some from the mystery meals) is to be found in those meals at all. He concludes: "Whatever may be said of its evolution, the origin of the Eucharist can hardly be sought in Paganism."[7] MacGregor himself argues for a background in the Sabbath *kiddush* rite. However, the *kiddush* lacks most of the covenantal overtones that are found in other Jewish meals like the Passover or the covenant-renewal meals themselves.

The phrase "cup of blessing" (v. 16) would certainly suggest a background in Jewish meals and particularly the Passover. Thus, Jeremias listed a number of aspects of the Lord's Supper found in Paul's accounts that he believed indicated that the meal was derived from the Passover meal.[8] Others have followed Jeremias.[9] In the light of Passover liturgies, some have commented on the link that Paul made between the "new covenant" and "blood" in the Christian meal (11:25; cf. 10:16) and have further suggested that the Passover was a form of "covenant meal." Segal, for example, suggests that in the confirmation of the covenant, a meal was eaten and that the blood ritual at the Passover had much in common with a covenant meal.[10] The link between the Lord's Supper and

5. Lietzmann, *An Die Korinther I–II*, 49–51, 57–58.

6. George C. H. MacGregor, *Eucharistic Origins: A Survey of the New Testament Evidence* (London: J Clarke, 1929), 23–28.

7. Ibid., 28.

8. Joachim Jeremias, *The Eucharistic Words of Jesus*, trans. Norman Perrin, New Testament Library (London: SCM, 1966); also see idem, "This is My Body," *ExpTim* 83 (1972): 196–203.

9. Thiselton, *1 Corinthians*, 756–60, has an extensive sum-

mary of the arguments in favor of viewing the Passover as background. Garland, *1 Corinthians*, 476n5, advises caution with this approach, warning that the early surviving Passover liturgies postdate the destruction of the temple and were "probably less uniform" in Paul's day.

10. J. B. Segal, *The Hebrew Passover: From the Earliest Times to A.D. 70*, London Oriental Series 12 (London: Oxford University Press, 1963), 105–6.

the Passover meal is, of course, established in the Gospel narratives (cf. Matt 26:17–28; Mark 14:16–24).

Since the covenant context in 1 Corinthians 10 is clearly important, there has been considerable discussion about whether the Passover can be readily identified as a "covenant meal." While it is certainly not a covenant meal *per se*, many agree that its context is broadly covenantal and sufficiently so for it to be useful to Paul in this context. Given the tendency to link the exodus, the Red Sea, and the wanderings in Sinai, it is not surprising that the Passover would also recall God's "covenant" dealings with his people. Nevertheless, it is also worth mentioning the meals in the Old Testament that were actually "covenant meals." Interestingly, one of the few clear examples is to be found in Exodus 24:11 where, following God's covenant with Israel, Moses took the blood of burnt offerings and threw it over the people. After this we read that Moses and Aaron and the elders "beheld God, and ate and drank" (vv. 9–11 ESV). God was regarded as present at the meal. The eating and drinking in the covenant God's presence helps establish and celebrate the covenant treaty. Just a few other meals were associated with specific covenants or treaties: Isaac and Abimelech, Jacob and Laban, Israel and Moab, Joshua and the Gibeonites.[11] Certainly it is possible that Paul had in mind these covenant meals (especially Exod 24) rather than pagan or other Jewish meals.

In summary, Paul probably regards the main background for the Supper as the Passover meal, since the Christian meal was itself instituted during Passover and the phrase "cup of blessing" seems to belong in that realm.[12] However, the category of the ancient Jewish covenant meals may also have enabled Paul to draw attention to the theology of "covenant participation." Finally, since Paul goes on to mention the Israelite participation in idolatrous meals and has already mentioned the incident of the golden calf by quoting Exodus 32:6 (1 Cor 10:7), this pagan meal may also be in mind as he thinks of how the Israelites who "sat down to eat and rose up to play" were then judged by the covenant Lord.

10:16 The cup of blessing that we bless, is it not a covenant participation in the blood of Christ? The bread[13] that we break, is it not a covenant participation in the body of Christ? (τὸ ποτήριον τῆς εὐλογίας ὃ εὐλογοῦμεν, οὐχὶ κοινωνία ἐστὶν τοῦ αἵματος τοῦ Χριστοῦ; τὸν ἄρτον ὃν κλῶμεν, οὐχὶ κοινωνία τοῦ σώματος τοῦ Χριστοῦ ἐστιν;). In v. 16 Paul once again turns to rhetorical questions to

---

11. Gen 26:28–30; 31:44, 51–54; Num 25:1–5; Josh 9:3–15.

12. See comments on 11:23c–24 for the parallels with Luke's account.

13. Grammatically, it is to be noticed that in the clause "the bread that we break," "the bread" (τὸν ἄρτον) is in the accusative as probably is "the cup" (τὸ ποτήριον). This is due to "inverse attraction" in which the antecedent is attracted to the case of the following relative pronoun.

make assertions. Here he makes claims about the nature and practice of the Lord's Supper that he assumes will meet with agreement among his readers. Though much has been written about various aspects of Paul's so-called "sacramental" theology in this verse, it must be remembered that Paul's intention here is to demonstrate the danger to Christians of taking part in pagan meals *from the example of* what takes place in the Lord's Supper. For the apostle, these types of religious meals, the Lord's Supper and pagan cult meals, are not mere "meals"—they are religious activities and are eaten in a context in which the presence of the divinity is assumed. These meals therefore speak of allegiance to the god being worshipped by his followers or subjects.

The origin of the phrase "the cup of blessing" (τὸ ποτήριον τῆς εὐλογίας) lies in the Passover, though whether it is the second, third, or fourth cup of the Passover meal that Paul has in mind is of minor interest. The "cup of blessing" is the cup over which a blessing or thanksgiving to God is prayed. The first plural (εὐλογοῦμεν) suggests that this may have been a prayer of thanksgiving in which the whole congregation joined. There is no sense here of the cup or wine itself being "blessed." In Jewish and Christian thought alike, it is God who is "blessed." As Ciampa and Rosner note: "The ancient and still traditional Jewish blessing begins, 'Blessed are you, O Lord, our God, King of the Universe, who brings forth food from the earth.'"[14] They also note how the Gospels' accounts "alternate between references to blessing bread and giving thanks for it, indicating that the references to blessing bread are to be understood as references to blessing or thanking God for it."[15] The genitive "of blessing" (τῆς εὐλογίας) is thus objective. It is

not the cup that *possesses* a blessing that the people receive when they drink from it but a cup for which a blessing, a thanksgiving, is given to God by the people who then drink from it.

As has been noted in various places in this epistle but especially in this chapter, Paul understands Christians to be members of the Christian community that stands in covenantal relationship with God in the same way as the wilderness generation did. The difference is, of course, that the covenant king's own blood has sealed the new covenant (11:25) and, as the covenant Lord, *he* interprets the covenantal relationship. The word Paul chooses to describe the participation in the new covenant and its many blessings is κοινωνία. As noted at 1:9,[16] this could simply mean "fellowship" or "association" or even "sharing."[17] We have opted to translate the word "covenant participation." Using the phrase "covenant participation" reminds us that the word κοινωνία is at the very heart of the gospel message and of what the church is all about (Acts 2:42). It also reminds us that on a number of occasions Paul uses the word in a context of Christ's lordship and the blessings or judgments that ensue from that lordship.

There is some discussion as to whether the clause "that we break" (ὃν κλῶμεν), "the fraction," as liturgists call it, has any significance. Clearly the action implies the start of the meal, and it also carries with it the idea of sharing, in that the bread is broken to be eaten by many. But does the actual "breaking" of the bread point further, that is, to the brokenness of Christ's body on the cross? The parallel structure in 11:24 and 25 makes this likely. In 11:24 we read: "He [the Lord] *broke* the bread and said, 'This is my body which is for you.'" In 11:25 we read: "[He took] also the cup after sup-

---

14. *First Corinthians*, 472.
15. Ibid., 472n201.

16. See at 1:9, "In Depth: The Meaning of the Word Κοινωνία."
17. BDAG 552.

per, saying, 'This cup is the new covenant in my blood.'" These parallels probably indicate that the act of breaking the bread is intended to be as much part of the visual representation of Christ's death (by which "the new covenant in my blood" is established) as is the wine in the cup.[18]

Given the covenantal ideas present in the context of chapter 10, Paul surely sees the Lord's Supper as a successor not just to the Passover but also to some of the covenant meals in the Old Testament. The fact that in 11:25 Paul states that "this cup is the new covenant [ἡ καινὴ διαθήκη] in my blood" also makes this likely. Here the parallelism between 10:16 and 11:24–25 is helpful. (Though note that in ch. 11 the bread precedes the wine in the more usual order of the modern Supper.) Willis lays it out like this:[19]

Cup = participation in the blood of Christ (10:16a)
= the new covenant in my blood (11:25)
Bread = participation in the body of Christ (10:16b)
= my body which is for you (11:24)

The body and blood of Christ are seen to be formative for the new covenant, again reinforcing the fact that covenant ideas dominate here. Even the word "cup" is likely drawn from this realm of ideas. In the LXX "cup" (ποτήριον) can be used metaphorically for what is portioned out and of which a person must then "partake." Although there is a "cup of salvation" and a cup that supplies God's faithful people (cf. Pss 16:4–5; 23:5; 116:13), it is the "cup of wrath" and of judgment that predominates in the word's metaphorical use (e.g., Pss 11:6; 75:8; Isa 51:17, 22; Jer 49:12; Lam 4:21; Ezek 23:33). It is worth noting that even in the Passover the cups are interpreted sometimes as pointing the Jewish people toward "consolation" and others toward "judgment": "The four cups correspond to the four cups of punishment which God will someday cause the nations of the world to drink . . . and corresponding to them God will some day cause Israel to drink four cups of consolations."[20] This concept of the dual sanctions of covenantal "blessings" and "curses" is found throughout God's covenant dealings with his people in the Old Testament.

All of this helps demonstrate that Paul understands that Christians have entered the new covenant by the blood of Christ and that the Lord's Supper reflects the forming of the covenant and the continuing membership of the covenant. In taking the bread and the wine, therefore, Christians proclaim "Christ's death," that is, they proclaim the event that established the new covenant and demonstrate that they are participating in this "new covenant." They take part in it in such a way that they establish their covenantal relationship with the Lord (the "vertical" aspect) *and* they establish their membership of the church, which is the covenant community (the "horizontal" aspect) and so share in its blessings. Later, however, Paul will show that drinking this covenant-indicating "cup" can also lead to judgment (11:27–29), thus revealing the dual sanctions even in the new-covenant meal.

10:17 Because [there is] one bread, we who are many are one body, for we all partake of the one bread (ὅτι εἷς ἄρτος, ἓν σῶμα οἱ πολλοί ἐσμεν, οἱ

---

18. For an exegetical examination of this from a Roman Catholic perspective, see Francis J. Moloney, *A Body Broken for a Broken People: Eucharist in the New Testament*, rev. ed. (Peabody, MA: Hendrickson, 1997), 159–77.

19. Willis, *Idol Meat in Corinth*, 206. Schema is his, while the translation is mine.

20. L. Goppelt, "ποτήριον," *TDNT* 6:150–51; see also Dan Cohn-Sherbok, "A Jewish Note on ΤΟ ΠΟΤΗΡΙΟΝ ΤΗΣ ΕΥΛΟΓΙΑΣ," *NTS* 27 (1981): 704–9; cf. J. Keir Howard, "Christ Our Passover: A Study of the Passover-Exodus Theme in I Corinthians," *EvQ* 41 (1969): 97–108.

γὰρ πάντες ἐκ τοῦ ἑνὸς ἄρτου μετέχομεν). A most wonderful benefit of the covenant formed with the shedding of Christ's blood is that of the community of Christ. This is so important that Paul will build on the idea in chapters 12 and 14 when he speaks to the right use of the gifts of the Spirit for the building up of this "body." The picture here is that one loaf of bread (εἷς ἄρτος), broken up for distribution so people can "partake" (μετέχω) of it, reveals the unity of the one people who belong to Christ and have been called by him. Those "who are many" (οἱ πολλοί) are revealed in fact to be "one body" (ἓν σῶμα). Thus, the meal directly opposes the divisions found in the church at Corinth. Once again, what the Corinthians have failed to discern is that the meal they enjoy together as the Lord's Supper involves the commitment of the *church* to the Lord of the covenant. It is no mere meal. Every time it is taken, God's people "proclaim the Lord's death until he comes," that is, they proclaim as a body their continued commitment to the covenantal relationship with the Lord established by his death. While Paul is not directly addressing here the divisions in the church at Corinth, his statement certainly addresses the matter indirectly. Divisions among God's people are a breach of the covenant community.

10:18 Consider the Israelites according to the flesh: Are not those who eat the sacrifices [covenantal] participants in the altar of sacrifice? (βλέπετε τὸν Ἰσραὴλ κατὰ σάρκα· οὐχ οἱ ἐσθίοντες τὰς θυσίας κοινωνοὶ τοῦ θυσιαστηρίου εἰσίν;). Covenantal participation with God is seen in the Lord's Supper, but now Paul resumes his argument, drawing on Israel by way of a *negative* example. With another rhetorical question, he insists that those who eat the sacrifices are "[covenantal] participants" (κοινωνοί) in the altar. For Paul, the Israelites of the wilderness generation allied themselves with demons. It is most likely that he still has in mind the golden-calf incident and the meal mentioned in v. 7. Once again the wilderness generation provides a *negative* example. It was their participation in the pagan meal that offers a direct parallel to what Paul encounters with the Corinthians, which is why in v. 20 he concludes, "I do not want *you* [emphatic] to become covenant participants with demons."

In terms of the *type* of "participation" that Paul believes was established between the Israelites and the idols, there is no suggestion that they had been involved in theophagy or that they had achieved union with the demons through some sort of "sacramentalism." Rather, in the meal they were celebrating the sacrifices made (e.g., burnt and peace offerings; Exod 32:6), and eating, drinking and "playing" before their created god, which is just what they were supposed to do in their sacrificial offerings "before Yahweh," the true covenant Lord (cf. Exod 29). However, this was a complete betrayal of Yahweh. The people were to be destroyed, and a new "great nation" was to be formed (Exod 32:10).

In evangelical church language, especially in America, "altar" has come to refer to a communion table. It is therefore important, as Thiselton notes, to talk of the "altar of sacrifice" since it is the sacrifice that is at issue here. It also clearly accounts for the fact that the Greek word is built around the word for "sacrifice" that Paul has just used (θυσίας . . . τοῦ θυσιαστηρίου).[21] The Corinthians are asked to "consider" what was occurring when the wilderness generation participated in pagan feasts (the word βλέπετε is used figuratively; hence, "consider"). Paul's point is that they became covenantally linked to the idol, just as happens in the Lord's Supper with believing Christians being covenantally linked to the Lord.

---

21. Thiselton, *1 Corinthians*, 772.

Some have questioned whether this is a negative example drawn from the past or whether Paul is simply referring generally to the fact that Israelite sacrifices, as ordained by God, involved a participation in and commitment to him. In this view, considerable weight is placed on the present tenses (ἐσθίοντες . . . εἰσίν) and, it is said, the reference is to the contemporary practice of Jews in the Jerusalem temple.[22] The implicit contrast is therefore between "Israel according to the flesh" (Jews) and "Israel according to the Spirit" (Christians).[23] Thus, it is held that Paul addresses three meals in these verses. There is the example of the Lord's Supper (vv. 16–17). There is a further *good* example in which he draws lessons from the godly sacrifices ordained for Israel (v. 18), and the third which is the pagan meal of v. 20. However, there are good reasons to take the meal of v. 18 as another in the list of negative examples that Paul has drawn from the wilderness generation of Israelites. First, while "according to the flesh" (κατὰ σάρκα) can simply refer to the historical flesh and blood of the people (Rom 4:1; 9:5; 11:14; cf. 2 Cor 5:16), it can also, in a religious sense, be used negatively by Paul (cf. Rom 8:5). Indeed, in 1 Corinthians 3:3 "flesh" (σαρκικός) has been used in just this way. Thus far in this chapter, Israel has been used consistently as a negative example. Lessons are still to be learned. The "fleshly" people of Israel still stand as a warning. Secondly, this view also makes sense of v. 19.

Instead of there being an unnatural jump between v. 18 and vv. 19–20, Paul is naturally thinking of the allegiance the Israelites formed at pagan idolatrous meals. This leads him to ask about the nature of idols. Thirdly, the allusions to Deuteronomy 32 that follow in vv. 20 and 22 refer in their original context to *sinful* Israel. In Deuteronomy 32:17 it is important to note that when it says "they sacrificed to demons, not God," the reference is to the *Israelites* (NRSV). Finally, the view taken here avoids the need to *import* a different subject into v. 20, where most translations add "the Gentiles" or "the pagans" when in fact there is simply a third-person, plural subject: "I state that what *they* sacrifice . . . ."[24]

10:19–20 What then do I affirm? That food offered to idols is anything or that an idol is anything? No, rather [I affirm] that what they sacrifice, they sacrifice to demons and not to God. I do not want you to become covenant participants with demons (τί οὖν φημι; ὅτι εἰδωλόθυτόν τί ἐστιν; ἢ ὅτι εἴδωλόν τί ἐστιν; ἀλλ᾽ ὅτι ἃ θύουσιν [τὰ ἔθνη],[25] δαιμονίοις καὶ οὐ θεῷ θύουσιν, οὐ θέλω δὲ ὑμᾶς κοινωνοὺς τῶν δαιμονίων γίνεσθαι). Verse 19 now follows perfectly and naturally as Paul's argument progresses. With another rhetorical question, Paul summarizes his thought: cult meals result in worship of and allegiance to demons. First, he must deal with a possible misunderstanding of what he is saying. Since participation in

---

22. In principle, these present tenses are likely to be gnomic. When asked to consider the practice of Israel as they "sat down to eat and drink and rose up to play," it may be asserted (by means of the rhetorical question) that people who do such things are indeed participants in the altar of sacrifice. This is a universal truth and timeless fact, precisely the point Paul wants to make!

23. Ciampa and Rosner, *First Corinthians*, 477–78 argue for this.

24. See next footnote.

25. The problem of the lack of subject for v. 20 is ancient. However, the textual evidence for including "the nations" (τὰ

ἔθνη) is inconclusive. It is largely Alexandrian (𝔓[46vid], א, A, C, P, Ψ, 33[vid], 81, etc.). The words are omitted by B, D, F, G, Ambst, and they were considered to be an "ancient gloss" by Tischendorf. The harder reading omits the subject and is probably the one to be accepted. This, together with our other reasons for regarding *Israel* as the subject, confirms us in the view that τὰ ἔθνη is a gloss. See Constantin von Tischendorf, *Novum Testamentum Graece* (Lipsiae: Tauchnitz, 1904), 518; also G. Zuntz, *The Text of the Epistles: A Disquisition upon the Corpus Paulinum* (London: Oxford University Press, 1953), 102; Metzger, *Textual Commentary*, 494.

an idol sacrifice (θυσία; v. 18) *does* achieve a covenant participation in the sacrifice, it is therefore a logical question to ask whether the special food (εἰδωλόθυτος) eaten in celebration *causes* the participation (κοινωνία) or whether this participation is achieved because the idol (god) is at the sacrifice? In other words, are "gods" present at the feast? Paul's answer to both these questions is "no." The answer to the problem of *how* Israel participated in heathen sacrifices lay not in the specific nature of the sacrificial food nor in the existence of the idol at the meal. Rather, "participation" lay in taking part in alien worship. Willis phrased it thus: "Just as one shows his master by whom he serves (Rom 6:16ff.), so also one shows allegiance by the worship in which he participates."[26]

Thus, v. 20 picks up the question of v. 19: "No, rather [I affirm] that what they sacrifice, they sacrifice to demons and not to God." Paul's indebtedness to Deuteronomy 32 is now explicit as he quotes 32:17 (LXX). This "song of Moses" offers one of the clearest descriptions in the Old Testament of the rebellion of God's covenant people as they worshipped other gods ("demons") despite God's faithfulness to them. It is worth citing part of this passage (vv. 5ff and vv. 15–18):

> They have dealt corruptly with him [v. 4, the Rock, the θεὸς πιστός [LXX]; cf. 1 Cor 10:13]; they are no longer his children. . . . The Lord's portion is his people, Jacob his allotted heritage. . . . The Lord alone guided him, no foreign god was with him. . . . You grew fat, stout, and sleek; then he forsook God who made him and scoffed at the Rock of his salvation. They stirred him to jealousy with strange gods; with abominations they provoked

him to anger. They sacrificed to demons that were no gods [and not to God—LXX] to gods they had never known. . . . You were unmindful of the Rock that bore you. (Deut 32:5–18 ESV)

Seen in this original context, it is clear just what an exceptional resource this passage is for the apostle at this point. It effectively provides an excellent summary of his whole argument in chapters 8–10. The Israelites became "unmindful of the Rock" (v. 18) because they presumed on God's gifts and became arrogant. This resulted in worship of other so-called lords and gods in the nature of demons (cf. 1 Cor 8:5). Such was Paul's message for the Corinthians who, he believed, had gone the same way as Israel "according to the flesh" and had become involved in showing allegiance to other lords. The passage draws attention to the fact that those who were "children" of God "are no longer" so; this is the point Paul has made as he has talked of "most of them" being judged (Deut 32:5; 1 Cor 10:5). Of course, the faithfulness of the covenant Lord remains for those who follow him (he is their "Rock" and "the faithful God"), but the sacrifices of the Israelites who broke this covenant relationship were "to demons that were no gods" (Deut 32:17 ESV). This caused the Lord to be "jealous" (Deut 32:21; cf. 1 Cor 10:22).

Paul strongly maintains biblical monotheism here. However, he acknowledges that as they worship idols, people are truly reflecting their allegiance to another lord or lords, who do indeed exist in the form of demons.[27] Neither the food itself is special, nor do the wooden or clay idols have any existence in themselves. Yet as the people worship and eat in direct disobedience of the one true

---

26. Willis, *Idol Meat in Corinth*, 192.

27. While Paul is adamant that there is only one God, he does recognize cosmic forces that are set against God. However, these are "doomed to come to nothing" (1 Cor 2:6). In Christ such forces have already been conquered, but there are

realms where they still persist with evil power. These realms are most clearly seen when people choose to worship that which is not the true God, but they also become visible as the gospel is preached and are probably to be equated with "the spiritual forces of evil in the heavenly realms" mentioned in Eph 6:12.

God and covenant Lord, they give a terrible reality to the meal. They truly worship demons. This is the fearful danger that faces the Corinthians if they do not take seriously the covenantal allegiances involved in these sacrificial meals. Since Paul will talk shortly about eating other types of food, it is important to see here that the whole logic of these verses is that Paul is concerned with the *worship* of idols/demons rather than simply the eating of the food that has been sacrificed to the idol. Thus, Paul begins his conclusion in v. 20b with a heartfelt appeal. He does not want them to become "covenant participants with demons" (κοινωνοὺς τῶν δαιμονίων). His message: it happened once, do not let it happen again!

10:21–22 You cannot drink the cup of the Lord and the cup of demons, and you cannot partake at the table of the Lord and at the table of demons. Or shall we make the Lord jealous? Are we stronger than he? (οὐ δύνασθε ποτήριον κυρίου πίνειν καὶ ποτήριον δαιμονίων· οὐ δύνασθε τραπέζης κυρίου μετέχειν καὶ τραπέζης δαιμονίων. ἢ παραζηλοῦμεν τὸν κύριον; μὴ ἰσχυρότεροι αὐτοῦ ἐσμεν;). With a clear assertion Paul insists that the Corinthians cannot worship at the Lord's Supper and then *also* at the sacrificial table (meal) of an idol. The issue is one of *allegiance*. The covenant Lord demands full and total allegiance from his people. The same principal is at work here as in the Lord's words about God and money: "'No servant can serve two masters; for either he will hate the one and love the other, or he will be devoted to the one and despise the other. You cannot serve God and mammon'" (Luke 16:13 RSV). It is important to see how Paul builds the contrast, *not* between the pagan and Christian meals but between the

Lord and demons. The deliberate repeated opposition of these words is often overlooked: (v. 20) "demons ... God ... demons"; (v. 21) "Lord ... demons ... Lord ... demons"; (v. 22) "Lord."

The "cup of demons" (ποτήριον δαιμονίων) probably stresses covenant participation just as the Christian "cup" did in v. 16. In using the phrase "table of demons" (τράπεζα δαιμονίων) Paul may have been thinking of the "sitting down to eat and drink" of v. 7. But there is also a possible linguistic dependence on Malachi 1:7, 12. There the prophet referred to the altar on which sacrifices were made to God.[28] Either way, it is the deity that is worshipped that is the issue. Demons must not be worshipped at idol feasts by someone who also claims covenant allegiance to the Lord.

"Lord" in vv. 21–22 refers to Christ, but it is mildly surprising that Paul did not use "Christ" as he did in vv. 4, 9, and 16. It is possible the choice of "Lord" is deliberate because Paul wished to stress the issue of *lordship* (cf. the contrast between "gods" and "lords" in 8:5 and "one God" and "one Lord" in 8:6). The role of Christ as covenant Lord and the one with full authority to bless and to judge cannot be far from Paul's mind here as he insists that dual allegiance is impossible.

Once it is understood that Paul has subsumed the whole content of worship under the phrases "cup of the Lord" and "table of the Lord," it becomes clear that Paul's thought ranged more widely than a specific act of sacrifice. His thought, as noted above, centered on the commitment to and identification with the one to whom the worship was offered. Thus, the penultimate rhetorical question of this section in v. 22 falls into place. Again it functions as a strong assertion. Paul does not expect people to differ with his logic. This "jealousy"

---

28. Cf. Ezek 44:16; T. Jud. 21:5; T. Levi 8:16. Leonhard Goppelt, "τράπεζα," *TDNT* 8:214, accepts a biblical background here. *Contra* Conzelmann, *1 Corinthians*, 174n47.

of the Lord is the jealousy of the covenant Lord of Deuteronomy 32:21. It is dangerous to provoke the Lord, for the result will be judgment of the sort Paul has written about in vv. 5–10.

Paul used the verb "to provoke to jealousy" (παραζηλόω) on four occasions, in Romans 10:19, 11:11, 14, and here. The verb, it seems, does not appear in secular Greek. But it doubtless derives from "zeal" (ζῆλος) for maintaining the Lord's honor. This zeal becomes operative against all worship that is not intended for him. In Ezekiel the zeal was likened to marital jealousy: a jealousy that brought wrath and judgment (Ezek 16:38; 23:25; cf. 2 Cor 11:2).

The final rhetorical question, "Are we stronger than he?" (μὴ ἰσχυρότεροι αὐτοῦ ἐσμεν) is ironic, even though Paul addresses all in the church and even himself with his use of the first-person plural.[29] The warning must be noted by all Christians, though it is only a certain number of them who are involved in these meals (ch. 8). The "weak" are not involved, but they find themselves near to "stumbling" as they are drawn into the feasts on spurious grounds. In this way Paul comes to the conclusion of this part of his discussion of "food offered to idols." Christians must be aware of the covenant allegiances indicated by the cult meals, on the one hand, and by the Lord's Supper on the other. To those who thought that they were secure enough before God to be able to eat meat in the idol temple (8:10), Paul has decisively responded, "Don't! Flee idolatry." Now, in the next section he will move on to address meat that is bought in the market place (10:25).

Theology in Application

Commitment to the Covenant Lord

Regarding Christ as the covenant Lord of his people is often overlooked in modern Christian circles, but it accurately describes the one who protects, loves, and cares for his people yet is also their judge. Often Christians, caught up in the glory of receiving God's saving grace through faith in Christ, forget his rule and lordship. He alone must be worshipped, and his commands are to be obeyed by a people he has called to be holy (1:2; cf. 1 Pet 1:13–15). Paul's emphasis on Christ as Lord has been consistent throughout his epistle (note especially the first nine verses of the book). His peoples' priorities must be his priorities. His thoughts are to be their thoughts. The prioritizing of the Lord's will in every area of life is Christ's desire for his people, but it should also be their desire to follow, obey, and serve him. Fleeing idolatry of all sorts must therefore be a primary focus of Christian life, for it is the other side of the primary and positive focus of pursuing Christ alone (cf. 1 Pet 4:3–5). 1 Corinthians 10:13 has already indicated that such a route is possible thanks to God's own faithfulness.

However, it is all too easy to rationalize idolatries and sin and even consider

---

29. This question can be ironic in its mention of being "stronger" since it is the "strong" who are causing the problem in the first place with their knowledge and elitism. But it is the whole community that is in danger of being drawn down the wrong path. This is why Paul has been talking about "stumbling blocks" and why he has identified with the "weak."

them to be "not so serious" because of God's amazing, life-giving grace in Christ. If Christians have noted how God has gifted them with grace-gifts, they can especially fall into this trap. A Christian's thinking can move all too easily from "I see God at work in my life" to "I see God at work in my life despite my sin; therefore, my sin can't be too important." It is perhaps not a matter of denying sin so much as not realizing what sin reveals about allegiance to the Lord (cf. Rom 6:1–4). Such an attitude is to presume upon God. In the end it is to reject him despite his love, and to let other "gods" become the focus. We have already touched on many ways in which "gods" rear their heads in today's world.

While gospel ministers and teachers will frequently and rightly teach about the evils of such "gods" (e.g., sexual immorality, material possessions, covetousness, sport, the family) and how they affect our lives and how we need to repent, there is a great need to present this in the context of the biblical theme of covenant account-ability to the Lord. When certain sins are singled out as having the power to control Christians without being placed in the context that Paul gives us in these verses, sin can become separated from the discussion of Christ's lordship. Then the greater spiritual background in which "demons" are real is obscured, and so the heinous, covenant-breaking nature of our idolatries is also diminished. It is crucial for all who claim to be part of Christ's church to understand that who or what they worship re-veals their heart and ultimately their position of standing or falling before the Lord. Fleeing idolatry should be a preoccupation that in itself will inevitably reveal a per-son's dependence on the Lord himself. There can be no dual loyalties. Having heard the strong warnings here, however, we also need to remember that those who truly belong to the Lord, though in serious danger of being led astray to or by false gods or demonic activity are actually "possessed" by the Holy Spirit (1 Cor 3:16; 2 Cor 5:5; Rom 8:14). It is important that Christians heed the warnings of Paul in this passage and others against temptations and idolatry and what lies behind idolatry. Yet it also is crucial that they recognise that the Spirit is the one who protects them and in the end upholds them and delivers them from a demonic takeover. It is significant that 10:13 with its promise that "God is faithful" comes before 10:14 and a section that deals with the dangers of idolatry.

One Bread, One Body

Paul says more about the Lord's Supper in chapter 11. Although in chapter 10 Paul is making a point about pagan meals by analogy with the Supper, it is import-ant to note how Paul draws attention to the unity of the body being revealed in the covenant meal. The Lord's presence at this meal is taken for granted as Paul makes his argument, but the emphasis on the unity of his people as a "body" is also vital. Later Paul will develop the "body" metaphor, but here he insists that the meal itself signifies the community's commitment to Christ as Lord. Often people see the Lord's

Supper, or communion, as about an individual's relationship with the Lord. It is certainly this, but this passage again draws attention to the fact that all individuals are part of the greater community. Eating and drinking together says something about the church's *united* commitment to each other in her service of the Lord.

This corporate dimension of covenant accountability is another teaching often obscured in the modern church impacted by a society in which individualism has taken on the nature of one of the "gods." In the church's table fellowship around the Supper, Christians express their "covenant participation" and accountability to the Lord alone as he spiritually sits with them. However, in doing this they express their accountability to one another and their care for one another. Here the church as a whole is reminded it is "one body" as its members seek to follow the Lord and rejoice in their redemption.

The loss in many churches of being given a piece of bread to eat from *one* loaf and of drinking from *one* larger cup has diminished something of the vivid picture that Paul here describes. Christ's death brought not just "me" to himself but all with whom I worship, and to whom I am now bound in covenant relationship under the same Lord. In this Supper I am reminded that together *we* must be a people who defy demons, who defy other "gods," and who worship the Lord Christ alone. Together we hold one another accountable for our worship; indeed, if we do not, the Lord will come to judge. The covenant judgment of the Lord on the church is vividly described as Jesus warns some of the seven churches in the book of Revelation that he will come and remove the "lampstand" (see Rev 1:20; 2:5, 16, 22–23; 3:3, 19).

1 Corinthians 10:23–11:1

Literary Context

The problem with idolatrous meals has been explained in covenantal terms. As happens for Christians in the Lord's Supper, when a religious meal is eaten as part of the worship of an idol an allegiance is affirmed. The main section started in 8:1 with the issue of food offered to idols. Paul has responded first by tackling the way the "knowers" or elitists have handled the matter. They have argued that their "knowledge" affirms their status in the community and allows them to eat any food in any situation. Paul points to the danger that others who follow them will end up stumbling and even being judged. As an apostle, he was prepared to give up his right to support, lest he should be seen to be putting a stumbling block in the way of the gospel (ch. 9). In chapter 10 Paul has drawn parts of chapters 8 and 9 together. Like the Corinthians, the Israelites of the wilderness generation received gifts from God, but these did not guarantee their security in the covenant community. Many of them became involved with the idolatry that surrounded them in the society of that day, and in the end God judged "most of them" (10:5). Those in the Corinthian church who "think they stand" (10:12) must therefore recognize that they may also "fall" should they too become involved in idolatrous meals. In this next section (10:23–11:1), Paul now speaks more generally. Bringing glory to God and building up one's neighbor provide general categories by which to approach the question of what (sacrificed) meat to eat. The theme of stumbling reappears in v. 32. Should the good of the other not be furthered, then it is better not to eat. In a link back to chapter 9, Paul concludes with a return to the first-person singular and urges that people imitate him as he imitates Christ. He especially recalls from that chapter how he seeks not his own advantage but that many may be saved.

Main Idea

Christians can eat food previously sacrificed to an idol when sold in the market, and they can eat the same food when invited to dinner at someone's house. However, the good of other Christians and the glory of God must be pre-eminent in all things. As in chapter 9, what is possible and not wrong may not be expedient, since not all things "build up."

Translation

1 Corinthians 10:23–11:1

23a	Quotation	**"All things are lawful,"**
b	Assertion (contrast)	but **not all things are beneficial.**
c	Quotation	**"All things are lawful,"**
d	Assertion (contrast)	but **not all things build up.**
24a	Exhortation	**Let no one seek their own [benefit], but**
b	Contrast	that of another.
25a	Exhortation	**Eat whatever is sold in the market**
b	Manner	without evaluating for the sake of self-awareness;
26a	Scriptural basis for 25a	for "the earth is the Lord's, and the fullness of it." [Ps 24:1]
27a	Condition (protasis)	If one of the unbelievers invites you and
b	Expansion	you want to go,
c	Exhortation (apodosis)	**eat everything put before you**
d	Manner	without evaluating for the sake of self-awareness.

28a	Condition (protasis)	But	if someone says to you,
b	Content/quotation		"This is sacrificed food,"
c	Exhortation		**do not eat**
d	Advantage		for the sake of the one who informed you, and
e			for the sake of self-awareness
29a	Explanation		—I do not mean *your* self-awareness, but theirs.
b	Basis for 28c–29a	For	**why should my freedom be judged by another's self-awareness?**
30a	Condition		If I participate by grace,
b	Question		**why am I defamed**
c	Cause		for that for which I give thanks?
31a	Summary of vv. 25–30	Therefore,	
b	Circumstance		whether you eat or
			drink, or
c	Circumstance		whatever you do,
d	Exhortation		**do all things to God's glory.**
32a	Exhortation		**Be no cause of stumbling**
b	Advantage/list		to Jews or
c	List		to Greeks or
d			to the church of God,
33a	Comparison		just as I strive to benefit everyone
b	Manner		in everything [I do],
c	Contrast		not seeking my own benefit, but rather
d			that of the many,
e	Purpose		in order that they may be saved.
11:1a	Exhortation		**Be imitators of me,**
b	Comparison		as I am of Christ.

Structure

The focus of this section is on the building up of other Christians, a theme that Paul has already spoken to and will continue to do so. This point is made at the start (v. 23) and the end of the section (v. 33) thus shaping a form of *inclusio*. This overarching theme is Paul's concern throughout the discussion of eating food offered to idols (8:1–11:1). The present section may be further broken down. In vv. 23–24 Paul repeats the principle that each should seek the other's benefit rather than their own. In vv. 25–26 Paul allows the eating of food sold in the market, offering biblical support. In vv. 27–29a Paul examines reasons both for and for *not* eating food provided in an unbeliever's house. Verses 29b–30 then address the nature of a Christian's liberty, with vv. 31–33 urging that all be done to God's glory. Then 11:1 provides a conclusion to the whole section from 8:1.

Exegetical Outline

VII. Status, Knowledge, Freedom, and Food Offered to Idols (8:1–11:1)

    A. Knowledge and Love Contrasted (8:1–3)

    B. Knowledge concerning the Existence of "gods" and "lords" (8:4–6)

    C. Knowledge regarding the Eating of Idol Food in an Idol Temple (8:7–13)

    D. Status and Rights Should Be Subordinated for the Sake of the Gospel (9:1–27)

    E. Israel's Abuse of Spiritual Gifts Provides a Warning (10:1–13)

    F. Covenant Allegiance Matters (10:14–22)

➡   **G. Seek Only the Neighbor's Good and Bring Glory to God (10:23–11:1)**

      1. When to Eat and When Not to Eat (10:23–30)

        a. Seek the Benefit of the Other Person (10:23–24)

        b. Eat Food Sold in the Market (10:25–26)

        c. Eat Food Offered at Dinner with an Unbeliever (10:27)

        d. Do Not Eat to Prove a Point! (10:28–29a)

        e. Understand the Nature of Your Liberty (10:29b–30)

      2. Do All to the Glory of God (10:31–11:1)

Explanation of the Text

10:23–24 "All things are lawful," but not all things are beneficial. "All things are lawful," but not all things build up. Let no one seek their own [benefit], but that of another (Πάντα ἔξεστιν, ἀλλ᾽ οὐ πάντα συμφέρει. πάντα ἔξεστιν, ἀλλ᾽ οὐ πάντα οἰκοδομεῖ. μηδεὶς τὸ ἑαυτοῦ ζητείτω ἀλλὰ τὸ τοῦ ἑτέρου). By reference to a Corinthian slogan, Paul returns to his call that building one another up should characterize a Christian community. Indeed, this becomes an arbiter of what may be deemed "beneficial" to a church. The Corinthian quotation has already appeared in 6:12. For a discussion of the statement "all things are lawful" and how Paul qualifies it, see the comments there. Paul has demonstrated that phrases and slogans that appear to the elitists to be "wise" must be examined most closely. First, the church at large must

remember that such wisdom does not authenticate anyone's membership in the Christian church or their superior "spiritual" status in the church (this is part of the issue in 10:27b–29). Secondly, what some may think is "wise" must be judged against a number of important theological "givens." As Paul will make clear in the pivotal chapter 13, since "love" is the defining marker of membership in the Christian community, it is unsurprising that Paul here, as in 6:12, tests the value of so-called "knowledge" by whether it is "beneficial" (συμφέρω) to the community. This will be one genuine test of whether the statement reveals true and godly wisdom. Paul's second qualification in 6:12, that no one should become enslaved to a way of life or a behavior that is ungodly, is not repeated here in chapter 10. Rather, there is a straightforward command: "Let no one seek their own [benefit]" (μηδεὶς τὸ ἑαυτοῦ ζητείτω).

The verb translated "are beneficial" (συμφέρω) implies a "bringing together." Yet as the context shows, its meaning is an outworking of Paul's repeated discussion in the letter of what "builds up." This entails what enables a godly and spiritual edification of the entire Christian community (not just a particular group). In 8:1 Paul clarified that this is summed up in the word "love" ("love builds up"). It is because love builds up that Paul demands in 6:12 and here that mature Christians should always be seeking the benefit of the neighbor or the other (τὸ τοῦ ἑτέρου) and so seeking to build that person up in Christ and in his church (see 13:5, "love is not self-seeking"; οὐ ζητεῖ τὰ ἑαυτῆς).

It is sometimes held that Paul agreed with the quotation "all things are lawful" despite his qualification of it, but this is to misunderstand the force of his argument both here and in chapter 6.[1] The force of "you cannot" (οὐ δύνασθε) in v. 21 has already demonstrated that such a saying could never have been accepted as an absolute.[2] Indeed, the qualifications of the saying found right here in vv. 23–24 were strong enough for the saying to be rendered effectively worthless. However, the assumption that essentially Paul agreed with what the strong were saying has had a forceful impact on the interpretation of this section of text. As a result, it is often believed that Paul was speaking to the "strong" about the attitude of *the weak* toward eating meat.[3] In fact, though, for Paul the slogan simply fails his test. He could not have agreed with it.

The theme of "building up" has undergirded the whole section but specifically augments what

Paul wrote in 8:1 and 8:10 (cf. 3:9). In 8:10 Paul was concerned that some Christians were "building up" the weak to get them to join them in eating in an idol's temple. Paul has shown how wrong and sinful this is. Instead of "building up" Christians to "stand" (10:12), it has led to "stumbling" and "falling" (8:13; 10:12). The opposite of "building up" the other person is to "sin against your brothers [and sisters]" (8:12). In chapter 14 Paul will further show how "building up" the community *should* take place. He will do this in the context of showing how God's grace-gifts should *actually* function in the community rather than the way they are functioning for the elitists (14:3–6). Paul's problem remains with anyone who, like the elitists, will eat food regardless of the spiritual and communal consequences of that action. The Greek of v. 24 literally reads: "Let no one seek that which is his, but that which is the other's." The meaning of this abbreviated construction is nevertheless clear given the preceding verse; hence the addition of the word "benefit" to our translation.

10:25–27 Eat whatever is sold in the market without evaluating for the sake of self-awareness; for "the earth is the Lord's, and the fullness of it." If one of the unbelievers invites you and you want to go, eat everything put before you without evaluating for the sake of self-awareness. (Πᾶν τὸ ἐν μακέλλῳ πωλούμενον ἐσθίετε μηδὲν ἀνακρίνοντες διὰ τὴν συνείδησιν, τοῦ κυρίου γὰρ ἡ γῆ καὶ τὸ πλήρωμα αὐτῆς. εἴ τις καλεῖ ὑμᾶς τῶν ἀπίστων καὶ θέλετε πορεύεσθαι, πᾶν τὸ παρατιθέμενον ὑμῖν ἐσθίετε μηδὲν ἀνακρίνοντες διὰ τὴν συνείδησιν). Paul has reset the scene so that the issue is clear: "Do these actions build up God's people in covenant

---

1. Willis, *Idol Meat in Corinth*, 224n1.

2. In a completely unnecessary deduction and misunderstanding of what Paul is saying here, Senft, *Première Épître de Saint Paul aux Corinthiens*, 136, sees the saying in 10:23 as evidence that the subject is now irreconcilable with v. 21.

3. So, e.g., Weiss, *Der erste Korintherbrief*, 263–64; H. A. W. Meyer, *Critical and Exegetical Handbook to the Epistles to the Corinthians, Vol. 1 (First Epistle, Ch. I–XIII)*, trans. D. D. Bannerman and W. P. Dickson (T&T Clark: Edinburgh, 1877), 307.

commitment to the Lord and to each other?" Since much of the food sold in markets in Corinth had probably earlier been offered as a sacrifice in a temple, this was a real and live issue for Christians. If idolatry is as serious as Paul has made out in the previous verses and if the eating of food is so central to that idolatry and personal identification with the idol, then what about that same food when it moves away from the place where it has been sacrificed and is sold in the market? Paul is clear that *this meat and food can be eaten.*

This is a further indication that Paul's real concern about eating such food is not the fact that it may, at some stage, have been sacrificed to an idol but the *context* in which it is eaten. Eaten in the temple itself (8:10), it is being eaten as part of the worship of that idol, and so the eater is caught up in the worship, and the results of that are what Paul has spoken about earlier in this chapter. Eaten in a nonreligious context simply as food rather than as the content of a sacrifice, there is nothing to worry about. Christians may eat this food. Paul gives a theological reason why, in principle, he is prepared to eat this meat, drawing on Psalm 24:1: "The earth is the Lord's, and the fullness of it." In other words, eating food when *not* as part of temple worship is simply to enjoy God's creation. It should be done with genuine thanksgiving to God, who supplies all food (v. 30).

In v. 27 Paul considers another similar situation. If a Christian is invited to dinner with an unbeliever, he will be served food and meat probably bought from the market.[4] Thus something of an in-between situation is posed. The food is eaten in the presence of an unbeliever, but not in a temple,

nor in a Christian home. In this situation, likewise, in principle Paul has no objection to the food being eaten. Thus far all is clear.

However, once again Paul qualifies what he is saying, and in both vv. 25 and 27 he does so with exactly the same clause. We have translated this as "without evaluating for the sake of self-awareness" (μηδὲν ἀνακρίνοντες διὰ τὴν συνείδησιν).[5] The view taken here is that Paul means that this food can be eaten, but this must not become a matter linked to proving or addressing a person's community status or "self-awareness." In other words, Paul is saying, "You can eat this food with thanksgiving because the earth is the Lord's and its fullness, but do *not* eat it to evaluate or 'judge' yours or someone else's community status. Do not let eating this food become a spiritual determining point among you." To do that would be to fly in the face of what Paul has just said in v. 24.

To arrive at this understanding, it is necessary to step back and return to matters that have already been addressed in this epistle and that help shed light on what is going on. These matters must also be related to the question of who Paul is addressing here or who he has in mind will be doing the judging or evaluating. The words "to evaluate" (ἀνακρίνω; vv. 25, 27) and "self-awareness" (συνείδησις) have already been examined and their importance for the whole of this epistle noted. For a discussion of the various words Paul uses in this epistle to further his discussion of spiritual evaluation and discernment or judging, see the comments on 2:14 (where ἀνακρίνω is used three times in 2:14–15).

The evaluating or judging that was going on

---

4. The nature of this dinner invitation is not clear. Was it to a home, a "restaurant" possibly associated with a temple, or was it to a "post-sacrificial meal at a pagan temple"? (Willis, *Idol Meat in Corinth*, 235–40). The latter is unlikely in view of ch. 8. Most commentators see this as a home invitation.

5. For "self-awareness," see "In Depth: The Meaning of the Word 'Conscience' (συνείδησις)" at 8:7. The word also appears in 8:10 and 8:12. This translation of the word is followed here by Thiselton, *1 Corinthians*, 785.

in the Corinthian community is clearly a "spiritual evaluation" emanating from the elitists, as was noted in chapter 2. They were the ones always seeking their own benefit (10:24). In 9:3 Paul comments on those who would even "judge" or "evaluate" (ἀνακρίνω) him! In the light of all that has been written in the epistle, the type of evaluation to which Paul refers cannot be set aside or treated as of no consequence to what he is saying here. It is something that the strong or "knowers" thought they were able to do properly and spiritually, but it is something that Paul had told them they were not doing properly (in ch. 2)! Note, there has been no suggestion that somehow the "weak" were judging the "knowers."

However, earlier, in looking at 8:7 and 8:10, we noted that a so-called "weak conscience" simply means having a lack of knowledge or self-awareness of oneself in relation to the community. Those "weak" in their "self-awareness" were people who, reflecting on their own actions and feelings, felt insecure as God's people. Their weakness was not in moral decision-making. The problem of self-awareness is one that has been seen among the weak. The question of what authenticates a person's status among Christ's people when someone has come out of idolatry has become a real concern for the weak. This is because the elitists have argued that this security comes from having certain grace-gifts from God, evidence for which was to be seen in doing things *like* eating meat offered to idols in an idol temple. Paul has shown this to be utterly wrong.

With these matters of "evaluation" and "self-awareness" in mind, Paul argues that it is fine to eat this meat at dinner or when bought in a market, *provided* it is not seen as a way of evaluating or judging anyone's self-awareness vis-à-vis the community. As long as eating this food is in no way done to make some point about being spiritually mature or having "knowledge," then it is fine. Thus Paul insists *twice* that eating can take place as long as it is "without evaluation for the sake of self-awareness."

Other views on this clause abound and cannot be examined in detail here. It is important, though, to note that most commentators assume that "conscience" means "moral conscience" and that "weak" converted *Jews* would have had the greatest problem with eating such meat.[6] Barrett sees Paul siding here with the strong and making a "clean break" with Judaism where "conscience demanded . . . the most searching inquiry before he might eat."[7] The statements in vv. 25 and 27 therefore involve Paul's hedging of his views "by reference to the conscience, not of the eater, or potential eater, but of his weak Christian brother."[8] Certainly a possible parallel to "examining" food lay in Jewish food laws where meat was examined carefully to discern its origin before being eaten. However, a Jewish background for the "weak" is unlikely, as argued above.

Some suggest Paul is directly addressing the "strong" here. The problem with this is simply that if the issue is a "moral conscience" about the eating, the strong clearly had no such conscience. After all, they ate in an idol temple! This also makes it difficult to see how Garland can be right in suggesting that Paul makes no distinction at all here between the so-called "strong" and "weak" and that Paul is addressing the whole community generally.[9] It is

---

6. Although cf. Fee, *1 Corinthians*, 530–32, who argues that the problem was Jewish-styled investigations into the origin of the food but that Paul was more concerned to show that such questions lay "outside the concerns of conscience altogether" than to deal with the weak.

7. Barrett, *First Corinthians*, 240.

8. C. K. Barrett, *Essays on Paul* (London: SPCK, 1982), 46.

9. Garland, *1 Corinthians*, 490: "In this case ignorance is bliss."

not that Paul's theology here depends on such a distinction but that clearly part of the problem for some (whom Paul has indicated see themselves as "strong") is that they have always felt they had the "right" or "freedom" to eat all such meat. They have never had a (moral) "conscience" about the matter. They have never accepted Paul's dictum that "not all things build up." In fact, even though Paul says "eat," with his talk of "self-awareness" or "conscience" he limits that right; he does not extend it. That Paul makes this distinction becomes clearer in v. 28 as he posits a hypothetical variation on the dinner invitation.

10:28–29 But if someone says to you, "This is sacrificed food," do not eat for the sake of the one who informed you, and for the sake of self-awareness—I do not mean *your* self-awareness, but theirs. For why should my freedom be judged by another's self-awareness? (ἐὰν δέ τις ὑμῖν εἴπῃ, Τοῦτο ἱερόθυτόν ἐστιν, μὴ ἐσθίετε δι᾽ ἐκεῖνον τὸν μηνύσαντα καὶ τὴν συνείδησιν—συνείδησιν δὲ λέγω οὐχὶ τὴν ἑαυτοῦ ἀλλὰ τὴν τοῦ ἑτέρου. ἱνατί γὰρ ἡ ἐλευθερία μου κρίνεται ὑπὸ ἄλλης συνειδήσεως;). Paul now asks hypothetically what a Christian is supposed to do if, at this unbeliever's house and while eating food previously offered to idols, "someone" makes an issue of the food. In other words, if someone draws attention to the nature of the food and to its provenance, does that change the previous advice that it is alright to eat such food at this unbeliever's house? In this third-class condition, Paul establishes this as a hypothetical question. In v. 27 he used a first-class condition, which assumes the condition to be true. Here, Paul is vaguer as he anticipates a potential situation.

Two main interpretive questions immediately surface here. Who is the "someone" (τις), the informant? And how and why might "their" conscience/self-awareness be affected? In the end, it is important to admit that the text gives very limited infor-

mation. Yet from what has gone before, it is likely to be the "knowers" who would draw attention to what was being eaten (cf. comments on 8:10). Since most food would have been sourced in sacrificial contexts, and all participants at any meal would have surely known this, the statement to which Paul refers must be more than simply announcing where the food came from! The information must have been given for a purpose that Paul clearly shows is related to "self-awareness." Consistently it is with the strong that Paul has taken issue on this matter. Therefore, it seems likely that here Paul is telling believers that even though this is not a religious context, if the eating is suddenly given religious *significance*, they should not eat. If a "strong" person makes a point of this eating, as if to say, "Look at this; this is us exercising our 'knowledge' and demonstrating our community status and security," then Paul says that the food should not be eaten. This is a *general* statement in that Paul is not simply telling the "weak" not to eat but any Christian who may be present. To eat at this stage would be to confirm the *informant* in his arrogance. It would be bad for *their* "self-awareness" and add to their false sense of confidence that is altogether based in the wrong things. This understanding of what Paul is saying allows the next rhetorical question in v. 29b to fit in logically. Given the situation of v. 28a, Paul would *not* eat simply to make a point for the sake of *another person's* understanding of self-awareness. Paul's "liberty" could never be "judged" or "evaluated" in this way.

For the sake of clarity we may paraphrase vv. 28–29 thus:

> If, at a meal with an unbeliever, one of the so-called "knowledgeable" Christians draws attention to the fact that idol meat is being eaten and that, therefore, this is a good occasion to make a point of your "freedom," then you should decline to eat. You do not want further to encourage this person

in *his or her* false understanding of self-awareness. Anyway, why should another (and false) type of self-awareness be allowed to decide whether or not I am "free"?[10]

While the above, to our mind, seems to make most coherent sense of the whole of vv. 27–29, many other suggestions have been made concerning who the "someone" is. These include that they were, variously, the pagan host,[11] another pagan guest,[12] or another believer either present at the meal[13] or, if absent, who knew about the invitation.[14] However, it is difficult to imagine how this information would have been given by a pagan host or even another pagan guest. How would it have helped the pagan if a Christian then refused to eat the meat (v. 28b)? And why would the pagan have said anything, anyway?[15] It seems far-fetched that a pagan would have invited a Christian to a meal with evil intent to make them eat something they did not want to eat![16] But it also seems to stretch the imagination to suggest, with Fee, that the pagan spoke from a "sense of moral obligation to the Christian," assuming Christians would not eat such food. If so, why invite the Christian in the first place? Also, the concept of a "noble"

motivation on the part of a pagan (to protect the "[moral?] conscience" of a Christian) is hardly how Paul speaks of pagans! Indeed, this approach makes v.29b almost unintelligible. As noted, many believe this exegetical problem is best solved by suggesting that the informant is another Christian present at the meal, who was drawing attention to the moral problem that needed to be confronted. But this still poses some problems. What would be their motivation? If the Christian were among the so-called "strong," why would they bother mentioning the food at all? Surely, he or she would not have had a problem with it? Then if the Christian was "weak" in the way most commentators take it, that is, weak in terms of having a tender "conscience" on these things, why would such a person have accepted the invitation in the first place? If such a Christian had been at the meal but was not going to eat the meat anyway, how would his or her conscience or consciousness have been hurt? In summary, assuming Paul is here talking of a (moral) "conscience" (συνείδησις) really provides no obviously satisfactory understanding of what Paul was addressing.

On the other hand, understanding Paul to be speaking of "self-awareness," especially with regard

---

10. Gardner, *Gifts of God*, 178. Cf. Bultmann's similar paraphrase: "No other person has the right to force his judgment upon me: 'for why is my freedom decided by any other conscience [than my own]?'" (*Theology of the New Testament*, 1:219).

11. Bultmann, *Theology of the New Testament*, 1:219; cf. Senft, *Première Épître de Saint Paul aux Corinthiens*, 138; Garland, *1 Corinthians*, 496.

12. J. J. Lias, *The First Epistle to the Corinthians*, Cambridge Bible for Schools (Cambridge: Cambridge University Press, 1881), 103; H. Osborn, "Συνείδησις," *JTS* 32 (1931): 178; Lietzmann, *An Die Korinther I–II*, 53.

13. Meyer, *Epistles to the Corinthians, Vol. 1*, 311; Robertson and Plummer, *First Corinthians*, 221; Barrett, *First Corinthians*, 242, among others. In this case the informant is normally assumed to have been a *weak* Christian.

14. Murphy-O'Connor, *Keys to First Corinthians*, 125, says it was a "weak Christian."

15. Garland (*1 Corinthians*, 497) seems to assume that once the pagan host has made the announcement that "this food is sacred," the Christian has no option but to cease from eating on three grounds: it would offer a tacit recognition of pagan gods and so compromise the confession of the one true God; it would confirm the unbeliever in his idolatrous beliefs and not lead him away from them; it would make the Christian censure of pagan gods seem hypocritical. But this does not really answer why a Christian would have felt they could go to the meal in the first place! That some of the food may have come from idol offerings was almost inevitable. No host would have needed to say this. It is possible, perhaps, that the Christian might arrive to discover that a more seriously religious meal has been organized by the host than they had anticipated and so they find themselves having to decline.

16. The suggestion of Chrysostom, *Homilies on First Corinthians*, homily 25.2.

to community identification, does make sense, as we have seen. The elitists might well have said, "This is meat offered to idols." In doing so they would have been making a *religious* point by applying their "knowledge" (γνῶσις) to the situation.[17] This eating in the presence of an unbeliever would be yet another occasion, arrogantly and without thought for others, to demonstrate their self-awareness as secure people. Finally, as noted above, one important result of viewing the issue in this way is that it makes sense of the "for" (γάρ) of v. 29b. Right through this whole section Paul has continued to apply his core principle that "love builds up" (8:1). He will never let any eat idol food in any situation or for any reason that might cause them to stumble (see his summary in v. 32).

10:30 If I participate by grace, why am I defamed for that for which I give thanks? (εἰ ἐγὼ χάριτι μετέχω, τί βλασφημοῦμαι ὑπὲρ οὗ ἐγὼ εὐχαριστῶ;). Paul continues his argument that he has the right to say "no" to eating should his eating not build up another or should it fail to bring glory to God. However, v. 30 has raised a number of further interpretative problems. If read in one way, it can appear that Paul is going back on virtually all he has said! Provided he rejoices when he eats, then why should anyone speak against him? However, difficult as this verse is, there is no reason to delete vv. 29b–30 as a "marginal gloss."[18] Neither is there a need to see these final rhetorical questions as following naturally on from v. 27, as if vv. 28–29a are simply an interruption in which Paul addresses a subsidiary matter. In any case, v. 30 would still

remain difficult to understand since Paul has spent much of the last three chapters insisting that liberty will *always* be subjected to qualification of what builds up others and what brings glory to God. Our view, in agreement with Bultmann[19] and Barrett,[20] is that Paul was continuing to defend a position of *not* eating. When Paul, or "anyone,"[21] participates in eating this food by God's grace, how can anyone defame him? In other words, neither the freedom to eat with thanksgiving *nor* the freedom Paul has just spoken about *not* to eat give anyone grounds to defame or revile him. As Paul has shown in chapter 9, freedom for him involves the right to say "no" as well as the right to say "yes," provided certain principles have been followed. These two great principles that have coursed their way right through chapters 8–10 are now summarized in vv. 31–32. (And which should never be separated from v. 30!) In v. 31 Paul returns to the principle of doing all "to God's glory," and in v. 32 he returns to the principle of what builds up, for nothing that is done must cause any group to "stumble."

10:31 Therefore, whether you eat or drink, or whatever you do, do all things to God's glory (Εἴτε οὖν ἐσθίετε εἴτε πίνετε εἴτε τι ποιεῖτε, πάντα εἰς δόξαν θεοῦ ποιεῖτε). "Therefore" (οὖν) has a strong rhetorical appeal and emphatically sums up what Paul has been talking about in the preceding verses as well as in the whole context of 8:1–11:1. "Or whatever you do" (τι ποιεῖτε) is elliptical but probably refers to the idea that at times a person may decide, for God's glory, *not* to eat or drink. As v. 28 and the immediate context have made clear, it

---

17. Though not adopting the position articulated here about who the informant was, Garland is right in saying that "the person who makes the announcement understands the food to be *religiously* significant" (*1 Corinthians*, 496, our emphasis).

18. Weiss, *Der erste Korintherbrief*, 266.

19. Bultmann (*Theology of the New Testament*, 1:219) paraphrases: "I am free to eat anything that I can eat with thanks-

giving . . . but I do not surrender my freedom either, if I decline out of consideration for another's conscience."

20. Barrett, *First Corinthians*, 243–44: "Paul is still justifying abstention by the strong."

21. "Anyone" since the "I" of v. 30a is probably representative of a class of people adopting Paul's position on eating this food.

can be just as glorifying to God *not* to eat or drink for the reasons given above because thinking of the benefit of the "other" also brings glory to God.

It is important to note that the opposite in this context of bringing "glory to God" is to "provoke the Lord to jealousy" and to suggest by their actions that "they are stronger than he" (v. 22). By the end of this lengthy section on meat offered to idols the idea that "all things are lawful" has clearly been discredited or at least qualified to the point that it's a meaningless dictum. Rather, God's glory and the benefit of his people must always be paramount. Of course, this is what "covenant participation" (κοινωνία) is all about, and Paul will go on to say that this is what it is to follow Christ (11:1). In his words of 9:21, this is precisely what it is to be under the law of Christ. Freedom and food and drink are God's. The earth is the Lord's. But all is to be enjoyed in a way that reveals the covenant commitment to be humble before the Lord and to love his people through seeking their edification rather than causing them to stumble.

10:32 Be no cause of stumbling to Jews or to Greeks or to the church of God (ἀπρόσκοποι καὶ Ἰουδαίοις γίνεσθε καὶ Ἕλλησιν καὶ τῇ ἐκκλησίᾳ τοῦ θεοῦ). Paul's summary is generalized. In 9:19–23 he has provided precise examples from his own life. To the Jew he became like a Jew. To the Greek he became like a Greek. Here, interestingly, he adds "to the church of God" (καὶ τῇ ἐκκλησίᾳ τοῦ θεοῦ). Not to cause a stumbling to the church would surely include all that Paul has been saying. The "weak" have nearly been caused to stumble (cf. comments on 9:22); indeed, the "strong" have stumbled by eating idol food in an idol's temple. Christians can

cause their own brothers or sisters to "stumble" in many ways and thus be in danger of judgment.

The opening imperative is often translated "give no offence," but in modern idiom this is hardly satisfactory. It sounds as if Paul is simply saying, "Be nice to them!" Neither is Paul thinking that they should be "blameless" in the day of Christ, which is how the word (ἀπρόσκοπος) is translated in Philippians 1:10 in the RSV, NRSV, ESV, and NIV. As Thayer makes clear, the word's semantic range is firmly entrenched in the idea of stumbling or falling and so can be translated, *"having nothing for one to strike against; not causing to stumble."*[22] Thus, the NIV translates: "Do not cause anyone to stumble." Paul's concern that no stumbling block be placed in the way of the gospel has been part of his argument throughout this section. Indeed, it has been part of the thrust of the epistle itself. The noun, "no cause of stumbling" (ἀπρόσκοπος), recalls his earlier use of the two nouns referring to a "stumbling block" (σκάνδαλον and πρόσκομμα). The theme was introduced in 1:23 where Christ himself was said to be a "stumbling block" to the Jews. (See at 1:23b, "In Depth: The Theme of Stumbling.") We noted that as Paul uses these ideas, *he sees the preaching of the crucified Christ as the tested stone, the article of belief.* Nothing else can replace this, for it will immediately become a "stumbling block" (see comments on 1:23). Here Paul summarizes that same message. "Rights" can be forsaken. Therefore, food offered to idols should not be eaten in certain situations, all because no one should encounter any hindrance to the gospel of Christ.

10:33 just as I strive to benefit[23] everyone in everything [I do], not seeking my own benefit, but

---

22. Thayer, *Greek-English Lexicon*, 70. See also LSJ ("not stumbling").

23. The word ἀρέσκω here connotes more than simply "to please" in the sense of giving pleasure or satisfaction. In 7:32–34 it is used in that way. Here its link with σύμφορον in

the contrasting clause that follows indicates that Paul's thought continues to involve accommodation of oneself in the interests of others (Thayer, *Greek-English Lexicon*, 72); hence, the translation "to benefit." Cf. Rom 15:2.

rather that of the many, in order that they may be saved (καθὼς κἀγὼ πάντα πᾶσιν ἀρέσκω, μὴ ζητῶν τὸ ἐμαυτοῦ σύμφορον ἀλλὰ τὸ τῶν πολλῶν, ἵνα σωθῶσιν). Finally, Paul returns to himself once more by way of example. The life he has lived before the churches is one that has modeled the desire to always build up his fellow Christians, striving to bring them spiritual benefit. His great desire in his dealings with the people of Corinth, whether believers or not,[24] has always been to ensure that they are a saved people. (The verse thus recalls 9:22.) In 13:5 love is defined as "not self-seeking" (οὐ ζητεῖ τὰ ἑαυτῆς), and this is what Paul has demonstrated in his life. He will put nothing between himself and the gospel of Christ.

11:1 Be imitators of me, as I am of Christ (μιμηταί μου γίνεσθε, καθὼς κἀγὼ Χριστοῦ). The traditional chapter division is unsatisfactory; 11:1 belongs with chapter 10. Christ himself is the great example of the one who obeyed his Father and who was a servant who gave even his life for his people. Christ was concerned first and foremost for the salvation of men and women and for their spiritual well-being. His life and death showed the depths of the love that drove him. Part of apostolic leadership was not only to teach the gospel truth of Christ but to model that truth in imitating the Lord. In 4:9–13, 16 (see comments) and in chapter 9, Paul has laid out some of the ways he has done this in practice, but the theme runs throughout his life and writings (Phil 3:17; 1 Thess 1:6; 2 Thess 3:7, 9). His final imperative (μιμηταί μου γίνεσθε) is thus a completely appropriate summary of all he has said in 8:1–11:1.

Theology in Application

Learning to See Ourselves through Others' Eyes

Paul began this section at 10:23 by repeating both the catchphrase and its strong qualification from 6:12: "'All things are lawful for me,' but not all things are beneficial" (πάντα [μοι] ἔξεστιν ἀλλ᾽ οὐ πάντα συμφέρει). Paul has affirmed certain Christians' "rights" as we have seen in chapters 8–9. Having insisted that meat cannot be eaten as part of a sacrificial meal to a so-called "god," he now affirms the liberty Christians have to eat other meat, even that which has been sacrificed to idols in other settings that are not religious. Meat sold in the market is, in this sense, neutral material. Eating it is neither right nor wrong in and of itself. However, once again Paul comes back to an abiding principle for the life of the believer: act in a way that will build people up in Christ. The difficulty with this is that it requires learning to see actions as others see them. Paul's concern is to "build up" people. This means knowing what is needed to build them up, but it also means knowing what may pull them down. Seeking the other's good (10:24) means more than insisting on certain theological truths (e.g., that "the earth is the Lord's and the fullness thereof"). It means looking at how actions are perceived by others to see if they can be misread

---

24. Garland, *1 Corinthians*, 502, is right to insist that "the many" refers to "the majority of people inside and outside the church."

or used as an expression of power to manipulate others. In chapter 9 Paul has already shown how he is prepared to give up much for the sake of building others up rather than insisting on what may be technically his "right." Understanding how our actions may affect people spiritually, emotionally, or psychologically requires a maturity in the faith, and it is this to which Paul points here. Christians should be careful not to act in ways that will end up leading another person into sin or away from the truth. Deciding whether to refrain from certain foods (and so possibly encourage another's legalism) or to eat certain foods (and so possibly encourage another's licentiousness) involves a spiritual awareness of the "other" that many Christians fail to employ. It is all too easy for others to give a false religious significance to our actions. Sometimes we will need to live with this, but at other times we should refrain lest we lead a person astray. Bringing glory to God (v. 31) will involve deep spiritual care for others and being prepared to change behavior for their sake.

The Affirmation of Creation

The quotation from Psalm 24:1, "the earth is the Lord's, and the fullness thereof," appears almost in passing in Paul's argument, and yet it contains a deep truth by which he lived his life. Of course, Paul had had to learn that this verse applied to all food, much as Peter had (Acts 10:14–15). As a Jew, he would have been used to this verse providing grounds for thanksgiving to God for food, but that food would have already been carefully vetted to ensure it met with Jewish dietary laws. Now Paul was using this general principle about all creation and applying it to all food (cf. 1 Tim 4:4). While people can abuse God's creation in multiple ways, including giving it religious significance it does not have, the creation has wholly been given to humanity to enjoy and for their benefit.

In some Christian circles today there remains an essentially Greek, dualistic view of the world. This should not come as a great surprise since Western education is largely built on this worldview where the "religious" is separated off as an altogether different discipline from, for example, the scientific enterprise. Such Christians today tend to view the material world as mostly evil or at least rather irrelevant to their faith, while what is "spiritual" or of "heaven," such as worship, prayer, and other "religious" activities, are regarded as good. The biblical worldview cuts right across this dualism. The created world, even in its fallen and distorted form (Rom 8:19–22), is good and should be approached as God's gift to humanity, which is to care for it, to have dominion over it, and to give thanks for it (Gen 1:26–30; Ps 147:7–20). This view of the world allows Paul to eat different foods, but it also allows him to move between cultures as he preaches to the world. To enjoy God's creation, including food and drink, is to bring glory to the Lord who created this for us. This can be done with Christian and unbelieving friends alike, without distinction.

This passage has occasionally been used as a support for the Christian need to be environmentally conscious and to work to protect creation. Generally speaking, such an argument can be made right from the creation account itself and through many pages of Scripture. However, in this particular context it is to stretch what Paul is saying too far. It is good to remember that Paul makes the argument, but then immediately offers a qualification: food cannot always be eaten as, for example, in settings where the eating involves idolatrous rites. In much thinking these days, the goodness of creation is distorted. For example, some treat creation with a reverence that even involves a worship that should be reserved only for God himself. Thus, just as there are times when refraining from eating certain foods may be necessary, so there are times when it may be necessary to distance ourselves from others who appear to believe in the "goodness" of nature, but give it a religious life of its own with no acknowledgment of the Creator.

The Imitation of Christ

In the matter of seeking always to bring glory to God, Jesus Christ stands as the supreme example. In always seeking to bring glory to God, Paul has shown how seriously he takes the question of a person "stumbling." To avoid this, he will put aside his rights, and in doing so he longs to see many saved (10:33). In Romans 15:2–3 Paul gives another insight into what this imitation means: "Let each of us please his neighbor for his good, to build him up. For Christ did not please himself, but as it is written, 'The reproaches of those who reproached you fell on me'" (ESV).

Paul's exhortation for people to follow him as he follows Christ may sound rather arrogant to modern ears. However, paradoxically, if it is understood in Paul's own terms, then it is a call to humility and to humiliation and obedience even to death. It is a life that seeks to live "the mind of Christ" (2:16). Paul describes the vital content of this in Philippians 2:4–8, where he appeals again for Christians to consider others first and then points to Christ doing just that when he "emptied himself," took "the form of a servant," and obeyed even to death on the cross (ESV). It is this self-emptying of pride and of the exercise of his "rights" in favor of the redemption of many people that is what Paul asks people to imitate. Paul did not claim perfection in his life, but this was his pattern and the one he calls all Christians to follow.

Sadly, the disjunction between what is taught by some Christian leaders and how they live is often well noted, especially in the media. Of course, throughout the history of the church this has been a problem. Jesus, Paul, and Peter warn strongly against hypocrisy seen in a life that does not match the words or the truth of Scripture (cf. Matt 23:13; Gal 2:13; 1 Pet 2:1). However, the fact that Christians will often fail in this endeavor must not deter them from seeking to live always in imitation of Christ and to do so with the Spirit's help. Indeed, the readiness to admit sin and failure is surely part of the demonstration of humility required of fallible sinful men and women. Church leaders especially must understand the need to offer their lives as a model of the gospel they preach in order that none should be caused to "stumble." It is worth recalling that God's people are in fact commanded to "consider" the conduct of their teachers and "imitate" them (Heb 13:7). No doubt this is one of the reasons James stresses the enormous weight of being a teacher in the church of Christ while also acknowledging that "we all stumble" (Jas 3:1–2).

1 Corinthians 11:2–16

Literary Context

Paul has addressed in some detail the matter of eating food offered to idols in 8:1–11:1. Through these chapters, he has gently but firmly remonstrated with those who are "puffed up" with their "knowledge" (8:1). Though the issue of eating food offered in an idol's temple is serious since it leads to a breach of covenant with the Lord, Paul has also proposed three guiding principles for all legitimate Christian behavior. Having shown from his own life how he lives by these principles in chapter 9, he has returned to summarize this in 10:31–33. Everything must be done for the glory of God, no "stumbling block" must be placed in the way of the gospel for any person, and Christians should seek the benefit or building up of other Christians rather than of themselves. Together these three principles can be summarized in the word "love," which is in fact the true marker of a Christian. Thus chapters 8:1–11:1 anticipate the wonderful summary chapter 13.

The section from 11:2–14:40 now addresses other specific issues that are causing debate and a breach of unity in the community. Paul continues to show how the answer to these different matters must be addressed in terms of God's glory, ensuring that no one is caused to "stumble," and in terms of "building up" others in the community. In chapter 12 Paul addresses in some detail the nature of the "grace-gifts." Having criticized the use of "knowledge" by those who claim great gifting, Paul here writes positively about the real function of such gifts from God's Spirit. They may have been abused by the elitists, but that does not mean they should be ignored. Paul addresses their tremendous value to the community when used as God intended to "build up" the community. In chapter 14 Paul returns to speak practically of how to use gifts such as prophecy and tongues in ways that lead not to pride but to building up others. Chapter 13 then summarizes all that is said in the whole epistle, but especially in 8:1–14:40. Not even the most amazing of the grace-gifts count for anything when put alongside the marker of all that is spiritually mature and to be sought after: love.

In 11:2–16, to which we now turn, Paul addresses a matter in which "rights" need to be examined in the light of care, respect, and love for one another. It seems that whatever the reason for the lack of head coverings on the part of some women, Paul is urging them to curtail what may appear to be a "freedom" or a "right" in a similar way to that which he has described in chapter 9, and to do so out of respect for others. Though the issue of head coverings clearly has to do with gender differences between men and women, and probably mainly between the married woman and her husband, if much of the congregation is distressed by what is going on, then for several reasons they should dress in a way that will "build up" and "benefit" others rather than drawing attention to themselves.

Paul adduces five arguments for the covering of a (married) woman's head in worship. He appeals, first, to the order seen in the relationship of God to Christ, to man, and to woman. Then, he appeals to socially acceptable norms regarding the headdress of men and women. Thirdly, he argues from the order in which man and woman were created in the account of Genesis. He then, and somewhat obscurely, makes an appeal: "because of the angels." Finally, he appeals to the common practice among other churches. This is followed in 11:17–32 by another matter relating to the corporate worship of the church. At issue is another flagrant violation of the principles of conduct he has enunciated. There is division at the heart of community activity, in the Lord's Supper itself. Again, some are acting in an elitist way, while others are being excluded.

VII. Status, Knowledge, Freedom, and Food Offered to Idols (8:1–11:1)

➡ **VIII. Status, Public Worship, Freedom, and Grace-Gifts (11:2–14:40)**

    A. The Conduct of Husbands and Wives in Public Worship (11:2–16)

    B. The Conduct of the Church at the Lord's Supper (11:17–34)

    C. Spiritual People and the Function of Their Grace-Gifts in the Church (12:1–31)

    D. The Status of Spiritual People Is Authenticated by Love (13:1–13)

    E. The Proper Function of Grace-Gifts in Public Worship (14:1–25)

    F. In Public Worship All Activity Must Build Up the Church (14:26–40)

Main Idea

Paul addresses head coverings in public worship and offers theological arguments to support the view that when they pray or prophesy in the church's gathering for worship, married women should wear headdress that reflects their respect for their husband's role as their "head," lest they bring shame upon him. Despite this, Paul insists on the interdependence of husband and wife. The practices he enjoins are to be found in the other "churches of God."

Translation

1 Corinthians 11:2–16

2a		Now
b	Assertion	**I praise you**
c	Basis	because you remember me in everything and
d	Basis	hold firmly the traditions
e	Expansion	just as I delivered them to you.
3a		Now
b	Assertion	**I want you to understand**
c	Content	that the head of every man is Christ, and
d	Content	the head of a wife is her husband, and
e	Content	the head of Christ is God.
4a	Assertion (Subject)	**Every man ...**
b	Description	who prays or prophesies
c	Manner	having [something] down from his head
d	Assertion	**... shames his head,**
	Contrast	but
5a	Assertion (Subject)	**every wife ...**
b	Description	who prays or prophesies
c	Manner	with uncovered head
d	Assertion	**... shames her head**
	Basis	since it is the same as if she were shaven.
6a		For
b	Condition (protasis)	if a wife will not cover herself, then
c	Exhortation (apodosis)	**let her shave herself.**
d	Contrast (protasis)	But if it is shameful for a woman to [have her hair] cut off or to be shaved,
e	Exhortation (apodosis)	**let her cover herself.**
		For
7a	Assertion	**a man ought not to cover his head**
b	Basis	since he is the image and glory of God.
c	Contrast	But **woman is the glory of man.**
8a	Basis (source, negative)	For **man is not from the woman** but
b	Source (positive)	**the woman from man.**
9a	Advantage (negative)	**Neither was man created for woman but**
b	Advantage (positive)	**woman for man.**

10a	Result of 7c	Because of this
b	Assertion	**the woman must have [a symbol of] authority on her head,**
c	Reason	because of the angels.
	Contrast	Nevertheless,
11a	Assertion	**woman is nothing** **apart from man,** **(A, woman)**
b	Contrast	**nor is a man anything** **apart from woman** **(B, man)**
c	Sphere	**in the Lord;**
12a	Basis (source)	**for as woman came** **from man** **(A)**
b	Series (source)	**so also man is born** **of woman,** **(B)**
c	Series (source)	**and all things are** **from God.**
13a	Exhortation	**Judge for yourselves:**
b	Rhetorical question	**Is it seemly for a wife to pray to God without a covering?**
14a	Rhetorical question	**Does not nature itself teach you**
b	Expansion	that if a man has long hair it is a dishonor to him, but
15a	Contrast	if a woman has long hair it is her glory?
b	Basis for 15a	For her hair is given to ↻
		her for a covering.
16a	Condition	If anyone thinks he will be contentious,
b	Assertion	**we have no such custom, nor do**
c	Assertion	**the churches of God.**

Structure

Paul begins by noting the church's adherence to the traditions he had left with them (v. 2). These no doubt included those relating to liturgical practice. A theological statement regarding "headship" relationships introduces the discussion of a woman's head covering in worship (v. 3). In vv. 4–5 the question of "shame" reveals the nature of Paul's concern. The reference to the "man" serves throughout as a rhetorical foil for this main issue. This becomes clear in v. 10 with the "for this reason" (διὰ τοῦτο) and with the rhetorical question concerning the woman in v. 13. Various theological arguments are then adduced in vv. 6–16, demonstrating the need to avoid shame and for women therefore to wear appropriate head covering in corporate worship.

Exegetical Outline

VIII. Status, Public Worship, Freedom, and Grace-Gifts (11:2–14:40)

➤ **A. The Conduct of Husbands and Wives in Public Worship (11:2–16)**

1. The Relationship of Husband and Wife in Public Worship (11:2–3)

2. Inappropriate Head Coverings Bring Shame to the "Head" (11:4–16)

a. A Husband's Shame to His "Head": Praying and Prophesying Covered (11:4)

b. A Wife's Shame to her "Head": Praying and Prophesying Uncovered (11:5–6)

c. Theological Reasons for the Differentiation of Head Coverings (11:7–16)

Explanation of the Text

11:2 Now I praise you because you remember me in everything and hold firmly the traditions just as I delivered them to you (Ἐπαινῶ δὲ ὑμᾶς ὅτι πάντα μου μέμνησθε καὶ καθὼς παρέδωκα ὑμῖν τὰς παραδόσεις κατέχετε). The link with what has gone before is carried both in the opening "now" (δέ) and in the content of this verse. Paul finished the last section by calling upon them to imitate him as he imitated Christ. This would mean listening to him and following him. Paul now "praises" (ἐπαινέω) them for remembering him and calling to mind what he has taught. As Mitchell has shown, this complimenting of the Corinthians is part of Paul's careful rhetoric as he prepares his audience to be receptive both to his advice and his critique of some of their behavior.[1] There is no need to regard Paul's expressed sentiment as ironic, nor is there any reason to see this kind approach to them as "surprising."[2] Paul still addresses his beloved brothers and sisters (4:14, 17; 10:14; 15:58) and seeks their spiritual benefit in all things. His relationship with the Corinthians is once again shown to be generally strong and constructive, despite some hard-hitting challenges to them and instruction for them.

The apostle speaks generally of "traditions" (τὰς παραδόσεις) at this point, not just about those traditions relating to men and women in their roles in worship. These traditions would have included the teaching of the gospel facts about Jesus as well as foundational Christian doctrine drawn from those facts (cf. 15:3). They would also have included instruction in the Christian way of life (cf. 2 Thess 3:6) and of corporate worship. This latter is how Paul uses the expression of himself in 11:23 as he speaks of handing down the way of celebrating the Lord's Supper. In 2 Thessalonians 2:15 he speaks of having delivered these traditions both verbally and in letter form. By referring to these traditions, Paul seems to be offering theological support for ideas that are common to the church at large (11:16) and that he had originally taught them. It is most unlikely that he is writing here to change practices from those that had been taught earlier, though it is certainly possible that the Corinthians had begun to question some aspects of what they had received.

At this point many commentaries seek to imagine the situation or questions that gave rise to this section of the epistle.[3] Does Paul address the matter

---

1. Mitchell, *Rhetoric of Reconciliation*, 260.
2. *Contra* Fee, *1 Corinthians*, 551.
3. Two recent commentaries both offer lengthy hypothet-

ical reconstructions of what the Corinthians may have been asking of Paul: Hays, *First Corinthians*, 182–83 and Ciampa and Rosner, *First Corinthians*, 501–2.

of women in worship because he has heard about problems, because the Corinthians have written to him asking for advice, or because there is confusion in Paul's teaching on these matters? In places like this where all we have is Paul's writing and no quotation from the Corinthians or direct interaction with things they may have said, all interpreters have to remain judiciously agnostic. The problem of "mirror reading," as it has been called, is always present. There is no reason why a careful reconstruction of what may have been happening in the congregation is not possible, but it will always be tentative. Some suggestions as to the precipitating events or questions that give rise to this section will be examined as we work through the text.

11:3 Now I want you to understand that the head of every man is Christ, and the head of a wife is her husband, and the head of Christ is God (Θέλω δὲ ὑμᾶς εἰδέναι ὅτι παντὸς ἀνδρὸς ἡ κεφαλὴ ὁ Χριστός ἐστιν, κεφαλὴ δὲ γυναικὸς ὁ ἀνήρ, κεφαλὴ δὲ τοῦ Χριστοῦ ὁ θεός). Paul begins to address the question of the place of married women in worship and in doing so first draws attention to a series of relationships involving Christ and God. "Now" (δέ) is simply continuative, though sometimes translated as mildly adversative ("but"). The recurring theme of "knowledge" and "understanding" is evident again, but now Paul writes neutrally. There is not the force here of the former "I do not want you to be ignorant" (10:1; 12:1) or the irony of "do you not know . . . ?" (3:16; 5:6; 6:2, etc.). Since Paul is about to expound on gender relationships in certain areas of corporate worship, it may be that the traditions that have been handed down are being questioned by the Corinthians, especially in relation to whether women can pray and prophesy (v. 5). It is remotely possible that some Corinthians have seen a conflict between these traditions

about women and their roles in worship and the teaching that is summarized in Galatians 3:28 with its emphasis on "no male and female, for you are all one in Christ Jesus" (ESV). Yet there is no direct evidence for this, and Paul's concern lies mostly elsewhere in this section.

What Paul writes in the next few verses has generated enormous discussion. In part, the debate is engendered simply by the complexity of an argument that is, to say the least, abbreviated for those of us who cannot be sure what exactly Paul wished to affirm or what behavior, if any, he wished to correct. Mostly, however, the volumes of writing about these verses have arisen because of the often heated debate in the modern church about the role of women in worship. At the outset, it is clear that Paul's assumption in v. 5 is that women *do* take part in some parts of worship, at least in prayer and prophesying. Thus, it is important to keep in mind that he speaks about what this may look like in the congregation rather than *whether* it should happen. As Paul speaks of whether women should pray and prophesy with or without head coverings,[4] he also says something about the relationship of men and women, or of husbands and wives, during worship. Throughout this difficult section and regardless of the view one takes concerning Paul's approach to the role of women in worship, it is highly unlikely that the section can properly be used to justify as much gender-related theology as some have wanted to argue for!

Verse 3 immediately raises two difficult questions of interpretation. First, what does the word usually translated "head" (κεφαλή) mean in this context? Secondly, should the word "man" (ἀνήρ) be translated as "husband" and "woman" (γυνή) as "wife"? Both words are ambiguous. We take this last matter first.

---

4. See below the discussion concerning the nature of head coverings.

IN DEPTH: Man and Woman or Husband and Wife?

There can be little doubt that in v. 3a "man" refers to all men or at least to all Christian men. The same is likely true in v. 4. Yet in v. 3b Paul could be referring to men and women generally (NIV, AV) or to husbands and wives—"the husband is the head of his wife" (NRSV, TEV). Usually the context helps the reader to make a decision. For example, in Ephesians 5:23 the context requires "husband" and "wife." Yet in 11:3b there is little help, leading Hays to write, "In the absence of any indicators to the contrary . . . it is preferable to understand Paul's directives here as applying to everyone in the community, married or unmarried: women should have covered heads in worship; men should not."[5] However, others suggest that there is some indication in the text that husbands and wives are in view. When these two words (ἀνήρ and γυνή) come together in Greek, they often refer to husband and wife (e.g., 1 Cor 7:2–16; Eph 5:23; Titus 1:6). If the issue addressed refers to women wearing veils (a matter we examine later), then Winter (see below) adds the argument that it was from among *married* Roman women that the issue of wearing and not wearing veils had entered the church and caused controversy. Furthermore, since there is an appeal in vv. 7–9 to the creation story of Genesis, it is noted that reference is to the first *married* couple. In light of this, the view adopted here is that Paul probably had married women and their husbands in mind. This does not negate the fact that Paul also makes general comments in this passage about all men and women. Finally, while we should not assume 14:35 speaks to the same issue raised here in 11:2–16, there is probably some clear relationship between these passages, and in chapter 14 it is evident that the matter addressed there has to do with the behavior of certain husbands and wives in corporate worship.

IN DEPTH: The Meaning of "Head" (Κεφαλή)

The meaning of the word "head" has traditionally been understood to involve a certain degree of authority or hierarchy when it is used metaphorically in v. 3 (it is used literally in v. 4). All lexicons support this metaphorical understanding of the word. Thus "head" is used to denote a "being of high status" or of "superior rank" (BDAG), and so it is taken to connote some form of authoritative relationship. Recently, the meaning of "source" (for κεφαλή) has attracted great

---

5. Hays, *First Corinthians*, 185. Conzelmann, *1 Corinthians*, 184, suggests that it is "not questions of marriage . . . but questions of community" that are being discussed here.

attention even though it is not acknowledged as a possible meaning in the major lexicons. An apparent exception to this appears in LSJ where "head" is said to have a literal meaning with physical objects in a reference to the "source" or "head" of a river. However, this dictionary definition offers no example of this being picked up in metaphorical usage. Rather, in this usage "head" is another application of the occasional and rather rare literal meaning of "end point" or "extremity" of an object.

The main reason the suggested meaning of "source" (for κεφαλή) has come to prominence in some modern writings is that it provides a way in which to avoid any connotation of "authority over" or hierarchy such as is normally assumed in this and other New Testament uses of the word. In theory, "source" can be as neutral as saying that one thing comes from another without regard for ideas of authority or control issuing from it. In a modern world where authority structures, especially in matters of gender, are highly suspect, if such a meaning can be substantiated then part of the perceived problem of Paul's male chauvinism would disappear. The original suggestion for this meaning of "source" seems to have begun with an article by Stephen Bedale,[6] who has since been followed by many who draw rather different conclusions from his work than he did![7] While much of what is argued in his short article has come in for strong and convincing criticism, it should be noted what Bedale himself actually concluded on 11:3:

> That is to say, the male is κεφαλή [head] in the sense of ἀρχή [beginning] relatively (*sic*) to the female; and, in St Paul's view, the female in consequence is 'subordinate.'. . . But this principle of subordination which he finds in human relationships rests upon the order of creation, and includes the 'sonship' of the Christ himself . . . while the word κεφαλή . . . unquestionably carries with it the idea of 'authority', such authority in social relationships derives from a relative priority (causal rather than merely temporal) in the order of being.[8]

Whether or not one accepts the argument about the word's meaning, at no time did Bedale imply that his interpretation removed the metaphorical connotation of "authority over." Given how prominent his article has become in some circles, it is strange how rarely his actual exegesis of 11:3 is recounted.[9]

---

6. Stephen Bedale, "The Meaning of κεφαλή in the Pauline Epistles," *JTS* 5 (1954): 211–16, esp. 215.

7. For example, Bruce, *1 and 2 Corinthians*, 103, takes the word to mean "source" and cites Bedale as his evidence, as does Barrett, *First Corinthians*, 248. Barrett also cites a plural occurrence of the word meaning the source of a river in Herodotus as well as an Orphic fragment in which Zeus is said to

be "Zeus the first, Zeus the middle, and from Zeus all things are completed."

8. Bedale, "The Meaning of κεφαλή," 215.

9. Cf. Bruce, *1 and 2 Corinthians*, 103; also Ben Witherington, *Women in the Earliest Churches*, SNTSMS 59 (Cambridge: Cambridge University Press, 1989), 84–85. Interestingly, one of the early and most influential popular articles

However, the case for viewing "source" as a possible meaning for "head" has been undermined in recent years. An initial article by Wayne Grudem in 1985 examined 2,336 uses of the word "head" in Greek literature and concludes that it never means "source."[10] This article received various responses, including a direct response by Richard Cervin in a later issue of the same journal.[11] His examination of Grudem's examples and his own lead him to conclude: "What does Paul mean by his use of the word *head* in his letters? He does not mean "authority over," as the traditionalists assert, nor does he mean "source" as the egalitarians assert. I think he is merely employing a head-body metaphor and that his point is *preeminence*."[12] Further interaction and responses to Grudem's work include several in a volume edited by Alvera Mickelsen.[13] In his major commentary, Gordon Fee also takes issue with Grudem's analysis, stating that "Paul's understanding of the metaphor . . . and almost certainly the only one the Corinthians would have grasped, is 'head' as 'source,' especially 'source of life.'"[14] Grudem responds to Cervin at considerable length and to all of these in his second article where, following Cotterell and Turner, he also strongly critiques Fee's argument for "source," essentially asking whether there is *any* evidence for what Fee asserts![15] A third article by Grudem in 2001 interacts at length with Catherine Kroeger and, more briefly, with Andrew Perriman, who, following Cervin, also proposes the meaning of "most prominent, foremost, uppermost, preeminent."[16] Joseph Fitzmyer has offered further evidence to demonstrate the inadequacy of the translation "source." He has argued that v. 3 lays out a "fundamental theological principle that will govern Paul's discussion in this pericope, a principle of headship or preeminence that prevails in the Christian community."[17]

advocating "source" cites no authority other than LSJ, which, as noted above, offers just one plural reference: Berkeley and Alvera Mickelsen, "Does Male Dominance Tarnish our Translations?" *Christianity Today* (5 October 1979): 23–29. See also Letha Scanzoni, *All We're Meant to Be: Biblical Feminism for Today*, 3rd ed. (Grand Rapids: Eerdmans, 1992).

10. Wayne Grudem, "Does Κεφαλή ("Head") mean 'Source' or 'Authority Over' in Greek Literature? A Survey of 2,336 Examples," *TrinJ* 6 (1985): 38–59. Grudem's examples are representative of the use of the word by different authors across different periods and different genres of literature. The word appears some twelve-thousand times in the Greek corpus.

11. Richard S. Cervin, "Does Κεφαλή Mean 'Source' or 'Authority' in Greek Literature? A Rebuttal," *TrinJ* 10 (1989): 85–112.

12. Ibid., 112.

13. Alvera Mickelsen, ed., *Women, Authority and the Bible* (Downers Grove, IL: InterVarsity Press, 1986).

14. Fee, *1 Corinthians*, 555.

15. Peter Cotterell and Max Turner, *Linguistics and Biblical Interpretation* (Downers Grove, IL: InterVarsity Press, 1989), 141–45, 316–25; Wayne Grudem, "The Meaning of Κεφαλή ('Head'): A Response to Recent Studies," *TrinJ* 11 (1990): 3–72.

16. Wayne Grudem, "The Meaning of Κεφαλή ('Head'): An Evaluation of New Evidence, Real and Alleged," *JETS* 44 (2001): 25–65. See C. Kroeger, "Head," in *Dictionary of Paul and his Letters*, ed. Gerald F. Hawthorne and Ralph P. Martin (Downers Grove, IL: InterVarsity Press, 1993); Andrew Perriman, "The Head of a Woman: The Meaning of Κεφαλή in 1 Cor. 11:3," *JTS* 45 (1994): 602–22.

17. Fitzmyer, *1 Corinthians*, 409–10. See also the extended discussion reaching similar conclusions in Jorunn Økland, *Women in Their Place: Paul and the Corinthian Discourse of Gender and Sanctuary Space*, JSNTSup 269 (London: T&T Clark, 2004), 174–83.

Finally, we should note that Perriman's conclusion that the word (κεφαλή) neither means "chief" nor "ruler" nor "source" has more recently been defended by David Garland, who suggests Perriman "has the best of the arguments."[18] In his brief article Perriman further criticized the understanding of "head" as "source," but also argued that the word does not mean "chief" or connote "authority." Arguing strongly that the main issue in the passage in 1 Corinthians 11 has to do with "honor" and "dishonor," he asserts that "what mars the headship relationship . . . is dishonor, not disobedience: so the woman praying or prophesying with her head uncovered 'dishonors her head' (v. 5)."[19] He states that the word "head" denotes (1) the physical top or extremity of an object, (2) that which is first (extreme); (3) what is prominent or outstanding; (4) that which is determinative or representative by virtue of its prominence. Thus, he sees the main content of the word in this context to reflect a representative headship: "The behavior of the woman reflects upon the man who as her head *is representative of her*, the prominent partner in the relationship, or that woman's status and value is summed up in the man."[20] Grudem has once again pointed to a number of problems with this view. He notes specifically three points: that no lexicons have supported this meaning; that the idea of prominence does not fit the context of 11:3; that in literary examples where prominence may be in evidence it is "derived from ruling authority or power that is possessed by (for example) the king of a nation or the head of a tribe, or from Christ's position as the head of the church."[21]

In this commentary we take the view that "head" does denote authority over. This seems to be fully justified on the basis of the available evidence from other Greek literature as all the lexicons and, recently, Grudem have demonstrated. However, this does not mean that there are not other nuances attached to the word, such as that of preeminence. Having said that, one of the main problems for believing that Paul used the word "head" to denote preeminence here in 11:3 is contextual. Paul's problem right through this epistle has been with people who think of themselves as above others, who "boast" and flaunt themselves as "puffed up" through their "knowledge." These are people who believe they are "strong" and who seek to influence others and laud it over them by their insistence on their rights, while taking no cognizance of what is happening spiritually in the lives of other brothers and sisters. This remains part of the problem Paul addresses here. To refer thus to relationships in which his first

---

18. Garland, *1 Corinthians*, 516.
19. Perriman, "The Head of a Woman," 621.
20. Ibid., 621 (emphasis added).

21. Grudem, "The Meaning of Κεφαλή: An Evaluation of New Evidence, Real and Alleged," 25–65.

idea is to stress the preeminence of men in relation to women, or of God to Christ, seems precisely to go against the tenor of his argument. The issue to be dealt with is this: given that the husband is "head" of his wife (and so has some authority), how should this be reflected in worship when all come together and all are involved in worship? In fact, Christ shows us in his relationship to the Father how "authority" structures can function in a godly, love-based fulfillment of roles of leadership and authority and roles of voluntary submission. It is one of the strange parts of the debate we have outlined that in the end it is surely hard to accept an equality of status in the community (which Paul affirms throughout) with the idea of *preeminence* if that is what Paul affirms here for the husband! On the other hand, it is not hard to conceive of a person voluntarily submitting to another or having authority over another without questioning equality of community status. Many obvious examples from common life spring to mind. One to be considered in church life is the call for a congregation to obey their spiritual leaders or elders (Heb 13:17; cf. 1 Pet 5:1–4). Such submission is voluntary, and the position of leadership is a role to which some of God's people are called. Yet no one brought up in the Christian tradition would ever question whether leader and flock have the same status as members of God's community and before God. Of course they do!

It should further be noted that one of the problems with some arguments is the "slippage" of ideas. First, it is assumed by many that to allow that "authority" is involved in a relationship must mean that one person is "inferior." Garland insists that taking the word to mean preeminent "does not connote inferiority." We would add, but *neither does taking the word to mean "authority" connote inferiority.*[22] Christ in his relationship to the Father is the example![23]

---

22. Bedale's words are especially revealing: "St. Paul makes it plain, of course (verse 2, cf. Gal. 3:28), that he is here speaking only of men and women in their respective sexual differentiation and function, not of their spiritual status or capacities" ("The Meaning of κεφαλή," 215).

23. It is troubling that some modern feminist writings have argued that any suggestion of "authority" in the Christ-God relationship is "subordinationist" and so is to be equated with the early Arian heresy. For example, Gilbert Bilezikian, *Beyond Sex Roles: What the Bible Says about a Woman's Place in Church and Family*, 3rd ed. (Grand Rapids: Baker Academic, 2006), 228, commenting on the traditionalist views of "authority" involved in the concept of headship, writes, "Such 'subordinationist' theories were propounded during the fourth century and were rejected as heretical." This is deeply to misunderstand subordination*ism*, which is indeed a heresy. In fact, it confuses two things that are often confused in the modern discussion about the roles of men and women. Today, it is undoubtedly difficult for some to understand that one can voluntarily submit to someone else and thus fulfill a different role or function that brings glory and elevates the "other" *without* regarding the "other" as thereby different in essence or even status. The functional subordination of Christ to the Father and of the biblical wife to her husband says nothing about the being or essence of either. Christ is equal with God in essence as orthodox Christianity has always maintained, but he submits himself to the Father as we have noted. Christian men and women are equal in being (in his image) and in status before God (there is neither male nor female), a point Paul clearly makes even in this passage in 11:11–12, but that does not mean that women cannot submit to the "authority" of a man should they choose to marry. See further comments on Christ's subordination to the Father in comments on 15:28.

One further comment must suffice. It is doubtful whether it is even possible to conceive of a "representative" relationship between people that does not connote some understanding of "authority." Surely this is *especially* true in this context. Much of this epistle has had to do with elitists who have been flaunting their leading roles over others. It is likely, as we shall see, that this section also has to do with a certain flaunting of "rights" among some women. But the apostle Paul has addressed this, especially in chapters 8–11, in "covenant" categories. Christ is the "Lord" who alone is to be worshipped. Having just read chapters 8–10, the idea that it would be possible to contemplate Christ as "head of every man" and *not* to attach some understanding of his lordship and authority over men seems to defy logic, or to suggest that what Paul now addresses has no relationship at all to what has just been said about the Lord.

To return now to the detail of v. 3, it is notable that the threefold statement (man, Christ, wife, husband, Christ, God) does not reveal a descending or ascending hierarchy. But this is not to say there is no hierarchy present. Paul is introducing the subject of how husbands and wives and then, more broadly, men and women should worship, given their created and social relationships to each other. Thus, as we look at the Greek word order, we see Paul laying the groundwork by talking of the head of "man" first and then the head of "woman" before concluding with the head of Christ. This third statement reminds the reader "that the hierarchy in which the man and woman find themselves continues all the way up to God the Father."[24] Since Paul is concerned about whether men "shame" their head or women in turn shame their head, the reference to God as the head of Christ is profoundly significant in a manner often missed by commentators. Paul wrote in 11:1, "Be imitators of me, as I am of Christ." This concluded a lengthy section on giving up one's rights, seeking the benefit of others, building up the community, and not flaunting oneself. Throughout, Paul had shown in his life that this is

what he had sought to do, and in doing so he was imitating "Christ crucified." With all the emphasis on status and rights established by gifts from God, Christ himself has provided Paul with the example. If people should ask about their rights or insist upon flaunting their status and being "puffed up" in relation to others, Christ provides the ultimate example to them. He who is the covenant Lord has revealed more clearly than anyone in history how headship and voluntary submission work without any diminishment of status. Christ will finally reveal his submission to the ultimate headship of the Father "when he delivers up the kingdom to [him who is] God and Father" (15:24, 28). The one of whom Paul can say in Colossians 2:10 that he is "the head over every power and authority," an authority given by the Father, submits himself and his church to the Father. As to Paul himself, when he says, "Be imitators of me, as I am of Christ," he has placed himself squarely into the clause, "the head of every man is Christ."

With arguments from creation and nature, Paul now discusses how husbands and wives should pray and prophesy within the gathered worshipping

---

24. Ciampa and Rosner, *First Corinthians*, 507.

community in such a way that public respect is paid to the nature of their relationship in which the husband is the head of his wife. Again, it is important to note that as Paul discusses head coverings, he is discussing *how* women will participate and not *if* they can participate. In this sense Paul is far removed from those in Judaism who would have forbidden a woman to take part verbally in corporate worship.

11:4–5 Every man who prays or prophesies having [something] down from his head shames his head, but every wife who prays or prophesies with uncovered head shames her head since it is the same as if she were shaven (πᾶς ἀνὴρ προσευχόμενος ἢ προφητεύων κατὰ κεφαλῆς ἔχων καταισχύνει τὴν κεφαλὴν αὐτοῦ· πᾶσα δὲ γυνὴ προσευχομένη ἢ προφητεύουσα ἀκατακαλύπτῳ τῇ κεφαλῇ καταισχύνει τὴν κεφαλὴν αὐτῆς· ἓν γάρ ἐστιν καὶ τὸ αὐτὸ τῇ ἐξυρημένῃ). In vv. 4–5 Paul argues that a man should not be covered [with long hair?] as he prays and prophesies, and a woman should be covered. To diverge from this "shames" his or her "head." Paul is not saying that somehow shame is brought to his or her literal head, that is, the head that is or is not covered. The scene has been set by v. 3. For the man to be "covered" brings shame to his head, that is, Christ. For the woman to be "uncovered," shame is brought to her head, her husband.

First, following the structure of v. 3, Paul addresses men, then women. The issue of head coverings is dealt with in the context of "shame" (καταισχύνω) or bringing dishonor upon the "head." Though men are also addressed in vv. 7a and 14, they are not Paul's main concern here.

However, Paul's reference to men does offer such a contrast with women that it becomes evident as the passage progresses that it is the distinction of the gender-related roles of husband and wife that is key.[25]

Both men and women were involved in praying and in prophesying in worship. This probably means that there were times of *extempore* worship in which individuals, moved by God's Spirit, could lead the congregation through prayer or prophecy. It is hard to define with any great precision what "prophecy" was in that early church's worship. More is said on this in the discussion of the subject in 12:10 and 14:1–3. A summary, based on what little may be determined from those passages, is that it was one of the ways that the Spirit "built up" the congregation spiritually. It especially involved the three elements of "encouragement," "consolation," and some degree of "teaching."[26] A prophecy always pointed to Christ (the purpose of grace-gifts) and would thus have been gospel focused and probably expository in nature, as Scripture was applied directly to a current matter in the church's or an individual's life. (Regarding what Paul is saying here about head coverings, see below, "In Depth: Hair or Veils?")

Though any decision as to whether Paul is referring here to the way hair itself is worn or to a woman wearing a veil must remain tentative; it seems more likely that the issue concerned the way the hair was worn or dressed. The references to having one's head "shaved" (ξυράω) in v. 6 and to "having long hair" (κομάω) in vv. 14–15 support this view, as does Paul's appeal to "nature."

What is not so tentative, though, is that the mat-

---

25. Økland, *Women in Their Place*, 178, writes: "A ritual setting is the proper place to make the places for men and for women and the boundary between them clear and distinct, as opposed to the fluent and confusing practices of everyday life."

26. For a detailed, contemporary discussion of the nature of "prophecy," see Wayne Grudem, *The Gift of Prophecy in the New Testament Today*, rev. ed. (Wheaton, IL: Crossway, 2000). For interaction with Grudem and others, see comments below on 12:10 and 14:1–3.

ter Paul addresses has to do with what is "seemly" (v. 13, πρέπω), and what reflects most aptly the role relationship between husband and wife when, as they worship publicly, they both pray and prophesy, and both have standing *in their own right* in the covenant community.

Whether or not this has to do with veils or with hairstyles, the point is that there can be no flaunting of social mores in such a way that attention is drawn to oneself. There is some evidence that the hair of adulterous women was sometimes shaved, as happens to this day in some cultures.[27] If this is what Paul is referring to, then it is likely that the "shame" involved for the husband is that the wife would be communicating her freedom, not just as a Christian worshipper but her "freedom" from her husband. A married woman would not be expected to wear her hair long or loose in public. This she might do for her husband at home, but in public (with Hurley and Murphy-O'Connor) the hair would be worn "up" or carefully dressed in a way that reflected her marriage status and her husband's status as "head."[28] (If the issue is a head scarf or shawl, then the same would be true. Not to wear one would be to publicly disregard her status as a married woman and so bring dishonor or "shame" to her "head," her husband.)

The next question to be raised is why wives or women would want to behave like this in the first place. At best this is speculation since the text does not tell us. It may be that some of the elite women simply brought pagan practices into the church without further thought. It may be that certain pagan cult practices, in which women did not wear headgear at worship, were being adopted by some.

But the passage indicates that this choice of how to wear hair was deliberate and "contentious" (v. 16), perhaps in a similar way to how some deliberately ate meat in an idol temple. Most commentators see the women's action as reflecting the belief that "in Christ" all, including women, are free people and that sexual relationships in worship before the Lord simply do not matter at all. Hurley's summary is useful: "It would seem quite likely that the Corinthian women had concluded that, having been raised with Christ (1 Cor 4:8–10), their new position in Christ and their resultant freedom to participate in the worship by prayer and prophecy was incompatible with wearing a sign of submission to their husbands! Paul defends their right to pray and prophesy, but does not see it as doing away with the marital relation. . . . Only at the resurrection will marital patterns be done away with completely (Matt 22:30). The Corinthians had not grasped the both/and of the present stage of the kingdom."[29]

As Paul writes it seems that, whatever the reason for the lack of head coverings on the part of some women, Paul is urging them to curtail what may appear to be a "freedom" or a "right" in a similar way to that which he has described in chapter 9. Though this action of wearing or not wearing a head covering clearly has to do with gender differences between men and women and probably mainly between the married woman and her husband, if much of the congregation is distressed by what is going on, then on several grounds they should dress in a way that will "build up" and "benefit" others rather than drawing attention to themselves.

---

27. Dio Chrysostom, *Orations* 64.3; other citations in Winter, *After Paul Left Corinth*, 128.

28. See discussion below in "In Depth: Hair or Veils?"

29. James B. Hurley, *Man and Woman in Biblical Perspective*

(Grand Rapids: Zondervan, 1981), 170. Cf. Barrett, *First Corinthians*, 247; J. P. Meier, "On the Veiling of Hermeneutics (1 Cor 11:2–16)," *CBQ* 40 (1978): 216–17; Hays, *First Corinthians*, 182–84.

IN DEPTH: Hair or Veils?

The exact nature of the head coverings to which Paul refers here has proved to be yet another much-debated matter. The problem starts with the Greek, which literally reads: "having down from the head" (v. 4; κατὰ κεφαλῆς ἔχων). The preposition (κατά) with the genitive usually means "down" or "down upon" or "against."[30] Thus an unintelligible translation might read: "Who prays and prophecies having down from the head." This could mean that he has long hair "down from his head" (cf. v. 14) or that he has a covering or veil of some sort "down from his head." Another problem right through the passage is that a "veil" is never actually mentioned, though the noun for "veil" or "head covering" (κάλυμμα) is used in 2 Corinthians 3:13–16 where the verb for "uncovered" (ἀνακαλύπτω) is also found and could mean uncovered with a veil, or a cloth, or headdress, or simply without a (seemly) covering of hair. In 1 Corinthians 11:15 a specific covering is mentioned (περιβόλαιον), but it may not refer to what we think of as a "veil"! The word more usually infers a "cloak" covering and so perhaps a cloth veil, but that verse is also difficult because many argue that it precisely says that a woman's *hair* is given her "in the place of" or "for" (ἀντί) the head covering.

The obscurity of meaning in this passage has been resolved traditionally by saying that the issue primarily related to women and that a covering placed on the head was the issue. Women therefore needed a "veil" or a cloth covering of some sort if they were to maintain decorum and show honor to their head (cf. NRSV, NEB).[31] This has recently been given considerably more weight through various discussions of the headdress among Roman and Greek men and women in public and at places of worship. Two approaches should be especially noted. The first, proposed by Winter, suggests that Paul is concerned about appropriate head coverings in public settings.[32] He argues that "all respectable married women would wear their veil outside the home, as Roman law and custom prescribed."[33] But Winter's main point is that by deliberately removing the veil in worship certain women were flouting convention and so making a "contentious" statement to the congregation (v. 16). He suggests they sought to reflect something of the so-called "new" Roman women, who embraced more liberal social mores than normal in Roman society and seem to have emerged "in the

---

30. Dana and Mantey, *Manual Grammar*, 107; BDF §225.

31. It is notable that it is highly unlikely that if a "veil" is in mind it was the sort that came down across the face like a modern bridal veil. The idea that public prayer or prophecy would take place *through* cloth and be delivered from an unseen face is far-fetched. If the word "veil" is used, we might be better to think of the garment as a sort of head scarf or shawl.

32. Winter, *After Paul Left Corinth*, 121–41. Much more material is added in his more technical work, *Roman Wives, Roman Widows: The Appearance of New Women and the Pauline Communities* (Grand Rapids: Eerdmans, 2003).

33. Winter, *Roman Wives*, 90.

late Roman Republic and early Empire."[34] Such women were fond of their new status and freedoms in society. They were especially found among the wealthier echelons of Roman society. These women sat light to family responsibilities and even to accepted norms "of marriage, fidelity and chastity."[35] In church life, women influenced by this secular world would seem immodest, and their behavior would have been seen as undermining both Roman social norms regarding marriage and a woman's relationship to her husband, but also biblical norms of modesty and of a wife's role relationship vis-à-vis her husband. This would make sense of Paul's statement that "it is the same thing as a woman who has been shorn" since women were shaven, Winter demonstrates, for adultery.[36] In other words, Paul says that the women who did not cover their heads were exhibiting a disregard for biblical and Roman sexual ethics and decorum such that they almost appeared as adulterers or prostitutes!

A second view argues that Paul's greater concern is in fact with the way head coverings were used in *Roman* worship. Roman men covered their heads in worship. Oster argues that the toga was pulled up over the head and "hung down," thus accounting for the language Paul uses here. Partially adopting this view, Garland concludes: "The shame to the 'head,' Christ, is caused by the associations of the headdress with pagan sacrifice."[37]

Others suggest that the head covering in view is that of the hair itself (building on vv. 14–15) and that to some degree the hair of *both* men and women is in view as Paul writes—a man should wear his hair short and a woman should have long hair. Hurley argues that the issue lies with the way hair itself is worn rather than any veiling. He also argues there is no evidence that veiling "was required by Jews at the time of Christ except perhaps among the wealthy of the large cities." He continues that among Greek, Roman, and Jewish *women* long hair mattered and that it was then "put up in different styles." Generally, in all cultures disheveled hair was regarded as a sign that the wearer was set off from the community.[38]

Murphy-O'Connor has also argued that hairstyles were the issue and that both men and women are being addressed here by Paul. He refutes the common view, adopted here, that the discussion of men should be seen as some sort of foil to Paul's main message about women and their head coverings. He points to various texts suggesting that in the Greco-Roman society of that day

34. Ibid., 5.

35. Ibid.

36. *After Paul Left Corinth*, 128–29.

37. Richard Oster, "When Men Wore Veils to Worship: The Historical Context of 1 Corinthians 11:4," *NTS* 34 (1988): 481–505. Garland, *1 Corinthians*, 518.

38. James B. Hurley, *Man and Woman in Biblical Perspective: A Study in Role Relationships and Authority* (Leicester: Inter-Varsity Press, 1981), 168–71. See the extended discussion in his Appendix, 254–71.

long hair on men was linked to homosexuality. Given Paul's already-mentioned views on that subject (cf. Rom 1:26–27; 1 Cor 6:9), this provides the reason for addressing men about their hair length. For the woman, long hair was expected as her "covering," but this should be feminine and "well-dressed in a conventional manner." A woman who did not conform to these conventions was seeking to become like a man, and so the differentiation of sexes expected of Christians in worship was not being respected.[39]

There is certainly no consensus view emerging at present with three relatively recent commentaries by Thiselton, Garland, and Fitzmyer all taking different positions! It is clear that Winter's and Oster's works highlight how significant people's attitudes were to hairstyles and headdress in the Roman and Greek cultures. Hurley did similar work, mainly regarding the Jewish background and the issue of the way hair itself was worn. In view of the repeated mention of the (literal) head and the explicit reference to a woman's head being completely "shaved" in v. 6, the specific reference to "long hair" in vv. 14–15, and other arguments noted both by Hurley and Murphy-O'Connor, we believe that the issue probably concerned the way hair was worn. Such a conclusion is decidedly tentative, however!

11:6 For if a wife will not cover herself, then let her shave herself. But if it is shameful for a woman to [have her hair] cut off or to be shaved, let her cover herself (εἰ γὰρ οὐ κατακαλύπτεται γυνή, καὶ κειράσθω· εἰ δὲ αἰσχρὸν γυναικὶ τὸ κείρασθαι ἢ ξυρᾶσθαι, κατακαλυπτέσθω). Paul is polemical as he argues that if a woman wishes to be regarded by those around as a "shaven" woman might be regarded, then that is how she should be: shaven! Paul insists that a married woman worshipping without her hair appropriately reflecting her marital status is shameful, and therefore she must (imperative) "cover herself" (κατακαλυπτέσθω) or wear her hair in an appropriate way that causes no concern to those in the assembly.

"Not cover herself" in the first clause of the verse seeks to convey the permissive middle form of the verb "to cover" (κατακαλύπτω), and "let her shave herself" is an aorist, middle imperative (κείρω). The context informs the reader that Paul has in mind the covering of the head. (Hence the ESV: "If a wife will not cover her head.") The use of two verbs translated "cut off" and "shaved" is stylistic, both referring to the same action of leaving the head clear of all hair. The noun "shameful" (αἰσχρός) does not come from the same root as the earlier verb "to shame" (καταισχύνω), but it connotes more directly that which is morally unacceptable (cf. Eph 5:12; Titus 1:11). The first-class condition assumes the truthfulness of what is being said. A woman not covering her head is indeed shameful.

---

39. Jerome Murphy-O'Connor, "Sex and Logic in 1Cor 11:2–16," *CBQ* 42 (1980): 482–500; see also idem, "1 Cor 11:2–16 Once Again," *CBQ* 50 (1988): 265–74.

Thus v. 6 adds power without adding to the content of what Paul has just written. Its persuasive force with its abbreviated form, its *argumentum ad absurdum* in the first clause, and its final imperative leaves the reader in no doubt as to the serious nature of what Paul is saying. The next three sections will further expand on this as Paul appeals to creation for what he is saying (vv. 7–12), then to nature (vv. 13–15), and finally to the common teaching of all the churches on the matter (v. 16).

11:7–9 For a man ought not to cover his head since he is the image and glory of God. But woman is the glory of man. For man is not from the woman but the woman from man. Neither was man created for woman but woman for man (ἀνὴρ μὲν γὰρ οὐκ ὀφείλει κατακαλύπτεσθαι τὴν κεφαλὴν, εἰκὼν καὶ δόξα θεοῦ ὑπάρχων· ἡ γυνὴ δὲ δόξα ἀνδρός ἐστιν. οὐ γάρ ἐστιν ἀνὴρ ἐκ γυναικός, ἀλλὰ γυνὴ ἐξ ἀνδρός· καὶ γὰρ οὐκ ἐκτίσθη ἀνὴρ διὰ τὴν γυναῖκα, ἀλλὰ γυνὴ διὰ τὸν ἄνδρα). Paul now expands on his reasons why a wife should cover her head when praying and prophesying and a man should not. He appeals to man as reflective of God's glory and to the creation order. That this is an expansion is seen in the Greek construction (μὲν γὰρ . . . δὲ). In the appeal to creation, the thought centers not on the word "image" (εἰκών) but on "glory" (δόξα). As Barrett notes, "Paul values the term image only as leading to the term glory."[40] It is notable that Paul does not say in v. 7c that woman is the "image" of man. Surely he was well aware that both men and women are created in the image of God (Gen 1:26–27). The perspective Paul brings to the question of covering the head and what does or does not bring honor is drawn both from Genesis 1:27 and 2:18–23. God created both man and woman in his image. Yet Paul's point is

more subtle. The man, who was created first and was in God's image, was brought into being by God to bring glory to him through serving, living, and acting for him in the world where he was placed. Woman, who was created second and was also in God's image, was brought into being by God to be a "helper fit for him [the man]" (Gen 2:18 ESV). God created her "from man" (ἐξ ἀνδρός) and for the purpose of serving the man. She was to bring "glory" to him through being with, enabling, and serving him. Thus the creation of woman was designed to bring glory to the man because, first she came from him (thinking of her being taken from his rib) and secondly because she was created *for* him (v. 9b; διά with the accusative gives *cause*).

The word "glory" (δόξα) is virtually a synonym here for "honor" in much the way it is used in Psalm 8:5: "Yet you have made him a little lower than the heavenly beings and crowned him with glory and honor" (8:6 LXX; δόξῃ καὶ τιμῇ ἐστεφάνωσας αὐτόν). That "glory" means more or less the same as "honor" is also to be seen in comparing vv. 14 and 15. In v. 14 it is a "dishonor" for a man to wear long hair (ἀτιμία; τίμιος means "held in honor" [BDAG]), while in v. 15 the woman's hair "is her glory" (δόξα αὐτῇ ἐστιν). As in Psalm 8 and in 1 Corinthians 11:14–15, Paul seems to use the words with similar meanings. At its core the word "glory" means that which intrinsically belongs to that person. Thus, to bring glory to someone is to honor them in the sense of revealing or pointing to who the person is in all their goodness. When Paul says, "Woman [was created] for man," he is indicating again that the wife's God-given role was to honor the one for whom she was created, while the man, created first, was created to bring honor/glory to God and not to the woman who was not

---

40. Barrett, *First Corinthians*, 252. Also, Morna D. Hooker, "Authority on Her Head: An Examination of 1 Cor. 11:10," *NTS* 10 (1964): 410–16. It is quite incorrect to suggest that Paul does not think of the woman as in the image of God.

yet created.[41] Whatever the reason for the head covering in terms of social mores at the time, Paul's point is that this created difference between husbands and wives has not changed simply because people have become Christians. The created order should still be respected. In this way, as worship takes place, it is ultimately only Christ to whom glory is given.

11:10 Because of this the woman must have [a symbol of] authority on her head, because of the angels (διὰ τοῦτο ὀφείλει ἡ γυνὴ ἐξουσίαν ἔχειν ἐπὶ τῆς κεφαλῆς διὰ τοὺς ἀγγέλους). This strange verse with its reference to angels actually helps us understand what is going on as the woman puts up her hair or wears a head scarf or shawl. A few structural comments on the place of this verse in the argument help set the scene for its interpretation. First, "because" (διὰ τοῦτο) looks back to the immediately preceding argument in which Paul has shown why a man "ought not" (οὐκ ὀφείλει) to be "covered" (v. 7). Verses 8–9 offered two arguments for this from the creation narrative: (1) "woman came from man," and (2) man was not created "for woman" but the other way around. It is thus "because" of this creation structure that a woman is now told what she ought to do. In other words, the strong command[42] implied by "ought to" or "must" for *both* men (v. 7) and women (v. 10) is defended from the argument of vv. 8–9. Secondly, the "nevertheless" (πλήν) of v. 11 indicates a strong contrast with what has just been said in v. 10, which is also significant for how we understand v. 10.

So what does Paul mean in v. 10 when he refers to a "woman hav[ing] [a symbol of] author-ity on her head" (ἐξουσίαν ἔχειν ἐπὶ τῆς κεφαλῆς)? Different translations add words, attempting to make this more comprehensible: "A symbol of . . ." (NASB 1995, ESV, NRSV, NKJV, NIV 2011); "a sign of" (NIV 1984); "a veil" (RSV); "have power on her head" (AV). Given the structure and the framework of the whole argument from v. 3, Paul is surely referring to the woman, or more probably still the wife, having her hair dressed (or covered) in a seemly and appropriate manner. But to what does the "[symbol of] authority" refer? Does it, as with most translations, refer to what the TEV describes periphrastically as "a covering over her head to show that she is under her husband's authority"? Undoubtedly, this has been the traditional way of regarding the passage. On this interpretation, the properly dressed hair of a woman is a requirement because this is the way she shows due honor to her husband while speaking in a public gathering. The covering is thus a symbol of the fact that she is a married woman under her husband's "authority."

Or does it, as Watson suggests, indicate instead that there was an issue with women distracting men from worship by the erotic attraction of a woman's hair and that, therefore, the woman should cover herself so she has control over her *own* (physical) head, ensuring that males are not "eyeing" her when she prays or prophesies? In this way Paul then allows her to exercise her full rights in the new-covenant community to be involved in worship.[43] One problem here, however, is that Paul has not addressed problems of sexual temptation thus far and his appeal to the creation order (prefall) does not lend itself to what would be a sudden

---

41. Proverbs 11:16a (LXX) says, "A gracious wife brings glory to her husband" (γυνὴ εὐχάριστος ἐγείρει ἀνδρὶ δόξαν). The opposite is the unrighteous woman, who is a "seat of dishonor" (ἀτιμίας).

42. Winter, *After Paul Left Corinth*, 130–31, points out that "the mild 'ought' . . . does not do justice to the powerful sig-

nificance represented by that term in Graeco-Roman society. Roman law devoted a whole section to *The Laws of Obligations*. . . . Obligations were binding and, according to Seneca, failure to meet them was 'a sin'" (emphasis added).

43. Francis Watson, "The Authority of the Voice: A Theological Reading of 1 Cor 11:2–16," *NTS* 46 (2000): 520–36.

change of emphasis. That theme seems generally inimical to the current context.

An alternative view has been suggested by Hooker. She argues that since the word "authority" (ἐξουσία) is always used in an "active" sense, it can hardly be someone else's authority that is addressed here but rather the woman's own. Rather, the head covering has to do with the authority *she* now has to pray and prophesy, *and* it serves to hide man's glory. The covering does not show the woman to be under the authority of her husband. It is argued that since the woman is the glory of *man* yet the object of worship is *God*, then the covering is needed in order to hide the "glory of man"; in this way, God's glory alone is the focus of worship.[44] In a significant article addressing the exegetical and theological issues of this section, Schreiner takes issue with Hooker on seven grounds.[45] The most important are these. This view does not adequately account for the fact that v. 10 is true "because" of what has been said in vv. 8–9. Verse 10 is parallel to v. 7. A command is being given here to women and how they must dress. The emphasis is not on their "right." If the focus were now on the "right or "authority" of women, "he would be contradicting what he has said in the preceding verses." It is "not at all strained," as some have suggested, "to see *exousia* in verse 10 as 'sign of authority' or 'symbol of authority.'" Indeed, Schreiner suggests it is straightforward to see how something worn on the head can become a sign or symbol of something. He gives the example of the dragon with its crowns in Revelation 12:3. Especially interesting is his reference to Diodorus of Sicily 1.47.5, who refers to a stone statue that has "three kingdoms on its head."

In the context, this is a reference to "three crowns, which are symbols for the governing kingdoms."[46] The example from Diodorus is then used again to demonstrate that Hooker has overstated her case that "authority" always refers to a person's *own* authority. He continues:

> The text describes a statue of the mother of King Osymandias, and reads as follows:
>
> There is also another statue of his mother standing alone, a monolith twenty cubits high, and it has three kingdoms on its head, signifying that she was both daughter and wife and mother of a king (1.47.5).
>
> Here the three crowns . . . all represent someone else's authority.[47]

In view of these arguments and the fact that the major change of direction in the argument appears not here but in the next verse with the word "nevertheless," we take it that the majority and traditional way of viewing this passage is probably correct. Paul has required the covering of the praying and prophesying woman through arguments drawn from the role relationships of the "headship" argument, but he has also argued this from *both* Genesis 1 and 2. The headship of the husband is one argument. The other relates to man as the source of woman. The covering pays due respect to these differences of gender. Though all may take part in worship, the roles of *husband* and *wife* in the marriage relationship should be respected. In Greco-Roman society, this was to be seen in the particular way a woman dressed her hair rather than letting it hang loose.

Finally, in this verse we come to the enigmatic phrase, "because of the angels" (διὰ τοὺς ἀγγέλους).

---

44. Hooker, "Authority on Her Head." She is followed by many; cf. Barrett, *First Corinthians*, 253; Cotterell and Turner, *Linguistics and Biblical Interpretation*, 326.

45. Thomas R. Schreiner, "Head Coverings, Prophecies and the Trinity: 1 Corinthians 11:2–16," in *Recovering Biblical Man-* *hood and Womanhood: A Response to Evangelical Feminism*, ed. John Piper and Wayne A. Grudem (Wheaton, IL: Crossway, 1991), 124–39.

46. Ibid., 135.

47. Ibid., 136.

A number of possible meanings have been put forward. Just three possibilities are mentioned here. Some have taken the word (ἄγγελος) to mean "messenger." For example, Winter suggests that women covering their heads is for the sake of messengers who have come from other churches and who might be horrified by women looking like the "new women" of Rome.[48] Others have believed that the reference goes back to an interpretation of Genesis 6 in which angels are said to have come down and had sexual relations with women. For example, Tertullian argued from Genesis 6 that women were vulnerable to the (bad) angels. He wrote, "'Because of the angels.' What angels? In other words, whose angels? If he means the fallen angels of the Creator, there is great propriety in his meaning. It is right that that face which was a snare to them should wear some mark of a humble guise and obscured beauty."[49] And so women should not "tempt" angels by leaving their heads uncovered.

Finally, some have seen a possible link to angels being enablers of worship and being guardians of order in worship.[50] For example, in Revelation 8:3 an angel mediates the prayers of the people. The presence of (good) angels in worship is reflected in Revelation 8:3 and Hebrews 1:6, and angels are seen to be aware of what is going on among God's people on earth (Luke 15:10). Moreover, angels are seen to be guardians of and mediators of the law (cf. Gal 3:19). So it seems likely that for Paul this provides simply another reason why women should dress their hair appropriately, not just for men and for others but because this is the way it should be done in worship where the angels themselves are involved. It may also be a reminder to women that they are truly part of that God-ordered society who worship him and who will one day be involved in judging the angels. This last view seems to us to make most sense of this tricky verse.

11:11–12 Nevertheless, woman is nothing apart from man, nor is a man anything apart from woman in the Lord; for as woman came from man so also man is born of woman, and all things are from God (πλὴν οὔτε γυνὴ χωρὶς ἀνδρὸς οὔτε ἀνὴρ χωρὶς γυναικὸς ἐν κυρίῳ· ὥσπερ γὰρ ἡ γυνὴ ἐκ τοῦ ἀνδρός, οὕτως καὶ ὁ ἀνὴρ διὰ τῆς γυναικός· τὰ δὲ πάντα ἐκ τοῦ θεοῦ). If there is a shift in this section in Paul's argument, it is here. Paul now stresses the interrelatedness of men and women. There is a deliberate contrast with what has gone before where Paul had appealed to the headship of a husband in his role relationship with the wife. His words are designed to counter the very sort of argument that we might hear today that therefore there must be something "inferior" about a woman or "superior" about a man. Paul will have nothing of this. "Nevertheless" (πλήν) offers a strong contrast with what has gone before. The argument is again carefully and structurally balanced (woman, man, woman, man), clarifying the contrast between what is said about woman and man. Men and women are interdependent as they live and work "in the Lord" (ἐν κυρίῳ). Just as woman came originally from man, now all men come through women (in the sense of being born of women). There is a mutual dependence here regarding their existence.

The argument for the headship of a husband to be reflected in the headdress of wives (while those women still fully participate in worship through prayer and prophecy) is qualified lest some should take the argument further than Paul intends. Bengel aptly summarizes Paul's intention, which is to qualify what he has just said: "Lest the man

---

48. *Roman Wives*, 91.
49. Tertullian, *Against Marcion* 5.8 (*ANF* 3:445).

50. Cf. Hays, *First Corinthians*, 188; Fitzmyer, *1 Corinthians*, 418–19, who especially references Qumran documents; Collins, *First Corinthians*, 412.

should exalt himself, or the woman think herself despised."[51] The danger might be that women are viewed as of less worth in the economy of God's kingdom or that men have some peculiar and more important status in the economy of the kingdom. Rather, says Paul, both men and women must never forget their interdependence. The one cannot do without the other and vice versa. There is probably considerable overlap in Paul's thinking here with his exposition of the "body" in chapter 12. There he insists that people functioning in the church in different ways with different gifts are in no way inferior to people with seemingly more significant gifts. For example, in 12:16 we read: "If the ear should say, 'Because I am not an eye, I do not belong to the body,' that would not make it any less a part of the body" (ESV). Once again we see that for Paul, describing role distinctions while insisting on equality of being and of standing before God are not contradictory ideas, for what matters is that all are "in the Lord."

While there has been some discussion about what Paul means by this phrase "in the Lord" (ἐν κυρίῳ), which can range from being a synonym for "Christian" through to a description of the representative work of the covenant Lord, here the meaning seems natural enough. It refers to those who are part of the Lord's new community, that is, those who "participate" in Christ (have κοινωνία with him; 1:9). Paul laid the basis for this as he addressed the Corinthian Christians in 1:3. He will build on this with the body metaphor of chapter 12.

Paul's conclusion that "all things are from God" (v. 12c; πάντα ἐκ τοῦ θεοῦ) reminds the Corinthians that in the end God is the source of all things and all glory must find its final focus in him. The statement is broad, indicating that all creation, not just those "in the Lord," have come from the cre-

ator God. Thus, as Paul points to the broadest of contexts in which all live, he also opens the way to talk about what "nature" may teach.

11:13–15 Judge for yourselves: Is it seemly for a wife to pray to God without a covering? Does not nature itself teach you that if a man has long hair it is a dishonor to him, but if a woman has long hair, it is her glory? For her hair is given to her for a covering (ἐν ὑμῖν αὐτοῖς κρίνατε· πρέπον ἐστὶν γυναῖκα ἀκατακάλυπτον τῷ θεῷ προσεύχεσθαι; οὐδὲ ἡ φύσις αὐτὴ διδάσκει ὑμᾶς ὅτι ἀνὴρ μὲν ἐὰν κομᾷ ἀτιμία αὐτῷ ἐστιν, γυνὴ δὲ ἐὰν κομᾷ δόξα αὐτῇ ἐστιν; ὅτι ἡ κόμη ἀντὶ περιβολαίου δέδοται [αὐτῇ]). Three final elements will conclude Paul's appeal to some of the Corinthians that they should respect the role differences of men and women and so women should dress their hair appropriately. First, he appeals to what is "seemly" (v. 13), then to "nature" (vv. 14–15), and finally in v. 16 to the practice of all the churches. The first two of these are normally seen as part of the same argument. In other words, we should know from "nature" (ἡ φύσις) what is "seemly" (πρέπον).

Once again, the woman is the focus in the woman-man-woman structure. An imperative introduces the opening rhetorical question (the first of three), which functions as an assertion. The assumed answer will be "no, it is not seemly." Paul's appeal here is to "nature." There is probably a degree of irony here or even sarcasm in the command to "judge" (κρίνατε). Many of these Corinthians believed they were indeed able to "judge" and "discern" things because of their wisdom or knowledge. Now these puffed-up people, who are prepared to throw over even the teaching of Scripture and to flaunt some supposed new status of some women, are challenged to make a judgment. The aorist imperative is not that common in this

---

51. Bengel, *Gnomon of the New Testament*, 281.

epistle and probably implies that they must come to a decision and not go on discussing the matter. As they judge for themselves, the answer should be utterly obvious. By implication Paul is asking why they have not seen how obvious this is and why they have ignored the "seemly" hairstyles or head coverings for wives.

The first question further helps the reader understand the issue. While Paul has shown from Scripture why there are role differences between men and women and how they are part of the created order to be reflected in public worship, the way this is shown or demonstrated in real life is culturally dependent. What is "seemly" is not something that is set in stone through the whole of this age. As Hurley, Winter, and others have shown, hairstyles and head coverings were changing. Jewish women of the day were used to different ways of wearing their hair to that seen among Greek women. Roman women saw things changing once again during the period. Indeed, Winter's evidence about the "new" Roman woman reveals this very trend. For Paul, therefore, the matter of whether something is "seemly" has to do with modesty and cultural ways of reflecting the status of being married and so bringing honor to the husband. The evidence Paul has mustered from the creation narrative reveals the facts of gender difference and the roles of men and women as they come to worship God publicly. How these roles will be reflected today will best be answered by submitting to the command again today: "Judge for yourselves . . ." (cf. 10:15).

The appeal to "nature" has generated further discussion. At one level it seems like Paul is returning to creation-narrative ideas; that is, men and women "by nature" or in accordance with the way

they were created know that men must have short hair and women long hair. However, as Blomberg correctly notes:

> Paul the Jew would have known of the Nazirites whom God blessed precisely because they did not cut their hair (of whom Samson was the most famous example; Judg. 13:5). In the Greek world, the Spartan men were known for their shoulder-length hair. But it was true, then as now, that most cultures maintained a relative difference in hair length between men and women.[52]

Blomberg therefore concludes, in line with many other commentators that

> "nature" is probably best understood here as that which is "almost instinctive because of long habit," a "long established custom."[53]

It is most unlikely that *in this context* Paul regarded "nature" as that which is intuitively understood by all human beings, nor did he see it as a description of something that belongs to the very essence of how men and women are created (e.g., as in Stoicism).

So the custom of Paul's day, and of most generations, is that a man with long hair brings dishonor on himself. Probably this has to do with conventions that long hair on a man, as in many contemporary societies, indicates effeminacy or that men are trying to look like women. Since gender roles matter, as Paul has shown from Scripture, then flouting of these established customs is shameful before the church and God as they gather to worship. It was noted above that this verse serves as further corroboration of the view that Paul has throughout been addressing the matter of what men and women do with their *hair* rather than with coverings of their hair.[54] Paul continues that a woman's

---

52. Blomberg, *1 Corinthians*, 213.

53. Ibid. Calvin, *1 Corinthians*, 235, writes: "[Paul] reckons as *nature* a custom that had come to be confirmed."

54. Bruce, *1 and 2 Corinthians*, 108, argues that the ample covering of hair given to a woman is made so that an "analogical inference" can be drawn that therefore she should have

long hair is her "glory." Barrett helpfully comments, "Obediently to be what God intended them to be is the highest glory that human beings can achieve. To wear her hair long, in a womanly fashion, is an outward sign that a woman is fulfilling her role in creation."[55] Appropriately and modestly dressed, this long hair that is *her* glory therefore truly brings glory to her head, her husband, for it reveals she is a wife, and it reveals her chosen way of humility in the congregation whereby she refuses to flaunt her "authority." Thus, Paul concludes, "Her hair is given to her for a covering." The perfect passive "is given" (δέδοται) is a reminder that it is not some impersonal force like "nature" that has given her the covering that is so important to this distinction of genders, but God himself who has given the woman her hair. What she does with what she is given will, according to Paul's arguments from Genesis, either bring glory to her husband or not. As she fulfills her duty and dresses her hair appropriately, she will be enabling the whole community, including herself as she prays and prophesies, to bring glory to God properly as they worship. The hair must be properly dressed, but it is her *hair* that is the God-given covering.

11:16 If anyone thinks he will be contentious, we have no such custom, nor do the churches of God (Εἰ δέ τις δοκεῖ φιλόνεικος εἶναι, ἡμεῖς τοιαύτην συνήθειαν οὐκ ἔχομεν, οὐδὲ αἱ ἐκκλησίαι τοῦ θεοῦ). In conclusion, Paul raises the matter of people being "contentious" (φιλόνεικος). The partial first-class condition assumes that such people may be around! The opening conditional clause is, as Fee notes,[56] one that has been seen previously at 3:18 and 8:2 and will be seen again in 14:37 (cf.

10:12). In each of those cases Paul takes up one of the Corinthian claims, either to be "wise" (3:18), or to be "knowledgeable" (8:2), or to be a "prophet or spiritual" (14:37). As in each of those cases, some were following the wrong path. So they are doing here. The challenge throughout to those who think they "think" rather well and knowledgeably is to "think again"!

This is another indicator, as we noted earlier, that it was only certain women who were praying "uncovered" and that were probably appealing to their "wisdom" or their "knowledge." There is little doubt that with the many different issues that Paul tackles in this letter, the people who differ from him do so from a *thinking* position. The arrogance of some might lead to them being "contentious" with what Paul has said. It is unlikely that the issue here is that they are contentious with each other. Paul is still involved in *his* desire to persuade them of a more biblical approach to the subject at hand. His final appeal now is to the practice of other churches (αἱ ἐκκλησίαι τοῦ θεοῦ). It is important that the Corinthians understand Paul is not asking things of them that are not generally taught and followed in the wider churches (see also at 7:17 and 14:33).

Brief Summary of Verses 12–16

Paul has offered a careful, multipronged argument for his position that the distinction of roles between husband and wife should be recognized as the married women take part in public worship. He has argued that culturally what is "seemly" in the worship setting will be seen, at least in part, in a woman's and a man's respective hairstyles. He has laid his groundwork with a statement of

---

such hair covered. This is far-fetched. Francis Watson in *Agape, Eros, Gender: Toward a Pauline Sexual Ethic* (Cambridge: Cambridge University Press, 2000), 86–87, followed by Ciampa and Rosner, *First Corinthians*, 540, move in the same direction. This makes Paul's argument unbearably complex. His appeal

is much more simply understood as an appeal to convention: the woman has long hair, the man has short hair; to one it is her glory and to the other, should it be long, it is a dishonor.

55. *First Corinthians*, 257.

56. Fee, *1 Corinthians*, 585n160.

various relationships that speak to headship. He has spoken about how, within these relationships, glory and honor must be given to the "head." He has shown that head covering is one way in which such honor is reflected between husband and wife. He has turned to the creation narrative to support this, then also to the general custom of "nature," then to the fact that a woman's hair itself has been given for this purpose before finally appealing to the general custom of the other churches. (Note that this appeal to other "churches" has been used in both 4:17 and 7:17.) Paul's argument has been strong and carefully constructed rhetorically. The section started with Paul's compliment to them on how they have held to the traditions he had delivered to them, and it finishes with an appeal to the traditions found in all "the churches of God." Yet, throughout this has been the argument of one who deeply cares for this church and longs to see them worshipping appropriately and in a God-honoring way. For this reason, it is entirely appropriate to finish with an appeal to other churches, for that is where other women can be seen praying and prophesying.

Theology in Application

There is no doubt that this section of the epistle has caused much debate in the modern era. It has been seen as a passage reflecting a patriarchal and even misogynistic view of worship and relationships within the church. Certainly any theological application to the contemporary church must keep in mind three points. First, cultural ways of expressing respect and honor between people, whether men or women, husband and wife, or young and old vary from generation to generation and from culture to culture. Secondly, it must be remembered that Paul's concern more generally in these chapters has to do with order, propriety, and peace in worship (11:13, 16, 33; 14:33, 40). Paul is not addressing *whether* women can pray or prophesy in worship settings. Rather, he is concerned with *how* they should do this. This will evoke caution as to how, later, we interpret 14:33–34. Thirdly, Paul is concerned that proper distinctions are maintained between men and women and therefore especially between husbands and wives. He has laid out various arguments to defend his position, but he is concerned that no cultural norms should be ignored in corporate worship that might undermine the headship of the husband in marriage and so bring shame upon him.

However, the carefully balanced structure of this passage, moving between the man and the woman, reminds us that it is also incumbent upon the man or husband to avoid any "shame" by ignoring cultural norms that differentiate between men and women. The role differentiation of husbands and wives finds its origin, Paul has argued, in creation itself. Together they image God, both individually but also in marriage. The relationship of the loving God to his people is often expressed biblically with the picture of marriage (Isa 54:5; Jer 3:20; Ezek 16; Hos 2:16). In that picture, as Ephesians 5:23–33 makes clear, roles may be different as the wife reflects the church and the husband reflects the Lord, but together they powerfully depict the loving relationship of Christ to the church (5:32).

Paul's concern is with how hair is worn because it seems that the breach of cultural norms on the length of hair (or how the head was covered) suggested women might be shaming their "head," their husbands. To blur the distinctions between husband and wife and the different ways they are to reveal the glory of their head is to distort and to misunderstand the freedom men and women have in Christ. Wives are to worship in prayer and prophesying as men do, but they are to do so in a way that continues to reflect, to all onlookers, their love and honor for their husband. Both husband and wife by being who they are and maintaining their gender distinctions, seen here in hairstyle, bring glory to their "head," which is what they were created to do.

It is probably true to say that there was a deliberate move among some women in Corinth to flaunt a certain status within the church that was inappropriate. The fact that the problem arose as these women possibly flaunted their Spirit-given gifts with a lack of consideration for others, and were failing to build up others in Christ, all point to this being another specific example of the "puffed-up" elitism that Paul has faced in other areas of this church's life.

In much of the modern church, men and women can participate in both praying and prophesying, but this activity must never be self-flaunting and should not obscure their different roles as husbands and wives in God's creation. Any deliberate breach of cultural ways of defining gender while worshipping the Lord is to shame the other and so to obscure the glory of God, of man, and of woman. In Western society head coverings will often not be the issue. However, there are still ways in which men and women can flaunt their disdain for convention and for gender differentiation and so draw attention to themselves rather than to the Lord and his created order. In fact, in some parts of Western culture today the disdain for gender-role differentiation has become so strong that the issue is more likely to arise in modern worship than in Paul's Corinth. In some places this may be with the exhibitionism of certain types of clothing, or with flaunting expensive jewelry, or with women appearing more like men and men more like women. Each person and each church in each different culture and age will need to determine how they are tempted to obscure in their behavior at worship the truth Paul affirms in v. 3: "I want you to understand that the head of every man is Christ, and the head of a wife is her husband, and the head of Christ is God."

CHAPTER 24

1 Corinthians 11:17–34

Literary Context

Chapter 11 had begun with Paul commending the Corinthians for maintaining the traditions he had handed down to them. The section from vv. 17–34 contrasts with this. Now Paul repeats twice that he does "not commend them" (vv. 17, 22). Paul continues addressing questions related to the church's corporate worship. Even in the Lord's Supper the church is seeing the horrendous results of an arrogant elitism that has remained uncorrected in the life of the church. On this occasion the divisions appear along socio-economic lines with the poorer members being left out of parts of the meal. As Paul examines these divisions in the church during worship, he takes them back to the instructions they had received for communion. He then returns to an earlier theme of self-judgment and examination as the only way forward if they are to avoid God's judgment for their sin at the table. In chapter 12 he will continue with matters of congregational worship. There, he will write from a more positive perspective as he shows them the right way to employ grace-gifts and how, when they function properly in the community, they build up the body rather than tearing it down.

Main Idea

The tendency of the Corinthian Christians to divide into factions is clearly seen in disgraceful behavior at the Lord's Supper. The poor were being excluded from elements of the Supper and so were humiliated. The church is to remember their common covenantal membership of the body as together they eat and drink the bread and the wine. Self-examination will avoid God's judgment.

Translation

(See pages 502–03.)

Structure

The passage divides into three parts. The first (11:17–22) begins and ends with the comment from Paul that he does not commend the Corinthians on their attitude to and behavior at the Lord's Supper. In the second section (11:23–26) he reminds his readers of the tradition he had passed on to them concerning the Lord's Supper, and in the third (11:27–34) he offers instruction on how to participate in the meal without running the risk of God's judgment. The emphasis on the importance of their corporate gathering for the Supper is carried through the section with the repetition of the verb "to come together" (συνέρχομαι) in verses 17, 18, 20, 33, and 34.

Exegetical Outline

    VIII. Status, Public Worship, Freedom, and Grace-Gifts (11:2–14:40)

       A. The Conduct of Husbands and Wives in Public Worship (11:2–16)

➡   **B. The Conduct of the Church at the Lord's Supper (11:17–34)**

          1. Divisions in the Church Are Revealed at the Lord's Supper (11:17–22)

          2. The Tradition of the Lord's Supper Received from the Lord (11:23–26)

          3. Instructions to Correct the Abuse of the Lord's Supper (11:27–34)

             a. The Guilt of Drinking in an "Unworthy Manner" (11:27)

             b. Self-Judgment Will Avert Final Judgment (11:28–32)

             c. Wait to Eat Together (11:33–34)

1 Corinthians 11:17–34

17a	Circumstance	Now	in giving these instructions

17a Circumstance — Now · in giving these instructions
  b Assertion
     (contrast with 11:2b) — **I do not praise you,**
  c Basis — for you gather together
  d Advantage — not for the better but
                for the worse.

18a Basis — For most significantly,
  b Time — when you gather together as a church,
  c Assertion — **I hear that** divisions exist among you,
  d Assertion — and in part **I believe** it.
19a Basis — For **it is necessary that there must also be factions among you,**
  b Purpose — so that those who are genuine may be shown up among you.

                For
20a Time — when you gather together,
  b Topic introduction
     (assertion) — **it is not to eat the Lord's Supper,**
21a Basis — for in eating **each one devours his own supper.**
  b Expansion — One goes hungry, and
                one is drunk.

22a Exclamation/
     rhetorical question — **What! Do you not have houses to eat and drink in?**

                Or
  b Rhetorical question — **do you despise the church of God and**
  c Series, questions — **shame those who have nothing?**
  d Series — **What shall I say to you?**
  e Series — **Shall I commend you?**
  f Assertion (negative) — **I will not commend you in this.**
23a Assertion — For **I received from the Lord**
  b Content — that which I also passed on to you,

  c Content of tradition — The Lord Jesus,...
  d Time — on the night on which he was betrayed,
  e Assertion — ... took bread and,

24a Time — when he had given thanks,
  b Assertion — he broke it and said,
  c Quotation — "This is my body which is for you;
                do this in remembrance of me."
                [Cf. Matt 26:26–28 and synoptic parallels]

25a Manner
     (ref. back to 23e–24) — In the same way
  b Assertion — [he took] also the cup
  c Time — after supper, saying,

d	Quotation		"This cup is the new covenant in my blood;
e	Quotation (cont.)		do this whenever you drink it, ↵
			in remembrance of me."
			[Cf. Matt 26:26–28 and synoptic parallels]

26a Explanation   For   whenever you eat this bread and drink this cup,
  b Assertion   **you proclaim the death of the Lord**
  c Time   until he comes.

27a Inference
       from vv. 23–26   Consequently,
  b Assertion (subject) **anyone who eats the bread or**
                                       drinks the cup of the Lord
  c Manner   in an unworthy manner
  d Assertion   **will be guilty of the body and blood ↵**
                                                                of the Lord.

28a Contrast   Rather,
  b Exhortation   **let a person examine himself** and in this way
  c Exhortation   **let him   eat of the bread and**
                                         drink of the cup.
29a Basis   For **the one who eats and**
                                drinks,
                                eats and
                                drinks   judgment on himself --------
  b Circumstance   if he does not discern the body. --------------

30a Inference   For this reason
  b Assertion   **many among you are   weak and**
  c List   **ill,**
  d List   and   **some are sleeping.**

31a Condition (protasis) But   if we were discerning about ourselves, ---------
  b Assertion (apodosis) **we would not be judged.** -------------

32a Time   But   when we are judged by the Lord,
  b Assertion   **we are disciplined**
    Purpose   so that we may not be condemned along with the world. -------

33a Conclusion   So then my brothers [and sisters],

  b Time   when you gather together to eat,
  c Exhortation   **wait for one another.**

34a Condition (protasis)   If anyone is hungry,
  b Exhortation (apodosis) **let him eat at home,**
  c Purpose   so that when you gather together it will not be for judgment. -------

  d Assertion   Now **I will put in order the other matters**
  e Time   when I come.

Explanation of the Text

11:17–18 Now in giving these instructions I do not praise you, for you gather together not for the better but for the worse. For most significantly, when you gather together as a church, I hear that divisions exist among you, and in part I believe it (Τοῦτο δὲ παραγγέλλων οὐκ ἐπαινῶ ὅτι οὐκ εἰς τὸ κρεῖσσον ἀλλὰ εἰς τὸ ἧσσον συνέρχεσθε. πρῶτον μὲν γὰρ συνερχομένων ὑμῶν ἐν ἐκκλησίᾳ ἀκούω σχίσματα ἐν ὑμῖν ὑπάρχειν, καὶ μέρος τι πιστεύω). Paul turns to address the divisive behavior of some Corinthian Christians as they gather together for worship and to take the Lord's Supper.[1] This meal, as Paul demonstrated in the illustration in 10:16–17, is supposed to signify their allegiance to the covenant Lord *and* his covenant people. Divisions at the meal thus undermine and make a mockery of the purpose of the Lord's Supper. It is likely that the problem had been raised with Paul through oral reports, as v. 18 indicates: "I hear that . . ." (ἀκούω). Yet the seriousness of the matter is reinforced by Paul's carefully judged and forceful rhetoric.

Paul introduces a deliberate contrast with the way he opened the previous discussion in v. 2. This time both at the start of the section (v. 17) and at the end of the first part of the section (v. 22), he says he does *not* praise them (οὐκ ἐπαινῶ). The contrasting rhetoric is then reinforced by the "not" (οὐκ) followed by the strong adversative "but" (ἀλλά) that introduce the two comparative adjectives "better" and "worse" respectively. Throughout this letter it has become clear that Paul wants the Corinthians to "build up" others and work for the benefit of others. It is this that Paul has in mind as he speaks of "not for the better but for the worse."

The "worse" means that people are being led away from the covenant relationship that the meal signifies rather than being built up in it. The "better," had it happened as it should have, would have meant that the meal was serving to confirm their covenant commitment to each other as well as to the Lord.

Verse 17 begins with a nominative construction in which "this" (Τοῦτο) could point backward, as it often does, or forward. Many translations add the word "following" to indicate that they believe Paul is looking forward to what he is about to say (e.g., NIV, ESV, NRSV). This is most likely, especially given the deliberate contrast with what has gone before. "Giving instructions" (παραγγέλλων; cf. 7:10; 1 Tim 1:5) is a present, *singular* participle in the Greek, hence "giving" and "this instruction" (AV, NASB), though making it plural reads better in English (RSV, NIV, ESV). "As a church" (ἐν ἐκκλησίᾳ) could be translated "in a church," but Paul does not have in mind a specific building given over to the purpose of worship. Rather, they are a church as they gather together. It is in their public worship, wherever it happens to be, that God's people are visible to all "as the church." Christians would have gathered either in larger buildings or in larger houses of the wealthy in the congregation. It is at least possible that the houses of Stephanas, Chloe, and Gaius, among others, were used (cf. 1:11, 14, 16; 16:15; Rom 16:23).

The rhetorical force of the adverbial phrase "most significantly" adds still further weight to the gravity of what Paul is saying. The Greek literally reads, "for firstly" (πρῶτον μὲν γάρ). However, there is no "secondly," and it is simply a way of af-

---

1. The word "gather together" (συνέρχομαι) appears five times in this section and then again in 14:23, 26. It makes it clear that Paul is speaking in these chapters about corpo-rate worship of "the church" that consists of the Christians at Corinth. Verse 18 "when you gather together" (συνερχομένων ὑμῶν) is a genitive absolute. Another appears in v. 20.

firming the importance of what follows (cf. Mark 12:28: "the most important" commandment).

The problem is "divisions" (σχίσματα). Though modern English draws the word "schisms" from this Greek background, the force of this English word is quite different from what Paul intends by this Greek word. "Schisms" usually refer to complete breaches in churches as people have walked out and gone to form another, or where people have founded other churches because of profound theological disagreements. Here the matter, though serious, is one of divisions among people at the Lord's Supper that are neither theological nor "schismatic" as we might think of it. There *are* theological issues at stake, but Paul knows that this can be put right and that they are still listening to him as a church. The strange addition of "and in part I believe it" (καὶ μέρος τι πιστεύω) may reflect Paul's pastoral caution. He knows that, once again, it is only some who are causing the problem and he does not wish to enter a confrontation with all.

11:19 For it is necessary that there must also be factions among you, so that those who are genuine may be shown up among you (δεῖ γὰρ καὶ αἱρέσεις ἐν ὑμῖν εἶναι, ἵνα [καὶ] οἱ δόκιμοι φανεροὶ γένωνται ἐν ὑμῖν). In an enigmatic further comment, Paul suggests that these factions at the Lord's Supper reveal those who are genuinely the Lord's and those who will stand under judgment. Initially it may seem the apostle has changed his mind about the evil of "divisions" in the church, but this is clearly unlikely.[2] He has spoken about how serious divisions are and how unity is essential in 1:10.

Some commentators have suggested that when Paul says these factions are "necessary" he may be indicating God's eschatological design. That is, Paul sees this sort of horrendous division as being part of God's way of revealing those who are truly his and those who are not. "It is necessary" (δεῖ) means that the divisions are part of God's sifting process. It is argued that this leads well into vv. 27–31 in which people will be judged by God on the basis of their behavior at the Lord's Supper. The "genuine" (δόκιμοι) are thus those who are righteous in this matter and not causing divisions at the Supper. Robertson and Plummer write, "Divine Providence turns this evil tendency to good account: it is the means of causing the trusty and true to become recognizable."[3] Certainly divisions are part of what are expected as signs of the end times. In various places Jesus himself foretold how people would be divided (Matt 10:34–37; 24:9–13).

More recently it has been suggested that the apostle is using mention of "the genuine" (δόκιμοι) in a negative way with a sense of "the dignitaries" or "the elite."[4] This would suggest a strong irony here. In this case the elitist group, who are probably the wealthier members who have separated themselves away from the poorer brothers and sisters when it comes to mealtime (see below), consider themselves "approved." Following Campbell, Garland translates this verse, "For it is necessary that there be factions among you in order that the elite may be evident among you."[5] The main support for this internally to the section itself is that later in his conclusion Paul exhorts the Corinthian Christian

---

2. There is no difference of meaning here between "divisions" (σχίσματα) and "factions" (αἱρέσεις). Just as the former did not mean "schism" in the modern sense of the word, so the latter does not mean "heresies," the modern English word that has its origin in the Greek (αἵρεσις).

3. Robertson and Plummer, *First Corinthians*, 240; cf. Bruce, *1 and 2 Corinthians*, 109.

4. R. Alastair Campbell, "Does Paul Acquiesce in Divisions at the Lord's Supper?," *NovT* 33 (1991): 61–70. Campbell cites Philo, *Joseph* 201 as one interesting example where "dignitaries" could be a correct translation of δόκιμοι ("other Egyptian dignitaries feasted with them").

5. Garland, *1 Corinthians*, 535–39; cf. Horsley, *1 Corinthians*, 159. Campbell, "Does Paul Acquiesce in Divisions at the Lord's Supper?," 61–70.

with the words "let him examine himself" (v. 28; δοκιμαζέτω). While this is an intriguing way of looking at a difficult text, it requires a number of assumptions. This would be a very rare use of the word normally meaning "approved" or "tested." This would make the pastoral caution we noted in v. 18 dissolve into a harsh sarcasm or irony!

However, the Lord's Supper has a strong eschatological aspect, and the verb "testing" (δοκιμάζω) has itself already been used in 3:13 in a definite eschatological context. Likewise, 11:28 is set within an eschatological context. The whole of 11:26–32 is written in the light of proclaiming the Lord's death "until he comes" when he will judge and "condemn" the world. It is this that Paul most likely has in mind here. He is referring with some pastoral caution to the fact that the covenant meal is sadly revealing, even as they eat, those who will be blessed and those who will be judged by the Lord, since the way they treat the Supper reveals their attitude toward others who are partakers of the covenant. Once again, it is only "some" who are in the wrong here, but this is a serious situation for them. Their behavior points to their eventual judgment rather than to the blessings they ought to be inheriting.

11:20–22 For when you gather together, it is not to eat the Lord's Supper, for in eating each one devours his own supper. One goes hungry, and one is drunk. What! Do you not have houses to eat and drink in? Or do you despise the church of God and shame those who have nothing? What shall I say to you? Shall I commend you? I will not commend you in this (Συνερχομένων οὖν ὑμῶν ἐπὶ τὸ αὐτὸ οὐκ ἔστιν κυριακὸν δεῖπνον φαγεῖν, ἕκαστος γὰρ τὸ ἴδιον δεῖπνον προλαμβάνει ἐν τῷ φαγεῖν, καὶ ὃς μὲν πεινᾷ, ὃς δὲ μεθύει. μὴ γὰρ οἰκίας οὐκ ἔχετε εἰς τὸ ἐσθίειν καὶ πίνειν; ἢ τῆς ἐκκλησίας τοῦ θεοῦ καταφρονεῖτε, καὶ καταισχύνετε τοὺς μὴ ἔχοντας; τί εἴπω ὑμῖν; ἐπαινέσω ὑμᾶς; ἐν τούτῳ οὐκ

ἐπαινῶ). With another genitive absolute, Paul introduces the problem he is now addressing. The Lord's Supper should have been the place that most clearly revealed the unity of the covenant community. It was the gathering in which the community's formation was remembered, its present existence with Christ as Lord was celebrated, and its future at the Lord's coming anticipated. However, this meal had become a place where the divisions between groups in the congregation were made evident. The poor and the rich were divided. Once again one group was acting in an elitist manner to the extent that the elite wealthy were drunk while others went hungry and suffered humiliation. Again, status-seeking by some has resulted in "shame" (καταισχύνω) for others.

The Lord's Supper is a celebration of the meal instituted by Jesus at the last Passover that the disciples celebrated before the crucifixion. Paul expounds on the inherited tradition from that "last supper" and explains what takes place at the communion meal in vv. 23–26. The Supper seems to have been taking place in the context of a communal meal to which people brought their own food. It was in this communal eating that the disparity between the rich and the poor became obvious. Paul's comment to the rich is that they eat their "own supper" (τὸ ἴδιον δεῖπνον) and "it is not the Lord's supper" (οὐκ ἔστιν κυριακὸν δεῖπνον). If the rich wanted to behave in this way, then they could go to their own homes and have gatherings for meals. The result of their action is that the church of God is despised and many Christians are shamed. Paul repeats how he started this section. With a rhetorical question expecting a clear response of "no," he asks ironically if he can commend them for this behavior. He will in no wise commend them.

The fact that some are wealthy in the congregation and that they are the ones who eat "their own supper" becomes clear when Paul indicates they have "houses" to eat and drink in (οἰκίας οὐκ ἔχετε εἰς τὸ ἐσθίειν). Only the wealthy would have had their own homes. Thus, his comment that people should eat at home if they are hungry is also addressed to the rich (v. 34). What seems to have been happening is that the rich facilitated the Lord's Supper in their homes where the home churches met. It seems that they may have had separate meals, with the rich eating and others coming later who could ill afford to bring food with them.[6] Murphy-O'Connor has described what these typical, reasonably wealthy houses may have looked like from the archaeological evidence. He shows that people invited to these homes to eat with their hosts would normally have eaten in the dining room (the Roman *triclinium*), which averaged about thirty-six square meters less any area used for couches. Since these people would have reclined to eat and would have been served their food by servants, it is unlikely they accommodated more than around nine or ten people. When the church gathered together, the rest would have had to sit in the atrium. In that setting, they might not have been served food at all, or perhaps they were served food of a different kind, suitable for people of a lower class or community status. The atrium in such houses might have seated somewhat less than fifty people.[7] There is some indication that even in the dining room itself the food may have been better, depending on how close to the host a guest was reclining. Status was generally an important factor in Roman dining. Thus, as with the matter of "wisdom" and "knowledge," which were so highly esteemed in that Corinthian society, here too those of status in the society at large found ways of import-

ing that into the church itself. Given that even the servants serving at the table would have been entitled to eat at the Lord's Supper in the same manner as those they normally waited on, it is easy to imagine what a social upheaval the Christian faith was causing. Given that the poorer classes would have had less time at their disposal, it is likely that they would have arrived later at the host's house for the Lord's Supper. Thus, the poorer people would not have been seated in the best room for eating but also would have arrived to find the status-seeking elite already eating or having "devoured" their food.[8] Paul uses hyperbole to make his point as he calls them "drunk."

Since all celebrations of the Lord's Supper would have been in the larger homes of wealthy Christians, the point Paul establishes is that when the church "gathers together" the space is no longer someone's home, it is a special space of worship. This is why, as we saw earlier, there may have been some confusion about the hairstyles the women would use—were they at home or in the gathering of the church? Was there in fact any difference for some of them? Paul's point is that there is indeed a difference. When a home is opened up for worship, then the rules of the gathered community apply as they eat and drink the Lord's Supper, not the social rules of Roman society. Furthermore, in light of this it is easier to understand why Paul said in v. 17 that "you gather together not for the better but for the worse."

The result of what is happening as the Corinthian church eats the Lord's Supper is that some are being shamed. Those who have no food are, as it were, having their faces rubbed in it. As they

---

6. Bruce W. Winter, "The Lord's Supper at Corinth: An Alternative Reconstruction" *RTR* 37 (1978): 73–82. See also Theissen, *Social Setting of Pauline Christianity*, 152–68.

7. Murphy-O'Connor, *St. Paul's Corinth*, 178–85. See also Witherington, *Conflict and Community*, 241–52.

8. We follow Winter's suggested translation ("The Lord's Supper at Corinth," 77). He suggests that the word (προλαμβάνω) normally translated as "eat first" (NASB) or "goes ahead with" (RSV, NIV, ESV) more likely means "devour." The προ suffix thus intensifies the "taking" (λαμβάνω).

come to worship as equals before the Lord, they find that they are treated as far from equal. In fact, the behavior that marked out those who claimed to be part of the elite is the very behavior that brings God's judgment upon them (vv. 27–30). The Christian rules, which he will now lay out, come directly from the Lord, reflect some of the attitudes of the Passover, and stand in stark contrast to Roman ideas of status.

11:23a–b For I received from the Lord that which I also passed on to you (Ἐγὼ γὰρ παρέλαβον ἀπὸ τοῦ κυρίου, ὃ καὶ παρέδωκα ὑμῖν). Paul proceeds to remind the Corinthians of the nature of the Lord's Supper. He appeals to the tradition that he had received from the Lord. The words "received" (παρέλαβον) and "passed on" (παρέδωκα) are virtually technical words in Jewish thought for the passing on of traditions of the fathers to later generations. Unlike the constantly fluid nature of social customs of eating and drinking, these instructions are given by the Lord and therefore are to be followed by all the churches.[9] Paul had delivered this tradition to the Corinthians probably when the church first became established under his leadership. It is likely that as soon as there were a few Christians in a city, Paul and the apostles would have taught about corporate worship of God and of Christ from Scripture, but at the heart of their teaching would be something that, though founded in the ancient Passover meal, was in fact a new institution from the Lord Jesus himself. This probably explains how it came to be called "the Lord's Supper." When Paul says he received it

"from the Lord," he is not saying that he personally received a special revelation, but simply that this tradition that he has passed on came directly from those who had indeed been present at the Supper's institution. It is therefore reliable and genuine tradition going back to the Lord himself.

The purposes for recounting the Supper tradition in this way are important. There are three. First, the Lord's focus in giving this "Supper" was quite different from the focus of the Corinthian meals. There was a simplicity to the eating and drinking at the Lord's Supper that should have overcome all social divisions. Secondly, the eschatological context of the meal relativizes any possibility of elitism. Thirdly, because of its status as a covenant meal, Paul emphasized that blessings and curses are attached to taking part in the meal.

Much has been written on the variations between the tradition to which Paul refers here and that found in the institution of the Supper in the Gospels: Matt 26:26–28; Mark 14:22–24; Luke 22:19–20. Paul is largely in line with Luke, but, interesting as this may be, the rhetoric of the transmission of tradition indicates that what Paul has taught is clearly pre-Pauline[10] and that its content is not in dispute with the Corinthians.[11]

11:23c–24 The Lord Jesus, on the night on which he was betrayed, took bread and, when he had given thanks, he broke it and said, "This is my body which is for you; do this in remembrance of me" (ὅτι ὁ κύριος Ἰησοῦς ἐν τῇ νυκτὶ ᾗ παρεδίδετο ἔλαβεν ἄρτον καὶ εὐχαριστήσας ἔκλασεν καὶ εἶπεν, τοῦτό μού ἐστιν τὸ σῶμα τὸ ὑπὲρ ὑμῶν· τοῦτο

---

9. Cullmann argues that "from the Lord" "can be understood as not only pointing to the historical Jesus as the chronological beginning and the first link of the chain of tradition, but to the exalted Lord as the real author of the whole tradition developing itself within the apostolic Church" (Oscar Cullmann, *The Early Church*, abridged ed. [London: SCM Press, 1966], 62, 67).

10. Jeremias, *Eucharistic Words of Jesus*, 103–4.

11. In examining the extent of the New Testament witness to the Supper, two works are well commended. Both examine the Gospel and Pauline traditions of the Lord's Supper, showing their relationship and discussing issues that arise concerning the nature of the meal, its theological background, and the significance of the Supper for the continuing church community. See I. Howard Marshall, *Last Supper and Lord's Supper* (Exeter: Paternoster, 1980) and Jeremias, *Eucharistic Words of Jesus*.

ποιεῖτε εἰς τὴν ἐμὴν ἀνάμνησιν). The tradition that Paul had delivered to them in the past is now laid out. The description of the night of betrayal places the origins of the tradition back in the Passover meal celebrated by Jesus and his disciples just before his arrest. It was at the meal, according to the Gospels, that Jesus announced that he would be betrayed (Matt 26:24–25; Mark 14:18–20; Luke 22:20–23). A descriptive imperfect tense,[12] "was betrayed" (παρεδίδετο), contrasts with the aorists of "he took . . . he gave thanks [aorist participle] . . . he broke." This passive verb can mean "handed over" or "betrayed." The use of the word in the Synoptic accounts of the Last Supper referring to the betrayal by Judas[13] suggests that "betrayed" is the more likely meaning.[14] However, the possibility remains that Paul was thinking somewhat more broadly of the way Jesus was "handed over" to the authorities and thus to his crucifixion. Elsewhere Paul speaks of God as the agent of the handing over. Thus, in Romans 4:25 we read that Jesus "was handed over to death for our trespasses and was raised for our justification" (NRSV). In Romans 8:32 Paul writes, "He who did not spare his own Son, but gave him up for us all. . . ." Hays suggests that there are "echoes" here of Isaiah 53:6 and 12b (LXX) with both verses using the same verb as here (παραδίδωμι): "And the Lord handed him over [or gave him up] for our sins. . . . He bore the sins of many, and on account of their iniquities he was handed over."[15] It may be that Paul does not distinguish these matters as he writes. For him salvation that comes through the death of Christ was always God's provision, but the betrayal was the act of one man, Judas.

Jesus's actions are the actions of any Jewish host at a dinner. In taking the bread and giving thanks, Jesus is saying a "blessing" for the bread, what we might call "saying grace." However, as Thiselton strongly states, there must be no theological confusion here. Whether the background to Jesus "giving thanks" is the standard *blessing* for the three cups at the Passover or simply a "grace at the meal," it is always *God* who is blessed or thanked and never the bread or meal itself. Thiselton's concluding statement is significant, given how some sacramental theology has developed. "Such modern versions of 'grace' as 'bless this food . . .' are not only alien to the meaning conveyed by giving thanks to God, whether in the context of Jerusalem, Jesus, or Paul, but also risk imposing at the earliest stage an overly explicit overtone of eucharistic 'consecration.'"[16] "When he had given thanks" (εὐχαριστήσας),[17] he broke the loaf of bread, and the meal would have commenced. However, to this action Jesus added his own interpretation of what he was doing, an interpretation that would be carried forward into generations of the church in the form of the "handed-down tradition."

The words "this is my body" (τοῦτό μού ἐστιν τὸ σῶμα) have caused much debate through the ages in terms of different sacramental theologies. Yet whether it be a Roman Catholic view of the transubstantiation of the bread in the Lord's Supper or the Lutheran view of consubstantiation, the Greek words of this verse alone cannot bear the weight of such theological ideas. The word "is" means simply "stands for" or "represents," and what the bread represents is the "body which is for you," that is, Jesus's own body that he gave over to death

---

12. The descriptive imperfect or progressive imperfect "speaks either of *vividness* or *simultaneity* with another action" (Wallace, *Greek Grammar*, 543).

13. Matt 26:15–25; Luke 22:4–6, 21–22, 48; Mark 14:10–11, 18–21.

14. As Fee says, the word's "proximity to the preceding παρέδωκα [I passed on] is probably completely fortuitous," *1 Corinthians*, 608n90; *pace* Hays, *First Corinthians*, 198.

15. Hays, *First Corinthians*, 198.

16. Thiselton, *1 Corinthians*, 871.

17. A temporal, aorist participle.

for the sake of his people. The further explanation "which is for you" (τὸ ὑπὲρ ὑμῶν) is abbreviated and not immediately easy to understand. Each Gospel account has the words "this is my body," but only Luke carries the additional words "which is given for you. Do this in remembrance of me" (v. 19 ESV; τὸ ὑπὲρ ὑμῶν διδόμενον· τοῦτο ποιεῖτε εἰς τὴν ἐμὴν ἀνάμνησιν). This is why some variants in 1 Corinthians 11:24, possibly imitating Luke or simply seeking to make the verse more intelligible, added "broken for you" or "given for you."[18]

"For you" (ὑπὲρ ὑμῶν) does not simply mean that this is food now "for you" to eat. The phrase has a vicarious sense. Given the allusion to Isaiah 53:6 mentioned above, the expression possibly draws upon Isaiah 53:12 where the Servant "bore the sin of many." The preposition "for," which in some contexts is rightly translated "on behalf of" (ὑπέρ), is used by Paul in several other places in its vicarious sense and often with the atoning sacrifice of Christ in mind (cf. 1 Cor 15:3; Rom 5:6, 8; 8:32; 2 Cor 5:14; Gal 3:13). However, it is the link of the Supper with the Passover meal that also helps clarify what is said here.[19] Indeed, even if the Last Supper was not itself a Passover celebration, we can affirm with Jeremias that "the last supper would still be surrounded by the atmosphere of the Passover even if it should have occurred on the evening before the feast."[20]

This Israelite meal was specifically a time for remembering. Exodus 12:14 says that the Passover day "shall be for you a memorial [LXX: μνημόσυνον]." Jesus took this aspect of the meal

and made it into a "remembrance of me" (εἰς τὴν ἐμὴν ἀνάμνησιν; cf. Luke 22:19). The Israelites were to remember their deliverance from Egypt. This had involved the sacrifice of a lamb in the place of the death of the firstborn sons of the Israelite families. The blood of the lamb was painted on the lintels and doorposts of the Israelite houses. As Jesus went on to speak of the "blood" of the covenant, he clearly thought of his giving of himself in sacrifice (Luke 22:20). As the Passover remembered the sacrifice with the death of a lamb, so the Supper looks to Jesus and remembers the deliverance of God's people by and through the sacrifice of Christ. Deuteronomy 16:1–8 describes the feast and reminds the Israelites that they were brought out of Egypt "by night" and are to celebrate it "in the evening," a point to which Paul draws attention in 1 Cor 11:23 ("on the night"; ἐν τῇ νυκτί). As the Israelites celebrated their deliverance annually, they told their story and explained aspects of the meal (Exod 12:26). Jeremias argues that this is the decisive factor in viewing the Lord's Supper as having its roots in the Passover. In the Passover the "interpretation of the special elements of the meal is a fixed part of the Passover ritual."[21] It is this that Jesus as the host takes to himself. His interpretation of the bread as representing his body given "for you" and his insistence that the meal is a remembrance make sense in this context. Furthermore, the Passover context is also one of sacrifice and substitution, for the lamb dies instead of the Israelites. (The Egyptians who do not sacrifice the lamb find their firstborn sons dying through

---

18. The variant "broken" (κλώμενον) is supported by ℵ² C³ D¹ F G K L P Ψ 81. 104. 365. 630. 1175. 1241. 1505. 1739ᵐᵍ. 1881. 2464 𝔐 sy. The word is missing from 𝔓⁴⁶ ℵ A B C° 6. 33. 1739ᵗˣᵗ vgˢᵗ; Cyp. The variant "given for you" is found only in the Vulgate and the Coptic (διδόμενον).

19. See above, following comments on 10:15 ("In Depth: Possible Backgrounds to the 'Meals' of 10:16–20"), for a fuller discussion of the Supper and its relationship to the Passover.

20. Jeremias, *Eucharistic Words of Jesus*, 88. In a lengthy section Jeremias argues that the Last Supper should be seen as taking place in the context of and deeply reflecting the nature of a Passover meal. He interacts at length with those who would disagree (ibid., 41–88).

21. Jeremias, *Eucharistic Words of Jesus*, 56 (and see larger discussion on 41–62).

the work of the destroying angel.) Once again, the "for you" does, in that context, take on a vicarious meaning. As Paul had made clear in 5:8, the identification of Jesus with the Passover lamb itself had already been made very early in the church's life. Interestingly, the later Passover liturgies looked forward to the messianic banquet and to the end-time, and this too has parallels with what Paul says here, for the meal, like the Passover, is a proclamation of the historic events but also has an end time. For the Supper will proclaim the Lord's death only "until he comes" (v. 26; ἄχρι οὗ ἔλθῃ).

The emphasis on remembering is strong with the phrase "in remembrance of me" (εἰς τὴν ἐμὴν ἀνάμνησιν) being repeated twice, once here with the bread and then also in v. 25 with the cup. Thus, the tradition of the Lord's Supper as it has been handed down from the Lord is one that now calls the Christian to remember the death of Christ in which he died "for you." But it is more than simply remembering an event for, at the Supper, the church proclaims the gospel and the people are drawn into those events, even as the family was drawn into the Passover meal by the words of interpretation and the breaking and distribution of the bread. Even as the bread is eaten, the church remembers Christ's sacrificial giving of his body "for" them. As with the Passover in which the participants remember their redemption when they take bread and bitter herbs and are able to say, "He brought *us* from bondage to freedom,"[22] so here the events are made real *in the present* and are recognized to be for all generations of Christians as they take the bread.

11:25 In the same way [he took] also the cup after supper, saying, "This cup is the new cove-nant in my blood; do this whenever you drink it, in remembrance of me" (ὡσαύτως καὶ τὸ ποτήριον μετὰ τὸ δειπνῆσαι, λέγων, Τοῦτο τὸ ποτήριον ἡ καινὴ διαθήκη ἐστὶν ἐν τῷ ἐμῷ αἵματι· τοῦτο ποιεῖτε, ὁσάκις ἐὰν πίνητε, εἰς τὴν ἐμὴν ἀνάμνησιν). As with the bread, Christians are to take the cup "in remembrance of me" (εἰς τὴν ἐμὴν ἀνάμνησιν). This is the way by which they will align themselves to the covenant Lord. As they drink, they will think of the covenant Lord himself, of the covenant he brought into being by his own blood, and the sacrifice through which they gain their forgiveness and justification (cf. Rom 5:8–9). This is the "covenant participation" (κοινωνία) at the heart of the meal that becomes part of the ongoing life of the covenant community.

"In the same way" (ὡσαύτως) refers back to Jesus taking and then verbally interpreting the bread. Now Jesus took the cup and interpreted it as well. This happened "after [the] supper,"[23] that is, after the main meal, and so raises the question of the order of events in the meal Paul describes. Whether this can be seen as the third or fourth cup of the Passover matters little.[24] The order provided is bread, followed by "supper," followed by the cup. To many this has suggested that in the early church's celebration of the Lord's Supper there was the initial breaking and distribution of the bread together with its interpretation, followed by a communal meal, the supper, followed by the drinking of the cup of wine. Certainly the words "after supper" do seem to require that a meal separated the bread from the cup. However, if this was the case, the tragedy of some eating early and well and getting drunk, while others were not eating, would have been even more keenly felt. It suggests the poorer

---

22. See m. Pesahim 10:5.

23. The aorist infinitive δειπνῆσαι is used with μετὰ τό indicating antecedent time. "After supper" means "after eating supper."

24. See above, "In Depth: Possible Backgrounds to the 'Meals' of 10:16–20" at 10:15.

people may not have actually been taking part in the full "Lord's Supper" at all but perhaps only arriving in time for the cup. They would thus miss a most significant aspect of the worship and the retelling of *their* story of salvation and deliverance.

In the interpretation of the cup, the Lord referred to the "covenant" (διαθήκη). As we have seen, especially in the comments on 10:16–17, this is of fundamental importance for all that Paul has been saying, especially when he was dealing with the idolatrous breaches of covenant. Here, the "covenant" being referred to is "new" (καινή), and it was formed as Jesus shed his blood on the cross for his people. The nature of the meal has been partly addressed above and was examined more closely under 10:15 above. It is important to remember that in 10:16 Paul had discussed in some detail the nature of the "cup" in terms of "covenant participation [κοινωνία] in the blood of Christ." It was suggested above that both the Passover and other "covenant meals" provided the background for understanding the cup and the emphasis on covenant. Here in chapter 11, Paul addresses the right use of the Christian covenant meal, which stands in stark contrast to the pagan meal.

The cup here most likely refers to the "the cup of blessing" in 10:16 and probably, as noted, looks back to the Passover meal. A covenant treaty normally required the death of an animal as an indication of commitment to the treaty's blessings (promises) and curses (the judgment if the treaty was broken). In effect, the blood of a covenant treaty, provided through the slaughter of an animal, became the sign that both sides were committed to the treaty on penalty of their own death (shedding of blood). However, when Jesus says, "This cup is the new covenant in *my* blood," he is first and foremost speaking of his own commitment to bringing the covenant into being. Jesus thus fulfills Jeremiah's prophecy that God himself would provide a

"new covenant" for his people that would involve the forgiveness of their iniquity and that he would "remember their sins no more" (Jer 31:31–34).

11:26 For whenever you eat this bread and drink this cup, you proclaim the death of the Lord until he comes (ὁσάκις γὰρ ἐὰν ἐσθίητε τὸν ἄρτον τοῦτον καὶ τὸ ποτήριον πίνητε, τὸν θάνατον τοῦ κυρίου καταγγέλλετε, ἄχρις οὗ ἔλθῃ). Those who identify with Christ's new covenant will "eat this bread and drink this cup." In doing this, not only do they participate in the blessings of the covenant and identify with the Lord himself, but they also "proclaim the death of the Lord" (τὸν θάνατον τοῦ κυρίου καταγγέλλετε). To paraphrase, the interpreted actions of eating and drinking at the meal announce to the church and the world that he gave his body and he shed his blood as he died for us, and this sacrificial death has brought us into his covenant and provided for our forgiveness.

The people of the new covenant are drawn into being and brought together through Christ and his death. The meal is thus to be taken by each member *together* as the community reaffirms its position as God's people. Their focus is on Christ and all that he has done for them, for his self-giving sacrifice in which all was done "for you." It is thus truly shameful that divisions have occurred at the very time when they were celebrating the coming into being of the one people of God by his grace.

This meal will continually be celebrated by God's people "until he comes" (ἄχρις οὗ ἔλθῃ). The Lord will return to his people, bringing both the promised blessings, that is, the consummation of their redemption, and judgment for those who break covenant. This eschatological aspect of the Lord's Supper is important in Paul's argument. In the next few verses Paul turns to the *present* judgment of the Lord upon his people, a judgment intended to "discipline" (v. 32). This discipline is necessary precisely so that the covenant people themselves may not get caught up in the judgment of the returning Lord. Throughout the epistle, Paul has frequently emphasized the eschatological aspect of the church's existence. Thiselton aptly writes, "Eschatology in this epistle serves to remind complacent groups within the congregation at Corinth of their fallibility, vulnerability, and status as travelers still *en route* to their final goal."[25] Notably this theme is present throughout the discussion of idol meat and rights in chapters 8–10. The danger of judgment looms over those who do not take the covenant commitment seriously (8:10–13; 9:24–27). In the Lord's Supper there is the reminder that the new covenant was attained at great price ("my body . . . my blood"). As Christians eat and drink, they retell *their* story that Christ died "for" them so they might be incorporated into the covenant community. Then, they also remind themselves that this Lord will return, at which point symbols will no longer be required, as he is seen "face to face" (13:12). Therefore, all who disgrace the Lord's Supper bring shame upon their Lord and open themselves up to his judgment. It is to this that Paul now turns.

11:27 Consequently, anyone who eats the bread or drinks the cup of the Lord in an unworthy manner will be guilty of the body and blood of the Lord (Ὥστε ὃς ἂν ἐσθίῃ τὸν ἄρτον ἢ πίνῃ τὸ ποτήριον τοῦ κυρίου ἀναξίως, ἔνοχος ἔσται τοῦ σώματος καὶ τοῦ αἵματος τοῦ κυρίου). "Consequently" (ὥστε) introduces the conclusions that Paul wishes to draw from the argument he has just laid out (see also 11:33). What he has said in vv. 23–26 has direct and important consequences for those in Corinth who have brought the Supper into disrepute. In this section Paul argues that those who thus drink "in an unworthy manner" (ἀναξίως) will themselves be guilty for the death of Christ (v. 27). Therefore, they should examine

themselves before participating in the Supper (v. 28). If they participate without "discerning the body," that is, without concern for the community *as a whole*, then they will eat and drink judgment upon themselves (v. 29). Already this has resulted in some experiencing illness and even death under the present judgment of the Lord (v. 30).

For a moment Paul moves from the second-person plural (v. 26; "you eat . . . drink") to the more general indefinite third singular, "anyone who eats" (ὃς ἂν ἐσθίῃ). This has the effect of softening an otherwise strong challenge to the Corinthians.

The word translated here as "in an unworthy manner" (ἀναξίως; cf. NRSV, NIV) is a *hapax legomenon* in the New Testament and has been also translated as "unworthily" (AV, NJB) and as "in a way that dishonors him" (TEV). The problem of how best to understand this adverb is significant. Often this verse has been taken out of context and incorrectly applied to those coming to the Lord's Supper. It is suggested that Paul writes to individuals who are somehow "unworthy" to come before the Lord at the communion because of their sin. This has led to seeing v. 28 as a call for a careful, introspective self-examination to see if there are any sins in one's life that need forgiveness immediately before taking the bread and wine. However, while that may be a valuable exercise and can be argued for biblically in other ways, in *this* context it is the manner of eating or the way in which people participate in the meal that is at issue (see below). Paul's concern is that there is an "appropriate" or right way of coming together to eat that involves the whole community coming on equal terms to participate in the Supper and an inappropriate or "improper" way of coming to eat the meal.[26] "The cup of the Lord" (τὸ ποτήριον τοῦ κυρίου) is simply another way of speaking of the *Lord's* Supper.

---

25. Thiselton, *1 Corinthians*, 888.

26. See L&N 66.7.

In the expression, "guilty of the body and blood of the Lord," the word "guilty" (ἔνοχος) could refer to the one against whom a crime has been committed, or to the crime itself, or to one who is liable for or answerable for the crime.[27] For this reason various translations propose "guilty of" (AV, NASB 1995), "guilty of sinning against" (NIV) and "answerable for" (NRSV, NJB). Since the word is "a technical legal term to express liability," then "answerable for" could be appropriate.[28] But this hardly connotes the legal severity of what is being said. To be held liable in law for some crime is to be found "guilty." But of what are they guilty?

Again, the apostle refers to the eating and drinking because *it is in the conduct surrounding the Lord's Supper that the sin of some Corinthians lies.* They are liable for "the body and blood of the Lord." This means they could simply be found guilty of profaning or bringing into disgrace the meal itself, but Paul's point goes deeper than this. The elitists who have eaten without regard for the poor have altogether missed the point of the meal. They have failed to reflect the fact that the covenant meal demonstrates the forgiveness and *oneness* of the people before the Lord. They have failed as a community to proclaim the death of Christ and the salvation that has come through his death "for" all of them. Fee thus correctly writes, "To 'profane' the meal as they are doing is to place themselves under the same liability as those responsible for that death in the first place. Thus to be 'guilty of his body and blood' means to be 'liable for his death.'"[29] The incredibly serious implications of what has been going on in the meal at Corinth are thus laid out and provide the clear framework for the repeated emphasis on judgment in the verses that follow.

11:28–29 Rather,[30] let a person examine himself and in this way let him eat of the bread and drink of the cup. For the one who eats and drinks, eats and drinks judgment on himself if he does not discern the body (δοκιμαζέτω δὲ ἄνθρωπος ἑαυτόν, καὶ οὕτως ἐκ τοῦ ἄρτου ἐσθιέτω καὶ ἐκ τοῦ ποτηρίου πινέτω· ὁ γὰρ ἐσθίων καὶ πίνων κρίμα ἑαυτῷ ἐσθίει καὶ πίνει μὴ διακρίνων τὸ σῶμα). Paul now exhorts any wealthy Corinthian man or woman who might abuse the Lord's Supper in the way that he has described and thus be "guilty" to "examine himself." On the meaning of the verb "to examine" (δοκιμάζω), see comments at 11:19. Since Paul is finally concerned about the eschatological impact of the improper participation in the Supper and the danger of God's judgment coming on them in the same way as it will on the rest of the world (v. 32), this self-examination should be seen in this light. The idea is that people should "test" or "examine" themselves in order that they should not be "tested" on the final day.

Once again Paul is urging discernment and right judgment upon the Corinthian elitists. The immediate problem here is summed up by Paul's insistence that they should "discern" properly the "body." The verb "discern" (διακρίνω), which may also be translated "judge," has been used previously in 4:7 and 6:5 and appears again in 11:31 and 14:29. The noun (διάκρισις) is found in 12:10. In its broader connotation the verb implies judging between two positions or differentiating matters, as can be seen in most of these examples. The elite and wealthy, who are so keen to show off their status as they recline at a meal while others go hungry, have not discerned the nature of the "body." Paul urges them to make a judgment about what

---

27. See BDAG 338.
28. Fee, *1 Corinthians*, 560.
29. Fee, *1 Corinthians*, 621.

30. "Rather" expresses the adversative nature here of the particle δέ.

the body is and what it is not and to understand its central place in the meaning of the Lord's Supper.

To what does "the body" (τὸ σῶμα) refer? Some have argued that Paul is urging the elite to discern between normal bread at normal meals and the "sacramental" Lord's body present in the bread at the Supper.[31] Paul, though, seems to have no concern for the *nature* of the bread or wine in this section or for some actual presence of the covenant Lord. The emphasis is on "remembrance." Another view, mostly found among Protestant commentators, is that Paul here speaks of discerning and properly understanding the church as the body of Christ. As they have eaten without concern for the poor in the church, so they have not discerned the body. They have forgotten that the one loaf speaks of the unity and equality before God of God's people (cf. 10:17). They must take into consideration how their actions affect their brothers and sisters in Christ, who are the body.[32] The main problem with this view is that the body as *people* has not been the subject that Paul has been addressing. It requires looking back to 10:17 to see the body as the people or looking forward to 12:12–31.

A third view suggests that the body is *the Lord's* body and blood ("my body . . . my blood"; vv. 24–25), but not in some sacramental sense. Rather, in the bread and the wine the one who died "for you" is signified together with all that his death meant. To "discern" this means therefore to distinguish this meal as different from a normal meal. Again, it is not that the bread is no longer bread (in some sacramental sense), but that in this meal, instituted by the Lord himself, something different is going

on from what might happen in a normal meal. The "remembrance" must happen! Christ died to bring forgiveness of sin and form a people who participate together in the covenant he guaranteed through his blood. If they "discerned" in this way, they would not mix up two different meals nor would they conduct the meal in a way that divides covenant members one from another. This latter view seems to make most sense of the immediate context.[33] The Lord's Supper is not just any meal! Even if the Lord's Supper is celebrated around a bigger meal, it will govern the nature of the bigger meal to ensure that the whole is "communal."

The result of eating and drinking while not discerning is stated strongly. That person eats and drinks "judgment on himself" (κρίμα ἑαυτῷ). In other words, God judges him or her. The use of present tenses suggests that Paul sees this as something that will go on in the community as and when such judgment is deserved, for it is a present reality. It is to this present judgment that Paul turns in the next verse (v. 30).

This discerning or differentiating what is indicated by the eating of the bread and the drinking of the cup is all part of the continuing issue of spiritual judgment. In fact, this whole section takes on a decidedly forensic tone from the moment the word "guilty" is used. It is difficult to show in English the play on words that Paul uses here. But the upshot is that discernment and judgment on the part of covenant members is vital if they are to take part in a meal that itself can be used by God to bring judgment. Thus, self-judgment may spare a person God's disciplining judgment so that he or she may be spared final judgment. The play on words

---

31. So a number of medieval commentators and, more recently, Lietzmann, *An Die Korinther I–II*, 59; Johan C. Beker, *Paul the Apostle: The Triumph of God in Life and Thought* (Philadelphia: Fortress, 1984), 253; Senft, *Première Épitre de Saint Paul aux Corinthiens*, 153.

32. Günther Bornkamm, *Early Christian Experience* (New York: Harper & Row), 149; Fee, *1 Corinthians*, 623–24; Hays, *First Corinthians*, 200.

33. Barrett, *First Corinthians*, 274–75. Cf. Ciampa and Rosner, *First Corinthians*, 555.

develops like this: v. 27, "guilty" (ἔνοχος); v. 28, "let a man examine himself" (δοκιμαζέτω); v. 29, "judgment" (κρίμα); "discern" (διακρίνων); v. 31, "discerning" (διεκρίνομεν), "be judged" (ἐκρινόμεθα); v. 32, "we are judged" (κρινόμενοι), "condemned" (κατακριθῶμεν); v. 34, "judgment" (κρίμα).

11:30 For this reason many among you are weak and ill, and some are sleeping (διὰ τοῦτο ἐν ὑμῖν πολλοὶ ἀσθενεῖς καὶ ἄρρωστοι καὶ κοιμῶνται ἱκανοί). The present tense of "dying" or "sleeping" (κοιμῶνται) follows the present participles of the previous verse where Paul talked of eating and drinking "judgment." The tenses remind us that this is what God is doing *at the moment* in the community.[34] Thus, the Lord's Supper is the place where, on an ongoing basis, Christians accept again the judgment verdict that they are sinners and that Christ has died to overcome that verdict. That there are serious present consequences to an abuse of the Lord's Supper, including physical ill health and even death ("sleeping"), provides a stern reminder of the need to treat this community event and covenant meal with the utmost respect since the covenant Lord is present among them.

Abuse of the sacrament, therefore, is tantamount to rejecting the death of Christ for sin and accepting that judgment will now come upon the rebellious person. This is why self-examination is so vital before taking the Supper. If this does not take place, then the Lord himself steps in and judges.[35] However, this judgment that Paul refers to is still not the final judgment. In fact, it is God disciplining precisely in order that the individual will be spared the final judgment (v. 32).

11:31–32 But if we were discerning about ourselves, we would not be judged. But when we are judged by the Lord, we are disciplined so that we may not be condemned along with the world (εἰ δὲ ἑαυτοὺς διεκρίνομεν, οὐκ ἂν ἐκρινόμεθα· κρινόμενοι δὲ ὑπὸ [τοῦ] κυρίου παιδευόμεθα, ἵνα μὴ σὺν τῷ κόσμῳ κατακριθῶμεν). In the Lord's Supper the future judgment of God is anticipated. Some of God's people have found themselves being judged by way of discipline (v. 30), but they will not finally be condemned as will be the world. Paul urges spiritual self-discernment or discipline since it would be better to avoid the Lord's discipline. It is difficult again to know how best to translate the word of self-judgment here. Many versions have "if we judged [διακρίνω] ourselves" for the protasis of this second-class condition (contrary to fact). This rightly helps the reader to see the continuing play on words with "we would not be judged [κρίνω]." However, the parallel with v. 29 ("discerning" the body; διακρίνω) is also significant. With this in mind, the translation above keeps "discerning" for both verses 29 and 31. The passive voice of the verbs reminds us that the judgment and disciplining of Christians takes place at the hand of the (covenant) Lord (ὑπὸ [τοῦ] κυρίου), who is among his people. The imperfect tenses of the second-class condition indicate it refers to the *present* time.[36] The fact is that they do *not* discern/examine themselves and are therefore in distinct danger of that future judgment.

The practice of "spiritual people" discerning/judging spiritual things was introduced by Paul in 2:14–16 in the context of jealousies and strife among the Corinthian Christians (3:3). Discerning their own situation before the Lord and within the covenant community is thus something that the spiritually mature will do (cf. 3:1–2). In the Lord's Supper especially, the mature Christian

---

34. The verb "to be" is assumed and the "weak" and "ill" are predicate nominatives.

35. See the discussion below in the Theology in Application section entitled, "The Lord's Supper and God's Judgment."

36. Wallace, *Greek Grammar*, 695–96.

will discern him or herself as a sinner in need of forgiveness rather than thinking about worldly status in the community or about when to eat a big meal. The Supper will truly humble godly men or women as they renew their acceptance of the verdict of "guilty" before the Lord and turn to him for the blessings of forgiveness and acceptance that only he can give. In that humbling and self-discernment, they will also realize afresh that they are part of a community of God's people, that each one has equal value and status before the Lord, and that each should be cared for and shown love as Christ first cared and showed love for his people.

In v. 32, however, Paul reminds us of the protecting aspect of God's side of the covenant. The temporal participle, "when we are judged" (κρινόμενοι), builds on the fact that this judgment "by the Lord" (ὑπὸ [τοῦ] κυρίου) is actually taking place among them right now. Yet it is a judgment designed to "discipline" (παιδεύω) rather than damn. Semantically the word incorporates the idea of children being castigated in order to mature into the adults they should be. For Paul, this is entirely appropriate. He could not speak to them as mature (3:1). God himself is determined to enable them to grow to become the spiritual people they should be. In Hebrews 12:5–11 the author speaks in detail of the purpose of God's discipline and the deep spiritual need for it. He says, "If you are not disciplined—and everyone undergoes discipline—then you are not legitimate, not true sons and daughters at all" (12:8).

There is a great need for the Corinthians as a church community to understand that God is working in their midst to discipline them and that his ultimate purpose is the purpose of a loving father "that [they] may not be condemned along with the world." Discipline now is designed to spare God's people from his judgment on the last day. The word "condemned" is another of the Greek words for judgment (κατακρίνω). This word always connotes the guilt of the one being judged and thus signifies the judgment of *sentence*.[37]

In summary, the way Christians take the Lord's Supper is itself part of the distinguishing work of God's Spirit between those who are truly his, and so are occasionally disciplined by a loving father, and those who are not the Lord's and so eat and drink judgment upon themselves. This verdict of the last day of "guilty" is read forward into the meal itself, just as the verdict of "righteous" is read forward for those who take in a properly discerning manner.

11:33–34c So then my brothers [and sisters], when you gather together to eat, wait for one another. If anyone is hungry, let him eat at home, so that when you gather together it will not be for judgment (ὥστε, ἀδελφοί μου, συνερχόμενοι εἰς τὸ φαγεῖν ἀλλήλους ἐκδέχεσθε. εἴ τις πεινᾷ, ἐν οἴκῳ ἐσθιέτω, ἵνα μὴ εἰς κρίμα συνέρχησθε). Paul's conclusion is now seen in terms of specific application to the problem outlined in vv. 17–22. The questions of how and when to eat and whether some people are being left out of parts of the meal are picked up, and the apostle gives direct instructions. They should eat together, being mindful of one another, or, if necessary, eat at home. The link with vv. 27–32 is also explicit since in following Paul's command they will avoid the judgment of which he has warned them. Once again, serious as the whole situation is, Paul speaks pastorally as he addresses them as "my brothers [and sisters]." When they gather together as the church "to eat" the Lord's Supper, they should think of the "other" and so wait until all are present. This will mean that those who gather for a main meal at the time of day when they are hungry should "eat at home"

---

37. BDAG 519.

(ἐν οἴκῳ ἐσθιέτω). Presumably Paul intends that people should come, having already eaten, so that they are not hungry and rush into the meal simply as "food," or that they should delay and eat after the Lord's Supper. Either way, the elitists, who are enjoying a significant meal while others go hungry, should regard the Lord's Supper as something different, as a "remembrance" meal in which all "gather together." (The emphasis on "gathering together" is clearly a focus with the threefold use of the verb [συνέρχομαι] in vv. 17–20 and twice in vv. 33–34.) There is nothing explicit here to suggest that all should gather first for the breaking of bread, then for a following meal (supper), to be followed by the cup (vv. 23–25). The precise way things are to be done is not discussed. Nevertheless, if Paul's injunctions were followed, it would either have meant that the main meal would no longer be part of the Lord's Supper or that food would be fully shared around with no distinctions of people. The point is that all, the poor and the rich alike, should eat side by side and eat the same thing at the same time. Certainly, there needed to be a deliberate effort to avoid any elitist behavior, and that would mean a full sharing of food and drink with those who were poor.

Coming together and eating in a way that understands the nature of the Supper and recognizes that all believers are equal at the Supper will mean they avoid coming together "for judgment" (εἰς κρίμα). God may overrule for good through the judgment of discipline for his people, but it is not something to be desired. Since the covenant Lord brings blessings and curses, they should clearly seek in every way that they can to live out the Lord's will and receive his blessings.

11:34d–e Now I will put in order the other matters when I come (Τὰ δὲ λοιπὰ ὡς ἂν ἔλθω διατάξομαι). What the other matters were, we do not know. Perhaps they were related to the Lord's Supper or to other less urgent matters of their practice in corporate worship.

Theology in Application

The Supper as a Community Event

In a hyper-individualized society, the communion service has often lost the emphasis Paul gives it here of being a community event. It can seem almost accidental that the Supper should only be held "when you come together." The concept of a people sitting down together in covenant participation, one with the other and all with their Lord, is missing. It was Christ himself who prayed that his people would become "perfectly one" (John 17:23 ESV) so that the love of God for his Son and for his people would be seen by outsiders. He said this just before he was betrayed and in proximity to taking the Passover meal with his disciples. The unity of the disciples and of those who would believe through them is a vital part of the gospel, and it is a unity won for them through Christ's death and resurrection. To hide this unity, or to behave in a way that seems to deny the "body" nature of God's people, is to "despise the church of God" (11:22) and potentially to "be guilty of the body and blood of the Lord" (11:27) and so face judgment.

In verses 28–29 Paul urges self-examination or self-judgment to avoid God's judgment. However, we must understand that more is going on here than simply an apostolic request for some modern Christianized form of individualized psychoanalysis. The call is to participate in a covenant meal in full recognition that we are sinners who needed Christ to die for us and that, in his death and resurrection, Christ brought us into the fellowship of his church. Christians who are properly discerning of themselves will see themselves *also* as part of the community established by one who gave his life for them. Personal self-examination for sin is indeed at the heart of what Paul is saying, but the modern individualist will often leave it there. In the Lord's Supper the personal identification of oneself as a sinner worthy of death also means identifying oneself as a participant in the covenant community and so discerning properly the body.

The Lord's Supper and God's Judgment

Verse 30 can sound shocking to modern ears that hate to hear of final judgment, let alone hear of any possible link between behavior now and God's *present* judgment of people. Yet, however a modern reader might react, Paul sees "many" in the church as ill and weak and some "sleeping" (that is, having died), and informs them that the reason is to be found in their lack of discernment at the Supper and the judgment God has attached to that. We may note that Paul does not suggest that all illnesses find their root in such sinful behavior. It is thoroughly illegitimate to build an argument from silence to suggest that somehow a person's sin produces *all* illness and that therefore turning from sin will lead to true health for all. However, we may also note that as God's judgment falls on his people all can be caught up in it, even if they personally are not guilty of certain, particular sins (cf. Josh 22:17).

Here Paul's approach to what is going on has to be understood within his covenantal theology. Covenant theology of the type that Paul espouses throughout his writing, but which he has especially described since chapter 8, assumes the presence of the covenant Lord in the midst of his people. The Lord offers his people protection and his loving care, but he also holds them accountable so that they may truly be the people they are supposed to be, that is, a people who image the covenant Lord himself to the world. Building on the Old Testament passages where Yahweh is among his people and brings blessings and curses (cf. Deut 11:26–28), Paul sees Jesus as the Lord who, likewise, blesses his people but also brings judgment when they rebel against him. He has already made this point in chapter 8. However, as Moule has clearly shown, it is in the sacraments especially where this dual sanction of God's covenant relationship with his people is shown to all Christians on a regular basis.[38] Starting with what he calls the "two absolutes," baptism and the last day,

---

38. C. F. D. Moule, "The Judgment Theme in the Sacraments," in *The Background of the New Testament and Its Escha-* *tology*, ed. W. D. Davies and D. Daube (Cambridge: Cambridge University Press, 1956), 464–81.

Moule describes the fact that while living in the reality of having died with Christ in baptism, Christians still find themselves sinning until that last day. Unlike "sectarian enthusiasts" who believe "the new creation is already complete" and unlike the "mockers" of 2 Peter 3:2 "who think that nothing has yet been altered," "Christian realists" "cling to the conviction that change has taken place" and yet live with the knowledge of their sin.[39] This calls for Christians to repent regularly of their sin lest they are judged along with the world. The judgment theme of the Lord's Supper dominates in this passage because it is here that Christians are reminded of the need to live in the light of Christ's death and follow him as their Lord. If Christians, participating in the Supper, do not acknowledge their sin and the just verdict of death, then they join with "the secular powers in pronouncing a sentence of 'Guilty' on Jesus" (v. 27).[40]

It is in the Lord's Supper where the baptismal commitment to the verdict of death for sin, taken for us by Christ, is renewed regularly until the last day. Without self-judgment and the repentance and changed life that must go with it, then judgment awaits, both present and future. Lack of spiritual discernment and consequent spiritual blindness truly come into focus as God's people take the Supper, replete as it is with the reminder that sin brings death. This is a terrible and awesome reminder of the nature of sin and the horror of God's judgment. In the light of the strength of this warning, it is remarkable that many in the modern church can treat the Lord's Supper so casually. Surely ministers serving communion should not only express the joy at the covenant blessings of forgiveness and peace with God seen in taking the Supper, but should also warn of the covenant judgment on those who would despise the body and breach the community.

---

39. Ibid., 468–69.   40. Ibid., 472.

1 Corinthians 12:1–31

Literary Context

In chapter 12 Paul returns to talk in some detail about the nature of the "grace-gifts." Having criticized the use of "knowledge" by those who claim great gifting, Paul now writes positively about the true function of gifts given by God's Spirit. Grace-gifts may have been abused by the elitists, but that does not mean they should be ignored. Paul addresses their great value to the community when used as God intended, that is, to "build up" the community. In the preceding discussion of the Lord's Supper, Paul described a covenantal understanding of Christ's lordship and of the potential judgment on those who despised the church of God (11:22, 27). Now he continues the theme as he insists that spiritual people will proclaim Christ as "Lord" (12:1–3). The Lord gives grace-gifts to build up the community. These gifts are not indicators of community status and must not be allowed to divide people or be used to distinguish between one group in the church and another. In chapter 12 the apostle begins to make his case (indicated in 1:4–9) for how the gifts are truly enriching for the church when understood correctly and allowed to function properly. Each person has a gift. Different people have different gifts, but all are empowered by "the same Spirit" (12:11), and the Spirit allocates them as he desires. No one must divide the body by saying or implying that one member is less useful or less gifted than another. Every believer must humble themselves to admit their need of the others. The grace-gifts must build up the body and unite the body rather than divide it (12:25, 27).

The following chapter (ch. 13), centering on the marker of "love," is then to be seen as an excellent summary of all that has been said about grace-gifts and their relative position alongside the Christian marker of "love." Where "knowledge" may puff up, love builds up (8:1). Not even the most amazing of grace-gifts is anything when placed alongside the marker of all that is spiritually mature and to be sought after: love.

VII. Status, Knowledge, Freedom, and Food Offered to Idols (8:1–11:1)
VIII. Status, Public Worship, Freedom, and Grace-Gifts (11:2–14:40)
    A. The Conduct of Husbands and Wives in Public Worship (11:2–16)
    B. The Conduct of the Church at the Lord's Supper (11:17–34)
➡   **C. Spiritual People and the Function of Their Grace-Gifts in the Church (12:1–31)**
    D. The Status of Spiritual People Is Authenticated by Love (13:1–13)
    E. The Proper Function of Grace-Gifts in Public Worship (14:1–25)
    F. In Public Worship All Activity Must Build Up the Church (14:26–40)

Main Idea

Spiritual people are those who possess the Holy Spirit and are thus enabled to affirm the total lordship of Christ. They must recognize their dependence on one another as the body of Christ, and each must build up the body of Christ as they employ the grace-gifts given them by the Spirit.

Translation

(See pages 524–25.)

Structure

In 12:1–3 Paul returns to the matter of knowledge and what the Corinthians must "know." Accepting the lordship of Christ indicates the presence of the Holy Spirit in a person's life and so reveals all such people to be "spiritual" people. A second section addresses the diversity of grace-gifts received as the Spirit apportions them (vv. 4–11). The repetition seen in the phrases "the same Spirit" (vv. 4, 9, 11), "the same Lord" (v. 5), and "the same God" (v. 6) reminds the reader that every Christian is blessed by God and enriched with grace-gifts in the same way. The gifts may differ, but that is because the Spirit allocates them as he wills (v. 11), with a view toward the edification of God's people (v. 7). In a third section (vv. 12–26), Paul speaks explicitly to the way in which gifts are to be used by all Christians to build up the body of Christ so that each member may care for the others and there may be no division among them. He argues for a mutual interdependence that must hold the body together. In a fourth and final section (vv. 27–31), Paul's focus is on the nature of the body of Christ, which must be understood if people are to understand the right and proper function of the gifts of the Spirit.

1 Corinthians 12:1–31

1a	Topic introduction	Now	concerning spiritual people, brothers [and sisters],
b	Desire		**I do not want you to be unaware.**
2a	Assertion		**You know that when you were pagans you were led astray** to mute idols,
b	Circumstance		however you were led.
3a		Therefore,	
b	Assertion		**I want to make known to you**
c	Confession		that no one speaking in the Spirit of God says, "Jesus is accursed,"
d	Confession		and no one can say, "Jesus is Lord,"
e	Means		except by the Holy Spirit.

4a	Assertion 1	Now **there are**	**different allocations of grace-gifts,** but
b	Assertion/source 2		**the same Spirit;**
5a	Series (1)	and **there are**	**different allocations of serving,** but
b	Series (2)		**the same Lord,**
6a	Series (1)	and **there are**	**different allocations of workings** but
b	Series (2)		**the same God**
c	Description		who works all things in all people.

7a	Assertion	Now	**to each one is given the manifestation of the Spirit**
b	Advantage		for the benefit [of all].

8a	Examples ...	For	to one **is given** a word of wisdom
b	Means		through the Holy Spirit, and
c	Series		to another a word of knowledge
d	Means		according to the same Spirit,
9a	Series		to another faith
b	Means		by the same Spirit,
c	Series		to another grace-gifts of healings
d	Means		by the one Spirit,
10a	Series		to another works of power,
b	Series		to another prophecy,
c	Series		to another the judging of spirits,
d	Series		to another [various] kinds of tongues, and
e	Series		to another the interpretation of tongues.

11a	Assertion	Now	**all these are empowered**
b	Agency		by the one and the same Spirit,
c	Expansion		who allocates to each one ↵ individually just as he wills.

Continued on next page.

Continued from previous page.

12a	Analogy (for vv. 4–11)	**For just as**
b	Assertion	**the body is one and**
c	List	**has many members, and**
d	List	**all the members of the body, being many, are one,**
e	Assertion	**so also is Christ.**
	Basis	For indeed
13a	Sphere	in one Spirit
b	Assertion	**we were all baptized into one body,**
c	Expansion	whether Jews or Greeks or slaves or free,
d	Assertion	and **all were made to drink of one Spirit.**
		For indeed
14a	Assertion	**the body is not one member** but
b	Contrast	**[is] many.**
15a	Illustrations ... condition	If the foot should say,
b	Direct speech	"Because I am not a hand I am not [a part of] the body,"
c	Rhetorical question	**is it for that reason not [a part of] the body?**
16a	Series of rhetorical questions	And
		if the ear says,
b		"Because I am not an eye, I am not [a part of] the body,"
c		**is it for that reason not [a part of] the body?**
17a	Series	If the whole body were an eye,
b	Rhetorical question	**where would be the hearing?**
c	Series	If the whole body were the hearing,
d	Rhetorical question	**where would be the sense of smell?**
		Now in fact
18a	Assertion	**God arranged the members,**
b	Expansion	each one of them,
c	Location	in the body
d	Manner	just as he willed.

19a	Rhetorical question	But if all were a single member,
b		**where would the body be?**
20a		Yet in fact
b	Assertion	**[there are]** **many members,** but
		one body.

21a	Illustration	Now **the eye cannot say to the hand,**
b	Content	"I do not have need of you,"
c	Restatement	nor again **the head to the feet**
d		"I do not have need of you."

22a	Contrast	On the contrary, even more,
b	Assertion	**the parts of the body that seem to be weaker are indispensable,**
23a	Assertion	and the members of the body
b	Description	that we suppose to be less honorable,
c		on these **we place the greater honor,**
d	Restatement	and **our unpresentable parts are given greater modesty,**
24a	Expansion	[of which] our more presentable ↺
		parts have no need.
		Rather,
b	Assertion	**God has composed the body,**
c	Expansion	giving greater honor to [the part] that feels it lacks it,
25a	Purpose (negative)	so that there may be no division in the body, but
b	Purpose (positive)	that the members may have the same care for one another.
		And
26a	Condition (protasis)	if one member suffers,
b	Assertion (apodosis)	**all the members suffer together;**
d	Condition	if one member is honored,
e	Assertion	**all rejoice together.**

27a	Summary	Now **you are the body of Christ** and
b	Restatement	individually members of it.

28a	Assertion	And **God has appointed in the church**
b	List	first apostles,
c	List	secondly prophets and thirdly teachers,
d	List	then [powerful] works,
e	List	then grace-gifts of healing,
f	List	helpful deeds, administrative supervision, [various] kinds of tongues.

29a	Rhetorical questions	**Are all apostles? Are all prophets? Are all teachers? Do all do powerful works?**
30a	Series	**Do all have grace-gifts of healing? Do all speak with tongues? Do all interpret?**
31a	Summary	Now **you are earnestly desiring the greater grace-gifts.**
b	Conclusion/ bridge to ch. 13	And **I am showing you a still more excellent way.**

Exegetical Outline

VIII. **Status, Public Worship, Freedom, and Grace-Gifts (11:2–14:40)**

    A. The Conduct of Husbands and Wives in Public Worship (11:2–16)

    B. The Conduct of the Church at the Lord's Supper (11:17–34)

➡   C. **Spiritual People and the Function of Their Grace-Gifts in the Church (12:1–31)**

        1. **Spiritual People Affirm Christ's Lordship (12:1–3)**

        2. **Spiritual People Receive Grace-Gifts as the Spirit Apportions (12:4–11)**

        3. **Spiritual People Use Grace-Gifts to Build Up the Body of Christ (12:12–26)**

           a. All Are Members of the One Body (12:12–14)

           b. All Are Necessary to the Body (12:15–16)

           c. All Depend on Others in the Body (12:17–21)

           d. All Must Care for Each Other (12:22–26)

        4. **Spiritual People Must Know Their Place in the Body of Christ (12:27–31)**

Explanation of the Text

12:1 Now concerning spiritual people, brothers [and sisters], I do not want you to be unaware (Περὶ δὲ τῶν πνευματικῶν, ἀδελφοί, οὐ θέλω ὑμᾶς ἀγνοεῖν). Again Paul begins a section of his epistle by referring to the letter the Corinthians had written to him. Now he addresses their concerns about the identification of spiritual people. The introductory words "now concerning" (περὶ δέ) appear on six occasions in the epistle (7:1, 25; 8:1; 12:1; 16:1, 12; cf. 8:4) and, in most cases, indicate the apostle is taking up issues identified by both parties as matters of concern. However, unlike 7:1 and 8:1 there is no quotation from the Corinthian letter. Though this is a new section, it quickly becomes evident that it has close links with the recent sections addressing aspects of corporate worship. Furthermore, it also relates closely to what Paul wrote about "spiritual matters" and "spiritual people" in 2:13–16. (See comments there for the discussion about what the word "spiritual" [πνευματικός] means for Paul in this letter.) As in 2:13 the first thing to be determined is whether Paul is speaking of "spiritual matters," perhaps the gifts of the

Spirit or other matters, or of "spiritual people." The substantival adjective (πνευματικός) can be either masculine or neuter. Most translations have opted for the neuter, and so they either translate as "spiritual *gifts*" (AV, RSV, TEV, NIV, NASB), or refer simply to "*gifts* of the Spirit" (REB, NJB).

The arguments for believing that here Paul addresses *gifts* rather than *people* are several, not least the fact that the apostle clearly begins a section on spiritual gifts in v. 4. However, there the word used is "grace-gifts" (χαρίσματα), a word also used earlier in the epistle (cf. 1:7 and 7:7). Elsewhere in his writings Paul usually uses the word "spiritual" of *things* that are spiritual, such as "the law" (Rom 7:14), the blessings that the Gentiles now inherit (Rom 15:27), and God's general blessings (Eph 1:3; cf. also Eph 5:19 and Col 3:16: "spiritual" songs). But in Galatians 6:1 where the word is again used as a substantive, Paul writes "you who are spiritual" (ESV).

Notably, in 2:15, 3:1, and 14:37 Paul speaks of spiritual people, and in the light of these verses and of the epistle as a whole, it is likely that here too he in fact refers to *people*.[1] Part of the problem, as chapters 2–3 indicated so clearly, is that people who think they are spiritual (the elitists) are not discerning spiritual *things*, including the grace-gifts, properly. In the more significant and immediate context of chapters 12–14, 12:2–3 goes on to speak of *people* in their spiritual beliefs and actions. Verse 3 has to do with coming to understand who the true spiritual *person* is and what, guided by the Spirit, he or she says about Jesus.[2] At the end of this section in 14:37, Paul returns to the question of spiritual *people*: "If someone thinks he is . . . spiritual." Since Paul is about to talk of the grace-gifts, it seems logical that he would start by speaking of "spiritual people" who are the only ones who can properly "discern" and "judge" them (see comments on 2:14–15). The question of just who is "spiritual" remains a dominant theme as it has in various ways throughout the epistle. Furthermore, chapter 14 is about *people* with certain gifts and how those people should act with due consideration for the nature of worship and others in the congregation. Chapter 13 speaks directly to the need for the mature Christian *person* to exhibit love and to consider this as more important than the grace-gifts, however wonderful they may be.

Since in this chapter Paul's teaching is also aimed largely at elitists who have not had proper concern for others in the church, the litotes "I do not want you to be ignorant" carries the same force that we noted when it was used in 10:1. Again there is a certain irony here, given that the spiritual people in Corinth believe they "know" (8:2)! Paul now turns to making known to them (v. 3; γνωρίζω ὑμῖν) the

difference between the pagan and the Christian influenced by the Spirit.

12:2–3 You know that when you were pagans you were led astray to mute idols, however you were led. Therefore, I want to make known to you that no one speaking in the Spirit of God says, "Jesus is accursed," and no one can say, "Jesus is Lord," except by the Holy Spirit (Οἴδατε ὅτι ὅτε ἔθνη ἦτε πρὸς τὰ εἴδωλα τὰ ἄφωνα ὡς ἂν ἤγεσθε ἀπαγόμενοι. διὸ γνωρίζω ὑμῖν ὅτι οὐδεὶς ἐν πνεύματι θεοῦ λαλῶν λέγει, Ἀνάθεμα Ἰησοῦς, καὶ οὐδεὶς δύναται εἰπεῖν, Κύριος Ἰησοῦς, εἰ μὴ ἐν πνεύματι ἁγίῳ). As Paul's discussion proceeds, he highlights the contrast between pagan spiritual identity, which is tied up with mute idols, and Christian spiritual identity, which depends upon the presence of the Holy Spirit and the recognition of Christ as Lord.

The sentence structure of v. 2 is complex with a missing finite verb. The Greek text reads, "When you were pagans being led astray to mute idols however you were led." Ellipsis is a relatively common feature with Greek participle constructions. Here it seems most natural to assume a second "you were." The repeated action of being led stray is emphasized in the Greek with the combination of the imperfect passive tense ("you were led"; ἤγεσθε) and the particle (ἄν).[3] To understand these opening verses better they need to be held together. Especially this is true of vv. 2 and 3, which many commentaries seem to separate from each other in a way that hides the progression of argument. Thus, before looking at alternative interpretations or at the language Paul uses, it is useful to see what

---

1. Schmithals, *Gnosticism in Corinth*, 172, translates 12:1 as "concerning the Pneumatics." However, though he is correct in identifying Paul's argument as being against the elitists who value "knowledge" as a marker "that distinguished them from the other members of the community," he argues, wrongly, that they are gnostics. See Introduction.

2. As discussed in 2:13–15, the word "spiritual," whether applied to people or things, has to do with the work of the Spirit and points specifically to *Jesus*.

3. Robertson, *Grammar of the Greek New Testament*, 974.

we believe the three verses *together* are saying and where Paul is leading the reader.

First, it is notable that each verse of vv. 1–3 is united by the theme of "knowing." Paul does not want them "to be unaware" (v. 1; ἀγνοεῖν). He states "you know" (v. 2; οἴδατε) and then says, "I want to make known to you" (v. 3; γνωρίζω ὑμῖν). There is a progression here. Starting with mild irony, Paul speaks to those who think they know all about what it is to be a "spiritual" person and says, "I do not want you to be unaware." He moves on to say something obvious about their past that they "know," before insisting that they need to "know" something more. The knowledge in all three verses has to do with the overriding theme of "spiritual people" and what defines them. Some in the community, as we have seen, believe that spiritual people are defined by their possession of various grace-gifts and have become arrogant and come to see themselves as somehow spiritually superior to others. However, as Paul has already argued in chapters 2 and 8, this is not the function of such gifts. Paul now wants them to "know" what does define spiritual people. Because it is not the grace-gifts, he will then go on from 12:4 to discuss the true purpose of the grace-gifts, a theme that he continues right through chapters 13 and 14.

So what is the content of Paul's argument? In v. 2 Paul addresses those with a specifically pagan background. They "know" the background they came from. They know its spiritual forms and activities since they used to worship idols. Paul is not telling them anything of which they were not already thoroughly aware. Definitions matter. What distinguished them as pagans was that they were led to "mute idols" (τὰ εἴδωλα τὰ ἄφωνα). They were led astray wherever that worship might lead. The point is obvious and simple, but is something they truly "know." Their pagan "spirituality" (though Paul never uses that word of either Chris-

tian or pagan activity) was defined for them by the spiritual powers that led them (astray) to idols. This is what gave them their pagan identity. These idols neither spoke to them nor gave them words to speak.

"Therefore" (v. 3; διό), Paul says, you (also) need to "know" what truly defines a spiritual person. The answer is that he or she is one who speaks "by the Spirit of God" (ἐν πνεύματι θεοῦ), and such people are the only ones who affirm "Jesus is Lord" (Κύριος Ἰησοῦς). The emphasis on this early acclamation, perhaps used in baptism settings, is highly suitable because it is an identification of "Jesus" as the covenant "Lord" and as the one who is to be obeyed and who has enabled his people to participate in his community. Significantly, then, Paul insists that this great acclamation can *only be made* by a person who speaks "in the Holy Spirit" (see further below). While others may say, "Jesus is accursed," no person led by the Holy Spirit ever will! Thus, by definition, spiritual people (i.e., Spirit-led people) are those who can make the basic faith declaration of submission to the covenant Lord. Conclusion: that means *all* Christians! For this reason, there can be no elite group. No group is more led "by the Spirit" than any other part of the Christian community, for the final evidence of spiritual status is the declaration of faithful covenant commitment itself. Suggestions of different levels of spiritual status between Christians are nonsense.

Having taken an overview of what it appears these verses are saying, it is important to note that much has been written on what Paul may have in mind here when he talks of being "led astray" and of "mute" (ἄφωνα) idols. The repetitive nature of their being led astray suggests that their common experience was to turn in their paganism to their idols for help. But these idols were "mute." Here Paul likely draws on an Old Testament view of idols and the gods they are supposed to represent. For example, Habakkuk 2:18 says, "What profit is an idol . . . ? For its maker trusts in his own creation when he makes speechless idols!" (ESV).[4] This is what defined them as pagans, that they were led to their gods who, as Paul notes, could offer no help or words of assistance. Their whole spiritual existence was bound up with deception!

However, some have suggested that Paul's emphasis on them being "mute" is a reference to the ecstatic experiences of some cult worshippers in the paganism of the day. Thus Fee writes: "Most likely, therefore, he is reminding them of what they well know, that in some of the cults 'inspired utterances' were part of the worship, despite the 'mute idols.'" Fee goes on to argue that this provides evidence for Paul that "'inspired utterances' in themselves are no sure guarantee that one is speaking by the Spirit."[5] However, there is nothing in the text to suggest that Paul has in mind these ecstatic experiences unless v. 3a is read in that way. The passive voice of the pagans "being led" does not require that they were being led into some trance or other experience that resulted in verbal, supernatural manifestations. Indeed, as Grudem has shown, the suggestion that the participle "carried away" (ἀπαγόμενοι) means being carried away in ecstatic experiences has "no support at all in the other uses of the word." Rather, it simply refers to travel *to* a point, and so Paul is saying that, as pagans, they were "under strong compulsion to attend idol temples."[6]

Though differing from Grudem, Terence Paige

has also argued that there is no sense here of being "led astray *by*" idols. Paul simply says that they were led *to* idols and that the "language of v. 2 evokes the image of a cultic festival procession."[7] Citing a number of ancient sources, he suggests these processions normally wound their way through the public streets, ending at the idol temple and with worship. Thus he argues that Paul writes here of the way, when they were pagans, they were led (through the streets) "to the images." The processions themselves became symbols of power within the pagan society. Paige concludes with a translation that does not require the insertion of another finite verb: "Whenever you were led [in the processions] you were [really] being carried away captive." Verse 2 is thus a reminder to the Corinthians that they were enslaved in their former life. Paul then proceeds in the rest of chapters 12–14 to explain "what it is to be really 'led' by God."[8] Attractive and innovative as this reading of the text is, it hinges too much on details that are not at all evident in the text. Moreover, in the following verses Paul does not build on a contrast between pagan enslavement and Christian freedom. He is making a point about what it is to be a "*spiritual* person."

The meaning of "Jesus is accursed" (taking the word ἀνάθεμα as a pronouncement) has also been much discussed. Thiselton delineates *twelve* different ways of understanding the words and what Paul intends here in v. 3![9] Here we touch on just a couple. Some, taking the view that Paul introduced the subject of pagan ecstatic speech in v. 2, suggest

4. Cf. Baruch 6:41 (Ep Jer 41): "If they shall see one dumb [idol] that cannot speak, they bring him, and intreat Bel that he may speak, as though he were able to understand" (Lancelot C. L. Brenton, *The Septuagint with Apocrypha: Greek and English* [London: Samuel Bagster & Sons, 1851; repr., Grand Rapids: Zondervan, 1993], 129 [Apocrypha section]). The whole of Baruch 6 (Ep Jer) is an extended polemic against the uselessness of idols.

5. Fee, *1 Corinthians*, 640. Also Conzelmann, *1 Corinthians*,

206; Weiss, *Der erste Korintherbrief*, 295–97; James D. G. Dunn, *1 Corinthians*, New Testament Guides (Sheffield: Sheffield Academic Press, 1995), 80–81.

6. Wayne A. Grudem, *The Gift of Prophecy in 1 Corinthians* (Washington, DC: University Press of America, 1982), 164.

7. Terence Paige, "1 Corinthians 12:2: A Pagan Pompe?" *JSNT* 44 (1991): 57–65.

8. Ibid., 64.

9. Thiselton, *1 Corinthians*, 918–27.

that under the influence of idols or demons people sometimes would pronounce curses on Jesus.[10]

Others have suggested that Paul here creates a hypothetical situation. It is said that no one actually said "Jesus be cursed." Imperial requests for Christians to curse Jesus (such as those referenced in Pliny's letters to Trajan) are anachronistic. Such persecution had not broken out at this time. The suggestions that some gnostic ecstatics might have cursed Jesus in the flesh are also utterly speculative and, anyway, would also be thoroughly anachronistic. Hays summarizes his view, writing that "Paul is simply using this dramatic fiction of cursing Jesus to emphasize that those who are inspired by the Holy Spirit will speak and act in ways that glorify the Lordship of Jesus."[11]

Still others have suggested that Paul has in mind unconverted *Jewish* people at this point. Having spoken of pagans, here he speaks of Jews, and then he speaks of Christians. This is argued on the grounds that pagans would have been most unlikely to curse Jesus, if they even knew who he was! Nevertheless, the apostle Paul's own personal history reveals the hatred of traditional Judaism at that time for those who would follow the Messiah (Acts 26:10–11). This they considered blasphemy, as Paul had done. Taking the clause not as an imprecation ("Jesus be cursed") but as a statement ("Jesus is cursed") would fit with the Jewish analysis of the (blasphemous) claims that Jesus is the Messiah.[12]

In our view, the clause "Jesus is accursed" (ἀνάθεμα Ἰησοῦς) must be understood in the light of the Christian confession "Jesus is Lord" that, in various forms, is so frequently seen in the New Tes-

tament and was clearly part and parcel of the identification of true Christians (cf. 8:6; Rom 10:9; Phil 2:9–11). It is *submission* to the lordship of Jesus that is key. Paul has made this clear in many ways through the epistle, but especially as he has contrasted this lordship with the activity and worship of demons in chapters 8 and 10. Any explanations of v. 2 that avoid the *compulsion* to follow idols implicit in the passive voice of "being led away" easily miss the contrast between v. 2 and v. 3 and fail to do justice to Paul's insistence that those who eat with idols "covenantally participate" with them (10:20). To follow another lord is to curse Jesus.

Paul may be posing a hypothetical exclamation in that it does seem hard to imagine even pagans, before becoming Christians, exclaiming "Jesus is accursed." Why he should suddenly be speaking of unconverted Jewish exclamations at this point is unclear, even if the word *anathema* itself probably has a Jewish background as Paul uses it. On the other hand, whether some pagans in some situations actually said it in so many words or not, the situation was one that would have rung true to converted pagans. In being specifically led to idols, they were led to another lord and so were turning their back on the true Lord. Only those who are led by the Spirit of the true God will say "Jesus is Lord." More importantly, especially given the examples of the wilderness generation in chapter 10, it is they alone who will *live* as submissive subjects to the covenant Lord. "Spiritual people" are all those who acknowledge Jesus as the (covenant) Lord and live this out in their daily life. This is something that Paul wants to make sure they "know." They know about their pagan background, but about this they cannot and

---

10. Chrysostom, *Homilies on First Corinthians*, homily 29.3, says that a person doing this was a "soothsayer." See Dunn, *1 Corinthians*, 80–81; Héring, *First Corinthians*, 125.

11. Hays, *First Corinthians*, 209. See also Jouette M. Bassler, "1 Cor 12:3: Curse and Confession in Context," *JBL* 101 (1982): 415–18.

12. Bengel, *Gnomon of the New Testament*, 293; Robertson and Plummer, *First Corinthians*, 261; Moffatt, *First Corinthians*, 179; Garland, *1 Corinthians*, 570–71.

must not remain uninformed. For the elitist "know-ers" who have been differentiating people by virtue of their gifts into the "spirituals" and not so spiritual, this is a serious challenge indeed.

Since it is only the person "led" by God and by his Spirit who can be defined as a "spiritual person," Paul will now build on this with the repeated, similar phrases "the same Spirit," "the same Lord," "the same God." But he will also make clear what has been implicit in these opening verses, namely, that *all* Christians experience the working and enabling of the Spirit of God within them, and so they cannot be distinguished in terms of their level of spirituality. Paul does this in the section that follows by reference to the God "who empowers them all in *everyone*" and his insistence that "to each" is given some working of the Holy Spirit.

Since we have suggested that the Corinthians had emphasized the gifts of wisdom and knowledge, it is noteworthy that these are, once again, the first two mentioned in a lengthy list starting at v. 8.

12:4–6 Now there are different allocations of grace-gifts, but the same Spirit; and there are different allocations of serving, but the same Lord, and there are different allocations of workings but the same God who works all things in all people (Διαιρέσεις δὲ χαρισμάτων εἰσίν, τὸ δὲ αὐτὸ πνεῦμα· καὶ διαιρέσεις διακονιῶν εἰσιν, καὶ ὁ αὐτὸς κύριος· καὶ διαιρέσεις ἐνεργημάτων εἰσίν, ὁ δὲ αὐτὸς θεός, ὁ ἐνεργῶν τὰ πάντα ἐν πᾶσιν). With the elitist group among the Corinthian Christians emphasizing specific gifts of the Spirit, notably those of wisdom and knowledge, in this section Paul is determined to make sure they know two important yet definitely related truths about the gifts. He will develop what he has already introduced, that *all* have gifts from the Spirit and so they cannot

be used to differentiate between Christians regarding spiritual status. Then, since they do not prove status, it is important for the Corinthians to be aware of the true purpose of the grace-gifts. Thus this section is not all about ecstatic verbal gifts, as some suggest. Nor is it primarily about prophecy or speaking in tongues, for they both are just an obvious example of the two main issues that Paul is addressing—that status is not differentiated by gifts and the *function* of the gifts must be understood properly. The *function* is laid out again clearly in v. 7, as Paul insists that though the gifts given by God to his people differ, *everyone* who is a Christian receives from him "for the benefit [of all]" (v. 7; πρὸς τὸ συμφέρον).

Paul insists three times here that there are "different allocations" (διαίρεσις) of grace-gifts given by God to his people. Immediately this emphasis on different allocations is a humbling challenge to the elite, who value a few gifts above others. The gifts of knowledge or wisdom, or even of tongues and prophecy, may seem grand and indicative of some superior spiritual status, but there are "varieties," "varieties," "varieties." The translation "varieties" is used by some versions (e.g., RSV, NRSV, ESV). This catches the connotation of the word (διαιρέσεις) relating to the differences between gifts, a point Paul will build on later. The NIV has "different kinds." However, this does not capture the sense of *God apportioning* the variety of gifts. For this reason we have translated the word as "different allocations." Others have sought to convey the same idea in a number of ways. Robertson and Plummer have spoken of "various distributions" and Thiselton of "different apportionings," which, as he says, seems stilted.[13] Garland has spoken of "allotments."[14] The meaning of the word (διαίρεσις) is helpfully further defined in v. 11 where the related verb is used and

---

13. Robertson and Plummer, *First Corinthians*, 258; Thiselton, *1 Corinthians*, 929.

14. Garland, *1 Corinthians*, 574–76. For the modern British reader, this may have unhelpful connotations.

Paul writes that "the same Spirit . . . apportions/distributes [διαιρέω] to each one."[15]

The structure is clear. It carefully emphasizes the *variety* of allocated gifts with each verse beginning with the word ("different allocations"). But the repetitious ending (the same Spirit/Lord/God) shows that Paul's point is only properly to be understood in the *combination* of God and his different allocations.

The Corinthians must understand that in the midst of a discussion of status, *God* gives and he allocates *differently*. The word "grace-gifts" (χαρίσματα) was defined at 1:7. The word contains within it the idea of gifting by "grace." "Serving" comes from the word sometimes translated as "ministries" (διακονία). Because it is plural, Paul has in mind the activity of serving, of which there are many different forms. Since "ministry" is often used in a more specific sense in church circles today, it is perhaps best to avoid the word here. Finally, the word "workings" is used (ἐνέργηματα). We might translate this as "what makes things happen." Many different things are effected by people in the life of the church.

It is important, though, not to make much of a distinction between the three types of gifts or services or workings. The distinction is simply a rhetorical device to ensure that the multiplicity of the different, gracious workings of God among his people is well understood. The second part of the structure of each verse centers on what we may call the trinitarian aspect of these grace-gifts. It is "the same Spirit," "the same Lord," and "the same God." Again, it is important not to imagine here that Paul implies the Spirit gives one set of gifts, the Lord another, and God a third. The overall point is that God is the source and gives gifts to all who are his. Nevertheless, a cautious differentiation of the sort

offered by Blomberg may be correct. He writes, "Paul elucidates spiritual gifts from three different angles: They are bestowed freely by the Spirit's grace (v. 4), are intended to be used in a Christ-like attitude of servanthood (v. 5), and are the result of God's powerful working in a person's life (v. 6)."[16]

Finally, at the end of v. 6 Paul adds about God that he is the one "who works all things in all people" (ὁ ἐνεργῶν τὰ πάντα ἐν πᾶσιν). God is the source of all the spiritual activity that goes on in the community of his church, and he empowers everyone. No one is left out. All have something to rejoice in and content with as they are given gifts by God to serve and honor him. At the end of the day, this recognition that all comes from God and is of his grace is a complete and full reminder of why Paul made that key statement early on in this epistle: "Let the one who boasts, boast in the Lord" (1 Cor 1:31; cf. 3:21; 4:7).

12:7 Now to each one is given the manifestation of the Spirit for the benefit [of all] (ἑκάστῳ δὲ δίδοται ἡ φανέρωσις τοῦ πνεύματος πρὸς τὸ συμφέρον). Paul has established that all Christians are "spiritual" on two grounds: (1) all proclaim that Jesus is Lord and can only do so "by the Holy Spirit," and (2) all are given different gifts by the same Spirit, that is, by God. Paul will move on to examine these different gifts, but for now he must return briefly to the second matter, that is, the purpose of the gifts. If they are provided to all Christians and are not given for the sake of indicating degrees of spirituality or status, then what are they given for? This verse offers a full answer that will be developed in detail as chapters 12–14 progress.

Gifts are given for the good of the community, that is, to build up the people of God. Here Paul uses a fourth word to follow "grace-gifts" (v. 4), "serving" (v. 5), and "workings" (v. 6). "The man-

---

15. See BDAG 229.   16. Blomberg, *1 Corinthians*, 243.

ifestation" (ἡ φανέρωσις) is, as Fitzmyer notes, "important, for Paul is not speaking only of the internal gifts of the Spirit but of the *external* signs of the presence and activity of the Spirit within the community."[17] The genitive "of the Spirit" (τοῦ πνεύματος) could be subjective or objective, and it is not possible to be sure here. Thus it could mean that the gift each person receives manifests or reveals the Spirit (objective) or it could mean that the Spirit manifests or distributes to each (subjective; cf. v. 11b). Possibly the latter is more likely in this context. "The manifestation" comes from the Spirit and is a broad summary word for the gifts and workings of the Spirit to which Paul has been referring.

The word "benefit" (τὸ συμφέρον) was first used in this epistle in 6:12 (see more detailed comments there). The idea of a spiritual advantage and benefit for people has been a strong theme throughout the epistle (cf. comments also on 10:23, 33). For Paul it is the determining factor for judging whether a person is "spiritual." It is the way of manifesting "love," the true marker of a person's spiritual standing (see ch. 13). This verse thus speaks to the question of the *purpose* of the grace-gifts within the community. The idea of "benefit" or "advantage" clearly has to do with bringing benefit to the whole church of God and so is almost synonymous with the other metaphor that Paul uses for this, which is "building up" the community. This is also developed in the chapters that follow. For example, it provides the basis for his discussion of the relative values of the gift of "prophecy" and of "tongues" in chapter 14.

We have added "of all" to the Greek to indicate the implied recipients of the benefit that comes from the workings of God's Spirit through his people. (The συμ- of συμφέρω points to the word's general meaning of "bringing together.") Some translations have rendered it "for the common good" (NASB, NRSV, ESV, NIV), but this is, perhaps, rather too impersonal both for the common use of the verb itself and for what Paul is saying here.

12:8 For to one is given a word of wisdom through the Holy Spirit, and to another a word of knowledge according to the same Spirit (ᾧ μὲν γὰρ διὰ τοῦ πνεύματος δίδοται λόγος σοφίας, ἄλλῳ δὲ λόγος γνώσεως κατὰ τὸ αὐτὸ πνεῦμα). Paul now illustrates his point about how the Spirit works among God's people by referring to different grace-gifts. The variety of these gifts is truly significant, and Paul does not imply at all that this list is exhaustive. Those in the modern church who have tried to see some list here that might define a group of so-called "charismatic" gifts have missed the point of what Paul is saying. It is precisely the *variety* of the different workings of the Spirit among *all* God's people that he now stresses with his repeated use of the words "to one . . . to another . . . to another." At the end of the list in v. 11 there is again a reminder that these grace-gifts, whatever they may be, are entirely allocated at the disposal of the Spirit, but he does allocate "to each one" (ἑκάστῳ). The fact that Paul then moves straight into a discussion of the "body" and how each member is needed is a further indication that Paul teaches that "all"—that is, each individual Christian—receive "a manifestation" of the Spirit, though not all receive the same one.

It is equally alien to Paul's thinking to speak of "supernatural gifts" or of the "miraculous" (as opposed to non-miraculous) gifts.[18] This is a legacy

---

17. Fitzmyer, *1 Corinthians*, 406 (emphasis added).

18. This is common practice in both "charismatic" circles and more "cessationist" circles. Thus, some cessationists argue that it is the "supernatural" or "miraculous" gifts that died out after the apostolic era. They propose various theological arguments for this, but the point here is simply that it is those

of Greek dualistic thinking that is unhelpful when seeking to understand how Paul (and Scriptures generally) thinks of God's gifts. Some gifts may well be thought of as more "extraordinary" than others, but *all* come from God. Indeed, the words of C. F. D. Moule remind us of the dangers of examining biblical texts with a dualistic worldview that sees the regularity of the material world to be decisive in determining that which God does "miraculously" and in a supernatural manner, and that which occurs naturally but under his general guidance. He writes, "If the ultimate *locus* of consistency is in the realm of the personal—in the character of a God who 'cannot deny himself'—then what is (in our present conditions) unusual need not be ultimately an intervention or an irruption or a dislocation or suspension of natural law: it need only be what normally happens—indeed what is bound to happen—on the rare and 'abnormal' occasions when a right relationship is achieved in the family of God."[19] While some gifts are self-evidently more conspicuous than others, and there is good reason to believe that these are what Paul chooses to refer to in this first list in vv. 8–12, they are not to be seen as qualitatively different from any other "manifestation" of the Spirit, some of which may be quiet, unseen, or less exceptional in the common way of seeing things. In Romans 12:3–8 this becomes quite clear where among the grace-gifts

(χαρίσματα) we find "acts of mercy" and "generosity" sitting side by side with "prophecy" (ESV).

In vv. 8–12 Paul is not interested in explaining what each gift might look like when used in the gathered, worshipping community, though there has been a great amount written about the nature of each gift mentioned.[20] Below we make only general comments about the different gifts since to do much more than this is usually to go beyond what the text says and certainly goes beyond Paul's intention in this text. However, many different attempts have been made to show, in these verses, a structure to Paul's list of the gifts. Some have suggested that there is a movement from gifts of teaching (words of wisdom, and knowledge) through "miraculous" gifts (faith, healing miracles) to inspired speech (prophecy, discernment, tongues and their interpretation). Carson cautiously suggests that the only useful distinction *might* be made on the basis of the change in the Greek terms for "another," a division suggested by Robertson and Plummer. Thus, when "another" (ἕτερος) is used it may introduce a new grouping of gifts. But, wisely, Carson concludes: "On balance it is best to treat the gifts one by one."[21]

"For" (γάρ) at the start of the verse indicates this follows from the previous verse where "to each . . . is given." Now Paul gives his illustration of the sort of gifts given "to each." First, in these four

that meet the criteria of being regarded as "miraculous" or "supernatural" that are the gifts they dispute arise in the modern church. They do not argue for the cessation of gifts such as teaching, preaching, or hospitality or administration. For example, see B. B. Warfield, *Counterfeit Miracles* (New York: Charles Scribner, 1918); cf. Kistemaker, *First Corinthians*, 421–22. Some charismatic theologians also argue for seemingly similar distinctions. Indeed, in some circles of popular charismatic worship there is a deliberate seeking after the "supernatural gifts" as evidence of a specific "blessing" of the Spirit. Often speaking in tongues is given an especially high profile in this. See, for example, G. Arekion, *The Power of Praying in Tongues: Unleashing the Supernatural Dimension in You* (Citta

Sant' Angelo, Italy: Evangelista Media, 2010).

19. C. F. D. Moule, ed., *Miracles: Cambridge Studies in Their Philosophy and History* (London: A. R. Mowbray, 1965), 16–17; see also the excursus on "The Vocabulary of the Miracle," 235–38.

20. See, for example, Arnold Bittlinger, *Gifts and Graces: A Commentary on I Corinthians 12–14*, trans. Herbert Klassen (London: Hodder & Stoughton, 1967), 27–53; also J. D. G. Dunn, *Jesus and the Spirit: A Study of the Religious and Charismatic Experience of Jesus and the First Christians as Reflected in the New Testament* (Philadelphia: Westminster, 1975), 199–258.

21. Carson, *Showing the Spirit*, 37.

verses Paul continues to insist on the Holy Spirit as the source and provider of these gifts, again specifically mentioning his activity three times in vv. 8–9 and summarizing it in v. 11. It is likely that the change of prepositions is simply stylistic ("through the Spirit"—διὰ τοῦ πνεύματος; "according to the Spirit"—κατὰ τὸ αὐτὸ πνεῦμα; "in the Spirit"—ἐν τῷ . . . πνεύματι). As we noted back in 1:4–7, Paul may have a problem with the way the elitists let the gifts of the Spirit *function* among them, but nowhere does Paul deny that "wisdom" or "knowledge" or any other highly visible gift is sourced from or enabled by the Spirit. Indeed, he specifically "thanks God" that these gifts have so "enriched" them (1:5). The Spirit is at work, Paul says.

Word of wisdom/knowledge. The first and second grace-gifts mentioned are "word of wisdom" (λόγος σοφίας) and "word of knowledge" (λόγος γνώσεως). "Word" in this context refers to the communication of the wisdom or knowledge that the person has received from the Lord. Thus, the NRSV translates as "utterance of wisdom" and "utterance of knowledge." In light of the epistle so far, it seems that these two gifts do not appear first because they are more significant than any other. That would be to contradict what Paul is seeking to teach. However, they are the two gifts that were obviously of great significance for the Corinthian elitists. Paul notes "knowledge" as his main example of their enrichment in his introduction. Yet the contrast between true and false "wisdom" also figures prominently in his introduction (1:17, 19; 1:21–2:13). Paul deliberately says that he has come to them "not with wisdom of speech [οὐκ ἐν σοφίᾳ λόγου] lest the cross of Christ should be made of no effect" (1:17). In 2:1 he also says, "I . . . did not come to you with loftiness of speech or wisdom" (οὐ καθ᾿ ὑπεροχὴν λόγου ἢ σοφίας καταγγέλλων ὑμῖν). In 2:5 he has argued that their faith was

not to be based "in the wisdom of men" (ἐν σοφίᾳ ἀνθρώπων).

The gift of "knowledge," as we have seen, has again become the focus through chapter 8 and into chapter 10. (See specific comments on the gift, its function, and its nature in the comments on 8:1–2.) In chapter 13 it is one of the specific gifts contrasted with "love." Probably, therefore, Paul first mentions the two gifts that have surfaced previously as points of discussion in this epistle and that have proved to be the most important for the prideful Corinthians. But the list of gifts itself demonstrates that they are but examples of a number of many diverse gifts that God's Spirit gives to his people.

Paul's use of "word of wisdom/knowledge" may signify that the gift was some public statement made to the church by the recipient of the gift that came from a specific, spontaneous work of the Spirit. The assumption by many commentators is that this is the case. Of course, the possibility of a prepared "word" must not be ruled out. It was probably a word (from God) that spoke to the immediate needs of the church, applying ideas or theology to a specific, required action by the people. We suggested earlier that it was perhaps by a "word of knowledge" (in that case a deficient one) that the elite were arguing for attendance at idol temples because "an idol is nothing" (8:4). One way or another both this and words of "wisdom" were most unlikely to be theoretical theology. Jewish wisdom literature is deeply practical and down-to-earth, and it is likely that words of knowledge and wisdom were also. They may well have been gifts in which the Spirit enabled the recipients to have deeper insights into Scripture itself. Certainly it seems people were expected to *do* something after hearing them. This was precisely the problem because the weak were thus being "built up" to go to idol temples! For Paul, there could be both good and bad knowledge and wisdom. There was the "wisdom of men" and of "this age" (2:5–6), and there was a "wisdom of God" (2:7). The need for "judging" and "discernment" is part of what it is to be "spiritual," as Paul has shown. Yet as Paul speaks in 12:8–11, he clearly assumes the wise or knowledgeable words spoken by church members are given by the Spirit. Here he assumes the best about the content, but he is more concerned that no one or two gifts are seen as more important, that all gifts come from God, and that all must build up his people. In the end we would be hard pressed, given the evidence from the epistle, to determine any real difference between "knowledge" and "wisdom."

12:9 to another faith by the same Spirit, to another grace-gifts of healings by the one Spirit (ἑτέρῳ πίστις ἐν τῷ αὐτῷ πνεύματι, ἄλλῳ δὲ χαρίσματα ἰαμάτων ἐν τῷ ἑνὶ πνεύματι). Though saving faith was clearly regarded by Paul as a gracious gift from God, it seems this is not what he refers to here.[22]

Faith. First Corinthians 13:2 helps define the word "faith" (πίστις) in this context of God's gifts— "faith, *so as to remove mountains.*" This probably draws upon Jesus's own words in Mark 11:23–24 where faith is directly linked with prayer: "Truly, I say to you, whoever says to this mountain, 'Be taken up and thrown into the sea,' and does not doubt in his heart, but believes that what he says will come to pass, it will be done for him. Therefore I tell you, whatever you ask in prayer, believe that you have received it, and it will be yours" (ESV). Carson writes of this gift, "It appears to be the God-given ability . . . to believe what you really do not believe, to trust God for a certain blessing *not* promised in Scripture—exactly as in the well-known case of George Muller of Bristol."[23] Dunn

suggests that Paul may have in mind "that mysterious surge of confidence which sometimes arises within a man in a particular situation of need or challenge and which gives him an otherly certainty and assurance that God is about to act through a word."[24]

Healings. As many note, "grace-gifts of healings" seem closely related to "faith." James 5:15 says, "The prayer offered in faith will make the sick person well; the Lord will raise them up." However, it is vital in the modern church to recognize that the gift is given to the one who will heal, and so it must be as we relate "faith" to this grace-gift. This is not a matter of the one who needs healing simply possessing enough "faith"! This gift probably relates to an individual being influenced by the Spirit on a specific occasion to pray for or lay hands on an individual in a manner that results in God's healing of that person. The apostles saw this happening from time to time in their ministry in various ways (cf. Acts 4:30), and of course it was a feature of Jesus's own ministry. This gift is mentioned again in vv. 28 and 30, and it always appears in the plural. Dunn is probably correct when he says of this gift, "The charisma is not a healing power which is effective for all (sorts of) illnesses; it is *the actual healing itself*."[25] It is certainly important to note that these gifts may be given to one person or to another, but this does not mean that someone who has experienced such a grace-gift is therefore a "healer."

12:10 to another works of power, to another prophecy, to another the judging of spirits, to another [various] kinds of tongues, and to another the interpretation of tongues (ἄλλῳ δὲ ἐνεργήματα δυνάμεων, ἄλλῳ [δὲ] προφητεία, ἄλλῳ

---

22. Cf. 1 Cor 6:11; Rom 8:9; Gal 3:2–5. For the role of the Spirit in conversion in Paul's writings, see Fee, *God's Empowering Presence*, 853–60; also Ridderbos, *Paul*, 226–28, 233–35.

23. Carson, *Showing the Spirit*, 38–39.
24. Dunn, *Jesus and the Spirit*, 211.
25. Ibid., 211 (emphasis original).

[δὲ] διακρίσεις πνευμάτων, ἑτέρῳ γένη γλωσσῶν, ἄλλῳ δὲ ἑρμηνεία γλωσσῶν).

Works of power. "Works of power" (ἐνεργήματα δυνάμεων) is another gift in the same vein as "faith" and "healings." It concerns someone receiving a grace-gift that produces a "work of power," that is, a work that is beyond what is normally expected, whether in "removing mountains" (13:2) or in healings. This category may simply be a "catchall" for those occasions when the Spirit gifts a person to be able to work in a way that is unexpected for the glory of God in the community. "Healings" may be assumed here, but this gift may have included, for example, exorcisms or even special discernments of the needs of others. Again, we see what these might look like in the work of the apostles (Acts 19:11; cf. Gal 3:5). Calvin comments, "I am however inclined to think that it is the power which is exercised against demons, and also hypocrites. Thus when Christ and the apostles authoritatively subdued demons or put them to flight, that was ἐνέργημα, effective working . . . and when Peter caused Ananias and Sapphira to fall dead upon the ground simply by speaking to them." He then notes a contrast: "The gifts of healing and miracles are both channels of God's goodness to us; but in His severity He uses miracles for the destruction of Satan."[26]

Our translation above is more literal than that seen in many versions where we read "working of *miracles*" (AV, RSV, NJB) or "*miraculous* powers" (NIV). The potential problem with the concept of "miracle" is its modern connotation. Broadly speaking, in the biblical worldview God is at work always in everything, but sometimes he works with "works of power," that is, he works in ways he does not normally work. The modern concept of "miracle" is much more closely related to the dualistic idea mentioned above that, for once, God has intervened in the regular course of life in a "supernatural" way. Moule's work on "the Vocabulary of Miracle"[27] provides a salutary reminder of how rare this sense of God's working is in the New Testament, if indeed it is ever present. The usual words for what could be called a "miracle" are either "(work of) power" (δύναμις) or "sign" (σημεῖον), the latter especially in John's Gospel (e.g., John 2:11). The occasional use of "wonders" or "portents" (τέρατα) appears, but only in the plural and only accompanied by the word "signs" (e.g., Acts 2:43). For the modern church, so invaded by a dualistic way of thinking in which the normal events of day-to-day life have little to do with God while the occasional, amazing experiences of so-called "answered" prayer or healings in the church are what "God has done," it is good to be reminded that God is *always* at work in the midst of his people. This is true even if sometimes, through his grace-gifts, his people see him working with "power" among them. Such powerful workings of God were part of what Paul expected as God's Spirit worked his grace-gifts among them.

Prophecy. "Prophecy" (προφητεία) is examined in more detail in 14:1ff.[28] In recent years much has been written on this gift,[29] mainly as it has become more prominent in charismatic churches. This is a verbal gift used in the gathered congregation. As we discover in more detail in chapter 14, while it is unlikely (usually) to be entirely spontaneous, its purpose is to build up the congregation through

---

26. Calvin, *First Corinthians*, 262–63.

27. Moule, *Miracles*, 235–38.

28. See a summary in comments at 14:1.

29. For extensive examinations of this phenomenon in Scripture and in the early church, see Dunn, *Jesus and the Spirit*, 170–76, 227–33; David E. Aune, *Prophecy in Early Christianity and the Ancient Mediterranean World* (Grand Rapids: Eerdmans, 1983); Grudem, *Gift of Prophecy in the New Testament*; Fee, *God's Empowering Presence*; Turner, *Holy Spirit and Spiritual Gifts*, 185–220, 315–28.

words of encouragement and consolation (14:3). This probably involved the direct application to the congregation of Scriptures relating to God's plan of salvation and his will for his church, in ways that would inform and edify Christians seeking to follow the Lord. Paul insists that it be exercised with due consideration of discipline. At least *functionally* in some modern worship, prophecy is granted the same or even greater status than Scripture. It is important to be clear as we read chapter 14 that there is not even a hint that prophecy replaces Scripture or that it is to be regarded as on the same level with Scripture in terms of inspiration. Indeed, it must, as with all the gifts, be tested against Scripture. As we have seen, this is part of what Paul means by "discernment" or "judging" things and so being truly "spiritual." In the light of chapter 14 we would agree with Grudem that, contrary to some popular theologies, "the primary function of prophecy is not guidance or prediction."[30]

Judging spirits. "Judging spirits" (διακρίσεις πνευμάτων) probably has to do with a gift of evaluation or discernment of spiritual activity. Once again, a fundamental theme of the epistle is encountered, namely, the right "spiritual" assessment of things and people. Of all the gifts, we may imagine Paul desiring more of this one at Corinth! The sort of question answered by those with this gift might be along the lines of "is this prophecy in line with Scripture?" or "is this false teaching or prophecy?" (cf. 1 Thess 5:20–21; 2 Thess. 2:1–2) or "is this truly a Spirit-given word of knowledge or wisdom or is it simply someone's (well-intentioned?) own thoughts?" The result of such evaluation and judgment might then lead to the denunciation of the false teacher. It should be added, though, that this gift is probably *not* what Paul refers to in 14:29

when he writes, "Let two or three prophets speak, and let the others judge," even though the same Greek verb is used in both places.

The gift may go further than this and involve judgments as to whether a person is demon possessed, thus asking the question, "Is this of the Lord or is this demonic activity?" Then the gift might lead on to the decision that exorcism is required. Thiselton's caution here, though, should be noted as he points out that if the word "spirits" means "evil spirits" this would be exceptional in Paul's writings since he never uses the word "spirit" or "spirits" of evil spirits.[31]

Kinds of tongues. "[Various] kinds of tongues" (γένη γλωσσῶν) is examined in detail in the comments on 14:2ff. and 14:10–11. This gift is, of course, always directed *to God* himself as part of a person's praise or prayer. This is still true even if the gift is used with interpretation in the gathered congregation (cf. 14:13 and 16–17). The communication with God is delivered in sounds or a language that cannot normally be understood. Three possible understandings of the nature of these tongues are discussed at 14:4.[32] These are, *first, "tongues" as the language of angels; second, "tongues" as real languages that are foreign to the one who speaks; third, "tongues" as some form of ecstatic speech.*

Interpretation of tongues. "The interpretation of tongues" (ἑρμηνεία γλωσσῶν) is a gift that does just what it says. Thiselton defines it as the "intelligible articulation of tongues-speech."[33] In the exegesis below of 14:5, it would seem that normally it is the same individual who has spoken in tongues who is expected to interpret. In other words, it is unnecessary to assume that different people are required to interpret from those who speak in tongues. On the

---

30. Grudem, *Gift of Prophecy in the New Testament*, 212.

31. Thiselton, *1 Corinthians*, 966 (though see 2 Thess 2:2 as a possible exception).

32. See at 14:4, "In Depth: What Was Paul's Attitude to 'Speaking in a Tongue' and What Is the Phenomenon?"

33. Thiselton, *1 Corinthians*, 970.

other hand, "to another" (ἄλλῳ) certainly implies that these gifts may be received separately.

12:11 Now all these are empowered by the one and the same Spirit, who allocates to each one individually just as he wills (πάντα δὲ ταῦτα ἐνεργεῖ τὸ ἓν καὶ τὸ αὐτὸ πνεῦμα, διαιροῦν ἰδίᾳ ἑκάστῳ καθὼς βούλεται). This concise summary verse draws out each aspect of Paul's argument. "All these" (πάντα) refers to all the gifts he has mentioned and, no doubt, others left unmentioned. This stands opposed to the Corinthian elitists, who have emphasized, at best, one or two gifts as indicating a spiritually superior status, which they therefore believe all should seek after.

These gifts are all "worked" by or "empowered by" (ἐνεργέω) the "one and the same Spirit" and are allocated of the Spirit's own volition (cf. v. 18). That he gives "to each one individually" (ἰδίᾳ ἑκάστῳ) also stands opposed to the elite who, *as a group*, believe they have received some special gifts that put them on a different plain. In the light of this it is absurd for them to take pride in a particular gift or to flaunt their prowess in knowledge or wisdom. Such gifting does not lie in their individual ability or in their level of "spiritual" maturity. Indeed, in order to discern "spiritual *people*" (12:1), the true working of the Holy Spirit must first be discerned.

12:12 For just as the body is one and has many members, and all the members of the body, being many, are one, so also is Christ (Καθάπερ γὰρ τὸ σῶμα ἕν ἐστιν καὶ μέλη πολλὰ ἔχει, πάντα δὲ τὰ μέλη τοῦ σώματος πολλὰ ὄντα ἕν ἐστιν σῶμα, οὕτως καὶ ὁ Χριστός). Paul now advances an extended metaphor (vv. 12–26) for the church that he describes as a human body. The intention of the metaphor is to demonstrate that every member of the church is vital and that the church will not function properly when one or more members are ignored or regarded as less useful or less valuable. The unity of the physical body, in which each part serves a different but important function, becomes a picture of how the body of the church ought to function and view its members. Once again, it provides Paul with another way of tackling the whole question of the elitism among some that has been based upon certain grace-gifts. The emphasis of v. 11 that the Spirit allocates these gifts "as he wills" (καθὼς βούλεται) is taken up again in v. 18 where it is "God" who has arranged the members of the body "as he chose" (καθὼς ἠθέλησεν). "For" (γάρ) indicates that he is offering a further explanation of the last section (vv. 4–11). God determines what the body looks like, how it functions, and the place of each person within it. Because of this, no one can view another as greater or lesser.

The metaphor itself was introduced, though not in detail, in 6:15–17 (see comments there). As he develops the picture here, though, it has more in common with 10:17 where Paul had talked of the unity of the covenant community as the "many [who] are one body," and the "one bread" of the Lord's Supper that pictures this. (The "body" of 11:29 does not refer to the church community, *pace* Fee. See comments at 11:29.) Calvin makes the point that the body metaphor would have been reasonably well known to the apostle from its use in the political sphere of his day. He says, "When Menenius Agrippa wanted to reconcile the Roman people to the senate, against whom they were rebelling, he told a fable, which bore some resemblance to what Paul is teaching here. But the situation is entirely different in the case of Christians, for they do not constitute a mere *body*-politic, but are the spiritual and mystical body of Christ, as Paul himself adds."[34]

---

34. Calvin, *First Corinthians*, 264. The account of how this Roman consul quelled a rebellion by using an illustration of the close relatedness and mutual dependence of the parts of the body can be read in Livy, *History of Rome* 2:32. But Calvin is

The "members" (τὰ μέλη) of the body are its constituent parts as the next verses make clear, thus feet, hands, ears, etc. It has "many" members, but together they make up "the body." The clause, "so also is Christ" (οὕτως καὶ ὁ Χριστός), is opaque, though its meaning becomes clear as Paul's argument progresses. Simply, as v. 27 indicates, it is an abbreviation for "the body of Christ," which is the church. As the body has many members but is one body, so it is with the church, the body of Christ.

As Hays comments, the question of whether Paul here presses "beyond mere analogy to make an ontological equation of the church with Christ" has been the subject of much discussion and debate.[35] From Schweitzer to Bultmann to Robinson to Stacey to Jewett, Gundry, and others, extended discussions that center on how Paul views this corporate entity that he calls the "body of Christ" have proliferated. Does Paul see some "mystical" concept of Christ's body revealed in the church? Does Paul look to the resurrected Christ as *in fact* the Christian community? Does baptism bring into being the body of Christ or bring people into a body that is preexistent? Such studies become exercises in seeking to understand Paul's anthropology, eschatology, and even ecclesiology and go far beyond the scope of this commentary.[36]

So, in these verses we encounter a fascinating metaphor that illustrates the way God has designed and brought into being a people who *together* become *his* society in which he dwells and that lives for his glory and to reflect him to the world. It is a body where, precisely in the grace-gifts that each individual employs for the benefit of the community, we find the *Spirit* working for the benefit of the Lord's covenant community. Thus, as Calvin correctly noted, "the case is different" from simply another group of comrades or a socio-political meeting of minds.

12:13 For indeed in one Spirit we were all baptized into one body, whether Jews or Greeks or slaves or free, and all were made to drink of one Spirit (καὶ γὰρ ἐν ἑνὶ πνεύματι ἡμεῖς πάντες εἰς ἓν σῶμα ἐβαπτίσθημεν, εἴτε Ἰουδαῖοι εἴτε Ἕλληνες εἴτε δοῦλοι εἴτε ἐλεύθεροι, καὶ πάντες ἓν πνεῦμα ἐποτίσθημεν). "For indeed" (καὶ γάρ; also in v. 14) has an intensifying force; thus what follows explains what has gone before. The basis of the *unity* of the body lies in the "one Spirit." Paul has repeatedly talked of "the same Spirit" in the preceding verses. This emphasis on the work of the Spirit remains vital to the argument. The question concerns "spiritual people" (12:1), and this means

---

right to say that with Paul "the case is different"! One of many roughly comparable examples is to be found in the works of Dio Chrysostom, *Orations* 1.32: "For whatever is the number of comrades one has acquired, so many are the eyes with which he can see what he wishes, so many are the ears . . . so many are the minds. . . . Indeed, it is exactly as if a god had given him, along with his one body, a multitude of souls all full of concern in his behalf" (also 3:104–7). For further illustrations from the ancients and detailed discussion about the likely and unlikely parallels between their usage and Paul's usage of the metaphor, see Mitchell, *Rhetoric of Reconciliation*, 159–64. On the "body of Christ" and specially its ethical significance and relationship to Greco-Roman ideas, see Yung Suk Kim, *Christ's Body in Corinth: The Politics of a Metaphor* (Minneapolis: Fortress, 2008).

35. Hays, *First Corinthians*, 213.

36. For those wishing to examine this aspect of Paul's general theological understanding of "personhood" and how the "body" fits into this, the literature is vast. Useful introductions are found in the articles on "Body" (by L. J. Kreitzer) and "Body of Christ" (R. Y. K. Fung) in *Dictionary of Paul and his Letters*, 71–82. One of the most extended treatises on the subject suggests that Paul develops his view of the person largely by responding to gnostic, Hellenistic opponents. See Robert Jewett, *Paul's Anthropological Terms: A Study of Their Use in Conflict Settings*, AGJU 10 (Leiden: Brill, 1971); see also Gundry, *SOMA in Biblical Theology*, and David Stacey, *The Pauline View of Man in Relation to Its Judaic and Hellenistic Background* (London: Macmillan, 1956). See also Michelle V. Lee, *Paul, the Stoics, and the Body of Christ*, SNTSMS 137 (Cambridge: Cambridge University Press, 2006).

discerning the work of the Holy Spirit among God's people. However, a number of exegetical questions that arise here must briefly be addressed.

The meaning of "in one Spirit" (ἐν ἑνὶ πνεύματι) may be locative (NRSV, ASV, REB) or instrumental. It could mean that the baptism into one body in which all have shared took place *by* the Spirit (AV, RSV, NIV, TEV, NASB).[37] However, as Carson notes, nowhere else in the New Testament is the Spirit the *agent* of baptism. Normally the "Spirit is the medium or sphere *in* which we are baptized." In discussions of baptism, he notes, it is the *medium* of the baptism that is expressed, using the preposition "in." The examples of baptism in water, fire, and cloud are noted.[38] Furthermore, it must be asked whether the verb "baptized" itself is a metaphor here referring to the incorporation of Christians *into* the body of Christ generally (namely, at conversion) or whether it refers to the water ceremony specifically. (The reference in the second half of the verse to "drinking" of one Spirit suggests to some that water baptism is what is in mind.) Some see little or no difference between these two possibilities. For them, water baptism is to be linked with conversion, at which time the Spirit comes upon the individual and he or she is incorporated into the church. Calvin, writing on this verse, says that Paul is teaching about the nature of (water) baptism that connects us with Christ's body: "However, so that no one might suppose that this is effected by the outward symbol, Paul adds that it is the work of the Holy Spirit."[39] Others see a clear distinction between this (metaphorical) Spirit baptism and water baptism. For them, baptism in the Spirit refers to regeneration and the incorporation of believers into the church. Water baptism may provide the analogy, but that is not what Paul is speaking of here. Still others see two sacraments represented in this one verse: baptism in the clause "baptized into one body" and the Lord's Supper in the clause "drink of one Spirit." In the end, there is not much in the text to make it clear which of these alternatives was in Paul's mind. We return later to the importance for this verse of Paul's analogical use of "baptism" as community entrance in 10:2.

However, taking "in the Spirit" to refer to the sphere of the Spirit in which people find themselves immersed and allied to the covenant community and seeing the triple emphasis in the verse on "one" (one Spirit, one body, one Spirit), reminds us that all are, to put it colloquially, "in the same place." All believers are "spiritual" people by virtue of being found in the realm of the Spirit and living under his special influence within the community of the church. Being part of the body of Christ is to move into the realm of the Spirit through the work of the Spirit, who draws people to God and to the Lord. "Baptism" is thus more likely simply by metonymy to be a reference to entering the church of Christ. The church is the sphere of the gracious, special working of the Holy Spirit for God's people. "Drinking of the same Spirit" probably indicates the common experience of all Christians of the enjoyment, refreshment, and abundant blessings or grace-gifts that the Spirit bestows on *all* the people of God. However, we should note that the two passive aorists, "were baptized" (ἐβαπτίσθημεν) and "were made to drink" (ἐποτίσθημεν) do not allow for seeing the "drinking" as a separate (later) event after conversion, as some modern charismatics have suggested.

It is interesting that though a few commentators mention 10:2–4 in passing, the links between what Paul says here and in chapter 10 remain largely

---

37. Among others, see Moffat, *First Corinthians*, 186; Oscar Cullmann, *Baptism in the New Testament*, trans. J. K. S. Reid, SBT 1 (London: SCM, 1952), 30.

38. Carson, *Showing the Spirit*, 47. See also Dunn, *Baptism in the Holy Spirit*, 127–29.

39. Calvin, *First Corinthians*, 265.

undeveloped. The main difference is Paul's move to the first-person plural in 12:13, but the former pas-

> and all were baptized into Moses
> in the cloud
> and all drank the same spiritual drink

We noted that being "baptized into Moses" described Israel's entrance into the covenant and its allegiance to the Lord (by analogy with baptized into Christ). "In the cloud" spoke of the active presence of God in the nation-forming event and his continuing protection of them. Drinking the same "spiritual drink" referred to *all* Israelites drinking of water in the wilderness that was given as a gift of the Holy Spirit (for details, see comments at 10:2–4). Now in 12:13 we would suggest something quite similar is being said. The earlier example of the wilderness generation was used negatively. Its teaching purpose was that though *all* were part of the covenant community and the presence of God in the cloud brought them into being as a separate people and *all* received the Spirit's gifts for their good, yet many rebelled and were judged. In 12:13, however, it is no longer an illustration and is now used positively. The Corinthian believers were baptized "into one body," that is, they all became part of the single covenant community of Christ. "In one Spirit" speaks of the active presence of the Spirit in the community-forming event but especially of his continuing protection of them, for they remain in his sphere. They are *all* caused to drink of one Spirit, that is, they enjoy the gifts that God gives them for their spiritual sustenance. Thus, the drinking of the Spirit, we believe, ties back well to how Paul viewed the water gift in the wilderness

sage can help elucidate this one here. The parallels may be seen like this:

> all were baptized into one body
> in one Spirit
> all were made to drink of one Spirit.

where the people "drank from the rock . . . and the rock was Christ" and to the Spirit's work in that provision for the Israelites.[40] One further point may be made. The passive (ἐποτίσθημεν) is rightly translated "made to drink." In its most common use in the LXX it refers to flocks and land that are "watered" in the sense of being given to drink. (The passive voice of the verb only appears in Gen 13:10 and Ezek 32:6.)

In summary, Paul thinks again of the community-forming nature of the Spirit's work into which *all* were brought at their conversion, since this happened through the Spirit's active presence. All also were given to drink of the blessings of the Spirit, namely, the grace-gifts that are the matter Paul addresses here. The passive voices remind us again it is all of the Spirit and not because of the work of "spiritual" individuals. Mention of "Jews or Greeks or slaves or free" once more stresses that all are in this together and that no one has been left out if they are "in the one Spirit." No one is better than another, nor is there any hierarchy of people or gifts.

12:14 For indeed the body is not one member but [is] many (καὶ γὰρ τὸ σῶμα οὐκ ἔστιν ἓν μέλος ἀλλὰ πολλά). As in v. 13, "for indeed" continues the explanation of v. 12. Paul now develops the analogy from the body, applying it to the church, the body of Christ. To say that this analogy allows Paul *first* to emphasize *diversity*, before later

---

40. Note that the Greek verb ποτίζω is used in Num 20:8 where water pours forth from the rock, so Paul himself would easily have related drinking water from the rock with the Spirit (as in 1 Cor 10:4). The link with Isa 29:10 (LXX) and the Lord making a rebellious people drink the "spirit of sleep" is far-fetched. Whatever the vision in Isaiah 29 means, it is not the Holy Spirit of which they drink (*pace* Carson, *Showing the Spirit*, 46).

stressing mutual *dependence*, is correct at one level. However, the overarching picture is more subtle. Paul's point is that each member cannot exist at all when it is separated from the body *and* that the body loses its functionality when members are cut off from it. The message of this verse summarizes this overview by insisting that the body "is not one member" but "[*is*] many [members]" (cf. AV, NASB). To say that it does not "consist of one member" (NRSV, ESV) or "is not made up of only one part" (TEV) does not quite convey the totality of the body in its essence. Without its members, there is no body.

12:15–17 If the foot should say, "Because I am not a hand I am not [a part of] the body," is it for that reason not [a part of] the body?[41] **And if the ear says, "Because I am not an eye, I am not [a part of] the body," is it for that reason not [a part of] the body? If the whole body were an eye, where would be the hearing? If the whole body were the hearing, where would be the sense of smell?** (ἐὰν εἴπῃ ὁ πούς, Ὅτι οὐκ εἰμὶ χείρ, οὐκ εἰμὶ ἐκ τοῦ σώματος, οὐ παρὰ τοῦτο οὐκ ἔστιν ἐκ τοῦ σώματος· καὶ ἐὰν εἴπῃ τὸ οὖς, Ὅτι οὐκ εἰμὶ ὀφθαλμός, οὐκ εἰμὶ ἐκ τοῦ σώματος, οὐ παρὰ τοῦτο οὐκ ἔστιν ἐκ τοῦ σώματος· εἰ ὅλον τὸ σῶμα ὀφθαλμός, ποῦ ἡ ἀκοή; εἰ ὅλον ἀκοή, ποῦ ἡ ὄσφρησις;). Paul now offers a clear encouragement to those who think they are left out or are lacking in their self-awareness and self-confidence as constituent members of the church. They are truly part of the body, whatever may be said. The third-class condition using an aorist subjunctive offers a hypothetical situation with the apodosis in the form of a rhetorical question. The phrase "for that reason" (παρὰ τοῦτο)[42] refers to the hypothetical point of

the apodosis. Paul's intent is to make it clear that simply because the foot might say it is not part of the body does not make the statement true. The foot can say that it is not a hand, but it is still part of the body. Under pressure from the elitists, some may feel like or even say that they do not possess the grace-gifts the elitists have and that they therefore do not belong. Yet the fact of the matter is that they *are* part of the body. Whatever the strong may imply about others or whatever the weak may feel about themselves, all *are* the body. Verse 16 repeats the same point as v. 15 but changes the body parts to ear and eye.

This leads in v. 17 to Paul beginning to apply the picture by referring to the functions of the last two examples, the eye and the ear. The body would not be a body if it only had one member, the eye, and so was all about seeing but had no hearing or smell, etc. This again functions to encourage those who lack self-awareness as community members and to humble those who see themselves as the most necessary or superior ones. Especially in the light of vv. 23–24 below, it is a tortuous argument here (*pace* Fee) to say that there is no indication that one person (or organ of the body) is thinking he or she is inferior or superior to the other.[43] Paul's insistence that all persons are needed for the body to function clearly answers a setting in which some are excluded or exclude themselves on the grounds of how they feel about their status.

12:18 Now in fact God arranged the members, each one of them, in the body just as he willed (νυνὶ δὲ ὁ θεὸς ἔθετο τὰ μέλη, ἓν ἕκαστον αὐτῶν, ἐν τῷ σώματι καθὼς ἠθέλησεν). Paul continues his application of the analogy. Each member's part in the body is determined by God. When Paul says,

---

41. We take this as a question, following the punctuation of NA[28].

42. Moule, *Idiom Book of New Testament Greek*, 51, com-

ments that the meaning of παρὰ τοῦτο is similar to ἐν τούτῳ of 4:4, and suggests the translation "for that reason."

43. Fee, *1 Corinthians*, 676.

"Now in fact,"[44] it is almost as though he decides to answer his own rhetorical questions. He will not allow any confusion over what he is saying in this whole section. God has arranged the parts of the body "as he willed." This translation seeks to make it clear that Paul is not just speaking of something God wanted to happen (all things being equal) but that in his sovereignty he "willed into being" (cf. 4:19; Jas 4:15). In this sense, it takes the reader back again to the emphasis that the whole way the body functions and what part different people play in the body is entirely due to God. In v. 6 Paul had said that all gifts are empowered by God and given by the Spirit (v. 8). In v. 11 the Spirit had allocated "as he wills" and empowered them all. Here again the members [of the body] have been arranged by God "as he willed" (ἠθέλησεν). While diversity in the body seems to be the main focus of this verse, once again that is far from all that Paul is saying as the argument builds. The picture as Paul applies it here says rather more. Paul is indicating that the body itself is brought into being and designed with its many members as *one* body. This is God's church, and this is the way he chose to build the body. The logic of the next verse carries this forward.

12:19–20 But if all were a single member, where would the body be? Yet in fact [there are] many members, but one body (εἰ δὲ ἦν τὰ πάντα ἓν μέλος, ποῦ τὸ σῶμα; νῦν δὲ πολλὰ μὲν μέλη, ἓν δὲ σῶμα). Paul's concern in the midst of his desire for understanding diversity is for the *body*. The body itself, as God has designed it, would not be a body if all were an eye or ear or whatever. In terms of the gifts, the body would not truly be the body that God has designed and brought into being if a member finds that membership is narrowed down to those possessing only one or two gifts. In putting

it this way, of course, we need to remember that Paul is not at all implying this is like membership in some club! He is talking about body parts, each of which enables the body to be fit for purpose, to function coherently, and to be the body God willed. Therefore, there is indeed diversity, but the focus is on the one body that God has brought into being (v. 20).

12:21 Now the eye cannot say to the hand, "I do not have need of you," nor again the head to the feet "I do not have need of you." (οὐ δύναται δὲ ὁ ὀφθαλμὸς εἰπεῖν τῇ χειρί, Χρείαν σου οὐκ ἔχω, ἢ πάλιν ἡ κεφαλὴ τοῖς ποσίν, Χρείαν ὑμῶν οὐκ ἔχω). On the one hand, this summary sentence chastises the elite who think they have arrived and boast of their wisdom and knowledge and perhaps other gifts of the Spirit. Their gifts are something to thank God for and in God's providence enrich the community (1:4–5), but they cannot be allowed to define the body. The body is defined only as the single unit God has intended the church to be by all its members working *together* as they should. Yet the verse perhaps primarily serves as an encouragement to those who feel insecure in their self-awareness as God's people. They need to hear the apostle say, in effect, "*It really does not matter what anyone else says; no part of the body can legitimately say it does not need you, for the body is only a body when you are part of it!*" It has been noted by some that the order in which Paul puts these examples is from the superior or uppermost member in the body to the lower; so eye to hand, and head to feet. That the next verse (v. 22) starts with a strong adversative, "on the contrary," and then speaks of the weaker and less honorable parts might give this idea some substance. It is clear Paul thinks of the elite disparaging the so-called weak,

---

44. The νυνί introduces the real situation following the hypothetical example (BDAG 682).

but whether it was his intention to further show this by the order in which he cites the body parts may be rather far-fetched.

It is important to note that throughout Paul continues to address "spiritual people" (12:1), not "spiritual gifts." Though there is much, as we have noted throughout the epistle, that suggests the gifts of the Spirit were being used in the appeal to elite status, the analogy is not about the gifts themselves but remains about the people. It is people who make up the body parts in this analogy and continue to do so, as Paul takes it still further. No one in the church has the right to say to any other person that he or she is not needed. In fact, the spiritual person is the one who recognizes the truth of what Paul is saying and recognizes him or herself to be a vital part of the body, but no more significant than any other member. Paul now makes this even clearer.

12:22–24a On the contrary, even more, the parts of the body that seem to be weaker are indispensable, and the members of the body that we suppose to be less honorable, on these we place the greater honor, and our unpresentable parts are given greater modesty, [of which] our more presentable parts have no need (ἀλλὰ πολλῷ μᾶλλον τὰ δοκοῦντα μέλη τοῦ σώματος ἀσθενέστερα ὑπάρχειν ἀναγκαῖά ἐστιν, καὶ ἃ δοκοῦμεν ἀτιμότερα εἶναι τοῦ σώματος, τούτοις τιμὴν περισσοτέραν περιτίθεμεν, καὶ τὰ ἀσχήμονα ἡμῶν εὐσχημοσύνην περισσοτέραν ἔχει, τὰ δὲ εὐσχήμονα ἡμῶν οὐ χρείαν ἔχει). Though Paul somewhat changes the picture now, it follows on naturally from the illustration he has been using. Here he compares those parts of the body *to which attention is drawn* with those to which attention is not drawn. This is the point of the word "presentable" (εὐσχήμων). In fact, the word is virtually synonymous with "honorable" but

with emphasis on what is public and visible. Thus, in Acts 13:50 we read of women of "high standing" (εὐσχήμονας), and Plutarch can describe a woman of "honorable estate" (εὐσχημόνων).[45] Paul contrasts this in v. 23 with the "modesty" of less honorable and "unpresentable" (ἀσχήμων) parts that are nevertheless also entirely necessary. The word "unpresentable" refers to that which is not worth looking at. It becomes clear that Paul is thinking of the genital area, which, as all know, functions in a variety of utterly essential ways. (Of note is that the word is used of illicit sexual activity in LXX Gen 34:7; Deut 24:1). The fact is that those parts of the body that seem "weaker" only "seem" to be so since they are actually indispensable. "On the contrary" (ἀλλά) is a strong adversative. "Even more" (πολλῷ μᾶλλον) is not translated in various translations (including RSV, TEV, NIV, and NRSV). But Paul uses the phrase to indicate a strengthening of his argument. A paraphrase might run: "We can go *even further than* what we have just said and say that the parts of the body. . . ."

This is another challenge to those who would outwardly flaunt and boast about their gifts. Just as with the body, where some members are noted and would even *seem* to be more "honorable" while some vital organs are hardly ever mentioned and are always covered up, so it is in the body of Christ. Those who *seem* to be less honorable, who are not often mentioned or talked about, who never flaunt themselves are, in fact, indispensable to the body if it is to be a body at all!

The meaning of "weaker" (ἀσθενέστερα) has been provided by the epistle as a whole. It is not about physical weakness but primarily about the flaunting of and claims of community status and spiritual superiority. It is about understanding or not understanding the purposes of God and his

---

45. *Moralia* 4.309.15 (LCL).

will in bringing into being the body of the church. In the end, it is to understand that the way of the cross, the way of Christ, is the way of the church as God willed it. Paul has used this comparison of "strength" and "weakness" in 4:9–10. There, with great irony he spoke to the elitists, calling them "wise" and contrasting them with himself and the apostles who were "fools" for Christ. He continued, "We are weak, but you are strong. You are held in honor, but we are dishonored" (v. 10).

It has been said that perhaps Paul wants his readers to deduce that the body could do without a hand but not without the genitals. But that seems to be stretching the picture too far and to undermine the overall teaching. Paul is not saying and has not said that any gift is unnecessary. Nor does he imply that because the "weaker" parts are "indispensable" that the other parts are not also indispensable. He has problems with those who flaunt knowledge and wisdom. Perhaps he has problems with the way some of the other gifts, like speaking in tongues, are used, but never once does he suggest that any person's gift is not needed. Rather, his point throughout is that each person has a gift and each person is needed if the body is to be the body because, as Paul goes on to say, *that's how God made it to be.*

12:24b–25 Rather, God has composed the body, giving greater honor to [the part] that feels it lacks it,[46] so that there may be no division in the body, but that the members may have the same care for one another (ἀλλὰ ὁ θεὸς συνεκέρασεν τὸ σῶμα τῷ ὑστερουμένῳ περισσοτέραν δοὺς τιμήν, ἵνα μὴ ᾖ σχίσμα ἐν τῷ σώματι, ἀλλὰ τὸ αὐτὸ ὑπὲρ ἀλλήλων μεριμνῶσιν τὰ μέλη). Paul returns to the fact that this is the way *God* put things together.

He has composed the body. Thus the church, like the physical body, is his creation. He can choose to make one part prominent and one not so, but the body cannot be divided on these grounds. The verb "compose" (συγκεράννυμι) may remind us in English of an orchestra in which all instruments are needed for the piece of music to be complete. The Greek word means "to effect a harmonious unit"[47] or to "mingle together" (cf. LXX Dan 2:43; 2 Macc 15:39).

Two purpose clauses round out Paul's definitive point that this is the way *God* designed things to be. The first expresses the negative, and the second a positive comparison. God did it this way "so that there may be no division" (ἵνα μὴ ᾖ σχίσμα) and that the members "may have the same care for one another" (τὸ αὐτὸ ὑπὲρ ἀλλήλων μεριμνῶσιν). The present active subjunctives indicate the enduring nature of this aspect of the body and what it was created for. Both clauses pick up on what has been said in many places through the epistle even as they specifically apply the body metaphor to the Corinthians. Paul has been concerned by one division in the church or another ever since 1:10–13. He has also been concerned to ensure that those whose actions seem to be dividing the church should realize that everything they do should be "building up" others in the church and for their "benefit." The divisive behavior characterizes those who, in Paul's eyes, are *not* "spiritual," even if they think they are. The behavior of caring for each other characterizes "spiritual people" in that it has to do with building people up. The verb translated "caring" (μεριμνάω) is normally used by Paul to mean "be anxious for" (cf. 7:32–34). Generally the verb connotes rather more urgency than the English word "care for."

---

46. We follow NA[28] in taking the middle voice ὑστερουμένῳ instead of the active ὑστεροῦντι. Thiselton, *1 Corinthians*, 1010, is surely correct in saying that this middle voice is significant "since Paul speaks of those who *feel inferior* or *feel* lacking; not

of those who *are* inferior, which would contradict his argument" (emphases original).

47. BDAG 951–52.

The TEV uses "concern for," which may capture this better (cf. Phil 2:20). The behavior that entails being concerned for the building up and caring of other members will be summed up in 13:1 with the word "love," as it was in 8:1.

12:26 And if one member suffers, all the members suffer together; if one member is honored, all rejoice together (καὶ εἴτε πάσχει ἓν μέλος, συμπάσχει πάντα τὰ μέλη· εἴτε δοξάζεται ἓν μέλος, συγχαίρει πάντα τὰ μέλη). Here Paul expands the point about members having "the same" deep concern for each other. This is what it will look like in a body where this is happening: when one suffers, all suffer, and when one is honored, all rejoice. A true covenant community where all "participate" is being described here. The individual members are so involved with one another that they react as one to what goes on in their midst. They identify with each other. This, of course, is far from what is actually happening in the church, whether at the Lord's Supper where the rich have no concern for what is happening to the poor or as the elitists altogether ignore and look down on those who do not share their particular grace-gifts.

12:27 Now you are the body of Christ and individually members of it (Ὑμεῖς δέ ἐστε σῶμα Χριστοῦ καὶ μέλη ἐκ μέρους). Paul directly addresses the people to whom he is writing in Corinth as he makes clear that they (emphatic "you") are indeed the "body of Christ" (σῶμα Χριστοῦ). While it is certainly possible to speak of the worldwide church as the "body of Christ," it is important to note that Paul sees each local church in this way. Each church will have a variety of gifts given by the Spirit to God's people, for this is how God composes the body. By implication this means that not all local churches will look alike or even

contain within them the exact same list of grace-gifts. God calls into being "the body of Christ" in its local representation as *he* sees fit and in ways that will lead to its greatest spiritual advantage. All individuals must therefore see themselves as part of this body, whatever grace-gift they have. This is about an individual's fundamental approach to *the nature of the church*. It involves the question of diversity of gifts in the church, but that is *not* what Paul is handling here. He will continue, as he has done already, to develop how different gifts may be used in the church and the need for unity, but his main concern is how the "spiritual person" views the "body of Christ" itself. It may involve that individual recognising more deeply what diversity looks like or an individual being more prepared to give honor to a member who was previously disregarded. But the key concern for both the elite and those lacking in self-awareness is the nature of the church as *the body of Christ*.

12:28 And God has appointed in the church first apostles, secondly prophets and thirdly teachers, then [powerful] works, then grace-gifts of healing, helpful deeds, administrative supervision, [various] kinds of tongues (καὶ οὓς μὲν ἔθετο ὁ θεὸς ἐν τῇ ἐκκλησίᾳ πρῶτον ἀποστόλους, δεύτερον προφήτας, τρίτον διδασκάλους, ἔπειτα δυνάμεις, ἔπειτα χαρίσματα ἰαμάτων, ἀντιλήμψεις, κυβερνήσεις, γένη γλωσσῶν). Garland rightly says that now "Paul lists a sampling of members that God has placed in the church body."[48] While Paul also then moves on to speak of the gifts (e.g., helpful deeds) rather than the people with gifts (e.g., teachers), it is possible to make too much of this. The rhetorical questions of vv. 29–30 reveal that in all examples Paul is concerned with the *people* who have these gifts. Some have some gifts, and some have others. Here he illustrates from their

---

48. Garland, *1 Corinthians*, 598.

own knowledge and experience of church life how God has indeed composed the body.

The fact that Paul uses the adverbs, firstly, secondly, and thirdly to modify the verb "appointed" has caused considerable discussion. Since his discussion has consistently argued against any group thinking they are superior or inferior to another, this seems initially to be a change of tack at least. If there is any form of "ranking" in order of importance here, it is only with the first three, and it could possibly be Paul's way of emphasizing the initial and continuing foundational ministry of the word without which the church could not long survive. This is the view of most commentators, who are also at pains to say with Collins that "placing the apostolate as the first of the charisms in 12:28 does not suggest that those who have this role have superior status within the community."[49] But true as this may be, it does seem to remove us from the way Paul has been arguing in this passage.

Those who suggest that Paul is beginning to move the argument on in a way that will not become fully evident until chapter 14 approach the question of ranking slightly differently. Paul, it is said, is beginning to demonstrate that though there is no distinction of persons in the church, all of whom have gifts from God, nevertheless, the gifts themselves can be distinguished in terms of how they "build up" the people. He will later show that "tongues" is less useful in this regard in the church than is prophecy, and so, it is said, this also explains why he lists it last in v. 28. Grudem argues in a similar way, suggesting the ranking has to do with

what Paul considers the "greater" gifts (12:31a). This, he says, is spelled out in 14:5b where the person who prophesies is said to be the "greater," because "greatness in this context measures usefulness to the church."[50] But all that seems a way ahead yet. It is not the point Paul actually makes in vv. 29–30 where the rhetorical questions reinforce the general argument of the whole chapter that not all *people* have all gifts. Rather God allocates to each *person* as he wills. If Paul is intending here to rank a few of these people in terms of their place in the community because of how they build up the people, he is distinguishing between people on the grounds of their gifts—precisely what he has argued against.

However, given the adverbial nature of the numerals modifying "God has appointed," it seems to us that Blomberg provides the right way forward that still does justice to the overall movement of the chapter. He writes, "It is best to see in this enumeration a chronological priority (cf. Eph 2:20). To establish a local congregation requires a church-planter. Then the regular proclamation of God's word must ensue. Next teachers must supplement evangelism with discipleship. . . . Only at this point does a viable Christian fellowship exist to enable all the other gifts to come into play."[51]

The gifts mentioned here overlap with 12:7–10 but are not identical. On the meaning of "apostle" see 1:1. As 15:7–9 make clear, Paul was able to distinguish between the type of "apostle" of which he was one (along with the disciples of Jesus, all of whom had to be witnesses to the risen Lord), and

---

49. Collins, *1 Corinthians*, 468.

50. Grudem, *Gift of Prophecy in the New Testament*, 53.

51. Blomberg, *1 Corinthians*, 247. Charles H. Talbert, *Reading Corinthians: A Literary and Theological Commentary on 1 and 2 Corinthians* (New York: Crossroad, 1987), 85, comments that Paul here "enumerates sequence" and there is "no ranking." Cf. Fitzmyer, *1 Corinthians*, 482. Grudem, *Gift of Prophecy in the New Testament*, 68, says the ranking "is certainly not chronological, for tongues are last here but came at the very beginning of the church (Acts 2:4)." Yet this begs a major question about the nature of tongues, since the tongues Paul refers to are for "building up the church" and in Acts 2 are given so the gospel might be heard among those who are not Christians. Whether or not they are the same gift, the function they performed undoubtedly was different.

the more general use of the word meaning messenger or even church planter. In this context, however, it is likely that Paul is thinking of the rather limited understanding of what might be called the "office" of apostle. It is his own type of apostleship that he has used by way of example in chapter 9, and there is no reason for thinking that this verse would be the only place in the epistle where he would use the word deliberately more broadly of all who might serve a missionary or church-planting role. "Prophecy" was described in 12:10, and more will be said in the comments on 14:1ff. Though this gift might be given *at the Spirit's will* to anyone in the congregation, it seems that some may have prophesied on a regular basis and thus become known as "prophets" in much the same way as with the third in the list. As any might teach at different times in the life of the church if the Spirit thus empowered them with a grace-gift, some were called and empowered to do so on a regular basis and were called "teachers." Since prophecy is likely to have involved the Spirit-given "knowledge" and "wisdom" to apply Scripture directly to the immediate needs of the church and would have required a good understanding of Scripture (against which it was no doubt to be "judged"; 14:29), then it is difficult to see how prophets would be regarded as of higher "rank" than teachers. Both groups are similar, and it is likely that teachers, who would have been responsible for ensuring apostolic tradition was properly understood and applied in the church, would have been involved in deciding whether what prophets said was in accordance with apostolic teaching. This provides a further reason for doubting that Paul enumerated these people in any ranking of importance.

On "[powerful] works" and "grace-gifts of heal-ing" see the comments above on vv. 9–10. "Helpful deeds" (ἀντίλημψις) is a rare word and a New Testament *hapax legomenon*. A verbal form of the word is found in Romans 8:26 where "the Spirit *helps* us in our weakness." In the LXX another verbal form is used of God's providential care in Isaiah 41:9 (ἀντιλαμβάνω). There is not much to help the reader know whether Paul has any specific "helps" in mind as he talks of those with this gift. Calvin thinks that it probably related to the type of helping done by deacons in the church. Thiselton takes the position that since it is in the plural, it refers to "kinds of administrative support."[52] He disagrees with those who would say that this assumes a later and more institutionalized church, pointing out that people with these gifts were needed and appointed in Acts 6:1–6. This would mean that part of the work people who had this gift were involved with probably included oversight of finances. "Administrative supervision" (κυβέρνησις) is a word that usually refers to a guiding "leadership," such as with the pilot of a ship (cf. LXX Prov 1:5; 11:14; 24:6). Only those who have a prior commitment to some division between so-called "supernatural" and other "natural" gifts would have any difficulty with seeing this as a vital grace-gift of the Spirit. Such a gift would help ensure the smooth running of even the smallest church. This gift is indispensable and a vital need for the body to be the body. In the modern church, a person with this gift might be called a "church administrator" as long as that role is understood to be one of guidance for the direction of the church itself.

"Various kinds of tongues" was discussed at 12:10.[53] The suggestion that this "gift comes last again" because it has caused "such problems in Corinth" is at the very least jumping the gun.[54]

---

52. Thiselton, *1 Corinthians*, 1020–22. He translates as "administrations."

53. Also see, "In Depth: What Was Paul's Attitude to 'Speak-ing in a Tongue' and What Is the Phenomenon?" following comments at 14:4.

54. Ciampa and Rosner, *First Corinthians*, 614.

However, it has little support within the text. The *interpretation* of tongues came last in v. 10, which is, as chapter 14 makes clear, an excellent and beneficial gift of the Spirit. Fee's comment that this gift "surely seems out of place after the preceding four items" betrays his conviction that some gifts "of utterance" are of an entirely different order as "extraordinary manifestations of the Spirit" from other, more normal gifts.[55] There is no evidence in the text that Paul thought like this even if, possibly, some of the elitist Corinthians did.

12:29–30 Are all apostles? Are all prophets? Are all teachers? Do all do powerful works? Do all have grace-gifts of healing? Do all speak with tongues? Do all interpret? (μὴ πάντες ἀπόστολοι; μὴ πάντες προφῆται; μὴ πάντες διδάσκαλοι; μὴ πάντες δυνάμεις; μὴ πάντες χαρίσματα ἔχουσιν ἰαμάτων; μὴ πάντες γλώσσαις λαλοῦσιν; μὴ πάντες διερμηνεύουσιν;). A list of rhetorical questions strongly asserts the one fact that *not* everyone has the same gift. *Not* all do the same things in the community. The questions begin with the word "not" (μή), which requires a negative response. This Greek is best translated with an affirmative question, since in English it is this that requires a negative response. In order to keep the Greek negative form, the questions would have to be phrased like this: "All are not apostles, are they?" As we have noted on a number of occasions, rhetorical questions like this are not functioning properly as real questions but as definite statements. *The fact is that no one does all these things because no one is given all the necessary gifts by the Spirit.* Once again Paul's focus is not on diversity or on unity *per se*. The focus is on the nature of the body, which must be understood if people are to understand the right and proper function of the gifts of the Spirit.

12:31 Now you are earnestly desiring the greater grace-gifts. And I am showing you a still more excellent way (ζηλοῦτε δὲ τὰ χαρίσματα τὰ μείζονα. Καὶ ἔτι καθ᾽ ὑπερβολὴν ὁδὸν ὑμῖν δείκνυμι). Paul summarizes the problem he is addressing, that some seek out "greater gifts," before he leads his readers back, in chapter 13, to an extended discussion on a "more excellent way" that is love. The problem that v. 31a poses to any reader is obvious. Is the verb "desire" (ζηλόω) to be taken as a present indicative or as an imperative? Since Paul has been speaking against those who pride themselves in possessing certain grace-gifts and has spent many verses insisting that the body is made up of people, all of whom have been given gifts by the Spirit for the sake of the body, what might he mean by now urging people to seek "greater" gifts (assuming an imperative)? Has he completely reversed his previous argument? Two related questions arise. What does "greater" mean here? And what does Paul mean when he writes of desiring such gifts? Commentators offer a number of different interpretations.

Firstly, it has been suggested that Paul once again picks up another quotation from the Corinthians, as he did in 8:1.[56] The problem with this is that there are no indicators in the text that he might be doing this. While a difficult text that seems out of place might be a quotation, this would usually be expected to have textual indicators, as we have noted in previous instances. It might also be expected that, as in 8:1, Paul would qualify the quotation with a sentence beginning with an adversative, such as "but" (e.g., δέ in 8:1 or ἀλλά in 6:12). Of course, as we see below, it is still possible to say that v. 31a reflects the opinion of the Corinthians without saying that it has to be a quotation.

---

55. Fee, *1 Corinthians*, 662, 688.

56. David L. Baker, "The Interpretation of 1 Corinthians 12–14," *EvQ* 46 (1974): 224–34.

Secondly, it is suggested that the whole of v. 31 is more an introduction to the theme of chapter 13 than a conclusion to chapter 12. Thus, instead of separating the verse with a paragraph marking between v. 31a and v. 31b, the true separation must come at the end of v. 30 as Paul does indeed turn his mind to an important and related subject, but one that is a distinct move away from what he has been saying. Now he moves to talk about the "greater" gifts that should be sought after, of which "love" is the key one because it is the one that builds up the community.[57] This has the great advantage of recognizing the severe change of direction in v. 31a. Yet problems arise with this view also. The "now" or "but" (δέ) that introduces v. 31a is at the very least continuative if not somewhat adversative. It is hardly likely that such an abrupt change in direction happens in this way. Moreover, this would be a highly confusing way to start a new section. "Spiritual people all have gifts as God has given, so don't view certain gifts as more important than others. *But* (or *now*) earnestly desire those that are greater!"[58] Furthermore, nowhere does Paul refer to love as a "grace-gift." Indeed, the whole context of chapter 13 reveals that it is something utterly distinct from the "grace-gifts." It is qualitatively different in a variety of ways. For Paul "love" is a "fruit of the Spirit," as he describes it in Galatians 5:22. Paul's point, as we shall see, is that love is something *all* Christians must exhibit because it is *the* authenticator of belonging to the covenant community. While *not* all have grace-gifts that are the *same* (though all have at least one), all *should* have love. This is why, unlike the grace-gifts, it

continues into eternity even after the "perfect" has come (13:10) and why it "abides" (13:13). Confusing "grace-gifts," which *differ* among the people as the Spirit wills, with "fruit," which *all* Christians are expected to show in their life, is the opposite of what Paul has in mind here and is precisely the problem he writes to correct. A variation on this view is offered by Fee, who also believes that with this whole verse "Paul is about to launch on his next argument, namely 14:1–25." This means he regards chapter 13 as an interruption and 14:1 as "resumptive." Chapter 13 sets the "proper framework" for the need for the "intelligible gifts."[59]

Thirdly, it is suggested that v. 31a is an ironic question or statement. Recently, Fitzmyer has argued that the first sentence should be taken as an ironic question. He comments and translates thus: "*But are you striving for the greater gifts?* I.e., for *charismata* that are superior . . . Paul with irony queries Corinthian Christians as he realizes that some of them covet important spiritual roles in the community."[60] He goes on to say that further irony is seen in the fact that what they are striving for is in reality a gift of the Spirit, love. While this latter comment seems unlikely in the light of what we said above, that Paul may be using irony has widespread support, though few have taken this as an interrogative, for which there seems little evidence. In a widely quoted article, Smit argues from rules of rhetoric that this verse must be seen to be irony, a view followed with modifications by Thiselton. He admits that there need to be contextual signals that such is the case, but argues that "contextual contradiction" is precisely the signal in this

---

57. Barclay, *Letters to the Corinthians*, 116; Horsley, *1 Corinthians*, 175: "12:31 . . . is more an introduction to . . . chapter 13 . . . than a conclusion." See also Talbert, *Reading Corinthians*, 108.

58. Interestingly, noting this problem, Chrysostom insists that Paul is not talking about "greater gifts but the *best*," which he then defines as all those that are of greater benefit to the

church. He continues that, for Paul, this did not mean specific gifts but "a *way*" that "is open in common to all." For, he says, this *way* of love is a "universal gift" (*Homilies on First Corinthians*, homily 32.3 [p. 441]).

59. Fee, *1 Corinthians*, 691–92.

60. Fitzmyer, *1 Corinthians*, 484.

passage.[61] Though Garland has questioned whether Paul would use irony, which he calls "mockery," to "introduce a discussion of love," there is no inherent reason why not (though irony is far from mockery) and certainly such a comment does not deal with the rhetorical argument that Smit proposes. Indeed, such a rhetorical device fits well with v. 30 and gives a weighted and clear introduction to the critical chapter 13. This is the view also of Martin, who also takes v. 31a as a question: "'You are seeking, then, the greater gifts, are you?' 'Well,' Paul replies, 'I will show you a still better way.'"[62]

Finally, a number of writers have suggested that the verb (ζηλοῦτε) should not be taken as an imperative but as an indicative (cf. REB). Thus it would read "now you desire the greater grace-gifts, and I will show you. . . ." Of course, this would fit well with those mentioned above who also speak of the irony of the statement whether imperative, interrogative, or indicative. *Yet, if correct, the indicative would offer a simple way forward.* Paul has spoken against a hierarchy of gifts or of any gift being better than another, and he will go on to develop this, but "you"—that is, the Corinthians—are desiring "greater gifts." For the reasons that Paul expounds in chapter 13, this they should not do. This approach has more modern proponents than is often recognized, though they can often vary in the detail of their argument.[63] The main objection to taking the verb as an indicative, cited in almost all commentaries that insist on an imperative, is that the same word is "clearly" imperative when used in 14:1 and 14:39. Carson, following Fee, further suggests that the indicative would require a much stronger adversative between v. 31a and v. 31b. He says that for consistency the conjunction "and" (καί) would have to be translated as "but," a meaning the word "very rarely" has. Much of the rest of his criticism of the indicative is, in fact, leveled at those who also insist there must be a Corinthian quotation here.[64]

In fact, there is no vital reason why v. 31a cannot read "now [δέ] you are earnestly desiring [present indicative, ζηλοῦτε] the greater gifts and I am showing you an even greater way." (Note that the verb "showing" [δείκνυμι] is a *present*-tense verb, and there is no need to take it as a present with a future connotation!) The first half of the sentence is not harsh irony, nor does it stand in an adversative contrast with v. 31b. It may have an ironic feel to it, as has much of what Paul has said ever since 8:1! But it is also simply a summary of where the argument of the last few chapters has got to and where it is going. The Corinthian elite "are earnestly desiring" certain gifts that they consider "greater" or "higher." That is a fact. Paul is showing them a different way. That is also a fact and rightly linked by the conjunction "and" (καί). Furthermore, unless chapter 13 is seen simply as an interlude or digression, there is no reason at all to suggest that

---

61. Joop Smit, "Two Puzzles: 1 Corinthians 12:31 and 13:3: A Rhetorical Solution," *NTS* 39 (1993): 246–64. Smit cites from a number of ancient rhetoricians, but notably on this matter he quotes Quintilian, *Institutio oratoria* 8.6.54, who argues that if "the nature of the subject . . . is out of keeping with the words, it at once becomes clear that the intention of the speaker is other than what he actually says" (ibid., 251n16). Cf. Thiselton, *1 Corinthians*, 1024–26, who says Paul writes "tongue in cheek."

62. Ralph P. Martin, *The Spirit and the Congregation: Studies in 1 Corinthians 12–15* (Grand Rapids: Eerdmanns, 1984), 35.

63. In English, see Bittlinger, *Gifts and Graces*, 73–75; Dunn, *Jesus and the Spirit*, 430n37; John S. Ruef, *Paul's First*

Letter to Corinth (Philadelphia: Westminster, 1977), 140–41; Talbert, *Reading Corinthians*, 85; Martin, *Spirit and the Congregation*, 34–35; J. P. Louw, "The Function of Discourse in a Sociosemiotic Theory of Translation Illustrated by the Translation of Zeloute in 1 Corinthians 12:31," *BT* 39 (1988): 329–35. Fitzmyer, *1 Corinthians*, 484, takes it as an interrogative indicative, "But are you striving for the greater gifts?" In German, a foundational article for this position is Gerhard Iber, "Zum Verstandnis von 1Cor 12:31," *ZNW* 54 (1963): 43–52; Andreas Lindemann, *Der Erste Korintherbrief*, HNT 9/1 (Tübingen: Mohr Siebeck, 2000), 278.

64. Carson, *Showing the Spirit*, 53–54.

14:1 *must* guide our understanding of 12:31a! Even if we allow that it *might* be a guide, a number of questions remain largely unaddressed by those who argue for this. For example, 14:1 starts with the imperative "pursue love," so a different context has now been established for the command. With this context, the imperative does not glaringly contradict what has just been said in the way it seems to in 12:31a. Secondly, 14:1 does *not* say "earnestly desire the greater grace-gifts [τὰ χαρίσματα]"; it actually says "earnestly desire spiritual things [τὰ πνευματικά]." These "things" may indeed be the grace-gifts (though see the comments on 14:1), but there is no hint of irony here and we note that the word "greater" is not present!

By way of summary, *either* this is an ironic imperative that both summarizes what has been said in chapter 12 and lays the way open to the introduction of the way of love in chapter 13, *or* this is an indicative as laid out above. In either of these views, Thiselton is surely correct in saying that Paul is in the process here of radically "subverting" the Corinthian view of what they see as the "greatest grace-gifts."[65] Our preference, however, is *to see the verb of v. 31a as indicative*. We do not believe that any of the arguments against this are substantial, and mostly they depend on a particular way of interpreting parts of chapter 14. Furthermore, we would argue that this way of looking at the statement also deals with many other problems with taking the verb as an imperative. Space prohibits further discussion, but, for example, an indicative as a statement of fact avoids the seeming contradiction of Paul saying "be *zealous* for [ζηλόω]" and then following that in 13:4 with love "is not zealous [οὐ ζηλοῖ]." It also avoids the problem of taking tongues, prophecies, knowledge, etc., which seem to be the "greater gifts" (or minimally "prophecy"

as a greater gift; 14:3) and "earnestly desired," only to have them systematically torn apart in the immediately following verses where Paul "successively demonstrates that these gifts are useless (v. 1–3), devoid of virtue (v. 4–7) and incomplete (v. 8–12)."[66]

Throughout this epistle, we have noted how the Corinthians have been seeking "spiritual things" (τὰ πνευματικά). We do not doubt the majority view that this is a word drawn from the Corinthian vocabulary, but it is not a word of which Paul is afraid. He simply does with it what he often does with ideas that emanate from a different thought world; he seeks to redefine it. Paul is concerned that "spiritual people" should discern "spiritual things" (ch. 2). The "grace-gifts" are spiritual things. Indeed, they *are* the spiritual things for all intents and purposes for the Corinthian elite. They are what define the elite as "spiritual" in their own eyes. For Paul, however, truly "spiritual people" will see things quite differently. They will be guided by and *identified by* the Christian marker of "love." They will be seeking all "spiritual things" with a view to what "builds up" and "benefits" the community. This is just what Paul had said in 8:1 and what he has addressed in chapter 12 and continues to address in chapters 13 and 14. "Spiritual people" are *defined* by love. This is why, even as they earnestly seek the "grace-gifts," that Paul can be showing them a more excellent way *in which to be the spiritual people they should be*.

The phrase "a still more excellent way" (ἔτι καθ᾽ ὑπερβολὴν ὁδόν) could be variously translated. "Still" (ἔτι) most likely links with "more excellent way" as we suggest, but it could also be linked to the conjunction "and" and so mean, "Moreover, I show you. . . ." "More excellent" (καθ᾽ ὑπερβολήν) can be taken adverbially since its common meaning

---

65. *1 Corinthians*, 1024.

66. Smit, "Two Puzzles," 250.

is "extremely" or "excessively," as in 2 Corinthians 1:18 ("burdened *excessively*"). (Remember this is where the English word *hyperbole* comes from, and it can mean the same in describing overstated arguments in Greek!) But here it is an adjectival phrase, qualifying "way." Paul says, "Now you are earnestly desiring the greater grace-gifts. And[67] I am showing you a still more excellent way."

At the start of this chapter we suggested the real issue was one of "spiritual *people*" and the place of the grace-gifts in the defining of those people. At the end of the chapter in both vv. 27–30 *and* v. 31 it is again clear that Paul is concerned for *people*.

One group argues that the grace-gifts define spiritual status in the community, while Paul points to a "more excellent way." For him, what counts is the pursuit of love.

He teaches that it is for those "who *love* [God]" that much has been prepared (2:9). It is the person who "*loves* [God]" who is "known [by God]" (8:3). Thus Paul *is showing* them a *more excellent way* by what he writes, by the way he lives (ch. 9), by reference to Scripture, and now by addressing once again the contrast between grace-gifts and love. Love authenticates those who are "spiritual," who are possessed by God's Spirit.

Theology in Application

The Proper Function of Grace-Gifts in the Church

Paul has addressed the value of the grace-gifts in terms of the community. They are for the building up and benefit of the church, and not for individual aggrandizement. Given the tendency for some Corinthians to appeal to certain gifts in ways that have built their spiritual pride and led to elitism, Paul has focused in this passage on the constructive benefit of the grace-gifts when they are allowed to function properly in the church. They should not divide people. They are not "markers" of spirituality but are given freely by God in his sovereignty to all Christians for the sake of the church as a whole (12:7, 11, 18).

In virtually all modern Christian churches there remains a great need to examine carefully the gifts of its members and to make use of them. This will mean each person, and no doubt especially the leadership, looking out for others and seeking out the gifts God may have given them so they may bring them to the community. For those who lead and have a tendency toward pride and self-sufficiency, it may be humbling to know that God wants them to depend on and be built up by others with different gifts. For others, though, this will mean accepting what God has given them and then living and working in the community for the benefit of the body, knowing that this is their God-given and Spirit-enabled duty to the body. Just as there is no place for pride, so there is no place for false humility.

---

67. It is possible that καί here is used to express something mildly noteworthy (not adversative). There are numerous examples of the conjunction meaning "and yet" or "in spite of that"; see BDAG 495. Cf. 1 Cor 5:2; 2 Cor 6:9. The sense here, which is grammatically possible but not essential to our argument, would be "you desire this . . . and yet I am showing you this."

Often in those churches that put so much emphasis on teaching and preaching that other gifts may be considered second-rate or even irrelevant, gifts are hardly being allowed to function in their great diversity for the building up of the people. On the other hand, many other churches put so much emphasis on the more extraordinary gifts, such as tongues or healing, that they too suffer as they fail to benefit from the wide and diverse gifting of all church members. Pragmatically, most church ministers will point out how difficult it is to discern the gifts of many people in any one church, even when they would like to do so. However, recognizing that the church is the messianic King's community, to which the King himself has graciously given gifts for their encouragement, building up, and consolation (14:3, 26), should motivate the attempt. If Joel 2:28–32 (cf. Acts 2:17–18) is truly fulfilled in and among the people of the new covenant, then they should be rejoicing in what has been poured out upon them and enabling one another to use their gifts that all may benefit. Whether this will be done in plenary times of worship, when time seems always to be limited, or in smaller home-style gatherings, or simply in small groups or one-to-one encounters, is not the issue. The issue is that God's Spirit has endowed each member of his church with gifts, and most churches rarely even know what they are, let alone seek to find ways of ensuring all are "built up" by one another as God has willed for them. The several lists in the New Testament of various such gifts reinforce the challenge. It is especially notable that three other lists of gifts (outside 1 Corinthians) do not arise in situations where they are being abused or where they have led to any form of pride or elitism. Each list takes it for granted that a unified body is strengthened by the multiplicity of gifts that God has given it. Thus we may note Romans 12:3–8; Ephesians 4:1–16; 1 Peter 4:8–11.

The Body and Close Christian Relationships

One of the remarkable aspects of this chapter is Paul's description of just how closely related to each other God's people should be. Since the Messiah's people are drawn from all nations and backgrounds and are baptized into "one body" (12:12–13, 27), diversity in the body is seen to be part of God's great plan for this people. In this way Paul indicates that diversity is integral to the nature of the church, to its well-being (12:12–13), and to its witness to the world. The body metaphor of chapter 12 makes it clear that diversity itself helps make the body stronger when it is properly understood and when it is developed in the context of love (8:1; ch. 13).

Sadly, in the modern Western world of individualism, this community identity seems missing altogether from many churches. The deficit is most remarkable when 12:25–26 is considered. Having shown that God has arranged the body so no part may believe it is more important than another (v. 24), and so that there will be no dissension (v. 25), Paul speaks about the mutual care there should be within the church. It is the staggering claim of v. 26 that surely challenges any church to consider whether, as a people, they have worked at and developed their unity. The proper use of grace-gifts will build up others. They are *other* focused. It is in that context that each member will come to know others and so "when one member suffers, all the members suffer together" (v. 26). If we do not see others as being able to benefit us and do not feel the need ourselves to benefit others as the Lord has gifted us to do, then we shall never suffer when others suffer since we shall not know their suffering. The members of the body are to be aware of other members and what they are feeling, as well as what they are saying and doing. The closeness of the community described here is the closeness of a good family relationship. The "body" metaphor suggests Paul sees it as even closer than the family metaphor might imply.

1 Corinthians 13:1–13

Literary Context

Paul has addressed multiple matters of concern among the Corinthians. The arrogance and elitism of those who claimed "wisdom" and "knowledge" and believed these grace-gifts distanced them from other Christians have given rise to serious problems in the church. In 8:1–3 Paul specifically contrasted "knowledge" with the marker of "love." The one "puffs up" and the other "builds up." Tragically, the divisions in this church have spilled over even into corporate worship. In 11:17–34 Paul had tackled the divisions occurring in the worship of the communion service. In chapter 12 Paul had been rather more positive, at last turning to the proper use of the grace-gifts, which should function to "build up" God's people. Chapter 13 begins with further commentary on these gifts. Now, however, the focus moves to "love" (ἀγάπη appears ten times in this chapter).

Chapter 13 forms a climax to Paul's discussion of the role of both grace-gifts and the marker of "love" in the community. As in 8:1–3, love is contrasted with the grace-gifts. For Paul "love" and "grace-gifts" must not be presented as an "either-or." He has argued, especially in chapter 12, that the grace-gifts are needed, and he has thanked God that this church is well blessed with them by God's Spirit (1:4–9). He will continue to discuss them in chapter 14. However, they only make sense when used in a context where people are marked out as the Lord's by "love." The gifts themselves, therefore, are not to be seen as community markers.

The links between 8:1–3 and chapter 13 are substantial. The contrast of knowledge with love from 8:1 is augmented by the statement of 13:4 that love is "not puffed up." The identification of love as a marker of status as one of God's people in 8:3 ("But if anyone loves [God], this one is known [by him]") is augmented by 13:12, "as I have been fully known." Paul will continue to build on these contrasts in his teaching in chapter 14 as he examines the use of the gift of speaking in tongues. Once again, he will emphasize that which builds up the community rather than the individual.

This chapter also offers a relatively clear use of epideictic rhetoric in that it eulogizes love. However, if, as has been noted, the epistle as a whole takes on something more akin to deliberative rhetoric, it is important not thereby to conclude that chapter 13 is to be seen as a digression. Rhetorical analyses within letters of this length must not be allowed to distance one section of material from another or to distance this chapter from the rest of the epistle.[1] For many reasons we have argued and will argue that this chapter is the climactic center of a prolonged and multi-pronged critique of the elitists in Corinth. However, Paul's more structured and poetic praise of love is seen to carry even greater weight if we understand that Paul uses epideictic rhetoric precisely to emphasize the centrality of love to his argument. In this his appeal to the Corinthians takes on an emotional content.

VII. Status, Knowledge, Freedom, and Food Offered to Idols (8:1–11:1)
VIII. Status, Public Worship, Freedom, and Grace-Gifts (11:2–14:40)
    A. The Conduct of Husbands and Wives in Public Worship (11:2–16)
    B. The Conduct of the Church at the Lord's Supper (11:17–34)
    C. Spiritual People and the Function of Their Grace-Gifts in the Church (12:1–31)
➡   **D. The Status of Spiritual People Is Authenticated by Love (13:1–13)**
    E. The Proper Function of Grace-Gifts in Public Worship (14:1–25)
    F. In Public Worship All Activity Must Build Up the Church (14:26–40)

Main Idea

Spiritual people are marked by their love rather than their grace-gifts. Love continues into eternity and must control all their actions and thoughts, while grace-gifts prove to be partial, temporal, and passing.

Translation

(See pages 559–60.)

---

1. See Ben Witherington, *New Testament Rhetoric: An Introductory Guide to the Art of Persuasion in and of the New Testament* (Eugene, OR: Cascade, 2009), 127–28.

1 Corinthians 13:1–13

[31b]	[Assertion/bridge from ch. 12]	[And **I am showing you a still more excellent way.**]
1a	Condition (protasis)	If I speak with the tongues of men and of angels, but
b	Contrast	do not have love,
c	Assertion (apodosis)	**I have become　a noisy gong or** **a clanging cymbal.**
2a	Condition	And if I have [the gift of] prophecy and
b	Series	I understand all mysteries and all knowledge, and
c	Series	if I have all faith
d	Result	so as to remove mountains, but
e	Contrast	do not have love,
f	Assertion (apodosis)	**I am nothing.**
3a	Condition (protasis)	And if I give away all my possessions and
b	Condition (protasis)	if I deliver up my body to be burned, but
c	Contrast	do not have love,
d	Assertion (apodosis)	**I gain nothing.**
4a	Assertion series	**Love is forbearing,**
b	Series	**love is kind,**
c		**it does not envy,**
d		**it does not boast,**
e		**it is not puffed up,**
5a		**it does not behave rudely,**
b		**it is not self-seeking,**
c		**it is not provoked to anger,**
d		**it does not record wrongs,**
6a		**it does not rejoice at evil**
b	Assertion (contrast)	but **rejoices at the truth.**
7a	Assertion	**Love　puts up with all things,**
b	Series	believes all things,
c		hopes all things,
d		endures all things.
8a	Assertion	**Love never fails.**
b	Contrasting examples	But　　　　if there be prophecies,
c	Assertion (apodosis)	**they　will be abolished;**
d	Series	if tongues,
e		**they　will cease;**
f	Series	if knowledge,
g		**it　will be abolished.**

Continued on next page.

Continued from previous page.

9a	Basis	For **we know in part**
b	Basis	and **we prophesy in part,**
10a	Time	but when the perfect comes,
b	Basis (contrast)	**the partial will be abolished.**
11a	Illustration for vv. 8b–10b	When I was a child,
b	Assertion	**I used to speak like a child,**
c	Series	**I used to think like a child,**
d		**I used to reason like a child;**
e	Contrast/time	when I became a man,
f	Assertion	**I got rid of childish things.**
12a	Analogy	For now **we see** **in a mirror dimly,**
b	Contrast (1)	but then [we shall see] face to face;
c	Assertion	now **I know partially,**
d	Contrast (2)	then **I shall know fully**
e	Assertion	even as I have been fully known.
		But now
13a	Conclusion/Assertion	**faith, hope, love remain,**
b		these three; but
c	Comparison	the greatest of these is love.

Structure

This chapter may be divided simply into three sections. In 13:1–3 Paul insists on the necessity of love, for it is love that authenticates spiritual people as truly the Lord's. They are "nothing" without it, even if they possess grace-gifts. In 13:4–7 we see how love among Christians may be recognized by its celebrated characteristics and how it must control their thoughts and actions. Then in 13:8–13 the apostle again addresses the authenticating function of love in the church of God as he shows how, unlike the grace-gifts, love continues into eternity (vv. 8, 13) and the time when we shall see "face to face" (v. 12). 13:13 provides a climactic summary.

Exegetical Outline

VIII. Status, Public Worship, Freedom, and Grace-Gifts (11:2–14:40)

    A. The Conduct of Husbands and Wives in Public Worship (11:2–16)

    B. The Conduct of the Church at the Lord's Supper (11:17–34)

    C. Spiritual People and the Function of Their Grace-Gifts in the Church (12:1–31)

➡   **D. The Status of Spiritual People Is Authenticated by Love (13:1–13)**

        1. Love Alone Authenticates Spiritual People (13:1–3)

        2. Love Controls the Thoughts and Actions of Spiritual People (13:4–7)

        3. Love Is Eternal and Complete, While Grace-Gifts Are Temporal (13:8–13)

Explanation of the Text

Since 12:31b not only concludes chapter 12 but also introduces chapter 13, a few more comments are offered here.

12:31b And I am showing you a still more excellent way (Καὶ ἔτι καθ' ὑπερβολὴν ὁδὸν ὑμῖν δείκνυμι). In many ways, as has been seen, Paul has been showing a "still more excellent way" (ἔτι καθ' ὑπερβολὴν ὁδόν) throughout this epistle. It is a biblical path that will bring the Christian to a proper maturity as a "spiritual person," and that will produce a person who is thus able to "discern" and to "judge" things and so see the difference between boasting in the Lord and boasting in oneself. It will produce the "spiritual person" who will care for the "other" and understand the nature of the body of Christ and their part in that body. It is fundamentally a path that follows "Christ crucified," that is, a path of humility and of giving up "rights," and a path that may lead to rejection and suffering. It is *not* a path of boasting nor a path that will get involved with the worship of idols. It is not a path of elite groups nor a path that sees the rich enjoying meals while the poor go hungry. This "more excellent way" has been the subject from the start of this letter, which is one of the main reasons for saying that the verb of v. 31b (δείκνυμι) should be given

its proper place as a true present tense: "And I am showing you a still more excellent way."

The truly remarkable nature of chapter 13 has made it stand out from almost all other Scripture. Here for all to understand is a succinct and clear description of the ultimate Christian marker, "love," yet it also remains directly related to the specific needs of the Corinthian church. "Love" is now contrasted directly with certain examples of the grace-gifts. In the contrast of these gifts with love, the gifts are presented in a light that seems negative. But that is too simplistic a view of what Paul is doing here.

Again, we must continue to remember that it is *people* and whether or not they stand before God and what marks them out as "spiritual" that Paul is concerned with. Therefore, the apparent negativity toward the gifts in this passage is, in fact, a negativity to the *function* of the gifts that some in the community seem to have been attributing to them. It is quite clear that Paul is not negative *per se* to the grace-gifts (cf. 1:4–9; 12:4–11, 28; 14:1–2, 18, 26, 29, 39). On the one hand, Paul can praise these Christians and thank God for their "enrichment" with a gift like "knowledge" (1:5), while, on the other, say that "knowledge puffs up" (8:1). This is another clear indication that the problem is not with "knowledge" but the way it *functions* among the Corinthians. It has become something that they take pride in, that separates them from others, and that divides rather than "benefits" or "builds up" the community. And it is this that Paul addresses. It is *love* that in biblical faith must function as the marker of the spiritually mature Christian. This is what reveals the *authentic* Christian and, of course, does so because it lasts into eternity (13:13).[2]

13:1 If I speak with the tongues of men and of angels, but do not have love, I have become a noisy gong or a clanging cymbal (Ἐὰν ταῖς γλώσσαις τῶν ἀνθρώπων λαλῶ καὶ τῶν ἀγγέλων, ἀγάπην δὲ μὴ ἔχω, γέγονα χαλκὸς ἠχῶν ἢ κύμβαλον ἀλαλάζον). As the apostle establishes the contrast in function between love and grace-gifts, he uses the first-person singular with three third-class conditional sentences. The first person no doubt serves rhetorically to soften what Paul says, but it also helps to clarify that Paul is not presenting an *either/or*. It is not *either* "I have gifts" *or* "I have love." In the way they are formulated, the "present general" conditional clauses themselves also serve to soften what Paul is saying because the protases express a hypothetical situation concerning gifts that we know from the epistle must have been important to the Corinthians: speaking in tongues, prophecy, and knowledge.[3] It has already become clear that knowledge was an important gift to the elitists, but as Paul introduces tongues and prophecy here in chapter 13 and develops most of the argument of chapter 14 around these two, they must also have had a high profile among the elitists.

Paul begins with the grace-gift of tongues. This was listed among the gifts in 12:10 and 12:30 and described in the comments at 12:10. Paul later says he is thankful that he has this gift (14:18), so the

foundation is laid for that later discussion. But that is not the concern here. The point is simple: the speaker makes a noise. If, in the church's life the gift of tongues is employed and yet the person speaking "does not have love," *that person* has become a noise! The person involved "is nothing," as v. 2 makes clear, and "gains nothing" (v. 3). In this first verse Paul does not go that far, but he makes the point that as a person he would simply be a useless maker of noise. This is a vital point to keep in mind through these three verses. It is the *person* who is simply a noise maker, the *person*, "I," who is "nothing." Far from speaking in tongues being evidence of spiritual status, as the elitists seem to believe, it was taking them nowhere because they were not exhibiting love.

Love, as Paul describes it here, is not an extra special grace-gift but is what marks *all* who are possessed by the Spirit. Gifts being exercised in a context where this is not present, where self is first and God and neighbor second or third, where status is sought rather than humility seen, make the person simply irrelevant spiritually. The person has become like random noise, which has no purpose or meaning. The verb meaning "to become" or "to be" (γέγονα) is in an intensive perfect. The present results are what matters to Paul. If this person spoke in this way, without love, then *he or she has become* or simply *is* a noisy gong. What Paul is saying is clear thus far.

However, other questions require attention. When Paul speaks of tongues "of men" (τῶν ἀνθρώπων) and "of angels" (τῶν ἀγγέλων), is he talking of two different types of "tongues"? If not, does the second simply serve to intensify the first by way of extending it? It has been suggested that "tongues of men" may refer to clever rhetorical speech. This could be the sort of speech referred to

---

2. See below, "In Depth: Love, Its Function and Background" at 13:3.

3. Wallace, *Greek Grammar*, 470–71.

by Paul in 2:1 (cf. 1:5) when he says: "I . . . did not come to you with loftiness of speech or wisdom, proclaiming the testimony from God." "Tongues of angels" would then be the same as those mentioned in 12:10 and that need interpretation. Attractive though this idea is, the only reference to "tongues" has concerned the "grace-gift" of tongues and it is this that is picked up again in chapter 14. While it is possible Paul has in mind two types of tongues, it is unlikely. It is more likely that "tongues of angels" serves to intensify the idea. It is possible that the Corinthians believed their "tongues" (which needed interpretation) were the languages spoken by angels. If this were the case, then it would further underscore the fact that they felt their gifts indicated that they had arrived and were indeed spiritual. It seems more likely that "tongues" refers to the "tongues" to be interpreted as in 12:10 and that "of angels" is added for emphasis. It does not matter how completely extraordinary the gift that a person may employ or what great value it is given by some in Corinth, without love the person is a "noisy gong." This leads to comments made recently about the analogy of musical instruments.

The word "gong" (χαλκός) more usually simply describes various types of metal, especially brass or bronze. It rarely has to do with music. This fact was reflected in the AV, which translates "I am become as sounding brass." In a brief article, Klein has suggested that this may be a reference to "acoustic vases" that were vases placed "in niches around the periphery of the theatre." They were used to help project the voices of actors and of music. The better translation therefore might be "echoing bronze" with these acoustic vases in mind. He concludes with this fascinating and perhaps enlightening comment: "Speaking in tongues is a sound all right; but it is a mere echo, a reverberation, an empty sound coming out of a hollow lifeless vessel."[4] "Noisy" is a translation of an adjectival participle (ἠχέω). It can mean simply "sounding" (AV) or "sounding out." Yet in Psalm 46:3 (45:4 LXX; cf. Jer 5:22) and elsewhere, it refers to the "roaring" of waves. It seems Paul's emphasis is on the sound itself, and so with the NASB, NRSV, and ESV we translate it as "noisy." The mention of a cymbal qualified by the participle "clashing" (ἀλαλάζον) adds to the hyperbole of Paul's comments. The word can refer to the loud wailing at a funeral wake. Such speaking in tongues without "love" is just a lot of noise!

13:2 And if I have [the gift of] prophecy and I understand all mysteries and all knowledge, and if I have all faith so as to remove mountains, but do not have love, I am nothing (καὶ ἐὰν ἔχω προφητείαν καὶ εἰδῶ τὰ μυστήρια πάντα καὶ πᾶσαν τὴν γνῶσιν, κἂν ἔχω πᾶσαν τὴν πίστιν ὥστε ὄρη μεθιστάναι, ἀγάπην δὲ μὴ ἔχω, οὐθέν εἰμι). Paul moves on to make the same point, but to do so in relation to other prominent grace-gifts. Whether Paul refers to four, three, or two different gifts is not entirely clear. It is possible that two main gifts are mentioned, prophecy and faith, and then to take "mysteries" (τὰ μυστήρια) and "knowledge" as a subset of prophecy. Another possibility is that the verb "understand" (εἰδῶ from οἶδα) stands separately with "mysteries" and "knowledge," which should be taken together.

As with tongues in the previous verse, we remain in the realm of the spoken grace-gifts until Paul moves to "faith." "Prophecy" has been described in the comments on 12:10 (see more in 14:1–2) and "knowledge" in the comments on 12:8 (cf. 1:5; 8:1–2). These gifts, given by the Spirit for the body of Christ, in various ways expound the

---

4. William W. Klein, "Noisy Gong or Acoustic Vase: A Note on 1 Corinthians 13:1," *NTS* 32 (1986): 286–89.

plans of God and of Christ to the congregation in ways that are practical, challenging, and encouraging. "Mysteries" probably draws on Jewish apocalyptic background and on passages such as Daniel 2:19–47 and 1 Enoch 63:3. Paul himself occasionally speaks of a revealed "mystery," though it usually refers to the way in which Gentiles are brought into God's people. In other words, what was a "mystery," namely, how God would bring the Abrahamic blessing to completion in reaching all people, has been revealed in Christ (Rom 11:25; 16:25; Eph 3:6; Col 1:26–27). In that sense the gospel itself is the revelation of "mysteries" disclosed in Christ (see comments on 2:7). But here, with the grace-gift, it is likely that Paul is speaking of some special gift that applies aspects of the plan of salvation to the life of the church. Perhaps it would involve some reemphasis or special insight into the benefits of salvation or of God's plans for the community. It is difficult to see much distinction between this and "all knowledge" (πᾶσαν τὴν γνῶσιν).[5] The threefold repetition of "all" indicates that Paul is deliberately overstating the position to make the point. Hyperbole continues. Of course, Paul does have prophetic gifts from the Spirit, and he does have "knowledge" and "understands" much of the "mysteries" of God. In Romans 16:25–26 Paul speaks of the gospel he has preached as a word of "revelation of the mystery hidden for long ages past" and of its disclosure "through the prophetic writings."

As Paul uses the first singular and people know that he shares grace-gifts that include prophecy, wisdom, and knowledge (2:9–10, 12–13; 4:1), the point

he makes becomes stronger. Even if *he* has all this but does not have love and even if *he* has the sort of faith that will move mountains but has not love, he says, "I am nothing" (οὐθέν εἰμι). This apodosis, short as it is compared with the previous verse, is a much more significant statement than often recognized. It cannot be understood without reference back to chapter 1. There Paul insists that he preaches Christ crucified and then asks the Corinthians to remember who they were when they were called to faith in Christ. They were nothing special in terms of either worldly wisdom or power. Indeed, he insisted that God "chose . . . the things *that are not*, in order to bring to nothing the things that are" (v. 28). Different words are used, but the contrast is significant. The elitists used to be worth nothing in the eyes of the world, even though they were so wedded to status in the church. Now, as they seek status in the church, they will end up once again being "nothing," but this time "nothing" in the church. What irony! Those who think they are "something" by virtue of their gifts were nothing before they came to faith and will find themselves once again "a nothing." Love must be the defining marker. As they became "something" when they encountered the crucified Christ, so they find their status and their being in becoming like him, summed up in this mighty word "love."

13:3 And if I give away all my possessions and if I deliver up my body to be burned, but do not have love, I gain nothing (κἂν ψωμίσω πάντα τὰ ὑπάρχοντά μου, καὶ ἐὰν παραδῶ τὸ σῶμά μου ἵνα καυχήσωμαι,[6] ἀγάπην δὲ μὴ ἔχω, οὐδὲν ὠφελοῦμαι).

---

5. After lengthy discussion, Dunn suggests the possibility that a "word of wisdom" (12:8) might be a gift involved in the proclamation of God's plan of salvation and so perhaps linked to an evangelist, while a "word of knowledge" may be a gift more likely to belong to a teacher. But, given such little evidence, any distinction between these gifts is difficult to define clearly. See Dunn, *Jesus and the Spirit*, 219–21.

6. The NA[28] shows the various textual variants associated with the editors' choice of the verb "to boast" (καυχήσωμαι: 𝔓[46] ℵ A B 048. 33. 1739* co; Hier[mss]). The alternative we use here is the verb "to burn" (καυθήσομαι: C D F G L 6. 81. 104. 630. 945. 1175. 1881* latt sy[hmg]; Tert Ambst). The balance of the evidence for the NA[28]'s choice is rated by Metzger (*Textual Commentary*, 497–98) as "C," meaning there is considerable

Paul's final illustration turns to an example of self-sacrifice and has become somewhat proverbial. Self-sacrifice on behalf of others to give food to the poor (or selling possessions in order to do so) is a well-known *noble* concept that would provide status in many societies whether in Roman Corinth or even in some Christians circles, where it is encouraged by a wealth of Old Testament writing and the words of Jesus himself. The word "to give away" (ψωμίζω) can mean to dole out bit by bit, but it can also mean "to feed" someone.[7] The word "poor" found in most translations is not present in the Greek. However, the idea is present in what Paul is saying. "And if," abbreviated in Greek (κἄν = καί ἐάν), again introduces the sentence with the aorist subjunctive continuing the hypothetical conditional clauses.

It may be that this giving away of food is part of the work that would be done by those with the grace-gift of "helpful deeds" (ἀντιλήμψεις) mentioned in 12:28. In Romans 12:8 Paul mentions the grace-gift of "giv[ing] generously." Either way, Paul supposes a situation in which a person gives away everything owned. Paul and his readers may have thought back to the story of Jesus's meeting with the man who asked what he needed to do to inherit eternal life. The response came: "You lack one thing: go, sell all that you have and give to the poor" (Mark 10:21 ESV). Paul's point is that even if he was actually to do this and give everything he had, still, if he was without love, it would be of no benefit.

With further hyperbole Paul adds, "And if I deliver up my body up to be burned." The series of examples culminates with this high point of his rhetoric. Even if Paul were to give himself to be burned, he would gain nothing if he did not have love. What Paul had in mind in saying this is not entirely clear. Some support their adoption of the verb "to boast" rather than "to burn" by arguing that there is considerable doubt whether "burning" was used as a form of punishment by the Romans in those days. However, the idea of being "burnt" for the faith is found in Daniel with the story of Shadrach, Meshach, and Abednego, who were thrown into the fiery furnace for their faith in and obedience to God (Dan 3). Whether of Jewish or Greek background, all Christians would have known this story as they studied Scripture. We know from Hebrews 11:33–34 that such great stories of faith from the Old Testament became common themes of encouragement to faith among Christians. Those, like Paul, who came from a Jewish background in the church at Corinth would probably also have been aware of the horrific

---

doubt whether the text contains the superior meaning. In spite of this, most main versions translate the word as "burn" (e.g., RSV; ESV; NIV 1984; TEV; REB; NJB). One notable exception is the NRSV, "if I hand over my body so that I may boast" (see also NIV 2011). Given that the external evidence is finely balanced, the internal evidence must be given weight. If "boast" is accepted, then the idea must be that Paul posits giving up his body and therefore having a "boast" on the final day. Thus, even *if Paul does something as wonderful as giving over his body to suffering in a way that gives him a boast before God but has not love, he gains nothing.* Fee (*1 Corinthians*, 703–4) cites Paul's boasting in bodily ailments in 2 Cor 11:23–29. Thus "boast" is seen positively, yet without love it gains nothing. However, Garland (*1 Corinthians*, 615) is surely right in responding: "Can one boast lovingly about giving up one's possessions and one's body? Hardly. Paul believes that he will have a boast at

the end-time judgment, but it is a boast in his churches, not of his great sacrifices, and it is a boast he can have only 'in Christ Jesus our Lord' (15:31)." Many other arguments are adduced to support "burn." Barrett, *First Corinthians*, 302, suggests that "to be burned" is parallel to "so as to remove mountains." He also points out that "handing oneself over" does not mean very much and needs a "supplementary clause." Handed over to what?—to be burned. Further arguments for and against this position may be found in Thiselton, *1 Corinthians*, 1042–44, who concludes by choosing "boast." Also see J. H. Petzer, "Contextual Evidence in Favour of ΚΑΥΧΗΣΩΜΑΙ in 1 Corinthians 13:3," *NTS* 35 (1989): 242–43.

7. BDAG 1100. Cf. Rom 12:20. Liddell and Scott, *An Intermediate Greek-English Lexicon* (New York: Harper & Brothers, 1889), 903, gives the meaning "to employ in feeding others."

stories of torture, some by fire, recounted in the books of the Maccabees (see 2 Macc 7:5; 4 Macc 9:22; 10:14). In the late fourth century, Chrysostom comments on giving the "body to be burned" in this way: "[Paul] names the most terrible of all deaths, being burned alive, and saith that even this without charity is no great thing." As Chrysostom expounds this, he refers back to Jesus's exposition of loving one's neighbor and his statement, "greater love hath no man than this, that a man lay down his life for his friends [John 15:3]."[8] Thus, with this final emotive illustration Paul concludes what he is saying. Without love, even dying under persecution would bring him no gain.

"I gain nothing" (οὐδὲν ὠφελοῦμαι) is exactly what we would expect as Paul finishes these illustrations. Status before God has been Paul's and the Corinthians' concern. The elite believe that their exercise of certain gifts does indeed "gain" them much and reveals their standing before God. Paul has been at pains to say this is not the case. "Food will not prove our standing before God," Paul had said in debate with them and their supposed "knowledge" back in 8:8. If they think they "stand," they should "take heed lest [they] fall" (10:12). The theology of the elite did indeed see gain in the exercise of the grace-gifts. Paul insists that if he were to do all that he has outlined he would still find no "gain" without love. The word "gain" often has connotations of financial debt, but here it is used metaphorically in a rhetorical argument from advantage. In the overall argument of the epistle, all "advantage" or benefit flows from God himself, who calls people to himself as he chooses—even "things that are not, in order to bring to nothing the things that are, so that no human being might boast in the presence of God" (1:28–29). It is love that flows from God, the love seen in Christ's own self-sacrifice and in his calling of his people, that alone demonstrates that one is known by him (8:3). Without love there is no benefit or gain of any sort before God. Paul thus completes a fascinating and progressive argument about the *person* who would claim status on the grounds of grace-gifts: "I am just a lot of noise!" "I am nothing!" "I gain nothing!"

IN DEPTH: Love, Its Function and Background

Love is a way of *being* as a person, a way of thinking, acting, and living. It is, in fact, *being* Christ-like or (given the first-person singular in 11:1) even *being* like Paul, who has shown us what this looks like in his own life in chapter 9 and so summoned the Corinthians to "be imitators of me" (4:16; 11:1). Love is the way of being that is so all invasive that it affects the whole of the way life is conducted.

The idea of "love," in contrast with "knowledge" and grace-gifts, is introduced in 8:1 and lies behind much of the discussion through to the end of chapter 14. Paul in 14:1 begins with the imperative "pursue love" (διώκετε τὴν ἀγάπην), before returning to the subject of grace-gifts, which must operate in a context of love. The magnificent poetry of chapter 13 contains the greatest exposition of love. However, the concept of love is present in these other chapters even when

---

8. Chrysostom, *Homilies on First Corinthians*, homily 32.8 (p. 444).

the word is not. The argument in 8:1 that "love builds up" (ἀγάπη οἰκοδομεῖ) reminds the reader that when Paul speaks of "building up" the church or the body he thinks of love in action in the community. The focus of love here is thus predominantly the believer or the church—the understood object of "to build up."

First Corinthians 8:3, however, provides a rare exception to this, where God is the object of the love. Since Paul rarely talks of love for God,[9] this first deserves comment. As Barrett writes, "It is more characteristic of Paul to describe man's response to God as faith rather than love."[10] However, we may recall that Paul has already talked of love for God in 2:9, and 8:3 appears deliberately to build on the teaching of chapters 1–3. There the emphasis was on the electing call of God (1:26–29), who had saved his people (1:18) by his power (2:5). Thus, love for God was seen to rest in God's prior work through his Spirit. Paul's understanding of the process involved here is most clearly expressed in Romans 5:5: "The love of God has been poured into our hearts by the Holy Spirit which has been given to us" (NJB).[11] This is why Paul regards love for God rather than wisdom or knowledge as evidence of having "not received the spirit of the world; rather we have received the Spirit of God" (2:12). This close relationship between love and the work of the Spirit no doubt provides a partial explanation for why in Paul, and in the early church more generally, love is seen as the authenticator or marker of a Christian. It is possession by the Spirit of God (who pours out God's love into believers' hearts) that indicates a person belongs to Christ (Rom 8:9–11).[12]

A further explanation of why love comes to function as the marker *par excellence* of the true believer lies in the imitation of Christ. Christ stands as the supreme example of love through the whole of his life, but specially in his death. In 1 Corinthians 1 the death of Christ was at the center of Paul's understanding of God's wisdom (his plan) to save his people. It was the "word of the cross" that was the power of God to those "being saved" (1:18). Supremely in Christ's death the love of God and of Christ was shown. The link is explicit in Romans 5:8: "God shows his love for us in that while we were still sinners, Christ died for us" (ESV). It is also clear in Ephesians 5:2: "Walk in love, as Christ loved us and gave himself up for us, a fragrant offering and sacrifice to God" (ESV). It is surely for this reason that in 1 Corinthians 8:11–12 the link is made between sinning against

---

9. Rom 8:28 is probably the only other verse where God is the object. Cf. 2 Thess 3:5.

10. Barrett, *First Corinthians*, 190.

11. This assumes τοῦ θεοῦ to be an objective genitive.

12. Although Barrett believes Paul would more normally have used the word "faith," we may suggest why he did not in 8:3. Galatians 5:6 helps clarify the distinction: "For in Christ Jesus neither circumcision nor uncircumcision has any value.

The only thing that counts is faith expressing itself through love." It is wrong simply to say here that faith is theory and love is practice, rightly noted by Hans D. Betz, *Galatians*, Hermeneia (Philadelphia: Fortress, 1979), 264. Rather, love is a description of faith in practice. As Ridderbos says: "Faith expresses itself, so to speak, in love" (Herman N. Ridderbos, *Galatians*, NICNT [Grand Rapids: Eerdmans, 1976], 191).

a brother or sister "for whom Christ died" and "sinning against Christ." For Paul, "brother" (or "sister") was a synonym for Christian, but his addition of "for whom Christ died" emphasized the centrality of the death of Christ as a motivation to love. As Paul summarized it in 2 Corinthians 5:14–15, "For Christ's love controls us . . . he died for all, that those who live should no longer live for themselves but for him who died and was raised again for them." Of course, it is in the words of Jesus, especially as recorded in John's Gospel, where Jesus speaks of his own love as the example that, if followed, would provide evidence of true disciple-ship. For example, we read in John 13:34–35, "A new commandment I give to you, that you love one another: just as I have loved you, you also are to love one another. By this all people will know that you are my disciples, if you have love for one another" (ESV; cf. 1 John 4:7–21).

A third explanation of why love comes to authenticate people of true Christian faith is surely to be found in the way the law is now understood to be written on the hearts of all Christians. Love, focused in two directions, was to be a defining marker of all God's people since the days of the Mosaic law. The first direction, repeat-edly stressed, is summed up in Deuteronomy 6:5 with the command to love "the LORD your God with all your heart and with all your soul and with all your might" (NRSV). The second direction is toward the neighbor (Lev 19:18). Jesus repeated this law and even expanded its horizons for the disciples in Matthew 5:43–44 with the command to love enemies. Indeed, Paul talked in Galatians 5:13–14 of the law being "fulfilled in one word, 'You shall love your neighbor as yourself'" (ESV).

None of these explanations need stand alone. Much of the whole of biblical theology is based on God and his love for his people and the response of love from his people. As the new-covenant people now saw themselves as endued with the Holy Spirit, as having the law on their hearts, and as called to obey Christ, it is not surprising that love develops even more clearly than it had been in the Old Testament into the defining marker of those who truly belong to Christ and follow him. No wonder Paul later speaks of love as the "greatest" when speaking of those Christian markers that will go forward in to all eternity (13:13c). For Paul, then, love for God is inevitably the sure sign that the person is "known [by God]" (8:3).

Finally, perhaps the great surprise of chapter 13 is the depth of intimacy of the love relationship Paul described. It is surely more than could have been imagined, especially as Paul looks forward to seeing "face to face" and writes, "Then I shall know fully even as I have been fully known" (v. 12). Gone, as it were, will be the love letters and the photographs and the messages, for "then," to use John's language, the bride and husband are together (Rev 18:3; 19:7). We shall know God, not in the sense of having the same omniscience as God has, but "even as" he has known us personally with such extraordinary depths of love.

13:4–6 Love is forbearing, love is kind, it does not envy, it does not boast, it is not puffed up, it does not behave rudely, it is not self-seeking, it is not provoked to anger, it does not record wrongs, it does not rejoice at[13] evil but rejoices at the truth (Ἡ ἀγάπη μακροθυμεῖ, χρηστεύεται ἡ ἀγάπη, οὐ ζηλοῖ, οὐ περπερεύεται, οὐ φυσιοῦται, οὐκ ἀσχημονεῖ, οὐ ζητεῖ τὰ ἑαυτῆς, οὐ παροξύνεται, οὐ λογίζεται τὸ κακόν, οὐ χαίρει ἐπὶ τῇ ἀδικίᾳ, συγχαίρει δὲ τῇ ἀληθείᾳ). Paul now describes what love looks like. Of course, in this description Paul continues to describe the attributes of a person who exhibits love in their life. Love is not some theoretical theological construct for Paul. It only has meaning when it is *seen* in action in the life of an individual or in the action of God in Christ Jesus. The verbs with which Paul chooses to describe love stress the *action* involved in Christian love. However, they are carefully chosen to relate specifically to the issues that Paul has been addressing in this epistle.

Love is forbearing. Paul builds the description first with the present, active verb meaning "to be forbearing" or "patient" (μακροθυμέω).[14] The person who "forebears" is the one who is able to wait for someone without complaining, to put up with another's weaknesses, foibles, and idiosyncrasies. Yet its substance in Paul's thinking probably derives from his understanding of God's own forbearance. In the Old Testament patience is often mentioned as one of God's great attributes, especially seen in his relationship with Israel; it is frequently linked to his love for his people, seen in his mercy and forgiveness. For example, Nehemiah 9:17 (LXX) states, "You, God, are merciful and compassionate, patient and very merciful" (cf. Ps 144:8; Joel

2:13). Paul describes God's "forbearance" as part of his kindness in giving time that will lead "to repentance" (Rom 2:4). The apostle Peter speaks similarly of God's forbearance in 2 Peter 3:9 as he describes the waiting for Christ's return as a time for more people to come to faith. The eschatological overtones that often accompany the verb are also seen in James 5:8 where we read, "You also must be patient [μακροθυμέω]. Strengthen your hearts, for the coming of the Lord is near" (NRSV; cf. Luke 18:7). The community and people that exhibit patience are a people of the last days who follow a God who has patience with them.

Love is kind. The present indicative of the verb (deponent middle) "to be kind to" or "to be merciful to" (χρηστεύομαι) here indicates a continuing action of the one who loves or a continuing attribute of love itself (if we treat what Paul says here as some kind of personification of love). Again, this finds its basis in God himself, as noted in Romans 2:4. God teaches kindness (Ps 118:66). Wisdom 15:1 states, "God you are kind [χρηστός] and true, forbearing [μακρόθυμος], and mercifully ordering all things." Frequently God's kindness is also linked, like his patience, with his forgiveness and mercy shown toward his rebellious people (Ps 25:7–8 [24:7–8 LXX; χρηστότης]; cf. 106:1 LXX). At the heart of Christian kindness will be a reflection of what the kindness of God and of Jesus look like. Certainly this will involve mercy, forgiveness, and compassion. Patience and kindness are joined together in the list of the fruit of the Spirit in Galatians 5:22 and in the "clothing" that should identify the believer in Colossians 3:12 (cf. 2 Cor 6:6). Some have noted also the remarkable comment by Tertullian, who wrote about the hatred of Christians

---

13. The preposition ἐπί can have many meanings. Here, with the dative it is a marker of presence or proximity (BDAG 363 [2.b.]). Thus, the translation "at" evil or "being in the presence of" evil. Rejoicing "at the truth" translates a simple dative.

As Barrett points out, "Not *with* [the truth]; *the truth* does not rejoice" (*First Corinthians*, 304, emphases his).

14. Wallace, *Greek Grammar*, 413, identifies this as a stative active, that is, "the subject exists in the state indicated by the verb."

in the last part of the second century, as he refers to the characteristics of Christians: "'Christian,' so far as translation goes, is derived from 'anointing.' Yes, and when it is mispronounced by you 'Chrestian' . . . it is framed from 'sweetness' or 'kindness.' So in innocent men you hate even the innocent name."[15] It is toward this sort of visible *identification* of Christians that Paul exhorts his readers, for many have been far from kind to their brothers and sisters in Christ and far from forbearing in their attitudes.

It does not envy.[16] A number of negative assertions about love are now made. At the heart of those who constantly compare themselves with others to see whether their status is superior or adequate is a "striving after" the things they think they need to achieve that status. The Greek verb "envy" here (ζηλόω) when used positively carries the idea of "earnest striving after." In English we might use the words "to have *zeal* for." But here Paul uses the word negatively. In effect, it describes having *zeal for* what others have or being jealous or envious in wanting to be like someone else. The implied object here is not someone else's possession but the person himself! In a status-loving community the striving to be like someone else or to belong to certain groups was no doubt part and parcel of social life. Sadly, it was a part of church life in Corinth. Paul's use of the same verb here, as in 12:31, may have an element of irony. The "still better way" that Paul is showing them is one that does not "strive after" people possessing the grace-gifts mentioned in chapter 12 and in the opening three verses of this chapter. The Christian life is to be marked out as part of what Paul elsewhere can call the "new creation" (2 Cor 5:17; Gal 6:15). This new sphere of existence in Christ that Christians inhabit puts others first and "does not envy."

It does not boast (οὐ περπερεύεται). This second negative statement is closely related to the previous matter of "striving after" or "envying." The elitists at Corinth strove after all the wrong things for the sake of status and authentication. When they felt they had found them, they "boasted" in them. This is not love! Paul has shown up their boasting and arrogance on a number of occasions in this epistle (3:21; 4:7; 5:6). This leads very naturally into the next statement.

It is not puffed up (οὐ φυσιοῦται). The section that started at 8:1 began with the statement, "knowledge puffs up but love builds up." As the status seekers exploit their grace-gift of "knowledge" and, no doubt, other gifts that Paul has mentioned in chapter 12 and the first three verses of chapter 13, they have become conceited. What Paul says here in his description of love becomes almost a reprise on 4:6–7. There Paul had held himself up by way of example, then continued to tell them not to be "puffed up one against another."[17] He reminded them that all they possess had come as a gift from God, much as he has argued in chapter 12. Therefore, there could be no grounds for "boasting" (4:7). On 8:1 we commented, "Being 'puffed up' (φυσιόω) involves the flaunting of something for one's own benefit or to stress one's own status. So . . . Paul offers a sober and deliberately *deflating* perspective on the way their 'knowledge' was functioning in the community." It is the flaunting implied by the use of the verb (φυσιόω) that is so significant. It also reminds us that these people were looking for visible evidence that they were superior or "spiritual." Something can only be "flaunted" if every-

---

15. *Apology* 3.5 (Glover and Rendall, LCL).

16. Textual variants here omit the third reference to "love" (ἀγάπη). It does not affect interpretation. The square brackets of NA[28] and UBS[5] indicate that a clear decision is not possible.

17. The verb "to be puffed up" (φυσιόω) occurs six times in 1 Corinthians and elsewhere only in Col 2:18 where it is used in the same negative sense.

one can see it! This then gives rise to the bragging that Paul captures with the verb "boast." The true marker of "love" will also be *seen*, but it will appear in an altogether different form that will involve no boasting, no flaunting of the individual, no status-seeking arrogance.

It does not behave rudely. The word Paul uses here (ἀσχημονέω) only appears in the New Testament here and in 7:36, where it refers to the behavior of a potential husband regarding a woman he may or may not be going to marry. With its moral overtone, Thayer is probably right to give it the translation "to act unbecomingly."[18] The adjective was used in 12:23 where it also has a sense of what is morally acceptable, referring to those parts of the body that are "unpresentable" (the genitals). In this context of 13:4–7, the word sits between "puffed up" and "self-seeking." This suggests that it probably relates to the sort of arrogant and therefore unseemly behavior that has been seen among the elitists in their dealings with their Christian brothers and sisters. The translation "behave rudely" leaves open the precise nature of the "rudeness." Love is always kind and patient and so is very different from the rude, exclusive behavior of arrogance.

It is not self-seeking (οὐ ζητεῖ τὰ ἑαυτῆς). Once again, Paul recalls previous comments to the elitists. In 10:24 Paul had picked up on the catchphrase "all things are lawful" but had insisted that not everything "build[s] up." He continued, "Let no one seek their own [benefit] [μηδεὶς τὸ ἑαυτοῦ ζητείτω], but that of another." Love is thus prepared to give up its rights, as we saw Paul doing in chapter 9. It is always prepared to put the other first. Once again Paul had held himself up by way of example in 10:33: "I strive to benefit everyone in everything [I do], not seeking my own benefit,

but rather that of the many, in order that they may be saved" (cf. Phil 2:4). Each of these negative descriptions fits the elitists whom Paul has addressed throughout the epistle. They seek their own benefit, while the one who loves seeks the benefit of others. In the end, of course, it is Christ who is to be imitated (11:1). Christ "emptied himself" and did not seek to grasp the status of "equality with God" for the benefit of those for whom he came to die (Phil 2:6–8).

It is not provoked to anger. The verb (παροξύνω) is in the passive voice. This is more than being "irritable" (RSV, NRSV), despite the use of the cognate noun in Acts 15:39 where Paul and Barnabas have a "sharp disagreement." Nor is "take offence" (REB, NJB) adequate, since the verb is stronger than this. The word's background in its nonmetaphorical usage is "to sharpen" (cf. Prov 27:17 LXX). LSJ suggests "to urge," "to spur on," or "to provoke," and in the light of its use in the LXX both negatively and positively this seems the better translation. Some versions read simply "is not provoked" (AV, NASB). The only other passive use of the verb in the New Testament is in Acts 17:16 where Paul was "provoked" to anger by a city given over to idolatry. In the LXX God is at times seen to be provoked to anger by the sin of the people (cf. Deut 9:22; 32:19; Isa 47:6). Patience and kindness both contribute to the characteristics of one who is not provoked to anger with someone else. Such a person exhibiting love in their life will not be quick to respond when hurt or attacked or even persecuted. Again, Jesus is the supreme example of someone who exemplified such love. Paul also modeled it.

It does not record wrongs. Here the Greek verb (λογίζομαι) can have a number of different meanings. It is primarily a mathematical or accounting term, but it can also relate to "cognitive processes."[19]

---

18. Thayer, *Greek-English Lexicon*, 82.

19. BDAG 597.

Thus it can mean "to count," to "make a record of," or even "to consider" in the sense of giving thought to a matter or devising a plan (hence AV's translation, "thinketh no evil"; cf. Zech 8:17 LXX). Here the sense is of counting and then recording the count of wrong or evil that has occurred against oneself (cf. TEV, NIV). Forgiveness has not therefore truly happened. Paul's comment in 6:7, "Why not rather suffer wrong? Why not rather be defrauded?" is his response to those who count the wrongs and take even their brothers and sisters to court. How different will be the attitude of love! Here the approach will be like that of God himself. Paul writes of how God "does not count sin" for the believer: "Blessed is the one whose sin the Lord will never count [λογίζομαι] against them" (Rom 4:8; cf. 2 Cor 5:19: "In Christ . . . not counting their trespasses against them" [ESV]). It is an indication of how all these characteristics of love hold together that a person who is easily provoked to anger will likely also be the one who keeps record of the ways they have been wronged. As they do this, they are, in effect, rejoicing in evil.

It does not rejoice at evil but rejoices at the truth. Paul completes this series of positive and negative statements about love with two statements that must be held together, one negative and one gloriously positive. The direct contrast of evil and truth is found in a number of places in the Bible (e.g., LXX Deut 32:4; Mal 2:6; cf. 1 Esdras 4:37: "There is no truth in them and in their unrighteousness they will perish" [NRSV]). The danger for many is that they come to rejoice or delight in that which is evil. This seems to have been the case among the elitists in a number of ways, perhaps with their bragging about their status, their eating food offered to idols in idol temples, or in their ignoring of their poorer brothers and sisters at the Lord's Supper. These are evil things and evil actions in which they have come to rejoice. Instead, "love" will turn away from evil and its presence wherever it is found and will rather rejoice "at the truth" (τῇ ἀληθείᾳ). This is a provisional summary statement in Paul's longer argument, but Fee is surely right when he writes, "Evil and truth, therefore, are probably thought of here in the larger sense of the gospel and all that is opposed to it."[20] The one who rejoices at the truth is the one who sees God at work in and through people and sees God being honored and obeyed. Such a person rejoices in the proclamation of even that which is a "stumbling block" to some and "folly" to others *because it is true* (1:23). Such a person will not even reject criticism if deserved *because it is true* (Gal 4:16). This leads to great rejoicing.[21]

These four verses paint a glorious picture of love personified. In many ways the description, beautiful and poetic as it is, interacts at an immediate level with the problems the church at Corinth faces and that Paul has highlighted. The many in the church, who are keen to designate themselves as "spiritual," need to look again at what should truly identify God's people. They should look at Paul (and at Jesus, 11:1) who in his actions and in his person has witnessed to the love that God's Spirit has poured into the hearts of all who believe (Rom 5:5).

13:7 Love[22] puts up with all things, believes all things, hopes all things, endures all things (πάντα στέγει, πάντα πιστεύει, πάντα ἐλπίζει, πάντα ὑπομένει). In carefully fashioned balance, Paul provides another list of four descriptions of love. Again, the beauty of the poetic form is striking with each sentence in the Greek beginning with "all things" (πάντα) and assonance provided

---

20. Fee, *1 Corinthians*, 708.
21. The prefix συν- intensifies the verb (συγχαίρω).

22. The subject of these verbs remains ἡ ἀγάπη from v. 4.

in the final sound of each of the four sentences. The word "all" is central to the construction and is usually taken to be the direct object of the four verbs, hence the famous AV translation, "[Love] beareth *all things*, believeth *all things*, hopeth *all things*, endureth *all things*." However, the word can also be taken adverbially, modifying each of the four verbs. Hence the NIV (cf. NJB) translates it all four times as "always": "[love] *always*. . . ." Both options are possible in the Greek. The construction of the sentence is also debated. For example, Garland, Fee, Hays, and others (all with minor variations) suggest that the structure is chiastic (ABBA). That is, the two verbs in the middle hang together and later form part of that which abides (13:13; thus perhaps they look to the future), while the first and the last are virtually synonymous, dealing with the present. They form an *inclusio*. Fitzmyer sees the first two as a pair followed by a second pairing. However, there is no need to separate out this list in this way. All four sentences help build the overall picture that Paul wants to paint of the active and deeply positive working of love in the life of the covenant community.

Firstly Paul says love "puts up with all things" (πάντα στέγει). In 9:12 Paul spoke of how he "put up with all things" (πάντα στέγομεν) lest "we put a stumbling block in the way of the gospel of Christ." Even though this is not a common meaning for the verb in other Greek literature, where it can mean "to cover up" or "keep silent about," it is most likely that in 13:7 Paul has in mind the way he has had to put up with the consequences of putting Christ and the gospel before all else. It has been noted how much of chapter 13 refers back to what has been written earlier in the epistle and especially to those places where Paul has used himself as an example. Love is prepared to give up rights (ch. 9) and

"put up with all things" that may happen as a result, including bearing with persecution and being dishonored. The burden may indeed be profound, as many Christians have experienced, even to the point of death. In the end this means that all life must be lived in the realization of the providence of God.

In the next two sentences Paul says love "believes all things, hopes all things" (πάντα πιστεύει, πάντα ἐλπίζει). Thiselton sounds a note of caution here in the light of the contemporary world and its possible *mis*understanding of "believes all things." He cites part of Nietzsche's and Marx's critique of Christian faith as they have understood it.[23] Yet even at the level of standard Christian conversations in this age, it is important not to misunderstand what is said here. To say that love *believes* all things is not somehow to imply that truth itself can be relativized or compromised! Part of Thiselton's answer is to translate the whole verse by "negating a series of negations." Thus he translates, "[Love] never loses faith, never exhausts hope."[24] We have not followed Thiselton in his translation, but recognise that his serious warning must be heeded and great care taken in explaining just what is meant by "believes all things." Furthermore, it is vital that love, as Paul describes it, not be thought to be credulous, naive, or undiscriminating.

The activity of believing and hoping all things implies that love will never stop having faith and will never lose hope.[25] It does not simply mean that love always tries to think the best about people. Paul has in mind the deep and total commitment to God that should characterize all Christians, together with their total commitment to the promises God has made to his people. Paul begins to remind his readers of the eschatological framework within which this sort of love must be set, something he

---

23. Thiselton, *1 Corinthians*, 1057.
24. Ibid. Cf. REB.
25. Cf. Fee, *1 Corinthians*, 709.

will develop in the next few verses. The "hope" referred to here is likely the confidence that God will protect the Christian now as they await God's future eternal blessings (cf. 15:19; Rom 8:24–25; Col 1:4–5). So much of what is faced by Christians in this age is transient and contingent. The faith and the hope of which Paul speaks are neither transient nor contingent as God pours out his love upon us. This is the commitment to Christ crucified who comes in glory rather than to the "wisdom of this age" and the folly of chasing spiritual status markers. The risk that Paul has already "put up with" for the sake of Christ and the "hope" in which he has trusted, even while being persecuted, is only possible as he believes all things and hopes all things.

Finally, Paul writes that love "endures all things." Whether there is any difference at all between the meaning of the verbs in the first and last of these four sentences (στέγω and ὑπομένω) is far from clear. (We have translated the words differently simply to reflect the different verbs in Greek.) It may simply be that different words are used for the sake of style within the careful poetic construction. If that is the case, then "believing" and "hoping" are the focal point enclosed by these two similar sentences. It is only with this total *believing and hoping* in the Lord that the Christian can put up with or endure all things that may come by way of affliction for Christ's sake. The concept of Christian endurance thus underlies the verse, an endurance to be discovered only in the life lived by, with, and through love.

13:8–10 Love never fails. But if there be prophecies, they will be abolished; if tongues, they will cease; if knowledge, it will be abolished. For we know in part and we prophesy in part, but when the perfect comes, the partial will be abolished (Ἡ ἀγάπη οὐδέποτε πίπτει. εἴτε δὲ προφητεῖαι,

καταργηθήσονται· εἴτε γλῶσσαι, παύσονται· εἴτε γνῶσις, καταργηθήσεται. ἐκ μέρους γὰρ γινώσκομεν καὶ ἐκ μέρους προφητεύομεν· ὅταν δὲ ἔλθῃ τὸ τέλειον, τὸ ἐκ μέρους καταργηθήσεται). The eschatological framework for understanding the distinction between the nature of love and of the grace-gifts is now developed. As Paul does this, it becomes clear that though love is so beautifully described in this chapter, Paul has "composed [it] to deal with the specific problem of the evaluation of spiritual gifts in the Corinthian community. Love is mentioned only in the beginning and the end of the unit."[26] He develops the contrast between love and the gifts on two levels. On the one hand there is the contrast between the eternal, status-identifying nature of love and the temporal nature of the grace-gifts that come to an end. On the other, there is the contrast between what is partial and what is complete or perfect. The *inclusio* formed by these two statements about love (in vv. 8, 13) makes the first point. Love "never fails" and "love abides." The grace-gifts are imperfect for they are "partial." On the last day they are gone for good, but even now they never provide a complete understanding of God's will. "Love," on the other hand, cannot be seen as partial for it is a revelation of the in-breaking of God's kingdom (the eternal) into the present. Love will never be gone. Rather, it will simply continue, as now, but in a world where the sin that wars against love is altogether removed. Whereas the gifts are "nothing" without love (vv. 1–3), love does not need the gifts for its full revelation.

Paul begins the section with a simple proposition that affirms the permanence of love: "love never fails." Significantly, however, the Greek verb used here usually means "to fall" (πίπτω). In 10:12 Paul had warned that some who think they will

---

26. Hays, *First Corinthians*, 228.

"stand" before God will in fact "fall." Love does not "fall," nor will it "fall" on judgment day (nor at any point before that).[27] This highlights the comparison between love that never fails (in the sense of marking out those who stand on the last day) and the grace-gifts that "will be abolished" (καταργέω) and "cease" (παύω) and so cannot offer such security of status. The context is of what happens at the Lord's coming. Love will indeed "put up with" and "endure" always, but especially *through* the final judgment and the face-to-face revelation of the Lord (13:12). It will remain a feature of those who inhabit the new earth as it is of those who are God's people in this age.

This never-failing permanence of love is contrasted with three of the grace-gifts mentioned earlier, prophecy, tongues, and knowledge. The nature of these gifts was examined above (12:8–10). Nevertheless, it should be noted that once again it is the *verbal*, public gifts that Paul contemplates, what Paul probably refers to in 1:5 as "all speech and all knowledge." These are the gifts that can be flaunted and appear powerful in their ability to coerce. Paul variously focuses in different ways on each of these gifts. Thus he writes at length of prophesying in chapter 11 and, by way of contrast with tongues, in chapter 14. He writes at length on tongues in chapter 14 and on knowledge in chapter 8 and, in part, in chapter 10.

Each of these gifts, considered so vital to the life of the Corinthian church and especially those who would claim to be "spiritual" and see themselves as further on the way, have within them the seeds of their own destruction. That is, in themselves they actually reveal their own *impermanence*. Each clause is introduced by "if there be . . ." (εἴτε). The use of this particle introduces a conditional sense to each clause that is often ignored in various translations. The NJB and NASB capture the conditional element with the words "if there are . . . ." This may perhaps confirm Paul's view of gifts, seen in chapter 12, where he insists that not all have the same gifts.[28] Therefore, "if there are prophecies" suggests that Paul thinks there may not be prophecies, at this time or that time, if the Spirit chooses not to give the gift. Paul seems to assume that all three of these gifts are not necessarily always evident in the church, but "if they are," then all must know that they will ultimately be abolished.

Prophecies and knowledge will be "abolished" (καταργέω). The verb was used in 1:28 of God bringing things to nothing so that there may be no boasting before God. In 2:6 it was used of God's final judgment of the rulers of this age who are "doomed to come to nothing" (cf. 6:13). In the context of the end of chapter 13 the passive voice presupposes that God is the agent by which this will happen (in 1:28, 2:6, and 6:13 God is the subject and the active voice is used). Paul does not distinguish in his argument here between what happens to prophecy and knowledge (which "will be abolished" or "brought to nothing") and what happens to tongues (which "will cease").[29] He is looking forward to the time of Christ's coming in glory and its perfection and argues that, as with the judgment of the rulers of this age, so even *good* Spirit-given

---

27. W. Michaelis, "πίπτω," *TDNT* 6:164–66. BDAG 815 notes that the word can refer to buildings and structures falling to pieces or collapsing, and so figuratively it can come to mean "to fail" or "come to an end." In Luke 16:17 the present infinitive (πεσεῖν) is used with this connotation (cf. Ruth 3:18 LXX).

28. There is no need to go so far as Robertson and Plummer, *First Corinthians*, 296, who says, "The repeated εἴτε is deprecatory; it suggests indifference as to the existence of gifts of

which the use was at best temporary."

29. What Paul says here regarding "tongues" raises again the question about what exactly they are. If they are a reflection in this age of heavenly languages, then they might be expected to survive into the next age! See at 14:4, "In Depth: What Was Paul's Attitude to 'Speaking in a Tongue' and What Is the Phenomenon?"

things will be abolished, for they are provisional and adapted by God for this age alone. Translations that talk of prophecies that "will pass away" (e.g., RSV) fail to establish *the God-ordained nature of what happens here to the grace-gifts*, which is carried by the passive voice.

Paul then says that tongues will "cease" or "stop." It is usually argued that the double passive voice associated with prophecies and knowledge influences the connotation of "cease." Thus, it is assumed that Paul means that *God causes tongues to "stop" as well*. However, this presumes that the future middle verb "to stop" (παύσονται) is deponent in form. A deponent middle is usually understood as describing a verb that has no active form but its middle form functions as if it were an *active* voice. However, Wallace makes a substantial *grammatical* case for this verb being a true middle and therefore reflexive in form. He translates: "If there are tongues, they will cease [on their own]."[30] Wallace argues this is probably simply stylistic. It has been argued by a few others that it implies tongues are different and they, as it were, simply dry up on their own while the other gifts finish at Christ's return. But, of course, the text says nothing at all about when they might cease on their own. A good argument could be made that no one would even try to speak in tongues when seeing face to face! Yet all this is stretching Paul's meaning too far. He is simply saying here that on that future day of the Lord's coming in glory when all things are made new, all such "speech" (1:5), whether prophecy,

knowledge, or tongues, will become redundant as all God's people come "to know" even as God has fully "known" them (v. 12).

Paul now lays out clearly the reason for the abolition of these grace-gifts of "speech" in terms of the difference between this age and the next. Returning to what was in the Corinthian view the key speech-gift, "knowledge," he comments on how even now *it is partial*.[31] The difference between now and then is that "then" is defined as the time "when the perfect comes" (v. 10; ὅταν δὲ ἔλθῃ τὸ τέλειον). Paul's argument is simple. As God ushers in all that is perfect and complete, he brings perfect and full knowledge. He will simultaneously abolish or do away with that which is not perfect, that is, anything that is partial (v. 9), or inappropriate, or unnecessary for the age of perfection. In v. 8 Paul says the same of prophecy. It may be reading too much into it to say that Paul speaks first to *their* favorite gift and then to his, since Paul has no favorites (he simply has the view that gifts must build people up). Nevertheless, Paul will go on to say good things about prophecy in contrast with tongues. Yet *even such a beneficial gift* as prophecy will not survive into the next age, for it "will be abolished" (v. 10b; note the same passive verb and form as in v. 8c).

"The perfect" (τὸ τέλειον) refers to the coming of Christ and the perfection of all things that is ushered in at the end of this age (v. 10). Many factors point in this direction. Probably the most significant is the statement "then I shall know fully

---

30. Wallace, *Greek Grammar*, 422–23. For a description of true deponent verbs, see his discussion on 428–30. However, compare Robertson, *Grammar of the Greek New Testament*, 355–57, who offers a more nuanced view of what some deponent middle verbs may look like. On the need for recovering an understanding of the middle voice see Jonathan T. Pennington, "Setting Aside 'Deponency' and Rediscovering the Middle Voice for New Testament Studies," in *Studying the Greek New Testament: Papers from the SBL Greek Language and Linguistics Section*, ed. Stanley Porter and Matthew Brook O'Donnell

(Sheffield: Sheffield Phoenix, 2009).

31. Fee (*1 Corinthians*, 714n379) is wrong to assert that the choice of prophecy and knowledge "does not 'mean' anything." It does, as we have noted. To say that "the argument of chap. 14, (esp. v. 6) refutes this" is utterly strange. Among many verses, 14:6 precisely indicates why Paul singles out these two! (See comments on 14:6.) Even two key gifts of *clear and beneficial* communication from God are, nevertheless, partial and will be abolished by God!

even as I have been fully known" in v. 12. It is hard to see how we can "know fully" as God has providentially "known" us until we see him face to face (cf. 8:3). The "perfect" is thus distinct from the partial knowing or seeing of this age. The eschatological use of the word "abolish" (καταργέω) in this epistle at the very least points toward the day of God's action in judgment. At his coming a new state prevails. Some things are done away with, but all that remains (such as love and our existence as the Lord's people) and all that is new is *permanent*. The sheer number of future tenses used throughout this passage speak against the view, for example, that it might refer to a time of "maturity." The contrast of "then" and "now" in the mirror analogy of v. 12 is one of "now" as opposed to "face to face" (πρόσωπον πρὸς πρόσωπον). This surely speaks of a face-to-face encounter with God, something the apostle John in later years regarded as one of the great blessings for God's people of the new earth (Rev 22:4: "They will see his face"), but which had its precursors in Scripture (cf. LXX Exod 33:20; Deut 5:4). As already noted, the use of the word "hope" in Paul's theology generally refers not just to a trust in God for the present but is trust in God's promised future blessings. The culmination of this is the revelation of Christ in his glory (cf. Rom 8:18–25). That is certainly the sense of "hope" in this chapter.

Paul has thus carefully woven together his two arguments about the difference in nature between grace-gifts and love. He has shown the contrast between the eternal nature of love, which never fails, and the temporal nature of the grace-gifts, which come to an end. He has then added to this the contrast between what is "the partial" and what is complete or "the perfect."

13:11–12 When I was a child, I used to speak like a child, I used to think like a child, I used to reason like a child; when I became a man, I got rid of childish things. For now we see in a mirror dimly, but then [we shall see] face to face; now I know partially, then I shall know fully even as I have been fully known (ὅτε ἤμην νήπιος, ἐλάλουν ὡς νήπιος, ἐφρόνουν ὡς νήπιος, ἐλογιζόμην ὡς νήπιος· ὅτε γέγονα ἀνήρ, κατήργηκα τὰ τοῦ νηπίου. βλέπομεν γὰρ ἄρτι δι᾽ ἐσόπτρου ἐν αἰνίγματι, τότε δὲ πρόσωπον πρὸς πρόσωπον· ἄρτι γινώσκω ἐκ μέρους, τότε δὲ ἐπιγνώσομαι καθὼς καὶ ἐπεγνώσθην). Paul's poetic chapter now incorporates one of the best-known examples of a classic rhetorical epistrophe in which the repeated phrase "like a child" finishes each sentence. In this way, Paul uses an analogy as he continues to reinforce the point he has been making. The repetition here of the verb "abolish" (καταργέω), though in the active voice in this verse, which we translate as "I got rid of,"[32] helps indicate the main purpose of the analogy. It is about one way of speaking and thinking being appropriate at one stage in a person's life and another way being appropriate at another stage in that life. In the later stage, there is a deliberate "getting rid of" the former way of living. It is a familiar analogy that is commonplace in literature. There was the "then" when, as a child, an individual spoke and thought "like a child," and a "now" when, as an adult, that person has deliberately "got rid of" childish ways of thinking and speaking. The change from imperfect tenses in the first part of the illustration to the perfect in the second makes the analogy clearer. During the time when "I was a child, I used to . . ." well captures in English the continuous nature of this way of being during that time of life when a child. The perfect captures the

---

32. The deliberative force of the verb (καταργέω), which we translated as "abolish" earlier, needs to be carried through here as well. It does not always denote "abolishing," but it does refer to bringing something to an end or to ensuring it no longer has existence or is wiped out (BDAG 525–26); hence our translation "got rid of."

deliberate decision taken on reaching adulthood to act like an adult. "I became . . . I got rid of" were decisive past actions, but the result is where the emphasis falls (intensive perfect).

However, the analogy should not be misunderstood. Paul is not suggesting that he thinks of speaking in tongues as childish and that the Corinthians should "mature" out of such things. The "then" and "now" does not describe the one who is immature spiritually and the one who is "spiritual," even though Paul uses an analogy of a child to make a point about maturity back in 3:1. As the whole context indicates and v. 12 makes especially clear, the picture of the child refers to how Christians are "now," and the picture of the adult refers to how Christians will be "then" when "the perfect" comes. On the other hand, of course, Paul is asking the Corinthians to contemplate adulthood when the perfect has come. He is asking them to think about things within this Christian eschatological framework. As they realize the *difference* between where they are today and the world that will be, they will begin to see that a whole way of speaking and thinking and evaluating things lies ahead. That way will be one that *no longer requires grace-gifts* to make it happen. Within this framework, the importance of their present grace-gifts will be relativized.

This analogy leads directly into another illustration. Verses 11 and 12a are linked by the word "for" (γάρ) so that the latter further amplifies the former. Paul changes from the first-person singular to the first plural here as he applies what he is saying to all who inhabit this age. The picture is of seeing indirectly in this age but then seeing "face to face" when the perfect has come and the new age has begun. The contrast of the ages is made twice with the words "at present" (ἄρτι) and "then" (τότε) in both v. 12a and v. 12b.

How the illustration of the mirror is understood depends on what is meant by the sentence translated here as "we see in a mirror dimly" (ἐν αἰνίγματι). Most will know from the AV the striking line: "For now we see through a glass, *darkly*." Certainly the phrase is used adverbially, but does it mean that a person seeing "in" the mirror (δι᾽ ἐσόπτρου; or is it "by" or "through"?) sees "darkly," that is, "dimly" (NRSV), or sees "only a reflection" (NIV), or "only reflections . . . mere riddles" (NJB), or "puzzling reflections" (REB), or "indirectly" (Thiselton).[33] First, it is simple, as Barrett contends, to see why Paul should write of seeing "through" a mirror.[34] An image looked at "in a mirror," as we would say, in fact appears to be the other side of it; hence the Greeks spoke of seeing "through a mirror." Secondly, some have suggested that since Roman mirrors were made of metal, the image was always clouded and somewhat distorted or darkened. In other words, it would hardly have been as clear as we might see today in a well-made glass mirror.[35] However, as some point out, mirrors were often of high quality. In fact, mirrors are sometimes used in the literature Paul would have known to speak of *clarity* of vision. Thirdly, the main word in the adverbial phrase translated here as "dimly" (ἐν αἰνίγματι) normally means "puzzling" or "riddle."[36] In this context, whatever its meaning, the word is set in contrast to the utter clarity of seeing "face to face."

There is a long-noted apparent parallel to v. 12a in Numbers 12:8 where God speaks of his relation-

---

33. Thiselton, *1 Corinthians*, 1027. This of course is one of those infrequent instances in which the modern English word ("enigma") carries much of the connotation of the Greek word from which it is drawn.

34. Barrett, *First Corinthians*, 307.

35. Cf. Robertson and Plummer, *First Corinthians*, 298, who write "the Corinthian mirrors were famous; but the best of them would give an imperfect and somewhat distorted reflection." Hays, *First Corinthians*, 230, "not false but indistinct."

36. BDAG 27; hence NJB and REB versions above.

ship with Moses and says that he speaks to him "mouth to mouth, clearly, and not in riddles" (ESV; LXX: οὐ δι' αἰνιγμάτων). The LXX continues, "And he sees the glory of the Lord" (Heb. "the form of the Lord"). For Paul, undoubtedly the issue is seeing or not seeing God. Of course, *speaking* "mouth to mouth" is not the same as *seeing* "face to face," and both Hebrew and Greek versions show their traditional caution here, unlike many modern commentators! The most detailed examination of the background to what Paul is saying here is found in J. Dupont's *magnum opus* on gnosis where he has a chapter dedicated to this verse.[37] Since that work, many commentators have followed at least parts or most of what he wrote. He accepts that Paul drew on Scriptures such as Numbers 12:6–8 for the background to prophets being given "knowledge" of God (v. 6) and Moses receiving more knowledge more clearly. However, he also examines Exodus 34:29–35. This is the main text, he says, from which the motif of "face" comes. In the account of Moses coming down from Mount Sinai, his face shone because he "had been talking with God." This made the people afraid, and after Moses had talked to them he put a veil on his face. The veil was removed whenever Moses spoke to the Lord. Then, when he "came out," he would tell the people what the Lord had said and the people would see "the shining of Moses's face." Then he would cover his face again. The text illuminates v. 12a because it directly relates to the "face" of Moses when words of the Lord are imparted. This has led some to the

view that Paul therefore equates Moses's experience of God, forbidden to the people, as a foretaste of what in the eschaton all God's people will experience. Attractive as this view is, Dupont points out that Paul has a much bigger "hope" in store, for even the vision of God that Moses receives is set firmly in the theological context of Exodus 33:20 where God says to *Moses*, "You cannot see my *face*, for no one may see me and live." Paul builds on this view that no person on earth can see God's face and live, not even Moses. To say that "mouth to mouth" (Num 12:8) is therefore the *same* as "face to face" begs a number of questions. Dupont insists that Paul therefore only uses Numbers 12:8 "loosely" to draw out the issue of God normally speaking through prophets "indirectly" or in a "puzzling way" (δι' αἰνιγμάτων). Yet Paul is going to say *more* than this.[38] His point centers on his eschatological hope that we shall see "face to face," something that not even Moses was allowed to do.

Even so, as Dupont notes, this does not explain the "mirror" analogy. For this he, like many, turns to various Hellenistic sources for an explanation. In fact, mirrors were widely regarded as "clear," and it was believed that a proper and right image could be seen in them. So the matter is not about seeing in some obscure fashion.[39] In some sources it is noted that a mirror, while giving a good reflection, in fact gives a "dim" or even "indirect" image. Many references can be found from Plato to Plutarch and beyond that incorporate the idea of a "mirror" into the way the gods or the noumenal can be perceived. Some undoubtedly describe this in terms of its *lack*

---

37. This is one of the most thorough and detailed examinations of the meaning of this illustration and its possible background in Hellenistic and/or Jewish and Old Testament background. J. Dupont, *Gnosis: La Connaissance Religieuse dans les Épîtres de Saint Paul*, Dissertationes ad gradum magistri in Facultate Theologica vel in Facultate Iuris Canonici consequendum conscriptae 2.40 (Louvain: Nauwelaerts, 1949), 106–48.

38. In 2 Cor 3:16–18 Paul uses similar material where the removal of the veil available to Moses is also available now to all who receive Christ. Here Christians are said, as was said of Moses, that they behold the glory of the Lord with "unveiled face" (ESV). This is *now*. The hope laid before Christians is much, much greater than what Moses had or what we have now.

39. Rather, in line with Platonic thought the issue is often whether the reflection in the mirror is "real" or "true." Cf. Plato, *Republic* 10.596E (Emlyn-Jones and Preddy, LCL).

of clarity, but others use the image to suggest a dim or *indirect* clarity and glory.[40] This is surely the picture that Paul desires here as he thinks of the "knowledge" that we are currently given for the benefit of God's church and the "knowledge" that we shall "then" experience (cf. 8:2). What we have now is true knowledge, just as what Moses received was true and amazingly detailed "mouth to mouth" knowledge from God. But *it was dim and partial.*[41]

The context in which Paul applies the analogy is set firmly in the biblical/Jewish context of "knowing God." Through the prophets, this has been possible by God's grace in a true but dim manner (because only partial). As Numbers 12:6 states, "If there is a prophet among you, I the LORD *make myself known* to him in a vision; I speak with him in a dream" (ESV). Moses received a brighter picture, but it was still specifically, as God makes clear, *not* "face to face" since he was told he *could not* see God's face. Paul is not making a point about Moses's revelation as opposed to that of other prophets. Rather, he makes a point that is explained by the Hellenistic analogy of the mirror, that all such revelation of God "now" is "indirect." The future is thus, as Dupont says, so far greater than even Moses knew. But Exodus 33:17–22 remains foundational. Everything in this world order, even for us "upon whom the ends of the ages have come" (1 Cor 10:11) in Christ and who have received gifts of God's Spirit, remains partial and indistinct compared with the glory to come.

Interestingly, as we move to the second half of 13:12, it should be noted that Exodus 33:17 began

with God saying to Moses, "You have found favor in my sight, and *I know you* by name" (ESV; LXX: "above all" [παρὰ πάντας]). This is what Paul now turns to. For him the most important matter is that Christians are known by God (cf. 8:3; Gal 4:9). As Moses was known first by God and then given a glorious but restricted vision of God, so it is with all God's people. As Paul reverts again to the first-person singular, he insists, "I have been fully known" (ἐπεγνώσθην). Yet, even so, he only knows "partially" (ἐκ μέρους). "Then," and only then, will he fully know even as he has been fully known. The first singular may again be Paul drawing attention to the fact that he, who is a prophet and an apostle and has knowledge and speaks in tongues, is in the same boat as all other Christians. The end result is that all grace-gifts are relativized in the light of what is to come. All are only indirect. All provide truth, but it is partial truth and partial sight and partial knowledge. "Partial" does not mean inadequate or wrong or poor. From Paul's perspective, such "knowledge" is from God and for the building up of the church. Yet when "the perfect" comes, it will be done away with. Who will want to see God indirectly or to know in part when the complete revelation is made and he can be known fully?

13:13 But now faith, hope, love remain, these three; but the greatest of these is love. (Νυνὶ δὲ μένει πίστις, ἐλπίς, ἀγάπη, τὰ τρία ταῦτα· μείζων δὲ τούτων ἡ ἀγάπη). The apostle completes this amazing passage with the frequently used triad of faith, hope, and love (1 Thess 1:3; 5:8; Rom 5:1–5; Col 1:4–

---

40. Cf. Plutarch, *Moralia* 10.781.F–782, here, drawing on Plato. He says of god being imaged in his creation: "As the sun, his most beautiful image, appears in the heavens as his mirrored likeness to those who are able to see him in it . . ." (LCL). Also cf. *Moralia* 5.382.A, where Plutarch reflects upon observing "the *riddle* [αἴνιγμα] of the divine in inanimate objects" but regards those beings with natures and souls, etc., as a "clearer mirror of the divine" (LCL).

41. This approach is far more satisfactory than an appeal to a midrashic wordplay on "vision" and "mirror" that brings together Ezek 43:3 and Num 12:8 (interpreted through Exod 38:8). See M. Fishbane, "Through the Looking Glass: Reflections on Ezek 43:3, Num 12:8 and 1 Cor 13:8," *HAR* 10 (1986): 63–75. Paul needs no wordplays. He simply builds on the Old Testament understanding of prophetic knowledge and the revelation of God's glory, which, even with Moses, was partial and deliberately dimmed behind the rock (Exod 33:22)!

5; Eph 4:2–5). This triad that "remains" provides a vivid contrast with the triad of prophecies, tongues, and knowledge in v. 8, each of which will be "abolished" or "disappear." The verse thus becomes a grand summary. That which lasts into eternity must also be the most valued in this present age. The words "but now" (νυνὶ δέ) indicate the logical progression of his argument as he wraps up this section. In the previous verse, Paul twice contrasted "then" and "now."[42] Here there is no longer a "then," for all three "remain." The superiority of love is firmly established even against faith and hope, which also continue through eternity. Paul has insisted that prophecy, knowledge, and tongues will be abolished, and it is perhaps that triad (a representative example of the grace-gifts) that gives rise to this further list of three *permanent* great identifiers of true Christian existence that Paul says "remain" (μένω; cf. NIV, TEV, NJB).[43] The matter of permanence versus impermanence, established in vv. 8–12, thus becomes one of the great ways of deciding what the true authenticators of Christian status really are. Yet, three exegetical matters require attention.

First, the meaning of each element of the triad requires attention. "Faith" (πίστις) here is not the grace-gift of faith that can remove mountains mentioned in v. 2. Rather, it is the summary word that Paul uses in a number of places in his writing. It refers to the full response to the saving gospel of Christ crucified.[44] This is especially seen in the passages noted above where the triad appears. This faith involves the acceptance of forgiveness through the death of Jesus and the judicial verdict of justification. As Paul says in Romans 10:6–10, it

is demonstrated in the confession "Jesus is Lord" and the experience of being "never put to shame" (judged). If this continues to eternity, as seems to be Paul's point, then "faith" characterises a life lived for all eternity in the sphere in which Christ's salvation is known and experienced and in which he continues forever to be acknowledged as Lord. The Christian's faith is then the eternal commitment of that person to the Lord, whom he or she will one day see face to face.

"Hope" (ἐλπίς) refers, similarly, to trusting God for the future. In the present, the Christian hope is mainly focused on Christ's coming in glory (cf. Gal 5:5; Col 1:5), but there is no reason to suggest that this cannot also go forward into eternity, for it is closely related to faith. Barrett captures this as he writes: "Like faith, hope presupposes and expresses a genuine and therefore unalterable truth about God. God is faithful (πιστός); that is, one in whom faith (πίστις) is properly reposed. Similarly, God is our hope; that is, one in whom hope is properly reposed. It is because they are thus rooted in the truth about God that faith and hope express a *permanent* truth about man."[45] As hope is contemplated in this way, we should especially remember 15:19: "If for this life only we are (even now) those who hope in Christ, we are more pitiable than all people." "Love" has already been described at 8:1–3.

Some take issue with the explanation above precisely because they do not see that "faith" and "hope" may continue on into eternity.[46] It is suggested that "but now" should be taken as fully temporal and refer to "this age" in the same way as the word "now" (ἄρτι) does in v. 12. The argument

---

42. Ciampa and Rosner, *1 Corinthians*, 664n238, examines whether the change of vocabulary from "now" (ἄρτι) in v. 12 to "now" (νυνί) in v. 13 is significant since the temporal connotation of the latter is sometimes missing. They conclude that this is unlikely but that there is a contrast in v. 13 with v. 12 that has a temporal aspect to it.

43. "Last for ever" (REB) or "abide" (NASB, NRSV, ESV; cf. AV ["abideth"]).

44. Fitzmyer, *1 Corinthians*, 501.

45. Barrett, *First Corinthians*, 309 (emphasis added).

46. See Calvin, *First Corinthians*, 283; Ruef, *Paul's First Letter to Corinth*, 145; Hays, *First Corinthians*, 230; Horsley, *1 Corinthians*, 179.

for taking "but now" as temporal is further supported by the suggestion that the logical meaning of "love is the greatest" is that *it alone* continues on into eternity.[47] Faith and hope, it is said, come to an end at the coming of Christ, for then neither will be necessary. Thus "faith" comes to an end when "sight" comes (2 Cor 5:7), and "hope" anticipates that "coming" and so disappears when we see face to face (Rom 8:24–25). Nevertheless, these objections to the explanation above do not seem weighty. As noted, it is possible to view both faith and hope as carrying forward beyond this age into the next alongside love. More than that, we may note from 13:7 that Paul has already bound up faith and hope into love. Thus love "believes all things" and "hopes all things."

Secondly it is important to ask what Paul means by calling love "the greatest."[48] This was addressed in the "In Depth" section on "Love" at 13:3. It is unlikely that it is the "greatest" because it is permanent while faith and hope die out. More likely it is the greatest because it is the true indicator that a person belongs to and is imitating God himself. Love belongs to God and is poured out upon Christians by the Holy Spirit (Rom 5:5). God himself does not possess "faith" or "hope." But he does possess love and gives it to all his people. The two great commands speak of loving God and loving the neighbor. Neither are possible without the love of God being poured out as the Spirit is given. Yet with Christ's arrival and the establishment of a new covenant in his blood, the Spirit has indeed been poured out on all flesh as Joel prophesied (Joel 2:28–32). Thus, *all* Christians can truly imitate the Lord (1 Cor 11:1). Paul himself has shown himself to be an example of this (ch. 9) As Barrett says,

"Love is an activity, the essential activity, of God himself, and when men love either him or their fellow-men they are doing (however imperfectly) what God does."[49]

Thirdly the meaning of "remain" must be considered. There is no great need to distinguish between the English words "abide" and "remain." The former may better indicate going on in this age, while the latter may perhaps better indicate the idea of the triad enduring beyond the ceasing of the grace-gifts into the new age. For those who take it that love's "greatest" aspect is the fact that it alone carries over into the future age, then when faith, hope, and love *remain* it means that they carry on in *this* age and endure until Christ's coming. The problem with this is simply that throughout the passage Paul has been building a contrast between love and the grace-gifts. The triad continues the contrast, and nowhere does Paul suggest that a grace-gift will not *also* "remain" (in that sense). The point of the contrast in vv. 8–12 is thus lost in the summary of v. 13, and the point of v. 13 is almost redundant, other than to say that love is somehow better than faith and hope!

Paul has clearly established the preeminence of love for the church's life and identity. Unlike grace-gifts that not all possess, it is the marker of true community membership. All who are Christians possess it. Since it is active, it can be worked at and imitated, and since it comes from God and reflects God, it remains forever.

The words of 14:1a, "pursue love" (διώκετε τὴν ἀγάπην), thus become a bridge between the end of this section and the start of the next. This is the "greater way" that truly will demonstrate authentic and mature community membership.

---

47. Chrysostom, *Homilies on First Corinthians*, homily 34.3 (p. 476), writes, "How then is charity the greater? In that those [faith and hope] pass away."

48. Here is an example of the occasional lack of distinction

between the comparative and the superlative by the time the New Testament was written. See BDF §244. See Wallace, *Greek Grammar*, 299–300, for detailed discussion.

49. *First Corinthians*, 311.

Theology in Application

Love As a Way of Life

Love as described in 1 Corinthians 13 is best understood as a way of life, lived in imitation of Jesus Christ, that is focused not on oneself but on the "other" and his or her good. This is why it is not altogether helpful to distinguish between love for God (8:3) and love for those who belong to the Lord. Love is about action, how a person lives for the Lord and obeys him and how a person lives for others and serves them. Yet it is also about *being*. This is because its foundation is in God who *is* love (2 Cor 13:14; cf. 1 John 4:8, 16), and in Christ who *shows* that love (Rom 5:8). The sense that this is about more than simply how people behave is seen in passages like Paul's prayer of Ephesians 3:14–19, particularly as he prays that Christians will be "rooted and grounded in love" (v. 17 ESV). To "know the love of Christ" is to experience his presence "through faith" in their "hearts" (vv. 17, 19 ESV). God's people are to look and become more and more like Christ, and it is this for which Paul prays here. It is because *being* and *actions* are so closely tied together in God and in Christ, first, but then also in his people, that Paul calls it a "more excellent *way*" (12:31b). It is the way of the new age that has been ushered in with the appearance of the Messiah, who has shown it in his life, passion, and death, but who has also exhibited it in his being. Love is the way of existence in the heavenlies. As this breaks into the present in Christ, his people, filled with the Spirit of Christ, are to take on this way of existence and develop a life where love guides their approach to all things. Of course, this will immediately be seen in *how* they live and speak and think. It is this that chapter 13 describes, especially in vv. 4–7. Even so, when all that is mentioned here is done, the meaning of love for the believer is by no means exhausted!

Paul's description of the action and behavior produced by love is distinctly countercultural. It speaks against the envy, pride, and self-centeredness of the Corinthian Christians, and in doing so speaks clearly to our own generation as well. In a society where so much is presented in terms of "self" (whether self-awareness, self-esteem, self-acceptance, self-image, self-realization, etc.), to present a way of existence in which a person lives for the other in a life of loving self-sacrifice will be highly provocative. Following the one who gave his life as a sacrifice for *us* will be humbling and undoubtedly costly in terms of human recognition and progress in life as secular society defines it.

As we have seen throughout, Christ has to remain the example. The envy, boasting, rudeness, arrogance, and anger of normal life will be turned upside down. Instead, patience and love and a rejoicing in truth are to mark out God's people. In line with the way Christ forgave our sin and no longer holds it against us, so our love is to hold no record of evil. Here, by way of example is surely one of the easiest ways in which Christians fail properly to handle the times when they are sinned against.

They forgive, but the hurt or pain remains at the back of their mind. Then, the next time they encounter that person who has wronged them, they remember and keep score. If something goes wrong again in the relationship, they may once again say "I forgive you," but they will then add the word "but." The *but* usually will hark back to the past and to the record that has been kept of previous hurts committed. We are reminded of Peter's question about how often to forgive his brother when he sins against him (Matt 18:21). The answer Jesus gives is that life must be lived as a forgiving life. Disciples of Christ will go on and on forgiving because it is part of who they are. Love is a most excellent *way.*

Love Is Not Soft

Many see love as little more than an attitude of "niceness" to everyone. This means that any dispute, any strong speaking over important matters, and any firm spiritual discipling or disciplining of another is *ab initio* to be regarded as unloving. In some churches this has even led to a watered-down Christian faith being preached with little emphasis on holiness lest some should feel condemned or unloved. The apostle Paul wrote of the dangers of letting the world's understanding of matters like this influence the church in 2 Timothy 4:3–4: "For the time is coming when people will not endure sound teaching, but having itching ears they will accumulate for themselves teachers to suit their own passions, and will turn away from listening to the truth and wander off into myths" (ESV). One of the modern myths so prevalent in our society is that love will tolerate all things, promote all things, and deny nothing. In Scripture love is beautiful and well defined for us in that God is love, and Jesus demonstrated this perfectly to us all. The New Testament writers, like Paul in this chapter, put further, down-to-earth flesh on the subject. Certainly, love is not soft. It will always seek to build up the other, but that does not mean turning a blind eye to sin or not calling out evil in another person. "It does not rejoice at evil" (13:6).

In fact, true love, since it is supremely seen in the gospel of Jesus Christ, will often divide people, for that is what happens as the gospel is preached and lived out. While Paul can urge patience and insist on kindness (v. 4), he sees no contradiction between this and possibly bringing a "rod" to the Corinthian church (4:21). He sees no conflict between his heavy sarcasm in 4:8 and being kind. Then neither does he see a conflict between God's love and God's severe discipline of his people (11:32; cf. Heb 12:6 where the Lord's discipline is seen as his love). It is critical when presenting the love inherent in the gospel of Jesus Christ that it not be reduced to meaningless platitudes and the "smiley face" of yesteryear.

1 Corinthians 14:1–25

Literary Context

Having spoken of the serious problems of practical theology that have developed in the church because of their abuse of the grace-gifts, Paul began in chapter 12 to look at the right use and right purposes for which God gave these gifts. They are for the building up of the body of Christ. Chapter 13 fits well in Paul's argument. There he specifically contrasts grace-gifts with the true authenticator of mature Christian faith: love. Paul had already indicated that the key to love is that it functions to build up the community (8:1). Then in chapter 13 he drew on some of the more exceptional or unusual gifts to make his point. It has been suggested that these gifts were among those that the elitists were probably promoting. Having shown that "love" is the only true authenticator of God's people and one that, unlike the grace-gifts, survives death itself, Paul now returns to the right and proper function of the gifts. Chapter 14 thus follows clearly and easily from chapter 13. The first verse of chapter 14 makes the transition with a summary of the thought of chapter 13 and a return to the matter of the gifts, specifically two of the gifts mentioned in 13:1–2.

Paul thus applies his teaching specifically by comparing the gifts of speaking in tongues and of prophecy. He demonstrates how one can function to build up the community and even outsiders, thus becoming an example of the love spoken of in chapter 13, while the other cannot normally serve this purpose. While there is good reason to assume that these gifts were highly esteemed among the elitist Corinthians, they serve for Paul to make the general point about the need for discernment and judgment about the things of the Spirit and how they should be allowed to function in the community.

Main Idea

Church members should pursue love, and this means desiring those grace-gifts that build up the church. This will lead to a prioritizing in public worship of gifts that build up the worshippers. The contrast between the gifts of speaking in tongues and prophecy help establish Paul's point.

Translation

1 Corinthians 14:1–25

1a	Exhortation	**Pursue**	**love,**
		and	
b	Exhortation	**earnestly desire**	**spiritual things,** but
c	Expansion		especially that you may prophesy.
2a	Basis for 1c, Assertion	For **the one who speaks in a tongue does not speak**	to men [or women] but
b			to God,
c	Basis for 2a	for **no one understands him,**	
d	Contrast	but **he speaks mysteries**	
e	Means	by the Spirit.	
3a	Contrast with 2a	But **the one who prophesies speaks**	to men [and women]
b	Advantage	for their	building up and
c			encouragement and
d			consolation.
4a	Assertion	**The one who speaks in a tongue**	**builds himself up,**
b	Contrast	but **the one who prophesies**	**builds up the church.**

5a	Desire (concession)	Now **I wish that you all would speak in tongues,** but
b	Comparison	to an [even] greater extent
c	Desire	**I wish you would prophesy;**
d	Assertion	and **the one who prophesies is greater than the one who speaks in tongues**
e	Exception	unless he interprets
f	Purpose	in order that the church may be edified.

6a	Explanation	Now it is like this, brothers [and sisters],
b	Hypothetical illustration (1)	if I come to you speaking in tongues,
c	Question	**what shall I benefit you**
d	Exception	unless I communicate to you
e	Instrumental	either by [some] means of revelation or knowledge, or
f	list	prophecy, or teaching?

7a	Hypothetical illustration (2)	Similarly,
b		lifeless instruments
		that produce a sound, whether
c		a flute or harp,
d	Condition	if they give no distinction ♫
		between sounds,
e	Question	**how will what is played on the flute or on the harp be recognized?**

8a	Hypothetical illustration (3)	Also, you see,
b	Condition	if the trumpet gives an indistinct sound,
c	Question	**who will get ready for battle?**

9a	Hypothetical illustration (4)	And so it is with you,
b	Condition (negative)	if with the tongue you do not give a clear word,
c	Question	**how will what is said be recognized?**
d	Reason	For **you will be speaking into thin air.**

10a	Condition (expressing	Though there may be many kinds of languages in the world and
b	possibility)	none without meaning,

11a	Condition (protasis)	if I do not know the meaning of the language,
b	Assertions (apodosis)	**I will be a foreigner to the speaker** and
c		**the one speaking a foreigner to me.**

12a	Series	And so it is with you,
b	Basis for 12c	since you are enthusiasts for inspirations of the Spirit,
c	Exhortation	**strive that you may abound in the building up of the church.**

Continued on next page.

Continued from previous page.

13a	Inference from vv. 6–12	Therefore,
b	Exhortation	**let the one who speaks in a tongue pray to interpret.**
14a	Condition	For if I pray in a tongue,
b	Assertion	**my spirit prays**
c	Contrast	but **my mind is unfruitful.**
15a	Rhetorical question	**What am I to do?**
b	Response (assertions)	**I will pray with my spirit,**
c		and **I will pray with my mind also;**
d	Series	**I will sing with my spirit**
e		and **I will sing with my mind also.**
16a		Otherwise,
b	Condition	if you give thanks
c	Means	by means of the Spirit,
d	Assertion	**how can the one …**
e	Description	who finds himself among those who do not understand
f	Assertion (cont.)	**… say the "amen" to your thanksgiving,**
g	Basis	since he does not know what you are saying?
17a	Inference	For **you may be giving thanks** well enough,
b	Contrast	but **the other person is not built up.**
18a	Assertion	**I thank God,**
b	Assertion (hyperbole)	**I speak in tongues** more than all of you.
19a		Nevertheless,
b	Location	in the congregation
c	Wish	**I would rather speak five words**
d	Means	with my mind
e	Purpose	to instruct others
f	Comparison	**than ten-thousand words**
		in a tongue.
20a		Brothers [and sisters],
b	Exhortation	**do not be children**
		in your thinking,
c	Contrast	but rather
d	Exhortation	**be children**
		in evil
e	Exhortation/contrast	and in your thinking
		be mature.
21a	Assertion	**In the law it is written,**
b	Quotation	"By people of strange tongues and by the lips of strangers
c		I will speak to this people,
d		and even then they will not listen to me, says the Lord."
		[cf. Isa 28:11–12]

22a	Inference	So then
b	Assertion	**tongues are a sign**
c	Negative	not for those who believe but rather
d	Advantage	for those who do not believe,
		and
e	Assertion	**prophecy is a sign**
f	Negative	not for those who do not believe but rather
g	Advantage	for those who believe.
23a	Elaboration on v. 22b–d	Therefore,
b	Condition (protasis)	if the whole church comes together
c	Place	in the same place and
d	Condition (cont.)	all speak in tongues and
e		outsiders or unbelievers should enter,
f	Rhetorical question	**will they not say that you are insane?**
24a	Elaboration on v. 22e–g	But if all prophesy and
b	Expansion	one who is an unbeliever or
c		who does not understand should enter,
d	Assertions	**he is convicted by all,**
e		**he is judged by all,**
25a		**the secrets of his heart are revealed**
		and so,
b	Manner	falling on his face,
c	Assertion	**he will worship God,**
		confessing,
d	Confession	"God is really among you."

Structure

This chapter divides into two main sections, with the command "earnestly desire" in v. 1 and v. 39 forming an *inclusio*. The first section (14:1–25) compares and contrasts the gifts of tongues and prophecy, since they offer Paul a good case study of the right function of the gifts in the community. Tongues that are unintelligible do not function to build up anyone, while prophecy that is clearly understood and intelligible to the hearer does indeed do so. The second section (14:26–40) is integrally related to the first part, but moves in a somewhat different direction. Speaking again specifically to matters of worship within the gathered congregation, these verses appeal for order in worship based on the fact that God himself is a God of order. Since he is the one worshipped and has provided the gifts, any spiritually mature person will readily recognize this. Total spontaneity in worship is not appropriate for a God of order, but also in itself it fails to reflect the driving force of love and the building up of the community that should happen in worship.

The first section divides into four parts. (1) 14:1–5 addresses the use of grace-gifts by examining two examples and their use in corporate worship. Note that Paul dealt with matters of worship in 11:17–34, and in chapter 12 he assumes that the Christians are gathered together as a body to receive God's gifts. The two examples of prophecy and tongues are directly contrasted in terms of their capacity to "build up" the church. (2) 14:6–12 develops further, with the use of two analogies, the reason why the gift of tongues may not build up the church. Rather, he urges the pursuit of gifts that "abound in the building up of the church" (v. 12; cf. 15:58). (3) 14:13–19 demonstrates how the gift of tongues fails to build up people within or without the church and stresses the necessity of intelligibility if building up is properly to take place. (4) 14:20–25 returns to the question of true spiritual maturity among the believers. As the whole church participates together in *intelligible* worship, even the outsider will be convicted and will acknowledge God's presence with his people and so be drawn to worship.

Exegetical Outline

VIII. **Status, Public Worship, Freedom, and Grace-Gifts (11:2–14:40)**
- A. The Conduct of Husbands and Wives in Public Worship (11:2–16)
- B. The Conduct of the Church at the Lord's Supper (11:17–34)
- C. Spiritual People and the Function of Their Grace-Gifts in the Church (12:1–31)
- D. The Status of Spiritual People Is Authenticated by Love (13:1–13)
- ➡ **E. The Proper Function of Grace-Gifts in Public Worship (14:1–25)**
  - 1. **Pursue Love and Strive for Gifts That Build Up the Worshippers (14:1–5)**
  - 2. **Tongues Can Be Problematic in Worship (14:6–12)**
    - a. Illustration from Musical Instruments and Application (14:6–9)
    - b. Illustration from Different Languages and Application (14:10–12)
  - 3. **Public Worship Should Be Characterized by Intelligibility (14:13–19)**
  - 4. **Prophecy Is More Beneficial Than Tongues in Public Worship (14:20–25)**

Explanation of the Text

14:1 Pursue love, and earnestly desire spiritual things, but especially that you may prophesy (Διώκετε τὴν ἀγάπην, ζηλοῦτε δὲ τὰ πνευματικά, μᾶλλον δὲ ἵνα προφητεύητε). The initial command summarizes the thrust of chapter 13 and returns to the matter of spiritual gifts, now to be understood in their relationship to the true mark of a Christian: love. Love must be pursued. There is an important, dynamic aspect to what Paul commands here. The present imperative is necessary because, as much as "love" is the mark of the Christian, it has to be worked at and developed. At least until the end of this age, love is not a "natural" attribute of Christians simply because they belong to the Lord. They are called to be like him, and certainly love is part of God's nature, yet as the apostle John puts it, it is not until "he appears [that] we shall be like him" (1 John 3:2).

Paul uses the verb "to pursue" elsewhere of the work in which believers must engage as they seek conformity to the will of God or Christ (Rom 14:19; Phil 3:12, 14; 1 Thess 5:15; 1 Tim 6:11). On the use of "spiritual things" (πνευματικά), see the discussion in 2:13–15. Despite their belief that they possessed and pursued spiritual things, it is Paul's contention that this is not at all what they have done, mostly because they have simply misunderstood the whole concept of what it is to be mature and spiritual. This is why Paul has called the Corinthians "babies" and been concerned with their lack of spiritual maturity (3:1). The great irony here is that the grace-gifts of God to his church should in fact promote growth in love, whereas their abuse by some of the Corinthians has led to the opposite occurring. The pursuit of love thus sets the right perspective, though not for seeking greater grace-gifts as if there is some hierarchy (12:31) but for seeking "spiritual things" (πνευματικά).

They are already eager for "spiritual things," and Paul now says that they are to "earnestly seek" (ζηλόω) them. However, as becomes clear in 14:12, it is *Paul*, not the elitists, who will define what is to be sought and why they should seek these particular things. "Spiritual things," as we noted in chapter 2, are things given by the Spirit that point to Christ. Thus, "prophecy" provides the example Paul needs. The definition of "prophecy" was touched on in 12:10. Though ultimately it is important to remain cautious as to the actual nature of this discourse in times of worship, the gift certainly receives a closer

definition. We shall see in the verses that follow that it is unlikely (usually) to be entirely spontaneous, that it builds up, encourages, and consoles the congregation, that it is exercised under discipline, and that it is always intelligible even to outsiders (vv. 3–4, 12, 19, 31, 40). "But especially" (μᾶλλον δέ) introduces immediately Paul's belief that prophecy is more significant in the life of the church than speaking in tongues.

14:2 For the one who speaks in a tongue does not speak to men [or women] but to God, for no one understands him, but he speaks mysteries by the Spirit (ὁ γὰρ λαλῶν γλώσσῃ οὐκ ἀνθρώποις λαλεῖ ἀλλὰ θεῷ, οὐδεὶς γὰρ ἀκούει, πνεύματι δὲ λαλεῖ μυστήρια). The gist of this verse is simply that the person who speaks "in a tongue" (γλώσσῃ) cannot be understood by normal people but only by God because what he speaks is a "mystery" given him by God's Spirit (πνεύματι; a dative of means).[1] The word translated "tongue" in Greek can, as in English, simply refer to the organ of speech, but the context here defines it more specifically. "Understands" (ἀκούω) could simply mean "hears," but the context again indicates that the real issue is not whether someone can be *heard* but whether what is heard is intelligible and therefore can be *understood*.[2] On the nature of speaking in tongues, see more on 12:10. In this chapter the detailed discussion allows aspects of this gift to be more clearly understood. As this verse shows, this gift is always directed *to God* as part of a person's praise or prayer. This is still true even if the gift is used

---

1. The NIV 1984 translates as "with his spirit" and so does not see it as a reference to the Holy Spirit. Cf. AV, ASV, NASB. (NIV 2011 has "Spirit.") Also see Héring, *First Corinthians*, 146, who follows Godet, *First Corinthians*, 2:266, and bases his argument on the fact that there is "no article nor preposition before the substantive." Thus, the clause is taken to mean that the one speaking in tongues "is carried away in an ecstasy" and it is *his* spirit from which the communication comes. However, the lack of an article probably suggests exactly the opposite.

Fee, *1 Corinthians*, 641n46 (cf. 727n442) rightly notes that "it is a Pauline idiosyncrasy that πνεῦμα in the dative is almost always anarthrous when referring to the Holy Spirit (see, e.g., Rom 8:9, 13, 14, surrounded by arthrous uses in other cases)." The arthrous use of "spirit" referring to a person's spirit here in 14:14 provides further evidence. Contextually, it seems that "Spirit" here is much more easily defined as the Holy Spirit in the light of 12:9.

2. BDAG 37 (sect. 7); cf. Mark 4:33; Gal 4:21.

with interpretation in the gathered congregation (cf. vv. 13 and 16–17). The communication with God clearly is delivered in sounds or a language that cannot normally be understood.

In 2:1 it was noted that Paul's usual use of the word "mystery" has to do with what has now been revealed in Jesus Christ (so also in 15:51). In other words, it focuses on the gospel, which can only be understood through the revelation and work found in Jesus Christ (cf. 4:1). However, in 13:2 we noted that the word may have rather broader connotations. Contextually, here in chapter 14 the word explicates "no one understands" (οὐδεὶς . . . ἀκούει) and hence indicates that the contents of the communication remain a "mystery" to the casual listener, for it is a language or message given by God's Spirit and addressed back to God. This is not to say that the usual Pauline semantic content is altogether missing. The whole point of Christ's coming is to *reveal* God, his purposes, and his love. For something therefore to be allowed to remain a "mystery" is distinctly *unChrist-like*! It is highly inappropriate for a gathered congregation, in which the gospel and its glories are articulated and in which constant praise is being given to God for his work through Christ, to have something spoken that remains unexplained.

14:3 But the one who prophesies speaks to men [and women] for their building up and encouragement and consolation (ὁ δὲ προφητεύων ἀνθρώποις λαλεῖ οἰκοδομὴν καὶ παράκλησιν καὶ παραμυθίαν). The apostle now returns to the building metaphor he used earlier in the epistle, especially in 8:1 (cf. 3:10; 8:10; 10:23). There he began this lengthy argument that "love builds up," while some "spiritual things" like "knowledge" mentioned in 8:1 and

"tongues" here in ch. 14 can fail to do so *if wrongly used*. For Paul the contrast between "tongues" and "prophecy" *as they are employed by the Corinthians* offers a key to understanding how "love" ought to be the controlling factor in discerning the function of "spiritual things" when used in the gathered community. The conjunction (δέ) is adversative here.[3] Rhetorically, Paul may be using alliteration as he speaks of prophecy that brings "encouragement" (παράκλησις) and "consolation" (παραμυθία).[4]

The concept of "building up" was examined at 8:1. Now further definition is added to the idea by use of the words "encouragement" (παράκλησις) and "consolation" (παραμυθία).[5] The two words seem to overlap in meaning. "Encouragement" (παράκλησις) often has to do with verbal exhortation (cf. 2 Macc 7:24; 1 Tim 4:13; Heb 12:5; 13:22) but also with offering comfort (Rom 15:4; 2 Cor 1:4–7; Phil 2:1). That Scriptures are sometimes said to be such "encouragement" indicates how Paul might have viewed prophecy: as doing in the congregation what Scriptures do by way of exhortation and challenge. (Though of course this says nothing about Paul's view of their relative authority!) As this passage progresses, it is possible to see what prophecy actually *does* and what Paul commends it for. It becomes evident that this encouragement is expected to lead, in some circumstances, to thanksgiving by the church (v. 16, something that cannot happen with speaking in a tongue). It involves the exhortation and encouragement that comes with the instruction of people (v. 19). It leads to conviction both for insiders and outsiders, who are called to account, and it finds the secrets of their hearts exposed (v. 24). Thus, this encouragement will lead to worship (v. 25). "Consolation" (παραμυθία) is a rare word appearing as a feminine noun only

---

3. See comments on this postpositive particle at 1:12.

4. The nominative participle with the article provides the subject of the verb (also in v. 4).

5. See also Grudem, *Gift of Prophecy in the New Testament*, 126–28.

here in the New Testament. Although the cognate, neuter noun appears once at Philippians 2:1 and the cognate verb only four times (John 11:19, 31; 1 Thess 2:12; 5:14), the meaning is largely reflected by the English verb "to console." It is about giving words of encouragement to those who have lost loved ones in death, or to standing alongside "the fainthearted," or helping those going through hard times (1 Thess 5:14).[6] These two words thus give a glimpse of what Paul means by "building up" through prophecy. It is about speaking words that challenge, or encourage, or console individuals in such a way that they are turned to the Lord and find their faith to be made stronger.

Since in 3:11 Paul has been explicit that the foundation is Jesus Christ and that any building must always be on that foundation, it is reasonable to assume that this "encouragement" and "consolation" is understood by Paul always to point in some way to Christ. This may be because he can bring full comfort to those in need, or will call people to repentance, or will challenge the lives of those who follow him. "Prophecy" is thus gospel focused and expository in nature.[7]

14:4 The one who speaks in a tongue builds himself up, but the one who prophesies builds up the church (ὁ λαλῶν γλώσσῃ ἑαυτὸν οἰκοδομεῖ· ὁ δὲ προφητεύων ἐκκλησίαν οἰκοδομεῖ). This verse now summarizes the contrast. All along Paul has been addressing the church. When some separate themselves from others on the basis of their supposed spiritual superiority or maturity, the closeness and love of God's people is lost and the church divided. The word "church" refers here to the gathering of God's people to worship (see v. 26: "Whenever you come together"; cf. 11:18; note also 1:2; 6:4; 12:5, 12, 19, 23, 28–35). Prophecy, by focusing on *others* rather than the individual who is speaking, helps express that unity and the concern each should feel for the other. It encourages the erection of an edifice on the foundation of Christ that begins to look *Christ-like*. When a person speaks in a tongue that is unintelligible to others, it may be good for the individual but it fails the "building" test for the community. It is as if the individual has used the wrong materials. Each Christian must understand that Paul's greatest desire is to see the whole body of Christ "edified" (v. 5).

IN DEPTH: What Was Paul's Attitude to "Speaking in a Tongue" and What Is the Phenomenon?

While it is clear that in chapter 14 Paul generally discourages the use of speaking in a tongue in corporate worship, save where there may be interpretation (v. 5), there is considerable debate about Paul's general attitude toward the phenomenon. In v. 4a he does talk of this activity as "building up" the individual who speaks. Is this simply a rhetorical device to make the contrast with what is right and good the more obvious? In this case the first use of "build up" in v. 4 may be a negative or even sarcastic comment by Paul, such that the person

---

6. The meaning of consolation in death or in hardship is borne out in both the neuter and feminine forms in examples in MM 488 and in Horsley, *New Documents*, 3:79.

7. The nature of New Testament prophecy is also discussed in the comments on 12:10. There we noted that the main purpose or function of prophecy in the New Testament is not to be seen in foretelling the future or offering specific guidance.

who speaks in a tongue "puffs himself up" (cf. 8:1). Is Paul's point that the one speaking in a tongue is concerned with self-aggrandizement rather than with the church and the body? Is this another example of how the elitists are becoming "puffed up" against others (4:16, 18–19; 5:2; 8:1), something to which "love" is utterly opposed (13:4)? Given Paul's use of sarcasm and deep irony in 4:7–13, it is not impossible that he does the same here. However, this does seem less likely. First, in v. 5 Paul either desires (see below) that all speak in tongues or offers a concession that many do. Secondly, in v. 18 Paul refers to speaking in a tongue himself and clearly contrasts this private speaking with his preference for speaking "five words with my mind" "*in the congregation.*" Paul would hardly admit to using this gift privately if he regarded it as an entirely self-serving activity that necessarily puffs up the individual.

Those from the more charismatic or Pentecostal traditions sometimes argue much the opposite from this text. That is, although Paul is mostly concerned here about "prophecy" and public worship, he in fact *encourages* speaking in a tongue. In this chapter v. 5 and v. 18 are pointed to, but the view is further supported by pointing to the fact that Paul admits its usage in worship if there is an "interpretation." He has spoken of "tongues" as a gift given by the Holy Spirit to certain people in 12:10. He has taken himself by way of example as one speaking in tongues in 13:1 and in 14:18 admits to speaking in a tongue more than all of them. Paul says nothing negative about this gift other than offering the important proviso that it should be interpreted when used in public worship. His negativity is aimed rather at the continued theme of self-aggrandizement. Grudem delivers a gentle swipe at "some Reformed and dispensational interpreters of this passage" who suggest Paul is wholly against the use of tongues. He points out that this is to generalize from the specific matter of *uninterpreted* tongues (the real issue) in an unwarranted manner. He writes, "Concerning the proper public function of the use of tongues plus interpretation, or the proper private function of speaking in tongues, Paul is elsewhere quite positive (1 Cor 12:10–11, 21–22, 14:4, 5, 18, 26–28, 39)."[8] This latter point is well taken. But it is also true that one can hardly build a whole (positive) theology of tongues-speaking around texts that mostly are delivered in a context of the discussion of a church's *abuse* of the gift. This is certainly a danger with some modern, popular theology that seeks to practice this gift and do so *without* interpretation. The lack of interpretation of tongues in many modern churches should certainly provide cause for concern among church pastors.[9]

---

8. Grudem, *Gift of Prophecy in the New Testament*, 177–78.
9. Carson expresses this deep concern, while not ruling out the use of the gift of tongues (*Showing the Spirit*, 87–88, 108–17).

However, a further significant question is raised by Paul's reference to this gift in 1 Corinthians. Simply stated, "What *are* gifts of 'speaking in tongues'?" The matter is further complicated exegetically by Paul's admission that "to another [various] *kinds* of tongues" (ἑτέρῳ γένη γλωσσῶν) may be given (12:10). What does Paul mean by "kinds"? Interpretations abound. Three views, in one form or another, have come to dominate the discussion. The first, in the light of 13:1, regards speaking in a "tongue" as an "angelic" language. This is not a human language but a heavenly or spiritual language similar to that used by the angels before the throne of God. In the second view some regard the gift as being related to real languages, that is, known human languages. The events recorded in Acts 2 when the apostles preached on the day of Pentecost and people heard the gospel in their own language are often cited as an example. In a third view some, probably the majority of modern commentators, regard speaking in a "tongue" as some form of "ecstatic utterance" or "unconscious" pouring out of emotion that can be interpreted in a way that makes the outpouring meaningful to those listening. Of course, there are many variations within each of these views.

"Tongues" as the language of angels. E. E. Ellis is among some who argue that Paul is speaking here of "angelic" languages, that is, of the languages referred to in 13:1 as "the tongues of angels," which are set in contrast with "tongues of men" (see comments on 13:1).[10] He proposes that it is the spirits of angels who stand behind the so-called "spiritual" people at Corinth. That is, these people would appeal to angels who act as "bearers and/or facilitators of the 'spiritual gifts' from the risen Lord."[11] Tracing this teaching about the role of angels in apocalyptic Judaism and especially certain texts at Qumran, such as 1QS 4:21–22, Ellis argues that the Old Testament prophets were also seen to receive their messages through angels (e.g., 1 Kgs 13:18). He suggests the Corinthians regard their gifts of prophecy as also emanating from angels (he takes the neuter plural of the word "spirit" (πνευμάτων) in 14:12 to refer to "spirits" understood as angelic spirits). Since the angels are the mediators of God's will and message, then it is natural, he argues, to assume that the "tongues" are angelic tongues, which can then be interpreted in order that all may understand. He and others cite the intensely dualistic apocryphal *Testament of Job* (48–50), which recounts the restoration of Job and his daughters, at which time they are transfigured,

---

10. Ellis, *Prophecy and Hermeneutic*, 63–71. See also Collins, *First Corinthians*, 456, 475, who refers to "parallels" in the Testament of Job; Dunn, *Theology of Paul*, 556–57, and idem, *Jesus and the Spirit*, 242–46.

11. Ellis, *Prophecy and Hermeneutic*, 37.

escape their bodies, and begin to sing and speak in the voices of angels, reflecting the mysteries of heaven. Of course, this latter example is highly speculative in its content. However, there are exegetical reasons for doubting that Paul has in mind the languages of angels when speaking of the gift of "tongues." It is unlikely that the neuter plural of the word "spirit" would refer to angels at 1 Corinthians 14:12.[12] Then, 13:1 can hardly offer help with understanding "tongues" as a gift since in that verse it is directly put alongside "tongues of men" (see on 13:1). Paul is making the point that it does not matter which language he speaks (that of men or of angels), for love is always a requirement. Indeed, "tongues of angels" may be added simply for the sake of hyperbole. Also, it is highly unlikely that languages spoken by angels would "cease" in the future (13:8), whereas the "grace-gifts" will surely do so (a point made strongly in ch. 13).

"Tongues" as real languages that are foreign to the one who speaks. This is a more widely held view. The need for "interpretation" itself suggests that a real language is at stake rather than something so ecstatic it might be little more than babble. In support of this it is said that the term "tongue" (γλῶσσα) used in this metaphorical sense means "language."[13] The phrase "tongues of men and of angels" in 13:1 seems to indicate two different languages or types of language. In 14:21 Paul quotes Isaiah 28:11–12 where clearly it is the spoken language of "foreigners" that is the issue. Then, it is also suggested that Acts 2:6–11 provides some evidence of what Paul had in mind. Among more recent interpreters to hold this view are Gundry and Forbes.[14] One of the matters that speaks to this is the function of the gift of "interpretation" (12:10; 14:26; ἑρμηνεία) and the meaning of the verb "to interpret" (12:30; 14:5, 13, 27; διερμηνεύω). This verb "normally refers to translating a language when used in such a context," says Gundry. The "association of Luke with Paul," he adds, "makes it very likely" that Luke's writing in Acts 2 reflects "Paul's own understanding of the phenomenon."[15] This position links Acts 2 and 1 Corinthians in this way. On the day of Pentecost many different nationalities were present. The gift of interpretation was not needed because the languages spoken were understood by those who spoke those languages. In Corinth, there would often have been people who spoke other languages present, and so speaking in tongues would have been beneficial for them. But when only local people were present, such a gift of speaking another

---

12. A detailed examination of Ellis's view and ultimately its firm rejection is offered by Grudem, *Gift of Prophecy in 1 Corinthians*, 120ff., especially the lengthy note 10.

13. This is the way it is used in Acts 2:6 where each hears "in his own language" (cf. Rom 14:11; Phil 2:11). See BDAG 201, sect. 2.

14. Robert H. Gundry, "Ecstatic Utterance (N.E.B.)," *JTS* 17 (1966): 299–307; Christopher Forbes, *Prophecy and Inspired Speech in Early Christianity and Its Hellenistic Environment* (Tubingen: Mohr Siebeck, 1995). See also Turner, *Holy Spirit and Spiritual Gifts*, 227–39.

15. Gundry, "Ecstatic Utterance," 305.

language was useless if no one speaking that language was present. It thus needed translating into the common language of the people present. This setting, it is argued, does away with any need to regard tongues as "ecstatic" simply because "interpretation" was needed. This position is also supported, then, by 14:10–11, which is not seen as an illustration from real languages concerning ecstatic speech, but rather as a straightforward statement about real languages of the sort being spoken in the assembly.

However, this view has also been widely challenged. If real languages are at stake here, then it is at best difficult to see the point of 14:2, 13–14, 18, 26. For example, why would God need to be *spoken to* (14:2) in a different language of this world to the one being spoken in the room? Paul has firmly established that the grace-gifts, of which this is one, are given for "building up" the community (and even outsiders). The problem with this gift is that it does not do that unless interpreted, so we are left asking what precisely would the point of the grace-gift have been. Why would Paul or anyone else need to speak to God in a different known language from his own? How would this build *him* up, except perhaps in the general sense that he would know some work of the Spirit was going on in or through him? If there is a parallel in Acts 2, then the purpose of the gift may indeed be seen as either evangelistic (people speaking different languages hear the gospel and understand) or as a sign of the dawning of the messianic age to those needing to be convinced that the Messiah has come. But it is difficult to see how either of these purposes would be of any benefit to an individual Christian. In fact, if this was the purpose, Paul might surely be saying of this gift almost the exact opposite of what he actually says. Surely he would argue that it is irrelevant to the individual who knows the gospel, but relevant to those who do not, or irrelevant to the one speaking the language of the gathered assembly, but relevant to those who do not.

"Tongues" as some form of ecstatic speech. The "second" view above has recently been largely formulated in opposition to the idea that the tongues of which Paul speaks are so-called "ecstatic" verbal manifestations of the Spirit's presence with an individual. When this gift is present, a person utters unintelligible sounds that must be interpreted. Some suggest the sounds seem to well up within a person almost beyond their ability to stop them. They are not speaking actual human languages that no one in the room understands, but have some sort of outpouring of sound that allows an individual from the depths of their being to express praise and thanksgiving to God. Different understandings have been suggested for "ecstatic" gifts. An older version arose out of the history-of-religions theologians, who argued that these "tongues" find a precedent in similar phenomena in the Greco-Roman world. Forbes's detailed

study of the available evidence finds no support at all for the phenomenon, as Paul describes it, within the Hellenistic mystery religions, and this need not detain us here.[16] Further, it is important to note that while "ecstatic" may mean that someone speaks during some form of trance or while going through some extraordinary spiritual experience and that the individual is out of control, the word *need* not imply this. The word itself has therefore sometimes caused unnecessary misunderstandings between different Christians. In modern, popular theology "ecstatic" is often used simply to mean that the speaker has an experience of God that appears to be direct and immediate, that is, more spontaneous than planned or prepared. However, even the deliberate decision to use this gift may be included in the understanding of "ecstatic." In fact, most modern uses of the gift of tongues usually fall into some category of this popular use of the word "ecstatic." It is extremely rare to hear of an incident in which a known language is supposed to have been spoken by someone who otherwise did not know that language. Usually modern speaking in tongues does involve the individual in some form of control over the gift's use, its length, its relationship to other individuals in the room, and so on. Such control is assumed by Paul in his treatment of speaking in "a tongue" in that he assumes it is possible to refrain from using the gift if no interpretation is present. Neither need the word "ecstatic" used in this manner mean that what is spoken is somehow gibberish. Having said this, there is a wide-ranging discussion as to whether such tongues-speaking can legitimately be seen as "cognitive" sound. All of this leads to the fact that in many modern groups there is a general assumption that their use of what they call "speaking in tongues" is both "ecstatic" but *also* may be defined as "the language of angels." For the purists this may seem to be a contradiction in terms: angels, presumably, completely control their speech and do not speak to each other or to God only while in some state of "ecstasy." In the current debate between some from more traditionally Reformed circles, some from dispensationalist circles, and modern charismatic circles, these seemingly small misunderstandings about how words are being used needs careful attention.

Having said this, the question of whether there can be a cognitive aspect to a language that might otherwise be considered "ecstatic" raises a matter of interest. Carson comments on this in the light of recent linguistic studies in relation to the practice of the modern experience of "tongues." He believes that "on balance" the gift was "a gift of real languages, that is, the languages were cognitive, whether of men or of angels."[17] But then he also points out

---

16. Forbes, *Prophecy and Inspired Speech*, especially chs. 5–7.

17. Carson, *Showing the Spirit*, 83.

that there is "universal" agreement that it is not any human language that is being spoken. Building upon Poythress's work on this subject, he cites four possible ways of understanding the phenomenon, given that it is "lexically uncommunicative." First, the sounds may be disconnected "ejaculations, and the like, that are not confused with human language." Secondly, they may be "connected sequences of sound that appear to be real languages unknown to the hearer . . . even though they are not." Thirdly, they can be a real language, "even if unknown to the hearer." To this Carson adds his own fourth possibility, which brings together the second and third possibilities above. The sounds may reflect complex speech patterns that "may bear all kinds of cognitive information in some coded array, even though these patterns are not identifiable as human language."[18] After using a couple of rather humorous examples, Carson's final simple point is that it is possible to imagine tongues-speaking as bearing cognitive information even if the result is not a human language. The interpreter in effect has to provide the interpretative code much like a computer programmer could do so for his program (Carson's example).

When stated like this, it seems little more than, in our experience, what many modern practitioners have always said of their tongues-speaking. However, this may go some way, which is clearly Carson's hope, to bring together those who see the only alternative to translatable "language" as gibberish. Of course, what Carson does not do in this particular part of his argument is directly speak to the matter of "tongues" as Paul spoke of them. But it does offer another example of what Paul may have in mind when he speaks in 12:10 of "to another, *kinds* of tongues." Thiselton makes a strong case for understanding "tongues" fairly broadly in the light of Paul's phrase (as he translates it), "species of tongues."[19] He also argues, importantly, that the gift of "interpretation" does not have to mean "translation," even if a language is involved. It may be a gift of "intelligible articulation of tongues-speech."[20] While in the end Thiselton views these tongues as most likely to be the articulation given by the Holy Spirit of "the unconscious released in 'Sighs too deep for words'" (Rom 8:26–27), this too can be incorporated under Carson's view that the interpreter then simply needs the "code" given by God.

Finally, then, what may be said? First, provided we understand "ecstatic" to mean "out of one's senses" only to the extent that a person is being filled at

---

18. Ibid., 83–85, expanding upon Vern S. Poythress, "The Nature of Corinthian Glossolalia: Possible Options," *WTJ* 40 (1977): 130–35; also Poythress, "Linguistic and Sociological Analyses of Modern Tongues-Speaking: Their Contributions and Limitations," *WTJ* 42 (1980): 367–88.

19. Thiselton, *1 Corinthians*, 970.
20. Ibid., 970, 974.

that moment with a cognitive communication from God, then there is surely little that is objectionable to the use of the word. Using the word in this sense is not to speak of something even remotely similar to a drug-induced haze or a trance-like state induced in some religious act more akin to voodoo than to biblical Christianity. Rather, it is to speak about the gracious activity of God among his people in which, for the grace fully to be appreciated by the church, the communication must have its code broken and an intelligible translation or "articulation" given. Then secondly, the logic of Paul's argument that "tongues" builds up the individual rather than the congregation must be kept in mind. How this building up might occur when the one speaking is unaware of the content of what he is saying is left unaddressed by Paul. It may be surmised that the individual is encouraged by a deeper sense of the Holy Spirit's work in his or her life.

14:5 Now I wish that you all would speak in tongues, but to an [even] greater extent I wish you would prophesy; and the one who prophesies is greater than the one who speaks in tongues unless he interprets in order that the church may be edified (θέλω δὲ πάντας ὑμᾶς λαλεῖν γλώσσαις, μᾶλλον δὲ ἵνα προφητεύητε· μείζων δὲ ὁ προφητεύων ἢ ὁ λαλῶν γλώσσαις ἐκτὸς εἰ μὴ διερμηνεύῃ, ἵνα ἡ ἐκκλησία οἰκοδομὴν λάβῃ). Initially this verse strikes the reader as particularly strange. Superficially, its meaning appears to indicate a change of heart from previous verses and even from some of the argument that follows. Why would Paul want "everyone" to speak in tongues when he has argued specifically that "not all" receive all the gifts? But also why would he want "everyone" to speak in tongues when he has argued that it is a gift that, without interpretation, does not fulfill the purpose of "building up"? To begin with, it is important to note that there is no need to assume that "all" means each individual in the sense

that Paul wanted every single individual to speak in tongues and also to prophesy. Paul clearly teaches that the distribution of all the gifts, including the two spoken of here, is at the complete, free discretion of God himself, who distributes them "as he wills" (12:11). Instead, many commentators rightly suggest that, taken together with the verb "I wish" (θέλω), this is a concession. Paul confirms that he is not against the gift of tongues *per se*. Yet surely the intent is also rather more positive than simply a concession. Paul clearly desires that "all" are built up. Probably he is here thinking of the positive effects for the building up of the individual *when in private*.[21] For Paul there can be no elitism in the church such as some have been promoting. All the gifts are for all people so that each individual and the whole church may be built up. In this sense Paul is able to desire all good things for all people, while still knowing that "all" as individuals may not experience the particular "good." Of course, in Paul's understanding of the body, "all" will *bene-*

---

21. Fee, *1 Corinthians*, 658. In effect, this view suggests that v. 5a parallels v. 4a with "builds himself up" being understood in v. 5a.

fit from interpreted tongues, prophecy, etc., even if they do not themselves individually possess that gift. A partial, parallel construction is provided by 7:7 where, speaking of being single, Paul writes, "I wish that all [of you] were as I myself am" (θέλω δὲ πάντας ἀνθρώπους εἶναι ὡς καὶ ἐμαυτόν). Because of the "good" that Paul can see in his own calling, he wishes that "all" might have that calling even while knowing and arguing for people to remain in the good calling to which they are called.

Thiselton, however, offers an important alternative view of these clauses. He examines the meaning of the verb we have translated as "to wish" (θέλω) and suggests it makes better sense in this context to be translated as "I take pleasure in."[22] He points out that when the verb occurs with the infinitive, as here, it can mean this. Mark 12:38 provides an example, with other instances cited in BDAG with an object following (cf. Matt 27:43, quoting Ps 21:9; Heb 10:5). This suggests that Paul speaks kindly of and "takes pleasure in" all speaking in tongues. Then he continues that he takes *greater* (μᾶλλον) pleasure in all who prophesy.

In our view, Paul expresses a general desire for "all" to experience the benefit of being built up individually when exercising the gift of tongues in private. Yet he wishes "to an [even] greater extent" that people should prophesy because that gift builds up the entire church. This coheres with his next statement that the one who prophesies "is greater than" the tongues-speaker, with one caveat: unless the tongues-speaker interprets his message for all to receive benefit. Paul is not going back on all that he has taught in this epistle concerning the problems of arrogance and pride, but speaks pragmatically. The greater person in the gathered congregation is the one whose gift *at that moment*

better builds up the congregation. This is normally going to be the prophet, though an exception occurs if the tongues-speaker interprets their speech. The primacy of prophecy in this section is further emphasized rhetorically with the clause "but to an [even] greater extent I wish you would prophesy" (μᾶλλον δὲ ἵνα προφητεύητε), forming the end of the *inclusio* that began with the same phrase in v. 1.[23]

One further matter requires attention. Who is Paul expecting to "interpret" or "put into words" (with Thiselton) the tongues-speaking?[24] Several versions insert the word "someone" ("unless someone interprets," e.g., ESV, NIV 2011). This interpolation helps to reflect the *differentiation* of the gifts of interpretation and tongues-speaking found in chapter 12. However, more accurately, especially in the light of 12:13, the NIV 1984 translates, "unless he interprets" (cf. AV: "except he interpret"). Verse 13 seems to require that, in this instance, *the one asked to interpret the "tongue" is the one who is currently employing the gift.* If we allow that there is a certain degree of being "carried away" in such a gift, especially in terms of praising and praying *to God*, then the individual is being asked to help the congregation and any outsiders present to understand at least something of the praises and prayers he or she articulates and so to be able to say, "Amen" (cf. v. 16).

The final clause, "in order that the church may be edified" (ἵνα ἡ ἐκκλησία οἰκοδομὴν λάβῃ) is a purpose clause expressing the goal of any gift, whether prophecy or tongues with interpretation. The fact that Paul desires the one gift *to an even greater extent* than another, and that he calls one person *greater* than another reminds the reader that this is the only criterion by which one may

---

22. Thiselton, *1 Corinthians*, 1097.

23. His shift from the verb "to wish" with the complementary infinitive in the first clause to a subjunctive in the second

clause (nonfinal use of ἵνα, as noted in v. 1 above) is surely deliberately stylistic to close out the *inclusio*.

24. Thiselton, *1 Corinthians*, 1098–1100.

judge the greater gifts (12:31). They are not the more flamboyant. They are not defined by being "ecstatic" (however we understand that word). They are defined as those that best "build up" the church. This will be the nub of Paul's argument through much of the rest of this chapter.

14:6 Now it is like this, brothers [and sisters], if I come to you speaking in tongues, what shall I benefit you unless I communicate to you either by [some] means of revelation or knowledge, or prophecy, or teaching? (Νῦν δέ, ἀδελφοί, ἐὰν ἔλθω πρὸς ὑμᾶς γλώσσαις λαλῶν, τί ὑμᾶς ὠφελήσω, ἐὰν μὴ ὑμῖν λαλήσω ἢ ἐν ἀποκαλύψει ἢ ἐν γνώσει ἢ ἐν προφητείᾳ ἢ ἐν διδαχῇ;). Verse 6 introduces the next subsection (vv. 6–12) in which Paul develops further, with the use of two analogies, the reason why the one gift builds up but the other does not. He concludes by urging the pursuit of gifts that "abound in building up the church" (v. 12; cf. 15:58). He begins by exhorting his readers as "brothers and sisters" and so sets his remarks firmly within the family of the church. This is not high polemic or confrontational rhetoric but careful and persuasive speech. The combination "but now" (νῦν δέ) carries both a continuative and explanatory sense. Given that Paul leads into hypothetical examples and analogies, the meaning is carried by a phrase such as "now it's like this. . . ." Paul then presents the first of four hypothetical illustrations. With considerable, cumulative rhetorical effect, all four have an identical grammatical structure and are presented in the form of a third-class condition, formed with an aorist subjunctive in the protasis and a future in the interrogative apodosis.[25] Each example focuses on intelligibil-

ity like the first. The second (v. 7) speaks of musical instruments not giving a clear sound, so *how* will anyone know what is played? The third (v. 8) speaks of an indistinct bugle, so *who* will get ready for battle? The fourth (v. 9) returns to the matter of the "tongue" which is not intelligible, so *how* will anyone understand what is said?

Underlying this whole argument of intelligibility is of course the "building up" of the community, which is the criterion by which the *greater* gifts must be assessed and by which the Corinthians should operate as they seek gifts for use in the congregation. Thus, Paul here reintroduces the concept of "bringing benefit to" (ὠφελέω). In doing so he recalls the contrast he made using the same word in 13:3 and so again alludes to his emphasis on love. He also looks back to the idea of each gift being given for the common good (12:7). Paul mentions speaking, and therefore bringing benefit, "by means of" (instrumental, ἐν) four types of *intelligible* communication.

"Revelation" (ἀποκάλυψις) usually in the New Testament refers to the gospel revelation found in Christ. This may simply be the preaching of the gospel, or it may refer to some special experience in which the gospel of Christ or some message from Christ came to a person (cf. Gal 1:12; 2:2; Rom 16:25; Eph 1:17; Rev 1:1). Here it may be a Spirit-given message from Christ, or, perhaps more likely, *about* Christ for the benefit of the church. It is followed in this passage by "knowledge" (γνῶσις; see above, 8:1). How these communicative speech activities differ is simply not evident from the text or from Paul's wider writings. The final two activities he mentions are "prophecy" and "teaching." "Prophecy" has been discussed above, and

---

25. Often the third-class condition is regarded as "future more probable." In this instance it simply offers a hypothesis that is, at best, *not* probable! The TEV translation "when I come" at v. 6b does not do justice to the form of the condition. Wallace, *Greek Grammar*, 470 (see 698 for 14:8), rightly

shows that, with the decline of the use of the optative between classical and Koine Greek, the fourth-class condition all but disappears and the third class takes on a "broad range of potentialities." Interestingly, one of the rare uses of the optative in the New Testament is found in 14:10!

"teaching" is plainly understood, probably referring to the teaching of the gospel and of Scripture within the congregation (see 12:28–29).

Returning to Paul's example here in 14:6, his point is this: should he himself come among them speaking in tongues—a gift they know he possesses (v. 18)—he asks what benefit he would be to them unless he communicated some intelligible message. It is the *intelligibility* of the "revelation," "knowledge," etc., that is at issue here rather than the specific style of each communication. The rhetoric, of course, expects the answer "none" to this question.

14:7 Similarly, lifeless instruments that produce a sound, whether a flute or harp, if they give no distinction between sounds, how will what is played on the flute or on the harp be recognized? (ὅμως τὰ ἄψυχα φωνὴν διδόντα, εἴτε αὐλὸς εἴτε κιθάρα, ἐὰν διαστολὴν τοῖς φθόγγοις μὴ δῷ, πῶς γνωσθήσεται τὸ αὐλούμενον ἢ τὸ κιθαριζόμενον;). Paul here introduces the second of his hypothetical examples. Whether it be a wind instrument, like the flute, or a stringed instrument, each is supposed to produce a good sound and must be played in a way that produces intelligible sound sequences. Only then will a tune be recognized for what it is. If these instruments are played in such a way that there is no attempt to distinguish sounds in a recognizable manner, then the whole production will be unrecognizable and pointless.

The construction in this verse is essentially the same as the previous verse, using a conditional clause followed by an interrogative. However, the vocabulary is undoubtedly interesting. "Similarly" (ὅμως) appears only twice in Paul's writings.[26] Then the words "lifeless" (ἄψυχος) and "flute" (αὐλός) appear only here in the New Testament. The neuter,

plural "lifeless" things (cf. NIV; AV) refer to the flute and the harp, and hence it is rightly often translated "lifeless instruments" (RSV, NRSV, ESV). The participle "produce" (διδόντα) agrees in number and case with "lifeless instruments" and so is perhaps best, though with difficulty, translated adjectivally as above. In the Greek the verb of the apodosis is in the singular.

14:8 Also, you see, if the trumpet gives an indistinct sound, who will get ready for battle? (καὶ γὰρ ἐὰν ἄδηλον σάλπιγξ φωνὴν δῷ, τίς παρασκευάσεται εἰς πόλεμον;). The point is made for a third time. The trumpet (cf. 15:52) must be played in a particular way to communicate a message that troops should be battle ready. An indistinct series of notes would say nothing to a soldier at a time when an important message needed to be communicated. The Greek structure is the same as in the previous two verses with a conditional clause followed by an interrogative. "For" (γάρ) could be left untranslated as a continuative particle, which adds nothing to "also" (καί). But the particle also often functions as a "marker of clarification," and that may be the case here; hence our translation, "you see."[27]

14:9 And so it is with you, if with the tongue you do not give a clear word, how will what is said be recognized? For you will be speaking into thin air (οὕτως καὶ ὑμεῖς διὰ τῆς γλώσσης ἐὰν μὴ εὔσημον λόγον δῶτε, πῶς γνωσθήσεται τὸ λαλούμενον; ἔσεσθε γὰρ εἰς ἀέρα λαλοῦντες). Maintaining the conditional form somewhat softens the impact of the challenge as Paul moves to more explicit application. He now effectively uses the word "tongue" (γλῶσσα) here of the physical organ to make his point. Just as a musical instrument must be played properly and proper notes sounded in

---

26. This word normally means "nevertheless," as in John 12:42. However, its use here seems to be different. BDAG 710 suggests this is probably a form of the earlier ὁμῶς that means

"likewise" or "equally." Of course, no accents would have been present originally.

27. BDAG 189 (sect. 2).

proper sequence for the music to mean anything, so the tongue must be controlled in a way that will produce clear and comprehensible speech. Without this clarity the sounds being made will be like speech going nowhere, a "speaking into thin air." Paul's first hypothetical condition involved himself as the subject (v. 6), his second and third involved "lifeless" instruments (vv. 7–8), but here in v. 9 he returns to the second-person plural, turning the hypothetical example into more of a general application. "So it is" (οὕτως) introduces this final hypothetical illustration as the apostle begins to make his application. The conditional structure with the aorist subjunctive and the following interrogative with a (periphrastic future, ἔσεσθε) future remains the same as in the previous verses, though the protasis is expressed with the negative "if . . . not." The phrase "into the air" is colloquial in Greek, hence the colloquial "thin air" of our English translation. "Clear" (εὔσημος) is another New Testament *hapax* and can also mean "readily recognizable."[28]

Interestingly, Paul does not say that "only God will hear." His application here cannot be watered down, nor is it hedged around with caveats. Elsewhere in the argument he has granted a positive use for speaking in tongues and has granted that, with interpretation, they have their purpose. Yet not here. He is adamant as he talks about the gathered assembly. Of greatest importance is that, whatever occurs at a congregational gathering, the whole content must be comprehensible to all. Even what is primarily addressed to God in praise (v. 2) must be done in a way that is meaningful to the whole worshipping body. To speak otherwise is to disregard the body.

14:10–11 Though there may be many kinds of languages in the world and none without meaning, if I do not know the meaning of the lan- **guage, I will be a foreigner to the speaker and the one speaking a foreigner to me** (τοσαῦτα εἰ τύχοι γένη φωνῶν εἰσιν ἐν κόσμῳ, καὶ οὐδὲν ἄφωνον· ἐὰν οὖν μὴ εἰδῶ τὴν δύναμιν τῆς φωνῆς, ἔσομαι τῷ λαλοῦντι βάρβαρος καὶ ὁ λαλῶν ἐν ἐμοὶ βάρβαρος). Another relevant illustration is advanced. Corinth was a thoroughly cosmopolitan port city, and *many* languages would have been heard on its streets, even if Greek and Latin dominated. Thus, almost everyone would regularly have heard the *sound* of other languages and not understood what was being said. The experience of being a "foreigner" in one's hometown would resonate well in any city where the nations gather for trade, and so it makes for a powerful illustration. This is Paul's point as he writes both that the speaker will be "a foreigner" and also that "I will be a foreigner to the speaker." The sense of frustration and time-wasting in such a situation is well depicted. For Paul it is unthinkable that "I," a member of the congregation, should be made to feel a foreigner in my own family. In this way Paul not only draws attention as before to the lack of intelligibility of "tongues" but also, now, to their divisiveness.

The verse begins with a rare, fourth-class condition with the optative (εἰ τύχοι, cf. 15:37), "though there may be," but the sentence is incomplete with no apodosis. In fact, there are no examples of a complete fourth-class condition in New Testament Greek. The clause thus simply functions to express the *possibility for the sake of argument* of what follows and perhaps somewhat restricts the impact of "*many* kinds of languages" (τοσαῦτα agreeing with γένη). The translation "though there may be many kinds" is an attempt to reflect the *possibility* and sense of slight *doubt* often present in the optative. "Languages" here does not translate the earlier word "tongues" (γλῶσσαι) but "sound" (φωνή; used in vv. 7–8), which can also refer to a language. Paul plays

---

28. BDAG 413.

on this word here where "without meaning" literally means "without *sound*" (ἄφωνον). Verse 11 is another third-class condition as in previous verses.

14:12 And so it is with you, since you are enthusiasts for inspirations of the Spirit, strive that you may abound in the building up of the church (οὕτως καὶ ὑμεῖς, ἐπεὶ ζηλωταί ἐστε πνευμάτων, πρὸς τὴν οἰκοδομὴν τῆς ἐκκλησίας ζητεῖτε ἵνα περισσεύητε). The noun "enthusiast" (ζηλωτής) is a cognate of the verb used in 12:31 and 14:1 meaning "to earnestly desire" or "be zealous for." These Corinthians are zealous for visible evidences of their spiritual competencies, but Paul again insists they should rather pursue the building up of the church. It is difficult to know exactly what Paul meant by using a word normally translated as "spirits" (πνεύματα; here translated "inspirations of the Spirit") when "grace-gifts" (χαρίσματα) or "spiritual things" (πνευματικά) might have been expected. In a similar way in 14:32 Paul refers to the "inspirations [lit., "spirits" (πνεύματα)] of the prophets" that are subject to prophets. Godet is probably correct in saying of the word, "It must be taken as a strong individualizing of the Holy Spirit, not in the sense of many personalities . . . but in the sense that the one Divine principle spoken of in ch. xii. manifested itself in transient and very various *breathing of inspirations* in the assemblies of the Church."[29]

Clearly from these chapters Paul saw the Holy Spirit as the one who gives all these manifestations and inspirations from God. Hence the translation above, "inspirations of the Spirit," seeks to reflect the source (the Spirit) but also the fact that, for the Corinthians, the issue is the visibility of the Spirit's workings in and through them. Since they regarded the gifts of the Spirit as indicators of their spiritual maturity, then they would have regarded each manifestation as an indication of the Spir-

it's personal presence with them in a special way at that moment. They were enthusiasts or zealots for this evidence of the Spirit's works among them. Paul indicates that they are wrong to desire such "inspirations," such "spirits," for their own sake. If they are earnestly to desire the Spirit's inspirations, then it should be for the one purpose for which they are given in the first place, which is to build up the church. Paul beseeches them to seek or "strive" after (ζητεῖτε) these inspirations in order that they may "abound" (περισσεύητε), that is, let their cup overflow excessively, for the building up of the church (cf. 15:58). So Paul summarizes his various examples.

14:13 Therefore, let the one who speaks in a tongue pray to interpret (Διὸ ὁ λαλῶν γλώσσῃ προσευχέσθω ἵνα διερμηνεύῃ). This verse begins the next section of vv. 13–19, which examines in more detail how the gift of tongues fails to build up people. Here again Paul stresses the necessity of intelligibility, if building up is properly to take place. Paul begins simply, saying in effect, "If speaking in a tongue, pray for an interpretation since only then will the church be built up." "Therefore" (διό) is strong. Sometimes the force of what Paul is saying here is missed. He insists that there is only one way forward if a person speaks in a tongue in the gathered congregation. That person is to pray to be able to "interpret" (see v. 5) or articulate comprehensibly what he or she is saying so that the congregation may be built up. In other words, Paul urges the tongues speaker to be doing something different! The Spirit's gift needed in the congregation is that an individual interpret *rather than* that he or she speak in a tongue.

14:14–15 For if I pray in a tongue, my spirit prays but my mind is unfruitful. What am I to

---

29. Godet, *First Corinthians*, 2:276.

do? I will pray with my spirit, and I will pray with my mind also; I will sing with my spirit and I will sing with my mind also (ἐὰν [γὰρ] προσεύχωμαι γλώσσῃ, τὸ πνεῦμά μου προσεύχεται, ὁ δὲ νοῦς μου ἄκαρπός ἐστιν. τί οὖν ἐστιν; προσεύξομαι τῷ πνεύματι, προσεύξομαι δὲ καὶ τῷ νοΐ· ψαλῶ τῷ πνεύματι, ψαλῶ δὲ καὶ τῷ νοΐ). The matter at hand is whether the congregation enjoys the fruit of the individual's prayers (or songs) or not. Since Paul says tongues are spoken *to God* (v. 2), it is not surprising that he would speak here in terms of praying in a tongue. He is not, however, speaking of two gifts as some have suggested (speaking in tongues and praying in tongues). Another third-class conditional clause sets up Paul's personal hypothetical example. "Unfruitful" (ἄκαρπός) well captures his intention.

The precise meaning of Paul's contrast between "my spirit" and "my mind" has provoked much discussion. Charles Hodge says of this verse, "Though the general meaning of this verse is thus plain, it is the most difficult verse in the whole chapter. What does Paul mean by saying his spirit prays?"[30] A number of comments may help. First, it is unlikely that Paul would refer to "my spirit" and have in mind the Holy Spirit. Paul does not personalize the Holy Spirit in this particular way, although it is just possible he has in mind his own personalized inspiration that comes from the Spirit (v. 12). Also the contrast with "*my* mind" suggests that Paul is talking of *his* own spirit, *my* spirit, not of

the Holy Spirit. Secondly, Paul does not work with a Platonic dualism. It is not that the "spirit" is what relates to God and the "mind" is what relates, unspiritually, to this world. Such dualistic thinking is entirely alien to Paul's worldview. Indeed, 14:15 in which Paul speaks of praying *both* with "spirit" and "mind" speaks against this dualism.[31]

Given the context, a third suggestion may be best. It is vital to see that Paul remains concerned with *intelligibility* (cf. vv. 16, 19). Thus it may be that Paul simply makes a distinction between, on the one hand, a person delivering some communication to God as a result of a thought process or, on the other hand, a person delivering some communication (inspired by God) that is spoken or received in such a way that it is not *understood*. The word "spirit" is thus not some definition of an aspect of personhood which, *as opposed to* "mind," can receive the things of the Spirit. Nor is "mind" used in such a way that leaves room only to describe "tongues" as entirely ecstatic or received only when in a state entirely *un*controlled (by the mind). The word "spirit," in this sense, simply describes the whole person in terms of his or her ability to relate to God or to spiritual things (cf. Rom 8:16; 12:11; 1 Cor 2:1; 5:3–4 [probably]; 5:5; 16:18). Thus, for the one receiving grace-gifts from the Spirit, this may simply be Paul's way of distinguishing that which may or may not be *understood* (which is one of the functions of the "mind"). For Paul the whole person, both mind and spirit, receives things

---

30. Hodge, *First Corinthians*, 287. We agree with Hodge also on the matter of lack of fruitfulness where he says, "By his understanding being unfruitful is therefore meant, that others did not understand what he said" (ibid., 288).

31. Thus references to Philo and other Hellenistic writers are of no more than passing interest in that they use similar terms to those used by Paul and with which the Corinthians would have been acquainted. But those references must not be allowed to define what Paul intends by these words any more than we have let Hellenistic philosophy define Paul's use of the word "spiritual." The most interesting aspect of comparing Philo on his use of "mind" and "spirit" with Paul and his use is to see just how much Paul differs from Philo in his own non-dualistic usage of these words. Of course, given Paul's argument, it is very possible that the Corinthians themselves thought of these things in a more dualistic way. Cf. on ecstasy Philo Vol. 4, *Quis Rerum Divinarum Heres (Who is the Heir of Divine Things)*, 249–267; on "mind" and "tongue" and their relationship to "ecstasy" specifically see 265–266: "For indeed the prophet, even when he seems to be speaking, really holds his peace, and his organs of speech, mouth and tongue, are wholly in the employ of Another, to shew forth what He wills."

of the Spirit. This is obvious even in this passage in the contrast between tongues and prophecy. However, it is possible in some circumstances for the "mind" not to interact with what is going on, in which case the gift that has been received bears no fruit within the congregation. Those speaking in tongues, always desiring to build up the church (12:7), should therefore be praying specifically that God will enable their minds to engage with the "tongue" in such a way that they may be able to explain, interpret, or put into words what has been received from the Spirit. Paul is content to affirm that prophecy and tongues-speaking well up, as it were, from the very core of the person (the person's spirit),[32] but this person should ensure that what is then spoken out loud to people around should benefit each one.

It is all too easy to disengage the mind from spiritual gifts or experiences, just as a Christian can all too easily disengage life practice from the content of a prophecy. But especially this would be true if already "tongues" are expressing things that are too deep for the mind immediately to articulate (as in the "sighs" of Rom 8:26–27). In fact, as a gift of the Spirit this disengagement of the mind *in the sense of intelligible communication* is, under certain circumstances (in private), God endorsed! However, a person will need to engage the mind either to choose to use the gift in private or, if in the congregation, immediately to pray that the Spirit will enable an *understandable* version so that all may be built up. The "mind" a Christian should have is "the mind of Christ" (2:16). It is a mind that is able to discern how a grace-gift should be used so that a person's whole life reflects Christ and the

whole church benefits (Rom 7:23–25; 12:2; 14:5; 1 Cor 1:10; Col 2:18). This is why in a context that goes on to speak of grace-gifts of the Spirit (Rom 12:6), Paul begins by saying, "Be transformed by the renewing of your minds" (Rom 12:2).

First Corinthians 14:15 must be kept with the previous verse. The rhetorical question, "What am I to do?" serves to introduce Paul's suggested way forward for the person who prays in a tongue. The possible separation of the "mind" and "spirit" does not set up an opposition. Paul will pray in the only way possible "with my spirit," from the very core of his person, but he will do so with his "mind" as well. He will do the same even as he sings praises.[33] Clearly Paul believes that he has a choice in this. He can pray for an "interpretation" that will allow him to build up the congregation or he can choose to keep quiet in the assembly.

Paul's reference to singing seems to refer to singing in tongues, though Paul is speaking of himself as an individual. The modern phenomenon of a congregation singing in tongues, beautiful and moving as it is, finds no support in this chapter. Indeed, this chapter indirectly may speak against it since everything in the assembly of Christians should be *understood*. Again, Paul insists that while such singing (in a tongue) may well up from the core of his person, he must sing praise in language that all can understand. This verb (ψάλλω) is widely used in the Psalms of the LXX and means "to sing" or "sing praise" whether or not accompanied by an instrument (e.g., Pss 7:18; 9:12; 107:4). Paul also uses the word in quoting the Psalms (Rom 15:9) and in Eph 5:19 (cf. Jas 5:13).[34] There is no doubt that the early church sang psalms and

---

32. Thiselton, *1 Corinthians*, 1110, helpfully paraphrases "spirit" in this context as the "innermost spiritual being." He warns, however, that "this risks misunderstanding in the direction of Plato or of idealist or Cartesian dualism."

33. BDAG 1096 (ψάλλω). It is wrong to contrast types of singing here as between that which is sung in a state of

"spiritual ecstasy" or sung "in full possession of one's mental faculties."

34. In Eph 5:19 Paul speaks of "singing to the Lord *with your heart*" (AT). "Heart" here seems to be virtually a synonym for "spirit." Ernest Best in his *Critical and Exegetical Commentary on Ephesians*, ICC (Edinburgh: T&T Clark, 1998), 513,

hymns regularly and through them expressed their praise and thanksgiving to the Lord. Thanksgiving is in Paul's mind here, as v. 16 makes clear. What is especially interesting is that in v. 26 (see comments below) "*each one* has a psalm." This provides a clear indication of the centrality of joyful singing in the worship of the early church. Verses 15 and 26 together remind us that singing is not just "to God" but also for building each other up. In other words, in the congregation Christians sing to God and to each other, for in singing to each other the *content* of what is sung will cause all to bring even greater praise and thanksgiving to the Lord and for all to be edified spiritually.

14:16–17 Otherwise, if you give thanks by means of the Spirit, how can the one who finds himself among those who do not understand say the "amen" to your thanksgiving since he does not know what you are saying? For you may be giving thanks well enough, but the other person is not built up (ἐπεὶ ἐὰν εὐλογῇς ἐν πνεύματι, ὁ ἀναπληρῶν τὸν τόπον τοῦ ἰδιώτου πῶς ἐρεῖ τὸ Ἀμὴν ἐπὶ τῇ σῇ εὐχαριστίᾳ, ἐπειδὴ τί λέγεις οὐκ οἶδεν; σὺ μὲν γὰρ καλῶς εὐχαριστεῖς, ἀλλ᾿ ὁ ἕτερος οὐκ οἰκοδομεῖται). Paul again returns to the reason behind what he is saying. He changes from first to second-person singular as he applies his teaching. Congregational worship is fundamentally *participatory*. Even saying "amen" is a way in which all can join by affirming or, as it were, adding their name to what is going on. The word "amen" is a transliteration of the Hebrew. In its verbal form in Hebrew it connotes "standing firm" and so in its liturgical setting comes to imply full and firm agreement or consent with what has been said or sung (cf. Deut 27:15–26 for such congregational

assent to the reading of certain laws). From an individual's perspective an endorsement with the word "amen" means "this is true and valid *for me*." The whole congregation must therefore be able to understand what the blessing or thanksgiving to the Lord means if they are to identify with the message! "If you give thanks" (ἐὰν εὐλογῇς) refers to blessing God or giving thanks to God (v. 17 uses "giving thanks" in the place of "bless"). What Paul has in mind here is no doubt closely paralleled by Asaph's singing of a song of thanksgiving to the Lord in 1 Chronicles 16:36. The LXX uses both the verb "to bless" (εὐλογέω) and the transliterated Hebrew "amen" (ἀμήν). As the song comes to an end, we read: "Blessed be the LORD. . . . Then all the people said, "Amen!" and praised the LORD" (ESV). As both verses make clear, if the thanksgiving is not understood, then it doesn't matter how good or well-intentioned the thanksgiving is. No one else is being edified.

Two matters need further examination. First, once again the question of the meaning of "spirit" (πνεῦμα) arises. The most obvious way forward would be to assume that it carries the same meaning as in the previous verse. In other words, Paul continues with the thought of the prayer welling up from *the core of a person's being* and being expressed in a "tongue" that is not understood by the congregation. However, there is an argument for saying that Paul is now speaking of the [Holy] Spirit as the means by which "you give thanks," that is, speak in a tongue (so NIV 2011). Many English versions add the word "your" (not present in the Greek) to "spirit" closing out this latter option (e.g., ESV, NIV 1984). It has been noted above that usually when Paul speaks of a person's "spirit" he uses the article and when he speaks of the Holy

---

says of singing coming from the "heart" in Eph 5:19 that "it comes from the deepest level of existence." Markus Barth, *Ephesians: Translation and Commentary on Chapters 4–6* (New

York: Doubleday, 1974), 583, likewise refers to the appeal to the heart as "an appeal to the center of man's intellect and will, even to the total man."

Spirit he does not. Here there is no article. Now, such factors are matters of style rather than rule and should not be pushed too far; further, there may always be exceptions to any writer's normal use of articles, particles, etc. Yet, this does provide possible evidence that the Holy Spirit is in mind here, and recently Wallace has given this suggestion a stronger grammatical base.[35] Further, in this verse Paul changes from the simple dative in v. 15 (τῷ πνεύματι), which we translated "with my spirit," to "*in* the spirit" in v. 16 (ἐν πνεύματι). Verse 15 is likely to be a dative of association; hence, "I will pray (in association) with my spirit . . . (in association) with my mind." Paul seeks, as it were, to draw his "mind" into the process of his praying. Verse 16, however, presents us with a dative governed by the preposition "in/by/with" (ἐν), and this could be a dative of means "you give thanks by means of the Spirit."[36] Contextually, if the Holy Spirit is in mind here, this need not be regarded as strange. All the way through the epistle Paul has acknowledged that all the grace-gifts, including tongues and prophecy, are made available to people by means of the Holy Spirit. Now Paul speaks of giving thanks as the Spirit enables ("by means of").

Secondly, the precise meaning of "who finds himself among those who do not understand" is unclear. The clause may be translated: "The one occupying the place of one who is a private citizen."[37] It is unlikely that Paul refers to a literal "place" in the assembly that was reserved for such people who were perhaps not yet members. Rather, it is to be taken figuratively. But what sort of person is this? Is this an "uninitiated person," or one who "does not understand," or an "outsider," or an "ordinary person," or one who is "not adept at speaking in tongues"?[38] It has been suggested that in the context of worship the word may mean "lay people" as against the "priest" or "leader," but in the Christian church this is surely anachronistic. "Uninitiated" is too technical and limiting for what Paul is saying here and rather depends on taking "fills the place of" literally as indicating some formal status. "Normal person" is more or less synonymous with "private citizen" and may fit the context here. Elsewhere in the New Testament the word is rare and means "ordinary" in Acts 4:13 or "untrained" in 2 Cor 11:6. Yet in the context of these verses, Schlier is surely correct to point out that this person is "expressly described" in this same verse as the one who does not know what is being said and who therefore cannot say "amen."[39] It seems to us, therefore, that the regularly encountered meaning of "private citizen" is not far removed from what

---

35. Wallace, *Greek Grammar*, 215, adds weight to Fee's suggestion (Fee, *1 Corinthians*, 671 and 578n43) by saying that "it is important to note that unless a noun is modified by a possessive pronoun or at least an article, possession is almost surely *not* implied." He cites Eph 5:18 where he argues that possession is *not* implied by ἐν πνεύματι and so it cannot mean "in your own spirit" but "in/with/by the Spirit." If Wallace is correct, the (Holy) Spirit must be in Paul's mind here in 1 Cor 14:16.

36. See BDF §219.1; and lengthy comments in Wallace, *Greek Grammar*, 373–74.

37. MM 299 cites examples where the dominant meaning is simply "private citizen." BDAG 468 gives this as one of the translations of ἰδιώτης but sees its likely meaning in this verse as referring to people who are "prospects for membership" or "relatively outsiders." This is based on the word's use in 1 Cor 14:23.

38. Thiselton translates it as "uninitiated" (*1 Corinthians*, 1114; NIV 2011 renders it "inquirer"; NRSV has "outsider"). Calvin renders it "normal person" (*First Corinthians*, 293; cf. REB); Horsley translates it as "not adept at" (*1 Corinthians*, 185).

39. H. Schlier, "ἰδιώτης," *TDNT* 3:217. However, he then links the word's meaning directly with its use in v. 23 where he (rightly in our view) says it means "unbeliever" and reads that back into v. 16, concluding that this "demands a reference to non-Christians." This conclusion is unnecessary and unlikely. The context is one of address to the church in which it is assumed that these people are worshipping believers who possess grace-gifts. They are being told how to worship and why "tongues" must be interpreted or not used at all in public worship.

Paul intends. This is a person who does not have the technical know-how that the specialist has. Paul thus simply uses the whole expression in a figurative sense for the one who does not understand. In church all are supposed to participate in worship and say "amen," but if one speaks in tongues and the rest do not understand they *all* find themselves in the position of being like a non-understanding "private person" who needs some technical know-how before they can join in. The issue remains one of intelligibility. All members, but the one tongues-speaker, thus find themselves *among those who do not understand* (with NIV 1984). They all become the other person who is not built up (v. 17). We see below that this understanding of who these people are does in fact fit with the use of the word (ἰδιώτης) in v. 23 as well. The idea that anyone should find themselves feeling like a "private" individual in the midst of what is supposed to be a functioning community where people are constantly building each other up with their God-given gifts is anathema to Paul. The church is hardly "church" anymore.

14:18–19 I thank God, I speak in tongues more than all of you. Nevertheless, in the congregation I would rather speak five words with my mind to instruct others than ten-thousand words in a tongue (εὐχαριστῶ τῷ θεῷ, πάντων ὑμῶν μᾶλλον γλώσσαις λαλῶ· ἀλλὰ ἐν ἐκκλησίᾳ θέλω πέντε λόγους τῷ νοΐ μου λαλῆσαι, ἵνα καὶ ἄλλους κατηχήσω, ἢ μυρίους λόγους ἐν γλώσσῃ). Paul reminds his readers that however strong and even harsh his condemnation of tongues spoken without interpretation has been, he does not rule them out altogether. The verse affirms that they are indeed a grace-gift since he thanks God that he has this gift. He uses hyperbole ("more than all of you"; πάντων ὑμῶν μᾶλλον) to make his point that this gift, when properly used, is something for which God is to be thanked. However, the benefit of tongues to the community remains central as he continues with

the strong adversative "nevertheless" (ἀλλά). Even a few words of instruction, spoken in association with his "mind" (as in vv. 14–15) and therefore intelligible, are far preferable to innumerable words spoken in a tongue.

Paul held himself up as a hypothetical example, but now he makes it clear that he really does speak in tongues frequently, while reserving this gift for private use. In the "church," by which he means the local assembly of Christians gathered for worship, he will always be seeking to teach in such a way that people will be built up in their faith and understanding.

14:20 Brothers [and sisters], do not be children in your thinking, but rather be children in evil and in your thinking be mature (Ἀδελφοί, μὴ παιδία γίνεσθε ταῖς φρεσίν, ἀλλὰ τῇ κακίᾳ νηπιάζετε, ταῖς δὲ φρεσὶν τέλειοι γίνεσθε). In this fourth part of the first section of this chapter, 14:20–25 returns to the question of true spiritual maturity among the believers. As the whole church participates together in *intelligible* worship, as opposed to suffering under uninterpreted tongues, so even the outsider will be convicted and will acknowledge God's presence with his people and so be drawn to worship. Paul's move now to speaking of "children" (παιδία) and the "mature" (τέλειοι) reminds the reader that the Corinthian abuse of the gift of tongues is yet another symptom of their underlying problem. Thinking they are superior and mature, they are simply acting as children and revealing that their gifts in themselves authenticate nothing. The relationship between spiritual maturity and the grace-gifts is tangential. To the extent that it exists, it is in how the gifts are *used*. If they are used in the context of *love*, then they will function to build up other Christians. It is in seeking to build up a fellow believer or to build up the church that a Christian will reveal *love* for the other and so spiritual maturity will be evidenced.

Paul has spoken of maturity and childishness in 2:6, 3:1, and 13:11–12. In the comments on 2:6 we dismissed the idea that Paul is drawing on Hellenistic mystery religions as he speaks of "the mature" (τέλειοι). For Paul the "mature" are the truly "spiritual" people, as he made clear in 3:1–2. All Christians are "spiritual" people, but the Corinthians have not behaved as such, and have thought that their spiritual prowess was evidenced in their gifts. In fact their behavior and attitudes reflected a spiritual childishness. Now Paul has to appeal to them again for the same reason. He urges that they not act as "children" (παιδία) in their "thinking" (φρεσίν, a dative of reference). That is, they must stop thinking of tongues as a marker of spiritual prowess. The pride and arrogance that goes with this type of thinking is nothing less than "evil" (κακία). With clever rhetoric, Paul turns it around and says that it is in this evil that they should be infants, but should become mature in their thinking. That is, they should begin to think like Paul and see "love" as the marker, ensuring that they let gifts *function* to build up others.

The analogy is a good one. Children, and especially very young children, are notoriously self-centered. They do not think about others and are concerned only to have their own way and, among other children, long to be the dominant one. This sort of behavior is not that of the mature person, who should be able to put others first and think about caring for others. The word "thinking" (φρήν) implies careful consideration or discernment and recalls the insistence in 2:14–16 that the mature person will discern or judge spiritual things in a godly way. See the discussion of this type of discernment or judgment (ἀνακρίνω and συγκρίνω) in comments on 2:14. This sort of "mature" Christian discernment about the gift of tongues will lead to a recognition of the limitation of the gift in terms of its community benefit. It will also recognize that such a gift cannot possibly be a marker of someone's degree of "spirituality." Paul's appeal here, as in 13:11, is that Christians should "give up childish ways" and reflect an understanding that if they are to be "something" rather than "nothing" (13:2), it will be as they exhibit love.

14:21 In the law it is written, "By people of strange tongues and by the lips of strangers I will speak to this people, and even then they will not listen to me, says the Lord" (ἐν τῷ νόμῳ γέγραπται ὅτι Ἐν ἑτερογλώσσοις καὶ ἐν χείλεσιν ἑτέρων λαλήσω τῷ λαῷ τούτῳ, καὶ οὐδ' οὕτως εἰσακούσονταί μου, λέγει κύριος). Motyer in his commentary on this section of Isaiah, quoted by Paul, writes, "The thrust is plain: the word of grace rejected becomes the word of condemnation."[40] It is this point that is the apostle's intention in his quotation. "The law" can denote the "prophets" as well as the Pentateuch (cf. 9:8, 9; 14:34; John 10:34), while the addition of "says the Lord" simply identifies the speaker in the original prophecy as God rather than the prophet. Here, then, Paul paraphrases Isaiah 28:11–12 and applies it to the Corinthian situation. Though the quotation varies in a number of ways from both the LXX and the Hebrew, it is clear how Paul uses Isaiah and that he does so with a mind to the original context. The Israelite leaders were indulging in food and much drink to the point where they stumbled and were unable to render judgment (vv. 7–8). The sophisticated leaders believed they had nothing to be taught and so mocked Isaiah (v. 14), who had preached a plain message (vv. 9–10). The words of v. 10 may simply indicate the careful,

---

40. J. Alec Motyer, *The Prophecy of Isaiah: An Introduction and Commentary*, TOTC (Leicester: Inter-Varsity Press, 1993), 231.

patient, line-by-line teaching of a teacher of young children, or it may simply reflect the noises that might be made to a baby. In 28:11 Isaiah foresees the message to which the leaders will eventually be forced to listen. These same leaders had heard and then rejected (v. 12) the simple message of the stone that had been offered as a resting place (v. 16). It is in this firm foundation that they should have trusted, but did not. In the end God's judgment will come through people who speak not the simple and childlike message of the Lord's protection, but rather who speak the foreign language of an invading army (the Assyrians).

Paul's paraphrase of a part of this story from Isaiah is well suited to his message for the Corinthians. It is not simply that the connection between Corinth and Isaiah is made through the phrase "speaking in tongues." Rather, Paul takes an example from "the law" in which the complex of languages, sophisticated elitism (the wisdom of this world), and the matter of intelligibility of a message all come together. The problem at Corinth was one of worldly elitism and a belief that they were "safe," yet they were in fact in danger of God's judgment (see discussion of 10:1–12). One of their favored gifts was speaking in tongues in the congregation. The lack of interpretation meant the whole congregation was *excluded* from participation or any degree of edification. Paul's point is that the simple, understandable prayer to God is to be preferred for everyone's sake, both for the believer and the unbeliever who might be present in the assembly. Isaiah faced the problem of an elitist group of leaders for whom a message presented in simple and intelligible language had meant nothing and had been disdained and rejected. Therefore, God would let them hear a more complicated language, and they would not understand, and it would lead to their destruction.

Those at Corinth who are so eager for the use of languages that necessarily exclude others must realize the seriousness of the consequences. They will be putting those who do not understand in a similar position to the Israelites when the Assyrians eventually entered the land. In God's economy an unintelligible message leads to judgment, and a simple and clear message leads to salvation. How can those who are supposed to "love" their fellow brothers and sisters "for whom Christ died" (8:11) even consider making those people feel that they are no longer at home and no longer "belong"? Those Christians will find themselves in the same place as other "outsiders" or unbelievers who stand under judgment. The end of all this is thus very like what was happening with the eating of idol meat, which some advocated on the grounds of their gift of "knowledge." This could lead to the weaker brother or sister being "destroyed" (8:11). It also parallels the problem enunciated in 10:1–12 where, again, those who consider spiritual gifts to be evidence of their status before God must be warned by examples from the Israelites that destruction may await them. The greatest irony is that the ones advocating such "tongue-speaking" without interpretation find *themselves* "left out" when one of their friends uses such a tongue. At that point they will discover that even they are no longer at home but rather are excluded and so are in danger of judgment. Just as the unintelligible tongues in Isaiah became a sign of God's judgment, so there is a real danger at Corinth. In short, God's gracious word of salvation is to be delivered in simple and understandable language. When unintelligible language is used among God's people, there should be a real fear of God's judgment, for he has used such language before to judge. Paul now moves to a further application of what he has been saying.

14:22 So then tongues are a sign not for those who believe but rather for those who do not

believe, and prophecy is a sign not for those who do not believe but rather for those who believe (ὥστε αἱ γλῶσσαι εἰς σημεῖόν εἰσιν οὐ τοῖς πιστεύουσιν ἀλλὰ τοῖς ἀπίστοις, ἡ δὲ προφητεία οὐ τοῖς ἀπίστοις ἀλλὰ τοῖς πιστεύουσιν). Tongues continue to be seen as a negative sign and are thus for unbelievers, while in his continuing contrast of these gifts Paul sees prophecy as a sign for those who believe precisely because it is intelligible and builds them up. Therefore, what Paul now writes is a clear inference from what he has just written ("so then" [ὥστε]). "Tongues are a sign" is the right translation (there is no need to say they "are for a sign").[41] Of course, the immediate question that arises is, "In what way are tongues a sign for unbelievers?" We shall see below that any answer to this is further complicated by the verses that follow.

It has been suggested by some that tongues function as a sign for unbelievers in the sense they did on the day of Pentecost in Acts 2, that is, as an evangelistic sign. However, this assumes that what Paul speaks of here is the same phenomenon, and above it has been argued that it is not. It also assumes that the tongues of Acts 2 served as an evangelistic tool, an assumption that is far from clear, though that cannot be addressed here.[42] Johanson believes that the *Corinthians* regarded "tongues" as having an apologetic intent and suggests v. 22 is part of *their* argument to which Paul responds in v. 23.[43] If this were a quotation, we might expect some indication in the text that this is the case. Even then, the idea falters on Paul's use of "therefore" in v. 23, suggesting that he is drawing consequences from what *he* has said, not from what others have said! Ruef has suggested that tongues here are a God-given sign

for (Gentile) unbelievers who become Christians and speak in tongues as a sign of their new identity, along the lines of apparent examples like Cornelius in Acts 11. But this position is hardly sustainable in this context and fails to give an adequate explanation of the mention of unbelievers in v. 23.[44] Barrett, and many others, conclude that Paul must be arguing that tongues serve "as a sign of judgment" on unbelievers. Broadly speaking, this must surely be the right way forward, though the question then arises as to whether the second half of the sentence about prophecy balances the first and also how it fits with v. 23.

Paul has already indicated that "signs" are something Jews demand over against the simplicity of the message of Christ crucified (1:22). While they were wrong to demand "signs" when presented with Christ, nevertheless, there has always been throughout Scripture the right and proper use by God of signs. In a detailed study of the word, Grudem states that a sign "can often mean an indication of God's attitude."[45] He goes on to demonstrate that these are often positive for those who believe and negative toward those who do not believe or who are disobedient to the Lord. He cites many examples of both kinds of signs (where the word σημεῖον is used in the LXX). For example, signs that are a positive sign for believers include the rainbow (Gen 9:1–14) and the blood on the doorposts (Exod 12:13). Signs that are negative also abound, often warning God's people to repent as, for example, with the bronze censers of the unfaithful Korah (Num 16:38 [17:3 LXX]) and Aaron's rod (Num 17:10 [17:25 LXX]). But Grudem also notes that many signs are *both* positive and

---

41. "Are a sign" (εἰς σημεῖόν εἰσιν) is an example of an expected predicate nominative with the verb "to be" that has been replaced with a preposition and the accusative (cf. Col 2:22; Jas 5:3). BDF §145.1.

42. See Carson, *Showing the Spirit*, 138ff.

43. Bruce C. Johanson, "Tongues, A Sign for Unbelievers? A Structural and Exegetical Study of 1 Cor 14:20–25," *NTS* 25 (1979): 180–203.

44. Ruef, *Paul's First Letter to Corinth*, 152.

45. Grudem, *Gift of Prophecy in the New Testament*, 148.

negative; that is, they express God's approval to his believing people and judgment on others.[46] Thus, for example, the plagues of the exodus are seen as a blessing for Israel and a judgment on Egypt (cf. Exod 10:1–4; Deut 4:34–35). The same is true in some instances in the New Testament, such as in Acts 2:22, 43, and 4:30, where a "sign" indicates God's approval and in Acts 2:19 where it indicates God's disapproval. Grudem concludes, Paul is using "sign" "in a familiar and well-established sense."[47]

In verse 22 it appears Paul has in mind both the positive and negative functions of the word. The function of the "strange *tongues*" in Isaiah was to warn of judgment, and so Paul uses the term "sign." Since signs for believers are positive and indicate God's blessing, Paul can equally think of *prophecy* as a positive sign that indicates God's presence in the community and his blessing on the assembly. Indeed, the withdrawal of prophecy is seen in the Old Testament as an indication of God's judgment (Ps 74:9; Isa 29:10).[48] With this background we may now turn to the structure of the verse, which is clear:

```
tongues are a sign
           not    for believers
                        but   for unbelievers
and prophecy [is a sign]
           not    for unbelievers
                        but   for believers
```

If we understand that Paul has already established by his quotation from Isaiah 28 that incomprehensible tongues are a negative "sign," then we know that they must be this for those who are "unbelievers," or at least to those who find themselves in the place of unbelievers. Precisely because they are a negative sign they are not for "believers." For believers we would expect a positive "sign," indicating God's attitude of blessing upon them. This is precisely what Paul has argued *is* provided by the gift of prophecy (14:3). Thus, the gift of prophecy is for "believers." All through this chapter in various ways, Paul argues for the priority in public worship of prophecy or indeed any *intelligible* gift since these function to build up the community, which, in turn, is an indication of God's blessing among them. Paul's argument, though perhaps strange to our ears, is reasonably clear *so far*. However, many commentators have regarded this verse as exceptionally difficult to understand.[49] The reason lies in the analogies found in the subsequent verses. Initially they appear to indicate the *positive* nature of prophecy for *un*believers.

14:23 Therefore, if the whole church comes together in the same place and all speak in tongues and outsiders or unbelievers should enter, will they not say that you are insane? (Ἐὰν οὖν συνέλθῃ ἡ ἐκκλησία ὅλη ἐπὶ τὸ αὐτὸ καὶ πάντες λαλῶσιν γλώσσαις, εἰσέλθωσιν δὲ ἰδιῶται ἢ ἄπιστοι, οὐκ ἐροῦσιν ὅτι μαίνεσθε;). For all the ways in which this verse seems difficult to relate to the previous verse, Paul regards what he now says *as a consequence* of what has been said ("therefore" [οὖν]). His intention is to ensure that unbelievers entering the church should be able to understand clearly what God may be saying to the church or to them. In another conditional clause, Paul speaks of the whole church coming together "in the same place" (ἐπὶ τὸ αὐτό; cf. Luke 17:35; Acts 2:1) and the hypothetical situation of "all" speaking in tongues. "All" cannot mean that he expects all to have this gift, but rather provides a graphic illustration.

The question arises then as to whether Paul

---

46. Ibid., 149.
47. Ibid.
48. Ibid., 148–54.

49. For example, Hays, *First Corinthians*, 239–40, refers to "great confusion. . . . Paul's argument is somewhat garbled."

signals two different groups when he speaks of "outsiders" (ἰδιῶται) and "unbelievers" (ἄπιστοι). As we noted, in v. 16 the word translated here as "outsiders" (ἰδιῶται) must apply to those who are already Christians but who find themselves like an outsider in not understanding what is going on. Here Paul may be using the word in a more technical religious sense. Yet it may simply be used as a synonym in this context for people who are not Christians, the "unbelievers." The point is that these people do not understand what they hear. The word thus has the same connotation as in v. 16, but now describes uncomprehending "unbelievers." Paul does not address two categories of people. Rather, he thinks of outsiders who are unbelievers and who are people who, therefore, do not understand what is being said.

If unbelievers enter and find that everyone speaks in an unintelligible language, they will simply think, says Paul, that "you are insane [or *crazy*]" (μαίνεσθε). While some have suggested that such unbelievers would have been well acquainted with the cult practices of the mystery religions, and so would simply take the gathering to be another group involved in the uncontrolled noises that seem to have been part of the fare in such a cult, this need not be the case. Indeed, we should not read too much of this into what Paul is saying here.[50] Nevertheless, the reaction of people then would have been similar to the reaction we might expect today. People would believe that they were witnessing religious fanatics and would walk out, not having been challenged at all by the gospel of Christ. The "sign" involved therefore for unbelievers is one of judgment (v. 22), as in Isaiah 28. Unbelievers walking into a group of worshipping Christians should encounter an intelligible challenge from God himself. This very naturally sets up the argument for v. 24.

14:24–25 But if all prophesy and one who is an unbeliever or who does not understand should enter, he is convicted by all, he is judged by all, the secrets of his heart are revealed and so, falling on his face, he will worship God, confessing, "God is really among you" (ἐὰν δὲ πάντες προφητεύωσιν, εἰσέλθῃ δέ τις ἄπιστος ἢ ἰδιώτης, ἐλέγχεται ὑπὸ πάντων, ἀνακρίνεται ὑπὸ πάντων, τὰ κρυπτὰ τῆς καρδίας αὐτοῦ φανερὰ γίνεται, καὶ οὕτως πεσὼν ἐπὶ πρόσωπον προσκυνήσει τῷ θεῷ ἀπαγγέλλων ὅτι Ὄντως ὁ θεὸς ἐν ὑμῖν ἐστιν). Paul continues to talk of unbelievers entering the church. We know how tongues is a sign for unbelievers (v. 23 has elaborated upon v. 22b–d), but now Paul reflects on how *prophecy* may impact unbelievers. Through prophecy an unbeliever may be challenged by God as their sin is exposed to judgment. This may result in a person turning to God in worship. Initially, the verse seems strange. As Paul now turns to prophecy the reader is expecting him to reflect on *believers* and so elaborate on how prophecy may be a sign for believers. However, the difficulty is not as acute as some suggest. The key lies in the final scriptural allusion, "God is really among you." This *is* the sign that prophecy can provide for *believers* of God's gracious presence in the community: *unbelievers* begin to worship. Verses 24–25 do indeed elaborate upon v. 22e–g. The beauty of the gift of prophecy and its edification of the church is thus seen in two ways: it produces fruit as the church is built up, but also its effects will be seen as some unbelievers become believers.

---

50. Conzelmann, *1 Corinthians*, 243, says that "the reader naturally thinks of the ecstatic cults." Hays, *First Corinthians*, 238, refers to outsiders regarding it as "a fit of religious ecstasy, common in that culture." Thiselton, *1 Corinthians*, 1127, and

Garland, *1 Corinthians*, 652, among many, warn against building too much on this background. "Insane" simply denotes the appearance of being out of one's mind (cf. Acts 26:25).

Some further details of these verses need attention. The same form of conditional sentence sets up this further hypothetical situation. The word translated as "convicted" (ἐλέγχω) can also mean to "expose" or "bring to light" (cf. Eph 5:11, 13), but in this context of judgment ("he is judged"; ἀνακρίνεται) "to convict" seems the best translation (cf. John 16:8; Jas 2:9). This function of the grace-gift of "prophecy," given by the Holy Spirit to his people, mirrors the work and role of the Spirit mentioned in John 16:8. In that passage Jesus promises to send the Spirit to the disciples, and his role will be to "convict the world concerning sin and righteousness and judgment" (ESV). Paul is indicating that if these Christians had eyes to see they would see the conversion of believers as evidence that the Spirit has come to them and is at work among them.

The unbeliever will be "judged by all" (ἀνακρίνεται ὑπὸ πάντων). In our examination of the theme of discernment and judgment, we noted that this word has a forensic tone to it (2:14). The work of prophecy means that the unbeliever, being convicted in his heart, also finds him or herself spiritually judged by all. It is not so much that individual believers who are prophesying judge anyone, but the message the Lord gives them leads some unbelievers to conviction. The divine nature of what is happening becomes clear as "the secrets of his heart are revealed" (τὰ κρυπτὰ τῆς καρδίας αὐτοῦ φανερὰ γίνεται). The "heart" refers to a person's inner self, which is laid bare by the word of the Lord in the prophecy. People's sinful inclinations, desires, and even motivations are opened up by the penetrating light that comes from the Spirit of God himself. There is no need to assume that by some special "revelation" a prophet speaks directly to an individual's heart.[51] Rather, in one form or another

the gospel is brought to bear in such a way that the unbeliever turns to fall in worship before the Lord.

Prostration (πεσὼν ἐπὶ πρόσωπον) is an act of worship that acknowledges the presence of God among the people (cf. 1 Kgs 18:39). Paul alludes to Isaiah 45:14 (LXX: ἐν σοὶ ὁ θεός ἐστιν) and possibly Zechariah 8:23 (LXX: ὁ θεὸς μεθ' ὑμῶν ἐστιν) as he puts words in the mouth of an unbeliever who has been so touched: "God is really among you" (ὄντως ὁ θεὸς ἐν ὑμῖν ἐστιν). It is noteworthy that in those two Old Testament contexts the declaration that God is among his people is spoken by foreigners to Israel. It was always God's intention to bring into being a people from all the nations. As the unbelievers acknowledge God's presence among his people in Corinth, they come in fulfillment of the great visions of the drawing in of the nations that were given to Isaiah and Zechariah and other prophets. In Zechariah 8:23 there is a specific reference to people of other nations and "tongues" coming to join God's people: "Thus says the LORD of hosts: In those days ten men from the nations of every tongue shall take hold of the robe of a Jew, saying, 'Let us go with you, for we have heard that God is with you'" (ESV). These words of the unbeliever here in 1 Corinthians 14:25 can be treated as direct speech.[52] "Really" (ὄντως) emphasizes the enormity of what these people discover through prophecy.

The first twenty-five verses of 1 Corinthians 14 have led to several conclusions, but the most important is that prophecy is the better gift to use in corporate worship than tongues. The former is intelligible and useful, but the latter, unless the person concerned interprets what he or she has said, does not benefit or build up the community. Prophecy not only builds up believers as they gather to worship and allows them all to participate

---

51. *Contra* Grudem, *Gift of Prophecy in the New Testament*, 142–43. Though, equally, there is no reason to ignore the possibility of a specific revelation that would be taken by an indi-

vidual as directly addressing their heart.

52. Taking ὅτι as recitative.

in affirming the message with the "amen" but also can lead to the conversion of those who may come in as unbelievers. These same people might walk out claiming Christians are insane should they simply encounter uninterpreted tongues. Yet Paul does not write off tongues completely. They can be interpreted for public use, and they remain useful for an individual who prays *to God* with them. As a sign, prophecy demonstrates God's favor on the community. But, generally, tongues that are not understood by those who are believers, or unbelievers, function as a sign of judgment.

Theology in Application

Seeking after Deeper Spiritual Experience

Each Christian longs to experience at an ever deeper level the knowledge of God and of Christ. That this knowledge can and should be one of the Christian's goals in this age, before "we see . . . face to face" (13:12), is certain. Paul surely drives toward this in his prayer for the Ephesians (Eph 3:14–19). He prays that the Spirit will strengthen them with power in their "inner being" (v. 16). He prays they will "know" the glorious extent of Christ's love for them, so they will be filled "with all the fullness of God" (v. 19; τὸ πλήρωμα τοῦ θεοῦ). There is no doubt that the experiential knowledge of God and his Spirit's power at work in the life of the believer has, at times in the church's history, received less emphasis than it should. So it is unsurprising that when some exhibit the more obvious workings of the Spirit, they may be respected as more spiritual or more mature in the faith than others. In some cases, individuals or groups will give themselves that status. This was a major part of the problem in the church at Corinth.

Paul's strong emphasis on *love* and *Christ crucified* provided an altogether different way of understanding the type of spiritual experience that Christians should seek. The path of humility before others and even suffering for their benefit is found in following the one who was crucified. The way of the cross was a path where the Savior gave himself completely for the benefit of his people. As Paul has urged the Corinthians to imitate Christ, he has summarized what this should look like with the word "love." He has especially noted how love is to be seen and focused on the *other*. For Paul, then, the most fulfilling experiential knowledge of God and of Christ will be found within the worshipping community where God's people will learn more of Christ's love but also then live out the life of Christ with one another. They will know more of Christ and his love as they seek the *other's* benefit and spiritual edification. As grace-gifts, which were poured out in the church by God's Spirit, are allowed to function properly in the community, then all will "grow in the grace and *knowledge* of our Lord and Savior Jesus Christ" (2 Pet 3:18). The intelligibility of what comes from the Spirit is thus of extraordinary importance, since it is only what is understood that can edify spiritually. Furthermore, it is only what is understood that can be properly *judged* or discerned to see whether it is of the Lord or not. Discernment of this sort will also help the church decide how best to benefit from what the Lord is saying or doing among his people. The question of "order" becomes essential to this process so that all, rather than just a few, may benefit.

Tongues, Prophecy, and Speech Gifts

It is one of the great sadnesses for the church throughout history, including in our own day and age, that so many believers look for God's "signs" in their *own* lives (such as speaking in tongues) to evidence their special gifting rather than looking for signs that clearly evidence the presence of God in the *community* and lead to the edification of the community. In 14:12 it is clear how much the Corinthians desired evidences in their own lives of "inspirations of the Spirit." Paul's response, as might be expected, is that they should strive for the benefit of the community. If there is to be any form of competition between Christians, then Paul says it must be centered in *others*: "Be devoted to one another in love. Honor one another above yourselves" (Rom 12:10). For Paul, the preferred and deepest spiritual experience for Christians is to be found in seeing others built up because in this they find themselves being drawn closer to the Christ who died for them. Paul caps this section with the joy that intelligible prophecy may even lead to the conversion of the unbeliever (14:25).

The contrast of tongues with prophecy has not been made with a view to replacing tongues with prophecy as a superior gift. Rather, prophecy is a good example of Paul's point that any gift that builds up the community should be given primacy over those that do not, like tongues (unless interpreted). However, in the modern church intelligibility and the spiritual building up of the people in line with God's will and purposes remains a pressing matter, whether or not there is speaking in tongues in a congregation. The poverty of sound teaching or preaching in much of modern Western Christianity is a serious matter if spiritual maturity is desired. The building up of God's people will happen as God's word is spoken intelligibly among them. It is especially in and through the use of the speech gifts such as teaching, preaching, and prophecy that God's people will mature spiritually. It is in the teaching, discussion, and discerning of the congregation as a whole that people will learn where they are too much conformed to this world and how better to live out the will of God. As Paul said in Romans 12:2, "Do not be conformed to this world, but be transformed by the renewing of your minds, so that you may discern what is the will of God—what is good and acceptable and perfect" (NRSV). The mind must be engaged with the truth of God (1 Cor 14:14, 19, 20). As so many long for spiritual experiences and chase around different churches trying to find something that makes them feel good, congregations need to be taught that they should strive to "abound in the building up of the church" (14:12). This means discerning the will of God found in his word.

For those seeking to witness the more spectacular workings of God in their midst, there is a need to recapture an understanding of conversion as a true miracle. As Paul contrasts tongues and prophecy, we can refreshingly be reminded that nowhere is God's activity to be seen more clearly than when he uses the very grace-gifts he has given the church in order that the *other* may also become a worshipper of the true God. If some Corinthians regarded the grace-gifts as a sign of their own spiritual superiority, then they needed to take their eyes off themselves and see how the gifts truly function. If they had done that, they would have seen that "prophecy" was a wonderful gift because it not only produced fruit among the Corinthian Christians themselves but led to the miracle of some coming to faith in Christ. What better clarity can there be that intelligible speech gifts should be preferred, especially in corporate worship, than in hearing *un*believers acknowledge, "God is among you."

1 Corinthians 14:26–40

Literary Context

Having examined the right use and purposes for which God provides the grace-gifts (ch. 12), Paul has turned to contrast tongues and prophecy (ch. 14). He writes in chapter 13 that love is the key marker of authentic faith. Now Paul develops what he has said about corporate worship. These verses give a small insight into the nature of worship in the gathered assembly, though they do not necessarily indicate that all worship followed this pattern in all the cities. In the section (14:26–40), Paul wants to ensure that there is order in the way worship is done. The order in worship is to reflect the fact that God himself is a God of order. It is clear here that Paul continues to strive for all corporate worship to edify all present. This will mean allowing people to speak and to be heard; it will mean taking time to judge what has been said to discern whether it benefits the community; it will mean avoiding any possibility of confusion; it will even mean paying attention to how men and women relate to one another. His conclusion then returns to the opening exhortation that they should "earnestly seek" gifts, though he now narrows it down to "prophecy," while still diminishing "tongues" (vv. 39–40). By use of these two gifts as examples, Paul successfully demonstrates what the "greater gifts" are. Thus Paul concludes the lengthy section that began at 11:2, which has examined a number of matters concerning public worship, the use of grace-gifts, and the status-authenticating nature of love.

Main Idea

The spiritual edification of God's people in public worship requires their orderly conduct in worship, the orderly use of the grace-gifts, and an eagerness especially for prophecy.

Translation

1 Corinthians 14:26–40

26a	Rhetorical question	**What shall we say then,** brothers [and sisters]?
b	Occasion	Whenever you come together,
c	Assertion	**each person has a psalm,**
d	List	**a teaching, a revelation,**
e		**a tongue, an interpretation.**
f	Assertion	[Well,] **all things [are] for the building up** [of the church].
27a	Condition	If someone speaks in a tongue,
b	Exhortation	**let only two or at most three [speak]** and
c		each in turn,
		and
d	Exhortation	**let that one interpret.**
28a	Condition	But if he is not an interpreter,
b	Exhortation (apodosis)	**let him [or her] keep silent …**
c	Place	in the church,
d	Contrast	but **speak**
		to himself and
		to God.
29a	Exhortation	Now **let two or three prophets speak,**
b	Exhortation	and **let the others judge,**
30a	Condition	and if a revelation is made to another
b	Description	who is sitting down,
c	Exhortation	**let the first person be silent.**
31a	Basis	For **you can all prophesy** one by one,
b	Purpose	in order that all may learn and
c	Purpose	all may be encouraged,
32a	Assertion	and **the inspirations of the prophets are subject to the prophets,**
33a	Basis	for **God is not [a God] of disorder** but
b	Contrast	**of peace.**

Continued on next page.

Continued from previous page.

c	Location	As in all the churches of the saints
34a	Assertion	**the wives [women] should keep silent**
b	Location	in the churches,
c	Basis	for **they are not permitted to speak,**
d	Expansion on 34a	but **let them subject themselves,**
e	Basis for 34d	as the law says.
35a	Condition	But if they wish to learn,
b	Expansion on 34a	**let them ask their own husbands** at home,
c	Basis	for **it is shameful for a wife [woman] to speak** in church.
36a	Reinforcement of vv. 29–35	So tell me,
b	Rhetorical question	**did the word of God come from you?**
c		Or tell me,
d	Rhetorical question	**did it come only to you?**
37a	Condition	If someone thinks he [or she] is a prophet or spiritual,
b	Exhortation	**let him [or her] acknowledge that the things I write to you are a command** ✍ **of the Lord.**
38a	Contrast	But if someone does not recognize this,
b	Exhortation	**let him [or her] not be recognized.**
39a	Inference	Therefore, my brothers [and sisters],
b	Exhortations	**earnestly desire to prophesy**
c	(Series)	and **do not forbid speaking in tongues.**
40a	(Series)	But **let all things be done properly and**
b	Manner	**in an orderly manner.**

Structure

This chapter has divided into two main sections with the command "earnestly desire" (ζηλοῦτε) in v. 1 and v. 39 forming an *inclusio*. The first section (14:1–25) contrasted the gifts of tongues and of prophecy. In the second section (14:26–40), Paul lets this theme take him back to his more general concern for the conduct of worship within the gathered congregation. The way that worship is conducted will itself reflect whether people have properly understood that all should have the goal of building up the church. This section may be divided into four parts. First, 14:26–33b reinforces again the need for "building up" (v. 26) before immediately speaking to the matter of order that will help enable this. He addresses necessary order for tongues-speaking (vv. 27–28) and then for prophecy (vv. 29–32). Secondly, 14:33c–36 addresses the conduct of certain women in public worship. Thirdly, 14:37–38 gives a warning to prophets. Finally, in 14:39–40 Paul adds an encouragement to use the grace-gifts appropriately while still maintaining order in worship.

Exegetical Outline

VIII. Status, Public Worship, Freedom, and Grace-Gifts (11:2–14:40)

    A. The Conduct of Husbands and Wives in Public Worship (11:2–16)

    B. The Conduct of the Church at the Lord's Supper (11:17–34)

    C. Spiritual People and the Function of Their Grace-Gifts in the Church (12:1–31)

    D. The Status of Spiritual People Is Authenticated by Love (13:1–13)

    E. The Proper Function of Grace-Gifts in Public Worship (14:1–25)

➡   **F. In Public Worship All Activity Must Build Up the Church (14:26–40)**

        1. The Orderly Use of Grace-Gifts in Worship Enables Edification (14:26–33a)

            a. Many Gifts Are Used to Build Up the Church (14:26)

            b. How Tongues-Speaking May Be Used (14:27–28)

            c. How Prophecy May Be Used (14:29–33b)

        2. The Conduct of Wives in Judging Prophecies (14:33c–36)

        3. Prophets Must Heed the Lord's Command (14:37–38)

        4. All Should Desire Prophecy and Maintain Order in Public Worship (14:39–40)

Explanation of the Text

14:26 What shall we say then, brothers [and sisters]? Whenever you come together, each person has a psalm, a teaching, a revelation, a tongue, an interpretation. [Well,] all things [are] for the building up [of the church] (Τί οὖν ἐστιν, ἀδελφοί; ὅταν συνέρχησθε, ἕκαστος ψαλμὸν ἔχει, διδαχὴν ἔχει, ἀποκάλυψιν ἔχει, γλῶσσαν ἔχει, ἑρμηνείαν ἔχει· πάντα πρὸς οἰκοδομὴν γινέσθω). Paul writes an abbreviated summary of what he is saying to them, once again returning to his key theme that all things are for building up. This remains the key determinant for all he says. He is not inflicting some "order" or universal worship "rule" on the Corinthians (and hence upon others throughout history). He suggests ways forward that will allow

the church to experience the full benefit of the grace-gifts in their function of "building up" the church (πάντα πρὸς οἰκοδομήν, cf. v. 12).[1] By allowing each to speak in turn, just as by insisting on intelligible communication, there will be no sense that some are part of the "in" crowd and others are left out. This ordering of worship, in fact, will reflect love in action as each person is heard and considered. The verse reveals a little more about what went on in the early worship gatherings of the community. Different people had different gifts, and clearly they were accustomed to these gifts being used during their assemblies. So this section from vv. 26–33a gives instructions about how best to conduct worship while ensuring that

---

1. "Well" in our translation is added simply to indicate the continuity implicit in the Greek. The intended verb ("are") and object ("the church") are also missing in the Greek but added for intelligibility.

the Spirit-given grace-gifts function in the way they are supposed to when several different people are each expecting to participate.

The opening question is a rhetorical device to maintain interest and press home the argument. "Whenever" (ὅταν) could simply be translated "when," but the present subjunctive indicates an indefinite temporal clause and a degree of repetition regarding time; hence "whenever."[2] "Each person" (ἕκαστος) does not imply that every single individual had something to say to the gathering (cf. 7:2) anymore than "all" implied every single person in v. 24. The various gifts mentioned here have appeared before either in this chapter or in 12:10–11, and the list is surely not exclusive. Paul has spoken in chapter 12 of other gifts, such as a "word of wisdom" or of "knowledge" or "discernment between spirits," so we may reasonably assume that they too were also used in congregational gatherings.

A further issue arises with the verb "has" (ἔχει) a psalm, etc. It might mean that people arrive prepared to present something that God has given them for the worship service or that they "receive" something spontaneously as they worship. Fee suggests that these must be spontaneous gifts of the Spirit arising in the midst of worship. The difficulty is that he draws this conclusion from some rather broad generalizations that may or may not be correct. For example, he writes, "Since the latter three are Spirit-inspired utterances [revelation, tongue, interpretation], and are therefore spontaneous, it is probable that the first two are to be understood in that way as well, although one cannot be certain."[3] The problem is that Spirit-inspired utterances are nowhere defined by Paul as being "spontaneous," though some, such as these last three, may well

have been so. Furthermore, the problem of the nature of these gifts can be exacerbated by the terminology people use. Many can speak of these gifts as "supernatural." Thus Fee writes that "the emphasis is on the supernatural"[4] But the word "supernatural" begs a host of questions and can sound thoroughly dualistic in a non-Pauline way. It requires the reader rather arbitrarily to decide what may or may not be placed in that category. For Paul, it is the Holy Spirit who is at work in the believer from beginning to end, and it is he who gives gifts for the building up of the community. Undoubtedly, some of those gifts were and are more "spectacular" than others. To listen to teaching is likely to be less noteworthy than suddenly hearing a person speaking in tongues, which may cause reactions simply because it is "spectacular" or just plain weird when it is not understood! A "revelation" or a "prophecy" may suddenly come to a person while someone else is speaking—at least this chapter implies that such may be the case—and so may at that moment appear more spectacular or more worthy of immediate attention. But *none* of this suggests that one is somehow "supernatural" and another not. All is from God if it builds up the church, whether teaching, preaching, or interpreting a tongue.

It has been our contention throughout this commentary that the Corinthians have probably taken the more spectacular gifts—those which do indeed perhaps seem more "spontaneous"—and have made them into indicators or markers of spiritual maturity. Throughout Paul has denied them this function. The issue is whether they build up or not. There is no clear reason to limit these gifts to complete spontaneity, even if some may have been given by God in this way. The text does not

---

2. See Wallace, *Greek Grammar*, 479. BDAG 730.

3. Fee, *1 Corinthians*, 765; see also 655, 658–660. Sadly and confusingly, given what the apostle actually says in this epistle, Fee also uses the word "charismatic" to indicate "that there

was general participation by all the members . . . and that there was considerable expression of the more spontaneous gifts of utterance" (ibid., 758).

4. Ibid., 655.

preclude some people standing up at will in the congregation with a prepared piece of "teaching."

"A psalm" (ψαλμός) may simply be an Old Testament psalm. In such a case it is possible that an individual started singing their own psalm while others were still talking, or that someone's suggestion of an appropriate song from Scripture was being ignored by the gathering. On the other hand, as noted in v. 15, it may refer to "singing in tongues," in which case v. 27 will qualify this gift as well, requiring the words to be made intelligible to the whole gathering. Most likely, to our mind, especially given verses like Ephesians 5:19 and Colossians 3:16 in which "psalms, hymns, and songs" (ψαλμοῖς καὶ ὕμνοις καὶ ᾠδαῖς) seem to be differentiated, Paul thinks of people ("spontaneously"?) praising God with the words of Scripture that the Spirit has brought to their mind.

We continue to use the word "interpretation" (ἑρμηνεία) here but understand that it can have a broad meaning that could include "putting into words" or even simply "making intelligible" whatever has come in a "tongue." It does not need to mean the same as what we might think of as a parallel "translation." Paul returns to tongues and how to apply what he has said to this particular gift.

14:27–28 If someone speaks in a tongue, let only two or at most three [speak] and each in turn, and let that one interpret. But if he is not an interpreter, let him [or her] keep silent in the church, but speak to himself and to God (εἴτε γλώσσῃ τις λαλεῖ, κατὰ δύο ἢ τὸ πλεῖστον τρεῖς, καὶ ἀνὰ μέρος, καὶ εἷς διερμηνευέτω· ἐὰν δὲ μὴ ᾖ διερμηνευτής, σιγάτω ἐν ἐκκλησίᾳ, ἑαυτῷ δὲ λαλείτω καὶ τῷ θεῷ).

What Paul now says about "tongues" puts a practical edge on how to implement what he has said in v. 26 about all to be done "for building up." Perhaps some in different places in the room had been speaking in tongues simultaneously. If this gift was specially regarded as a marker of a deeper degree of spirituality, then this need not be a surprise. It would be a way in which, all at once, a number of people could be "noted" by those around. Since in many modern "charismatic" churches there are times when a number speak or sing in tongues all at once, it is important not to assume that this is what Paul faced. Too little is said in this passage for us to draw conclusions as to what the Corinthian practice may have looked like.

Paul is clear, though, in his instructions. First, only "two or at most three" (κατὰ δύο ἢ τὸ πλεῖστον τρεῖς) may speak. Paul limits the total number of such communications in any gathering. It is unlikely this has anything at all to do with the length of a service, for that is far too modern an issue. Rather, it expresses some of Paul's considerable reservation about the public use of this gift of "tongues." Secondly, they should speak "each in turn" (ἀνὰ μέρος). This is part of Paul's concern for order in worship but also for intelligibility. Each one must be heard by the whole congregation. Thirdly, the "one" speaking must interpret,[5] picking up on what he has said above in 14:5, 13. All three of these instructions make it clear that however the word "ecstatic" might be used of some gifts and however they might be regarded as "spontaneous," they can always be controlled *by the one speaking*. The speaker has choices when employing the grace-gifts, and Paul directs that these choices

---

5. "Let that one interpret" seeks to do justice to the Greek use of "one" (εἷς). It is possible, of course, that this sentence would allow for another "one" to be doing the interpreting rather than the one who has spoken in tongues him or herself. But as BDF §247 makes clear, the use of this word (εἷς) can simply indicate "someone" or an indefinite "person" (τις) rather than indicate the numeral (cf. Matt 19:16; Mark 10:17). Here it could simply mean "if someone speaks . . . let [that] someone interpret."

should focus on love for the community, even if it means choosing to curtail the use of a gift so that others may speak, or so that the community may be better built up.

Paul begins with another conditional clause in 14:28. The verb in the apodosis is in the present imperative. Should the individual not be able to interpret, "let him keep silent" (σιγάτω). Though Paul exhorts the Corinthians pleasantly with the introductory "brothers [and sisters]" (v. 20), this instruction is forceful enough. The protasis could be translated more generally as "if there is no interpreter" (NIV) or "if there is no one to interpret" (NRSV). However, our choice, "if he is not an interpreter," seeks to maintain the continuity with what has gone before and allow the "one" of the previous clause to become the subject of the verb "to be" here.[6] It avoids translating the noun (διερμηνευτής) in a verbal form and perhaps makes better sense of the following imperative, which is in the singular and appears to be addressed to the very one who is speaking.

While this imperative is restrictive, it is closely qualified by the apostle. He is concerned with what happens "in the church" (not outside and not in private). He allows for a private conversation between the speaker and God to continue (in silence) or perhaps when the public worship is over. Paul contemplates uninterpreted tongues in the way he did earlier. They are spoken "to God" (θεῷ, here and in v. 2) and are thus referred to as "praying" in (v. 14). But they are also very much individualized and so about "oneself" and God (ἑαυτοῦ is used here and in v. 4). Of course, Paul does not negate the self-to-God relationship in any way, but he is concerned to guide their worship so that all can be built up and all can say "amen" (v. 16).

14:29–31 Now let two or three prophets speak, and let the others judge, and if a revelation is made to another who is sitting down, let the first person be silent. For you can all prophesy one by one, in order that all may learn and all may be encouraged (προφῆται δὲ δύο ἢ τρεῖς λαλείτωσαν, καὶ οἱ ἄλλοι διακρινέτωσαν· ἐὰν δὲ ἄλλῳ ἀποκαλυφθῇ καθημένῳ, ὁ πρῶτος σιγάτω. δύνασθε γὰρ καθ᾽ ἕνα πάντες προφητεύειν, ἵνα πάντες μανθάνωσιν καὶ πάντες παρακαλῶνται). With another present imperative Paul moves on to address the prophets and encourages two or three of them to speak. As with tongues, there is an appropriate way of conducting this in worship "in order that" (ἵνα, indicating purpose) maximum benefit and edification may take place for the whole congregation through learning and encouragement.

Intelligibility is still an issue even if the words spoken by an individual can be understood. They are told to prophesy "one by one" (καθ᾽ ἕνα). Whether they were in fact allowing multiple different "prophecies" in the gathering at the same time is unclear. Paul is concerned that all should hear clearly the enunciation of the prophecy or the "revelation" (ἀποκαλύπτω).

Further, Paul expects prophecy to be "judged" (διακρίνω) by others. There has been repeated emphasis in this epistle that "spiritual" people must pursue right "judgment" and "discernment." This involves making an assessment of what is godly and right and what builds up the congregation in Christ (see comments on 2:10–16; 3:1–4; 4:3–13; and ch. 9). Paul has used various words from the same root verb "to judge" (κρίνω; συγκρίνω; διακρίνω) and has given them slightly different nuances. Here he uses the word "judge" (διακρίνω). It is used in 6:5 of settling legal disputes between brothers and in

---

6. Barrett, *First Corinthians*, 328, is right to say that a subject "is required in order to avoid ambiguity." But he puts this in the second clause, hence: "Let the man who would speak in tongues keep silence." This seems unnecessarily pedantic.

11:29, 31 of judgment and the Lord's Supper. There can be little doubt that Paul expects whatever is prophesied to be "judged" during the assembly. This "judgment" is probably an assessment made by "others" concerning, first, whether this is truly of the Lord and, second, how the word delivered by the prophet should be applied to those present. Indeed, though this is not necessarily in view here, this process of judging and discernment is so vital to the well-being of a church that there is a grace-gift of "discernment" or "judging the spirits" (διακρίσεις πνευμάτων; 12:10).

It is difficult to know how this judging would have taken place. In our age, in some traditional Pentecostal churches, the elders sit at the front and listen to prophecies and judge them then and there, either saying that something is perhaps not of the Spirit or urging the congregation to take note and to take to heart what has been said as being from the Lord. But again, we should not move from contemporary practice back to what Paul might have experienced. Though the usual forensic context of the verb suggests that possibly a rather formal "judgment" took place in the congregation, this may be to read too much into the situation. Whatever the way that the judgment or assessment was made, the word suggests the decision was final and followed by both the assembly and the prophet concerned. Given the grace-gift that has been mentioned in 12:10, it may simply have been "other people" who would exercise their gift in assessing the nature and value of what the prophet had just spoken. Such judgment would surely have reflected the type of judgment Paul had urged back in chapters 2–4. Are God's people humbled before Christ crucified? Is an individual self-centered or boastful with the message, bringing glory to themselves rather than to God? Does the message encourage an understanding of the depths of God's purposes and plans for his people and the world around? And, therefore, in light of the immediate context of v. 31, can it be said that these prophecies enable God's people to "learn" and be "encouraged"? Such discernment and judging would no doubt have been based first and foremost on the conformity of the message with Scripture itself, with the gospel of Christ, and with apostolic teaching.[7]

There is some discussion about who the "others" are. Some have suggested it is the "other prophets."[8] The strongest argument for this is taken from v. 32 where the "inspirations of the prophets" are said to be "subject to the prophets." But, as noted below, v. 32 more probably means that the prophets can and must control their own use of the gift of prophecy in the way Paul has outlined. The manifestation of the gift is subject to the prophets. Also, it seems unlikely that Paul would have used "the others" if he was thinking of the prophets. Moreover, as Grudem notes, in various places Paul seems to grant that the whole congregation can be involved in judging what is going on in the congregation (e.g., 1 Cor 12:3; 1 Thess 5:20–21; cf. 1 John 4:1–6).[9] While others might be those with the grace-gift of "discernment between spirits" (12:10),[10] that grace-gift probably has a much broader reference than simply judging prophecies. It likely refers to discerning generally whether something is of the Lord or of an evil spirit. Passages such as 1 Thessalonians 5:19–21 and even the general appeal to maturity of discernment in chapters 2–3 in this epistle suggest that "others" refers to the whole congregation present. While Paul leaves this "judging" open to

---

7. See 14:37–38; cf. Acts 17:11; Gal 1:8.

8. Calvin, *First Corinthians*, 302; Horsley, *1 Corinthians*, 187.

9. Grudem, *Gift of Prophecy in the New Testament*, 60–61; cf. Godet, *First Corinthians*, 2:303.

10. Dunn, *Theology of Paul*, 581.

the whole congregation, it is inconceivable that any apostles or teachers present would not have had a substantial role in this process.

Thirdly, the one prophesying should give way if another has something revealed to him or her. The construction in Greek here is not easy to translate. The Greek reads, "If to another who is seated [dative participle] is revealed [aorist passive subjunctive], let the first sit down" [present imperative]." The conditional clause explains the subjunctive aorist. But what is being revealed? Is this a "revelation" of the sort mentioned in v. 26 that then takes precedence over a "prophecy," which is what some English translations imply? Or is it simply that one prophet has something revealed and so must speak it out while the first (prophet) sits down? Since v. 30 sits between a sentence about how prophets should speak and have their message judged (v. 29) and an injunction that all may prophesy "one by one" (v. 31), it seems more likely that what "is revealed" here is another prophecy.

A small insight into the conduct of worship is given here in that it seems that those speaking in the assembly stood to do so, otherwise they were seated while others addressed them. What Paul is saying is that if, while one is prophesying, another has something revealed to him or her, the first should sit down and let the next one stand to speak. The agent of the passive verb is the Spirit of God. In some ways this is a remarkable statement, for it seems to indicate that Paul was prepared to miss the message of one prophecy for the sake of another. If this is the case, it provides another indication that prophecy in the New Testament is

to be distinguished from the almost absolute authority granted prophecy in the Old Testament.[11] Paul was probably so committed to the view that the Spirit freely distributes gifts as he wills that he was prepared to allow God sovereignly to control these events. Of course, the event would also be controlled locally by the process of judging the prophecy itself. "The others" might have discerned whether such an interruption was of the Lord or not. Again, there is a danger of reading too much into a text like this. Paul may simply have in mind the organizing of the worship in such a way that an opening was given for the next prophet to speak. In other words, perhaps by some indication as we might see in any meeting today, a person wishing to prophesy would let the current speaker know. That first speaker then understands he or she should begin to "wrap it up" so another can speak.[12] This would still allow the first speaker to summarize what they had received but to do so with due consideration for those waiting to come next.

14:32–33b and the inspirations of the prophets are subject to the prophets, for God is not [a God] of disorder but of peace (καὶ πνεύματα προφητῶν προφήταις ὑποτάσσεται, οὐ γάρ ἐστιν ἀκαταστασίας ὁ θεὸς ἀλλὰ εἰρήνης). This sentence follows directly on from the previous as Paul talks about orderly worship. To be effective, prophetic messages must be offered humbly and in an ordered way so all may benefit. Once again there is the difficulty of Paul's use of the word "spirits" (πνεύματα). Here we take the word in the way it is used in v. 12 as "inspirations of the Spirit."[13] In

---

11. Grudem, *Gift of Prophecy in the New Testament*, 68–69.

12. This more nuanced understanding is reflected in Turner, *Holy Spirit and Spiritual Gifts*, 203, when he refers to a prophet being given "*almost* immediate hearing" (my italics) and the other who is speaking at the time being "able to bring his speech to a close."

13. See comments above on v. 12 and v. 14. The main alternative understanding of "spirits" in v. 32 is to see this as a reference to the "spirits" of those who speak. But this makes little sense here since Paul could simply have said "the prophets are subject to the prophets." Cf. Grudem, *Gift of Prophecy in the New Testament*, 97–98.

this sense "spirits" refers to the results of the Spirit in his inspiring of the prophets. These "inspirations," given by the Spirit and welling up within the prophets, are to be subjected to (ὑποτάσσω) or controlled by the discipline of which Paul speaks. Paul expects the prophets themselves to have this degree of self-control over what they do. Of course, it is quite possible that the elitist Christians in Corinth felt that a certain lack of self-control indicated their spiritual prowess. Paul has already spoken of their need for self-control in using himself as an example in 9:25. Here their insistence on standing and speaking, even if others were doing so, reflected no more than their own self-delusion, but it may have arisen from the belief that "control" was less "spiritual" than lack of control. It is no less a work of the Spirit for prophets to control their prophecy than it is to receive it in the first place "because" (γάρ introduces the reason) they are inspired by God who is a God "not of disorder but of peace."

Paul has been clear that "love" is the marker that authenticates true Christian existence. The spiritually mature person exhibits love because he or she will reflect the image of God. So Paul returns to the character of God himself. God is a God of "peace" and hence not of "disorder." Nowhere should this "imaging" of God be more clearly seen than in the worship of the gathered congregation. As Paul ends this section, therefore, his concern remains for the building up of the body of Christ even when he is talking about an especially useful gift like prophecy. All the good learning and encouragement (v. 31) that should come from a prophecy comes to nothing if the presentation of the prophetic messages is not ordered in a humble and peaceable way. Paul will say more about the prophets in 14:37–38, but his comments on order in worship now turn to the matter of "the women."

14:33c–35 As in all the churches of the saints the wives [women] should keep silent in the churches, for they are not permitted to speak, but let them subject themselves, as the law says. But if they wish to learn, let them ask their own husbands at home, for it is shameful for a wife [woman] to speak in church (Ὡς ἐν πάσαις ταῖς ἐκκλησίαις τῶν ἁγίων, αἱ γυναῖκες ἐν ταῖς ἐκκλησίαις σιγάτωσαν· οὐ γὰρ ἐπιτρέπεται αὐταῖς λαλεῖν· ἀλλὰ ὑποτασσέσθωσαν, καθὼς καὶ ὁ νόμος λέγει. εἰ δέ τι μαθεῖν θέλουσιν, ἐν οἴκῳ τοὺς ἰδίους ἄνδρας ἐπερωτάτωσαν, αἰσχρὸν γάρ ἐστιν γυναικὶ λαλεῖν ἐν ἐκκλησίᾳ). These verses raise a number of difficult exegetical issues. Our view, in summary, is that wives are told not to judge or question publicly any prophecies emanating from their own husbands. Such action might bring shame upon the marriage. Rather, if they have questions they should raise them at home.

Structurally, these next two-and-a-half verses (vv. 33c–36) make a second unit in this half of the chapter as Paul continues teaching concerning conduct and order in gatherings for church worship. The text, which is difficult to translate, has become particularly challenging in more recent years, given the heightened sensitivity to gender-related issues in the modern church. Below, the interpretation taken of this section is that it speaks to wives (though it could be women more generally) and their relationship in public worship to their husbands (though it could be men more generally). In the process of judging and weighing prophecies, as Paul advocates in v. 29, the conduct of peaceable order in God's church indicates that wives should not challenge their husbands publicly. Therefore, we do not see the section as an interpolation or as a quotation from the Corinthians (vv. 34–35) answered by Paul sarcastically in v. 36. We do *not* believe it forbids all women from speaking in the gathered assembly, and therefore we *do* believe it coheres with 11:2–16. The complexity of the issues involved in interpretation is substantial.

IN DEPTH: Three Key Questions in the Interpretation of 14:33c–35

(1) *Does v. 33c belong with what follows* (so most English versions) *or what precedes it* (so AV and NIV 2011)? Hays takes v. 33c ("As in all the churches of the saints") with what has gone before and sees it as Paul's "withering sarcasm."[14] This he does by rejecting vv. 34–35 as an interpolation and constructing a view that sees Paul arguing with the Corinthian enthusiasts who wish to overturn "community discipline in worship." He paraphrases Paul's response: "That's funny: in all the other church of the saints, it seems that God is a God of order and peace. Or [v. 36] perhaps you are the only ones who really have heard the word of God?"[15] As we see below, from a text-critical point of view the text should be read as it stands without deleting these verses. If this is done, then the idea of linking v. 33c with v. 33a–b, as opposed to what follows, seems a nonsense: "For God is not [a God] of disorder but of peace, as in all the churches of the saints." One is tempted to reply, "Well, of course! We can hardly imagine God being a God of disorder somewhere else!" Fee likewise places this second clause with the preceding clause.[16] Again, the first reason he gives is that he regards vv. 34–35 as "not authentic," then argues that it fits well with the rhetorical questions of v. 36.[17] His argument that this is the fourth similar kind of appeal in the letter (4:17; 7:17; 11:16) simply fails to address the fact that the other instances make logical and grammatical sense in their own contexts, while here neither sense is at all obvious. He also fails to point out that while Paul does at times reinforce teaching by saying that it is common to the churches, it is more likely that he would do so with reference to the manner of behavior in church than with reference to the character of God! Grammatically it is forced, if not impossible, to make "as" (ὡς) relate to the whole previous discussion about "order" when an intervening sentence has provided an interim summary with a statement about *God*. Either "as" should relate to what immediately precedes or to what immediately follows. If it is related to what immediately precedes, then, again, at best such a statement would be banal if not meaningless.

Having said this, if v. 33c looks forward directly to v. 34, as in most translations, there remains an issue. It seems redundant to say, "As in *all the churches*

---

14. Hays, *First Corinthians*, 244.

15. Ibid. Others place v. 33c with what precedes but do not see any sign of sarcasm while generally admitting the difficulty (e.g., Robertson and Plummer, *First Corinthians*, 324; Barrett, *First Corinthians*, 330; Horsley, *1 Corinthians*, 188; Fitzmyer, *1 Corinthians*, 527).

16. Fee, *1 Corinthians*, 772–73.

17. See below on the text-critical issues that arise with vv. 33–35.

of the saints the wives should keep silence *in the churches.*" The redundancy in English may be avoided by speaking of "churches" in the first clause and "assemblies" or "congregations" in the second.[18] However, this fails to address the issue of the seeming redundancy of what Paul wrote. Ralph Martin's suggestion possibly makes most sense. He suggests that Paul here places an *emphasis* on "churches" that he wishes his readers to note.[19] It is not entirely clear why Paul would want to emphasize the "churches," but perhaps he is preparing the ground for the important contrast he makes explicit in v. 35 between what happens "in the church" (ἐν ἐκκλησίᾳ) and what happens "in the home" (ἐν οἴκῳ).

(2) *Do verses 34–35 belong here? The text-critical issues.* For example, the NRSV puts vv. 33c–36 in parentheses.[20] Of course, this is not simply a question of external textual witnesses, though we start with that. Various commentators remove these verses, at least from this position in the text, on the basis also of internal exegetical issues. The overwhelming and earliest evidence favors the positioning of the verses where they are in our English versions. (There are a number of other minor variants within these verses, but these do not affect the positioning of the text.) From the early 𝔓[46] (about AD 200), through the fourth-century codex Sinaiticus (ℵ), and the fifth-century Alexandrinus (A), including B, Ψ, 33, the old Syriac translations, the Vulgate editions, and indeed most of the Byzantine witnesses, there is no indication of the transposition of these verses to a location after v. 40 or to anywhere else. In fact, it is easier simply to refer to the few manuscripts, mostly in the Western tradition of the text, that have this transposition, namely the sixth-century codex Bezae Claromontanus (D), the ninth-century codex Augiensis (F) and G. (The latter two follow almost directly the variants found in D.) Also a few Old Latin manuscripts and Ambrosiaster are cited. The last is the earliest evidence of the transposition (late fourth century). In a technical article, Philip Payne has sought to show from this evidence that the transposition reveals the text is an interpolation.[21] He speculates why these

---

18. E.g., NIV 1984, "congregations . . . churches" and TEV, "churches . . . meetings." Collins, *First Corinthians*, 520–21, takes the "assemblies of the saints" (ταῖς ἐκκλησίαις τῶν ἁγίων) as having a "formulaic" quality and so suggests that the first clause refers in fact to the practices of the synagogues where, he says, women were not allowed to speak. Yet, given that Paul addresses this church as "called saints" (κλητοῖς ἁγίοις) in 1:2, that there is no other reference to synagogues in the epistle, and that this church has a predominantly Gentile background, this seems a far-fetched way to deal with an apparent redundancy.

19. Martin, *Spirit and the Congregation*, 83.

20. It is not at all clear why NRSV should include v. 36 in this. It is also interesting that in the introduction to the NRSV the editors point out that the apparatus that was shortly afterwards printed as UBS⁴ was available and used by the translators of the New Testament. Yet the UBS⁴ in the apparatus rates vv. 34–35 in their current position (rather than after v. 40) with a "B," which it says means "the text is almost certain." Metzger, *Textual Commentary*, 499, says of the "chiefly Western" transposition: "Such scribal alterations represent attempts to find a more appropriate location in the context for Paul's directive concerning women." No textual variants are listed relating to the positioning v. 36. To our knowledge the NRSV does this nowhere else with a "B"-rated text.

21. Philip B. Payne, "Fuldensis, Sigla for Variants in Vaticanus, and 1 Cor 14:34–35," *NTS* 41 (1995): 240–62.

verses may have originally been a marginal gloss, suggesting they may have been added to counter "the appropriation by women of 'you can all prophesy' in 14:31."[22] Curt Niccum provides a detailed refutation of this view and also brings some balance to some of Fee's strong assertions that "the entire Western tradition" supports the textual transposition.[23] Niccum writes, "Far from being the reading of the entire Western tradition, the transposition is the product of a local text." He concludes by reminding his readers that "no extant MS [manuscript] offers evidence of an original omission of 1 Cor 14.34–35" and points out that the so-called "balance" of witnesses between Eastern and Western readings is simply not there. The traditional order has the only claim to being "original."[24] In her major work on the Corinthian women prophets, Antoinette Wire also tackles the textual evidence and concludes that the traditional reading is the right one but posits a number of possible explanations as to why this text might have become transposed in a few manuscripts. Interestingly, because she writes as a self-professed feminist, one suggestion she makes is that a scribe might have excluded these verses for "ideological" reasons such as a desire to "omit a passage silencing women."[25] Finally, it may be noted that even if the text were displaced, it need not mean it was an interpolation.

Other arguments are also advanced for regarding the verses as an interpolation. The most significant is that this text does not sit well in its context since it contradicts 11:2–16, where the participation of women in worship is assumed. It is said that these verses reflect "later" thinking of the sort that is found in 1 Timothy 2 when, supposedly, the limitations on women participating in worship became stricter. Language parallels are also noted between this passage and that section of Timothy.[26] The appeal to "the law" is said to be unlike Paul. Furthermore, it is argued that this section of vv. 33c–35 or vv. 34–35 interrupts the main theme of prophecy, tongues, and community edification and addresses only women, with no apparent concern for the grace-gifts. If these verses are omitted, it is said, then the text reads fluently and is left uninterrupted. Further comments seeking to bolster the suggestion of an interpolation include the view that though there is some vocabulary overlap with the surrounding section, the words are used differently and here the injunction to silence is ab-

---

22. Ibid., 252.

23. See Fee, *1 Corinthians*, 780.

24. Curt Niccum, "The Voice of the Manuscripts on the Silence of Women: The External Evidence for 1 Cor 14:34–35," *NTS* 43 (1997): 242–55. For Fee's assertions on the external argument and his rather superficial dismissal of Niccum and others, see his *1 Corinthians*, 780–85.

25. Antoinette C. Wire, *The Corinthian Women Prophets: A Reconstruction through Paul's Rhetoric* (Minneapolis: Fortress, 1990), 149–58 (quote from 152). Appendix 11 should also be noted.

26. We shall briefly speak to the relationship between 11:2ff and this section following our own exegesis.

solute.[27] However, none of these arguments is convincing enough to warrant calling the text an "interpolation," especially when the external textual evidence is lacking. The fact is that two undoubtedly difficult verses need to be read and, if possible, understood *in situ*. From a text-critical perspective, the more difficult reading may be more likely to be right. If later the text was moved to v. 40, it may have been to make v. 36 read a little more easily after v. 33. Placing it after v. 40 would simply have made it another subject that Paul wanted to address between prophecy and tongues on the one hand and the resurrection on the other. Only the exegesis of these verses in their context will show whether sense can be made of the more difficult reading; that is, of taking the verses in their traditional position.

(3) Are vv. 34–35 a quotation from the Corinthians that is then hotly contradicted by Paul in v. 36? In principle, this might be possible. Other quotations have been identified, for example, at 8:1 and 8:4. The clearest exposition of this view is given by Odell-Scott in three articles, the intention of which is revealed in the title of the first.[28] His main argument is that v. 36 starts with the word "or" (ἤ), which is to be seen as a strong disjunctive particle. Thus v. 36 is regarded as responding to and negating what has gone before. What has gone before in this case is the unit of text represented by vv. 34–35. The rhetorical questions of v. 36, it is argued, are then an attack on the *men* who were forbidding women to speak in the assemblies.[29] *Men* as the object of Paul's attack are identified by the masculine form used in the words "you alone" (ὑμᾶς μόνους). In this way, it is argued that Paul remains in line with the freedom he gave women in 11:2–13 and attacks those who would limit women in the congregation. A number of responses may be given to this. First, it is nonsense to suggest that the masculine form of "you alone" requires Paul to be addressing men. How else could he have addressed all men *and women*? The word is gender inclusive. It is much more likely in the context that Paul continues to address the whole church as he did in v. 33 but *also* as he did in vv. 34–35. There he is guiding the whole

---

27. Fee, *1 Corinthians*, 780–85, offers one of the most comprehensive summaries of reasons to regard this section as an interpolation. Conzelmann, *1 Corinthians*, 246, does not give weight to the textual evidence but in customary succinct style lists reasons for regarding this as an interpolation. Murphy-O'Connor, "Interpolations in 1 Corinthians," *CBQ* 48 (1986): 81–94, also examines these verses.

28. David W. Odell-Scott, "Let the Women Speak in Church: An Egalitarian Interpretation of 1 Cor 14:33b–36," *BTB* 13 (1983): 90–93. See also *BTB* 17 (1987): 100–103 and *BTB* 30 (2000): 68–74.

29. Ibid., 91. Odell-Scott argues that 11:20–22 is "structurally identical" to this passage. But surely this is not the case. In 11:20–21 Paul is *already* commenting on what is going on among the Corinthians. It is not a quotation (even Odell-Scott does not argue for that), but neither is it a simple summary of a Corinthian position. It is Paul's reflection on what he sees in their midst, an entirely different idea to the one he proposes for 14:34–35.

church (whatever he might mean by this guidance).[30] Apart from the problem just mentioned, the main issue with this approach is the huge weight put on the disjunctive particle. The particle (ἤ) appears a number of times in this epistle, but it only once seems to follow a Corinthian quotation, and that is in 1:13b where Paul makes it quite clear that he is quoting them with the clause "each one of you says. . . ." In that verse and in 6:2 the particle introduces rhetorical questions that may even be sarcastic and are certainly confrontational to the Corinthian position, but this proves nothing. Moreover, the questions *reinforce* the point that has just been made; they do not negate it.[31] Most of the texts that are taken by various commentators to be quotations have no such disjunctive particle (e.g., 6:12–13; 8:1, 4). Rightly or wrongly, it is the immediate indicators such as "now concerning" in 8:1 or "now concerning what you wrote" in 7:1 that suggest that a quotation may be in view. Generally speaking, it is worth noting that where scholars are reasonably and widely agreed that a quotation exists, it is usually virtually explicit (with an indicator such as a recitative ὅτι or indicators like those just mentioned) *and* it is short *and* it is followed by a (sometimes lengthy) rebuttal *and* the response is clearly pertinent to the quotation and unambiguous.[32] It seems to us that Odell-Scott's view fails at most points. However, an appeal to a quotation becomes entirely unnecessary, for in the exegesis we see both themes and vocabulary that strongly indicate these instructions belong to Paul himself.

Here these verses are now examined as they exist, in the traditional position. An apparent redundancy of the phrase "in the churches" arises with Paul's addition of "of the saints" (τῶν ἁγίων). This is unique in Paul's writings, but he has already said that he writes "to the church" "called [to be] saints" (κλητοῖς ἁγίοις) in 1:2 and "to those sanctified [ἡγιασμένοις] in Christ Jesus." He has written, "the temple of God is holy [ἅγιος], and you are the temple." He has also referred to the church as "the saints" in 6:1 (cf. 6:2; 7:14), so the phrase itself should not surprise us. Although it is tempting to resolve the apparent redundancy by saying that Paul has in mind different settings or places, such as a large public gathering or a small gathering in peoples' homes, this is not entirely obvious in the text. Rather, in the context Paul is surely concerned to draw attention to something that is

---

30. It is another assumption that Odell-Scott makes to suggest that vv. 34–35 are "*about* the women addressed *to* the men" (ibid., 92; emphasis original). Even accepting this as a quotation, it could still have been *about* women and addressed to men *and* women. Conjecture is added to conjecture here simply, it seems, to promote the "egalitarian interpretation" referred to in his title. Of course, an egalitarian view of this passage need not depend on this being a quotation, anyway!

31. See D. A. Carson, "'Silent in the Churches': On the Role of Women in 1 Corinthians 14:33b–36," in *Recovering Biblical Manhood and Womanhood: A Response to Evangelical Feminism*, ed. John Piper and Wayne Grudem (Wheaton, IL: Crossway, 1991), 151. Carson makes the observation that "in every instance in the New Testament where the disjunctive particle in question is used in a construction analogous to the passage at hand, its effect is to reinforce the truth of the clause or verse that precedes it."

32. Ibid., 148.

followed across the church at large, not just in a local congregation. If "of the saints" has any particular significance here, and it may not, then perhaps Paul is concerned to draw attention to the faithful (or holy) who worship in these congregations as if to say, "This is what God's holy people do." The injunction that follows is a present imperative, "let the women keep silent [σιγάω] in the churches" and is explained with an explanatory "for" (γάρ) and a passive verb "they are not permitted" (ἐπιτρέπεται). The latter implies at least some kind of received wisdom, if not a generally understood rule, that "all the churches" accept for conduct in worship (except some at Corinth).

The second half of the sentence points to what Paul means, starting with a strong adversative, "but" or "rather" (ἀλλ᾽) and a middle imperative verb, "let them subject themselves" (ὑποτασσέσθωσαν). The vocabulary reflects words already used in the previous verses. This at least suggests continuity of ideas and a flow of thought, but it also helps with the meaning of words. The words to be noted are "to speak" (λαλέω; vv. 14, 23, and thirteen other times in the preceding verses of this chapter), "to be silent" (σιγάω; vv. 28, 30), "to be subject to" (ὑποτάσσω; v. 32), and "in the church" (ἐν ἐκκλησία; vv. 28, 35).

"To speak" (λαλέω) ranges in meaning from denoting normal speaking to making a sound, chattering, asserting, proclaiming, telling, and so on. Thayer notes that whereas "to say" (λέγω) normally refers to the content of what is spoken, this verb (λαλέω) often refers to the sound of words, the actual "speaking," as it were.[33] This verb was also used at 13:1 ("if I speak with") where it referred to forms of inspired speech (cf. 13:11). In this chapter it has also been used of two forms of inspired speech, tongues (vv. 2, 4, etc.) and prophecy (vv. 2, 4, etc.),

and it has been used of normal speech of the sort a teacher might give (v. 19). It has been used of legal or judgment speech (v. 21) and also of a private communication with God (vv. 2 understood and v. 28). When we come to v. 34, any of these meanings could be possible. For example, it might be that the women are forbidden to "speak" prophecy or to "speak" in tongues. However, this is unlikely, given the deliberate emphasis on "all" speaking or prophesying (vv. 23–34). Though the "all" does not mean each individual present, it is precisely a reference to the *possibility* of anyone (male or female) so speaking, with no one being superior or having priority over anyone else. It is likely that Paul simply has in mind some normal speech, but what sort of speaking and in what context does he envisage "silence"? Since "all" does not seem to exclude some speaking of women, confirming 11:5, then however bald the imperative may sound and whatever "permission" they do not have, it must surely be limited.

The verb "to be silent" (σιγάω; cf. vv. 28 and 30) can mean to be silent, to become silent, to say nothing, or to hold one's peace. Nowhere in the New Testament does it refer to total silence (cf. Luke 18:39; Acts 12:17; 15:12). It may refer to silence for a time, or keeping quiet about a specific matter, or becoming quiet as others speak. This we have seen is the case in vv. 28, 30 where the silence enjoined refers to being quiet while someone else speaks.

In this context, almost everyone is being limited in their speech in some fashion or another, all under the rubric of what "builds up." If a person cannot interpret, "let each one keep silent" and "speak to himself and to God" (v. 28). If prophets speak, let two or three speak, then let the judging begin! If a person has something revealed to him, let the prophet currently speaking be silent (v. 30).

---

33. Thayer, *Greek-English Lexicon*, 368. BDAG 582 gives multiple meanings. See Rom 3:19 for the two words together.

This is because "order" and "conduct" in worship is the issue at hand for Paul. In fact, the type of "normal" speaking that Paul has in mind and that he argues is "shameful" (to be examined below) is indeed limited. Verse 35 tells us that "asking" questions should not be done "in the churches" but "in the home" and asked of their husbands. We shall develop this point shortly.

One clear limitation on speech follows in v. 34. Paul says "let the women subject themselves" (ὑποτασσέσθωσαν). There is no indirect object here. We are not told to what they are supposed to subject themselves, although the following reference to asking their husbands at home (v. 35) suggests that silence is being enjoined as part of their voluntary subjection of themselves to their husbands. The strong adversative "but" in "*but* let the women" suggests that the women were somehow not being respectful of or caring enough for their husbands. It is possible that Paul here thinks of Genesis 3:16 and the position of Eve who was told that her "desire will be for your husband." This could account for Paul's comment "as the law says."[34] However, since neither Genesis 3:16 nor any other verse in the Old Testament tells a woman to be silent, it might be that Paul is simply thinking more generally about women not officiating in the tabernacle or temple worship. It is perhaps more likely, however, that Paul again appeals to the cre-

ation narrative (Gen 2:20b–24). In this narrative God's creation *order* is being described. He appealed to these *pre*-fall narratives in 11:3–12 when talking about *how* men and women should pray and prophesy. He has appealed to the ordered relationship between God, Christ, man, and women and so he expects that this God, whose "Holy Spirit creatively transforms chaos into order,"[35] should be worshipped in a manner that reflects that he is "not a God of disorder but of peace" (14:33). However, the differentiation of roles between men and women has become distorted and sin-ridden following the fall (Gen 3), and so Paul argues that they "should submit themselves" in line with the law, that is, with Scripture and its account of the created order. He does so, as Hurley notes, "alongside the new freedom of women to participate in the worship."[36] This self-subjection, though, is to men or probably to husbands (v. 35). It is not simply to a set of rules.

Verse 35 addresses the fact that women will indeed have questions and want to discuss what they have heard, but Paul now insists that they should "ask their own husbands at home." Clearly the "at home" (ἐν οἴκῳ) contrasts with and helps define "in the churches" (ἐν ταῖς ἐκκλησίαις). Two different situations are referred to. Whereas it is improper for women to speak in a certain defined situation in the gathered assembly, this does not mean that

---

34. This is not as strange an expression as some have suggested. Paul has already spoken of the law in this immediate context in 14:21 but also in 9:8, explained as the "law of Moses" in 9:9. Cf. D. A. Carson, *Exegetical Fallacies* (Grand Rapids: Baker, 1984), 37–40.

35. Thiselton, *1 Corinthians*, 1154. On pp. 1153–55 Thiselton observes that the issue is not so much about the submission of a woman to a man but about the "very large issue of whether 'order' still applies to a charismatic gospel community" (partly quoting Antoinette Wire). Thiselton translates ὑποτασσέσθωσαν as "let them keep to their ordered place." Thiselton is surely right to insist that we are not here dealing with the issues of *submission* that arise from Gen 3:16 with

all their tensions and sinfulness on the part of both men and women. However, to try to remove this, as Witherington does, from actual practical matters of women subjecting themselves to men as they seek to reflect this "order" is to abstract the theology altogether from its context in the worshipping community. Witherington suggests that women are being told to "submit themselves" not to their husbands but "to the principle of order in the worship service" (*Women and the Genesis of Christianity* [Cambridge: Cambridge University Press, 1990], 179). To sustain this, it is necessary to create a detailed argument (for which there is almost no evidence) explaining why *women* would need to be told this more than men.

36. Hurley, *Man and Woman in Biblical Perspective*, 192.

they should refrain from "speaking" altogether. The use of the word "shameful" (αἰσχρός) used in 11:6 of a woman cutting her hair implies that an action is socially or morally unacceptable (Titus 1:11) or culturally embarrassing (Eph 5:12). And this may give an indication of why the behavior of some women has been singled out here. If, as Paul says, "all the churches" had this limitation on speech, there would have been no need to repeat it here unless something was going wrong. In fact, the forceful adversative (ἀλλά) *"but let them sub-ject themselves"* suggests that in some way their speech was inappropriate, especially in relation-ship perhaps to their husbands. It is this that is "shameful."

It is at this point that clear sense of the passage begins to take shape. If simply prophesying or praying in church is not automatically "shameful" (αἰσχρός), provided the women have appropriate head covering (11:10–15), then the limitation on their speech at this point must be even further con-textually restricted. Verse 29 began a more detailed examination of the conduct of prophecy within the gatherings for worship. Prophecies are to be "judged" by "the others," which we have suggested was everyone else. All are encouraged to prophesy so that all may learn and be encouraged (no restric-tion on women is mentioned). The prophets are to control their inspirations to comply with these rules of conduct because this is what God himself wants. It is only the weighing or judging of proph-ecy that remains for further qualification. It is pre-cisely here that it would be possible for the order of creation to be abused, if women were found to be sitting in judgment, or contesting, or arguing with other men in the congregation, especially with their husbands. This would bring "shame" on the family, but also it would bring shame on the congregation as a whole. Some would say, proba-bly correctly, that only wives and husbands are in

view here as Paul writes. Certainly, "the women" (αἱ γυναῖκες) can be translated "the wives." "Hus-bands" (τοὺς . . . ἄνδρας) could be translated "men," but this meaning is highly unlikely given that Paul refers to "their own" (ἰδίους) men.

Finally, we can return to the structure of these verses to see that this explanation does make sense of the flow of the passage as a whole. Under the heading of "conduct of prophets," v. 29 indicates that prophets should order their prophetic utter-ances so that two or three speak and then others "judge" what is said. The first clause of v. 29 is addressed in vv. 30–33. Having only two or three speak means that people prophesy "one by one" (v. 31) and that the prophets themselves are to con-trol and order their inspirations appropriately (v. 32). The second clause of v. 29 is addressed in vv. 33c–36. "Let others judge what is said. . . . Let the women keep silent," or, in this context, "refrain from speaking" (σιγάω). This view of the passage takes full account of the local context, but it also makes sense of the broader context. There is no contradiction with Paul allowing women to proph-esy and to pray in 11:5. They have not been asked here to refrain from speaking prophecies. In fact "all" have been encouraged to do so. Rather, they have been asked to refrain from speaking during the "judging" of those prophecies and, perhaps specifically, during the judging of the prophecies of their own husbands.

14:36 So tell me, did the word of God come from you? Or tell me, did it come only to you? (ἤ ἀφ᾽ ὑμῶν ὁ λόγος τοῦ θεοῦ ἐξῆλθεν, ἤ εἰς ὑμᾶς μόνους κατήντησεν;). In contrast to "all the churches" (v. 33c) Paul sarcastically points out that the Corinthi-ans are ploughing their own furrow, as if God had only spoken to them. The disjunctive particle (ἤ) does not introduce a retort to the supposed Corin-thian position of vv. 34–35. In fact, as a rhetorical device these questions serve to reinforce what Paul has been saying. We have translated the particle as "so tell me." The word simply means "or," but the disjunction introduces questions that are almost sarcastic in their forcefulness, and so some English phrase is needed to make this point. Paul has used rhetorical questions on numerous occasions in this epistle, starting with 1:13. In 12:29–30 he finished summarizing his discussion of the various grace-gifts and their place in the body of the church with another series of such questions. So this rhetorical structure is not unexpected. This verse looks back to the whole section talking about prophecy that began at v. 29. Paul probably anticipated some pushback from the elitists in the church. For them, speaking in tongues and prophesying were more about status than about building people up and encouraging all in the church.

It is unlikely they encouraged "all" to prophesy. In fact, Paul's teaching has "democratized" the gifts, especially prophecy. The elitists do not have a monopoly on the truth. As Paul demonstrated in the early chapters and in chapter 12, the grace-gifts are part and parcel of the gospel itself, and that gospel (the "word of God") did not "come from" (ἐξῆλθεν) them! Order in worship remains the issue. Paul sees this as embedded in Old Testament Scripture, but even more deeply he sees it as embedded in the character of God himself (v. 33). If prophets all prophesy at once so no one is "built up" or encouraged, if they do not wait for their prophecies to be "judged" by the others, if wives sit in judgment, publicly, on the prophecies of their husbands, then these Corinthians are putting themselves above Scripture. In doing so, they ignore the fact that many other churches have heard the word of

God and have understood it and applied it in the way Paul has described. The phrase "you alone" (ὑμᾶς μόνους) refers to both the men and women at Corinth and stands in rhetorical contrast to "in all the churches of the saints" (v. 33). How can the Corinthians ignore the wider church as if they alone were the ones who knew how to worship?

14:37–38 If someone thinks he [or she] is a prophet or spiritual, let him [or her] acknowledge that the things I write to you are a command of the Lord. But if someone does not recognize this, let him [or her] not be recognized (Εἴ τις δοκεῖ προφήτης εἶναι ἢ πνευματικός, ἐπιγινωσκέτω ἃ γράφω ὑμῖν ὅτι κυρίου ἐστὶν ἐντολή· εἰ δέ τις ἀγνοεῖ, ἀγνοείτω). The apostle insists that the accuracy of what he has written will be acknowledged by people who are truly "spiritual." Those who do not agree with Paul's view on these matters should not be recognized by the church as prophets or spiritual persons. He uses a first-class condition and so assumes the truth of the protasis. He addresses all who think of themselves as "prophets" or "spiritual."

In v. 38 a textual variant is notable. Some texts have a passive of the verb "recognize" (ἀγνοεῖται) and some have the third-person, present imperative (ἀγνοείτω). The imperative is adopted here.[37] Though we have separated these two verses into a third section in this second half of the chapter, this verse closely follows the thought of the previous. Paul has argued that all he has said of prophecy, its conduct and ordering, is from the Lord and simply reflects the Lord's own character as a God of peace and order rather than disorder. Therefore, a true prophet will recognize this. A truly "spiritual"

---

37. The imperative has earlier and stronger support, including 𝔓⁴⁶, ℵ², Aᶜ, B, D¹, Ψ, Byz, Syriac, Origen, Chrysostom. This is followed by AV, TEV. The passive indicative has support that includes ℵ*, A*ᵛⁱᵈ, D*, 048, 0243, 6, 33, Coptic. This is followed by NIV, NJB, RSV, ESV. A number of modern commentators

follow the passive indicative, suggesting it is in line with the grammatical structure of 8:3 and that it is the harder reading. The earlier and wider support for the imperative is the reason we have taken this reading. We also note with Zuntz, *Text of the Epistles*, 107–8 that 7:15 offers a similar syntax.

person will always submit to the Lord's will and instructions.

Therefore, as Paul draws his discussion to a close, he offers part of a definition of what it is to be "spiritual" person in a statement that summarizes much that he has said throughout the epistle. On two previous occasions, Paul has challenged those claiming to be "spiritual," using the same phrase: "If someone thinks . . ." (εἴ τις δοκεῖ; 3:18; 8:2). He has challenged their self-centered elitism focused on "wisdom," "knowledge," and here on "prophecy/tongues." In 3:18 the clause is followed by another imperative as Paul wrote, "If anyone among you thinks he is wise . . . let him become a fool." In 8:2 he wrote, "If anyone thinks that he knows, he does not yet know. . . ." If people are truly "spiritual" people (πνευματικός), they will submit to the Lord and to his word in Scripture. It is not just the *content* of what prophets say that must be judged in the light of Scripture, but it is also the prophets' *conduct*. Will they be humble and let others speak when someone else has an inspiration from the Lord? Will they let their prophecies be judged and questioned by all? Will they pay true attention to order in worship, seeking to reflect the word of God and the character of God? The harsh but important truth is that if they are not prepared to be obedient to this "command of the Lord," then the church is given a clear command to reject such people and ensure that they are not listened to by the congregation.

To some extent Paul is elaborating here on what it is to let the others "judge" (v. 29). It is more than simply assessing the content of a prophecy. It is about looking at the prophet's whole approach to what they are doing. In v. 37 Paul says, "Let [the prophet] acknowledge [ἐπιγινώσκω]." The Greek word can mean simply to "know" or to "under-

stand," but it can also mean to "acknowledge" or "give recognition to."[38] Paul insists that the genuinely spiritual among the people will acknowledge this is the Lord's word. The imperative carries a sense here of a formal assessment, in the style of the "judging" that we noted in v. 29. Much as a person might be "recognized" in a debate today and so be allowed to speak, Paul is saying these people are not to be "recognized," that is, allowed to speak. However, these are still grace-gifts that the Spirit may spontaneously inspire. "All" may speak, and Paul has encouraged them to do so. Nevertheless, Paul knows there are some who should not even be allowed to speak if, in their arrogance, they refuse to acknowledge the God-given rules of order for the assembly.

One further question arises. Is it the *church* that is not to recognize the disobedient individual or is it *God*? Above it is taken to be the church. This seems likely in the light of v. 29. It is the only way in which the imperative truly makes sense. If it is a passive verb ("he is not recognized"), then the agent could be either people in the church or God. While some have spoken of how "harsh" the text would be if God were the agent of a passive verb, it is rather forced to make too great a distinction. When the church refuses to recognize someone who is disobedient to God's word, it does so in the name of God or in obedience, as here, to the apostolic word of the Lord. The fact of the matter is that the church has a highly privileged position as the people of God, who act for him and in obedience to him. If the church of the saints does "not recognize" someone, they are acting according to God's instructions through the apostolic word. This perhaps reminds us of Jesus's own teaching to his disciples in Matthew 18:18: "Whatever you bind on earth will be bound in heaven." If men and women

---

38. BDAG 369; Thayer, *Greek-English Lexicon*, 237.

refuse to follow the "command of the Lord" regarding his church, then they will not reap the benefits of his church. The irony of this is obvious. The very thing the elitists most wanted—to be "recognized" as mature, spiritual people—will be the very thing that they are denied by the community. The command orders the community to act on this and take it seriously.

14:39–40 Therefore, my brothers [and sisters] earnestly desire to prophesy and do not forbid speaking in tongues. But let all things be done properly and in an orderly manner (ὥστε, ἀδελφοί [μου], ζηλοῦτε τὸ προφητεύειν, καὶ τὸ λαλεῖν μὴ κωλύετε γλώσσαις· πάντα δὲ εὐσχημόνως καὶ κατὰ τάξιν γινέσθω). With three imperatives Paul now applies his teaching. Thus this fourth section of the second half of the chapter serves to summarize the key points and becomes an encouragement and exhortation to all. Paul had started in 14:1 by telling them to "pursue love," the marker of authentic Christian life, and to "earnestly desire spiritual things." The *inclusio* formed by the word "earnestly desire" (ζηλοῦτε) is thus completed here. It is Paul who has now defined what is to be earnestly desired and why.

They must "earnestly desire to prophesy." The building up of the church is to carry on until the return of Christ when it will be perfected (13:10, 12). Prophecy is one of the grace-gifts that the Spirit has provided to achieve this. In line with 14:31, all are encouraged in this final exhortation to desire this gift for the church. The second imperative also reflects the tenor of the previous argument.

Clearly, priority is given to prophecy over tongues for all the reasons Paul has spelled out in chapter 14, which explains why the imperative seems almost half-hearted, "do not forbid" (κωλύετε). In the light of Paul's great caution regarding tongues, there may well have been an immediate reaction from some to actually forbid tongues-speaking. Paul will not go that far since, once interpreted, it does become intelligible and can thus edify. In this way Paul has now defined for his readers what the "greater" gifts are and why they are greater.

The third imperative (v. 40) provides a climax to the whole argument. "Let all things," that is, all that happens in the worship of the gathered congregation of God's people, "be done properly [εὐσχημόνως]." This adverb is used in Romans 13:13 and 1 Thessalonians 4:12 of Christians walking or living "decently" or respectfully before outsiders. The adjective has been used in 7:35 to denote what is "seemly" in terms of marriage and singleness (cf. 12:24). There is a right and proper way for Christians to live before outsiders that reflects who they are and who they worship. The word is used here not in a moral context of life lived before outsiders but in a church context of worship before God. There is a right way to behave and a wrong way. Paul has described the right way for people to conduct themselves in corporate worship, and so all things must be done "properly" (or "decently"). To this Paul adds, "and in an orderly manner." This has been the key point. Since God is a God of peace and not confusion and since he brings order to everything, all must be done in a way that reflects him "in an orderly manner" (κατὰ τάξιν).[39]

---

39. The noun τάγμα is employed in 15:23 where Paul is talking of the way in which the resurrection is "ordered" by rank: "Each one in his own *order*: Christ the firstfruit, then those who belong to Christ at his coming."

Theology in Application

Form and Freedom

Sometimes today in the church's worship there is a tendency to set "order" against so-called "freedom"; the former is considered less spiritual or less Spirit-led. However, it is important to note that "self-control" (ἐγκράτεια) is listed as a fruit of the Spirit in Galatians 5:23 and appears in a number of places in the New Testament as a characteristic of a mature Christian (e.g., Acts 24:25; 2 Pet 1:6; cf. Titus 1:8). Paul talked in 9:25 of exercising self-control like an athlete for the sake of the gospel in his life. It is not surprising therefore that Paul called for people to exercise self-control in worship. He did so for the sake of gospel intelligibility and for the spiritual building up of the many. Exhibiting such love for the other and for the building up of the community was a driving force.

Whether in Corinth spontaneous "tongues" or "prophecies" or "revelations" were treated as more "spiritual" than a regular and more prepared form of worship is uncertain. This chapter does not address this matter directly, but it does give clear guidelines by which a church may judge its worship. Worship cannot be left to simple spontaneity, for this fails to reflect the driving force of love and the edification of the community that should happen in worship. Worship cannot be about everyone "doing their own thing" whenever they feel so inclined. First, worship is not about one individual edifying themselves. Secondly, God called his people to image him. Since he is a God of peace and of order, this should be reflected in worship. Thirdly, all that is said and done in worship must be subject to the discerning judgment of all the people, and this too will require order and at least some degree of form.

This does not mean that Paul patronizingly insists on some authoritarian structure for worship. His perspective is that if truly the Spirit is present among the believers, then this will inevitably lead to the community being built up in love, faith, and knowledge of God. If the Spirit is truly present, then there will be peace and order even in the midst of "spontaneity." The people as a whole, not just certain individuals, will be edified spiritually. Moreover, the whole people will be involved in discerning the Lord's will in what has been taught or spoken, with the goal of renewing their minds in conformity to that will. Finally, if the Spirit is truly present, then individuals will be happy to exercise self-control and refrain from speaking when it furthers love in their midst.

In chapter 12 Paul taught that God "orders" the working of his Spirit among the congregation. Paul showed the nature of God's carefully structured church with his use of the "body" analogy. The ordering of the people of God reflects God's desire to see every individual having an impact on all the others. No one person is superior to another. No one part of the body can do without another, for each must build the other up. Even with varied grace-gifts, it is the constant presence of the Holy Spirit that unites and enables each to bring glory to God. Thus, when Paul speaks against disorder, it is because this is not *who* God is, but it is also not what God has revealed he wants for his church. In the church at Corinth where selfish elitism existed and seems to have caused much disorder, the words of James further explain why peace is so essential. He argues that "bitter envy and selfish ambition" are the symptoms of a worldly wisdom and are of the devil (Jas 3:14–15). This will bring forth "disorder" (ἀκαταστασία) and "every evil practice" (v. 16). This contrasts with a "wisdom from above" that is "peaceable, gentle, open to reason, full of mercy and good fruits, impartial and sincere. And a harvest of righteousness is sown in peace by those who make peace" (vv. 17–18 ESV). If gifts are to be employed in a spontaneous manner in corporate worship, then they are to be circumscribed carefully. In some modern churches where there is an emphasis on the "ecstatic," there is little or no discipline or order. In some modern, noncharismatic churches there is no room given for "discerning judgment" of what has been preached or taught at any point in the gathering. It seems Paul points to a balance, not often seen today, in which many members of the body could participate in aspects of worship and in which order and form are helpful to ensure that the spiritual building up of the body takes place.

Further Reflections on Prophecy

Four further comments may be made about prophecy. First, prophecy is not exempt from criticism (v. 29). It is to be judged by the congregation. The words of a prophet are not beyond censure. In an age where some have elevated the gifts of tongues and prophecy to a higher status than should be done, it is important for all to see that measures are in place to ensure proper intelligibility of what is said and proper conformity to the will of God as revealed in the Scriptures. Secondly, such "judgment" does not confirm someone in the role of "prophet" as if he or she would no longer be subject to any further "judging" (v. 19; διακρίνω). Each prophecy is judged on its own terms, for theological trustworthiness, and for what it brings to the congregation. Thirdly, especially for those in modern churches where no such gifts are used, it is worth noting that Paul allows that "all can prophesy one by one" (v. 31). As we have seen before, "all" does not mean that everyone would have been able to prophesy, but it does indicate that Paul was content for all who had this gift to employ it in the worship service, subject to the constraints he has laid out. Whereas Paul had a distinct coolness toward tongues, there is no such reticence in 14:29–33 regarding the gift of prophecy. Fourthly, prophecy is given "in order that all may learn and all may be encouraged" (v. 31). "Learning" suggests that the content of prophecy is not far removed from what a teacher or preacher might do. Indeed, Calvin suggests that prophets are those who "are (1) outstanding interpreters of Scripture; and (2) men endowed with extraordinary wisdom and aptitude for grasping what the immediate need of the Church is, and speaking the right word to meet it. That is why they are, so to speak, messengers who bring news of what God wants."[40] It is likely that some of what was said by the pastors, teachers, and apostles was automatically viewed as prophecy and subject to judgment and discussion among the people. The idea of encouragement is also part of the work of a pastor and teacher. Again, all this suggests we would do well to maintain the fluidity between these different gifts that seems to be present in the New Testament and not to pit "teacher" against "prophet" or "prophet" against "pastor." Paul was much more concerned with edification than who was speaking when and what precise gift they seemed to be exercising at the time!

Wives Judging Their Husbands' Prophecies

As we have seen, much has been written on this subject, and the interpretation of the passage has been much debated. In the end, we have opted for the view that the issue concerns the relationship between husbands and wives and the possibility of a wife being "shamefully" seen to challenge her husband in public worship. Paul calls for order and a degree of self-control on the part of the wife. She should voluntarily refrain from speaking at the time of judgment on the prophecies, especially in the judgment of her own husband's prophecy. Whatever some might think of this in the modern era, it is of note that Paul is concerned that the creation order of Genesis 2 is reflected in worship. Whatever *submission* may look like between a husband and a wife today, Paul was concerned that breaching the cultural norms of his day in worship would lead to wrong conclusions about how husbands and wives should relate to each other. Today, at least in the West, neither the type of head-covering (ch. 11) nor the fact that a wife speaks in church necessarily indicates a lack of submission or a breach of the created order. However, in an age when any idea of *order* is despised if it refers to gender-role differentiation, it will be necessary to work at other ways of modeling what is distinctly countercultural. That is, if discussion and judgment of what is said in worship is allowed in our worship, then it will still be necessary to ask whether husbands and wives are modeling together their love and respect for each other and how best their role differentiation may be acknowledged.

---

40. Calvin, *First Corinthians*, 271.

1 Corinthians 15:1–11

Literary Context

First Corinthians 15 can appear at first sight to sit at a distance from the rest of this epistle. It is one of Paul's longest expositions on one particular subject in all his writings and deals with the resurrection of Jesus and the consequent resurrection of those who belong to him. Without doubt this chapter has always been regarded as of crucial importance for the whole of the Christian faith in the way it spells out the facts of the faith and develops the subject of the resurrection with all its implications for Christians. However, its links to the rest of the book are clear and must not be overlooked. Paul began the epistle with an emphasis on God's grace given to the Corinthian church in Christ. They had received grace-gifts from God, but only as part of God's gracious calling of them to be his people. Paul repeatedly drew his readers back to their commitment to Christ as Lord (e.g., 1:2, 10, 31; 2:8; 5:4; 8:6; 10:21–22), to an understanding of the implications of their belief in Christ crucified (1:17–25; 5:7; 6:20; 11:17–32), and to the recognition that until "the end," the "day of the Lord" (e.g., 1:7–8; 3:13; 4:5), they are sustained by God's grace (1:4; 3:10) because God is faithful (1:9; 10:13). He has repeatedly demonstrated that they must live, knowing that the present age will come to an end in judgment and resurrection (1:2, 7–8; 2:9; 6:2–3, 13; 7:29; 9:24; 10:11). Therefore, it is always to the "faith," the "gospel" of Jesus Christ, that Christians must constantly return.

God has done something radical in history by sending his Son Jesus to be born, to live, to die on the cross, to be raised from the dead, to be seated in glory, and then to come in glory to reign forever on this earth. It is this whole message that drives all that Paul has been teaching. It is belief in this view of the world, a world in which Christ is Lord of all and in which God calls people to himself "in Christ," that must guide the way believers live and think and worship. It will guide their relationship to the rest of the pagan world around, as well as their relationship to each other in community. It will guide their understanding of what must happen to them in their relationship with God as they live and die and are then raised from the dead. In a church where many boasted of their grace-gifts and believed they had "arrived" spiritually, the resurrection especially reminds them that their only "boast" can be in the

Lord (1:31) and that their whole existence is determined by God's grace alone (4:7). They are not yet fully transformed into the people they will be.

In rhetorical terms, it is suggested that the opening verses of this chapter seem to function as a *narratio*.[1] That is, they provide a narrative account of what has happened and explain the case that will be addressed. Verse 12 may be said to provide the *propositio* as it lays out the controversy. This is followed by a form of *refutatio* in 15:13–19.[2] Thus, it is not until 15:12 that the reader discovers there was some question among the Corinthians concerning the nature of the resurrection and that it is from 15:13 onward that Paul develops his arguments against those who are denying the resurrection.

In 15:1–12 Paul reminds his readers of the basic tenets of the faith that he had preached and that they had believed. After referencing the death and burial of Jesus, he writes at greater length of the physical appearances of Jesus after his resurrection, allowing him to reference his own witness to Jesus and to the astounding grace of God revealed in his calling. This leads him into the subject that he will develop: the case for the resurrection, its theological significance, and its implications for Christian life and thinking.

VIII. Status, Public Worship, Freedom, and Grace-Gifts (11:2–14:40)

➧ **IX. The Gospel of the Resurrection of Christ and His People (15:1–58)**

    A. The Facts of the Gospel Secured by the Resurrection of Christ (15:1–11)

    B. The Truth of the Resurrection (15:12–34)

    C. The Resurrection Body: Continuity and Discontinuity (15:35–49)

    D. The Necessity of the Transformation of the Body (15:50–58)

X. Closing Instructions and Comments (16:1–24)

Main Idea

Before moving to an extended discussion of the theology of the resurrection, Paul reminds the Corinthians of the content of the gospel that he preached among them. What he preached was the same as all the apostles had preached. He then focuses on the resurrection and various witnesses to the risen Lord.

---

1. The use of such terms is mainly useful for seeing how Paul carefully develops his argument in stages. The terms themselves come from the traditions of classical oration and are described in various places, for example, in Quintilian's *Institutio Oratoria*.

2. For a slightly different and more detailed examination of Paul's rhetorical techniques in ch. 15, see Thiselton, *1 Corinthians*, 1176–78.

Translation

1 Corinthians 15:1–11

1a	Reminder	Now **I want to remind you brothers [and sisters],**
b	Content	of the gospel
c	Description	I preached to you,
d		which you received and
e	Expansion	on which you stand and
2a	Instrument	through which you are being saved,
b	Condition	if you hold fast to the word that I preached to you,
c	Exception	unless you believed in vain.
3a	Assertion	For **I delivered to you as of first importance what I also received,**
b	Creedal assertions	"Christ died for our sins
c	List	according to the Scriptures, and
4a		he was buried, and
b		he was raised on the third day
c		according to the Scriptures, and
5a		appeared
		to Cephas, and then
b		to the Twelve."
6a	Time (Sequence)	Then
b	Assertion	he appeared
		before five hundred brothers [and sisters] at once,
		of whom many remain alive until now, but
c	Expansion	
d	Contrast	some have fallen asleep.
7a	Time (Sequence)	Then
b	Assertion	he appeared
		to James and additionally
c		to all the apostles.
8a	Time (Sequence)	Last of all,
b	Circumstance	as if to a stillborn child,
c	Assertion	he also appeared to me.
9a	Basis for v. 8	For **I am the least of the apostles,**
b	Expansion	and am not worthy to be called an apostle,
c	Basis	because I persecuted the church of God.

10a	Means	By the grace of God ··············
b	Assertion	**I am what I am,**
c	Assertion	and **his grace toward me was not in vain;** ··········
d	Assertion	rather, **I worked harder than all of them,** though ···
e	Concession	it was not I but
f	Means	the grace of God with me.
11a	Condition	Whether then it is I or they, ···············
		so
b	Summary assertion	**we preach,**
		and you believed.

Structure

This chapter follows a clear progression of argument. This first section (15:1–11) lays out the basic gospel message of the resurrection and provides the *narratio*. In four parts it provides the common ground of Christian belief between Paul and those to whom he writes. (1) In vv. 1–2 Paul reminds his readers that the gospel brought them salvation. (2) In vv. 3–5 he affirms the facts of the gospel faith, culminating in the resurrection. (3) In vv. 6-8 Paul elaborates on the second and focuses on the resurrection as he speaks of witnesses to the risen Lord (vv. 6–8). (4) In vv. 9–11 Paul reminds them that the gospel, though mediated to them through his own apostolic ministry, comes to all (both apostles and Corinthian believers) entirely by "the grace of God." An *inclusio* is formed as Paul writes in v. 1 and v. 11 of what was "preached" and "received"/"believed."

Exegetical Outline

IX. The Gospel of the Resurrection of Christ and His People (15:1–58)

➡ **A. The Facts of the Gospel Secured by the Resurrection of Christ (15:1–11)**

　　1. A Reminder of the Gospel and Its Results (15:1–2)

　　2. The Content of the Gospel That Was Preached and Received (15:3–5)

　　3. Witnesses to the Resurrected Christ (15:6–8)

　　4. Paul Preached the Same Gospel as Other Apostles with the Same Result (15:9–11)

Explanation of the Text

15:1–2 Now I want to remind you, brothers [and sisters], of the gospel I preached to you, which you received and on which you stand and through which you are being saved, if you hold fast to the word that I preached to you, unless you believed in vain (Γνωρίζω δὲ ὑμῖν, ἀδελφοί, τὸ εὐαγγέλιον ὃ εὐηγγελισάμην ὑμῖν, ὃ καὶ παρελάβετε, ἐν ᾧ καὶ ἑστήκατε, δι' οὗ καὶ σῴζεσθε, τίνι λόγῳ εὐηγγελισάμην ὑμῖν εἰ κατέχετε, ἐκτὸς εἰ μὴ εἰκῇ ἐπιστεύσατε). Paul begins a remarkable chapter that will discuss in detail the nature of the resurrection by reminding the Corinthians of the content of the gospel that he first preached to them. He intends them to understand that they received the gospel through his preaching and owe their present status as saved people to their reception of the message. Unless they have failed properly to believe the gospel, then they should accept that they hold in common with Paul the gospel facts laid out in vv. 3–7.

"I want to remind you" (Γνωρίζω) might normally be translated as "I make known to you," but the context makes it clear that Paul is recalling what he once preached to them. The content of what he had preached is summarized by the word "gospel."[3] This noun or its verbal form (εὐαγγέλιον or εὐαγγελίζω) has been used on several occasions in this epistle already (1:17; 4:15; 9:12–23). However, for Paul the content aspect of the good news can never be separated from the power inherent in the gospel as the word of God that brings salvation. This is God's message that is in itself a performative action. The gospel is a speech act with perlocutionary force. Thus, it is that God's gracious

act in Jesus Christ is both the content of the gospel and the power of the gospel in producing salvation (Rom 1:16). For this reason, in v. 2 Paul can see the gospel as *instrumental* ("*through which* you are being saved," δι' οὗ καὶ σῴζεσθε) in maintaining the salvation of the believer.

The two clauses, "the gospel I preached" (τὸ εὐαγγέλιον ὃ εὐηγγελισάμην) and "the word that I preached to you" (τίνι λόγῳ εὐηγγελισάμην ὑμῖν) explicate each other. Paul's use of "the word" for the message that was preached probably refers back to 14:36 where he refers to "the word of God." In Colossians 1:5 the word "gospel" is found in apposition to "the word of truth." Elsewhere Paul can speak of "the word of the cross" (1:18), or "the word of Christ" (Rom 10:17 ESV), or "the word of the Lord" (1 Thess 1:8 ESV), or "the word of truth" (Eph 1:13 ESV). In each place he points to the gospel that was preached or the gospel message that was heard and received. Yet here the reader has to wait for the content of the preaching until vv. 3–4.

Prior to that Paul qualifies "gospel" with four subordinate clauses. Initially, he reminds them that it was he who preached to them. Paul has already made it clear that God had required this preaching of him (9:16) and that this was his passion for which he had relinquished all (9:21–23). It was the whole focus of his work at Corinth (1:17). Then he impresses upon them that this is the gospel that they "received."[4] He thus establishes the summary basis for the following discussion, which should be a matter of common belief between him and the Corinthian believers. The third clause, "on which you stand,"[5] means that because of God's gracious

---

3. See at 1:17, "In Depth: The Gospel."

4. The use of "received" (παρελάβετε) provides a good example of the perfective aspect of the Greek aorist. Seen by Paul from outside, they "received" the gospel. The aorist functions

by way of "summary." See Campbell, *Basics of Verbal Aspect*, 84–86.

5. The perfect frequently communicates a state of being and here has a present reference (ἑστήκατε). On the frequent cove-

working through the preached word, the gospel provides the locus for their current status as part of the church of Christ. Verse 2 then begins with the fourth clause, which shows the gospel to be instrumental in salvation (see above). Paul can speak of salvation in past, present, and future tenses, but here the present tense (passive) reminds us that God's grace continues to "save" in order that in the future this salvation may be complete at the judgment day.

The conditional clause "if you hold fast . . ." (εἰ κατέχετε) looks back to the saving gospel that they received and have believed. Paul describes the same idea when he says, "Stand firm in the faith" (16:13). Whether Paul truly believed there were those who were not "holding fast" to what he had preached is not clear.[6] Either way the clause that follows ("unless[7] you believed in vain") serves as a reminder of the opposing reactions to the gospel. The one produces those who "are being saved," and the other produces those who "are perishing" (1:18).[8] The theological question that is frequently raised from what Paul says here is well articulated by Kistemaker: "Can a Christian receive God's good news, take a stand for Jesus Christ . . . and yet still believe in vain?"[9] Schreiner places this conditional clause firmly in the context of the way Paul warns

Christians. Of this verse he writes, "Warnings and admonitions are a constituent part of the Pauline gospel. . . . Eschatological salvation is conditioned on perseverance in the gospel. Paul never views faith as a static reality that cancels out the need for present and future faith."[10]

Since Paul has just said he is going to summarize the facts of the gospel that have been preached, the exception clause most likely speaks to these facts. If what he now summarizes is not true, then their believing has indeed been in vain. He will go on to say just this with specific application to the resurrection in vv. 13–14. The first issue is not that Christians might lose their faith; rather, it is that the whole idea of this faith will have been pointless. He is going to remind the Corinthians of the theological and practical import of the resurrection and the danger of denying it (vv. 12–19).

15:3 For I delivered to you as of first importance what I also received, "Christ died for our sins according to the Scriptures (παρέδωκα γὰρ ὑμῖν ἐν πρώτοις, ὃ καὶ παρέλαβον, ὅτι Χριστὸς ἀπέθανεν ὑπὲρ τῶν ἁμαρτιῶν ἡμῶν κατὰ τὰς γραφάς). "For" (γάρ) marks the continuity of what follows with the preceding statements, as Paul now summarizes that which was most important in his teaching by means of a confessional formula.[11] "I delivered . . .

---

nantal implications of the verb "to stand" (ἵστημι), see 1 Cor 8:7 and "In Depth: The Theme of Stumbling" at 1:23b.

6. In 11:2 he uses the same word (κατέχετε) and commends them for "holding fast" to the traditions that he had handed down to them.

7. "Unless" translates ἐκτὸς εἰ μὴ; see on 14:5.

8. Thiselton, *1 Corinthians*, 1186, argues that the adverb "in vain" (εἰκῇ) should be read as "without due consideration" or "thoughtlessly" (cf. BDAG 281). He suggests the problem Paul highlighted was one of a "confused appropriation of the gospel" that had led to an incoherent grasp of the "practical entailments for eschatology or for practical discipleship."

9. Kistemaker, *First Corinthians*, 527. This is part of his response: "Paul says that the Corinthians are saved. Elsewhere he

teaches that salvation is a process which, on the one hand, the believers must work out fully, and on the other, God accomplishes by working within them (Phil. 2:12–13). This means that the believers are being saved provided they hold on to the gospel and apply it to their lives. God is at work in the process of salvation and holds on to the believers. He wants them to hold on to him by obeying his Word. Paul writes a conditional clause, 'if you hold fast,' but he knows that the activity of holding fast is a fact."

10. Schreiner, *Paul, Apostle of God's Glory in Christ*, 291.

11. As with the English adjective "first," so the Greek adverb (πρῶτος) can have a temporal reference: "Firstly, I delivered." Or it can indicate prominence. The context here suggests the latter: "Of first importance."

what I also received" is language that reflects the passing on of tradition. The words (παρέδωκα and παρέλαβον) are almost identical to those in 11:23 where they are discussed in more detail. Each clause of the confession of faith is introduced by "that" (ὅτι; recitative use). This serves in this context to introduce direct speech; hence the translation above, which simply uses quotation marks instead of translating the word "that."[12] The frequently appearing perfective aspect and punctiliar function of the aorist tense is seen in three of the verbs in the confession: "died" (ἀπέθανεν), "buried" (v. 4; ἐτάφη), "appeared" (v. 5; ὤφθη). But Paul uses the perfect tense for the resurrection (v. 4; ἐγήγερται). The use of the perfect here no doubt reflects the tense's regular "stative" function. That is, the tense points not simply to the point of Christ's resurrection but to the state of having been raised. Christ remains raised. Clearly a different agent is implied in the uses of the passive voice. Christ was buried by his friends and raised by God.[13]

In these verses three questions of interpretation have attracted attention. The first concerns the nature and form of the tradition to which Paul refers. The second concerns the clause "died for our sins," and the third relates to the twice-repeated phrase "according to the Scriptures."

The tradition. That Paul is passing on received tradition is clear in his use of the verbs "I *delivered* . . . what I also *received*." See comments on 11:23. It is therefore reasonable to assume that he is using very early creedal-type statements that summarize the faith and probably go back to the early Jerusalem church. Peter's sermon in Acts 2, for example, contains the same essential detail as appears here regarding the death of Christ, his resurrection, and its relationship to the sin of men and women, but the formula would have been established sometime subsequent, probably in the Gentile mission. A great deal has been written on the nature of early Christians creeds and much on vv. 3–5 as indicative of such early creedal formulae. J. N. D. Kelly's older work[14] remains important in its assessment of the development of creeds within Scripture and beyond, though he warns that "in the proper sense of the terms, no creed, confession or formula of faith can be discovered in the New Testament." He notes their development from early existence as little more than "catchwords" or "miniature creeds" to more "detailed confessions," and he classes 15:3–7 as one of the more significant examples of the latter category.[15] Though he is surely not correct in asserting that this text evinces a "defensive apologetic note" by listing the witnesses, nevertheless his suggestion that it is drawn up as a summary suitable for catechetical or preaching purposes is helpful.

Unlike Galatians 1:11–12 where Paul argues that he did not receive his gospel from any "man" but through a "revelation" (referring to his conversion on the Damascus road), here he asserts that he has "received" what he hands down. Garland suggests that in the Galatians passage Paul probably has in mind less the historical facts of 15:3–7 and more the "interpretation of what those facts mean."[16] However, we may assume with Dunn that Paul regarded the "kerygmatic tradition" as confirming his own convictions and giving useful (and widely known?) form to his own beliefs.[17] Nevertheless, these discussions of possible backgrounds for the

---

12. Dana and Mantey, *Manual Grammar*, 252. BDF §395.5.

13. "Appeared" (ὤφθη) in v. 5 is an aorist passive translated with an active meaning (see BDF §313; an intransitive-deponent from ὁράω).

14. J. N. D. Kelly, *Early Christian Creeds*, 2nd ed. (London: Longmans, 1960).

15. Ibid., 16–18. Also Dunn, *Theology of Paul*, 174–77.

16. Garland, *1 Corinthians*, 684.

17. James D. G. Dunn, *Unity and Diversity in the New Testament: An Inquiry into the Character of Earliest Christianity* (London: SCM, 1977), 66–67.

formula, the questions raised by some concerning its unity, and debates about the extent of the quotation,[18] all reveal the impossibility of any certainty as to its original form or provenance.[19] It is probably best simply to insist on what we know from the text: Paul himself taught the gospel in this way and these are facts of greatest importance, forming the essence of Paul's saving gospel of grace.

"Died for our sins." This is the first affirmation of the formula. At the heart of the Christian faith is the fundamental assertion that Christ died on the cross, and it is this "Christ crucified" that Paul says he proclaims (1:23; 2:2, 8; 8:11). The fact that the name "Christ" is used on the four occasions in this epistle where he speaks of the crucifixion or death of Jesus is a further indication that the name carried messianic connotations rather than simply being, as it were, the second name for Jesus. The Messiah comes as king to his people in line with Old Testament hope for the salvation of God's people. His kingship implies a representative role on behalf of his people, much as is found in 2 Corinthians 5:14: "For the love of Christ controls us, because we have concluded this: that one has died for all, therefore all have died" (ESV; see also Gal 2:20). A similar representative theology is to be seen in 1 Cor 15:21–22 (see below) where Adam represents one group in death and Christ represents another group in life. It is, in part, this corporate and representative role of the Messiah that provides an understanding of what is meant by the phrase "for our sins" (ὑπὲρ τῶν ἁμαρτιῶν).

In this epistle there is virtually no explanation of the origins of sin or the way it can be forgiven. Sin is discussed in chapters 6–8 in the context of the church's ethics and the danger of a life that does not reflect Christ. Otherwise, as here in 15:3, that Christ comes to deal with sin in his death on the cross is a given for the Christian community. Thus, solely from this text there is an inevitable limit on what we may determine about the manner in which Christ deals with sin. The theological context in Paul's writings is that the death of all people is the undoubted outcome for the people of a world in which "all have sinned and fall short of the glory of God" (Rom 3:23). It is this death, the result of the judgment of God (Rom 5:9; 6:23), that is overcome in the person and work of Christ for all who will believe in him. It is this death that, above all, reveals the love of God being extended to all the nations (Rom 5:8).

Grammatically, the weight that may be put on the word "for" (ὑπέρ) has been key to many discussions. However, the semantic value of these prepositions is remarkably fluid in Koine Greek. With the genitive of a person this preposition could mean "for our advantage" (cf. Phil 2:13). Yet, later in this same chapter (1 Cor 15:29; cf. Isa 43:3–4 LXX) it clearly means "on behalf of" in a substitutionary sense.[20] With the genitive of a "thing" (as with "sin" in this case) similar meanings are evident. Moreover, the preposition is almost indistinguishable at times from two others (περί and ἀντί; cf. Rom 8:3; 11:15).[21] This is notable in 1:13 where our text reads, "Was Paul crucified for you [ὑπὲρ ὑμῶν]?" and a variant in 𝔓⁴⁶ reads, "Was Paul

---

18. For example, Héring, *First Corinthians*, 158, says the quotation ends at v. 4. Fitzmyer, *1 Corinthians*, 541, regards v. 5b to v. 7 as a part of a list of early eyewitnesses to the risen Christ and that the original "fragment of the kerygma" ends with v. 5a. Most see the formula extending to the end of v. 5. However, the direct speech (introduced by καὶ ὅτι) comes to an end with v. 5a. The clauses that follow in vv. 5b, 6a, 7a, and 7b begin with "then" (εἶτα and ἔπειτα).

19. Cf. Conzelmann, *1 Corinthians*, 251; also John S. Kloppenborg, "An Analysis of the pre-Pauline formula in 1 Cor 15:3b-5 in Light of Some Recent Literature," *CBQ* 40 (1978): 351–67; J. Murphy-O'Connor, "Tradition and Redaction in 1 Cor 15:3–7," *CBQ* 43 (1981): 582–89.

20. BDF §231.

21. BDF §229.1.

crucified for us [περὶ ἡμῶν]?" In short, the intent of the preposition must be determined from the immediate context, which in 15:3 offers no direct help except that it is part of what is intended in the discussion of Christ's death. Therefore, the general significance of Christ's death in Paul's writings must be brought to bear on the discussion. The closest parallel in his writings is in Galatians 1:4, in which Paul speaks of Christ's death "for our sins, to rescue us from the present evil age." Here the context is eschatological and has largely to do with the transfer of lordships or kingdoms. Yet, in Paul Christ's death is most often spoken of in a sacrificial context. For example, in Romans 8:3 (where περὶ ἁμαρτίας is used) the context is most likely one of Christ's sacrifice.[22] Partly this may be seen in the fact that in the LXX this phrase translates the Hebrew "sin offering," or in Isaiah 53:10 it translates "guilt offering." Furthermore, Paul's references to Christ's blood usually refer to some aspect of sacrifice. This is apparent in one of Paul's clearest statements about the death of Christ, Romans 3:23–26. In 1 Corinthians 5:7 Paul spoke of Christ as "our Passover lamb" that has been sacrificed. In 2 Corinthians 5:14–15 Paul speaks of Christ as "one" who has died "for all" (ὑπὲρ πάντων), and this leads into the discussion at v. 21 that is clearly based in ideas drawn from sacrificial theology. With a likely allusion to Isaiah 53:4–6, Paul speaks of God making the sinless Christ "sin for us" (ὑπὲρ ἡμῶν), surely implying substitution, yet one that in some sense goes both ways since we "become the righteousness of God."[23]

If we take it that Paul often, if not usually, thinks of Christ's death in terms of some form of sacrifice, then as we look for parallels in the Old Testament we find a number, some of which are mentioned above. But here in 15:3 the most notable parallel that possibly provides the basis for the expression "for our sin," especially given the following phrase "according to the Scriptures," lies in Isaiah 53 LXX. Many commentators throughout the centuries have seen the Servant Songs of Isaiah, especially Isaiah 52:13–53:12, as providing the most likely background for Paul's thought here,[24] though this approach has not met with universal agreement.[25]

---

22. For a more detailed discussion see Dunn, *Theology of Paul*, 216.

23. For a detailed discussion of the role of sacrifice in Paul's understanding of Christ's work of salvation, see Stephen Finlan, *The Background and Content of Paul's Cultic Atonement Metaphors*, AcBib 19 (Atlanta: SBL Press, 2004).

24. Cf. Ambrosiaster, quoted in *Ancient Christian Commentary on Scripture, 1–2 Corinthians*, ed. Gerald Bray (Downers Grove, IL: IVP Academic, 1999), 146; Calvin, *First Corinthians*, 314. See Fee, *1 Corinthians*, 803–4.

25. Of those who argue against this background for this text, see Morna D. Hooker, *Jesus the Servant: The Influence of the Servant Concept of Deutero-Isaiah in the New Testament* (London: SPCK, 1959). Fitzmyer, *1 Corinthians*, 546, doubts the value of the servant songs but offers no alternatives. Garland, *1 Corinthians*, 685, is also disinclined to see the servant songs as the primary background but concludes, "Christians found scriptural antecedents and associations with Jesus' death in a broad range of Scripture." But see Martin Hengel, *The Atonement: The Origin of the Doctrine in the New Testament* (Philadelphia: Fortress Press, 1981), 36–38, 58–61. Hengel argues that Christ's death from the earliest church was regarded as an atoning sacrifice and that Isa 43 and 53 seem to provide considerable background in understanding how this theology developed.

IN DEPTH: "For Our Sins" and Isaiah 53

Perhaps the strongest argument against regarding Isaiah 53 as the (main) background is that it would appear that no direct link had been made in Jewish theology between the Messiah and the suffering servant in the pre-Christian era.

Nevertheless, since the apostle Paul often thinks of the death of Christ in sacrificial terms, there is no reason to suppose that he could not have drawn on Isaiah 53 to explain Christ's sacrificial giving of himself in the place of men and women, whether or not this interpretation had a pre-Christian history. He surely did so in Romans 4:25 where he talks of Jesus being "delivered over to death for [because of] our sins" (cf. 53:12 LXX: διὰ τὰς ἁμαρτίας αὐτῶν παρεδόθη).[26] In 2 Corinthians 5:21, as mentioned above, it is also likely that he is alluding to Isaiah 53:6. Others draw attention to the likelihood that Christ's suffering and death were linked to the suffering servant by this stage in the Gentile mission, given Peter's lengthy quotation from Isaiah 53 when using Christ as an example in a discussion on suffering (1 Pet 2:21–25; see also 3:18, περὶ ἁμαρτιῶν). But it is also quite possible that this link with Christ and Isaiah 53 can be traced back to Jesus's own lifetime (many would say that this can be seen in Mark 10:45, 14:24, and Luke 22:37). Furthermore, the very use of the word "gospel," as seen above, is surely drawn from Isaiah, especially the Servant Song in Isaiah 52:13–53:12, thus also indicating a likelihood that it was but the next step to see the "gospel" of Jesus and the servant of Isaiah as linked. It is therefore worth examining the LXX of Isaiah 53 in a little more detail since it is often glossed over by commentators.

Isaiah 53:4 speaks of the one who has carried "our sins" (τὰς ἁμαρτίας ἡμῶν, the same words occur in v. 5; see also v. 6) and been in pain "for us" (περὶ ἡμῶν). In v. 5 we read, "He is made sick for our sins" (where the preposition is διά), in v. 11 "He shall bear their sins" and in v. 12 he was given up "for their sins" (διὰ τὰς ἁμαρτίας αὐτῶν). However, the closest parallel to 1 Corinthians 15:3 lies in v. 10 where we read, "If he would give himself for sin [περὶ ἁμαρτίας]." Here the Hebrew refers to the servant giving himself as "a guilt offering." Three points are worth noting from Isaiah 53 that may help us see more of what Paul means in 1 Corinthians 15:3. First, Isaiah 53 is speaking of the world of sacrifice. The LXX of 53:10 speaks of the servant's soul being given for sin under the will of the Lord. This lines up with the intention of the phrase "according to the Scriptures"; that is, the death of Christ was intended and willed by God. Secondly, it suggests that

---

26. James D. G. Dunn, *Romans*, WBC 38A (Dallas: Word, 1988), 225, argues that we "probably" have here a Greek version "of one of the earliest theological reflections about Jesus' death."

the idea of Christ's death being understood, at least partly, as a substitutionary atonement where "our sins" were laid on him (53:6) and where he "bore the sin of many" (53:12) would have been nothing radical on Paul's part. Thirdly, this passage more clearly than any other in (Old Testament) Scripture speaks of a *person* (as opposed to an animal) as a "guilt offering" (53:10 NASB; LXX: περὶ ἁμαρτίας, where περί is virtually interchangeable with the ὑπέρ of 1 Cor 15:3). This too bears on the fullness of what Paul understands by "Christ died for our sins."

Precisely because this sentence in 15:3 is part of a summary formula of the faith, it is inherently likely that it is a shorthand for a full-fledged teaching about Christ's sacrificial death. For Paul, this death was "according to the Scriptures" and so fulfilled, no doubt, all the various sacrifices, including sacrifices of atonement, those with a representative connotation, and those that were more evidently vicarious and substitutionary. The forgiveness of sins was understood, but, given the similar words in Galatians 1:4, we may also assume that Paul could hardly think of the atonement without also thinking in terms of a transfer of lordships and deliverance from the "present evil age" (Gal 1:4).

"According to the Scriptures." This phrase appears twice in Paul's creedal formula, suggesting that it was probably part of the original formula Paul is citing. The use of "the Scriptures" implies a canon in the sense of a defined body of texts that are assumed to be from God. Thus Paul can talk of "the holy Scriptures" in Romans 1:2 and the "oracles of God" in Romans 3:2 (ESV). For Paul, reflecting back on Scripture in the light of Christ reveals that they had spoken in advance of the facts of the gospel as given here in 1 Corinthians 15 and, in fact, of everything to do with Christ and salvation. Thus they showed how a sinner might be justified (Rom 4:3) and even how the church of Christ should live and conduct itself in the apostolic and subsequent eras (Rom 15:4). As Paul

quotes multiple Scriptures (at least a hundred) and alludes to many more, he reveals his understanding that the (Old Testament) Scripture points forward to Christ. This enables him to see implications in the gospel that would not otherwise be understood. Furthermore, Paul's view of Scripture allows him to read back his Christ-centered focus into the older texts and enable them to be understood in a manner that could not otherwise be known. Thus, for example, Paul sees the gospel being preached in advance to Abraham in such a way that Abraham becomes an exemplar of a man of faith. He also understands that the preaching of the gospel fulfills God's promise to Abraham to bless all the nations, thus explaining the mission to the Gentiles (Gal 3:8).

The twice-repeated phrase ("according to the Scriptures"; 1 Cor 15:3–4) therefore serves in both instances to affirm that all this happened according to God's plan and according to his promises (cf. Acts 2:23) and helps explain Christ's death and resurrection. On the first occasion it is used to corroborate the teaching of Christ's death for sin. We have seen how Scripture may help explain this enigmatic idea of death for sin. While Isaiah 53 may provide substantial background, the reference is no doubt broader than simply one text and refers to the broad flow of Scripture regarding punishment for sin and related sacrifices resulting in God's mercy being shown and forgiveness received.

15:4–5 "and he was buried, and he was raised on the third day according to the Scriptures, and he appeared to Cephas, and then to the Twelve" (καὶ ὅτι ἐτάφη, καὶ ὅτι ἐγήγερται τῇ ἡμέρᾳ τῇ τρίτῃ κατὰ τὰς γραφὰς, καὶ ὅτι ὤφθη Κηφᾷ, εἶτα τοῖς δώδεκα). "He was buried" (ἐτάφη) is key to this summary of the faith. The statement has a finality to it. Jesus was literally "dead and buried," and thus the discussion of Christ's death is completed. Any talk after this of "resurrection" requires that the tomb would have to be empty. While the majority of commentators recognize that Paul (and the early church) must have believed in an empty tomb to spell things out in the way he does, some have suggested that there is no evidence here for such a belief.[27] While the list of eyewitnesses that follows is not an apologetic for a physical resurrection, that so many reliable people saw the resurrected Lord certainly adds to the evidence of what the early church believed. Together with the Gospel writers, they surely believed that the tomb was empty and that the risen Lord, in his body, was seen walking around by many people.

The emphasis on the burial accentuates the fact and the glory of the resurrection. Given the early date of this epistle, it is unlikely that this was an example of a partial polemic against docetism, though Thiselton quotes Ignatius (ca. AD 108), who appears to refer to some who claimed Christ's sufferings were merely "seeming."[28]

The second reference to the "Scriptures" qualifies the resurrection and also perhaps "on the third day" (τῇ ἡμέρᾳ τῇ τρίτῃ). This too has been the subject of some discussion. Does Paul have specific Scriptures in mind or, again, a general flow of prophecy linked with many texts about God creating life? Once more the answer is probably "both." Since the passive voice ("was raised") makes it clear

that God is the agent of the resurrection (cf. Rom 8:23) and since the whole is a summary of the gospel, then probably Paul thinks of the general flow of Scriptures relating to the merciful and gracious God who brings life, especially where once there was death (Deut 32:47; Pss 16:9–11; 21:1–7; 103:4; 116:8; 119:25, 50; Isa 66:22; Dan 12:1–3). Several people from as far back as Pelagius have suggested that Paul has in mind Hosea 6:2 here. In its context that verse speaks of God's people returning to the Lord and being restored: "After two days he will revive us; on the third day he will raise us up, that we may live before him" (ESV). It is also notable that two other Scriptures are explicitly linked to resurrection passages elsewhere in the New Testament. Jonah 1:17 is mentioned by the Lord regarding his death and resurrection (Matt 12:40). Psalm 16:9–11 is used by Peter in the sermon at Pentecost in Acts 2:27–28. These two examples show at least how individual verses came to be used to support the resurrection. However, Thiselton is no doubt correct when he says that isolating certain texts like this amounts to an "unintended reductionism and constraint," for the resurrection is seen as the great climax of God's sovereign plans and the vindication of his grace.[29]

More specifically, the phrase "on the third day" is an expression used of Christ's resurrection in Matthew 16:21, 20:19, and Luke 9:22, 24:46 and elsewhere in these two Gospels. It also appears in Acts 10:40. The three days are usually accounted for by counting the day in which he was put in the grave, the day following, and the day of the resurrection. Jesus himself had taught in Luke 24:46–48 that the resurrection on the third day following suffering was according to the Scriptures. While the three days is, no doubt, simply factual (this is the time Jesus was buried), it is also of note that a

---

27. Conzelmann, *1 Corinthians*, 255; Bultmann, *Theology of the New Testament*, 1:292–306.

28. Thiselton, *1 Corinthians*, 1192.
29. Ibid., 1195.

number of important actions of God throughout history involve a time period of three days. While too much should not be made of this, God may have intended to draw attention to this as another, but the greatest, of his saving acts of power. In Genesis 40:12–13 Pharaoh's chief cupbearer was restored to service in three days, prophesied in a God-given dream, that would eventually lead to God's positioning of Joseph in a place where he could save God's people. Three days was the time of preparation before the Israelites crossed the Jordan (Josh 1:11). Jonah and the fish is an example already noted, and others may be cited. Hosea 6:2 provides another possible example.

In summary, it is likely that from the earliest days, not just Paul but the Christian community as a whole regarded the summary of the gospel faith as an exposition and explanation of Old Testament Scripture, for the Christ was none other than the long-promised and long-awaited Savior.

The addition of the reference to the appearance to Cephas (the Aramaic name for Peter, also at 1:12, 3:22, and 9:5) is unsurprising. The Gospels record Jesus's appearance to this apostle as one of the first appearances (Mark 16:7; Luke 24:34), but he was already prominent as a witness in the early church, having been the one who identified Jesus as the Messiah (Matt 16:15–20). It is likely that this was part of the original formula and reflects the significant role that Peter played in the early church in proclaiming the gospel and Christ's resurrection on the day of Pentecost (Acts 2:14–36). He was also prominent in the work among the Samaritans (Acts 8:14–17), and among Gentiles (Acts 10:40).

"To the Twelve" (τοῖς δώδεκα) completes the formula, though it may have been added here by Paul himself. It is not introduced as the previous clauses by an indicator of direct speech (καὶ ὅτι). Rather it is introduced by "then" or perhaps better simply

"and to the Twelve" (εἶτα; see comments on v. 7 below). The Twelve were the disciples who were the earliest witnesses and who led the early church in Jerusalem. Again, this forces the statement of faith right back into those early gatherings of the Jerusalem church and thus gives it great weight for all time. At the end of Jesus's life, Matthew writes about the "eleven" disciples (Matt 28:16), so the use of "Twelve" suggests that the replacement described at the start of Acts was well known even though we hear nothing further about this particular "Twelve" in the New Testament. Since the original "Twelve" did not all witness the resurrection, and here Paul is clearly not including himself, this number most likely includes Matthias. The main criterion for the replacement apostle was that he had to come from among the small group of men who had witnessed the resurrection (Acts 1:22).

15:6–7 Then he appeared before five hundred brothers [and sisters] at once, of whom many remain alive until now, but some have fallen asleep. Then he appeared to James and additionally to all the apostles (ἔπειτα ὤφθη ἐπάνω πεντακοσίοις ἀδελφοῖς ἐφάπαξ, ἐξ ὧν οἱ πλείονες μένουσιν ἕως ἄρτι, τινὲς δὲ ἐκοιμήθησαν· ἔπειτα ὤφθη Ἰακώβῳ, εἶτα τοῖς ἀποστόλοις πᾶσιν). The argument and evidence for the resurrection continues with mention of further appearances of Jesus. "Then" (ἔπειτα) implies sequence on both occasions of its use here. Though the word "additionally" (εἶτα) is usually also translated as "then," it is unlikely to express a further point in the sequence; rather, it simply signals another addition to what has just been said. If this is the case, then Paul refers to James *and* the apostles, without implying sequence. The same is likely to be true in v. 5, where he appears to Cephas *and* the Twelve. Since we do not know from any other source when this appearance to five hundred happened, we should not speculate why they are mentioned here before James. This

James is almost certainly the Lord's brother on whom Jesus's resurrection clearly had a profound impact. Paul regarded this James as an apostle (Gal 1:18–21) and he was a leader (a "pillar," Gal 2:9) of the church in Jerusalem and so would have been widely known throughout the early church. Paul's mention of the apostles, as distinct from the "Twelve," reveals Paul's wider use of the term to describe those leaders regarded as witnesses to Christ's resurrection in the early church, who took the gospel message out to the world.[30] Mention of five hundred "at once" (ἐφάπαξ), together with the other people mentioned, adds weight to the truth of the witness. Too many had seen the risen Christ for the story to have been fabricated, and, as Paul makes clear, "many remain alive" (οἱ πλείονες μένουσιν) and so can be checked for the accuracy of their witness. To "fall asleep" (κοιμάω) is a regular euphemism for dying, but it is highly appropriate since it implies an eventual waking up and therefore helps lead naturally into the discussion about the resurrection.

Perhaps the brevity of the reference to the five hundred to whom Jesus appeared, like the references to James and to the "apostles" that follow, suggests that these various incidents and even the order of the stories were well known and had consistently been described in the preaching of the gospel. Paul is deliberately developing his argument by promoting a series of witnesses that culminates with himself.

15:8–9 Last of all, as if to a stillborn child, he also appeared to me. For I am the least of the apostles, and am not worthy to be called an apostle, because I persecuted the church of God (ἔσχατον δὲ πάντων ὡσπερεὶ τῷ ἐκτρώματι ὤφθη

κἀμοί. Ἐγὼ γάρ εἰμι ὁ ἐλάχιστος τῶν ἀποστόλων, ὃς οὐκ εἰμὶ ἱκανὸς καλεῖσθαι ἀπόστολος, διότι ἐδίωξα τὴν ἐκκλησίαν τοῦ θεοῦ). It now becomes clear why Paul drew attention to a temporal sequence among the witnesses to the resurrection that he has just listed. It draws attention to Paul's own witness that is "last of all" (in time). While no less genuine, since he did encounter the risen Lord on the road to Damascus, it was a strange appearance. The word for "stillborn child" (ἔκτρωμα) is a New Testament *hapax legomenon*, but Paul's intention in using the word here is not obvious. The word appears in LXX Numbers 12:12, Job 3:16, and Ecclesiastes 6:3 where it refers to a stillborn child, but it can also designate an aborted foetus.[31] In each of the passages cited, a stillborn birth is used to describe a dreadful and wretched situation in which people find themselves. It is possible that this was some horrible term of abuse that Paul's opponents hurled at him as an insult, and that he now picks up and acknowledges to emphasize the glory of the grace that he had received from the Lord. Yet Paul does not seem to be concerned here with opponents.[32] Another possibility is that it is the suddenness and unexpected nature of a stillborn birth that causes Paul to use this term of his own calling. A third alternative is that Paul uses the word as a vivid picture of his wretched state much as it is used in the LXX. Given v. 10 and Paul's insistence that as an apostle he is what he is by God's grace, it may be best to understand him as drawing attention to his state as all but "dead" save for the sovereign redeeming work of Christ that gave him a new and purposeful life (2 Cor 5:16–18).

So wretched was Paul's state that he can only describe himself as "the least of the apostles" (cf. Eph 3:7–8). That is, he is the most unlikely candidate

---

30. See comments on 1:1.

31. See J. Munck, "Paulus tanquam abortivus, I Cor 15:8," in *New Testament Essays: Studies in Memory of Thomas Walter*

Manson, ed. A. J. B. Higgins (Manchester: Manchester University Press, 1959), 180–93.

32. *Contra* Fee, *1 Corinthians*, 814.

for the work. His place among the apostles, more clearly than for any of the others, is an indication that such a calling depends entirely upon God's grace. The other apostles had lived with Jesus and heard him teaching. Pentecost had surely been a complete revelation for them that allowed them to finally understand all that they had been taught over the previous months and years, but they had already been disciples. For Paul, life was entirely different. He reminds his readers that he persecuted the church of God. He was not a disciple before his conversion, but the opposite, intent on destroying the church of God (Acts 9:1–2; 22:3–5; 26:9–11). Certainly, his position was utterly wretched before God. Though he had thought of himself as righteous (Gal 1:13–16), he was "stillborn" until God intervened dramatically.

15:10 By the grace of God I am what I am, and his grace toward me was not in vain; rather, I worked harder than all of them, though it was not I but the grace of God with me (χάριτι δὲ θεοῦ εἰμι ὅ εἰμι, καὶ ἡ χάρις αὐτοῦ ἡ εἰς ἐμὲ οὐ κενὴ ἐγενήθη, ἀλλὰ περισσότερον αὐτῶν πάντων ἐκοπίασα, οὐκ ἐγὼ δὲ ἀλλὰ ἡ χάρις τοῦ θεοῦ [ἡ] σὺν ἐμοί).[33] Paul is emphatic. God's grace is primary. Whatever he may have been, now God's grace has made him what he is. The neuter "what" (ὅ) may be used in a general sense, but more likely refers to his apostleship. By God's grace Paul is an apostle, and he has lived up to this calling. This grace was not "in vain," that is, it was not to no purpose (κενή). Paul uses this word again in vv. 14, 58, and in 2 Corinthians 6:1 where he appeals to the Corinthians not to receive God's grace "in vain." God's grace is manifest through fruit in God's service. This fruit involves work, and Paul says that he has worked "harder"

(περισσότερον) than all of the other apostles. His concern is not to compare himself with the other apostles but to compare his present work with his former work. Paul was always a hard worker. Formerly he had been working against the Lord, but now he works even harder than other apostles *for* the Lord. However, even his hard work to fulfill his calling is not about him "but" (ἀλλά, the adversative makes the point forcefully) has been achieved entirely by God extending his grace "toward" (εἰς ἐμέ) him. The repetition of "grace" three times in this sentence puts the emphasis firmly where Paul wants it in his discussion here. If Paul has a boast, it is not in himself, his apostleship, or his hard work but "in the Lord" (1:31).

This section lays the groundwork for part of Paul's argument yet to come in v. 14, where he talks about the possibility of preaching "in vain" and so also of the possibility of the Corinthians' having believed "in vain." At the end of this section, in v. 58, Paul will urge the Corinthians to "abound in the work of the Lord" and so ensure that their own "labor is not in vain."

15:11 Whether then it is I or they, so we preach and you believed (εἴτε οὖν ἐγὼ εἴτε ἐκεῖνοι, οὕτως κηρύσσομεν καὶ οὕτως ἐπιστεύσατε). Paul's point here is that the gospel he has restated was not and is not proclaimed in any different way by the other apostles. The same message is what all have as the common base for Christian commitment. The opening condition (εἴτε . . . εἴτε) needs the verb supplied (cf. 3:22), while the use of the present tense of "preach" (κηρύσσομεν) has a progressive function. Both Paul and the other apostles (hence "we") continue to preach this same gospel, the one on which they "believed" when they came to faith

---

33. Concerning the phrase [ἡ] σὺν ἐμοί, ἡ is omitted in ℵ* B, D*, F, G, 0243, 0270*. The text is found in 𝔓46, ℵ2 A, D1, Ψ, 33, 1881, 𝔐 among others. The inclusion is not certain and may reflect an assimilation to ἡ εἰς ἐμέ in the first part of the verse. Again, probably by assimilation to the earlier phrase, 𝔓46 changes οὖν to εἰς.

in the first place (the ingressive aorist, ἐπιστεύσατε, indicates that their belief started them on a new course in life). Nothing has changed! The same gospel continues to be preached.

Paul thus summarizes what he has been saying in the opening verses of this chapter. The preaching looks back to vv. 1–3. The same gospel tradition has been handed down to him and preached by him as has been preached by all the apostles. Whether they wish to acknowledge him is un-important. They are where they are because they received and believed the gospel that he and the apostles and the Corinthians hold in common. At the heart of that gospel is God's sovereign grace, something Paul has experienced as deeply as anyone to whom he writes. That grace is seen in the preaching of the gospel and especially in the death of Christ for his people, followed by his resurrection. Paul will now expound upon the nature of the resurrection and its implications for Christians.

Theology in Application

Preaching the Full Gospel of Christ

The centrality of the gospel as a body of received truth that must be believed for salvation is evidenced in all Paul's epistles. As noted above ("In Depth: The Gospel" following comments on 1:17), the substance of his gospel has its roots far back in the plan and will of God. In the Old Testament it is especially Isaiah who picks up the idea that the saving work of God is "good news" to be announced far and wide (cf. Isa 52:7; 61:1–2), and Paul quotes and alludes to the prophecy on a number of occasions (cf. Rom 10:15). Time and again Paul refers to the need to "preach" or "proclaim" the gospel (e.g., Rom 1:9, 15; 15:20; 1 Cor 1:17; 9:14; 15:1; 2 Cor 10:16). The preaching is, above all, the proclamation of the King who is Christ the Lord and of the power of God in him for the salvation of all who believe. If this gospel is to be properly preached, then it can never be divorced from its historical location. This is not just a matter of affirming the historicity of the resurrection, but is a matter of understanding that salvation and the forgiveness of sins are achieved in and through the historical acts of Jesus as he lived, suffered, died, was buried, and was raised from the dead for his exaltation and our justification.

In the modern church, where once again many question or outright deny the facts of Jesus's life, it is essential that this gospel not be sold short by those who believe it. Preaching it fully, as Paul outlined it, led to the Corinthians believing in Christ (15:11), as it does for so many around the world today. However, as Paul writes in Romans 10:14, "How can they believe in the one of whom they have not heard? And how can they hear without someone preaching to them?" He insists that "faith comes from hearing, and hearing through the word of Christ" (Rom 10:17 ESV). Often the whole concept of proclamation is missing in church life. The frequent avoidance of the mention of sin renders vacuous the point of Jesus's death, however much the kindness and love of Jesus is discussed. The failure to speak of the judgment of God on sinful people empties the resurrection of Jesus of its victory (over sin and death.) Too many Christians today, even in some evangelical churches, are reduced to having to listen to Christ's death and atonement presented in little more than exemplary terms. For many, this easily leads to a moralistic religion, and in the end to a form of legalistic righteousness centered on the self. Paul's commitment to and consequent suffering for this proclamation at all times and in all places surely remind us of the challenge. Christians have an obligation to pass on the gospel *intact* and *in full* to the world, wherever God has placed them.

According to the Scriptures

Throughout his writings, Paul builds the edifice of his theology on Scripture. His conversion on the Damascus road did not change his great commitment as a Pharisee to the Scriptures as divinely inspired writings and oracles.[34] Yet his conversion did involve a change in hermeneutic. From that point on, the "Lord" was Jesus, and he was the Messiah (king). Thus, Scripture had to be interpreted in the light of God's plan of salvation for Jew and Gentile provided for in the person of Christ, especially through his life, death, resurrection, and exaltation. This is what is emphasized in 15:2–3. As Paul appeals to Scripture, he does of course appeal to specific verses in many of his theological discussions. Here in chapter 15 several texts are quoted. However, there is much more to what Paul is doing here than simply finding proof texts from the prophets to show that God had foreseen and foreordained Christ's saving activity. For Paul, these gospel events are the climax of the long Scripture story of God and humanity, of a relationship broken by sin, of God's promises of salvation and forgiveness, of his calling into being a people, Israel, and of the possibility of salvation and reconciliation. Just as Adam sinned and was expelled from the garden under God's judgment, just as Noah sinned after witnessing terrible judgment for sin, so did Israel, even after it was called out by God and graciously given God's law and a land in which to rest and enjoy peace. Time after time as God showed grace, the people worshiped him for a while, but before long they fell back into rebellion and sin and were judged. On the cross, this story reaches a climax. In Jesus's representative role (the last Adam) his death sees God's judgment on Adam, and also on Israel, for he is her king/Messiah. Yet in his resurrection all humanity can come to this king in faith, whether Jew or Gentile, and receive forgiveness. All of this was part of the expectation of the story of Scripture: both Israel and the nations would find salvation in God. It is this whole story that forms the backdrop to the good news of God's salvation. Christ was the king who would not just live for one generation

---

34. Dunn, *Theology of Paul*, 169–77, examines both the place of Scripture for Paul and his use of Christian creedal formulae.

before things fell apart yet again but who would himself be raised to live forever, representing all his believing people in righteousness and holiness. So this long story of "the Scriptures" comes to its climax in the messianic King. As Wright so well describes this, "Jesus does not have an independent 'story' all on his own."[35]

It is surely critical that this larger story be understood by Christians of all ages. Such teaching of Jesus "according to the Scriptures" will not only enable God's people to see grace in greater depth but will also allow them to find their place within that story. They will be able to pass the story on in ways that will help explain what it means to call Jesus "the Christ," "the Lord," and "the King." The more Scriptures are used to contextualize the whole story, the more a modern generation will come to be passionate about the gospel and the King. To see the salvation "in which you stand" is indeed "of first importance." It takes effort to engage people in any other story than their own, immediate story. Helping Christians to see that "the Scriptures" describe Jesus's story in a way that helps us understand our own story in relation to God will surely deepen our faith and worship.

---

35. Wright, *Paul and the Faithfulness of God*, 521.

1 Corinthians 15:12–19

Literary Context

Paul now moves to a discussion of the resurrection and its implications for the Corinthian Christians. It is only in 15:12 that Paul introduces the reader to his reason for writing about the resurrection. Rhetorically, this could be termed the *propositio*. He is deeply disturbed that some deny the resurrection. Having written of the common ground in thinking between Corinthian Christians and himself by recounting the gospel as it has been handed down and preached (the *narratio*—15:1–11), Paul now moves through the *propositio* to what is technically probably the *refutatio*.[1] He argues for the truth of the resurrection, first, by asserting the absurdity of the position held by those who deny the resurrection (15:13–19). The rhetoric is terse and to the point as Paul lays out the consequences of such a denial. This section is followed by a *confirmatio* (15:20–28) in which Paul affirms the veracity of Jesus's resurrection by assessing its results and merits for believers. In 15:29–34 Paul returns to the problems inherent in denying the resurrection.

The resurrection of Jesus is the great climax of the gospel. This is what gives meaning to Christ's death. There is no gospel unless there is also resurrection. However, the death also gives meaning to the resurrection, for in this is seen the sovereign work of God in the vindication of Christ and of his people. Furthermore, the resurrection of Christ is what guarantees the fact of resurrection life that is available to all through Jesus Christ. Where he has gone before, there his people also will go. In this way, the resurrection can be seen to bring about the great eschatological hope and to fulfill all the great covenant promises.

---

1. See Mitchell, *Rhetoric of Reconciliation*, 177, 283. Thiselton, *1Corinthians*, 1177, 1214. Witherington, *Conflict and Community*, 292, calls this the *propositio*.

VIII. Status, Public Worship, Freedom, and Grace-Gifts (11:2–14:40)

IX. The Gospel of the Resurrection of Christ and His People (15:1–58)

  A. The Facts of the Gospel Secured by the Resurrection of Christ (15:1–11)

➡   **B. The Truth of the Resurrection (15:12–34)**

  C. The Resurrection Body: Continuity and Discontinuity (15:35–49)

  D. The Necessity of the Transformation of the Body (15:50–58)

 X. Closing Instructions and Comments (16:1–24)

Main Idea

Denying the resurrection implies that Christ has not been raised and therefore that faith is futile, God is misrepresented, Christians remain in sin, and the dead cannot be raised.

Translation

1 Corinthians 15:12–19

12a	Condition	Now	if Christ is proclaimed as raised from the dead,
b	Rhetorical question	**how do some among you say** that	there is no resurrection of the dead?
13a	Condition (premise)	but	if there is no resurrection of the dead, then
b	Assertion (consequence)	**not even Christ has been raised.**	
14a	Condition (premise)	Now	if Christ has not been raised, then
b	Consequence 1	**our preaching is also in vain**	
c	Consequence 2	and **your faith is in vain.**	
		And	
15a	Consequence 3	**we are found to be false witnesses of God**	
b	Basis	because we testified about God	
c	Content	that he raised Christ,	
d		whom he did not raise	
e	Condition	if it is true that the dead are not raised.	
16a	Condition (premise)	For	if the dead are not raised, then
b	Consequence	**not even Christ has been raised.**	
17a	Condition (premise)	Now	if Christ has not been raised,
b	Consequence	**your faith is futile,**	
c	Apposition	**you are still in your sins;**	
18a	Consequence	then also **those who have fallen asleep in Christ have perished.**	

Continued on next page.

19a	Condition (premise)	If for this life only we are (even now) those who hope in Christ,
b	Consequence	**we are more pitiable than all people.**

Continued from previous page.

Structure

In his reminder of the gospel, Paul has especially emphasized the resurrection as being "according to the Scriptures" (15:4) and having been witnessed by many (15:5–8). As he builds his argument in support of the historical fact of the bodily resurrection of Jesus, Paul begins with a rhetorical question in v. 12 that links back to what he has just written and lays out the subject to be discussed. If Christ's resurrection is what has been preached, how can some of the Corinthians now deny it? In what follows in vv. 13–19, Paul takes his premises from the perspective of those who may deny the resurrection. The series of conditional clauses that follow thus provide *false* premises, which Paul then demonstrates have certain logical consequences. Each consequence then becomes the basis for the next premise. The basic premise, "if there is no resurrection of the dead" (v. 13) is repeated in v. 16, "if the dead are not raised." The consequence, which becomes the next premise, "not even Christ has been raised" (v. 13) is repeated in v. 16b. The consequence of the vanity of faith is repeated in vv. 14 and 17. The argument builds to a climax as Paul shows that sin therefore must still remain (v. 17) and those who have died must have perished (v. 18). The final conditional clause provides the climactic false premise: "If for this life only we are (even now) those who hope in Christ." The consequence is that people must therefore be pitied (v. 19). For those claiming to be Christians, the negative argument of these verses becomes a form of *reductio ad absurdum*. In 15:20 Paul will move to a positive argument based on the facts of the resurrection.

Exegetical Outline

IX. The Gospel of the Resurrection of Christ and His People (15:1–58)

  A. The Gospel Facts Are Secured by the Resurrection of Christ (15:1–11)

  B. The Truth of the Resurrection (15:12–34)

➡   **1. The Absurdity of Denying the Resurrection (15:12–19)**

      a. Christ Has Not Been Raised (15:12–13)

      b. Preaching and Faith Are in Vain (15:14–16)

      c. Sin Remains and the Dead Have Perished (15:17–19)

Explanation of the Text

15:12 Now if Christ is proclaimed as raised from the dead, how do some among you say that there is no resurrection of the dead? (Εἰ δὲ Χριστὸς κηρύσσεται ὅτι ἐκ νεκρῶν ἐγήγερται, πῶς λέγουσιν ἐν ὑμῖν τινες ὅτι ἀνάστασις νεκρῶν οὐκ ἔστιν;). Paul begins by asserting what he has just taught: that Christ is proclaimed as having been "raised" (ἐγήγερται), but he presents the idea in the form of a conditional question. The assertion that "some among you" (ἐν ὑμῖν τινες) deny the resurrection suggests disagreements, not only with the apostle but also among themselves on this vital and core teaching.[2] It is this denial of the resurrection that explains for the first time why Paul has spent time on the subject when laying out the gospel in vv. 1–11.

Paul's question is rhetorical and functions more like an exclamation: "How [πῶς] can this be!"[3] The protasis is a first-class or simple condition and assumes the truth of the statement that Christ is proclaimed as raised. The rhetorical flourish indicates it is inconceivable for Paul that anyone should deny the resurrection. The logic is simple. If Christ was raised from the dead, it follows that there must be such a thing as the resurrection of the dead. As Paul proceeds, he will assume there is no resurrection of the dead and so argue that there cannot be a resurrection of Christ. He continues by showing the consequences of such a position.

The particular position some Corinthians held with regard to the resurrection has been much debated. Reconstructing their theology on this matter involves a degree of "mirror reading." That is, we read Paul's statements against a position that he disapproves of and that he does not explain and then try to decide what his opponents taught. Such work can be precarious.[4] Nevertheless, the attempt has been made by many with some results that are partially persuasive. Six major though often related views surface among commentators: (1) Some Corinthians, converted largely from within a Greek, dualistic worldview, believed in the immortality of the soul but rejected a bodily resurrection. This reflects the dualism that sees a division between the material and the spiritual, the phenomenal and the noumenal. Since the body is material it would not inherit that which is spiritual. (2) Some who were converted from a Hellenistic-Jewish background took a position similar to that of the Sadducees, who denied the bodily resurrection (on similar grounds to [1] above; see Matt 22:23; Acts 23:6). (3) Some Corinthians had been influenced by Epicurean philosophy and, it is said, this philosophy denied life after death altogether. This view may be reflected in Paul's comments in 15:19, "If for this life only we are (even now) those who hope in Christ, we are more pitiable than all people," and also in 15:32 where he quotes Epicureans: "Let us eat and

---

2. Fee, *1 Corinthians*, 713, suggests there is nothing in what Paul says that indicates the Corinthians differ among themselves in their view of the resurrection. However, this does no justice to the clear meaning of "some," as opposed to "all," "among you" (ἐν ὑμῖν τινες). Nor, given the possible suggestions as to why they should have denied the resurrection, does it take into account the possibility that a mixed Jewish and Gentile church may have been divided on the nature of the resurrection (see below). We know from Acts 18:7–8 and from this epistle (see Introduction) that there were converted Jews in this church, though most of the congregation was Gentile in origin.

3. The word πῶς is used like this also in 14:7, 9. BDAG 900.

4. We note cautions against "mirror reading" in J. M. G. Barclay, "Mirror-Reading a Polemical Letter: Galatians as a Test Case," *JSNT* 31 (1987): 73–93. Barclay's warnings are mainly aimed at the interpretation of Galatians where many have attempted to reconstruct the position of a *third* party. Here in 1 Corinthians, the attempt is to reconstruct the view of those to whom Paul writes *directly* (for more detail on possible reconstructions in 1 Corinthians, see Gardner, *Gifts of God*, 11–12).

drink, for tomorrow we die." (4) Some Corinthians believed that the resurrection had already taken place (an over-realized eschatology). Christians have a new "spiritual" existence already through faith in Christ. When they die, it is this spiritual state that continues. There is no need to talk of a further resurrection in any meaningful way. Some see the reference in 2 Timothy 2:18 as evidence that such views did exist (Hymenaeus and Philetus say that "the resurrection has already taken place"). (6) Some Corinthians were influenced by gnostic views. Again, based in Greek dualism, this view suggests that the "spiritual" or "wise" were already "raised" to a spiritual life. However, the existence of Gnosticism as early as this is thoroughly unlikely.

It is our view that some Corinthians, deeply dependent on the general dualism of Greek thought, probably denied the resurrection on the grounds of some form of a realized eschatology that misunderstood what it is to be "spiritual." Paul's point here in v. 12 is that Christ was raised *from* the dead (ἐκ νεκρῶν, also in v. 20). This has started something new. It will later be described in v. 20 as the "firstfruits." Dunn writes concerning the period of the last days ushered in by Christ's resurrection that "this new era was marked as final, climactic, in the unfolding purpose of God."[5] As Christ is raised *from* the dead, Paul's logic insists, so the resurrection *of* the dead must be a given.

15:13 but if there is no resurrection of the dead, then not even Christ has been raised (εἰ δὲ ἀνάστασις νεκρῶν οὐκ ἔστιν, οὐδὲ Χριστὸς ἐγήγερται). If there is no resurrection *of* the dead, then it follows that Christ cannot have been raised. Verse 13a takes v. 12b as its starting point with another first-class condition. The statement, "there is no resurrection of the dead," is assumed true for the sake of argument.

15:14 Now if Christ has not been raised, then our preaching is also in vain and your faith is in vain (εἰ δὲ Χριστὸς οὐκ ἐγήγερται, κενὸν ἄρα [καὶ] τὸ κήρυγμα ἡμῶν, κενὴ καὶ ἡ πίστις ὑμῶν). The rhetorical use of the conditional clauses continues in a deliberative manner, as Paul seeks to demonstrate the absurdity of the denial of the resurrection while still holding to any semblance of the gospel as it has been taught. The postpositive connectors (δέ and ἄρα) reveal the progression of the argument ("now if . . . then"). Once again, taking the second half, the apodosis, of the previous sentence as its starting point and assuming its truth, Paul speaks of various consequences. First, *the preaching has been futile.* That is, the whole gospel he and others have preached (vv. 1–3, 11) is rendered vacuous of both content and effect. Since the gospel is understood as God's active word that brings about saving faith and since the core of that faith is that "Christ died for our sins" and "was raised from the dead," denying the truth of the message renders it also devoid of performative effect. Hence Paul adds a *second consequence that their faith is in vain.* It is not just that they have believed in something that is not true but that faith devoid of belief in the resurrection of the dead achieves nothing in the life of an individual. The gospel is a sham.

15:15–16 And we are found to be false witnesses of God because we testified about God that he raised Christ, whom he did not raise if it is true that the dead are not raised. For if the dead are not raised, then not even Christ has been raised (εὑρισκόμεθα δὲ καὶ ψευδομάρτυρες τοῦ θεοῦ, ὅτι ἐμαρτυρήσαμεν κατὰ τοῦ θεοῦ ὅτι ἤγειρεν τὸν Χριστόν, ὃν οὐκ ἤγειρεν εἴπερ ἄρα νεκροὶ οὐκ ἐγείρονται. εἰ γὰρ νεκροὶ οὐκ ἐγείρονται, οὐδὲ Χριστὸς ἐγήγερται). Paul now adduces a *third consequence that the messengers must have been false*

---

5. Dunn, *Theology of Paul*, 240.

witnesses because (ὅτι is causal) the original gospel preached by Paul and the apostles included the witness statements (15:5–8) that God had raised Christ. Thus, if there is no resurrection, then that witness *about God* must be false (τοῦ θεοῦ is an objective genitive). It is not just the fact of the possibility of resurrected life that is at stake here but the truth or not of God's action in that resurrection. The apostolic witness was to the action of God raising Jesus, and so God himself has been misrepresented if there is no resurrection. As in v. 12, the argument proceeds on the assumption that the specific resurrection of Jesus is a subset of a general acceptance of the resurrection of the dead, and so v. 16 repeats the argument of v. 13.

15:17–18 Now if Christ has not been raised, your faith is futile, you are still in your sins; then also those who have fallen asleep in Christ have perished (εἰ δὲ Χριστὸς οὐκ ἐγήγερται, ματαία ἡ πίστις ὑμῶν, ἔτι ἐστὲ ἐν ταῖς ἁμαρτίαις ὑμῶν. ἄρα καὶ οἱ κοιμηθέντες ἐν Χριστῷ ἀπώλοντο). The repetition of ideas from v. 13 sets Paul up for two further consequences of the denial of the resurrection of the dead, once again introduced by a rhetorical conditional clause identical to that found in v. 14. *A fourth consequence is that faith is futile.* In v. 14 the preaching was said to be "in vain" and here "futile." The Greek words are not the same, but their semantic range clearly overlaps (κενός and μάταιος). Paul may have used different words simply for stylistic reasons. However, the futility of faith is explained with the appositional clause, "you are still in your sins." The plural (ἐν ταῖς ἁμαρτίαις) recalls the confession of v. 3. Faith in the dead, buried, and *raised* Christ achieves the forgiveness of sin. Do away with the fact of the resurrection and the achievement disappears. But worse is to come, for

a corollary of this leads to a *fifth consequence that those who have died in Christ have perished*. The point of v. 13 is made again but with direct application to those who would call themselves Christian. No resurrection of Christ means no resurrection for any who have died.

Of course, even this is not the end of the matter for the dead will otherwise "perish" (ἀπόλλυμι). Men and women remain in a relationship with God in terms of sin, as Barrett carefully notes.[6] Justification is still required, and this would be no longer available in Christ, for his sacrifice would bring no atonement, no forgiveness, and no freedom from bondage, which things are directly related in Paul's theology to the resurrection (1 Cor 15:1–11; cf. Rom 4:24; 5:10; 6:4; 1 Thess 1:10). The aorist, passive participle (κοιμηθέντες) has an active meaning, "have fallen asleep" and is ingressive in function. For those in Christ, the sleep of death implies a route to being awake once more. But if there is no resurrection, then there is entry into death and a state of destruction (see 1:18; 8:11). To be "in Christ" (see v. 22) is to be represented by him and united with him. If he has not been raised, then all are represented by and united with Adam and so "all die" (v. 21). Some Corinthians may have felt that the death of those who believe in Christ has led to a new, "spiritual," non-bodily experience of God. For Paul, this is not an option. Either one exists in a (bodily) resurrected state like Christ or in a state of death and perishing like Adam (v. 22). There is no future even for any so-called believers who deny the resurrection of Christ.

15:19 If for this life only we are (even now) those who hope in Christ, we are more pitiable than all people (εἰ ἐν τῇ ζωῇ ταύτῃ ἐν Χριστῷ ἠλπικότες ἐσμὲν μόνον, ἐλεεινότεροι πάντων ἀνθρώπων

---

6. Barrett, *First Corinthians*, 349, writes: "The sin you commit determines God's judgment upon you . . . with a vain faith in a dead Christ you continue in your sins, death retains its victory."

ἐσμέν). If those who have died are without a future other than one described in terms of "perishing," then the Corinthians who believe there is no resurrection must understand that their present faith is without significance. Paul has given all the reasons for this in the last few verses. Thus, in yet another conditional clause Paul develops his line of reasoning a step further. A periphrastic perfect is used (ἠλπικότες ἐσμὲν) with intensifying force, "we are (even now) those who hope."[7] It is difficult to know for certain to what the word "only" (μόνον) refers. The majority of versions link it with "this life," though technically, since it comes at the end, it may refer to the whole clause. Paul uses the first-person plural since, if for the sake of argument this is true, then it must be as true for him and the other apostles as it is for the Corinthians. His writing continues, forcefully building to the climax of the

apodosis that expresses the tragedy of the position: "we are more pitiable than all people" (ἐλεεινότεροι πάντων ἀνθρώπων ἐσμέν). The genitive is one of comparison following the comparative.

For Paul the consequences of denying the resurrection are severe and many. These are as much found in the present as they are in the future. People's faith right now is in vain. The present preaching of the gospel is vacuous without the resurrection. Christ is not alive now if he has not been raised, and this means that right now people are still in their sins with no atoning sacrifice having availed anything on their behalf. Even those who are now dead have not gained anything but have perished. Thus, v. 19 functions as a powerful summary. It is utterly pitiable to think of believing in Christ only for this life since all believers then have is a dead Christ.

Theology in Application

The Resurrection: More Than a Happy Ending

The centrality of the resurrection to the gospel is here established by the consequences of *not* believing in resurrection. Paul has argued that Christ was raised "according to the Scriptures" (15:4). As we noted, this probably refers to the general flow of Scriptures and to the merciful and gracious works of God to bring life to his people. Specific texts such as Hosea 6:2, Jonah 1:17, and Psalm 16:9–11 may have added to the general acceptance that the resurrection of Christ was indeed indicated in the Old Testament. Paul insists that the full authority of Scripture and the authority of still-living eyewitnesses speak to the veracity of the claim. However, the theological consequences of *not* believing in the possibility of a bodily resurrection are critical to Paul's argument. In essence, he argues that the whole of Christian faith as he has outlined it in his gospel summary (vv. 1–8) is null and void.

Christian faith, as it has been understood historically and is described here in Scripture, depends upon a risen Christ. Without that, there is no resurrection hope for Christians. Since death is the punishment for and the end result of sin, there can be no escaping sin without the resurrection. In Adam, the representative head of all

---

7. On the intensifying aspect of the periphrastic participle, see Dana and Mantey, *Manual Grammar*, 232; BDF §352.

humanity, all die. If Christ died and remains dead, he is no different from anyone else represented by Adam. He remains under judgment, and those whom he supposedly represents also remain under judgment and are no better off than they were without him. Any who have died already have therefore "perished." This link of the resurrection with the fact of Christ's death "for our sins" (15:3) must not and cannot be avoided. This is why Paul can go on to speak of "victory" over death (vv. 54–57). For Paul, it is a pitiable thing to imagine people who call themselves Christians going through all the suffering that may entail, only to find they remain "in Adam." Why would he have given up his "rights" (9:15) and his community and friends, and why would he urge anyone to believe if it were all "futile" (v. 17)? In what meaningful sense could the message of Christ be considered "good news," and why would there be a "compulsion" to preach (9:16)?

In the last few decades much of evangelicalism has spoken more of living this life than of the future when the new earth will be inherited and God's people will enjoy resurrected bodies. Perhaps the problem for some has arisen because of an overemphasis in previous generations on some rather slippery concept of "heaven." For many even today, the final goal for humanity is regularly portrayed more as an eternal choir than as a gloriously created world to be worked and enjoyed and for which our bodies are prepared. The future had become too much of a "spiritual" idea. Indeed, there are remarkable assumptions in some parts of evangelicalism shared in common with some forms of liberal theology that cannot imagine a "bodily" existence beyond this age! What Paul argues is that the resurrection is a critical belief enabling us to live in this age and helping us comprehend the goal of our existence. We cannot experience peace with God now if there is no resurrection since then we remain in our sins. We have no gospel to proclaim if Christ, the King, is not even now reigning as Lord.

Some Christians strongly proclaim the atoning death of Christ and that he died "for our sins" and yet seem to reduce the resurrection to little more than "the happy ending to the story." Understanding what Paul says here—that without the resurrection faith is futile, that Christ himself is not raised, and that believers who have died have perished—is a somber reminder that all who speak and preach the gospel must preach the *whole* of God's work in Christ.

There is no doubt the resurrection is a difficult concept. Like the necessary gospel emphasis on the need for sin to be forgiven, this will never be an easy message. However, in the preaching of this message lies the power of God to salvation (2:5), and for the many reasons Paul outlines here it can and must be preached.

1 Corinthians 15:20–28

Literary Context

Paul now affirms the veracity of the resurrection of Jesus and leads from that into affirming the resurrection for all believers. In these verses, he assesses the results and merits of the Lord's resurrection for those who believe in him. Where the previous section had demonstrated the absurdity of the denial of a bodily resurrection for Christian faith, this section explains the theological and practical benefits for believers who trust in Christ's resurrection. Building on ideas of the respective representative headships of Adam and Christ, Paul shows how death gives way, in Christ, to life. This life is seen in its fullness now in "Christ the firstfruits" and will be seen at his coming among all "who belong to Christ" (v. 23). The resurrection guarantees the destruction of "the last enemy . . . death" (v. 26) and culminates in all things being in subjection under God (vv. 27–28). In terms of the rhetoric of the argument, this should probably be seen as the *confirmatio*, that is, the main body of Paul's argument in which logical proofs for the wisdom of his position are offered.

Main Idea

Christ has indeed been raised and, by God's clear design, leads the way through death to resurrection for all who are in him. Christ destroys death and rules his kingdom until he finally delivers all to the Father.

Translation

1 Corinthians 15:20–28

20a	Contrast with vv. 12–19	But, in fact
b	Assertion	**Christi** **has been raised from the dead,**
c	Apposition	the firstfruits of those who have fallen asleep.
		For
21a	Assertion	**since death** **[came] through a man, so also**
b		**resurrection of the dead [came] through a man;**
		for
22a	Assertion	**just as** **in Adam all die,**
b	Comparison	**in the same way in Christ all are made alive.**
23a	Assertion	But **each one in his own** **order:**
b	Series	Christ the firstfruits, then
c		those who belong to Christ at his coming.
24a	Assertion	**Then [is] the end,**
b	Description of 24a	when he delivers up the kingdom
c	Recipient	to [him who is] God and Father,
d	Description of 24a	when he has destroyed every rule and
e	List	every power and authority.
25a	Basis for 24a	For **he must reign**
b	Time	until such time as he shall put all enemies under his feet.
26a	Assertion	**The last enemy [that is] being brought to nothing [is] death.**
27a	Quotation/ explanation of 26a	For "he has put all things in subjection under his feet." [cf. Ps 8:7 LXX]
		But
b	Circumstance	when it says,
c	Quotation	"All things are put in subjection,"
d	Assertion	**it is clear that he is excepted**
e	Identification	who put all things in subjection to him.
28a	Time	But when everything has been subjected to him, then also
b	Assertion	**the Son himself will be subjected to him**
c	Identification	who subjected everything to him,
d	Purpose	in order that God may be all in all.

Structure

The structure of this text falls into two main sections, vv. 20–24a and vv. 24b–28. The first section begins with Paul starting a new part to his argument, this time from a positive perspective as he lays out the true proposition that Christ has been raised from the dead and that he is the firstfruits of a great harvest to come. Centered around this idea of firstfruits, Paul briefly develops an Adam-Christ typology in vv. 21–22 in a structure that forms an ABAB pattern. It begins with the description of death coming into the world, "by a man" and "in Adam" (A); and ends with resurrection and life (B).

A For since   through a man

[came] death (v. 21a)

B so also   through a man

[came] resurrection of the dead (v. 21b)

A¹ For just as in Adam

all die (v. 22a)

B¹ so also   in Christ

all are made alive (v. 22b)

Verses 23–24a, "each in his own order . . . then [is] the end," concludes this point and sets up a second section.

In vv. 24b–28 a further structure may be seen (ABCBA). It begins and ends (A) with what the Son does for the Father. He delivers the kingdom (v. 24b) and he subjects himself to the Father (v. 28). Within that (vv. 25, 27) Paul speaks of the subjection of all things to Christ (B), with the center point of his argument (v. 26) being the destruction of death itself (C).[1]

A Christ delivers the kingdom to God the Father (v. 24)

B He [Christ] must reign until all enemies are subjected (v. 25) (with appeal to Ps 110)

C The last enemy is death (v. 26)

B¹ He [God] subjects all things under his [the Son's] feet (v. 27) (with appeal to Ps 8)

A¹ Christ himself is subjected to the Father (v. 28)

---

1. For a detailed and extended version of this structure, see C. E. Hill, "Paul's Understanding of Christ's Kingdom in 1 Corinthians 15:20–28," *NovT* 30 (1988): 301–2.

Exegetical Outline

IX. The Gospel of the Resurrection of Christ and His People (15:1–58)

   A. The Facts of the Gosepl Secured by the Resurrection of Christ (15:1–11)

   B. The Truth of the Resurrection (15:12–34)

      1. The Absurdity of Denying the Resurrection (15:12–19)

➡   **2. Christ Has Been Raised, So in Him Shall All Be Made Alive (15:20–28)**

         a. As in Adam All Die, in Christ All Are Made Alive (15:20–22)

         b. The Risen Christ Comes for Those Who Belong to Him (15:23–24a)

         c. Christ Delivers the Kingdom to the Father (vv. 24b–25)

         d. Sin Is Destroyed (v. 26)

         e. Christ Subjects Himself to the Father (vv. 27–28)

Explanation of the Text

15:20 But, in fact Christ has been raised from the dead, the firstfruits of those who have fallen asleep (Νυνὶ δὲ Χριστὸς ἐγήγερται ἐκ νεκρῶν, ἀπαρχὴ τῶν κεκοιμημένων). The sentence begins a new section with a strong contrast with what has gone before as Paul now speaks of Christ's resurrection as "firstfruits" (ἀπαρχή; the word is singular). Christ is the first example of one who is raised from the dead. This first clause thus begins the *confirmatio* in which Paul presents a further, careful, and logical argument. This time he argues for the veracity of Jesus's resurrection and, in doing so, assesses its results and merits for believers. The Greek translated "in fact" (νυνί) is normally an adverb of time. Occasionally, as here, it follows a clause that states an unreal situation—in this case a series of conditional clauses—by introducing the real (see 12:18; cf. Heb 9:26). The contrast between having "been raised" and having "fallen asleep" is drawn from the previous verses (vv. 15–18). Again,

the passive sense of the verb (ἐγήγερται) speaks to God having raised Christ, and the perfect has a stative aspect, the past action initiating a present state (AV: "But now is Christ risen from the dead").

BDAG suggests that in this instance "the original meaning [of the word "firstfruits" (ἀπαρχὴ)] is greatly weakened," so that it comes simply to mean "first."[2] But this barely does justice to the way in which Paul is thinking.[3] Finlan's warning is timely that "a metaphor need not have the same reference in every case: 'first fruits' can refer to converts, to Christ, or to the Holy Spirit (1 Cor 6:15–20; 5:7; 2 Cor 7:1)."[4] The gospel summary has spoken of Christ as a sacrifice "for our sins." Paul is about to enter the realm of representational theology as he speaks of Adam and Christ. It is therefore probable that Paul has a deliberate purpose in using this word, the origins of which lie in the grain harvest in Leviticus 23:10–12.[5] The fact that it is often assumed that the resurrection of Jesus occurred on

---

2. BDAG 98.

3. Wrongly in our view, Fee, *1 Corinthians*, 749, says, "Paul's interest [in the word] is not in its biblical overtones." For him the emphasis is on Christ being the "first" but also therefore as the guarantee of what is to come.

4. Finlan, *Atonement Metaphors*, 162.

5. In 1 Cor 5:7–8 Paul referred to the festival of unleavened bread to draw attention to the need for cleaning out the leaven for the sake of sincerity and truth.

the Sabbath on which the sheaf offering would be made (that is, the day after the regular Sabbath), may also provide grounds for Paul's use of the metaphor here.[6]

It was suggested above that Paul regarded all the Old Testament offerings and sacrifices as being fulfilled in Christ. This provides another example. The first sheaf of the harvest, probably a sheaf of barley, was to be brought to the priest as an offering. This was a community offering rather than one brought by an individual.[7] As the sheaves are "waved" or elevated before the Lord by the priest, so the offering becomes one of praise to Yahweh, who has supplied food for his people. In this sense the image does justice to Paul's constant emphasis through this chapter that God is the one who raised Jesus and that as "firstfruit" Jesus brings glory to God. Of note from Leviticus is the fact that the people may not eat of the harvest themselves until the firstfruit has been offered to God, but once the offering has been made, the people may participate in the enjoyment of the harvest as well. Paul may have this strict order in mind as he develops his argument here that Christ must rise first and then those who are "in Christ" (v. 23). The offering also looks forward with expectation to the Lord supplying a full harvest. Indeed, the dedicated firstfruit comes to be regarded as the guarantee of the full harvest. In this sense, it takes on the same idea as the "deposit" or "guarantee" (ἀρραβών) that is reflected in Paul's discussion of the work of the Spirit, who secures "what is to come" (2 Cor 5:5).

In Paul's thought, however, there may be one further aspect to this reference to the offering of "firstfruits" that is easily overlooked. Part of the firstfruits offering specifically involved a "burnt offering to the LORD" that had to be a "male lamb . . . without blemish" (Lev 23:12 ESV). It was to be offered on the same day as the sheaf waving. Some have argued that a burnt offering (or "whole offering") symbolized submission to the Lord or an act of homage, but many note that it involves atonement for sin (Lev 1:3–4; 14:20; 16:24).[8] Could Paul be thinking so broadly, as he speaks here of "firstfruits," that he is also thinking of sin having been dealt with? Possibly so. Notably, he has built and is building his whole argument on the creedal formula in which he talked of Christ dying "for our sins" (see above)—a clearly sacrificial idea. Moreover, he has just argued in v. 17 that "if Christ has not been raised . . . you are still in your sins." Now he says, "In fact, Christ has been raised from the dead, the firstfruits. . . ." Furthermore, his conclusion to this section talks of the final defeat of sin.

Perhaps where modern commentators so desire to see a particular thought attached to a sacrificial allusion, Paul would have thought of several attendant circumstances, as he did with the Passover offering in 5:7–8. If that is so in this case, then "firstfruits" is full of meaning: Christ is the firstfruits offering to God to whom alone is glory due; he is the first in order, and the full harvest will follow; and (perhaps) he is the unblemished lamb who accompanies the firstfruits offering as

---

6. This depends on how we understand the order of the days of the offerings in Leviticus 23: the sheaf offering is to be given on the day after the Sabbath after the Passover feast. But see Barrett, *First Corinthians*, 351, who finds some support for this in Philo, but then rightly adds that "this however cannot be positively affirmed." See Gordon J. Wenham, *The Book of Leviticus*, NICOT (Grand Rapids: Eerdmans, 1979), 306, for a summary of the traditional view of how the important redemptive events in Jesus's life paralleled principal Old Testament feasts, and 304 for a discussion of the meaning of the "day after the Sabbath."

7. So John E. Hartley, *Leviticus*, WBC (Dallas: Word, 1992), 385.

8. R. E. Clements, "Leviticus," in *Leviticus–Ruth*, The Broadman Bible Commentary (Nashville: Broadman, 1970), 11; Wenham, *Leviticus*, 57. Hartley, *Leviticus*, 18, writes that "the frequent presentation of whole offerings enabled the covenant community, despite the human proneness to sin, to maintain fellowship with the Holy God."

an atonement offering dealing with sin. This is the Christ who has been raised by God from the dead and who is the subject and content of the gospel.

15:21–22 For since death [came] through a man, so also resurrection of the dead [came] through a man; for just as in Adam all die, in the same way in Christ all are made alive (ἐπειδὴ γὰρ δι᾽ ἀνθρώπου θάνατος, καὶ δι᾽ ἀνθρώπου ἀνάστασις νεκρῶν. ὥσπερ γὰρ ἐν τῷ Ἀδὰμ πάντες ἀποθνήσκουσιν, οὕτως καὶ ἐν τῷ Χριστῷ πάντες ζῳοποιηθήσονται). In these verses Paul states the truth as opposed to the fantasy some Corinthians seemed to have believed. Death came through a man, Adam. Only resurrection can deal with this, and it too has come through a man, Christ. In the true world of God and his Son Jesus Christ, all who belong to Christ will be made alive. "Since" (ἐπειδὴ) is causal as in 1:21, 22. In v. 21 "Through a man" (δι᾽ ἀνθρώπου) is instrumental and the verb is understood. Because in v. 22 Paul speaks generally of *all* death in principle being attributable to Adam, Paul uses the verb "to die" (ἀποθνήσκω) rather than "fall asleep" (κοιμάω). He uses the latter on several occasions, but only when speaking of believers who have died (11:30; 15:6, 18, 51; 1 Thess 4:13–15). Adam's death was long ago, but its result is ongoing death, hence Paul's use of the present tense "die" (ἀποθνήσκουσιν). Christ's resurrection also happened in the past, but Paul here speaks of the resurrection of believers that will happen "at his coming" (ἐν τῇ παρουσίᾳ αὐτοῦ; v. 23) and so uses the future passive "are made alive" (ζῳοποιηθήσονται). The passive indicates that Christians are raised by God, as Christ is raised by God. What is true of Christ is true of God's people "in Christ." "Just as . . . in the same way" (ὥσπερ . . . οὕτως καί) makes the comparison between those "in Adam" and those "in Christ."

It is important, though, to note just how the correspondence in these two verses functions. The dead with whom Paul is concerned have been identified in v. 18. They are those who are "in Christ" who, on the Corinthian view, would seem to have perished. In fact, however, they will be "made alive." Paul is not suggesting that all die and all rise. The key identifiers are "in Adam" and "in Christ." All in Adam die, and all who are "in Christ" are made alive. Paul is not therefore thinking of the *same* people. Nor is he thinking of the general resurrection, a point made forcefully by Héring: "Not all men, but Christians only who belong to the body of Christ form the new humanity."[9] Rather, he is thinking of the true future that believers possess and that he sums up in vv. 51–55. So Paul now asserts the true facts and explains the logic of v. 21 in v. 22 in the ABAB structure noted above.

Adam was the first man, and his sinful actions brought death into the world. Paul's argument here, as in Romans 5, depends on a historical Adam. Through this man death came to *all* people (Rom 5:12), for he represents all human beings. That is, the physical death related to God's judgment on sin is experienced by all people and is to be traced back to Adam. Though Paul does not explain this here, it is precisely for this reason that Christ's dealing with sin must go hand in hand with his bringing life and resurrection (15:3, 17, 56; 2 Cor 5:19, 21).

Paul uses the phrase "in Christ" on a number of occasions in this epistle and regularly throughout his epistles. His expression "in Adam" is by analogy. Christ stands at the head of his people. They are represented by him as their king and so, as it were, are caught up into him in a manner that allows the apostle generally to say of Christ's people anything that is true of Christ as king. In the messianic community, because it is true that Christ is raised from the dead, so it is true that all who are

---

9. Héring, *First Corinthians*, 165.

his (who "belong to Christ," v. 23) will be like him. By analogy Adam too functions as the representative head of all human beings. He died, so all die.

What is so staggering in Paul's argument here is that he emphasizes that Christ is truly "a man" (like Adam) and yet "in Christ" something so remarkable happens that the representative headship of Adam is broken. This is climactically seen in the resurrection. Even Christ was to be identified with Adam as a human being, for certainly these verses will not allow anyone to argue that Jesus was not a human being (δι' ἀνθρώπου). However, that Adamic humanity should have led to death. It did, but *it didn't end there*. By the action of God in Christ, at last, linkage to Adam's representational headship has been broken. How it is that God was able, in Christ, to break this linkage is well summed up in 2 Corinthians 5:21: "God made him who had no sin to be sin for us, so that in him we might become the righteousness of God." Thus, as head of *his* covenant people, the linkage to Adam is broken for his people as well. To ensure their resurrection, Christ identifies with their humanity and even their death, not just the physical death of age but the death of judgment by God. A few verses earlier, in 2 Corinthians 5:17, Paul uses a dynamic metaphor to describe the astonishing fact of this radical transformation of identity. He writes: "If anyone is in Christ, he is a new creation" (ESV).

15:23 But each one in his own order: Christ the firstfruit, then those who belong to Christ at his coming (ἕκαστος δὲ ἐν τῷ ἰδίῳ τάγματι· ἀπαρχὴ Χριστός, ἔπειτα οἱ τοῦ Χριστοῦ ἐν τῇ παρουσίᾳ αὐτοῦ). Paul continues to think here of Jesus as the representative head of his people; that is, in his role

as messianic King, the Christ. Where Christ goes first, his people follow. His resurrection life makes possible their resurrection life. The genitive (τοῦ Χριστοῦ) implies "belonging to" or being "owned by" and finds an interesting parallel in the use of the genitive Καίσαρος ("of Caesar") in describing slaves who belonged to the Emperor.[10] The word "order" (τάγμα) is a strange word for Paul to use here and could easily be translated "rank." Its primary denotation is of a military grouping such as a division or detachment of soldiers or a ranking among soldiers. It is a New Testament *hapax legomenon*[11] and may come to Paul's mind because of the military image he is about to attach to Christ's rule that leads to the destruction of his enemies (v. 25). Additionally, he probably already has in mind the allusions he is about to make to the messianic Psalms 110 and 8 in vv. 25 and 27. The fact of the matter is that Paul deals in these verses with an "ordering" of events and people as he builds to his climax that "God may be all in all" (v. 28). This understanding of an "ordering" and ranking by God in what is happening is reflected further in the six occurences of the verb "to be subject to" (ὑποτάσσω) in vv. 27–28.

The singular ("in his own order," ἐν τῷ ἰδίῳ τάγματι) is used to refer to the two separate orders: Christ, and those who are Christ's. The order Paul describes is one of *rank*. The first in rank is the Messiah, who leads the way and represents his people. He is then followed by "those who belong to Christ" (οἱ τοῦ Χριστοῦ). His people rank second in order to their king. It is from *this* fact that we also find an inevitable *temporal* order of Christ's resurrection needing to precede that of his people.

---

10. Evidenced in papyri of the first-century BC to the first-century AD. See Adolf Deissmann, *Light from the Ancient East: The New Testament Illustrated by Recently Discovered Texts of the Graeco-Roman World*, rev. ed. (New York: George H. Doran, 1927), 382.

11. Cf. 2 Sam 23:13 LXX, a "detachment" (τάγμα) of Philistines; 1 Clem. 37:3, "not all are soldiers or captains . . . but each has his own place" (ἐν τῷ ἰδίῳ τάγματι). A related word (τάξις) is used in 1 Cor 14:40 to describe "orderliness" in worship.

He is the firstfruit, and this continues the idea from v. 20. They will be raised at Christ's "coming."

Christ's "coming" also has strong and clear kingly connotations. Paul speaks of Christ's "coming" (παρουσία) only here and in 1 and 2 Thessalonians (1 Thess 2:19, 3:13; 4:15; 5:23; 2 Thess 2:1, 8). The word has a number of meanings.[12] In Philippians 2:12 there is an example of the word simply meaning "being present at." At other times it can mean "arrival" much like we might talk of a friend "coming this afternoon" (cf. 2 Cor 7:6; Phil 1:26). Two other more technical senses of the word also appear in Greek literature. Firstly, there is the use of the word to describe the coming of a "hidden divinity, who makes his presence felt by a revelation of his power, or whose presence is celebrated in the cult."[13] Then it also becomes "the official term for the visit of a person of high rank" like emperors and kings visiting their dominions. There is even reference to some being taxed to pay for an Emperor's "coming," which would be a time of great extravagance.[14] This is not dissimilar to the idea of Zechariah 9:9 where people are urged to come out and shout and rejoice as the king, mounted on a donkey, comes to his people (though παρουσία is not used in the LXX of this verse).

Paul is concerned that the people who have not seen the resurrection understand the way things are to happen. Christ has been raised, and this makes possible the resurrection of his people. However, this will happen at his "coming," that is, when he appears as king.[15] The fact that Paul speaks of Christ "coming" in this way is a direct challenge to the Imperial cult.[16] At the arrival of the King *all* other powers will be defeated, including the power of the Caesars to whom so many "belong" and who have been used to arriving among people surrounded by pomp and grandeur. So Paul speaks of the time of Christ's return.

15:24 Then [is] the end, when he delivers up the kingdom to [him who is] God and Father, when he has destroyed every rule and every power and authority (εἶτα τὸ τέλος, ὅταν παραδιδῷ τὴν βασιλείαν τῷ θεῷ καὶ πατρί, ὅταν καταργήσῃ πᾶσαν ἀρχὴν καὶ πᾶσαν ἐξουσίαν καὶ δύναμιν). The resurrection of God's people happens at Christ's "coming," as the kingdom is delivered to God. All others who claim to have dominion, such as the imperial Roman authorities, will be destroyed. There is no need to see "then" as introducing a third matter in the "order" above, as some have suggested. The ordering or ranking has to do with Christ and his people in v. 23, not with temporal sequence. "Then" (εἶτα) often has some sense of following on logically from what has just been said. This was noted in vv. 5 and 7 above. So there is no need to see a gap of time between the end of v. 23 and the start of v. 24. As we shall see below, some suggest that because there is a time gap between Christ's resurrection and the resurrection of those "in Christ," there is also a time gap between that resurrection and the final handing over of the kingdom by Christ to God (see toward the end of comments

---

12. BDAG 780–81.

13. Ibid. Cf. Josephus, *Ant.* 3.80; 9.55.

14. BDAG 781. Deissmann, *Light from the Ancient East*, 372–75, notes considerable evidence of this use of the word. See also more recently Horsley, *New Documentss*, 4:167–68.

15. A question arises as to whether Paul's view of the timing of the resurrection of those who have died in the faith developed between his writing here in ch. 15 and his writing in 2 Cor 5, where he appears to suggest that the resurrected body is given immediately upon death rather than all having to wait

for the parousia. For a useful summary of the arguments on both sides of this debate, see P. Woodbridge, "Time of Receipt of the Resurrection Body—A Pauline Inconsistency?," in Burke and Elliott, *Paul and the Corinthians*, 241–58. Woodbridge concludes there is no inconsistency and that 2 Cor 5 can also be understood to mean that the resurrection of all Christians is at the parousia.

16. On Christ's coming, see also N. T. Wright, *Surprised by Hope* (London: SPCK, 2007), 136–49.

on vv. 25–26 below). There is little, if any, evidence within this text to support such a view.

The matter at hand remains Paul's concern to demonstrate to "some" Corinthians that there *is* a resurrection of the dead. That this happens through the resurrection of Christ has been explained, but self-evidently people still die, and so the question of "when" is critical to his argument. The answer is simple: it happens at his "coming." This is a time for which Christians are now waiting. As Paul put it in 1:7–8, "while awaiting the revealing of our Lord Jesus Christ . . . on the day of our Lord Jesus Christ" (see comments there). This time of Christ's "coming" is the "end" (τέλος), meaning the close of things as we now know them. When the resurrection of believers happens, the end comes and a new age begins, as Paul describes so vividly elsewhere (Rom 8:21–23).[17] Though we have the firstfruits in Jesus Christ, the final harvest at the conclusion to this age is awaited, and those who deny the resurrection must understand that this age must be waited out. Paul will go on to address the matter of those "in Christ" who die before the "coming" in vv. 51–55. After all, "death" has yet to be "swallowed up in victory" (v. 54).

However, that end time, though coinciding with Christ's "coming," is not known, and so Paul uses the indefinite "when" (ὅταν) with the present subjunctive (παραδιδῷ). We could translate this as "whenever," but that is simply too vague. Paul knows when it is going to happen in terms of what events accompany it, but he doesn't know the time. This will happen "when [Christ] has destroyed [καταργήσῃ, an aorist subjunctive]" all rivals, another event that is anticipated but the time

of which is unknown. The two subordinate clauses thus describe further what happens at the end at the "coming" and tells us that Christ "must reign" until these things happen.

It is important to keep Paul's careful structure in mind as we examine his flow of thought through v. 28:

A Christ delivers the kingdom to God the Father (v. 24)
   B He [Christ] must reign until all enemies are subjected (v. 25) (with appeal to Ps 110)
      C The last enemy is death (v. 26)
   B[1] He [God] subjects all things under his [the Son's] feet (v. 27) (with appeal to Ps 8)
A[1] Christ himself is subjected to the Father (v. 28)

First, then, we see what Paul expects to happen, before returning to ask in what sense Christ "reigns." The first clause speaks of when Christ "delivers up the kingdom to [him who is] God and Father."[18] The "kingdom" has been mentioned in 4:20 and 6:9–10.[19] Here it refers to God's rule of this earth that has been exercised by Christ since the resurrection and exaltation. Since there is debate (see below) about the timing of Christ's rule and the extent of that rule, it is important to see that Paul assumes this rule is already in place in the way described in Ephesians 1:21 where Christ has been given "all rule and authority." First Corinthians 15:27–28 also makes it clear that God has indeed subjected all things to Jesus and his rule. Even the second clause here in v. 24 implies this, for it is Christ who will have "destroyed every rule and every power and authority" as the end comes. This final exercise of Christ's judgment is the final great act of *this* age and becomes one of the clear

---

17. Lietzmann, *An Die Korinther I–II*, 81, argues unsuccessfully that Paul has in mind a third matter in the "order" when he speaks of the "end" (τέλος). The first is Christ's resurrection, the second is the resurrection of those in Christ, and the third is the resurrection of the "rest" (which is how he translates

τέλος). This word cannot bear that weight.

18. The Greek here is ambiguous: "to God and to Father" (τῷ θεῷ καὶ πατρί).

19. See further, "In Depth: The Kingdom of God" following comments on 6:9a.

evidences that the "end" has come. It is heralded with a trumpet (see on 15:52 below), death is finally vanquished, and the dead will be raised.

The end comes when he "has destroyed" (καταργέω) every rule. Paul has used this verb on seven previous occasions (1:28; 2:6; 6:13; 13:8 [2x], 10, 11). He will use it again at 15:26. It can mean "to bring to nothing" or "to destroy" and is used in this epistle consistently in a firmly eschatological context of the passing of "this age" (1:20). In this sense it relates to the final judgment, as we saw in 2:6 where Paul has already shown that the "rulers of this age are doomed to come to nothing." Being "brought to nothing" is what will happen to all people and things that belong to "this age" when this age is brought to an end at the "coming" of Christ. In 1:28 it will be all the accoutrements that go with "those who are perishing," their wisdom, pride, and so on, that will be brought to nothing. In 2:6 it is the "cross," that is, the gospel, that leads to the rulers "of this age" being brought to nothing. In chapters 1–2 it becomes clear that this is what is also meant, when applied to people, by the word "perishing" (1:18). Throughout, Paul works with the schema that "this age" is one that is "passing away" (7:31) and that the things and people and rulers of this age will come to nothing. The crucifixion and resurrection of Christ have inaugurated the dawning of the new age. The verdict of the end is already felt in the present as some "are perishing," and God, through Christ, is already tearing down the wisdom of this age. For this reason, the translation "has annihilated" is not unreasonable.[20] However, the word rarely if ever seems to have this

strength elsewhere in Greek,[21] and so here it has been translated as "to bring to nothing" or "to destroy" (see also 13:8–11).

The object of this work of Christ is "every rule and every power and authority" (πᾶσαν ἀρχὴν καὶ πᾶσαν ἐξουσίαν καὶ δύναμιν). It is most likely that in 2:6–8 ("rulers of this age"; cf. Rom 8:38), Paul has already shown us what he has in mind (see comments there). There it was seen that Paul was concerned with the ruling authorities who are set against God and his plans in Christ. Given the contrast that Paul surely draws between Christ as king and the imperial authorities of Rome, this makes sense of v. 24. These are the ones who "crucified the Lord of glory" (2:8), leaders who are "in Adam." Yet, while both Paul and the Corinthians are likely to think immediately of their current rulers, the statement is so broad that Paul may also be thinking of the powers of Satan that lie behind the rulers. This may even include the evil powers of injustice often incorporated into this world's political, legal, and economic structures. Indeed, the final enemy to be "brought to nothing" is "death" (v. 26).[22]

15:25–26 For he must reign until such time as he shall put all enemies under his feet. The last enemy [that is] being brought to nothing [is] death (δεῖ γὰρ αὐτὸν βασιλεύειν ἄχρι οὗ θῇ πάντας τοὺς ἐχθροὺς ὑπὸ τοὺς πόδας αὐτοῦ. ἔσχατος ἐχθρὸς καταργεῖται ὁ θάνατος). Christ already reigns and does so until his enemies are finally subjugated and death is vanquished. That he "must reign" reminds the reader that all this is carried out under God the Father's sovereignty over all things. Indeed, Scripture witnesses to this, as Paul alludes to Psalm 8:1

---

20. Conzelmann, *1 Corinthians*, 271; Thiselton, *1 Corinthians*, 1231.

21. The examples in MM 331 use the word in a much weaker sense, such as to "hinder" or to "make idle." See also BDAG 525.

22. Fee, *1 Corinthians*, 754, goes far beyond the evidence in insisting that Paul uses this terminology to refer to "spiritual powers" and that v. 25 makes it "certain" that the defeat of the "powers" referred to is death. If that is all Paul had meant, why did he use such broad terminology and why refer to "all his enemies"?

in v. 27. "Until such time as he shall put" attempts to convey the meaning of the relative pronoun followed by the aorist subjunctive (ἄχρι οὗ θῇ). The aorist subjunctive is often employed to convey a summary and/or punctiliar verbal aspect, while the fact that the timing itself remains indefinite is also conveyed by the subjunctive. The present, passive "being brought to nothing" (καταργεῖται) is also difficult to convey in English without it simply sounding like it has a perfective rather than imperfective aspect.[23] Paul probably wishes to convey that though the climax of Christ's reign is the final defeat of death, this is an action that began with Christ's death and resurrection.[24] The above translation "being brought to nothing" seeks to reflect the continuous sense of the verb.

Paul alludes to Psalm 110:1 (it is not an exact quotation, though very close to Ps 109:1 LXX).[25] This text is used elsewhere in the New Testament and had already been regarded as a messianic psalm well before the time of Christ. In the psalm, God subjects the enemies to the "Lord," who is the Davidic king. This raises the question about who the subject is of the verb "shall put" (θῇ) in 15:25. The most natural understanding logically and grammatically in the light of v. 24 is that this is Jesus Christ. However, in the light of Psalm 110:1 some have suggested that the reference here is to God himself.[26] Christ reigns until God subjects Christ's enemies, as in Psalm 110. In v. 28 Paul is explicit, as he quotes Psalm 8, that God is involved in subjecting things to Christ. In the end, it is perhaps best to take the more natural grammatical

reading and assume that Christ is the subject. The very fact that Paul does not *quote* Psalm 110 may support this.

From these verses it is clear that in the movement of history toward "the end," Christ already reigns. Verse 25 adds that "he must reign" (δεῖ . . . αὐτὸν βασιλεύειν) until his enemies are destroyed, thus addressing the time leading up to the delivering of the kingdom to God. This raises the next question of whether there is a gap between the time of v. 24 and v. 25 and when this reign of Christ begins. We have already suggested that grammatically there is no time lapse indicated. It has also been clear throughout this epistle that Christ is Lord *now* and that he rules *now*. The "coming" indeed is not a coming to be Lord but the arrival or appearance of the one who is the King.

So Paul focuses his argument in v. 26. The resurrection (and exaltation) of Christ has established his rule. He will continue to rule until he has subdued all his enemies and brought to nothing all those who are set against God. The final enemy to which this will apply is death itself. To those who deny the resurrection Paul is clear: no resurrection of Christ, no kingly rule, no lordship, no defeat of God's enemies, and no defeat of death (so no resurrection for anyone). Death would then remain victorious. But the fact is that Christ has been raised, does reign, and will defeat all of God's enemies including death, thus guaranteeing resurrection for those who are "in Christ." In v. 27 Paul will now expand this a little further as he adduces still more scriptural evidence, this time from Psalm 8.

---

23. Campbell, *Basics of Verbal Aspect*, 72–73.

24. Calvin, *First Corinthians*, 324: "Although that has begun to be fulfilled under the rule of Christ, it will not, however, be brought to absolute completeness until the last day."

25. On the use of Psalm 110 see Donald M. Hay, *Glory at the Right Hand: Psalm 110 in Early Christianity*, SBLMS (Nashville: Abingdon, 1973).

26. Barrett, *First Corinthians*, 358; Fitzmyer, *1 Corinthians*, 573, among others.

IN DEPTH: Is There Support for the Idea of Three Resurrections in 1 Corinthians 15:23–28 (Christ, Those in Christ, the Others Who Have Died)?

Some commentators approach this text from what is sometimes called a "premillennial" perspective. This perspective broadly teaches that when the risen Christ returns, his people are raised to rule with him on earth. He then rules on this earth for a thousand years, which may or may not be a figurative period of time, in line with the so-called "millennium" of Revelation 20. Then comes the time when those who are not the Lord's are raised for judgment, and death is vanquished. In Revelation 20:4 we read, "Also I saw the souls of those who had been beheaded for the testimony of Jesus. . . . They came to life and reigned with Christ for a thousand years" (ESV). This is described as the "first resurrection" (v. 5). At the end of that time Satan will be defeated publicly, and those who are "dead" are judged (v. 13). Then "death and Hades were thrown into the lake of fire" (v. 14). This is not the place to explain Revelation 20,[27] nor is it the place to comment on whether or not the author of Revelation saw the final defeat of death as at a separate time from the time of Christ's second coming. The question we face is whether this schema may be seen here in 1 Corinthians 15:20–28.

D. K. Lowery, in a brief commentary on 1 Corinthians, sums up how he and others read v. 24: "Following the resurrection of the church, another period intervenes until the end when Christ will deliver His kingdom to God the Father" (cf. Matt 13:42–43).[28] He then allows that some "dispute" any interval but is convinced that "chronological sequences" are involved that "may indeed be almost momentary (1 Cor 15:5) but then again they may be prolonged (cf. v. 23). If about 2000 years can elapse between the first and second phases . . . a millennium, between the second and third phases should cause no consternation."[29] Since Paul makes no mention at all of a thousand-year rule of Christ in this context of 1 Corinthians 15 and has no discussion at all of the resurrection of those who are not "in Christ" but rather clearly indicates that Christ's resurrection means that he rules and is Lord now, then it also would become necessary to ask how Christ's lordship now and then (in the millennial kingdom) would differ. Some argue that the second aspect of the lordship in the future is that he comes

---

27. For a simply stated amillennial perspective on Rev 20, see my commentary *Revelation: The Compassion and Protection of Christ*, Focus on the Bible (Ross-shire, UK: Christian Focus, 2008), 269ff.

28. D. K. Lowery, "1 Corinthians," in *The Bible Knowledge Commentary: An Exposition of the Scriptures by Dallas Seminary Faculty*, ed. John F. Walvoord and Roy B. Zuck, New Testament edition (Wheaton: Victor, 1983), 544.

29. Ibid.

visibly to reign on this earth with those who are "in him" and have been raised from the dead *before* "the end," when the new earth is finally ushered in. But if this picture emerges in this form in Scripture, it does not do so in this passage.

A detailed exegetical argument in support not of premillennialism *per se* but of a messianic kingdom *after* the resurrection of those "in Christ," and *before* "the end" and the final defeat of death is offered by Larry J. Kreitzer. He concludes that this passage "probably does reflect belief" in a "temporary, Messianic Kingdom . . . though this does mean that it is a modification to the rest of Paul's teaching on the matter."[30] His exegesis, however, has been well challenged by many, including Joseph Plevnik and especially C. E. Hill.[31] Hill argues that the temporary reign of Christ begins at Christ's ascension. Hill points to the references to Psalms 110 and 8, where the Lord is on the throne until the enemies are defeated and that he has been set over creation. He shows how these two psalms are brought together in several other contexts in the New Testament and consistently assume the *present status* of Christ as Lord. Exegetically he argues that v. 24 and v. 25 "cannot be seen as the beginning point of the reign" precisely because "he must reign *until*"![32] At the end of a detailed examination of this passage Hill concludes, "Christ's own resurrection . . . thus begins his heavenly session, and the resurrection of his people marks the completion of this victory and the closure of the work of his royal dispensation. When . . . the last stronghold of opposition is removed, a tranquilized universe is presented to God the Father by the victorious Son. . . . Then indeed will God be all in all."[33] One further comment may be added. Difficult as v. 26 is to translate, the verb is in the present tense, which, if nothing else, at least conveys here an imperfective aspect.[34] The last enemy, which will ultimately be brought to nothing at *the end*, is even now *being* brought to nothing. Paul intends us to understand that this began with Jesus's own death and resurrection and continues *while Christ reigns* (for he *must* go on reigning, v. 25) until the end.

How this passage fits in with a premillennialist position will need to be determined by those adopting that view.[35] But its apparent support for a "third

---

30. Larry J. Kreitzer, *Jesus and God in Paul's Eschatology*, JSNTSup 19 (Sheffield: JSOT, 1987), 168. For supporting exegesis, see 142–64.

31. Joseph Plevnik, *Paul and the Parousia: An Exegetical and Theological Investigation* (Peabody, MA: Hendrickson, 1997). Hill, "Paul's Understanding of Christ's Kingdom," 297–320. See also the extended discussion of 15:23–28 in Ridderbos, *Paul*, 556–62.

32. Hill, "Paul's Understanding of Christ's Kingdom," 315.

33. Ibid., 320.

34. More accurately in the Greek: "The last enemy being destroyed [is] death." Thiselton, *1 Corinthians*, 1234, conveys this continuous sense with "doomed to be brought to nothing."

35. Darrell L. Bock, *Jesus according to Scripture* (Grand Rapids: Baker, 2002), 588–90, offers a useful overview from a premillennial perspective. He seeks to demonstrate how, drawing on Rev 20, the "setting up [of] an intermediate kingdom before the new heaven and earth" may take its place alongside Paul's teaching in 1 Cor 15:25–28 and Rom 11.

stage," a temporary kingdom of rule on this earth for a millennium *after* the parousia, is perhaps exegetically unconvincing.

15:27 For "he has put all things in subjection under his feet." But when it says, "All things are put in subjection," it is clear that he is excepted who put all things in subjection to him (πάντα γὰρ ὑπέταξεν ὑπὸ τοὺς πόδας αὐτοῦ. ὅταν δὲ εἴπῃ ὅτι πάντα ὑποτέτακται, δῆλον ὅτι ἐκτὸς τοῦ ὑποτάξαντος αὐτῷ τὰ πάντα). Paul explains that it is God who "has put all things in subjection." In his "ordering" of all, God is the one who raises the dead, and Christ is working out God's plans for the subjection of all things and the resurrection of all "in Christ" to the crowning glory that should be theirs, as Psalm 8 points out. "It says" (εἴπῃ) could be "he says." "It" refers to "Scriptures" and "he" would refer to "God." God speaks in Scripture so Paul could use either (cf. Rom 11:12; Gal 4:30 with Rom 10:8; Eph 5:14). Paul quotes here from Psalm 8:6 (8:7 LXX).[36] In terms of structure he returns to the matter raised in v. 25 that all things must be subjected to him (see outline above in "Structure"). The last part of the quotation repeats exactly the words Paul has used in v. 25b, which suggests that Paul has, in part, employed Psalm 8 to show again that what he is saying is "according to the Scriptures."

Psalm 8 speaks to the rule of created humanity over creation itself. Humankind has been crowned with glory and honor by God, and the psalmist says in praise of God: "You have put all things under his feet" (v. 6 ESV). However, as the author to Hebrews notes in quoting Psalm 8 at much greater length,

"We do not yet see everything in subjection to him" (Heb 2:8 ESV). However, "we do see Jesus . . . now crowned with glory and honor" (2:9). What was prophesied for humanity is now seen in one man, Jesus. Paul is working with the same Adam-Christ schema. Where Adam failed, Christ succeeds. In Ephesians 1:20–23 where Psalms 110 and 8 are again brought together, it is expressly laid out that in this role, as the one to whom all things have been subjected, Christ represents his people. He is "head over everything *for* the church" (Eph 1:22).

In a real sense, the giving of such complete dominion by God the Father to Jesus Christ is God's own fulfillment of his purposes described in Genesis 1:27–30 and in Psalms 8 and 110. "In Christ" humanity has had all things put in subjection to it. But one seemingly unnecessary caveat remains. Paul writes "It is clear that" (δῆλον ὅτι) God himself is excluded from this subjection of all things to Christ. At no point is God the Father's ultimate and total sovereignty over all things and all people ever to be questioned. It is not that "in Christ" humanity comes to have sovereignty even over the Father himself.

There has been some speculation as to why Paul felt it necessary to say something this obvious. More than likely it is simply because he is moving to his conclusion of these ideas in v. 28 and to the nature of the end goal. What will *the end* look like? It is not that God the Father will be subject to the one representing all raised humanity but that

---

36. Paul has changed the second-person singular of the LXX ("you have put all things") to a third-person singular for the sake of his argument.

all "in Christ" will, together with their king, be subjected to God. Structurally this is where v. 28 now leads as we return to the ideas of v. 24. There Christ's goal is to deliver the kingdom to God the Father. Here in v. 28 Christ, to whom all has been subjected, fulfills the Father's goal that all will be subjected to God, including Christ as representative king of all God's people.

15:28 But when everything has been subjected to him, then also the Son himself will be subjected to him who subjected everything to him, in order that God may be all in all (ὅταν δὲ ὑποταγῇ αὐτῷ τὰ πάντα, τότε [καὶ][37] αὐτὸς ὁ υἱὸς ὑποταγήσεται τῷ ὑποτάξαντι αὐτῷ τὰ πάντα, ἵνα ᾖ ὁ θεὸς [τὰ] πάντα ἐν πᾶσιν). Paul now describes the ultimate goal of Christ's victory over his enemies, sin and death. Christ will, at the last, present all to the Father, including himself, in a final subjection or subordination that brings ultimate and total glory to God.[38] "Everything" seeks to keep the singular in English with the third-singular verb (ὑποταγῇ). As in v. 24 above, the fact is certain that all things will be subjected to God, but the timing is uncertain (ὅταν). This is the only place where "Son" is found in the absolute. It is likely Paul deliberately uses "Son," in contrast with "God and Father" in v. 24, for two reasons.

First, vv. 24 and 28 form "A" in the structure and so contrast well with each other:

A. Christ delivers the kingdom to *God the Father* (v. 24)

. . . . .

A. The Son [Christ] himself is subjected to *him* [the Father] (v. 28)

More importantly, Paul probably deliberately wishes to clarify the distinction of the roles in the Godhead within the contrast of these two verses. There is no subordination*ism* implied here. Paul refers to the sovereign God's plans to win a people for himself and deliver them to a kingdom that is entirely his. Christ's role, as Son, reveals something of the inner workings of the one true God. The Father "subjects" all to the Son but is then also the agent of the subjection of the Son to the Father: "The Son himself *will be subjected* to him" (ὑποταγήσεται, future passive). Of course, at the completion of Christ's work, Christ is willingly involved in the subjection of all things, including himself, to the Father, just as he has been throughout his work of redemption. However, it does seem to us that Paul is pointing us to a fascinating aspect of the nature of Christ's sonship. That sonship (noting again the absolute use of "Son") is, in the end, to submit always to the Father. (See further below.) Sampley is surely right to say, "As he sketches the grandeur of God's culminating purposes, Paul's language drifts toward doxology."[39]

The meaning of the purpose clause "in order that God may be all in all" (ἵνα ᾖ ὁ θεὸς [τὰ] πάντα

---

37. The καί is omitted by B D* F G 0243, 33, 1175, 1739, Vulgate (among others); it is found here in ℵ A D² K L P Ψ and in several miniscules and 𝔐. Here it would either mean "also" or "even" ("then even the Son").

38. We have already noted the idea of God's "ordering" in 15:23. The verb "to subject to" (ὑποτάσσω) appeared in 14:32, 34. In that context, as here in 15:28, the idea of the "ordering" of things is also clearly present. Thiselton, *1 Corinthians*, 1235, writes: "The important point, however, is its connection with τάσσω and τάγμα or τάξις, *that which is ordered*, with ὑπό, i.e., *sub-ordinate*." The repetition of this verb (six times in vv. 27–28) is initiated by the scriptural quotation, but reflects

Paul's concern with the ordering of these events and people and the eventual "subordination" of all to the Father. As Wright says, "Of course, the fact that Paul says 'the son himself will be placed in proper order under the one who placed everything in order under him' can be summarized with the *word* 'subordination' without implying the overtones which that word later came to carry" (Wright, *Paul and the Faithfulness of God*, 737n353).

39. J. Paul Sampley, "The First Letter to the Corinthians," in *The New Interpreter's Bible*, ed. Leander E. Keck, 12 vols. (Nashville: Abingdon, 2002), 10:982.

ἐν πᾶσιν) is not immediately clear though the intent seems clear enough. The goal of all Christ's work, the conquest of all God's enemies and the resurrection of the dead, is that all may truly be subordinated to God for God's great glory. At the end of this age all things, that is, "everything" (neuter, τὰ πάντα) in the universe including all God's people, like the Son himself, will be subordinated to the Father. All evil will be defeated, and God's people will live in the presence of and for the God who has so loved them. Nothing ever again will challenge the rule of God.

This section started by saying, "In fact Jesus Christ has been raised." The end result of God's overcoming death in Christ, and of Christ's vanquishing all God's enemies, is that God reigns supreme. If there is no resurrection of the dead, it is the very reign of God himself that has been denied.

IN DEPTH: The Subjection of the Son

Verse 28 has given rise to much discussion concerning the relationship of the Father and the Son. As we have noted, the absolute use of "Son" draws attention to the differentiation of these persons of the Trinity. In v. 24 the Son "delivers" the kingdom to "God the Father." In v. 25 that he "must reign until . . ." points to the necessity of the Son to fulfill the Father's will. It is the Father in v. 27 who subjects all things to the Son. It is once all this has happened that "then the Son himself will be subjected," where, once again, the Father is the agent of the subjection. The complexity of the argument for trinitarian theology has been noted by many. Here it must suffice simply to note the theological issues that have sometimes been raised and to comment briefly.

Undoubtedly, the subjection of the Son to the Father in these verses must not be ignored. These verses at least imply and have traditionally been used to help argue for the functional subordination of the Son to the Father, beyond simply the time of his redemptive work on this earth. In other words, it is argued that in v. 28 the Son is seen to be subjected to the Father in all eternity; that is, it is part of what it is for Jesus to be the "Son" that he has a relationship of submission to the Father. Of course, even if this is the case, most commentators[40] who address this rapidly go on to affirm with orthodox Christianity across the centuries that the Son is revealed as one in "substance, power, and eternity" with the Father (*Westminster Confession of Faith* 2.3). In orthodox and Nicene terms the further affirmation is necessary of the belief in the "one Lord Jesus Christ, the only begotten Son of God, begotten of the Father before all worlds,

---

40. There are, of course, some who believe that in this verse and elsewhere the apostle teaches the "essential," eternal subordination of the Son to the Father and so some form of apparent subordinationism. For example, Hay's view approaches this when he says, "It is impossible to avoid the impression that Paul is operating with what would later come to be called a subordi-nationist christology" (*First Corinthians*, 266). John V. Dahms, "The Subordination of the Son," *JETS* 37 (1994): 351–64, argues against the view that the "subordination is merely economic" and affirms "that it is essential and eternal." Sometimes there is no doubt a confusion of terms when the word "essence" and "essential" are used in such discussions.

God of God" (Nicene Creed). The question highlighted by v. 28 in particular is, then, whether it is part of that eternal (*functional*) relationship of the Son to the Father that the Son is subjected by the Father to the Father. Fee, for example, though arguing otherwise, admits, "It could easily be argued that [vv.25–28] implies some form of 'eternal submission' of the Son to the Father."[41] Barrett writes of this verse that "man's dominion is being restored, but its security lies only in *the unvarying submission of Jesus the Son to his Father*."[42]

The alternative to this is to see this subjection only in terms of Christ's *role* as Savior and thus limited to matters of the redemption of his people and his incarnation. However, as Charles Hodge notes in his extended wrestling with these verses as to how the Son can be coequal with the Father (as described above) and yet be subject to the Father, this latter view may be inadequate as an explanation of what Paul is saying.[43] The problem v. 28 especially gives rise to in such discussions is that it seems to describe the end of time and the *eternal* future in which the Son is in "subjection." That subjection seems to be part and parcel of the eternal future in which God is "all in all." Hodge insists: "We know that the verbally inconsistent propositions, the Son is subject to the Father, and, the Son is equal with the Father, are both true. In one sense he [Christ] is subject, in another sense he is equal. The son of a king may be the equal of his father in every attribute of his nature, though officially inferior. So the eternal Son of God may be coequal with the Father, though officially subordinate."[44]

It seems to us that J. I. Packer captures both the general biblical teaching, but especially the position at least hinted at in 1 Corinthians 15:24–28 when he cites John 5 and John 8 and writes:

> It is the nature of the second person of the Trinity to acknowledge the authority and submit to the good pleasure of the first. That is why He declares Himself to be the Son, and the first person to be the Father. Though co-equal with the Father in eternity, power and glory, it is natural to Him to play the Son's part, and find all His joy in doing the Father's will, just as it is natural to the first person of the Trinity to plan and initiate the works of the Godhead and natural to the third person to proceed from the Father and the Son to do their joint bidding. Thus the obedience of the God-man to the Father while He was on earth was not a new relationship occasioned by the incarnation, but the continuation in time of the eternal relationship between the Son and the Father in heaven.[45]

---

41. Gordon Fee, *Pauline Christology: An Exegetical-Theological Study* (Peabody, MA: Hendrickson, 2007), 113. He goes on to say that "it is unlikely that Paul is thinking of Christ's *person* here, but rather of his *role* in salvation history."

42. Barrett, *First Corinthians*, 361 (emphasis added).

43. Hodge, *First Corinthians*, 333–36.

44. Ibid., 334.

45. J. I. Packer, *Knowing God* (London: Hodder and Stoughton, 1973), 64. For a wider defense of the view that the Son is eternally subordinate to the Father, see Steven D. Kovach and

Unfortunately, this genuinely interesting and important discussion has become obscured recently in an argument between those who have sought to use the subordination of the Son to the Father, or lack of it, in arguments for or against the highly emotive debate about the subordination of women to men. Since the question of the subordination of women to men is clearly *not* the subject of 15:24–28, it is important to examine the texts for what they actually say. Only then should those who wish to do so move on to argue for possible applications of the resultant teaching. Either way, it is clearly incorrect to label those who see v. 28 pointing to an eternal *functional* role of the Son in his submission to the Father as necessarily espousing the early heresy of "subordination*ism*." Such is to misunderstand the early heresy and to dismiss too easily the serious theological wrestling that is needed as we approach a text like this.

In the end, Robertson and Plummer may have stated the obvious: "The passage is a summary of the mysteries which our present knowledge does not enable us to explain, and which our present faculties, perhaps, do not enable us to understand."[46] We would add that perhaps all one can do with certainty after reading 15:28 is to follow where Paul would take us and to bow in awe before the Father, for we yet await the time when *we shall know fully, even as we have been fully known* (13:12).

Theology in Application

The Conquering King

That death is the great "enemy" of all people has been clear since Genesis 3. Normal existence experiences death as a great enemy. It may be death in old age or death that comes as a result of illness or natural disaster. It may be death in war or at the hands of a murderer, or even judicial death, but it is always and for all the great enemy. Its power is precisely that all who are human beings "in Adam" are under its grip. Even for those who suffer and see death as possibly an "escape" from torment, death is still the final and terrible end. Paul's central statement in this section, that the last enemy that must be dealt with is death (v. 26), is almost a truism. Yet here Paul addresses this head-on and appeals to the risen Lord as the one who overcomes this enemy.

The relationship between life and death and righteousness and evil is found frequently in the Old Testament. Ezekiel 18 provides an extended prophetic word on

---

Peter R. Schemm Jr., "A Defense of the Doctrine of the Eternal Subordination of the Son," *JETS* 42 (1999): 461–76.

46. Robertson and Plummer, *First Corinthians*, 357.

death and life and on God as the king who judges and so determines death and life. In that passage the great heart of God is revealed as a heart that does not desire to see death (18:23, 32). He desires that people should turn from sin and live. Passages and discussions like this in Scripture contribute background to Paul's teaching here. In 1 Corinthians 15:20–28 God, who is judge of all, is determined "in Christ" to see sin dealt with and life extended to many, as life has been extended to Christ in the resurrection. Where Christ has gone, his people will go. In his resurrection the possibility of resurrection for his people is secured.

Paul insists that the "order" here is critical. Christ is the firstfruits, so this means there will be others at the time of the king's "coming." The verses are replete with such references and allusions to Christ's kingly rule. We see it in Paul's repetitious use of "Christ" (Messiah) four times in four verses. It is seen in his representative function ("in Christ") for those who "belong" to him and in the references to the "kingdom." Yet all this is used by Paul in this section to build up to his description of the climactic battles the king will fight and win. He rules even now as he destroys and will finally destroy powers and authorities. Finally, he will even destroy death itself. This leads to the talk of his rule over all things and his final great "victory," perhaps recalling King David's words concerning the Lord's power, victory, and kingdom (1 Chr 29:10–11). For Paul, the result of the victory is that the king who has been the obedient Son submits himself and all things to the Father.

Talk of Christ's destruction of all that is evil and of victory and subjugation is countercultural in the present world. Furthermore, it is difficult to talk meaningfully of Christ's return and of his victory and glory, if sin itself has been treated too lightly in the presentation of the gospel. Yet the joy of this great picture that Paul paints of Christ's final victory over sin and death must be understood against the backdrop that Paul provides. The glory of that day when Christ the King has conquered death and leads his people to the Father in complete surrender is like none other presented in Scripture. In a world where people fear evil, fear their government, fear disease, and fear so much in general, it is vital we preach again of sin and death in order that the need for and joy of resurrection and glory may be understood. It is vital that people clearly hear that the goal of the resurrection is "that God may be all in all."

1 Corinthians 15:29–34

Literary Context

Having argued positively for the resurrection and laid out its end goal, in this section Paul returns to a similar form of argument to that seen in 15:13–19. He speaks of the absurdity of denying the resurrection in relation to two matters.[1] The first concerns the practice of baptism for the dead, which would be pointless if there is no resurrection. The second is more personal, in which Paul uses the first-person singular and argues that his own preparedness to sacrifice his life for the gospel would be utterly in vain if there is no resurrection. Paul's summary in vv. 32b–34 then applies this to the way life should be lived in this age. If there is no resurrection, then sacrifice of life is useless and people might as well live in whatever way they wish: "Let us eat and drink, for tomorrow we die" (v. 32). At last Paul shows clearly how teaching about the resurrection relates back even to the ethical issues that he has addressed earlier in the letter. The resurrection of necessity requires the believer to take sin seriously. In an ironic gesture to a subject that has preoccupied him through much of this epistle, Paul returns to those who would claim superior "knowledge" and says in v. 34, "Do not sin, for some have no *knowledge* of God. I say this to your shame." The resurrection therefore must have a direct impact on how Christians live in the present. In 15:35–49 Paul will return to a defense of the resurrection and do so in the form of responding to questions.

---

1. This may be regarded as a second *refutatio*.

Main Idea

If there is no resurrection of the dead, then much of what Christians do is foolish. Even upright moral living is foolish, so Christians must sober up and retreat from such stupidity and sin.

Translation

1 Corinthians 15:29–34

29a		Otherwise,
b	Rhetorical question	**what will those who are baptized for the sake of the dead do?**
c	Condition (protasis)	If the dead are not raised at all,
d	Rhetorical question	**why then are they baptized for their sake?**
30a	Expansion of v. 29	Likewise,
b	Rhetorical question	**why are we in danger every hour?**
31a	Oath	**Every day I die!**
b		**[This I swear] by my pride in you,**
c	Description	which I have in Christ Jesus our Lord.
32a	Condition	If, for merely human reasons, I fought with wild animals ⤵ in Ephesus,
b	Rhetorical question	**what gain would there be for me?**
c	Condition	If the dead are not raised,
d	Proverb (assertion)	"Let us eat and drink, for tomorrow we die." [Isa 22:13]
33a	Exhortation	**Do not deceive yourselves:**
b	Proverb (assertion)	**bad companionships corrupt good ways.**
34a	Exhortation	**Sober up,**
b	Circumstance	as is fitting,
c	Exhortation	and **do not sin,**
d	Basis	for **some have no knowledge of God.**
e	Assertion	**I say this to your shame.**

Structure

This section divides into three as Paul further demonstrates the absurdity of Christians denying the resurrection of the dead. This time he makes his argument from the potential consequences of such a denial. (1) Paul appeals to the nature of baptism (v. 29). The whole idea of baptism is a nonsense if there is no resurrection of the dead. (2) He appeals to his own suffering for the sake of the gospel (vv. 30–32b). There is no point at all in "dying every day" if there is no resurrection. He might as well simply live for today without regard for the gospel. (3) He appeals to them to live lives appropriate to those who believe in the resurrection (vv. 32c–33). (4) He orders them to stop sinning (v. 34).

Exegetical Outline

IX. **The Gospel of the Resurrection of Christ and His People (15:1–58)**

  A. The Facts of the Gospel Secured by the Resurrection of Christ (15:1–11)

  B. **The Truth of the Resurrection (15:12–34)**

    1. The Absurdity of Denying the Resurrection (15:12–19)

    2. Christ Has Been Raised, So in Him Shall All Be Made Alive (15:20–28)

➡   3. **Practical Consequences of Denying the Resurrection (15:29–34)**

      a. There Is No Point in the Practice of Baptism for the Dead (15:29)

      b. There is No Point in Suffering for the Gospel (15:30–32b)

      c. The Conduct of Christian Life Matters (15:32c–33)

      d. Application: Do Not Go on Sinning (15:34)

Explanation of the Text

15:29 Otherwise, what will those who are baptized for the sake of the dead do? If the dead are not raised at all, why then are they baptized for their sake? (Ἐπεὶ τί ποιήσουσιν οἱ βαπτιζόμενοι ὑπὲρ τῶν νεκρῶν; εἰ ὅλως νεκροὶ οὐκ ἐγείρονται, τί καὶ βαπτίζονται ὑπὲρ αὐτῶν;). Paul returns to the discussion of vv. 12–19 and points out further consequences of adopting the position of some Corinthians that there is no resurrection of the dead. The first argument is to demonstrate the complete futility in "baptism for the dead." The point Paul is making is clear. Baptism has to do with new life and resurrection (cf. Rom 6:3–4; Gal 3:27–29; Col 2:12). To deny the resurrection makes this prac- tice of baptism for the dead redundant and even foolish superstition. The first rhetorical question in this *ad hominem* argument uses the future tense (ποιήσουσιν) and may mean "what will those who are baptized . . . do?"; that is, what will they do once they have understood that the baptism is meaningless if there is no resurrection of the dead. A second alternative is that it may mean "what will they achieve by this baptism?"

Since the point is clear, it is tempting to leave this verse without further comment, for there have been too many pages written about this practice of baptism for the dead, when it must be admitted that there is remarkably little to go on other than speculation. Some of this speculation is fanciful, and some perhaps a little more persuasive. The fact is that we have no certain idea as to what practice Paul was referring, and there is no attempt in the text to explain it. Here the discussion will necessarily be brief and only cover three general categories of the more popular suggestions of the meaning of the phrase "baptism for the dead" (βαπτιζόμενοι ὑπὲρ τῶν νεκρῶν).[2]

The first is perhaps the best known because it is the most obvious reading of the text; namely, that Paul refers to a practice of vicarious baptism. People were being baptized on behalf of those who were already dead. Whether the baptism of the dead was understood to carry with it some mystical sense of unity or whether people were baptized on behalf of dead relatives who were Christians but had died without baptism, this position views Christians as standing in baptism *in the place of* others. Most writers who take this view of the text immediately qualify it, insisting that the apostle does not advocate this proxy baptism. Indeed, they point out that in the early church the Fathers strongly condemned such vicarious baptisms. Today this interpretation is well known because many are aware that Mormons practice some form of baptism for the dead. Since often neither this practice nor its purpose is understood, just as 15:29 itself is not understood, this leads simply to an avoidance of the text altogether. However, there has been strong scholarly support that Paul has in mind vicarious baptism through most of the twentieth century.[3]

This makes easy grammatical sense of ὑπὲρ τῶν νεκρῶν, understood as a vicarious action. Despite a number of different explanations of what might have been going on in this vicarious baptism, it is generally suggested that Paul simply uses the practice to comment on how ridiculous the rite would be if there is no resurrection.

Since some see an exaggerated sacramentalism as part of the Corinthian problem (a point we have rejected in our discussion of ch. 10 above), they find no difficulty in assuming that the Corinthians could have adopted this teaching, perhaps from attitudes to the dead in the surrounding culture. Most unconvincingly, it has even been suggested that this may have its roots in pagan Corinthian rites of passage from life to death.[4] The greatest problem with this view remains the fact that Paul appears to refer to a strange practice, of which he cannot have approved, and does so without any negative or explanatory comment at all. Furthermore, if some form of sacramentalism was involved, Paul would never have tolerated it and would never have allowed people to misunderstand him, even implicitly, on such an important matter. In a more recent monograph on v. 29, Hull has examined most possible backgrounds for the existence of any form of vicarious baptism, whether in Greco-Roman Corinth and its ancient religions, or in any indication anywhere in Paul's own writings, other than this verse, and found no "historical foundation whatsoever."[5]

The second position sees this as baptism for

2. For more lengthy discussions of many alternative views on this baptism see the following: Thiselton, *1 Corinthians*, 1242–49, who lists thirteen views after omitting those which "scarcely deserve thought." Also Adam C. English, "Mediated, Mediation, Unmediated: 1 Corinthians 15:29: The History of Interpretation, and the Current State of Biblical Studies," *Rev-Exp* 99 (2002): 419–28; Beasley-Murray, *Baptism in the New Testament*, 185–92; Rudolf Schnackenburg, *Baptism in the Thought of St. Paul: A Study in Pauline Theology*, trans. G. R. Beasley-Murray (Oxford: Blackwell, 1964), 95–102.

3. Fitzmyer, *1 Corinthians*, 577–80; Hays, *First Corinthians*, 267; Collins, *First Corinthians*, 557; Barrett, *First Corinthians*, 362–64; Conzelmann, *1 Corinthians*, 275–77.

4. Richard E. DeMaris, "Corinthian Religion and Baptism for the Dead (1 Corinthians 15:29): Insights from Archaeology and Anthropology," *JBL* 114 (1995): 661–82.

5. Michael F. Hull, *Baptism on Account of the Dead (1 Cor 15:29): An Act of Faith in the Resurrection*, AcBib 22 (Atlanta: SBL Press, 2005).

those who are "dead bodies" in the sense of "near to death," so that they may receive resurrection. Again, the actual theological point Paul makes would be the same. If people are quickly baptized because their bodies are near to death and they have not as yet been baptized, then what is the point if they will never be raised from the dead (because baptism and resurrection are intimately linked)? Grammatically this makes "for the dead" in effect mean "for the sake of their (nearly) dead bodies." Some Greek Fathers held to this view and others more recently. Talbert paraphrases like this: "What will those being baptized accomplish for the corpses? If corpses are not raised at all. . . ."[6] This same view that sees the corpses or dead bodies as the issue is adapted by some to be a metaphorical reference to those who are dead or dying "in their sin." The main problem here is that Paul has spoken of the "dead" as more than "corpses" (vv. 13, 15, 16, 20, 21). The "dead" (νεκροί) are a category of people who become evidence, if none are raised from the dead, that death has not been vanquished and God is not ultimately sovereign. Baptism, for Paul, is that visible commitment to death "in Christ" and hence to the expectation of resurrection "in Christ" through faith (Rom 6:4).

A third view takes "for the dead" in a final sense, that is, "for the sake of the dead" or even "because of the dead." This would, in other words, give the purpose for the baptism. Several suggestions have been made as to what this purpose might be. One of the more persuasive suggestions, followed by a number of commentators, is that the purpose is to be reunited at the time of the resurrection with relatives who have died. Perhaps for some at Corinth,

the death of those of faith had become a motivation for their relatives to be baptized. To see their relatives again, people take up the Christian faith that alone teaches of one who has risen from the dead. If there is no resurrection of the dead, then this whole exercise is pointless. One disadvantage of this suggestion is that it makes the desire to see relatives after death a motivation for coming to faith in Christ. But there are various motivations to faith in Scripture, and being faced with death among friends or family is surely a reminder of one's own mortality that can be used by God as he calls people to himself. This suggestion as to the meaning of this rhetorical question also has the advantage of fitting well with the next couple of verses. There Paul offers himself by way of example. He is prepared to be thrown to the beasts so that he may be raised (vv. 30–32). Furthermore, it adequately explains the use of the third person, the future tense (ποιήσουσιν), and the middle voice (βαπτιζόμενοι): what will they gain from it, those who "*have themselves baptized* for the sake of the dead"?[7] It is not that this "baptism" has been an issue for many at Corinth. It simply provides an easily understood illustration that is not controversial (as opposed to a vicarious baptism, which surely would have been controversial, at least for the apostle). People have come to faith because of their appreciation of the wonder of the resurrection and the possibility of seeing their relatives again. This would be all to no avail if there is no resurrection of the dead.

Closely related to this third view is another suggestion extensively argued by Hull. In short, he suggests that Paul refers to those being baptized by

---

6. Talbert, *Reading Corinthians*, 99. Chrysostom, *Homilies on First Corinthians*, homily 40.2; Martin, *Spirit and the Congregation*, 118–21; J. C. O'Neil, "1 Corinthians 15:29," *ExpTim* 91 (1980): 310–11.

7. Thiselton, *1 Corinthians*, 1248, offers this translation, rightly arguing that it maintains the impact of the present mid-

dle form of the verb (βαπτιζόμενοι). For others who follow a final sense for ὑπὲρ τῶν νεκρῶν see Joachim Jeremias, "Flesh and Blood Cannot Inherit the Kingdom of God (I Corinthians 15:50)," *NTS* 2 (1956): 155; Schnackenburg, *Baptism*, 102; J. Keir Howard, "Baptism for the Dead: A Study of 1 Cor 15:29," *EvQ* 37 (1965): 137–41.

way of a good example for those who seem to doubt the resurrection. His reading of the text is generally rather straightforward. These people are probably the newer and younger Christians in the congregation. Following the teaching of the gospel, they are baptized. Their baptism is precisely to identify with the Christian faith. They do actually believe what some seem to doubt, that Jesus was raised from the dead and that those who die in the faith will likewise be raised. The resurrection of Christ and the resurrection of the dead (their own resurrection) is why they have, in faith, committed themselves to baptism. He thus translates the phrase (ὑπὲρ αὐτῶν) as "on account of" or "because of the dead." Hull suggests Paul is making an intense appeal for the validity of the resurrection of the dead based on an "ordinary" understanding of baptism. Paul is thus saying something like, "Look at those eager baptismal candidates. Look at their faith . . . they do not doubt that those among us who have fallen asleep will rise on the last day . . . it is their firm faith in the resurrection of Christ and of his dead that moves them to baptism . . . that is what you once believed. Come back to your senses!"[8]

In conclusion, it seems to us, with Schnackenburg, Howard, Thiselton, and others, that the third option is the clearest and has the least problems, though Hull's work (rid of some of its more sacramentalist comments) is also helpful in showing that the whole text can be read in a more straightforward manner. However, it is important to remember where this started. The actual point that Paul is making is clear enough: *What is the point of baptism, related as it is to the death of a believer, if there is no resurrection?* The death symbolized in the waters of baptism is experienced in the hope of the resurrection.

15:30–32 Likewise, why are we in danger every hour? Every day I die! [This I swear] by my pride in you, which I have in Christ Jesus our Lord. If, for merely human reasons, I fought with wild animals in Ephesus, what gain would there be for me? If the dead are not raised, "Let us eat and drink, for tomorrow we die" (Τί καὶ ἡμεῖς κινδυνεύομεν πᾶσαν ὥραν; καθ᾽ ἡμέραν ἀποθνῄσκω, νὴ τὴν ὑμετέραν καύχησιν, [ἀδελφοί,][9] ἣν ἔχω ἐν Χριστῷ Ἰησοῦ τῷ κυρίῳ ἡμῶν. εἰ κατὰ ἄνθρωπον ἐθηριομάχησα ἐν Ἐφέσῳ, τί μοι τὸ ὄφελος; εἰ νεκροὶ οὐκ ἐγείρονται, Φάγωμεν καὶ πίωμεν, αὔριον γὰρ ἀποθνῄσκομεν). The apostle now moves on to use himself and his life to make the point that everything he does is born of the assumption of a resurrection. If there is no resurrection, it makes his whole life's work meaningless. "Likewise" (καί) indicates the addition that Paul now makes to the previous argument. "We" probably reflects Paul's identification with the apostles and their sufferings for the gospel rather than with the sufferings of some Corinthians, especially with his emphasis that these sufferings are uninterrupted ("every hour," πᾶσαν ὥραν). He and they are in constant danger. Hyperbole, "every day I die" (καθ᾽ ἡμέραν ἀποθνῄσκω), functions rhetorically to further strengthen the force of the argument he is about to make. To paraphrase: "Every hour of every day we are in danger to the point of death, and to what end if the dead are not raised?"

There is some difficulty in translating v. 31. The particle "by" (νή) followed by the accusative of the thing or person being invoked introduces a strong statement or an oath.[10] Here Paul invokes his "pride" (καύχησις) in the Corinthians as he insists on his daily suffering: "Every day I die" is what Paul is "swearing." Thus we have added for clarification

---

8. Hull, *Baptism on account of the Dead*, 229–56.

9. The omission of "brothers" by 𝔓[46], D, F, G, L Ψ 𝔐 and others is probably the correct reading. There would have been

no reason for dropping the word had it been in the traditions of the texts being copied.

10. BDAG 670; MM 426.

in English, "[This I swear]." It is, therefore, with an emphatic oath that Paul insists that this is how he lives, in daily fear of death. His pride in the Corinthians lies in the fact that they have come to faith, but this is not ultimately either a pride in them as people or in himself as the one who brought the gospel to them. It is a pride in the Lord Jesus Christ and his gospel ("which I have in Christ Jesus our Lord"). By adding this clause, Paul fulfills his own injunction of 1:31 that a person should only boast "in the Lord" (cf. 9:14–16). For Paul, the Christian faith that these Corinthians have is one of his greatest joys. It serves as a confirmation of his ministry, and it makes his gospel service to the Lord worthwhile despite the risks of suffering and death. He invokes the very thing that gives purpose to his ministry, that people should hear the gospel and receive Christ as Lord. This is a clever and important argument. Paul has preached, and the Corinthians have believed, and the glory is to be given to Christ. How can some deny that the goal of this is the resurrection? Why would he go through all this suffering if there is no resurrection?

The dying to which Paul appeals is not to be taken metaphorically, though undoubtedly Paul sees his suffering as following in the footsteps of Jesus (2 Cor 4:9–11). The word "die" (ἀποθνῄσκω) has been used already in this epistle and refers to real death, whether Christ's death on the cross (8:11) or his own death (9:15). Paul's concern is that they must know he faces physical death at any time and that without hope of the resurrection his life and ministry would be meaningless. Lest any

should doubt that he is prepared to give his life for the gospel of Christ and the resurrection of the dead, he takes an example from his own life.

Two first-class conditional clauses framed within rhetorical questions help develop Paul's *persuasive* rhetoric. In the first, Paul speaks of his having fought wild animals at Ephesus. Questions immediately arise as to whether this is meant literally or metaphorically. Since this is a first-class condition, the Greek would normally require that the protasis be assumed to be true, though it could be taken as true simply for the sake of the argument. The question arises because it seems unlikely that the apostle had ever been thrown to the arena in Ephesus and faced real lions. It is just possible that he refers to rumors that this might happen, given the uproar he had caused in the city (Acts 19:23–41), but this would require seeing the protasis as a hypothetical condition that was *not* true. The first-class condition and the aorist indicative (ἐθηριομάχησα) speak against that. Furthermore, anyone who was thrown to the arena lost Roman civil rights,[11] and this does not seem to have happened for Paul, who could still appeal to Rome as a Roman citizen (Acts 22:25–29). Also, it is unlikely that anyone would actually survive the arena, unless God had intervened in a miraculous way. In 2 Corinthians Paul lists many actual sufferings to make his argument and would surely have listed this one, if it had happened (2 Cor 9:23–27). Given this, many suggest that a metaphorical use of the expression "to fight with wild beasts" makes best sense of this verse.[12] That is, Paul refers to his

---

11. Theodor Mommsen, ed., *Digesta Iustiniani Augusti*, vol. 1 (Berolini: Apud Weidmannos, 1870), 28.1.8.4.

12. Guy Williams has argued that Paul's confrontation with "beasts" refers to confrontations with evil spirits who possessed the magicians and idol worshippers of the city. He suggests this because beasts and animals sometimes symbolically represented evil spirits in Judaism. Within the confines of Scripture itself the clearest example perhaps of what is in mind is

found in 1 Peter 5:8 where the devil is described as a "roaring lion." G. Williams, "An Apocalyptic and Magical Interpretation of Paul's 'Beast Fight' in Ephesus (1 Corinthians 15:32)," *JTS* 57 (2006): 42–56. Clint Arnold also takes this view that "the beast fight reflects the spiritual warfare struggle" and develops this argument further in his introduction to his commentary (Arnold, *Ephesians*, 38–39).

battles with and sufferings at the hands of men and women in Ephesus (cf. 16:6–9) as "fighting with wild beasts." Coffin goes further and suggests that it could be paraphrased "contending with beasts in human form" (taking κατὰ ἄνθρωπον as meaning "in human form").[13]

However, apart from the grammar, in favor of a real situation is the way Paul described his experiences in Ephesus in 2 Cor 1:8–10. There he speaks that he "despaired of life itself" and felt he had "received the sentence of death." His Roman citizenship only ever helped him partially, and in a riot situation he might well have received an illegitimate judgment against him. Moreover, it was not unheard of for people to survive the arena. While it is perhaps more likely that Paul speaks metaphorically of the spiritual battles he faced, the persuasive form of Paul's rhetoric in this section assumes that Paul's point will be well understood.

The only other matter in the first part of v. 32 that needs explanation is the phrase translated by the RSV and ESV as "humanly speaking" (κατὰ ἄνθρωπον; cf. 3:3). The phrase qualifies the fighting with beasts. Paul is alluding to the motivation for fighting with beasts. He gains nothing if it was all merely for human ambitions. It would be pointless to go to death with no resurrection ahead. Thus, correctly in our view, the NRSV translates "with merely human hopes" and the NIV "with no more than human hopes." As in 3:3 the contrast in Paul's mind is the way things are viewed, whether spiritually and in the light of the gospel or simply at a human level. If Paul fought wild animals "for merely human reasons," then there would be no benefit for him at all. The benefit or profit Paul is looking for is not about personal gain. His concern is to see the purposes of God fulfilled in bringing

the gospel to all nations. The resurrection is the pinnacle of this as people from the whole world are raised from the dead to receive their inheritance in Christ and to experience the full gracious rule of the sovereign God and Father. Such "gain" (ὄφελος) or "profit" entirely disappears if there is no resurrection, providing yet more proof of the truth of what Paul has been arguing throughout this passage. A suffering, Christ-following life would be so pointless that an entirely different approach to life would be preferable. Paul sums this up in a saying: "Let us eat and drink, for tomorrow we die" (φάγωμεν καὶ πίωμεν, αὔριον γὰρ ἀποθνήσκομεν).

These words are directly quoted from LXX Isaiah 22:13. In that passage the Israelites were suffering under the siege of the Assyrians, but they still refused to repent as the Lord had demanded. In fact, as they faced their almost certain conquest and annihilation, they held festivities and parties, killing oxen and eating and drinking. Since in their view they had no future and God did not figure in their thinking, they might as well party before dying. This is the alternative Paul himself would confront. Faced with death and nothing more, he might as well "eat and drink" before dying. Since the saying is in the plural, Paul is thus able to draw in all the Corinthians who take the view that there is no resurrection of the dead.

15:33 Do not deceive yourselves: Bad companionships corrupt good ways. (μὴ πλανᾶσθε· φθείρουσιν ἤθη χρηστὰ ὁμιλίαι κακαί). Paul begins with the same imperative he used in 6:9 (cf. 3:18 where the meaning is the same though the words different). Here the problem is different, but the danger the same. Christians can always deceive themselves into thinking that wrong is right and

---

13. Charles P. Coffin, "The Meaning of 1 Cor 15:32," *JBL* 43 (1924): 172–76. For a summary of arguments for and against the metaphor and a suggestion from Hebrew sources that sug-

gests a metaphorical use, see Robert E. Osborne, "Paul and the Wild Beasts," *JBL* 85 (1966): 225–30.

right wrong. They may deceive themselves, but God is never deceived. A saying follows, which may have been a well-known proverb by Paul's day. In fact, it is a quotation from the playwright Menander (from the play *Thais*), but that is not to say that Paul had necessarily read the comedy. Presumably Paul is talking to the "some" who have been denying the resurrection. Their denial of the resurrection has perhaps already led to the sort of behavior that Paul has warned of at the end of the previous verse. Perhaps these people had become altogether too careless about how they live in the present, given that they believe there is no resurrection.

The warning itself needs some examination. "Companionships" translates a word (ὁμιλία) that refers to a group of people and then, by extension, to the associations and conversations in which the group participates.[14] "Good ways" (ἤθη χρηστά) refers to the customs or habits of a people. It is more than simply "morals" (NRSV, ESV). Paul is concerned with the way certain people are living, and there is a real danger that mixing with the wrong crowd leads to the ruin of good (godly) habits. We have seen how the apostle has been disturbed throughout the epistle by the behavior of some of the Corinthians who, we have suggested, claim to have gifts of the Spirit, especially gifts of wisdom and knowledge. They claim to be "spiritual," yet their behavior is far from godly. If such people also fraternize with or even support those who deny the resurrection (because they have already "arrived" spiritually), then it is easily understandable that they would find themselves morally corrupted.

15:34 Sober up, as is fitting, and do not sin, for some have no knowledge of God. I say this to your shame (ἐκνήψατε δικαίως καὶ μὴ ἁμαρτάνετε,

ἀγνωσίαν γὰρ θεοῦ τινες ἔχουσιν· πρὸς ἐντροπὴν ὑμῖν λαλῶ). For all their supposed "knowledge" and "wisdom," Paul states his thesis more clearly than ever: "Some have no knowledge of God" (ἀγνωσίαν ... θεοῦ τινες ἔχουσιν). They must cease their sin and should be ashamed that Paul has to write to them in this way. Paul is now expanding his exhortation. In an indication that the "bad companionships" (ὁμιλίαι κακαί) are those made with people who deny the resurrection, Paul refers back to the eating and *drinking* of v. 32, as he tells them to "sober up" (ἐκνήψατε) from the partying, as it were. The aorist imperative is used to issue a specific command, though it is not punctiliar. This is something to be done immediately, but, as the present imperative "do not sin" (ἁμαρτάνετε) indicates, it must produce a continued sobriety that involves not getting involved in sin. "Sin" is a broad category here and generally in Paul's thought. Although sometimes he is concerned for specific "sins" (6:18; 15:3) he often contemplates sin, as here, in terms of all that reflects a lack of knowledge of God and his ways. The Westminster Shorter Catechism probably has this broader definition about right when it says: "Sin is any want of conformity unto, or transgression of, the law of God" (question 14). The word translated "as is fitting" (δικαίως) can mean "righteous" (1 Thess 2:10), or "justly" (1 Pet 2:23). The adjective can signify "right" and "fitting," and so perhaps this adverbial form is best translated "as is fitting," that is, as is appropriate to those who claim to be followers of Christ.

The word translated as "no knowledge" (ἀγνωσία) refers not to intellectual understanding of God but to a true, spiritual experience of God. For all their claims to spirituality and to deeper experiences, they actually are to be identified with

---

14. BDAG 705; also examples in MM 448.

pagans who have no knowledge of God! (Cf. Rom 1:21, 24–32.) Never could there be a better example of the inanity of the slogan "all of us possess knowledge" (8:1). Here are people who are so "puffed up" they need "sobering up." No wonder Paul adds that this is "to [their] shame." As seen in 6:5, the word is not just a "put down" in terms of their status in Corinthian society, though it is surely that, but probably has behind it the Old Testament view that this "shame" is also a "shame" before God. These people should surely be ashamed before God as they are caused to think about whether they have any true knowledge of him at all as they deny the resurrection and "party" to the end.

In this way Paul draws his carefully constructed and hard-hitting argument to an end. The gospel that has been preached among them by Paul and the apostles (vv. 1–11) is supposedly held in common between them, yet some deny the resurrection. Paul has demonstrated in two sections (vv. 12–19 and 29–34) the absurdity of this position, using deliberative rhetoric with full persuasive and *ad hominem* arguments. He has also set before them the contrary position, which is the truth (vv. 20–28). Christ has been raised, he reigns, and he will vanquish death so that all "in Christ" will also be raised from the dead. In the next section, therefore, Paul turns to address the questions, "How will this happen?" and, "What will the resurrection look like?"

Theology in Application

The Resurrection as Goal and Motivation

As has repeatedly been seen in this epistle, the so-called "strong" or elitists who flaunt their spiritual gifts of "knowledge" and "wisdom" have to be humbled and made to refocus on Christ. Now, as Paul addresses the question of the resurrection, he argues that its denial will reveal that the "some" (v. 2) who take this position have "no knowledge of God" (v. 34).[15] Once again it is a cutting comment. The knowledgeable should have realized that a denial of the resurrection inevitably would render redundant, as Paul has so carefully pointed out in vv. 12–19 and vv. 29–34, the whole point of the gospel faith. Since the goal of the faith is found in the resurrected Christ and his glory, then the resurrection is part of that goal. God's people must become like Christ. Just as Christ's life and death were not simply historical facts but had to do with his identification with humanity and their sin and death, so his resurrection has to do with their eternal existence in the presence of God. Seeing "face to face" and "fully knowing" (13:12) are part of the Christian's goal in their relationship with God. If this future is not to be experienced, then "today" is all there is left (15:32). However, this future also functions as a motivation for life in the present.

While Scripture knows multiple motivations for godly living in this age,[16] the

---

15. Notably, Jesus's conversation with the Sadducees concerning their denial of the resurrection involved him accusing them of knowing "neither the Scriptures nor the power of God" (Matt 22:29 ESV).

16. For example, love for God, the imitation of Christ, and the call to obedience all figure as motivations to a godly life.

final victory over sin and death evidenced in Christ's resurrection is surely one. Living with the certainty that sinners will face the resurrected Christ himself as he comes in judgment provides a motivation of fear (2 Pet 3:9–10). Yet it also provides a great motivation of excited anticipation (2 Pet 3:14–15). Christ comes as the King who has defeated death, so his people look forward to overcoming death. He has defeated sin, so they anticipate lives without sin in bodies made ready for eternal existence. Life today is to be lived in obedience to Christ, all the while anticipating the day when full obedience is realized and the Christian's own perfection is established. The race is worth running, but only if the end is Christ and sharing in his resurrection and his glory. Otherwise, Christians are left to the world that "is passing away" (7:29–31). Sadly, some at Corinth, as so often in the church today, seem to be sleepwalking into ruin as they evidence "no knowledge of God" (15:34). With no anticipation of the resurrection, they mix too readily with those who, likewise, have no great hope for the future. Most seriously they have dramatically underestimated the power of God to raise the dead.

CHAPTER 33

1 Corinthians 15:35–49

Literary Context

Paul's defense of the resurrection of the body as integral to the gospel message continues as he insists it is essential to all aspects of the Christian faith in a second *confirmatio*. Without a resurrection of the body death alone remains. Now he tackles the question of the form of that resurrection body. With a degree of sarcasm, he addresses the person who might ask such a question as a "fool" (v. 36). Once again, the allusion to the comparison Paul has made earlier in the epistle between those who are "wise" and those who are "foolish" is obvious. As Witherington notes, this "fool" is "the one who fails to take into account God's actions."[1] This "fool" is akin to that found in the Psalms and the biblical wisdom literature, a point that was noted with Paul's earlier use of the contrast between "folly" and "wisdom."

The image of a seed being sown and growing is now employed to further the argument. First, the apostle stresses the extraordinary work of God in bringing about a body of his choosing from something as small and insignificant as a seed before arguing that bodies differ according to what God chooses to bring into being. Having established how different "bodies" can be, Paul then returns to the picture of the seed and how it provides a picture of the resurrection. The transformation of the "seed" into the "body that is to be" (v. 37) is like the resurrection. The perishable and dishonorable body is raised imperishable and glorious. Such is the contrast between the "natural" and the "spiritual," between the first man, Adam, and the last, Jesus. All believers will find that what is true of Jesus in his resurrection will be true of them as well. There is therefore continuity and discontinuity as the form of resurrection bodies are considered. The main scriptural background for Paul remains Genesis 1–2.

---

1. Witherington, *Conflict and Community*, 307.

Main Idea

At the resurrection, the natural body in the image of Adam will give way to a spiritual body in the image of Christ. That body is appropriate for the eternal realm of existence.

Translation

1 Corinthians 15:35–49

35a	Assertion	Nevertheless, **someone will ask,**		
b	Rhetorical question		"How are the dead raised?" and	
c	Rhetorical question		"With what kind of body do they come?"	
36a	Exclamation (bridge)	**You fool!**		
b	Assertion	**What you sow is not brought to life**		
c	Contingency		unless it dies.	
37a	Expansion of 36b	And	as for what you sow,	
b	Assertion	**you do not sow**	**the body that is to be,** but	
c	Contrast		a naked grain, or	
d	List		perhaps of wheat or	
e			something else.	
38a	Contrast with 36b, 37b	But **God gives it a**		**body**
b	Manner		just as he has willed and	
c			to each of the seeds its own	body.
39a	Proposition (for analogy)	**Not all flesh is the same;**		
b	Explanation	on the contrary,		
c	Assertion	**there is**	**one belonging**	**to humans,** and
d	Series		**another flesh belonging**	**to animals,** and
e			**another flesh belonging**	**to birds,** and
f			**another**	**to fish.**

Continued on next page.

Continued from previous page.

40a	Proposition (for analogy)	**Now there are heavenly bodies** and
b		**earthly bodies.**
c		Nevertheless,
d	Assertion	**the glory of the heavenly is of one kind,** and
e	Assertion	**the glory of the earthly is another.**
41a	Expansion (of 40d)	Indeed, there is
		one glory of the sun and
b	Series	another glory of the moon, and
c		another glory of the stars;
d	Expansion	for star differs from star in glory.

42a	Summation	And **so it is with the resurrection of the dead.**
b	Assertion (negative)	**What is sown is perishable,**
c	Contrast (positive)	**what is raised is imperishable;**

43a	Expansion of 42b, c	
	Assertion (negative)	**it is sown in dishonor,**
b	Contrast (positive)	**it is raised in glory;**
c	Series	**it is sown in weakness,**
d		**it is raised in power;**
44a		**it is sown a natural body,**
b		**it is raised a spiritual body.**
	Summary	
c	Condition (protasis)	If there is a natural body,
d	Assertion (apodosis)	**there is also a spiritual [body].**
45a	Proof	Just as it is written,
b	Quotation	"The first man Adam became a living being," [Gen 2:7]
c	Assertion	the last Adam a life-giving Spirit.

46a	Assertion (contrast)	Indeed **the spiritual is not the first,**
b	Sequence	but rather the natural, then
c	Sequence	the spiritual.

47a	Assertion	**The first man is from the earth, made of dust,**
b	Assertion	**the second man is of heaven.**

48a	Comparison	As was the man made of dust,
b	Assertion	so also are those who are made of dust;
c	Comparison	and as is the man of heaven,
d	Assertion	so also are those who are of heaven.

49a	Comparison	And just as we have borne the image of the man made of dust,
b	Exhortation	**let us also bear the image of the man of heaven.**

Structure

The apostle begins this section with two questions about the resurrection, the answers to which he believes all Christians ought to know (v. 35). The text then divides into two further main sections in which Paul lays out his answers. In the first Paul introduces the illustration of a seed being planted and growing (vv. 36–44). In the second, Paul compares the "natural" man Adam with the resurrected Christ (vv. 45–49). The first section may be further divided, revealing the progress of the discussion. The work of God in the process of determining what the seed will become is emphasized (vv. 36–38), leading Paul to offer further examples of different "bodies" that exist for different settings and have different "glories" and purposes (vv. 39–41). A conclusion to this part of the argument is offered in vv. 42–44. The resurrected body is raised in a way appropriate to its setting. It is thus different from the natural body that was sown. This leads into the second main argument in vv. 45–49 that involves a comparison between Adam and Christ. Adam is from this earth, while Christ is from heaven (vv. 45–47). Thus, it may be deduced that believers in the present age are like Adam with his natural body, but at the resurrection they will be like Christ with his resurrected body (vv. 48–49).

Exegetical Outline

IX. The Gospel of the Resurrection of Christ and His People (15:1–58)

    A. The Facts of the Gospel Secured by the Resurrection of Christ (15:1–11)

    B. The Truth of the Resurrection (15:12–34)

➡   **C. The Resurrection Body: Continuity and Discontinuity (15:35–49)**

       1. Two Questions about the Resurrection Body (15:35)

       2. The Sowing of a Seed Illustrates the Answer to the Questions (15:36–44)

          a. The Seed Dies in Becoming a Plant (15:36–37)

          b. God Determines the Body Each Seed Will Become (15:38)

          c. Different Bodies Exist for Different Settings (15:39–41)

          d. Application: A Natural Body That Dies Is Raised a Spiritual Body (15:42–44)

       3. Adam and Christ Compared (15:45–49)

          a. Adam Was from This Earth, Christ Is from Heaven (15:45–47)

          b. Christians, Presently in Adam's Image, Will Bear Christ's Image When Raised (15:48–49)

Explanation of the Text

15:35 Nevertheless, someone will ask, "How are the dead raised? and "With what kind of body do they come?" (Ἀλλὰ ἐρεῖ τις, Πῶς ἐγείρονται οἱ νεκροί; ποίῳ δὲ σώματι ἔρχονται;). While the subject is directly related to what has gone before, it now takes a new turn as Paul examines the nature of a *bodily* resurrection. The strong adversative (ἀλλά) thus marks the start of this new section of Paul's discussion of the resurrection rather than a contrast with what preceded, hence our translation "nevertheless." Diatribe-style answers to some of the questions that, it may be presumed, were being discussed in Corinth are now presented. It may have been that those who denied the resurrection asked these questions with sarcasm: "So if you believe in a resurrection, how is it going to happen and what are these resurrected people going to look like?" This is made likely by the fact that rhetorical questions beginning with "how?" (πῶς) are often used to "call an assumption into question or reject it altogether."[2] On the other hand, it may be that such was the Greek philosophical influence among some that these were genuine questions from people who could not envisage a spiritual realm in which real "bodies" existed. Either way, Paul provides the clearest description in Scripture of what the resurrection of the *body* (σῶμα) is all about and how it should be understood.

The present tense "do they come" (ἔρχονται) may infer that the questioners are relating the resurrection of the dead to the "coming" of Christ. If Christ is "coming" (v. 23), how will the dead "come"? Though the word "coming" (παρουσία) is used in v. 23, the verb used here in v. 35 is unrelated (ἔρχομαι). While this verb is also occasionally used of Christ's "coming" (cf. John 4:25; Heb 10:37), it

is probably more likely that the questioners, rather than thinking of Christ's return, are thinking of what a resurrected body might look like. Thus, by linking the second question closely to the first question, we might paraphrase: "So, with what kind of body do the resurrected dead *show up*?" The question relates to the form of the physical body, should it rise from the dead. Whether Paul expands the meaning of the word "body" as he expounds his theology has been the subject of many of the discussions relating to the next few verses.

15:36–38 You fool! What you sow is not brought to life unless it dies. And as for what you sow, you do not sow the body that is to be, but a naked grain, or perhaps of wheat or something else. But God gives it a body just as he has willed and to each of the seeds its own body (ἄφρων, σὺ ὃ σπείρεις οὐ ζῳοποιεῖται ἐὰν μὴ ἀποθάνῃ· καὶ ὃ σπείρεις, οὐ τὸ σῶμα τὸ γενησόμενον σπείρεις ἀλλὰ γυμνὸν κόκκον εἰ τύχοι σίτου ἤ τινος τῶν λοιπῶν· ὁ δὲ θεὸς δίδωσιν αὐτῷ σῶμα καθὼς ἠθέλησεν, καὶ ἑκάστῳ τῶν σπερμάτων ἴδιον σῶμα). Paul now sets out his initial response to these two questions, employing three analogies in vv. 36–41, and applying these to the resurrection of the dead in vv. 42–44. In these verses he establishes that death leads to resurrection and that resurrection bodies are, at some level, different from the body that has died. The whole process is entirely an outworking of God's will.

"You fool" (ἄφρων) is a strong vocative and is to be taken with "you" (σύ); hence the different punctuation from NA[28]. Paul is not thinking here of the "foolishness" of this age or of the "fools" that Christians appear to be in the eyes of the world (cf. 3:18 and 4:10). This is the rhetoric of exclama-

---

2. BDAG 900.

tion. Christians who ask this sort of question are without sense! The exclamation thus, in rhetorical terms, introduces an "obvious" example.

The first analogy (vv. 37–38) concerns the planting of a seed and the full-grown plant. Christ has been described as the "firstfruits" (v. 20), and it is this that gives rise to the illustration from seed and the grown wheat. Paul speaks of a seed as having a *body*. This is not without precedent in Greek writings, though it is rare,[3] but it is the only place in Scripture where plant life is described as having a body. He uses the word deliberately to make his illustration intelligible; that is, that this does provide an analogy for a *person's* body in its death and resurrection. It also opens the way for the next two analogies that there are many different "bodies" in creation and these have different "glories."

Paul sets up the contrast between life and death—"is not brought to *life* unless it *dies*" (οὐ ζωοποιεῖται ἐὰν μὴ ἀποθάνῃ). The contingency causes the subjunctive, while the aorist tense has a present meaning. It might also be translated "unless it should die," giving the verb the somewhat more common sense of future contingency. That science demonstrates a seed does not really die is not an issue here. While science in today's world is able to describe in detail what happens when a seed is put into the ground, germinates, and grows to the plant, the fact of the matter is that this illustration remains a good one even today. It is a remarkable thing that what appears to be a hard and lifeless pip can be put in the ground and grow to something full of life. By analogy, Paul says that the death of a human being and their resurrection must be regarded in a similar way. Of course, this

is somewhat more than analogy in one sense, for we have Jesus to look at since he is the "firstfruits."

It is important to see that this whole section remains rooted in the gospel confession of vv. 1–8. It is an exposition of part of that confession in the light of its denial by some. Just as Jesus died and was buried before he came to life, so will those "in Christ" die and then be raised (except for those who are still alive at Christ's coming; see vv. 51–52). Paul's picture therefore enables us to look again at what has happened with Jesus, who walked and talked and lived on this earth and was witnessed by many (vv. 4–7). He died and was "buried," just as one might bury a seed. Then he was alive. This first contrast is one that speaks to radical discontinuity. Death is followed by life. The seed is followed by a plant.

Next Paul contrasts "you sow" (σπείρεις) with "God willed" (ἠθέλησεν; v. 38). Verse 36 has already set this up with the verb "is brought to life." The present passive here (ζωοποιεῖται) may be termed a "divine" passive.[4] God is the assumed life-giver, a point clearly made in v. 38.[5] In fact, the contrast is emphatic. Three times, once in v. 36 and twice in v. 37, Paul says "*you* sow." This is often lost in translation. In v. 37 he writes, "And as for what[6] *you* sow, *you* do not sow the body that is to be but . . ." (NRSV). In v. 37 the RSV and ESV ignore the first occurrence of the verb altogether. The NIV changes the second occurrence of the verb to "plant" and makes the first into a temporal clause: "When you sow, you do not plant. . . ." But the repetition is important as a rhetorical device that leads into the important contrast in v. 38, "But *God* gives it a body. . . ." Paul is not denying that God

---

3. A few examples are given in BDAG 984; MM 620–21.

4. Fitzmyer, *1 Corinthians*, 588.

5. In a number of places it is God who is the subject of "to bring to life" with the verb in the active voice (John 5:21; Rom 4:17; contrast the law that cannot bring life in Gal 3:21). In 15:22 we have already seen a passive use of the verb where

God is the implied agent and the dead are brought to life "in Christ." Cf. N. T. Wright, *The Resurrection of the Son of God*, Christian Origins and the Question of God 3 (Minneapolis: Fortress, 2003), 244ff.

6. An accusative relative pronoun of respect.

also gives the pre-resurrection body in his creative purposes. Indeed, Paul's illustration of planting seed and watching it grow is surely a continuing allusion to the creation narrative of Genesis as God created the plant world (Gen 1:11–12; 2:9), a world over which God had given Adam dominion (Gen 1:28).[7] Thus Paul assumed that, looked at from a human point of view, "you" put the body in the grave. That is all you do or can do, so any resurrection depends on something that only God can do. As with Christ, it is God who raises people from the dead, and so clearly it must be God who gives the body. The radical and what we would call "miraculous" power of God must take over from the "you" for resurrection to happen. If some Corinthians deny the resurrection, they must first see that there is a radical discontinuity between this life and the resurrected life. Yet they must also see that only the power of God can deliver this. In fact, this is really what is assumed in the word "sow." There is an assumption that something amazing will happen. We sow with confidence that a plant will grow. God will bring fruit from what is sown; therefore, we sow the body with the same expectation.

Paul then sets up a further contrast (similar to one found in in 2 Cor 5:3) between what is "naked" and what is "clothed" (v. 37, γυμνὸν κόκκον; vv. 53–54, ἐνδύω [4x]). The picture is at once apparent. The seed seems dull and lifeless as if with no clothes. Today, a person is often dressed before being put in a coffin, but the action is simply done to make an otherwise repulsive truth more palatable, that this person is now simply a bare body of skin and bones. Whatever takes place for the dead in Christ to be raised, a new clothing will be needed that turns out to be, as Paul expounds it, a differ-

ent mode of existence. However, *this picture speaks of continuity*. Being naked and then being clothed does not involve ceasing to exist, but it does involve ceasing to be naked! This is further explained in v. 38b. God has determined that each kind of seed should have the body God gives it.[8] In other words, seed appears to be dead, but because of God's will any seed is already pointing toward a future body that is appropriate to it. Just as the wheat seed will bring forth wheat,[9] so from the dead human body God brings to life a resurrected *human* body. As Paul puts it, each kind of seed receives its "own body" (ἴδιον σῶμα). The creedal formula has reminded the Corinthians that because Christ has been raised and *seen* we can have confidence that such a "body" exists and is recognizable. This is as much an exposition of Christ in his resurrection as it is of "dead Christians" in their resurrection.

15:39 Not all flesh is the same; on the contrary, there is one belonging to[10] humans, and another flesh belonging to animals, and another flesh belonging to birds, and another to fish (οὐ πᾶσα σὰρξ ἡ αὐτὴ σάρξ, ἀλλὰ ἄλλη μὲν ἀνθρώπων, ἄλλη δὲ σὰρξ κτηνῶν, ἄλλη δὲ σὰρξ πτηνῶν, ἄλλη δὲ ἰχθύων). Now Paul indicates the necessary appropriateness of a body to its environment, and he does so by introducing his second analogy.

The second analogy (vv. 39–41) concerns different bodies existing for different settings. Because God has determined what the resurrected body will be like and is the one who gives the body to the seed, it is important to understand that this body, like any other "body," will be appropriate to its environment and circumstances. This will be Paul's conclusion in vv. 42–49 where what is raised

---

7. Wright, *Resurrection of the Son of God*, 341.

8. The plural partitive genitive refers to particular seeds out of many, while the singular "seed" refers to all the seed that is sown collectively.

9. εἰ τύχοι "perhaps of" is a rare use of the potential optative. See also at 14:10. BDF §385.2.

10. The genitives in this verse are subjective; hence the translation "belonging to."

is raised in a different form from the form in which it died. That form will be appropriate for an age and a world in which nothing perishes. The analogy now moves the reader toward this conclusion. Paul's affirmative proposition is that "not all flesh is the same" (οὐ πᾶσα σὰρξ ἡ αὐτὴ σάρξ). We look around at God's cosmos; every part of creation has a different form or what Paul calls "flesh" (σάρξ). Paul begins with the apex of creation, humanity, and moves to the less intricate (animals, birds, fish) in the reverse order of what we find in Genesis 1:20–25.

The introduction of the new word "flesh" needs explanation here. Paul has not moved into the realm of the very dualism he abhors! He is not contrasting the "spiritual body" with "flesh" understood as material and nonmaterial. Neither does he simply have in mind "flesh" as we might use it when we say "he is all flesh and bones." Rather, he has in mind here the outward appearance or outward "dress" of animate beings (note he does not use "flesh" of the sun or moon in v. 41). Looked at from outside, a human being is different from other animals, and a bird is different from a fish. Both have physical bodies that are clothed with appropriate "flesh" for their environment. In this case the different "flesh" of the bird would be its feathers and wings that allow it to cope in its environment by flying.[11]

Paul grounds his example solidly in the creation story of Genesis 1:11–12 where God created vegetation and trees and plants, and the passage speaks of each plant bringing forth seed "which is their seed, each according to its kind" (ESV). Even the differentiation where a seed will only produce its particular kind of plant is part of God's creative purposes. The future lies with God, and he will see to it that the seed of the human who has died will be brought to life in the form and physical body appropriate to the realm or environment in which it will then be living. (There is nothing wrong with using the word "physical" at this point, for Paul is dealing with a real resurrection of substance that is in continuity with the physical body that has died, but which has a different "flesh" or outward form. There is nothing in anything that Paul says that would lead us to believe physicality as such has gone; in fact, this very use of the word "flesh" militates against this.)

So Paul has set up two analogies. The first analogy, which involves three contrasts, was the seed that dies and then is brought to life. This gave rise to the first contrast between life and death, which was followed by the second between what "you sow" (that is, what human beings put in the ground) and what God has determined will be right for the future in the age of the resurrection. A further, third contrast is seen in the seed that seems naked as it is put in the ground and the body that will be clothed at the resurrection. The second analogy concerns different bodies being determined by God for different purposes and gives rise to Paul's fourth contrast between different bodies that are created with different "flesh" by God for different environments. The sum of it all is that the resurrected body will be different from the body

---

11. The problem encountered with the word "flesh" is that Paul uses this word in a variety of different ways. It can denote the physical body as it more or less does in this case (cf. 6:16). It is perhaps best known in its metaphorical use in which "flesh" is seen as that which is opposed to God's ways (cf. Rom 7:18; 8:6). The reference in 1 Cor 10:18 to "Israel according to the flesh" (see comments there) refers to their humanity but carries with it spiritual implications, for Paul implies that there is another Israel (cf. Rom 9:6). "Flesh" thus also has moral connotations in some contexts, and so Paul can talk of "the desires of the flesh" and "the works of the flesh" (Gal 5:17, 19 ESV). For various approaches and summaries of Paul's uses of this word, see Dunn, *Theology of Paul*, 62–73; Bruce, *Paul*, 203–11; Ridderbos, *Paul*, 93–95, 102–3, 548–51; Stacey, *Pauline View of Man*, 154–73.

that dies yet continuous with it, for the body that is buried can only produce one type of resurrected body, the one God has determined. It will be appropriate for the resurrected life and environment. It will be continuous with what has gone before.

15:40–41 Now there are heavenly bodies and earthly bodies. Nevertheless, the glory of the heavenly is of one kind, and the glory of the earthly is another. Indeed, there is one glory of the sun and another glory of the moon, and another glory of the stars; for star differs from star in glory (καὶ σώματα ἐπουράνια, καὶ σώματα ἐπίγεια· ἀλλὰ ἑτέρα μὲν ἡ τῶν ἐπουρανίων δόξα, ἑτέρα δὲ ἡ τῶν ἐπιγείων. ἄλλη δόξα ἡλίου, καὶ ἄλλη δόξα σελήνης, καὶ ἄλλη δόξα ἀστέρων· ἀστὴρ γὰρ ἀστέρος διαφέρει ἐν δόξῃ). Paul's argument now moves on a stage. Different created entities have different "flesh" for different situations and environments. Therefore, we may understand that the resurrected body will be different, though organically related to the original body, because it will be appropriate to the new way of being that is the resurrected life. Now Paul demonstrates that other created entities also have different "glories," thus providing a further analogy. The great cosmic lights offer an example. Again, he progresses from the greater to the lesser, the sun to the moon and then to the stars, recalling creation itself where precisely this differentiation takes place at the hands of the creator God (cf. Gen 1:14–18). Not only do heavenly bodies like the sun and the moon differ from earthly bodies like plants, but even within the heavenly structures themselves there is a difference between the sun and the moon and the stars. Even stars differ from each other in their "glory" (δόξα).

"Heavenly bodies"(σώματα ἐπουράνια) in v. 40 is defined in v. 41. Paul is speaking of the sun, moon, and stars.[12] Paul is no doubt thinking of the splendor or brightness of the sun and stars. Daniel 12:2–3 may lie behind this. There the prophet speaks of those who die ("sleep in the dust of the earth") but who will awake to "everlasting life." He continues: "Those who are wise will shine like the brightness of the heavens, and those who lead many to righteousness, like the stars forever and ever." This is not to say at all that Paul thinks (as modern popular mythology does) that those who die become shining stars that look down on those they have left behind. Rather, it is part of what Paul has been saying right through. There is a new "glory," a new form of existence that is appropriate for the resurrected believer. There is something about the resurrected body that will reflect a greater glory and a greater brightness that is a result of seeing God "face to face" (cf. 13:13; Rev 22:4).

The word "glory," however, means more than simply splendor and light. The comments on this word in 1 Corinthians 11:7 are useful here as well. There it was noted that any "glory" attached to a person was derived first from the "glory" attached to God. With God the word points to all that is uniquely true about him. It no doubt involves his brightness and existence as "light." God is revealed in a "pillar of fire" in the exodus, the "cloud" that surrounds him seems to be there to protect humankind from death, and it is understood even from the blinding that happened to Paul as he saw

---

12. A few commentators have demurred. Morris, *First Corinthians*, 225, takes the view that Paul speaks here of heavenly beings for whom, Paul is saying, God created appropriate bodies. Héring regards the "heavenly bodies" as "the living bodies of certain angels which appear to us in the form of stars." Paul's point, he says, is that they are "of other matter than earthly bodies" (*First Corinthians*, 174). But this fails to take into account Paul's reliance on the distinctions and differentiations in Gen 1 and the way that v. 40 forms a pivot between two categories that Paul himself explains, never mentioning the possibility of angels! The fact is that the mention of angels here would have been thoroughly confusing. It would have implied, in line with dualistic thinking, that the resurrected "body" would be an unrelated and less than a "physical" body.

Christ in his "glory" on the Damascus road. When it is applied to men and women, as in 11:7, we suggested that "glory" was to be understood in close relationship with being in God's image and so reflecting glory back to him as the worship of their lives (cf. 2 Cor 4:6). "Glory" therefore becomes that which sums up the person as God created them. Glory is that which belongs to the person and, in this case by extension, the created entity that reflects his, her, or its creator.

Paul's point therefore becomes stronger. Like their earthly counterparts, all these celestial bodies have a created purpose, a glory that God has given them. Just as this glory differs between them since each has a different purpose (as Gen 1 makes clear), so it will be with the resurrection. The resurrected body will reflect a "glory" that appropriately reflects the image of God and the role that humanity has in the new age. So beautiful and different in its "glory" will this be that it may be compared with the "dishonor" of the sowing of the dead body in v. 43. This is not to suggest that humanity has no glory now but that the contrast between the dead body, which has for a while appeared to lose its "glory," and the resurrected body that reflects God will be magnificent.

15:42–44b And so it is with the resurrection of the dead. What is sown is perishable, what is raised is imperishable; it is sown in dishonor, it is raised in glory; it is sown in weakness, it is raised in power; it is sown a natural body, it is raised a spiritual body (Οὕτως καὶ ἡ ἀνάστασις τῶν νεκρῶν. σπείρεται ἐν φθορᾷ, ἐγείρεται ἐν ἀφθαρσίᾳ· σπείρεται ἐν ἀτιμίᾳ, ἐγείρεται ἐν δόξῃ· σπείρεται ἐν ἀσθενείᾳ, ἐγείρεται ἐν δυνάμει· σπείρεται σῶμα ψυχικόν, ἐγείρεται σῶμα πνευματικόν). "And so it is" (οὕτως, v. 42a) draws together all that has been argued so far: the continuity, the differentiation

of diverse "flesh" and "bodies," the different "glories," and also the sovereign determination of God to create these bodies for his designed purposes. These new bodies Paul now calls "spiritual." "The dead" (νεκροί) are the dead "in Christ." This category of dead persons is marked throughout this chapter by the use of the article (cf. vv. 35, 42, 52), whereas the dead as a whole, all humanity in death, is anarthrous (cf. vv. 12, 15, 16, 21, 29). Paul thus provides the interim conclusion to the question, "With what kind of body do they come?" But Paul has more to say.

He now embarks on a more detailed description of the nature of the body that belongs to those raised by God from death. The subject of the verb "is sown" is not present and must be supplied. The "what" or "it" that is sown seems obvious enough: the body that is put into the ground, dead. The verb continues to have a passive connotation, meaning that the "you" of v. 36 is still probably in mind as the sower and that God is still the one who raises a body. Indeed, the final couplet in v. 44a states that the "body" is what is sown. Paul refers again to the great difference between the body that dies and that which is brought to life. The one was perishable and died. The other is "imperishable" and will never die (see 15:53–55; cf. Rom 8:38). Then three further couplets are provided in which there are specific and clear contrasts between the perishable body and the resurrected, imperishable body: dishonor/glory, weakness/power, and natural/spiritual.

It is these next three couplets that have caused some commentators to ask whether the "it" or "what" of v. 42b is really as obvious as it might seem. The main concern, as Garland outlines it, is that sowing "in dishonor" and "in weakness" "do not seem applicable descriptions of interment."[13] In

---

13. Garland, *1 Corinthians*, 732–33.

other words, it seems strange to speak of a lifeless, dead body as being "weak." It also seems unlikely that a dead body would be referred to by Paul as a "soulish [ψυχικός] body" (quoting Edwards), because a "dead body . . . is soulless." Edwards argues further and forcibly that "it is impossible" to apply the second couplet to the interment of a body and "still more impossible to apply the term *psychical*, 'moved by a soul,' in ver. 44, to the body which is laid in the tomb."[14] Godet suggests that "the word *sow* embraces all the phases of the body's existence, which beginning with the first dawn of being, terminates in committal to the earth." For him "dishonor" refers to the general miseries of this life experienced by the body. Moving backward through life, "weakness" refers to the moment of birth, and the final term "Psychical" (his translation of ψυχικός) refers to that moment when "the breath of life" comes to the "soul" (ψυχή) and its development begins.[15]

However, there is no need to assume that Paul is speaking here of the body *qua* corpse. Paul moved on from this in v. 38 when he broadened his thought to an examination of God's creative purposes, showing that God designed *different* bodies suitable for different environments. Here Paul speaks of the body of a Christian prior to the resurrection and after that great event. He continues to draw attention to the "kind of body" with which they will come. In doing so, he again shows the distinction between the two states, but it is still the "body," as v. 44a makes clear. What is sown a "natural body" (see below) is raised a "spiritual body."

But it is a *body*. Prior to the resurrection, it is "perishable" (ἐν φθορᾷ). That is, it is always becoming corrupt and gradually decomposing. Paul uses the word in Romans 8:21 where he describes creation itself in bondage to this corruption. In that passage Paul describes the future as a world where creation will be freed from this when God's people receive "the redemption of our bodies" (v. 23). Death is therefore the final result of the present, perishable "body." The converse is that the resurrected body will be of a nature that is "imperishable." It will not have within it that which leads to decay and death.

The second couplet picks up the idea of "glory" from vv. 40–41. The state of the resurrected Christian's body will be one to which glory belongs; that is, it will be a body that finds complete fulfillment in God's design and purpose to bring him "glory." The person with the resurrected body is the person as God created him or her to be, without intrusion of sin or decay. In contrast to this, Paul speaks of the body that is sown in "dishonor." Philippians 3:21 may reflect a similar idea: Christ "will transform our lowly bodies so that they will be like his glorious body." In Philippians 3:21, Christ's resurrected body provides the pattern for what all future resurrected bodies will be like. If Philippians 3:21 is allowed to be the guide, then Paul has in mind here the contrast between the present and lowly body, with all its impermanence and suffering that leads eventually to death, and the glory of the perfection that lies ahead. But the prior "dishonor" may reflect also a type of "bondage." Paul describes elsewhere how the old body is held captive by sin (Rom 6:6,

---

14. Thomas C. Edwards, *A Commentary on the First Epistle to the Corinthians* (London: Hodder and Stoughton, 1885), 438–40, uses "soulish body" to translate σῶμα ψυχικόν. Many commentators discuss the difficulty of interpreting this Greek phrase. The usual, "natural body" (ESV, NIV) or "physical body" (RSV, NRSV) does not seem to connote the fullness of the Greek expression. Calvin, *First Corinthians*, 337, says Paul "compares the time of this present life metaphorically to seed-

time, and that of the resurrection to the harvest; and he says that now our body is indeed subject to death and dishonor, but then it will be glorious and incorruptible." See also Jeffrey R. Asher, "Σπείρεται: Paul's Anthropogenic Metaphor in 1 Corinthians 15:42–44," *JBL* 120 (2001): 101–22, though see Fitzmyer's criticism (*1 Corinthians*, 595).

15. Godet, *First Corinthians*, 2:412.

12) and how the mind is set on "earthly things" (Phil 3:19). This brings "shame" and dishonor to men and women before the community but also before God (1 Cor 6:5; 15:34). As Héring says, Paul describes "a body freed from corruption, i.e., realizing the fullness of the eternal and completed life willed by the Creator."[16]

The third couplet compares the body that is sown "in weakness" (ἐν ἀσθενείᾳ) and raised in "power" (ἐν δυνάμει). In 1 Corinthians 1 Paul has spoken of the reversal of normal human values by speaking of the "word of the cross" as "the power of God" (1:18). "God chose the weak things of the world to shame the strong" (1:27), and it is this weakness that he has in mind. It is a weakness that the body of the Christian has constantly experienced. However, it is more than simply the weakness of the frailty of the human body, for it is also the apparent weakness in the world's eyes of living for Christ and being shamed and humiliated for Christ (4:9–10). The body that is raised will be Christlike and without fault, but it will also be vindicated in its new demonstration of the power of God.

The three couplets thus encourage the Corinthian Christians and exhort those who might deny the resurrection that the new state of the body will be quite different. All that has seemed to define Christians in their existence in this world will be reversed. Just as the gospel shone a light on these reversals in chapter 1, and Christ does so as the firstfruits, so all this awaits those who will be raised from the dead.

Finally, a fourth couplet in v. 44a provides a pivot. It concludes the series and serves to introduce a comparison of the natural and the spiritual. Our thinking is so saturated by the influence

of Greek dualism that it is all too easy to think of the main difference between the "natural body" (σῶμα ψυχικόν) and the "spiritual body" (σῶμα πνευματικόν) as the difference between that which has a tangible and substantial body versus that which is ghostly and nontangible. Moreover, v. 50, which says that "flesh and blood are not able to inherit the kingdom of God," has further complicated matters and made some even more convinced that the issue is one of corporeality (see below). Yet all that Paul has been saying thus far has spoken against that as a way of seeing things. The body that has been raised will be different, but it will be a real body. It will be powerful, glorious, and imperishable. Perhaps the closest we can get to a modern way of describing what Paul is talking about is to speak of another "dimension." The fact that a body looks glorious and functions in a better way and is imperishable makes it no less a body. Though Paul does not directly refer to this here, the example that we have before us remains the one spoken of at the start of this chapter: the Lord Jesus Christ (15:4). The witnesses to his resurrection saw this sort of *body*.

With this in mind, the two words "natural" (ψυχικός) and "spiritual" (πνευματικός) need examining. Against the RSV, NRSV, TEV, etc., the word "natural" (ψυχικός) should not be translated as "physical." Just as the previous three couplets were not dealing with the substance or matter of the body but rather with the *way* or *mode* of existence of the body (perishing, imperishable, etc.), so here. We are dealing now with what animates the body. The first speaks of what we might call the normal or "natural" (ψυχικός) manner of existence of the body that is common to all human beings; hence our translation "natural" (with AV, NIV

---

16. Héring, *First Corinthians*, 175. An examination of the resurrected body and the Christian hope of the resurrection is found N. T. Wright, *Surprised by Hope*, esp. 55ff, 167ff. In

much greater detail see also Wright, *Resurrection of the Son of God*, 277–374.

2011, ESV).[17] The second speaks of the "spiritual" (πνευματικός) manner of existence that Christ's *resurrected* body now enjoys. It is this contrast that is being made here, a contrast that is also seen in terms of the present and the future, as it has been throughout this chapter (cf. v. 49). The contrast was also seen in 2:13–14 when both these words were used of the way the Corinthians behave in their lives. The word "spiritual" helps us define the intent of the word "natural," but only in so far as we understand that Paul uses the word "spiritual" in a consistent way that points to the Holy Spirit and, above all, reveals more about Christ. The -ικός ending itself in Greek regularly denotes characteristics or ways of being. The Christian who has died is raised *bodily* (there is a spiritual body, v. 44), but this means that his or her body must enter a manner of existence that is animated by the Holy Spirit who points toward Christ; indeed, who makes their body like Christ's. The Spirit who raised Christ from the dead gives life to mortal bodies through his Spirit (Rom 8:11).

Of course, all this is more intelligible when we remember that Paul remains concerned with the fact that death is conquered, a theme to which he returns (vv. 54–55). For death to be conquered the body must be raised. Put another way, there must be an empty tomb. The body will be truly transformed, but both the before and the after are Man (Adam), as v. 45 goes on to discuss. For those who considered they had "arrived" spiritually and saw themselves as mature, spiritual people, this would have been jarring. Paul is saying that the fullness of what it is to be "spiritual" must await the "spiritual body." Meanwhile, any "spiritual" life, a life Paul longs that all believers should have, is provisional.

Throughout this chapter, Paul has never moved far in his thinking from the account of creation in Genesis 1–2, and it may well be that Genesis 2:7 lies behind Paul's use of "natural." There it is said that the newly created Adam is the man who "became a living soul" (ψυχή). For Paul Adam characterizes that which is of the first creation. His is a body formed for a "soul." He has been created to live on this earth as it now is (v. 47). But the raised Christ must have a different body since he lives in the realm of the Spirit (or "heaven" vv. 47–49). So Paul will turn back to Gen 2:7 to make his point.

15:44c–45 If there is a natural body, there is also a spiritual [body]. Just as it is written, "The first man Adam became a living being," the last Adam a life-giving Spirit (εἰ ἔστιν σῶμα ψυχικόν, ἔστιν καὶ πνευματικόν. οὕτως καὶ γέγραπται, Ἐγένετο ὁ πρῶτος ἄνθρωπος Ἀδὰμ εἰς ψυχὴν ζῶσαν· ὁ ἔσχατος Ἀδὰμ εἰς πνεῦμα ζῳοποιοῦν). First, then, the apostle offers a summary in v. 44c that also becomes the thesis he will develop. Assuming there is a natural body, then there must also be a spiritual body. All should accept the protasis that there is a "natural body" (first-class condition), that is, a "living being" (v. 45) appropriate to the world God created. Yet, as Paul has shown, this must mean that the resurrection body has to be a "spiritual body" appropriate, not to some celestial realm but to the world to be inhabited by the raised bodies. Adam and Christ once more provide the picture with a parallelism being provided between v. 44c–d and v. 45. To the quotation from Genesis 2:7 Paul simply adds the word "first." The first Adam was a "living being" (and so had a "natural body"). The "last Adam" became a "life-giving Spirit" (and so has a "spiritual [body]"). Paul's point of comparison here lies in seeing both Adam and Christ in their representative roles. Where they have gone first, others followed or will follow. Yet this is not

---

17. BDAG 1100 gives the main meaning as "pertaining to the life of the natural world" in contrast to that whose central characteristic is the Spirit. Then, strangely, 1 Cor 15:46 is cited as the "physical" in contrast to the spiritual.

straightforward. Clearly, all who follow Adam are also human souls, "living beings," but not all "in Christ" become a "life-giving Spirit." (Even if we take it as "spirit" with a small 's'!) So how is the comparison being made?

Dunn is surely right to suggest that the last Adam is regarded as "the *progenitor* of a new kind of humanity—resurrected humankind. It is the *uniqueness* of the risen Christ's role as 'life-giver' which is in view."[18] But to understand the comparison it is important to see that Paul builds on the *uniqueness* of Adam's role as well. In his representative role as the first Adam, *he brings death.* Christ is the last Adam *and brings life.* At the head of each group of people, those "in Adam" and those "in Christ," stands one who is unique. As Paul has been demonstrating, in his role Christ fulfills the determined purposes of God. He brings to all whom he represents the life-giving power of the Spirit of God (as opposed to Adam who brought death). As has already been expressed in v. 22: "In Adam all die," "in Christ all are made alive." Thus each "Adam" in his own right begins a whole new stage in God's history; Jesus's resurrection is seen as the start of something radically new, just as Adam's sin changed everything that followed.

It is noteworthy that the typology of Adam and Christ seen in 15:21–22 and here in vv. 45–47 points toward the development of the theme in Romans 5:12–19. In that passage the representative role of Adam is clearly expressed ("just as sin entered the world through one man" and "death reigned"; vv. 12, 14). Indeed, in Romans 5:14 Paul speaks of Adam as "a type of the one who was to come" (ESV). Paul also makes it clear that one of the ways the two representatives are set apart is by their action (vv. 18–19). Adam's act ("one act of sin") led to condemnation for all. Christ's "one act

of righteousness" leads to "justification and life for all." Throughout this exposition Paul stresses the "how much more" (v. 15) of Christ. While the typology is there, what Christ does is so far superior to what has happened previously that it truly bears no comparison, and so Paul can also say, "The gift is *not* like the trespass" (v. 15). This is where Paul will lead the reader in 1 Corinthians 15 as well. In the end there is no comparison, for God gives a victory in Christ in which death is "swallowed up" and destroyed (vv. 54–57).

Before moving on, more must be said of v. 45 and the representative role of Christ, for here it is easy to miss the fact that *Jesus* is called "Adam" (albeit the "last Adam"). Paul sees Jesus not only as starting something new and making resurrection possible but also as being part of the old order of things. Jesus becomes truly "Adam"—not only in the sense of heading a people but in becoming truly *human.* He knows what it is to inhabit a perishable, dishonorable, and weak "natural body." In other words, even *before* his death Jesus takes on a representative roll, no doubt specifically because he is the Messiah King (Rom 1:3). Thus, in his death he represents all who are his as much as he does in his resurrection (cf. Rom 8:3–4; Gal 4:4–6; 2 Cor 5:21). It is for this reason that Paul can say elsewhere that we must die with him to rise with him (Rom 6:4–5, 8; cf. Col 2:12; 2 Tim 2:11).

Thus in vv. 44c–45 attention is once again drawn to the difference between the "natural body" and the "spiritual body," but this time with reference to Adam, that is, to the different representative roles fulfilled by the first and last Adam. As Genesis is quoted, we are reminded again that God's creative power is sovereign in all this. As the one was created by God from the dust of the earth, so the second was raised by God from the grave.

---

18. Dunn, *Theology of Paul,* 261. Also Morris, *First Corinthians,* 228–29.

15:46 Indeed the spiritual is not the first, but rather the natural, then the spiritual (ἀλλ᾽ οὐ πρῶτον τὸ πνευματικὸν ἀλλὰ τὸ ψυχικόν, ἔπειτα τὸ πνευματικόν). Verse 46 now uses the previous sentence as a basis for reminding the Corinthians that God's plan has still *ordered* the way things will happen (15:23–24). It is not the "spiritual" [body] that is first but the natural [body] that is followed by the spiritual. Paul uses the strong adversative (ἀλλά) twice to make the contrast emphatic, and so the translation here seeks to grasp this ("indeed . . . but rather"). "Spiritual" and "natural" are both substantival adjectives in the neuter here, and so it is probably best to assume an agreement with "body," though it is possible that Paul thinks more broadly of Adam and Christ in their respective bodily existence. The adverb "first" is to be understood here as temporal. Of course, Christ himself provides the evidence for understanding this in temporal terms. He was "Adam" (though the "last Adam"), who "became a life-giving Spirit."

It is important to reiterate that this says nothing negative about the physicality of the *bodily* experience described. It is not that a "body" is first and a "spirit" is second. Neither is it that Jesus was once human but is now a spirit. Rather, Jesus once had a body that fully experienced the natural world and is now raised with a new and transformed body that fully experiences the realm of the Spirit, *his realm*, the realm of God. And this is what it will be like for those who are "in Christ." Paul thus encourages people that the weakness and perishability that each experiences now has its place and its time, but it will pass. Even being a mature and spiritual person "in Christ" now, with all the benefits that come with this and all the "grace-gifts" that are given to God's people, is nothing to what is held in store for the future. Each one will come

to experience the work of Christ and the Spirit in a "life-giving" way appropriate for the new order. Paul makes the same point by way of summary in v. 49: At the moment we are like Adam, bearing his image, but we *shall* bear Christ's image.

15:47 The first man is from the earth, made of dust, the second man is of heaven (ὁ πρῶτος ἄνθρωπος ἐκ γῆς χοϊκός, ὁ δεύτερος ἄνθρωπος ἐξ οὐρανοῦ). Paul does not now move into some considered, christological discussion on the origins of Christ or his preexistence, as if to suggest he always came *from* heaven. The "primary reference" is not "to our Lord's heavenly origin."[19] Indeed, that could hardly be the case given that Paul is making the point that the "man of heaven" is second in order. Rather, Paul continues to describe what is characteristic of the two men. Although Paul uses the rare adjective "made of dust" (χοϊκός), the intention is clear. He returns to Genesis 2:7 and the integral relationship between "man" and earth. Previously Paul had quoted Gensis 2:7b, but now he alludes to 2:7a: "God formed the man from the dust of the earth" (LXX: ἔπλασεν ὁ θεὸς τὸν ἄνθρωπον χοῦν ἀπὸ τῆς γῆς). Paul is thinking of Adam as described in the creation account of Genesis. Adam is made by God of the dust of the *earth*, which characterizes him as one made to exist on this *earth*. In fact Genesis 2:7 itself reveals the closeness of this link between the created man and the earth he is to inhabit. "Man" (*adam*; אָדָם) is formed from the "earth" (*adamah*; אֲדָמָה). Indeed *Adam*, who was taken from *adamah*, must work the *adamah* and will eventually return to the *adamah* (Gen 3:19, 23). To say that Adam is "of the earth" therefore also includes the idea that he is to die and will return to dust.

Paul's allusion to Genesis 2:7 is thus critical to

---

19. *Contra* Morris, *First Corinthians*, 230; see also Martin, *Spirit and the Congregation*, 137. Nor is there any myth of a "primal man" lying in the background (cf. Conzelmann, *1 Corinthians*, 284–86; Barrett, *First Corinthians*, 377).

his discussion here of the difference of "bodies." Adam was created to be integrally linked to "earth." Similarly, the man Christ has now been raised in such a way that he is integrally related to the new realm of his existence. He is described as "of heaven," characterizing him as one made fit for existence in the presence of God and the realm of the Spirit of God. His body is one that does not perish but reflects God's own glory and power. Indeed, it is well summarized in v. 43 with the words "power" and "glory." The type of body that is now Christ's is the same body into which the bodies of all "in Christ" will one day be transformed (Phil 3:21). It is possible, given Paul's mention of his own witness to the risen Lord (v. 8), that Paul thinks of Christ who, having died and been raised, appeared to him in glory on the Damascus road.

15:48 As was the man made of dust, so also are those who are made of dust; and as is the man of heaven, so also are those who are of heaven (οἷος ὁ χοϊκός, τοιοῦτοι καὶ οἱ χοϊκοί, καὶ οἷος ὁ ἐπουράνιος, τοιοῦτοι καὶ οἱ ἐπουράνιοι). This verse now applies this teaching, first, to all people "in Adam" and then to those who are "in Christ." As Adam was "of dust [of the earth]" and so had a "natural body" and died (v. 22), so it is with all like him, including Christ. But those who are "in Christ"—"the man of heaven"—are "of heaven." Their complete transformation belongs to the future resurrection as Paul has been saying, but it is even now who they are. It is thus appropriate to insert a present tense in both v. 48b and v. 48d, instead of a future tense, as some do, in v. 48d.[20]

15:49 And just as we have borne the image of the man made of dust, let us also bear the image of the man of heaven (καὶ καθὼς ἐφορέσαμεν τὴν εἰκόνα τοῦ χοϊκοῦ, φορέσομεν καὶ τὴν εἰκόνα τοῦ ἐπουρανίου). "And just as" (καὶ καθώς) indicates that Paul continues the application of his teaching and sets up once again a contrast between those represented "in Adam" and those "in Christ." The ingressive aorist of the first clause speaks to men and women who, because of his representative role, have found themselves in perishable bodies like Adam. They "have borne" the image of Adam now as a result of their being human. The Greek word (φορέω, *not* φέρω) picks up the idea of "wearing the clothes" appropriate to this earth (cf. TEV: "Just as we wear the likeness of the man." See comments on vv. 53–54 below).

On occasion as Paul thinks of the transformation of those who are in Christ, he uses the word "image" (as he does the word "glory").[21] In chapter 15 he has been primarily thinking of the future resurrection when people will image Christ in their full "spiritual" bodies, but he rarely speaks on the future without also urging that Christians should image Christ now as well. Paul sees this as moving from "glory" to "glory" in 2 Corinthians 3:16–18 (cf. Rom 8:29; Col 3:10; Eph 4:24). This is what Paul does here as he exhorts the Corinthians at the end of this section to "bear the image of the man of heaven." Just as Adam represents us and we come to be like him in sin and death, so as Christ represents us we should come to be like him in righteousness and life.

---

20. Calvin, *First Corinthians*, 341, writes: "This is not an exhortation, but teaching, pure and simple." See Garland, *1 Corinthians*, 737. He argues that in v. 48 Adam and Christ set "the pattern" for those who follow them. Thus, "the Last Adam sets the pattern for all who *will* be resurrected and given a spiritual body" (emphasis added). This misses the fact that Paul has been talking of Adam and Christ's representative roles, which are far more than simply setting a "pattern." What is true of

the Messiah is true of his people *now*, even though, as Paul has been teaching, it will not be fully revealed until "the end." That Paul is still working here with a representative understanding of "the man of the earth" and "the man of heaven" is further clarified in the next verse. There, we take the much-debated verb "to bear the image" (of the man of heaven) as a hortatory subjunctive rather than a future tense; see below.

21. E.g., Rom 8:29; 2 Cor 3:18.

A textual variant of the verb in the second clause has caused some debate. Should v. 49b read "we shall also bear" (a simple future, φορέσομεν) or "let us also bear" (aorist subjunctive, φορέσωμεν)? As we have shown above, we believe that Paul intends the latter subjunctive form (with NET). But it is to be acknowledged that the former fits simply and easily with what Paul has been saying. The new likeness, the likeness of Christ, is something that comes to all who are "in him" in the future, at the end. However, taking the verb as a hortatory subjunctive ("let us bear") means the intent of the sentence is rather different. Paul is asking the Corinthians to begin to prepare for what will come. This thus becomes another example of Paul thinking of the present implications of being "in Christ" and being prompted to do so by his reflection on the final "glory" of the resurrection. Christians are asked to become Christlike in this age, even though their bodies and the perfection of the Christlikeness still lies in the future at "the end." Even though this exhortation is less amenable to the present context, where Paul has been speaking to the facts of the resurrection and the type of body with which people will eventually be clothed, it does fit generally quite well in the epistle as a whole.[22]

For the future tense, which is used in the majority of modern translations, the textual evidence is, as Metzger puts it, "rather slender."[23] Alternatively, the subjunctive form has early and consistent witness.[24] In spite of the textual evidence, a majority of commentators follow the main versions in reading the future tense. Godet sums up the general view by saying: "It is demanded by the context, which does not admit of an exhortation any more than

in the case of Rom 5:1. The object is simply to conclude the argument begun in v. 39."[25] The "o" sound in both verbs, which is all that distinguishes the two forms, probably sounded identical in spoken Greek, and this could easily account for change from omega to omicron. Of course, this argument could be made the other way round (o to ω). Nevertheless, the fact is that the more difficult reading (the aorist subjunctive) maintained an unbroken and uncorrected history through a variety of traditions. Either is of course possible. Above we have chosen the more difficult reading and the better-supported reading, in line with the usual guidelines of textual criticism. It is also theologically in line with what Paul often does in moving from the future hope to the present life.

However, there is one further reason as to why the subjunctive *may* have been used here. This also provides at least a partial answer to those who have insisted that *context* must determine which form of the verb was original. Paul may be deliberately contrasting this exhortation with the earlier hortatory subjunctive of v. 32. There, the exhortation came in the form of the refrain, "Let us eat and drink." This was the appropriate behavioral response for those who deny the resurrection of the dead. In fact, Paul concluded the argument of vv. 29–34 with a series of imperatives (see vv. 33–34). Now, as Paul expounds on the reality of the resurrection life in vv. 42–49, it is not unreasonable to suppose that he would also end this section with an exhortation. This exhortation is to an appropriate behavioral response for those who are "of heaven." They are to look like Christ, the man of heaven. Christians must behave now as the eschatological people of

---

22. Cf., e.g., Paul's exhortations in the early verses of 1 Cor 3 or 10.

23. Metzger, *Textual Commentary*, 502. The NA[28] gives only B, I, 6, 630, 945 (variant), 1881, and Sahidic.

24. This includes 𝔓[46], ℵ, A, C, D, F, G, Ψ, various other uncials and miniscules, 𝔐, etc.

25. Godet, *First Corinthians*, 2:431. See Metzger, *Textual Commentary*, 502, who supports the future with a "B" rating because of "exegetical considerations" regarding the context as "didactic, not hortatory."

God; they must "put on" Christ now and be conformed to his image.[26] The next section, which brings the whole chapter to a conclusion, also ends with explicit exhortation (v. 58). We take it that exhortation is what Paul intends here. In this way Paul draws this section to a provisional close, although he will develop some of these thoughts further in the next few verses.

Theology in Application

Paul has used the story of creation, especially Genesis 2:7, to show that a resurrected body is a radical new creation involving a great transformation of the perishable body. If it is asked of the resurrected, "With what kind of body do they come?" then the development of seed to grain and the picture of the two Adams help illustrate the matter. Christ as the "last Adam" has revealed in his resurrected being what it is to be one of the renewed people who now find themselves living with imperishable and incorruptible *bodies*, prepared for the new earth. The resurrected Christ is the start of the new way of being, but it is still *physical* being with an appropriately transformed body.

At the heart of it all is the fact that dishonor, weakness, and what is "natural" and right for this earth's existence is raised in glory and power and becomes what is "spiritual" and right for existence in the spiritual or eternal realm. That eternal realm consists in "a new heavens and a new *earth*" (Isa 65:17; see 2 Pet 3:13; Rev 21:1). This new body is ready to inhabit that new earth. Denying the resurrection fails to see that Jesus himself is not only the firstfruits but is also the bestower on others of the "spiritual body." He is this, says Paul, because he became a "life-giving Spirit" (v. 45). Again, the comparison with Adam reminds us that Paul is building on Genesis and sees what is happening as being a new or, better, renewed creation. Thus, those who are "in him" will become fully like him. Yet Paul also makes the point that as Christ is now, so, at least in some sense, are his people now. The goal is yet to be attained, but the new order has already begun. The perfection of the image of Christ is yet to be achieved in the resurrection of the body, but still we are to bear his image even now.[27] For now Paul simply exhorts the Corinthians to be clothed with Christ's image while they await this radical transformation. Thus, the impact of this theology of the resurrection must be seen clearly in the lives we live now on this earth.

The body and what we do with it is not less significant than "the spirit." We must and can bring glory to God with our whole lives, borne along by the knowledge that the Spirit indwells *this* body, even while we long for the perfection of the resurrected

---

26. This principle underlies 2:12–16, cf. 1 Thess 5:23–24. This argument for a hortatory subjunctive is given greater support if we suppose, as we did above, that Paul has already moved to a consideration of the *present* state of people "in Christ" in v. 48b.

27. It is here, as has been seen through this epistle, that Paul sees the purpose of the gifts of the Spirit. They enable God's people to become more Christlike while awaiting the parousia.

body and its life. In the struggles of this life, which often seem to limit how we can serve the Lord—struggles such as those we encounter with illness or age or other suffering—the knowledge and hope of the resurrection motivate and encourage this present Christian life. In a real sense, the life lived by Christians in the body fit for this age becomes a preparation for that future life and body.

Of course, given the dualistic view of the world held by so many today, the teacher must wrestle hard with how to convey the fact that the picture Paul gives is drawn from creation and the relationship of God's Spirit to humanity within that creation. The temptation to jump from speaking of the man or woman in whom the Spirit dwells as "spiritual" and from that to speaking of their eventual spiritual existence as a nonphysical existence is extreme. It is vital that the continuity between the creation and renewed creation is taught alongside discontinuity. This will help put away unbiblical views of what it is to be "spiritual." As Paul puts it in Romans 8:11, "If the Spirit of him who raised Jesus from the dead dwells in you, he who raised Christ Jesus from the dead will also give life to your mortal bodies through his Spirit who dwells in you" (ESV). In this way we can begin to argue, as Paul has done, that "just as we have borne the image of the man of dust, let us also bear the image of the man of heaven." In a number of ways Paul has taught that there is continuity of bodily existence but discontinuity in that this bodily existence is transformed for eternity into that which is incorruptible and imperishable. What that might look like can hardly be imagined other than to look again at the descriptions of the risen Jesus himself.

1 Corinthians 15:50–58

Literary Context

At the heart of what the Corinthians must understand about the resurrection is the matter of continuity and discontinuity. It is this, which Paul has partially described in the preceding verses, that he now argues for in more detail. Continuity there certainly is: Christians are themselves raised from the dead. Yet, there is also great discontinuity. Thus, Paul continues his answer to the question of v. 35, "How are the dead raised?" and, "With what kind of body do they come?" while also moving the reader on to examining the resurrection itself. Verse 50 acts as a transitional verse as Paul's argument progresses. There is an extraordinary and miraculous, God-ordained change that must take place at the resurrection if victory over death is finally to be established. Paul looks back to Isaiah and Hosea as he develops the idea of victory over death. Whether dead or alive at the coming of Christ, all believers will be "changed" (v. 51). This change, as the dead are raised and all are given incorruptible bodies, is the final evidence that death has been defeated, that the power of sin has been broken, and that God's victory has been won "through our Lord Jesus Christ" (vv. 54–57). The final appeal in v. 58 reminds the Corinthians once again that Paul is not discussing the theology of the resurrection for its own sake but because true belief and trust in the resurrection has immediate and powerful implications for the present. It means that faithful and steadfast commitment to the Lord and his calling is not in vain.

Main Idea

The dead will be raised. All will be changed in an instant, and God's victory over sin and death will be evident to all. Since the outcome is assured, Christians should live and work hard for the Lord in the present.

Translation

1 Corinthians 15:50–58

50a	Affirmation	Now **this I state, brothers [and sisters],**
b	Content	"flesh and blood are not able to inherit the kingdom of God,
c	Content	neither does the perishable inherit the imperishable."
51a	Assertion	**Behold! I tell you a mystery:**
b	Content	we shall not all sleep, but
c	Contrast	we shall all be changed,
52a	Time	in a moment,
b	Restatement	in the blink of an eye,
c	Simultaneous	at the last trumpet.
d	Assertion	For **the trumpet will sound**
e	Series	and **the dead will be raised imperishable**
f		and **we shall be changed.**
53a	Basis for 51–52	For **this perishable [body] must put on imperishability**
b	Restatement	and **this mortal [body] put on immortality.**
54a	Time	Now when this perishable [body] has put on the imperishable and
b	Restatement	this mortal [body] has put on immortality,
c	Assertion	then **the saying that is written shall come to pass:**
d	Content/quotation	"Death was swallowed up in victory. [Isa 25:8]
55a		Oh death, where is your victory? Oh death, where is ⤶ your sting?" [cf. Hos 13:14]
56a	Expansion of 55	Now **the sting of death is sin,** - - - - - -
b		and **the power of sin is the law.**
57a	Thanksgiving	But **thanks be to God,**
b	Description	who gives us the victory
c	Agency	through our Lord Jesus Christ.
58a	Inference	Therefore, my beloved brothers [and sisters],
b	Exhortation	**be steadfast,**
c	Exhortation	**unmovable,**
d	Exhortation	**always abounding in the work of the Lord,**
e	Basis for 58b–c	because you know that your labor is not in vain in the Lord.

Structure

This section of Paul's discussion of the resurrection and the nature of the bodily transformation that must take place culminates in Paul's great statements on the victory over sin and death that is gained "through our Lord Jesus Christ." It may be divided into two main sections and a final exhortation. In the first division (vv. 50–53), Paul outlines a theological understanding of what must happen if people are to "inherit the kingdom of God." The mortal and perishable body must give way to the immortal and imperishable. All will be changed, whether they have already died or are alive at Christ's coming. The second division demonstrates, with the use of Old Testament Scripture, that such radical transformation of the body will be evidence of God's victory in Christ over sin and death (vv. 54–57). The final verse of this chapter (v. 58) concludes the discussion of the resurrection with the positive insistence that, in view of this future resurrection and the inheritance that awaits them, Christians should devote themselves fully to the Lord's work and know that this work is not in vain.

Exegetical Outline

IX. The Gospel of the Resurrection of Christ and His People (15:1–58)

 A. The Facts of the Gospel Secured by the Resurrection of Christ (15:1–11)

 B. The Truth of the Resurrection (15:12–34)

 C. The Resurrection Body: Continuity and Discontinuity (15:35–49)

➡ **D. The Necessity of the Transformation of the Body (15:50–58)**

  1. The Mortal Must Take on Immortality (15:50–53)

  2. All Will See Christ's Victory over Sin and Death (15:54–57)

  3. Be Steadfast in the Lord's Work: It Is Not in Vain (15:58)

Explanation of the Text

Verse 50, though a transitional verse, serves to introduce a new and most glorious passage that draws together, but also considerably adds to, what has been said before. It begins with a strong affirmation that radical change is necessary if people, whether dead or alive at the time of Christ's coming, are to "inherit" the covenant promises of the defeat of death. Radical transformation will happen at the parousia and will be instant. Paul paints a picture of how things will appear when God's power is seen and the resurrection of multitudes is witnessed. This is the decisive, complete, and powerful end of a great battle as death is defeated and the consequences of sin overcome. The emphasis is on the victory of God in this great event that is announced with a trumpet as the King triumphs on behalf of his people. God is to be thanked. And today makes sense in the light of that great event (v. 58).

15:50 Now this I state, brothers [and sisters], "flesh and blood are not able to inherit the

kingdom of God, neither does the perishable inherit the imperishable" (Τοῦτο δέ φημι, ἀδελφοί, ὅτι σὰρξ καὶ αἷμα βασιλείαν θεοῦ κληρονομῆσαι οὐ δύναται, οὐδὲ ἡ φθορὰ τὴν ἀφθαρσίαν κληρονομεῖ). Believers cannot inherit all the wondrous covenant promises summarized in the final rule of God in a kingdom of peace and righteousness if they are not appropriately clothed. "Flesh and blood" is inappropriate because it is frail and decaying in its propensity to sin, and it is not righteous and glorious. Moreover, as Paul has said before, the "perishable" must be replaced by the "imperishable" (15:42). "Now" implies a degree of continuity with what has gone before. The transitional verse looks forward with the strong "this I state" (φημί). This verb has a number of meanings. It sometimes introduces a quotation (e.g., 6:16), and can occasionally be used to explain what has been said before (as in 10:19). However, it also regularly introduces direct discourse, which is why inverted commas (quotation marks) have been used here. The strength of this affirmation may suggest, as noted in v. 35, that Paul responds to a certain degree of sarcasm or at least an element of disagreement with what he is about to say. Despite the continuation of the previous theme, this affirmation does introduce a new matter that is expounded in the following verses (vv. 51–57). This new matter moves the readers be-

yond the question of the resurrection of the dead and the body that people will have to the resurrection event itself. What happens to those who have died, and what happens to those who are alive when Christ comes? Paul insists that both those still alive in decaying and frail bodies and those whose bodies are already dead must be radically "changed" (v. 51; ἀλλάσσω). To better understand how v. 50 introduces these matters, three subjects need some comment.

(1) *"Flesh and blood"* (σὰρξ καὶ αἷμα). This phrase certainly refers to the human body *as it now is*. It is perishable and decaying and a body that suffers and is decidedly mortal. Flesh corrupts, and blood stops flowing as men and women die. As noted earlier, Paul's statement about "flesh and blood" has been used by some to explain v. 44 in a dualistic manner. That is, it is taken that "flesh and blood" refers to what is physical and describes "the natural body." This physical body cannot inherit "the kingdom of God" since only a "spiritual" (i.e., nonmaterial) body can. Yet we have already seen that Paul has not been concerned with the question of what is or is not *physical*. Rather he has spoken of how different realms of existence require different types of (physical) bodies.

Key to the interpretation of this verse is the parallelism between the first half and the second half.

| flesh and blood | are not able to | inherit | the kingdom of God |
| the perishable | does not | inherit | the imperishable |

Is v. 50c simply another way of saying the same thing as v. 50b or does it complement or even contrast with the first statement? In an influential examination of this phrase, Jeremias has argued that the parallelism presents a contrast as Paul, having dealt with the question of "with what kind of

body do they come?" now turns to the question of "how are the dead raised?" (v. 35). In doing so he addresses the situation of the living and how they must be changed by putting on immortality. This happens at the same time as the dead are raised.[1] He further argues that the phrase "flesh and blood"

---

1. Joachim Jeremias, "'Flesh and Blood Cannot Inherit the Kingdom of God' (1 Cor. xv. 50)," *NTS* 2.3 (1956): 151–59. On slightly different grounds Godet, *First Corinthians*, 2:434, ends

up with a similar position to Jeremias: v. 50a speaks of those who are alive at Christ's coming and v. 50b speaks of those already dead at the coming of Christ.

"denotes the natural man as a frail creature in opposition to God."[2] That is, the phrase implies not simply the physical frailty experienced by the human body but the sinful frailty of *living* men and women who are sinners before a holy God. He argues that the phrase is not used to speak of the dead, as if in some crude form the resurrection simply means the resuscitation of a body.

It is not necessary to conclude with Jeremias that the phrase "flesh and blood" speaks to the living (who will be changed), and the "perishable," by way of contrast, speaks of the "dead." Such a view is difficult to sustain, given that "perishable" (ἡ φθορά) is a true description of the living body as much as it is of a dead body. However, neither is it then necessary to assume that the parallelism must be synonymous.[3] Jeremias's view that "flesh and blood" may refer more broadly to frailty but especially with respect to God, that is, that it incorporates the idea of sinfulness, may be supported in three ways. First, there is partial, though rather weak support, from the use of the phrase in Sirach 17:31. There the phrase is clearly linked to sin: "Flesh and blood devise evil" (NRSV; cf. Sir 14:18).[4] Secondly, and more significantly, sin is clearly in Paul's mind *in this context* (vv. 55–56) as that which must be dealt with in the resurrection. The resurrection is most certainly about God's victory over what gave rise to death, namely, sin. Thirdly, the phrase is immediately followed by mention of "the kingdom of God" (see below), and this includes the idea of God's righteous and holy kingdom (that cannot be inherited by that which is under the power of sin).

It is reasonable therefore to say that Paul probably was thinking of men and women in their frail human bodies, together *with* their propensity to sin. After all, his example has been Adam, by whom sin entered the world and because of whom death came. When Paul reflected on the extraordinary and miraculously powerful change that must happen to someone of "flesh and blood," if they are to become like the resurrected Christ, then God's resurrection must not only create a body suitable for the new environment but a body that has undergone "full deliverance from sin to a disposition of holiness."[5]

(2) The verb "*inherit*" (κληρονομέω) merits consideration. In the normal turn of events, inheritance involves surviving to the point where a person receives from, most often, a relative that which has belonged to the relative. Usually, at least in some sense, an inheritance is something that has been legally promised. The biblical idea of inheritance is not far removed from this way of thinking. Through Scripture God has made promises for which the people of God await fulfillment. Many promises have received at least provisional fulfillment in the incarnation of Jesus Christ and his death and resurrection, but Scriptures reveal that the full inheritance awaits the end, the time when, as Paul puts it in 15:28, "God will be all in all." The promises include that fact that all God's enemies will be vanquished. Paul has already demonstrated that this will happen along with the destruction of death itself at the coming of Christ (15:26–28). The famous Old Testament prophecies that speak of inheritance usually refer to the "land" or "earth" (אֶרֶץ) and see it as God's to give (Deut 4:21; Ps 25:13 [24:13 LXX]). Yet closely related to this is God's promise of "peace" (שָׁלוֹם; Ps 35:20,

---

2. Jeremias, "Flesh and Blood," 152.

3. Collins, *First Corinthians*, 579, suggests the parallelism is synonymous, with the first phrase embedded in Jewish apocalyptic thought and the second repeating the same idea from within a Hellenistic philosophical framework.

4. Despite frequent reference to the LXX for the background to this phrase, in fact it only appears in this form in these two Sirach references.

5. Thiselton, *1 Corinthians*, 1291.

27), which has to do with the vanquishing of enemies and a land of righteousness where his people
will know God's steadfast love. This can be summarized in the word "salvation" (יֵשַׁע; Ps 85:8–10).
With this background Paul sees the inheritance as
what is given by the Lord to his people on the last
day. In Ephesians this is an inheritance received
"in [Christ]" (1:11; also called "salvation" in 1:13),
whose Spirit believers have received as "the guarantee of our inheritance until we acquire possession of it, to the praise of his glory" (1:14 ESV). As
Paul uses the verb "to inherit" here in 15:50, the
context is also clearly eschatological.

(3) The phrase *the kingdom of God* (βασιλεία
θεοῦ).[6] This summarizes the inheritance of which
we have been speaking. It functions as a shorthand
referring to the fulfillment of all the covenant
promises when at the end Christ, in his "coming"
as King, will bring peace and righteousness on
earth and all God's enemies including death are
vanquished. This is the time spoken of in 15:23–27.
At this time, God's people are under Christ's rule
and will eventually encounter the fullness of the
Father's total rule of glory.

The body must be changed and radically transformed before such wonders can be inherited.
This view of the end is reflected in similar terms
in Philippians 3:20–21. There too Paul says that
we await the Savior who is to come and writes of
the transformation of our bodies at that time when
we shall indeed be made to "be like his glorious
body." There too he talks of the extraordinary
power involved in that transformation and sees
it as the same power that is at work as God subjects all things to himself. Always it is Christ in his
resurrected glory who stands before Paul as the
reminder of what Christians will one day be like.

Only then will they be properly able to experience
the kingdom of God.

**15:51–52 Behold! I tell you a mystery: we
shall not all sleep, but we shall all be changed,
in a moment, in the blink of an eye, at the last
trumpet. For the trumpet will sound and the
dead will be raised imperishable and we shall
be changed** (ἰδοὺ μυστήριον ὑμῖν λέγω· πάντες οὐ
κοιμηθησόμεθα, πάντες δὲ ἀλλαγησόμεθα, ἐν ἀτόμῳ,
ἐν ῥιπῇ ὀφθαλμοῦ, ἐν τῇ ἐσχάτῃ σάλπιγγι· σαλπίσει
γὰρ, καὶ οἱ νεκροὶ ἐγερθήσονται ἄφθαρτοι, καὶ ἡμεῖς
ἀλλαγησόμεθα). Paul normally uses the word "mystery" (μυστήριον) of things pertaining to God's wisdom and his plan of salvation in Christ (2:7; 4:1; cf.
Rom 11:25; 16:25; Eph 1:9; 3:3, 4, 9). In fact, generally speaking, the "mystery" is something that *has
now been revealed* in Christ. As was noted in the
last verse, Paul *saw* Christ in his resurrected glory.
The mystery revealed is therefore that all who are
to inherit the kingdom of God will be changed to
be like Christ. *What this will be like has been revealed in Christ, who has been seen in this changed
condition by all the witnesses established at the start
of this chapter.* In this specific instance, Paul speaks
now of those who will be alive at his coming and of
the radical change that will occur for all.

The verb "to sleep" is a euphemism for dying,
though, as noted in v. 18, *for those in Christ, the
sleep of death implies a route to being awake once
more* (cf. v. 6). The clause "we shall not all sleep"
(πάντες οὐ κοιμηθησόμεθα) cannot mean that no
one will die before the last trumpet, for Paul has
already spoken much of "the dead," meaning those
who have died in Christ. However, now he opens
the subject of the impact of Christ's return on those
who are still alive at his coming. That Paul anticipated the return of Christ at any time is made clear

---

6. See "In Depth: The Kingdom of God" following comments on 6:9a.

in several passages, but little can be made of the fact that Paul uses the first-person plural here. It is going too far to build on this use of the "we" a view that Paul certainly expected that some of his own generation, if not himself, would still be alive at Christ's coming. Perhaps he thought this, perhaps not, though he surely lived every day as in the presence of Christ and ready for his appearance. Primarily, though, Paul uses "we" here because he is one of those who will be "changed," whether dead and needing to be raised or alive at the coming.[7] The passive voice of "be changed" (ἀλλαγησόμεθα) recalls yet again that only God can possibly be the agent of this work.

The radical and extraordinary nature of the change that the body must undergo, whether alive at Christ's coming or needing to be raised from the dead, is emphasized strongly by the speed of its happening. "In a moment" is a fraction of time so small that it cannot be cut (ἄτομος). The "blink" (ῥιπή) of an eye reinforces the same point.

The "trumpet" sound accompanies the arrival of the King. The idea is also found in Second Temple apocalyptic literature, yet it is a commonplace in cultures of all ages for the arrival of a potentate. In biblical thought its pedigree is ancient. A trumpet is sounded as Solomon is anointed king (1 Kgs 1:39); trumpets are used to summons armies and peoples (Neh 4:20; Isa 27:13); trumpets are used to alert people to danger (Hos 5:8; Joel 2:1). Perhaps closer to Paul's intention here is the fearful sounding of the trumpet that accompanied God's descent onto mount Sinai (Exod 19:16, 19; cf. Ps 47:2–5). Indeed, it is probably this that gives rise to the trumpet of apocalyptic texts that speak of God's

appearing with the sound of a trumpet (e.g., Zech 9:14; cf. 1 Thess 4:16).

At that sound, as Christ the King comes, in a moment and the blink of an eye, the great transformation will take place for *all* of God's people. For the dead that change involves them being raised; for those who are alive it means being "changed." The end result is that all will be the same: their bodies changed to bodies suitable for their new environment of glory. Even here Paul would never have anyone forget that this is the same change that happened with Christ when he was raised, for we are to be like Christ, *fully* bearing the image of the man of heaven (v. 49).

15:53 For this perishable [body] must put on imperishability and this mortal [body] put on immortality (δεῖ γὰρ τὸ φθαρτὸν τοῦτο ἐνδύσασθαι ἀφθαρσίαν καὶ τὸ θνητὸν τοῦτο ἐνδύσασθαι ἀθανασίαν). The change "must" happen (cf. 15:25), just as the apostle has been insisting in the previous verses. The change is primarily about that move from what dies to what does not die, but the word "perishable" denotes that which is dying or wasting away in decay. Thus "for" (γάρ) introduces a further explanation of the change required to inherit the kingdom of God. The two clauses of v. 53 are synonymous as they are in the parallel v. 54. Two neuter adjectives are used as substantives referring to the "perishable" (φθαρτός) and "mortal" (θνητός) body. The English verb "to waste away" captures well the difference between the old and the new as Paul describes them. Thus, the new body not only will not be subject to death but also will not "waste away" or gradually become less and less fruitful until finally it expires. Even if there may possibly

---

7. There is nothing here that forces Conzelmann's conclusion that "underlying what he says is the expectation that he will personally live to see the parousia" (*1 Corinthians*, 290). Some have tried to use this text along with 1 Thess 4:15 and a few others to suggest that there is an eschatological develop-ment in Paul's thought from these early texts to a more settled position in his later eschatology (e.g., Charles H. Dodd, *The Meaning of Paul for Today* (New York: Meridian, 1965), 40–41. This has been forcibly repudiated by many. Cf. Plevnik, *Paul and the Parousia*, 276–81; Dunn, *Theology of Paul*, 310–15.

be a sense of "growing old" in this eternal kingdom (though there is no indication that even this sense will be present), there will be no sense of "aging" as we know it in this world, no sense of becoming gradually weaker and less able to do the work for which we were created. Rather, our bodies will be changed in such a way that we will live without any wasting decay.

However radical this change must be, the fourfold repetition of "this" in vv. 53–54 demonstrates the continuity between old and new. It is "this" (present) body that "puts on" imperishability. It would be incorrect to argue from this passage that a person's personal identity lies in their disembodied "spirit," even though that spirit can exist separately from the body after this body has died and before the "change." Nevertheless, human beings are created both for this world and the next to be embodied persons, and the continuity between the two forms of bodily existence is expressly stated here. There is no Greek notion here that the spirit needs to escape the body if it is to be perfected.

In the days of science fiction and many stories written of people who are supposedly "immortal," it is important to recognize how different Paul's description is here. Here, both the aspects of continuity and discontinuity are important as God's history anticipates a "new earth" and the "change" that will take place. The bodily continuity is established, but the discontinuity is also significant. These *changed* bodies are, as we have seen through this chapter, prepared for a new order of existence where righteousness dwells and peace reigns. These bodies are the only appropriate form of existence for people who are now living for all eternity in a kingdom where everything and everyone has

been subjected to God himself, that he may "be all in all" (v. 28).

15:54–55 Now when this perishable [body] has put on the imperishable and this mortal [body] has put on immortality, then the saying that is written shall come to pass: "Death was swallowed up in victory. Oh death, where is your victory? Oh death, where is your sting?" (ὅταν δὲ τὸ φθαρτὸν τοῦτο ἐνδύσηται ἀφθαρσίαν καὶ τὸ θνητὸν τοῦτο ἐνδύσηται ἀθανασίαν, τότε γενήσεται ὁ λόγος ὁ γεγραμμένος, Κατεπόθη ὁ θάνατος εἰς νῖκος. ποῦ σου, θάνατε, τὸ νῖκος; ποῦ σου, θάνατε, τὸ κέντρον;). Paul now anticipates the change of the mortal body to the immortal. It will wondrously and finally evidence the defeat of death. "When" (ὅταν) introduces an uncertainty as to the time when this change will happen; hence the subjunctive verb. But that is not to say that the fact of this change is uncertain. The idea of "putting on" (ἐνδύσηται) immortality suggests being clothed in a different way or being *additionally* clothed. The aorist middle infinitive of v. 53 is ingressive (ἐνδύσασθαι), meaning that this one occasion in which, in a moment, all will be raised and reclothed starts a new era. The idea of "putting on" new clothes is used on a few occasions in the New Testament in a similar metaphorical way. Second Corinthians 5:1–5 describes the new existence as being *fully* clothed" (v. 4) or having clothing put on *over* other clothing (ἐπενδύομαι), also suggesting continuity.[8]

However, this new clothing implies an ethical transformation as well. These bodies will be prepared for a place where sin has been vanquished. They will not be liable to the very sin that led in the first place, through the judgment of God, to "perishability" and death. The quotation that follows

---

8. Cf. Phil 3:21 which speaks of "transforming" (μετασχηματίζω) "our lowly bodies" to be "like his glorious body."

establishes this. Furthermore, the idea noted in v. 42 above remains present here. Though for those "in Christ" there is already no condemnation (Rom 8:1), yet the bondage to decay described by Paul in that chapter is also a bondage to sin (vv. 10–11). Ever since God's judgment on humanity in Genesis 3, the two were part and parcel of each other. To have a human bodily existence is to have an existence that leads to decay and eventual death *because* the human existence as it now pertains is an existence inescapably involved with and under the dominion of sin. The believer consequently longs for the new clothes that provide immortality but also exhibit no remaining stain of sin. This is why in Romans 8:23 Paul can speak of the transformation of the body also as "the redemption of our bodies" (τὴν ἀπολύτρωσιν τοῦ σώματος ἡμῶν). The change involves a transformation from that which is capable of and regularly involved with sin to that which is not.

This ethical dimension of the transformation is of course entirely consistent with Paul's use in v. 50 of the phrase "the kingdom of God" since the phrase, especially in the Pauline correspondence, is often used in ethical contexts. In these contexts, Christians are reminded that their behavior should reflect that they are part of this kingdom (e.g., Rom 14:17; 1 Cor 4:20; 6:9–10; 1 Thess 2:12).[9] The continuity of the body is thus established, but the nature of the discontinuity is again explicit. The body will be changed so that it no longer suffers death, wastes away, or has any part in the realm of sin, for it will be perfected in every way for the kingdom of God.

When this change has taken place, when the King has come, then the word which is written will come true (v. 54): "Death is swallowed up in victory."[10] Paul now draws together two Old Testament texts. The first he takes from the Hebrew rather than the LXX. As Hays writes, "Paul is reading the prophetic text with careful attention to its original context."[11] In Isaiah 25:8 the prophet looks forward to the time when God will wipe the tears from his people's eyes and "will swallow up death forever." For Isaiah this is the day of the Lord's "salvation" for which his people have been waiting; it is set firmly in the context of God's conquest over his enemies (25:9–12). The whole context of this part of Isaiah 25 provides an insight into Paul's understanding of the conquest of death. Thus, while the word "victory" is not present in either the Hebrew or the Greek of Isaiah 25, it is this original context that gives rise to Paul's use of the word. For Paul the word "victory" sums up what Isaiah anticipates. The bringing down of the proud and rebellious opponents of God's people, and hence the conquest of death itself is now, for Paul, to be seen in the light of Christ and his work. This quotation is especially interesting because it is the only place that Paul quotes Scripture where he still anticipates its fulfillment in the future.

The second quotation in v. 55 (though perhaps "allusion" is a better word) confirms both the glory of the day when death has been vanquished and also specifically serves to remind the reader of the link between death and sin on which Paul elaborates in v. 56. The words are drawn from Hosea 13:14, though again Paul makes changes. The Hebrew asks, "O Death, where are your plagues?" and asks, "O Sheol, where is your sting?" (ESV). The LXX asks, "Oh Death, where is your punishment?" and "Where is your sting, Oh Hades?" Paul thus changes the "plagues" of the Hebrew or the

---

9. For a further examination of the kingdom of God in Paul, see ch. 3 in Kreitzer, *Jesus and God in Paul's Eschatology*, 131–64.

10. The aorist passive (κατεπόθη) is gnomic, having a perfective aspect but expressing a general truth. It is therefore probably best translated as present in English.

11. Hays, *First Corinthians*, 295.

"punishment" of the Greek to "victory" and addresses both questions to Death personified. The vocative, "Oh Death" (θάνατε) is one of only two examples in the New Testament where something rather than someone is addressed in the vocative.[12] The personification is striking. The conquest of death is in the end the conquest of an enemy as Paul has shown in v. 26. The origin of Paul's use of the word "victory" here continues to be debated among the commentaries, as it was in v. 54. Hays suggests that Paul "changes" the "penalty" of the LXX to "victory" (δίκη to νῖκος), but adds that Paul probably did this in the light of Hosea's "larger message of God's ultimate mercy."[13] Whether its origin lies in various Greek translations or mistranslations, it is surely Paul's point that the personified enemy Death has been defeated and hence "victory" accomplished. Paul goes on in v. 57 to show that this "victory" is won by the Lord Jesus Christ.

The "sting" (κέντρον) is the *deathly* sting that may be found in a scorpion or a venomous insect or animal (cf. Rev 9:10). Thus the link between sin and death is firmly established once again. As Paul shows in v. 56, it is sin that has *stung* its victims in a way that has led to death. And so the rhetorical questions of v. 55 are little more than a taunt to Death. Its sting has gone. Indeed, where once it seemed to conquer all in its path, it no longer has any victory. As the last trumpet is sounded and the perishable puts on the imperishable, all Death's power has been rendered useless. So certain is this that even though the Christian still has a perishable body, the sting has already been drawn, much as one might suck the poison from the bite of a snake or the sting of a scorpion. The taunts are thus presented in the present tense as Paul demonstrates to

his readers that all of this is possible through the finished work of Christ on the cross. This is perhaps the greatest of the glories of the "word of the cross" for the believer and why Paul can talk of Christians, even now, as "us who are being saved" (1:18).

15:56 Now the sting of death is sin, and the power of sin is the law (τὸ δὲ κέντρον τοῦ θανάτου ἡ ἁμαρτία, ἡ δὲ δύναμις τῆς ἁμαρτίας ὁ νόμος). At first glance v. 56 seems to be anticlimactic and almost a diversion from the substance of Paul's argument in this section. However, it serves both to explain the cause of the "sting" in the first place and so also to introduce the extraordinary nature of Christ's victory, a victory for which grateful thanks must be given to God (v. 57) and to which the Christian must respond with a life of service (v. 58). For the sting of death to be dealt with, sin must be dealt with. For Paul the biblical understanding of death as God's judgment upon the sin of humanity is a given (cf. Rom 1:32). Genesis 3 narrates the expulsion of Adam and Eve from the garden and the fulfillment of the promise of death (Gen 2:17) as Adam is told he will return to the dust of the earth (Gen 3:19). That Paul has this judgment of God in mind as he thinks of death has been noted above when he expounded upon Adam and sin and death (1 Cor 15:21–22; cf. Rom 5:17–19). It is vital to see here that *sin* is the ultimate problem, not death itself. The latter is a divine consequence of the former (Rom 6:23a). This also has been part of Paul's discussion in various parts of this epistle, but especially earlier in this chapter. The creedal formula speaks of Christ's death "for our sins" (v. 3). If Christ has not been raised, then, he has argued, people are still in their sins (v. 17). Thus resurrection, specifically Christ's res-

---

12. Cf. "Oh heaven" in Rev 18:20.

13. Hays, *First Corinthians*, 276. For detailed discussion on how Paul may have been using the texts here, see Christo-

pher D. Stanley, *Paul and the Language of Scripture: Citation Technique in the Pauline Epistles and Contemporary Literature* (Cambridge: Cambridge University Press, 1992), 209ff.

urrection, means that sin has been dealt with (Rom 4:25), while no resurrection means sin retains its power to bring death. This also explains Paul's regular appeal in his epistles for Christians to stop sinning or to live Christ-like lives (6:8; 8:12; 15:34), for their lives should reflect their present situation as recipients of Christ's victory over sin.

The second clause in this verse is more difficult because it is so abbreviated. It speaks of the relationship of sin and the *law*. This relationship of sin and the law (and death) is addressed in much greater detail in Romans 5:8–21, 6:12–23, 7:7–14 and in Galatians 3–5. There is no reason to suppose that Paul later developed his thinking about the law and sin when he came to write Romans. The abbreviated comment here suggests that Paul had preached about this and taught it and so his meaning would be plain to his readers. For Paul the law was a gracious gift of God that was "holy," "righteous," and "spiritual" (Rom 7:12, 14). Indeed, in Romans 7:13 Paul explicitly says that "that which is good" (the law) did *not* "become death to me." Rather, it was sin that produced death, and the law revealed that sin. For Paul the law functioned in a number of ways. The most important for consideration here in v. 56 is the function of revealing God's covenantal demands and the enumerating of covenant sanctions on lawbreakers.[14] In other words, the law reveals God's will and hence the revelation of sin in all people, because all fail to live up to its demands, while it also functions to reveal the (righteous) covenantal judgment of God on all sinners. To speak then, as here, of "the power of sin" (ἡ δὲ δύναμις τῆς ἁμαρτίας) as "the law" is to describe the way in which sin uses the law to draw attention

to disobedience and the failure of a person to obey the Lord. In effect, its power is to "imprison" or "shut up" all people "under sin" (Gal 3:22 ESV). It reveals sin and even encourages sin in the defiant and rebellious sinner, but it is unable to achieve the forgiveness and expiation of sin so needed if death is to have no sting (Gal 3:21). In fact, it reveals the hopelessness of people in their inability to obey and so confirms the justice of their judgment (2 Cor 3:6). Thus, sin truly has a power that is legitimated by the very law of God itself. It is a power to hold any sinner captive to death.

15:57 But thanks be to God who gives us the victory through our Lord Jesus Christ (τῷ δὲ θεῷ χάρις τῷ διδόντι ἡμῖν τὸ νῖκος διὰ τοῦ κυρίου ἡμῶν Ἰησοῦ Χριστοῦ). The opening "but" (δέ) sets up the contrast between death, sin, and law and the victory in Christ. It is only in the light of all that Paul has said about sin, death, the perishable body, and the essential transformation that is needed to escape sin's power that the true wonder of the "good news" "through which [we] are being saved" (vv. 1–2), and the staggering impact of the phrase "Christ died for our sins" (v. 3), can truly be appreciated. Only as it is truly understood that the resurrection of Jesus reveals a total and radical shattering of the power of sin do we come to see what praise is due to the one "who gives us" (τῷ διδόντι) this victory over sin and death. The present tense of the participle reminds us that though the transformation is future the work is already done. This is a *gift* of God in Jesus. It is not something that the law could give, though the law pointed clearly to the need for the forgiving grace

---

14. For further examination of this use of "law" in the light of 2 Cor 2:14–4:6 see Frank Thielman, *Paul & the Law: A Contextual Approach* (Downers Grove, IL: IVP Academic, 1995), 107–18. For further, reasonably accessible and extended discussions on the use and function of "law" in Paul's correspondence, see Thielman (above), also Brian S. Rosner, *Paul and the*

Law: Keeping the Commandments of God, NSBT 31 (Downers Grove, IL: InterVarsity Press, 2013); Dunn, *Theology of Paul*, 128–61; Stephen Westerholm, *Justification Reconsidered: Rethinking a Pauline Theme* (Grand Rapids: Eerdmans, 2013); Seyoon Kim, *Paul and the New Perspective: Second Thoughts on the Origin of Paul's Gospel* (Grand Rapids: Eerdmans, 2002).

of God. It is not something that could be earned by a person's works. But it is a victory given by God and that happens "through" (διά) Christ. He is the agent by whom God's gracious gift of victory over sin and death comes to his people. If the power of sin is the law (15:56), the power and wisdom of God is Christ (1:24). When the power of God is set against the power of sin, there is no contest (cf. 2:5). Christ is the victor. God has ensured that indeed he is the source of their life in Christ (see comment at 1:30a). "Through" is thus a shorthand for all that has been said elsewhere in this epistle about God's work in Christ in saving his people and especially his work on the cross (1:18, 23–24).

Never will Paul allow his readers to forget that Christ's death was "for our sins." The sting of death has been drawn, but at great cost. In Christ's death the believer finds life, for it was there that the righteous judgment of God on sin was carried out. It is here that the sinner encounters all the gracious wonder of the divine compact to save a people for God who would be his possession forever. In Christ's resurrection, as Paul has portrayed it, the believer contemplates the firstfruits of a harvest in which later he or she also takes part. Meanwhile, though the believer awaits "the end" for the final resurrection, he or she right now discovers God "gives" the victory in such a certain way that Death can be taunted with the new reality, and God's people can rest in confidence that the power of sin has been destroyed by the infinitely greater power of God. So, *"thanks be to God!"* (τῷ δὲ θεῷ χάρις).

15:58 Therefore my beloved brothers [and sisters], be steadfast, unmovable, always abounding in the work of the Lord, because you know that your labor is not in vain in the Lord (Ὥστε, ἀδελφοί μου ἀγαπητοί, ἑδραῖοι γίνεσθε, ἀμετακίνητοι, περισσεύοντες ἐν τῷ ἔργῳ τοῦ κυρίου πάντοτε, εἰδότες ὅτι ὁ κόπος ὑμῶν οὐκ ἔστιν κενὸς ἐν κυρίῳ). Paul ends this section of teaching, as so

often (cf. vv. 34, 49), in exhortation to the Lord's service. The exhortation is a consequence of what has been said, "Therefore" (ὥστε, cf. 7:24; 11:33). Polemic has gone, and Paul reminds his readers that he loves them as family, setting his exhortation within this context of affectionate love (ἀγαπητοί; a vocative). As we have seen before (1:10–11, 26; 2:1, etc.), the use of "brothers" has a broader semantic range here than just male members of the community; hence "brothers [and sisters]." This is the community he loves, and he urges them first to be "steadfast" and "unmovable." In vv. 1–2 he had spoken of the gospel "on which you stand" and added "if you hold fast to the word I preached, unless you believed in vain." In the light of all he has said about the resurrection and the victory over death, Paul now reflects back on the start of this chapter. They must not let the doubt and skepticism of some about the resurrection sway them. The present imperative (γίνεσθε) governs both adjectival nouns and the following clause. The first adjectival noun speaks to conviction or firmness of direction ("steadfast," ἑδραῖοι; cf. 7:37), and the second speaks to their tendency to be "shifting" or "swaying" in that conviction (ἀμετακίνητοι; "be unmovable"). This latter idea is also seen in Colossians 1:23 where a related verb refers to not "shifting" from "the hope of the gospel" (ESV), which is much what the adjectival noun means here. Paul affirms that it is this gospel of hope in the death of Christ for sins and in his resurrection and victory over death on which they must continue to take their stand just as they did when they received it originally (15:3).

The next clause also forms the third part of Paul's exhortation. This could be translated as "and abound in. . . ." The Corinthians are to respond to the Lord's grace in Christ with the work to which they have been called and for which they have been gifted by the Holy Spirit. The use of the word "abounding" may indicate that Paul has in mind once again the needful, loving work of Christians to build up the church of Christ. It is this that he urged of the Corinthians as they sought to use their grace-gifts in 14:12: "Since you are enthusiasts for inspirations of the Spirit, strive that you may *abound* [ζητεῖτε ἵνα περισσεύητε] in the building up of the church" (cf. 1 Thess 3:12; 4:1, 10). The idea of "abounding" carries with it a sense of eagerness and excess. With such a staggering salvation in front of them and with the glorious prospect of the resurrection body, the response of Christians to God's gracious work in Christ should be one that "pours over" in almost excessive enthusiasm and dedication.

The genitive "of the Lord" (τοῦ κυρίου) is objective. The work in which Christians are to abound is *for* the Lord.[15] And it is for this reason that they should know, just as Paul knew of his own work (15:14), that such labor for him is not "in vain" (κενός). The final clause provides the reason for all the exhortations, not just the last one ("because you know"). Their work will stand before the Lord and not be burned up (3:12–15). After all, they have certainly not "believed in vain" (εἰκῇ; 15:2). Of course, the fact that such work will not be "in vain" must be attributed entirely to God himself. As noted so often in this epistle, God has given his grace-gifts to achieve such work. The fact of the matter is that if the Christian's work is not to be in vain, then it is ultimately due only to the fact that

God's grace to the Christian is itself "not in vain," as Paul shows so clearly (15:10; κενός). Truly, God gives it all: the "victory" is his, and any response that the believer may offer is provided for and enabled by him.

This chapter thus concludes on one of the great themes that courses through this epistle: the theme of God's grace. The whole chapter, though dealing with a specific issue, namely, the denial of the resurrection, has in fact reminded the reader again and again of God's grace: his grace in the story of salvation summarized in the creedal formula; his grace in providing the preaching of the gospel (vv. 9–11); his grace in raising Christ from the dead as the firstfruits of all who die in faith; his grace in drawing all things to himself as Christ reigns and conquers all God's enemies, even death; his grace in providing an appropriate body for a person's continued existence at "the end" at Christ's coming; his grace in enabling frail human beings to bear the image of the man of heaven; his grace in ensuring that both those who have died before the coming and those still alive at the coming will benefit from the transformation and resurrected life; his grace in providing for an appropriate response in this age to such wonders awaiting the believer in the next. In the end, this chapter has been a detailed analysis of the results of the gospel proclamation of "Christ crucified." As Paul stated in 1:31, "'He who boasts, let him boast in the Lord,'" and this is precisely what he does in v. 57.

---

15. In 16:10 the "work of the Lord" in which Paul and Timothy are involved is more likely to be the work of evangelism (cf. 16:9). It may be that this is also in Paul's mind for the whole church at Corinth as they "abound" in it, but this is less likely.

Theology in Application

The Now and the Not Yet

Some Corinthians were claiming to be "spiritual" over against other Christians, whom they deemed either unspiritual or, at best, less so. Paul has argued throughout this epistle that all God's people possess the Holy Spirit and so are "spiritual," and he has carefully defined what such a person should look like since, though spiritual, they were behaving like infants. It appears their great emphasis on and understanding of what it is to be "spiritual" had led some even to deny the bodily resurrection. Paul has insisted that the indwelling Spirit of Christ is the one who raises the dead in renewed, transformed, and imperishable bodies suitable for eternity. To this Paul has now attached a brief mention of the inheritance of the kingdom of God. This, we have argued, is for Paul a summary way of describing the experience of the fulfillment of all God's covenant promises. While in this age, God's people must reflect in their life the fact that they are already possessed by God's Spirit and must live lives appropriate to the kingdom. It is not until the final victory over death is seen, and the full number of God's people are raised to glory, that they will experience all that God has promised. Even now Christians enjoy the presence of God with them and covenant participation in Christ with all his people. They enjoy their gifts of the Spirit, and they experience peace with God and his steadfast love. Yet more awaits them.

In today's church there is much misunderstanding about what can be experienced in this age of all that God has promised and what is still yet to come. The lack of emphasis on the bodily resurrection (because the church so often defaults to a nebulous form of spiritual existence in heaven as the goal) has meant that many Christians have failed to see that they are expecting too much in this age. Some teach that with enough faith all can be healed from illness. Some teach that the promises of wealth and even land found in many places in Scripture can be experienced in this age. Of course, Scriptures teach that the indwelling Holy Spirit is the guarantee of this inheritance. They also give a clear understanding that we can enjoy now the firstfruits of that final kingdom inheritance. The grace-gifts the church enjoys do give an advance taste of what will follow. There is continuity. Yet much is missing still, and this is summarized perhaps best in Paul's words "perishable" and "imperishable." It is only when the body has become imperishable that the full kingdom of God can be enjoyed and God's promises entirely fulfilled. Those promises do include land (the new earth), full healing (imperishable and immortal bodies), and full peace with God (sin and death have been vanquished). Among those who come to expect too much now, there is often a poor understanding of all that is implied by the bodily resurrection and the coming of the King in glory. For those who simply criticize such theology, it might be better to urge a greater examination of this argument in 1 Corinthians 15. For Christians to inherit the imperishable kingdom of God, they must, like Christ, be raised from the dead or be fully "changed" (15:51, 52). An overrealized eschatology will almost invariably lead to a diminished emphasis on the Christian's resurrection and the perfection of the renewed creation.

Living in the Present with Eager Anticipation of the Future

Throughout Scripture God's people are encouraged by God for their present existence as he holds before them their future. Abraham was encouraged with the promised land as he set out from Mesopotamia. Moses and the wilderness generation were encouraged in the same way. The prophets looked forward to the peace of God's covenant people and their inheritance of the land. Above all, the coming of the Davidic king and his rule was held before the people as encouragement that God would indeed save and restore his people. At the same time, the experience of God's judgment when his people rebelled against him became a warning and challenge pointing to the future judgment (10:1–13; cf. 3:12–15). Paul draws these various themes together in the epistle with this great, climactic presentation of the resurrection. The future directly impacts the present. The return of the resurrected Lord means that God's people must be *prepared*. Their existence must *witness* to that future. And their *identification* with God's people, as those who *stand* rather than fall, must be affirmed.

The presence of God's Holy Spirit in the lives of his people means they are truly spiritual people though, as yet, still with perishable bodies. However, the Spirit provides for them in the present in terms of the power to live for God. His presence also provides for their true identification as spiritual people who have been redeemed in Christ crucified. He guarantees their standing before God rather than their shaming or falling (10:12). This identification will be authenticated in a Christian's life as it is lived out in love (ch. 13). Such people must not and do not have to wait for the end of this age to be "spiritual." They are that already and must reflect in this age what that means. Their lives must "abound" in all this (15:58).

While the wisdom of this age with its idolatry, self-centered pride, and immorality currently sits alongside the wisdom of God that his people have come to know in Christ, it is the resurrection that reveals how the two wisdoms will eventually be separated entirely. The church's continued existence as God's people in these overlapping ages is only possible through the sustaining power of the indwelling Spirit. He empowers them to live a holy, separated, Christ-focused life in anticipation of the perfection of their future existence. But the present is thus made all the more important. What is done now and how life is lived now anticipates the future. Life is to be lived as a foretaste of what is to come. Those who are the Lord's now, while mortal and perishing, find themselves thoroughly affirmed in their present lives by the Spirit's presence. They await the Lord's return and their own resurrection, for then they will be able to serve and to imitate Christ and live holy lives as immortal and imperishable beings from whom all sin has been removed.

The lack of eagerness for Christ's return in the modern church has been noted above. However, it is important to see how much poor theology in how many areas has led to this. Whether it has been a reaction against a false heavenly eschatology of people becoming forever non-physical spiritual beings, or the preaching of an over-realized eschatology, God's people need to lift their eyes again to the resurrected Lord and see their future in him. But other problems have further hindered a healthy understanding of living now in anticipation of this future. The Western church has become so comfortable that many in the Christian community do not even see or feel much of the "pain" of the fallen world. Many are so happy with the now that they see no point in thinking much of the resurrection and are unsure what might be better about a new earth. There has been a failure to preach the covenant promises of God and to teach the depths of what the kingdom of God means in all its fullness in Christ. Being aware of the persecuted and suffering church worldwide may help gain a better perspective on this. Returning to preaching a biblical call for holiness and the need to flee idolatry and immorality may also help as people become more aware of their sinfulness and their struggle in this age for holiness of life. Teaching clearly, as Paul does, that those who fail to follow the Lord will not "inherit" the kingdom of God (1 Cor 6:9–10; Gal 5:21) may also encourage Christians in the need to serve and in the knowledge that their labor in the Lord is not in vain.

1 Corinthians 16:1–24

Literary Context

Chapter 16 sees the apostle drawing his lengthy epistle to an end. Paul begins by briefly addressing the subject of the collection for the saints that had probably been raised by the Corinthians in a letter to him (vv. 1–4). While there is no direct link between these opening verses and the chapter on the resurrection, Paul's reference in 15:58 to "always abounding in the work of the Lord," rather naturally leads into the generosity of spirit that Paul seeks with regard to the collection. In 2 Corinthians 8:2, 7 and 9:12 where the offering is in mind Paul uses the same word of "abounding" in good work (περισσεύω). Paul's commitment to living out the implications of "covenantal participation" (κοινωνία) in the gospel with the saints at Corinth is reflected in his personal comments, reflections on his travel plans, pastoral concern for them and for Timothy, and in his request that they pray for an open door for effective ministry (v. 9). As he urges the congregation to learn from the example of Stephanas and give recognition to those such as him and Fortunatus and Achaicus, the emphasis on unity and wise leadership is stated positively and contrasts with the opening chapter in which names are used to illustrate divisions. In the final personal greeting (vv. 21–24), Paul returns to the central thought of the epistle, that "love" is the authenticator of any faithful Christian. Negatively, Paul speaks of judgment on those who do not show love (v. 22) and, positively, affirms his love for this church in v. 24. The final verse, with its emphasis on Paul's own love for this people, indicates that Paul in fact imagines coming to them not "with a rod," but "in love" (4:21). It is an altogether appropriate ending for an epistle that has insisted that "love builds up" (8:1) and has urged that all should "pursue love" (14:1).

Main Idea

The Corinthians should raise a collection for Jerusalem. Other miscellaneous plans, comments and exhortations climax with farewell greetings and a final appeal for love.

Translation

1 Corinthians 16:1–24

1a	Topic introduction	Now	concerning the collection for the saints,
b	Circumstance		as I directed the churches of Galatia,
c	Assertion		**so you also are to do.**

2a	Time		On the first day of each week
b	Exhortation		**let each of you lay aside something**
c	Purpose		to save up,
d	Circumstance		however one may prosper,
e	Result		so that ...
f	Time		whenever I may come
g	Result		... there should not be collections
			then.

3a	Time	Now	when I arrive,
b	Identification for 3c		whomever you approve,
c	Assertion	these	**I will send** with authorizing letters
d	Purpose		to carry your gift to Jerusalem.

4a	Condition (protasis)	And	if my going also seems advisable,
b	Assertion (apodosis)		**they can go with me.**

5a	Assertion	Now **I will visit you**
b	Time	after I have passed through Macedonia—
c	Cause	**for** I am going through Macedonia—
6a	Assertion	and **perhaps I will stay with you or**
b	Time	**even spend the winter,**
c	Purpose	so that you may send me on my way wherever I may go.
7a	Assertion (negative)	For **I do not want to see you now**
b	Circumstance	just in passing,
c	Basis	for **I hope to remain with you**
d	Time	for some time,
e	Desire	if the Lord permits.
8a	Assertion	But **I will remain in Ephesus**
b	Time	until Pentecost,
9a	Basis for 8	because a wide and effective door has opened to me, and
b		there are many adversaries.
10a	Time	Now
		whenever Timothy may arrive,
b	Exhortation	**see to it that he is without fear among you,**
c	Reason	for he is carrying out the work of the Lord, even as I am.
	Inference	Therefore,
11a	Exhortation	**let no one disdain him,**
b	Exhortation (contrast)	but **send him on his way in peace,**
c	Purpose	so that he may return to me,
d	Basis	for **I am expecting him,** with the brothers [and sisters].
12a	Topic introduction	Now concerning our brother Apollos,
b	Assertion	**I greatly urged him to visit you**
c	Circumstance	with the brothers [and sisters],
d	Assertion (negative)	but **it was by no means his wish at this time to come.**
e	Contrast (positive)	But **he will come**
		when he has the opportunity.
13a	Exhortations (1)	**Be alert,**
b	List (2)	**stand firm in the faith,**
c	(3)	**be brave,** [and]
d	(4)	**be strong.**
14a	(5)	**Let all that you do be done in love.**

Continued on next page.

Continued from previous page.

15a	Assertion	Now **I exhort you** brothers [and sisters]
b	Basis for 16	—you know that the household of Stephanas is the firstfruits ↺ of Achaia, and
c		that they devoted themselves to the service of the saints—
16a	Complement to 15a	also to subject yourselves to such people and
b		to all who share together in the work and
c		labor hard.
17a	Assertion	And **I rejoice at the arrival of Stephanas and Fortunatus and Achaicus,**
b	Cause	because they have made up for your absence;
18a	Basis for 17b	for **they refreshed my spirit**
b	Comparative	even as [they have] yours.
c	Exhortation	Therefore, **give recognition to such people.**
19a	Greeting	**The churches of Asia greet you.**
b	Greeting	**Aquila and Prisca warmly greet you** in the Lord,
c		together with the church in their house.
20a	Greeting	**All the brothers [and sisters] greet you.**
b	Greeting	**Greet one another**
c	Manner	with a holy kiss.
21a	Greeting	**[I send] this greeting**
b	Manner	with my own—Paul's—hand.
22a	Condition	If anyone does not love the Lord,
b	Curse formula	**let that one be anathema.**
c	Prayer	**Our Lord come!**
23a	Blessing	**The grace of the Lord Jesus be with you.**
24a		**My love be with you all in Christ Jesus.**

Structure

The final chapter may be divided relatively straightforwardly into five or six parts. The collection for the saints is a self-contained section (vv. 1–4), which also serves to introduce Paul's own travel plans. Paul's plans and ministry opportunities are then developed in the second section (vv. 5–9). Some include vv. 10–12 in this section as well since they continue to address matters of travel concerning Timothy and Apollos. Here, we treat this separately as forming a third section. The fourth section (vv. 13–18) incorporates a number of exhortations concerning the faith and life of the church. The fifth section consists largely of greetings (vv. 19–24). For our purposes this last section has been divided into two: the first being greetings from others (vv. 19–20), followed by Paul's personal greetings and closure centered on the theme of "love" (vv. 21–24). We shall later note a further, useful breakdown of the structure of vv. 13–24 provided by Weima.[1]

Exegetical Outline

➡ **X. Closing Instructions and Comments (16:1–24)**

    A. Instructions for the Collection (16:1–4)

        1. Put Aside Gifts Each Week (16:1–2)

        2. Paul Will Collect and Deliver the Gifts (16:3–4)

    B. Paul's Travel Plans (16:5–9)

        1. Plans to Visit Corinth (16:5–7)

        2. His Immediate Plans (16:8–9)

    C. Note about Timothy and Apollos (16:10–12)

    D. Various Exhortations (16:13–18)

    E. Greetings in the Lord from Others (16:19–20)

    F. Paul's Own Closure to the Letter (16:21–24)

Explanation of the Text

16:1 Now concerning the collection for the saints, as I directed the churches of Galatia, so you also are to do (Περὶ δὲ τῆς λογείας τῆς εἰς τοὺς ἁγίους, ὥσπερ διέταξα ταῖς ἐκκλησίαις τῆς Γαλατίας, οὕτως καὶ ὑμεῖς ποιήσατε). Paul changes the subject and addresses a financial collection for God's people. There is some discussion about whether "now concerning" (περὶ δέ) here and in v. 12 introduces a further matter arising from the Corinthian correspondence or not. Previously in 7:1, 25, 8:1, and 12:1, it has seemed to do this. Certainly it is used rhetorically to introduce a new subject, and contextually it seems likely that these final comments from Paul do indeed pick up at least two minor matters from the Corinthian letter to Paul: the "collection" and a question relating to Apollos.

The nature of a question regarding the collection must be treated with the usual caution when we try to reconstruct what the Corinthians wrote from what *Paul* wrote. There are two clear possibilities. It may be that they had heard about Paul's collection for "the saints" in Jerusalem (v. 3) from other churches, such as those he mentions in Galatia, and were asking if they could take part. However, it is likely Paul already would have sought to involve churches as urgently as possible in such a collection. It seems more likely, especially from what Paul says here, that they had asked about how the money would be handled and perhaps how they could make sure it was kept safe and delivered to the right people by the right people.[2] In fact, Paul's unique use of this word for "collection" (λογεία)

---

1. Jeffrey A. D. Weima, *Neglected Endings: The Significance of the Pauline Letter Closings*, JSNTSup 101 (Sheffield: JSOT, 1994), 203–8.

2. Verlyn D. Verbrugge suggests that Paul has heard that

the Corinthians are reluctant to stay involved in the project and that he writes to command them to do so. He cites the continuing trouble Paul seems to have had with the Corinthians over the collection (though much of this hypothesis is

may suggest the word originates in Corinth. The word, not used elsewhere in the New Testament, can refer to contributions or "non-regular" occasional taxes or to a collection for religious purposes.[3] Here it is clear that the latter is in mind. Indeed, Thiselton suggests that Paul's use of the word is deliberate because he wished "to avoid any implication that it is to be regarded as a kind of 'tax,' and certainly not as a repeated tax."[4] Elsewhere Paul uses a variety of words to speak of the collection or offering for Jerusalem. For example, in v. 3 he refers to it as a "grace" (χάρις), while in 2 Corinthians 8:4 and 9:1, 12, 13 he calls it a "service" (διακονία).

Little is known of the true reasons behind this collection for Jerusalem, though much has been written about it, especially in relation to the references to a collection in Galatians 2:10 and the extended discussion of 2 Corinthians 8–9.[5] It seems likely that the Council of Jerusalem recorded in Acts 15 may lie behind what is going on. Some years after that, Paul refers back to what was agreed there as he writes in Galatians 2:10 and says, "All they asked was that we should continue to remember the poor, the very thing I was eager to do."

However, three significant points should be noted. First, giving is a subject to which Paul returns in each of the major epistles of Romans, 1 and 2 Corinthians, and Galatians. This suggests that it figures in his thinking at a deeper level than simply his concern for poorer Christians in Jerusalem. Secondly, it is possible that the special poverty of the church in Jerusalem, partly noticed

in Acts 15 and Galatians 2, may have been due to the special role its early members had fulfilled at the start of the mission of the church shortly after the day of Pentecost. For a while they sold their possessions and had things in common (Acts 4:32, 34–36). This may have led to considerable poverty among many, even if there were other reasons why this poverty had later become more serious. If this were the case, then part of Paul's concern is to ensure that the churches that had been founded since those early days should recognize the debt of love they owed to the Jerusalem church, without whose sacrifice, financial and in other ways, the early church might well have floundered.

Thirdly, though Paul can speak of various motivations for giving, in 2 Corinthians 8:9–10, 24 Paul speaks of it as a test of and evidence of "love." In 1 Corinthians much has been said of "love" as the marker of authentic Christians. Even though Paul does not build on this at this point in chapter 16, it is not far from his mind as we see in vv. 14, 22, 24. The link he makes in 2 Corinthians provides a general theological background that explains why giving is such an important theme for Paul. *This is a way of reflecting the grace of the gospel itself and membership in God's people.* The Lord is the example: "You know the grace of our Lord Jesus Christ, that though he was rich, yet for your sake he became poor, so that you through his poverty might become rich" (2 Cor 8:9). Such a response to the Lord's grace and love is the evidence of love in the believer, and so in 8:8 Paul writes, "I am *testing the genuineness of your love*" (NRSV). Similarly in 8:24,

---

dependent upon a reconstruction based on detail from 2 Corinthians). He further points to the rhetoric of the "commanding letter" of vv. 1–2, the aorist imperatives, and other evidence. See Verbrugge, *Paul's Style of Church Leadership Illustrated by His Instructions to the Corinthians on the Collection* (San Francisco: Mellen Research University Press, 1992), 60ff.

3. For papyri evidence, see MM 377. See also BDAG 597; G. Kittel, "λογεία," *TDNT* 4:282.

4. Thiselton, *1 Corinthians*, 1318–19.

5. Verbrugge, *Paul's Style of Church Leadership*, 60ff. Among many on this subject, see also D. Georgi, *Remembering the Poor: The History of Paul's Collection for Jerusalem* (Nashville: Abingdon, 1992); G. W. Peterman, *Paul's Gift from Philippi: Conventions of Gift Exchange and Christian Giving*, SNTSMS 92 (Cambridge: Cambridge University Press, 1997).

speaking of Titus and other administrators of the offering, he writes, "Therefore show these men *the proof of your love* and the reason for our pride in you, so that the churches can see it." In 1 Corinthians 13 Paul highlighted the centrality of love and has consistently contrasted it with the abuse of the grace-gifts by the elitists. Though this may seem a minor matter at the end of the letter, for Paul it remains vital because giving is just one of those very public ways a church can show that it truly loves in a way that builds others up.

This approach of Paul to giving, centered in the need of others and the mutual fellowship across churches and focused in the Christ who gave himself for his people, is undoubtedly different from how giving and receiving gifts were regarded in Greco-Roman society. The apostle's observations on giving may touch upon the recurring issue of elitism in 1 Corinthians. It seems that giving almost universally involved obligation in the Greco-Roman world. Giving and receiving was part of "social reciprocity," much as is still seen in many cultures today. If a gift is received, there was often an obligation to give back.[6] The one who gives is regarded as the "socially superior" unless reciprocity can be maintained. Honor will be gained by the one who can gain the upper hand in these exchanges of gifts.[7] To speculate, not unreasonably perhaps, it may be that some of the Corinthians were quite concerned about who delivered the gift and who was seen to be involved in the transaction of gift giving since this helped indicate their social status. This would fit with their general concern throughout every area of the church's life to evidence "status" of one sort or another. Paul's theological understanding of giving, therefore, though not laid out here in this brief paragraph, provides a radically different perspective on giving from that which perhaps was driving the elite, wealthy Corinthian Christians. For him there is no expectation at all of reciprocity. Rather, Paul exhorts them strongly with an aorist imperative to "do" the same as he had "directed" the Galatian churches (cf. Acts 13–14).

16:2 On the first day of each week let each of you lay aside something to save up, however one may prosper, so that whenever I may come there should not be collections then (κατὰ μίαν σαββάτου ἕκαστος ὑμῶν παρ᾽ ἑαυτῷ τιθέτω θησαυρίζων ὅ τι ἐὰν εὐοδῶται, ἵνα μὴ ὅταν ἔλθω τότε λογεῖαι γίνωνται). This verse offers straightforward instructions to enable the collection to happen efficiently. "Each one" (ἕκαστος) is to give. They are to "lay aside" (τίθημι) money regularly each week (the present imperative suggests the continuity of this action) with the purpose of saving, so it can then be given when Paul comes.[8] Paul does not want to launch a brief (what we might call) "fund drive" that would really only allow the wealthy with extra money to participate. Allowing a period of time to accumulate some savings lets everyone become involved in the gift as "one may prosper." The verb "to prosper" (εὐοδόω) derives from the idea of being led well along a road. In Romans 1:10 it is used of Paul "succeeding" in travelling to Rome (see ESV). Here it comes to refer metaphorically to one whose pathway has prospered (cf. LXX Ezra 5:8; Tob 4:19). The clause is indefinite, though the switch to the third person from the second plural sounds strange in English: "However one might prosper" (ὅ τι ἐὰν εὐοδῶται). Paul's arrival is also indefinite. It is unclear when he was writing or when he would arrive. The fact that

---

6. For the most thorough examination of "gift" and giving in Paul's writings, set against and within the cultural context of that age, see Barclay, *Paul and the Gift*, 24–30, 183–88, 576–80.

7. Peterman, *Paul's Gift from Philippi*, 51–89. Also, Barclay, *Paul and the Gift*, 432–39.

8. The participle (θησαυρίζων) is probably correctly regarded as indicating "purpose" (so Wallace, *Greek Grammar*, 637).

he suggests each week may indicate that it may be quite a while until he eventually comes.

Paul probably hopes to achieve two results from what he says here. The first is a large offering through steady giving over a period of time. The second is the participation of all who are able to take part. The only exception would be those who for one reason or another were unable to join in, perhaps through unemployment or old age, or perhaps being an unpaid slave or servant. Though for Paul it is simply an aside to what he is saying, his reference to setting aside this money "on the first day of the week" (κατὰ μίαν σαββάτου) provides an interesting historical reflection. In Acts 20:7 there is a reference to worshipping with the breaking of bread and preaching on the first day of the week. The day seems to have become the main worship day quite early in the church's life. It is also referred to as "the Lord's Day" in Revelation 1:10 and frequently among second-century writers.[9]

16:3–4 Now when I arrive, whomever you approve, these I will send with authorizing letters to carry your gift to Jerusalem. And if my going also seems advisable, they can go with me (ὅταν δὲ παραγένωμαι, οὓς ἐὰν δοκιμάσητε, δι᾽ ἐπιστολῶν τούτους πέμψω ἀπενεγκεῖν τὴν χάριν ὑμῶν εἰς Ἰερουσαλήμ· ἐὰν δὲ ἄξιον ᾖ τοῦ κἀμὲ πορεύεσθαι, σὺν ἐμοὶ πορεύσονται). Paul now addresses the way in which the letter will be delivered and the part the Corinthians themselves may play in this process. As in the previous verse he refers to his coming to Corinth at some time soon (cf. 4:19; 11:34), though the timing is uncertain. Back in chapter 4 this talk of his coming had felt more like a threat. Here it is neutral. While he is with them, he will receive, presumably in the home(s) where they worship,

the offering that each has saved up at home. Since this is Paul's undertaking, he remains in control. But he explains that he is prepared to have whomever the Corinthians consider suitable for this important task take the money to Jerusalem. He will send letters of authorization with them. Such letters would have introduced the Corinthians to the leaders at the church of Jerusalem and made it clear that they travelled with Paul's authority and were to be trusted. The fact is that security was probably a serious concern both for Paul and the Corinthians. This may even have been part of the question raised with Paul in their letter and why he says that some of them will be involved in the delivery of the gift. For such an important job as this, Paul looks for people who are "approved" by the Corinthians. Their trustworthiness and maturity as Christians, no doubt, will be part of the recommendation Paul is seeking. The verb "approve" (δοκιμάζω) is one Paul used in 3:13 and 11:28. In 11:19 the cognate noun is used. In each case, the word carries connotations of a testing as it relates to standing before God and to the final day. While it does not necessarily connote all this here, it does likely refer to those who are mature Christians and so tested as *trusted Christians.*

The Greek translated as "with authorizing letters" (δι᾽ ἐπιστολῶν) is ambiguous. It is possible to read this as meaning that Paul will send those whom *the Corinthians accredit with letters* (AV, ESV). The more usual reading, and most likely, is that Paul intends to write letters of accreditation to accompany those whom the Corinthians trust and thus commend them to the Jerusalem church (TEV, NASB, REB).

Paul adds in v. 4 that if it seems "advisable" (ἄξιον) he will travel but they, the trusted Corin-

---

9. For a full discussion of the first day of the week, the "Lord's Day," and the reason for choosing the first day, which almost certainly has to do with the day of the resurrection, see R. J. Bauckham, "The Lord's Day" in *From Sabbath to Lord's Day: A Biblical, Historical, and Theological Investigation*, ed. D. A. Carson (Grand Rapids: Zondervan, 1982), 221–50.

thians, will travel with him. Once again this suggests that it is possible they were concerned with security: "Would their gift get there?" On the other hand, if they were concerned with status in gift-giving, Paul still allows that some of their own people will be allowed to accompany him. It is possible that the problem in Jerusalem itself might make it important for Paul to travel there. It may also be that Paul was wondering whether it was simply too dangerous for him to go there. While other passages may give a glimpse into what Paul was thinking, there is nothing in the text here to give any indication of Paul's concerns that would either cause him to wish to go or not to go. By the time of writing 2 Corinthians 1:15–16 it seems that Paul had decided he would accompany the gift to Jerusalem (cf. Rom 15:25–27).

Little would better establish the "covenant participation" (κοινωνία) of all God's people, Jew and Gentile, than the apostle Paul's accompanying of Gentiles back to Jerusalem with a gift from the next generation of churches populated with many converted pagans. Paul is able to see the beauty of the churches as individual churches when he writes to them, but as he speaks of his travels he reveals how clearly he also sees the beauty of their interrelatedness.

16:5–9 Now I will visit you after I have passed through Macedonia[10]—for I am going through Macedonia—and perhaps I will stay with you or even spend the winter, so that you may send me on my way wherever I may go. For I do not want to see you now just in passing, for I hope to remain with you for some time, if the Lord permits. But I will remain in Ephesus until Pentecost, because a wide and effective door has opened to me, and there are many adversaries (Ἐλεύσομαι δὲ πρὸς ὑμᾶς ὅταν Μακεδονίαν διέλθω· Μακεδονίαν γὰρ διέρχομαι· πρὸς ὑμᾶς δὲ τυχὸν παραμενῶ ἢ καὶ παραχειμάσω, ἵνα ὑμεῖς με προπέμψητε οὗ ἐὰν πορεύωμαι. οὐ θέλω γὰρ ὑμᾶς ἄρτι ἐν παρόδῳ ἰδεῖν, ἐλπίζω γὰρ χρόνον τινὰ ἐπιμεῖναι πρὸς ὑμᾶς, ἐὰν ὁ κύριος ἐπιτρέψῃ. ἐπιμενῶ δὲ ἐν Ἐφέσῳ ἕως τῆς πεντηκοστῆς· θύρα γάρ μοι ἀνέῳγεν μεγάλη καὶ ἐνεργής, καὶ ἀντικείμενοι πολλοί). In vv. 5–12 Paul talks about various travel plans and how these will affect the Corinthian church. In vv. 5–9 he specifically talks about his own plans, then in v. 10–11 he speaks of Timothy, and in v. 12 of Apollos. As Paul lays out his plans, it is clear that he thinks strategically for the sake of the gospel. A number of points may be noted about his approach to travel.

First, he always submits himself to the will of the Lord. All his work and travels are conditional upon the Lord's own plans for him (hence the conditional clause with its subjunctive). The word "permits" (ἐπιτρέπω) carries considerably more force than the expression James uses in James 4:15, "If the Lord wills [θέλω]." Among English-speaking Christians it has become commonplace to say, "The Lord willing," but it is often little more than a pious platitude. Paul knows that he is under "compulsion" (9:16) to preach and that this calling comes from the Lord who directs his every journey and every choice for the sake of the mission of the gospel. Thus this is not a throwaway "Christian" sentence; it speaks to Paul's understanding of obedience to the one who will permit or "allow" him to do some things and not others (cf. Rom 1:13; 1 Thess 2:18).

Secondly, subject to the Lord's permission, Paul operates pragmatically in the light of the priority of the gospel. A door, which is described almost anthropomorphically, has opened for Paul that is "wide and effective" (μεγάλη καὶ ἐνεργής). Paul

---

10. Macedonia was a large Roman province in the north of Greece, including the cities of Thessalonica and Philippi.

means that the ministry in Ephesus is thriving because God has opened a door for ministry[11] that is seeing fruit and therefore "effective" (ἐνεργής).[12] His mission constantly appears to be flexible even while being carefully planned, and when opportunities for the gospel open up he takes full advantage of them. Thus, he intends to remain in Ephesus for some time,[13] that is, until Pentecost. The mention of Pentecost assumes that the Corinthians from all backgrounds know Scripture and the Jewish feast times.[14] Rather than a specific date here, Paul may have in mind a period around Pentecost in late spring, much as we might say, "I will come at Easter."

Thirdly, Paul also strategically plans on the basis of *pastoral* needs. The relationship with Corinth was proving complex, to put it mildly! This letter itself is proof of that. There is no complete certainty to be had on how many letters Paul sent to them, or even how many visits Paul eventually made to them. But here Paul is indicating that this important and strategic church needed a lengthier stay than simply one of "passing through." He says he does "not want to see [them] *just in passing*" (ἐν παρόδῳ) and hopes to remain "some time" with them (v. 7). Part of the reason for staying with them is that they may send him on his way "wherever I may go" (οὗ ἐὰν πορεύωμαι; v. 6). While Paul did not take money during his stay in Corinth as he worked among them, he was prepared to take funds as he travelled elsewhere on his missionary journey. This may have been part of what he was expecting, but he would also have looked for their prayers and general support. He leaves it open as to where he may be going next, though we know he has in mind probably going to Jerusalem if "it seems advisable" (v. 4). His pastoral work at Corinth, when eventually he did go, seems to have met with considerable difficulty as well as some success. He probably ended up returning from Corinth, via Macedonia, to Ephesus (2 Cor 2:12–13).[15]

Fourthly, Paul is aware that he is fighting a spiritual battle. There are many "adversaries" (ἀντικείμενοι). The word here indicates those who are opposed both to him personally and to the message he proclaims.[16] Paul has already experienced life-threatening situations for the sake of the gospel. Perhaps he had already experienced this in Ephesus (see comments on 15:32). We get some understanding of how vicious some of these opponents could be when we read of the riot in Ephesus in Acts 19. Though this incident may have been later, the currents of ill will were probably with him throughout his stay in Ephesus.

These verses give a fascinating, brief insight into the way Paul made his plans and thought about his work and his travel. In the end the reader encounters an apostle who was prepared to give himself emotionally, physically, and spiritually to the task

---

11. Paul refers to an open "door" for ministry also in 2 Cor 2:12. In Col 4:3 he prays that God will "open to us a door for the word" (NRSV). In other words, Paul refers to God opening up opportunities for proclaiming the gospel of Christ (cf. Acts 14:27).

12. Also see Phlm 6 where Paul prays that "the sharing of your faith" may be "effective" (NRSV).

13. The prefix ἐπί intensifies the verb ἐπιμένω.

14. Pentecost refers to the Feast of Weeks. Whether Paul intentionally decides to wait for Pentecost for the sake of the Corinthians cannot be known. The most likely reason for choosing to travel then is that travel would be much easier

than in winter. However, his emphasis on the offering might also be part of his decision. The Feast of Weeks was known for its special freewill offering and was to be given, much as Paul describes above, "as the LORD your God blesses you" (Deut 16:10 ESV). Certainly the outpouring of the Holy Spirit commemorated by Christians at Pentecost would provide positive incentive for special offerings.

15. For a detailed attempt at reconstructing Paul's visits, see Jerome Murphy-O'Connor, *Paul: His Story* (Oxford: Oxford University Press, 2004), 291–332, 341–51.

16. Cf. Phil 1:28.

of preaching to which he had been called. In all this he was aware that if doors were opened for the gospel, it was the Lord's work. His task of itinerant apostle, though, also involved him in clear pastoral roles as he travelled, and so he could remain flexible about the amount of time he was needed in the various places he visited. Thus he knew he would need more time with the Corinthians at his next visit than he might have expected. Meanwhile, he is constantly aware of the spiritual battle he faces in the form of adversaries as he does "the work of the Lord" (v. 10).

16:10–11 Now whenever Timothy may arrive, see to it that he is without fear among you, for he is carrying out the work of the Lord, even as I am. Therefore, let no one disdain him, but send him on his way in peace, so that he may return to me, for I am expecting him, with the brothers [and sisters] (Ἐὰν δὲ ἔλθῃ Τιμόθεος, βλέπετε, ἵνα ἀφόβως γένηται πρὸς ὑμᾶς, τὸ γὰρ ἔργον κυρίου ἐργάζεται ὡς κἀγώ· μή τις οὖν αὐτὸν ἐξουθενήσῃ. προπέμψατε δὲ αὐτὸν ἐν εἰρήνῃ, ἵνα ἔλθῃ πρός με, ἐκδέχομαι γὰρ αὐτὸν μετὰ τῶν ἀδελφῶν). In 4:17 Paul had given the reason for Timothy being "sent,"[17] which was to "remind you of my ways in Christ." Clearly Paul held Timothy in high regard and sent him on various missions in his place, but here he emphasizes that Timothy is carrying out the Lord's work *even as Paul does*. Since Timothy is already on his way to the Corinthians, the indefinite clause better relates to the timing of his arrival than to whether he is actually travelling to Corinth. The difficulties of travel in those days frequently would create uncertainty as to the time of arrival. Timothy will stand before the Corin-

thians in the apostle's place, and there is a danger in that for him. Even though Paul's insistence on this point could make matters worse for Timothy, it is important that the Corinthians understand the authority with which Timothy will come. He comes as one who, like Paul, does the work of the Lord no matter what people might feel about him. What Paul fears is that some might take out their arrogant frustration with Paul on his messenger. Paul's letter has been strongly critical of the elitists in this church, and Timothy's expressed purpose for this visit is to reinforce Paul's teaching (4:17). In 4:18 Paul had again mentioned the arrogance of the Corinthians. Paul will come to confront them (4:19), but Timothy will get there first as Paul's ambassador. Therefore, Paul appeals to his readers that Timothy should not be given reason for any uneasiness as he comes to them. He asks them to send Timothy back to him and the other brothers and sisters in Ephesus with the same practical care and support that he himself will expect when he passes through (16:6).[18] "In peace" (ἐν εἰρήνῃ) does not refer to matters of reconciliation but is simply a polite form of dismissal, much as it can be a polite form of address.

Given all this, Paul urges the Corinthians to honor this younger man, who had been involved in planting the church with Paul in the first place (Acts 18:5). They should not "disdain" (ἐξουθενέω) him, a word that implies regarding him as of no account (cf. 1:28; 6:4). They should heed what he has to say as Paul's ambassador.

16:12 Now concerning our brother Apollos, I greatly urged him to visit you with the brothers [and sisters], but it was by no means his wish at

---

17. See the comments on 4:17 about Timothy as Paul's coworker.

18. There is a possibility that the brothers and sisters mentioned were travelling with Timothy, but in Acts 19:22 only Erastus appears to have been with him, so it is probably more

likely that Paul refers to those with him in Ephesus. Having said that, it is not entirely clear on the information given in this text that Paul expects Timothy to come back to him in Ephesus, though we take this as the most likely scenario.

this time to come. But he will come when he has the opportunity (Περὶ δὲ Ἀπολλῶ τοῦ ἀδελφοῦ, πολλὰ παρεκάλεσα αὐτόν ἵνα ἔλθῃ πρὸς ὑμᾶς μετὰ τῶν ἀδελφῶν· καὶ πάντως οὐκ ἦν θέλημα ἵνα νῦν ἔλθῃ, ἐλεύσεται δὲ ὅταν εὐκαιρήσῃ). "Now concerning" introduces the final matter from the Corinthian letter that Paul decides to address. It seems that some of the Corinthians were especially keen to see Apollos visit them again.[19] Paul's comment is exceedingly brief. The readers are given no indication as to why Apollos did not think it right to visit at this time, either with Timothy or perhaps later with Paul, but Apollos's determination definitely *not* to go ("by n̶̶̶̶̶̶̶̶̶" ̶̶̶̶̶̶ως οὐκ ἦν θέλημα),[20] sugge̶̶̶̶̶   ̶̶ a significant reason. While it is important to caution against over-speculation, it is at least possible, as others have suggested, that Apollos feared his presence would further foment the factionalism that Paul has addressed in this letter (1:11–13). However, if that was the case, Paul obviously thought otherwise since he insisted he had "greatly urged" Apollos to make the visit.[21] Undoubtedly Paul believes what he has affirmed in 3:9, that he and Apollos are God's fellow workers. Paul's words here confirm that he does not feel threatened by the one he has already acknowledged "watered" where he had "planted" (3:6).

16:13–14 Be alert, stand firm in the faith, be brave, [and] be strong. Let all that you do be done in love (Γρηγορεῖτε, στήκετε ἐν τῇ πίστει, ἀνδρίζεσθε, κραταιοῦσθε· πάντα ὑμῶν ἐν ἀγάπῃ γινέσθω). A series of imperatives drawn together

in the command to do all "in love" continues Paul's concluding remarks. Weima describes vv. 13–24 as the "letter closing of 1 Corinthians."[22] His outline, below, provides a useful structure for examining Paul's concluding remarks to this lengthy epistle.

vv. 13–16   Hortatory Section
   vv. 13–14   Five imperatives
   vv. 15–16   παρακαλέω unit
vv. 17–18   Joy Expression
vv. 19–21   Greetings
   vv. 19–20a   Greetings
   v. 20b   Kiss greeting
   v. 21   Autograph greeting
v. 22   Hortatory Section
   v. 22a   Curse formula
   v. 22b   Eschatological prayer formula
v. 23   Grace Benediction
v. 24   Postscript: Word of assurance

Rhetorically, vv. 13–18 probably reflect a *peroratio*, as Witherington suggests.[23] That is, they review, with some emotion, aspects of the main thesis of the whole letter. Five imperatives follow that are deeply related to the content of the letter.

Be alert. This verb (γρηγορέω) is sometimes used in eschatological contexts (cf. Luke 12:37–39; 1 Thess 5:6) and could be an appeal here to remain vigilant for the coming of Christ in glory. However, it is more likely to refer to being alert against temptation and against being drawn into sin (cf. Acts 20:31; 1 Pet 5:8; Rev 3:2). Paul has spent much time addressing the sin of some of the Corinthian Christians in areas of sexual morality through to idolatry. Here the imperative is similar to the im-

---

19. A previous visit of Apollos to Corinth is mentioned in Acts 18:24–28 and 19:1.

20. While the clause "by no means [the] wish" is impersonal in the Greek, the most natural antecedent is Apollos. This is how it is translated above: "By no means his [Apollos's] wish." Another possibility would be that it was not *God's* will (cf. Barrett, *First Corinthians*, 391) for Apollos to make the journey.

21. The word πολλά is used adverbially as in 16:19. While

this adverb can mean "many times" or "repeatedly," the absence of the article suggests otherwise; cf. Rom 15:22.

22. Weima, *Neglected Endings*, 203–8. Given the imperative at v. 18 the section "Joy Expression" could well be included under "Hortatory Section."

23. Witherington, *Conflict and Community*, 318. The *peroratio* in Greek rhetoric would form a summary of an argument and usually include pathos or an appeal to emotions.

perative "take heed" (βλεπέτω) in 10:12 where the danger of idolatry is being addressed. The following imperative suggests that watchfulness against sin is indeed what Paul has in mind.

Stand firm in the faith (στήκετε ἐν τῇ πίστει). In 15:1 Paul talked of standing firm in the gospel. As there, Paul is speaking of the body of belief that determines what it is to be a Christian, much of which is summarized in the early verses of chapter 15. It is worth noting that in Philippians 4:1 and 1 Thessalonians 3:8 Paul also speaks of the need to "stand firm in the Lord" (στήκετε ἐν κυρίῳ). Given the seeming interchangeability of these ideas, it is important to remember that for Paul "standing" frequently has connotations of the covenant "standing" or "falling" we noted in 1 Corinthians 10:12. "Standing firm" therefore surely means more than affirming the creeds of the church regularly in worship. For Paul, it means following the whole will of the Lord regarding how those who are in covenant fellowship with him should live. There should be no separation here between affirming from the heart an allegiance to the gospel facts as recounted in, for example, 15:3–11 and an allegiance to the Lord himself who is thus proclaimed.

Be brave, [and] be strong (ἀνδρίζεσθε, κραταιοῦσθε). The last three commands probably draw upon LXX Psalm 30:24–25 (31:23–24 ET). "Love the Lord, all his saints: for the Lord seeks for truth and abundantly repays those who work with pride. Be brave [ἀνδρίζεσθε], and let your heart be strong [κραταιοῦσθε], all who hope in the Lord."[24] Here the psalmist writes of God saving him as he trusts in the Lord, while he calls on the Lord to shame the proud. The emphasis on pride, shame, and on the love of the Lord, reflecting so clearly certain themes in Paul's letter, surely makes this an appropriate psalm to which to allude in his conclusion.

Whatever the temptations, Paul calls upon the Corinthians to "act like men" (ἀνδρίζεσθε), that is to say, "be brave" and "be strong." Paul has amply laid out the pressures of a pagan society to which this church is being subjected: from the proud elitists with their vaunted "wisdom" and "knowledge" through to problems with sexual immorality and idolatry. These require true courage and a reliance upon the Lord to overcome.

Let all that you do be done in love (ἐν ἀγάπῃ γινέσθω). This final command stands out from the previous four commands in both its length and the fact that it is placed in the third-singular rather than the second-person plural. It reminds the readers that love is the true authenticator of the "spiritual" person. It points back to the central thesis of 8:1–3 that is so beautifully developed in chapter 13. While "love builds up," "knowledge puffs up" (8:1). Paul returns twice more to this crucial subject in vv. 22 and 24. As we see below, the comments on the household of Stephanas also serve to reinforce Paul's teaching on the necessary humility and service incorporated in the idea of love. It is notable that the emphasis on love is largely absent from the other endings of Paul's letters.

The Corinthians are thus reminded in this final exhortation that there can be no place for pride or elitism, no place for some setting themselves up as more "spiritual" than others, and no place for the divisions that seem to pervade the church. It reminds them of the call to act as "one body" and of their covenant commitment to love one another even as the Lord loves them.

16:15–18 Now I exhort you brothers [and sisters]—you know that the household of Stephanas is the firstfruits of Achaia, and that they devoted themselves to the service of the saints—also to

---

24. These two verbs are also found together in 2 Sam 10:12 LXX.

subject yourselves to such people and to all who share together in the work and labor hard. And I rejoice at the arrival of Stephanas and Fortunatus and Achaicus, because they have made up for your absence; for they refreshed my spirit even as [they have] yours. Therefore, give recognition to such people (Παρακαλῶ δὲ ὑμᾶς, ἀδελφοί· οἴδατε τὴν οἰκίαν Στεφανᾶ, ὅτι ἐστὶν ἀπαρχὴ τῆς Ἀχαΐας καὶ εἰς διακονίαν τοῖς ἁγίοις ἔταξαν ἑαυτούς· ἵνα καὶ ὑμεῖς ὑποτάσσησθε τοῖς τοιούτοις καὶ παντὶ τῷ συνεργοῦντι καὶ κοπιῶντι. χαίρω δὲ ἐπὶ τῇ παρουσίᾳ Στεφανᾶ καὶ Φορτουνάτου καὶ Ἀχαϊκοῦ, ὅτι τὸ ὑμέτερον ὑστέρημα οὗτοι ἀνεπλήρωσαν, ἀνέπαυσαν γὰρ τὸ ἐμὸν πνεῦμα καὶ τὸ ὑμῶν. ἐπιγινώσκετε οὖν τοὺς τοιούτους). These verses offer a final exhortation within the *peroratio*. Verses 15–16 are disjointed in Greek. Verse 16 is the complement to Paul's appeal, "Now I exhort you. . . ." Paul urges a submission to his friends who were probably leaders in the church. The intervening sentence, "you know that . . . ," forms the basis for his appeal.

In 1:16 Paul had mentioned his participation in the baptism of the household of Stephanas, which he now describes as "the firstfruits of Achaia."[25] The "firstfruits" may indicate that this household was the first or among the first of such households to be converted in that region.[26] Since the apostle Paul himself had only baptized very few in Corinth, among whom was this household (1:14–17), "firstfruits" likely carries the idea that since then many have been baptized by others. These verses raise the interesting possibility that this man and his household, being core or founding members of the church, had not taken up with the elitists but had truly stood firm in the faith Paul had originally preached. Since the word "firstfruits" can carry the connotation of *quality* (the best is offered to the Lord) as well as chronological sequence, then this is more likely.[27]

The second reason Paul gives for urging the Corinthians to submit to "such people" is that the household of Stephanas "devoted themselves to the service of the saints." The word "devoted" (ἔταξαν) refers to the ordering or arranging of matters or people.[28] That is, this household determined that they would dedicate themselves to the service of God's people. On many occasions Paul has indicated that service and humility are needed among the Corinthians and that these great attributes stand in stark contrast to those who are proud and elitist in their attitudes and behavior toward others. To "subject yourselves to such people" (ὑποτάσσω) in all their hard work of service for the church of Christ is surely to follow their lead. This is the leadership of servants whose way of life reflects the attitude of heart and mind that Paul has advocated throughout the letter.[29] Families like this see no room for pride or distinctions among people as they work together with other workers for the benefit of the saints and the Lord (cf. 2 Cor 8:23). There is an irony here that the Corinthians are called upon to submit themselves to people who already devoted themselves to serving the Corinthians! Such is the way of God's people, for "love does not boast . . . [and] is not self-seeking" (13:4–5)!

In verse 17 Paul additionally refers to Fortunatus

---

25. Achaia was the Roman province to the south of Macedonia (cf. Acts 19:22), covering the whole of southern Greece (the area of the Peloponnesus) and incorporating the main cities of Corinth and Athens.

26. Cf. RSV, REB, NRSV, ESV, NIV: "First converts." Cf. Rom 16:5 and 2 Thess 2:13.

27. See BDAG 98. When Christ is called the "firstfruits of those who have fallen asleep" (15:20), it is primarily chronol-

ogy that is in mind, but the quality of his cultic self-offering as the holy one cannot be ignored. See also Rev 14:4. If he has in mind this cultic imagery (cf. Num 18:29–32 LXX), then Paul is greatly honoring these people and indicating one reason why he calls upon the Corinthians to give them "recognition."

28. BDAG 991.

29. See esp. 9:19 and 13:5.

and Achaicus, who have come with Stephanas. Paul rejoices since "they have made up for your absence" (τὸ ὑμέτερον ὑστέρημα οὗτοι ἀνεπλήρωσαν).[30] Stephanas, Fortunatus, and Achaicus have been able to bring the news that Paul was unable to hear and see for himself. Paul expresses again his affection for the Corinthians. Truly he has felt the lack of contact with "his dearly loved children" (4:14; cf. 15:58) and no doubt would have preferred to speak to them rather than write to them.

Paul has been "refreshed" by the news these three have brought from the church (v. 18).[31] Despite its problems, they have probably brought Paul news of new converts, of people growing in the faith, and perhaps of the congregation's love for Paul himself. Paul also indicates that the Corinthian church has had its spirit refreshed by these three men.[32] The sense in which spirits might have been refreshed is discussed in detail by Thiselton, who concludes that the least ambiguous translation may be the REB's "they have raised my spirits."[33] All in all, as news is carried by these three men in both directions, both Paul and the Corinthians find encouragement and joy.

Paul concludes this brief section with the imperative "give recognition" (ἐπιγινώσκετε), insisting that it is people such as these who should be acknowledged. Unlike what is happening in some sections of the Corinthian church where recognition is given on the grounds of status, wisdom, wealth, etc., Paul seeks recognition for people on the grounds of their humble and generous service offered to himself and to the Corinthian church for the Lord's sake.

16:19–21 The churches of Asia greet you. Aquila and Prisca warmly greet you in the Lord, together with the church in their house. All the brothers [and sisters] greet you. Greet one another with a holy kiss. [I send] this greeting with my own— Paul's—hand. (Ἀσπάζονται ὑμᾶς αἱ ἐκκλησίαι τῆς Ἀσίας. ἀσπάζεται ὑμᾶς ἐν κυρίῳ πολλὰ Ἀκύλας καὶ Πρίσκα σὺν τῇ κατ᾽ οἶκον αὐτῶν ἐκκλησίᾳ. ἀσπάζονται ὑμᾶς οἱ ἀδελφοὶ πάντες. Ἀσπάσασθε ἀλλήλους ἐν φιλήματι ἁγίῳ. Ὁ ἀσπασμὸς τῇ ἐμῇ χειρὶ Παύλου). Paul now proceeds to pass on greetings from himself and other friends of the church. As noted above, Weima usefully divides this "greetings" section into three parts. There are some general greetings in vv. 19–20a, followed by what he calls the "kiss greeting" and then Paul's own greeting, v. 21.[34] As in modern English where a person might add to a letter or email, "My wife also sends her greetings," so in Hellenistic letter writing it was the norm to conclude letters with greetings both from the writer and others. Mullins states that "the greeting was a distinct literary form which was intended to establish a bond of friendship."[35] Here Paul adds three sets of greetings beyond his own. Since Paul writes from Ephesus in the Roman province of Asia,[36] he sends greetings from this wider group of churches, though he does not indicate whether certain churches had specifically asked him to do this. In Acts 19:10 we read of the rapid expansion of the church in the province of Asia. Such a greeting may have owed much to convention, but it also reminds the modern reader of the close association between these early Christian churches and

---

30. Cf. NJB: "They have made up for your not being here." The NIV translates more closely to the Greek: "They have supplied what was lacking from you."

31. "To refresh" (ἀναπαύω) or "to cause to rest" (BDAG 69) is used in the same way in 2 Cor 7:13 and Phlm 7.

32. Lit., "and the [spirit] of you" (καὶ τὸ ὑμῶν).

33. Thiselton, *1 Corinthians*, 1340–41.

34. In a fashion similar to Fee (*1 Corinthians*), Weima considerably overplays the tension between Paul and the Corinthian church.

35. Terence Y. Mullins, "Greeting as a New Testament Form," *JBL* 87 (1968): 418–26.

36. The Roman province of Asia covered most of what we would now call western Turkey. Ephesus was its capital city. The seven churches of Rev 1:11 were all part of this province.

how much news was carried backward and forward as they prayed for each other and learned together to "stand firm in the faith" in a pagan society where many faced various degrees of persecution.

Secondly, Paul writes of "warm"[37] greetings to Corinth from Aquila and Prisca, who are referred to elsewhere at times as Aquila and Priscilla (Acts 18:2, 18, 26). Their Latin names suggest that Rome may have been their original home, and some speculate that they were freed slaves. It seems that this married couple was fairly widely known in the early church since they are also mentioned in Acts 18:2–3 when Paul first went to Corinth. Like Paul, they were "tentmakers," and so he stayed with them and worked at their trade with them.[38] In Acts 18 Aquila is referred to as a Jew who, with his wife, had been subject to the general expulsion of Jews from Rome under the Emperor Claudius in AD 49. Since that expulsion involved some who followed Christ, most commentators assume that the couple were already Christians when they met Paul. If not, then it would have been as Paul spoke week by week in the synagogue in Corinth that this couple came to faith in Jesus Christ (Acts 18:4). As Paul writes this epistle to Corinth from Ephesus, it may be assumed that this couple, well known to the Corinthian Christians, were now with him in Ephesus. In Romans 16:3–5 Paul refers to these two as his "fellow workers in Christ," and comments on his gratitude and the gratitude of "all the churches of the Gentiles" for the way they had "risked their necks" for Paul's life (ESV). By the time Paul travelled to Ephesus, Acts 18:26–27 tells us that Priscilla and Aquila were already there. Their knowledge of the Christian faith, no doubt learned day by day as

they worked together with the apostle, meant they were able to advise Apollos and help him deepen his understanding of the faith as he continued his powerful preaching ministry (Acts 18:24–28).

This outstanding Christian couple, who were such a great help to Paul and to the churches he planted, may have fulfilled a role something akin to modern "church planting" as we now know of it, in which further house churches would be established as the Christian faith spread through a city. Of course, these churches would not have been independent of each other as is often the case in the modern church. In any case, the greetings Paul sends come from not just the couple but also from "the church in their house." Even toward the end of his life Paul remembers to send Prisca and Aquila greetings (2 Tim 4:19).

Finally, Paul sends a greeting from "all the brothers" (οἱ ἀδελφοὶ πάντες). This likely refers to all Christians, men and women, who had had contact with the church in Corinth and were currently living in Ephesus. It is perhaps a final catch-all that further indicates the close relationship between churches and their love for one another (cf. 1:2).

Paul now speaks of greeting "one another with a holy kiss" (also Rom 16:16; cf. 2 Cor 13:12; 1 Thess 5:26). Since churches met in homes and Christians saw themselves as a family of brothers and sisters in Christ, this may have reflected a practice of greeting commonly used in society as family visited family in their homes. Peter refers to a "kiss of love" (1 Pet 5:14). More generally, the kiss appears not to have been widely used in society at large as a greeting.[39] While it is certainly true that later the "kiss of peace" became a formal part of the

---

37. The word πολλά usually means "many." Here it is used adjectivally and would equate to "*warm* greetings" in modern English. Mullins, "Greeting as a New Testament Form," 422, suggests that πολλά is the most frequently used modifier of greetings in the papyri and is used "to intensify the warmth of the greeting."

38. Murphy-O'Connor, *Paul: His Story*, 83–84, describes what Paul's work in a small city shop in Corinth might have looked like as he spoke to customers coming to purchase the leather work.

39. For an extended study of the "holy kiss," see William Klassen, "The Sacred Kiss in the New Testament: An Example

liturgy of the communion service as it is in many churches today, it is surely anachronistic to read that later stylized liturgical kiss back into Paul's words here.[40] It is better simply to understand that within the church the kiss indicates a depth of love and intimacy that, through joint "participation in Christ," all Christians have with one another. The personal warmth of the sign would additionally have helped diminish other societal marks of status, power, or ethnicity, say, between slaves and free or the wealthy and the poor.

A final, abbreviated greeting from the apostle himself reminds us that the letter has been written by an amanuensis and Paul now picks up the pen to sign it himself. Here, as in the letters to the Galatians (6:11) and 2 Thessalonians (3:17), Paul used a secretary to write at his dictation. In Romans 16:22 it is the secretary himself who draws attention to this fact: "I Tertius, who wrote down this letter, greet you in the Lord."

When seen as a whole, these three verses do more than simply conclude a letter with greetings. They draw attention to the close unity and love between these early churches of the Roman provinces of Asia, Macedonia, and Achaia and the close fellowship shared by individual Christians with one another and with the apostle Paul.

16:22 If anyone does not love the Lord, let that one be anathema. Our Lord come! (εἴ τις οὐ φιλεῖ τὸν κύριον, ἤτω ἀνάθεμα. Μαράνα θά). Verse 22 seems almost to be an afterthought, and yet for the second of three occasions in these closing verses Paul returns to his concern that love must mark out those who profess faith in Christ. Indeed, if anyone had doubted that Paul was saying that *all* true believers possess this marker or characteristic, this final pronouncement of a curse formula should banish such doubts. Nowhere else in the conclusions to Paul's letters is such a strong statement of this sort made.[41] This "anathema" or pronouncement of curse[42] is similar to the one that Paul pronounces in Galatians 1:8 where we read: "If we or an angel from heaven should preach to you a gospel contrary to the one we preached to you, let him be accursed [ἀνάθεμα ἔστω]" (ESV).

The calling down of God's judgment on a person helps make sense of the immediately following "our Lord come!" (μαράνα θά). It is at Christ's coming that the final standing or falling of those who claim to belong to the covenant community of Christ will be revealed. At the heart of the Old Testament covenant law was the command to love the Lord and to love neighbor. Disobedience to the covenant led to curse, while obedience led to blessing.[43] We noted how much of chapter 10 made just this point from God's judgment (and blessings) on the Israelites in the wilderness. In the LXX the word "anathema" (ἀνάθεμα) is regularly employed

---

of Social Boundary Lines," *NTS* 39 (1993): 122–35. Referring to the "holy kiss" of the early church he writes: "Nothing analogous to it is to be found among any Greco-Roman societies, nor indeed at Qumran" (ibid., 128).

40. J. A. T. Robinson, *Twelve New Testament Studies* (London: SCM, 1962), is one of a number of writers who have argued that Paul's epistle was read aloud in the context of the gathered church's worship and that the ending manifests aspects of an early eucharistic liturgy. He claims that there is a "striking resemblance" between "what appears to be [the] dialogue shape" of Didache 10:6 and 1 Cor 16:22 (154). He argues that "the salutations, the kiss, the peace, the grace are all rich with the overtones of worship" (156). But it is especially the

link between judgment and the prayer, "Our Lord, Come!" that draws commentators' attention to the similarities between the Didache's description of the eucharistic liturgy and this passage. Chapter 10 of the Didache concerns the prayer after communion. Part of that reads: "Let grace come, and this world pass away. Hosanna to the Son of David! If any one is holy, let him come; if any one is not, let him repent. Maranatha. Amen." Cf. also Bornkamm, *Early Christian Experience*, 169–76; Talbert, *Reading Corinthians*, 106–7; G. Stählin, "φιλέω," *TDNT* 9:138–40.

41. A less strong statement is made in 2 Thess 3:14.
42. "Let him be cursed" is a reasonable translation.
43. See, e.g., Deut 30:19; Josh 8:34.

to indicate the most solemn "devotion of things or people to destruction" when God's law has been broken (e.g., Deut 7:26; Josh 7:12).

The Aramaic formula μαράνα θά was undoubtedly a very early prayer in the church calling upon the Lord to come in his great glory to rule on this earth as Scripture had promised.[44] It is a prayer that "all things" will be "put in subjection" to God as the Son "delivers up the kingdom to [him who is] God and Father, when he has destroyed every rule and every power and authority" (15:24, 27). Thus the prayer itself involves a call both for blessing and curse, that is, that God's people and his own name will finally be vindicated.

In this way the final emotional appeal of the *peroratio* looks forward to the glorious coming of Christ and to the extreme danger for some of that day of judgment. The choice is curse or blessing. The choice is to "fall" (10:8, 12) before God's judgment as so many Israelites did in the wilderness or to "stand" before him (10:12–13). The cup of demons and the cup of the Lord cannot be drunk together (10:21). In the Adamic terms of 15:22, the question is whether people find themselves "in Adam," and so are judged at Christ's "coming," or "in Christ" and so look forward to being "made alive." Love is not a minor matter of disagreement between Christians. Judgment or blessing depends on getting this right. Love for the Lord means blessing and an absence of fear as the church prays, "Our Lord come!"[45] "If anyone does not love the Lord," then judgment awaits.[46]

16:23–24 The grace of the Lord Jesus be with you. My love be with you all in Christ Jesus (ἡ χάρις τοῦ κυρίου Ἰησοῦ μεθ᾽ ὑμῶν. ἡ ἀγάπη μου μετὰ πάντων ὑμῶν ἐν Χριστῷ Ἰησοῦ). Weima's separation of vv. 23–24 is perhaps unnecessary.[47] Paul's benediction and final word are integrally tied to what he has just written. "Grace" may be a common greeting at the start and end of Paul's letters, but it is much more than this. For Paul knows that it is God's grace alone that will bring these Christians to mature faith. The grace that alone brought them salvation is the same grace that they need as they continue their path to maturity as Christians, a path that reaches its end only when they see "face to face" (13:12). Progress in the Christian life requires the ongoing, faithful, and merciful love of Christ and of the Father, and so Paul leaves them in the Lord's hands.

His final words indicate his own commitment to the principles of which he has spoken. For all his concern for them, this is a people he deeply loves in Christ. They are his "dearly loved children," and he is the one who became their "father" in Christ Jesus through the gospel (4:14–15). This love is "in Christ Jesus." Once again Paul reminds them that they are in covenant fellowship with the Lord himself. This is the one who has loved them even to his death. This is the one they imitate as they seek to love God and to love neighbor, and so identify with their covenant Lord. A final "amen" concludes and affirms the letter and Paul's final prayer for these people whom he loves so much.

44. The Aramaic *maranatha* could be read as "our Lord has come" (*maran atha*) or as "come, Lord!" (*marana tha*). See BDAG 616. The context suggests final judgment.

45. Note the blessing of Eph 6:24, "Grace be with all who love our Lord Jesus Christ with love incorruptible" (ESV), the encouragement of 1 Cor 8:3, "If anyone loves [God], this one is known [by him]," and of 13:8, "Love never fails."

46. Thiselton, *1 Corinthians*, 1348–51, building on Eriksson, describes in detail the covenant framework that governs Paul's thinking here. See Anders Eriksson, *Traditions as Rhetorical Proof: Pauline Argumentation in 1 Corinthians*, ConBNT 29 (Stockholm: Almquist and Wiksel, 1998), especially the chapter, "Maranatha in the Letter's *Peroratio*," 279–98.

47. Weima, *Neglected Endings*, 203–8.

Theology in Application

The Collection

The giving of gifts for the support of the church and its ministries, as in this case, to help those in need, has always been a feature of Christian worship. The roots of such giving are found in the various Old Testament sacrifices, in the commands to tithe and in freewill offerings, as well as in commands to help the neighbor. Theologically, as we have noted in 1 Corinthians 16, they have always been regarded as a tangible expression of the believer's or the community's love for God and love for neighbor. In that sense such giving is a response to the two great commands as Jesus noted them (Luke 10:27; cf. Lev 19:18; Deut 6:5). Yet such giving must be traced back still further, for in biblical faith it is fundamentally a response of worship before the God who first loved us (1 Chr 16:29–34). This is especially observed as the freewill offerings are seen to increase exponentially at times of revival (2 Chr 29–31; 34–35).

If "the collection" of 16:1 is to be compared with the Old Testament, it is neither a tithe nor a tax, but more in line with the freewill offerings at such times of revival or of special Sabbaths (cf. Exod 36:3; Lev 23:37–38; 1 Chr 29:6–8). Christ's own emphasis on giving reinforces the Old Testament teaching of such offerings being genuine, unforced, and from the heart (Matt 12:41–43; cf. Exod 35:22, 29; 1 Chr 29:17). Since Paul sees this offering as part of the exhibition of community "love," he looks for genuineness.

In the modern church, the "collection" or "offering" at a Sunday service is often separated from corporate worship in a variety of ways. In some churches (and especially in some countries) the legalistic idea of the "tithe" as a duty has virtually removed all sense of a genuine, unforced, heart-gift to the Lord who first loved us. The community understanding of corporate giving is rarely discussed, as individuals see their giving as an intensely private affair. There is no doubt that both the regularity of giving and the involvement of each person provide guidance for all successful church giving, and Paul urges this on the Corinthians. However, when combined, these ideas should make the offering a whole-community event and something that should be thought about each week. It should therefore regularly be brought to the attention of the church. The proportionality of giving to which Paul refers is another reminder that the church has always assumed that giving is "as the Lord prospers." Therefore, the godly wealthy will give more than the poor, and some poor may not be able to give. There is an inherent freedom and joy in the giving that Paul addresses here, even if he has to urge it upon them. Church ministers should be unashamed to urge giving upon their congregations as Paul does. To do so will lead many into a new, joyful response to the Lord and a renewed attention to the physical needs of the church, especially of poor and needy brothers and sisters.

Disciplined Flexibility

"If the Lord permits" (16:7) reminds the reader that ultimately God controls the itinerary of even the greatest of evangelists and apostles. Throughout Scripture it is a feature of the great people of faith that they have been prepared to go where the Lord wants them to go, even when it means a change of their well-intended plans. Whether it be Abraham who "by faith" obeyed and travelled to the promised land (Heb 11:8; see Gen 12:1–4) or Paul who, though fearful for his life and probably desirous of leaving Corinth, in fact stayed there a further eighteen months because he had a dream in which the Lord told him to stay put (Acts 18:6–11). In Romans 1:13 Paul speaks of having been "prevented" from travelling to visit the church in Rome. The passive voice likely indicates he saw this as God preventing him from making that journey. Even more clearly, Luke tells us that Paul and others were "forbidden by the Holy Spirit to speak the word in Asia" (Acts 16:6 ESV).

In this final section of 1 Corinthians as Paul spells out his travel plans, a clear example is provided of a disciplined person who has a plan of action for his ministry. His intentions are good and honorable and have to do with proclaiming the word and building up the churches. Yet, at the same time there is a genuine flexibility borne of knowing that he can only know so much and the Lord might have other plans for him.

In the modern church it often seems that only two alternatives are available. In many cases it seems church "programs" or the most detailed, careful planning of mission trips can never be challenged or changed. Often such decisions are based on the previous "success" of the program or a previous trip that was handled in just this way and so must be done in the same way again. The lack of flexibility probably implies that the prayers accompanying the work are more along the lines of "Lord bless our plans" than "if the Lord permits." On the other hand, Paul does show us that he carefully planned his mission trips. He planned out the people that he wanted to see and who he wanted to come to him. He did not simply wait to see whether, through some supernatural dream or vision, he would know where to go or what to do, as if such was a more spiritual approach! With both our personal as well as our church plans, it is critical to work toward the balance Paul exhibits between strategic and purposeful planning and appropriate flexibility. It is about following God's calling, using the grace-gifts that we have been given, and doing so always in an attitude of prayer for the Lord's guidance to rule.

Love for the Saints

Much has been said in this epistle and this commentary on love as the marker or authenticator of mature Christian faith. It is thus right, just as Paul himself does, to finish by reminding ourselves of its importance. Jeremiah, speaking of the new covenant, foretells the day when the law will be written on the hearts of God's people (Jer 31:31–34). The law is summed up in the two great commands of loving God and neighbor. Theologically, it is thus utterly to be expected that those with the law now written on their hearts will show that in their lives and worship. In the last verses of 1 Corinthians 16, Paul draws attention to the need for all faithful action to arise from and reflect a commitment to love (vv. 13–14). He also draws attention to the greatest command (v. 22) as he insists that love for the Lord functions as the marker of that which he has been writing. If the Lord is not loved, then that person stands condemned. In an age in which love is little more than some feeble romantic and idealistic concept, it is critical for the church to examine what love for the world and love for the Lord really means. As Paul reveals in his own dealings with the Corinthians in this epistle, it is often hard hitting and direct in its application, but in the end love is always about participation in Christ. It is about imitating Christ, and that involves obedience. Paul may not quote the Lord's words, but he exemplifies one who seeks at all points to obey Jesus's statement to his disciples: "If you love me, you will keep my commandments" (John 14:15–24 ESV).

Theology of 1 Corinthians

While many will instinctively seek for Paul's main theological concerns first in epistles such as Romans or Galatians, 1 Corinthians also provides many insights into his theology. In fact, one of the great joys of studying Paul's theology through the lens of this epistle is that we learn much of it as Paul applies it to specific matters in the church's life. This helps to bring his theology alive but also to demonstrate how consistent he is in those matters that he considers most important. We have noted throughout the commentary what we believe are the main issues the church faces, but as Paul seeks to encourage or rectify their theology, he does so by further expounding his own theological priorities. The sections below are by no means exhaustive of the many theological matters raised in the epistle, nor are they in a necessary order of priority in terms of importance, but they are perhaps Paul's theological headlines in relationship to this particular church.

God

Paul speaks of God (θεός) on multiple occasions in this epistle. Indeed, the name appears twice as often as the name "Christ" (Χριστός). Though Paul offers no systematic development of a doctrine of God, there is much to be gleaned of how he understood God. God is the ultimate creator and sovereign, whose will is being worked out especially through the Lord Jesus Christ. Thus, from the outset we read that Paul is an apostle of Christ Jesus "through the will of God" (1:1). In 8:4, building on the *Shema*, Paul maintains biblical monotheism and insists there is one "God," who is "the Father" (8:6). The familial background of naming God as Father is occasionally seen in the Old Testament (Pss 68:5; 89:26; Isa 9:6) and seems mainly to arise from God's compassionate care for his people Israel, whom he has "created" (Mal 2:10) and who can be called his "son" (Exod 4:22; Hos 11:1). The idea comes to the fore especially in the New Testament teaching of Christ who calls God his Father (e.g., Mark 8:38; 14:36; Luke 10:21). However, this intimate appellation is taken by Jesus and effectively given or "revealed" to his own disciples (Mark 11:25; Luke 10:22; see especially Matt 5:44–6:33). As a name for God in 1 Corinthians, "Father" is used to describe the God who has created a people for himself whom he loves (1:3) and to describe the God to whom Christ will deliver his people at the end (15:24). For God's people, the Father is the creator and sustainer of all things and the one for whom they exist (8:6). Elsewhere Paul speaks of God as the Father of Jesus (2 Cor 1:3; 11:31; Eph 1:17), and this teaching is implicit in 1 Cor 3:23 and 11:3.

God is viewed as the Savior of his people in and through the Lord Jesus Christ, but it is notable how frequently it is "God" to whom Paul refers in 1:18–2:5 as he describes the calling and salvation of the Christians in the Corinthian church. It is by God's "power" (vv. 18, 24) and God's "wisdom" (v. 24) and God's choice that they find salvation (vv. 18, 21). God's decretal sovereignty in salvation is further seen in Paul's contrast between the wisdom of this world and the wisdom and power of God (2:7–9).

In this epistle Paul especially draws attention to God's faithfulness (1:9; 10:13; cf. 2 Cor 1:18) as he draws on Deuteronomy 7:9 and 32:4 (LXX). It is this faithfulness that establishes his people and enables them to be found "unimpeachable" at the last day (1:8). What some have called the "Emmanuel principle," that is, that God is always with his people, is also a focus of Paul's thinking. Throughout Scripture, God dwells in the midst of his people whether in the garden of Eden, the tabernacle, or the temple. Paul understands God's people themselves as forming "the temple of God" and indwelt by his Spirit (3:16–17). This temple (the church, see below) is defended by God, who will destroy any who would seek to destroy his people (v. 17). In 6:19 God provides the Holy Spirit to indwell the individual believer's body.

Finally, in Paul's discussion of the resurrection (see below) it is God who raised Christ from the dead (15:15), and so it is also God who will raise "us," that is, those who belong to him (6:14). It is to God the Father that eventually the victorious Christ will deliver the "kingdom" (15:24–25). God, having put all in subjection to Christ, eventually receives all things that "God may be all in all" (15:28).

The Lordship of Christ

In the opening ten verses of the epistle Paul emphatically established the theological centrality of Jesus as the "Christ" and "Lord." The fact that in these few introductory verses Paul speaks of "Christ Jesus" (three times) and designates him as "Lord" with the repeated title "Lord Jesus Christ" (five times), and "Jesus Christ our Lord" (once), and "his Son, Jesus Christ our Lord" (once) indicates the importance that he will attach to Christ's rule and authority in this epistle. The attachment of "Christ" to Jesus's lordship is a good indication that Paul thought of "Christ" in kingly terms, that is, as the messianic king. In Romans 10:9 Paul states that acknowledging Christ as Lord is necessary for salvation. In 1 Corinthians 12:3 a spiritual person is defined as one who "in the Spirit of God" affirms "Jesus is Lord," suggesting that the brief statement probably formed part of the earliest Christian confessions. The use of the full title "Lord Jesus Christ" in the greetings and the benedictions of most of the epistles also suggests a pre-Pauline general acceptance in the early church of this designation, and an early association of that lordship with Jesus's messianic status as the Christ. In 1 Corinthians 16:22 the Aramaic *maranatha* ("our Lord come") also points to the use of the title prior to Paul's writings. In places Paul uses *kyrios* (κύριος) in translating or alluding to the Old Testament Scriptures. In the LXX the word often substitutes for the Hebrew Yahweh. In 1 Corinthians 3:20 and 14:21 *kyrios* refers to God as Psalm 94:11 and Isaiah 28:11 are quoted, respectively. However, Paul also takes Old Testament passages referring to Yahweh (LXX *kyrios*) and applies them to Christ. First Corinthians 1:31 and 10:26 are examples of this where, respectively, Jeremiah 9:23–24 and Psalm 24:1 are used. In 1 Corinthians Paul's appeal to the lordship of Christ is most notably seen in three contexts.

In the context of addressing idolatry. Paul appeals to the lordship of Christ as he addresses idolatry in chapters 8 and 10. Fee rightly asserts that 8:6 provides "an extraordinary christological moment."[1] In 8:5 Paul writes of the "many 'gods'" and "many 'lords'" that are worshipped by idolatrous pagans. He then appeals to the Jewish confession of monotheism in the *Shema* to undermine their belief system but adapts the confession precisely to designate Christ as Lord. Without undermining his commitment to monotheism, Paul affirms the unity of the Father and Christ by dividing the Scripture into two parts. In the first part, the affirmation of one God (εἷς θεός) is attributed to the Father, and in the second half the affirmation of one Lord (εἷς κύριος) is attributed to the Lord, Jesus Christ. Just as God the Father stands opposed to any other "gods," so the Lord, Jesus Christ, stands opposed to any other "lords." In saying this Paul affirms that the Father has created and the Lord is the agent of that creation and the one through whom redemption is accomplished ("through whom are all things and through whom we [come to God]"). What is equally astounding as Paul writes is that this Christ, who stands as *the* Lord opposed to all other "lords," is also the Messiah crucified (see below).

As Paul insists that "for us" there is only one "Lord Jesus Christ," he contrasts Christ with the lords of those caught up in idolatry. Thus, Paul's earlier contrasts between the "wisdom of this age" or "of this world," and the wisdom of God and of Christ, are seen to be a subset of the much bigger picture in which two kingdoms are set against each other, the kingdom of Christ and of darkness (Col 1:3; Eph 5:5–8). However, it is not until 10:20–22 that Paul expands on this in more detail by showing that people either have allegiance to the one Lord and drink his cup and sit at his table, or have allegiance to demons. An appeal to the Old Testament idea of the "jealousy" of the Lord makes it clear that Paul sees these two kingdoms set against each other, with the true Lord as the one who rules and must be obeyed. It is also

---

1. Fee, *Pauline Christology*, 89.

Christ as Lord in whom Christians finally find their victory over the power of sin and death (15:54–57). It is this contrast between "lords" and the "Lord Jesus Christ" that makes the creedal acclamation "Jesus is Lord" so foundational to Christian belief (12:3). Such identification of the covenant Lord of old with Christ as Lord speaks to the preexistence of Jesus as well as to his authority and power over the demons worshipped by idolaters.

In eschatological contexts. From the start Paul sets his epistle in the context of the returning Lord and the judgment that accompanies him. Thus in 1:7–8 Paul sees church life as existing in the context of awaiting "the revealing of our Lord Jesus Christ," a day which is a day of judgment and referred to as "the day of our Lord Jesus Christ" (drawing from the "day of the Lord" in Old Testament texts, see commentary). Standing or falling before the judge is a recurrent theme (See "In Depth: The Theme of Stumbling" at 1:23). It is thus essential that believers understand that it is the Lord Jesus Christ who himself will sustain them guiltless on that day of judgment and glory (v. 8). The excommunication in chapter 5 is precisely so that the person concerned may ultimately be saved "in the day of the Lord" (5:5). Paul also talks of the Lord's present judgment on the community as "discipline" in order that on the final day they will be spared judgment (11:31–32). As the importance of Christ's resurrection is explained so also the eschatological lordship and kingly authority of Christ are highlighted. "In Christ" all will be raised, and he will deliver the kingdom to the Father. His lordship will finally be revealed to all as he destroys every rule and power and authority (15:23–24). On that day the world will see that "he [has] put all his enemies under his feet" (v. 25), before finally himself being subjected to the Father as the representative King and Lord of all his people (v. 27). It is again the lordship of Christ that is the focus as Paul rejoices in v. 57, "Thanks be to God, who gives us the victory through our Lord Jesus Christ." The *maranatha* (16:22) well summarizes the centrality to Paul's Christology that Christ is the Lord who will return as King, Savior, and Judge.

In Ethical Contexts. It is Christ's lordship that drives Paul's ethical challenges to the Corinthians. Since the church has received the grace of God summarized in "Christ crucified" and since Christ is their Lord and they "belong" to him (3:23), Paul insists they serve and obey their Lord. This is variously seen by Paul as a response of gratitude and of obligation. The appeal to all that Christ's lordship implies for the church begins in 1:10 where Paul writes, "I urge you, brothers [and sisters], in the name of our Lord Jesus Christ, that you all agree." Since all that they are and have is by God's grace "in Christ Jesus," their "boast" is to be in him alone (1:30–31). The appeal to Christ as the foundation of the church and to his coming is used as a motivation to Christ-like living (3:11–15), and Paul offers himself and the apostles as examples of what it is to be "servants of Christ" (4:1). It is therefore his Lord who alone can judge how he performs in his task of stewardship (v. 4). Since Christ is

Lord and all that Christians have and are is subject to him, Paul can say that immorality is wrong. The body is, after all, "*for* the Lord" (6:13). Pleasing the Lord becomes a matter of concern as Paul writes about whether people should marry or remain unmarried, for the better course is "an undivided devotion to the Lord" (7:35). It is clear that those who belong to the Lord are to live their lives in obedience to his law, "Christ's law" (9:21). It is in the light of who the Lord is and his eschatological victory that Paul can summarize chapter 15 by urging Christians to be "always abounding in the work of the Lord, because you know that your labor is not in vain in the Lord" (15:58).

The Christ Crucified

In this epistle Paul carefully holds together the lordship of Christ with his emphasis on Christ crucified (cf. Rom 14:9). Yet his appeal to the theological motif of the crucified Jesus may be separately noted. Paul's talk of Christ crucified is a shorthand for Christ's saving work through his death and resurrection. Indeed, Paul says that "if Christ has not been raised, then our preaching is also in vain and your faith is in vain" (15:14). Nevertheless, emphasis on the death of Christ still serves to remind the reader of Paul's commitment to the humanity of the Messiah who truly died and was then raised bodily. For Paul, Christ's death provides the grounds of faith (Rom 5:6; Gal 3:1; 2 Cor 5:14–15). It is the grace of God manifest (Rom 5:8; Col 1:22). It is evidence of the justice of God (Rom 3:21–26; 5:17–18; Gal 2:21) and much more, but in this epistle Paul especially uses this foundational teaching of the faith in a variety of practical, pastoral situations.

Christ "crucified" (1:22) has been the substance of Paul's preaching among the Corinthians (2:2). Paul draws attention to the scandal that the teaching of a crucified Christ is to Jews who seek messianic signs and the folly that such a message is to Greeks who prefer human wisdom and its designs (1:23). Thus Paul acknowledges that his message inevitably turns upside down all human expectations. In contrast to what may be expected, Paul refers to the *power* of the cross of Christ, to the "word of the cross" as "the *power* of God" for salvation (1:18). In terms of human wisdom, Christ crucified provides the fulfillment of Old Testament ideas that God will destroy it (1:19). Yet in the same message lies the power of God for salvation.

In these opening verses, Paul appeals to this message in five main ways. Firstly, it reminds the Corinthians that salvation is all of God's power and his grace (1:17). Secondly, it reminds the Corinthians that the person of Christ and the message of the gospel are divisive. There will be those who are saved and those who perish (vv. 21–24). Thirdly, Paul employs this message as a reminder that arrogance on the part of Christians cannot be tolerated (vv. 26–31; cf. 4:17–21). Fourthly, Paul justifies his lifestyle and manner of communication among the Corinthians as one that reflects the message of humiliation and servanthood inherent in the teaching of Christ crucified (1:17; 2:1–5; cf. 4:8–13; 9:12). The Corinthians should follow suit. Fifthly, it is used to bolster the appeal to Christ's lordship in some of Paul's ethical appeals (5:7; 8:10–13; 10:14–22; 11:23–30).

In other words, this foundational gospel theology of Jesus the Messiah, crucified and dying for his church, becomes a multifaceted theological theme. It should humble the believer, change the believer's way of living, and destroy any vestiges of boastful pride. It is, from a human perspective, utterly weak and powerless, and yet it is in fact the proclamation of the one who is the "one Lord, Jesus Christ, through whom are all things and through whom we [come to God]" (8:6). The centrality of this captivating theology is nowhere seen more clearly than in the communion service of the gathered church instituted by "the Lord Jesus" (11:23). There the weakness of Christ's death and the glory of the deliverance and salvation achieved for the church by that death is proclaimed week by week. There too, even as Christ crucified is remembered in the bread and wine, his judgment as Lord is recalled (v. 32). As Paul says, "Whenever you eat this bread and drink the cup, *you proclaim the death of the Lord* until he comes" (v. 26).

The Holy Spirit

The work of the Holy Spirit is prominent in this epistle, especially in chapters 2 and 12. His work is at the heart of the preaching of the gospel. Paul insists that though he did not come to the Corinthians with lofty speech or wisdom but rather with a simple message of Christ crucified, nevertheless, this became a demonstration of the Spirit and of power (2:4). It is the Spirit who is seen to be God's agent in revealing the wisdom of God to men and women, for the Spirit alone comprehends the "depths of God," and it is he who enables God's people to understand what God has for them in the gospel (2:9–13). It is the Spirit who thus defines who a "spiritual" person is. Such a person possesses the Spirit, who enables him or her to understand the gospel, that is, the work and word of God in Jesus Christ and him crucified. Through the Spirit, the Christian can come to have "the mind of Christ," while "the unspiritual person does not receive the things of the Spirit of God for they are foolishness to him" (2:14–16; cf. Rom 8:9). This is well summarized by Paul's insistence that it is only "in the Spirit" that anyone can say "Jesus is Lord" (12:3).

The Spirit is seen to come from God to his people and thus to demonstrate that they belong to God (6:19; cf. Rom 8:14, 16; 2 Cor 1:22; 5:5). Indeed, it is in the realm of the Spirit that all were baptized into one body (see commentary on 12:13). Thus, his work is seen in each stage of the life of God's people: in their hearing and understanding of the gospel, in their incorporation into the covenant community, in their sanctification, in their security, and in their equipping for life as members of the body of Christ. In this epistle Paul's understanding of the Spirit's role in sanctification is hinted at in verses such as 3:16 and 12:3, but it is not developed in the way found elsewhere in his writings (cf. Rom 8:2–4, 12–14; Gal 5:16–23). However, the Spirit's activity in bringing God's gifts to his church does become a central focus of the letter.

Gifts of the Spirit

In the opening to the letter (1:4–7) Paul thanks God for the grace given to the Corinthians "in Christ Jesus" such that they have been enriched and are not lacking in any gift (χάρισμα). These grace-gifts are set in the context of living as God's people while awaiting "the revealing of our Lord Jesus Christ." Their purpose is to enable them to live together as the local church, each being enabled by God to "build up" the church (14:12). The source of these gifts in the opening verses is God. As Paul develops the theme in chapter 12, they are variously ascribed to God and Christ, but in the end are seen to be provided by the Holy Spirit. In this chapter Paul variously refers to diverse allocations among the people of "grace-gifts" (χαρίσματα), "serving(s)" (διακονίαι), and "workings" (ἐνεργήματα), but all are for the building up of the church (12:4–6). In these verses Paul refers to "the same Spirit," "the same Lord," and "the same God." However, in vv. 8–11 the Spirit is shown to be the source and provider of the gifts. His agency in the distribution of the gifts is specifically mentioned four times in vv. 8–9. In the summary of v. 11 the Spirit is the source of the power of the gifts and is the one who determines who receives which gift. Thus the Spirit is the one who enables the body to function in unity and for the common good until such time as the church sees "face to face" (13:12). As we have seen through the exegesis of the epistle, it is the very diversity of the gifts and their allocation by the Spirit to whom he wills that provides the final theological reason why the grace-gifts cannot function as boundary markers in the way "love" can. What Paul elsewhere calls one of the fruits of the Spirit is expected to be found in all in whom the Spirit dwells (Gal 5:22).

The grace-gifts also highlight the Spirit's role in the worship of the congregation. The gathered worshipping community is inhabited by the Spirit, who enables and empowers the gifts that will be used as they gather. Paul speaks especially about the gifts of speaking in tongues and prophecy and gives specific instructions for how they should be used appropriately in corporate worship, that all may be done in order (chs. 12, 14). Teaching is also a gift enabled by the Spirit (12:28). Even the prayer and singing of the church is enabled and empowered by the Spirit (14:15–17, 26; cf. Eph 5:18–19; 6:18; Col 3:16).

The Church

Paul's extensive teaching on the church in this epistle may broadly be divided into two great themes.[2] In the first place, the church is the place where God's Spirit dwells. Then, secondly, each individual has a part to play in the church, which Paul teaches may be likened to a "body." The importance of the church becomes clear in the letter's opening (1:2). Paul writes "to the church of God that is in Corinth." The church belongs to God, who called it into being. In this sense it is not a human institution, association, or club, to which it is so often reduced in the modern era, but a divinely created community. This is immediately expanded on with appositional clauses that draw attention to the holy status of the people who belong to this community. Paul begins his letter with statements about the church that help accentuate his later arguments against divisions and a party spirit among them. The singular "church" and the fact that it belongs to God speak both to the source and unity of the community. In the appositional clauses the plural draws attention to the many members who make up this singular community known as the "church." In Paul's writings, "church" generally refers to the gathering of the people of God in a particular house or meeting place. In this epistle this may be seen in expressions such as "when you gather together as a church, I hear that divisions exist among you" (11:18), or in clauses such as "the one who prophesies builds up the church," "when you come together," and "let him [or her] keep silent in the church" (14:4, 26, 28). In the light of the reference to the "whole church" gathering at the house of Gaius in Corinth (Rom 16:23), it is likely that the normal practice was to gather in smaller house "churches."

Though it is probably anachronistic to talk of Paul referring to the "universal" church in 1 Corinthians,[3] he certainly has a deep commitment to seeing the various churches, with which he has had dealings, following the same standards in polity and worship and recognising their interdependence. He thus refers to what he teaches "everywhere in every church" in 4:17 and of how he orders "things in all the churches" (7:17). In 11:16 he writes of "the churches of God" and of "all the churches of the saints" in 14:33–34.

Church as Temple

In arguing decisively against divisions and quarrels in the church at Corinth, Paul appeals to the church as a *temple* (3:16). It is the place where God dwells by his Spirit (ναὸς θεοῦ ἐστε καὶ τὸ πνεῦμα τοῦ θεοῦ οἰκεῖ ἐν ὑμῖν). If disunity was to be overcome,

---

2. The word "church" (ἐκκλησία) in either the plural or singular appears twenty-two times in this epistle, substantially more frequently than in other Pauline letters.

3. Using 4:17 as an example, Whiteley writes that "the *thought of* the universal church is sometimes conveyed by a phrase which includes the *word* in its local signification" (*Theology of St. Paul*, 188–89, emphasis his).

then the people had to understand the significance of the *church*. The key to this is that the Spirit is among them. Paul can even say that when they gather together they experience "the power of our Lord Jesus" (5:4). God has always dwelt among his people, first in the garden of Eden, then in a tabernacle and later in a temple, but now he dwells by his Spirit in the congregation of the saints. The significance of the church of God's people being the place where the Holy Spirit dwells cannot be underestimated as Paul speaks of it in this epistle. Witherington writes, "Remarkably, Paul believes that even these badly mixed up Christians are still God's temple where God still dwells."[4] Nowadays many Christians think first only of their individual salvation. Thus, emphasis on the gathered, local community as the temple of God needs great attention. Such attention to the church as *temple* will inevitably lead to seeing the church in "building" terms (3:9–12). Hence Paul's frequent emphasis on "building up" the people of God (14:12, 26, etc.), something especially achieved in the exercise of love (8:1).

Church as Body

In using the metaphor of a "body" to describe the church, Paul again addresses unity and interdependence among the "saints" who compose the church. The idea is introduced in 10:16–17 in the context of the Lord's Supper. The product of the shed blood of Christ and the broken bread, reflecting the body given for his people in Christ's death, is a covenant community: the church. The "one loaf" is broken so that all may participate and recall the covenant-forming event into which they have been drawn by the Lord himself. In this way, those "who are many" are revealed in fact to be "one body" (ἓν σῶμα). The body is thus seen to belong to the covenant Lord, who gave himself for a people who would be unified in their belonging to him and in their worship and service of him. Yet the picture of the body serves as more than a reminder of the cost by which the church came into being and more than simply a further appeal to unity. In 11:27–29 the picture of the "body" is used to urge a proper concern for how the whole church takes part in the meal. The whole community must eat and drink together if the body is being "discerned" correctly. Indeed, the judgment that may come on them if they do not do this is further evidence that Paul still thinks in covenantal terms and of the judgment of the Lord (1:29–32).

In chapter 12, Paul develops the idea further. There he employs the body image to further his purpose to reverse the priorities of worldly thinking in favor of having the mind of Christ. As he emphasizes the diversity of gifts among the members of the body, he also develops the ideas of the more "presentable" and not so "presentable" parts and their relative significance (12:22–24). There is a reminder here of Paul's comments about the socio-economic makeup of the church in 1:26–29. It is God

---

4. Witherington, *Conflict and Community*, 134.

who has composed the body. Once again, it is the lowly and humble who are to be viewed as of great significance. Each part of the body needs the other parts: "God has composed the body, giving greater honor to [the part] that feels it lacks it, so that there may be no division in the body, but that the members may have the same care for one another" (12:24–25). In an age in which once again the church has been seriously influenced by the ideas of individualism and a status-seeking society, the need for churches to teach afresh the nature of "church" and to do so in understandable and popular terms must surely be critical. As traditional churches still depend on the one or two pastors for most of what goes on in church and as many modern churches depend on the "professionals" up front, Paul calls on all to recognize the extraordinary nature of a covenant community gifted to fulfil God's calling together in unity.

Idolatry and Demonology

This epistle contains Paul's most detailed discussion of idolatry. The subject was of great concern throughout the early church with many converts coming from Gentile backgrounds in which they had been accustomed to worshipping idols (8:7; cf. 1 Pet 4:3; Rev 2:20). His theological approach to the issue of idolatry involves several important points. In the first place, he examines the nature of idols and their relative position vis-à-vis the one true God. Secondly, he explains why idolatry is so dangerous for Christians. Thirdly, he addresses the practical matter of eating meat that has been offered to idols. Each part of Paul's exposition on idolatry involves a theological reflection that appeals to Scripture for support.

First, Paul considers idols alongside the Christian understanding of the nature of God. He insists that for Christians there is only one God, and appeals to the *Shema*. This God is the one who has created all things and for whom all exist. Furthermore, there is also only one Lord, who is the Lord Jesus Christ, "through whom are all things and through whom we [come to God]" (8:6). Access to God is thus provided through the one Lord (and not through any other "lords"). This emphasis on one God and one Lord allows Paul to speak of the "many 'gods'" and "many 'lords'" worshipped by idolaters (8:5). While initially this may seem to be a *non sequitur*, 10:14–22 helps explain Paul's thinking. While no other God exists, demons do exist and are the entities being worshipped behind the idols who themselves are "nothing in the world" (8:4; see 10:20–22). Paul demonstrates that in the case of idolatry, an appeal to the biblical truth that there is only one God and that idols are nothing does not give the whole story. Scripture says more than that. His appeal is mainly to Deuteronomy 32:17–18.

Secondly, Paul gives reasons for considering idolatry to be so dangerous for Christians. Christians only come to God through the covenant Lord, that is, the Lord Jesus Christ (8:6). Destruction awaits those who turn to idols (8:11; 10:5–7).

This is an especially serious warning for those who once were pagans and who may be drawn back into idolatry (8:10). Those who may lead others in the church astray so that they return to idolatry need to know that they are causing the stumbling of one for whom Christ died, and that they not only sin against the brother or sister but also against Christ himself (8:12). There is particular danger in taking part in religious meals within idol temples since this brings about a union with the demons.

Finally, Paul expands upon the theology governing the practice of eating meat that has been offered to idols. Here his argument is carefully nuanced. Eating food in a temple dedicated to an idol is unacceptable (8:10). Apart from the problem of Christians being led back to idolatry, in chapter 10 Paul returns to the question of lordships. These meals in a religious context are to be regarded as covenant meals. Paul offers the Lord's Supper by way of example. In that meal there is a "covenant participation" with the Lord (10:16). Therefore, they must understand that the same holds true for idolatrous meals in the context of the idol temple (10:16–18). Using Israel as yet another *negative* example in this chapter, Paul argues that the Israelites became participants with idols when they participated with idolaters (cf. Mal 1:7, 12). Christians cannot belong to the Lord and then "participate" with demons at their "table" (10:18, 20–21). The role of Christ as covenant Lord with full authority to bless and judge is assumed as Paul insists that dual allegiance is impossible. He even appeals to the Lord's "jealousy" (10:22; see Deut 32:21). However, meat offered to idols but on sale in the marketplace may be eaten (10:25). This general proposition is supported from Scripture since "the earth is the Lord's, and the fullness of it" (10:26, quoting Ps 24:1). Yet even this is set in the context of one of Paul's key theological themes in the epistle: all things should be done with consideration as to whether brothers and sisters in Christ are being "built up" (10:23). It is this theology that must then guide the question of specific instances of eating such meat, such as when a person makes an issue of the fact that the food being eaten has been offered to idols (10:27–31; see commentary). Though it is in Ephesians 5:5 where Paul most directly links idolatry with greed, in 1 Corinthians 5:10–11 and 6:9 he moves close to this. Idolatry is in the end for Paul anything that takes the place of the Lord or intrudes upon his purposes for humanity.

Immorality and Sexual Ethics

Throughout Scripture idolatry and immorality are closely linked. Both indicate a breach with the Lord. Paul clearly regards all sin, especially sexual immorality, as having its roots in idolatry (Rom 1:21–32). When Paul lists some of the various sins of those outside the church in 1 Corinthians 5:10–11 and 6:9–10, idolatry, sexual immorality, and greed are closely linked. The link became explicit at various times in Israel's history. In the incident of the golden calf narrated in Exodus 32, the account referred to by Paul in 1 Corinthians 10:7, idolatry leads directly into sexual immorality. The same is true in Israel's relationship with the Moabites in Numbers 25–26 (cf. 1 Cor 10:8). However, the link is also established in the Bible as faithful marriage is used as a picture of God's faithful love for his people, while unfaithful and adulterous relationships are taken up as a picture of a people going after other gods. The story of Hosea makes this picture explicit as the prophet is asked to seek out his wife, who has become a prostitute, and make her his wife again. In doing this Hosea's marriage reflects Israel's sin and judgment, and the reconciliation reflects God's restoration of Israel. Many other passages draw on this picture in one form or another and so link idolatry and immorality. In 1 Corinthians 6:9 sins relating to immorality appear either side of the sin of idolatry (cf. Rom 2:2). In 5:9 Paul reminds the Corinthians that he had previously written to them, telling them not to associate with sexually immoral people in their own midst. In the same way, he tells the people in the church that they cannot sit at the table of demons (idols) and at the table of the Lord (10:21). His commands to "flee sexual immorality" (6:18) and to "flee from idolatry" (10:14) mirror each other.

Theologically, it is the fact that the church consists in those who are "sanctified in Christ Jesus" and "called [to be] saints" (1:2) that drives the appeal to avoid sexual immorality. Christians are to be differentiated from those around in their holiness of life (cf. Eph 5:3). They are to reflect the new reality that they are in Christ and "one spirit" with the Lord (6:17) and that their bodies are the temple of the Holy Spirit (6:19). In 1 Thessalonians 4:3–4 Paul makes it clear that this was part of his core instruction to the churches: their "sanctification" is God's will, and therefore they are to abstain from immorality and learn how to control their bodies "in holiness and honor" (ESV). For the Corinthians, many of whom had been sexually immoral before conversion (6:9), the call to holiness meant a radical transformation in their behavior.

Sexual ethics are to be determined by trying to discern what "pleases the Lord" (Eph 5:10) and recalling that the death of Christ as Passover lamb has cleansed out the old "leaven" (1 Cor 5:6–8 ESV). Sexual ethics are also to be worked out in the light of the resurrection (6:14). Behavior and life now should be a preparation for the resurrection and reflect the resurrected Christ's priorities for his holy people.

Thus, as we noted in the commentary, Paul lists five reasons why sinning against the body is altogether wrong for believers, who should understand the body is for the Lord (6:13–20). The body that God has created was designed to be "joined to the Lord" (v. 17) and for bringing God glory (v. 20). It must not be used for immoral purposes. Under the lordship of Christ the body, in its sexual activity, has a purpose that cannot be destroyed. This purpose is to reflect certain aspects of the image of God, including his faithfulness to his people and his love and commitment to them (and theirs to him). The body must be used to God's glory, that is, "*for* the Lord" (6:13).

The Resurrection of Christ and of His People

As we have seen in the commentary, chapter 15 of this epistle offers the most extended exposition of the resurrection not only in Paul's writings but in the whole of Scripture. Here it is only necessary to summarize some aspects of what has been said in the explanation of the text. Again, Paul's theology arises from the questioning or misunderstandings of some in the Corinthian church whose views were affecting the whole church. The resurrection of God's people depends upon the resurrection of Christ. If the latter is doubted or denied, then Paul insists that there can be no resurrection at all, with the result that people are "still in [their] sins" and their "faith is futile" (15:17). Paul begins the chapter with his account of the gospel, which reaches its climax with the resurrection of Jesus. Christ's sacrificial death "for" the sins of the people only makes sense with the resurrection. This is the gospel: sin has been overcome and death vanquished. The resurrection of Christ thus comes to guarantee the fact of resurrection life itself and to make that life available to all through Jesus Christ. As Christ is raised *from* the dead, Paul's logic insists, so the resurrection *of* the dead must be a given.

As we argued earlier, the problem at Corinth probably emanated from some form of dualism (see comments on 15:12). Paul counters with teaching on the resurrection that, at its heart, offers a masterful examination of the present age in contrast with the future. The former has bodies prepared for this age, and the age to come has new bodies prepared for the new age. Paul seems deliberately to be recalling Genesis 1–3 as he develops this teaching. Building on ideas of the respective representative headships of Adam and Christ, Paul shows how death gives way, in Christ, to life. This life is seen in its fullness now in "Christ the firstfruits" and will be seen at his coming among all "who belong to Christ" (15:23). Thus resurrection guarantees the destruction of "the last enemy . . . death" (15:26) and culminates in all things being in subjection under God (15:27–28).

As Paul contrasts the two bodies, he is not distinguishing between that which is physical (the body of this age) and that which is "spiritual" in the sense of being nonphysical in the age to come. For Paul both bodies are, for want of a better word, "real" bodies, but the one is created and prepared by God in a way that enables it to live on this earth in this age, while the latter is created and prepared by God, through God's powerful work of resurrection, to live in the age to come. The former is "perishable" and "mortal," and the latter is "imperishable" and "put[s] on immortality" (vv. 50–54). Paul's appeal to different types of bodies for different entities dramatically reinforces this point. God creates appropriate "bodies" for existence in different spheres or worlds, whether it be stars in the heavens or plants on earth or birds that fly (vv. 37–42). Again, it is Paul's contrast between Adam and Christ (v. 45) that elucidates his reasoning, as he deliberately draws attention to Genesis 2:7: "'The first man Adam became a living being,' the last Adam a life-giving Spirit" (v. 45). Adam, Paul writes, is "from the earth" and Christ, the last Adam, is "of heaven" (v. 47).

In the final verses of 1 Corinthians 15, Paul masterfully indicates the extraordinary work of God in the transforming nature of the resurrection (vv. 53–55) but concludes with an appeal that in fact underscores the continuity between the now and the not yet (v. 58). It is the future face of humanity in Christ, living in bodies prepared to see "face to face" and ready to inhabit eternity and the new earth, that gives Paul grounds to appeal to the Corinthians to abound "in the work of the Lord" *now*. All Christians today must continue to take their stand on this gospel of hope in the death of Christ for sins and his resurrection and victory over death, just as the Corinthians did when they originally received it (15:3).

Scripture Index

Jeremiah

Lamentations

Ezekiel

Daniel

Galatians

Other Ancient Literature Index

Subject Index

as real languages foreign to the speaker, 596–97

as some form of ecstatic speech, 597–98

a sign for unbelievers, 612–13, 614

will be abolished, 574–76, 581

without intelligible communication, futility of, 602–3

traditions

Pauline, 477, 478, 479, 498, 500, 508, 649n6

wilderness, 66n42, 425–31, 433, 434, 438, 439, 445–46

transubstantiation, 509

trusting

that God is faithful to his church, 73–74

the power of God's Word, 90–91

typology, 421–24, 433, 672, 713

unbelief, 313, 314

unity

of the body revealed in the covenant meal, 457–58

lack of (in the Corinthian church), 75, 77, 79–80, 89, 92

the ultimate argument for, 180

unmarried, the, 294, 295, 302–3, 304–5, 307, 308, 310, 321, 330, 339, 342–44, 346, 350–57

contrast between the married man and, 350, 351–52

veils. See hair; head

virginity, 343

virgins, 339, 342, 343–44

warnings against self-deception, 188–89, 259

washing of believers. See repentance

weak, the, 408–9

Western education, 471

Westminster Confession of Faith, 685

widows, 293, 295, 304, 307, 310, 312, 342, 352n20, 357–58, 359

wilderness traditions, 66n42, 425–31, 433, 434, 438, 439, 445–46

Paul's use of the 428–30

will of God, the law reveals the, 729

winning (people): what it means, 405–6

wisdom

defined, 86

gift of (word of), 36, 62, 81, 117, 143, 194, 205, 217, 220, 244, 245, 362, 409, 531, 533, 534, 536, 539, 544, 546, 557, 697, 698

Greeks' seeking after, 99, 100, 106, 129

of speech versus the cross of Christ, 85–87

the test of true, 277

true wisdom and the wisdom of the age, contrasted, 136–42, 146

of the wise, 96–98, 103, 139, 141, 148, 381

word(s) of, 533–34, 535, 564n4, 624

"wisdom theology," 80

"wise person," 86, 97

wish-prayer, Paul's, 58, 59–60

wives

and husbands

conduct in public worship, 474–99

relation of, in public worship, 478–86

judging their husbands' prophecies, 637, 643

Man and woman, or husband and wife? (1 Cor 11), 480

on the silence of (in the church), 629–37

subordination of, 484n23

woman and man, 494–95 and passim. See hair; head; husband; wives

wonders, signs and, 105, 429, 537

word of the cross

defined, 96

versus the wisdom of speech, the, 85–87

word(s) of knowledge, 374, 533–54, 535, 538, 564n5, 624

women

on the silence of (in the church), 629–37

subordination of, 687. See also head; husband

works

to be revealed by fire, 174–76

of power (grace-gift), 536–37, 549

worship

the conduct of husbands and wives in public, 474–99

the relationship of husband and wife in public, 478–86

Author Index